BLAIR WHEATON
489-3484.

Basic Studies in Social Psychology

Basic Studies

Published for the Society for the
Psychological Study of Social Issues

in Social Psychology

edited and with introductions by

Brooklyn College of the
City University of New York

HAROLD PROSHANSKY

BERNARD SEIDENBERG

HOLT, RINEHART AND WINSTON
NEW YORK · CHICAGO · SAN FRANCISCO · TORONTO · LONDON

July, 1966
Copyright © 1965 by Holt, Rinehart and Winston, Inc.
All Rights Reserved
Library of Congress Catalog Card Number: 65–14870
27198–0115
Printed in the United States of America

FOREWORD

Many members of the Society for the Psychological Study of Social Issues identify themselves primarily as social psychologists. The Society's membership also includes, however, many psychologists in a variety of other areas of specialization, as well as social scientists from other disciplines, all of whom share the conviction that psychological analyses can contribute to the understanding and solution of pressing social problems. It is reasonable to assume that Society members—regardless of their own specialties—view social pychology as the central body of knowledge from which systematic psychological contributions to the study of social issues can be derived. Understandably, therefore, the Society has taken an active interest for many years in the development of social psychology as a discipline, and in the improvement of teaching, empirical research, and theory-building in this field.

A major contribution to this enterprise was the publication, under the sponsorship of the Society, of the *Readings in Social Psychology* in 1947. This volume, edited by Theodore M. Newcomb and Eugene L. Hartley, soon became widely recognized as a valuable tool in the teaching of social psychology. A revised edition, edited by Guy E. Swanson, along with Newcomb and Hartley, was published in 1952. A third edition was prepared by Eleanor E. Maccoby, again together with the original editors. All three editions have been, to quote Nevitt Sanford's foreword to the third edition, "a continuing source of pride and satisfaction" to the Society.

The field has continued to grow, however, and at an increasingly rapid rate. A committee, chaired by Theodore Newcomb and including Martin Hoffman, Edward Jones, Robert Kahn, Harold Proshansky, and M. Brewster Smith, was therefore appointed to consider the possibility of a new edition and the general policy questions that this raised. In considering a new volume, the Committee was faced with two apparently contradictory requirements: inclusion of enough of the classical studies in the field so as to provide historical continuity and inclusion of enough of the current research so as to reflect the present state of the field. To do justice to both of these needs, the Committee recommended replacement of the original *Readings* with two companion volumes: the present volume, *Basic Studies in Social Psychology,* which is designed to illustrate the types of research —mostly published before 1958—in which current work in the field is rooted; and *Current Studies in Social Psychology,* edited by Ivan D. Steiner and Martin E. Fishbein, which is designed to exemplify very recent developments.

The Society owes an enormous debt of gratitude to Harold Proshansky and Bernard Seidenberg, who undertook the arduous task of editing this volume and performed it with great dedication. Not only did they make an extensive survey of the field as a basis for selecting the readings but they also prepared introductory materials for the book as a whole and for each major section. This innovation helps considerably in providing a context for the individual selections and facilitating their integration. We are also grateful to Morton Deutsch, Daniel Katz, Theodore Newcomb, and Brewster Smith, who served as the Editorial Committee for this volume, as well as for its companion, and who were always ready to share their considerable wisdom with the editors.

HERBERT C. KELMAN
President
Society for the Psychological Study
of Social Issues

March 1965

PREFACE

The editor's role in the preparation of a book of readings is never an enviable one. There is a seemingly endless number of mundane tasks that follow once the final selection of papers to be included in the volume has been made. In retrospect, however, these demands represent a welcome relief from the pain and torment of deciding what these selections should be. Inasmuch as the objective in the present instance was to provide a volume of readings on empirical research for the entire field of social psychology, the selection problem was especially acute. Not only have new subfields emerged since the period following World War II but other more traditional ones (for example, public opinion) have now achieved the status of specialized fields in their own right. What confronted the editors was the seemingly insurmountable task of selecting a very small number of investigations—four or five at the most—from the many hundreds of them reported in the published literature for *each* of these subfields both new and old.

Our difficulties in this respect, however, were eased to some extent by a number of considerations. First, in the planning for a sequel to the three editions of *Readings in Social Psychology*, the SPSSI Readings Revision Committee took the view that it was no longer possible to represent adequately empirical research in the various topical areas of social psychology in a single volume. Thus, a companion volume to the present one, *Current Studies in Social Psychology*, edited by Ivan Steiner and Martin Fishbein, draws on research reported during the period from about 1958, whereas the present editors assumed the task of sampling investigations for the period from the early 1930s through 1958. While the temporal boundary between the two volumes could not always be maintained, the extent of overlap between them in this respect involves no more than a few investigations in each instance.

The task of choosing published studies for the present volume was also facilitated by the fact that it was intended primarily for use by undergraduates in general courses in social psychology. For this reason otherwise excellent investigations which involved highly complicated research designs and/or statistical procedures were in most instances excluded from consideration. While most, if not all, of the studies reported here make use of elementary statistics in the presentation of their findings, those students who are least prepared in this respect may still require some help in understanding some of the measures employed, for example, correlation coefficients, p values, and so on. On the other hand, it was impossible to avoid completely the problem of specialized terminology and somewhat abstract, theoretical presentations which characterize some

vii

of the selections. It was assumed that the editors' introduction to each general problem area would overcome this difficulty for the beginning student.

Focusing on relatively less technical investigations published no later than 1958 still left us with far more investigations than could be included in a single volume. At this point still other criteria were reluctantly invoked in order to reduce the number of selections on our list. It was decided, for example, to eliminate purely methodological investigations as well as those of the personality-social type which were primarily personality oriented. Although we had decided from the beginning to concentrate on empirical investigations—we did not feel that we could do justice to both research reports and theoretical essays—it was our intention to include a small number of significant papers that were exclusively theoretical. The latter was abandoned in the belief that the introductions to each general section and the theoretical discussions provided by the authors of many of the reprinted studies would serve as a reasonable substitute. Finally, since for any single problem area, for example, attitude change, interpersonal influence, and so on, we desired breadth of coverage rather than depth on any single issue or problem, we eliminated many worthy investigations which either duplicated or extended the findings of an equally superior study that was published earlier. In at least two instances, however, where an earlier pioneering investigation was refined, clarified, or superseded by a recent study, we decided to include both the original investigation and the one that grew out of it. While this same procedure would have been desirable in a number of other instances, space limitations prevented the selection of both studies for the volume. However, of the two, we selected the one which was more appropriate for inclusion as a separate reading, and established its continuity with the other by discussing both in the introduction to the general problem area.

After invoking the second set of criteria we found for some problem areas that not only were we left with a greatly reduced number of selections, but that deciding which among them should be included in the volume was not too difficult a task if we considered such additional criteria as methodological soundness, a critical demonstration of the validity of existing concepts, the nexus of a wide range of subsequent empirical work, and others. On the other hand, the application of these final criteria to other problem areas still left us with far more studies than space would permit. To help resolve this difficulty as well as to provide a check on those decisions we had already made with certainty, the editors turned to various groups of their colleagues in social psychology.

A four-man SPSSI Editorial Committee had agreed to work with us at every phase in the preparation of the volume. Their judgments of what investigations should be included in the volume confirmed many of our own, made us reexamine still others that we had made, and in general helped narrow down the number of choices in areas for which we had an "abundance" of excellent choices. No less helpful in these respects were the opinions of some thirty of our colleagues in social psychology who indicated their selections for the volume in a mailed questionnaire. Finally, we also gave very serious consideration to the empirical selections made by the various editors of the three editions of *Readings in Social Psychology* published in 1947, 1952, and 1958, respectively. The fact, for example, that a particular investigation was selected for inclusion in all three editions was in itself regarded as an important reason for giving it serious thought.

That we relied on the judgments made by our colleagues goes without saying. Of course, while we found relatively high agreement in their choices for some problem areas, there were also considerable differences of opinion among them for others. In both instances, however, it was the editors who weighed all of the factors for and against the inclusion of each study, and on this basis arrived at the final set of selections. While very much satisfied with these choices, they could not help but regret the omission of many studies for reasons which in no way cast doubt on the excellence of the research involved.

The subject matter of social psychology can be organized in many different ways. As yet there is no single conceptual scheme which stands above all others in its capacity to explain and integrate a variety of social phenomena. It is primarily for this reason that courses and textbooks in social psychology vary in the emphasis given to particular concepts or theoretical orientations and, therefore, in the way the findings of different empirical investigations are related to each other. The organization of the present volume of researches avoids taking sides or emphasizing a particular point of view. A variety of concepts, theoretical orientations, and methodological strategies are represented by these works, and we have employed commonly used topical headings and subheadings in organizing these studies for the student. In all probability, other familiar sets of categories could have been employed just as effectively. However, since no single set of categories could accommodate the considerable diversity of approach taken by teachers of social psychology, we were guided in all aspects of the organization of the volume by what seemed simple, straightforward, and most convenient in terms of our intention to write brief but informative introductions to each major division of the book. We found it simpler, for example, to discuss ethnic prejudice as a problem in Stress and Conflict in Group Life (Part VI), than to incorporate it into a discussion of the nature and development of Attitudes and Opinions (Part III).

Generally speaking, the sequence of general headings which we employ here is similar to what can be found in a number of widely used textbooks of social psychology. After an initial discussion of the nature and problems of the field, basic psychological processes are considered (motivation and cognition), followed by investigations and a discussion of more complex psychological structures (attitudes and values). The findings, concepts, and principles derived from these two sections of the book, then provide a basis for the introduction of still other analytical tools required in a consideration of both the content and structure of group life at various levels of social organization. As for the ordering of the subheadings in each division and the particular investigations covered by a particular subheading, there is little question that in many instances our decisions were arbitrary; on the other hand, in some other cases it was relatively clear as to which subtopics or studies had to be presented first in order to prepare the student for subsequent presentations, for example, *motivation and cognition* before *the per-*

ception of people. Regardless, however, of the general and specific nature of the organization of the various studies employed here, it is evident that they can be regrouped when assigned to students in any number of ways thereby meeting the needs of a wide variety of teachers.

The importance of writing both a general introduction and introductions to the broad problem areas covered by the volume was agreed on by the two editors from the start. Regarding the latter we do far more than summarize the various studies presented for each such area; we discuss the general nature of the problem area under consideration, define and elaborate relevant concepts and principles, discuss the significance and implications of some of the research reported here in the light of the findings of other investigations which are not presented as readings, and finally, wherever possible, clarify important theoretical issues or approaches which guide the empirical directions taken by researchers in a given problem area. The major purpose of these discussions is to provide the student with a conceptual scaffold for understanding and *relating* the investigations subsumed by each such area. For this reason we allowed the significant concepts and issues of the general problem area to determine when particular studies would be discussed rather than the fact that they were grouped together under a familiar subtopical heading. Each introductory discussion, in effect, ranges freely across the various subcategories used to organize the presentation of the studies themselves under the general problem area; and indeed in some instances they draw on investigations categorized by other major problem areas in the volume.

Whatever our initial aspirations regarding the completeness and amount of detail to be given in the introductions, we were clearly limited in what we could do by considerations of available space. The discussions of concepts and critical theoretical issues are selective, brief, and to the point. In order to insure clarity under these circumstances, in many instances we either quoted or paraphrased the presentations of other social psychologists. For certain general and specific problem areas we relied on one or more general or specialized texts in social psychology as well as the relevant journals. For example, in the case of the introduction to Part V, we often checked and added to our own conceptions by turning to those presented in the second edition of *Group Dynamics,* written and edited by D. Cartwright and A. Zander. Such volumes were invaluable in the attempt to define and elaborate for the student the conceptual and empirical character of social psychology as a science.

A book of readings, perhaps more than any other kind of academic work, depends on the efforts of many other people besides the editors. We are especially indebted to the SPSSI Editorial Committee whose assistance and guidance throughout this endeavor lightened our burden considerably. We would also like to thank those of our colleagues who willingly gave up their time to give us their judgments regarding what selections they believed should be included in the volume. We undoubtedly owe much to Eugene L. Hartley, Theodore M. Newcomb, Eleanor E. Maccoby, and Guy E. Swanson who, as editors of one or more of the three editions of *Readings in Social Psychology,* clearly established the directions we were to take in organizing and making selections for the book. We are also very grateful to Mrs. Mona Carp, Miss Sandra Leiblum, Mrs. Etta Proshansky, Miss Marilyn Sale, and Miss Marilyn Streisand who gave their time unstintingly in one or another of the many time-consuming and tedious tasks involved in the preparation of a book of readings. Finally we would like to express our appreciation to the authors and publishers who granted us permission to reprint their articles in this volume.

H.M.P.
B.S.

Brooklyn, New York
March 1965

CONTENTS

Foreword   v

Preface   **vii**

PART I   THE FIELD OF SOCIAL PSYCHOLOGY   1

Introduction: Problems of Theory and Method   3

PART II   BASIC PSYCHOLOGICAL PROCESSES   19

Introduction   **21**

A. Motivation and Cognition   **32**

FREDERIC CHARLES BARTLETT   *Social Factors in Recall*   **32**

EDWARD E. JONES *and* JANE ANESHANSEL   *The Learning and Utilization of Contravaluant Material*   **39**

GORDON W. ALLPORT *and* LEO J. POSTMAN   *The Basic Psychology of Rumor*   **47**

ELIZABETH DOUVAN   *Social Status and Success Strivings*   **58**

B. The Perception of People   **65**

HAROLD H. KELLEY   *The Warm-Cold Variable in First Impressions of Persons*   **65**

ALBERT PEPITONE   *The Determinants of Distortion in Social Perception*   **71**

JOHN W. THIBAUT *and* HENRY W. RIECKEN   *Some Determinants and Consequences of the Perception of Social Causality*   **81**

PART III   ATTITUDES AND OPINIONS   **95**

Introduction   **97**

A. The Nature of Attitudes and Attitude Change   **111**

EUGENE L. HOROWITZ   *Development of Attitude toward Negroes*   **111**

IRVING SARNOFF, DANIEL KATZ, and CHARLES
MC CLINTOCK   Attitude-Change Procedures and Motivating
Patterns   121

M. BREWSTER SMITH   The Personal Setting of Public Opinions:
A Study of Attitudes toward Russia   129

HERBERT C. KELMAN   Compliance, Identification, and
Internalization: Three Processes of Attitude Change   140

MILTON J. ROSENBERG   Cognitive Structure and Attitudinal
Affect   149

B. Communication and Persuasion   157

IRVING L. JANIS and SEYMOUR FESHBACH   Effects of
Fear-arousing Communications   157

CARL I. HOVLAND and WALTER WEISS   The Influence of
Source Credibility on Communication Effectiveness   175

CARL I. HOVLAND, O. J. HARVEY, and MUZAFER SHERIF
Assimilation and Contrast Effects in Reactions to Communication
and Attitude Change   186

ELIHU KATZ   The Two-step Flow of Communications:
An Up-to-date Report on an Hypothesis   196

C. Reference Groups   210

HAROLD H. KELLEY   Two Functions of Reference Groups   210

THEODORE M. NEWCOMB   Attitude Development as a
Function of Reference Groups: The Bennington Study   215

ALBERTA ENGVALL SIEGEL and SIDNEY SIEGEL
Reference Groups, Membership Groups, and Attitude Change   225

PART IV   CULTURE CONTEXT AND THE INDIVIDUAL   231

Introduction   233

A. Language and Meaning   244

ROGER W. BROWN and ERIC H. LENNEBERG   Studies in
Linguistic Relativity   244

ROGER W. BROWN   Linguistic Determinism and the
Part of Speech   253

W. E. LAMBERT, J. HAVELKA, and C. CROSBY   The
Influence of Language-Acquisition Contexts on Bilingualism   259

DANIEL KATZ and KENNETH W. BRALY   Verbal Stereotypes
and Racial Prejudice   266

B. Socialization of the Child   273

JEAN PIAGET   Social Factors in Moral Development   273

JOHN W. M. WHITING, RICHARD KLUCKHOHN, and ALBERT ANTHONY   The Function of Male Initiation Ceremonies at Puberty   283

MARIAN R. WINTERBOTTOM   The Relation of Need for Achievement to Learning Experiences in Independence and Mastery   294

KENNETH B. CLARK and MAMIE P. CLARK   Racial Identification and Preference in Negro Children   308

C. Social Stratification   318

ALLISON DAVIS, BURLEIGH B. GARDNER, and MARY R. GARDNER   The Class System of the White Caste   318

RICHARD CENTERS   The American Class Structure: A Psychological Analysis   326

PHILIP E. CONVERSE   The Shifting Role of Class in Political Attitudes and Behavior   339

URIE BRONFENBRENNER   Socialization and Social Class through Time and Space   349

AUGUST B. HOLLINGSHEAD and FREDERICK C. REDLICH Social Stratification and Psychiatric Disorders   366

PART V   PATTERNING OF SOCIAL INTERACTION IN GROUPS AND ORGANIZATIONS   375

Introduction   377

A. Interpersonal Influence   393

S. E. ASCH   Effects of Group Pressure upon the Modification and Distortion of Judgments   393

MORTON DEUTSCH and HAROLD B. GERARD   A Study of Normative and Informational Social Influences upon Individual Judgment   402

KURT W. BACK   Influence through Social Communication   411

KURT LEWIN   Group Decision and Social Change   423

EDITH BENNETT PELZ   Some Factors in "Group Decision"   437

LESTER COCH and JOHN R. P. FRENCH, JR.   Overcoming Resistance to Change   444

B. Norms, Roles, and Role Conflict   461

MUZAFER SHERIF   Formation of Social Norms: The Experimental Paradigm   461

LEON FESTINGER, STANLEY SCHACHTER, and KURT BACK The Operation of Group Standards   471

SEYMOUR LIEBERMAN   *The Effects of Changes in Roles on the Attitudes of Role Occupants*   **485**

NEAL GROSS, ALEXANDER W. MC EACHERN, and WARD S. MASON   *Role Conflict and Its Resolution*   **494**

LEWIS M. KILLIAN   *The Significance of Multiple-group Membership in Disaster*   **505**

C. Leadership   **511**

HELEN HALL JENNINGS   *Leadership and Sociometric Choice*   **511**

WILLIAM FOOTE WHYTE   *Leader-Follower Relations in Street-corner Society*   **519**

RONALD LIPPITT and RALPH K. WHITE   *An Experimental Study of Leadership and Group Life*   **523**

FRED E. FIEDLER   *The Contingency Model: A Theory of Leadership Effectiveness*   **538**

D. Group Structure and Process   **552**

MORTON DEUTSCH   *The Effects of Cooperation and Competition upon Group Process*   **552**

HAROLD J. LEAVITT   *Some Effects of Certain Communication Patterns on Group Performance*   **577**

GEORGE CASPAR HOMANS   *Group Factors in Worker Productivity*   **592**

PART VI   STRESS AND CONFLICT IN GROUP LIFE   **605**

Introduction   **607**

A. The Individual under Stress   **620**

ALEXANDER MINTZ   *Nonadaptive Group Behavior*   **620**

BRUNO BETTELHEIM   *Individual and Mass Behavior in Extreme Situations*   **628**

EDGAR H. SCHEIN   *Reaction Patterns to Severe, Chronic Stress in American Army Prisoners of War of the Chinese*   **638**

B. Prejudice and Intergroup Tension   **646**

MORTON DEUTSCH and MARY EVANS COLLINS   *The Effect of Public Policy in Housing Projects upon Interracial Attitudes*   **646**

MARIAN RADKE YARROW, JOHN D. CAMPBELL, and LEON J. YARROW   *Interpersonal Dynamics in Racial Integration*   **657**

ELSE FRENKEL-BRUNSWIK, DANIEL J. LEVINSON, and R. NEVITT SANFORD   *The Authoritarian Personality*   **670**

SHIRLEY A. STAR, ROBIN M. WILLIAMS, JR., and
SAMUEL A. STOUFFER   Negro Infantry Platoons in
White Companies   **680**

BRUNO BETTELHEIM and MORRIS JANOWITZ   Ethnic
Tolerance: A Function of Social and Personal Control   **685**

C. Group Conflict and International Tension   **694**

MUZAFER SHERIF   Superordinate Goals in the Reduction of
Intergroup Conflict   **694**

ROBERT R. BLAKE and JANE S. MOUTON   Loyalty of
Representatives to Ingroup Positions during Intergroup
Competition   **702**

BJORN CHRISTIANSEN   Attitudes towards Foreign Affairs
as a Function of Personality   **706**

Index   **719**

Basic Studies in Social Psychology

PART I

The Field of
Social
Psychology

INTRODUCTION:

PROBLEMS OF THEORY

AND METHOD

The focus of the present volume is on empirical research. The major headings and subheadings that organize the various investigations reported here indicate the kinds of human problems that have been of concern to the social psychologist during the last three decades. In the introduction preceding each of the major sections we consider briefly some of the basic concepts and questions involved in the various problem areas covered by that section, and thereby attempt to establish a framework for relating the various investigations. The purpose of the present section is more general in scope. The objective is to spell out the essential nature of the field of social psychology by asking, first, What are its distinguishing properties?—and in this respect its relationship to psychology proper and to other behavioral science disciplines is noted; and, second, What are some of the major problems and issues which characterize it as a scientific discipline?

Defining Social Psychology

Existing definitions of social psychology tend to be remarkably similar in both their substance and form (Asch, 1952; Krech, Crutchfield, and Ballachey, 1962; Newcomb, 1950; Sherif and Sherif, 1956; and others). By "form" we mean the kind of definition employed, in the sense of whether it is descriptive or theoretical in nature. Descriptive definitions of a field of inquiry simply point to or designate in either specific or general terms the kinds of events (as distinguished from other kinds of events) which are being subjected to analysis and study. Theoretical definitions, on the other hand, are more abstract in character. They designate sets of basic concepts and principles that have a firm empirical basis and that are employed to order and explain a variety of observed phenomena. Arriving at this

3

level of development of a field depends not only on significant and appropriate theoretical developments but no less importantly on advances in methods of observation and experimentation that permit the necessary empirical tests of derived hypotheses and predictions.

At the present time social psychology cannot be defined in theoretical terms.[1] This is not to suggest that social psychologists have either neglected or eschewed the development of concepts or theories, but rather that they have not been able to agree upon or establish empirically a common conceptual scheme for the analysis of social behavior. The reasons for this will be considered at a subsequent point in our discussion. Here we would only like to take note of the fact that as a scientific discipline social psychology has a rich heritage but a short history. As Allport (1954) indicates, many of its conceptual attempts to resolve fundamental human problems have their roots in the thinking of the Greek philosophers and the political and social philosophers of the seventeenth and eighteenth centuries, for example, Hobbes and Bentham. What distinguishes social psychology from these earlier approaches is its attempt to subject these problems to a systematic conceptual analysis that at every step must demonstrate its validity through appropriate empirical tests.

It is true, however, that scientific disciplines do not emerge fullgrown. They achieve maturity on the basis of slow and painstaking advances in theory and method over many generations; and even then, as has been well demonstrated in the physical sciences, each major advance in understanding brings with it a new set of problems that may challenge existing achievements. Social psychology was born at the turn of the century—although there are some who would argue that real signs of life were not apparent until the 1930's; hence there should be little cause for despair over the present relatively inchoate level of its development as a scientific discipline.

At this point, then, we must be content with a descriptive definition of social psychology. As we noted above, there is considerable agreement among existing definitions of the field in substance as well as form. What is emphasized in most, if not in all, of these statements is, first, the behaving *individual* (including what he experiences), and, second, the context in which this behavior takes place, that is, the *social setting*—other individuals or groups. When taken together these two elements of the definitions imply a number of important distinguishing properties of social psychology as a scientific approach to man's social behavior.

If the nexus of the social psychologist's concern with social process is the behavior and experience of the individual, then it follows that his level of analysis must be *psychological* in nature, expressed in terms of human perceptions, emotions, attitudes, values, and the like. And in this respect his orientation can be distinguished from the orientations of the sociologist, anthropologist, political scientist, and other social scientists. In these disciplines the primary unit of analysis is not the individual but groups of individuals, social organizations, and even larger, insti-

---

[1] This is true of most, if not all, other fields of psychology as well as of the other behavioral science disciplines, for example, sociology, anthropology, and political science.

tutional structures. In contrast to the psychological properties of the person noted above, the analysis of collectivities of all kinds and sizes (for example, the family or socioeconomic classes) involves such properties as cultural traditions, group atmosphere, and role systems.

It is evident that social psychology has no corner on the behavioral market. Sociologists, anthropologists, and other behavioral scientists are no less concerned with human behavior. The difference, however, is that the other approaches study behavior (for example, voting, prejudice, or buying) as it applies to specific groups of people rather than to the individual. In making the distinction between these two levels of analysis, it cannot be stressed too strongly that neither can claim any inherent superiority in approach over the other, although for certain kinds of problems one may have more to offer or be more appropriate than the other. It is now widely held (Allport, 1954; Selltiz, Jahoda, Deutsch, and Cook, 1959; Sherif and Sherif, 1956) that any given social phenomenon is a function not of any single sovereign determinant, but of *many interacting* determinants reflecting the influence of psychological, sociological, historical, and other kinds of factors.[2] If it is found that antiminority attitudes in the individual are related to a tendency to displace feelings of hostility, then we are provided with a psychological fact which in no way precludes or contradicts the equally reasonable sociological fact that the high degree of ethnic prejudice in a community tends to be inversely related to the social class level of its members. It would be quite erroneous, however, as Krech and Crutchfield (1947) suggest, to explain the existence of prejudice in a particular member of the community on the basis of his lower class status. To ask why a person is prejudiced is a psychological question and therefore requires a psychological answer, that is, in terms of the needs, cognitions, and feelings of the individual; it cannot be answered by reference to an established sociological fact.

This does not mean, however, that we should ignore the possible linking relationships that may and should be established between psychological and sociological facts. Let us carry the example given above further. If, on the one hand, it can be demonstrated that for some lower-class individuals their experiences of economic deprivation and social rejection provoke strong feelings of frustration accompanied by hostility, and, on the other, that because of particular personality factors and/or social conditions they are unable to express their hostility toward the actual sources of frustration, then to some extent a possible relationship between our original psychological and sociological facts begins to take shape. The fact that not all lower-class individuals exhibit antiminority group prejudices, even those who experience frustration accompanied by hostility and who cannot express the latter directly, clearly suggests that other determinants at both these levels of analysis are undoubtedly at work. Perhaps what deserves the greatest emphasis in this illustration is the fact that it reveals the critical interdependency between the

[2] It should be noted that the principle of multicausality refers to the interaction of determinants not only at different levels of human organization but within the same level of organization.

two disciplines. The finding that ethnic prejudice may be more characteristic of the lower class is better understood if the underlying psychological mechanisms are revealed; by the same token, the knowledge that prejudice in some individuals may be fostered by tendencies to displace hostility is deepened and extended if we know the social conditions which both establish and maintain this relationship.

The task of establishing functional relationships between the properties of the physical world and man's basic psychological processes (cognitive, emotional, and motivational) has typically been the province of general psychology.[3] It is a simple enough matter, then, to distinguish this orientation from the focus of social psychology, where the concern is with the functional relationship between these same processes in the person and the properties of his social world. The difficulty with this distinction is that its meaning is easily misconstrued unless the exact nature of the relationship between the two approaches is clarified.

Their locus of conceptualization is the same, namely, the behavior and experience of the individual. However, the fact that this behavior and experience is observed in the context of the physical world, on the one hand, and in a social context, on the other, is not and should not be construed to mean that a valid distinction can be made between a social man and a nonsocial man; or, perhaps what is more important, that two sets of concepts and principles are necessary to explain the behavior of the individual in each of these contexts, respectively.

Krech, Crutchfield, and Ballachey (1962) argue cogently that the distinction between a social and a nonsocial man is a fiction: ". . . every man lives in a social world, and no psychologist can study the behavior of an asocial man" (p. 7). The isolated individual observing or responding to a flash of light in the laboratory, they would contend, is no exception to this view. Be that as it may, it still may be argued that in the laboratory the effects of social factors are minimized or held constant, and that essentially the properties of the basic psychological processes in relation to the physical world are revealed. In the realm of social psychology just the reverse is true and, therefore, carrying this argument to its logical conclusion, only the "social properties" of the basic psychological functions are determined. This view is no less fallacious than the attempt to distinguish between a social and a nonsocial man. An essential truth is ignored. Whatever the characteristics of man's basic psychological processes as revealed in the laboratory setting, their influence on the individual's behavior and experience is ubiquitous. Whether he is experiencing a point of light in isolation or the behavior of another person in a social situation, the same underlying principles are involved. Nor should we overlook the equally important fact that the ability of the person to react to complex social stimuli is rooted in his capacities to respond to the physical world. An under-

---

[3] The introductory course in psychology is focused primarily on what for want of a better name is called "general psychology," which subsumes perception, thinking, learning, attention, motivation, and other psychological processes. The student is presented with the concepts, methods, and empirical findings for each of these processes, and in most instances these have been derived from highly controlled laboratory investigations involving the manipulation of physical stimuli in relation to the behavior and experience of the individual.

standing of the social behavior of man must begin with an understanding of the nature of his adaptation to the array of physical stimuli which impinge on him.

It should be evident by now that social psychology as a field of inquiry is by no means an autonomous discipline. It bears a close and intimate relationship to general psychology, seeking to erect a science of social behavior which is grounded in our fundamental knowledge of how individuals think, perceive, and act.

As Asch (1952) has noted, there are some psychologists who would agree with the final analysis given above of man's relation to his physical and social environment, but arrive at a quite different conclusion. Since there is only one set of psychological functions, they would argue, and inasmuch as man's social behavior and experience depend on his capacities to adapt to his physical environment, the need for a science of social psychology may be more apparent than real. It is assumed that if we understand his adjustments to the physical world—his perceptions, motivations, and the way he learns—we would then have a set of principles which would be both necessary and sufficient to explain all of man's behavior in any context, simple or complex. Most of the dilemmas of modern, present-day social psychology could be resolved by the application of these principles to man in society.

There are a number of underlying assumptions involved in this position which cast considerable doubt on its validity. First, it ignores the real possibility that critical psychological factors may occur in more complex social settings which are not included or observed in the laboratory situation. There is a real need then to "test" existing principles in complex settings in order to determine their efficacy. Krech, Crutchfield, and Ballachey (1962) point out that these principles "may . . . have to be modified before they can be applied to the understanding and prediction of social behavior" (p. 9). An even stronger case can be made against the view. If we assume the validity of existing psychological principles developed under nonsocial conditions, then what is seriously open to question is whether they are *both* necessary and sufficient to explain the complexities of human behavior at increasing levels of social organization. It hardly seems likely, as Asch (1952) suggests, that we can acquire "a knowledge of the facts and principles of social action by extrapolation from observations of non-social conditions" (p. 33). The essential similarities that may be involved in the perception of a light flash and the perception of the behavior of a person have no inherent priority over the essential differences that also may be involved in these two events. Only direct study of the second kind of event and others like it can help us to understand fully the nature of social behavior and experience. It is more than a question of modifying or correcting existing principles of perception, motivation, and learning based on man's relation to his physical environment. It is very likely that additional principles will be required in order to comprehend fully the nature of human social existence.

One other difference in orientation between social psychology and general psychology should be emphasized. Typically the study of basic psychological processes in relation to physical stimuli has required a segmented approach in which perception, learning, thinking, and other psychological processes are subjected to analysis as if they were independent of each other. The understanding of social behavior and experience, on the other hand, requires that the "psychological integrity" of the individual be maintained. The individual behaves in response to other persons or other social stimuli as an intact organism in which the interrelatedness of his motives, perceptions, and feelings is an unassailable fact. It is the whole person and not discrete psychological processes that is the locus of attention for the social psychologist. It is true, of course, that conceptual formulation and empirical investigation require that particular aspects of this whole be extracted for analysis. However, the understanding of these selected processes or attributes depends not only on their established functional relationships with external conditions but also on the nature of their interrelatedness with other states or properties of the person.

Some Problems and Issues

Early in the previous discussion we took note of the fact that theoretical developments in social psychology were symptomatic of the "growing pains" of a science still in its infancy. As yet there is no common language of descriptive or explanatory concepts that all theorists will agree upon. Diversity of concepts and theories is the order of the day, a fact which emerges all too clearly from the studies reported here. Ostensibly, one reason for this diversity is to be found in the scope and complexity of the problems which the social psychologist seeks to understand: role conflict, intergroup hostility, leadership, attitude change, and many others. Furthermore, each one of these problems constitutes a complex of more specific problems, which, not unlike the larger problem areas themselves, usually involve very different phenomena or variables being observed in a variety of social situations. A concern, for example, with attitude change in groups requires a consideration of such variables as group cohesiveness, group goals, and pressures toward conformity. On the other hand, the problem of attitude change as a function of mass media draws attention to the context of the messages communicated, the credibility of the source, the order of presentation, and so on. To the extent, then, that different investigators focus on different problems (and thereby different social settings and individuals), we can expect that they will stress different variables and explanations in their theorizing.

Theory, however, is not simply a function of what problems are studied but also of who studies them. By this we mean that different social psychologists may attack the very *same* problem and still end up with very different descriptions and explanations. Whatever the reasons, the fact remains that varying concepts and theories emerge because different researchers or investigators make quite different assumptions about the essential psychological processes and states necessary to understand the social behavior of the person. Indeed, as we noted above, different social problems are likely to generate different concepts and theories. But it is no less likely that different theorists may be attracted to just those social events or aspects of the very same events that involve phenomena that are congruent with their basic preconceptions.

The latter can be easily illustrated if we consider, for example, how different *psychological* theorists would describe the behavior of a prejudiced person. Psychoanalytically oriented investigators would be primarily concerned with the existing affective tendencies of the individual as indicators of unconscious psychodynamic conflicts. Reinforcement theorists, on the other hand, would give far more attention to the instrumental nature of the prejudiced person's behavior as a means of acquiring rewards or avoiding punishments. For the cognitive theorists emphasis would be on that person's perceptions of the minority group member, the nature of his beliefs about them, and the extent to which there are distortions in these cognitions. And, finally, those investigators who stress the individual's group memberships as a source of his attitudes will be concerned with the individual's group identifications and the prevailing norms of these groups. Similarly, as Cartwright and Zander (1960) have noted, the observation of the same *group* by different researchers can lead to considerable diversity in the descriptions which emerge, depending on whether one has an interactionist, psychoanalytic, field-theoretical, sociometric, or cognitive orientation.

The fact that the same specific problem or observed event can be subjected to analysis in different ways is not a serious issue in and by itself. If it were clear that each of the approaches noted was in fact describing a different phenomenon in the prejudiced person or in a particular group, then in time we could expect to overcome this difficulty. The fundamental task is no different from what must occur for the diversity of concepts and theories that exist for different problems or observed events. The empirical and conceptual relationships among different phenomena will have to be determined. However, Cartwright and Zander (1960) take note of the fact that "it is not always clear to what degree these different descriptions may be different ways of talking about exactly the same thing" (p. 46). Certainly social psychologists are by no means ready to decide this issue. The need for more refined measuring instruments as well as for more precise definitions of existing concepts in order to solve this problem is clearly indicated. What is needed at the moment is research endeavors in which the same individuals or groups are studied by means of a variety of techniques reflecting the various conceptual orientations to which we referred.

Apart from the problem noted above, it should be pointed out that in other instances it is quite evident that existing differences in terminology are just that. Investigators are aware that at times they are using different terms to describe the same behavior or process. The influences on the theoretical thinking of social psychologists come from general psychology, personality, sociology, anthropology, and, to a lesser extent, economics and political science. In this sense, then, we should expect to find different terms employed to describe the same events: motivational processes as needs, motives, wishes, and drives. And it is also true—and perhaps it is a more serious problem—that the same concepts may be readily employed by different theorists which refer to different phenomena. "Role" as used by some individuals refers to normative behaviors that are prescribed for various positions in a social system, whereas others readily apply it to describe the actual behavior of persons occupying these positions in the system. As Allport (1943) notes in his now classic paper, the concept "ego" has a number of underlying referents depending on what theorist is employing the term. Needless confusion results from both the use of diverse concepts to describe the same phenomenon and the application of the same concept to different events. Again the need for precise definition supplemented by appropriate measuring instruments is evident.

Theoretical diversity in the analysis of man's social behavior is rooted in still another issue that distinguishes the thinking not only of social psychologists but of behavioral scientists in general. Differences in the substantive assumptions made about the basic determinants of man's social behavior often reflect differences among researchers in their approach to science. The acquisition of a scientific body of knowledge depends on two kinds of activities: the collection of verifiable data and the ordering of these data in a theoretical system. In a mature or well-developed science these two activities achieve a balanced interdependence in the progress of research. Observations lead to hypotheses and theories which initiate new observations, and these in turn lead to a revision of the original hypotheses and theories, and again new observations are undertaken, and so the scientific process continues. The consequence of this process is the emergence of a more comprehensive theoretical system (or systems) that rests on a firm empirical foundation.

Before a science reaches this level of development, however, the proper relationship between theory construction and data collection emerges as a focal point of contention. Evidence of this controversy can be found in social psychology as well as in most if not all of the other behavioral sciences. The problem can be stated in simple terms. For some investigators the primary task of the social psychologist at the present time should be the description of social phenomena achieved by the careful development of measuring instruments and research techniques. Theorizing at this time may be a premature activity that will lead to wasted research efforts. Hypotheses are to be derived only after the facts are in and the basic dimensions for describing individual and group phenomena have been established. The factor analytic approach in the study of individuals and groups illustrates this point of view (Cattell, 1948). The empirical approach is also characteristic of the efforts of Bales (1950) and his associates, who began their study of face-to-face groups by developing a standardized observational system for categorizing the interactions of the members of these groups.

In opposition to this view are those that argue against data collection as the "royal road" to theory. Research is to be determined by formulated problems in which the essential variables of a given hypothesis or theory are defined. Only then can the investigator know what kind of events he should study, and therefore the kinds of empirical techniques and methods he will require. Field theorists, cognitive theorists, and those investigators who are psychoanalytically oriented give evidence of this kind of scientific approach.

In no sense, however, do we wish to suggest that researchers can be easily classified in terms of this dichotomy. There are various shades of opinion about how to proceed in the analysis of human behavior. Furthermore, there are other dichotomies of scientific orientation that may cut across both of these approaches to scientific research. For example, among those who espouse the importance of theory can be found differences in the nature of concepts to be employed. Some theorists advocate the use of concepts in theories or hypotheses that are to be defined as much as possible in terms of observable events. Others tend to employ more abstract conceptions which go beyond observable events and are tied to these events only indirectly by a network of other concepts and assumptions. For those of the empirical persuasion who have already moved from description to theory, similar differences can be found in the nature of their induced conceptions.

It should be evident that the "empirical" and "theoretical" orientations may each have different consequences as far as what specific phenomena are selected for study and what methods are to be employed in the research. Exploratory studies lend themselves to determining what are the essential variables in or dimensions of some phenomenon, whereas the test of a hypothesis derived from some theory may require a more rigorous experimental study in which one or two variables are systematically varied. It is also likely that the latter will involve problems that have been sufficiently researched to allow theory development; the former, in turn, may be more prone to consider new and undeveloped problem areas.

Notwithstanding these differences, the fact remains that the two approaches are not irreconcilable. Each has a contribution to make if for no other reason than that it serves as a check on the other. Theoretically minded psychologists are prone to point out the underlying psychological assumptions involved in the use of standardized measuring instruments designed to "merely describe." To the extent that these assumptions are tenable the obtained data can help to formulate theory. On the other hand, those who are data-oriented are quick to point out the limitations of specifically designed instruments used to test specific hypotheses, and to stress the need for standardized instruments and procedures as a basis for making comparisons of one investigation with another.

We turn our attention now to problems of empirical methodology in the study of social behavior. Social psychologists may employ any one of a number of methods in the conduct of their research. Which method they use depends on the objectives of their investigations. Well represented in the present volume are *experimental laboratory studies* in which the primary purpose was to manipulate isolated variables under highly controlled conditions. Investigations of both individuals (see Jones and Aneshansel, IIA, and Hovland and Weiss, IIIB) and groups (see Sherif, VB, and Lippitt and White, VC) have been undertaken in the setting of the laboratory and in most instances college students have been used as subjects. Groups in this setting are actually created by the experimenter and then are required to function in situations carefully controlled by him.

In contrast to the experimental laboratory investigation, the *field study* focuses on aggregates of individuals or organized groups in real-life settings. Under these circumstances individuals or groups are usually studied without any attempt to manipulate their behavior or introduce experimental variables. Although social psychologists have increasingly turned to field research during the last two decades, it has been and continues to be the primary research method of the sociologist and the anthropologist. Variations in the use of this general method again depend on the objectives of the investigator. In some instances his desire may be to observe and record as accurately as possible the day-to-day behavior and experiences of an organized group or community. The emphasis is usually on obtaining qualitative data and what emerges is a detailed study of selected aspects of the life of a group (see Whyte, VC) or an entire community (see Davis, Gardner, and Gardner, IVC). In other field studies the description of group life may be combined with an attempt to obtain quantitative data on specific variables through the use of standardized interviews, questionnaires, or other measurement techniques (see Newcomb, IIIC). Relationships among these variables are then studied by appropriate statistical procedures. Finally, other field studies focus exclusively on the task of obtaining quantitative data on particular dependent variables from aggregates of individuals with given demographic characteristics—such as age, sex, or social class, and other kinds of characteristics—such as psychiatric features, social attitudes, or particular experiences (see Centers, IVC, and Hollingshead and Redlich, IVC). Other variations within this kind of field study are possible, such as the use of control populations.

In recent years research methods that combine to some degree the features of the controlled laboratory investigation and the field study have been adopted. In the *natural experiment* the investigator takes advantage of changes which occur in the normal course of events of a real-life setting. Some change in policy or a critical event in a community or an industrial setting may occur that affords him the opportunity to determine its effects on the individuals or organized groups in question (see Lieberman, VB, and Deutsch and Collins, VIB). The Supreme Court decision of 1954 ordering white and Negro segregated schools in the nation to integrate has permitted researchers to study the effects of this change on the behavior and attitudes of white and Negro children. What should be stressed is that the experimental variable is not introduced by the experimenter but rather occurs as part of the day-to-day existence of individuals in their natural setting. Furthermore, the investigator must institute appropriate controls or checks in order to be sure that the observed effects are indeed the result of the "naturally" instituted change.

The problems involved in instituting such controls in the natural experiment as well as certain practical problems (knowing when such "natural" changes will occur, for example), have led to the development of a research method known as the *field experiment*. The distinguishing feature of this methodological approach is the fact that changes are deliberately introduced into the natural setting by the investigator in cooperation with those in authority. Changes may be introduced to test some hypothesis or to determine the effectiveness of some new procedure or policy. As a controlled experiment the particular change to be instituted is determined by the requirements of the research problem, and its effects are measured under conditions that permit the necessary controls to be employed in the comparison of properly equated groups (see Coch and French, VA).

One variation of the field experiment is the *natural laboratory experiment* in which individuals or groups are moved from their usual social context into a more restricted setting over which the experimenter has even greater control. To a large extent the typical laboratory investigation is duplicated except for the fact that the psychological and social attributes of the subjects or, if groups are being studied, the relationships among the group members, do not have to be created in the laboratory. In effect this method is of value when and if the variables under investigation are difficult to establish artificially in the laboratory setting, for example, friendly and hostile relationships among individuals (see Pepitone, IIB, and Homans, VD).

Although each of these methods has its advantages and disadvantages, the use of any one of them must be evaluated in the light of the research objectives of the investigator. It is only in this special sense that one method can be regarded as superior to another. On the other hand, the fact that the most appropriate method has been selected by an investigator for a given set of research objectives does not mean that he can afford to ignore its inherent limitations. The meaning and validity of his findings eventually must be assessed in the light of these factors as well as others. Here we take note of some general issues with respect to social psychological research and in the process reveal some of the important advantages and disadvantages of the laboratory method and the various field-study methods.

The extent to which generalizations are possible from a set of research findings is a continuing problem for those engaged in studies of human behavior. A research method optimally suited to a set of research objectives in no way obviates the possible limits imposed on making generalizations by the answers to the questions of who, how, and where were the subjects studied. The major advantage of the laboratory experimental method lies in the experimenter's ability to control variables and thereby to determine *which* of a number of simultaneously operating variables are the cause of an observed effect. During the last two decades social psychologists have demonstrated by their research designs and techniques considerable ingenuity in establishing such controls over individuals and groups in the laboratory setting. By the same token these methodological advances have not mitigated the persistent and nagging question about how much generalization is possible from their laboratory findings to individuals and groups in society.

One important consideration is the kind of subjects that have been employed in the laboratory experiment. It is undoubtedly true that the study of the fundamental properties of the various perceptual functions—brightness discrimination, and perhaps other psychological functions, for example—do not pose any serious problem in generalizing from the responses of college students to individuals in general. The same cannot be said, however, when social motivation, prejudice, interpersonal relations, conformity, and other complex social processes are the focus of investigation. The very fact that college students have been available as subjects has probably contributed in part to the success in establishing even greater controls in the laboratory setting. Ostensibly, one of the reasons that social psychologists have turned to field experiments and natural laboratory investigations has been to test their hypotheses and theories with more heterogeneous subject populations, or at least to test them with individuals or groups other than college students.

It has often been argued that the laboratory is a world unto itself, that the control of variables is achieved at the expense of creating an artificial setting which bears little resemblance to the "real" social context. In answer to this criticism it should be stressed that it is seldom the objective of the experimenter to duplicate exactly in the laboratory events found in the outside world, but rather to study the effects which result from variations in more or less abstract variables. Furthermore, these experimenters are often ready to defend the "artificiality" of their research on the grounds that it is only by means of such a high degree of control that variables which commonly occur together in the normal course of events can be isolated from each other and their separate effects studied.

It is true, however, that the ability to generalize in research depends not only on who is studied but in what context. The fact remains that in the laboratory study, many significant social variables are deliberately held constant while only a few others are varied systematically. This means that whatever effects are observed are a function not only of the latter but of the other prevailing conditions, that is, the levels at which the controlled variables are held constant. Given other combinations of these same variables, it may well be that not only will the observed effects change (either grow stronger or disappear) but new or quite different relationships may emerge. It follows, therefore, that extreme care must be exercised in generalizing laboratory findings to more complex social settings where other conditions prevail which have not been studied. That the context of research makes a difference is evident from the fact that attitude change produced in the laboratory (see Hovland and Weiss, IIIB) as a function of various communication variables tends to be greater than what has been found in the community setting by means of field-research approaches. As Hovland notes (1959), many conditions that prevail in laboratory studies of attitude change do not occur in the more realistic research setting: the time interval between the presentation of the communication and the measured change, the degree of the subject's personal involvement in the kinds of attitudes measured, and so on. It is important to note, however, that the systematic exposure of the differences between these two research settings in the study of attitude change has served to reconcile what would otherwise represent a set of conflicting findings.

Assuming no other sources of error in the collection of data, it is obvious that generalizing the findings of a field study to "real life" presents no problem to the investigator. Although he is free of this particular generalization difficulty, however, he is still confronted with another. An important issue is the extent to which the particular setting studied—either quantitatively or qualitatively—is representative of other settings. The extent to which the investigated setting is typical will determine the degree to which he can apply his findings to other situations. This is also a problem in the natural experiment and the field experiment. The ideal situation lies in field investigations that study individuals or groups in a representative sample of settings.

We should also take note of the difficulties often involved in interpreting the direction of causality in quantitative field studies in which correlations are obtained, for example, a positive relationship between the extent to which individuals are attracted to each other and the degree of similarity in their political attitudes. This limitation, of course, does not always hold, especially where information regarding the temporal sequence of the variables is available or where existing knowledge provides a basis for making a valid inference regarding the direction of causality. In the natural experiment, establishing the direction of causality is much less of a problem. However, although the sequence of events may be clear, there are other problems relevant to establishing experimental controls, for example, finding a control situation. Of particular importance is the possibility that a change introduced in the natural course of events by individuals or groups in authority may be far less responsible for the observed effects than other factors which induced those in authority to act in the first place.

By its attempt to combine the best features of the field study and the experimental method, the field experiment, in principle, avoids most of the limitations we described above. In practice, however, the investigator must contend with the serious problem of first gaining permission to undertake his research and, in the event that this permission is granted, with being able to effect the changes required by the design of his research, say, getting supervisors to behave in a democratic fashion. If both problems are overcome there is still another difficulty inherent in all kinds of field research but perhaps more so in the field experiment. To what extent does the *intrusion* of the research process into the normal activities of a social situation contribute to the observed effects? In many kinds of field experiments it is not a simple matter to collect data in a social setting without the manipulated individuals or groups being aware of what is occurring. Individuals are sensitive to unexpected and novel changes in their environments, and their awareness that they are being subjected to study creates expectations which may contribute to the observed changes as much as do the independent variables being manipulated. Obviously field researchers take precautions to minimize these kinds of uncontrollable effects. For example, the actual research activity itself is begun only after the investigator and his paraphernalia have become commonplace in the social setting. Of course this procedure and others do not completely solve the problem in principle since, commonplace or not, his presence (even under conditions of anonymity of purpose and role) does represent a change in the actual situation. Unfortunately, the common use of the placebo in drug research as a means of controlling for this kind of influence would be an extremely costly procedure in social research.

By definition the experiment in the laboratory disturbs the normal routine of the individual or group. But in these circumstances there is still another kind of problem that, although not unique to the laboratory, assumes special importance in this setting because, in the main, experimenters tend to ignore it. The subject and the experimenter each have expectations about and attitudes toward the other that emerge by virtue of the special nature of their relationship in the research setting. As Riecken (1962) so ably states it, the experimenter and the subject make "assumptions and inferences . . . about the social character of each other and about the nature of the experiment as a social situation" (p. 26). It is not unlikely that these underlying interpretations and expectations represent unintended influences on the collection of data in the laboratory setting. For example, the "real-life" relationship between subject and experimenter was found to make a difference in the subject's behavior in the experiment. In one investigation it was found that a faculty experimenter induced higher performance levels in subjects than did a graduate student experimenter (Birney, 1958). Undoubtedly these kinds of unintended influences are present in field studies as well. However, because investigators in this kind of research are generally more sensitive to the whole question of their intrusion into the social setting, at the very least they are more likely to be aware of them. Clearly there is a need for research into the consequences of these uncontrolled influences in both the laboratory and the field settings.

At the very beginning of our discussion we examined the definition of social psychology and in the process revealed its relationships to general psychology, on the one hand, and other social sciences, on the other. By way of concluding our comments in this section it is important to take note of another issue relating to the approach of some sociologists and some social psychologists.

Newcomb (1950b; 1954) has pointed out the existence of two kinds of social psychologies, one with a psychological orientation and the other with a sociological orientation. Both are involved with problems of the behavior of individuals in the social setting and with group process. The essential difference between them lies in the kinds of determinants that are stressed to explain social behavior with respect to individuals or with respect to groups. For the psychological social psychologist the behavior of individuals or the interaction between them is sought in intraindividual processes or psychological events rather than in the properties of the social interaction situation. The essence of the approach is succinctly expressed by Newcomb (1954) when he states, "There is no harder lesson for the psychologist to learn, probably, than that of viewing persons as functionaries in a group structure rather than as psychological organisms" (p. 241). The sociologically oriented social psychologist, on the other hand, gives greater emphasis to the properties of the social system in which the individual is contained. The behaviors of persons as well as groups are determined by their positions and functions in these systems. For the sociologist the hard lesson is viewing the person as a psychological organism rather than as the occupant of a position in a role system.

At the present time there are sociologists and social psychologists who seek to integrate these two approaches rather than view them as mutually exclusive. Each approach obviously touches on a significant source of variation; but the success of each approach will depend on the extent to which it adopts the perspective of the other in the development of its own concepts. Psychological processes are rooted not only in the biological character of the individual but also in the structured social world in which he develops and acts. Psychological descriptions of the individual, therefore, must be defined in terms that imply the operation of both kinds of determinants. Similarly, the conceptual schemes of interactions and social systems must take account of the underlying psychological processes that provide the basis for normative social relationships.

The goal is not a homogenization of the two approaches in which the identity of each is lost. On the contrary, what is required is the vigorous development of each in the light of the contributions that can be made by the other. Psychological and sociological concepts established on this basis will reduce considerably the difficulty involved in the long-range goal of conceptually linking psychological process with social process.

References

ALLPORT, G. W. The ego in contemporary psychology. *Psychol. Rev.*, 1943, *50*, 451-478.

ALLPORT, G. W. The historical background of modern social psychology. In G. Lindzey (Ed.), *Handbook of social psychology*, Vol. 2. Reading, Mass.: Addison-Wesley, 1954.

ASCH, S. *Social Psychology.* Englewood Cliffs, N.J.: Prentice-Hall, 1952.

BALES, R. F. *Interaction process analysis: a method for the study of small groups.* Reading, Mass.: Addison-Wesley, 1950.

BIRNEY, R. C. The achievement motive and task performance: a replication. *J. abnorm. soc. Psychol.*, 1958, *56*, 133-135.

CARTWRIGHT, D., and ZANDER, A. *Group dynamics,* 2d Ed. New York: Harper & Row, 1960.

CATTELL, R. B. Concepts and methods in the measurement of group syntality. *Psychol. Rev.*, 1948, *55*, 48-63.

HOVLAND, C. I. Reconciling conflicting results derived from experimental and survey studies of attitude change. *Amer. Psychol.*, 1959, *14*, 8-17.

KRECH, D., and CRUTCHFIELD, R. S. *Theory and problems of social behavior.* New York: McGraw-Hill, 1947.

KRECH, D., CRUTCHFIELD, R. S. and BALLACHEY, E. L. *Individual in society.* New York: McGraw-Hill, 1962.

NEWCOMB, T. M. Social psychological theory. In J. H. Rohrer and M. Sherif (Eds.), *Social psychology at the crossroads.* New York: Harper & Row, 1950b.

NEWCOMB, T. M. *Social psychology.* New York: Holt, Rinehart and Winston, 1950a.

NEWCOMB, T. M. Sociology and psychology. In J. Gillin (Ed.), *For a science of social man.* New York: Macmillan, 1954.

RIECKEN, H. W. A program for research on experiments in social psychology. In N. F. Washburne (Ed.), *Decisions, values, and groups,* Vol. 2. New York: Macmillan, 1962.

SELLTIZ, C. JAHODA, M., DEUTSCH, M., and COOK, S. W. *Research methods in social relations.* New York: Holt, Rinehart and Winston, 1959.

SHERIF, M., and SHERIF, C. W. *An outline of social psychology.* New York: Harper & Row, 1956.

PART II   *Basic*
Psychological
Processes

INTRODUCTION

Human motivation and cognition are problems of central concern to the social psychologist. What moves men to act in their social world and how they order and give meaning to this world are fundamental questions he asks in his quest for an understanding of social behavior. Attempts to answer these questions, as we noted in the preceding introduction, must encompass the existing knowledge of how men adapt to their physical world. The inherent properties of man's capacities to be moved to action and to be guided in this action by what he sees, thinks, and believes have influence on any and all of his behavior regardless of the context.

Man is capable of thinking, reasoning, perceiving, remembering, and imagining, as well as reacting in still other kinds of cognitive ways. Although each of these psychological processes has certain properties that distinguish it from the others, all of them show considerable similarity in the experience of the individual. It is by no means a simple matter to tell where, for example, the person's perception of an object leaves off and his ideas or thoughts about it begin. The presence of the object he views in no way precludes the possibility that these other processes are involved in his "perceptions" of it. Furthermore, existing evidence suggests that all cognitive processes tend to obey the same general principles or laws. Many of the factors that determine our perceptions of an immediately given object also seem to influence our thoughts, memories, and judgments about it. In the discussion that follows we will speak primarily about perception, but it should be understood that the analysis provided is no less applicable to other cognitive processes.

It is now generally agreed that the formation of human percepts is rooted in two classes of determinants: *stimulus factors* and *behavioral factors*. Stimulus factors refer to the properties of the stimulus itself, and the stimuli may be other people, pictures, a social setting, or words. Behavioral factors, on the other hand, refer to any and all internal psychological states or processes of the individual: his needs, values, attitudes, past experiences, and so on. It is interesting to note that this approach to cognition reflects the general orientation of most social psychologists to understanding social behavior that we noted at the end of our general introduction. How people act depends on inner psychological processes and the nature of the external setting.

The social psychologist's special concern with the problem of how people perceive has led to the use of the term "social perception." Oddly enough, until recently it was employed with two different connotations (MacLeod, 1950). For some investigators the concept implied the operation of social factors in the person, that is, the behavioral factors noted above; for others it meant the perception of the social. Neither view is correct if it ignores the significance of the determinants in the perceptual process advocated by the other. What must be stressed is the general and important assumption underlying the investigations in the next two sections, namely, that percepts flow from the *interaction* of behavioral and stimulus factors. However, to understand the role of each of these classes of determinants in perception it has been necessary to separate them in both analysis and investigation. As it turns out, far more attention in research has been given to the operation of behavioral determinants than to stimulus determinants. Let us consider the former first.

If perceiving an external object or event (or even oneself) means attributing meaning to it—a view held by many social psychologists—then it should be evident that the past experience of the person is a critical behavioral determinant in perception. His past experience sensitizes him not only to particular categories of meaning, but also to particular kinds of events in his social setting. Whether we are dealing with an experience that has occurred only recently or with an enduring accumulation of many previous experiences, the person becomes sensitized or set to perceive in given ways. The individual who has recently had a pleasant experience with a new acquaintance is more likely to view him on the next occasion of their meeting in positive terms than the individual whose experience with him has been unpleasant. Similarly, the word "capsule" seen in isolation is likely to have a very different meaning for an astronaut on the one hand and a physician on the other.

Bartlett's (IIA) classic study focuses on the broadest and most pervasive context of the individual's experience: culture. The significance of culture in the development and socialization of the individual is considered in Part IV. Here we need only note the important role it plays in sensitizing its members to given sets of events which have particular meanings for them. Thus, Bartlett's British students remembered, organized, and elaborated the elements of a story from another culture in terms that reflected what was salient in their own cultural experiences.

To understand the influence of culture or past experience generally on the perceptions or memories of the individual it is important to take note of an essential aspect of human experience. The experiences of the person are neither lost nor registered as isolated events. His commerce with objects, events, and people becomes organized into enduring systems of percepts, ideas, and beliefs, which as continuing *cognitive structures* have influence on his subsequent cognitive reactions, and therefore on his overt behavior. It is in this sense that the cultural experiences of Bartlett's subjects influenced their memories. They simplified, elaborated, and accentuated specific elements of the stories in a manner which was consistent with their own view of the world.

Cognitive structures are not always neutral. They often involve beliefs and ideas about objects or events which are evaluative in character. The belief that foreigners are dirty is an example. As a consequence such structures often lead to or become associated with particular emotional responses toward the object, for example, anger or fear, as well as predispositions to act toward the object in given ways, say, to punish it. "Attitudes" are cognitive, affective, and behavioral components of experience that have become interrelated in this fashion. This is a problem that will concern us in the next section.

Another class of behavioral determinants that influence cognitive processes is the motivations of the person. What individuals want and feel also sensitize them to particular aspects of an object or a situation. Attitudes, as we described them above, as well as the person's values and interests, are psychological states that can impel the individual to act by virtue of their motivational properties; as a consequence they also exert influence on what he sees, thinks, and remembers. It should be clear at this point that a basic aspect of human psychological functioning is the interrelatedness of motivations, cognitions, and actions. Men's actions are guided by cognitions that reflect the influence of the internal forces that drive them to act in the first place. However, this relationship flows in both directions. The social stimulus world of the person has influence on his cognitions, which, in turn, serve to modify his directive states.

If the desires or feelings of the individual sensitize him to given aspects of an object or an event, then it is evident that his perceptions of these stimuli may not always be accurate. Under certain conditions it is often the case that people see, think, and remember what is congruent with their wants or fears. The studies by Allport and Postman (IIA) and Pepitone (IIB) show how the needs or fears of the individual can distort his perceptions. In the Pepitone investigation high school boys, varying in the extent to which they wanted to obtain a free ticket to a basketball game, were asked to rate three judges who interviewed them and who exhibited varying degrees of friendliness but the same degree of power during the interview. Adult observers confirmed that the judges were reflecting the two attributes at the required levels. Under these conditions the friendliest judge was seen as having the most power and the least friendly judge as having the least power. In the former instance high-motivation subjects distorted significantly more than low-motivation subjects. Hence distortion took place in the direction of goal achievement and to some extent it was related to the degree to which the individual was motivated.

In the Allport and Postman paper the cognitive distortions that are typical in rumor transmission are analyzed in terms of the ambiguity of significant events and the consequent fear and anxiety aroused in the individual. Rumors circulate, Allport and Postman suggest, because they explain and relieve the motivational tensions that are developed under these conditions. In this circulation the mechanisms of leveling, sharpening, and assimilation lead to distortions that are congruent with the interests, fears, and desires of the person. These same three mechanisms to some extent are used to account for the distortions found by Bartlett in his subjects' reproductions of a culturally alien story.

A number of studies have demonstrated the influence of attitudes and values on human learning. Thus, an early investigation by Levine and Murphy (1943) found that pro-Communist and anti-Communist students learned and retained relevant statements that were congruent with their attitudes better than they did statements that ran counter to their attitudes. Must attitudinal biases always lead to congruent effects in their influence on cognitive process? The study by Jones and Aneshansel (IIA) asks this same question and provides evidence that under appropriate conditions the person may better learn material that runs counter to his values than do individuals who actually agree with this material. As these investigators demonstrate, where the individual has to learn contravaluent material (opposite to his views) because he has to be ready to argue from this viewpoint at a later time, he will learn it better than will those who agree with the material and therefore already have such arguments in hand. It would appear, then, that the influence of enduring attitudes and values on cognitive processes may be overridden by more immediate situationally determined needs.

What this suggests, and what most of us know from our own experiences, is that gross cognitive distortion is by no means the rule of everyday life. It should be evident from the previous discussion that motivational determinants are more or less likely to lead to distortion, depending on the degree of ambiguity of the stimulus situation. Where significant events are unclear or complex, or where we are removed from the events themselves and must depend on others for information, it is not unlikely that distortion will occur. But even here note that we have described the events as "significant." In situations where our values, attitudes, and interests are not engaged, their immediate influence on perceiving relevant stimuli is likely to be minimal. And where these processes are aroused we must consider the intensity of the motivation experienced and who is experiencing it.

Individuals learn to handle their needs in many different ways, which is another way of saying that they cope with reality in consistent and predictable fashions. Whether or not distortion occurs may also depend on the nature of these underlying personality patterns. Since we assume the interrelatedness of all psychological processes, then it follows that cognitive processes too may be shaped along given lines by these basic dispositions. Indeed, there is now evidence that "cognitive styles" exist in the ways individuals order and give meaning to the external world. The research on the "authoritarian" personality (see VIB), for example, has revealed that the authoritarian has difficulty with ambiguous situations, and that he tends to structure them in absolute, either-or terms. Since many situations, individuals, and events are neither simple nor unambiguous, the possibility of distortion in his cognitions is evident.

At one level of analysis the stimulus determinants that influence the perception of complex social stimuli are not difficult to specify. A written message, the overt behavior of a person, a discussion between two people, a television debate, and so on, have physical properties that may influence our perceptions. What we have learned in the experimental perception laboratory about significant physical stimulus properties applies equally well to the social setting. Intensity, novelty or contrast, repetition, movement, and other physical characteristics of social stimuli can and do orient the direction of our perceptions. For example, a Negro child among a group of all-white children will readily be seen; the loudest voice in a group discussion may at first attract our attention. For certain kinds of social events, for example, influencing large groups of individuals via mass media or educating the young, some of these properties are obviously important considerations in the preparation of stimulus materials. These factors only initiate and sustain the cognitive process; other stimulus properties, for example, order of presentation, as well as behavioral determinants will determine the final nature of what is perceived.

There are also organizational properties of stimuli that have consequences for our perceptions of social objects. We know that inanimate objects that have spatial or temporal *proximity* or that have *similar* properties—color, size, and so on—tend to be viewed as belonging together. Certainly individuals also may be perceived as belonging together because of their physical proximity (for example, people living in the same house), or because of their physical similarity (for example, people having the same hair color). Of far greater significance, of course, for the way we group social objects is the nature of our experience in society. Since skin color is emphasized, Negroes are distinguished from whites. The social attributes of persons—their occupations, religious denominations, and many others—also provide important criteria for such groupings. It can be seen that how we select and organize a great variety of social objects into meaningful cognitive structures depends on the individual's cultural experience.

The proximity and similarity of stimuli also have important consequences for our perceptions of cause and effect relationships. How we behave is determined in many instances by how we organize particular causes with particular effects. Similarity or proximity may lead us to attribute the responsibility for or the cause of an event to another person (Heider, 1944). A person whom we favor is more likely to be associated with a favorable than with an unfavorable act. It should be stressed that beyond these two stimulus determinants of the perception of cause and effect, we learn to relate particular causes with particular effects. We learn to expect that people in given roles or social categories will behave in certain ways. When such behavior or its consequences occur under ambiguous circumstances we are more likely to attribute it to the person from whom it is typically expected than to someone else. The disappearance of the teacher's pocketbook from her desk is more likely to be attributed to a lower-class youth than to a youth of higher social status.

The problem of the stimulus properties of another person is far more complex than the above discussion would seem to suggest. This is especially true in a social interaction situation in which A first responds to B's response, B in turn responds to A's response, and so on. Social interaction flows smoothly by virtue of the fact that each individual is able to comprehend the responses of the other person, and then respond accordingly. But what he comprehends are not simply the overt responses of the other but their meaning in terms of the latter's feelings, desires, conceptions, and other inner psychological characteristics. What makes for difficulty for the psychologist is that the perception of this meaning cannot be coordinated with the physical properties of the other's behavior or with any single social cue. Each social cue exists in a context of other cues, and these in turn are embedded in still larger patterns of stimuli. What the perceived person says and does, his known social attributes, and the nature of the social situation in which the interaction occurs provide a pattern of stimuli which creates an almost insurmountable problem when a systematic analysis is attempted of what stimuli contributed to the perceptions of the perceiver.

Perhaps what requires emphasis as a critical stimulus determinant in the perception of others is *context*. The meaning of particular stimuli or patterns of stimuli depends on the context of other stimuli in which they occur. The same comment or gesture will vary in meaning, depending on who said it, when, and in what situation. The studies reported by Thibaut and Riecken (IIB) are of some interest in this respect. Their concern, among other things, was with the nature of perceived causality in a person who successfully influences other people who vary in status. The question they asked was to whom does the person making a successful influence attempt attribute the change when the person who changes is of low status as opposed to one of high status. Where the person was of low status the perceiver attributed the compliance of the other to his own coercive efforts; in the case of the high-status person the change was seen as emanating from the high-status person himself, that is, as being due to his goodwill. The context of the perceived status of each clearly led to quite different interpretations as to how and why the change occurred. In the earlier mentioned study by Pepitone the contextual effect of one behavior on another is also evident. Although objectively the three judges acted with the same "medium power," the objective variations in their friendliness toward the high school student led him to perceive them as varying in their degree of power.

In a study by Asch (1946) subjects were presented with a list of discrete trait names—warm, intelligent, and so on—and were asked to write their impressions of a fictitious person with these attributes. Asch found that the resulting impressions tended to be unified and complete such that any contradictions and inconsistencies among the stimulus elements were minimized. Although it has not always been found that subjects exhibit such consistency, the mutual influence of traits on each other in the perceiver's impressions has been confirmed in many other investigations. Particular traits have greater organizing power, greater influence on other traits, and therefore greater effect on the resulting impression.

A study by Kelley (IIB) tested some of Asch's formulations in an ongoing interaction setting. College students wrote brief impressions and rated a "new instructor" after a twenty-minute class period, prior to which half the students had been told that the instructor was a "rather cold" person, and the other half that he was a "very warm" person. The warm–cold variable made a difference in both their written impressions and their ratings of the instructor in the expected directions. Furthermore, their preinteraction cognitions of him made a difference in their class behavior. Those who received the favorable impression participated in the class discussion more frequently than did those who were told that he was a "rather cold" person.

It should not be assumed, of course, that knowledge about a new acquaintance gained prior to the initial interaction will necessarily dominate our cognitions of him during and after the first meeting. Given the very brief interaction period in Kelley's study, in which the stimulus person's behavior was limited to a specific role, there was little in the situation that could have competed with the previously established knowledge of the instructor. We are all aware of the fact that first impressions of persons may either grow stronger or reverse themselves as interaction continues over an extended period of time. The nature of the impression and the changes that occur in it will depend not only on the behavior of the other but also on many behavioral determinants in the perceiver—his values, immediate needs, and so on—that are relevant to the interaction context. This suggests that some types of behaviors or cues in the stimulus person will be attended to more readily than others. Thus, in the case of an anxious person being interviewed for a new job, we can expect that he will be far more sensitive to cues in the interviewer that tell him what the latter thinks of him or whether he likes him, than to cues which will tell him just what kind of person his future employer may be. To be liked or well thought of in this case means increased probability of goal attainment.

The focal nature of the problem of human motivation for the social psychologist is self-evident. Any attempt to describe and explain the social behavior of the individual must take into account the forces that initiate and sustain his behavior in a given direction. The existence of these forces is inferred on the basis of what persons do and say in a given set of circumstances. They may occur in a "pure state" as desires, likes, dislikes, fears, and so on, or they may be embedded in more complex psychological structures, such as attitudes, values, and interests. In both instances there is the capacity to arouse and maintain goal-directed activity.

The diversity of concepts, hypotheses, and theories that characterize modern social psychology is perhaps no more evident than in its attempts to understand human motivation. Approaches to this problem range far and wide, extending from the broad theoretical conceptions of the sociologist and the anthropologist to the highly specialized and precise formulations of the experimental learning theorist. In between these two approaches, and perhaps having greater effect, are to be found the influences of the psychoanalytic theorist, the field theorist, the cognitive theorist, and others. It is not our intention nor is it possible within the scope of this introduction to treat any of these approaches in any detail. In the discussion that follows we shall briefly consider some of the general dimensions of the problem of human motivation that have guided the thinking and research of social psychologists. In the process it will become evident to the student that in part the existing diversity of concepts and methods reflects a difference in emphasis among investigators as to which should be the critical dimension.

Clearly a fundamental aspect of the problem of motivation is the question of its origin and development. Early in the development of the field of social psychology considerable attention was given to establishing the "fundamental nature" of all men. Influenced by Darwinian theory, the concept of "instinct" reigned supreme in accounting for man's behavior. Not only the biological drives of man (hunger, thirst, sex, and so on) but, indeed, all complex social motives were, at root, inherited impulses to action. Developments in sociology and anthropology which clearly indicated that there were considerable variations among men in the nature of their complex social motives soon led to the demise of the instinct approach. It was replaced by the contemporary view of "man in culture" in which the fundamental assumption was that most, if not all, of man's enduring motivations were learned; and the task of explaining the exact nature of the learning process was left to the learning theorist.

In response to this assumption, two approaches emerged, both of which are in evidence in the present volume. The first seeks to determine the existing differences in needs, attitudes, and values as a function of variations in the group experiences of the individual. Of importance are not merely comparisons of individuals from different cultures but also of individuals within the same culture. Aside from its major objective, the study by Douvan (IIA) contributes to the already existing data that middle-class youth have greater achievement motivation (the desire to excel or do well for its own sake) than lower-class youth. Studies of this kind point to the significant social sources of variation in the behavior and motivations of individuals. The second approach is genetic in its orientation. It seeks to trace the development of a given need or attitude and to establish the actual conditions that foster its emergence. Other research on achievement motivation, for example, has provided evidence that differences in achievement motivation between lower- and middle-class youth can be traced to differences in child rearing and particularly in the independence training given the child (see Winterbottom, IVB).

Both psychoanalytic theory and anthropology have given considerable impetus to the genetic approach in the study of complex social motives. Each, of course, has made significant contributions to our understanding of motivational development; the former by its emphasis on the very early interaction experiences of the child in the family setting; and the other in focusing attention on the determining influence of the larger social setting in conditioning both the structure and the content of these interaction experiences. By the same token it is important to point out one consequence of this general approach, which for some time contaminated the general problem of analyzing the motivational basis of a person's behavior.

The consequence involves an unwarranted fusion between a motivational analysis of the behavior of a person in a given situation and the problem, as we stated it above, of understanding the development of the motivations of this person. For example, this would be the case if we attempted to explain the anti-Negro behavior of a person as we viewed it in the present by reference to the attitudes toward Negroes that prevailed in his family setting when he was a child. As Lewin (1936) has pointed out, only present conditions can have influence in the present. Furthermore, it should be stressed that motivations in the early life of the person undergo change and therefore are not identical with their occurrence in the person as an adult. Obviously a genetic analysis is important if we are to understand what motivations are characteristic of the person. However, the understanding of how these motivations influence behavior in the present requires an analysis of them as they exist in the present in relation to both the person and the existing social context.

This brings us to a second important consideration in the approach to motivation which has become increasingly characteristic of modern social psychology. The efficacy of the person's motive patterns, enduring or otherwise, in determining his behavior lies in their capacity for arousal by appropriate situational conditions. The prediction of the individual's behavior, therefore, requires a knowledge of both the person's motives or needs and the characteristic situational cues which give rise to them. In middle-class youth, for example, as the Douvan study demonstrates, the arousal of achievement motivation depends on the presence of cues that relate to success and failure experiences; in lower-class youth, on the other hand, such arousal shows a greater tie to cues relevant to obtaining material rewards for one's performance. In the situation in which both kinds of cues existed there was no difference between the two groups in the degree to which achievement motivation was aroused. There is, of course, still another question to be asked: Once aroused, what consequences does achievement motivation have for the behavior of the person? We would expect, for example, that performance in a task would be better under high achievement motivation than under low. This finding was, in fact, reported by McClelland, Atkinson, Clark, and Lowell (1953).

It should now be evident that, as distinguished from a genetic approach, a situational analysis of a need involves, on the one hand, establishing the conditions or factors in the situation which characteristically give rise to the need and, on the other, determining its effects on the behavior of the person. That each of these approaches to understanding motivation provides important leads for the other is well demonstrated by a series of studies of the need for affiliation reported by Schachter (1959). He found that, in a high-anxiety condition as compared with a low-anxiety condition, the individual had a stronger desire to affiliate with others who were similarly exposed. Furthermore, the affiliative tendency evoked by high anxiety was found to be significantly more characteristic of students who were first-born or only children than students who were later-born children. On the basis of this finding and additional analyses Schachter was able to suggest some important leads regarding the developmental factors that determine the intensity of affiliation under high-anxiety conditions.

So far we have discussed the development of needs and their influence on behavior in relevant situations. An important question to be asked is what needs should be studied. What are the important needs for understanding behavior in a complex society? Social psychologists have typically been concerned with the *content* of motivation. In general psychology, especially with regard to the approach of the learning theorist, motives are treated as functionally interchangeable, differing only in degree of intensity. The emphasis is on process rather than on content. Without denying the importance of process for the problem of understanding social behavior, the kind of motive involved in the person's behavior is no less significant. Knowledge about achievement motivation enables us to understand behavior in certain kinds of contexts, whereas for other contexts it may be more important to consider the person's need for power, or affiliation, or status. All these needs as well as others have been subjected to some degree of systematic study, and their selection is not by chance. Each has some importance for understanding the behavior of the person in relation to other individuals or in the group context, patently a major concern of the social psychologist.

The needs of a person do not exist in isolation from each other. The arousal of one need may have consequences for the arousal of others, as evidenced by Schachter's study wherein strong anxiety provoked a desire in a person to affiliate with other individuals in the same situation. Which needs are significant for the person and how they are related to each other depend on how the person conceives of himself as a social being. The concept of "self" has assumed increasing importance in the theory and research of the social psychologist. The person's early experiences with others in a variety of group settings lead him to conceive of himself in given ways, depending on what is demanded of him and how these others evaluate his responses to these demands. In brief, the person himself becomes the core of a cognitive structure that defines and evaluates who he is, what he is, and what he can do. Different individuals have different group experiences, and as a consequence variations occur in their conceptions of self and in their standards for evaluating themselves. The higher achievement motivation in middle-class youth reflects the influence of a self-conception in which doing well generally or for its own sake becomes the critical standard of self-evaluation. For individuals in the same group setting we also find important differences as well as similarities in these respects since they differ in their abilities and capacities, there previous success and failure experiences, and their status in the group. This means in turn that they will vary in the levels of success that they will pursue. The successes of one person may represent the failures of another.

Both psychoanalytic theory and experimental learning theory have had extensive influence on the thinking of psychologists in all fields about the nature of human motivation. Complex social motives are seen as rooted in the inherent bodily tensions of the organism, tensions, in effect, which provide the energy for all of man's social pursuits. In recent years, this view has been challenged on a number of grounds, one of which points to its limited conception of the nature of motivational process. In particular, the view ignores the cognitive capacities of man and their potential as a source of needs that move the individual to behave. What has been posited by a number of social psychologists is not only a need to know but, more importantly, a need for cognitive consistency (Festinger, 1957; Heider, 1958; Newcomb, 1959). A number of "balance theories" have emerged, which assume that discrepancies in the cognitions of the perceiver create "dissonance" or "strain" which motivates the person to think and behave in ways which will result in greater cognitive consistency. For example, a person's knowledge of the facts on smoking and lung cancer and his awareness that he himself smokes, represent inconsistent cognitions which may lead him to give up smoking, deny the validity of the facts on smoking and cancer, and so on. In recent years there has been a proliferation of investigations which have established the validity of the assumption that cognitive inconsistency may indeed motivate the behavior of the person. To what extent this kind of conception can explain the many complexities of social behavior and social interaction remains to be seen.

References

Asch, S. E. Forming impressions of personality. *J. abnorm. soc. Psychol.*, 1946, *41*, 258-290.

Festinger, L. *A theory of cognitive dissonance.* New York: Harper & Row, 1957.

Heider, F. Social perception and phenomenal causality. *Psychol. Rev.*, 1944, *51*, 358-374.

Heider, F. *The psychology of interpersonal relations.* New York: Wiley, 1958.

Levine, J. M., and Murphy, G. The learning and forgetting of controversial material. *J. abnorm. soc. Psychol.*, 1943, *38*, 507-517.

Lewin, K. *Principles of topological psychology.* New York: McGraw-Hill, 1936.

MacLeod, R. B. The phenomenological approach to social psychology. In J. H. Rohrer and M. Sherif (Eds.), *Social psychology at the crossroads.* New York: Harper & Row, 1950.

McClelland, D. C., Atkinson, J. W., Clark, R. A., and Lowell, E. L. *The achievement motive.* New York: Appleton-Century-Crofts, 1953.

Newcomb, T. M. Individual systems of orientation. In S. Koch (Ed.), *Psychology: a study of a science,* Vol. 3, *Formulations of the person and the social context.* New York: McGraw-Hill, 1959.

Schachter, S. *The psychology of affiliation: experimental studies of sources of gregariousness.* Stanford, Calif.: Stanford Univer. Press, 1959.

A. MOTIVATION

AND COGNITION

Social Factors in Recall ❧ Frederic Charles Bartlett

Experiments on Remembering: The Method of Repeated Reproduction

I have selected for special consideration a story which was adapted from a translation by Dr. Franz Boas (1901) of a North American folk-tale. Several reasons prompted the use of this story.

First, the story as presented belonged to a level of culture and a social environment exceedingly different from those of my subjects. Hence it seemed likely to afford good material for persistent transformation. I had also in mind the general problem of what actually happens when a popular story travels about from one social group to another, and thought that possibly the use of this story might throw some light upon the general conditions of transformation under such circumstances. It may fairly be said that this hope was at least to some extent realized.

Secondly, the incidents described in some of the cases had no very manifest interconnection, and I wished particularly to see how educated and rather sophisticated subjects would deal with this lack of obvious rational order.

Thirdly, the dramatic character of some of the events recorded seemed likely to arouse fairly vivid visual imagery in suitable subjects, and I thought perhaps further light might be thrown on some of the suggestions regarding the conditions and functions of imaging arising from the use of *The Method of Description.*°

Fourthly, the conclusion of the story might easily be regarded as introducing a supernatural element, and I desired to see how this would be dealt with.

The original story was as follows:

THE WAR OF THE GHOSTS

One night two young men from Egulac went down to the river to hunt seals, and while they were there it became foggy and calm. Then they heard war-cries, and they thought: "Maybe this is a war-party." They escaped to the shore, and hid behind a log. Now canoes came

° A method used earlier in the book, and not excerpted here.

From F. C. Bartlett, *Remembering* (Cambridge, England: Cambridge University Press, 1932). Reprinted by permission of the author and publisher.

up, and they heard the noise of paddles, and saw one canoe coming up to them. There were five men in the canoe, and they said:

"What do you think? We wish to take you along. We are going up the river to make war on the people."

One of the young men said: "I have no arrows."

"Arrows are in the canoe," they said.

"I will not go along. I might be killed. My relatives do not know where I have gone. But you," he said, turning to the other, "may go with them."

So one of the young men went, but the other returned home.

And the warriors went on up the river to a town on the other side of Kalama. The people came down to the water, and they began to fight, and many were killed. But presently the young man heard one of the warriors say: "Quick, let us go home: that Indian has been hit." Now he thought: "Oh, they are ghosts." He did not feel sick, but they said he had been shot.

So the canoes went back to Egulac, and the young man went ashore to his house, and made a fire. And he told everybody and said: "Behold I accompanied the ghosts, and we went to fight. Many of our fellows were killed, and many of those who attacked us were killed. They said I was hit, and I did not feel sick."

He told it all, and then he became quiet. When the sun rose he fell down. Something black came out of his mouth. His face became contorted. The people jumped up and cried.

He was dead.

Each subject read the story through to himself twice, at his normal reading rate. Except in the case which will be indicated later, the first reproduction was made 15 minutes after this reading. Other reproductions were effected at intervals as opportunity offered. No attempt was made to secure uniformity in the length of interval for all subjects; obviously equalizing intervals of any length in no way equalizes the effective conditions of reproduction in the case of different subjects. No subject knew the aim of the experiment. All who were interested in this were allowed to think that the test was merely one for accuracy of recall.

I shall analyze the results obtained in three ways:

First, a number of reproductions will be given in full, together with some comments;

Secondly, special details of interest in this particular story will be considered;

Thirdly, certain general or common tendencies in the successive remembering of the story will be stated and discussed more fully.

Some Complete Reproductions Together with Comments

After an interval of 20 hours subject H produced the following first reproduction:

THE WAR OF THE GHOSTS

Two men from Edulac went fishing. While thus occupied by the river they heard a noise in the distance.

"It sounds like a cry," said one, and presently there appeared some men in canoes who invited them to join the party on their adventure. One of the young men refused to go, on the ground of family ties, but the other offered to go.

"But there are no arrows," he said.

"The arrows are in the boat," was the reply.

He thereupon took his place, while his friend returned home. The party paddled up the river to Kaloma, and began to land on the banks of the river. The enemy came rushing upon them, and some sharp fighting ensued. Presently someone was injured, and the cry was raised that the enemy were ghosts.

The party returned down the stream, and the young man arrived home feeling none the worse for his experience. The next morning at dawn he endeavoured to recount his adventures. While he was talking something black issued from his mouth. Suddenly he uttered a cry and fell down. His friends gathered round him.

But he was dead.

In general form (1) the story is considerably shortened, mainly by omissions; (2) the phraseology becomes more modern, more "journalistic," e.g., "refused, on the ground of family ties"; "sharp fighting ensued"; "feeling none the worse for his adventures"; "something black issued from his mouth"; (3) the story has already become somewhat more coherent and consequential than in its original form.

In matter there are numerous omissions and some transformations. The more familiar "boat" once replaces "canoe"; hunting seals becomes merely "fishing"; Egulac becomes Edulac, while Kalama changes to Kaloma. The main point about the ghosts is entirely misunderstood. The two excuses made by the man who did not wish to join the warparty change places; that "he refused on the ground of family ties" becomes the only excuse explicitly offered.

Eight days later this subject remembered the story as follows:

THE WAR OF THE GHOSTS

Two young men from Edulac went fishing. While thus engaged they heard a noise in the distance. "That sounds like a war-cry," said one, "there is going to be some fighting." Presently there appeared some warriors who invited them to join an expedition up the river.

One of the young men excused himself on the ground of family ties. "I cannot come," he said, "as I might get killed." So he returned home. The other man, however, joined the party, and they proceeded in canoes up the river. While landing on the banks the enemy appeared and were running down to meet them. Soon someone was wounded, and the party discovered that they were fighting against ghosts. The young man and his companion returned to the boats, and went back to their homes.

The next morning at dawn he was describing his adventures to his friends, who had gathered round him. Suddenly something black issued from his mouth, and he fell down uttering a cry. His friends closed around him, but found that he was dead.

All the tendencies to change manifested in the first reproduction now seem to be more marked. The story has become still more concise, still more coherent. The proper name Kaloma has disappeared, and the lack of arrows, put into the second place a week earlier, has now dropped out completely. On the other hand a part of the other excuse: "I might get killed," now comes back into the story, though it found no place in the first version. It is perhaps odd that the friend, after having returned home, seems suddenly to come back into the story again when the young man is wounded. But this kind of confusion of connected incidents is a common characteristic of remembering.

Experiments on Remembering: The Method of Serial Reproduction

Methods for studying remembering often deal with factors influencing individual observers. They help to show what occurs when a person makes use of some new material which he meets, assimilating it and later reproducing it in his own characteristic manner. Already it is clear, however, that several of the factors influencing the individual observer are social in origin and character. For example, many of the transformations which took place as a result of the repeated reproduction of prose passages were directly due to the influence of social conventions and beliefs current in the group to which the individual subject belonged. In the actual remembering of daily life the importance of these social factors is greatly intensified. The form which a rumor, or a story, or a decorative design, finally assumes within a given social group is the work of many different successive social reactions. Elements of culture, or cultural complexes, pass from person to person within a group, or from group to group, and, eventually reaching a thoroughly conventionalized form, may take an established place in the general mass of culture possessed by a specific group. Whether we deal with an institution, a mode of conduct, a story, or an art-form, the conventionalized product varies from group to group, so that it may come to be the very characteristic we use when we wish most sharply to differentiate one social group from another. In this way, cultural characters which have a common origin may come to have apparently the most diverse forms.

The experiments now to be described were designed to study the effects of the combination of changes brought about by many different individuals. The results produced are not entirely beyond the range of experimental research, as I shall show, and the main method which I have used is best called *The Method of Serial Reproduction.*

In its material form this method is simply a reduplication of *The Method of Repeated Reproduction.* The only difference is that A's reproduction is now itself reproduced by B, whose version is subsequently dealt with by C, and so on. In this way chains of reproduction were obtained: (1) of folk-stories, (2) of descriptive and argumentative prose passages and (3) of picture material. The folk-stories were used, as before, because they are predominantly a type of material which passes very rapidly from one social group to another; because most subjects regard them as interesting in themselves; because stories can easily be chosen which were fashioned in a social environment very different from that of any social group that is likely to yield subjects for a given experiment; and because, both as to form and as to content, they undergo much change in the course of transmission. The descriptive and argumentative passages were used be-

cause they represent a type of material with which all the subjects of these experiments were already familiar, so that they would provide some kind of check, or control, upon the results with the folk-tales. The picture material was used, because the transmission of picture forms has constantly occurred in the development of decorative and realistic art, and in order to see whether the same principles of change would operate in spite of the difference of medium dealt with.

In the case of the verbal passages, each subject read the material twice through, to himself, at his normal reading pace. Reproduction was effected after a filled interval of 15-30 minutes. In the case of the picture forms, a subject was allowed adequate time for observation, and he effected his reproduction after a similar interval.

So far as the two chains of reproduction already considered go, it appears that, under the conditions of the experiment, the following are the main types of transformation likely to occur:

1. There will be much general simplification, due to the omission of material that appears irrelevant, to the construction gradually of a more coherent whole, and to the changing of the unfamiliar into some more familiar counterpart.
2. There will be persistent rationalization, both of a whole story and of its details, until a form is reached which can be readily dealt with by all the subjects belonging to the special social group concerned. This may result in considerable elaboration.
3. There will be a tendency for certain incidents to become dominant, so that all the others are grouped about them.

It also seems probable that a cumulative form of story favors the retention of the general series of incidents with little change, and that whatever causes amusement is likely to be remembered and preserved. It may be to this last factor that the preservation of the novel in a commonplace setting is largely due.

Social Psychology and the Matter of Recall

First, then, I propose to consider a few typical cases in which memory appears to be directly influenced by social facts. I shall discuss the psychological explanation of these instances, and, following this, I shall draw certain tentative conclusions bearing upon the psychological significance of social organization, so far as remembering is concerned.

Some years ago the Paramount Chief of the Swazi people, accompanied by several of his leading men, visited England for the purpose of attempting to obtain a final settlement of a long-standing land dispute. When the party returned, there was naturally some curiosity among the British settlers in Swaziland concerning what were the main points of recall by the native group of their visit to England. The one thing that remained most firmly and vividly fixed in the recollection of the Swazi chiefs was their picture of the English policeman, regulating the road traffic with uplifted hand.

Why should this simple action have made so profound an impression? Certainly not merely because it was taken as a symbol of power. Many other illustrations of power, far more striking to the European mind, had been seen and, for all practical purposes, forgotten. The Swazi greets his fellow, or his visitor, with uplifted hand. Here was the familiar gesture, warm with friendliness in a foreign country, and at the same time arresting in its consequences. It was one of the few things they saw that fitted immediately into their own well-established social framework, and so it produced a quick impression and a lasting effect.

I take another case from the same community. Even acute observers often assert of the Swazi the same kind of observation that has been made of the Bantu in general: "The Bantu mind is endowed with a wonderful memory (Junod, 1927)." Yet this sort of statement never seems to have been submitted to any careful experimental test.[1] If such tests were carried out, it would most certainly be found that individual differences are about as pronounced as they are in a European community, and, a fact more to our present purpose, that the lines of accurate and full recall are very largely indeed, just as they are with us, a matter of social organization, with its accepted scales of value.

I myself, having listened to numerous stories about the marvelous word-perfect memory of the Swazi from his childhood up, and having been credibly informed that I could test these stories, with complete certainty of confirmation, upon any person I liked, arranged a simple experiment. Choosing at random a boy of eleven or twelve years of age, a native interpreter and myself concocted a brief message of about twenty-five words which the boy was to take from one end to another of a village. The journey took him about two minutes. The message was given to him very carefully twice over, and he did not know that he was being kept under observation. He was given a lively inducement to be accurate. He delivered the message with three important omissions, doing certainly no better than an English boy of the same age might do. Several times also I tried, with natives of varied ages and both sexes, common observation and description tests, something like the ones I have already recorded in this book, but with modifications so as to make them of greater intrinsic interest to a native observer. The results were much the same as they would have

[1] It seems very curious that, while a mass of excellent experimental observation has been carried out upon the special sense reactions of relatively primitive people (see, e.g., *Report of the Cambridge expedition to the Torres Straits*, Cambridge, 1903), little controlled investigation has been made upon their higher mental processes. Yet the latter would almost certainly reveal many extremely interesting results, and might go far to correct current views with regard to profound differences of mental life between civilized and uncivilized peoples.

been for similar tests in a typical European group, neither better nor worse.

Nevertheless, it is not difficult to show that the common belief has some ground. For example, once, when I was talking with a prominent Scottish settler in Swaziland who has an extensive and sound knowledge of the native, he repeated the usual stories of exceedingly accurate and detailed memory. I told him of my own tests, and he at once agreed that his assertions held good only provided the native were taken in his own preferred fields of interest. Now most Swazi culture revolves around the possession and care of cattle. Cattle are the center of many of the most persistent and important social customs. The settler himself suggested a test case. He guaranteed that his herdsman would give me a prompt and absolutely literal description of all the cattle which he, the owner, had bought a year earlier. The herdsman had been with him while the transactions were completed, and had then driven the beasts back to the main farm. Immediately after the purchase, the cattle had been dispersed to different places and the herdsman had seen them no more. The settler himself had his own written records of the deals, and naturally could not himself remember the details without looking them up. It was arranged that he should not himself look at his records, or interview the herdsman. At the moment, the native was found to be at a "beer-drink," and inaccessible in more ways than one. The next day, however, the man was sent to me. He walked some twenty miles and brought with him the sealed book of accounts, which, in any case, he was not able to read. He knew nothing whatever of the reason for his journey. I asked him for a list of the cattle bought by his employer the year previously, together with whatever detail he cared to give. Squatting on the ground, apparently wholly unmoved, he rapidly recited the list. This was as follows:

> From Magama Sikindsa, one black ox for £4;

> From Mloyeni Sifundra, one young black ox for £2;

> From Mbimbi Maseko, one young black ox, with a white brush to its tail, for £2;

> From Gampoka Likindsa, one young white bull, with small red spots, for £1;

> From Mapsini Ngomane and Mpohlonde Maseko, one red cow, one black heifer, one very young black bull for £3 in all;

> From Makanda, one young gray ox, about two years old, for £3;

> From Lolalela, one spotted five year old cow, white and black, for £3, which was made up of two bags of grain and £1;

> From Mampini Mavalane, one black polly cow, with gray on the throat, for £3;

> From Ndoda Kadeli, one young red heifer, the calf of a red cow, and with a white belly, for £1.

My notes, made at the time, say that the herdsman, a native of something over forty years, "showed no hesitation, no apparent interest, and certainly no excitement. He seemed to be reciting a well-known exercise and in no way reconstructing the deals on the basis of a few definitely remembered details."

The list was correct in every detail but two. The price of the second black ox mentioned was £1. 10s., and the "black" heifer from Mpohlonde Maseko was described in the book as "red." Against these trifling errors, it must be remembered that the herdsman had himself no say in the price of the beasts, and had merely overheard the bargains made by his master; and further that native color names are apt to be rather widely ambiguous.

It seems certain that this was in no way an isolated and remarkable case. The Swazi herdsman has generally an accurate and prodigiously retentive capacity to recall the individual characteristics of his beasts. An animal may stray and get mixed up with other herds. It may be away for a very long time. However long the interval, if the owner comes with a description of the missing beast, his word is almost never questioned, and he is peaceably allowed to drive the animal back. It is true, that, in spite of this, cattle were formerly all earmarked—a custom that appears to have fallen into disuse except in the case of the Royal herds— but altogether apart from these special marks, by common consent, the native herdsman always remembers his beasts individually.

And why should he not? Just as the policeman's uplifted hand was noteworthy because of the familiar social background, so the individual peculiarities of the cattle can be recalled freshly and vividly, because herds, and all dealings with them, are of tremendous social importance.

We can now see the general psychology underlying the way in which social conditions settle the matter of individual recall. Every social group is organized and held together by some specific psychological tendency or group of tendencies, which give the group a bias in its dealings with external circumstances. The bias constructs the special persistent features of group culture, its technical and religious practices, its material art, its traditions and institutions; and these again, once they are established, become themselves direct stimuli to individual response within the group. Perhaps, in some so far unexplained way, the social bias of the group may work its way, by actual inheritance, into at least some of the individual members; perhaps all that happens is that it appears in the individual through the pervasive influence of one of the many forms of social suggestion. In any case, it does immediately settle what the individual will observe in his environment, and what he will connect from his past life with this direct response. It does this markedly in two ways. First, by providing that setting of interest, excitement and emotion which favors the development of specific images, and secondly, by providing a persistent framework of institutions and customs which acts as a schematic basis for constructive memory.

Social Psychology and the Manner of Recall

I shall state briefly three principles. I do this with great hesitation. Others could perhaps be derived from the general discussion. In an uncharted realm like the present one, any tentative expression of laws can do no more than form a basis for a further exploration of the relevant facts. The principles, such as they are, must stand or fall as more facts become known. What is beyond dispute is that remembering, in a group, is influenced, as to its manner, directly by the preferred persistent tendencies of that group.

1. In whatever field, where social organization has no specifically directed organizing tendencies, but only a group of interests, all about equally dominant, recall is apt to be of the rote recapitulatory type. This very often is the case over a wide field of daily happenings in the primitive group.
2. Whenever there are strong, preferred, persistent, specific, social tendencies, remembering is apt to appear direct, and as if it were a way of reading off from a copy, and there is a minimum of irrelevance. It may perhaps be that this is due to the adoption of a direct image type of recall, supplemented by the help of prevailing social "schemata" which take the form of persistent customs.
3. Whenever strong, preferred, persistent, social tendencies are subjected to any form of forcible social control (e.g., are disapproved by an incoming superior people, or are opposed to the general immediate trend of social development in the group), social remembering is very apt to take on a constructive and inventive character, either wittingly or unwittingly. Its manner then tends to become assertive, rather dogmatic and confident, and recall will probably be accompanied by excitement and emotion.

Each of these principles has found illustration in the preceding discussion. Obviously they all stand in need of further differentiation before, some day, the whole story of the social control of remembering can be written.

References

BOAS, F. Kathlamet texts. *Bulletin 26, Bureau of American Ethnology,* 1901, 182-184.

JUNOD, H. A. *The life of a South African tribe,* Vol. II. London: Macmillan, 1927.

The Learning and Utilization ❧ Edward E. Jones

of Contravaluant Material ❧ Jane Aneshansel

During the past two decades, there have been several attempts to investigate the effects of attitude, set, and frame of reference on the learning of meaningful prose material. The general form of these studies has involved the comparison by various measures of immediate and delayed recall, of groups known or presumed to differ in their attitude toward the content of the material to be learned. In an early study, Laird (1923) found that optimistic Ss recall significantly more pleasant items than did pessimistic Ss. Widely separated studies by Clark (1940) and Alper and Korchin (1952) have both explored differences between the recall by males and females of controversial prose material presumably relevant to attitudes determined by sex identification. Both studies resulted in differences between recall scores of males and females which were interpretable in terms of the material presented. Watson and Hartmann (1939) found that theistic and atheistic students tended to remember better material supporting their "attitudinal frame," although most of the differences in their study

were not statistically significant. With a larger group of Ss and a more sensitive method of quantitative analysis, Edwards (1941) came to the same general conclusion with regard to Ss differing in their attitude to the New Deal. The most familiar study in this vein is the clear-cut demonstration by Levine and Murphy (1943) that prose which is congenial either to pro-communists or to anti-communists is more rapidly learned and more slowly forgotten than prose which presents arguments running counter to the S's attitudinal bias.

In general, considering the difficulties involved in the reliable assessment of relevant attitudes, the assumption that we more easily learn that which is congenial to our own views appears to have fairly solid empirical support. While previous authors have generally been cautious in generalizing their findings to other attitudes in other learning situations, it has become convenient to stress the autistic nature of meaningful learning at the expense of other motivational effects which may operate to inhibit or actually reverse the outcome predicted by a simple

From the *Journal of Abnormal and Social Psychology,* 1956, 53, 27-33. Reprinted by permission of the authors and the American Psychological Association.

autism theory. This paradox has been recognized by many of the students of social perception who have explored the polar mechanisms of perceptual defense and perceptual vigilance. To resolve this paradox, the functionalist might suggest that we examine the total context in which perception (or learning) takes place, in an effort to determine those conditions which promote lowered thresholds for threatening material (perceptual vigilance) and those which promote heightened thresholds (perceptual defense). On the basis of our analysis of these conditions we should be able to decide whether defense or vigilance will have greater functional utility in a given situation, and to predict the corresponding direction in threshold variation.

If we assume a continuity between perception, learning, and retention (and we would be in good company in doing so), there must be conditions under which the learning counterpart of perceptual vigilance will occur. It is somewhat surprising that as yet no one has thought to explore the conditions under which uncongenial or contravaluant material is successfully learned. It is rather easy to think of exceptions to the proposition that our minds are furnished largely with covaluant ideas. One need merely think of the political campaigner digging into his opponent's record, or the intelligence agent plotting the course of Soviet diplomacy, or the liberal who quotes *Time* magazine with shocked bitterness, to appreciate that we do not always surround ourselves with ideological yes-men. It is obviously an important psychological question, however, whether our pains to learn an opponent's views are rewarded with accurate learning and retention, and whether the conditions under which such learning is facilitated may be specified.

The present paper attempts to evaluate the effectiveness of a particular set of conditions in promoting the learning of contravaluant or uncongenial prose sentences. In brief outline, we propose to test the hypothesis that Ss who are presumed to disagree with a set of statements will actually learn them better than Ss who agree when retention of the statements serves a particular function in a later part of the experiment. Specifically, when Ss are told that they will be asked to provide appropriate counterarguments for prosegregation statements, prosegregation Ss will learn a set of antisegregation statements *better* than antisegregation Ss. In keeping with the traditional argument, however, antisegregaion Ss should learn more antisegregation statements when there is no anticipation of a counterargument task.

Method

Subjects. A 10-item Likert-type scale was devised for the experiment as a measure of attitudes toward segregation. The scale was pretested on 151 introductory psychology students and one item was subsequently modified because it showed a poor correlation with total score. The final form of the scale was administered to 147 different introductory students and the scores ranged from 61 (out of a theoretically possible high of 70) to 15 (out of a possible low of 10). The distribution of scores was approximately normal for both groups. While the segregation questionnaires were filled out anonymously, the 20 highest and 20 lowest Ss were reliably identified by other data and were successfully approached to serve as Ss in the apparently unrelated experiment. The scores of the prosegregation Ss (hereafter called "pros") ranged from 61 to 38; the scores of the antisegregation Ss (hereafter called "antis") ranged from 15 to 22.

Segregation Attitude Scale. Each of the 10 items of the segregation scale was explicitly related to the segregation issue. Although the scale itself was unlabeled, no special pains were taken to disguise intent because of the nature of our sample. The origins of the Duke student body are geographically diverse (with slightly over half coming from states in which segregation is sanctioned and practiced), the issue of segregation is a lively one on the campus, and there is no clearly specified college norm which would promote the uniform denial of prosegregation statements. Five of the scale items were slanted in the prosegregation direction (e.g., "Any attempt to deal with segregation ignores the oft proven maxim that you can't legislate morals") and five were slanted in the antisegregation direction (e.g., "The Negroes' major concern is with equal educational and economic opportunities. They have no intentions of interfering with the social patterns of the white community").

The validity of the scale is one of the issues at stake in the experiment itself, of course, but there are two independent sources of evidence that suggest that the scale is sufficiently valid for the purposes of the study. The original pretest group of 151 Ss was simultaneously administered a combined version of the California Ethnocentrism and Anti-Semitism scales (with some additional pro-Semitic items included to break any response set). This combined scale—the majority of whose items deal with attitudes towards Jews—correlated .41 with the segregation scale. Perhaps more revealing, in terms of validity, is the finding that the mean segregation-scale score of Northerners (29.7) differs significantly ($p < .01$) from the mean segregation score of Southerners (35.4). This contrast is in spite of the fact that the general prejudice scores of the two groups are indistinguishable (89.5 vs. 89.6). It would seem legitimate to assume that the Ss selected for the experiment itself had rather consistent beliefs either for or against segregation.

Experimental Procedure. Each of the 40 Ss individually attempted to learn 11 brief statements which were clearly loaded in the direction of arguing against segregation. The statements were printed on individual cards, and each S was instructed to read each card aloud at normal reading speed. After all 11 statements had been read in this manner, the S was asked to reproduce as many statements as he could remember.

This identical procedure was repeated for a total of five trials. The order of the statements differed randomly on each trial, but the order was constant across Ss. All attempts at reproduction were transferred verbatim to specially devised recording sheets in order to minimize recording error. In addition, the experimenter was usually unaware of whether a particular S was pro- or antisegregation.

After the five learning trials, each S was presented with a list of 11 prosegregation statements, and asked to provide appropriate counterarguments for each statement as rapidly as possible. Finally, each S was asked to match each pro- with each antisegregation statement, and told to indicate which of the statements came closer to his own beliefs.

While all of the Ss followed this same general procedure, half of the Ss (10 "pros" and 10 "antis") were forewarned that they would be asked to provide counterarguments for prosegregation statements. These Ss will be hereafter designated as the *experimental group.* Since the precise nature of the instructions to this group is important in evaluating the experiment, they are reproduced below:

"This is going to be an experiment to see how well you can think up appropriate counterarguments for controversial statements. You will be presented with a number of statements which all argue more or less in favor of segregation. Your task will be to look at each statement in turn, read it aloud, and then give me an appropriate counterargument. . . . (They were then provided with an example of a statement and its counterargument.) . . . Before getting on with the main part of the experiment, I am first going to show you some antisegregation statements like the ones you may want to use as counterarguments. Your first job is to learn *these* statements as quickly and completely as you can. Remember, you may want to use some of the statements in the main part of the experiment later on, so it will pay to learn these statements."

The other half of the Ss (the *control group*) were simply instructed to learn the antisegregation statements. No reference was made to the possible use of these statements in a subsequent part of the experiment. As indicated above, however, all Ss actually were eventually placed in the same position of using the statements as counterarguments.

The following examples illustrate the kind of statements which the Ss were originally asked to learn. Each antisegregation statement is followed by its appropriate counterargument (as determined by the consensus of several graduate student judges). The counterargument, of course, only appeared along with other counterarguments during the second phase of the experiment.

1. The issue of Negro-White integrated education has nothing to do with racial intermarriage. *Counterargument:* The Negro mulatto is a symbol of what would happen after desegregation.
2. The Negro points up the greatest disparity between the theory and our practice of democracy. *Counterargument:* The democratic philosophy includes the right to associate with whomever you please.

No claims need be made for the logical or empirical validity of any of these statements since they were intentionally stated in somewhat controversial form.

Results

THE LEARNING OF CONTROVERSIAL STATEMENTS

The major analysis involved scoring for accuracy each reproduction attempt for each S for each trial. The 11 antisegregation statements were broken down into 22 idea units and these in turn were scored for accuracy in terms of the following three categories: 1, the idea unit is identical to the original, or modified only in some incidental way (e.g., the S says "because of" whereas the original reads "a function of"); 2, the idea unit is identical in meaning to the orig-

inal, though it may vary in phraseology, through the use of synonyms, etc. (e.g., the S says "integrating the Negroes with the whites in education" whereas the original reads "Negro-White integrated education"); 3, the idea unit clearly conveys a different meaning than was intended by the original. Ten randomly selected response protocols (consisting of 632 idea units) were independently scored by a second rater. There was 89 per cent agreement on item placement.

The major hypothesis to be tested is that the Experimental "pros" will learn more idea units than the Experimental "antis," and the Control "antis" will learn more idea units than the Control "pros." In order to test this hypothesis, units learned were placed in a 2 (for replicated Ss) by 2 (for conditions) by 5 (for trials) factorial design and, following Lindquist (1953), a Type III analysis of variance was conducted. Three separate analyses were made, covering respectively the number of units exactly reproduced (Scoring Category 1), those which were reproduced with unchanged meaning (Category 1 + 2), and total units tried (1 + 2 + 3). These three analyses were conducted in order to test the hypothesis under investigation at different levels of accuracy.

Turning first to the analysis based on the very stringent accuracy criterion of Category 1, the over-all means (combining trials) indicate a slight tendency toward the predicted interaction but the F ratio is far from significant. As Table 1 shows, however, there is a significant triple interaction between Ss, trials, and conditions. Figure 1 reveals that this is a function of clear-cut fluctuations in the relations between the four cell means from trial to trial. Trials 3 and 5 provide the clearest example of the predicted interaction between Ss and conditions, but separate single analyses of variance for these trials result in moderate but nonsignificant interactions.

When Category 1 is combined with Category 2 to provide a still meaningful but less stringent measure of accuracy of reproduc-

TABLE 1

Learning at Three Levels of Accuracy
("Pros" vs. "Antis" under Experimental and Control Conditions,
Analysis of Variance)

Source	df	Stringency of Accuracy Criterion					
		Score 1		Score 1 + 2		Score 1 + 2 + 3 (Total Tried)	
		MEAN SQUARE	F	MEAN SQUARE	F	MEAN SQUARE	F
Between Ss	39						
A: Conditions	1	9.68	—	19.84	—	30.42	—
B: Attitude	1	.02	—	.24	—	1.62	—
A × B	1	52.00	1.10	315.01	6.39°	233.28	6.42°
Error	36	47.34		49.34		36.35	
Within	160						
C: Trials	4	465.09	112.48°°	687.49	214.18°°	674.28	156.93°°
A × C	4	.84	—	1.73	—	.66	—
B × C	4	2.34	—	1.01	—	.63	—
A × B × C	4	12.45	3.01°	5.12	1.60	1.42	—
Error	144	4.13		3.21		4.30	
Total	199						

° $p < .05$.
°° $p < .01$.

tion, the analysis of variance provides positive confirmation of the main hypothesis. As Table 1 and Fig. 1 show, at every trial Ex-

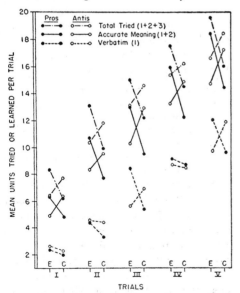

Fig. 1. Mean units tried or learned at two levels of accuracy per trial. Prosegregationists vs. antisegregationists under experimental (E) and control (C) conditions.

perimental "pros" learn more antisegregation units than Experimental "antis," and Control "pros" learn *less* than Control "antis." Except for the marked improvement in score as a function of trials, no other interaction or main effect is significant, and the application of Bartlett's test shows that the variances in each cell are homogeneous. Within conditions, t tests reveal a significant ($p < .05$) difference between "pros" and "antis" under experimental but not under control conditions.

Since the second analysis of variance resulted in a significant interaction, it is only of incidental importance that the third analysis of variance (dealing with the total number of units tried) resulted in almost identical F ratios for all main effects and interactions, and the main effect of trials plus the conditions by Ss interactions are again the only significant sources of variance. A glance at Fig. 1 tells us that Ss seldom responded incorrectly if they responded at all, and the fact that the slopes indicating the shift in mean as a function of conditions are uniformly parallel suggests that nothing would have been gained by devising a ratio score reflecting the percentage of accurate reproductions out of the total tried. In other words, reproduction errors were apparently distributed randomly across trials, conditions, and S groups.

In general, then, the analyses offer strong support for the main hypothesis of the study if we use a "meaningful" rather than a strictly verbatim criterion of accuracy. One apparent reason why the predicted interaction is significant under the lenient but not the stringent criterion of accuracy is that summing Categories 1 and 2 naturally results in a greater range of scores than Category 1 alone, thus providing a more reliable quantitative estimate of recall. However, a more purely psychological factor may also be operating to attenuate the predicted interaction under stringent accuracy conditions. Doob (1953) found that whereas Ss tended to recall an equivalent number of congruent vs. incongruent paragraphs, a percentage measure of recall accuracy based on individual statements showed that items with which the S agreed were recalled more correctly than incongruent statements. Thus it may be that strict accuracy of recall is determined largely by one's attitude toward the material and is not as subject to modification by variation in motivating instructions as the total amount learned as judged by less stringent criteria. Nevertheless, it should be pointed out that the more lenient $(1 + 2)$ measure of accuracy, which results in confirmation of the prediction in the present case, is very much a measure of "effective accuracy" since the meaning of the statement had to be preserved without modification to receive a score of 2.

In any event, conditions may apparently be established which can effectively reverse the customary conclusion that Ss will show better learning of congenial than uncongenial material. It is remotely possible that the present results reflect sampling errors in recruiting 10 Ss for each cell. It may be, for example, that the "pros" who ended up in the Experimental group were more intelligent, or more rapid and retentive readers than the Control "pros." This would not appear to be the case, if we can place any confidence in Total ACE scores as a measure of intelligence. While the "pros" do differ reliably from the "antis" in Total ACE (the difference between scores favoring the "antis," $p < .05$), there are no such differences in reading skill, or in either reading or total scores of the Experimental versus the Control "pros."

THE UTILIZATION OF STATEMENTS AS COUNTERARGUMENTS

The primary purpose for presenting prosegregation statements to the Ss and eliciting appropriate counterarguments was to fulfill the conditions of the experiment for the Ss. However, we thought it was possible that "pros" and "antis" would differ in the appropriateness of the argument chosen, and that perhaps the "antis" would show a less heavy reliance on the antisegregation statements learned. A scoring system similar to that used on the learning data was applied to the counterarguments chosen by the Ss. Five instead of three scoring categories were devised in an attempt to gain a more sensitive measure of variations in the kind of statement chosen as a counterargument:

1. Entire statement essentially correct;
2. In spite of changes in phrasing, the meaning of the statement is correct;
3. The statement is appropriate but novel or creative;
4. An earlier learned statement is inappropriately applied;
5. Nonsense statements and garbled versions are produced.

A series of 2×2 analyses of variance were conducted for each category and for various meaningful combinations of them, and the results are inconclusive. In eight separate analyses, not a single main effect or interaction was significant. There is a consistent, but never significant, tendency for the antisegregationists to be more "creative" under experimental conditions. Aside from this, there is little consistency in these data.

When the Ss were permitted to examine both lists of statements simultaneously and asked to match appropriate counterarguments, there were only a few "errors" in the entire sample of 40 Ss. The fact that 24 out of 40 Ss had completely correct matches supports the validity of our a priori selection of meaningful opposites. Perhaps because of the over-all high level of accuracy, there were no significant group differences in matching errors.

The final task for the Ss, it will be remembered, involved circling the alternative in each pair of counterarguments which best reflected their attitude. It should be noted that whether or not a "pro" indicates a preference for prosegregation statements is a relevant but far from decisive test of the validity of the segregation scale and the appropriateness of the statements to be learned. The task of circling the preferred statement was completed under conditions of surveillance and nonanonymity, and furthermore, the statements were generally stated in an extreme form, so a clear-cut reflection of true attitude would not be expected. It is not surprising, therefore, that the modal number of Ss circled 9 antisegregation statements and 2 prosegregation statements. With the exception of the 9 out of 40 Ss in this modal group, however, there is practically no overlap between "antis" and "pros." Application of the nonparametric Median Test results in a highly significant difference between prosegregation and antisegregation Ss in the relative tendency to check prosegregation statements. The fact that this difference appeared is encouraging evidence for the validity of the attitude scale and also for our assumption that the statements would be relatively more congenial to one group than to the other.

Discussion

The results of the present experiment indicate that under certain conditions, Ss who disagree with a set of statements will actually learn them better than Ss who agree with the statements. This conclusion complicates the picture presented by those who favor consistent explanations in terms of need-relevant perceptual and mnemonic selectivity. The traditional interpretations of meaningful learning which stress autism, perceptual selectivity, or congruence with the learner's frame of reference, receive support under the standard control conditions of the present experiment, but a rather slight modification in experimental instructions is sufficient to reverse the conventionally predicted relationship. It would appear, then, that we tend to be autistic in the retention of congenial material under conditions of low motivation and circumscribed time span. When the stakes are raised and the context of behavior is enlarged by increasing the instrumental significance of learning contravaluant material, something like vigilance appears. For the prosegregationist under the experimental conditions, the comfort of surrounding himself with congenial ideas is pitted against the comfort of performing well the stated experimental task. In this particular instance the latter factor won out. When the contravaluant material is given a new utility for the learner, the wish that is otherwise autistically pampered is supplanted by more powerful motives of ego-enhancement (subsuming implicit competition with other Ss as well as the hope of a kind word of reward from the experimenter). While this interpretation supplements the restricted theories of autism and covaluant selectivity, it neither supplants nor contradicts such theories. In particular, the present results support the functionalistic or pragmatic notion that we learn best that which is instrumental to adaptation and survival.

The interpretation outlined above would hold equally well if the predicted differences observed between "pros" and "antis" in the Control group were merely eliminated under the experimental instructions. But why should the "pros" actually surpass the "antis" in the learning of antisegregation material? The clue to this paradox, we suggest, lies in the general contention that different individuals can be differentially motivated by the same set of instructions. We assume that both "pros" and "antis" are about equally motivated to do well in the experiment—i.e., they both want to prepare themselves for the task of countering prosegregation arguments with appropriate antisegregation statements. While the "antis" presumably come trained and primed for such a task, the "pros" face the prospect of adducing contravaluant arguments like a nervous understudy rushed on stage to play an unfamiliar character type. Since the "anti" comes to the experiment more confidently familiar with the arguments which favor his cause, he is less inclined to view the initial learning task as a critical prerequisite for the fulfillment of the main experimental requirement. The "pro," on the other hand, is forced to rely on rote learning in order to comply with the experimental task and therefore he does a better job in memorizing the presented antisegregation statements. There is some empirical support for this otherwise plausible interpretation in the fact that the "antis" did tend to be more "creative" in their final rebuttals than the "pros," but this tendency was neither striking nor statistically reliable.

If we had introduced a third condition in which an extrinsic monetary reward was promised for successful learning, the same results would not be predicted. Assuming that the proposed monetary reinforcement was sufficient to raise the level of motivation to a high level in all Ss, we would predict an absence of any differences in learning between the two attitudinal groups—or rather, those differences that did exist would be a function of ability ceiling and not attitude. The reversal effect obtained in the present experiment is dependent on more subtle reinforcement potentials intrinsically relevant to the task at hand. What we apparently have in the present case is the operation of self-instructions or covert sets (Postman and Senders, 1946) which involve different interpretations of the overt instructions. The "pros" and the "antis" are both motivated to attain the same goal, but they tell themselves different ways to achieve it.

Summary

The assumption that we tend to learn statements that we agree with better than statements with which we disagree must be placed in the broader context of the learner's over-all purpose in the task. An experiment was conducted in which prosegregation and antisegregation Ss were asked to learn a series of antisegregation statements. Half of the Ss proceeded under the assumption that these same statements could well be used as counterarguments for prosegregation statements to be presented in a subsequent portion of the experiment. The remainder of the Ss were simply asked to learn the statements as well as possible. The results demonstrate quite conclusively that prosegregationists will learn antisegregation statements *better* than antisegregationists when a subsequent debate is anticipated. Without such an anticipation, however, the customary finding holds—i.e., the antisegregationists make better progress than the prosegregationists in learning the congenial material. No significant differences were found with regard to the utilization of antisegregation counterarguments in the debating task. The results were interpreted in terms of the differential availability of means to complete the experimental task. Since the antisegregationists are initially better prepared to fulfill the ultimate experimental requirement, they are less highly motivated to learn the congenial statements when a debate is anticipated.

References

ALPER, THELMA G., and KORCHIN, S. J. Memory for socially relevant material. *J. abnorm. soc. Psychol.*, 1952, 47, 25-37.

CLARK, K. B. Some factors influencing the remembering of prose material. *Arch. Psychol.*, N. Y., 1940, 36, No. 253.

DOOB, L. W. Effects of initial serial position and attitude upon recall under conditions of low motivation. *J. abnorm. soc. Psychol.*, 1953, 48, 199-205.

EDWARDS, A. L. Political frames of reference as a factor influencing recognition. *J. abnorm. soc. Psychol.*, 1941, 36, 34-50.

LAIRD, D. A. The influence of likes and dislikes on memory as related to personality. *J. exp. Psychol.*, 1923, 6, 294-303.

LEVINE, J. M. and MURPHY, G. The learning and forgetting of controversial material. *J. abnorm. soc. Psychol.*, 1943, 38, 507-515.

LINDQUIST, E. F. *Design and analysis of experiments in psychology and education.* Boston: Houghton Mifflin, 1953.

POSTMAN, L., and SENDERS, VIRGINIA L. Incidental learning and generality of set. *J. exp. Psychol.*, 1946, 36, 153-165.

WATSON, W. S., and HARTMANN, G. W. The rigidity of a basic attitudinal frame. *J. abnorm. soc. Psychol.*, 1939, 34, 314-335.

The Basic Psychology of Rumor ❧ Gordon W. Allport

❧ Leo J. Postman

Rumors in Wartime

During the year 1942, rumor became a national problem of considerable urgency. Its first dangerous manifestation was felt soon after the initial shock of Pearl Harbor. This traumatic event dislocated our normal channels of communication by bringing into existence an unfamiliar and unwelcome, if at the same time a relatively mild, censorship of news, and it simultaneously dislocated the lives of millions of citizens whose futures abruptly became hostages to fortune.

This combination of circumstances created the most fertile of all possible soils for the propagation of rumor. We now know that *rumors concerning a given subject-matter will circulate within a group in proportion to the importance and the ambiguity* of this subject-matter in the lives of individual members of the group.

The affair of Pearl Harbor was fraught with both importance and ambiguity to nearly every citizen. The affair was important because of the potential danger it represented to all of us, and because its aftermath of mobilization affected every life. It was ambiguous because no one seemed quite certain of the extent of, reasons for, or consequences of the attack. Since the two conditions of rumor—importance and ambiguity—were at a maximum, we had an unprecedented flood of what became known as "Pearl Harbor rumors." It was said that our fleet was "wiped out," that Washington didn't dare to tell the extent of the damage, that Hawaii was in the hands of the Japanese. So widespread and so demoralizing

From *Transactions of the New York Academy of Sciences*, Series II, 1945, VIII, 61-81. Reprinted by permission of the authors and publisher.

were these tales that, on February 23, 1942, President Roosevelt broadcast a speech devoted entirely to denying the harmful rumors and to reiterating the official report on the losses.

Did the solemn assurance of the Commander in Chief restore the confidence of the people and eliminate the tales of suspicion and fear? It so happens that a bit of objective evidence on this question became available to us almost by accident. On the twentieth of February, before the President's speech, we had asked approximately 200 college students whether they thought our losses at Pearl Harbor were "greater," "much greater," or "no greater" than the official Knox report had stated. Among these students, 68 percent had believed the demoralizing rumors in preference to the official report, and insisted that the losses were "greater" or "much greater" than Washington admitted. Then came the President's speech. On February 25 an equivalent group of college students were asked the same question. Among those who had not heard or read the speech the proportion of rumor-believers was still about two thirds. But among those who were acquainted with the President's speech, the number of rumor-believers fell by 24 percent. It is important to note that, in spite of the utmost efforts of the highest authority to allay anxiety, approximately 44 percent of the college population studied were too profoundly affected by the event and by the resulting rumors to accept the reassurance.

The year 1942 was characterized by floods of similar fear-inspired tales. Shipping losses were fantastically exaggerated. Knapp records one instance where a collier was sunk through accident near the Cape Cod Canal. So great was the anxiety of the New England public that this incident became a fantastic tale of an American ship being torpedoed with the loss of thousands of nurses who were aboard her (1944).

Such wild stories, as we have said, are due to the grave importance of the subject for the average citizen and to the ambiguity

to him of the objective situation. This ambiguity may result from the failure of communications, or from a total lack of authentic news, a condition that often prevailed in war-torn countries or among isolated bands of troops who had few reliable sources of news. Again, the ambiguity may be due to the receipt of conflicting news stories, no one more credible than another; or it may be due (as in the case of the Pearl Harbor rumors) to the distrust of many people in the candor of the Administration and in the operation of wartime censorship. As the war progressed, a higher degree of confidence in our news services was rapidly achieved, and rumors concurrently subsided.

In addition to the fear-rumors of 1942, which persisted until the tide of victory commenced to turn, there was a still more numerous crop of hostility-rumors whose theme dealt always with the shortcomings, disloyalty, or inefficiency of some special group of cobelligerents. The Army, the Navy, the Administration, our allies, or American minority groups were the most frequent scapegoats in these rumors. We were told that the Army wasted whole sides of beef, that the Russians greased their guns with lend-lease butter, that Negroes were saving icepicks for a revolt, and that Jews were evading the draft.

These hostility rumors were the most numerous of all. An analysis of 1,000 rumors collected from all parts of the country in 1942 (Knapp, 1944) revealed that they could be classified fairly readily as:

Hostility (wedge-driving)
    rumors   = 66 percent
Fear (bogey) rumors   = 25 percent
Wish (pipe-dream) rumors = 2 percent
Unclassifiable rumors   = 7 percent

To be sure, the proportion of fear and wish rumors soon altered. As victory approached, especially on the eve of V-E and V-J day, the whirlwind of rumors was almost wholly concerned with the cessation of hostilities, reflecting a goal-gradient phenomenon whereby rumor under special conditions hastens the completion of a desired event. But, throughout the war and continuing to the present, it is probably true that the majority of all rumors are of a more or less slanderous nature, expressing hostility against this group or that.

The principal reason why rumor circulates can be briefly stated. It circulates because it *serves the twin function of explaining and relieving emotional tensions felt by individuals.*[1]

The Pearl Harbor rumors, for example, helped to *explain* to the teller why he felt such distressing anxiety. Would his jitters not be justified if it were true that our protecting fleet was "wiped out" at Pearl Harbor? Something serious must have happened to account for his anxiety. Families deprived of sons, husbands, or fathers vaguely cast around for someone to blame for their privation. Well, the Jews, who were said to be evading the draft, were "obviously" not doing their share and thus the heavy burden falling on "good citizens" was explained. True, this draft-evasion charge did not last very long, owing, no doubt, to the inescapable evidence of heavy enlistments among Jews and of their heroic conduct in the war. But when shortages were felt, the traditional Jewish scapegoat was again trotted out as a convenient explanation of the privations suffered. Their operation of the black market "explained" our annoying experiences in the futile pursuit of an evening lamb chop.

To blame others verbally is not only a mode of explanation for one's emotional distress, but is at the same time a mode of *relief*. Everyone knows the reduction of tension that comes after administering a tongue lashing. It matters little whether the victim of the tongue lashing is guilty or not. Dressing down *anyone* to his face or behind his back has the strange property of temporarily reducing hatred felt against this person or, what is more remarkable, of reducing hatred felt against any person or thing. If you wish to deflate a taut inner tube you can unscrew the valve or you can make a puncture. Unscrewing the valve corresponds to directing our hostility toward the Nazis or Japanese, who were the cause of our suffering. Making a puncture corresponds to displacing the hostility upon innocent victims or scapegoats. In either case, the air will escape and relaxation follow. To blame Jews, Negroes, the Administration, brass hats, the OPA, or the politicians is to bring a certain relief from accumulated feelings of hostility, whatever their true cause. Relief, odd as it may seem, comes also from "bogey" rumors. To tell my neighbor that the Cape Cod Canal is choked with corpses is an easy manner of projecting into the outer world my own choking anxieties concerning my son or my friends in combat service. Having shared my anxiety with my friend by telling him exaggerated tales of losses or of atrocities, I no longer feel so much alone and helpless. Through my rumor-spreading, others, too, are put "on the alert." I therefore feel reassured.

---

[1] This brief formula leaves out of account only the relatively few rumors which seem to serve the purpose of "phatic communication"—a form of idle conversation to facilitate social intercourse. When a lull occurs in a conversation, an individual may "fill in" with the latest bit of gossip that comes to mind, without being motivated by the deeper tensions that underlie the great bulk of rumor mongering.

In this paper we cannot enter into a fuller discussion of the reasons why people believe some rumors and not others. This question is carefully studied by F. H. Allport and M. Lepkin, "Wartime rumors of waste and special privilege: why some people believe them," *J. abnorm. soc. Psychol.*, 1945, *40*, 3-36.

Experimental Approach

Leaving now the broader social setting of the problem, we ask ourselves what processes in the human mind account for the spectacular distortions and exaggerations that enter into the rumor-process, and lead to so much damage to the public intelligence and public conscience.

Since it is very difficult to trace in detail the course of a rumor in everyday life, we have endeavored by an experimental technique to study as many of the basic phenomena as possible under relatively well controlled laboratory conditions.

Our method is simple. A slide is thrown upon a screen. Ordinarily, a semidramatic picture is used containing a large number of related details. Six or seven subjects, who have not seen the picture, wait in an adjacent room. One of them enters and takes a position where he cannot see the screen. Someone in the audience (or the experimenter) describes the picture, giving about twenty details in the account. A second subject enters the room and stands beside the first subject who proceeds to tell him all he can about the picture. (All subjects are under instruction to report as "accurately as possible what you have heard.") The first

of the rumor by comparing the successive versions with the stimulus-picture which remains on the screen throughout the experiment.

This procedure has been used with over forty groups of subjects, including college undergraduates, Army trainees in ASTP, members of community forums, patients in an Army hospital, members of a Teachers' Round Table, and police officials in a training course. In addition to these adult subjects, children in a private school were used, in grades from the fourth through the ninth. In some experiments, Negro subjects took part along with whites, a fact which, as we shall see, had important consequences when the test-pictures depicted scenes with a "racial angle."

Fig. 1. A sample of pictorial material employed in the experiments. Here is a typical terminal report (the last in a chain of reproductions): "This is a subway train in New York headed for Portland Street. There is a Jewish woman and a Negro who has a razor in his hand. The woman has a baby or a dog. The train is going to Deyer Street, and nothing much happened."

subject then takes his seat, and a third enters to hear the story from the second subject. Each succeeding subject hears and repeats the story in the same way. Thus, the audience is able to watch the deterioration

All of these experiments took place before an audience (20-300 spectators). By using volunteer subjects, one eliminates the danger of stage fright. There was, however, a social influence in all the audience situations. The magnitude of this influence was studied in a control group of experiments where no one was present in the room excepting the subject and the experimenter.

At the outset, it is necessary to admit that in five respects this experimental situation fails to reproduce accurately the conditions of rumor-spreading in everyday life. (1) The effect of an audience is considerable, tending to create caution and to shorten the report. Without an audience subjects gave on the average twice as many details as with an audience. (2) The effect of the instructions is to maximize accuracy and induce caution. In ordinary rumor-spreading, there is no critical experimenter on hand to see whether the tale is rightly repeated. (3) There is no opportunity for subjects to ask questions of his informer. In ordinary rumor-spreading, the listener can chat with his informer and, if he wishes, cross-examine him. (4) The lapse of time between hearing and telling in the experimental situation is very slight. In ordinary rumor-spreading, it is much greater. (5) Most important of all, the conditions of motivation are quite different. In the experiment, the subject is striving for *accuracy.* His own fears, hates, wishes are not likely to be aroused under the experimental conditions. In short, he is not the spontaneous rumor-agent that he is in ordinary life. His stake in spreading the experimental rumor is neither personal nor deeply motivated.

It should be noted that all of these conditions, excepting the third, may be expected to enhance the accuracy of the report in the experimental situation, and to yield far less distortion and projection than in real-life rumor-spreading.

In spite of the fact that our experiment does not completely reproduce the normal conditions for rumor, still we believe that all essential changes and distortions are represented in our results. "Indoor" rumors may not be as lively, as emotionally toned, or as extreme as "outdoor" rumors, and yet the same basic phenomena are demonstrable in both.

What happens in both real-life and laboratory rumors is a complex course of distortion in which three interrelated tendencies are clearly distinguishable.

Leveling

As rumor travels, it tends to grow shorter, more concise, more easily grasped and told. In successive versions, fewer words are used and fewer details are mentioned.

The number of details *retained* declines most sharply at the beginning of the series of reproductions. The number continues to decline, more slowly, throughout the experiment. Figure 2 shows the percentage of the details initially given which are retained in each successive reproduction.

The number of items enumerated in the description from the screen constitutes the

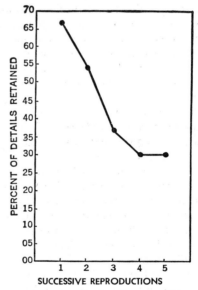

Fig. 2. Percentage of details originally given which are retained in each successive reproduction.

100 percent level, and all subsequent percentages are calculated from that base. The curve, based on 11 experiments, shows that about 70 percent of the details are eliminated in the course of five or six mouth-to-

mouth transmissions, even when virtually no time lapse intervenes.

The curve is like the famous Ebbinghaus curve for decline in individual retention, though in his experiments the interval between initial learning and successive reproductions was not as short as under the conditions of our experiment. Comparing the present curve with Ebbinghaus's, we conclude that *social memory accomplishes as much leveling within a few minutes as individual memory accomplishes in weeks of time.*

Leveling (in our experiments) never proceeds to the point of total obliteration. The stablization of the last part of the curve is a finding of some consequence. It indicates (1) that a short concise statement is likely to be faithfully reproduced; (2) that when the report has become short and concise, the subject has very little detail to select from and the possibilities of further distortion grow fewer; (3) that the assignment becomes so easy that a virtually rote memory serves to hold the material in mind. In all cases, the terminal and the anteterminal reports are more similar than any two preceding reports.

The reliance on rote is probably more conspicuous in our experiments than in ordinary rumor-spreading, where accuracy is not the aim, where time interval interferes with rote retention, and where strong interests prevent literal memory. There are, however, conditions where rote memory plays a part in ordinary rumor-spreading. If the individual is motivated by no stronger desire than to make conversation, he may find himself idly repeating what he has recently heard in the form in which he heard it. If a rumor has become so crisp and brief, so sloganized, that it requires no effort to retain it in the literal form in which it was heard, rote memory seems to be involved. For example:

The Jews are evading the draft;
The CIO is communist controlled;
The Russians are nationalizing their women.

We conclude that whenever verbal material is transmitted among a group of people whether as rumor, legend, or history, change will be in the direction of greater brevity and conciseness. Leveling, however, is not a random phenomenon. Our protocols show again and again that items which are of particular interest to the subjects, facts which confirm their expectations and help them to structure the story, are the last to be leveled out and often are retained to the final reproduction.

Sharpening

We may define sharpening as the selective perception, retention, and reporting of a limited number of details from a larger context. Sharpening is inevitably the reciprocal of leveling. The one cannot exist without the other, for what little remains to a rumor after leveling has taken place is by contrast unavoidably featured.

Although sharpening occurs in every protocol, the same items are not always emphasized. Sometimes, a trifling detail such as a subway advertising card becomes the focus of attention and report. Around it the whole rumor becomes structured. But, in most experiments, this same detail drops out promptly, and is never heard of after the first reproduction.

One way in which sharpening seems to be determined is through the retention of odd or attention-getting words which, having appeared early in the series, catch the attention of each successive listener and are often passed on in preference to other details intrisically more important to the story. An instance of this effect is seen in a series of protocols where the statement, "there is a boy stealing and a man remonstrating with him" is transmitted throughout the entire series. The unusual word "remonstrate" somehow caught the attention of each successive listener and was passed on without change.

Sharpening may also take a *numerical*

turn, as in the experiments where empha-sized items become reduplicated in the tell-ing. For example, in reports of a picture containing the figure of a Negro, whose size and unusual appearance invite emphasis, we find that the number of Negroes re-ported in the picture jumps from one to "four" or "several."

There is also *temporal* sharpening mani-fested in the tendency to describe events as occurring in the immediate present. What happens *here* and *now* is of greatest interest and importance to the perceiver. In most in-stances, to be sure, the story is started in the present tense, but even when the initial de-scription is couched in the past tense, imme-diate reversal occurs and the scene is con-temporized by the listener. Obviously, this effect cannot occur in rumors which deal specifically with some alleged past (or fu-ture) event. One cannot contemporize the rumor that "the *Queen Mary* sailed this morning (or will sail tomorrow) with 10,000 troops aboard." Yet it not infre-quently happens that stories gain in sharp-ening by tying them to present conditions. For example, a statement that Mr. X bought a chicken in the black market last week and paid $1.50 a pound for it may be (and usu-ally is) rendered, "I hear they *are* charging $1.50 a pound on the black market for chicken." People are more interested in today than in last week, and the temptation, there-fore, is to adapt (assimilate) the time of oc-currence, when possible, to this interest.

Sharpening often takes place when there is a clear implication of *movement*. The fly-ing of airplanes and the bursting of bombs are frequently stressed in the telling. Simi-larly, the falling flower pot in one picture is often retained and accented. Indeed, the "falling motif" may be extended to other ob-jects such as the cigar which a man in the picture is smoking. In one rumor, it is said to be falling (like the flower pot), though in reality it is quite securely held between his teeth.

Sometimes sharpening is achieved by as-cribing movement to objects which are really stationary. Thus, a subway train, clearly at a standstill at a subway station, is frequently described as moving.

Relative size is also a primary determi-nant of attention. Objects that are prominent because of their size tend to be retained and sharpened. The first reporter calls attention to their prominence and each successive lis-tener receives an impression of their large-ness. He then proceeds to sharpen this im-pression in his memory. The large Negro may, in the telling, become "four Negroes," or may become "a gigantic statue of a Ne-gro."

There are verbal as well as physical de-terminants of attention. Thus, there is a pro-nounced tendency for *labels* to persist, espe-cially if they serve to set the stage for the story. One picture is usually introduced by some version of the statement, "This is a battle scene," and this label persists throughout the series of reproductions. An-other story usually opens with the state-ment, "This is a picture of a race riot."

To explain this type of sharpening, we may invoke the desire of the subject to achieve some spatial and temporal schema for the story to come. Such orientation is es-sential in ordinary life and appears to con-stitute a strong need even when imaginal material is dealt with.

An additional factor making for preferen-tial retention of spatial and temporal labels is the *primacy* effect. An item that comes first in a series is likely to be better remem-bered than subsequent items. Usually, the "label" indicating place and time comes at the beginning of a report and thus benefits by the primacy effect.

Sharpening also occurs in relation to fa-miliar symbols. In one series of reports, a church and a cross are among the most fre-quently reported items, although they are relatively minor details in the original pic-ture. These well-known symbols "pack" meaning and are familiar to all. The subject feels secure in reporting them because they have an accustomed concreteness that the other details in the picture lack. Retention of familiar symbols advances the process of conventionalization that is so prominent an aspect of rumor-embedding. In two of our pictures are a night stick, symbol of police authority, and a razor, stereotyped symbol of Negro violence. These symbols are always retained and sharpened.

Explanations added by the reporter to the description transmitted to him comprise a final form of sharpening. They represent a tendency to put "closure" upon a story which is felt to be otherwise incomplete. They illustrate the "effort after meaning" which customarily haunts the subject who finds himself in an unstructured situation. Such need for sharpening by explanation becomes especially strong when the story has been badly distorted and the report contains implausible and incompatible items. As an example, one subject who received a badly confused description of the subway scene (Fig. 1) inferred that there must have been "an accident." This explanation seemed plausible enough to successive listeners and so was not only accepted by them but sharpened in the telling.

In everyday rumors, sharpening through the introduction of specious explanations is very apparent. Indeed, as we have said, one of the principal functions of a rumor is to explain personal tensions. To accept tales of Army waste or special privilege among OPA officials could "explain" food shortages and discomfort. Such stories, therefore, find wide credence.

Here, perhaps, is the place to take issue with the popular notion that rumors tend to expand like snowballs, become overelaborate, and verbose. Actually, the course of rumor is toward brevity, whether in the laboratory or in everyday life. Such exaggeration as exists is nearly always a sharpening of some feature resident in the original stimulus-situation. The distortion caused by sharpening is, of course, enormous in extent; but we do not find that we need the category of "elaboration" to account for the changes we observe.

Assimilation

It is apparent that both leveling and sharpening are selective processes. But what is it that leads to the obliteration of some details and the pointing-up of others; and what accounts for all transpositions, importations, and other falsifications that mark the course of rumor? The answer is to be found in the process of *assimilation*, which has to do with the powerful attractive force exerted upon rumor by habits, interests, and sentiments existing in the listener's mind.

ASSIMILATION TO PRINCIPAL THEME

It generally happens that items become sharpened or leveled to fit the leading motif of the story, and they become consistent with this motif in such a way as to make the resulting story more coherent, plausible, and well-rounded. Thus, in one series of rumors, the war theme is preserved and emphasized in all reports. In some experiments using the same picture, a chaplain is introduced, or people (in the plural) are reported as being killed; the ambulance becomes a Red Cross station; demolished buildings are multiplied in the telling; the extent of devastation is exaggerated. All these reports, false though they are, fit the principal theme—a battle incident. If the reported details were actually present in the picture, they would make a "better" *Gestalt*. Objects wholly extraneous to the theme are never introduced—no apple pies, no ballet dancers, no baseball players.

Besides importations, we find other falsifications in the interest of supporting the principal theme. The original picture shows that the Red Cross truck is loaded with explosives, but it is ordinarily reported as carrying medical supplies which is, of course, the way it "ought" to be.

The Negro in this same picture is nearly always described as a soldier, although his clothes might indicate that he is a civilian partisan. It is a "better" configuration to have a soldier in action on the battlefield than to have a civilian among regular soldiers.

GOOD CONTINUATION

Other falsifications result from the attempt to complete incompleted pictures or to fill in gaps which exist in the stimulus field. The effort is again to make the resulting whole coherent, and meaningful. Thus, the sign, "Loew's Pa . . . ," over a moving picture theater is invariably read and reproduced as "Loew's Palace" and Gene *Antry* becomes Gene *Autry*. "Lucky Rakes" are reported as "Lucky Strikes."

All these, and many instances like them, are examples of what has been called, in *Gestalt* terms, "closures." Falsifications of perception and memory they are, but they occur in the interests of bringing about a more coherent, consistent mental configuration. Every detail is assimilated to the principal theme, and "good continuation" is sought, in order to round out meaning where it is lacking or incomplete.

ASSIMILATION BY CONDENSATION

It sometimes seems as though memory tries to burden itself as little as possible. For instance, instead of remembering two items, it is more economical to fuse them into one. Instead of a series of subway cards, each of which has its own identity, reports sometimes refer only to "a billboard," or perhaps to a "lot of advertising" (Fig. 1). In another picture, it is more convenient to refer to "all kinds of fruit," rather than to enumerate all the different items on the vendor's cart. Again, the occupants of the car come to be described by some such summary phrase as "several people sitting and standing in the car." Their individuality is lost.

ASSIMILATION TO EXPECTATION

Just as details are changed or imported to bear out the simplified theme that the lis-

tener has in mind, so also many items take a form that supports the agent's habits of thought. Things are perceived and remembered the way they *usually* are. Thus a drugstore, in one stimulus-picture, is situated in the middle of a block; but, in the telling, it moves up to the corner of the two streets and becomes the familiar "corner drugstore." A Red Cross ambulance is said to carry medical supplies rather than explosives, because it "ought" to be carrying medical supplies. The kilometers on the signposts are changed into miles, since Americans are accustomed to having distances indicated in miles.

The most spectacular of all our assimilative distortions is the finding that, in more than half of our experiments, a razor moves (in the telling) from a white man's hand to a Negro's hand (Fig. 1). This result is a clear instance of assimilation to stereotyped expectancy. Black men are "supposed" to carry razors, white men not.

ASSIMILATION TO LINGUISTIC HABITS

Expectancy is often merely a matter of fitting perceived and remembered material to preexisting verbal clichés, which exert a powerful influence in the conventionalization of rumors. Words often arouse compelling familiar images in the listener's mind and fix for him the categories in which he must think of the event and the value that he must attach to it. A "zoot-suit sharpie" packs much more meaning and carries more affect than more objective words, such as, "a colored man with pegged trousers, wide-brimmed hat, etc." (Fig. 1). Rumors are commonly told in verbal stereotypes which imply prejudicial judgment, such as "draft dodger," "Japanese spy," "brass hat," "dumb Swede," "long-haired professor," and the like.

More Highly Motivated Assimilation

Although the conditions of our experiment do not give full play to emotional tendencies underlying gossip, rumor, and scandal, such tendencies are so insistent that they express themselves even under laboratory conditions.

ASSIMILATION TO INTEREST

It sometimes happens that a picture containing women's dresses, as a trifling detail in the original scene, becomes, in the telling, a story exclusively about dresses. This sharpening occurs when the rumor is told by groups of women, but never when told by men.

A picture involving police was employed with a group of police officers as subjects. In the resulting protocol, the entire reproduction centered around the police officer (with whom the subjects undoubtedly felt keen sympathy or "identification"). Furthermore, the nightstick, a symbol of his power, is greatly sharpened and becomes the main object of the controversy. The tale as a whole is protective of, and partial to, the policeman.

ASSIMILATION TO PREJUDICE

Hard as it is in an experimental situation to obtain distortions that arise from hatred, yet we have in our material a certain opportunity to trace the hostile complex of racial attitudes.

We have spoken of the picture which contained a white man holding a razor while arguing with a Negro. In over half of the experiments with this picture, the final report indicated that the Negro (instead of the white man) held the razor in his hand, and several times he was reported as "brandishing it widely" or as "threatening" the white man with it (Fig. 1).

Whether this ominous distortion reflects hatred and fear of Negroes we cannot definitely say. In some cases, these deeper emotions may be the assimilative factor at work. And yet the distortion may occur even in subjects who have no anti-Negro bias. It is an unthinking cultural stereotype that the Negro is hot tempered and addicted to the use of razors as weapons. The rumor, though mischievous, may reflect chiefly an assimilation of the story to verbal-clichés and conventional expectation. Distortion in this case may not mean assimilation to hostility. Much so-called prejudice is, of course, a mere matter of conforming to current folkways by accepting prevalent beliefs about an out-group.

Whether or not this razor-shift reflects deep hatred and fear on the part of white subjects, it is certain that the reports of our Negro subjects betray a motivated type of distortion. Because it was to their interest as members of the race to deemphasize the racial caricature, Negro subjects almost invariably avoided mention of color. One of them hearing a rumor containing the phrase, "a Negro zoot-suiter," reported "There is a man wearing a zoot suit, *possibly* a Negro."

For one picture, a Negro reporter said that the colored man in the center of the picture "is being maltreated." Though this interpretation may be correct, it is likewise possible that he is a rioter about to be arrested by the police officer. White and Negro subjects are very likely to perceive, remember, and interpret this particular situation in quite opposite ways.

Thus, even under laboratory conditions, we find assimilation in terms of deep-lying emotional predispositions. Our rumors, like those of everyday life, tend to fit into, and support, the occupational interests, class or racial memberships, or personal prejudices of the reporter.

Conclusion: The Embedding Process

Leveling, sharpening, and assimilation are not independent mechanisms. They function simultaneously, and reflect a singular subjectifying process that results in the autism and falsification which are so characteristic of rumor. If we were to attempt to summarize what happens in a few words we might say:

Whenever a stimulus field is of potential importance to an individual, but at the same time unclear, or susceptible of divergent interpretations, a subjective structuring process is started. Although the process is complex (involving, as it does, leveling, sharpening, and assimilation), its essential nature can be characterized as an effort to reduce the stimulus to a simple and meaningful structure that has adaptive significance for the individual in terms of his own interests and experience. The process begins at the moment the ambiguous situation is perceived, but the effects are greatest if memory intervenes. The longer the time that elapses after the stimulus is perceived the greater the threefold change is likely to be. Also, the more people involved in a serial report, the greater the change is likely to be, until the rumor has reached an aphoristic brevity, and is repeated by rote.

Now, this three-pronged process turns out to be characteristic not only of rumor but of the individual memory function as well. It has been uncovered and described in the experiments on individual retention conducted by Wulf, Gibson, Allport,[2] and, in Bartlett's memory experiments carried out both on individuals and on groups (1932).

Up to now, however, there has been no agreement on precisely the terminology to use, nor upon the adequacy of the three functions we here describe. We believe that our conceptualization of the three-fold course of change and decay is sufficient to account, not only for our own experimental findings and for the experiments of others in this area, but also for the distortions that everyday rumors undergo.

[2] Conveniently summarized in K. Koffka, *Principles of Gestalt psychology* (New York: Harcourt, Brace & World, 1935).

For lack of a better designation, we speak of the three-fold change as the *embedding* process. What seems to occur in all our experiments and in all related studies is that each subject finds the outer stimulus-world far too hard to grasp and retain in its objective character. For his own personal uses, it must be recast to fit not only his span of comprehension and his span of retention, but, likewise, his own personal needs and interests. What was outer becomes inner; what was objective becomes subjective. In telling a rumor, the kernel of objective information that he received has become so embedded into his own dynamic mental life that the product is chiefly one of projection. Into the rumor, he projects the deficiencies of his retentive processes, as well as his own effort to engender meaning upon an ambiguous field, and the product reveals much of his own emotional needs, including his anxieties, hates, and wishes. When several rumor-agents have been involved in this embedding process, the net result of the serial reproduction reflects the lowest common denominator of cultural interest, of memory span, and of group sentiment and prejudice.

One may ask whether a rumor must always be false. We answer that, in virtually every case, the embedding process is so extensive that no credibility whatever should be ascribed to the product. If a report does turn out to be trustworthy, we usually find that secure standards of evidence have somehow been present to which successive agents could refer for purposes of validation. Perhaps the morning newspaper or the radio have held the rumor under control, but when such secure standards of verification are available, it is questionable whether we should speak of rumor at all.

There are, of course, border-line cases where we may not be able to say whether a given tidbit should or should not be called a rumor. But if we define rumor (and we herewith propose that we should), as *a proposition for belief of topical reference, without secure standards of evidence being present*—then it follows from the facts we have presented that rumor will suffer such serious distortion through the embedding process, that *it is never under any circumstances a valid guide for belief or conduct.*

References

BARTLETT, F. C. *Remembering.* Cambridge, England: Cambridge University Press, 1932.

KNAPP, R. H. A psychology of rumor. *Pub. Opin. Quart.,* 1944, 8, 22-37.

Social Status and Success Strivings ❧ Elizabeth Douvan

Systematic differences between child-training procedures employed in the two major social classes have been reported by several investigators (Davis, 1944; Duvall, 1946; Ericson, 1947). These differences cluster in two related areas of training: development of internalized controls and learning of achievement motivation. Davis (1944) has noted the critical role of anxiety as a reinforcement for achievement strivings in the middle class training scheme, and Ericson's study (1947) reveals a picture of the environment of the middle class child as making early and consistent demands for personal attainment.

Since middle class society not only places great stress on accomplishment, but imposes demands earlier than does the working class (Ericson, 1947), we would expect the need for achievement to be more generalized in middle class children than in children of lower status.[1] Success-failure cues in any situation should, among middle class children, elicit a relatively consistent reaction, irrespective of the reward conditions of the specific situation. Since working class children are taught achievement strivings neither so early nor so systematically their reactions to success-failure cues should be more responsive to changes in the reward potential of the situation in which such cues occur.

The present study was designed to contrast members of the two social groups with respect to the degree of achievement motivation they manifest in two success-failure situations which differ in reward potential. In one situation success was defined as achieving an abstract norm; in the other successful performance offered, in addition, a material reward. The specific hypothesis to be tested was that working class youth would manifest a significantly greater difference in achievement strivings under the two reward conditions than would youngsters from the middle class.

Method

SUBJECTS

The Ss for this experiment were adolescents in the senior year of high school in a medium-sized midwestern community. Of the original group of 336, 23 were excluded

[1] The importance of time of training has been highlighted by McClelland (1951). He hypothesizes that behavior patterns learned in the preverbal period will be particularly generalized and intractable since the original learning cues are unavailable to consciousness.

From the *Journal of Abnormal and Social Psychology,* 1956, 52, 219-223. Reprinted by permission of the author and the American Psychological Association.

from the analysis because of incompletions in at least one of the measures used in the study.

School children were used as Ss because the schools provide established groups of individuals from both social classes under similar objective conditions. In addition Ss of this age were especially suitable because of the likelihood of finding among them a substantial proportion who had been subject to the influences of their class subcultures during the crucial early training period.

The schools in which the study was done provided a good cultural setting for an investigation of class differences. The social situation in these schools is characterized by relatively good apparent chances for mobility and by strong pressures exerted toward mobility by teachers and by the middle class satisfactions reflected in the well-kept and expensive homes surrounding the schools. Working class students who do not yield to such pressures—who identify with the working class even in this situation—should be stable representatives of people with working class values and goals.

MEASURES AND CONTROLS

Class Membership. Two types of indices were used in defining Ss' class position. The first was an occupational index based on data derived from school records and a questionnaire in which S was asked to describe his father's work and conditions of employment. The second index was a subjective class assignment based on a variation of Centers' technique.[2] Only those Ss for whom the two indices agreed on the middle or working class were used in the test of the study's central hypothesis.

[2] In addition to the Centers' question, and preceding it, Ss were asked: "Which one of the following social classes (middle, lower, working, upper) would you like to be a member of?" and "Which one . . . do you think you'll be a member of in ten years?" By including these questions, it was hoped to reduce elements of fantasy and aspiration in Ss' answers to the question on present class membership.

Independent placements of each S on the basis of father's occupation were made by two judges, with a percentage agreement of .95. The criteria for assigning occupations to the two classes are listed below.[3]

Middle Class

a. Addresses self to people.
b. Exerts control over people either in a disciplinary capacity within the business power unit, or as an active agent of control over people outside the business unit. In either case the exertion of control serves the interest of the business unit.
c. Income can be increased through individual efforts—some degree of effect on the market for his services and skills.

Working Class

a. Addresses self to tools.
b. Exerts control over no one in the job situation.
c. Income relatively fixed. No control over market for his labor, the only source of his income.
d. Easily replaceable skill.

Most occupations were relatively easily placed by means of these criteria. If a job met two of the three criteria for the middle class, it was assigned this position. Most commonly discrepancies occurred between the first criterion and later ones. Thus a surgeon might be said to address himself primarily to tools, but he exerts control over others (patients, nurses, secretarial help) and has some power over the market for his skills. The factory set-up man represents the opposite case of this discrepancy. Fewer than five per cent of the occupations rated revealed any such inharmonious elements.

Need Achievement. McClelland, Atkinson, and co-workers have developed a method for measuring achievement motivation based on a special scoring of an

[3] The rationale for this classification system is presented fully in the original report from which this article is drawn (1951). Placements made on the basis of this scheme have been shown to correlate highly with those based on Warner's more complex system (Ort, 1952).

adapted TAT. Their measure, which made possible an experimental test of the hypothesis of the present study, is presented in detail in a recent publication (1953).

Scoring was done by two judges, trained by a psychologist experienced in the use of the system. A number of indices of agreement were obtained between each judge and the instructor and between the two judges. Percentage agreements on scoring specific categories ranged from .83 to .96; eight rank-order correlations between total scores assigned by two judges to twenty-five Ss all yielded values above .91. Score-rescore reliabilities computed on 150 protocols were .87 for one judge and .94 for the other.

PROCEDURE

The Ss were assigned by a system of random numbers to one of the two motivation conditions. Limitation of funds for material rewards dictated the decision to distribute the sample two-to-one in favor of the symbolic reward condition.

The Ss were given tests, tasks, and questionnaires in the following order:

a. Questionnaire on subjective class identification
b. Anagrams "test"
c. Motor "test"
d. Need Achievement measure
e. Questionnaire on father's occupation

The experiment was introduced in the following manner in all groups:

A group of psychologists is administering a series of tests to high school students in different parts of the country. These tests tell us about various abilities of people. We're going to give the tests to you now. I'll describe the ability each test measures . . . before we give it. After each test I'll give you the average score of high school students on that test, so you'll know how you're doing as we go along.

In the material reward condition this introduction was followed by a short statement concerning the fact that we had found that students often did not do as well as they might because they didn't always try hard. For this reason, they were told, ten dollars would be given to any student whose over-all score on the tests reached a certain value:

We'll announce the winning scores tomorrow, but in the meantime, you'll have the average scores of students we've already tested in (name of city) so you'll know how you're doing.

The effectiveness of this device for increasing motivation was attested by the excitement which followed the announcement. A questionnaire asking each S to estimate the relative magnitude of his own and others' desire for the prize corroborated the impression of the Es.

The anagrams and motor tasks were used to create failure experiences and thus establish a nonsatiated state of the achievement motive. Before each of the "tests," Ss were told what it measured and how much time they would be given. They were admonished against any discussion during the testing period, and also against "giving up" if they did poorly on early tests. Since the important thing was the over-all score, success on later tests might compensate for humble beginnings.

Following a 4-minute trial on each "test," a falsely high average was announced for "high school students in your city," and we guided Ss rapidly into the next experimental step.

The n Achievement "test" was dissociated from the two previous ones. A different E administered it, and Ss were told that this test would not be counted in their scores. It was introduced as a test of creative imagination, and the instructions conformed closely to those used by McClelland et al. (1953).

At the end of the testing period it was necessary to relieve anxieties created by the experimentally induced failure. The previously announced high school norms were inaccessibly high, and our desire was to substitute for them more reasonable standards which would leave Ss with the feeling that they had performed well relative to their peers. To effect this substitution, a minor drama was staged.

An experimental assistant came into the room near the close of the hour and hurriedly whispered something to Es. Following this communication, one E announced with obvious embarrassment that because of a last-minute rush in preparations, he had by mistake been given supplies intended for the team of psychologists giving the tests at the local college. The norms he had previously announced for the tests had not, therefore, been the scores of a high school group, but were scores obtained by college students. He now had the correct high school norms, and would read them to Ss.

These belated but "correct" norms were quite moderate, having been established on the basis of pretest experience to be within the near-reach of even the slow high school senior. A free question and discussion period followed and concluded the experiment.

Results

Summary data for tests of hypotheses are presented in Table 1. There is, we see, a significantly greater difference between the n Achievement scores of working class Ss under the two reward conditions than between those of middle class Ss. This finding confirms our hypothesis that middle class youngsters would manifest more generalized achievement strivings, thus showing themselves more impervious to immediate situational demands.

One might ask whether the greater relative shift in striving among working class children does not simply reflect the fact that money is scarcer in their environment and therefore more highly desirable to them. The material reward offered might, according to this argument, be sufficient to trigger additional motivation in the working class child but insufficient to bring into play in the middle class youth any comparable increment of striving.

Results of the questionnaire on the desirability of the ten dollar reward oppose this interpretation—there was no class difference in conscious desire for the reward. The sum of ten dollars was used specifically to guard against differential subjective responses to the material reward.

The n Achievement scores of the class groups under the two reward conditions can be viewed in another way. The fact that under the material reward condition there is substantially no difference in the mean scores of the two class groups ($t = .27$; $p > .30$) indicates that the measure of n Achievement as such is not seriously class

TABLE 1

ACHIEVEMENT MOTIVATION OF WORKING CLASS, MIDDLE CLASS, AND MARGINAL Ss UNDER TWO REWARD CONDITIONS

Class	Material Reward						D_1-D_2	SE of Diff.	t	p
	Present			*Absent*						
	N	M	SD	N	M	SD				
Working	34	8.06	3.61	53	4.89	2.89				
							2.43°	1.05	2.31	.02
Middle	37	8.30	3.71	73	7.56	3.76				
							.60†	1.14	.53	.25
Marginal	36	7.85	3.72	71	7.71	4.93				

° Here D_1 refers to the mean difference for working class Ss under the reward conditions, D_2 to the mean difference for middle class Ss.
† In this case D_1 refers to the mean difference for middle class Ss, D_2 to mean difference for marginals.

biased. We might consider the condition of material reward a control situation designed to establish the applicability of the n Achievement measure to both groups. On this interpretation, results in the situation characterized by the absence of material reward can be generalized thus: In response to a failure, defined as not achieving an abstract standard, middle class individuals manifest a significantly higher need to achieve than working class individuals ($t = 4.3$; $p < .01$).

Since each S knew only his own scores, success did not entail any immediate gratification of prestige strivings or needs for recognition from the group. This extreme limitation of the satisfactions to be gained by success in the nonreward situation leads to the conclusion that the manifestation of a high need to achieve under such conditions attests to the independent and central nature of success as a motivating factor in the individuals responding in this manner.

MARGINALITY

The results reported to this point were obtained when social class was defined on the basis of both objective occupational criteria and a subjective measure. Possibly the most provocative groups defined by this dual scheme are those comprising individuals whose self-assigned social class differs from their objective position in the social structure. From the present analysis it is not possible to make even tentative remarks about downward identifying middle class Ss, since there were too few of these cases. Consider, however, upward identifying working class Ss.

Because of the variety of factors which may underlie such a misidentification (e.g., ambiguity in the status structure, simple ignorance, status anxiety, defensive resistance against one's actual position), no specific predictions were made about the relative achievement motivation of this group under the two reward conditions. However, several general possibilities were explored.

Steiner (1948) found a tendency for these marginal cases to behave like middle class individuals, but more extremely. The present study posed two questions relating to this observation: (a) Do marginals obtain higher n Achievement scores than middle class Ss under low reward conditions? and (b) Do marginals react to the two reward conditions with more consistent achievement motivation than middle class Ss?

This analysis did not yield any significant findings. While the mean n Achievement for the marginal group under the symbolic reward condition is higher than the mean of the middle class group (Table 1), the difference is not reliable ($t = .20$; $p > .40$). Nor do the marginals show greater consistency in response to the two situations. There was substantially no difference between middle class and marginals Ss with respect to the relative shift in achievement strivings ($t = .53$; $p > .25$).

Another inquiry into the behavior of this group followed from Davis' distinction (1944) between original socialization and adaptive acculturation, and his description of the differential demands and effects of these two kinds of learning. Since the marginal Ss were probably not uniformly socialized in the middle class value pattern, wide variation was anticipated in the extent and accuracy of their incorporation of middle class behavior patterns. Some might have overlearned, some not yet have learned the accepted middle class responses to success-failure cues in a symbolic reward situation. Greater heterogeneity should therefore be manifested in the responses of this group under the condition of absence of material reward.

The findings confirm this expectation. The standard deviation of the marginal group was not compared to that of the working class group, since their means were too different to allow the assumption that the groups derived from the same universe. But the test which could be made—between middle class and marginal variances—reveals that the marginal group is significantly less homogeneous than the middle class group (F ratio $= 1.6$; $p < .05$).

Discussion

The extent and nature of achievement responses have been shown to depend on social class membership. More autonomous and generalized success strivings characterize members of the middle class, while achievement motivation of working class individuals is more highly dependent on the reward loading of the task situation.

The present results, in conjunction with observations made by others (Centers, 1948; Davis, 1946; Hollingshead, 1949; Lynd and Lynd, 1929; Whyte, 1943), suggest that the nature of achievement motivation among adolescents in the two classes is functional to the dominant values and behavior expectations of the class subcultures. The occupational role of the middle class adult requires a high degree of competitive performance, the product is individual, and responsibility for success and failure is personal. To meet these demands successfully the individual must be equipped with generalized and stable internal motivation to achieve. The industrial manual worker, on the other hand, is more familiar with nonpersonal causality and the effect of external factors (e.g., layoffs) on individual goal attainment. His labor contributes to a group product, and the value of personal competitiveness is minimal in his occupational role. Success and failure are less highly personalized so there is little need to strive unless success involves some meaningful and apparent reward (Davis, 1946).

A caveat should be entered against overinterpretation of these findings. They are not concerned with the way in which achievement striving fits into the total psychological structure of the individual. Thus while Davis (1944) attributes to anxiety a major role in the determination of success strivings in the middle class, the present data do not permit conclusions about the kind of learning process which underlies them. Nor are assertions justified about the relative rationality, efficiency, or rigidity of the two patterns of behavior observed, since the psychological economics of individual Ss have not been studied. In any case Brown (1953) has pointed to the danger that terms like efficiency may serve as screens for evaluation.

The conclusion is warranted, however, that achievement motivation is conditioned by and appropriate to the cultural context in which it develops. The middle class child is urged to individual achievement, is compared to age mates by his parents, and is taught to respond to symbolic as well as material rewards. He develops, accordingly, strong and well-internalized desires for accomplishment, and responds consistently to success-failure cues even when achievement offers little or no substantial reward. The working class child, on the other hand, is not pressed for individual attainment as early or as consistently, and his motivation to succeed in a given task is more clearly related to the rewards such success entails. These differential patterns of response conform to values and life conditions in the two subcultures and to the behavior expectations which will be imposed when the subjects of this study reach adult status in their respective class cultures.

Summary

Previous research has indicated that the two major social classes differ with respect to norms and values in the area of personal achievement. Middle class parents, in rearing their children, assert demands for individual success earlier and more regularly than do parents in the working class. On this basis it was anticipated that achievement striving would be a more central motivational factor in middle class children, and that their responses to situations containing success-failure cues would be relatively consistent despite variations in rewards offered for success. Since children in working class homes are not so vigorously urged to personal attainment, it was hypothesized that their motivation to succeed would vary more directly with changes in the reward potential of task situations.

High school students from both social classes were given a series of tasks under two reward conditions. In one reward was limited to personal satisfaction derived from attaining a norm; in the other a material reward was added to this satisfaction. Following failure experiences (to induce deprivation) Ss in each condition were given McClelland's projective test for achievement motivation.

As predicted, the mean n Achievement scores for working class Ss under the two reward conditions showed greater variation than did the means for middle class Ss. Though members of both class groups responded similarly to the material reward condition, the achievement strivings of working class Ss dropped significantly when the material reward was absent, while the motivation of middle class Ss remained at approximately the same high level.

The Ss who were placed by an objective criterion in the working class, but identified themselves as middle class, were considered marginal and were excluded from the main analysis. It was predicted that the n Achievement scores of these Ss under the symbolic reward condition would be marked by greater variability than those of other groups. The prediction was confirmed.

From the results it is concluded that the pattern of achievement motivation a child develops depends on the class subculture in which he is trained, and is functional to the values and behavior requirements with which he will be confronted as he assumes adulthood within that setting.

References

Brown, R. W. A determinant of the relationship between rigidity and authoritarianism. *J. abnorm. soc. Psychol.*, 1953, 48, 469-476.

Centers, R. Attitude and belief in relation to occupational stratification. *J. soc. Psychol.*, 1948, 27, 159-185.

Davis, A. Socialization and adolescent personality. *Adolescence, Forty-third Yearbook, Part I.* Chicago: National Society for the Study of Education, 1944.

Davis, A. The motivation of the underprivileged worker. In W. F. Whyte (Ed.), *Industry and society.* Chicago: Univer. of Chicago Press, 1946. Pp. 84-106.

Douvan, Elizabeth. The influence of social class membership on reactions to failure. Unpublished doctor's dissertation, Univer. of Michigan, 1951.

Duvall, Evelyn M. Conceptions of parenthood. *Amer. J. Sociol.*, 1946, 52, 193-203.

Ericson, Martha C. Social status and child rearing practices. In T. M. Newcomb and E. L. Hartley (Eds.), *Readings in social psychology.* New York: Holt, Rinehart and Winston, 1947. Pp. 494-501.

Hollingshead, A. B. *Elmtown's youth.* New York: Wiley, 1949.

Lynd, R. S., and Lynd, Helen M. *Middletown.* New York: Harcourt, Brace & World, 1929.

McClelland, D. C. *Personality.* New York: Sloane, 1951.

McClelland, D. C., Atkinson, J. W., Clark, R. A., and Lowell, E. L. *The achievement motive.* New York: Appleton-Century-Crofts, 1953.

Ort, R. S. A study of role-conflicts as related to class level. *J. abnorm. soc. Psychol.*, 1952, 47, 425-432.

Steiner, I. A theory and an empirical study of the role of reference groups. Unpublished master's thesis, Univer. of Michigan, 1948.

Whyte, W. F. *Street corner society.* Chicago: Univer. of Chicago Press, 1943.

B. THE PERCEPTION OF PEOPLE

The Warm-Cold Variable
in First Impressions of Persons ❧ Harold H. Kelley

This experiment is one of several studies of first impressions (Kelley, 1948), the purpose of the series being to investigate the stability of early judgments, their determinants, and the relation of such judgments to the behavior of the person making them. In interpreting the data from several nonexperimental studies on the stability of first impressions, it proved to be necessary to postulate inner-observer variables which contribute to the impression and which remain relatively constant through time. Also some evidence was obtained which directly demonstrated the existence of these variables and their nature. The present experiment was designed to determine the effects of one kind of inner-observer variable, specifically, *expectations* about the stimulus person which the observer brings to the exposure situation.

That prior information or labels attached to a stimulus person make a difference in observers' first impressions is almost too obvious to require demonstration. The expectations resulting from such preinformation may restrict, modify, or accentuate the impressions he will have. The crucial question

is: What changes in perception will accompany a given expectation? Studies of stereotyping, for example, that of Katz and Braly (1947), indicate that from an ethnic label such as "German" or "Negro," a number of perceptions follow which are culturally determined. The present study finds its main significance in relation to a study by Asch (1946) which demonstrates that certain crucial labels can transform the entire impression of the person, leading to attributions which are related to the label on a broad cultural basis or even, perhaps, on an autochthonous basis.

Asch read to his subjects a list of adjectives which purportedly described a particular person. He then asked them to characterize that person. He found that the inclusion in the list of what he called *central* qualities, such as "warm" as opposed to "cold," produced a widespread change in the entire impression. This effect was not adequately explained by the halo effect since it did not extend indiscriminately in a positive or negative direction to all characteristics. Rather, it differentially transformed the other qualities, for example, by changing their relative

From the *Journal of Personality*, 1950, 18, 431-439. Reprinted by permission of the author and publisher.

importance in the total impression. Peripheral qualities (such as "polite" versus "blunt") did not produce effects as strong as those produced by the central qualities.[1]

The present study tested the effects of such central qualities upon the early impressions of *real* persons, the same qualities, "warm" vs. "cold," being used. They were introduced as preinformation about the stimulus person before his actual appearance; so presumably they operated as expectations rather than as part of the stimulus pattern during the exposure period. In addition, information was obtained about the effects of the expectations upon the observers' behavior toward the stimulus person. An earlier study in this series has indicated that the more incompatible the observer initially perceived the stimulus person to be, the less the observer initiated interaction with him thereafter. The second purpose of the present experiment, then, was to provide a better controlled study of this relationship.

No previous studies reported in the literature have dealt with the importance of first impressions for behavior. The most relevant data are found in the sociometric literature, where there are scattered studies of the relation between choices among children having some prior acquaintance and their interaction behavior. For an example, see the study by Newstetter, Feldstein, and Newcomb (1938).

Procedure

The experiment was performed in three sections of a psychology course (Economics 70) at the Massachusetts Institute of Technology.[2] The three sections provided 23, 16, and 16 subjects respectively. All 55 subjects were men, most of them in their third college year. In each class the stimulus person (also a male) was completely unknown to the subjects before the experimental period. One person served as stimulus person in two sections, and a second person took this role in the third section. In each case the stimulus person was introduced by the experimenter, who posed as a representative of the course instructors and who gave the following statement:

> Your regular instructor is out of town today, and since we of Economics 70 are interested in the general problem of how various classes react to different instructors, we're going to have an instructor today you've never had before, Mr. ——. Then, at the end of the period, I want you to fill out some forms about him. In order to give you some idea of what he's like, we've had a person who knows him write up a little biographical note about him. I'll pass this out to you now and you can read it before he arrives. *Please read these to yourselves and don't talk about this among yourselves until the class is over so that he won't get wind of what's going on.*

Two kinds of these notes were distributed, the two being identical except that in one the stimulus person was described among other things as being "rather cold" whereas in the other form the phrase "very warm" was substituted. The content of the "rather cold" version is as follows:

> Mr. —— is a graduate student in the Department of Economics and Social Science here at M. I. T. He has had three semesters of teaching experience in psychology at another college. This is his first semester teaching Ec. 70. He is 26 years old, a veteran, and married. People who know him consider him to be a

[1] Since the present experiment was carried out, Mensh and Wishner (1947) have repeated a number of Asch's experiments because of dissatisfaction with his sex and geographic distribution. Their data substantiate Asch's very closely. Also, Luchins (1948) has criticized Asch's experiments for their artifical methodology, repeated some of them and challenged some of the kinds of interpretations Asch made from his data. Luchins also briefly reports some tantalizing conclusions from a number of studies of first impressions of actual persons.

[2] Professor Mason Haire of the University of California provided valuable advice and help in executing the experiment.

rather cold person, industrious, critical, practical, and determined.

The two types of preinformation were distributed randomly within each of the three classes and in such a manner that the students were not aware that two kinds of information were being given out. The stimulus person then appeared and led the class in a twenty-minute discussion. During this time the experimenter kept a record of how often each student participated in the discussion. Since the discussion was almost totally leader-centered, this participation record indicates the number of times each student initiated verbal interaction with the instructor. After the discussion period, the stimulus person left the room, and the experimenter gave the following instructions:

Now, I'd like to get your impression of Mr. —— ——. This is not a test of you and can in no way affect your grade in this course. This material will not be identified as belonging to particular persons and will be kept strictly confidential. It will be of most value to us if you are completely honest in your evaluation of Mr. ——. Also, please understand that what you put down will not be used against him or cause him to lose his job or anything like that. This is not a test of him but merely a study of how different classes react to different instructors.

The subjects then wrote free descriptions of the stimulus person and finally rated him on a set of 15 rating scales.

Results and Discussion

1. INFLUENCE OF WARM-COLD VARIABLE ON FIRST IMPRESSIONS

The differences in the ratings produced by the warm-cold variable were consistent from one section to another even where different stimulus persons were used. Consequently, the data from the three sections were combined by equating means (the S.D.'s were approximately equal) and the results for the total group are presented in

Table 1. Also in this table is presented that part of Asch's data which refers to the qualities included in our rating scales. From this table it is quite clear that those given the "warm" preinformation consistently rated the stimulus person more favorably than do those given the "cold" preinformation. Summarizing the statistically significant differences, the "warm" subjects rated the stimulus person as more considerate of others, more informal, more sociable, more popular, better natured, more humorous, and more humane. These findings are very similar to Asch's for the characteristics common to both studies. He found more frequent attribution to his hypothetical "warm" personalities of sociability, popularity, good naturedness, generosity, humorousness, and humaneness. So these data strongly support his finding that such a central quality as "warmth" can greatly influence the total impression of a personality. This effect is found to be operative in the perception of real persons.

This general favorableness in the perceptions of the "warm" observers as compared with the "cold" ones indicates that something like a halo effect may have been operating in these ratings. Although his data are not completely persuasive on this point, Asch was convinced that such a general effect was *not* operating in his study. Closer inspection of the present data makes it clear that the "warm-cold' effect cannot be explained altogether on the basis of simple halo effect. In Table 1 it is evident that the "warm-cold" variable produced differential effects from one rating scale to another. The size of this effect seems to depend upon the closeness of relation between the specific dimension of any given rating scale and the central quality of "warmth" or "coldness." Even though the rating of intelligence may be influenced by a halo effect, it is not influenced to the same degree to which considerateness is. It seems to make sense to view such strongly influenced items as considerateness, informality, good naturedness, and humaneness as dynamically more closely related to warmth and hence more perceived

TABLE 1

COMPARISON OF "WARM" AND "COLD" OBSERVERS IN TERMS
OF AVERAGE RATINGS GIVEN STIMULUS PERSONS

Item	Low End of Rating Scale	High End of Rating Scale	Average Rating		Level of Significance of Warm-Cold Difference	Asch's Data: Per Cent of Group Assigning Quality at Low End of Our Rating Scale°	
			Warm $N = 27$	*Cold* $N = 28$		*Warm*	*Cold*
1	Knows his stuff	Doesn't know his stuff	3.5	4.6			
2	Considerate of others	Self-centered	6.3	9.6	1%		
3†	Informal	Formal	6.3	9.6	1%		
4†	Modest	Proud	9.4	10.6			
5	Sociable	Unsociable	5.6	10.4	1%	91%	38%
6	Self-assured	Uncertain of himself	8.4	9.1			
7	High intelligence	Low intelligence	4.8	5.1			
8	Popular	Unpopular	4.0	7.4	1%	84%	28%
9†	Good natured	Irritable	9.4	12.0	5%	94%	17%
10	Generous	Ungenerous	8.2	9.6		91%	08%
11	Humorous	Humorless	8.3	11.7	1%	77%	13%
12	Important	Insignificant	6.5	8.6		88%	99%
13†	Humane	Ruthless	8.6	11.0	5%	86%	31%
14†	Submissive	Dominant	13.2	14.5			
15	Will go far	Will not get ahead	4.2	5.8			

° Given for all qualities common to Asch's list and this set of rating scales.
† These scales were reversed when presented to the subjects.

in terms of this relation than in terms of a general positive or negative feeling toward the stimulus person. If first impressions are normally made in terms of such general dimensions as "warmth" and "coldness," the power they give the observer in making predictions and specific evaluations about such desparate behavior characteristics as formality and considerateness is considerable (even though these predictions may be incorrect or misleading).

The free report impression data were analyzed for only one of the sections. In general, there were few sizable differences between the "warm" and "cold" observers. The "warm" observers attributed more nervousness, more sincerity, and more industriousness to the stimulus person. Although the frequencies of comparable qualities are very low because of the great variety of descriptions produced by the observers, there is considerable agreement with the rating scale data.

Two important phenomena are illustrated in these free description protocols, the first of them having been noted by Asch. *Firstly,* the characteristics of the stimulus person are interpreted in terms of the precognition of warmth or coldness. For example, a "warm" observer writes about a rather shy and retiring stimulus person as follows: "He makes friends slowly but they are lasting friendships when formed." In another instance, several "cold" observers describe him as being ". . . intolerant: would be angry if you disagree with his views . . ."; while several "warm" observers put the same thing this way: "Unyielding in principle, not easily influenced or swayed from his original attitude." *Secondly,* the preinformation about the stimulus person's warmth or coldness is evaluated and interpreted in the light of the direct behavioral data about him. For example, "He has a slight inferiority complex which leads to his coldness," and "His conscientiousness and industriousness might be mistaken for coldness." Examples of these two phenomena occurred rather infrequently, and there was no way to evaluate the relative strengths of these countertendencies. Certainly some such evaluation is necessary to determine the conditions under which behavior which is contrary to a stereotyped label resists distortion and leads to rejection of the label.

A comparison of the data from the two different stimulus persons is pertinent to the last point in so far as it indicates the interaction between the properties of the stimulus person and the label. The fact that the warm-cold variable generally produced differences in the same direction for the two stimulus persons, even though they are very different in personality, behavior, and mannerisms, indicates the strength of this variable. However, there were some exceptions to this tendency as well as marked differences in the *degree* to which the experimental variable was able to produce differences. For example, stimulus person A typically appears to be anything but lacking in self-esteem and on rating scale 4 he was generally at the "proud" end of the scale. Although the "warm" observers tended to rate him as they did the other stimulus person (i.e., more "modest"), the difference between the "warm" and "cold" means for stimulus person A is very small and not significant as it is for stimulus person B. Similarly, stimulus person B was seen as "unpopular" and "humorless," which agrees with his typical classroom behavior. Again the "warm" observers rated him more favorably on these items, but their ratings were not significantly different from those of the "cold" observers, as was true for the other stimulus person. Thus we see that the

strength or compellingness of various qualities of the stimulus person must be reckoned with. The stimulus is not passive to the forces arising from the label but actively resists distortion and may severely limit the degree of influence exerted by the preinformation.[3]

2. INFLUENCE OF WARM-COLD VARIABLE ON INTERACTION WITH THE STIMULUS PERSON

In the analysis of the frequency with which the various students took part in the discussion led by the stimulus person, a larger proportion of those given the "warm" preinformation participated than of those given the "cold" preinformation. Fifty-six per cent of the "warm" subjects entered the discussion, whereas only 32 per cent of the "cold" subjects did so. Thus the expectation of warmth not only produced more favorable early perceptions of the stimulus person but led to greater initiation of interaction with him. This relation is a low one, significant at between the 5 per cent and 10 per cent level of confidence, but it is in line with the general principle that social perception serves to guide and steer the person's behavior in his social environment.

As would be expected from the foregoing findings, there was also a relation between the favorableness of the impression and whether or not the person participated in the discussion. Although any single item yielded only a small and insignificant rela-

[3] We must raise an important question here: Would there be a tendency for "warm" observers to distort the perception in the favorable direction regardless of how much the stimulus deviated from the expectation? Future research should test the following hypothesis, which is suggested by Gestalt perception theory (Krech, D., and Crutchfield, R. S., 1948, pp. 95-98): If the stimulus differs but slightly from the expectation, the perception will tend to be *assimilated* to the expectation; however, if the difference between the stimulus and expectation is too great, the perception will occur by contrast to the expectation and will be distorted in the opposite direction.

tion to participation, when a number are combined the trend becomes clear cut. For example, when we combine the seven items which were influenced to a statistically significant degree by the warm-cold variable, the total score bears considerable relation to participation, the relationship being significant as well beyond the 1 per cent level. A larger proportion of those having favorable total impressions participated than of those having unfavorable impressions, the biserial correlation between these variables being .34. Although this relation may be interpreted in several ways, it seems most likely that the unfavorable perception led to a curtailment of interaction. Support for this comes from one of the other studies in this series (Kelley, 1948). There it was found that those persons having unfavorable impressions of the instructor at the end of the first class meeting tended less often to initiate interactions with him in the succeeding four meetings than did those having favorable first impressions. There was also some tendency in the same study for those persons who interacted least with the instructor to change least in their judgments of him from the first to later impressions.

It will be noted that these relations lend some support to the autistic hostility hypothesis proposed by Newcomb (1947). This hypothesis suggests that the possession of an initially hostile attitude toward a person leads to a restriction of communication and contact with him which in turn serves to preserve the hostile attitude by preventing the acquisition of data which could correct it. The present data indicate that a restriction of interaction is associated with unfavorable preinformation and an unfavorable perception. The data from the other study support this result and also indicate the correctness of the second part of the hypothesis, that restricted interaction reduces the likelihood of change in the attitude.

What makes these findings more significant is that they appear in the context of a discussion class where there are numerous *induced* and *own* forces to enter the discussion and to interact with the instructor. It seems likely that the effects predicted by Newcomb's hypothesis would be much more marked in a setting where such forces were not present.

Summary

The warm-cold variable had been found by Asch to produce large differences in the impressions of personality formed from a list of adjectives. In this study the same variable was introduced in the form of expectations about a real person and was found to produce similar differences in first impressions of him in a classroom setting. In addition, the differences in first impressions produced by the different expectations were shown to influence the observers' behavior toward the stimulus person. Those observers given the favorable expectation (who, consequently, had a favorable impression of the stimulus person) tended to interact more with him than did those given the unfavorable expectation.

References

Asch, S. E. Forming impressions of personality. *J. abnorm. soc. Psychol.*, 1946, *41*, 258-290.

Katz, D., and Braly, K. W. Verbal stereotypes and racial prejudice. In T. M. Newcomb and E. L. Hartley (Eds.), *Readings in social psychology.* New York: Holt, Rinehart and Winston, 1947. Pp. 204-210.

Kelley, H. H. First impressions in interpersonal relations. Ph.D. thesis, Massachusetts Institute of Technology, Cambridge, Mass. Sept., 1948.

Krech, D., and Crutchfield, R. S. *Theory and problems of social psychology.* New York: McGraw-Hill, 1948.

Luchins, A. S. Forming impressions of personality: a critique. *J. abnorm. soc. Psychol.*, 1948, *48*, 318-325.

Mensh, I. N., and Wishner, J. Asch on

"Forming impressions of personality": further evidence. *J. Pers.*, 1947, *16*, 188-191.

NEWCOMB, T. M. Autistic hostility and social reality. *Hum. Relat.*, 1947, *1*, 69-86.

NEWSTETTER, W. I., FELDSTEIN, M. J., and NEWCOMB, T. M. *Group adjustment: a study in experimental sociology.* Cleveland: Western Reserve University, 1938.

The Determinants of Distortion
in Social Perception ❦ Albert Pepitone

Social perception as an area for focused experimental investigation has been recognized in recent years to be of first-rank importance. How individuals estimate or interpret the actions, intentions and personality attributes of other individuals and how they size-up groups, social classes, "atmospheres," and variously ordered social symbols suggest many significant problems to the social psychologist. Perhaps the primary importance of social perception derives from the assumption that overt forms of social behavior are "steered" by the perception of the social environment just as many actions in the physical environment are assumed to be regulated by the perception of physical objects (Lewin, 1948). If such a close relation exists between perception and action, inappropriate or maladaptive social behavior could be supposed to depend upon incorrect or distorted perceptions of the social situation. From this point of view, many problems of interpersonal relations may turn out to be in some measure the consequence of perceptual distortion.

The problem of distortion in perceiving real social stimuli has received relatively little attention in the literature. By and large, studies have been concerned with the distorting effect of attitude on the interpretation of picture stimuli (Frenkel-Brunswik and Sanford, 1945; Proshansky, 1943;

Seeleman, 1940), the biasing effect of "needs," values and emotions on the estimation of such characteristics as the size of physical objects (Bruner and Goodman, 1947; McClelland and Atkinson, 1948) or on the attribution of maliciousness and other characteristics to photographs (Murray, 1933) and so on.

The experiment to be reported in this paper grew out of an earlier exploratory investigation designed to determine the effects of motivation upon the estimation of power and approval in real "stimulus" people. The results of this study suggested that an increment of motivation brings about estimates of other persons' attributes which are beneficial or "facilitative" with respect to the perceiver's goal achievement. In other words, social perception under such conditions describes a better state of affairs for the individual than actually exists. The present experiment was designed to isolate crucial variables and to yield a more exact hypothesis of facilitative distortion.

Procedure

SUBJECTS

Eighty-eight high school Sophomore males were used as subjects (Ss). On the basis of their responses to a specially con-

This article has been adapted by the author especially for this book from "Motivational Effects in Social Perception," *Human Relations*, 1949, *3*, 57-76. Reprinted by permission of the author and publisher.

structed "Attitude toward Sports" questionnaire, it was possible to classify Ss as to their interest in observing championship basketball games, particularly a Conference game in which the University team was to participate. Generally speaking this was a highly desirable goal for such a sample.

Four days prior to the experiment the physical training instructors announced in the Sophomore gym periods that three coaches from the University were coming the following week to interview some of the boys individually as part of a statewide survey on student opinions in sports. The students to be queried would be selected at random from their study periods. It was said that if the coaches found a boy's ideas and opinions worthwhile, they would award him a free ticket to "some basketball game." This procedure standardized expectancies concerning the experimental procedure and minimized the possibility of resistance and confusion when a boy was approached in his study hall the following week.

THE INDUCTION OF MOTIVATION

Whether a High or Low level of motivation was induced depended upon the preclassification of the particular S.[1] The standard procedure followed by the experimenter (E) was to take an S of known interest potential from the study hall and informally make a set of remarks which had been carefully designed to arouse or dampen motivation. If the S belonged to a group of high interest potential, the following was said:

Do you know what this is about? Did you hear an announcement in your gym period last week about the three coaches

[1] Admittedly, the assignment of Ss to High and Low motivation conditions on the basis of their interest in and knowledge of basketball may have introduced into the later social perception measurement situation relevant variables other than experimentally induced motivational tension with respect to a specific goal. The relatively imprecise procedure was adopted, however, to insure the creation of a large differential between experimental treatments.

who are coming to the high school? These fellows, who are here now, are from the University where they are training to be coaches. They're making a statewide survey to get the students' viewpoints on sports. They're going to ask you a few questions. If they think your opinions are worthwhile, they will award you a ticket to a first-rate basketball game. How would you like to go to one of the Michigan games?. . . . There are only a few of these tickets and if you tell your friends then everybody will want one. You have to promise not to mention this to anyone.

If the S belonged to the low interest group, E told him the following, this time in a manner designed to dampen any interest in the ticket:

Do you know. . . . etc. (first part same as above). . . . If they think your opinions are worthwhile, they might give you a ticket to some basketball game—probably some high school game. Nothing very exciting about it, but it's the best they can do. Sounds pretty dull to me.

THE MEETING WITH THE COACHES

After the attempt to induce High or Low motivation, the S went directly into a small anteroom where three coaches introduced themselves and commenced to ask simple questions concerning present and proposed regulations in basketball and football. The questions were structured so that neither special ability nor information was needed for an adequate and "reasonable" answer. At the close of the ten-minute meeting, one of the coaches mentioned that "one of the men in your gym department wants to see you downstairs right away. I don't know what it's about." The S was then directed to a small office on the floor below where he was met by the Interviewer.

THE POSTMEETING INTERVIEW

The Interviewer, a graduate student trained in open-ended interviewing techniques, introduced himself as one closely affiliated with the physical training department and now co-operating with them on a study of leadership. He carefully explained that the "department" wanted to find out how "you fellows react to different kinds of leadership like the three coaches upstairs," that such information would be very useful when the high school wanted to employ an additional athletic director. He stated that this interview had absolutely nothing to do with getting a ticket, that "we are not as rich as the University and, therefore, cannot give out prizes." The Ss were fully cooperative and responded readily in what seemed to be an unbiased manner. No S expressed suspicion that any part of the procedure was an experiment.

THE STIMULUS SITUATIONS

What the coaches said in questioning and responding to each S as well as their manner of interaction with him originated in three prepared scripts. In each script, three roles were established so that each player displayed a given degree of *power* in relation to the others and indicated a given degree of *approval* of the S. In order to equate knowledge and skill factors, the questions were the same for each script, differing only in the manner in which they were asked and to a certain extent in the particular context out of which they arose. Generalized descriptions of the power and approval roles as expressed in each script are as follows:

The Friendly-Hostile (F-H) Situation

Mr. Friendly: maximum approval, medium power. Agrees wholeheartedly with the S's opinions and indicates that he has unusual insight, smiles warmly and acceptingly at him, always refers to him by first name.

Mr. Neutral: non-evaluative, medium power. Neither agrees nor disagrees with the S's answers but regards them matter-of-factly, makes no reference to him by name, makes no reference to his knowl-

edge, does not smile or frown at him but remains straightfaced.

Mr. Negative: disapproving, medium power. Disagrees openly with most of the S's answers, comments that S doesn't know too much about athletics and continually frowns in mild contempt at him.

The Friendly-Neutral (F-N) Situation

Mr. Friendly: maximum approval, medium power. Same as in F-H condition.

Mr. Moderate: moderately approving, medium power. Generally agrees with the S's opinions but points out additional problems, smiles warmly at him on occasion, makes no reference to him as person, has a rather general problem orientation.

Mr. Neutral: non-evaluative, medium power. Same as in F-H condition.

In both the Friendly-Hostile and Friendly-Neutral situations the three coaches expressed a medium degree of power. A general description of this attribute is as follows:

Each coach gives an authoritative opinion about athletics with which the other two coaches fully concur and gives an authoritative opinion about athletics with which the other two coaches openly disagree. A brief discussion held at the beginning of the meeting makes it clear that the order of questioning will be rotated arbitrarily, giving the impression that the coaches are equated in authority. Two interludes within the script describe a fictitious "boss" under whom the three coaches work and who is ultimately responsible for this project thus placing them in an equal power position under someone else's direction.

The Friendly-Authority (F-A) Situation

Mr. High Power: maximum power, moderate approval. Introduces "his" staff: refers to Mr. Medium Power as his "first assistant," and Mr. Low Power as a "fellow from Detroit Office here to help us out." Is seated in middle position at table, more formally attired than other two coaches, directs proceedings, order of questioning, gives others permission to ask questions.

Mr. Medium Power: medium power, moderate approval. Acts as Mr. High Power's amanuensis, e.g., vetoes an attempt by Mr. Low Power to ask a question, tells Mr. Low Power to make sure to "pick up some data" for Mr. High Power, acknowledges a correction by Mr. High Power, corrects an opinion given by Mr. Low Power, referring to Mr. High Power as a criterion.

Mr. Low Power: low power, moderate approval. Assumes most casual "unofficial" manner of all three coaches, asks permission of the other two coaches for questioning the subject; his attempt at questioning the subject is vetoed by Mr. Medium Power.

The three coaches expressed a moderate degree of friendliness toward the S. The empirical description of moderate friendliness corresponds approximately to the role of Mr. Moderate in the F-N condition described earlier.

A SAMPLE SCRIPT

Some idea of the flavor of the interaction between the S and the three coaches can be given by the following:

Mr. Friendly: Billie, do you think there should be longer rest periods for the players between halves? If yes: That's a good point. You're suggesting that basketball is played at such a fast clip that in a few minutes many players are completely exhausted. You're perfectly right—rest periods should be extended. If no: That's a good point. You're suggesting that basketball is such an exciting game because it *is* played at such a furious pace. To increase the rest period would have the effect of deadening the game. You're perfectly right there—rest periods should not be extended.

Mr. Negative: (With contempt.) They've been talking a lot about breaking a tie game. Do you think they should be played off in extra periods—like they do now—or in post-season games like in baseball? If S is for the extra period: You realize that in an extra period the game is won by only one or two points, which doesn't really tell you how good the winning team is. Hmph. . . . The game might be won by chance. But I'll put down your opinion. . . . (shakes head negatively).

Mr. Neutral: Formerly when a substitute was sent into the game, he first had to report to the referee on the floor. Now the new rules say that all he does is tell the scorer on the side, and then he goes in. Do you think that this is an improvement over the old procedure? I see (factually). Some have said that before. I'd like to think about that. I suppose in some ways it's an improvement, in other ways not.

STIMULUS CONTROLS

Various controls were employed in order to maintain maximum validity of the stimulus situation. The coaches were trained on all three scripts and on the three roles within each script to a high level of proficiency. During the two-week training period several independent observers came to essential agreement that the roles were being recited with the intended quality and intensity. During the experiment itself (while waiting for the next S) the coaches evaluated and corrected their roles. The individual personalities and physical appearances of the coaches were presumably balanced out by having each coach play a given role approximately the same number of times in any stimulus condition. There was also an attempt to equate the frequency of the three roles by each individual coach under each level of motivation. Although equal role frequency under the two motivational levels was not achieved, there were no differences in Ss' reactions which could be traced to the influence of any individual coach. To guard against fatigue of the coaches and the Ss as related to time of day, and to control against the non-random nature of study periods, the stimulus situations were presented in simple alternation. Thus, the three situations were represented about equally often at any given period during the school day. Finally, because the position of the coaches at the table might influence the Ss' estimations of power two of the coaches assumed the three table positions with about equal frequency. Mr. Friendly, the doubly approving coach, however, was purposely *not* seated at the middle position to make certain that this factor was completely non-influential in the estimation of his power.

THE EFFECTIVENESS OF THE MOTIVATION INDUCTION

In addition to serving as stimulus conditions, the coaches made ratings of the behavioral manifestations of each S's motivation. The observation form contained eight categories of motivational symptoms. Appropriate categories were checked independently by the three coaches directly after the meeting. Then, the S's motivational level was rated on a six-point scale. Table 1 contains the mean of the pooled coaches' ratings given to the Ss in the High and Low motivation conditions. The coaches did not know, of course, which treatment the S had been given.

TABLE 1

MEAN MOTIVATION RATINGS OF Ss IN HIGH AND LOW MOTIVATION CONDITIONS

Group	Stimulus Situation		
	F-H	F-N	F-A
High (n = 46)	14.20	14.81	14.56
Low (n = 42)	8.15	11.13	9.65
	$t = 5.106$	$t = 3.249$	$t = 5.367$
	$p < .01$	$p < .01$	$p < .01$

Table 1 indicates clearly that two levels of motivation had been created by E's remarks to the preclassified Ss. Regardless of the stimulus situation the boys who were given the High motivation treatment were observed to be more highly motivated than those who were given the Low treatment.

THE ESTIMATION OF POWER AND APPROVAL

The interview procedure first encouraged an expression of feelings concerning the general characteristics of the coaches and then examined the Ss' perceptions of power and approval. The main questions used at this stage were: *Who do you think has the most to say about whether you get a ticket? In other words, who is the boss. . . . Who runs things up there?* and *Which one of those fellows likes you best?* The same questions were then asked to ascertain which coach exhibited least power and least approval. The S was next to supply reasons for his choices. Finally, Ss made quantitative estimates on the following scales:

Power

8. He has everything to say about it (in the decision to award the ticket).
7. He has almost everything to say about it.
6. He has a whole lot to say about it.
5. He has pretty much to say about it.
4. He has something to say about it.
3. He has just a little to say about it.
2. He has almost nothing to say about it.
1. He has nothing to say about it.

Approval

8. He liked me very, very much.
7. He liked me a whole lot.
6. He liked me pretty much.
5. He liked me a little.
4. He disliked me a little.
3. He disliked me pretty much.
2. He disliked me a whole lot.
1. He disliked me very, very much.

THE MEASUREMENT OF DISTORTION

It was mentioned previously that during the lengthy training of the coaches judgments were made by several independent observers in order to validate the expressions of power and approval at the desired levels of intensity. The training, in fact, was aimed at making the behavior of power and approval correspond to intervals on the above scales. Thus, equated power was judged to lie in the interval between 4 and 5 on the interview scale and equated approval in the interval between 5 and 6. Distortion in the Ss' estimation of these equated attributes could thus be measured in terms of the numerical deviation from the "reality" intervals.

Concerning the attributes which were varied in the three stimulus situations, there was less certainty among judges in assigning the objective behavior to scale intervals. Where approval varied it was judged that Mr. Friendly liked the S at least "a whole lot" (scale point number 7) and that Mr. Negative disliked the S at least "a little" (scale point number 4). Mr. Neutral's objective behavior was placed between scale points 4 and 5. Mr. Moderate's degree of approval, on the other hand, was judged to be at least point 5 on the interview scale— "He liked me a little"—and very likely not more than 7—"He liked me a whole lot." Similarly where the attribute of power was made to vary objectively, the judged scale position was not more precise than statements as to minimum and maximum values.

It is important to recognize that, regardless of the exactitude with which the objective-subjective coordinations could be made, differences between the High and Low motivation conditions are likely to indicate distortion on the part of one or both groups. The problem in such an event would be to specify which group is distorting at all or distorting to a greater degree.

Results

THE ESTIMATION OF VARIED STIMULUS ATTRIBUTES

Table 2 contains the mean ratings representing the Ss' estimations of those attributes which varied in the three stimulus situation. In the F-H and F-N conditions, approval is the variable stimulus attribute, while in the F-A condition power is varied.

It can be seen that in each stimulus situation where either power or approval varied objectively across coaches, the estimation of that attribute varied correspondingly. The correspondence between subjective and objective estimates holds for Ss in both motivation groups. One cannot conclude from this

TABLE 2

MEAN ESTIMATES OF VARIED STIMULUS ATTRIBUTES BY HIGH AND LOW MOTIVATION Ss

	Approval (F-H Sit.)		Approval (F-N Sit.)		Power (F-A Sit.)	
	High Motiv. (N = 10)	Low Motiv. (N = 10)	High Motiv. (N = 18)	Low Motiv. (N = 15)	High Motiv. (N = 18)	Low Motiv. (N = 17)
Mr. Friendly[1] (Mr. High Power)	7.40 $t = 3.250$[2]	6.50[3]	7.06 $t = .094$	7.03[3]	6.44 $t = .912$	6.18[3]
Mr. Moderate (Mr. Medium Power)			6.22 $t = 1.552$	5.83	4.61 $t = .690$	4.79
Mr. Neutral (Mr. Low Power)	6.00 $t = 2.539$[2]	5.22	4.72 $t = 1.494$	5.17	3.67 $t = .760$	3.88
Mr. Negative	5.00 $t = .728$	4.50				

[1] In the F-A situation the coaches are Mr. High Power, Mr. Medium Power and Mr. Low Power.
[2] Differences between motivation conditions are significant at the 3% confidence level or better.
[3] The differences among the vertically arranged means, pooling both motivation groups, are all statistically reliable at least at the one percent confidence level.

result, however, that there was no perceptual distortion in the Ss' estimates. Only a detailed examination of the results within each stimulus situation can tell.

THE F-H SITUATION

First, in the F-H condition both motivation groups appear to have overestimated the approval of Mr. Negative. This disagreeable and mildly contemptuous coach was judged by the High group to like them "a little," and although the Low's estimate is somewhat below this, it is not so low as to be considered a realistic estimation. The distortion by the High motivation Ss of Mr. Negative's approval is striking when it is noted that they estimated more approval of them on the part of this coach than did the corresponding High motivation Ss on the part of Mr. Neutral in the F-N situation!

Both motivation groups of the F-H condition also seem to have overestimated the approval of Mr. Neutral. The High group average rating—"He liked me pretty much" —is probably more than this non-committal and neutral coach actually expressed. It is a significantly higher estimate than that made by the Low group.

As for the estimation of Mr. Friendly's approval, it will be recalled that, according to observations made during the training of the coaches, his approval was about "a whole lot"—that is, a scale rating of 7. Considered as a whole, the High Ss' ratings of Mr. Friendly, of Mr. Neutral and of Mr. Negative were distorted in an upward direction, and more so than the ratings of the Low motivation Ss.

THE F-N SITUATION

This stimulus situation is identical with the F-H situation except that, instead of including both Mr. Negative and Mr. Neutral, it contains only the latter role and substitutes Mr. Moderate for the former. Plainly, it can be regarded as a more favorable stimulus environment as far as the subject's

reaching his goal is concerned. Less distortion of it is noted in general.

Both motivation groups perceived the approval of Mr. Friendly to be about the level judged to be objective, and there is clearly no difference between the two groups.

There also appears to be little or no distortion with respect to Mr. Moderate; both groups estimated his approval at about his actual level of expression.

Concerning Mr. Neutral's approval, it seems as if the High group was more *sensitive* than the Low group. Their estimate corresponds to a level between "He liked me a little" and "He disliked me a little" which, according to objective definitions, best describes Mr. Neutral's actual behavior. That the High group was more accurate in estimating the differences between Mr. Moderate and Mr. Neutral is perhaps indicated by the significantly larger discrepancy in their ratings of these two coaches than that shown by the Low group ($t = 2.739$, $p < .01$). It is not unreasonable to suppose that when the stimulus environment is less restraining—as it is in the F-N condition relative to the F-H condition—High motivation sensitizes the individual to real differences in approval.

THE F-A SITUATION

According to the judgments adopted for the definition of objective behavior, there was practically no distortion of the coaches' power in the F-A condition. Both motivation groups estimate this behavior to be at levels which more or less correspond to their objective expressions. And, although no differences between the two motivation groups are significant, the larger over-all discrepancy between Mr. High Power and Mr. Low Power by the High group again suggests that motivation makes for increased sensitivity. This, of course, rests on the admittedly speculative assumption that numerical spread in the estimates of power can be coordinated to perceptual sensitivity.

THE ESTIMATION OF EQUATED STIMULUS ATTRIBUTES

We now consider the estimations of attributes which are constant for the three coaches. In the F-H and F-N situations all three coaches have medium power, while in the F-A stimulus situation, moderate approval remains constant for the three coaches. Table 3 contains the mean ratings of these attributes given by the High and Low motivation groups under each stimulus situation.

each of the three stimulus situations the attribute which was objectively equated was estimated by both motivation groups to vary in direct correspondence with the attribute which was not equated. In the F-H condition, the most approving coach—Mr. Friendly—was estimated to display most power and the disapproving coach—Mr. Negative—the least power. Similarly, in the F-N situation, Mr. Friendly appeared to possess most power and Mr. Neutral least. The results of the F-A situation in which approval is equated show that the most ap-

TABLE 3

Mean Estimates of Equated Stimulus Attributes by High and Low Motivation Ss

	Power (F-H Sit.)		Power (F-N Sit.)		Approval (F-A Sit.)	
	High Motiv. (N = 10)	Low Motiv. (N = 10)	High Motiv. (N = 18)	Low Motiv. (N = 15)	High Motiv. (N = 18)	Low Motiv. (N = 17)
Mr. Friendly (Mr. High Power) [1]	6.60	5.40[3]	6.06	6.47[3]	6.53	6.44[3]
	$t = 2.199$[2]		$t = 1.154$		$t = .274$	
Mr. Moderate (Mr. Medium Power)			4.86	5.13	6.14	5.82
			$t = .922$		$t = 1.081$	
Mr. Neutral (Mr. Low Power)	4.20	4.10	3.42	4.03	5.44	5.06
	$t = .292$		$t = 1.913$[2]		$t = 1.354$	
Mr. Negative	3.90	3.60				
	$t = .479$					

[1] In the F-A situation the coaches are Mr. High Power, Mr. Medium Power and Mr. Low Power.
[2] Differences between motivation conditions are significant at the six percent confidence level or better.
[3] The differences among the vertically arranged means, pooling both motivation groups, are significant at least at the five percent level. An exception is the mean difference between Mr. Negative and Mr. Neutral in the F-H condition.

The data shown in Table 3 can be readily interpreted if it is recalled that medium power was judged to lie within the interval "He has something to say about it" (i.e., awarding the ticket) and "He has pretty much to say about it"—between scale points 4 and 5. The medium or "moderate" degree of approval expressed in the F-A condition was judged to lie between "He liked me a little" and "He liked me pretty much"— between scale points 5 and 6.

The means in Table 3 indicate that in

proval was perceived in Mr. High Power while Mr. Low Power was seen as least approving. Pooling the two motivation groups, all the differences among the coaches in the F-N and F-A situation were statistically significant. The difference between Mr. Neutral and Mr. Negative in the F-H condition, however, was not.

It seems evident, then, that considerable distortion took place. Again a detailed analysis of each stimulus situation is necessary in order to determine more precisely the amount and direction of the distortion which occurred in the two motivation groups.

THE F-H SITUATION

Reference to the reality interval of equated power (between 4 and 5) indicates that both motivation groups have estimated Mr. Negative's power to be less than it was in actuality, that is, less than "something to say about it." The difference between High and Low groups is not statistically significant, however.

It is apparent, on the other hand, that both motivation groups overestimated the power of Mr. Friendly. More distortion occurred in the High group; they perceived this coach as displaying more than "a whole lot" of power. While the Low group also distorts upward, their estimate is just about the upper limit of the reality interval, i.e., about "pretty much to say about it." The difference between the motivation groups is statistically significant.

Granting the definition of the reality interval, there was no distortion with respect to Mr. Neutral's power.

THE F-N SITUATION

Both motivation groups overestimated the power of Mr. Friendly, having seen at least "a whole lot of power" in this coach. The difference between the High and Low groups, however, is not statistically significant.

Only the High group distorts the power of Mr. Neutral. This coach's power is estimated to be at a level considerably below the lower limit of the reality interval, that is, Mr. Neutral is perceived as displaying less than "something to say" about awarding the ticket. The difference between the High and Low group with respect to Mr. Neutral's power is statistically significant.

Apparently, no appreciable distortion occurred in the perception of Mr. Moderate's power—the estimates of both groups having been within or very close to the reality interval.

THE F-A SITUATION

Considering now the estimation of approval in the F-A situation—where the reality interval was judged to exist between ratings 5 and 6—it is apparent that neither motivation group distorted as much as the corresponding groups of Ss in the two other situations. Both groups, however, did overestimate the approval of Mr. High Power, placing it at a level above the postulated reality interval. It may also be noted that the High group slightly overestimated the approval of Mr. Medium Power.

A Theory of Facilitative Distortion

To formulate a general theoretical statement about distortion it is necessary to examine closely the nature of the distortions that have been identified above. Whether we consider the estimations made of varied or of equated stimulus attributes the distortions indicated have been in a "facilitative" direction. Tables 2 and 3 show that in the F-H condition Mr. Negative's approval is overestimated and his power underestimated by both the High and Low motivation groups. To regard Mr. Negative as less disagreeable than he actually is and to regard the same coach as having less power than he actually appeared to express tend to describe an optimal state of affairs for the S. Distortions in the other stimulus situations can be similarly interpreted as facilitative.

It has previously been suggested that the stimulus situations can be represented as three different points along a dimension of "restraint-against-goal-achievement." Considering first the data presented in Table 3 in terms of this dimension, it is apparent that the magnitude of facilitative distortion is related complexly to the level of motivation and the degree of stimulus restraint.

Fig. 1 illustrates how distortion in the estimation of equated stimulus attributes is affected by simulus restraint and level of

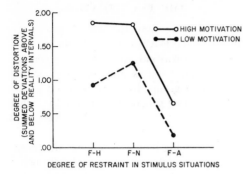

Fig. 1. Distortion of equated attributes by High and Low motivation groups in the three stimulus situations.

motivation. Considering the High group's estimates of all three coaches in the stimulus situation, the magnitude of distortion—based upon the sum of all the deviations in both directions from the assumed reality interval—decreases as the stimulus environment becomes less restraining.[2] Considering the High motivation Ss, distortion reaches its highest point in the F-H situation, falls off very slightly in the F-N condition, and then drops sharply in the most friendly condition. As for the Low motivation group, in the most restraining F-H situation there is comparatively little distortion. When stimulus restraint is diminished the amount of distortion increases sharply. Finally, when the stimulus environment offers maximum promise of goal achievement, the Low group exhibits the least amount of facilitative distortion. In the F-H situation, where the chances of reaching the goal presumably look bleak, S seems to have given up. It is

[2] It should be kept in mind, of course, that the equated attribute in the F-A condition (approval) is not the same as the equated attribute in the other two conditions (power). However, at this point there is no reason to believe that there would be inherently less distortability in one or the other of these attributes.

as if he "does not bother" to distort when the environment is too restraining; it is, perceptually, "not worth it." Such an interpretation emphasizes the subtle interdependence between person and environment in relation to perceptual organization. We may state the hypothesis:

The magnitude of facilitative distortion regarding equated stimulus attributes is a complex functon of the level of motivation and the degree to which the stimulus offers restraint against reaching the goal.

Concerning objectively varied attributes, it will be recalled that in the F-H condition upward distortion of approval occurred and that the High group appeared to show the stronger tendency. In the F-N condition, on the other hand, there was relatively little distortion. Moreover, the High group seemed to have perceived the attribute of approval more precisely in line with the observer estimates of the coaches' behavior. Similarly, in the F-A condition facilitative distortion was at a minimum and again there was some suggestion that the High group was more sensitive to the "real" levels of power expressed by the coaches. Thus, where we are dealing with the perception of varied attributes, facilitative distortion is most strongly demonstrated under conditions of relatively severe restraint in the objective stimulus environment. And since under these conditions the greater amount of distortion is noted in the High group, the hypothesis we have already formulated to cover the perception of equated stimulus attributes also covers the perception of varied attributes. In the milder ranges of stimulus restraint, however, not only is distortion greatly reduced but we find that the High group's estimates are more realistic than the Low group's. This fact points to a rather fundamental distinction between equated and varied stimulus attributes in regard to the amount of facilitative distortion and respecting the function of motivation in producing distortion. Research should address itself to this matter.

References

BRUNER, J. S., and GOODMAN, C. C. Value and need as organizing factors in perception. *J. abnorm. soc. Psychol.*, 1947, 42, 33-44.

FRENKEL-BRUNSWIK, E., and SANFORD, R. N. Personality factors in antisemitism. *J. Psychol.*, 1945, 20, 271-291.

LEWIN, K. Conduct, knowledge and acceptance of new values. *Resolving Social Conflicts*. New York: Harper & Row, 1948.

McCLELLAND, D. C., and ATKINSON, J. A. The projective expression of needs: the effect of different intensities of the hunger drive on perception, *J. Psychol.*, 1948, 25, 205-222.

MURRAY, H. A. The effect of fear upon estimates of maliciousness of other personalities. *J. soc. Psychol.*, 1933, 4, 310-339.

PROSHANSKY, H. M. A projective method for the study of attitudes. *J. abnorm. soc. Psychol.*, 1943, 38, 393-395.

SEELEMAN, V. The influence of attitudes upon the remembering of pictorial material. *Arch. Psychol.*, New York, 1940, No. 258.

Some Determinants and Consequences

of the Perception of Social ❊ John W. Thibaut

Causality ❊ Henry W. Riecken

It is a generally accepted finding of research on group cohesiveness that increased social interaction in a setting of reward or success leads to heightened interpersonal acceptance (Festinger and Kelley, 1951; Gilchrist, 1952; Homans, 1950; Riecken and Homans, 1954). It is not entirely clear, however, in just what ways social interaction is responsible for increasing liking between individuals. We shall describe below two experiments in which we have attempted to isolate some simple determinants of the ways in which interaction may be perceived, and to study the consequences of such perceptions for changes in interpersonal acceptance.

A basic determinant of acceptance is the perception that one's instrumental communications (e.g., attempts to influence an-

other) have controlled the recipient. This statement is based on our assumption that vertical perception of such control signalizes goalward locomotion and good predictability of the social environment. Thus, if person X sends influence attempts of equal strength to persons Y and Z, and if Y is perceived to comply while Z is perceived as not complying, then X will tend to accept Y and to reject Z. The authors have reported a preliminary experiment (Thibaut and Riecken, 1955) in which it was arranged that X would perceive Y as complying and Z as not complying in the influence attempt. The predicted relative acceptance of Y and rejection of Z were obtained. This relationship between perceived control and acceptance can also be formulated in terms of the perception of social causality. X perceives that

This article was adapted by the authors especially for E. E. Maccoby, T. M. Newcomb, and E. L. Hartley (Eds.), *Readings in Social Psychology*, 3d Ed. New York: Holt, Rinehart and Winston, 1958, from *Journal of Personality*, 1955, 24, 113-133. Reprinted by permission of the authors and publishers.

his influence attempt (instrumental communication) "causes" a compliant change in behavior or attitude in Y, and not in Z. X accepts Y and rejects Z.

The foregoing statement is restricted to situations where X perceives that his communication has caused compliance from one person but failed to produce it from another. When we consider the case in which two or more persons respond favorably following a communication from X, a new range of problems is introduced, for X may not necessarily perceive his communication as causing the compliance in each case. A comment by Heider (1944) notes this possibility. "When we see a moving object A, we can attribute the movement either to A itself or to another object B. In the first case we see the movement as a spontaneous act of A, in the second as passive movement induced by B." In his studies of the perception of mechanical causality, Michotte (1946) has described the experimental conditions under which two phenomena quite similar to those noted by Heider can be observed. In "l'effet Lancement . . . les observateurs voient l'objet A donner un choc à l'objet B et le chasser, le lancer en avant, le projeter, lui donner une impulsion." Although this "launching" of B is not the same as perceiving B's movement as self-caused, it begins to approximate the perception that B's movement was merely "occasioned" by A. Michottes "l'effet Entraînement" corresponds very closely to the perception that B is passive and inert, being "carried along" by A. In terms of the perception of social causality, any change in Y's behavior or attitude in a direction conforming to X's instrumental communication may be perceived by X to have been caused by Y himself or by X (or his communication). In this case Y's "compliance" is perceived to be either spontaneous and self-caused or coerced by X. This corresponds to the Lewinian distinction between "own force" and "induced force": X may perceive Y's "compliance" as motivated either by Y's "own force" or by an "induced force" from X.

We suggest that the main factors determining the two types of perceptual attribution are the *power* relations between X and Y and between X and Z. Suppose that: (1) X perceives that Y has relatively high power[1] and that Z has relatively low power, (2) X sends the same (or equally "strong") instrumental communications to Y and Z, (3) X perceives that both Y and Z comply with the communication, and (4) in complying, Y and Z are not behaving as they would have been in the absence of the influence attempt. If the foregoing conditions are met, X will tend to perceive the cause of Y's compliance as located "inside" Y (self-caused) and the cause of Z's compliance as located "outside" Z (i.e., a consequence of coercion by the induced force of X).

The results of these differences in attributions of power and causality are that X will credit Y with motives of friendliness and succorance, whereas Z will be regarded as merely responding passively to coercive power. X will tend to say of Y, "He likes me" or "He's a nice guy"; and of Z, "He had to do it" or "I forced him." Hence, as a result of this experience, X will tend to accept Y more than he does Z.

It should be noted that the predictions immediately above may seem to contradict the earlier statement relating perceived control to acceptance. We began by saying that X prefers Y to Z when X's communication is perceived to cause Y's compliance. We concluded by saying that X prefers to Y to Z when X's communication is perceived *not* to cause Y's compliance. A moment's reflection, however, will show that the contradiction is only apparent. When an individual is confronted by a controllable and an uncontrollable other, he will tend to accept or prefer the controllable other, because of the rele-

[1] Power is used here in the special sense of ability to resist social influence. It is believed, however, that the generalization applies to power from all sources (authority, personal competence, physical strength, etc.) except where the basis is itself liking or admiration as e.g., where X perceives that Z's low strength to resist is based on Z's cathexis of him.

vance of control to goalward locomotion. On the other hand, when both (or all) others show compliance, discriminations in acceptance will be made on some basis other than the instrumental capacities of the other for satisfying the individual's needs. Since this point may not be immediately obvious, we should like to discuss it in broader outline here.

An individual ordinarily wants to control his social environment in order to gratify his needs. Complete intractability on the part of another increases the chances of deprivation and consequently leads to rejection or dislike of the other. In order to insure a tractable social environment it may behoove an individual to take steps to increase his social power. As his power position improves, his social environment becomes more manageable, but at the same time the individual begins to lose a type of information. What he tends to lose is perceptual evidence concerning the degree to which the compliance of his subordinates is motivated by spontaneous good will and loyalty. We may assume that the perception of autonomous affection for oneself is *per se* gratifying to most individuals, but perhaps of equal importance are the consequences of spontaneous affection and loyalty for improved social prediction. Any controllable person is predictable, but only when compliance is perceived to be caused by spontaneous good will is prediction possible in the absence of the application of power. If compliant behavior is perceived to be contingent on continuous surveillance and coercion, an upward spiraling might be expected in which the absence of any evidence of loyalty and reliability leads to more vigorous applications of power, which in turn reduces the monitor's ability to perceive any spontaneity in the acquiescence. This may be a common affliction of tyrannical governments.

We shall now restate the hypotheses being tested in the present experiments. From the foregoing discussion it is clear that we are supposing a situation in which the individual is confronted with stimulus persons having relatively high and relatively low power and that, in response to the individual's communications, the stimulus persons will indicate compliance by altering their behavior. Our discussion has suggested two closely related hypotheses.

Hypotheses 1: The individual will perceive the causal locus for compliance as "internal" to the high-power stimulus person and as "external" to the low-power stimulus person.

Hypothesis 2: When an individual rates a person before and after a successful influence attempt, there will be a greater positive (or smaller negative) change in ratings of acceptance of the high-power stimulus person than of the low-power stimulus person.

Measurement Techniques

The measurement techniques were virtually identical to those used in an earlier study (Thibaut and Riecken, 1955), which contains a list of the rating-scale items, a statement of the scoring procedures, and the subscale reliabilities. The "opinion survey" administered to all Ss attempts to measure "authoritarianism" and is constituted of the 30-item California F-Scale (forms 40 and 45) (Adorno, Frenkel-Brunswik, Levinson, and Sanford, 1950) and 11 additional items.

A 19-item rating scale was administered to all Ss before the experiment proper had begun and again at the close of the experiment. This scale contains items of two types. Thirteen of the items are designed to measure the degree to which another person is liked, admired, cathected, accepted. In this part of the rating scale, called the "acceptance scale," the items were evaluatively toned questions about a variety of personal attributes, such as: "Is he good-natured or irritable?" Each question was followed by six alternatives from which S chose "the one that best describes" the ratee. These alternatives offered three degrees of "favorable" and three of "unfavorable" judgment. This "acceptance scale" is the same as that used in the earlier study except for the addition of two new items.

The remaining six items in the rating scale are called the "resistance scale." They attempted to measure the degree to which another person is perceived as being able to resist social influence. The same format as above was used in the "resistance scale," which contained three items in which the "strong" end of the continuum was "favorably" connoted ("forceful," "firm," and "strong-minded") and three items in which the "strong" end was "unfavorably" connoted ("stubborn," "obstinate," and "resistant"). This "resistance scale" is the same as that used in the earlier study except for the inclusion of two new items.

Postexperimental interviews were also conducted, but since the form of these differed slightly in the two experiments, these will be described separately in presenting the experimental findings.

Experimental Procedure

The two experiments to be reported are of the same general form. The S meets two stimulus persons (confederates of E) one of whom is of considerably higher status than the other. This manipulation of status is intended to produce perceived differences in the power of the stimulus persons. Immediately after meeting them, S makes an initial evaluation of them on the "acceptance" and "resistance" scales. During the experiment S repeatedly attempts to influence the behavior of the two confederates. Eventually both confederates comply. S again evaluates the two confederates on the "acceptance" and "resistance" scales and is interviewed. This is the basic form of the two experiments, but since the two sets of procedures and manipulations were different, we will describe the experiments separately.

THE NORTH CAROLINA EXPERIMENT

The Ss were 20 male "volunteers" from the introductory course in psychology at the University of North Carolina. Ss were scheduled to arrive singly at the experimental room, their arrival coinciding with that of two experimental confederates who were instructed to behave as though they were also "naïve" Ss. When S and the two confederates were assembled, E asked them to fill out an "opinion survey" (F-Scale plus related items).

The confederates had been rehearsed in advance to insure that they would conduct themselves in standard fashion. After E had briefly introduced himself and the three "subjects" to one another, E casually questioned each of the three about his background and present status. By prearrangement, one of the confederates said that he had just received the Ph.D. degree and was now a member of the instructional staff. This "high-status confederate" (HSC) was neatly dressed and always wore both coat and tie. The other confederate was in shirt-sleeves, without tie, and said that he had just finished his freshman year of undergraduate study. The two confederates exchanged statuses with every new S. That is, for half of the Ss confederate A was the HSC; for the other half of the Ss confederate B was the HSC. To make plausible the evident similarity of the confederates' ages, this "low-status confederate" (LSC) also said that he was an Army veteran.

E then described the task that the three were to perform. One of the three would be selected to serve as the communicator and the other two as audience. The communicator would attempt to influence the audience to donate blood for a Red Cross blood drive. The role of communicator was filled by drawing lots and it was contrived that S would invariably draw this assignment. Once the roles had been assigned, the confederates (audience) were asked to wait in an adjoining room for further detailed instructions which they would receive as soon as the communicator had been instructed. In his role as communicator, S was told that he would be evaluated on his ability to plan and execute a strategy of persuasion. The materials with which he must work were 38 previously prepared messages, from which he must select and send the ten that he thought would be most effective in persuading the audience to donate blood. The 38 messages varied considerably in forcefulness. Three examples are: "Please consider this request very carefully"; "I sincerely believe that you ought to participate in this drive"; and "I am in no mood to trifle with any refusals."

In order to give some apparent substance to the task, S was told that he would be evaluated on the "quality of the ten messages he selected," the sequence in which he sent the messages, and the pattern of temporal intervals between messages. Rules governing the communication procedure were that, although the audience would be located in the same room with S, all messages must be written, that E would deliver the messages on a signal from S, and that S must send the *same* message at the same time to both members of the audience. Finally S was told that the audience would be permitted no feed-back communication to him until he had finished sending the ten messages, at which point the members of the audience would individually indicate whether or not they had decided to donate blood.

When S had received his instruction, E explained that to evaluate S's strategy of persuasion it would be necessary to find out what kinds of people S perceived his audience to be. This pretext served to introduce the "acceptance" and "resistance" scales, which were then administered to S. In filling out these scales, S was required to discriminate between the two members of the audience on each item, i.e., for any given item the two members of the audience must be located at different points on the six-point scale.

When S commenced this initial rating, E

left the room on the pretext that he must instruct the members of the audience. As soon as S had finished making his ratings, E and the confederates returned to the experimental room and the message-sending began. At the conclusion of the message-sending period, both confederates indicated that they had been effectively influenced. Shortly thereafter they were thanked and dismissed. S then filled out the same "acceptance" and "resistance" scales as before, except that the order of the items was scrambled. Finally S was interviewed. Before S left the room, the purpose of the experiment was explained to him, all deceptions were described, and any questions he had were answered.

THE HARVARD EXPERIMENT

The Ss were 21 sophomore and junior male undergraduates at Harvard University, hired through the student employment service and paid at an hourly rate. Each S reported for a preliminary interview with E one or two days before the actual experimental session. He was given the F-Scale and interviewed on the subjects of family background, education, extracurricular activities, and "experience in groups and in positions of leadership." The resulting information was not used, but this interview served to make plausible to the S the occurrence of similar interviews between E and two confederates which S "accidentally" overheard at the beginning of the actual experimental session. The experiment was explained somewhat vaguely as a study of comparative productivity of individuals and groups in which individuals of different ability worked together. An incidental feature of the experiment, S was told, was that E was interested in using "first-impression" ratings as measures of how well individuals could size each other up as work partners. Therefore, E had arranged matters so S would meet two other men at the experiment who would probably be strangers to him and about whom he would later be asked to give his judgment or rating on certain traits. Thus forewarned, S was dismissed until the experimental session.

When he returned for the experimental session, S was ushered into the experimental room, where he apparently interrupted an interview between E and the high-status confederate (HSC). E apologized for being behind schedule, introduced HSC as one of S's partners in the experiment, and resumed the "interview" in the full hearing of S. The HSC's responses to E's questions revealed that he had attended a well-known private school, an Ivy League University where he had been editor of the daily newspaper, had had command responsibilities in naval combat service, and was currently a Harvard Law School student. The HSC was dressed in a manner appropriate to the stereotype of his background and was poised and confident.

This interview concluded, E left the room momentarily. While he was gone, HSC addressed a standard question and a standard remark to S indicating that he (HSC) expected to find the experiment interesting. This was the only direct interaction S had with HSC. Before the conversation could develop, E returned with the low-status confederate (LSC), whom he introduced and then interviewed. It turned out that LSC was a freshman at a nearby institution of considerably lower prestige (by S's presumed standards), had graduated from a little-known high school in a drab mill town, had never participated in extracurricular activities, and had, as his only "leadership experience," been secretary of his high-school camera club. His socioeconomic status seemed to be "lower," he was rather untastefully dressed, and appeared to be nervous, apologetic about his "background," and self-effacing.

The HSC and LSC were always introduced to S in this manner and in this order, but the two laboratory assistants who played the parts alternated roles so that half of the Ss confronted one person in the HSC role, the other half a second person. The interviews were carefully rehearsed and were as standard as possible; the "facts" purveyed to S were carefully chosen to accord with stereotypes of high- and low-prestige individuals that are current in the undergraduate population from which the Ss came.

Following the interviews, E explained that the trio's task was to construct crossword puzzles; today each would work alone, in order to determine their skill as individuals, and later they would be brought together to work as a group, whose leader would be the man who constructed the best puzzle alone. Further incentives were offered, and detailed instructions given. The three "subjects" were told they would work in separate rooms but could communicate by written notes that E would deliver. Finally, E displayed two copies of a "crossword-puzzle dictionary," talked about how helpful it was in the task, and concluded by saying: "There are only two copies of this special dictionary. I'm sorry there aren't more, but you can pass them around if you want to. You do not have to trade off if you do not want to and you might even enjoy working without the dictionary for a while. But you will find it a tremendous help." With that E gave one copy of the dictionary to each of the confederates. After answering any questions, E led the two confederates out, ostensibly to their separate rooms.

When E returned a few minutes later, he conducted a brief, open-ended interview on S's "first impressions" of his "partners." Following the interview, S rated the two confederates on the "acceptance" and "resistance" scales that have already been described. Rating procedure was identical to that in the North Carolina experiment. When the ratings had been completed, S began work on the crossword-puzzle construction.

At the end of about ten minutes E interrupted him. Pointing out that one of the purposes of the experiment was to study how well individuals learned to work together as a group, E said he was especially interested in the cooperativeness of HSC and LSC, as demonstrated by their willingness to share the dictionary with S. Since 15 or 20 minutes had gone by without any spontaneous demonstration of cooperativeness from the other two, *E* now wanted S to send messages to the others trying to persuade them to share the dictionary. To that end, *E* had prepared an array of standard messages (in order to "standardize conditions" from group to group) from which S could choose what he wished to send. The only requirement was that S had to send the same message to both other men. *E* spread the 28 messages out on the table and asked S to choose one and to make two copies of it. As in the previous experiment, these messages varied in forcefulness. Three examples are: "If you are not using the dictionary now, may I please have it?"; "I hope you are going to be cooperative about sharing the dictionary"; and "You have had your share of time with the dictionary. Give it to me."

E took these notes and left the room presumably to deliver them to the confederates. He returned in three or four minutes without a reply, saying that the confederates had made no acknowledgment. He instructed S to continue work on the puzzle and to send another message in five minutes. In reply to the second message, *E* brought back two standard notes, the authorship of which was assigned randomly to each confederate. One of these read: "I am still using it"; the other, "I need it now." S usually produced interesting material in reacting to these notes; and *E*, after chatting with him for a few minutes, then pointed out that the experiment was more than half over, and asked him to send another message. Upon his return from this trip, *E* brought back two dictionaries, evidence that both confederates had complied. After getting S's comments, *E* suggested that he might want to return one of the dictionaries, and to whom did he want to return it?

Before setting out on this trip, *E* asked S to rate his two "partners" again, now that he had further information about their personalities and behavior. The same rating scales, with items scrambled in order, were represented to S, and he was again instructed to employ the forced-choice technique. Finally, S was reinterviewed at length regarding his interpretation of the refusals and the ultimate compliance of HSC and LSC.

When the formal procedure of the experiment had been concluded, the purposes and the methods of the various deceptions were explained to the S and all his questions answered. No S left with curiosity unsatisfied and none seemed displeased at having been deceived. All promised not to reveal the workings of the procedure and seem to have kept their word.

Results

EFFECTIVENESS OF THE MANIPULATION

Since the primary purpose of introducing the role-playing confederates was to create a perception of difference between the two confederates in their power to resist influence, our first concern is whether or not our procedure was effective. Table 1 provides data on this point from both experiments. The data are shown for each confederate separately in each role, since there were evident differences in the ability of the two confederates in each experiment to play the two roles. The entries in Table 1 were obtained by subtracting the sum of the rating on the six-item "resistance" scale accorded the LSC from that given to the HSC on S's initial rating of the two confederates.

On the whole the manipulation was effective in both experiments (although less impressively so in the North Carolina experiment); and, as a group, Ss found themselves in the intended situation—facing a relatively strong and a relatively weak person, while sending the same persuasive messages to both.

We will return later on to a discussion of initial differences in the ratings of HSC and LSC on the "acceptance" scale. Right now we would like to move directly into a dis-

TABLE 1

DIFFERENCE BETWEEN DEGREES OF POWER TO RESIST EXTERNAL INFLUENCE
ATTRIBUTED INITIALLY TO HIGH- AND LOW-STATUS CONFEDERATES

Status of Confederates	North Carolina			Harvard		
	A High B Low (N = 10)	B High A Low (N = 10)	Combined (N = 20)	C High D Low (N = 11)	D Low C Low (N = 10)	Combined (N = 21)
Mean difference*	+3.40	+3.60	+3.50	+10.00	+8.20	+9.14
S.D.	6.50	7.59	6.89	4.92	4.57	4.73
t	1.65	1.50	2.27	6.71	5.66	8.87
p†	.07	.08	< .02	< .001	< .001	< .001

* The plus sign indicates that the high-status confederate was perceived as better able to resist than the low-status confederate.
† One-tailed test.

cussion of the results bearing on the main hypothesis of the study.

PERCEIVED LOCUS OF CAUSALITY

Our major hypothesis is simply stated in two parts. The first proposition states: When an individual is attempting to persuade two others, of unequal (perceived) power (to resist influence), the communicator will attribute "internal" reasons for compliance to the person of higher power and "external" reasons to the person of lower power. The second proposition is: When compliance has occurred, the communicator's liking for the others will increase more (or decrease less) if the other is seen as complying for "internal" reasons than if he is seen as complying for "external" reasons.

In this section we will report the data relevant to the first part of the hypothesis. Since in both experiments the status of the confederate appeared to create the appropriate differences in attributed power, our first proposition can be restated as follows: Ss will perceive the locus of causality for compliance as "internal" to HSC and "external" to LSC.

Perceived locus of causality was inferred in both experiments from responses to a question in the postexperimental interview. In the North Carolina experiment the question was as follows: "Suppose you had to decide that one of the members of the audience said 'yes' (i.e., complied) because you forced him to (that is, put pressure on him) and the other said 'yes' because he just naturally wanted to anyway. Which one would you say you forced and which one just wanted to anyway?" This forced discrimination yielded answers consistent with the hypothesis. Table 2 shows that of the 19 Ss that were able to make the decision, 18 reported that HSC was the one who "just wanted to anyway" (internal causality) and that LSC was the one who was "forced" (external causality).

In the Harvard experiment, perceived causality for compliance was inferred from responses to an interview question that was similar to the one above, except that a discrimination between the confederates was not forced. Instead, the S was allowed to decide separately for each confederate, when he was asked: "Do you think that (HSC) gave you the dictionary because he is a nice guy and just wanted to help you, or did he give it to you because you put pressure on him?" The question was then repeated for the other confederate, with the order of confederates and of alternatives being varied from S to S. Table 2 again shows the results from the interview responses. It will be seen, in the first place, that a little more than one half of the Ss behaved in exactly the predicted way, four Ss behaved in

TABLE 2

Locus of Causality for Compliance Attributed to High-
and Low-status Confederates

Status of Confederates	HSC Internal LSC External	HSC External LSC Internal	HSC Internal LSC Internal	HSC External LSC External
North Carolina				
A High / B Low (N = 10)	10	0		
B High / A Low (N = 9*)	8	1		
Harvard				
C High / D Low (N = 11)	8	1	1	1
D High / C Low (N = 10)	4	3	1	2

* One S was unable to make a decision.

a fashion exactly contradictory to the hypothesis, and the remaining five Ss failed to distinguish a difference in locus of causality.

These last Ss create some difficulties in interpretation. They do not support our first proposition, but it is not clear that they refute it, since the proposition assumes that Ss will make a discrimination in locus of causality between the two confederates. These five Ss who failed to perceive such a difference cannot be used to test our prediction; their behavior does not meet the conditions required by the proposition. We have been unable to discover anything in the behavior of these Ss that would help account for their failure to perceive differences in causality. It may be that they did not understand the question or that they are not accustomed to thinking in terms of "internal" versus "external" causes of behavior. Or possibly they perceived no difference in the overt behavior of the two confederates.

This sample of four Ss who perceived the locus of causality in exactly the opposite fashion from that hypothesized is equally interesting. These four Ss also perceived HSC as considerably stronger in power to resist influence than LSC, but apparently did not associate the compliance of strong individuals with "internal" motivation.

With the foregoing qualifications in mind

we can test our first proposition against the 16 cases in which the Ss' behavior met the requirements of our first proposition (i.e., there was a perceived difference in power in one direction or the other). The binomial expansion provides us with the information that the likelihood of obtaining 12 confirmatory cases out of 16, by chance, is .04. With the limitations previously stated, we can consider our first proposition satisfactorily demonstrated.

We must comment, however, on the striking effect of differences in the personal characteristics of the two confederates, and their relative success in inducing the expected perception of their motivation for compliance. Table 1 showed that when Confederate C played the high-status role, the attributed differences in strength to resist influence (initial rating) between HSC and LSC was slightly greater than when Confederate D played this role. Correspondingly, we must note that Confederate C gave an impression of greater formality and sternness of manner, whereas D was comparatively warm and relaxed, being given significantly higher (initial) acceptance ratings in the HSC role than C received. Thus, when C took the role of HSC the difference between the HSC and LSC was exaggerated, but when D played the same role it was minimized. The complicating effect of these "person-carried" characteristics is clearly demonstrated in Table 2, where it can be seen that Confederate C was considerably more successful at inducing the perception that he had complied for "internal" reasons than Confederate D was.

Before going on to the second part of the hypothesis it may be advisable to pause to consider whether the results relevant to perceived locus of causality may not be explained with equal plausibility by another mechanism. The data appear to confirm the hypothesized relationship between differential power of stimulus persons and the locus of causality for their compliance. But it could be asked: Might the data not equally well support the hypothesis that S initially will prefer HSC to LSC, that this preference will lead S to see HSC as liking him (S), and that in consequence S will perceive HSC's compliance as "internally" caused?

There are two pieces of evidence against this alternative hypothesis. Table 3 shows that only when Confederates A and D

the 16 cases where Ss discriminated locus of causality, there was no significant difference in initial acceptance between the confederate perceived as complying for "internal" reasons and the one seen as "externally" motivated. Differences are at chance levels (with p values ranging from .85 to .25) for the two confederates considered separately and combined. In 11 of these 16 cases the S showed higher acceptance initially for the confederate to whom he subsequently attributed "external" reasons for compliance.

CAUSALITY AND CHANGE IN ACCEPTANCE

While the first proposition in our hypothesis was concerned with the attribution of "inner" and "outer" reasons for compliance to individuals of different status, the second proposition dealt with the consequences of such attribution—i.e., with the change in acceptability of, or liking for, the compliant person. Specifically, we predicted that an individual's acceptability would increase

TABLE 3

DIFFERENCES BETWEEN DEGREES OF INITIAL ACCEPTANCE OF HIGH-
AND LOW-STATUS CONFEDERATES

Status of Confederates	North Carolina		Harvard	
	A High B Low (N = 10)	B High A Low (N = 10)	C High D Low (N = 11)	D High C Low (N = 10)
Mean Difference°	+6.10	−2.80	+0.09	+8.80
S.D.	6.94	10.83	7.30	9.68
t	2.79	0.82	0.04	2.88
p †	<.05	....	....	<.02

° The plus sign indicates that the high-status confederate was preferred to the low-status confederate.
† Two-tailed tests.

played the high-status role was there a clear initial preference for HSC. Yet in the North Carolina experiment, "internal" causality for compliance was attributed in a highly uniform way not only to Confederate A as HSC but also to Confederate B as HSC (see Table 2). In the Harvard experiment, for

more (or decrease less) if he was perceived as complying for "internal" reasons.

In the North Carolina experiment for virtually all cases HSC was perceived as complying for "internal" reasons, and LSC as complying for "external" reasons. Hence, the hypothesis leads to the prediction that the increase from initial to final rating in S's prediction of HSC will be greater than the increase in acceptance of LSC. Table 4 presents the data relevant to this prediction. Although when Confederate B is HSC the

TABLE 4

DIFFERENTIAL CHANGE IN ACCEPTANCE
FROM INITIAL TO FINAL RATINGS
(CHANGE IN ACCEPTANCE OF HSC MINUS
CHANGE IN ACCEPTANCE OF LSC;
NORTH CAROLINA DATA ONLY)

Status of Confederates	Mean Difference in Change	S.D.	t	p*
A High, B Low (N = 10)	+3.30	5.38	1.94	< .05
B High, A Low (N = 10)	+1.60	3.69	1.37	.10
Combined (N = 20)	+2.45	4.57	2.40	< .02

* One-tailed test.

predicted relationships merely approach statistical significance, the results for confederate A as HSC and for the combined data appear to be satisfactory. On the whole, the hypothesis appears to be confirmed in this experiment.

Table 5 presents the data on change in acceptance (between initial rating and final

dicted discrimination, who made the opposite discrimination, and who made no discrimination at all in locus of causality. For the total group of 21 Ss, the mean level of acceptance of the confederates declined between initial and final rating. The 12 Ss who made the predicted discrimination, however, show a significant *increase* in liking for HSC compared to LSC, while the four Ss who reversed the hypothesized discrimination show an even greater *decrease* in liking for HSC. Since these latter four attribute "external" motivation for compliance to HSC and "internal" to LSC, it is reasonable to reverse the sign of the changes in their acceptance ratings. We thus consider the total of 16 cases in which the confederate was seen as complying for "internal" reasons (regardless of the status he occupied in the experimental manipulation). Change in acceptance (in the predicted direction) is significant at the .01 level for the group of 12 and at the .02 level for the group of four separately. Combined, the change is significant in the predicted direction at the .001 level (see Table 6, bottom row).

Here again personal differences in the two confederates seem to affect the differential amount of change in acceptance accorded by the Ss. If we consider only the 16 Ss who perceived a difference between the

TABLE 5

DIFFERENTIAL CHANGE IN ACCEPTANCE FROM INITIAL TO FINAL RATINGS
(CHANGE IN ACCEPTANCE OF HSC MINUS CHANGE IN ACCEPTANCE
OF LSC; HARVARD DATA ONLY)

	HSC Internal LSC External (N = 12)	HSC External LSC Internal (N = 4)	HSC Internal LSC Internal (N = 2)	HSC External LSC External (N = 3)
Mean difference in change	+ 3.42	− 11.50	− 5.00	− 5.33
S.D.	0.94	2.22	2.00	2.35
t	3.64	5.18		
p*	< .01	< .02		

* One-tailed test.

rating) in the Harvard experiment. The mean change in acceptance is tabulated separately for those Ss who made the pre-

two confederates in their reasons for compliance and reorder the data, we obtain Table 6. The entries in this table were ob-

TABLE 6

Change in Acceptance of "Internally Complying" Confederate Minus "Externally Complying" Confederate (When S Discriminated Reasons for Compliance; Harvard Data Only)

Status of Confederate	Mean Difference in Change of Acceptance	S.D.	t	p[*]
C High, D Low (N = 11)	+ 6.18	5.29	3.86	< .01
D High, C Low (N = 5)	+ 3.80	4.21	2.02	< .10
Combined (N = 16)	+ 5.44	4.96	4.38	< .001

[*] One-tailed test.

tained by subtracting the change in acceptance score of the confederate perceived as having complied for "internal" reasons from the change score of his opposite number (who, in these cases, was seen as complying because of "external" pressure). Ss' acceptance of the former confederate tends to increase (or to decrease less), thus adding support to our second proposition, and the observed difference is significant at the .001 level for both confederates combined.

OTHER RESULTS

We might extend to the present Harvard-North Carolina study an earlier interpretation (Jones, 1954; Thibaut and Riecken, 1955) that as the S's authoritarianism (F-Scale score) increases his sensitivity to the power of a stimulus person will also increase when the power cues originate in "external" sources such as status. From this we would predict a positive relationship between F-Scale score and perceived initial difference in power to resist and would also expect high authoritarians to perceive locus of causality for compliance in the predicted direction more consistently than low authoritarians. Finally, we would expect a positive relationship between F-Scale score and differential change in acceptance of confederates.

The results in both experiments show none of these expected relationships in any consistent fashion. A possible explanation of these generally negative findings may be that our manipulation of status produced not only "external" cues (to which high authoritarians may be more sensitive) but also numerous correlated "internal" person-produced cues such as differences in ability, personal competence, and the like (to which, if the earlier interpretation is correct, low authoritarians are more sensitive).

Discussion

DIFFERENCES BETWEEN THE TWO EXPERIMENTS

Besides the superficially different nature of the task confronting the Ss in these two experiments, there is probably a more influential difference in the relationship between the S and the two confederates. There was a clear tendency of Ss in the North Carolina experiment to increase their acceptance of both confederates between initial and final rating, and an equally clear trend for Ss in the Harvard experiment to decrease their acceptance. These contradictory tendencies probably can be traced to differences in the Ss' expectations about getting compliance, and to the effect of refusals to comply. In the North Carolina experiment, Ss do not expect to know whether the confederates will comply until after all of the messages have been sent; in effect, they make a single, sustained attempt to persuade two others and are successful. The only feedback they receive is compliance. On the other hand, Ss in the Harvard experiment are led to expect at least the possibility of compliance after each of the three messages they send, but they receive two refusals followed by compliance on the third round. To the extent that frustration in an influence attempt leads to annoyance, this difference in the experimental procedures satisfactorily accounts for the over-all differences in acceptance-rejection.

Hence, it may be that these two refusals, encountered by the Harvard Ss, introduce a kind of error or variability into our results. To the extent that Ss expect HSC to comply quickly with their request because they consider him intelligent, able, and better educated, they will tend to resent his noncompliance and to rate him down, while forgiving LSC for noncompliance because they feel he has a greater genuine need for the dictionary. There is some evidence that such a view of the situation was common among the Ss. After they had received both dictionaries, following the third message, they were asked: "Since you don't need two dictionaries, would you like to return one of them? To whom?" Twelve of the 21 Ss chose to return a dictionary to LSC "because he needs it more." These 12 tended to show greater negative change in their acceptance ratings of HSC than of LSC—about 2.5 scale points, on the average. This interpretation of the situation of two confederates and their reasons for noncompliance tends to work against our hypothesis that HSC will be more accepted than LSC.

On the other hand, to the extent that Ss view LSC as a presumptuous nonentity who has no chance in the crossword-puzzle contest and ought to yield at once to their request, one would expect Ss to rate him down (show differentially less acceptance) more than they would HSC. Again, the fragmentary data support this interpretation. Six of our Ss chose to return the surplus dictionary to HSC, usually giving their reason that "He will do a better puzzle," or that he would make more effective use of the dictionary. Compared to the 12 Ss who chose the opposite course, these six tend to show a slight differential in acceptance in favor of HSC. This tendency, of course, works in favor of our major hypothesis, but it should be emphasized that it occurs in many fewer cases than does the contrary trend.

The striking fact is that in spite of the variability introduced by the tendency to perceive LSC's situation sympathetically

and thus attenuate the predicted tendency to dislike him (or like him less), the weight of the data supports our hypothesis regarding differential acceptance.

One final difference between the experiments must be noted. In the North Carolina experiment, the influence attempts were made in the name of altruism; the giver-receiver relationship was not immediately present and not identified directly with the interests of the S, who was attempting the influence. On the contrary, in the Harvard experiment, the S was in direct competition with the confederates for a scarce resource. Their refusal to comply labeled them not only resistant, but selfish—and, most important, selfish toward the influencer (and rater). Thus, to the failure to be influenced by two messages is added the strong implication that the confederates are hostile, or at least indifferent, to the welfare of the S. It is not surprising that he would tend to rate them down on "acceptance" items following such a display of coldness toward him.

Summary

Two experiments were designed to test an hypothesis concerning the relationships among the amount of power attributed to a stimulus person, the perceived locus of causality for his complying following an influence attempt, and the consequent relative acceptance of him. In both experiments individual Ss were confronted with two stimulus persons (paid confederates) who played roles having different degrees of status or prestige. In a series of communications S attempted to influence the behavior of the two confederates. Eventually and simultaneously both confederates indicated their compliance. The data relevant to the hypothesis were obtained from a final interview and from the S's initial and final ratings of the two confederates on two scales: a "strength of resistance" scale and an "acceptance" scale.

In general the hypothesis was confirmed

in both experiments, although in one of them the test of the hypothesis was not straight-forward. The main findings may be stated in terms of the two parts of the hypothesis:

1. S perceives the causal locus for compliance as "internal" to the high-status stimulus person and as "external" to the low-status stimulus person.

2. The increase from initial to final rating in S's acceptance of the high-status stimulus person is greater than the increase in acceptance of the low-status stimulus person.

References

ADORNO, T. W., FRENKEL-BRUNSWIK, E., LEVINSON, D. J., and SANFORD, R. N. *The authoritarian personality.* New York: Harper & Row, 1950.

FESTINGER, L., and KELLEY, H. H. *Changing attitudes through social contact.* Ann Arbor, Mich.: Univer. of Michigan, Research Center for Group Dynamics Institute for Social Research, 1951.

GILCHRIST, J. C. The formation of social groups under conditions of success and failure. *J. abnorm. soc. Psychol.,* 1952, 47, 174-187.

HEIDER, F. Social perception and phenomenal causality. *Psychol. Rev.,* 1944, 51, 358-374.

HOMANS, G. C. *The human group.* New York: Harcourt, Brace & World, 1950.

JONES, E. E. Authoritarianism as a determinant of first-impression formation. *J. Pers.,* 1954, 23, 107-127.

MICHOTTE, A. *La perception de la causalité.* Vrin: Institut Supérieur de Philosophie, Univ. de Louvain, 1946.

RIECKEN, H. W., and HOMANS, G. C. Psychological aspects of social structure. In G. Lindzey (Ed.), *Handbook of social psychology.* Reading, Mass.: Addison-Wesley, 1954.

THIBAUT, J. W., and RIECKEN, H. W. Authoritarianism, status, and the communication of aggression. *Hum. Relat.,* 1955, 8, 95-120.

Attitudes

and

Opinions

INTRODUCTION

An *attitude* is a complex tendency of the person to respond consistently in a favorable or an unfavorable way to social objects in his environment. The existence of an attitude is inferred from the individual's behavior on the basis of how he acts toward or what he says about the attitudinal object or referent. Individuals have not one but many attitudes, and, in general, social psychologists have given greatest attention to those attitudes directed at the major belief systems, institutional practices, and social groups of the society. Attitudes toward political groups and candidates, minority groups, education, medicine, sex, marriage, and religion, as well as many others, have been the subjects of investigation.

The adaptive significance of an attitude for the person lies in the fact that it orders and gives meaning to the social setting in which he moves. Making appropriate responses to other persons, groups, or issues depends on the degree to which such social stimuli can be identified and evaluated. The fact that he shares these same identifications and evaluations with some other individuals, but not with all persons, attests to the influence of the specific social context in the substantive patterning of these psychological processes. Social attitudes, in effect, represent a fundamental psychological link between the person's ability to perceive, feel, and learn and his continuing experience in a complex social environment. For Allport (1954) it "is probably the most distinctive and indispensable concept in contemporary American social psychology" (p. 43).

Systematic investigations of the attitudes of the individual have been guided by three interrelated questions: What are the distinguishing properties of attitudes? How are they developed or formed? Under what conditions will they change? All the studies reported in the following three sections touch on one or more of these problems.

Perhaps the most striking aspect of an attitude is its evaluative character. The person is "for" or "against" something, and individuals may be distinguished not only in terms of what side of the evaluative dimension they are on, but also with respect to the degree to which they are favorably or unfavorably disposed. It should be apparent, however, that this kind of knowledge tells us little about the nature of the attitude itself. Evaluations are indicated by the nature of the individual's beliefs and feelings about, and behavioral dispositions toward, the attitudinal object. Thus, attitudes are structured psychological tendencies consisting of *cognitive, affective,* and *behavioral* components. Each of these components may be examined in terms of its *content* and *structure* and in this way some of the critical properties of an attitude are revealed.

The cognitive component of the attitude consists of the person's perceptions of and beliefs about the object. Not only are racial groups, for example, conceived of in terms of the color of their skin and other external attributes, but the individual usually has beliefs concerning the intellectual and social characteristics as well as the institutions commonly associated with each group; for example, the Catholic creed calls for loyalty to the church first, and to one's country second. The object in question need not be a person or a group of persons. Individuals may have beliefs about democracy, socialized medicine, unemployment, and other social issues and events.

The affective elements of an attitude are defined by the person's feelings toward the object. Although two individuals may both have unfavorable attitudes toward an object, their personal feelings about it may be quite different. One may fear the object and the other may feel hostility or contempt for it. It is important not to confuse these affective responses with what might be called the person's over-all evaluative response toward the object as represented on the pro–con dimension that is characteristic of various techniques of attitude measurement. On the basis of the person's test score he is described as more or less hostile or friendly toward the group. Where such test scores are derived from a multitude of diverse test items (affective, cognitive, and behavioral), they may actually obscure the individual's predominant emotional response toward the object (Harding, Kutner, Proshansky, and Chein, 1954).

The behavioral aspects of an attitude consist of tendencies to react toward the object in given ways. If the person has negative beliefs about the members of a group, then he may tend to avoid or punish them; with positive beliefs, he may be predisposed to help and reward them. Closely related to behavioral components of attitudes are cognitive elements that can be described as *action beliefs.* These are beliefs about what should be done to and for the object, how it should be treated or dealt with. A person, for example, may be predisposed to avoid particular minority group members and also believe they should not be allowed to vote or even that they should be sent out of the country.

It should be noted that some investigators employ the concept "opinion" to refer to the person's cognitive reactions to an object as distinguished from an "attitude," which is reserved for his motivational or drive tendencies in relation to the object, that is, his feelings and behavioral tendencies (Hovland, Janis, and Kelley, 1953).

The approach taken here does not make this distinction since it assumes that opinions or beliefs are an integral part of every attitude. There are, however, beliefs and belief systems that do not involve affective and behavioral components, and therefore are to be distinguished from attitudes. In this respect the above distinction may have some validity.

If we examine the cognitive, affective, and behavioral components of the attitudes of different individuals then obviously we learn a great deal about how the contents of their attitudes differ. This, however, is not all that we can learn. There are important comparisons that can be made with respect to the structural properties of the various components. One individual's attitude may involve a detailed and extensive belief system about the object, but the same attitude in another person may be limited to the minimum knowledge necessary to identify the object and distinguish it from others. Similarly, affective tendencies and behavioral dispositions may vary in the extent to which they are *differentiated*. A person, for example, may have a single diffuse feeling of like or dislike for an object or he may experience many specific emotional reactions to it. Other structural properties may be employed in the analysis of the three attitudinal components, for example, the degree of integration (the extent to which the elements are organized).

An inevitable but important question concerning the three attitudinal components is the extent to which they are consistently related to each other. Do negative beliefs necessarily entail negative feelings and behavioral dispositions? If the person's affective responses are highly differentiated can we also expect to find an elaborate belief system? Some data with respect to the consistency of attitudinal components are provided in the studies reported by Smith (IIIA) and by Horowitz (IIIA). The three pictorial tests employed by Horowitz to measure attitudes toward the Negro in children touched on the affective and behavioral components of these attitudes. Of interest is the fact that for groups of children ranging in age from five to fourteen years the intercorrelations among the three tests, computed separately for each age group, increased with advancing age. Although the intercorrelations are small, they suggest greater consistency among intergroup attitudinal components with increasing maturity. In Smith's investigation of adults' attitudes toward Russia, various dimensions of the affective, cognitive, and policy orientation (behavioral tendencies involving beliefs about what should be done) aspects of these attitudes were systematically studied. Here again consistency among cognitive and affective elements was found. For example, Smith was able to demonstrate that positive feelings toward Russia could cause the development of an erroneous but attitudinally consistent belief.

Although a high level of consistency in attitudinal components has been demonstrated in a number of studies, other studies have reported somewhat less association among them (Bettelheim and Janowitz, 1950; MacKenzie, 1948; Katz and Braly, IVA). What does seem more certain is a finding reported by Bettelheim and Janowitz (1950). Greater consistency will occur among those persons who have extreme positive or negative attitudes. The person who feels hatred toward an object is very likely to have very negative beliefs about it and to be predisposed to aggressive action or repressive measures against it.

Investigations of the similarity of the structural properties of the three attitudinal components are almost nonexistent. Katz and Stotland (1959), however,
provide an insightful analysis of five possible attitude types based on the extent to
which one or two of the components are structurally dominant. For example, to
cite just two of the types, a person may have strong positive or negative affect
toward an object and at the same time have very little knowledge about it and a
minimum or no action orientation toward it (affective associations); other attitudes may involve extensively developed beliefs and feelings, but lack any action
tendencies (intellectualized attitudes). Two important implications can be drawn
from this kind of attitude typology: first, that the ability to predict a person's overt
behavior from his attitudes will depend on the type of attitude involved or, more
specifically, on the extent to which the behavioral or action component is developed; and second, that attitude change procedures will have to take account of,
among other things, the type of attitude to be changed. Information campaigns to
modify particular attitudes are likely to have little effect on persons who have
strong feelings and are ready to act in given ways, but whose knowledge and
beliefs about the object are only minimally developed.

The task of describing the properties of an attitude has also involved the significant question of the extent to which different attitudes in the person are related to
each other. All of the individual's attitudes may be specific and unrelated to each
other or they may form a unified system in which each attitude influences and is
influenced by the others. The occurrence of either of these extremes is undoubtedly rare. Attitudes tend to cluster and therefore be related to each other in terms
of some abstraction regarding a more general class of events. Thus, a person who
believes in religious orthodoxy is likely to have a set of related attitudes concerning
the education of the young, intermarriage, family life, religious rituals, and so on,
and these attitudes in turn may be related to other sets of attitudes, say, ethics in
behavior. Each of these organized sets of attitudes may reflect the operation of an
underlying value, that is, a generalized conception of what is "good" or "bad," and
all these values and attitudes, by virtue of their interrelatedness, may be described
as the person's religious *value system.* Smith's study, which we referred to earlier,
and Rosenberg's study in the same section (IIIA) are two of the few investigations
that have explored the relationships between the values of a person and his attitudes.

It has been found that attitudes tend to cluster in terms of the major groups and
institutions of a society, political, social, religious, and others. In Newcomb's study
of Bennington college girls (IIIC), their attitudes toward a number of social and
economic issues were measured as a basis of determining the degree of their conservatism. It should be emphasized, however, that for any one person attitudes
may cluster or be related to each other in ways which do not correspond to the
major institutional categories of a society. Furthermore, individuals vary in the
degree of consistency that characterizes their attitudes in any given cluster. We
would expect an individual opposed to government controls over big business also
to be opposed to labor unions, but this need not necessarily occur. Much depends
on the importance or salience of the individual's underlying political or economic

values. To the extent that they are not important values he may not even recognize that there is an inconsistency. It is also possible that each of these attitudes may be strongly and consistently embedded in other attitude clusters.

Earlier we noted that one implication of the Katz and Stotland (1959) attitude typology was that the ability to predict a person's behavior would depend on the structural features of his attitudes. If there is little action orientation in a particular attitude then there is little reason to expect any degree of consistency between the direction of his beliefs and feelings and how he will actually behave. The question of the relationship between attitudes and behavior is a complex one. Although social psychologists have given considerable attention to it, the amount of research generated has been relatively small. An early study by La Piere (1934) dramatically demonstrated a lack of consistency between the attitudes of the individual and his actual behavior. Approximately 93 percent of the proprietors of sleeping establishments and 92 percent of the owners of restaurants indicated in a mailed questionnaire that they would not accommodate Chinese people. The qustionnaire was mailed to these individuals after their establishments had been visited by La Piere and a Chinese couple, at which time they were refused service only once. In general, other studies of the relationship between intergroup attitudes and behavior have revealed similar inconsistencies (Kutner, Wilkins, and Yarrow, 1952; Minard, 1952; Saenger and Gilbert, 1950).

To expect a simple, consistent relationship between a person's attitude and his behavior is to ignore the complexity of persons and situations. We have already suggested that some attitudes may have a greater potential for overt behavior than others, and therefore consistency between attitudes and behavior must be considered in the light of this attitudinal characteristic. However, even where the attitude in question is developed in all of its components, there are many other factors which limit the assumption of consistency. Very important is the fact that attitudes have consequences for behavior only to the extent that they are aroused by appropriate situational cues. If a situation is not attitudinally relevant for the person there is little reason to expect that his behavior will reflect this attitude. No less significant is the fact that even in situations where an attitude has been aroused, there may be situational factors that lead to the arousal of stronger, competing attitudes or needs, thereby preventing the first attitude from influencing the person's behavior.

Early in our discussion we indicated that an individual's attitudes may be shared by others as a consequence of common group experiences. Organized groups have a characteristic ideology or a set of beliefs and values that are expressed in more specific terms by the norms of the groups: its standards of behavior and thought. Because the norms of a group reflect its essential values, there are strong pressures on group members to conform to them. Not only do the group members act in appropriate ways, but conformity to the norms of the group requires that they think, feel, and believe in certain ways about relevant objects and events, which, in effect, means the formation of appropriate attitudes. Having the "right" attitudes brings rewards in the form of support and acceptance by the other members of the group; the "wrong" attitudes bring pressures to conform or even punishment.

The influence of the norms of the group on the formation of attitudes is in part illustrated by Horowitz's study of white children's attitudes toward the Negro (IIIA). Although he tested children from New York City, Tennessee, and Georgia who had had varying degrees of contact with Negro children, Horowitz found little difference between New York City and Southern children in their attitudes. What emerged as the significant determinant was not contact with the Negro but contact with the *prevalent attitude* toward the Negro. Ostensibly, in the North as well as in the South children are exposed to primary group settings in which prejudice toward the Negro is the appropriate attitude.

The significance of primary or face-to-face group influence on the attitudes of the person is also revealed in Katz's (IIIB) detailed analysis of a number of large-scale panel studies. The panel technique involves the repeated interviewing of a small sample of individuals. Its use in an early study of voting behavior by Lazarsfeld, Berelson, and Gaudet (1948) led to the "two-step flow of communication" hypothesis. It was suggested that influences from mass media on voting behavior were indirect: they first reach "opinion leaders," who then communicate what they have heard and read to day-to-day associates over whom they have some influence —family, friends, or co-workers, for instance. The later investigations reported by Katz attempted more direct tests of this hypothesis not only with respect to voting behavior, but also with respect to decision making in other activities, for example, consumer buying. Although the original hypothesis was confirmed, in and by itself it merely indicates that interpersonal relationships serve as a network of communications, thereby enabling mass media to influence decision making. But from the various studies reviewed, Katz concluded that interpersonal relationships have two other kinds of influences on decision making: first, they are sources of pressure to conform to the group's way of thinking and acting; and, second, they serve as sources of social support for the individual.

The development of attitudes in the individual is related to his membership in not one social group but in many such groups. Our discussion up to this point has focused on the person's membership groups, that is, groups to which the person belongs and in which he has face-to-face contacts with the other members. However strong the pressures to conform to the norms of this kind of group, the extent to which it can influence the person depends on the degree to which he identifies with it. Attitudes are not simply poured into the person. On the contrary, he responds selectively, guided by a complex of his own needs and values. Even where the individual cannot leave the group and thus can be punished by it for failure to adhere to its norms—an example is a child in the family—his lack of identification with the group may lead to a superficial behavioral conformity which is not congruent with his underlying attitudes. Furthermore, under these circumstances a person may identify with a group to which he does not belong, and as a consequence his attitudes may be anchored more in this group than in the one in which he has membership. It is for this reason that the concept *reference group* is employed to designate those groups, membership groups or not, with which the individual identifies and thereby seeks to gain or maintain acceptance. A person's membership group is also his reference group to the extent that he identifies with it and wants to remain in it.

What of those many instances in which individuals are influenced in their attitudes by groups (or individuals) with whom they do not identify or wish to gain or maintain acceptance? This significant question is raised by Kelley in his discussion of "Two Functions of Reference Groups" (IIIC). According to Kelley, attitude change in these instances arises out of the fact that individuals use other groups as standards for *comparison* in evaluating their own behavior and the behavior of others. Conformity arises not out of normative pressures or desires to belong, but rather out of the individual's need to evaluate the appropriateness of his own behavior and that of others against the standards of particular groups. Thus groups may have a normative function for the person, a comparison function, or both. It will be recalled that in his analysis of the role of interpersonal relations in decision making, Katz (IIIB) reported "group pressure" and "social support" influences. It is not unlikely that these influences reflect the normative and comparison functions of reference groups, respectively.

In Newcomb's study of changes in attitudes of Bennington College girls (IIIC), it is evident that "reference group" is being used in its normative sense. Yet, as his data reveal, even this particular kind of influence on attitude formation and change cannot be conceived of in a simple, all-or-none fashion. Individuals may want to be accepted by the group (positive reference group) or they may actively reject it as their membership group (negative reference group), or they may do neither, in which case the group is not a reference group for them at all. Even greater complexity is introduced by the fact that, depending on what attitudes or behaviors are involved, a group may have all three of these characteristics for the person. Finally, for still other behaviors and attitudes, the college community undoubtedly served as a comparison group for all the girls regardless of their normative orientations.

In the natural field experiment by Siegel and Siegel (IIIC), it is clear that "reference group" is also being used in its normative sense. Women students at a university campus participated in a "drawing" to determine where they would live for the following year. Attitude information was available to the investigators before the girls were assigned to their living quarters and again at the end of the year. At the beginning, all the girls had the same membership group (freshman dormitory) and the same reference group (a "Row" house). Those girls whose choices were realized, and therefore whose reference group also became their membership group (Row house), showed little change in attitudes. Of more significance is the fact that where such convergence of membership and reference groups did not occur, the girls showed changes in their attitudes that reflected the influence of their membership group (non-Row house). Ostensibly, a membership group which has no reference group value for the person may still exert influence on his attitudes.

In our discussion of social influences on attitude formation we have focused on normative group influences. There are also other kinds of influences in the social setting. Mass media expose individuals to a variety of facts and opinions. Information is also a source of influence on the development of attitudes. Of course, as we have seen, group experiences and interpersonal relationships may either counteract or reinforce this information, depending on existing values and norms. The fact remains that this is not always the case, and that individuals may simply learn a great deal that also has consequences for the kind of attitudes they hold. Finally, it is important to remember that normative and comparison influences, as well as the effect of mass media, are all conditioned by the fundamental values and social structure of the larger society.

It is only in recent years that social psychologists have ceased to treat the attitudes of the individual as if they existed in limbo. As we have noted, attitudes are not simply "absorbed" by the person. He responds selectively in terms of his own unique needs and values, and as such the influence of groups on his attitude development requires the use of such concepts as reference group and group identity. Furthermore, not all his attitudes can be traced to the normative influences of groups, as the concept of comparison reference group indicates. This, in turn, suggests that the development or formation of attitudes may be a function of various kinds of motives in the person. What has emerged as a commonly accepted view is that all attitudes have a functional basis. They are developed and maintained because they satisfy the basic motive patterns of the person.

That this view has taken hold is clearly evident in many of the studies reported in this major section. The paper by Sarnoff, Katz, and McClintock (IIIA) provides a classification of the functions of attitudes that has implications for the way such attitudes can be changed. Some attitudes may be rooted in the person's need for knowledge about his external world. In some instances, then, the extent of information available to the individual regarding a particular object may determine his attitude toward it. Other attitudes may be adopted as a consequence of externally applied rewards and punishments. This brings us back to the role of normative group influences on attitude formation. Individuals may conform to the norms of the group because of its immediate reward potential. Accepting these norms may mean achieving increased status, material rewards, or increased feelings of security. Attitudes may also express the underlying values or value systems of the person and in this respect they are rewarding to him. However, these attitudes tend to be of greater significance to the person since, as expressions of his values, they maintain his conception of himself as a certain kind of individual.

The value-expressive function of attitudes is clearly revealed in the study reported by Rosenberg (IIIA). The attitudes of college students toward freedom of speech for Communists were found to be significantly related to their perceptions of the instrumental value of the attitude for achieving goals that were important to them. Where this attitude was perceived as a means of achieving the student's values or goals it was evaluated positively; if, on the other hand, it was seen as blocking these satisfactions it was not endorsed by the student.

Finally, Sarnoff, Katz, and McClintock (IIIA) point out that some attitudes may be ego-defensive in their function. The focus here is on underlying unconscious conflicts in which attitudes, in the same manner as symptoms, help in expressing unacceptable impulses without the person's becoming aware of them. The study of "The Authoritarian Personality" (VIB) conceives of antiminority group attitudes in these terms. The authoritarian cannot accept his own hostile and sexual impulses and therefore projects them onto others, thereby satisfying these impulses without the pain of recognizing them as his own.

It should be stressed that any single attitude may be instrumental for all the motivational patterns noted above. Furthermore, in the same person, one motivational pattern may underlie one set of attitudes, and another pattern may determine the acquisition of still other attitudes. These patterns are undoubtedly operative in all individuals, but as Sarnoff, Katz, and McClintock note, it is not unlikely that some types of individuals will be more prone to acquire attitudes as a consequence of one of these kinds of motivating patterns than will other individuals.

The problem of modifying or changing the attitudes of a person is directly related to much of our previous discussion. The ability to bring about such changes depends on a knowledge of the structural properties of the attitude itself, the group affiliations of the person, and the functional bases of the attitude. The important point to be stressed is that the method of bringing about an attitude change will require that all three of these factors be considered.

Earlier in our discussion we raised the question of consistency among attitudinal components. One would expect a consistent attitude structure to be a more stable system, since beliefs, feelings, and behavioral orientations tend to support each other. It may be that where there is inconsistency and therefore greater instability among components, change may be easier if the attempt is made to achieve greater consistency. It should be noted that the kind of change desired—making existing positive or negative attitudes more positive or negative (same-direction change) as opposed to making positive or negative attitudes less positive or negative or even reversing their signs (opposite-direction change)—will determine the ease or difficulty of making such a change. This can be demonstrated with respect to another structural property of an attitude: its interrelatedness with other attitudes. In general, an isolated attitude may be easier to change than those which are consistently integrated with others. However, it is still easier to change an isolated attitude if the objective is to make it more positive or negative than to make an opposite-direction change. On the other hand, effecting an opposite-direction change in an integrated attitude is even more difficult, whereas making the attitude more positive or negative in line with other positive or negative supporting attitudes should be relatively easier.

Still another structural factor is the importance of the value or value system underlying the attitude. Here again the direction of change plays a role. The more important the value the easier it is to effect a same-direction change, and the more difficult it is to produce an opposite-direction change. Among other structural properties of the attitude that determine the extent to which it can be changed are the degree of differentiation and organization of its basic components and the number and intensity of underlying needs it serves for the person.

The significance of the individual's group affiliations in effecting attitude change was suggested earlier. Where the person's group identity is rooted in deep-seated underlying needs rather than in immediate rewards and punishments, then changing his attitudes may be especially difficult. Of course, given this strong identification any change that can be made in the perceived norms of the group will bring corresponding changes in his attitudes. However, identification with the group may not be of this deep-seated kind but instead may involve immediate rewards and punishments, such as changes in status. The extent to which his attitudes can be changed will depend on the number and nature of the rewards and punishments involved. Attempts to change attitudes by manipulating rewards and punishments for the person are considered below.

The three types of attitude functions suggested by Sarnoff, Katz, and McClintock (IIIA) imply different approaches to attitude change. Obviously, where attitudes reflect the individual's search for meaning and understanding, then attitude change will require the introduction of new information about the attitudinal object. As we pointed out earlier, individuals do form attitudes on the basis of what they hear and see. To the extent that these attitudes are predominantly rooted in the need to know and understand, then exposure to new information is an important instrument for change. However, attitude change under these circumstances is also conditioned by a host of other classes of variables relevant to the communication process. Here we can only take note of a few of these.

A number of these classes of variables have been studied in detail by Hovland and his associates (Hovland, Janis, and Kelley, 1953; Hovland, Lumsdaine, Sheffield, 1949; and so on). Communications designed to instigate attitude change may differ greatly in the form, medium, source, and content of the presentation. For example, persuasive communications may be presented via speeches, lectures, movies, or newspaper clippings, and in other ways. Indeed, there is evidence that television is a particularly important and influential form of presenting persuasive communications (Campbell, Gurin, and Miller, 1953).

Communications also may vary in terms of the prestige or credibility of the source to which they are attributed. Hovland and Weiss (IIIB) presented identical communications to groups of subjects who were given varying information as to the source of the information. Although the groups did not differ in the amount of factual information learned, opinion change was significantly greater in the case of a trustworthy source as compared with a less trustworthy one. However, measures obtained four weeks after the influence attempt gave evidence of a "sleeper effect." The degree of change found earlier for the high-credibility source decreased; correspondingly, the amount of change for the low-credibility source increased.

The effects of the form and content of communications on attitude change have also been explored. For instance, to facilitate change, should arguments be presented on one or both sides of the question? Experiments investigating this problem have shown that an increase in the strength of an attitude is facilitated by a one-sided communication (Hovland, Lumsdaine, and Sheffield, 1949), whereas two-sided communications are more effective in producing attitude change in an opposite direction. Other studies have demonstrated that two-sided communications are more effective, first, in individuals of higher intelligence and, second, in creating resistance in subjects to counterpropaganda (Lumsdaine and Janis, 1953). If two opposing arguments are to be presented, it seems logical that the order of presentation might have some influence on attitude change. Various studies have focused on this issue (Hovland, Janis, and Kelley, 1953; Lund, 1925; McGuire, 1957). Generally, arguments presented first usually have greater influence (primacy), this being true not only in the case of persuasive communications but also in the case of forming impressions of people.

The content of communications may also vary in a number of ways. Very important is the amount of change advocated. In a study by Hovland and Pritzker (1957), communications were presented to students whose opinions on specific topics were known. Generally, the more the change advocated in the communication, the greater the change produced. That this simple relationship may not hold over a wide range of situations was recognized by Hovland and Pritzker.

In another study (Hovland, Harvey, and Sherif, IIIB), subjects having definite and ego-involved attitudes toward a controversial issue (prohibition in a dry state) were presented with communications that were very different or somewhat different from their own attitudes. The investigators report that the way in which the communication is viewed (fair and factual vs. propagandistic and unfair) is a function of the discrepancy between the subject's attitude and that conveyed by the communication. Furthermore, an increase in the discrepancy between the subject's attitude and the stand espoused by the communication did not lead to change. In fact, only subjects with moderate positions close to that taken by the communications changed their views. Communications which differ widely from the subject's own attitude are more likely to produce a change if the attitude is not ego-salient for him.

Earlier in the discussion we pointed out that attitudes may be instrumental in the satisfaction of specific needs. They may be the means by which the person achieves rewards or avoids punishments. It follows, therefore, that to the extent that the person's needs can be intensified or new needs created, we can expect changes in his attitudes (Katz, 1960). Increased economic dissatisfaction may produce a shift in the political orientation of the person; or a factory worker who has allegiance to his labor union because of the derived economic benefits may have a change of heart once he has been promoted to a supervisory position. However, producing changes in the needs of the person as a means of changing instrumental attitudes is admittedly a difficult procedure. Attempts at changing such attitudes are bound to be more successful if the individual's perceptions of their functional value in satisfying his needs are changed. In other words, attitudes are more likely to change when the person recognizes that his need satisfactions may be improved or better accomplished by changes in his existing attitudes. For example, opposition to school segregation by individuals whose status needs are involved, may be reduced if they perceive the economic benefits to be derived (lower taxes) from not maintaining separate school systems. Whether such a change will occur, of course, will depend on the relative importance of the two needs for the person.

It should be possible to change attitudes by means of threats of punishment or other harmful consequences for the person. Katz (1960) points out, however, that the use of this procedure is more difficult than the use of rewards. The success of the punishment technique depends on whether "there is clearly available a course of action that will save the individual from undesirable consequences" (p. 179). The study by Janis and Feshbach (IIIB) vividly illustrates this requirement. They employed three levels of fear appeal in lectures and pictures designed to coerce children to improve their dental habits. Contrary to expectations they found an inverse relationship between the degree of fear in the appeal and the amount of change that resulted. Janis and Feshbach explain the ineffectiveness of the strong fear appeal in terms of the fact that it provoked an intense emotional reaction which was not relieved by the reassuring recommendations in the communication; this in turn caused the subjects to reject or minimize the significance of the threat. Katz (1960) suggests that the children did not perceive a clear-cut relation between the recommended practices for brushing one's teeth and avoiding the dire consequences shown in the pictures used in the strong fear condition—old people with very severe dental conditions.

It follows from our previous discussion that changes in value-expressive attitudes must involve either changes in the values themselves or changes in the perceived validity of the attitudes in expressing the values of the person. The value system of a person may change following periods of extreme frustration or failure, or where the value structure is systematically undermined by brain-washing techniques (see Schein, VIA). Value change may also occur when the social setting undergoes rapid social and economic change, thereby rendering the value system of the person inadequate in maintaining a favorable self-image for him. Under these circumstances, however, it is more likely that the individual will find the attitudes expressing his values, rather than the values themselves, as no longer adequate or appropriate. If the person does perceive the inappropriateness of his value-expressive attitudes or if they are seen as running counter to other values that he may have, then a change in attitudes is possible. Carlson (1956) has shown that negative attitudes toward minority groups can be modified by demonstrating the significance of more positive attitudes for such values as American international prestige and the democratic way of life.

Finally, we turn to the question of changing ego-defensive attitudes, that is, those attitudes rooted in the unconscious emotional conflicts of the person. Inasmuch as they are critical mechanisms in the basic adjustment of the person, it follows that attempts to modify them by appeals to reason or by the use of reward and punishment will only intensify the amount of threat experienced by the individual. Not only are such techniques of attitude change ineffective, but, as Sarnoff, Katz, and McClintock (IIIA) point out, they "may actually reinforce" the existing attitudes of the individual. What is required are techniques that will minimize threat and reduce tension, thereby minimizing the person's need to act defensively: a supporting and permissive atmosphere, the use of emotional catharsis, and, finally, means for enabling the individual to achieve insight into the ego-defensive character of his attitudes. The study reported by Sarnoff, Katz, and McClintock, comparing rational persuasion with a self-insight procedure in modifying ego-defensive attitudes, indicated the superiority of the latter in changing these kinds of attitudes.

It follows from the preceding discussion that attitude change may involve very different underlying processes. The adoption of an attitude because of the possible reward and punishment consequences cannot be equated with the adoption of the same attitude because the individual now perceives it as more appropriate to his value system. Not only is the nature of the change different in these two instances but the differences imply differences in the properties and the subsequent expressions of these attitudes. The paper by Kelman (IIIA) is a significant attempt to conceptualize the different processes that may underlie attitude change. His formulation involves three types of attitude change: compliance, identification, and internalization. Each is analyzed with respect to the attitude-change conditions which produce it and its consequences for the subsequent expression of the attitude. For example, compliance refers to attitude changes resulting from expected rewards or the avoidance of punishments under conditions where the power of the influencing agent is based on his control over such effects. We would expect, therefore, that the content of the attitude will have little importance to the person, and that it will be expressed in behavior under conditions of surveillance by the power figure. Similar analyses with respect to identification and internalization provided the basis for a series of hypotheses that were largely supported by Kelman's findings. The broader significance of this research lies in its implications for understanding when attitude change will and will not make a difference in the subsequent actions of the individual. Compliance, for example, clearly suggests that attitude changes may involve public conformity without private acceptance.

References

ALLPORT, G. W. The historical background of modern social psychology. In G. Lindzey (Ed.), *Handbook of social psychology*, Vol. 2. Reading, Mass.: Addison-Wesley, 1954.

BETTELHEIM, B., and JANOWITZ, M. *Dynamics of prejudice: a psychological and sociological study of veterans.* New York: Harper & Row, 1950.

CAMPBELL, A., GURIN, G., and MILLER, W. E. Television and the election. *Sci. Amer.*, 1953, *188*, 46-48.

CARLSON, E. R. Attitude change through modification of attitude structure. *J. abnorm. soc. Psychol.*, 1956, 52, 256-261.

HARDING, J., KUTNER, B., PROSHANSKY, H., and CHEIN, I. Prejudice and ethnic relations. In G. Lindzey (Ed.), *Handbook of social psychology*, Vol. 2. Reading,

Mass.: Addison-Wesley, 1954.

HOVLAND, C. I., JANIS, I. L., and KELLEY, H. H. *Communication and persuasion.* New Haven, Conn.: Yale Univer. Press, 1953.

HOVLAND, C. I., LUMSDAINE, A. A., and SHEFFIELD, F. D. *Experiments in mass communication.* Princeton, N.J.: Princeton Univer. Press, 1949.

HOVLAND, C. I., and PRITZKER, H. A. Extent of opinion change as a function of amount of change advocated. *J. abnorm. soc. Psychol.*, 1957, 54, 257-261.

KATZ, D. The functional approach to the study of attitudes. *Publ. Opin. Quart.*, 1960, *24*, 163-204.

KATZ, D., and STOTLAND, E. A preliminary statement to a theory of attitude structure and change. In S. Koch (Ed.), *Psychology: a study of a science*, Vol. 3,

Formulations of the person and the social context. New York: McGraw-Hill, 1959.

KUTNER, B., WILKINS, C., and YARROW, P. R. Verbal attitudes and overt behavior involving racial prejudice. *J. abnorm. soc. Psychol.*, 1952, *47*, 649-652.

LaPIERE, R. T. Attitudes vs. actions. *Soc. Forces*, 1934, *13*, 230-237.

LAZARSFELD, P. F., BERELSON, B., and GAUDET, H. *The people's choice.* New York: Columbia Univer. Press, 1948.

LUMSDAINE, A. A., and JANIS, I. L. Resistance to "counter-propaganda" produced by one-sided and two-sided "propaganda" presentations. *Publ. Opin. Quart.*, 1953, *17*, 311-318.

LUND, F. H. The psychology of belief: IV. The law of primacy in persuasion. *J. abnorm. soc. Psychol.*, 1925, *20*, 183-191.

McGUIRE, W. J. Order of presentation as a factor in "conditioning" persuasiveness. In C. I. Hovland, et al., *The order of presentation in persuasion.* New Haven, Conn.: Yale Univer. Press, 1957.

MACKENZIE, B. K. The importance of contact in determining attitudes toward Negroes. *J. abnorm. soc. Psychol.*, 1948, *43*, 417-441.

MINARD, R. D. Race relationships in the Pocahontas coal field. *J. soc. Issues*, 1952, *8*, 29-44.

SAENGER, G., and GILBERT, E. Customer reactions to the integration of Negro sales personnel. *Int. J. Opin. Attitude Res.*, 1950, *4*, 57-76.

A. THE NATURE OF ATTITUDES

AND ATTITUDE CHANGE

Development of Attitude

toward Negroes ✲ Eugene L. Horowitz

At present, approximately every tenth man in the United States is a Negro. Against one tenth of the total population of this country there exists today an attitude which finds expression in social derogation, judicial discrimination, and severe circumscription of educational and industrial opportunities. Ample justification for the study of the attitude toward the Negro in the United States may be found in the consequence of its functioning, as well as in the needs of a scientific social psychology. Our problem, specifically stated, was *to study systematically in an objective fashion the development in white children of attitudes toward Negroes.*

Current theories accounting for race prejudice are phrased chiefly in terms of sexual factors, in terms of the historical derivation of the Negro's present status, and in terms of the present economic organization of society. Attempts at control, in view of these theories, were made by testing boys only, with boys' materials; testing quite young children; testing groups from different social and economic levels. Three tests were developed and applied to several hundred

boys in New York City, in an all-white school (with a retest after six months) and in one grade in a mixed school, and in a small group of communist children; in urban Tennessee; and in urban and rural Georgia. The data were analyzed so as to shed light on the process of the development of race prejudice as well as to compare the effects of the factors operative in the various groups tested on the degree of prejudice.

The Tests

Our plan was to test the attitude of white boys—kindergarten through the eighth grade, in New York and in the South—toward Negro boys.

The objective means employed in this study were three tests specially devised and standardized for the investigation. All three tests involved the presentation of pictorial material to children and the recording of responses to the standardized situations.

Two kinds of materials were used for the three tests. The two tests which will here be

This article was adapted by the author especially for T. M. Newcomb and E. L. Hartley (Eds.), *Readings in Social Psychology*, New York: Holt, Rinehart and Winston, 1947, from *Archives of Psychology*, 1936, No. 194. Reprinted by permission of the author and publishers.

called the "Ranks" and the "Show Me" tests utilized the same page of children's faces. Photographs of posed social situations served for the "Social Situations" test.

The page of faces used for the Ranks and the Show Me tests was a half-tone cut, which presented twelve boys' faces, three rows of four faces in a row. Directly underneath each face was an identifying letter, from A to L.

From a photographic canvass of several settlement houses in New York City, a large number of faces was collected. These were then judged for racial typicality and general pleasantness by four white people, adults, who had had wide contact with the Negro race. The same judges rated a group of white faces which had been collected during the same survey for equivalent qualities. Without statistical elaboration, four white faces and eight Negro faces were selected on the basis of the judgments, twelve faces which were deemed to be racially typical and pleasant by the adults who did the rating. The faces do not represent adequately the varieties which are to be found in both groups; it was sufficient for the purposes of the study that the racial character of each face be unequivocal.

The task involved in the Ranks test was ranking the faces in the order in which they were liked—"Pick out the one you like best, next best, next best," and so on until they were all ranked.

For the Show Me test, the children selected companions for a variety of imagined situations. On each occasion, no limit was placed on the selections; as many boys could be chosen as the child might want; and on successive occasions, the same or different boys might be selected. For this test the situations were:

1. Show me all those that you want to sit next to you on a streetcar.
2. Show me all those that you want to be in your class at school.
3. Show me all those that you would play ball with.
4. Show me all those that you want to come to your party.
5. Show me all those that you want to be in your gang.
6. Show me all those that you want to go home with you for lunch.
7. Show me all those that you want to sit next to in the movies.
8. Show me all those that you would go swimming with.
9. Show me all those that you'd like to have for a cousin.
10. Show me all those that you want to be captain of the ball team.
11. Show me all those that you want to live next door to you.
12. Show me all those that you like.

Scoring the Ranks test was by summing the ranks assigned the four white faces. If these faces were ranked 1, 2, 3, 4, the score was $1 + 2 + 3 + 4 = 10$; if they were ranked 1, 2, 5, 9, the score was 17. The lower the score, the greater the preference for the white faces. The possible range was from 10 to 42. If the ranking had been done by chance, the score might be expected to be 26. Deviation from the chance expectancy may be taken as indicative of the operation of a bias.

Scoring the Show Me test was by finding the relative frequency with which the white faces were selected for all activities, expressed as a percent. The number of companions selected for all twelve items of the test was determined, then the number of those selections which were of the white boys (maximum, of course, 48); the frequency of the white choices was then computed as a percent of the total number of selections. Since of twelve faces, four were white, if the selections of companions were made on a chance basis, the score might be expected to be 33⅓ percent. Deviation from the chance expectancy may be taken as indicative of the operation of a bias.

On these two tests, the interpretation of the scores is this: on the Ranks test, scores below 26 show preference for white as compared with Negroes (the smaller the score, the greater the preference); on the Show Me test, scores above 33⅓ percent show prejudice for white as compared with Negroes (the higher the score, the greater the prejudice against Negroes).

The third test used, the Social Situations test, in its original form consisted of a set of thirty photographic prints, later increased by nine. The purpose of the test was to discover whether children would reject participation in an activity because of the inclusion of a Negro. Fifteen posed situations were photographed twice, once posed by four white boys, and once again, without other change, substituting a Negro lad for one of the original group. The thirty photographs were then arranged in an order such that in eight of the fifteen situations the mixed group preceded the all-white group; while for the remaining seven, it followed. The general order was such that the situations appeared in random order, paired photographs being widely separated, in general.

The situations photographed might be briefly characterized: marbles, choosing sides for baseball, hand-wrestling, sitting around weary outdoors, lavatory, workshop, playing piano, radio, checkers, museum, library, school, in ice cream parlor, at home eating dinner. The task for the child on this test was to look at each picture, separately, each in its turn, and report whether or not he wanted "to join in with them and do what they're doing along with them." The children had the option of saying "Yes," "No," or registering an indeterminate attitude. This test was scored by assigning points on the basis of desire to participate: each "Yes" was awarded three points, the "?" two points, and the "No" one point. Summation was then made of the score for desire to participate in the fifteen all-white situations, and separately for the fifteen situations which included the one colored boy. The numerical differences between the summations so derived were taken to represent prejudice scores. For the fifteen situations, the difference between the all-white groups

and those with one colored boy might range from zero to plus or minus thirty, depending on degree and nature of prejudice. If the responses of the children were without bias, the prejudice score would be, of course, zero; the children would respond, in general, on the basis of the activities so that variations introduced in composition of the groups would not matter.

The three tests thus give three measures, each permitting a response by the test subjects which would or would not show the operation of a bias, a direct index of response on the basis of the racial characters of the test-situations. "Experimental controls" were introduced into the tests to permit reading off a "prejudice" score.

Results

The interest in this study was chiefly in the development of social attitudes. Group differences in school grade were taken to correspond to group differences in age. The analysis of the test scores, from the point of view of genetic development, was made by fitting regression lines by a least-squares fit to the original scores and testing the coefficients for significance. The equations describe the curves formed by the test scores when studied from the point of view of regression of prejudice on age (grade). The adequacy of the equations is indicated by the standard errors of the coefficients (S_a, S_b, etc.). This form of analysis permits a precise mathematical test of the goodness of the fit of the derived curves. Table 1 presents this analysis. [A "first order" equation of the general form $y = a + bx$ represents a straight line. A "second order" equation of the general form $y = a + bx + cx^2$ represents a negatively accelerated curve. In Table 1, y is the symbol for the individual's test score; a is the symbol for the constant which describes the general score level of the curve; b is the essential slope or angle of the curve; c is the coefficient which, when significant, defines the tend-

TABLE 1

REGRESSION EQUATIONS FOR THE THREE TESTS

y = score $\bar{x} = 4.078$
x = grade n = degrees of freedom

First order $y = a + b(x - \bar{x})$

Test	a	b	s_a	s_b	b/s_b	n
Ranks	14.9	.04	.955	.12	.33	470
Show Me	65.0	2.27	.953	.39	5.8	470
Social Situations	1.303	.300	.215	.088	3.42	470

Second order $y = a + b(x - \bar{x}) + c(x - \bar{x})^2$

Test	a	b	c	s_a	s_b	s_c	b/s_b	c/s_c	n
Show Me	69.65	1.89	−.78	1.39	.39	.17	4.8	4.6	469
Social Situations	1.28	.30	.004	.318	.090	.039	3.33	.10	469

ency of the curve to "flatten out," x represents the individual's school grade and $\bar{x}$ is the mean grade position of the entire sample (4.078). Thus the expression $(x - \bar{x})$ stands for the child's grade position as a deviation from the mean; n represents the degrees of freedom, derived from the number of cases and the form of analysis; s is the standard error for the coefficient in the equation indicated in its subscript. A coefficient divided by its standard error (e.g., b/s_b) is a "critical ratio" which provides the basis for an estimate of the probability of finding a like-sized coefficient "by chance." Where b (roughly, the slope coefficient) is more than three times its standard error (s_b) we can assume the curve meets the customary requirements of statistical tests of significance and the regression equation represents a curve with a "significant" slope; where the coefficient is relatively small in the light of its standard error, we can have little confidence in its significance (thus, in Table 1, the second order equation for the Social Situations test shows a reliable slope, $b/s_b = 3.33$, and an unreliable "flattening," $c/s_c = 0.10$; while the Show Me test has both a reliable slope, $b/s_b = 4.8$, and a reliable flattening, $c/s_c = 4.6$).]

These equations demonstrate that the Ranks test scores yield a growth curve which can best be described as a straight line with no reliable slope. The Show Me test scores yield a negatively accelerated curve. The scores of the Social Situations test conform to a curve which is a straight line with a reliable positive slope.

Investigating the difference in the shapes of the curves, regression lines were fitted to the reduced score differences among the curves. The various coefficients were found to be reliable, as Table 2 presents, indicating that there were reliable differences in the shapes of the curves.

Differences in percentage representing the number of children showing prejudice on comparable items confirms the suggestion from the curve analysis that there is a real difference between the tests. Ranking faces in the order that you like them is a task in which there is greater proneness to display prejudice than one in which children are asked to show all those that they like. Also, there is more proneness to display prejudices in selecting playmates for an activity than in expressing a desire to refrain from participating in an activity because of the participation of unwanted individuals.

These and other analyses tend to lend credence to the view that the tests are intrinsically different, though they all are designed to measure attitudes of children toward Negroes. The interpretation of these differences is discussed below.

TABLE 2

REGRESSION EQUATIONS FITTED TO REDUCED SCORE DIFFERENCES AMONG THE CURVES

$y =$ difference $\quad \bar{x} = 4.078$
$x =$ grade $\quad n =$ degrees of freedom

First order

Difference	a	b	s_a	s_b	a/s_a	b/s_b	n
Show Me-Ranks	.00055	.1064	.0415	.0170	.0130	6.259	469
Soc. Sit.-Ranks	.00081	.0562	.0575	.0235	.0140	2.389	469
Show Me-Soc. Sit.	.00066	.0507	.0658	.0269	.0100	1.884	469

Second order

Difference	a	b	c	s_a	s_b	s_c	a/s_a	b/s_b	c/s_c	n
Show Me-Ranks	.1398	.0952	−.0232	.0609	.0172	.0075	2.296	5.535	3.093	468
Soc. Sit.-Ranks	−.0943	.0636	.0156	.0851	.0240	.0105	1.108	2.650	1.486	468
Show Me-Soc. Sit.	.2289	.0320	−.0390	.0965	.0272	.0119	2.372	1.176	3.281	468

With the differences between the tests demonstrated, the next consideration is of the intercorrelations of the tests. These correlation coefficients were tested for trend by fitting regression lines to their z-function equivalents and testing the coefficients of the regression lines for reliability. This is presented in Table 3.

primarily, for the sake of permitting comparisons. To facilitate such comparison, the performance on the Show Me test is presented graphically in Figure 1. The comparative aspects of this test are representative of the performance on the other tests.

The children in the New York group showed no less prejudice as measured by the

TABLE 3

FIRST ORDER REGRESSION EQUATIONS FITTED TO THE z-FUNCTION EQUIVALENTS OF COEFFICIENTS OF INTERCORRELATION

$y = z \quad x =$ grade $\quad \bar{x} = 4.0701$

Tests Correlated	a	b	s_a	s_b	a/s_a	b/s_b	n
Ranks and Show Me	.7036	.0475	.0326	.0134	21.58	3.545	7
Ranks and Soc. Sit.	.1534	.0321	.0476	.0195	3.222	1.645	7
Show Me and Soc. Sit.	.2320	.0482	.0378	.0155	6.137	3.112	7

In the table the a/s_a column indicates that the tests are all reliably intercorrelated. From the b/s_b column we see that two of the three curves have a reliable slope, while in the third case, the tendency for the correlation to increase is not reliable. It is felt that this evidence warrants the generalization that though the tests are different, they tend to increase in intercorrelations with increase in the ages of the individuals studied.

Presentation of the results of the testing in the various groups sampled is of interest,

tests than did the children in the South. Comparison of the three Southern groups showed no differences among them, in spite of differences in mode of living represented by sampling rural and urban communities. White boys in a mixed school showed as much prejudice as did white boys elsewhere. The colored boys in the mixed school showed a preference for white faces reliably less than did their white classmates (Show Me, $t =$ 2.93), yet their mean score was significantly above the "chance" score (Show Me, $t =$

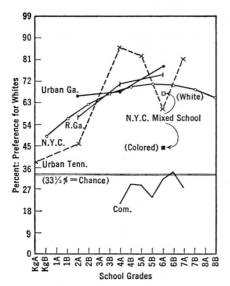

Fig. 1. Prejudice in different groups. Graphic comparison of performance on the Show Me test. Curve for New York City groups is smoothed, from regression equation.

been treated as a unit throughout but actually they came from two schools. One school was tested from kindergarten through the 6B grade (its highest grade) with the thoroughness just described as being generally sought. Another school, located nearby, to which many of the children went after completing the sixth grade work, was used to increase the age range of the subjects. Samples were drawn from the 6B, 7B, and 8B grades. Comparison was made of the means and sigmas of the distributions of the 6B samples from the two schools; their agreement was such as to justify combining the groups and served as basis for adding the 7B and 8B grades and treating the entire range as a whole in the subsequent analyses. The intensive analysis of the developmental trends discussed in the first part of this section was undertaken with data supplied by these children.

2.45). The children of communists showed no particular prejudice against the Negroes; if anything there seems to be a slight preference for, rather than prejudice against.

It might be well to conclude this section, presenting the results of a complicated testing program, with a few words about the subjects. In the interests of "representative sampling," whenever possible, *all* the boys of the desired grade level were taken. Whenever not possible, care was taken that all the boys in the chosen classes were tested, and further care was taken that the classes tested were selected as being representative rather than especially good or bad. The only nonschool group tested, the communist children, were selected by arranging, in a cooperative dwelling in New York City run under communist auspices, to test children attending a regular meeting of a representative club conducted as part of the cultural program of the establishment. On the designated night, all boys attending the meeting were tested. Assurances were received that the attendance was representative.

The New York City children, ranging from kindergarten through the eighth grade, have

Development of an Attitude

Previous sections have demonstrated our inability to present an equation representing the ultimate growth curve of an attitude. For the three tests developed, three different curves have been traced: the Ranks test, a straight line with an unreliable slope; the Show Me test, a negatively accelerated curve; and the Social Situations test, a straight line with a reliable slope.

First, the question of a generalized growth curve may be considered. The data presented need not be considered as conflicting with the applicability of the concept of the S-shaped curve as the generalized description of growth, so fruitfully developed in other fields of psychology as well as in cognate sciences. The three curves derived in this study may merely represent segments from different parts of three S-shaped curves. The tests may be representative of different aspects of the attitude under consideration, each aspect having a different parameter descriptive of its development.

The demonstrated increase in intercorrelations of the tests represents the approach to the adult condition in which the growth of the several aspects has achieved completion. The higher intercorrelation between the Ranks and the Show Me tests than between either of these tests and the Social Situation test may be due largely to the identity of stimulus materials and the similarity of the type of response elicited, but may be partially accounted for by the relative maturity of the aspects tested (see Fig. 2).

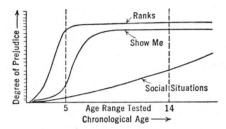

Fig. 2. Theoretical growth curves of attitude.

Two hypotheses for the interpretation of the "aspects" may be considered: the "aspects" may represent aspects of the testing situations, the attitude being a unitary phenomenon; the "aspects" may represent aspects of the responding organism, different response modalities being elicited by the different tests with increased development of the organism resulting in increased integration. It must be remembered that the test performance is a psychological function and the demonstration of differences between the tests means demonstration of psychologically different functions. That the tests are reliably, though not highly, intercorrelated, demonstrates that the functions are psychologically related, though not very closely. The two hypotheses attempting to account for the differences in psychological function both relate to the whole testing situation on each test. There is no attempt made to abstract either the test or the child from the reality of the responding-in-the-test-situation.

It seems likely that adequate description of attitudinal responses must involve consideration of both hypotheses. The concept of threshold of response seems particularly helpful in considering the differences here

discussed; but the involvement of different response modes seems no less important. Differences in developmental trends of responses to different groups of questions reported by Minard (1931) where the general threshold of the test situation involved response of a verbal sort on a questionnaire, seem best accounted for chiefly through different combinations of modalities involved. The gross differences reported by LaPiere (1934) between verbal and overt behavior with reference to racial attitudes and reactions of hotel keepers and restaurateurs (who accepted Chinese guests, but on a questionnaire said they would not) involve consideration of the differences in threshold of response, as well as the response modalities, required for display of prejudice on a questionnaire and overtly in a business situation.[1]

For the specific description of the process of development of attitudes toward Negroes, it is suggested that attractiveness of Negroes, individually and collectively, is reduced in the course of time below the various thresholds involved for inclusion in life's routine. This diminution probably occurs in almost all activities of the individuals of the population considered; the various response modalities are ultimately all conditioned to approximately similar degrees of prejudice and the result is a relatively integrated attitude.

Attitudes toward Negroes

This suggested description of the development of an attitude involves a continuous process; with reference to attitude toward Negroes, a diminution of the attractiveness of those considered Negroes. Precisely at what age such diminution begins cannot be ascertained from the data at hand. It is apparent, however, that the development of prejudice against Negroes begins very, very

[1] There are other considerations which may be raised concerning LaPiere's findings, e.g., had the questionnaire gone into more explicit verbal description of the scene, there might have been somewhat closer agreement between the expression and the act.

early in the life of the ordinary child. Most of the boys of the "younger" kindergarten, boys barely over five years of age, demonstrated a preference for the whites on the Ranks test, the most sensitive of the three tests to small amounts of prejudice. Some few attempts at testing special cases at three and four years of age elicited such comments as (from a three-year-old) "I don't like black boys," and (from a four-year-old) "I don't like colored boys."

Beginning very early in life, the attitude develops gradually. The growth curves, as far as they are plotted, show no sharp breaks, such as might be expected if the attitude depended on the sudden maturation of some physiological aspect of the organism. The suggested theory of the course of development does not preclude unevenness in the process. In individual cases or in some communities, events may be such that for a given time the process is greatly accelerated. For none of the groups tested was there any indication of other than a gradual growth (for some groups the data were insufficient to give any index). The specific evidence of the correlation coefficients computed from a pairing of original scores and a six-month retest on the several grades in the New York City school where such retest was conducted demonstrates more of a constancy of attitude, relative to other members of the grade, than would be expected if the development were other than gradual as an individual as well as a group phenomenon. Not only were group averages going up regularly, but relative position of children within groups was being maintained.

Beginning early and developing gradually, attitudes are derived from diffuse sources, being the result of the interplay of many diverse environmental factors. The lack of importance of specific experiences in the formation of attitudes is amply illustrated by the lack of difference in amount of prejudice displayed by groups with such varied contacts with Negroes as were tested: (1) with practically no personal contacts except for some few children in whose homes there were occasional Negro cleaning women; (2)

with school contact with one popular Negro lad for about four months; (3) with the great deal of contact implicit in attendance at a mixed school in New York City. No differences were found between children in New York and children in the supposedly very different South from which samples were drawn. No differences were found between the samples from urban and rural Georgia.

Yet that the prejudices are derived from social sources rather than through biologically transmitted traits is rather clearly demonstrated by consideration of the results from the communist sample. Most of the white children in the various comparable samples showed a very marked preference for white as compared with Negro boys. The Negro lads tested showed a slight preference for whites, whereas the averages for the communist children hovered about the chance line. The unfavorably prejudiced attitude is attributed to environmental forces, not to specific experience with Negroes, but to such social forces as apply with about equal pressure to children North and South, to children with little contact with Negroes and to those with much contact, to children in prosperous urban Georgia and to children in impoverished rural Georgia—social forces which extend to the Negro community and develop even there a preference for white as compared with colored lads, social forces which do not, however, penetrate, or are negated by, the training given to the communist-trained children.

The attitude derived from diverse sources is expressed diversely. Apparently the prejudiced attitude is displayed toward any Negro identified as such, independent of specific details. Exceptions, of course, might be such identifications as would remove the individual from the general category of Negro to some specific other category, such as "Joe." The attitude expressed toward this diversity of stimuli is not expressed in specific activities alone. Children displayed prejudice in imagined activities in which they were too young to participate in reality. Rural children responded in a fashion similar to their urban cousins in situations which could exist for them only in the realm of unreality. Among the youngest children, a general set to accept or reject is of importance even when comprehension of individual questions is lacking. Very young children, at the close of individual examinations, were not infrequently asked, as if a postscript to the Show Me test, to indicate those that "jabberwocky goldfish" and those youngsters that had been excluding the Negro boys from their selections would generally once again choose the whites.

In apparent contrast to this diffuse expression of prejudice independent of the specific activity, is the specificity of the responses dependent upon the general nature of the situation discussed in the [original monograph] when the difference between the tests was analyzed. Prejudice may be displayed diffusely through the different activities included in one type of situation and very specifically or perhaps not at all in another type of situation. In the course of time, as the increasing intercorrelations of the tests demonstrate, the expression of the attitude becomes more and more integrated internally, and, as may be generally observed, more and more integrated into the general community pattern of relations.

In summary, within the limitations imposed by the population sampled, attitudes toward Negroes are equally unfriendly among children of varied backgrounds. The prejudice begins very early in the life span, develops gradually, is not innate but is formed by the continued impact of widespread social forces, is expressed diffusely, and in the early stages may appear as lacking the integration which it gradually achieves. The social forces may nevertheless be controlled and an impartial attitude developed.

Conclusion

Validity in tests of personality, the degree to which a measurement describes what it is supposed to describe, is frequently mentioned, occasionally discussed, and rarely demonstrated to be high. Yet once a standardized measure is found to have adequate reliability for discussion, the naming of the measure raises the question of validity. Judgments by experts directly on the material or submission to objective test on criteria satisfactory to experts is the customary procedure for demonstrating validity. Since it is essential that experts agree on what they designate by commonly used terms, this is a satisfactory arrangement. The problem of demonstrating validity statistically in a field in which there are no recognized experts is indeed a difficult one, especially when people who might be expected to render judgment based on accurate observation disagree on major points.

In justification of naming the test responses in the present study "measure of attitude toward Negroes," the original precautions in test construction may be referred to. In addition, some incidental comments by test subjects, unsystematically recorded during the administration of individual examinations, are presented:

Selma, aged four years, was tested informally with the Ranks test. The four white boys were ranked 1, 2, 3, 4. Selma then halted.

Examiner: "Now which one do you like best?"

Selma: "I don't like colored boys."

Examiner: "Which are the colored boys?"

And Selma unerringly indicated the eight faces she had systematically excluded in the Show Me test preceding.

A Southern seven-year-old, when asked to show "all those that you would go swimming with," hesitated, then spoke up: "Where I go swimming I don't think they allow colored people, . . . oh yes, they do, on Tuesdays and Thursdays, for about two hours in the afternoon. But supposing they *could* go with me, I'd want him and him and him."

Another Southerner, eight years old, at the beginning of the Ranks test, pointing to one of the Negro pictures, said, "I like that one best; he's just like our chauffeur's boy."

That the responses of children were realistic may be seen in such comments as:

(Show Me—go home for lunch) "None of them. My mother would like to have them come for lunch, but we don't have enough to eat for ourselves."

(Show Me—come to your party) "Come all the way to A——?"

(Show Me—live next door to you) "All of them. I'm the super's boy. . . . My father's the superintendent where we live."

(Show Me—live next door to you) "They can't. There is no room. There's just a lot on one side and somebody lives on the other."

(Show Me—captain of the ball team) "Can I pick more than one?"

(Social Situations test: school) "What're they doing? Arithmetic, no, I don't want to join in."

(Social Situations test: eating) "What's that? Roast beef? Yes, I want to join in."

Since in the original construction of the test only those pictures were used which were chosen by people of experience as "racially characteristic" and ambiguous cases were discarded, and the scoring scheme was based entirely on the principle of comparative response to white and colored faces on scenes of all white or mixed groups, and since the children's comments were such as to indicate they were recognizing the racial aspect of the test and responding realistically, it is felt that the use of the term "measures of attitude toward Negroes" is justified; in other words, that the tests are valid.

Summary

1. An attempt was made to study the development of attitudes toward Negroes.
2. Three tests were developed which made possible objective recording of attitudes.
3. The tests were administered to boys from kindergarten through the eighth grade in various types of communities, a retest after six months being conducted in some samples in New York City.
4. An intensive statistical analysis was made of the data collected from New York City samples.
5. Analysis of the data for trends revealed that each test had a characteristic form of growth curve for the period investigated.
6. The tests, though each was considered valid, were demonstrated to differ significantly, from the point of view of growth, in the results yielded.
7. The intercorrelations among the tests increased with advance in age.
8. Boys were tested in urban Tennessee, urban Georgia and rural Georgia, and in comparing these groups with each other, no differences were discernible.
9. The Southern groups tested showed no more prejudice than that showed by the children in New York City.
10. A small group of white boys in a mixed school in New York City showed about as much prejudice as did the boys in the all-white schools.
11. The Negro boys in the mixed school gave evidence of having accepted, in part, the standards of the white (majority) group.
12. A small group of communist children tested in New York City showed no apparent prejudice against the Negro.
13. The results from the testing program are discussed with reference to the process of development of an attitude and with reference to attitudes toward Negroes.

Underneath the disguise of statistical manipulation, an effort has been made to present data of significance to students of interracial attitudes and to students of personality. Concerning none of the many issues dealt with has the present investigator felt the material presented is conclusive. The interpretations presented are but tentatively offered in the hope that they may not be entirely devoid of value.

In the course of this presentation, it has been found necessary to contradict many of the oft-repeated clichés current in the discussions of the race problem. Young children were found to be not devoid of prejudice; contact with a "nice" Negro is not a universal panacea; living as neighbors, going to a common school, were found to be insufficient; Northern children were found to differ very, very slightly from Southern children. It seems that attitudes toward Negroes are now chiefly determined not by contact with Negroes, but by contact with the prevalent attitude toward Negroes.

References

LaPiere, R. T. Attitudes vs. actions. Soc. Forces, 1934, 13, 230-237.

Minard, R. D. Race attitudes of Iowa children. Univ. of Iowa Stud.: Stud. in Character, 1931, 4, No. 2.

Attitude-Change ❀ Irving Sarnoff

Procedures and Motivating ❀ Daniel Katz

Patterns ❀ Charles McClintock

A major difficulty in the field of attitude research has been the oversimplification of problems in terms of a narrow theory of motivation. The perceptual model of the Gestalt school sees the situation as one in which people strive toward a more inclusive and stable organization of the psychological field; thus the individual tries to reconcile conflicting impressions, seeks to know what the world is like, and to make sense of it. According to this model, individuals will change their attitude in rational fashion if they are presented with facts and reasons which accord with their own beliefs and assumptions. Another motivational model has followed the reward-punishment pattern and has seen attitudes as part of an adaptive response to the social world. Group norms become of first importance since the individual must have acceptance and support from his group. Finally, the personality theorist and clinician emphasize the internal dynamics underlying attitudes in which the individual's need to preserve his self-image and self-integrity become more important than external reward and punishment.

THE RATIONAL MODEL: THE
SEARCH FOR MEANING

This approach emphasizes the fact that people seek to understand their world and to achieve a consistent picture of its complexities. They attempt to deal with the realities of the matter which are within the framework of their own experiences and to deal with these realities in an understanding fashion. The blind emotionalism and the stupid irrationalities of a person are not necessarily as blind or as irrational if we took the trouble to understand his particular set of experiences and his frame of reference. "Emotional processes are as a rule under the direction of cognitive factors, and are controlled by a

This article was adapted by the authors for D. Katz, A. M. Lee, S. Eldersveld, and D. Cartwright (Eds.), Public Opinion and Propaganda (New York: Holt, Rinehart and Winston, Inc., 1954), from "The Motivational Basis of Attitude Change," Journal of Abnormal and Social Psychology, 1954, 49, 115-124. Reprinted by permission of the authors and the American Psychological Association.

trend to find relevant relations." (Asch, 1948).

It is assumed that every person has a need to explore, to know about the external world. This need may be observed in the meanderings of naive children, as well as in the controlled experiments of trained scientists. Often this quest for information seems to be a curiosity which is entirely self-contained. At other times, it appears to be in the service of other motives, such as survival or the desire to master the environment.

Considered in this light, attitudes may sometimes be a function of the range of information which has been accessible to the individual in regard to certain target objects. Let us assume, for example, that a curious child has heard of the word *Negro* for the first time. He goes to his parents for information and is told, among other things, that Negroes are bad people, stupid, dirty, animal-like. Assuming that he has heard no information to the contrary, that he has had no actual experience with Negroes, and that his parents have always supplied him with reliable facts about things, it follows that he will be inclined to accept this statement about Negroes. Even if the child is entirely free of other motivational needs to maintain this attitude, it is likely to persist until his contact with Negroes indicates to him that not all of them are stupid or until he is confronted by contrary information which he considers to be more reliable than that which his parents gave him.

REWARD AND PUNISHMENT

Some of the principles of learning theory may be applied to certain types of attitude formation. Specifically, these principles are involved when attitudes are adopted as a consequence of externally applied rewards and punishments. A white youngster in rural Mississippi may begin life on very favorable terms with his Negro playmates. Still, as he matures, his adjustment to and acceptance by the white community depend in some measure upon the extent to which he has come to share the prevalent anti-Negro biases. If he rejected these biases, he might be vulnerable to social ostracism and even more severe manifestations of disapproval.

EGO DEFENSE

In his social relationships every individual attempts to gratify his basic physiological needs and the socially acquired ones. Some individuals, because of the strength, maturity, and integration of their egos, are able to perceive and tolerate the existence of their inner drives, including those which may be socially taboo. Such a person can, in terms of a realistic assessment of the social situation, decide which impulses to express and which ones to suppress. It is possible for him to approach others in a straightforward manner; to react to them in terms of how they, as unique individuals, actually fulfill or frustrate his needs. His social attitudes are likely to be appropriate since he is able to differentiate clearly between what is going on inside him and what is emanating from others.

At the other end of the scale of ego strength there are persons who are obliged to use devious means of gratifying their impulses. In an attempt to resolve inner conflict, they minimize or obliterate certain aspects of their emotional life. This deflection of impulse from conscious awareness does not destroy it. On the contrary, it continues to press for overt expression and requires the individual to expend considerable energy in keeping it below the threshold of consciousness. Despite the most strenuous counter measures (repression and other mechanisms of defense), the impulse tends to attain at least partial expression and gratification. This expression is achieved by means of symptom formation, a device which, however incapacitating it may be, serves a dual and somewhat paradoxical function:

1. It permits expression of the unconscious impulse.

2. It prevents the individual from becoming aware of the existence of the unconscious impulse.

Attitudes may thus function as ego defenses, and may be viewed as symptoms. For example, the type of bigot described in the California studies is one who cannot accept his own hostile impulses (Adorno, Frenkel-Brunswik, Levinson, and Sanford, 1950). By projecting them onto others, he gains gratification of his impulses while maintaining the fiction that these impulses originate in others rather than in himself.

Rather than attempting to elaborate any one of these three models to take account of all psychological phenomena concerned with attitudes, it seemed wiser to us to accept their essential contributions and to specify the conditions under which one or another of the theories best accounts for the phenomena under investigation. We feel that all people develop and alter their attitudes in terms of all three motivational contexts. Certain types of people, however, will be more likely to acquire attitudes on the basis of one kind of motivational pattern than will other people. Moreover, attitudes formed in the service of a given type of motivation will tend to show different characteristics than attitudes acquired in the interests of other motivational sources. In general, to take one important example, the dimension of the appropriateness or inappropriateness of an attitude, i.e., the amount of gross distortion of the target or referent of the attitude, will be related to the third type of motivation, ego defensiveness. Since the attitude has the function of protecting the individual from facing his internal conflicts, it will not be referred to the external world for reality testing. Moreover, any prediction of change or any attempts to modify attitudes must take account of these different motivational bases: (1) attitudes may be acquired in the interest of rationally structuring the individual's world and of testing what the world is like; (2) they may be formed as an adaptation to rewards and punishments imposed by the so-

cial situation; and (3) the attitude may be a function of the ego defensive needs of the individual. It follows that the processes which produce a change in the first type of attitudinal structure will not necessarily be operative for the second or third types of structure. Where the individual's attitude is based upon his search for meaning, his attitude can be changed by giving him more information about the cognitive object. Where the attitude is based, however, upon a motive like group approval or desire to advance in the group, additional information which opposed this attitude may have no impact. Where the attitude reflects the individual's manner of resolving his inner conflicts, he will resist changes which would be in his own self-interest.

It should be noted, moreover, that attempts to change the ego defensive individual which are based upon the logic of the first two approaches may actually reinforce his old attitudes. These appeals really assume either (a) the individual is interested in a more accurate and more complete knowledge of the world, or (b) he is primarily concerned with maximizing the satisfaction of his conscious needs. If, however, he is primarily concerned with avoiding a direct facing of his own internal conflicts, then he will protect himself from such a possibility the moment he senses an attempt to make him change. The well-known phenomenon of resistance is an example in point. The resistance generated to protect the ego results in a blanket rejection of the change situation, a perceptual distortion of what it is like and an emotional reinforcement of the attitude. Though we recognize the importance of resistance in other contexts, we have slighted its role in attitude change. Hence, persuasion and propaganda can have negative rather than positive effects.

It is not our thesis, however, that ego defenses cannot be breached, but that different procedures are involved in dealing with these defenses than with non-conflicted motives.

Adapting Change-Procedures to the Motivational Basis of Attitude

I. CHANGING ATTITUDES THROUGH ATTACKING THE COGNITIVE OBJECT AND THE FRAME OF REFERENCE IN WHICH IT IS PERCEIVED: THE RATIONAL APPROACH

Inappropriate attitudes, though more characteristically acquired as ego defense, can also be acquired (a) in the interests of social rewards and punishments and (b) in the functioning of the perceptual-cognitive process itself. In the last mentioned instance, the assumption is that the individual acquires beliefs either out of intellectual curiosity, reality-testing, or a desire for cognitive structure in terms of having to know what his world is really like. The belief or attitude may be inappropriate because the individual comes into contact with only a limited aspect of reality. In practice, of course, a number of these processes occur simultaneously. The individual takes on certain attitudes because he wants to be accepted as a group member, but the beliefs he acquires must make sense to him with respect to being accurate pictures of the world he knows.

The theory would be that when new facts are presented they result in cognitive reorganization rather than exclusion or blocking. In addition, sophisticated cognitive theory assumes that perception occurs in a frame of reference which is the momentary product of a number of possible forces. Pressing internal needs or the objective nature of the situation may result in a temporary frame in which things are perceived in relation to that frame. Since people already possess definite standards for perceiving Negroes,[1] it is important, if we are to change their perceptions, to be sure that the dominant frame of reference at the time the materials are introduced is not the product of these old

standards. Essentially, this calls for the activation of a "new" frame without any reference to the old standards. Once the "new" frame is operative, material bearing upon the old cognitive object can be introduced without the old standard operating as a censor. Specifically this can be accomplished through experimentation in the form of the creation of a frame of cultural relativity and cultural causation, and then the introduction of information about Negroes.

II. CHANGING ATTITUDES THROUGH THE APPLICATION OF SOCIAL REWARDS AND PUNISHMENTS

1. *The Use of Group Norms.* One of the major reasons for attitude change is the desire to gain the social approval of others. It is natural that experiments in social psychology have concentrated heavily upon the manipulation of group norms. The desire for social approval is a broad term, however, covering both deep-lying affiliation needs and the immediate rewards of adapting to the group situation. We are concerned here primarily with this latter type of conformity, namely the acceptance of group standards because of their immediate reward character. For example, the individual who accepts the values of the group has increased his chances of being liked by his fellows, of moving up in the group structure or of sharing in the returns from group effort. In these terms, it would first be necessary to find out what the individual's relation to the group is and what types of satisfaction he derives from group membership. If we know these facts, then we are in a better position to predict changes in attitude as a result of a changed perception of group norms. Similarly we could predict those individuals who would tend to maintain their attitudinal position independent of the group. The assumption here is at the simple level that the more the rewards and the greater the sanctions the group has, the more effective will a changed perception of the group position be. In the persuasion pattern the attempt is

---

[1] Attitudes toward Negroes were the dependent variable in our experimental program.

made to achieve cognitive restructuring through making the individual see new possibilities in achieving his goals. In the use of group norms, the change is more external in that the group norm is changed and the individual merely moves with it.

2. *Restructuring the Individual's Value Systems.* The great bulk of the efforts to change attitudes in the world of affairs is through persuasion and argumentation, in which an appeal is made to existing value structures. Some value system, other than that to which the target object is ordinarily connected, is invoked, and the necessity of meeting its requirements is stressed. In inducing change in the manner described under the *rational* approach, the emphasis was placed upon the perceptual side of the process, in getting people to look at the old object in a new frame of reference. Thus subjects would have had to take the further step of restructuring their attitudes themselves. No direct attempt would be made to suggest that they should not pursue a discriminatory policy toward Negroes. In this second type of experiment, however, the attempt will be to restructure their attitudes for them through making the specific connections between the target object and a different set of values. This can be done (1) through exploiting a very powerful system, (2) through utilizing more different values for the change than existed for the old attitudinal structure, and (3) through showing how the values tied to the target are blocked by social reality and are not in fact being achieved. In practice, all three methods are combined to produce change. From the point of view of content, the persuasive technique frequently relies upon demonstration of a fusion between the individual's self-interest and socially desirable goals. It further shows the feasibility of the alternative suggested, as contrasted to the impracticality of all other alternatives. These relationships have been systematically formulated and experimentally demonstrated by H. Peak and her colleagues (Carlson, 1953; Rosenberg, 1953).

The theory implicit in these persuasive techniques is that the individual will restructure his psychological field to maximize the attainment of his goals and values. Personality theorists have suggested that this theory is correct within limitations, namely, that when ego needs are threatened, the individual will respond to persuasive efforts by blocking and resistance. The resistance may result in more strongly reinforced attitudes than was true before the attempted persuasion. Again, the prediction is that the change attempts will have differential effects, depending upon the personal needs of the subject. Moreover, since the appeal to values operates more at the motivational than the perceptual level, the prediction is that for non-ego defensive people there will be more change than in the first and second series of experiments. For the ego defensive people there will be less change because of the phenomenon of resistance.

III. Changing Attitudes by Attacking Ego Defensive Forces through the Use of Catharsis and Direct Interpretation

Two techniques widely employed in psychotherapy which have possible application to group situations are permissive catharsis and direct interpretation. The basic objective is to help the individual attain insight and to restructure his attitudes accordingly.

1. *Permissive Catharsis.* The free ventilation of thought and feeling in an accepting interpersonal atmosphere is an integral part of virtually all schools of psychotherapy. It is generally assumed that this type of expression helps the patient to change in the following ways:

(a) It offers him relief from the tension of burdensome affects such as guilt and hostility. The very act of expressing these feelings is supposed to drain off energy which would necessitate the formation of various somatic and psychic symptoms.

(b) It permits him to verbalize and hence objectify his inner conflicts. Such objectification leads to clearer self-perception. This clarification in turn makes it possible for him to utilize his intellect more effectively in choosing among alternative means of resolving his conflicts.

2. *Direct Interpretation.* This technique uses a combination of logic and suggestion; patients are confronted with psychological explanations of their behavior. These explanations are supposed to give them immediate insight into the internal factors (motivation) which determine their overt behavior. The patient is then to bring the weight of his own common sense to bear upon the proffered insight and to change his behavior in the light of this newly acquired knowledge. Thus, the lengthy process of uncovering is short-circuited and the patient is directly informed about the underlying motives of which he had previously been unaware. In employing this sort of approach, the therapist is generally obliged to rely upon the degree of authoritativeness with which the patient invests him and the sources (research findings, theory) on which he bases his interpretation.

It is granted, however, that these techniques will not be effective for all ego defensive people. In some cases resistances may still be too strong to be affected, either by catharsis or by direct interpretation. The assumption is made, therefore, that people who already have enough insight to be concerned about their own conflicts and to be dissatisfied with some of their own behavior will respond to these techniques. Just as individual therapy can make little headway with patients who do not want to be helped, so group procedures will affect only those group members who are dissatisfied with their self-image, even though they do not understand the basis of their conflict.

In this type of experiment the direct interpretation can consist of psychological explanations of the dynamics of scapegoating and of displaced and repressed hostility. The objective will be to give self-insight. Individuals who are more insightful at the start will apply the interpretation to themselves more readily than individuals lacking insight. One

advantage of the technique of direct interpretation is that it can be used in printed materials and is not confined to interpersonal communication.

Some Experimental Findings

A. RATIONAL PERSUASION COMPARED WITH AUTHORITARIAN SUGGESTION

An experiment was devised by M. Wagman to test the proposition that different personality types would respond differentially to various kinds of change procedure (1953). It was postulated that non-authoritarian people would be more affected by rational persuasion than would authoritarian people, whereas the authoritarian personality would be more responsive to suggestion from power figures than would the non-authoritarian person. It was predicted that even when the influence exerted was in the direction of greater tolerance for minority groups, the authoritarian type of individual would be moved more by suggestion coming from authoritative sources than by a reasoned presentation of facts and arguments.

The measure of authoritarianism was the F scale developed by Frenkel-Brunswik and her colleagues, an instrument designed to give degrees of authoritarian character structure. The authoritarian suggestion consisted of statements attributed to power figures, which emphasized institutional values of efficiency and orderliness for their own sake, rather than as means to ends. The rational persuasion consisted of materials presenting facts and reasons based upon scientific study and historical and anthropological considerations of racial differences.

The subjects, 250 University of Michigan undergraduates, were given pre-measures at the first session, the influence attempt at a second session, and post-measures at a third session. In the first session they were given not only the attitude scales, as measures of the dependent variable, but also the F scale and the Michigan completion test as measures of personality characteristics. In the second session, different influence treatments were used. Approximately 70 subjects received the authoritarian suggestion which was designed to move them in a less prejudiced direction; 70 subjects were given the rational persuasion materials, again directed toward movement toward less prejudice; a third group of 70 subjects was given the authoritarian suggestion designed to move them in a more prejudiced direction. Finally, 40 subjects served as a control group. In a third session, post-measures were taken which repeated the original attitude scales. The influence attempt was separated from the pre- and post-measures by the use of different experimenters and by structuring the situation as part of a different investigation.

The results of this experiment can be summarized as follows:

1. The rational persuasion materials were more effective in producing more favorable attitudes toward Negroes for the non-authoritarian than for the authoritarian subjects.
2. A number of the authoritarian subjects showed greater prejudice after the persuasion attempt than they had originally shown.
3. The authoritarian suggestion, when used to produce more favorable attitudes toward Negroes, had greater success for authoritarian subjects than did the rational persuasion.
4. The authoritarian suggestion, when used to produce less favorable attitudes, was more successful with the authoritarian than the non-authoritarian subjects.
5. A number of non-authoritarian subjects reacted negatively to the authoritarian suggestion designed to move them away from a liberal position, i.e., they became even more liberal.

B. Rational Persuasion Compared with Self-insight

The limitations of both prestige suggestion and rational persuasion are implied in the above experiment. These attempts are dif-ferentially effective and if used with certain types of people can actually have negative effects. Moreover, authoritarian suggestion in one direction may produce change only as long as counter suggestions do not occur. In a second experiment, rational persuasion was compared with the technique of direct interpretation.

The subjects were 300 women students at the Michigan State Normal College at Ypsilanti, divided into their own sorority and dormitory groupings. The experiment was in three stages. In stage one, all subjects took a battery of personality tests and filled out a number of measures designed to test their beliefs, feelings, and attitudes toward relations with minority groups. The personality measures consisted of: (1) The Bender Gestalt test, (2) the F scale of Authoritarian Character Structure, (3) the Michigan Completion Test, scored for patterns of ego defensiveness, (4) a specially constructed thematic apperception test designed to get at hostility toward Negroes, and (5) fairly direct questions about the nature and kind of felt internal conflict. The attitude measures consisted of stereotyped statements about Negro characteristics, a revised Bogardus Social Distance scale, and twelve specific action issues. In addition, the subjects indicated their perception of the group position on two of the issues. In the second session, influence attempts to change attitudes were introduced and the attitude scales were repeated at the end of the session. In the third session some six weeks later, the attitude measures were administered at the start of the session, then different feed-back procedures were employed, and finally some of the attitude scales were repeated before the groups were dismissed.

The primary change manipulation took place during the second session. Two different experimental procedures were employed. One consisted of the rational persuasion materials, very similar in nature to the experiment already described in this section. The purpose here was to give the individual an opportunity to restructure his beliefs in relation to factual and logical materials. The second influence procedure used on comparable groups of subjects employed the technique of direct interpretation. A case study was presented of a girl who had never acquired insight into her own hostilities and inadequacies and who developed in consequence certain social prejudices. The case was presented sympathetically and with sufficient similarity of background to the subjects so that they would have little difficulty in identifying with her. They were asked specifically after reading the case story to indicate how relevant they thought this analysis was to the problem of prejudice in general. They were also asked whether they found themselves employing any of the psychological mechanisms which the girl in the story unconsciously utilized. The rationale for this procedure was that it might give some degree of insight to girls who already were not wholly satisfied with their own behavior. Thus, if they could see how all of us use defense mechanisms to buttress our own egos at the expense of other people, they might restructure some of their beliefs which have a defensive function.

The major purpose of the third session (some six weeks later) was to obtain a measure over time of stability of changes which had been produced in the second session. Since the girls had to be assembled for the taking of this test, their coming together was also used for trying different feed-back procedures to produce further change. The measures of the dependent variable (the attitude scales) were given at the very beginning of the meeting. Then some groups were merely given a reinforcement of the original

procedure they had been subjected to. Other groups were influenced further through the use of three group variables: (1) presentation of group norms, (2) a discussion of the treatment of Negroes in relation to the value of national security, (3) a similar discussion carried to the point of commitment to specific propositions about the problem. In both the second and third sessions measures were taken of perception of group consensus.

Though the analysis of all the data in this experiment has not been completed, these findings can be reported:

1. The interpretation materials produced more liberal attitudes toward Negroes than did the rational persuasion attempt.
2. The changes produced by direct interpretation were more permanent than were the changes produced by rational persuasion. After the six-week period there was more of a tendency to move back toward original position for people subjected to rational persuasion than for people subjected to direct interpretation.
3. The subjects who originally saw themselves as very much like the group persisted in estimating the group as close to their own position during the whole change process. This confirms T. Newcomb's concept of a fairly constant tolerance by the individual for his own nonconformity (White, 1953). People with a narrow limit either conform to changing group attitudes or autistically distort their perception of where the group is. And the most significant finding here is that this behavior during the attitude experiments was related to personality measures of conformity obtained from the Michigan Completion Test and the California F scale (Barlow, 1953).

References

ADORNO, T. W., FRENKEL-BRUNSWIK, E., LEVINSON, D. J., and SANFORD, R. N. *The authoritarian personality.* New York: Harper & Row, 1950.

ASCH, S. E. The doctrine of suggestion, prestige, and imitation in social psychology. *Psychol. Rev.*, 1948, 55, 250-276.

BARLOW, M. F. Security and group approval as value systems related to attitude change. Ph.D. dissertation, Univer. of Michigan, 1953.

CARLSON, E. R. A study of attitude change and attitude structure. Ph.D. dissertation, Univer. of Michigan, 1953.

ROSENBERG, M. J. The experimental investigation of a value theory of attitude structure. Ph.D. dissertation, Univer. of Michigan, 1953.

WAGMAN, M. An investigation of the effectiveness of authoritarian suggestion and non-authoritarian information as methods of changing the prejudiced attitudes of

relatively authoritarian and non-authoritarian personalities. Ph.D. dissertation, Univer. of Michigan, 1953.

WHITE, M. S. Attitudes change as related to perceived group consensus. Ph.D. dissertation, Univer. of Michigan, 1953.

The Personal Setting of Public Opinions: A Study of Attitudes toward Russia ❖ M. Brewster Smith

Underlying the rapid growth of public opinion research in the last decade has been the fruitful conception of public opinion as a sum or resultant of the opinions of individual members of the public. Such a conception leads immediately to the question, "What are Smith, Jones, Brown, and all the other members of the public actually thinking on a given subject?"—a question to which the techniques of the sampling survey are providing increasingly adequate answers. When our interest extends to the formative and directing influences on public opinion, the same approach leads us to ask, "Why do Smith, Jones, etc. think as they do?" "Depth interviewing" and its modifications have been developed to press this attack. If we are to take seriously the productive assumption that public opinion is most effectively studied on the individual level, an important source of insights into the dynamics of opinion should be found in the study of opinions as they reflect the personalities of the individuals who hold them. The relatively few studies that have made forays into this area have not attempted a systematic formulation of the ways in which opinions are grounded in the personality.

To develop and test such a coherent psychological approach to public opinion, the intensive methods of clinical personality study and the broader but shallower methods of the polling survey were brought to a focus in a cooperative study of attitudes toward Russia.[1] The study as a whole will be reported elsewhere. Here some of the main findings of a part of the project—a panel survey of attitudes toward Russia among a cross-section of adult men in a New England community—will be described with two ends in view: first, to illustrate the main lines of an attempt to formulate systematically the nature of opinion and its relation to personality factors, and second, to throw some incidental light on the important problem of American attitudes toward Russia.

The initial formulations underlying the opinion surveys emerged from the related clinical study of a small number of individuals, whose personalities and opinions were investigated in the course of over thirty hours of individual interviewing and testing. Our objective in the opinion surveys was to refine and test the generality of formulations

[1] This study was made possible by support from the Harvard Laboratory of Social Relations. The writer is particularly indebted to Dr. J. S. Bruner for his participation and guidance in the planning and analysis of the survey phase of the project.

From *Public Opinion Quarterly*, 1947, 11, 507-523. Reprinted by permission of the author and publisher.

that had proved important in understanding the opinions of the individual cases studied by intensive methods.

A "panel" representing adult men in the community was interviewed personally at the men's homes, first in March and then in May, 1947.[2] The first series of interviews, which systematically explored the men's attitudes toward Russia, comprised 319 men. Of these, 250 were re-interviewed in order to obtain information about their personalities. The smaller group taking part in both interviews did not differ markedly in demographic characteristics from the initial group.

Two general approaches were employed in the design of the interviews and in their analysis. The first of these sought to provide a systematic *descriptive analysis* of attitudes toward Russia. Here the attempt was made to delineate an "anatomy" of attitudes that would provide an adequate basis for the "physiology" of a subsequent *functional analysis*. The latter was concerned with the interplay of opinions and other manifestations of the personality.

Principal Concepts of a Descriptive Analysis

Descriptively we may fruitfully distinguish how a respondent *feels* about Russia —the *affective* aspect of his attitudes—and what he *thinks* about it—their *cognitive* aspect. On the affective side, there are the familiar factors of *direction*, defined in terms of his approval or disapproval of Russia as a whole or of such features as he may differentiate, and *intensity*, his degree of concern. On the cognitive side, the *informational context* of his attitudes may be distinguished as the structure of his beliefs and knowledge that affect his opinions, and their *times perspective* as his expectations concerning future developments in regard to Russia.

2 We are indebted to Dr. Alvin Zander and Dr. Seth Arsenian for their kind cooperation in facilitating the field work. Mr. Henry Riecken and the author trained the interviewers, and Mrs. Lopez supervised the interviewing.

Both the cognitive and affective elements of a person's attitudes patently have much to do with what he wants to *have done* about Russia. The latter aspect we singled out as the individual's *policy orientation:* the measures toward Russia that he supports and opposes. Policy orientation has the most direct political relevance of the various descriptive categories, but is probably bound more closely than the others to the issues of the moment. All of these categories seem necessary for an adequate description of the attitudes comprising public opinion. A brief consideration of some of our findings may serve to indicate the utility of this scheme, as well as to introduce some necessary elaborations.

DIRECTION, INTENSITY, AND ORGANIZATION

Probably the first problem to be faced in a description of public opinion toward Russia is its direction: are people favorable or unfavorable? As one might expect, the direction of opinion was found to vary according to the aspect of the problem in question. Direction was therefore studied in terms of the lines along which attitudes toward Russia were commonly differentiated. In most respects, unfavorable opinions prevailed. The extent of disapproval showed marked variation, however, and in regard to Russia's part in World War II, the proportion of respondents who indicated unqualified approval considerably exceeded the disapproving group.

Aspect of Russia	Per Cent Indicating Approval
Russia's part in World War II [3]	46%
Russia's international role[4]	14
Russian system of government[5]	6

3 The question was: "Looking back on it now, what would you say about Russia's part in the war?" Data are for respondents indicating unqualified approval.

4 Based on the card question: "Now, about Russia's part in the world today—do you think it has been mostly good, more good than bad, about half good and half bad, more bad than

One need not rest, however, with the statement that attitudes are predominantly favorable in some respects and unfavorable in others. The different aspects of Russia involved in the men's attitudes had different weight in determining their over-all evaluation of Russia and their policy orientation. Table 1 shows, for example, that when the respondents were asked to pick out what was most important (among 12 things listed) in making them feel about Russia the way they did, only 9 per cent cited "the part Russia played in World War II," as compared with 23 per cent who selected "Russia's part in spreading world Communism" and 21 per cent who mentioned "the lack of freedom and democracy inside Russia."

Attitudes toward Russia can therefore be conceived as hierarchically *organized.* The aspects in regard to which Russia was likely to be viewed with relative favor turn out only rarely to have had determinative importance for the respondents. This finding suggests the danger of looking to poll results from single questions for an assessment of the over-all direction of opinion. It is vital to know whether direction of opinion in regard to a given aspect is consequential or trivial in the organization of the respondent's attitudes. The conception of the heirarchical organization of a person's attitudes makes it possible to speak consistently of his being favorable to Russia in some respects and unfavorable in others, at the same time that we ascribe to him a generally favorable—or unfavorable—attitude toward Russia.

It is not enough to know the direction of attitudes toward Russia; we must also know their intensity. It seems likely, in fact, that the just-considered hierarchical organization of a person's over-all attitude depends directly on the intensity of his component attitudes. Thus, those features of Russia about

good, or mostly bad?" Data are for respondents giving the first two answers.
[5] Based on the question: "How do you feel about the Russian system of government? What is good and what is bad about it?" Data are for respondents giving favorable answers, with or without qualification. All three questions were asked in the March, 1947, survey.

TABLE 1

RELATIVE IMPORTANCE ATTRIBUTED BY RESPONDENTS TO VARIOUS ASPECTS OF RUSSIA[*]

Aspects of Russian Foreign Relations		52%
Russia's part in spreading world Communism	23%	
The possibility of war with Russia	11	
The part Russia played in World War II	9	
Russia's treatment of small countries	9	
Aspects of Russian Internal Affairs		46
The lack of freedom and democracy inside Russia	21	
The lack of free enterprise inside Russia	12	
Russia's treatment of the church and religion	7	
Russia's concern for the welfare of her people	5	
The equality given all races and minority groups in Russia	1	
Russian planning and efficiency	†	
Russian backwardness and inefficiency	†	
Russia's point of view on morality and the family	0	
No opinion		2
Total		100%
Number of respondents		250

[*] The question, asked in May, 1947, was: "As you know, we're interested in the way people look at Russia, what they see in her. I wonder if you could tell me which of these things you think is most important in making you feel about Russia the way you do?" [Show card.]
† Less than 0.5 per cent.

which he feels most strongly determine his over-all evaluation of Russia and have most to do with his policy orientation toward the country. Support for this plausible view is found in the survey data. When asked which things were most important and which next most important in making them feel as they did about Russia, some respondents indicated two aspects both of which could be classed under "Russian foreign relations" (see Table 1 for the classification), while others named aspects both in the area of "Russian internal affairs." When these extreme groups are compared in respect to the intensity of their attitudes toward Russia's international role, 75 per cent of the former group as against 56 per cent of the latter are found to have said that they were at least "quite a lot" concerned.[6] In this case, then, intensity of opinion was higher with respect to the dominant area in the organization of the respondents' attitudes. If we want to find the keystones of opinion on a topic, according to this view, we should look for the areas in which the intensity of opinion is highest.

TIME PERSPECTIVE

A study limited to the affective side of opinion—its direction and intensity—would give at best an incomplete understanding of opinion phenomena. The person's beliefs and expectations form the premises for his evaluation and policy orientation. In this regard, the complex pattern of expectations that constitutes the time perspective of a person's attitudes is of major importance. For some, the meaningful future extends little beyond the practical concerns of tomorrow. The opinions of such persons with narrow time perspective surely take form under different influences and have different meaning from those of persons whose broad time perspective includes a careful balancing of future possibilities. Another important distinction is between "short run" and "long run" perspectives. In the long run perspective, the constraint of reality may be more lax than in the short run, while the implications of threat or benefit to the individual are less immediate. Discrepancies between the two views may therefore be expected.

Results from our survey seem to require this distinction between the short and long run. When the respondents were asked,

"Do you think the United States and Russia will get along together better, worse, or about the same in the next few years?"

[6] The question, asked in the May survey, was: "How concerned are you about Russia's part in the world today—a great deal, quite a lot, not so much, or none at all?" There were 71 and 59 respondents in the two groups, respectively.

44 per cent said relations would get "better," while only 15 per cent indicated that they would get "worse." These optimistic findings must be contrasted with the results for the following question:

"Do you expect the United States to fight in another war within the next 50 years? [If 'yes,' 'perhaps,' or 'don't know'] Are there any particular countries that you think we might fight against?"

Here 51 per cent of the sample said they definitely expected another war, and named Russia as the probable enemy, while an additional 13 per cent thought that if there were to be another war it would be with Russia.

Rather than providing a relatively unbiased assessment of expectations in regard to possible war with Russia, this question appears to have tapped the stereotyped assumption of the inevitability of future wars, a belief that entails little personal threat when held in the relatively remote time perspective of the long run. The high proportion who mentioned Russia as the probable enemy did not necessarily foresee war with Russia; rather, they expected another war eventually and regarded the country with which American relations were most problematic as the most likely candidate. In the short run, nearly half of the respondents expected improvement in relations between the countries at the time of the survey.

INFORMATIONAL CONTEXT

Time perspective is only a part of the important cognitive aspect of attitudes. There remains to be considered their informational context—the entire complex of beliefs and knowledge that bears on a person's opinions. At the core of the informational context of our respondents' attitudes toward Russia lay the picture of Russia that they had formed for themselves. The degree of factually correct information—or *informational level*—is only one aspect of the informational context, and not the most important one.

Several questions revealed the prevalent stereotype of Russia among our respondents as one of a dictatorship engaged in spreading world Communism for purposes of self-aggrandizement. The economic aspect of Communism took a relatively secondary place, while considerations of social welfare figured scarcely at all. Beliefs concerning moral and religious practices were marginal to the stereotype, but those that prevailed were still mostly unfavorable in purport. The picture of Russia formed by our respondents was of course intimately related to the direction and policy orientation of their attitudes.

In regard to informational *level*, however, as estimated from scores on a series of seven "fact questions" on Russia, there was practically no relation to the direction of their opinions about Russia's international role nor to their policy orientation. On the other hand, the better informed men were distinctly more optimistic in their time perspective in regard to relations with Russia. They were less likely to pick Russia as a probable enemy in a future war, and, as Table 2 illustrates, they were more likely to expect United States-Soviet relations to improve.

TABLE 2

EXPECTATIONS ABOUT UNITED STATES-SOVIET RELATIONS, IN RELATION TO INFORMATIONAL LEVEL

Question: "Do you think the United States and Russia will get along together better, worse, or about the same in the next few years?"	Well Informed Respondents	Poorly Informed Respondents
Relations will get *better*	53%	35%
Relations will stay the *same*	28	36
Relations will get *worse*	14	16
No opinion	5	13
Total	100%	100%
Number of respondents	155	164

Results such as these call into question the conclusion of Walsh in 1944 that "the decisive factor in American opinion toward Russia appears to be neither class, nor religion,

nor political preference, but information" (Walsh, 1944). If we re-examine the data as summarized by Walsh, we find that it is again time perspective—expectations about post-war relations—that is related to informational level. It may have been that the extent of information about Russia was also related to the direction and policy orientation of opinion at that time, but the poll results that he quotes do not provide the necessary data. The present scheme has the merit of calling attention to distinguishable aspects of attitudes that warrant separate consideration.

POLICY ORIENTATION

The cognitive and affective aspects of attitudes both underlie their policy orientation, which we have defined as the measures, in this case toward Russia, that the respondent supports and opposes. From the standpoint of the individual as well as from that of political relevance, policy orientation represents in a very real sense the point or focus of his attitudes. Behind the persistent tendency of most people to evaluate the salient features of their world is the need to know where one *stands*, to know in at least a rudimentary way the course of action one would take if the occasion should demand it. In the case of political attitudes on topics of public concern, policy orientation consists for the most part in alignment in terms of publicly defined issues.

At the time of our first survey (just before the President's "Truman Doctrine" speech), the following question provided the principal information on our respondents' policy orientation:

"Some people say that the United States should try to do everything possible to cooperate with Russia and others say that we've got to be tough with Russia. Which do you agree with most?"

Fully 53 per cent said that the United States should be "tough" with Russia, while only a third (33 per cent) favored a policy of "cooperation." In itself, such a finding is not too informative. Further questions revealed, for example, that the majority could not further specify the policies they would favor, while many of those favoring "cooperation" appeared to have had relatively stern policies in mind. In addition, the supporters of a "tough" policy proved to be less easily dislodged from their position, and were more likely to indicate that policy toward Russia would make a difference in their vote for a presidential candidate. Such matters of liability and passivity of policy orientation need investigation to give meaning to the bare proportions found in support of different policies.

ILLUSTRATIVE RELATIONSHIPS

The descriptive features of attitudes that have been distinguished cannot of course be conceived in isolation. The study of their relationships is itself informative, and raises significant problems for functional interpretation. Two examples may serve to emphasize the complexity of the processes involved.

Intensity of concern about Russia was found to be associated with a high level of information about Russia. Among the relatively well-informed respondents, 71 per cent said they were at least "quite a lot" concerned about Russia's part in the world today, in comparison to 52 per cent among the poorly informed group. The respondents who were higher in intensity were found to have had more frequent and adequate contact with the press, radio, and magazines. Presumably the relationship is a reciprocal one: knowledge leads to concern, while concern leads to receptivity to information. This reciprocal relation between intensity and informational level has an important consequence: holders of the most narrowly stereotyped unfavorable views were not particularly likely to show the intensity that their beliefs might be supposed to warrant. The ignorance underlying their unfavorable stereotypes was part of a complex interaction that also involved their relative lack of concern about Russia.

Another close relationship held between the direction of a person's opinions and the nature of the beliefs forming his informational context. There is good evidence that the interplay here was also reciprocal. The influence of beliefs on the direction of opinion needs no special supporting evidence. The reverse influence is neatly documented by Table 3. There it may be seen that re-

TABLE 3

BELIEFS CONCERNING RUSSIAN ENTRY INTO THE WAR AGAINST JAPAN, IN RELATION TO DIRECTION OF OPINION TOWARD RUSSIA

Belief	Favorable Respondents°	Unfavorable Respondents°
Russia declared war in 1941	4%	4%
Russia declared war shortly before the first atomic bomb was dropped	49	35
Russia declared war shortly after the first atomic bomb was dropped	38	45
Russia never declared war	4	9
Don't know	5	7
Total	100%	100%
Number of respondents	45	109

° The question, asked in March, 1947, was "Now about Russia's part in the world today—do you think it has been mostly good; more good than bad, about half good and half bad; more bad than good, or mostly bad?" Data for the first two and the last two categories are compared here.

spondents who were relatively favorable toward Russia were more likely than unfavorable respondents to decide erroneously that Russia declared war on Japan shortly before the first atomic bomb. In this case it seems quite clear that the direction of opinion was causally prior to the belief. It is unlikely that many of the respondents had heard or read the erroneous assertion as a fact, while virtually all of the respondents must have been aware of the true succession of events when they were occurring. In all likelihood, those who answered the question incorrectly had no belief on the matter prior to the asking of the question, and created on the spur of the moment a belief consistent with the direction of their attitudes.

Functional Aspects of Attitudes toward Russia

One cannot pursue the study of attitudes far, however, without inquiring about their function in personality. The correspondence, for example, between the informational context and direction of an attitude can only be understood in terms of the values activating the individual's over-all view of Russia. That is to say, the correspondence between the conception of Russia as a dictatorship and unfavorable attitudes is only "natural" in a public sharing democratic values to which dictatorship is repugnant. Several ways in which attitudes are enmeshed with personality factors emerged from the study. They may reflect or express the person's central values (their *value* function). They may show consistency with his characteristic ways of reacting (their *consistency* function), or perhaps gratify indirectly his basic needs (their *gratification* function). They may form part of his attempt to construct for himself a stable and meaningful world within which he can order his life (their *meaning* function). Finally, they may serve to express his identification with and promote his acceptance by his favored social groups (their *conformity* function).

PERSONAL VALUES AND ATTITUDES

TOWARD RUSSIA

The nature of a person's central values was found to be important for his attitudes toward Russia in several respects. In the first place, the scope of his interests is of primary importance in determining the intensity of his attitudes toward Russia. Secondly, the particular values that he holds dear sensitize him to corresponding aspects of Russia and provide him with standards of judgment. Finally—a consequence of the second point—

the nature of his value system has much to do with the hierarchical organization of his attitudes toward Russia.

As might be expected, men with broader interests were much more likely than others to show a relatively high level of intensity in their concern about Russia. We took as one rough index of breadth of interests whether a respondent said that he usually preferred "to be with people who are quite a lot concerned about what is going on in the world, or with people who are mostly interested in their homes and families." Men who gave the former response were also more likely than others to place high value on participation in community affairs and on taking an interest in national and world affairs. As Table 4 shows, 80 per cent of the men with

TABLE 4

INTENSITY OF ATTITUDES TOWARD RUSSIA, IN RELATION TO BREADTH OF INTERESTS

Question: "How concerned are you about Russia's part in the world today? . . ."	Respondents with Broad Interests°	Respondents with Narrow Interests°
. . . a great deal	40%	23%
. . . quite a lot	40	28
. . . not so much	19	43
. . . none at all	1	4
No opinion	0	2
Total	100%	100%
Number of respondents	73	110

° The question, asked in May, 1947, was: "By and large, do you usually prefer to be with people who are quite a lot concerned about what is going on in the world, or with people who are mostly interested in their homes and families?"

broader interests said that they were at least "quite a lot" concerned about Russia's part in the world. Only 51 per cent of the group with narrower interests, on the other hand, showed this level of intensity. Intensity of attitudes toward Russia thus formed part of a more general tendency to take an interest in the world beyond hearth and home. A respondent may have prided himself on a range of interests that involved concern about Russia; or, his broader range of interests may have led him to enrich his information about Russia to an extent that he saw its relevance to values that were important to him.

The part played by the person's central values in determining the hierarchical organization of his attitudes toward Russia may be illustrated by the case of the value of *liberty*. Respondents who gave a response classifiable under this value when asked what things in life were most important to them[7] (62 cases) were compared with all others (188 cases) in regard to the aspect of Russia that they said had most to do with their feelings. Of the group stressing liberty, 36 per cent selected "the lack of freedom and democracy inside Russia," compared with 17 per cent of the remaining respondents—and this was the only notable difference in the responses of the two groups. The degree to which a value is important to the individual can thus determine which aspect of Russia plays the key part in the organization of his attitudes.

The correspondence between a person's central values and the features of Russia around which his attitudes are organized is, however, by no means direct. Some values of greatest importance to him may fail entirely to *engage* with his conceptions of Russia. A good example of this was the value of economic security. The most frequent responses elicited by the open-ended question on personal values referred to economic security—matters like a steady job, good pay, etc. A naive application of the present approach might therefore lead one to expect that individual economic security as espoused by Russia would play an important part in the attitudes toward Russia formed

[7] The question was: "We've been talking about some of your present opinions. We are also interested in finding out what sorts of things people think are important in life. I have a question here about what you think is important in life. It's a little hard to put in words right off, I know, but from your experience, what would you say are the most important things to you? What sort of things mean the most to you?"

by the men stressing this value. Actually, nothing of the kind was observed. There was no association between economic security as a value and emphasis on corresponding aspects of Russia.

Two facts that are probably sufficient to account for this finding have major implications for a general formulation of the relation between personal values and the organization of attitudes. In the first place, the information in terms of which the respondents might have seen the relevance of Russia to economic security was simply not available in the current media of communication. While it is probably true that the holding of a value sensitizes a person to perceive and digest information that pertains to it, there is a limit to the extent that he will actively seek out information that is not readily available. In this case, the resultant informational context furnished no basis for the *engagement* of the value. Secondly, the value of economic security was likely to entail a rather narrow scope of interests, in the form in which it was important to most of our respondents. Men who cited it as a central value were likely to show relatively little interest in current events or community participation. Their interests tended to center more exclusively around the daily concerns of a minimal existence. There was therefore small occasion for them to apply the value of economic security in their judgments of Russia.

For a value to enter into a person's attitudes on a topic, then, there are at least two necessary conditions: the scope of the value must be broad enough to apply to the topic, and the information available to the person must contain at least some basis for engaging his value. Taking these limitations into consideration, we may tentatively extend our principle of the organization of attitudes. It was previously suggested that the hierarchical organization of a person's attitudes on a complex topic depends directly on their relative intensity. Now we may say that *intensity is a function of the extent to which a personal value is engaged and of the importance of this engaged value in the hierarchy of the person's central values.*

Other functional relationships to the personality doubtless also enter into the determination of intensity. Here it may be noted that the present statement goes far to clarify the reciprocal relationship found to exist between informational level and intensity. A more adequate informational context permits the person's values to engage more fully with Russia.

PERSONALITY TRAITS AND ATTITUDES TOWARD RUSSIA

A person's attitudes are formed so as to be consistent with his characteristic modes of reaction, and may be pressed into service for the indirect gratification of underlying personality strivings. Although there is a serious limit to the kinds of personality data obtainable from door-to-door interviews, one can, nevertheless, get at some important personality factors in field interviewing. An illustration of the consistency of personality traits with attitudes toward Russia is a case in point.

People characteristically respond to a frustrating situation, according to Rosenzweig (1934), in one of three ways: they may turn aggressively on others ("extrapunitive reaction"), or on themselves ("intrapunitive reaction"), or they may ignore the frustration ("impunitive reaction"). It seemed likely that these characteristic types of reaction might carry over into their opinions. A rough indicator of the first two of these tendencies was provided by responses to the following question:

"When things go wrong, are you more likely to get sore at other people or to feel bad and blame yourself for the situation?"

Table 5 compares the men who said that they usually "get sore at" others with those who said they blamed themselves. It may be seen that those who blame others—the "extrapunitive" group—were somewhat more

TABLE 5

OPINIONS ABOUT RUSSIA, IN RELATION TO REPORTED REACTION TO FRUSTRATION

Opinion	Tends to Blame Others	Tends to Blame Self
Blames Russia for U.S.-Soviet disagreement°	74%	63%
Expects U.S.-Soviet relations to stay the same or deteriorate	76	49
Favors "tough" U.S. policy toward Russia	67	57
Number of respondents	46	127

° The question, asked in May, 1947, was: "Do you think that the present disagreements between the United States and Russia are *entirely* Russia's fault, *mostly* Russia's fault, the fault of the *United States,* or do you think that *both* countries are equally to blame?" Data are for respondents giving the first two answers. The other questions have already been quoted.

likely than the "intrapunitive" respondents to blame Russia for United States-Soviet disagreements and to support a "tough" United States policy toward Russia. This is what one would expect if their attitudes were to be consistent with the rest of their personality tendencies. They were also considerably more likely to expect United States-Soviet relations to stay the same or deteriorate. The latter finding appears to have been an *indirect* consequence of the distinguishing personality characteristic. Perhaps a greater tendency to blame oneself and the groups with which one was closely identified required a defensive sanguineness from the intrapunitive group. Or, on the other hand, those who saw the United States as at least partly implicated in the blame may have been more likely to think the disagreements between the countries remediable.

ATTITUDES TOWARD RUSSIA AS A SOURCE OF MEANING AND STABILITY

On *a priori* grounds one might suppose that a person's attitudes toward any topic serve the important function of sorting out his world of experience into a predictable order that can provide the background for an orderly existence. It is necessary to postulate some such function in order to interpret the constraint that knowledge places on wishful thinking. The present data on attitudes toward Russia provide several illustrations of the tendency of a person's beliefs and expectations to conform to the direction of his attitude. But, not surprisingly, the more informed respondents were less likely to let their feelings enter into their beliefs. For example, of the well-informed group (155 cases), 55 per cent said that they expected the world to become more communistic, compared with 41 per cent of the poorly informed group (164 cases). Here was an expectation that was surely distasteful to a large majority of the respondents but was accepted by a majority of the well-informed.

That knowledge imposes a constraint on wishful thinking is an obvious fact, but one which should not be neglected. This constraint would seem to depend on the likelihood that beliefs subject to contradiction in the normal course of experience may jeopardize the stability of one's world picture. It is possible to fend off some of the implications of experience, but the need for stability places limits on the development of one's private world.

This formulation leads to an hypothesis regarding the balance between differentiation and consistency in a person's attitudes. An undifferentiated attitude, depicting Russia as all black or all white, has the advantage of simplicity, posing fewer problems of decision than one compounded of shades of gray. But in order that a person's picture of the world may seem trustworthy and have the stability desirable in a map from which he takes his bearings, it must also take into account the situation as he understands it. The extent that a person's attitudes are differentiated, then, may represent the compromise between the need for simplicity and the need for adequacy that best fulfills his requirement of a stable and meaningful conception of his world.

SOCIAL CONFORMITY AND ATTITUDES TOWARD RUSSIA

The functional relationships thus far illustrated propose relatively basic relations between the structure and content of attitudes and personality factors. But the content of a person's attitudes may also be taken over more or less bodily from his associates or from prestigeful persons as a way of expressing identification with them and facilitating their acceptance. This pressure toward conformity is rooted in the person's basic needs for acceptance and approval. It is not, however, the sole or perhaps even the principal source of influence promoting relative uniformity of opinion within face-to-face groups. In addition there is the fact that members of such groups are likely to have common informational contexts on a topic, both because they share similar sources of information and because members of the group are themselves major sources of information for one another. Furthermore, they are also likely to have acquired from one another and from similar life experiences a relatively similar value outlook.

The survey findings were in keeping with the supposition that conformity plays an important role in the determination of a person's attitudes. Our data also suggest the interesting possibility that the need for conformity may favor *shifts* in the total distribution of opinion. A simple comparison of the men's own opinions with those that they ascribe to their friends reveals a tendency for the friends to be considered slightly more anti-Russian.[8] [See table opposite.]

Such a finding may be characteristic of a state of affairs in which the "anti" position is more strongly and vociferously held than the "pro"—as our data indicate was certainly the case in regard to Russia at the time of the

[8] Data are for the May, 1947, survey.

Evaluation of Russia's International Role	Own Opinions	Estimate of Friends' Opinions
Mostly good or more good than bad	11%	7%
About half good and half bad	29	21
More bad than good or mostly bad	59	66
No opinion	1	6
Total	100%	100%
Number of respondents	250	250

survey. To the extent that the need for approval creates real pressure toward conformity, conformity must be toward the opinions of others *as the person understands them.* When one direction of opinion has relatively higher "audibility" than the other, conformity may be expected to lead not merely toward uniformity but toward uniformity in the direction of the more audible opinion.

Conclusions

While the individual attitudes underlying public opinion on any topic are indeed complex, their complexity need not preclude systematic analysis. All too often, investigations

of public opinion have proceeded to devise questions about this or that aspect of a public issue on a hit-or-miss basis. A framework for the description of attitudes is clearly needed.

The descriptive scheme that has been developed here in connection with attitudes toward Russia should prove generally useful. Cognitive and affective elements as well as policy orientation can be fruitfully distinguished in most political attitudes. A systematic approach of this sort throws into perspective important relationships among attitudinal features from which a more adequate understanding of opinion processes may be attained.

Such an adequate understanding, however, requires insight into the functions that opinions serve in the psychological economy of the person who holds them—the ways in which opinions are embedded in personality. We have illustrated in connection with attitudes toward Russia a first approximation toward an analysis of these functions. Further investigations embodying a functional approach should add to the understanding of the dynamics of opinion on particular topics and in different publics, and be a promising source of advance in the theory of public opinion.

References

Rosenzweig, S. Types of reaction to frustration. *J. abnorm. soc. Psychol.*, 1934, 29, No. 3, 298-300.

Walsh, W. B. What the American people think of Russia. *Publ. Opin. Quart.*, 1944, 8, No. 4, 513-522.

Compliance, Identification,
and Internalization: Three
Processes of Attitude Change ❧ Herbert C. Kelman

A crucial issue in communication research relates to the *nature* of changes (if any) that are brought about by a particular communication or type of communication. It is not enough to know that there has been some measurable change in attitude; usually we would also want to know what kind of change it is. Is it a superficial change, on a verbal level, which disappears after a short lapse of time? Or is it a more lasting change in attitude and belief, which manifests itself in a wide range of situations and which is integrated into the person's value system? Or, to put it in other terms, did the communication produce public conformity *without* private acceptance, or did it produce public conformity coupled with private acceptance? (Festinger, 1953; Kelman, 1953.) Only if we know something about the nature and depth of changes can we make meaningful predictions about the way in which attitude changes will be reflected in subsequent actions and reactions to events.

These questions about the nature of attitude changes are highly significant in the study of international attitudes. For example, we may have observed changes in opinion toward certain international issues—e.g., aspects of foreign policy, international organization, or disarmament—among the population of a given country. The implications that we draw from these changes will depend on their depth and on the psychological meanings that can be assigned to them. Let us assume that we find an increase in favorable attitudes toward the United Nations among the population of the United States at a particular juncture. This change in attitude may be due primarily to recent pronouncements by high-placed figures and may thus represent an aspect of "social conformity." On the other hand, the change may result from a series of international events which have led large segments of the population to reevaluate American foreign policy and to ascribe a more central role to the UN. Depending on which of these *motivational processes* underlies the change in attitude, we would make different predictions about the manifestations and consequences of the new attitudes: about their durability, about the number of different attitudinal areas that will be affected by them, and about the ways in which they will be translated into action and will determine reactions to international events. Similarly, our predictions about the subsequent history of the new attitudes will depend on their *cognitive links*, i.e., the par-

From the *Journal of Conflict Resolution*, 1958, 2, 51-60. Reprinted by permission of the author and publisher. An earlier draft of this paper was written while the author was with the Laboratory of Psychology, National Institute of Mental Health, and was read at the annual meeting of the American Psychological Association in Chicago on August 30, 1956. The experiment reported here was conducted while the author was at Johns Hopkins University as a Public Health Service Research Fellow of the National Institute of Mental Health. Additional financial support was received from the Yale Communication Research Program, which is under the direction of Carl I. Hovland and which is operating under a grant from the Rockefeller Foundation. The author is particularly grateful to James Owings for his help in running the experiment; to Ramon J. Rhine and Janet Baldwin Barclay for their help in analysis of the data; and to Roger K. Williams, Chairman of the Psychology Department at Morgan State College, for the many ways in which he facilitated collection of the data.

ticular attitude structure within which the new attitude toward the UN is imbedded. For example, Americans may have become more favorable toward the UN because an important resolution sponsored by the United States delegate has been accepted. The new attitude toward the UN is thus an aspect of attitudes toward one's own nation and its prestige and international success. On the other hand, favorableness toward the UN may have increased because UN action has successfully averted war in a very tense conflict situation. In this case, the new attitude toward the UN is imbedded in an attitude structure revolving around the whole question of war and effective means of preventing its outbreak. Again, we would draw different implications from the changed attitudes, depending on which of these attitude areas was primarily involved in the occurrence of change.

The same considerations apply when we interpret the effects of international communications. For example, if we find changes in the way in which nationals of different countries perceive one another, it would be important to know at what level these changes have occurred and to what motivational and cognitive systems they are linked. These questions are important not only for the analysis of changes in attitude toward various international issues, objects, or events which may have occurred as a result of various kinds of communication or experience but also for the development of propositions about the conditions for change. In international relations, as in other areas of social behavior, one of our ultimate concerns is the exploration of the conditions under which lasting changes occur, changes which are generalized to many situations and which represent some degree of value reorganization.

In the present paper I should like to describe briefly an experimental study which is concerned with some of the conditions that determine the nature of attitude changes produced by communications on social issues. The specific content of the attitudes that were investigated in this study was in the area of race relations rather than international relations. The hypotheses refer, however, to general processes of attitude change, irrespective of the specific attitudinal area. Relationships found should be equally applicable, therefore, to the analysis of international attitudes.

I. Theoretical Framework

The experiment reported here grows out of a broader theoretical framework concerned with the analysis of different processes of attitude change resulting from social influence. It is impossible to present this framework in detail in the present paper, but I should like to outline its main features.

The starting point of the theoretical analysis is the observation discussed in the preceding paragraphs, i.e., that changes in attitudes and actions produced by social influence may occur at different "levels." It is proposed that these differences in the nature or level of changes that take place correspond to differences in the *process* whereby the individual accepts influence (or "conforms"). In other words, the underlying processes in which an individual engages when he adopts induced behavior may be different, even though the resulting overt behavior may appear the same.

Three different processes of influence can be distinguished: compliance, identification, and internalization.[1]

Compliance can be said to occur when an individual accepts influence because he hopes to achieve a favorable reaction from another person or group. He adopts the induced behavior not because he believes in its content but because he expects to gain specific rewards or approval and avoid specific punishments or disapproval by conforming. Thus the satisfaction derived from compliance is due to the *social effect* of accepting influence.

[1] A similar distinction, between four processes of conformity, was recently presented by Marie Jahoda (1956).

Identification can be said to occur when an individual accepts influence because he wants to establish or maintain a satisfying self-defining relationship to another person or a group. This relationship may take the form of classical identification, in which the individual takes over the role of the other, or it may take the form of a reciprocal role relationship. The individual actually believes in the responses which he adopts through identification, but their specific content is more or less irrelevant. He adopts the induced behavior because it is associated with the desired relationship. Thus the satisfaction derived from identification is due to the *act* of conforming as such.

Internalization can be said to occur when an individual accepts influence because the content of the induced behavior—the ideas and actions of which it is composed—is intrinsically rewarding. He adopts the induced behavior because it is congruent with his value system. He may consider it useful for the solution of a problem or find it congenial to his needs. Behavior adopted in this fashion tends to be integrated with the individual's existing values. Thus the satisfaction derived from internalization is due to the *content* of the new behavior.

The three processes represent three qualitatively different ways of accepting influence. A systematic treatment of the processes might, therefore, begin with an analysis of the determinants of influence in general. These determinants can be summarized by the following proposition: The probability of accepting influence is a combined function of (*a*) the relative importance of the anticipated effect, (*b*) the relative power of the influencing agent, and (*c*) the prepotency of the induced response. A variety of experimental findings can be cited in support of this proposition.

Compliance, identification, and internalization can each be represented as a function of these three determinants. For each process, however, these determinants take a qualitatively indifferent form. Thus the determinants of the three processes can be distinguished from one another in terms of the

nature of the anticipated effect, the *source of* the influencing agent's power, and the *manner* in which the induced response has become prepotent.

In other words, each process is characterized by a distinctive set of *antecedent* conditions, involving a particular qualitative variation of a more general set of determinants. Given the proper set of antecedents, then, influence will take the form of compliance, identification, or internalization, respectively. Each of these corresponds to a characteristic pattern of internal responses (thoughts and feelings) in which the individual engages while adopting the induced behavior.

Similarly, each process is characterized by a distinctive set of *consequent* conditions, involving a particular qualitative variation in the subsequent history of the induced response. Responses adopted through different processes will be performed under different conditions, will be changed and extinguished under different conditions, and will have different properties.

Since each of the three processes mediates between a distinct set of antecedents and a distinct set of consequents, the proposed distinctions between the three processes can be tested by experiments which attempt to relate the antecedents postulated for a given process to the consequents postulated for that process. The present experiment was designed to vary one of the antecedents—the source of the influencing agent's power—and to observe the effects of this variation on one of the consequents—the conditions of performance of the induced response.

Power is defined as the extent to which the influencing agent is perceived as instrumental to the achievement of the subject's goals. The sources of the agent's power may vary (French, 1956). The following hypotheses are offered regarding the variations in source of power:

1. To the extent to which the power of the influencing agent is based on means-control, conformity will tend to take the form of compliance.
2. To the extent to which the power of the influencing agent is based on attractive-

ness, conformity will tend to take the form of identification.

3. To the extent to which the power of the influencing agent is based on credibility, conformity will tend to take the form of internalization.

Now let us look at the consequent side. One of the ways in which behaviors adopted through different processes can be distinguished is in terms of the conditions under which the behavior is performed. The following hypotheses are offered regarding the conditions of performance:

1. When an individual adopts an induced response through compliance, he tends to perform it only under conditions of surveillance by the influencing agent.
2. When an individual adopts an induced response through identification, he tends to perform it only under conditions of salience of his relationship to the agent.
3. When an individual adopts an induced response through internalization, he tends to perform it under conditions of relevance of the issue, regardless of surveillance or salience.

II. Procedure

The subjects in this experiment were Negro college Freshmen in a border state. The experiment was conducted in the spring of 1954, just prior to the announcement of the Supreme Court decision on desegregation in the public schools. The social influence situation to which the students were exposed consisted of a fixed communication designed to change their attitudes on an issue related to the impending Court decision. Specifically, each of the communications employed in the study presented essentially the following message: If the Supreme Court rules that segregation is unconstitutional, it would still be desirable to maintain some of the *private* Negro colleges as all-Negro institutions, in order to preserve Negro culture, history, and tradition. Preliminary testing indicated that a large majority of the subjects would initially oppose the message presented in the communication.

The communications were tape-recorded interviews between a moderator and a guest (the communicator). They were presented to the subjects as recordings of radio programs which we were interested in evaluating. By varying the nature of these communications, it was possible to manipulate experimentally the source and degree of the communicator's power, while keeping the message of the communication constant. Four different communications were used, as can be seen from Table 1, which outlines the basic design of the experiment (see left-hand column).

TABLE 1°

DESIGN OF THE EXPERIMENT AND PREDICTIONS

Experimental Groups: Variations in Communicator Power	Questionnaires: Variations in Conditions in Performance		
	Questionnaire I *Surveillance* *Salience* *Issue-Relevance*	*Questionnaire II* *Non-surveillance* *Salience* *Issue-Relevance*	*Questionnaire III* *Non-surveillance* *Non-salience* *Issue-Relevance*
High power, based on means-control	H	L	L
High power, based on attractiveness	H	H	L
High power, based on credibility	H	H	H
Low power	L	L	L

° H = high probability that attitude will be expressed; L = low probability that attitude will be expressed.

In one communication the attempt was made to present the communicator in such a way that he would be perceived as possessing high means-control. He was introduced as the president of the National Foundation for Negro Colleges. In the course of the interview it became evident that his foundation had been supporting the college in which the study was being conducted; that he had almost complete control over the funds expended by the foundation; and that he was the kind of person who would not hesitate to use his control in order to achieve conformity. He made it clear that he would withdraw foundation grants from any college in which the students took a position on the issue in question which was at variance with his own position.

In the second communication the communicator was presented in such a way that he would be perceived as possessing high attractiveness. He was introduced as a Senior and president of the student council in a leading Negro university. He was also chairman of his university's chapter of an organization called Student Poll, which recently did a study on the attitudes of Negro college Seniors on issues relating to the Supreme Court decision. He presented the same message as the first communicator, but he made it clear that he was presenting not simply his own opinions but the overwhelming consensus of opinion of the college students represented in the polls. He was portrayed as a representative of one of the subjects' reference groups and as a person who was in a position to supply valid information on the group norms.

In the third communication the communicator was presented in such a way that he would be perceived as possessing high credibility. He was introduced as a professor of history in one of the country's leading universities. In the course of the interview, it became evident that he was one of the top experts on the history and problems of minority groups; that he was highly respected both by his colleagues and by members of minority groups; and that he had a profound concern for the welfare of the American Negro community. He presented the same position as the other speakers, but he made it clear that this position was based on his research and on the evidence of history.

For purposes of comparison, a fourth communication was used in which the communicator was presented in such a way that he would be perceived as possessing low power, that is, as being low in means-control, attractiveness, and credibility. He was introduced as an "ordinary citizen," who had no control over the subjects and no special knowledge about the topic. His attractiveness and credibility were further undermined by the fact that he was portrayed as a white man with a southern accent, who had recently come from Mississippi and who did not clearly dissociate himself from a pro-segregation point of view.

Each of the four communications was presented to a different experimental group. There was also a control group, which was not exposed to any communication at all. This group provided a base line for post-communication attitudes, since we did not obtain before-scores from the experimental subjects.

After exposure to the communication, the subjects in each experimental group filled out attitude questionnaires, designed to measure the extent of their agreement with the communicator. The questionnaire consisted of eighteen statements which were directly or indirectly related to the central message of the communication. Subjects were asked to respond to each item on a six-point scale. Scores for each item ranged from 1 for extreme disagreement with the communicator's position to 7 for extreme agreement (the score of 4 was not used, since the scale did not contain a neutral position). A total score for each subject was computed by adding up the individual scores on the 18 items. Thus the range of possible total scores was from 18 (complete disagreement) to 126 (complete agreement).

To vary the conditions of performance, we presented these eighteen statements to each subject on three separate questionnaires. As can be seen from Table 1, it is assumed that issue-relevance was present on all three questionnaires, since the attitude items dealt with the issues involved in the communication. The questionnaires differed, however, with respect to surveillance and salience.

Questionnaire I was completed under conditions of salience and surveillance. In order to maximize the salience of the communicator and the communication, the questionnaire was administered immediately after the communication. In order to maximize surveillance by the communicator, it was made clear—both by the appearance of the questionnaire and by the instructions—that this questionnaire was being administered at the communicator's request and that he would see each subject's answers. Moreover, the subjects were asked to sign their names and to give other identifying information.

Questionnaire II was completed under conditions of salience and non-surveillance. In order to maximize salience, the questionnaire was administered immediately after Questionnaire I, so that the relationship between the questionnaire and the communication was still clearly apparent. In order to minimize surveillance, Questionnaire II was anonymous, and it was made clear to the subjects that their responses would not be seen by the communicator or by anyone other than the research staff.

Questionnaire III was completed under conditions of non-salience and non-surveillance. In order to minimize the salience of the communicator and the communication, the questionnaire was administered from one to two weeks after the communication session, in a different place, under different auspices, and by a different experimenter. The questions were imbedded in a large number of other attitudinal items; and no mention of the communication was made. In order to minimize surveillance, Questionnaire III was anonymous and was in no way tied in to the communication.

III. Hypotheses

The specific hypotheses that were tested were as follows:

1. Attitudes adopted from a communicator whose power is based on means-control will tend to be expressed only under conditions of surveillance by the communicator. The mediating process postulated here is compliance.

   The specific prediction can be noted in Table 1. In the means-control group there will be a greater amount of acceptance of the communicator's position on Questionnaire I than on Questionnaires II and III, since Questionnaire I is the only one completed under conditions of surveillance. There should be no significant difference between Questionnaires II and III.

2. Attitudes adopted from a communicator whose power is based on attractiveness will tend to be expressed only under conditions of salience of the subject's relationship to the communicator. The mediating process postulated here is identification.

   Specifically, it is predicted that in the attractiveness group there will be a smaller amount of acceptance of the communicator's position on Questionnaire III than on Questionnaires I and II, since Questionnaire III is the only one completed under conditions of non-salience. There should be no significant difference between Questionnaires I and II.

3. Attitudes adopted from a communicator whose power is based on credibility will tend to be expressed under conditions of relevance of the issue, regardless of surveillance or salience. The mediating process postulated here is internalization.

   The specific prediction for the credibility group is that there will be no significant differences between the three questionnaires, since they were all completed under conditions of issue-relevance.

IV. Results

Before proceeding to examine the data which bear directly on the hypotheses, it was necessary to check on the success of the experimental variations. Did the subjects really perceive each of the variations in communicator power in the way in which we intended it? To provide an answer to this question, Questionnaire II included a series of statements about the speaker and the communication to which the subjects were asked to react. An analysis of these data indicated that, by and large, the experimental manipulations succeeded in producing the conditions they were intended to produce, thus making possible an adequate test of the hypotheses.

The findings which are directly relevant to the hypotheses are summarized in Tables 2 and 3. Table 2 presents the mean attitude

there is no significant difference between the scores on Questionnaires II and III. In the attractiveness group, the mean score on Questionnaire III is significantly lower than the mean scores on Questionnaires I and II; and there is no significant difference between the scores on Questionnaires I and II. In the credibility group, there are no significant differences between the three questionnaires.

While these results are all in line with the hypotheses, examination of the means in Table 2 reveals that the findings are not so clear-cut as they might be. Specifically, we should expect a relatively large drop in mean score for the means-control group from Questionnaire I to Questionnaire II. In actual

TABLE 2

Effects of Variations in Communicator Power on Acceptance of Induced Attitudes under Three Conditions of Measurement

Groups	N	Mean Attitude Scores		
		Quest. I	Quest. II	Quest. III
Means-control (compliance)	55	63.98	60.65	58.04
Attractiveness (identification)	48	56.81	55.94	49.67
Credibility (internalization)	51	59.51	56.39	56.10
Low Power	43	49.33	50.58	53.35

Summary of Significance Tests

Groups	Sources of Variation	F	p
Means-control	(1) Between Questionnaires	3.6	<0.05
	(2) I versus II and III	5.8	<0.05
	(3) II versus III	1.4	n.s.
Attractiveness	(1) Between Questionnaires	7.2	<0.01
	(2) I and II versus III	14.2	<0.01
	(3) I versus II	0.2	n.s.
Credibility	Between Questionnaires	2.3	n.s.
Low Power	Between Questionnaires	2.0	n.s.

scores for the four experimental groups on each of the three questionnaires. All subjects who had completed the three questionnaires were used in this analysis.

It can be seen from the summary of the significance tests that all the experimental predictions were confirmed. In the means-control group, the mean score on Questionnaire I is significantly higher than the mean scores on Questionnaires II and III; and

fact, however, the drop is only slightly higher than that for the credibility group. This might be due to the fact that the analysis is based on *all* subjects, including those who were not influenced by the communication at all. The hypotheses, however, refer only to changes from questionnaire to questionnaire for those people who *were* initially influenced.

It was not possible to identify the subjects

who were initially influenced, since there were no before-scores available for the experimental groups. It was possible, however, to approximate these conditions by using only those subjects who had a score of 60 or above on Questionnaire I. If we make certain limited assumptions (which I cannot spell out in this brief report), it can be shown that the use of a cutoff point of 60 "purifies" the experimental groups to some degree. That is, the subsamples selected by this criterion should have a higher ratio of influenced to uninfluenced subjects than the total groups from which they were selected. It was anticipated that an analysis based on these subsamples would provide a better test of the hypotheses and would yield more clear-cut results. This did, in fact, happen, as can be seen from Table 3.

tor is relatively high on Questionnaire I and declines on Questionnaires II and III. In the attractiveness group, agreement is high on Questionnaires I and II and declines on Questionnaire III. In the credibility group, changes from questionnaire to questionnaire are minimal. Analyses of variance clearly confirmed all the experimental predictions.

V. Conclusions

It would be premature to accept the hypotheses tested in this experiment as general principles that have been proved. The experiment does, however, lend considerable support to them. To the extent to which the hypotheses were substantiated, the experiment also gives support to the theoretical frame-

TABLE 3

EFFECTS OF VARIATIONS IN COMMUNICATOR POWER ON ACCEPTANCE OF
INDUCED ATTITUDES UNDER THREE CONDITIONS OF MEASUREMENT*

Groups	N	Mean Attitude Scores		
		Quest. I	Quest. II	Quest. III
Means-control (compliance)	30	78.20	70.76	67.56
Attractive (identification)	23	71.30	69.57	59.70
Credibility (internalization)	26	73.35	71.04	69.27

SUMMARY OF SIGNIFICANCE TESTS

Groups	Sources of Variation	F	p
Means-control	(1) Between Questionnaires	5.2	<0.01
	(2) I versus II and III	9.4	<0.01
	(3) II versus III	0.9	n.s.
Attractiveness	(1) Between Questionnaires	14.5	<0.01
	(2) I and II versus III	28.4	<0.01
	(3) I versus II	0.6	n.s.
Credibility	Between Questionnaires	1.1	n.s.

* Data based on a selected sample, containing a higher proportion of influenced subjects. Criterion for selection was a score of 60 or above on Questionnaire I.

Table 3 presents the mean attitude scores for the three high-power groups, using only those subjects who had scores of 60 or above on Questionnaire I. Examination of the means reveals a pattern completely consistent with the hypotheses. In the means-control group, agreement with the communica-

work from which these hypotheses were derived. The mediating concepts of compliance, identification, and internalization seem to provide a unified and meaningful way of organizing the present experimental findings and of relating them to a more general conceptual framework.

The framework presented here can be applied directly to the analysis of the effects of various communications and other forms of social influence on attitudes and actions in the international sphere. In the study of public opinion, for example, it should help us identify some of the conditions which are likely to produce one or another of these processes and predict the subsequent histories and action implications of attitudes adopted under these sets of conditions. This framework may also be helpful in the study of the social influences which affect decision-making processes and negotiations on the part of various elites.

Some of the concepts presented here might be useful not only for the study of change but also for the analysis of existing attitudes and their motivational bases. Let us take, for example, people's attitudes toward their own country's system of government. Even if we look only at those individuals who have favorable attitudes, various distinctions suggest themselves. For some individuals, acceptance of their system of government may be based largely on compliance; they may go along with the accepted norms in order to avoid social ostracism or perhaps even persecution. For others, attitudes toward their government may be largely identification-based: their relationship to their own nation and its major institutions may represent an essential aspect of their identity, and acceptance of certain political attitudes and beliefs may serve to maintain this relationship and their self-definition which is anchored in it. For a third group of individuals, belief in the country's system of government may be internalized: they may see this political form as fully congruent and integrated with their value systems and likely to lead to a maximization of their own values. Our evaluation of the meaning of "favorable attitudes" on the part of a particular individual or group or subpopulation and our prediction of the consequences of these attitudes would certainly vary with the motivational processes that underlie them. The conditions under which these attitudes are likely to be changed, the kinds of actions to which they are likely to lead, and the ways in which they are likely to affect reactions to particular events will be different, depending on whether these attitudes are based on compliance, identification, or internalization.

References

FESTINGER, L. An analysis of compliant behavior. In M. Sherif and M. O. Wilson (Eds.), *Group relations at the crossroads.* New York: Harper & Row, 1953.

FRENCH, J. R. P., JR. A formal theory of social power. *Psychol. Rev.,* 1956, *63*, 181-194.

JAHODA, MARIE. Psychological issues in civil liberties. *Amer. Psychologist,* 1956, *11*, 234-240.

KELMAN, H. C. Attitude change as a function of response restriction. *Hum. Relat.,* 1953, *6*, 185-214.

Cognitive Structure

and Attitudinal Affect ❧ Milton J. Rosenberg

Understanding of the related processes of attitude learning and attitude change will probably be advanced by the investigation of structural relationships between attitudes and beliefs about the objects of attitudes. The present research is an attempt to verify a set of hypotheses about such relationships. These hypotheses have much in common with some that have already been presented by Cartwright (1949), Hilliard (1950), Smith (1949), Tolman (1951), and Woodruff (1942, 1948). However, they differ from these earlier formulations in attempting to delineate more explicitly certain variables that are assumed to covary with attitude (here defined as *relatively stable affective response to an object*). One of these variables is the intensity of a person's values. A second is the perceived importance of the attitude object in leading to or blocking the attainment of his values.

The general theoretical view underlying the present study includes the following points: (*a*) When a person has a relatively stable tendency to respond to a given object with either positive or negative affect, such a tendency is accompanied by a *cognitive structure* made up of beliefs about the potentialities of that object for attaining or blocking the realization of valued states; (*b*) the sign (positive or negative) and extremity of the affect felt toward the object are correlated with the content of its associated cognitive structure. Thus strong and stable positive affect toward a given object should be associated with beliefs to the effect that the attitude object tends to facilitate the attainment of a number of important values,

while strong negative affect should be associated with beliefs to the effect that the attitude object tends to block the attainment of important values. Similarly, moderate positive or negative affects should be associated with beliefs that relate the attitude object to less important values or, if to important values, then with less confidence as to the existence of clear-cut instrumental relationships between the attitude object and the values in question.

From this view, three specific hypotheses were formulated for experimental test:

1. The degree and sign of affect aroused in an individual by an object (as reflected by the position he chooses on an attitude scale) vary as a function of the algebraic sum of the products obtained by multiplying the rated importance of each value associated with that object by the rated potency of the object for achieving or blocking the realization of that value.
2. The degree and sign of affect aroused in an individual by an object (as reflected by the position he chooses on an attitude scale) vary as a function of the algebraic sum of his ratings of the potency of that object for achieving or blocking the realization of his values (when the importance of these values is held constant).
3. The degree and sign of affect aroused in an individual by an object (as reflected by the position he chooses on an attitude scale) vary as a function of the algebraic sum of his ratings of the importance of the values whose attainment or blocking he perceives to be affected through the instrumental potency of that object (when the instrumental potency of that

From the *Journal of Abnormal and Social Psychology*, 1956, 53, 367-372. Reprinted by permission of the author and the American Psychological Association. This study was supported by the U.S. Air Force, Human Resources Research Institute, under contract #AF33-(038)-26646. The advice of Professor Helen Peak was of great value during all phases of the investigation.

object for attaining or blocking each of these values is held constant).

Method

SUBJECTS AND ATTITUDE MEASURE

One hundred and twenty Ss, recruited from undergraduate courses at the University of Michigan and the Ypsilanti State Teachers College, took an attitude questionnaire that contained, among other items, one dealing with the issue of "whether members of the Communist Party should be allowed to address the public." Each S checked his first choice among five alternative statements. Seventeen Ss chose the alternative indicating extreme opposition to allowing members of the Communist Party to address the public, 31 Ss the alternative indicating moderate opposition, 44 Ss that indicating moderate approval, and 25 Ss that indicating extreme approval. Only three Ss chose the alternative indicating "neutrality" on the issue, and, because of their small number, were excluded from the research population. In a retest of 95 Ss on this measure after an interval of at least two months, a reliability coefficient of .72 was obtained ($p < .001$).

VALUE MEASURES

Three to five weeks after the administration of the attitude measure two card-sorting tasks were administered individually. These tasks required S to categorize each of a group of value items in terms of (a) *value importance*, i.e., its importance to him as a "source of satisfaction" and (b) *perceived instrumentality*, i.e., his estimate as to whether, and to what extent, the value in question would tend to be achieved or blocked through the "policy of allowing members of the Communist Party to address the public."

The pack of value-cards included 35 items constructed in the light of White's value-analysis technique (1951) and Murray's

analysis of major needs (1938). (The value items used are given in Table 1.) In addition

TABLE 1

VALUE ITEMS USED IN CARD-SORTING TASKS°

1. People sticking to their own groups.
2. People looking out for the welfare of others.
3. Being looked up to by others.
4. Change and variety; having new kinds of experience.
5. Sticking to a difficult task; solving difficult problems.
6. Making one's own decisions.
7. People being strongly patriotic.
8. Serving the interests of the group to which one belongs.
9. Giving expression to feelings of anger or hostility.
10. Keeping promises made to others.
11. Having one's family approve of one's views.
12. The uncompromising administration of punishment to anyone who deserves it.
13. Having interesting work to do.
14. Having power and authority over people.
15. Being well-informed about current affairs.
16. Having the value of property well protected.
17. People of different backgrounds getting to know each other better.
18. All human beings having equal rights.
19. Being good-looking; having attractive face, body, or clothes.
20. Having a steady income.
21. Believing in a relationship between the individual and some higher spiritual power.
22. America having high prestige in other countries.
23. Being liked or loved by the opposite sex or associating with the opposite sex.
24. Getting advice on important problems.
25. People having the right to participate in making decisions which will affect them.
26. Achieving superiority over others in such things as knowledge, work, or sports.
27. Complying with the wishes of persons in authority.
28. Being like others in general; having the same interests.
29. People being well educated.
30. People having strict moral standards.
31. The open expression of disagreement between people.
32. Everyone being assured of a good standard of living.
33. Being allowed to maintain the privacy of one's opinions and beliefs.

34. Being with other people; socializing.
35. Letting others make their own decisions.

---

* This list does not include the "salient" value items specially constructed for each S.

to these 35 items, the pack of cards presented to each S also contained value terms that had been coded out of his questionnaire answer to a verbal probe in conjunction with the item on "allowing members of the Communist Party to address the public." For most Ss the total number of such "salient" values came to two or three, the range among all Ss extending from zero to six.

For the "value importance" measure S was asked to rank each card so as to indicate how much satisfaction he gets, or would get, from the value state that it described. Each value was to be judged independently in terms of 21 categories ranging from "gives me maximum satisfaction" (Category +10) through "gives me neither satisfaction nor dissatisfaction" (Category 0) to "gives me maximum dissatisfaction" (Category −10). For the measure of "perceived instrumentality" he was asked to judge and place each card in terms of 11 categories ranging from "the condition (value described on the card) is completely attained by allowing admitted Communists to address the public" (Category +5) through "whether or not admitted Communists are allowed to address the public is completely irrelevant to the attainment of the condition" (Category 0) to "the condition is completely blocked by allowing admitted Communists to address the public" (Category −5). In each of the two card-sorting tasks S was required, after the initial categorization was completed, to rank the cards *within* each category in terms of "value importance" and "perceived instrumentality" respectively.

The test-retest reliability of these two measures was studied with a subpopulation of 12 Ss, the second administration following the first by from four to five weeks. For each of these Ss Spearman's rho was computed as an estimate of the degree of correlation be-

tween the ranks assigned to the separate values on the first and second administrations respectively. For the measure of value importance, the median rho was .89 ($p < .01$); for that of perceived instrumentality, it was .74 ($p < .01$).

From the data obtained through the two card-sorting tasks ten indices were computed to permit testing the major hypotheses. Operational definitions of these indices are given in Tables 2-4.

Results and Discussion[1]

Each hypothesis was tested by chi square,[2] computed from a 3 × 4 table. In each such table the four groups in terms of attitude position (extremely favorable, moderately favorable, moderately unfavorable, and extremely unfavorable toward "allowing members of the Communist Party to address the public") were cross classified in terms of a threefold categorization of the Ss on one of the indices derived from the card-sorting value measures.

HYPOTHESIS 1

All of the four indices used to test Hypothesis 1 provide, as the hypothesis requires, for representation of both the importance to the individual of some set of values and his perceptions as to how these values are affected (with regard to their attainment

---

[1] All of the results reported in this section have been successfully replicated with regard to the attitude area of "allowing Negroes to move into white neighborhoods." The replication was based on an analysis exactly parallel to the one described in the present report and upon identical measurement operations.

[2] This technique was used rather than correlational methods because it was felt that the assumptions required by correlational methods (particularly the assumptions of normality and equal-interval scales) were not fully met by the data. The method used for computing chi square was the "maximum likelihood test" of Mood (1950) which is applicable to data plots with low cell counts.

or blocking) through the instrumental agency of the attitude object (the policy of "allowing members of the Communist Party to address the public"). By algebraically summing the importance-instrumentality products for each of the values it is possible to represent appropriately the interaction between positive and negative values on the one hand and perceptions of positive and negative instrumentality on the other. Thus a positive value (rated, say, as +7 in its capacity to satisfy the S) may be perceived as being attained through the policy of "allowing members of the Communist Party to address the public" (to the extent, say, of a rating of +3 on "instrumentality"). In this case the product would be +21. If on the other hand, the same value were rated as being *blocked* by the policy of "allowing members of the Communist Party to address the public" (for example a rating of −3 on "instrumentality") the resultant product would be −21. Similarly, a value rated as yielding dissatisfaction and thus bearing a minus sign on "value importance" would yield a negative product if multiplied by a rating of positive instrumentality and a positive product if multiplied by a rating of negative instrumentality. By summing all such products for a given set of values a single algebraic quantity is obtained representing the total import of the S's pattern of beliefs about the influ-

ence of the attitude object upon attaining or blocking various states that he values to differing degrees.

Since all four of the indices used to test Hypothesis 1 were found to be significantly related to attitude position (see Table 2), the hypothesis would appear to have been confirmed at an acceptable level. These findings, to generalize, lend support to the view that beliefs associated with an attitudinal affect tend to be congruent with it; i.e., that there exists within the individual an "organization" of the affective and cognitive properties of his total pattern of response to what is, for him, an "attitude object."

One possible objection to such an interpretation might hold that the way in which S sorts the cards may reflect not his actual cognitive structure but rather an attempt to demonstrate to the experimenter and to himself that his beliefs are consistent with his attitudes. If striving for cognitive-affective consistency accounts in part for relationships obtained during the testing session, however, it seems appropriate to assume that similar motivation had been in operation before the testing session, i.e., that the motive to "rationalize" one's attitudes plays a role in the natural history of attitude development.

Still another line of evidence that limits the significance of this objection arises from the findings obtained with Index 3. This in-

TABLE 2

RELATIONSHIPS BETWEEN "VALUE IMPORTANCE × PERCEIVED
INSTRUMENTALITY" (INDICES 1-4) AND ATTITUDE POSITION
($N = 117$)

Index	Description of Index	Chi Square	Probability*
1	Algebraic sum of importance-instrumentality products for all value items	26.33	.001
2	Algebraic sum of importance-instrumentality products for the twenty values ranking highest on importance	30.82	.001
3	Algebraic sum of importance-instrumentality products for all "salient" values	45.09	.001
4	Algebraic sum of importance-instrumentality products for all "non-salient" values	15.10	.02

* Examination of the actual data plots reveals that all of these significant chi squares are due to positive, monotonic relationships.

dex is based solely upon the "value importance" and "perceived instrumentality" ratings of the S's "salient" values, which were coded out of his own verbal defense of his stated attitude position. Certainly the individual's estimates of the importance of these values and the ways in which their realization would be influenced by the attitude object must have had *pre-experimental* reality to have been given expression in response to the questionnaire probe.

It should be noted, however, that the historical relationship between affective and cognitive processes in the development of attitudes is not approachable through analysis of the present data. The province of the present study is to examine the relationships between cognitive and affective processes at a point in time after an attitude has been acquired and stabilized. Nevertheless, the present hypotheses may, if confirmed, suggest further hypotheses about the processes of attitude learning and attitude change.

HYPOTHESES 2 AND 3

While the data just reviewed confirm the existence of a relationship between a measure of affect toward an object and a measure based upon both the "importance" and "perceived instrumentality" of values associated with it, the question may be raised as to whether each of these two latter variables may be demonstrated to covary with affect when the other is held constant. Hypotheses 2 and 3 assert the existence of such relationships. Indices 5-10 are based upon procedures for obtaining separate estimates of the "value importance" and "perceived instrumentality" variables. To isolate the one variable, it was possible to hold the other constant since the original card-sorting tasks had required S to rank the values *within* each of the categories used in sorting.

Thus, to test the relationship between "perceived instrumentality" of values and affect toward the attitude object, four indices (5-8) were developed, all of which have in common being based upon a summation of the "perceived instrumentality" ratings of a group of values defined and chosen in terms of their "value importance" ranks. Index 5 for example is obtained by choosing the value items ranked 1-20 by the S on the dimension of "value importance" and then obtaining the algebraic sum of the "perceived instrumentality" ratings of these same 20 values.

A similar procedure was employed with regard to the indices (9 and 10) used to test the relationship between "value importance" and affect toward the attitude object. These two indices are both based upon the "value importance" ratings of a group of values defined and chosen in terms of their "perceived instrumentality" ranks. Index 9 for example is obtained by choosing the five values ranked highest on "perceived positive instrumentality" and then obtaining the algebraic sum of the "importance" ratings of these same five values. Index 10 is identical except that it is computed from the five values ranked highest on "perceived negative instrumentality."

The results reported in Table 3 indicate that all four of the indices of "perceived instrumentality" are significantly related to attitude position. Furthermore it should be noted that the hypothesis has been verified at a number of different levels of "value importance" control, each of the four indices representing a different level. On the basis of these findings Hypothesis 2 appears to have been confirmed. To generalize, other things (particularly "value importance") being equal, extreme attitudinal affects are associated with perceptions of close positive or negative instrumental connection between the attitude object and related values, while moderate attitudinal affects are associated with perceptions of less clear-cut instrumental relationships. In terms of attitude theory this finding suggests the existence of a distinguishable and important dimension of attitude-related cognitive structures. Recent research (Carlson, 1956) based upon the present study lends confirmation to the existence of this dimension as a separate and

TABLE 3

RELATIONSHIPS BETWEEN "PERCEIVED INSTRUMENTALITY" (INDICES 5-8)
AND ATTITUDE POSITION ($N = 117$)

Index	Description of Index	Chi Square	Probability*
5	Algebraic sum of the instrumentality ratings of the values ranking 1st-20th on importance	35.51	.001
6	Algebraic sum of the instrumentality ratings of the values ranking 11th-30th on importance	21.27	.001
7	Algebraic sum of the instrumentality ratings of the values ranking 1st-10th on importance	20.82	.01
8	Algebraic sum of the instrumentality ratings of the values ranking 11th-20th on importance	38.47	.001

* Examination of the actual plots reveals that all of the significant chi squares are due to the presence of positive, monotonic relationships.

manipulable one and indicates that attitude-change effects (in the sense of affective change) may be achieved through its manipulation.

The results reported in Table 4 indicate that both of the indices of "value importance" are significantly related to attitude position. On the basis of these findings, Hypothesis 3 appears to have been confirmed.

Although the relationships reported in Table 4 reach an acceptable level of significance, however, their significance level is lower than most of the relationships reported in Tables 2 and 3. The present data leave it an open question as to whether this is an artifact of the measurements or computations employed or whether, on the other hand, "perceived instrumentality" actually controls more variance in attitudinal affect than does "value importance." The generalization is nevertheless supported that other things (particularly "perceived instrumentality") being equal, extreme attitudinal affects are associated with values of high importance while moderate attitudinal affects are associated with values of less importance. For attitude theory, these results suggest the existence of a second distin-

TABLE 4

RELATIONSHIPS BETWEEN "VALUE IMPORTANCE" (INDICES 9 AND 10)
AND ATTITUDE POSITION ($N = 117$)

Index	Description of Index	Chi Square	Probability*
9	Algebraic sum of the importance ratings of the values ranking 1st-5th on positive instrumentality (attainment of values)	12.75	.05
10	Algebraic sum of the importance ratings of the values ranking 1st-5th on negative instrumentality (blocking of values)	16.46	.02

* Examination of the actual plots reveals that the significant chi square in the case of Index 9 is due to the presence of a positive monotonic relationship, while the significant chi square in the case of Index 10 is due to the presence of a negative monotonic relationship, both as predicted.

guishable and important dimension of attitude-related cognitive structures. Further research is needed to determine whether the individual's assessment of the importance of his values is manipulable and whether, if it is, such manipulation is sufficient to produce change in affect toward an object seen as having instrumental influence upon the attainment or blocking of these values.

FURTHER IMPLICATIONS FOR
ATTITUDE THEORY

It has been suggested that attitudinal affect toward an object may be altered by the prior modification of value importance and perceived instrumentality. A related implication is that one way in which attitudes may originally develop is through the prior acquisition of beliefs about the value-attaining or value-blocking powers of particular objects, be those objects individuals, groups, political proposals, or commercial products. Such a view, even if it has not been systematically elaborated, seems to underlie the attitude-creating and attitude-changing communication techniques of many propagandists in such fields as advertising, teaching, psychological warfare, and child-rearing.

A less obvious implication of the present findings suggests at least one other type of sequential process leading to the establishment of stabilized affective-cognitive patterns. It seems plausible that much original attitudinal learning (the acquisition of a stable affective response where none existed previously) may originate in experiences of being rewarded or punished for imitation or rehearsal of expressions of affect provided by others. A case in point may be found in the data on the acquisition of the anti-Negro attitude as reported by Horowitz (1936). With an affect, or its beginnings, established through reinforcement procedures, something like a need for affective-cognitive consistency may set the person to acquire socially available beliefs that "rationalize" the acquired affect. When such beliefs are unavailable in the person's communicative surround, he may invent them. In real-life situations where attitudes are being instilled, there are generally available both cognitive supports for the advocated affect and direct reinforcements for its expression.

Recent research by the investigator seems to indicate that the production of *change* in an already established attitude may be obtained without any direct attempt to modify the associated cognitive structure, but rather through direct assault (with hypnotic techniques) upon the established affect. Such assault produces in some Ss a temporary affective reversal, and along with this reversal, a spontaneous, self-directed modification of the related cognitive structure.

Summary

An attitude questionnaire on the issue of "allowing members of the Communist Party to address the public" was administered to 117 Ss. Three to five weeks later each S took a card-sorting test which required him to rate and rank each of a group of value items in terms of (a) the importance of the value as a source of satisfaction and (b) his perception as to the extent to which the value tends to be attained or blocked through the instrumental agency of the attitude object.

The data thus gathered were used in testing three hypotheses concerned with the relationships between stable affective response (attitude) toward an object and beliefs about that object. These hypotheses were derived from a general proposition to the effect that the sign and extremity of affect toward an object are functions both of whether it is perceived as facilitating or blocking the attainment of values and of whether or not the values involved are important ones. All three hypotheses were confirmed. Some of the data were interpreted as suggesting that "value importance" and "perceived instrumentality" are separate and possibly manipulable dimensions of attitude-related cognitive structures.

Some suggestions were presented as to the implications of the present study with regard to the phenomena of attitude learning and attitude change.

References

CARLSON, E. R. Attitude change and attitude structure. *J. abnorm. soc. Psychol.*, 1956, *52*, 256-261

CARTWRIGHT, D. Some principles of mass persuasion. *Hum. Relat.*, 1949, *2*, 253-268.

HILLIARD, A. E. *The forms of value.* New York: Columbia Univer. Press, 1950.

HOROWITZ, E. L. The development of attitude toward the Negro. *Arch. Psychol.*, 1936, No. 194.

MOOD, A. E. *Introduction to the theory of statistics.* New York: McGraw-Hill, 1950.

MURRAY, H. A. *Explorations in personality.* New York: Oxford Univer. Press, 1938.

ROSENBERG, M. J. The experimental investigation of a value theory of attitude structure. Unpublished doctor's dissertation, Univer. of Michigan, 1953.

SMITH, M. B. Personal values as determinants of a political attitude, *J. Psychol.*, 1949, *28*, 477-486.

TOLMAN, E. C. A psychological model. In T. Parsons and E. A. Shils (Eds.), *Toward a general theory of action.* Cambridge, Mass.: Harvard Univer. Press, 1951.

WHITE, R. K. *Value analysis: the nature and use of the method.* Society for the Psychological Study of Social Issues, 1951.

WOODRUFF, A. D. Personal values and the direction of behavior. *Sch. Rev.*, 1942, *50*, 32-42.

WOODRUFF, A. D., and DiVESTA, F. J. The relationship between values, concepts, and attitudes. *Educ. psychol. Measmt*, 1948, *8*, 645-660.

B. COMMUNICATION AND

PERSUASION

Effects of Fear-arousing ❊ Irving L. Janis

Communications ❊ Seymour Feshbach

It is generally recognized that when beliefs and attitudes are modified, learning processes are involved in which motivational factors play a primary role. Symbols in mass communications can be manipulated in a variety of ways so as to arouse socially acquired motives such as need for achievement, group conformity, power-seeking, and the more emotion-laden drives arising from aggression, sympathy, guilt, and anxiety.

The present experiment was designed to study the effects of one particular type of motive-incentive variable in persuasive communications, namely, the arousal of fear or anxiety by depicting potential dangers to which the audience might be exposed. Fear appeals of this sort are frequently used to influence attitudes and behavior. For example, medical authorities sometimes try to persuade people to visit cancer detection clinics by pointing to the dangerous consequences of failing to detect the early symptoms of cancer; various political groups play up the threat of war or totalitarianism in an attempt to motivate adherence to their political program. Our interest in such attempts is primarily that of determining the condi-

tions under which the arousal of fear is effective or ineffective in eliciting changes in beliefs, practices, and attitudes.

Implicit in the use of fear appeals is the assumption that when emotional tension is aroused, the audience will become more highly motivated to accept the reassuring beliefs or recommendations advocated by the communicator. But the tendency to accept reassuring ideas about ways and means of warding off anticipated danger may not always be the dominant reaction to a fear-arousing communication. Under certain conditions, other types of defensive reactions may occur which could give rise to highly undesirable effects from the standpoint of the communicator.

Clinical studies based on patients' reactions to psychiatric treatment call attention to three main types of emotional interference which can prevent a person from being influenced by verbal communications which deal with anxiety-arousing topics.

1. When a communication touches off intense feelings of anxiety, communicatees will sometimes fail to pay attention to what is being said. Inattentiveness may be a mo-

From the *Journal of Abnormal and Social Psychology*, 1953, *48*, 78-92. Reprinted by permission of the authors and the American Psychological Association.

tivated effort to avoid thoughts which evoke incipient feelings of anxiety. This defensive tendency may be manifested by overt attempts to change the subject of conversation to a less disturbing topic. When such attempts fail and anxiety mounts to a very high level, attention disturbances may become much more severe, e.g., "inability to concentrate," "distractibility," or other symptoms of the cognitive disorganization temporarily produced by high emotional tension (Hanfmann, 1950).

2. When exposed to an anxiety-arousing communication, communicatees will occasionally react to the unpleasant ("punishing") experience by becoming aggressive toward the communicator. If the communicator is perceived as being responsible for producing painful feelings, aggression is likely to take the form of rejecting his statements.

3. If a communication succeeds in arousing intense anxiety and if the communicatee's emotional tension is not readily reduced either by the reassurances contained in the communication or by self-delivered reassurances, the residual emotional tension may motivate defensive avoidances, i.e., attempts to ward off subsequent exposures to the anxiety-arousing content. The experience of being temporarily unable to terminate the disturbing affective state elicited by a discussion of a potential threat can give rise to a powerful incentive to avoid thinking or hearing about it again; this may ultimately result in failing to recall what the communicator said, losing interest in the topic, denying or minimizing the importance of the threat.

The above reaction tendencies, while formulated in general terms, take account of three specific types of behavior observed during psychoanalytic or psychotherapeutic sessions (Alexander and French, 1946; Dollard and Miller, 1950; Fenichel, 1941). The first two refer to immediate reactions that often occur when a therapist gives an interpretation which brings anxiety-laden thoughts or motives into the patient's focus

of awareness: (a) attention disturbances, blocking of associations, mishearing, evasiveness, and similar forms of "resistance"; and (b) argumentativeness, defiance, contempt, and other manifestations of reactive hostility directed toward the therapist. The third refers to certain types of subsequent "resistance," displayed during the later course of treatment, as a carry-over effect of the therapist's disturbing comments or interpretations.

Although the three types of defensive behavior have been observed primarily in clinical studies of psychoneurotic patients (whose anxiety reactions are generally linked with unconscious conflicts), it seems probable that similar reactions may occur among normal persons during or after exposure to communications which make them acutely aware of severe threats of external danger. Nevertheless, it remains an open question whether such sources of emotional interference play any significant role in determining the net effectiveness of fear-arousing material in mass communications, especially when the communications are presented in an impersonal social setting where emotional responses of the audience are likely to be greatly attenuated.

The present experiment was designed to investigate the consequences of using fear appeals in persuasive communications that are presented in an impersonal group situation. One of the main purposes was to explore the potentially adverse effects which might result from defensive reactions of the sort previously noted in the more restricted situation of psychotherapy.

Method

The experiment was designed so as to provide measures of the effects of three different intensities of "fear appeal" in a standard communication on dental hygiene, presented to high school students. The influence of the fear-arousing material was investigated by means of a series of questionnaires which provided data on emotional reactions to the communication and on changes in dental hygiene beliefs, practices, and attitudes.

THE THREE FORMS OF
COMMUNICATION

A 15-minute illustrated lecture was prepared in three different forms, all of which contained the same essential information about causes of tooth decay and the same series of recommendations concerning oral hygiene practices. The three (recorded) lectures were of approximately equal length and were delivered in a standard manner by the same speaker. Each recording was supplemented by about 20 slides, which were shown on the screen in a prearranged sequence, to illustrate various points made by the speaker.

The three forms of the illustrated talk differed only with the respect to the amount of fear-arousing material presented. Form 1 contained a strong fear appeal, emphasizing the painful consequences of tooth decay, diseased gums, and other dangers that can result from improper dental hygiene. Form 2 presented a moderate appeal in which the dangers were described in a milder and more factual manner. Form 3 presented a minimal appeal which rarely alluded to the consequences of tooth neglect. In Form 3, most of the fear-arousing material was replaced by relatively neutral information dealing with the growth and functions of the teeth. In all other respects, however, Form 3 was identical with Forms 1 and 2.

The fear appeals were designed to represent typical characteristics of mass communications which attempt to stimulate emotional reactions in order to motivate the audience to conform to a set of recommendations. The main technique was that of calling attention to the potential dangers that can ensue from nonconformity. For example, the Strong appeal contained such statements as the following:

If you ever develop an infection of this kind from improper care of your teeth, it will be an extremely serious matter because these infections are really dangerous. They can spread to your eyes, or your heart, or your joints and cause secondary infections which may lead to diseases such as arthritic paralysis, kidney damage, or total blindness.

One of the main characteristics of the Strong appeal was the use of personalized threat-references explicitly directed to the audience, i.e., statements to the effect that "this can happen to you." The Moderate appeal, on the other hand, described the dangerous consequences of improper oral hygiene in a more factual way, using impersonal language. In the Minimal appeal, the limited discussion of unfavorable consequences also used a purely factual style.

The major differences in content are summarized in Table 1, which is based on a systematic content analysis of the three recorded lectures. The data in this table show how often each type of "threat" was mentioned. It is apparent that the main difference between the Strong appeal and the Moderate appeal was not so much in the total frequency of threat references as in the variety and types of threats that were emphasized. The Minimal appeal, however, differed markedly from the other two in that it contained relatively few threat references, almost all of which were restricted to "cavities" or "tooth decay."

One of the reasons for selecting dental hygiene as a suitable topic for investigating the influence of fear appeals was precisely because discussions of this topic readily lend themselves to quantitative and qualitative variations of the sort shown in Table 1. Moreover, because of the nature of the potential dangers that are referred to, one could reasonably expect the audience to be fairly responsive to such variations in content—the teeth and gums probably represent an important component in the average person's body image, and, according to psychoanalytic observations, the threat of dam-

TABLE 1

Content Analysis of the Three Forms of the Communication:
References to Consequences of Improper Care of the Teeth

Type of Reference	Form 1 (Strong Appeal)	Form 2 (Moderate Appeal)	Form 3 (Minimal Appeal)
Pain from toothaches	11	1	0
Cancer, paralysis, blindness, or other secondary diseases	6	0	0
Having teeth pulled, cavities drilled, or other painful dental work	9	1	0
Having cavities filled or having to go to the dentist	0	5	1
Mouth infections: sore, swollen, inflamed gums	18	16	2
Ugly or discolored teeth	4	2	0
"Decayed" teeth	14	12	6
"Cavities"	9	12	9
Total references to unfavorable consequences	71	49	18

age to the teeth and gums can sometimes evoke deep-seated anxieties concerning body integrity. In any case, by playing up the threat of pain, disease, and body damage, the material introduced in Form 1 is probably representative of the more extreme forms of fear appeals currently to be found in persuasive communications presented via the press, radio, television, and other mass media.

The fear appeals did not rely exclusively upon verbal material to convey the threatening consequences of nonconformity. In Form 1, the slides used to illustrate the lecture included a series of eleven highly realistic photographs which vividly portrayed tooth decay and mouth infections. Form 2, the Moderate appeal, included nine photographs which were milder examples of oral pathology than those used in Form 1. In Form 3, however, no realistic photographs of this kind were presented: X-ray pictures, diagrams of cavities, and photographs of completely healthy teeth were substituted for the photographs of oral pathology.

SUBJECTS

The entire freshman class of a large Connecticut high school was divided into four groups on a random bases. Each of the three forms of the communication was given to a separate experimental group; the fourth group was used as a control group and was exposed to a similar communication on a completely different topic (the structure and functioning of the human eye). All together there were 200 students in the experiment, with 50 in each group.

The four groups were well equated with respect to age, sex, educational level, and IQ. The mean age for each group was approximately 15 years and there were roughly equal numbers of boys and girls in each group. The mean and standard deviation of IQ scores, as measured by the Otis group test, were almost identical in all four groups.

ADMINISTRATION OF THE QUESTIONNAIRES

The first questionnaire, given one week before the communication, was represented to the students as a general health survey of high school students. The key questions dealing with dental hygiene were interspersed among questions dealing with many other aspects of health and hygiene.

One week later the illustrated talks were

given as part of the school's hygiene program. Immediately after the end of the communication, the students in each group were asked to fill out a short questionnaire designed to provide data on immediate effects of the communication, such as the amount of information acquired, attitudes toward the communication, and emotional reactions. A follow-up questionnaire was given one week later in order to ascertain the carry-over effects of the different forms of the communication.

Results

AFFECTIVE REACTIONS

Evidence that the three forms of the illustrated talk differed with respect to the amount of emotional tension evoked during the communication is presented in Table 2.

consistently falls in an intermediate position but does not, in most instances, differ significantly from the other two groups.

Further evidence of the effectiveness of the fear-arousing material was obtained from responses to the following two questions, each of which had a checklist of five answer categories ranging from "Very worried" to "Not at all worried":

1. When you think about the possibility that you might develop diseased gums, how concerned or worried do you feel about it?
2. When you think about the possibility that you might develop decayed teeth, how concerned or worried do you feel about it?

Since these questions made no reference to the illustrated talk, it was feasible to include them in the pre- and postcommunication questionnaires given to all four groups.

TABLE 2

FEELINGS OF WORRY OR CONCERN EVOKED DURING THE COMMUNICATION

Questionnaire Responses	Strong Group (N = 50)	Moderate Group (N = 50)	Minimal Group (N = 50)
Felt worried—a "few times" or "many times"—about own mouth condition	74%	60%	48%
Felt "somewhat" or "very" worried about improper care of own teeth	66%	36%	34%
Thought about condition of own teeth "most of the time"	42%	34%	22%

Immediately after exposure to the communication, the students were asked three questions concerning the feelings they had just experienced "while the illustrated talk was being given." Their responses indicate that the fear stimuli were successful in arousing affective reactions. On each of the three questionnaire items shown in the table, the difference between the Strong group and the Minimal group is reliable at beyond the .05 confidence level.[1] The Moderate group

---

[1] All probability values reported in this paper are based on one tail of the theoretical distribution, since the results were used to test specific hypotheses which predict the direction of the differences.

Systematic comparisons were made in terms of the percentage in each group who reported relatively high disturbance (i.e., "somewhat" or "very worried") in response to both questions. The results, presented in Table 3, show a marked increase in affective disturbance among each of the three experimental groups, as compared with the control group. Paralleling the results in Table 2, the greatest increase is found in the Strong group. The difference between the Moderate and the Minimal groups, however, is insignificant.

In order to obtain an over-all estimate of the relative degree of emotional arousal evoked by the three forms of the communi-

TABLE 3

PERCENTAGE OF EACH GROUP WHO REPORTED FEELING SOMEWHAT
OR VERY WORRIED ABOUT DECAYED TEETH AND DISEASED GUMS

	Strong Group (N=50)	Moderate Group (N=50)	Minimal Group (N=50)	Control Group (N=50)
One week before the communication	34	24	22	30
Immediately after the communication	76	50	46	38
Change	+42%	+26%	+24%	+8%

RELIABILITY OF DIFFERENCE*

Group	CR	p
Strong vs. Control	3.06	<.01
Strong vs. Minimal	1.59	.06
Strong vs. Moderate	1.37	.09
Moderate vs. Control	1.54	.06
Moderate vs. Minimal	0.17	.43
Minimal vs. Control	1.43	.08

* The statistical test used was the critical ratio for reliability of differences in amount of change between two independent samples, as described by Hovland, Lumsdaine, and Sheffield (1949, p. 321).

cation, a total score was computed for each individual in each experimental group, based on answers to all five questions: two points credit was given to each response specified in Tables 2 and 3 as indicative of high disturbance; one point credit was given to intermediate responses on the checklist; zero credit was given for the last two response categories in each checklist, which uniformly designated a relative absence of worry or concern. Hence individual scores ranged from zero to ten. The mean scores for the Strong, Moderate, and Minimal groups were 7.8, 6.6, and 5.9 respectively. The Strong group differs reliably at the one per cent confidence level from each of the other two groups ($t = 2.3$ and 3.6). The difference between the Moderate and Minimal groups approaches reliability at the .08 confidence level ($t = 1.4$).

In general, the foregoing evidence indicates that after exposure to the communications, the Strong group felt more worried about the condition of their teeth than did the other two groups; the Moderate group, in turn, tended to feel more worried than the Minimal group.

INFORMATION ACQUIRED

Immediately after exposure to the illustrated talk, each experimental group was given an information test consisting of 23 separate items. The test was based on the factual assertions common to all three forms of the communication, including topics such as the anatomical structure of the teeth, the causes of cavities and of gum disease, the "correct" technique of toothbrushing, and the type of toothbrush recommended by dental authorities. No significant differences were found among the three experimental groups with respect to information test scores. Comparisons with the Control group show that the three forms of the dental hygiene communication were equally effective in teaching the factual material.

ATTITUDE TOWARD THE COMMUNICATION

The questionnaire given immediately after exposure to the illustrated talk included a series of seven items concerning the students' appraisals of the communication.

TABLE 4

PERCENTAGE OF EACH GROUP WHO EXPRESSED STRONGLY FAVORABLE
APPRAISALS OF THE COMMUNICATION

Appraisal Response	Strong Group ($N = 50$)	Moderate Group ($N = 50$)	Minimal Group ($N = 50$)
The illustrated talk does a very good teaching job.	62	50	40
Most or all of it was interesting.	80	68	64
It was very easy to pay attention to what the speaker was saying.	74	36	50
My mind practically never wandered.	58	46	42
The slides do a very good job.	52	20	22
The speaker's voice was very good.	66	56	58
The illustrated talk definitely should be given to all Connecticut high schools.	74	58	70

From the results shown in Table 4, it is apparent that the Strong group responded more favorably than the other two groups.[2]

These findings imply that interest in the communication and acceptance of its educational value were heightened by the Strong appeal. But this conclusion applies only to relatively impersonal, objective ratings of the communication. Additional evidence

One of the additional questions was the following: "Was there anything in the illustrated talk on dental hygiene that you disliked?" Unfavorable ("dislike") answers were given by a reliably higher percentage of students in the Strong group than in the Moderate or Minimal groups (first row of Table 5). A tabulation was also made of the total number of students in each group who gave complaints in their answers to either of

TABLE 5

PERCENTAGE OF EACH GROUP WHO EXPRESSED COMPLAINTS ABOUT
THE COMMUNICATION

Type of Complaint	Strong Group ($N = 50$)	Moderate Group ($N = 50$)	Minimal Group ($N = 50$)
Disliked something in the illustrated talk.	28	8	2
The slides were too unpleasant ("horrible," "gory," "disgusting," etc.).	34	2	0
There was not enough material on prevention.	20	2	8

presented in Table 5, based on questions which elicited evaluations of a more subjective character, reveals a markedly different attitude toward the communication among those exposed to the Strong appeal.

[2] The Strong group differs significantly ($p < .05$) from the Minimal group on five of the seven items and from the Moderate group on three items; the Moderate group does *not* differ reliably from the Minimal group on any of the items.

two open-end questions which asked for criticisms of the illustrated talk. The results on complaints about the unpleasant character of the slides are shown in row two of Table 5; the difference between the Strong group and each of the other two groups is reliable at the .01 confidence level. Similarly, a reliably higher percentage of the Strong group complained about insufficient material on ways and means of preventing tooth and gum disease (row three of Table 5).[3] The latter type of criticism often was accompanied by the suggestion that some of the disturbing material should be eliminated, as is illutrated by the following comments from two students in the Strong group: "Leave out the slides that show the rottiness of the teeth and have more in about how to brush your teeth"; "I don't think you should have shown so many gory pictures without showing more to prevent it." Comments of this sort, together with the data presented in Table 5, provide additional evidence of residual emotional tension. They imply that the Strong appeal created a need for reassurance which persisted after the communication was over, despite the fact that the communication contained a large number of reassuring recommendations.

The apparent inconsistency between the results in Tables 4 and 5 suggests that the Strong appeal evoked a more mixed or ambivalent attitude toward the communication than did the Moderate or Minimal appeals. Some of the comments, particularly about the slides, help to illuminate the differentiation between the individual's *objective* evaluation of the communication and his *subjective* response to it. The following illustrative excerpts from the Strong group were selected from the answers given to the open-end question which asked for criticisms and suggestions:

I did not care for the "gory" illustrations of decayed teeth and diseased mouths but I really think that it did

make me feel sure that I did not want this to happen to me.

Some of the pictures went to the extremes but they probably had an effect on most of the people who wouldn't want their teeth to look like that.

I think it is good because it scares people when they see the awful things that can happen.

Such comments not only attest to the motivational impact of the Strong appeal, but also suggest one of the ways in which the discrepancy between subjective and objective evaluations may have been reconciled. In such cases, the ambivalence seems to have been resolved by adopting an attitude to the effect that "this is disagreeable medicine, but it is good for us."

CONFORMITY TO DENTAL HYGIENE RECOMMENDATIONS

The immediate effects of the illustrated talks described above show the type of affective reactions evoked by the fear-arousing material but provide little information bearing directly on attitude changes. The questionnaire administered one week later, however, was designed to measure some of the major carry-over effects of fear appeals, particularly with respect to changes in dental-hygiene practices, beliefs, and preferences. The results provide an empirical basis for estimating the degree to which such communications succeed in modifying attitudes.

Personal practices were investigated by asking the students to describe the way they were currently brushing their teeth: the type of stroke used, the amount of surface area cleansed, the amount of force applied, the length of time spent on brushing the teeth, and the time of day that the teeth were brushed. The same five questions were asked one week before the communication and again one week after. These questions covered practices about which the following specific recommendations were made in all

[3] In row three of Table 5, the difference between the Strong and Moderate groups is reliable at the .01 confidence level, and the difference between the Strong and Minimal groups is significant at the .08 level. Other types of criticisms, in addition to those shown in Table 5, were also tabulated. Most of these involved minor aspects of the presentation (e.g., "a movie would have been better than slides") and were given by approximately equal percentages of the three groups. The vast majority of students in the Moderate and Minimal groups expressed approval of the illustrated talk or stated that they had no criticisms.

three forms of the illustrated talk: (a) the teeth should be brushed with an up-and-down (vertical) stroke; (b) the inner surface of the teeth should be brushed as well as the outer surface; (c) the teeth should be brushed gently, using only a slight amount of force; (d) in order to cleanse the teeth adequately, one should spend about three minutes on each brushing; (e) in the morning, the teeth should be brushed after breakfast (rather than before).

Each student was given a score, ranging from zero to five, which represented the number of recommended practices on which he conformed. Before exposure to the communication, the majority of students in all four groups had very low scores and the group differences were insignificant. By comparing the score that each individual attained one week after the communication with that attained two weeks earlier, it was possible to determine for each group the percentage who changed in the direction of increased or decreased conformity.

The results, shown in Table 6, reveal that the greatest amount of conformity was produced by the communication which contained the least amount of fear-arousing material. The Strong group showed reliably less change than the Minimal group; in fact, the Strong group failed to differ significantly from the Control group, whereas the Minimal group showed a highly reliable increase in conformity as compared with the Control group. The Moderate group falls in an intermediate position, but does not differ reliably from the Strong or Minimal groups. Although there is some ambiguity with respect to the relative effectiveness of the Moderate appeal, the data in Table 6 show a fairly consistent trend which suggests that as the amount of fear-arousing material is increased, conformity tends to decrease. In contrast to the marked increase in conformity produced by the Minimal appeal and the fairly sizable increase produced by the Moderate appeal, the Strong appeal failed to achieve any significant effect whatsoever.

One cannot be certain, of course, that the findings represent changes in overt behavioral conformity, since the observations are based on the Ss' own verbal reports. What remains problematical, however, is whether the verbal responses reflect only "lip-service" to the recommendations or whether they also reflect internalized attitudes that were actually carried out in action. The results, nevertheless, demonstrate that the

TABLE 6

EFFECT OF THE ILLUSTRATED TALK ON CONFORMITY TO DENTAL HYGIENE RECOMMENDATIONS

Type of Change	Strong Group ($N = 50$)	Moderate Group ($N = 50$)	Minimal Group ($N = 50$)	Control Group ($N = 50$)
Increased conformity	28%	44%	50%	22%
Decreased conformity	20%	22%	14%	22%
No change	52%	34%	36%	56%
Net change in conformity	+8%	+22%	+36%	0%

RELIABILITY OF DIFFERENCE

Group	CR	p
Control vs. Minimal	2.54	<.01
Control vs. Moderate	1.50	.07
Control vs. Strong	0.59	.28
Strong vs. Moderate	0.95	.17
Strong vs. Minimal	1.96	.03
Moderate vs. Minimal	0.93	.18

Strong appeal was markedly less effective than the Minimal appeal, at least with respect to eliciting verbal conformity.

Further evidence in support of the same conclusion comes from responses pertinent to a different type of dental hygiene behavior which had also been recommended in the illustrated talk.[4] The students were asked to give the approximate date on which they had last gone to a dentist. The percentage in each group whose answers indicated that they had gone to the dentist during the week following exposure to the illustrated talk were as follows: 10 per cent of the Strong group, 14 per cent of the Moderate group, 18 per cent of the Minimal group, and 4 per cent of the Control group. The percentage difference between the Minimal group and the Control group was found to be statistically reliable at the .04 confidence level; none of the other comparisons yielded reliable differences. Although not conclusive evidence, these findings are in line with those in Table 6: the Minimal appeal again appears to have been superior with respect to eliciting conformity to a recommended practice.

BELIEFS CONCERNING THE "PROPER" TYPE OF TOOTHBRUSH

The illustrated talk presented an extensive discussion of the "proper" type of toothbrush recommended by dental authorities. Four main characteristics were emphasized: (a) the bristles should be of medium hardness, (b) the brush should have three rows of bristles, (c) the handle should be completely straight, and (d) the brushing surface should be completely straight. Personal beliefs concerning the desirability of these four characteristics were measured by four

[4] In all three forms of the illustrated talk, an explicit recommendation was made concerning the desirability of obtaining advice from a dentist about one's own toothbrushing technique. In addition, several references were made to the importance of going to a dentist for prompt treatment of cavities, before the decay spreads to the inner layers of the tooth.

questions which were included in the pre-communication questionnaire as well as in the questionnaire given one week after the communication. The main finding was that all three experimental groups, as compared with the Control group, showed a significant change in the direction of accepting the conclusions presented in the communication. Among the three experimental groups, there were no significant differences with respect to net changes. Nevertheless, as will be seen in the next section, the fear-arousing material appears to have had a considerable effect on the degree to which the students adhered to such beliefs in the face of counteracting propaganda.

RESISTANCE TO COUNTERACTING PROPAGANDA

In addition to describing the four essential characteristics of the "proper" toothbrush, the illustrated talk contained numerous comments and illustrations to explain the need for avoiding the "wrong" kind of toothbrush. Much of the material on cavities and other unpleasant consequences of tooth neglect was presented in this context. *The importance of using the proper kind of toothbrush* was the theme that was most heavily emphasized throughout the entire communication.

The key questionnaire item, designed to determine initial attitudes before exposure to the communication, was the following:

Please read the following statement carefully and decide whether you believe it is true or false.

It does not matter what kind of toothbrush a person uses. *Any sort of toothbrush* that is sold in a drugstore will keep your teeth clean and healthy—if you use it regularly.

Do you think that this statement is true or false? (Check one.)

One week after exposure to the communications, the question was asked again, in essentially the same form, with the same

TABLE 7

EFFECT OF THE ILLUSTRATED TALK ON REACTIONS TO SUBSEQUENT
COUNTERPROPAGANDA: NET PERCENTAGE OF EACH GROUP WHO
CHANGED IN THE DIRECTION OF AGREEING WITH THE STATEMENT
THAT "IT DOES NOT MATTER WHAT KIND OF TOOTHBRUSH
A PERSON USES"

Type of Change	Strong Group (N = 50)	Moderate Group (N = 50)	Minimal Group (N = 50)	Control Group (N = 50)
More agreement	30	28	14	44
Less agreement	38	42	54	24
No change	32	30	32	32
Net change	−8	−14	−40	+20
Net effect of exposure to the illustrated talk	−28	−34	−60	

RELIABILITY OF THE DIFFERENCES IN NET CHANGE

Group	CR	p
Control vs. Minimal	3.66	<.001
Control vs. Moderate	2.05	.02
Control vs. Strong	1.71	.05
Strong vs. Moderate	0.36	.36
Strong vs. Minimal	2.03	.02
Moderate vs. Minimal	1.66	.05

checklist of five answer categories (ranging from "Feel certain that it is true" to "Feel certain that it is false"). But in the post-communication questionnaire, the question was preceded by the following propaganda material which contradicted the dominant theme of the illustrated talk:

A well-known dentist recently made the following statement:

Some dentists, including a number of so-called "experts" on dental hygiene, claim it is important to use a special type of toothbrush in order to clean the teeth properly. But from my own experience, I believe that there is no sound basis for that idea. My honest opinion, as a dentist, is that it does not matter what kind of toothbrush a person uses. Any sort of toothbrush that is sold in a drugstore will keep your teeth clean and healthy —if you use it regularly.

That this propaganda exposure had a pronounced effect is revealed by the attitude changes shown by the Control group. A statistically reliable change in the direction of more agreement with the counterpropaganda was found in the Control group.[5]

How effective were the three forms of the illustrated talk in preventing students from accepting the propaganda to which they were exposed one week later? Did the fear appeals augment or diminish the students' resistance to the counteracting propaganda? A fairly definite answer emerges from the results in Table 7, which shows the percentage of each group who changed in the direction of agreement or disagreement with the counterpropaganda statement.

Before exposure to the illustrated talk, the

[5] In the Control group, the percentage who disagreed with the statement dropped from 54 to 34. This change proved to be significant at below the .02 confidence level, according to the formula described by Hovland, Lumsdaine, and Sheffield (1949, p. 319). The Control group did not show any significant change on other questions dealing with dental hygiene beliefs, preferences or practices, all of which were presented in the final questionnaire before the propaganda material was introduced. Consequently, it seems fairly safe to conclude that the propaganda exposure was responsible for the significant change displayed by the Control group.

TABLE 8

TYPES OF REFUTATION GIVEN BY STUDENTS WHO DISAGREED WITH THE
COUNTERPROPAGANDA

Type of Refutation	Strong Group (N = 30)	Moderate Group (N = 29)	Minimal Group (N = 39)	Control Group (N = 18)
Explicit reference to the illustrated talk as an authoritative source for the opposite conclusion	7%	14%	18%	0%
One or more arguments cited that had been presented in the illustrated talk	43%	38%	59%	28%
One or more arguments cited that contradicted the content of the illustrated talk	0%	0%	0%	22%
No answer or no specific reason given	50%	52%	36%	50%

group differences were negligible: approximately 50 per cent of the students in each of the four groups agreed with the statement that "it does not matter what kind of toothbrush a person uses." But two weeks later (immediately after exposure to the counterpropaganda) there were marked and statistically reliable differences which indicate that although all three forms of the illustrated talk had some influence, the Minimal appeal was most effective in producing resistance to the counterpropaganda. Thus the results suggest that under conditions where people will be exposed to competing communications dealing with the same issues, the use of a strong fear appeal will tend to be less effective than a minimal appeal in producing stable and persistent attitude changes.

Some clues to mediating processes were detected in the students' responses to an open-end question which asked them to "give the reason" for their answers to the key attitude item on which the results in Table 7 are based. A systematic analysis was made of the write-in answers given by those students who had disagreed with the counterpropaganda. In their refutations, some of the students made use of material that had been presented one week earlier, either by referring to the illustrated talk as an authoritative source or by citing one of the main arguments presented in the illustrated talk. From the results presented in the first two rows of Table 8, it is apparent that such refutations were given more frequently by the Minimal group than by the other experimental groups. The comparatively low frequency of such answers in the Strong and Moderate groups was not compensated for by an increase in any other type of specific reasons, as indicated by the results in the last row of the table.[6]

Although the group differences are not uniformly reliable, they reveal a consistent trend which suggests an "avoidance" tendency among the students who had been

[6] On the first type of reason (reference to the illustrated talk), the only difference large enough to approach statistical reliability was that between the Minimal group and the Control group ($p = .08$). On the second type of reason (arguments cited from the illustrated talk), the difference between the Minimal group and the Control group was found to be highly reliable ($p = .03$) while the difference between the Minimal and Moderate groups approached statistical reliability ($p = .08$). The Control group differed reliably from each of the experimental groups (at beyond the .10 confidence level) with respect to giving arguments which contradicted those contained in the illustrated talk (row three of the table). None of the other percentage differences in Table 8 were large enough to be significant at the .10 confidence level. (In some columns, the percentages add up to more than 100 per cent because a few students gave more than one type of refutation.)

exposed to the fear appeals. Apparently, even those who resisted the counterpropaganda were inclined to avoid recalling the content of the fear-arousing communication.

Discussion

The results in the preceding sections indicate that the Minimal appeal was the most effective form of the communication in that it elicited (*a*) more resistance to subsequent counterpropaganda and (*b*) a higher incidence of verbal adherence, and perhaps a greater degree of behavioral conformity, to a set of recommended practices. The absence of any significant differences on other indicators of preferences and beliefs implies that the Moderate and Strong appeals had no unique positive effects that would compensate for the observed detrimental effects.

Thus, the findings consistently indicate that inclusion of the fear-arousing material not only failed to increase the effectiveness of the communication, but actually interfered with its over-all success.

The outcome of the present experiment by no means precludes the possibility that, under certain conditions, fear appeals may prove to be highly successful. For instance, the Strong appeal was found to be maximally effective in arousing interest and in eliciting a high degree of emotional tension. The evocation of such reactions might augment the effectiveness of mass communications which are designed to instigate prompt audience action, such as donating money or volunteering to perform a group task. But if the communication is intended to create more sustained preferences or attitudes, the achievement of positive effects probably depends upon a number of different factors. Our experimental results suggest that in the latter case, a relatively low degree of fear arousal is likely to be the optimal level, that an appeal which is too strong will tend to evoke some form of interference which reduces the effectiveness of the communication. The findings definitely contradict the

assumption that as the dosage of fear-arousing stimuli (in a mass communication) is increased, the audience will become more highly motivated to accept the reassuring recommendations contained in the communication. Beneficial motivating effects probably occur when a relatively slight amount of fear-arousing material is inserted; but for communications of the sort used in the present experiment, the optimal dosage appears to be far below the level of the strongest fear appeals that a communicator could use if he chose to do so.

Before examining the implications of the findings in more detail, it is necessary to take account of the problems of generalizing from the findings of the present study. The present experiment shows the effects of only one type of communication, presented in an educational setting to a student audience. Until replications are carried out—using other media, topics, and fear-eliciting stimuli, in a variety of communication settings, with different audiences, etc.—one cannot be certain that the conclusions hold true for other situations. The results from a single experiment are obviously not sufficient for drawing broad generalizations concerning the entire range of fear-arousing communications which are currently being brought to the focus of public attention. Nor can un-replicated results be relied upon for extracting dependable rubrics that could be applied by educators, editors, public relations experts, propagandists, or other communication specialists who face the practical problems of selecting appropriate appeals for motivating mass audiences.

Nevertheless, the present experiment helps to elucidate the potentially unfavorable effects that may result from mass communications which play up ominous threats, alarming contingencies, or signs of impending danger. For instance, the findings tend to bear out some of the points raised concerning the need for careful pretesting and for other cautions when warnings about the dangers of atomic bombing are presented in civilian defense communications that are intended to prepare the public for coping with wartime emergencies (Janis, 1951). Moreover, despite our inability to specify the range of communications to which our conclusions would apply, we can derive tentative inferences that may have important theoretical implications with respect to the dynamics of "normal" fear reactions.

We turn now to a central question posed by the experimental findings: Why is it that the fear-arousing stimuli resulted in less adherence to recommended practices and less resistance to counterpropaganda? Although our experiment cannot give a definitive answer, it provides some suggestive leads concerning potential sources of emotional interference.

In the introduction, we have described three forms of "resistance" frequently observed in psychotherapy that might also occur among normal personalities exposed to mass communications which evoke strong fear or anxiety: (a) inattentiveness during the communication session, (b) rejection of the communicator's statements motivated by reactive aggression, and (c) subsequent defensive avoidance motivated by residual emotional tension. We shall discuss briefly the pertinent findings from the present experiment with a view to making a preliminary assessment of the importance of each of the three types of interfering reactions.

1. Our results provide no evidence that a strong fear appeal produces inattentiveness or any form of distraction that would interfere with learning efficiency during the communication session. The three forms of the communication were found to be equally effective in teaching the factual material on dental hygiene, as measured by a comprehensive information test given immediately after exposure to the communication. Beliefs concerning the desirable characteristics of the "proper" type of toothbrush were also acquired equally well. One might even surmise (from the results in Table 4) that the Strong appeal may have had a beneficial effect on attention, because a significantly higher percentage of the Strong group re-

ported that (a) it was very easy to pay attention to what the speaker was saying and (b) they experienced very little "mind-wandering."

The absence of any observable reduction of learning efficiency is consistent with numerous clinical observations which imply that normal personalities can ordinarily tolerate unpleasant information concerning potential threats to the self without manifesting any marked impairment of "ego" functions. Our findings definitely suggest that the use of fear-arousing material of the sort presented in the illustrated talks would rarely give rise to any interference with the audience's ability to learn the content of the communication.

It is necessary to bear in mind, however, that in the present experiment the communication was given to a "captive" classroom audience. When people are at home listening to the radio, or in any situation where they feel free to choose whether or not to terminate the communication exposure, the use of strong emotional appeals might often have drastic effects on sustained attention. Consequently, the tentative generalization concerning the low probability of inattentiveness would be expected to apply primarily to those fear-arousing communications which are presented under conditions where social norms or situational constraints prevent the audience from directing attention elsewhere.

Even with a "captive" audience, it is quite possible that under certain extreme conditions a strong fear appeal might interfere with learning efficiency. For instance, the same sort of temporary cognitive impairment that is sometimes observed when verbal stimuli happen to touch off unconscious personal conflicts or emotional "complexes" might also occur when a mass communication elicits sharp awareness of unexpected danger, particularly when the audience immediately perceives the threat to be imminent and inescapable. Hence, the inferences from our experimental findings probably should be restricted to fear appeals which deal with remote threats or with relatively familiar dangers that are perceived to be avoidable.

2. The fact that the Strong group expressed the greatest amount of subjective dislike of the illustrated talk and made the most complaints about its content could be construed as suggesting a potentially aggressive attitude. But if the aggressive reactions aroused by the use of the Strong fear appeal were intense enough to motivate rejection of the conclusions, one would not expect to find this group giving the most favorable appraisals of the interest value of the illustrated talk, of the quality of its presentation, and of its over-all educational success. Thus, although the possibility of suppressed aggression cannot be precluded, it seems unlikely that this factor was a major source of emotional interference. In drawing this tentative conclusion, however, we do not intend to minimize the importance of aggression as a potential source of interference. In the present experiment, the communication was administered as an official part of the school's hygiene program and contained recommendations that were obviously intended to be beneficial to the audience. Under markedly different conditions, where the auspices and intent of the communication are perceived to be less benign, the audience would probably be less disposed to suppress or control aggressive reactions. The low level of verbalized aggression observed in the present study, however, suggests that in the absence of cues which arouse the audience's suspicions, some factor other than reactive hostility may be a much more important source of interference.

3. Subsequent defensive avoidance arising from residual emotional tension seems to be the most likely explanation of the outcome of the present study. We have seen, from the data on immediate affective reactions, that the disturbing feelings which had been aroused during the illustrated talk tended to persist after the communication had ended, despite the reassuring recommendations which had been presented. The analysis of complaints made by the three experimental groups (Table 5) provides additional evidence that the need for reassurance persisted primarily among the students who had been exposed to the Strong appeal. Such findings support the following hypothesis: *When a mass communication is designed to influence an audience to adopt specific ways and means of averting a threat, the use of a strong fear appeal, as against a milder one, increases the likelihood that the audience will be left in a state of emotional tension which is not fully relieved by rehearsing the reassuring recommendations contained in the communication.* This hypothesis is compatible with the general assumption that when a person is exposed to signs of "threat," the greater the intensity of the fear reaction evoked, the greater the likelihood that his emotional tension will persist after the external stimulus has terminated.

Whether or not the above hypothesis is correct, the fact remains that "unreduced" emotional tension was manifested immediately after the communication predominantly by the group exposed to the Strong appeal. Our findings on subsequent reactions provide some suggestive evidence concerning the consequences of experiencing this type of residual tension. In general, the evidence appears to be consistent with the following hypothesis: *When fear is strongly aroused but is not fully relieved by the reassurances contained in a mass communication, the audience will become motivated to ignore or to minimize the importance of the threat.* This hypothesis could be regarded as a special case of the following general proposition which pertains to the effects of human exposure to any fear-producing stimulus: other things being equal, the more persistent the fear reaction, the greater will be the (acquired) motivation to avoid subsequent exposures to internal and external cues which were present at the time the fear reaction was aroused. This proposition is based on the postulate that fear is a stimulus-producing response which has the functional properties of a drive (Dollard and Miller, 1950; Mowrer, 1950).[7]

In the context of the present experiment, one would predict that the group displaying the greatest degree of residual fear would be most strongly motivated to ward off those internal symbolic cues—such as anticipations of the threatening consequences of improper dental hygiene—which were salient during and immediately after the communication. This prediction seems to be fairly well borne out by the evidence on carry-over effects, particularly by the finding that the greatest degree of resistance to the subsequent counterpropaganda was shown by the group which had been least motivated by fear. The use of the Strong appeal, as against the Minimal one, evidently resulted in less rejection of a subsequent communication which discounted and contradicted what was said in the original communication. In effect, the second communication asserted that one could ignore the alleged consequences of using the wrong type of

[7] In the sphere of human communication, the key communication, the key theoretical assumption could be formulated as follows: If rehearsal of the reassuring statements contained in a communication fails to alleviate the emotional tension elicited by the use of a fear appeal, the audience will be motivated to continue trying out other (symbolic or overt) responses until one occurs which succeeds in reducing fear to a tolerable level. Thus, a strong fear appeal which is intended to motivate the audience to take account of a realistic threat of danger could have the paradoxical effect of motivating the audience to ignore the threat or to adopt "magical," "wishful" or other types of reassuring beliefs that are antithetical to the communicator's intentions. Moreover, according to the same theoretical assumption, when a communication produces a high degree of persistent fear, the audience will be motivated to engage in overt escape activities, some of which may prove to be incompatible with the protective actions recommended by the communicator. Unintended effects of this kind can be regarded as spontaneous "defensive" reactions which are motivated by residual emotional tension. In the present experiment, it would be expected that, in addition to the tendency to avoid thinking about the threat, other defensive reactions would also occur. For example, following exposure to the Strong appeal, some of the students may have succeeded in alleviating their residual emotional tension through spontaneous interpersonal communication with fellow students.

toothbrush, and, in that sense, minimized the dangers which previously had been heavily emphasized by the fear-arousing communication.

The results obtained from the students' reports on their dental hygiene practices could be interpreted as supporting another prediction from the same hypothesis. It would be expected that those students who changed their practices, after having heard and seen one of the three forms of the illustrated talk, were motivated to do so because they recalled some of the verbal material which had been given in support of the recommendations, most of which referred to the unfavorable consequences of continuing to do the "wrong" thing. In theoretical terms, one might say that their conformity to the recommendations was mediated by symbolic responses which had been learned during the communication. The mediating responses (anticipations, thoughts, or images) acquired from any one of the three forms of the illustrated talk would frequently have, as their content, some reference to unpleasant consequences for the self, and consequently would cue off a resolution or an overt action that would be accompanied by anticipated success in warding off the threat. But defensive avoidance of the mediating responses would reduce the amount of conformity to whatever protective action is recommended by the fear-arousing communication. Hence the prediction would be that when rehearsal of statements concerning potential danger is accompanied by strong emotional tension during and after the communication, the audience will become motivated to avoid recalling those statements on later occasions when appropriate action could ordinarily be carried out. An inhibiting motivation of this kind would tend to prevent the students from adopting the recommended changes in their toothbrushing habits because they would fail to think about the unpleasant consequences of improper dental hygiene at times when they subsequently perform the act of brushing their teeth.

Much more direct evidence in support of

the "defensive avoidance" hypothesis comes from the analysis of spontaneous write-in answers in which the students explained why they disagreed with the counterpropaganda (Table 8). Those who had been exposed to the least amount of fear-arousing material were the ones who were most likely to refer to the illustrated talk as an authoritative source and to make use of its arguments. The relative absence of such references in the spontaneous answers given by those who had been exposed to the Moderate and Strong appeals implies a tendency to avoid recalling the content of the fear-arousing communication.

Although the various pieces of evidence discussed above seem to fit together, they cannot be regarded as a conclusive demonstration of the defensive avoidance hypothesis. What our findings clearly show is that a strong fear appeal can be markedly less effective than a minimal appeal, at least under the limited conditions represented in our experiment. Exactly which conditions and which mediating mechanisms are responsible for this outcome will remain problematical until further investigations are carried out. Nevertheless, so far as the present findings go, they consistently support the conclusion that the use of a strong fear-appeal will tend to reduce the over-all success of a persuasive communication, if it evokes a high degree of emotional tension without adequately satisfying the need for reassurance.

Summary and Conclusions

The experiment was designed to investigate the effects of persuasive communications which attempt to motivate people to conform with a set of recommendations by stimulating fear reactions. An illustrated lecture on dental hygiene was prepared in three different forms, representing three different intensities of fear appeal: the Strong appeal emphasized and graphically illustrated the threat of pain, disease, and body damage; the Moderate appeal described the same dangers in a milder and more factual manner; the Minimal appeal rarely referred to the unpleasant consequences of improper dental hygiene. Although differing in the amount of fear-arousing material presented, the three forms of the communication contained the same essential information and the same set of recommendations.

Equivalent groups of high school students were exposed to the three different forms of the communication as part of the school's hygiene program. In addition, the experiment included an equated Control group which was not exposed to the dental hygiene communication but was given a similar communication on an irrelevant topic. Altogether there were 200 students in the experiment, with 50 in each group. A questionnaire containing a series of items on dental hygiene beliefs, practices, and attitudes was administered to all four groups one week before the communications were presented. In order to observe the changes produced by the illustrated talk, postcommunication questionnaires were given immediately after exposure and again one week later.

1. The fear appeals were successful in arousing affective reactions. Immediately after the communication, the group exposed to the Strong appeal reported feeling more worried about the condition of their teeth than did the other groups. The Moderate appeal, in turn, evoked a higher incidence of "worry" reactions than did the Minimal appeal.

2. The three forms of the illustrated talk were equally effective with respect to (a) teaching the factual content of the communication, as assessed by an information test, and (b) modifying beliefs concerning four specific characteristics of the "proper" type of toothbrush. The evidence indicates that the emotional reactions aroused by the Strong appeal did not produce inattentiveness or reduce learning efficiency.

3. As compared with the other two forms of the communication, the Strong appeal evoked a more mixed or ambivalent attitude

toward the communication. The students exposed to the Strong appeal were more likely than the others to give favorable appraisals concerning the interest value and the quality of the presentation. Nevertheless, they showed the greatest amount of subjective dislike of the communication and made more complaints about the content.

4. From an analysis of the changes in each individual's reports about his current toothbrushing practices, it was found that the greatest amount of conformity to the communicator's recommendations was produced by the Minimal appeal. The Strong appeal failed to produce any significant change in dental hygiene practices, whereas the Minimal appeal resulted in a reliable increase in conformity, as compared with the Control group. Similar findings also emerged from an analysis of responses which indicated whether the students had gone to a dentist during the week following exposure to the illustrated talk, reflecting conformity to another recommendation made by the communicator. The evidence strongly suggests that as the amount of fear-arousing material is increased, conformity to recommended (protective) actions tends to decrease.

5. One week after the illustrated talk had been presented, exposure to counterpropaganda (which contradicted the main theme of the original communication) produced a greater effect on attitudes in the Control group than in the three experimental groups. The Minimal appeal, however, proved to be the most effective form of the illustrated talk with respect to producing resistance to the counterpropaganda. The results tend to support the conclusion that under conditions where people are exposed to competing communications dealing with the same issues, the use of a strong fear appeal is less successful than a minimal appeal in producing stable and persistent attitude changes.

6. The main conclusion which emerges from the entire set of findings is that the over-all effectiveness of a persuasive communication will tend to be reduced by the use of a strong fear appeal, if it evokes a high degree of emotional tension without adequately satisfying the need for reassurance. The evidence from the present experiment appears to be consistent with the following two explanatory hypotheses:

a. When a mass communication is designed to influence an audience to adopt specific ways and means of averting a threat, the use of a strong fear appeal, as against a milder one, increases the likelihood that the audience will be left in a state of emotional tension which is not fully relieved by rehearsing the reassuring recommendations contained in the communication.

b. When fear is strongly aroused but is not fully relieved by the reassurances contained in a mass communication, the audience will become motivated to ignore or to minimize the importance of the threat.

References

ALEXANDER, F., and FRENCH, T. M. *Psychoanalytic therapy.* New York: Ronald, 1946.

DOLLARD, J., and MILLER, N. E. *Personality and psychotherapy.* New York: McGraw-Hill, 1950.

FENICHEL, O. *Problems of psychoanalytic technique.* New York: Psychoanalytic Quart., 1941.

HANFMANN, EUGENIA. Psychological approaches to the study of anxiety. In P. H. Hoch and J. Zubin (Eds.), *Anxiety.* New York: Grune & Stratton, 1950, 51-69.

HOVLAND, C. I., LUMSDAINE, A. A., and SHEFFIELD, F. D. *Experiments on mass communication.* Princeton, N.J.: Princeton Univer. Press, 1949.

JANIS, I. L. *Air war and emotional stress.* New York: McGraw-Hill, 1951.

MOWRER, O. H. *Learning theory and personality dynamics: selected papers.* New York: Ronald, 1950.

The Influence of Source
Credibility on Communication ❦ Carl I. Hovland
Effectiveness ❦ Walter Weiss

An important but little-studied factor in the effectiveness of communication is the attitude of the audience toward the communicator. Indirect data on this problem come from studies of "prestige" in which subjects are asked to indicate their agreement or disagreement with statements which are attributed to different individuals (Sherif, 1935; Lewis, 1941; Asch, 1948). The extent of agreement is usually higher when the statements are attributed to "high prestige" sources. There are few studies in which an identical communication is presented by different communicators and the relative effects on opinion subsequently measured without explicit reference to the position taken by the communicator. Yet the latter research setting may be a closer approximation of the real-life situation to which the results of research are to be applied.

In one of the studies reported by Hovland, Lumsdaine and Sheffield (1949), the effects of a communication were studied without reference to the source of the items comprising the opinion questionnaire. They found that opinion changes following the showing of an Army orientation film were smaller among the members of the audience who believed the purpose of the film was "propagandistic" than among those who believed its purpose "informational." But such a study does not rule out the possibility that the results could be explained by general predispositional factors; that is, individuals who are "suspicious" of mass-media sources may be generally less responsive to such communications. The present study was designed to minimize the aforementioned methodological difficulties by experimentally controlling the source and by checking the effects of the source in a situation in which the subject's own opinion was obtained without reference to the source.

A second objective of the present study was to investigate the extent to which opinions derived from high and low credibility sources are maintained over a period of time. Hovland, Lumsdaine and Sheffield showed that some opinion changes in the direction of the communicator's position are larger after a lapse of time than immediately after the communication. This they refer to as the "sleeper effect." One hypothesis which they advanced for their results is that individuals may be suspicious of the motives of the communicator and initially discount his position, and thus may evidence little or no immediate change in opinion. With the passage of time, however, they may remember and accept *what* was communicated but not remember *who* communicated it. As a result, they may then be more inclined to agree with the position which had been presented by the communicator. In the study referred to, only a single source was used, so no test was available of the differential effects when the source was suspected of having a propagandistic motive and when it was not. The present experiment was designed to test differences in the retention, as

From the *Public Opinion Quarterly*, 1952, 15, 635-650. Reprinted by permission of the authors and publisher. This study was done as part of a coordinated research project on factors influencing changes in attitude and opinion being conducted at Yale University under a grant from the Rockefeller Foundation. (See C. I. Hovland, "Changes in Attitude through Communication," *Journal of Abnormal and Social Psychology*, 1951, 46, 424-437.) The writers wish to thank Professor Ralph E. Turner for making his class available for the study.

well as the acquisition, of identical communications when presented by "trustworthy" and by "untrustworthy" sources.

Procedure

The overall design of the study was to present an identical communication to two groups, one in which a communicator of a generally "trustworthy" character was used, and the other in which the communicator was generally regarded as "untrustworthy." Opinion questionnaires were administered before the communication, immediately after the communication, and a month after the communication.

Because of the possibility of specific factors affecting the relationship between communicator and content on a single topic, four different topics (with eight different communicators) were used. On each topic two alternative versions were prepared, one presenting the "affirmative" and one the "negative" position on the issue. For each version one "trustworthy" and one "untrustworthy" source was used. The topics chosen

were of current interest and of a controversial type so that a fairly even division of opinion among members of the audience was obtained.

The four topics and the communicators chosen to represent "high credibility" and "low credibility" sources were as follows: In some cases the sources were individual writers and in others periodical publications, and some were fictitious (but plausible) and others actual authors or publications.

The "affirmative" and "negative" versions of each article presented an equal number of facts on the topic and made use of essentially the same material. They differed in the emphasis given the material and in the conclusion drawn from the facts. Since there were two versions for each topic and these were prepared in such a way that either of the sources might have written either version, four possible combinations of content and source were available on each topic.

The communication consisted of a booklet containing one article on each of the four different topics, with the name of the author or periodical given at the end of each article. The order of the topics within the

	"High Credibility" Source	"Low Credibility" Source
A. Anti-histamine Drugs: Should the anti-histamine drugs continue to be sold without a doctor's prescription?	*New England Journal of Biology and Medicine*	Magazine A° [A mass circulation monthly pictorial magazine]
B. Atomic Submarines: Can a practicable atomic-powered submarine be built at the present time?	Robert J. Oppenheimer	*Pravda*
C. The Steel Shortage: Is the steel industry to blame for the current shortage of steel?	*Bulletin of National Resources Planning Board*	Writer A° [A widely syndicated anti-labor, anti-New Deal, "rightist" newspaper columnist]
D. The Future of Movie Theaters: As a result of TV, will there be a decrease in the number of movie theaters in operation by 1955?	*Fortune* magazine	Writer B ° [An extensively syndicated woman movie-gossip columnist]

° The names of one of the magazines and two of the writers used in the study have to be withheld to avoid any possible embarrassment to them. These sources will be referred to hereafter only by the later designations given.

booklets was kept constant. Two trust-worthy and two untrustworthy sources were included in each booklet. Twenty-four different booklets covered the various combinations used. An example of one such booklet-combination would be:

Topic	Version	Source
The Future of Movie Theaters	Affirmative	*Fortune*
Atomic Submarines	Negative	*Pravda*
The Steel Shortage	Affirmative	Writer A
Anti-histamine Drugs	Negative	*New England Journal of Biology and Medicine*

The questionnaires were designed to obtain data on the amount of factual information acquired from the communication and the extent to which opinion was changed in the direction of the position advocated by the communicator. Information was also obtained on the subject's evaluation of the general trustworthiness of each source, and, in the after-questionnaires, on the recall of the author of each article.

The subjects were college students in an advanced undergraduate course in History at Yale University. The first questionnaire, given five days before the communication, was represented to the students as a general opinion survey being conducted by a "National Opinion Survey Council." The key opinions bearing on the topics selected for the communication were scattered through many other unrelated ones. There were also questions asking for the subjects' evaluations of the general trustworthiness of a long list of sources, which included the critical ones used in the communications. This evaluation was based on a 5-point scale ranging from "very trustworthy" to "very untrustworthy."

Since it was desired that the subjects not associate the experiment with the "before" questionnaire, the following arrangement was devised: The senior experimenter was invited to give a guest lecture to the class during the absence of the regular instructor, five days after the initial questionnaire. His remarks constituted the instructions for the experiment:

Several weeks ago Professor [the regular instructor] asked me to meet with you this morning to discuss some phase of Contemporary Problems. He suggested that one interesting topic would be The Psychology of Communications. This is certainly an important problem, since so many of our attitudes and opinions are based not on direct experience but on what we hear over the radio or read in the newspaper. I finally agreed to take this topic but on the condition that I have some interesting live data on which to base my comments. We therefore agreed to use this period to make a survey of the role of newspaper and magazine reading as a vehicle of communication and then to report on the results and discuss their implications at a later session.

Today, therefore, I am asking you to read a number of excerpts from recent magazine and newspaper articles on controversial topics. The authors have attempted to summarize the best information available, duly taking into account the various sides of the issues. I have chosen up-to-date issues which are currently being widely discussed and ones which are being studied by Gallup, Roper and others interested in public opinion.

Will you please read each article carefully the way you would if you were reading it in your favorite newspaper and magazine. When you finish each article write your name in the lower right hand corner to indicate that you have read it through and then go on to the next. When you finish there will be a short quiz on your reaction to the readings.

Any questions before we begin?

The second questionnaire, handed out immediately after the booklets were collected, differed completely in format from the earlier one. It contained a series of general questions on the subjects' reactions to the articles, gradually moving toward opinion questions bearing on the content discussed in the articles. At the end of the questionnaire there was a series of fact-quiz items. Sixteen multiple choice questions, four on each content area, were used together with a question calling for the recall of the author of each of the articles.

An identical questionnaire was administered four weeks after the communication. At no prior time had the subjects been forewarned that they would be given this second post-test questionnaire.

A total of 223 subjects provided information which was used in some phase of the analysis. Attendance in the history course was not mandatory and there was considerable shrinkage in the number of students present at all three time periods. For the portions of the analysis requiring before-and-after information, the data derived from 61 students who were present on all three occasions were used. Thus for the main analysis a sample of 244 communications (four for each student) was available. Since different analyses permitted the use of differing numbers of cases, the exact number of instances used in each phase of the analysis is given in each table.

Results

Before proceeding to the main analyses it is important to state the extent to which the sources selected on *a priori* grounds by the experimenters as being of differing credibility were actually reacted to in this manner by the subjects. One item on the questionnaire given before the communication asked the subjects to rate the trustworthiness of each of a series of authors and publications. Figure 1 gives the percentages of subjects who rated each of the sources "trustworthy."

The first source named under each topic had been picked by the experimenters as being of high credibility and the second of low. It will be observed that there is a clear differentiation of the credibility in the direction of the initial selection by the experimenters. The differences between members of each pair are all highly significant (*t*'s range from 13 to 20). The results in Figure 1 are based on all of the subjects present when the preliminary questionnaire was administered. The percentages for the smaller sample of subjects present at all three sessions do not differ significantly from those for the group as a whole.

DIFFERENCES IN PERCEPTION OF COMMUNICATION OF VARIOUS AUDIENCE SUB-GROUPS

Following the communication, subjects were asked their opinion about the fairness of the presentation of each topic and the extent to which each communicator was justified in his conclusion. Although the communications being judged were *identical*, there was a marked difference in the way the sub-

Topic	Source	N	Percent Rating Source as Trustworthy
Anti-Histamines	New Engl. J. Biol. & Med.	208	94.7%
	Magazine A	222	←5.9%
Atomic Submarines	Oppenheimer	221	93.7%
	Pravda	223	←1.3%
Steel Shortage	Bull. Nat. Res. Plan. Bd.	220	80.9%
	Writer A	223	←17.0%
Future of Movies	Fortune	222	89.2%
	Writer B	222	←21.2%

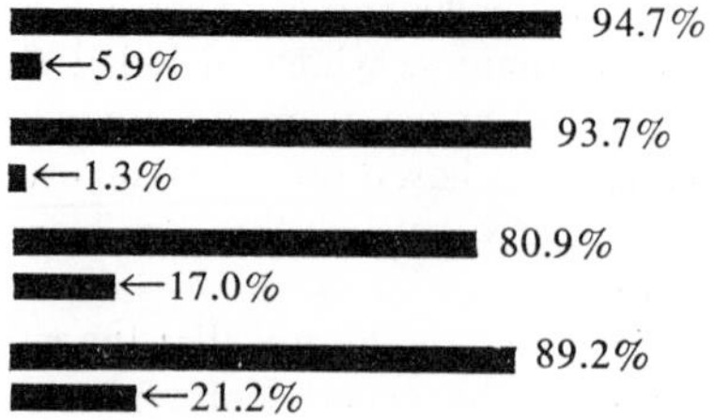

Fig. 1. Credibility of sources.

TABLE 1

Evaluation of "Fairness" and "Justifiability" of Identical Communications When Presented by "High Credibility" and "Low Credibility" Sources among Individuals Who Initially Agreed and Individuals Who Initially Disagreed with Position Advocated by Communicator

A. Per Cent Considering Author "Fair" in His Presentation[*]

Topic	High Credibility Source		Low Credibility Source	
	Initially Agree	Initially Disagree (or Don't Know)	Initially Agree	Initially Disagree (or Don't Know)
Anti-histamines	76.5%	50.0%	64.3%	62.5%
Atomic Submarines	100.0	93.7	75.0	66.7
Steel Shortage	44.4	15.4	12.5	22.2
Future of Movies	90.9	90.0	77.8	52.4
Mean	78.3%	57.9%	60.5%	51.9%
N =	46	76	43	79

B. Per Cent Considering Author's Conclusion "Justified" by the Facts[†]

Topic	High Credibility Source		Low Credibility Source	
	Initially Agree	Initially Disagree (or Don't Know)	Initially Agree	Initially Disagree (or Don't Know)
Anti-histamines	82.4%	57.1%	57.1%	50.0%
Atomic Submarines	77.8	81.2	50.0	41.2
Steel Shortage	55.6	23.1	37.5	22.2
Future of Movies	63.6	55.0	55.6	33.3
Mean	71.7%	50.0%	51.2%	36.7%
N =	46	76	43	79

[*] Question: Do you think that the author of each article was fair in his presentation of the facts on both sides of the question or did he write a one-sided report?
[†] Question: Do you think that the opinion expressed by the author in his conclusion *was* justified by the facts he presented or do you think his opinion *was not* justified by the facts?

jects responded to the "high credibility" and "low credibility" sources. Their evaluations were also affected by their personal opinions on the topic before the communication was ever presented. Audience evaluations of the four communications are presented in Table 1. In 14 of the 16 possible comparisons the "low credibility" sources are considered less fair or less justified than the corresponding high credibility sources. The differences for the low credibility sources for the individuals initially holding an opinion different from that advocated by the communicator and those for the high credibility sources for individuals who initially held the same position as that advocated by the communicator are significant at less than the .004 level.[1]

[1] The probability values given in the table, while adequately significant, are calculated conservatively. The two-tailed test of significance is used throughout, even though in the case of some of the tables it could be contended that the direction of the differences is in line with theoretical predictions, and hence might justify the use of the one-tail test. When analysis is made of *changes*, the significance test takes into account the internal correlation (Hovland, Lumsdaine and Sheffield, 1949, pp. 318ff.), but the analyses of cases of post-communication agreement and disagreement are calculated on the conservative assumption of independence of the separate communications.

TABLE 2

MEAN NUMBER OF ITEMS CORRECT ON FOUR-ITEM INFORMATION QUIZZES ON EACH OF
FOUR TOPICS WHEN PRESENTED BY "HIGH CREDIBILITY" AND "LOW CREDIBILITY"
SOURCES (TEST IMMEDIATELY AFTER COMMUNICATION)

Topic	Mean Number of Items Correct			
	High Credibility Source		Low Credibility Source	
Anti-histamines	(N = 31)	3.42	(N = 30)	3.17
Atomic Submarines	(N = 25)	3.48	(N = 36)	3.72
Steel Shortage	(N = 35)	3.34	(N = 26)	2.73
Future of Movies	(N = 31)	3.23	(N = 30)	3.27
Average	(N = 122)	3.36	(N = 122)	3.26
Per cent of items correct		84.0		81.5
$p$diff. M.			.35	

Effect of Credibility of Source on Acquisition of Information and on Change in Opinion

INFORMATION

There is no significant difference in the amount of factual information acquired by the subjects when the material is attributed to a high credibility source as compared to the amount learned when the same material is attributed to a low credibility source. Table 2 shows the mean number of items correct on the information quiz when material is presented by "high credibility" and "low credibility" sources.

OPINION

Significant differences were obtained in the extent to which opinion on an issue was changed by the attribution of the material to different sources. These results are presented in Table 3. Subjects changed their opinion in the direction advocated by the communicator in a significantly greater number of cases when the material was attributed to a "high credibility" source than when attributed to a "low credibility" source. The difference is significant at less than the .01 level.

From Figure 1 it will be recalled that less than 100 per cent of the subjects were in agreement with the group consensus concerning the trustworthiness of each source. The results presented in Table 3 were reanalyzed using the individual subject's own evaluation of the source as the independent variable. The effects on opinion were studied for those instances where the source was rated as "very trustworthy" or "moderately trustworthy" and for those where it

TABLE 3

NET CHANGES OF OPINION IN DIRECTION OF COMMUNICATION FOR SOURCES CLASSIFIED
BY EXPERIMENTERS AS "HIGH CREDIBILITY" OR "LOW CREDIBILITY" SOURCES *

Topic	Net Percentage of Cases in Which Subjects Changed Opinion in Direction of Communication			
	High Credibility Sources		Low Credibility Sources	
Anti-histamines	(N = 31)	22.6%	(N = 30)	13.3%
Atomic Submarines	(N = 25)	36.0	(N = 36)	0.0
Steel Shortage	(N = 35)	22.9	(N = 26)	−3.8
Future of Movies	(N = 31)	12.9	(N = 30)	16.7
Average	(N = 122)	23.0%	(N = 122)	6.6%
Diff.			16.4%	
$p$diff.			<.01	

* Net changes = positive changes minus negative changes.

TABLE 4

NET CHANGES OF OPINION IN DIRECTION OF COMMUNICATION FOR SOURCES JUDGED
"TRUSTWORTHY" OR "UNTRUSTWORTHY" BY INDIVIDUAL SUBJECTS

| Topic | Net Percentage of Cases in Which Subjects Changed Opinion in Direction of Communication | | | |
	"Trustworthy" Sources		"Untrustworthy" Sources	
Anti-histamines	(N = 31)	25.5%	(N = 27)	11.1%
Atomic Submarines	(N = 25)	36.0	(N = 36)	0.0
Steel Shortage	(N = 33)	18.2	(N = 27)	7.4
Future of Movies	(N = 31)	12.9	(N = 29)	17.2
Average	(N = 120)	22.5%	(N = 119)	8.4%
Diff.		14.1%		
ᵖdiff.		<.03		

was rated as "untrustworthy" or "inconsistently trustworthy." Results from this analysis are given in Table 4. The results, using the subject's own evaluation of the trustworthiness of the source, are substantially the same as those obtained when analyzed in terms of the experimenters' *a priori* classification (presented in Table 3). Only minor shifts were obtained. It appears that while the variable is made somewhat "purer" with this analysis this advantage is offset by possible increased variability attributable to unreliability in making individual judgments of the trustworthiness of the source.

Retention of Information and Opinion in Relation to Source

INFORMATION

As was the case with the immediate post-communication results (Table 2), there is no difference between the retention of factual information after four weeks when presented by high credibility sources and low credibility sources. Results in Table 5 show the mean retention scores for each of the four topics four weeks after the communication.

OPINION

Extremely interesting results were obtained for the retention of opinion changes. Table 6 shows the changes in opinion from immediately after the communication to those obtained after the four-week interval. It will be seen that compared with the changes immediately after the communication, there is a *decrease* in the extent of agreement with the high credibility source, but an *increase* in the case of the low credibility source. This result, then, is similar to the "sleeper effect" found by Hovland,

TABLE 5

MEAN NUMBER OF ITEMS CORRECT ON FOUR-ITEM INFORMATION QUIZZES ON EACH OF
FOUR TOPICS WHEN PRESENTED BY "HIGH CREDIBILITY" AND "LOW CREDIBILITY"
SOURCES (RECALL FOUR WEEKS AFTER COMMUNICATION)

| Topic | Mean Number of Items Correct | | | |
	High Credibility Source		Low Credibility Source	
Anti-histamines	(N = 31)	2.32	(N = 30)	2.90
Atomic Submarines	(N = 25)	3.08	(N = 36)	3.06
Steel Shortage	(N = 35)	2.51	(N = 26)	2.27
Future of Movies	(N = 31)	2.52	(N = 30)	2.33
Average	(N = 122)	2.58	(N = 122)	2.67
Per cent of items correct		64.5		66.7
ᵖdiff.		.46		

TABLE 6

NET CHANGES OF OPINION FROM IMMEDIATELY AFTER COMMUNICATION TO FOUR
WEEKS LATER IN DIRECTION OF "HIGH CREDIBILITY" AND "LOW
CREDIBILITY" SOURCES

Topic	High Credibility Source (A)		Low Credibility Source (B)		Difference (B-A)
Anti-histamines	(N = 31)	− 6.5%	(N = 30)	+ 6.7%	+13.2%
Atomic Submarines	(N = 25)	−16.0	(N = 36)	+13.9	+29.9
Steel Shortage	(N = 35)	−11.4	(N = 26)	+15.4	+26.8
Future of Movies	(N = 31)	− 9.7	(N = 30)	− 6.7	+ 3.0
Average	(N = 122)	−10.7%	(N = 122)	+ 7.4%	+18.1%
$p$diff.					.001

Lumsdaine and Sheffield (1949). The results derived from Tables 3 and 6 are compared in Figure 2, which shows the changes in opinion from before the communication to immediately afterwards and from before to four weeks afterwards.

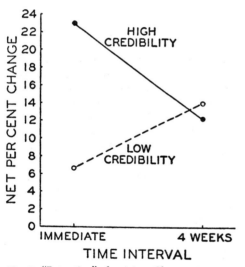

Fig. 2. "Retention" of opinion. Changes in extent of agreement with position advocated by "high credibility" and "low credibility" sources.

The loss with the "trustworthy" source and the gain with the "untrustworthy" source are clearly indicated. A parallel analysis using the individual's own evaluation of the source credibility (similar to the method of Table 4) showed substantially the same results.

RETENTION OF NAME OF SOURCE

One hypothesis advanced for the "sleeper effect" involved the assumption that forgetting of the source would be more rapid than that of the content. This is a most difficult point to test experimentally because it is almost impossible to equate retention tests for source and for content. It is, however, possible to make a comparison of the retention of the name of the source where the subjects initially agreed with the source's position and considered the communicator a "trustworthy" source, and those where they disagreed and considered the source "untrustworthy." Data on this point are presented in Table 7.

No clear differences are obtained immediately after the communication, indicating comparable initial learning of the names of the different sources. At the time of the delayed test, however, there appears to be a clear difference in the retention of the names of "untrustworthy" sources for the group initially agreeing with the communicator's position as compared with that for the group disagreeing with the communicator's position ($p = .02$). Since the "sleeper effect" occurs among the group which initially disagrees with an unreliable source (but subsequently comes to agree with it), it is interesting to note that among this group the retention of the source name is poorest of all. Too few subjects were available to check whether retention was poorer among

TABLE 7

RECALL OF SOURCE IMMEDIATELY AFTER COMMUNICATION AND AFTER FOUR WEEKS

Recall	Trustworthy Source		Untrustworthy Source	
	Individuals Initially Holding Position Advocated by Communicator	Individuals Not Initially Holding Position Advocated by Communicator	Individuals Initially Holding Position Advocated by Communicator	Individuals Not Initially Holding Position Advocated by Communicator
Immediately after communication	93.0% (N = 43)	85.7% (N = 77)	93.0% (N = 43)	93.4% (N = 76)
Four weeks after communication	60.5 (N = 43)	63.6 (N = 77)	76.7 (N = 43)	55.3 (N = 76)

the very subjects who showed the "sleeper effect," but no clear-cut difference could be seen from the analysis of the small sample.

Discussion

Under the conditions of this experiment, neither the acquisition nor the retention of factual information appears to be affected by the trustworthiness of the source. But changes in opinion are significantly related to the trustworthiness of the source used in the communication. This difference is in line with the results of Hovland, Lumsdaine and Sheffield (1949), who found a clear distinction between the effects of films on information and opinion. In the case of factual information they found that differences in acquisition and retention were primarily related to differences in learning ability. But in the case of opinion, the most important factor was the degree of "acceptance" of the material. In the present experiment, this variable was probably involved as a consequent of the variation in source credibility.

The present results add considerable detail to the Hovland-Lumsdaine-Sheffield findings concerning the nature of the "sleeper effect." While they were forced to make inferences concerning possible suspicion of the source, this factor was under experimental control in the present experiment and was shown to be a significant determinant of subsequent changes in opinion. In terms of their distinction between "learning"

and "acceptance," one could explain the present results by saying that the content of the communication (premises, arguments, etc.) is learned and forgotten to the same extent regardless of the communicator. But the extent of opinion change is influenced by both learning and acceptance, and the effect of an untrustworthy communicator is to interfere with the acceptance of the material ("I know what he is saying, but I don't believe it"). The aforementioned authors suggest that this interference is decreased with the passage of time, and at a more rapid rate than the forgetting of the content which provides the basis for the opinion. This could result in substantially the same extent of agreement with the position advocated by trustworthy and by untrustworthy sources at the time of the second post-test questionnaire. In the case of the trustworthy source, the forgetting of the content would be the main factor in the decrease in the extent of opinion change. But with an untrustworthy source the reduction due to forgetting would be more than offset by the removal of the interference associated with "non-acceptance." The net effect would be an increase in the extent of agreement with the position advocated by the source at the time of the second post-communication questionnaire. The present results are in complete agreement with this hypothesis; there is a large difference in extent of agreement with trustworthy and untrustworthy sources immediately after the communication, but the extent of agreement with the two types of source is almost identical four weeks later.

The Hovland-Lumsdaine-Sheffield formulation makes forgetting of the source a critical condition for the "sleeper" phenomenon. In the present analysis the critical requirement is a decreased tendency over time to reject the material presented by an untrustworthy source.[2] This may or may not require that the source be forgotten. But the individual must be less likely with the passage of time to associate spontaneously the content with the source. Thus the passage of time serves to remove recall of the source as a mediating cue that leads to rejection.[3]

It is in this connection that the methodological distinction mentioned earlier between the procedure used in this experiment and that customarily employed in "prestige" studies becomes of significance. In the present analysis, the untrustworthy source is regarded as a cue which is reacted to by rejection. When an individual is asked for his opinion at the later time he may not spontaneously remember the position held by the source. Hence the source does not then constitute a cue producing rejection of his position. In the usual "prestige" technique, the attachment of the name of the source to the statement would serve to reinstate the source as a cue; consequently the differen-

tial effects obtained with the present design would not be expected to obtain. An experiment is now under way to determine whether the "sleeper effect" disappears when the source cue is reinstated by the experimenter at the time of the delayed test of opinion change.

Finally, the question of the generalizability of the results should be discussed briefly. In the present study the subjects were all college students. Other groups of subjects varying in age and in education will be needed in future research. Four topics and eight different sources were used to increase the generality of the "source" variable. No attempt, however, was made to analyze the differences in effects for different topics. Throughout, the effects of the "Atomic Submarine" and "Steel Shortage" communications were larger and more closely related to the trustworthiness of source variable than those of the "Future of Movies" topic. An analysis of the factors responsible for the differential effects constitutes an interesting problem for future research. A repetition of the study with a single after-test for each time interval rather than double testing after the communication would be desirable, although this variation is probably much less significant with opinion than with information questions. The generality of the present results is limited to the situation where individuals are experimentally exposed to the communication; i.e., a "captive audience" situation. An interesting further research problem would be a repetition of the experiment under naturalistic conditions where the individual himself controls his exposure to communications. Finally for the present study it was important to use sources which could plausibly advocate either side of an issue. There are other combinations of position and source where the communicator and his stand are so intimately associated that one spontaneously recalls the source when he thinks about the issue. Under these conditions, the forgetting of the source may not occur and consequently no "sleeper effect" would be obtained.

[2] In the present analysis the difference in effects of trustworthy and untrustworthy sources is attributed primarily to the *negative* effects of rejection of the untrustworthy source. On the other hand, in prestige studies the effects are usually attributed to the *positive* enhancement of effects by a high prestige source. In both types of study only a difference in effect of the two kinds of influence is obtained. Future research must establish an effective "neutral" baseline to answer the question as to the absolute direction of the effects.

[3] In rare instances there may also occur a change with time in the attitude toward the source, such that one remembers the source but no longer has such a strong tendency to discount and reject the material. No evidence for the operation of this factor in the present experiment was obtained; our data indicate no significant changes in the evaluation of the trustworthiness of the sources from before to after the communication.

Summary

1. The effects of credibility of source on acquisition and retention of communication material were studied by presenting identical content but attributing the material to sources considered by the audience to be of "high trustworthiness" or of "low trustworthiness." The effects of source on factual information and on opinion were measured by the use of questionnaires administered before, immediately after, and four weeks after the communication.

2. The immediate reaction to the "fairness" of the presentation and the "justifiability" of the conclusions drawn by the communication is significantly affected by both the subject's initial position on the issue and by his evaluation of the trustworthiness of the source. Identical communications were regarded as being "justified" in their conclusions in 71.7 per cent of the cases when presented by a high credibility source to subjects who initially held the same opinion as advocated by the communicator, but were considered "justified" in only 36.7 per cent of the cases when presented by a low credibility source to subjects who initially held an opinion at variance with that advocated by the communicator.

3. No difference was found in the amount of factual information learned from the "high credibility" and "low credibility"

sources, and none in the amount retained over a four-week period.

4. Opinions were changed immediately after the communication in the direction advocated by the communicator to a significantly greater degree when the material was presented by a trustworthy source than when presented by an untrustworthy source.

5. There was a *decrease* after a time interval in the extent to which subjects agreed with the position advocated by the communication when the material was presented by trustworthy sources, but an *increase* when it was presented by untrustworthy sources.

6. Forgetting the name of the source is less rapid among individuals who initially agreed with the untrustworthy source than among those who disagreed with it.

7. Theoretical implications of the results are discussed. The data on post-communication changes in opinion (the "sleeper effect") can be explained by assuming equal *learning* of the content whether presented by a trustworthy or an untrustworthy source but an initial resistance to the *acceptance* of the material presented by an untrustworthy source. If this resistance to acceptance diminishes with time while the content which itself provides the basis for the opinion is forgotten more slowly, there will be an increase after the communication in the extent of agreement with an untrustworthy source.

References

ASCH, S. E. The doctrine of suggestion, prestige, and imitation in social psychology. *Psychol. Rev.* 1948, 55, 250-276.

HOVLAND, C. I. LUMSDAINE, A. A., and SHEFFIELD, F. D. *Experiments on mass communication.* Princeton, N.J.: Princeton Univer. Press, 1949.

LEWIS, H. B. Studies in the principles of judgments and attitudes: IV. The operation of prestige suggestion. *J. soc. Psychol.* 1941, *14*, 229-256.

SHERIF, M. An experimental study of stereotypes. *J. abnorm. soc. Psychol.* 1935, *29*, 371-375.

Assimilation and Contrast Effects ❊ Carl I. Hovland

in Reactions to Communication ❊ O. J. Harvey

and Attitude Change ❊ Muzafer Sherif

This paper presents an experiment on reactions to communication and on attitude changes by individuals whose initial stands on a controversial social issue diverged in varying degrees from positions advocated in communication. Study of the relationship between subject's (S's) attitude and the position advocated in communication may help resolve some apparently contradictory effects of communication aimed at changing attitudes.

Attempts to change attitudes in the direction advocated by communication on a social issue at times produce shifts in the direction opposite to that intended—the "boomerang effect." While numerous investigators have reported shifts of average test scores in the direction of communication (Hovland, 1954), a fairly common finding, even in these studies, is that some individuals shift their stand *away* from that presented in communication. Several studies reporting both positive and negative shifts in attitudes toward out-groups following communication are summarized by Williams (1947).

Thus, at times, persuasive communication produces a bi-modal distribution of attitude scores (Murphy, Murphy, and Newcomb 1937, pp. 874-875). For example, Remmers

(1938) obtained positive shifts on average scores following communications on conservation, social insurance, and labor unions, but the latter communication "sharply divided the group into two opposing tents" (Remmers, 1938, p. 201). In Knower's study prior to repeal of prohibition, "wet" communication to generally "dry" Ss and "dry" communication to generally "wet" Ss resulted in shifts in both positive and negative directions in each group (Knower, 1935). A rather striking instance of such opposing effects was reported by Wilke (1934), whose antiwar communication was presented at a time when the student population from which Ss were drawn was divided in controversy over this very issue.

A few studies, such as those by Manske (1937) and Russell and Robertson (1947), have found group shifts in the direction opposite to the stand presented in communication. A related finding reported by Williams and Remmers (1939) following communication on a rural issue was reduced variability and a comparatively less favorable stand by a group of rural youth in contrast to the increased variability in an urban group. Some authors who have obtained results in the direction away from communication in-

From the *Journal of Abnormal and Social Psychology,* 1957, 55, 242-252. Reprinted by permission of the authors and the American Psychological Association. This investigation was conducted as part of the Yale Communication Research Program. This series of studies, devoted to an analysis of factors related to attitude and opinion formation, is financed by a grant to Carl I. Hovland from the Rockefeller Foundation, whose support is gratefully acknowledged. Thanks are extended to Dr. Charles Shedd, now of Berea College, Mr. William Smith, and Mr. Richard Disney who participated in developing the procedures and in writing the communications used. We are also grateful to Dr. Laurence H. Snyder, Dean of the Graduate College, University of Oklahoma, for necessary administrative arrangements, and to Drs. Irving L. Janis, Robert P. Abelson, and Jack W. Brehm for suggestions made in the course of reading the manuscript.

sert the suggestion that too great divergence between S's stand on the issue and the stand presented in communication may have been responsible.

On the other hand, data from several recent studies suggest that the extent of influence increases as a function of the distance between position of communication and position of the recipient. Goldberg (1954) reports that the greater the discrepancy between an announced group norm and the S's own judgment the greater the change produced. In a still unpublished paper, French and Gyr (summarized in French, 1956) found a positive correlation between the degree of deviation between inducer and inductee and the amount of change. In a perceptual task, Lubin and Fisher (1956) obtained an increase in conformity to a partner's judgment as the distance increased up to a point where with great distance the proportion of movement declined. Hovland and Pritzker (1957) have shown that the larger the change in opinion advocated the greater the amount of change produced. The issues that were employed did not pertain to strongly rooted attitudes, but represented opinions on rather factual topics. The communicators used were authorities respected by the recipients.

A comprehensive analysis may be necessary to handle the above findings as well as results of studies employing communication on controversial social issues which suggest that too great a distance between S's attitude and the position advocated in communication produces "boomerang effects." One possible approach is through analysis of processes underlying judgments of motivationally neutral material, exemplified by psychophysical stimuli, as well as ego-involving verbal material, exemplified by controversial social issues. Investigations of judgmental processes and their theoretical relevance for the study of reaction to communication and attitude change will be presented in a forthcoming volume.

One set of findings suggests that S's position shifts toward the stand advocated in communication when the topic is not highly ego-involving and S's position does not diverge in the extreme from the stand advocated. This result seems akin to extension of an established reference scale in judgment of weights or inclinations following introduction of anchoring stimuli near the end stimulus of the series, as reported by Rogers (1941), Heintz (1950), and others. Sherif, Taub, and Hovland (Mimeo. Rep.) demonstrated this extension toward the anchor ("assimilation effect") as well as the effect of more remote anchors beyond either end of the stimulus series in constricting the reference scale of judgment and displacing judgment away from the anchor ("contrast effect"). Contrast phenomena may also appear in reaction to communication on an issue which is not highly involving for S if the position advocated is removed sufficiently from S's position, as the Lubin and Fisher results seem to indicate.

The above analysis based on findings from judgment studies suggested the further possibility that when Ss have established attitudes and are personally involved in a controversial social issue, their "own stand" functions as the major anchorage affecting reaction to and evaluation of communication. In this case, communication near S's stand would be assimilated to it, while communication at variance with S's own stand would be displaced still further away ("contrast effect"). Whether assimilation or contrast effects appear would be a function of the relative distance between S's own stand and the position of communication.

Accordingly, in the present experiment communications representing two opposite extremes and one moderate position on an ego-involving issue were presented to Ss whose initial stands on the issue ranged from one extreme to the other. The following hypotheses were formulated in terms of the effect of the relative distance between S's own stand and the position advocated upon evaluation and placement of communication as well as acceptance-rejection of that position:

1. Reactions to a communication will decrease in favorableness as the distance between S's own stand and the position advocated in the communication increases.
2. In evaluations by S of what position is advocated by a communication, the greater the distance between S's own stand and the position advocated in the communication, the greater the displacement *away* from S's position ("contrast effect"). When only a small discrepancy in position exists there will be a tendency for displacement *toward* S's stand ("assimilation effect").
3. With small distances between the position of the communication and that of the S, changes in S's opinion in the direction advocated by the communication will occur. With large distances between the stands taken by communication and by S, opinion changes in the direction advocated will be infrequent.

Method

ISSUE AND COMMUNICATIONS

The problem required that a controversial issue be selected, that Ss' stands on the controversy be ascertained, and that communications advocating various positions be presented to Ss with differing stands on the issue.

The issue chosen was the controversy over prohibition and repeal in a "dry" state. Shortly before the study began, a referendum was held to determine the fate of existing prohibition laws. The vote favored prohibition by a narrow margin.

In order to differentiate existing stands on the issue, representative statements made during the referendum campaign were collected from leading newspapers in two large cities. In addition, statements were obtained from 500 people in several localities on a random basis. These statements from public and private sources were sorted by 20 judges to secure clearly differentiated stands actually taken in the state. As a result, eight statements were chosen representing prevailing stands ranging from strong advocacy

of prohibition to strong advocacy of repeal. One additional "wet" statement was added as a logical counterpart of the most extreme "dry" stand, giving a total of nine statements. These statements are as follows, (I) being the additional item:

(A) Since alcohol is the curse of mankind, the sale and use of alcohol, including light beer, should be completely abolished.

(B) Since alcohol is the main cause of corruption in public life, lawlessness, and immoral acts, its sale and use should be prohibited.

(C) Since it is hard to stop at a reasonable moderation point in the use of alcohol, it is safer to discourage its use.

(D) Alcohol should not be sold or used except as a remedy for snake bites, cramps, colds, fainting, and other aches and pains.

(E) The arguments in favor and against the sale and use of alcohol are nearly equal.

(F) The sale of alcohol should be so regulated that it is available in limited quantities for special occasions.

(G) The sale and use of alcohol should be permitted with proper state controls, so that the revenue from taxation may be used for the betterment of schools, highways, and other state institutions.

(H) Since prohibition is a major cause of corruption in public life, lawlessness, immoral acts, and juvenile delinquency, the sale and use of alcohol should be legalized.

(I) It has become evident that man cannot get along without alcohol; therefore, there should be no restriction whatsoever on its sale and use.

Three communications of equal length were prepared, each requiring approximately 15 minutes for delivery. Arguments were those actually made by prohibition and repeal advocates during the referendum campaign. Arguments in the three communications were arranged in the same order, but from the viewpoint of the different parties to the controversy. One communication presented an extreme "dry" stand; one an extreme "wet" stand; and one a moderately wet stand, as typified in statement (F) above. All communications were presented by tape recording. The same voice was used in recording wet and dry communications.

PROCEDURE

In the first session, data on Ss' attitudes were obtained. At the time, Ss were not told that an additional session would be held. A schedule on "public issues" was presented with assurance of anonymity to Ss. Following a "dummy" issue (college football) Ss responded to the nine representative statements on prohibition. The following instructions were printed on the schedule and read aloud by the experimenter (E):

Below are some statements recently made concerning the wet-dry issue in this region.
Please read *all* of the statements carefully first before making any marks on this page.
Now that you have carefully read all the statements, *underline* the *one* statement that comes closest to your own point of view on the topic.
There may be other statement or statements which you find not objectionable from your point of view. Put a circle around the letter in front of such a statement or statements which are *not objectionable* to you.
Now cross out that one statement which is *most objectionable* from your point of view.
There may be other statement or statements which you find *objectionable* from your point of view. Cross out the letter in front of such a statement or statements which are *objectionable* to you.

These procedures yielded data on S's stand and also on the range of his tolerance for other stands in the series (*latitude of acceptance*), the range of stands he rejected (*latitude of rejection*) and those stands which he did not consider either acceptable or unacceptable. Thus the procedures gave S an opportunity not to take a stand in rela-

tion to items which he did not include in his latitude of acceptance or latitude of rejection, rather than requiring artificial "indifference" or "neutral" checkings.

From 1-3 weeks after the first session, a communication was presented by tape recording. Arrangements for its presentation were made through a member of the group being exposed and it was introduced as a talk actually made by a proponent of the stand advocated. The wet (repeal) communication was presented to extreme dry Ss and unselected Ss. The dry (prohibition) communication was presented to extreme wet and unselected Ss. The moderate communication was presented to wet, dry, and unselected Ss. The Ss participated in both "before" and "after" sessions in small groups of 10-30 under close supervision.

Following the communication, the same questionnaire for securing S's stand, latitudes of acceptance and rejection was filled in a second time. Reactions to the communication presented were obtained through ratings on like-dislike, reasonable-unreasonable, biased-unbiased, propaganda-fact dimensions. The Ss in the moderate communication groups also checked on a graphic rating scale ranging from extreme dry (A) to extreme wet (I) positions what they thought to be the stand taken in the communication itself.

SUBJECTS

Since the objective was to secure Ss who were definitely ego-involved, a special point was made of obtaining Ss with established and publicly committed dry or wet stands as a validity check of the paper-and-pencil checkings. It was not difficult to select Ss in the dry groups on the basis of known information concerning their stand. Two small samples from Women's Christian Temperance Union groups were obtained and a group of Salvation Army workers. The four remaining dry groups were students in preparation for the ministry or in strict denominational colleges. A total of 183 dry Ss participated in both sessions. It was much more difficult to obtain Ss whose position was known to be wet. However, on the basis of cases personally known to the Es or their assistants, 25 wet Ss were secured. For comparison, 290 additional Ss were obtained representing more moderate positions on the issue. These were college students secured from classes in journalism, speech, education, chemistry, etc. All Ss were residents of the dry state where prohibition was a lively topic of controversy at the time of the study. For the reason indicated, it was not possible to match the age levels of Ss in the three categories.

Results

EVALUATION OF THE COMMUNICATION

A five-item scale was used to measure the audience's evaluation of the fairness and impartiality of the communication. In Figure 1, the percentages of Ss in each group

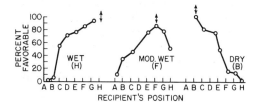

Fig. 1. Percentage of favorable evaluations of wet (H), moderately wet (F), and dry (B) communications for Ss holding various positions on prohibition (based on mean acceptable statement). (Positions of communications indicated by arrow.)

whose reactions were favorable are graphed for the three communications. On the abscissa the stands of the recipient (mean of statements checked acceptable) are presented and on the ordinate the percentage of favorable evaluations. It will be observed that there is an extremely close relationship between the individual's own stand on the issue and his evaluation of communication.

The two communications advocating extreme positions have their peak of favorable responses among those holding corresponding extreme positions. The maximum favorable reaction for the moderate communication is found among those holding a moderate position. The data provide quantitative information to support the expectation from earlier studies (Hovland, Janis, and Kelley, 1953; Weiss and Fine, 1955) that individuals who are in favor of the opinion advocated will consider the communication fair and unbiased, but that those with an opposed stand will regard an identical communication as propagandistic and unfair.

PLACEMENT OF THE POSITION OF THE COMMUNICATION

The principal results of the experiment are those pertaining to the recipient's perception of the stand advocated in the communication. We asked S to indicate on a graphic scale, ranging from extreme dry position to extreme wet position, what he thought to be the position of the moderately wet communication (at F). From our previous study on assimilation-contrast effects with psychophysical data we predicted that positions differing only slightly from one's own would be "assimilated," while larger differences between one's own position and that of the communication would be exaggerated, showing a "contrast" effect. In Figure 2, results concerning this prediction are presented. The S's own position is indicated on the abscissa and along the ordinate the average rating of the position of the communication is given for the speech in which a moderately wet position (about F) was advocated. The dots indicate the mean placement of the position of the communication for Ss who indicate each particular position as their own stand. The squares represent the mean placement of the position advocated when S's position is estimated from the mean of the acceptable positions

checked. The dotted line indicates a hypothetical relationship in which Ss holding the
same position as the communication report
its position accurately (at F), those a small
distance removed assimilate it to their own
position, and those still further removed exaggerate the position revealing a contrast
effect.

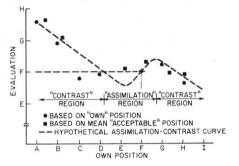

Fig. 2. Average placements of position of moderately wet communication (F) by Ss holding
various positions on the issue, plotted against
hypothetical assimilation-contrast curve.

The expectation is fulfilled that those at
the wet end judge that the communication
advocated a drier position than it did and
those at the dry end judge that it was advocating a wetter position than it did. Those
nearer the position of the communication reported it more objectively. The evidence
concerning assimilation deviates somewhat
from the theoretical curve. There were too
few Ss with intermediate positions to enable
us to determine these positions adequately.

ACCEPTANCE-REJECTION OF STANDS

Each S was asked to indicate not only the
stand which best represented his, but also
other stands which were more or less acceptable (i.e., his latitude of acceptance), the
stand most clearly opposed to his position,
and others not acceptable (i.e., his latitude
of rejection). From these data, we find that
Ss with more extreme positions tend to reject more frequently positions not within
their latitude of acceptance. The Ss with

middle positions are more apt to rate positions removed from their own as indifferent.
In Table 1, data are presented showing the

TABLE 1

ACCEPTABILITY OF STATEMENTS IN RELATION
TO EXTREMITY OF SUBJECTS' POSITION
ON ISSUE

S's Positions	N	Mean Number of Items Accept-able	Mean Number of Items Not Checked	Mean Number of Items Re-jected
1. Extreme (A, B, G, H, I)	193	2.81	1.48	4.71
2. Intermediate (C, D, E, F)	37	3.05	2.24	3.70
p				<.03

mean number of items rated "also acceptable," "unacceptable" and "neither acceptable nor unacceptable" by Ss with strong
positions (A, B, G, H, I) as compared with
those by Ss with more moderate positions
(C, D, E, F). It will be observed that a significantly greater number of items are
judged unacceptable by Ss with extreme
stands. Smaller differences between the
groups exist in the number rated acceptable.
These results tie in with our earlier studies
(Hovland and Sherif, 1952; Sherif and Hovland, 1953) in which we found that Ss with
extreme positions and considerable ego-
involvement in an issue have raised thresholds of acceptance and lowered thresholds
of rejection in placing items concerning that
issue, resulting in smaller latitudes of acceptance and greater latitudes of rejection than
for Ss with moderate positions. These findings can be used in constructing the expected latitudes of acceptance and rejection
of the individual for an ego-involving issue
once his own position is ascertained and
possibly in predicting evaluation of communication which stands at a given distance
from his own position. An attempt in this
direction is presented in the discussion.

CHANGES IN OPINION FOR GROUPS
WITH DIFFERENT STANDS
ON THE ISSUE

Finally, it would be expected on the basis of the considerations previously discussed that those holding a position at great variance with that being presented in the communication would be relatively little modified in their opinion. The index of opinion change was based on the mean position of the statements checked by Ss as being "acceptable" to them. A value of 1 indicates the extreme dry end in which only statement A was checked. Correspondingly, a value of 9 is at the wet end with only statement I checked. The positions of the three speeches at B, F, and H would thus be represented by values of 2, 6, and 8, respectively.

Table 2 gives the mean position for five

TABLE 2

OPINION CHANGE—CHANGES IN MEAN
ACCEPTABLE STATEMENT FOR Ss WITH
DIFFERING INITIAL STANDS

Group	N	Before Comm.	After Comm.	Change in Direction of Comm.
Wet Communication (H)				
Drys	69	2.39	2.34	− .05°
Unselected	92	5.10	5.65	+ .55°
Dry Communication (B)				
Wets	25	6.70	6.74	− .04
Unselected	87	5.90	5.78	+ .14
Moderately Wet Communication (F)				
Drys	114	2.17	2.26	+ .09

° Difference between changes: $p = < .03$ (one tail).

criterion groups before and after the communication, together with the average amount of change. Only the unselected group exposed to the wet communication should be expected to show sizeable change. The four other groups all have initial positions quite removed from the position being advocated. While the dry and unselected

groups exposed to the wet communication do differ substantially in their initial positions, the positions of the wet and unselected groups are similar, since the unselected group (college students) initially holds a rather wet position.

As predicted, there is a significantly greater change for the unselected group given the wet communication than for the dry group $(p = < .03)$. As in all studies in which the variable with which we are concerned cannot be directly manipulated, the possibility must be considered that there are factors other than position on the issue which are correlated with it and provide the basis for the relationship obtained.

In Table 3, results are presented for the

TABLE 3

OPINION CHANGE—PERCENTAGE OF Ss
CHANGING IN DIRECTION OF COMMUNICATION
OR IN OPPOSED DIRECTION

Group	N	Change in Direction of Comm.	No Change	Change in Direction Opposed to Comm.	Net Change
Wet Communication (H)					
		%	%	%	%
Drys	69	27.5	49.3	23.2	+ 4.5°
Unselected	92	52.2	23.9	23.9	+28.3°
Dry Communication (B)					
Wets	25	24.0	56.0	20.0	+4.0
Unselected	87	40.2	33.4	26.4	+13.8
Moderately Wet Communication (F)					
Drys	114	31.6	49.1	19.3	+12.3

° Difference between changes: $p = < .04$ (one tail).

same groups in terms of the percentage of Ss who are influenced either in the direction advocated by the communication or in the direction opposed to it. The net change column represents the differences between those changed in the direction advocated and those changed in the opposite direction. The net change is greater among the unselected group than among the drys when a wet communication is presented ($p = <.04$). Twenty-eight per cent of the former and only four per cent of the latter changed in the direction advocated. It will also be seen that the amount of change produced among the drys by a moderately wet communication (at F) is greater than that produced by the more extreme wet communication (at H). The net proportion changed by the former is 12 per cent, while it is only 4 per cent for the latter. This difference, however, is not statistically significant and, in any case, it is difficult to establish that the two different communications were inherently equivalent in persuasiveness.

It will be noted that by confining our comparisons to groups who were initially selected as having known differences in their stand on the issue (either wet or dry) we were able to avoid the regression effects often found in studies where amounts of change are compared for groups differentiated solely on the basis of initial scores on the attitude measure. Under the latter conditions, those with more extreme scores often regress toward the mean and this can either obscure the effect or produce a relationship artifactually.

Finally, it will be noted from Table 3 that the predominant response among Ss holding extreme positions is to remain uninfluenced by the communication. Even where Ss in these groups were influenced, changes were seldom found in the item they checked as best representing their own position. Instead, there was typically only an increase in the number of other statements intermediate between their own position and that of the communication which they would check as "also acceptable."

Discussion

The results presented lend support to the three hypotheses pertaining to evaluation and placement of communication and attitude change as a function of the relative dis-

tance between S's stand and the position of communication on an ego-involving issue. Our findings suggest that the relative distance between Ss' attitudes and position of communication may be useful in explaining apparently contradictory effects of communication in producing attitude change in the intended direction, no change, and change in the opposite direction. This approach seems to have predictive value for S's reactions to other positions on an issue and susceptibility to change once his own stand is ascertained.

On the basis of results in Table 1 and evidence from previous studies (Hovland and Sherif, 1952; Sherif and Hovland, 1953), we can formalize the pattern of acceptance and rejection for various positions by Ss holding each initial position. In Table 4, the

TABLE 4

HYPOTHETICAL LATITUDES OF ACCEPTANCE AND REJECTION OF Ss HOLDING EACH POSITION

(Columns show latitude of acceptance (strongly accept plus accept), latitude of rejection (strongly reject plus reject) and positions neither acceptable nor unacceptable to Ss holding given positions.)

Rating Positions	Own Position								
	A	B	C	D	E	F	G	H	I
A	√√	√	0	×	×	××	××	××	××
B	√	√√	√	0	×	×	×	×	×
C	0	√	√√	√	0	×	×	×	×
D	×	0	√	√√	√	0	×	×	×
E	×	×	0	√	√√	√	0	×	×
F	×	×	×	0	√	√√	√	0	×
G	×	×	×	×	0	√	√√	√	0
H	×	×	×	×	×	0	√	√√	√
I	××	××	××	××	×	×	0	√	√√

Code: √√ = strongly accept; √ = accept; 0 = neither accept nor reject; × = reject; ×× = strongly reject.

Mean frequencies in above table:

	A,B,G,H,I	C,D,E,F
√ and √√	2.7	3.0
0	1.3	2.0
× and ××	5.0	4.0

expected response to each opinion item is given for Ss checking positions from A to I as their most acceptable stand. The S's own stand is indicated by $\sqrt{}\sqrt{}$, "also acceptable" with $\sqrt{}$, completely unacceptable with $\times\times$, other stands unacceptable with $\times$, and not clearly acceptable or unacceptable with 0. Thus, the table presents a hypothetical pattern for the "latitude of acceptance" (consisting of S's own position and other acceptable positions) and "latitude of rejection" (consisting of all unacceptable positions) for Ss holding each position. Where sufficient numbers of Ss are available for a given stand, the empirical distributions of responses show a close correspondence to these hypothetical patterns.

This model for latitudes of acceptance and rejection can be used to explicate results on reaction to communication. By comparison with Figure 2, showing placement of the position advocated in the moderate communication, it can be seen that "contrast effects" begin to appear when the position advocated falls within S's latitude of rejection, an area far removed from his own stand. If the position advocated in communication falls at the limits or slightly beyond the latitude of acceptance, it would be more likely to be assimilated to the latitude of acceptance, although this trend is less clear in the present study.

If we assume that evaluation of communication on an issue in which S is personally involved depends on two factors: (a) what the position of communications is perceived to be and (b) what segment of the acceptance-rejection range is associated with the perceived position, we can predict from Fig. 2 and Table 4 the degree of favorableness of evaluations of the communication (Fig. 1). When the communication falls within the latitude of acceptance ($\sqrt{}$ or $\sqrt{}\sqrt{}$), it is judged fair and unbiased. As the perceived position of communication moves outside the latitude of acceptance into the latitude of rejection ($\times$), it is increasingly considered unfair and propagandistic. For example, an individual checking B as his most acceptable

stand displaces the F communication to G ("contrast effect") which, according to Table 4, is clearly in his latitude of rejection; an S checking A as his own stand places the F communication between G-H, still further toward the extreme end of the latitude of rejection, and the percentage of favorable evaluations of the communication declines still further (cf. Fig. 1).

Two general problems are suggested by the present analysis. Since S's stands on an issue of personal concern produce variation in reaction to communication and attitude change, the effect of the degree of ego-involvement in issues needs exploration. It is expected that latitudes of acceptance and rejection will vary as a function of the degree of ego-involvement, and these variations may affect the ranges in which assimilation and contrast effects in judging communication occur. A person strongly committed on an issue will be more discriminating in accepting stands (raised threshold of acceptance) while one who is less committed will be willing to consider a larger number of alternative positions (lowered threshold of acceptance). Corresponding effects on extent of opinion change with different distances between S and communication are to be expected. With low involvement issues one would anticipate increase in opinion change with increased separation over a considerable range, whereas with high involvement issues one would expect opinion change over only a narrow range of separation, with resistance to acceptance of the communication for the remaining distances.

Finally, an interesting problem remains as to the role of the communicator in influencing the range of assimilation. In the Hovland-Pritzker study (1957) the communicator was an authority respected by Ss on the issue presented. There the greater the distance between communicator position and that of S, the greater the opinion change. In the present study, on the other hand, the communicator was an anonymous individual whose acceptability might be determined by the stand taken by him on the issue under discussion. If he differed in position only slightly from S he would be regarded as fair and authoritative and bring about a shift in opinion, but if he differed greatly he would be regarded as incompetent and biased and fail to influence S's opinion. To explore this factor and the one of involvement mentioned in the preceding paragraph, a factorially designed experiment will be required in which type of communicator (positive, negative, and neutral), type of issue (high involvement and low involvement), and distance between the communicator's stand and S's own stand are all systematically varied to permit analysis not only of the main effects but also of the more interesting interaction effects.

Summary

The relationship between the attitude of the recipient and the position advocated in a communication was studied under conditions where a communicator not known to S presents a point of view on a controversial issue which differs from that of S by varying amounts.

The topic discussed was prohibition of alcohol. The Ss came from a dry state where this was a lively issue. Each S indicated for a series of nine statements ranging from extreme dry to extreme wet: (a) the position most acceptable to him, (b) other acceptable positions, (c) the position most objectionable to him, and (d) other objectionable positions. Groups of Ss were selected whose stands on the issue were known (e.g., WCTU members) for comparison with unselected groups of college students. In all, 514 Ss were used. In a subsequent session "wet" groups received a "dry" or "moderately wet" communication; "dry" groups received a "wet" or "moderately wet" communication; unselected groups received a "dry," "wet," or "moderately wet" communication. After the communication, opinion measurements and reactions to communication were obtained. The findings were as follows:

1. When the distance between S's own stand and the position advocated in communication is small, the communication is judged favorably, as fair and factual. With increasing distance, the favorable reaction is sharply reduced and the communication perceived as propagandistic and unfair.
2. The Ss whose own stands diverge widely from the position advocated perceive the communication as further removed from their own stand than it is ("contrast effect"). The present results indicate, though less clearly, that Ss whose own stands are close to the position advocated perceive the communication as closer to their own stand than is the case ("assimilation effect").
3. The most frequent result for Ss whose own stand diverges widely from that advocated in communication is to remain unchanged in their initial attitudes. More Ss with moderate positions closer to the stand in communication changed in the direction advocated.

It is suggested that the relative distance between S's own attitude and communication along with S's latitudes of acceptance and rejection for various stands on the issue may provide a basis for predicting reactions to communication and susceptibility to change. Further research varying degree of ego-involvement in issues and attitudes toward the communicator is suggested.

References

FRENCH, J. R. P., JR. A formal theory of social power. *Psychol. Rev.*, 1956, 63, 181-194.

GOLDBERG, S. C. Three situational determinants of conformity to social norms. *J. abnorm. soc. Psychol.*, 1954, 49, 325-329.

HEINTZ, R. The effect of remote anchoring points upon judgments of lifted weights. *J. exp. Psychol.*, 1950, 40, 584-591.

HOVLAND, C. I. Effects of mass media of communication. In G. Lindzey (Ed.), *Handbook of social psychology*, Vol. 2. Reading, Mass.: Addison-Wesley, 1954.

HOVLAND, C. I., JANIS, I. L., and KELLEY, H. H. *Communication and persuasion.* New Haven: Yale Univer. Press, 1953.

HOVLAND, C. I., and PRITZKER, H. Extent of opinion change as a function of amount of change advocated. *J. abnorm. soc. Psychol.*, 1957, 54, 257-261.

HOVLAND, C. I., and SHERIF, M. Judgmental phenomena and scales of attitude measurement: item displacement in Thurstone scales. *J. abnorm. soc. Psychol.*, 1952, 47, 822-833.

KNOWER, F. H. Experimental studies of changes in attitudes: I. A study of the effect of oral argument on change of attitude. *J. soc. Psychol.*, 1935, 6, 315-347.

LUBIN, A., and FISHER, S. Distance as a determinant of influence in a two-person continuous interaction situation. E.P.A. Talk. Title in *Amer. Psychologist*, 1956, 11, 491.

MANSKE, A. J. The reflection of teachers' attitudes in the attitudes of their pupils. In G. Murphy, L. B. Murphy, and T. M. Newcomb (Eds.), *Experimental social psychology*. New York: Harper & Row, 1937.

MURPHY, G., MURPHY, L. B., and NEWCOMB, T. M. *Experimental social psychology.* New York: Harper & Row, 1937.

REMMERS, H. H. Propaganda in the schools: do the effects last? *Publ. Opin. Quart.*, 1938, 2, 197-210.

ROGERS, S. The anchoring of absolute judgments. *Arch. Psychol.*, 1941, No. 261.

RUSSELL, D. H., and ROBERTSON, I. V. Influencing attitudes toward minority groups in a junior high school. *Sch. Rev.*, 1947, 55, 205-213.

SHERIF, M., and HOVLAND, C. I. Judgmental phenomena and scales of attitude measurement: placement of items with individual choice of number of categories. *J. abnorm. soc. Psychol.*, 1953, 48, 135-141.

SHERIF, M., TAUB, D., and HOVLAND, C. I. Assimilation and contrast effects of anchoring stimuli on judgments. (Mimeo. Rep.)

WEISS, W., and FINE, B. J. Opinion change as a function of some intrapersonal attributes of the communicatees. *J. abnorm. soc. Psychol.*, 1955, 51, 246-253.

WILKE, W. H. An experimental comparison of the speech, the radio, and the printed page as propaganda devices. *Arch. Psychol.*, 1934, No. 169.

WILLIAMS, A. C., and REMMERS, H. H. Persistence of attitudes concerning conservation issues. *J. exp. Educ.*, 1939, 40, 354-361.

WILLIAMS, R. M., JR. *The reduction of intergroup tensions.* New York: Soc. Sci. Res. Council, Bull. 57, 1947.

The Two-step Flow of Communication: An Up-to-date Report on an Hypothesis ❧ Elihu Katz

Analysis of the process of decision-making during the course of an election campaign led the authors of *The People's Choice* to suggest that the flow of mass communica- tions may be less direct than was commonly supposed. It may be, they proposed, that influences stemming from the mass media first reach "opinion leaders" who, in turn, pass

From *Public Opinion Quarterly*, 1957, *21*, 61-78. Reprinted by permission of the author and publisher. This is an abridged version of a chapter in the author's "Interpersonal Relations and Mass Communications: Studies in the Flow of Influence," unpublished Ph.D. thesis, Columbia University, 1956. The advice and encouragement of Dr. Paul F. Lazarsfeld in the writing of this thesis are gratefully acknowledged.

on what they read and hear to those of their every-day associates for whom they are influential. This hypothesis was called "the two-step flow of communication" (Lazarsfeld, Berelson, and Gaudet, 1948).

The hypothesis aroused considerable interest. The authors themselves were intrigued by its implications for democratic society. It was a healthy sign, they felt, that people were still most successfully persuaded by give-and-take with other people and that the influence of the mass media was less automatic and less potent than had been assumed. For social theory, and for the design of communications research, the hypothesis suggested that the image of modern urban society needed revision. The image of the audience as a mass of disconnected individuals hooked up to the media but not to each other could not be reconciled with the idea of a two-step flow of communication implying, as it did, networks of interconnected individuals through which mass communications are channeled.

Of all the ideas in *The People's Choice*, however, the two-step flow hypothesis is probably the one that was least well documented by empirical data. And the reason for this is clear: the design of the study did not anticipate the importance which interpersonal relations would assume in the analysis of the data. Given the image of the atomized audience which characterized so much of mass media research, the surprising thing is that interpersonal influence attracted the attention of the researchers at all.[1]

In the almost seventeen years since the voting study was undertaken, several studies at the Bureau of Applied Social Research of Columbia University have attempted to examine the hypothesis and to build upon it. Four such studies will be singled out for review. These are Merton's (1949) study of interpersonal influence and communications behavior in Rovere; the

Decatur study of decision-making in marketing, fashions, movie-going and public affairs, reported by Katz and Lazarsfeld (1955); the Elmira study of the 1948 election campaign reported by Berelson, Lazarsfeld, and McPhee (1954); and, finally, a very recent study by Katz and Menzel on the diffusion of a new drug among doctors (1955).

These studies will serve as a framework within which an attempt will be made to report on the present state of the two-step flow hypothesis, to examine the extent to which it has found confirmation and the ways in which it has been extended, contracted and reformulated. More than that, the studies will be drawn upon to highlight the successive strategies which have been developed in attempting to take systematic account of interpersonal relations in the design of communications research, aiming ultimately at a sort of "survey sociometry." Finally, these studies, plus others which will be referred to in passing, will provide an unusual opportunity to reflect upon problems in the continuity of social research.[2]

Findings of The People's Choice

The starting point for this review must be an examination of the evidence in the 1940 voting study which led to the original formulation of the hypothesis. Essentially, three distinct sets of findings seem to have been involved. The first had to do with *the impact of personal influence*. It is reported

---

[1] For the discussion of the image of the atomized audience and the contravening empirical evidence, see Katz and Lazarsfeld (1955, pp. 15-42), Friedson (1953), and Janowitz (1952).

[2] Other authors who have drawn upon the concepts of opinion leadership and the two-step flow of communication, and developed them further, are Riley and Riley (1951), Eisenstadt (1952, 1955), Riesman (1952), and Handel (1950). The program of research in international communications at the Bureau of Applied Social Research has given considerable attention to opinion leadership; see Glock (1952-1953), Stycos (1952), and the forthcoming book by Daniel Lerner, Paul Berkman and Lucille Pevsner, *Modernizing the Middle East*. Forthcoming studies by Peter H. Rossi and by Robert D. Leigh and Martin A. Trow are also concerned with the interplay of personal and mass media influences in local communities.

that people who made up their minds late in the campaign, and those who changed their minds during the course of the campaign, were more likely than other people to mention personal influence as having figured in their decisions. The political pressure brought to bear by everyday groups such as family and friends is illustrated by reference to the political homogeneity which characterizes such groups. What's more, on an average day, a greater number of people reported participating in discussion of the election than hearing a campaign speech or reading a newspaper editorial. From all of this, the authors conclude that personal contacts appear to have been both more frequent and more effective than the mass media in influencing voting decisions (Lazarsfeld, Berelson, and Gaudet, 1948).

The second ingredient that went into the formulation of the hypothesis concerned *the flow of personal influence*. Given the apparent importance of interpersonal influence, the obvious next step was to ask whether some people were more important than others in the transmission of influence. The study sought to single out the "opinion leaders" by two questions: "Have you recently tried to convince anyone of your political ideas?", and "Has anyone recently asked you for your advice on a political question?" Comparing the opinion leaders with others, they found the opinion leaders more interested in the election. And from the almost even distribution of opinion leaders throughout every class and occupation, as well as the frequent mention by decision-makers of the influence of friends, co-workers and relatives, it was concluded that opinion leaders are to be found on every level of society and presumably, therefore, are very much like the people whom they influence (Lazarsfeld, Berelson and Gaudet, 1948).

A further comparison of leaders and others with respect to mass media habits provides the third ingredient: *the opinion leaders and the mass media*. Compared with the rest of the population, opinion leaders were found to be considerably more exposed to the radio, to the newspapers and to magazines, that is, to the formal media of communication.

Now the argument is clear: If word-of-mouth is so important, and if word-of-mouth specialists are widely dispersed, and if these specialists are more exposed to the media than the people whom they influence, then perhaps "ideas often flow from radio and print to opinion leaders and from these to the less active sections of the population" (Lazarsfeld, Berelson, and Gaudet, 1948).

Design of the Voting Study

For studying the flow of influence as it impinges on the making of decisions, the study design of *The People's Choice* had several advantages. Most important was the panel method which made it possible to locate changes almost as soon as they occurred and then to correlate change with the influences reaching the decision-maker. Secondly, the unit of effect, the decision, was a tangible indicator of change which could readily be recorded. But for studying that part of the flow of influence which had to do with contacts among people, the study design fell short, since it called for a random sample of individuals abstracted from their social environments. It is this traditional element in the design of survey research which explains the leap that had to be made from the available data to the hypothesis of the two-step flow of communication.

Because every man in a random sample can speak only for himself, opinion leaders in the 1940 voting study had to be located by self-designation, that is, on the basis of their own answers to the two advice-giving questions cited above.[3] In effect, respond-

[3] Strictly speaking, of course, if a respondent reports whether or not he is a leader he is not speaking for himself but for his followers, real or imagined. Furthermore, it ought to be pointed out for the record that it is sometimes possible for a respondent to speak for others besides himself. The voting studies, for example, ask respondents to report the vote-intentions of other family members, of friends, of co-workers, though this procedure is of undetermined validity.

ents were simply asked to report whether or not they were opinion leaders. Much more important than the obvious problem of validity posed by this technique is the fact that it does not permit a comparison of leaders with their respective followers, but only of leaders and non-leaders in general. The data, in other words, consist only of two statistical groupings: people who said they were advice-givers and those who did not. Therefore, the fact that leaders were more interested in the election than non-leaders cannot be taken to mean that influence flows from more interested persons to less interested ones. To state the problem drastically, it may even be that the leaders influence only each other, while the uninterested non-leaders stand outside the influence market altogether. Nevertheless, the temptation to assume that the non-leaders are the followers of the leaders is very great, and while *The People's Choice* is quite careful about this, it cannot help but succumb.[4] Thus, from the fact that the opinion leaders were more exposed to the mass media than the non-leaders came the suggestion of the two-step flow of communication; yet, manifestly, it can be true only if the non-leaders are, in fact, followers of the leaders.

The authors themselves point out that a far better method would have been based on "asking people to whom they turn for advice on the issue at hand and then investigating the interaction between advisers and advisees. But that procedure would be extremely difficult, if not impossible, since few of the related 'leaders' and 'followers' would happen to be included in the sample (Lazarsfeld, Berelson, and Gaudet, 1948). As will be shown immediately, this is perhaps the most important problem which succeeding studies have attempted to solve.

Designs of Three Subsequent Studies

To this point, two aspects of the original statement of the two-step flow hypothesis have been reviewed. First of all, the hypothesis has been shown to have three distinct components, concerning respectively the impact of personal influence; the flow of personal influence; and the relationship of opinion leaders to the mass media. The evidence underlying each has been examined. Secondly, the design of the study has been recalled in order to point up the difficulty that arises from attempting to cope with the fundamentally new problem of incorporating *both* partners to an influence transaction into a cross-sectional study.

From this point forward, the major focus will turn to those studies that have succeeded *The People's Choice.* We will first report the different ways in which three of the four studies selected for review approached the problem of designing research on interpersonal influence.[5] Thereafter, the substantive findings of the several studies will be reviewed and evaluated so as to constitute an up-to-date report on the accumulating evidence for and against the hypothesis of the two-step flow of communication.

1. THE ROVERE STUDY

Undertaken just as the 1940 voting study was being completed, the earliest of the three studies was conducted in a small town in New Jersey. It began by asking a sample of 86 respondents to name the people to whom they turned for information and advice regarding a variety of matters. Hun-

---

[4] There is an alternative procedure which is something of an improvement. Respondents can be asked not only whether they have given advice but whether they have taken advice. This was done in the Decatur and Elmira studies which are cited below. Thus the non-leaders can be classified in terms of whether or not they are in the influence market at all, that is, whether or not they are "followers."

[5] The Elmira study will be omitted at this point because its design is essentially the same as that of the 1940 voting study except for the important fact that it obtained from each respondent considerably more information about the vote-intentions of others in his environment, the kinds of people he talks with, etc., than was done in *The People's Choice.*

dreds of names were mentioned in response, and those who were designated four times or more were considered opinion leaders. These influentials were then sought out and interviewed (Merton, 1949).

Here, then, is the initial attempt, on a pilot scale, to solve the problem of research design posed by *The People's Choice*. To locate influentials, this study suggests, begin by asking somebody, "Who influences you?" and proceed from the persons influenced to those who are designated as influential.

Two important differences between this study and the 1940 voting study must be pointed out. First, there is a difference in the conception of opinion leadership. Whereas the voting study regards any advice-giver as an opinion leader if he influences even one other person (such as a husband telling his wife for whom to vote), the leaders singled out by the criterion employed in Rovere were almost certainly wielders of wider influence.

Secondly, the voting study, at least by implication, was interested in such questions as the extent of the role of interpersonal influence in decision-making and its relative effectiveness compared to the mass media. The Rovere study took for granted the importance of this kind of influence, and proceeded to try to find the people who play key roles in its transmission.

A final point to make in connection with the design of this study is that it makes use of the initial interviews almost exclusively to *locate* opinion leaders and hardly at all to explore the *relationships* between leaders and followers. Once the leaders were designated, almost exclusive attention was given to classifying them into different types, studying the communications behavior of the different types and the interaction among the leaders themselves, but very little attention was given to the interaction between the leaders and the original informants who designated them.

2. THE DECATUR STUDY

[The Decatur study], carried out in 1945-46, tried to go a step further.[6] Like the voting study, but unlike Rovere, it tried to account for decisions—specific instances in which the effect of various influences could be discerned and assessed. Like Rovere, but unlike the voting study, it provided for interviews with the persons whom individuals in the initial sample had credited as influential in the making of recent decisions (in the realms of marketing, movie-going, and public affairs). The focus of the study this time was not on the opinion leaders alone, but (1) on the relative importance of personal influence and (2) on the person who named the leader as well as the leader—the adviser-advisee dyad.

Ideally, then, this study could ask whether opinion leaders tended to be from the same social class as their followers or whether the tendency was for influence to flow from the upper classes downwards. Were members of the dyads likely to be of the same age, the same sex, etc.? Was the leader more interested in the particular sphere of influence than his advisee? Was he more likely to be exposed to the mass media?

Just as the dyad could be constructed by proceeding from an advisee to his adviser, it was also possible to begin the other way around by talking first to a person who claimed to have acted as an adviser, and then locating the person he said he had influenced. The Decatur study tried this too. Using the same kind of self-designating questions employed in the voting study, persons who designated themselves as influential were asked to indicate the names of those whom they had influenced. By "snowballing" to the people thus designated, there arose the opportunity not only to study the interaction between adviser and advisee but also to explore the extent to which people who designated themselves as influential

[6] See Katz and Lazarsfeld (1955).

were confirmed in their self-evaluations by those whom they allegedly had influenced. Proceeding in this way, the researchers hoped to be able to say something about the validity of the self-designating technique (Katz and Lazarsfeld, 1955).[7]

The authors of *The People's Choice* had said that "asking people to whom they turn and then investigating the interaction between advisers and advisees . . . would be extremely difficult if not impossible." And, in fact, it proved to be extremely difficult. Many problems were encountered in the field work, the result of which was that not all the "snowball" interviews could be completed.[8] In many parts of the analysis of the data, therefore, it was necessary to revert to comparisons of leaders and non-leaders, imputing greater influence to groups with higher concentrations of self-designated leadership. Yet, in principle, it was demonstrated that a study design taking account of interpersonal relations was both possible and profitable to execute.

But about the time it became evident that this goal was within reach, the goal itself began to change. It began to seem desirable to take account of chains of influence longer than those involved in the dyad; and hence to view the adviser-advisee dyad as one component of a more elaborately structured social group.

These changes came about gradually and for a variety of reasons. First of all, findings from the Decatur study and from the later Elmira study revealed that the opinion lead-

ers themselves often reported that their own decisions were influenced by still other people (Berelson, Lazarsfeld, and McPhee, 1954). It began to seem desirable, therefore, to think in terms of the opinion leaders of opinion leaders (Katz and Lazarsfeld, 1955). Secondly, it became clear that opinion leadership could not be viewed as a "trait" which some people possess and others do not, although the voting study sometimes implied this view. Instead, it seemed quite apparent that the opinion leader is influential at certain times and with respect to certain substantive areas by virtue of the fact that he is "empowered" to be so by other members of his group. Why certain people are chosen must be accounted for not only in demographic terms (social status, sex, age, etc.) but also in terms of the structure and values of the groups of which both adviser and advisee are members. Thus, the unexpected rise of young men to opinion leadership in traditional groups, when these groups faced the new situations of urbanization and industrialization, can be understood only against the background of old and new patterns of social relations within the group and of old and new patterns of orientation to the world outside the group.[9] Reviewing the literature of small group research hastened the formulation of this conception (Katz and Lazarsfeld, 1955).

One other factor shaped the direction of the new program as well. Reflecting upon the Decatur study, it became clear that while one could talk about the role of various influences in the making of fashion *decisions by individuals,* the study design was not adequate for the study of fashion in the aggregate—*fashion as a process of diffusion* —as long as it did not take account of either

---

[7] About two-thirds of the alleged influences confirmed the fact that a conversation had taken place between themselves and the self-designated influential on the subject matter in question. Of these, about 80 per cent further confirmed that they had received advice. The extent of confirmation is considerably less in the realm of public affairs than it is in marketing or fashion.

[8] Partly this was due to inability to locate the designated people, but partly, too, to the fact that original respondents did not always know the person who had influenced them, as is obvious, for example, in the case of a woman copying another woman's hat style, etc.

[9] See, for example, the articles by Eisenstadt (1952, 1955) and Glock (1952-1953). The Rovere study, too, takes careful account of the structure of social relations and values in which influentials are embedded, and discusses the various avenues to influentiality open to different kinds of people.

the content of the decision or the time factor involved. The decisions of the "fashion changers" studied in Decatur might have cancelled each other out: while Mrs. X reported a change from Fashion A to Fashion B, Mrs. Y might have been reporting a change from B to A. What is true for fashion is true for any other diffusion phenomenon: to study it, one must trace the flow of some specific item over time. Combining this interest in diffusion with that of studying the role of more elaborate social networks of communication gave birth to a new study which focused on (1) a specific item, (2) diffusion over time, (3) through the social structure of an entire community.

3. THE DRUG STUDY

This study was conducted to determine the way in which doctors make decisions to adopt new drugs. This time, when it came to designing a study which would take account of the possible role of interpersonal influence among physicians, it became clear that there were so few physicians (less than one and one-half per 1000 population) that it was feasible to interview all members of the medical profession in several cities. If all doctors (or all doctors in specialties concerned with the issue at hand) could be interviewed, then there would be no doubt that all adviser-advisee pairs would fall within the sample. All such pairs could then be located within the context of larger social groupings of doctors, which could be measured by sociometric methods.

Doctors in the relevant specialties in four midwestern cities were interviewed. In addition to questions on background, attitudes, drug-use, exposure to various sources of information and influence, and the like, each doctor was also asked to name the three colleagues he saw most often socially, the three colleagues with whom he talked most frequently about cases, and the three colleagues to whom he looked for information and advice (Menzel and Katz, 1955).

In addition to the opportunity of mapping the networks of interpersonal relations, the drug study also provided for the two other factors necessary for a true diffusion study: attention to a specific item in the course of gaining acceptance, and a record of this diffusion over time. This was accomplished by means of an audit of prescriptions on file in the local pharmacies of the cities studied, which made it possible to date each doctor's earliest use of a particular new drug—a drug which had gained widespread acceptance a few months before the study had begun. Each doctor could thus be classified in terms of the promptness of his decision to respond to the innovation, and in terms of other information provided by the prescription audit.

Altogether, compared with the earlier studies, the drug study imposes a more objective framework—both psychological and sociological—on the decision. First of all, the decision-maker himself is not the only source of information concerning his decision. Objective data from the prescription record are used as well. Secondly, the role of different influences is assessed not only on the basis of the decision-maker's own reconstruction of the event, but also on the basis of objective correlations from which inferences concerning the flow of influence can be drawn. For example, doctors who adopted the new drug early were more likely to be participants in out-of-town medical specialty meetings than those who adopted it later.

Similarly, it is possible to infer the role of social relations in doctor's decision-making not only from the doctor's own testimony concerning the role of social influences but also from the doctor's "location" in the interpersonal networks mapped by the sociometric questions. Thus, on the basis of sociometric data, it is possible to classify doctors according to their integration into the medical community, or the degree of their influence, as measured by *the number of times* they are named by their colleagues as friends, discussion partners, and consultants. They can also be classified according to their membership in one or another network or clique, as indicated by *who* names them. Using the first measure makes it possible to investigate whether or not the more influential doctors adopt a drug earlier than those who are less influential. From the second kind of analysis one can learn, for example, whether or not those doctors who belong to the same sub-groups have similar drug-use patterns. In this way, it becomes possible to weave back and forth between the doctor's own testimony about his decisions and the influences involved, on the one hand, and the more objective record of his decisions and of the influences to which he has been exposed, on the other hand.

Note that the networks of social relations in this study are mapped "prior" to the introduction of the new drug being studied, in the sense that friendship, consultation, and so on, are recorded independently of any particular decision the doctor has made. The study is concerned with the potential relevance of various parts of these sociometric structures to the transmission of influence. For example, it is possible to point to the parts of the structure which are "activated" upon the introduction of a new drug, and to describe the sequence of diffusion of the drug as it gains acceptance by individuals and groups in the community. While the Decatur study could hope to examine only the particular face-to-face relationship which had been influential in a given decision, the drug study can locate this relationship against the background of the entire web of *potentially* relevant relationships within which the doctor is embedded.

The Findings of Studies Subsequent to The People's Choice

Having examined the *designs* of these studies, the next step is to explore their *findings* insofar as these are relevant to the hypothesis about the two-step flow of communication. It will be useful to return to the three categories already singled out in discussing *The People's Choice:* (1) the impact of personal influence; (2) the flow of personal influence; and (3) opinion leaders

and the mass media. Evidence from the three studies just reported, as well as from the 1948 Elmira study (Berelson, Lazarsfeld, and McPhee, 1954) and from others, will be brought together here; but in every case the characteristics of each study's design must be borne in mind in evaluating the evidence presented.

A. *The Impact of Personal Influence*

1. PERSONAL AND THE MASS MEDIA INFLUENCE

The 1940 study indicated that personal influence affected voting decisions more than the mass media did, particularly in the case of those who changed their minds during the course of the campaign. The Decatur study went on to explore the relative impact of personal influences and the mass media in three other realms: marketing, fashions and movie-going. Basing its conclusions on the testimony of the decision-makers themselves, and using an instrument for evaluating the relative effectiveness of the various media which entered into the decisions, the Decatur study again found that personal influence figured both more frequently and more effectively than any of the mass media (Katz and Lazarsfeld, 1955).

In the analysis to date, the drug study has not approached the problem of the relative effectiveness of the various media from the point of view of the doctor's own reconstruction of what went into the making of his decision. Comparing mere frequency of mention of different media, it is clear that colleagues are by no means the most frequently mentioned source. Nevertheless, exploration of the factors related to whether the doctor's decision to adopt the drug came early or late indicates that the factor most strongly associated with the time of adoption of the new drug is the extent of the doctor's integration · in the medical community. That is, the more frequently a doctor is named by his colleagues as a friend or a discussion partner, the more likely he is to be an innovator with respect to the new drug. Extent of integration proves to be a more important factor than any background factor (such as age, medical school, or income of patients), or any other source of influence (such as readership of medical journals) that was examined.

Investigation of why integration is related to innovation suggests two central factors: (1) interpersonal communication—doctors who are integrated are more in touch and more up-to-date; and (2) social support—doctors who are integrated feel more secure when facing the risks of innovation in medicine.[10] Thus the drug study, too, provides evidence of the strong impact of personal relations—even in the making of scientific decisions.

2. HOMOGENEITY OF OPINION
IN PRIMARY GROUPS

The effectiveness of interpersonal influence, as it is revealed in the studies under review, is reflected in the homogeneity of opinions and actions in primary groups. The medium of primary group communication is, by definition, person-to-person. Both of the voting studies indicate the high degree of homogeneity of political opinion among members of the same families, and among co-workers and friends. The effectiveness of such primary groups in pulling potential deviates back into line is demonstrated by the fact that those who changed their vote intentions were largely people who, early in the campaign, had reported that they intended to vote differently from their family or friends (Lazarsfeld, Berelson, and Gaudet, 1948; Berelson, Lazarsfeld, and McPhee, 1954).

The drug study, too, was able to examine the extent of homogeneity in the behavior of

---

[10] On the relationship between social integration and self-confidence in a work situation, see Blau (1955, pp. 126-129).

sociometrically related doctors, and was able to demonstrate that there were situations where similar behavior could be deserved. For example, it was found that, when called upon to treat the more puzzling diseases, doctors were likely to prescribe the same drug as their sociometric colleagues. The study also showed that, very early in the history of a new drug, innovating doctors who were sociometrically connected tended to adopt the new drug at virtually the same time. This phenomenon of homogeneity of opinion or behavior among interacting individuals confronting an unclear or uncertain situation which calls for action has often been studied by sociologists and social psychologists.[11]

3. THE VARIOUS ROLES
OF THE MEDIA

The 1940 voting study explored some of the reasons why personal influence might be expected to be more influential in changing opinions than the mass media: It is often non-purposive; it is flexible; it is trustworthy. It was suggested that the mass media more often play a reinforcing role in the strengthening of predispositions and of decisions already taken. Nevertheless, it was assumed that the various media and personal influence are essentially competitive, in the sense that a given decision is influenced by one *or* the other. The Decatur study tended toward this assumption too, but at one point the study does attempt to show that different media play different parts in the decision-making process and take patterned positions in a sequence of several influences. The drug study elaborates on the roles of the media even further, distinguishing between media that "inform" and media that "legitimate" decisions. Thus in doctors' deci-

---

[11] That men, faced with an unstructured situation, look to each other to establish a "social reality" in terms of which they act, is a central theme in the work of Durkheim, Kurt Lewin and his disciples, H. S. Sullivan ("consensual validation"), and in the studies of Sherif, Asch and others.

sions, professional media (including colleagues) seem to play a legitimating role, while commercial media play an informing role.

B. The Flow of Personal Influence

The 1940 voting study found that opinion leaders were not concentrated in the upper brackets of the population but were located in almost equal proportions in every social group and stratum. This finding led to efforts in subsequent studies to establish the extent to which this was true in areas other than election campaigns and also to ascertain what it is that *does* distinguish opinion leaders from those whom they influence.

The first thing that is clear from the series of studies under review is that the subject matter concerning which influence is transmitted has a lot to do with determining who will lead and who follow. Thus, the Rovere study suggests that within the broad sphere of public affairs one set of influentials is occupied with "local" affairs and another with "cosmopolitan" affairs (Merton, 1949). The Decatur study suggests that in marketing, for example, there is a concentration of opinion leadership among older women with larger families, while in fashions and movie-going it is the young, unmarried girl who has a disproportionate chance of being turned to for advice. There is very little overlap of leadership: a leader in one sphere is not likely to be influential in another unrelated sphere as well.[12]

Yet, even when leadership in one or another sphere is heavily concentrated among the members of a particular group—as was the case with marketing leadership in Decatur—the evidence suggests that people still talk, most of all, to others like themselves. Thus, while the marketing leaders among the older "large-family wives" also influenced other kinds of women, most of their

influence was directed to women of their own age with equally large families. In marketing, fashions, and movie-going, furthermore, there was no appreciable concentration of influentials in any of the three socioeconomic levels. Only in public affairs was there a concentration of leadership in the highest status, and there was some slight evidence that influence flows from this group to individuals of lower status. The Elmira study also found opinion leaders in similar proportions on every socioeconomic and occupational level and found that conversations concerning the campaign went on, typically, between people of similar age, occupation, and political opinion.

What makes for the concentration of certain kinds of opinion leadership within certain groups? And when influential and influencee are outwardly alike—as they so often seem to be—what, if anything, distinguishes one from the other? Broadly, it appears that influence is related (1) to the *personification of certain values* (who one is); (2) to *competence* (what one knows); and (3) to *strategic social location* (whom one knows). Social location, in turn, divides into whom one knows within a group; and "outside."

Influence is often successfully transmitted because the influencee wants to be as much like the influential as possible.[13] That the young, unmarried girls are fashion leaders can be understood easily in a culture where youth and youthfulness are supreme values. This is an example where "who one is" counts very heavily.

But "what one knows" is no less important.[14] The fact is that older women, by virtue of their greater experience, are looked to as marketing advisers and that specialists in internal medicine—the most "scientific" of

---

[12] For a summary of the Decatur findings on the flow of interpersonal influence, see Katz and Lazarsfeld (1955, pp. 327-334).

[13] That leaders are, in a certain sense, the most conformist members of their groups—upholding whatever norms and values are central to the group—is a proposition which further illustrates this point. For an empirical illustration from a highly relevant study, see Marsh and Coleman (1954).

[14] The distinction between "what" and "whom" one knows is used by Merton (1949, p. 197).

the practicing physicians—are the most frequently mentioned opinion leaders among the doctors. The influence of young people in the realm of movie-going can also be understood best in terms of their familiarity with the motion picture world. The Elmira study found slightly greater concentrations of opinion leadership among the more educated people on each socioeconomic level, again implying the importance of competence. Finally, the influence of the "cosmopolitans" in Rovere rested on the presumption that they had large amounts of information.

It is, however, not enough to be a person whom others want to emulate, or to be competent. One must also be accessible. Thus, the Decatur study finds gregariousness—"whom one knows"—related to every kind of leadership. The Rovere study reports that the leadership of the "local" influentials is based on their central location in the web of interpersonal contacts. Similarly, studies of rumor transmission have singled out those who are "socially active" as agents of rumor (Allport and Postman, 1943).

Of course, the importance of whom one knows is not simply a matter of the number of people with whom an opinion leader is in contact. It is also a question of whether the people with whom he is in touch happen to be interested in the area in which his leadership is likely to be sought. For this reason, it is quite clear that the greater interest of opinion leaders in the subjects over which they exert influence is not a sufficient explanation of their influence. While the voting studies as well as the Decatur study show leaders to be more interested, the Decatur study goes on to show that interest alone is not the determining factor (Katz and Lazarsfeld, 1955). In fashion, for example, a young unmarried girl is considerably more likely to be influential than a matron with an equally great interest in clothes. The reason, it is suggested, is that a girl who is interested in fashion is much more likely than a matron with an equally high interest to know other people who share her preoccupation, and thus is more

likely than the matron to have followers who are interested enough to ask for her advice. In other words, it takes two to be a leader—a leader and a follower.

Finally, there is the second aspect of "whom one knows." An individual may be influential not only because people within his group look to him for advice but also because of whom he knows outside his group.[15] Both the Elmira and Decatur studies found that men are more likely than women to be opinion leaders in the realm of public affairs and this, it is suggested, is because they have more of a chance to get outside the home to meet people and talk politics. Similarly, the Elmira study indicated that opinion leaders belonged to more organizations, more often knew workers for the political parties, and so on, than did others. The drug study found that influential doctors could be characterized in terms of such things as their more frequent attendance at out-of-town meetings and the diversity of places with which they maintained contact, particularly far-away places. It is interesting that a study of the farmer-innovators responsible for the diffusion of hybrid seed-corn in Iowa concluded that these leaders also could be characterized in terms of the relative frequency of their trips out of town (Ryan and Gross, 1942).

C. The Opinion Leaders and the Mass Media

The third aspect of the hypothesis of the two-step flow of communication states that opinion leaders are more exposed to the mass media than are those whom they influence. In *The People's Choice* this is supported by reference to the media behavior of leaders and non-leaders.

---

[15] It is interesting that a number of studies have found that the most integrated persons within a group are also likely to have more contacts outside the group than others. One might have expected the more marginal members to have more contacts outside. For example, see Blau (1955, p. 128).

The Decatur study corroborated this finding, and went on to explore two additional aspects of the same idea (Katz and Lazarsfeld, 1955). First of all, it was shown that leaders in a given sphere (fashions, public affairs, etc.) were particularly likely to be exposed to the media appropriate to that sphere. This is essentially a corroboration of the Rovere finding that those who proved influential with regard to "cosmopolitan" matters were more likely to be readers of national news magazines, but that this was not at all the case for those influential with regard to "local" matters. Secondly, the Decatur study shows that at least in the realm of fashions, the leaders are not only more exposed to the mass media, but are also more affected by them in their own decisions. This did not appear to be the case in other realms, where opinion leaders, though more exposed to the media than non-leaders, nevertheless reported personal influence as the major factor in their decisions. This suggests that in some spheres considerably longer chains of person-to-person influence than the dyad may have to be traced back before one encounters any decisive influence by the mass media, even though their contributory influence may be perceived at many points. This was suggested by the Elmira study too. It found that the leaders, though more exposed to the media, also more often reported that they sought information and advice from other persons (Berelson, Lazarsfeld, and McPhee, 1954).

Similarly, the drug study showed that the influential doctors were more likely to be readers of a large number of professional journals and valued them more highly than did doctors of lesser influence. But at the same time, they were as likely as other doctors to say that local colleagues were an important source of information and advice in their reaching particular decisions.

Finally, the drug study demonstrated that the more influential doctors could be characterized by their greater attention not only to medical journals, but to out-of-town meetings and contacts as well. This finding has already been discussed in the previous section treating the *strategic location* of the opinion leader with respect to "the world outside" his group. Considering it again under the present heading suggests that the greater exposure of the opinion leader to the mass media may only be a special case of the more general proposition that opinion leaders serve to relate their groups to relevant parts of the environment through whatever media happen to be appropriate. This more general statement makes clear the similar functions of big city newspapers for the Decatur fashion leader; of national news magazines for the "cosmopolitan" influentials of Rovere; of out-of-town medical meetings for the influential doctor; and of contact with the city for the farmer-innovator in Iowa[16] as well as for the newly risen, young opinion leaders in underdeveloped areas throughout the world.[17]

Conclusions

Despite the diversity of subject matter with which they are concerned, the studies reviewed here constitute an example of continuity and cumulation both in research design and theoretical commitment. Piecing together the findings of the latter-day studies in the light of the original statement of the two-step flow hypothesis suggests the following picture.

Opinion leaders and the people whom they influence are very much alike and typically belong to the same primary groups of family, friends and co-workers. While the opinion leader may be more interested in the particular sphere in which he is influential, it is highly unlikely that the persons influ-

[16] Ryan and Gross (1942) choose to explain "trips to the city" as another index of the non-traditional orientation of which innovation itself is also an index. In the case of the out-of-town meetings, trips to out-of-town centers of learning, etc., the latter were also mentioned as key sources of advice by doctors who were innovators and influentials.

[17] See the forthcoming book by Lerner et al. cited above.

enced will be very far behind the leader in their level of interest. Influentials and influencees may exchange roles in different spheres of influence. Most spheres focus the group's attention on some related part of the world outside the group, and it is the opinion leader's function to bring the group into touch with this relevant part of its environment through whatever media are appropriate. In every case, influentials have been found to be more exposed to these points of contact with the outside world. Nevertheless, it is also true that, despite their greater exposure to the media, most opinion leaders are primarily affected not by the communication media but by still other people.

The main emphasis of the two-step flow hypothesis appears to be on only one aspect of interpersonal relations—interpersonal relations as channels of communication. But from the several studies reviewed, it is clear that these very same interpersonal relations influence the making of decisions in at least two additional ways. In addition to serving as networks of communication, interpersonal relations are also sources of pressure to conform to the group's way of thinking and acting, as well as sources of social support. The workings of group pressure are clearly evident in the homogeneity of opinion and action observed among voters and among doctors in situations of unclarity or uncertainty. The social support that comes from being integrated in the medical community may give a doctor the confidence required to carry out a resolution to adopt a new drug. Thus, interpersonal relations are (1) channels of information, (2) sources of social pressure, and (3) sources of social support, and each relates interpersonal relations to decision-making in a somewhat different way.[18]

The central methodological problem in each of the studies reviewed has been how to take account of interpersonal relations and still preserve the economy and representativeness which the random, cross-sectional sample affords. Answers to this problem range from asking individuals in the sample to describe the others with whom they interacted (Elmira), to conducting "snowball" interviews with influential-influencee dyads (Decatur), to interviewing an entire community (drug study). Future studies will probably find themselves somewhere in between. For most studies, however, the guiding principle would seem to be to build larger or smaller social molecules around each individual atom in the sample.[19]

---

[18] These different dimensions of interpersonal relations can be further illustrated by reference to studies which represent the "pure type" of each dimension. Studies of rumor flow illustrate the "channels" dimension; see, for example, Moreno (1953, pp. 440-450). The study by Festinger, Schachter, and Back (1950) illustrates the second dimension. Blau (1955, pp. 126-129) illustrates the "social support" dimension.

[19] Various ways of accomplishing this have been discussed for the past two years in a staff seminar on "relational analysis" at the Bureau of Applied Social Research. The recent study by Lipset, Trow, and Coleman (1956) illustrates one approach in its study of printers within the varying social contexts of the shops in which they are employed. The study by Riley and Riley (1951) is another good example.

References

ALLPORT, G. W., and POSTMAN, L. J. *The psychology of rumor.* New York: Holt, Rinehart and Winston, 1943.

BERELSON, B. R., LAZARSFELD, P. F., and McPHEE, W. N. *Voting: a study of opinion formation in a presidential campaign.* Chicago: The Univer. of Chicago Press, 1954.

BLAU, P. M. *The dynamics of bureaucracy.* Chicago: The Univer. of Chicago Press, 1955.

EISENSTADT, S. N. Communication systems and social structure: an exploratory study. *Publ. Opin. Quart.*, 1955, *19*, 153-167.

EISENSTADT, S. N. Communications processes among immigrants in Israel. *Publ. Opin. Quart.*, 1952, *16*, 42-58.

FESTINGER, L., SCHACHTER, S., and BACK, K.

Social pressures in informal groups. New York: Harper & Row, 1950.

FRIEDSON, E. Communications research and the concept of the mass. *Amer. sociol. Rev.*, 1953, *18*, 313-317.

GLOCK, C. Y. The comparative study of communications and opinion formation. *Publ. Opin. Quart.*, 1952-1953, *16*, 512-523.

HANDEL, L. A. *Hollywood looks at its audience*. Urbana, Ill.: Univer. of Illinois Press, 1950.

JANOWITZ, M. *The urban press in a community setting*. New York: The Free Press of Glencoe, 1952.

KATZ, E., and LAZARSFELD, P. F. *Personal influence: the part played by people in the flow of mass communications*. New York: The Free Press of Glencoe, 1955.

LAZARSFELD, P. F., BERELSON, B., and GAUDET, H. *The people's choice*. New York: Columbia Univer. Press, 1948 (2d edition).

LIPSET, S. M., TROW, M. A., and COLEMAN, J. S. *Union democracy*. New York: The Free Press of Glencoe, 1956.

MARSH, C. P., and COLEMAN, A. L. Farmers' practice adoption rates in relation to adoption rates of leaders. *Rural Soc.*, 1954, *19*, 180-183.

MENZEL, H., and KATZ, E. Social relations and innovation in the medical profession. *Public Opin. Quart.*, 1955, *19*, 337-352.

MERTON, R. K. Patterns of influence: a study of interpersonal influence and communications behavior in a local community. In P. F. Lazarsfeld and F. N. Stanton (Eds.), *Communications research, 1948-1949*. New York: Harper & Row, 1949.

MORENO, J. L. *Who shall survive*. Beacon, N.Y.: Beacon House, 1953.

RIESMAN, D. *The lonely crowd*. New Haven: Yale Univer. Press, 1952.

RILEY, M., and RILEY, J. A sociological approach to communications research. *Publ. Opin. Quart.*, 1951, *15*, 445-460.

RYAN, B., and GROSS, N. *Acceptance and diffusion of hybrid seed corn in two Iowa communities*. Ames, Iowa: Iowa State College of Agriculture and Mechanic Arts, Research Bulletin 372, 1942.

STYCOS, J. M. Patterns of communication in a rural Greek village. *Publ. Opin. Quart.*, 1952, *16*, 59-70.

C. REFERENCE GROUPS

Two Functions

of Reference Groups ❧ Harold H. Kelley

A considerable number of every person's attitudes are related to or anchored in one or more social groups. The nature of this social anchorage of attitudes is by no means clear or simple. On the one hand, it is apparent that a person's attitudes are related to the attitudes commonly expressed within groups to which he belongs (his membership groups[1]). On the other hand, studies of prestige influence, opinion leadership, rejection of membership groups by underprivileged persons, and the influence of outgroups upon levels of aspiration have indicated that attitudes are often related to nonmembership groups.

In recognition of this fact, the term *reference group*, first used by Hyman (1942), has come into use to denote *any* group to which a person relates his attitudes. Paralleling this usage has been the development of a general theory of reference groups, largely the work of Sherif (1948), Newcomb

[1] Here we follow T. M. Newcomb's definition of a membership group as ". . . one in which a person is recognized by others as belonging. . . ." (1955, p. 225).

(1950), and Merton and Kitt (1950), which is designed to take account of anchorage in both membership and nonmembership groups. Although this theory is still in the initial stages of development, because of the problems it formulates it promises to be of central importance to social psychology. In particular, it is important to those social scientists who desire to interpret the development of attitudes, to predict their expression under different social conditions, to understand the social basis of their stability or resistance to change, or to devise means of increasing or overcoming this resistance.

The purpose of the present paper is to clarify certain aspects of "reference group theory" by drawing a distinction between two major functions which reference groups play in the determination of an individual's attitudes. This distinction is necessary because the term *reference group* has heretofore been applied to two rather different phenomena, each of which poses its own theoretical and research problems. However, the ultimate usefulness of the distinction should be, first, to indicate that a more com-

This article was written especially for G. E. Swanson, T. M. Newcomb, and E. L. Hartley (Eds.), *Readings in Social Psychology*, Rev. Ed., New York: Holt, Rinehart and Winston, 1952. Reprinted by permission of the author and publisher.

plete theory of reference groups must integrate a variety of perceptual and motivational phenomena and, second, to outline the kinds of concepts and research problems that are necessary for an analysis of reference groups.

1. Current Usages of "Reference Groups"

The concept "reference group" has been used to describe two kinds of relationships between a person and a group. *The first usage* has been to denote a group in which the individual is motivated to gain or maintain *acceptance*. To promote this acceptance, he holds his attitudes in conformity with what he perceives to be the consensus among the group members. Implicit here is the idea that the members of the reference group observe the person and evaluate him.

An example of this usage is found in Merton's reinterpretation of relevant material in the two volumes of *The American Soldier*, prepared by the Research Branch, Information and Education Division of the War Department (Stouffer et al., 1949).

EXAMPLE I

Three soldier populations were interviewed about their willingness to go into combat. They were: (1) inexperienced soldiers in units composed wholly of their own kind, (2) inexperienced soldiers who were replacements in units otherwise composed of combat veterans, and (3) the veterans themselves in the latter units. Other data indicated that combat veterans generally felt that "combat is hell" and had a strong group code against any tendencies to glamorize it or express eagerness for combat. In this comparison, it was found that while 45 percent of the men in completely unseasoned units were "ready to get into an actual battle zone," only 15 percent of the veterans felt ready. The important fact for our pur-

poses was that green replacements in combat units were intermediate between the two groups mentioned, with 28 percent expressing readiness. In this and other attitudinal areas, it appeared that the replacements had to some degree assimilated the attitudes of the veterans. Merton interprets this result as follows (Merton and Kitt, 1950, p. 76):

[Our] hypothesis drawn from reference group theory would lead us to anticipate that the replacements, *seeking affiliation* with the authoritative and prestigeful stratum of veterans, will move from the civilianlike values toward the more tough-minded values of the veterans. . . . For replacements, the assumed function of *assimilating the values* of the veterans is to find more ready acceptance by the higher-status group, in a setting where the subordinate group of replacements does not have independent claims to legitimate prestige.

Newcomb's use of "reference group" clearly falls into this category. Other persons are said to constitute a reference group for a person if his attitudes are influenced by a set of norms which he assumes he shares with them. The motivational aspects of this usage are emphasized in his distinction between positive and negative reference groups. A positive reference group is defined as one in which the person is motivated to be accepted and treated like a member. A negative reference group is one which the person is motivated to oppose or in which he does not want to be treated as a member. Sherif's usage is also of this variety. He emphasizes the individual's striving to maintain his standing in his reference groups and points out that the norms of the reference group become the person's attitudes.

The second usage of "reference group" has been to denote a group which the person uses as a reference point in making evaluations of himself or others. Examples are found in Hyman's paper on the "psychology of status."

EXAMPLE II

Defining status as the relative position of individuals, Hyman points out that the person's conception of his own position depends upon which other persons he considers. These other persons with whom a person compares himself in judging his status form a reference group for him. Hyman demonstrates that changes in judgments of one's own status can be brought about by changes in the reference group used. For instance, his subjects were first asked to indicate the proportion all of adults *in the U.S.* who are lower than they in economic status. This judgment was compared with that of the proportion of people *in their occupation* who are lower economically than they.

In this type of example, any evaluation of the person by members of the reference group is largely irrelevant. A group may become a reference group because *other persons* compare the individual with it. Hyman gives this example.

EXAMPLE III

"[If] a woman goes for a job as a model and her physical attractiveness is the desideratum, it may be irrelevant to the situation what her physical attractiveness is in relation to her friends, Hottentot women, etc. The relevant reference group is composed of the available women models" (Hyman, 1942, p. 47). In other words, the relevant reference group is the one with which she'll be compared by her prospective employers.

Whereas in the foregoing examples the reference group is a collection of persons to which the individual belongs, in one of Merton's examples that fits this general category this is not the case.

EXAMPLE IV

A survey of the morale attitudes of noncombat soldiers overseas revealed more expressed satisfaction with their lot than was expected. The interpretation of the authors of *The American Soldier,* in which Merton concurs, is that the noncombat soldiers overseas compared themselves with men in combat and consequently found their own circumstances to be relatively good. In this instance an outside, nonmembership group presumably served as a reference group.

In both Hyman's and Merton's examples the reference group is used in making self-evaluations. However, there would seem to be no reason why we should not also consider as reference groups those collections of persons who are used as reference points in judging others. In fact, it seems likely that the reference groups used in judging one's self would frequently be used in making judgments of others.

2. *Two Functions of Reference Groups*

From the foregoing it is apparent that the term *reference group* is used to describe two quite different kinds of groups. In the first case (Example I) the group is in a position to award recognition to the person or to withhold it. In the second (Examples II, III, and IV) the group is merely a standard or checkpoint which the person uses in making judgments. This dual usage of the term suggests that reference groups can play different functions in the determination of a person's attitudes.

The first of these is that of setting and enforcing standards for the person. Such standards are usually labeled *group norms,* so we shall call this the *normative function* of reference groups. A group can assume this function of norm-setting and norm-enforcement whenever it is in a position to deliver rewards or punishments for conformity or nonconformity. A group functions as a normative reference group for a person to the extent that its evaluations of him are based upon the degree of his conformity to certain standards of behavior or attitude and to the extent that the delivery of rewards or punishments is conditional upon these evaluations. In Example I above, the veterans in combat units presumably defined certain attitudes as being "correct," evaluated how well each replacement accepted these standards, and accordingly rewarded him with acceptance or punished him by withholding any recognition or acceptance.

The second of these functions is that of *serving as* or *being* a standard or comparison point against which the person can evaluate himself and others. We shall refer to this as the *comparison function* of reference groups. A group functions as a comparison reference group for an individual to the extent that the behavior, attitudes, circumstances, or other characteristics of its members represent standards or comparison points which he uses in making judgments and evaluations. In Example II the particular comparison group which Hyman suggested to his subjects (e.g., all adults in the U.S., one's friends and acquaintances, or the persons in one's occupational group) was a comparison point for each person to use in judging his own status. In Example IV, the combat soldiers served as a comparison reference group for the overseas noncombat men in their evaluations of their own situation.

These two functions, the normative and comparison functions, will frequently be served by one and the same group. This will usually be the case with membership groups. In Example I the combat veteran's attitudes provided comparison points for the replacements' self-evaluations (the comparison function), while at the same time the veterans defined these attitudes as "proper" and awarded acceptance and approval on the basis of their adoption (the normative function). The example well illustrates the integrated character of these functions: the veterans' attitudes served as comparison points primarily *because* the veterans also functioned in the normative or sanction-applying role. Both functions are also frequently served by nonmembership groups in which membership is desired. For the undergraduate who hopes eventually to be tapped by a senior fraternity that group acts both as a standard (the behavior and attitudes of its members provide examples for the aspirant) and as the source of sanctions related to conformity to these standards (since it may invite membership or withhold it). On the other hand, normative and comparison functions need not be localized within a single group. A membership group may define an external group as the standard of behavior (the parents may insist that their child model his behavior after that of other children in the neighborhood) or it may subdivide its members in such a way that the same norms do not apply to all (pledges vs. full fraternity member).

3. Implications

The distinction between the two functions suggested above is important because it makes explicit the two main aspects of reference-group theory: the motivational and the perceptual. A more complete theory of reference groups must consist of at least two parts, one having to do with groups as sources and enforcers of standards and the other having to do with groups as the standards themselves. These two parts of reference-group theory should prove to be merely special cases of more general theories about the *sources* and *nature* of standards which, in turn, should ultimately derive from fundamental theories of motivation and perception. The normative functions of reference groups may be expected to become part of a general theory of goal-setting and motivation which will also include other social determinants of standards (such as important individuals having the power to reward or punish), nonsocial factors in motivation, and the processes of self-motivation whereby social influences become internalized and operate through self-delivery of reward and punishment. The comparison functions of reference groups will be part of a general theory of perception and judgment such as is presently represented by the psychological theories of frames of reference. Comparison groups are, after all, only one of many kinds of comparison points within referential frameworks. Hyman found that individuals (as well as groups) are often the points against which a person compares himself in judging his status. Other standards would be inanimate objects or units of measurement (e.g., a child may use a table or a yardstick to judge his height) and impersonal descriptions of desired behavior (e.g., legal formulations of group norms).

Finally, a consideration of the normative and comparison functions of reference groups points to two major areas of research for students of reference-group behavior. In the study of *normative* reference groups such problems as the following will come under consideration: What is the motivational relationship between the person and each of his various reference groups? How much does he value his membership or, in the case of a nonmembership group, how much does he desire to become a member? What kind of motives are involved in his membership aspirations? What are the consequences of different kinds and degrees of motives? What factors permit a group member to resist the group pressures toward conformity without being rejected? With respect to what issues do norms develop within groups? What are the peculiar patterns of standards and norms associated with various special roles or offices within the group? What kind of sanctions are applied to produce conformity and what are the consequences of different kinds? How are these sanctions related to the degree of nonconformity? What factors in the person's relation to the group promote internalization of the group norms?

A study of *comparison* reference groups will involve different questions having largely to do with perceptual and judgmental processes. The following are some examples: What kind of stimulus does the comparison group present to the individual? Does it provide a highly structured and definite comparison point or is it an ambiguous stimulus capable of a variety of interpretations? What are the consequences of these different cases? In self-evaluations, what factors affect the size of the discrepancy the person perceives to exist between himself and the group norms? What are the effects of extremely high or low standards or comparison points? What is the nature of the scale along which comparisons are made?

Reference-group theory will be advanced by the answers to these and similar questions. Through the research and conceptual development necessary to yield these answers we may expect great advances in our understanding of the social basis of attitudes.

References

Hyman, H. H. The psychology of status. *Arch. Psychol.*, 1942, 269.

Merton, R. K., and Kitt, A. S. Contributions to the theory of reference group behavior. In R. K. Merton and P. F. Lazarsfeld (Eds.), *Studies in the scope and method of "The American Soldier."* New York: The Free Press of Glencoe, 1950, pp. 40-105.

Newcomb, T. M. *Social psychology.* New York: Holt, Rinehart and Winston, 1950.

Sherif, M. *An outline of social psychology.* New York: Harper & Row, 1948.

Stouffer, S. A., et al. *The American soldier*, Vols. I and II of *Studies in social psychology in World War II.* Princeton, N.J.: Princeton Univer. Press, 1949.

Attitude Development as a
Function of Reference Groups:
The Bennington Study ❧ Theodore M. Newcomb

Membership in established groups usually involves the taking on of whole patterns of interrelated behavior and attitudes. This was one of the hypotheses pursued in the study which is reported here in part. The group selected for study consisted of the entire student body at Bennington College—more than 600 individuals—between the years 1935 and 1939. One of the problems to be investigated was that of the manner in which the patterning of behavior and attitudes varied with different degrees of assimilation into the community.

Not all of the attitudes and behaviors that are likely to be taken on by new members, as they become absorbed into a community, can be investigated in a single study. A single, though rather inclusive, area of adaptation to the college community was therefore selected for special study, namely, *attitudes toward public affairs.* There were two reasons for this selection: (1) methods of attitude measurement were readily available; and (2) there was an unusually high degree of concern, in this community at this time, over a rather wide range of public issues. This latter fact resulted partly from the fact that the college opened its doors during the darkest days of the depression of the 1930's, and its formative period occurred in the period of social change characterized by the phrase "the New Deal." This was also the period of gathering war clouds in Europe. Underlying both of these circumstances, however, was the conviction on the part of the faculty that one of the foremost duties of the college was to acquaint its

somewhat oversheltered students with the nature of their contemporary social world.

In a membership group in which certain attitudes are approved (i.e., held by majorities, and conspicuously so by leaders), individuals acquire the approved attitudes to the extent that the membership group (particularly as symbolized by leaders and dominant subgroups) serves as a positive point of reference. The findings of the Bennington study seem to be better understood in terms of this thesis than any other. The distinction between membership group and reference group is a crucial one, in fact, although the original report did not make explicit use of it.

The above statement does not imply that no reference groups other than the membership group are involved in attitude formation; as we shall see, this is distinctly not the case. Neither does it imply that the use of the membership group as reference group necessarily results in adoption of the approved attitudes. It may also result in their rejection; hence the word *positive* in the initial statement. It is precisely these variations in degree and manner of relationship between reference group and membership group which must be known in order to explain individual variations in attitude formation, as reported in this study.

The essential facts about the Bennington membership group are as follows: (1) It was small enough (about 250 women students) so that data could be obtained from every member. (2) It was in most respects self-sufficient; college facilities provided not

This article was written especially for G. E. Swanson, T. M. Newcomb, and E. L. Hartley (Eds.), *Readings in Social Psychology,* Rev. Ed., New York: Holt, Rinehart and Winston, 1952. Reprinted by permission of the author and publisher.

only the necessities of living and studying, but also a cooperative store, post office and Western Union office, beauty parlor, gasoline station, and a wide range of recreational opportunities. The average student visited the four-mile-distant village once a week and spent one week end a month away from the college. (3) It was self-conscious and enthusiastic, in large part because it was new (the study was begun during the first year in which there was a senior class) and because of the novelty and attractiveness of the college's educational plan. (4) It was unusually active and concerned about public issues, largely because the faculty felt that its educational duties included the familiarizing of an oversheltered student body with the implications of a depression-torn America and a war-threatened world. (5) It was relatively homogeneous in respect to home background; tuition was very high, and the large majority of students came from urban, economically privileged families whose social attitudes were conservative.

Most individuals in this total membership group went through rather marked changes in attitudes toward public issues, as noted below. In most cases the total membership group served as the reference group for the changing attitudes. But some individuals changed little or not at all in attitudes during the four years of the study; attitude persistence was in some of these cases a function of the membership group as reference group and in some cases it was not. Among those who did change, moreover, the total membership group sometimes served as reference group but sometimes it did not. An oversimple theory of "assimilation into the community" thus leaves out of account some of those whose attitudes did and some of those whose attitudes did not change; they remain unexplained exceptions. A theory which traces the impact of other reference groups as well as the effect of the membership group seems to account for all cases without exception.

The general trend of attitude change for the total group is from freshman conserva-

tism to senior nonconservatism (as the term was commonly applied to the issues toward which attitudes were measured). During the 1936 presidential election, for example, 62 percent of the freshmen and only 14 percent of the juniors and seniors "voted" for the Republican candidate, 29 percent of freshmen and 54 percent of juniors and seniors for Roosevelt, and 9 percent of freshmen as compared with 30 percent of juniors and seniors for the Socialist or Communist candidates. Attitudes toward nine specific issues were measured during the four years of the study, and seniors were less conservative in all of them than freshmen; six of the nine differences are statistically reliable. These differences are best shown by a Likert-type scale labeled Political and Economic Progressivism (PEP) which dealt with such issues as unemployment, public relief, and the rights of organized labor, which were made prominent by the New Deal. Its odd-even reliability was about .9, and it was given once or more during each of the four years of the study to virtually all students. The critical ratios of the differences between freshmen and juniors-seniors in four successive years ranged between 3.9 and 6.5; the difference between the average freshman and senior scores of 44 individuals (the entire class that graduated in 1939) gives a critical ratio of 4.3.

As might be anticipated in such a community, *individual prestige was associated with nonconservatism.* Frequency of choice as one of five students "most worthy to represent the College" at an intercollegiate gathering was used as a measure of prestige. Nominations were submitted in sealed envelopes by 99 percent of all students in two successive years, with almost identical results. The nonconservatism of those with high prestige is not merely the result of the fact that juniors and seniors are characterized by both high prestige and nonconservatism; in each class those who have most prestige are least conservative. For example, ten freshmen receiving 2 to 4 choices had an average PEP score of 64.6 as compared with

72.8 for freshmen not chosen at all (high scores are conservative); eight sophomores chosen 12 or more times had an average score of 63.6 as compared with 71.3 for those not chosen; the mean PEP score of five juniors and seniors chosen 40 or more times was 50.4 and of the fifteen chosen 12 to 39 times, 57.6, as compared with 69.0 for those not chosen. In each class, those intermediate in prestige are also intermediate in average PEP score.

Such were the attitudinal characteristics of the total membership group, expressed in terms of average scores. Some individuals, however, showed these characteristics in heightened form and others failed to show them at all. An examination of the various reference groups in relation to which attitude change did or did not occur, and of the ways in which they were brought to bear, will account for a large part of such attitude variance.

Information concerning reference groups was obtained both directly, from the subjects themselves, and indirectly, from other students and from teachers. Chief among the indirect procedures was the obtaining of indexes of "community citizenship" by a guess-who technique. Each of twenty-four students, carefully selected to represent every cross section and grouping of importance within the community, named three individuals from each of three classes who were reputedly most extreme in each of twenty-eight characteristics related to community citizenship. The relationship between reputation for community identification and nonconservatism is a close one, in spite of the fact that no reference was made to the latter characteristic when the judges made their ratings. A reputation index was computed, based upon the frequency with which individuals were named in five items dealing with identification with the community, minus the number of times they were named in five other items dealing with negative community attitude. Examples of the former items are: "absorbed in college community affairs," and "influenced by com-

munity expectations regarding codes, standards, etc."; examples of the latter are: "indifferent to activities of student committees," and "resistant to community expectations regarding codes, standards, etc." The mean senior PEP score of fifteen individuals whose index was +15 or more was 54.4; of sixty-three whose index was +4 to −4, 65.3; and of ten whose index was −15 or less, 68.2.

To have the reputation of identifying oneself with the community is not the same thing, however, as to identify the community as a reference group for a specific purpose—e.g., in this case, as a point of reference for attitudes toward public issues. In short, the reputation index is informative as to degree and direction of tendency to use the total membership group as a *general* reference group, but not necessarily as a group to which social attitudes are referred. For this purpose information was obtained directly from students.

Informal investigation had shown that whereas most students were aware of the marked freshman-to-senior trend away from conservatism, a few (particularly among the conservatives) had little or no awareness of it. Obviously, those not aware of the dominant community trend could not be using the community as a reference group for an attitude. (It does not follow, of course, that all those who are aware of it are necessarily using the community as reference group.) A simple measure of awareness was therefore devised. Subjects were asked to respond in two ways to a number of attitude statements taken from the PEP scale: first, to indicate agreement or disagreement (for example, with the statement: "The budget should be balanced before the government spends any money on social security"); and second, to estimate what percentage of freshmen, juniors and seniors, and faculty would agree with the statement. From these responses was computed an index of divergence (of own attitude) from the estimated majority of juniors and seniors. Thus a positive index on the part of a senior indicates the degree to which her own responses are more conservative than those of her classmates, and a negative index the degree to which they are less conservative. Those seniors whose divergence index more or less faithfully reflects the true difference between own and class attitude may (or may not) be using the class as an attitude reference group; those whose divergence indexes represent an exaggerated or minimized version of the true relationship between own and class attitude are clearly not using the class as an attitude reference group, or if so, only in a fictitious sense. (For present purposes the junior-senior group may be taken as representative of the entire student body, since it is the group which "sets the tone" of the total membership group.)

These data were supplemented by direct information obtained in interviews with seniors in three consecutive classes, just prior to graduation. Questions were asked about resemblance between own attitudes and those of class majorities and leaders, about parents' attitudes and own resemblance to them, about any alleged "social pressure to become liberal," about probable reaction if the dominant college influence had been conservative instead of liberal, etc. Abundant information was also available from the college personnel office and from the college psychiatrist. It was not possible to combine all of these sources of information into intensive studies of each individual, but complete data were assembled for (roughly) the most conservative and least conservative sixths of three consecutive graduating classes. The twenty-four nonconservative and nineteen conservative seniors thus selected for intensive study were classified according to their indexes of conservative divergence and of community reputation. Thus eight sets of seniors were identified, all individuals within each set having in common similar attitudes scores, similar reputations for community identification, and similar degrees of awareness (based upon divergence index) of own attitude position relative to classmates. The following descrip-

tions of these eight sets of seniors will show that there was a characteristic pattern of relationship between membership group and reference group within each of the sets.

1. *Conservatives, reputedly negativistic, aware of their own relative conservatism.* Four of the five are considered stubborn or resistant by teachers (all five, by student judges). Three have prestige scores of 0, scores of the other two being about average for their class. Four of the five are considered by teachers of psychiatrist, or by both, to be overdependent upon one or both parents. All of the four who were interviewed described *their major hopes*, on entering college, *in terms of social rather than academic prestige;* all four felt that they had been defeated in this aim. The following verbatim quotations are illustrative:

E2

Probably the feeling that (my instructors) didn't accept me led me to reject their opinions. (She estimates classmates as being only moderately less conservative than herself, but faculty as much less so.)

G32

I wouldn't care to be intimate with those so-called "liberal" student leaders. (*She claims to be satisfied with a small group of friends.* She is chosen as friend, in a sociometric questionnaire responded to by all students, only twice, and reciprocates both choices; both are conservative students.)

F22

I wanted to disagree with all the noisy liberals, but I was afraid and I couldn't. *So I built up a wall inside me against what they said. I found I couldn't compete, so I decided to stick to my father's ideas. For at least two years I've been insulated against all college influences.* (She is chosen but once as a friend, and does not reciprocate that choice.)

Q10

(who rather early concluded that she had no chance of social success in college) It hurt me at first, but now I don't give a damn. *The things I really care about are mostly outside the college.* I think radicalism symbolizes the college for me more than anything else. (Needless to say, she has no use for radicals.)

For these four individuals (and probably for the fifth also) the community serves as reference group in a *negative* sense, and the home-and-family group in a positive sense. Thus their conservatism is dually reinforced.

2. *Conservatives, reputedly negativistic, unaware of their own relative conservatism.* All five are described by teachers, as well as by guess-who judges, to be stubborn or resistant. Four have prestige scores of 0, and the fifth a less than average score. Each reciprocated just one friendship choice. Four are considered insecure in social relationships, and all five are regarded as extremely dependent upon parents. In interviews four describe with considerable intensity, and the fifth with more moderation, precollege experiences of rebuff, ostracism, or isolation, and all describe their hopes, on entering college, in terms of making friends or avoiding rebuff rather than in terms of seeking prestige. All five felt that their (rather modest) aims had met with good success. Each of the five denies building up any resistance to the acceptance of liberal opinions (but two add that they would have resented any such pressure, if felt). Three believe that only small, special groups in the college have such opinions, while the other two describe themselves as just going their own way, *paying no attention to anything but their own little circles and their college work.* Typical quotations follow:

Q47

I'm a perfect middle-of-the-roader, neither enthusiast nor critic. I'd accept anything if they just let me alone. . . . I've made all the friends I want. (Only one of her friendship choices is reciprocated.)

Q19

In high school I was always thought of as my parents' daughter. I never felt really accepted for myself. . . . I wanted to make my own way here, socially, but independence from my family has never asserted itself in other ways. (According to guess-who ratings, she is highly resistant to faculty authority.)

L12

What I most wanted was to get over being a scared bunny. . . . I always resent doing the respectable thing just because it's the thing to do, but I didn't realize I was so different, politically, from my classmates. At least I agree with the few people I ever talk to about such matters. (Sociometric responses place her in a small, conservative group.)

Q81

I hated practically all my school life before coming here. I had the perfect inferiority complex, and I pulled out of school social life—out of fear. I didn't intend to repeat that mistake here. . . . I've just begun to be successful in winning friendships, and I've been blissfully happy here. (She is described by teachers as "pathologically belligerent"; she receives more than the average number of friendship choices, but reciprocates only one of them.)

For these five individuals, who are negativistic in the sense of being near-isolates rather than rebels, the community does not serve as reference group for public attitudes. To some extent, their small friendship groups serve in this capacity, but in the main they still refer such areas of their lives to the home-and-family group. They are too absorbed in their own pursuits to use the total membership group as a reference group for most other purposes, too.

3. *Conservatives, not reputedly negativistic, aware of their own relative conservatism.* Three of the five are described by teachers as "cooperative" and "eager," and none as stubborn or resistant. Four are above average in prestige. Four are considered by teachers or by guess-who raters, or both, to retain very close parental ties. All four who were interviewed had more or less definite ambitions for leadership on coming to college, and all felt that they had been relatively successful—though, in the words

of one of them, none ever attained the "really top-notch positions." All four are aware of conflict between parents and college community in respect to public attitudes, and all quite consciously decided to "string along" with parents, feeling self-confident of holding their own in college in spite of being atypical in this respect. Sample quotations follow:

Q73

I'm all my mother has in the world. It's considered intellectually superior here to be liberal or radical. This puts me on the defensive, as I refuse to consider my mother beneath me intellectually, as so many other students do. Apart from this, I have loved every aspect of college life. (A popular girl, many of whose friends are among the nonconservative college leaders.)

Q78

I've come to realize how much my mother's happiness depends on me, and the best way I can help her is to do things with her at home as often as I can. This has resulted in my not getting the feel of the college in certain ways, and I know my general conservatism is one of those ways. But it has not been important enough to me to make me feel particularly left out. If you're genuine and inoffensive about your opinions, no one really minds here if you remain conservative. (Another popular girl, whose friends were found among many groups.)

F32

Family against faculty has been my struggle here. As soon as I felt really secure here I decided not to let the college atmosphere affect me too much. Every time I've tried to rebel against my family I've found out how terribly wrong I am, and so I've naturally kept to my parents' attitudes. (While not particularly popular, she shows no bitterness and considerable satisfaction over her college experience.)

Q35

I've been aware of a protective shell against radical ideas. When I found several of my best friends getting that way,

I either had to go along or just shut out that area entirely. I couldn't respect myself if I had changed my opinions just for that reason, and so I almost deliberately lost interest—really, *it was out of fear of losing my friends.* (A very popular girl, with no trace of bitterness, who is not considered too dependent upon parents.)

For these five the total membership group does not serve as reference group in respect to public attitudes, but does so serve for most other purposes. At some stage in their college careers the conflict between college community and home and family as reference group for public attitudes was resolved in favor of the latter.

4. *Conservatives, not reputedly negativistic, not aware of their own relative conservatism.* All four are consistently described by teachers as conscientious and cooperative; three are considered overdocile and uncritical of authority. All are characterized by feelings of inferiority. All are low in prestige, two receiving scores of 0; all are low in friendship choices, but reciprocate most of these few choices. Two are described as in conflict about parental authority, and two as dependent and contented. All four recall considerable anxiety as to whether they would fit into the college community; all feel that they have succeeded better than they had expected. Sample statements from interviews follow:

D22

I'd like to think like the college leaders, but I'm not bold enough and I don't know enough. So the college trend means little to me; I didn't even realize how much more conservative I am than the others. *I guess my family influence has been strong enough to counterbalance the college influence.* (This girl was given to severe emotional upsets, and according to personnel records, felt "alone and helpless except when with her parents.")

M12

It isn't that I've been resisting any pressure to become liberal. The influences here didn't matter enough to resist,

I guess. *All that's really important that has happened to me occurred outside of college,* and so I never became very susceptible to college influences. (*Following her engagement to be married, in her second year, she had "practically retired" from community life.*)

Q68

If I'd had more time here I'd probably have caught on to the liberal drift here. But I've been horribly busy making money and trying to keep my college work up. *Politics and that sort of thing I've always associated with home instead of with the college.* (A "town girl" of working-class parentage.)

Q70

Most juniors and seniors, if they really *get excited about their work, forget about such community enthusiasms as sending telegrams to Congressmen.* It was so important to me to be accepted, I mean intellectually, *that I naturally came to identify myself in every way with the group which gave me this sort of intellectual satisfaction.* (One of a small group of science majors, nearly all conservative, who professed no interests other than science and who were highly self-sufficient socially.)

For none of the four was the total membership group a reference group for public attitudes. Unlike the nonnegativistic conservatives who are aware of their relative conservatism, they refer to the total membership group for few if any other purposes. Like the negativistic conservatives who are unaware of their relative conservatism, their reference groups for public attitudes are almost exclusively those related to home and family.

5. *Nonconservatives, reputedly community-identified, aware of their relative nonconservatism.* Each of the seven is considered highly independent by teachers, particularly in intellectual activities; all but one are referred to as meticulous, perfectionist, or overconscientious. Four are very high in prestige, two high, and one average; all are "good group members," and all but one a

"leader." None is considered overdependent upon parents. All have come to an understanding with parents concerning their "liberal" views; five have "agreed to differ," and the other two describe one or both parents as "very liberal." All take their public attitudes seriously, in most cases expressing the feeling that they have bled and died to achieve them. Interview excerpts follow.

B72

I bend in the direction of community expectation—almost more than I want to. I constantly have to check myself to be sure it's real self-conviction and not just social respect. (An outstanding and deeply respected leader.)

M42

My family has always been liberal, but the influences here made me go further, and for a while I was pretty far left. Now I'm pretty much in agreement with my family again, but it's my own and it means a lot. It wouldn't be easy for me to have friends who are very conservative. (Her friendship choices are exclusively given to nonconservatives.)

E72

I had been allowed so much independence by my parents that I needed desperately to identify myself with an institution with which I could conform conscientiously. Bennington was perfect. I drank up everything the college had to offer, including social attitudes, though not uncritically. I've become active in radical groups and constructively critical of them. (Both during and after college she worked with C.I.O. unions.)

H32

I accepted liberal attitudes here because *I had always secretly felt that my family was narrow and intolerant, and because such attitudes had prestige value.* It was all part of my generally expanding personality—*I had never really been part of anything before.* I don't accept things without examining things, however, and I was sure I meant it before I changed. (One of those who has "agreed to differ" with parents.)

Q43

It didn't take me long to see that liberal attitudes had prestige value. But all the time I felt inwardly superior to persons who want public acclaim. Once I had arrived at a feeling of personal security, I could see that it wasn't important —it wasn't enough. *So many people have no security at all. I became liberal at first because of its prestige value.* I remain so because the problems around which my liberalism centers are important. What I want now is to be effective in solving the problems. (Another conspicuous leader, active in and out of college in liberal movements.)

The total membership clearly serves as reference group for these individuals' changing attitudes, but by no means as the only one. For those whose parents are conservative, parents represent a negative reference group, from whom emancipation was gained via liberal attitudes. And for several of them the college community served as a bridge to outside liberal groups as points of reference.

6. *Nonconservatives, reputedly community-identified, not aware of their own relative nonconservatism.* The word *enthusiastic* appears constantly in the records of each of these six. All are considered eager, ambitious, hard-working, and anxious to please. Four are very high in prestige, the other two about average. None is considered overdependent upon parents, and only two are known to have suffered any particular conflict in achieving emancipation. Each one came to college with ambitions for leadership, and each professes extreme satisfaction with her college experience. Sample quotations follow:

Qx

Every influence I felt tended to push me in the liberal direction: my underdog complex, *my need to be independent of my parents, and my anxiousness to be a leader here.*

Q61

I met a whole body of new information here; I took a deep breath and plunged. When I talked about it at home my family began to treat me as if I had an adult mind. *Then too, my new opinions gave me the reputation here of being open-minded and capable of change.* I think I could have got really radical but I found it wasn't the way to get prestige here. (She judges most of her classmates to be as nonconservative as herself.)

Q72

I take everything hard, and so of course I reacted hard to all the attitudes I found here. I'm 100-percent enthusiastic about Bennington, and that includes liberalism (but not radicalism, though I used to think so). Now I know that you can't be an *extremist if you're really devoted to an institution,* whether it's a labor union or a college. (A conspicuous leader who, like most of the others in this set of six, *judges classmates to be only slightly more conservative than herself.*)

Q63

I came to college to get away from my family, who never had any respect for my mind. Becoming a radical meant thinking for myself and, figuratively, thumbing my nose at my family. *It also meant intellectual identification with the faculty and students that I most wanted to be like.* (She has always felt oppressed by parental respectability and sibling achievements.)

Q57

It's very simple. *I was so anxious to be accepted that I accepted the political complexion of the community here.* I just couldn't stand out against the crowd unless I had many friends and strong support. (Not a leader, but many close friends among leaders and nonconservatives.)

For these six, like the preceding seven, the membership group serves as reference group for public affairs. They differ from the preceding seven chiefly in that they are less sure of themselves and are careful "not to go too far." Hence they tend to repudiate "radicalism," and to judge classmates as only slightly less conservative than themselves.

7. *Nonconservatives, not reputedly community-identified, aware of own relative nonconservatism.* Each of the six is described as highly independent and critical-minded. Four are consistently reported as intellectually outstanding, and the other two occasionally so. All describe their ambitions on coming to college in intellectual rather than in social terms. Four of the five who were interviewed stated that in a conservative college they would be "even more radical than here." Two are slightly above average in prestige, two below average, and two have 0 scores. Three have gone through rather severe battles in the process of casting off what they regard as parental shackles; none is considered overdependent upon parents. Sample interview excerpts follow:

Q7

All my life I've resented the protection of governesses and parents. What I most wanted here was the intellectual approval of teachers and the more advanced students. Then I found you can't be reactionary and be intellectually respectable. (Her traits of independence became more marked as she achieved academic distinction.)

Q21

I simply got filled with new ideas here, and the only possible formulation of all of them was to adopt a radical approach. *I can't see my own position in the world in any other terms. The easy superficiality with which so many prestige-hounds here get "liberal" only forced me to think it out more intensely.* (A highly gifted girl, considered rather aloof.)

C32

I started rebelling against my pretty stuffy family before I came to college. I felt apart from freshmen here, because I was older. Then I caught on to faculty attempts to undermine prejudice. I took sides with the faculty immediately, against the immature freshmen. I crusaded about it. *It provided just what I needed by way of family rebellion,* and bolstered up my self-confidence, too. (A very bright girl, regarded as sharp tongued and a bit haughty.)

J24

I'm easily influenced by people whom I respect, and the people who rescued me when I was down and out, intellectually, gave me a radical intellectual approach; they included both teachers and advanced students. *I'm not rebelling against anything.* I'm just doing what I had to do to stand on my own feet intellectually. (Her academic work was poor as a freshman, but gradually became outstanding.)

For these six students it is not the total membership group, but dominant subgroups (faculty, advanced students) which at first served as positive reference groups, and for many of them the home groups served as a negative point of reference. Later, they developed extracollege reference groups (left-wing writers, etc.). In a secondary sense, however, the total membership group served as a negative point of reference—i.e., they regarded their nonconservatism as a mark of personal superiority.

8. *Nonconservatives, not reputedly community-identified, not aware of own relative nonconservatism.* Each of the five is considered hard-working, eager, and enthusiastic but (especially during the first year or two) unsure of herself and too dependent upon instructors. They are "good citizens," but in a distinctly retiring way. Two are above average in prestige, and the other three much below average. None of the five is considered overdependent upon parents; two are known to have experienced a good deal of conflict in emancipating themselves. All regard themselves as "pretty average persons," with a strong desire to conform; they describe their ambitions in terms of social acceptance instead of social or intellectual prestige. Sample excerpts follow:

E22

Social security is the focus of it all with me. I became steadily less conservative as long as I was *needing to gain in personal security, both with students and with faculty.* I developed some resentment against a few extreme radicals who don't really represent the college viewpoint, and that's why I changed my attitudes so far and no further. (A girl with a small personal following, otherwise not especially popular.)

D52

Of course there's social pressure here to give up your conservatism. I'm glad of it, because for me this became the *vehicle for achieving independence from my family.* So changing my attitudes has gone hand in hand with two *very important things: establishing my own independence and at the same time becoming a part of the college organism.* (She attributes the fact that her social attitudes changed, while those of her younger sister, also at the college, did not, to the fact that she had greater need both of family independence and of group support.)

Q6

I was ripe for developing liberal or even radical opinions because so many of my friends at home were doing the same thing. So it was really wonderful that I could agree with all the people I respected here and the same time move in the direction that my home friends were going." (A girl characterized by considerable personal instability at first, but showing marked improvement.)

Qy

I think my change of opinions has given me *intellectual and social self-respect at the same time.* I used to be too timid for words, and I never had an idea of my own. As I gradually became more successful in my work and made more friends, I came to feel that it didn't matter so much whether I agreed with my parents. It's all part of the feeling that I really belong here. (Much other evidence confirms this; she was lonely and pathetic at first, but really belonged later.)

These five provide the example *par excellence* of individuals who came to identify themselves with "the community" and whose attitudes change *pari passu* with the growing sense of identity. Home-and-family groups served as supplementary points of reference, either positive or negative. To varying degrees, subgroups within the community served as focal points of reference. But, because of *their need to be accepted, it was primarily the membership group as such which served as reference group for these five.*

Summary

In this community, as presumably in most others, all individuals belong to the total membership group, but such membership is not necessarily a point of reference for every form of social adaptation, e.g., for acquiring attitudes toward public issues. *Such attitudes, however, are not acquired in a social vacuum. Their acquisition is a function of relating oneself to some group or groups, positively or negatively.* In many cases (perhaps in all) the referring of social attitudes to one group negatively leads to referring them to another group positively, or vice versa, so that the attitudes are dually reinforced.

An individual is, of course, "typical" in respect to attitudes if the total membership group serves as a positive point of reference for that purpose, but "typicality" may also result from the use of other reference groups. It does not follow from the fact that an individual is "atypical" that the membership group does not serve for reference purposes; it may serve as negative reference group. Even if the membership group does not serve as reference group at all (as in the case of conservatives in this community who are unaware of the general freshman-to-senior trend), it cannot be concluded that attitude development is not a function of belonging to the total membership group. The unawareness of such individuals is itself a resultant adaptation of particular individuals to a particular membership group. The fact that such individuals continue to refer attitudes toward public issues primarily to home-and-family groups is, in part at least, a result of the kind of community in which they have membership.

In short, the Bennington findings seem to support the thesis that, in a community characterized by certain approved attitudes, the individual's attitude development is a function of the way in which he relates himself both to the total membership group and to one or more reference groups.

Reference Groups, Membership Groups, and Attitude Change ❋ Alberta Engvall Siegel ❋ Sidney Siegel

In social psychological theory, it has long been recognized that an individual's *membership groups* have an important influence on the values and attitudes he holds. More recently, attention has also been given to the influence of his *reference groups:* the groups in which he aspires to attain or maintain membership. In a given area, membership groups and reference groups may or may not be identical. They are identical when the person aspires to *maintain* membership in the group of which he is a part; they are disparate when the group in which the individual aspires to *attain* membership is one in which he is not a member. It has been widely asserted that both membership and reference groups affect the attitudes held by the individual (Sherif and Sherif, 1953).

The present study is an examination of the attitude changes which occur over time when reference groups and membership groups are identical and when they are disparate. The study takes advantage of a field experiment which occurred in the social context of the lives of the subjects, concerning events considered vital by them. The subjects were not aware that their membership and reference groups were of research interest; in fact, they did not know that the relevant information about these was available to the investigators.

The field experiment permitted a test of the general hypothesis that both the amount and the direction of a person's attitude change over time depends on the attitude norms of his membership group (whether or not that group is chosen by him) and on the attitude norms of his reference group.

This hypothesis is tested with subjects who shared a common reference group at the time of the initial assessment of attitudes. They were then randomly assigned to alternative membership groups, some being assigned to the chosen group and others to a nonchosen group. Attitudes were reassessed after a year of experience in these alternative membership groups with divergent attitude norms. During the course of the year, some subjects came to take the imposed (initially nonpreferred) membership group as their reference group. Attitude change af-

From the *Journal of Abnormal and Social Psychology*, 1957, 55, 360-364. Reprinted by permission of the author and the American Psychological Association. This study was supported by grants from the Committee for the Study of American Values at Stanford University and from the Stanford Value Theory Project. We wish to acknowledge with gratitude the assistance given by Davis W. Thompkins, Marilyn Sanchez-Corea, and Coleen Baker in the execution of this study, and the generous administrative cooperation of Elva Fay Brown, Dean of Women at Stanford University, and her staff.

ter the year was examined in terms of the membership group and reference group identifications of the subjects at that time.

The Field Experiment

The Ss of this study were women students at a large private coeducational university. The study was initiated shortly before the end of their freshman year, when they all lived in the same large freshman dormitory to which they had been assigned upon entering the university. At this university, all women move to new housing for their sophomore year. Several types of housing are available to them: a large dormitory, a medium-sized dormitory, several very small houses which share common dining facilities, and a number of former sorority houses which have been operated by the university since sororities were banished from the campus. These latter are located among the fraternity houses on Fraternity Row, and are therefore known as "Row houses." Although the Row houses are lower in physical comfort than most of the other residences for women, students consider them higher in social status. This observation was confirmed by a poll of students (Siegel, 1954, p. 205), in which over 90 per cent of the respondents stated that Row houses for women were higher in social status than non-Row houses, the remaining few disclaiming any information concerning status differences among women's residences.

In the Spring of each year, a "drawing" is held for housing for the subsequent year. All freshmen must participate in this drawing, and any other student who wishes to change her residence may participate. It is conducted by the office of the Dean of Women, in cooperation with woman student leaders. Any participant's ballot is understood to be secret. The woman uses the ballot to rank the houses in the order of her preference. After submitting this ballot, she draws a number from the hopper. The rank of that number determines the likelihood that her preference will be satisfied.

In research reported earlier (Siegel, 1954), a random sample was drawn from the population of freshman women at this university, several tests were administered to the Ss in that sample, and (unknown to the Ss their housing preferences for the forthcoming sophomore year were observed by the investigator. The Ss were characterized as "high status oriented" if they listed a Row house as their first choice, and were characterized as "low status oriented" if they listed a non-Row house as their first choice. The hypothesis under test, drawn from reference group theory and from theoretical formulations concerning authoritarianism, was that high status orientation is a correlate of authoritarianism. The hypothesis was confirmed: freshman women who listed a Row house as their first choice for residence scored significantly higher on the average in authoritarianism, as measured by the E-F scale (Adorno, Frenkel-Brunswik, Levinson, and Sanford, 1950; Gough, 1951) than did women who listed a non-Row house as their first choice. The present study is a continuation of the one described, and uses as its Ss only those members of the original sample who were "high status oriented," i.e., preferred to live in a Row house for the sophomore year. In the initial study (Siegel, 1954) of the 95 Ss whose housing choices were listed, 39 were "high status oriented," i.e., demonstrated that the Row was their reference group by giving a Row house as their first choice in the drawing. Of this group, 28 were available to serve as Ss for the follow-up or "change" study which is the topic of the present paper. These women form a homogeneous subsample in that at the conclusion of their freshman year they shared a common membership group (the freshman dormitory) and a common reference group (the Row). These Ss, however, had divergent experiences during their sophomore year: nine were Row residents during that year (having drawn sufficiently small numbers in the housing drawing to enable them to be assigned to the group of their choice) and the other 19 lived in non-Row houses during that year (having drawn numbers too large to enable them to be assigned to the housing group of their choice).

E-F scores were obtained from each of the 28 Ss in the course of a large-scale testing program administered to most of the women students at the university. Anonymity was guaranteed to the Ss, but a coding procedure permitted the investigators to identify each respondent and thereby to isolate the Ss and compare each S's second E-F score with her first.

To prevent the Ss from knowing that they were participating in a follow-up study, several procedures were utilized: (a) many persons who had not served in the earlier study were included in the second sample, (b) the testing was introduced as being part of a nation-wide study to establish norms, (c) the test administrators were different persons from those who had administered the initial tests, (d) Ss who informed the test administrator that they had already taken the "Public Opinion Questionnaire" (E-F scale) were casually told that this did not disqualify them from participating in the current study.

The Ss had no hint that the research was in any way related to their housing arrangements. Testing was conducted in classrooms as well as in residences, and all procedures and instructions were specifically designed to avoid any arousal of the salience of the housing groups in the frame of reference of the research.

The annual housing drawing was conducted three weeks after the sophomore-year testing, and, as usual, each woman's housing ballot was understood to be secret. In this drawing, each S had the opportunity to change her membership group, although a residence move is not required at the end of the sophomore year as it is at the end of the freshman year. If an S participated in this drawing, the house which she listed as

her first choice on the ballot was identified by the investigators as her reference group. If she did not, it was evident that the house in which she was currently a member was the one in which she chose to continue to live, i.e., was her reference group. With the information on each S's residence choice at the end of her freshman year, her assigned residence for her sophomore year, and her residence choice at the end of her sophomore year, it was possible to classify the subjects in three categories:

A. Women ($n = 9$) who had gained assignment to live on the Row during their sophomore year and who did not attempt to draw out of the Row at the end of that year;

B. Women ($n = 11$) who had not gained assignment to a Row house for the sophomore year and who drew for a Row house again after living in a non-Row house during the sophomore year; and

C. Women ($n = 8$) who had not gained assignment to a Row house for the sophomore year, and who chose to remain in a non-Row house after living in one during the sophomore year.

For all three groups of Ss, as we have pointed out, membership group (freshman dormitory) and reference group (Row house) were common at the end of the freshman year. For Group A, membership and reference groups were identical throughout the sophomore year. For Group B, membership and reference groups were disparate throughout the sophomore year. For Group C, membership and reference groups were initially disparate during the sophomore year but became identical because of a change in reference groups.

As will be demonstrated, the Row and the non-Row social groups differ in attitude norms, with Row residents being generally more authoritarian than non-Row residents. From social psychological theory concerning the influence of group norms on individuals' attitudes, it would be predicted that the different group identifications during the sophomore year of the three groups of Ss would result in differential attitude change. Those who gained admittance to a Row house for the sophomore year (Group A) would be expected to show the least change in authoritarianism, for they spent that year in a social context which reinforced their initial attitudes. Group C Ss would be expected to show the greatest change in authoritarianism, a change associated not only with their membership in a group (the non-Row group) which is typically low in authoritarianism, but also with their shift in reference groups, from Row to non-Row, i.e., from a group normatively higher in authoritarianism to a group normatively lower. The extent of attitude change in the Ss in Group B would be expected to be intermediate, due to the conflicting influences of the imposed membership group (non-Row) and of the unchanged reference group (Row). The research hypothesis, then, is that between the time of the freshman-year testing and the sophomore-year testing, the extent of change in authoritarianism will be least in Group A, greater in Group B, and greatest in Group C. That is, in extent of attitude change, Group A < Group B < Group C.

Results

GROUP NORMS

From the data collected in the large-scale testing program, it was possible to determine the group norms for authoritarian attitudes among the Row and the non-Row women at the university. The E-F scale was administered to all available Row residents ($n = 303$) and to a random sample of residents of non-Row houses ($n = 101$). These Ss were sophomores, juniors, and seniors. The mean E-F score of the Row women was 90, while the mean E-F score of the non-Row was 81. The E-F scores of the two groups were demonstrated to differ at the $p < .001$ level ($x^2 = 11.1$) by the median test (Siegel, 1956, pp. 111-116), a nonparametric test, the data for which are shown in Table 1.

TABLE 1

FREQUENCIES OF E-F SCORES ABOVE AND BELOW COMMON MEDIAN FOR ROW AND NON-ROW RESIDENTS

	Residents of Non-Row Houses	Residents of Row Houses	Total
Above Median	36	166	202
Below Median	65	137	202
Total	101	303	404

ATTITUDE CHANGE

The central hypothesis of this study is that attitude change will occur differentially in Groups A, B, and C, and that it will occur in the direction which would be predicted from knowledge of the group norms among Row and non-Row residents in general. The 28 Ss of this study had a mean E-F score of 102 at the end of their freshman year. The data reported above concerning authoritarianism norms for all women residing on campus would lead to the prediction that in general the Ss would show a reduction in authoritarianism during the sophomore year but that this reduction would be differential in the three groups; from the knowledge that Row residents generally are higher in authoritarianism than non-Row residents, the prediction based on social group theory would be that Group A would show the smallest reduction in authoritarianism scores, Group B would show a larger reduction, and Group C would show the largest reduction. The data which permit a test of this hypothesis are given in Table 2. The Jonckheere test (Jonckheere, 1954), a nonparametric k-sample test which tests the null hypothesis that the three groups are from the same population against the alternative hypothesis that they are from different populations which are ordered in a specified way, was used with these data. By that test, the hypothesis is confirmed at the $p < .025$ level.

TABLE 2

FRESHMAN-YEAR AND SOPHOMORE-YEAR
E-F SCORES OF SUBJECTS

| Group | E-F Score | | Difference |
	End of Freshman Year	End of Sophomore Year	
A	108	125	−17
	70	78	−8
	106	107	−1
	92	92	0
	80	78	2
	104	102	2
	143	138	5
	110	92	18
	114	80	34
B	76	117	−41
	105	107	−2
	88	82	6
	109	97	12
	98	83	15
	112	94	18
	101	82	19
	114	93	21
	104	81	23
	116	91	25
	101	74	27
C	121	126	−5
	87	79	8
	105	95	10
	97	81	16
	96	78	18
	108	73	35
	114	77	37
	88	49	39

Discussion

Substantively, the present study provides experimental verification of certain assertions in social group theory, demonstrating that attitude change over time is related to the group identification of the person—both his membership group identification and his reference group identification. The hypothesis that extent of attitude change would be different in the three subgroups of Ss, depending on their respective membership group and reference group identifications, is confirmed at the $p < .025$ level; in extent of change in authoritarianism, Group A < Group B < Group C, as predicted.

Another way of looking at the data may serve to highlight the influence of membership groups and reference groups. At the end of the freshman year, the Ss in Groups A, B, and C shared the same membership group and the same reference group. During the sophomore year, the Ss in Group A shared one membership group while those in Groups B and C together shared another. From membership group theory, it would be predicted that the extent of attitude change would be greater among the latter Ss. This hypothesis is supported by the data (in Table 2): by the Mann-Whitney test (Siegel, 1956, pp. 116-127), the change scores of these two sets of Ss (Group A versus Groups B and C together) differ in the predicted direction at the $p < .025$ level. This finding illustrates the influence of *membership* groups on attitude change. On the other hand, at the conclusion of the sophomore year, the Ss in Groups A and B shared a common reference group while those in Group C had come to share another. From reference group theory, it would be predicted that attitude change would be more extensive among the subjects who had changed reference groups (Group C) than among those who had not. This hypothesis is also supported by the data (in Table 2): by the Mann-Whitney test, the change scores of these two sets of Ss (Groups A and B together versus Group C) differ in the predicted direction at the $p < .05$ level. This finding illustrates the influence of *reference* groups on attitude change. Any inference from this mode of analysis (as contrasted with the main analysis of the data, by the Jonckheere test) must be qualified because of the nonindependence of the data on which the two Mann-Whitney tests are made, but it is mentioned here to clarify the role which membership and reference groups play in influencing attitude change.

The findings may also contribute to our understanding of processes affecting attitude change. The imposition of a membership group does have some effect on an individual's attitudes, even when the imposed group is not accepted by the individual as his reference group. This relationship is shown in the case of Group B. If the person comes to accept the imposed group as his reference group, as was the case with the Ss in Group C, then the change in his attitudes toward the level of the group norm is even more pronounced.

Methodologically, the study has certain features which may deserve brief mention. First, the study demonstrates that it is possible operationally to define the concept of reference group. The act of voting by secret ballot for the group in which one would like to live constitutes clear behavioral specification of one's reference group, and it is an act whose conceptual meaning can be so directly inferred that there is no problem of reliability of judgment in its categorization by the investigator. Second, the study demonstrates that a field study can be conducted which contains the critical feature of an experiment that is usually lacking in naturalistic situations: randomization. The determination of whether or not a woman student would be assigned to the living group of her choice was based on a random event: the size of the number she drew from the hopper. This fact satisfied the requirement that the treatment condition be randomized, and permitted sharper inferences than can usually be drawn from field studies. Third, the test behavior on which the conclusions of this study were based occurred in a context in which the salience of membership and reference groups was *not* aroused and

in which no external sanctions from the relevant groups were operative. This feature of the design permitted the interpretation that the E-F scores represented the Ss' internalized attitudes (Sherif and Sherif, 1953, p. 218). Finally, the use of a paper-and-pencil measure of attitude and thus of attitude change, rather than the use of some more behavioral measure, is a deficiency of the present study. Moreover, the measure which was used suffers from a well-known circularity, based on the occurrence of pseudo-low scores (Adorno, Frenkel-Brunswik, Levinson, and Sanford, 1950, p. 771; Siegel, 1953, pp. 221-222).

Summary

In the social context of the lives of the subjects, and in a natural social experiment which provided randomization of the relevant condition effects, the influence of both membership and reference groups on attitude change was assessed. All subjects shared a common reference group at the start of the period of the study. When divergent membership groups with disparate attitude norms were socially imposed on the basis of a random event, attitude change in the subjects over time was a function of the normative attitudes of both imposed membership groups and the individuals' reference groups. The greatest attitude change occurred in subjects who came to take the imposed, initially nonpreferred, membership group as their reference group.

References

ADORNO, T. W., FRENKEL-BRUNSWIK, ELSE, LEVINSON, D. J., and SANFORD, R. N. *The authoritarian personality.* New York: Harper & Row, 1950.

GOUGH, H. G. Studies of social intolerance: I. Some psychological and sociological correlates of anti-Semitism. *J. soc. Psychol.,* 1951, 33, 237-246.

JONCKHEERE, A. R. A distribution-free k-sample test against ordered alternatives. *Biometrika,* 1954, 41, 133-145.

SHERIF, M., and SHERIF, CAROLYN W. *Groups in harmony and tension.* New York: Harper & Row, 1953.

SIEGEL, S. Certain determinants and correlates of authoritarianism. *Genet. Psychol. Monogr.,* 1954, 49, 187-229.

SIEGEL, S. *Nonparametric statistics: for the behavioral sciences.* New York: McGraw-Hill, 1956.

PART IV

Culture
Context and
the Individual

INTRODUCTION

The human social environment is complex and diverse. To make conceptual sense out of it theorists typically have focused on its structure and content. The problem of structure, or the organization of social interactions, will concern us in the next major section. The emphasis here is on the content of these social interactions or, more particularly, on what occurs during interaction both in terms of how people behave and in reference to what social objects or events. Individuals think, feel, and act in determined ways with respect to specific social stimuli and under given sets of circumstances. All these substantive elements of the social environment reflect the pervasive and inexorable influence of *culture*.

From birth onward the individual lives and develops in a social context that determines much of what may appear to the naïve observer to be matters of his own choice. How he is reared, what he eats, the language he speaks, the nature of his interpersonal relationships, what his life's work shall be, and, indeed, the response to and the meaning of his death are all determined. True, this determination is always reflected in a range of possibilities presented by the culture rather than in terms of highly specific and precise requirements; it is a determinism nevertheless.

Culture is an abstraction employed by the anthropologist. Actually he uses the concept in two ways, each of which helps us to make sense out of the relationship between behaving individuals and the setting in which this behavior occurs (Kluckhohn, 1954). The existence of culture is inferred on the basis of the observed regularities in the behavior of specific individuals and from the multitude of cultural artifacts that derive from this behavior. Culture in this sense is defined in terms of its external, directly observable effects. To explain these effects or the observed regularities of behavior, anthropologists also assume the existence of an inner culture, the internalized representation of these behaivor patterns in the form of norms, beliefs, values, and needs. It should be evident that the anthropologist's "implicit culture" is the modal psychological factors which characterize the members of a given social setting.

Culture as a determinant of human behavior has not always been viewed with the significance it now has in modern social science. Early prescientific conceptions of man endowed him with any number of universal traits or motives to explain his behavior in a wide range of situations. Hobbes's cruel and selfish man seeking power, Bentham's "ethical hedonism," and Adam Smith's "economic man" are all instances of such formulations; many others can be cited. What should be stressed is the fact that these assumptions about the nature of man invariably reflected the prevailing values or social ethos of the society in which they arose. Behavioral science disciplines were no less free of this kind of influence in their inital conceptions of the nature of man. Here, too, were to be found culture-bound explanations in which Western man became the prototype of all men. It is only in recent times, and primarily because of the field studies of anthropologists, that the idea has been accepted that customs and ways of life other than our own are no less valid as expressions of "human nature."

It is not uncommon to view "cultural differences" in terms of the sharply defined variations that emerge when modern Western society is compared with existing preliterate groups, for example, the Arapesh and the Kwakiutl. Yet, it should be evident from our previous discussions that the very complexity of our own society creates significant differences as well as similarities in the cultural forces that shape the existence of Western man. Comparisons between different nations, or between social classes and racial groups within the same nation, are based on what is a readily observed fact: variations in culture occur at many levels of social organization. In general, the more encompassing the level of social organization at which the comparison is made the greater the range of cultural differences to be expected.

The usefulness of the concept of culture in understanding social behavior requires that it be viewed in its proper perspective. The pervasiveness of culture in the existence of man does not endow it with a conceptual sovereignty in explaining the behavior of individuals or groups of individuals. There are limits to the influence of culture and it is important that they be specified from the beginning.

The influence of culture on any single individual is always conditioned by the nature of his unique biological makeup. Individual differences in this respect, among other things, account for the range of variability among individuals in the same social setting. Furthermore, no individual is exposed to all the significant processes and events that comprise a cultural system. He experiences only selected aspects of this system, and a great deal of what he experiences, especially in development, is mediated by specific persons. The child is not influenced by culture in the abstract but by persons who are carriers of culture, persons whose own behavior embodies the existence of culture. By the same token these agents of culture reflect the sanctioned ways of the society as experienced and interpreted by them, which, in effect, means still another source of variability in the prescriptions of the culture. It should now be evident that the description of the culture of a society is not a description of any actual person in the society. It is a description of the modal member of that society.

The concept of "cultural relativism" achieved considerable importance with the demise of instinct theory and the advent of the view that man is a creature of culture. In its extreme form it viewed any number of behaviors as possible in a given situation; which one was employed was a matter of the cultural setting. These behaviors were equivalent and substitutable; hence the possibility of universals among men was ignored if not denied. What this conception overlooked was the fact that what appears to be the very same situation often varies in its functional meaning with the cultural context, and as a consequence the responses made to these situations are by no means equivalent. What this suggests is that, given functionally equivalent situations in different cultures, we can expect to find some commonality in the way men respond to and evaluate these situations. It is highly unlikely, for example, that any culture would value cowardice and disparage courage, although definitions of cowardly and courageous behavior may differ widely.

From the social psychologist's point of view the study of different cultures or subcultures becomes the basis for understanding the factors that underlie the origin and development of different motives, beliefs, interests, and values in different groups of individuals. On the other hand, it cannot be stressed too strongly that the study of different cultural settings provides a basis for determining not only what is different among men, but also what is common to human experience. In this respect, the concern is not merely with similarities in content, but, more importantly, with the determination of the extent to which concepts and theories of psychological process have validity in a variety of human settings. The universal characteristics of men go beyond hunger, thirst, sex, and the other primary drives. They include such human reactions as fear, conflict, anxiety, and self-image, as well as many others. That each of these may be expressed and experienced differently and be related to very different social conditions in no way reduces their significance as characteristic human reactions. The very fact that cultures can be compared along given dimensions suggests the existence of fundamental similarities in the human situation.

Human society rests on man's capacity to use words. It is his use of language that makes possible the communication of meaning and the sharing of experience. These factors, in turn, enable him to establish an enduring society characterized by a distinctive culture. Language for the individual is clearly the substance of his phenomenal world. He thinks, feels, and understands by means of, and within the limits imposed on him by, the content and structure of the language he speaks. It follows, therefore, that the study of language is important, on the one hand, for what it can reveal about the psychological functioning of man that is unique to him as a species; and, on the other, for what it can tell us about the nature of and variation in the cultural influences that act on him.

Languages differ in many respects. Even in the case of such closely related languages as English and German, many meanings cannot be translated precisely from one language into the other. In the case of languages that are completely unrelated, English and Hopi, for example, the structural differences are great enough for the same events to tend to be categorized or perceived differently by individuals in the two cultures. It is generally agreed that the language of a people reflects the central concerns and interests of their culture. But what of the influence of language on culture? Whorf (1940) contends that differences in content and structure between languages have differential consequences for the way individuals using them perceive and think about their external world. In his now classic example, he points to the fact that the Eskimo language has three distinct words for three varieties of snow—"falling snow," for example—all of which are included under the broad term "snow" in the English language. However, the fact that linguistic differences (vocabulary and grammatical form) exist between two languages in and by itself does not permit us to conclude that this results in differences in cognitive behavior. It is for this reason that a number of investigators have attempted to determine experimentally whether linguistic structure does in fact influence the cognitive behavior of the person.

Brown and Lenneberg (IVA) present evidence that demonstrates that both vocabulary and phonological differences in languages have consequences for the way individuals perceive their world. In the vocabulary study it was first shown that 24 colors differed in their "codability," that is, some colors were quickly responded to with a single-word name, whereas others produced blocking and compound-word names in being identified. Subjects were first shown 4 of these colors at a time and were then asked to pick out of a chart of 120 colors the 4 they had just seen. It was found that colors with simple, common names were recognized more accurately than the colors that were low in codability. Brown and Lenneberg also studied a group of Zuñi Indians and here again found a relationship between the codability of colors and the ability to recognize these colors.

The grammatical structure of a language as well as its vocabulary affects the individual's cognitive behavior. In a study of preschool children, Brown (IVA) found that the grammatical character or class of an artificial or nonsense word— for example, the verb "to sib"—enabled the child to identify correctly a relevant event in a series of pictures. In other words, when asked where he saw "sibbing" in any of three pictures, the child was more likely to select a picture in which a person was doing something, for example, someone drinking, than a picture in which an object was shown. On the other hand, if he was asked to select a picture with a "sib," the latter choice was more likely to occur.

Studies of the influence of structural differences in unrelated languages on cognitive behavior have also provided some support for the Whorfian hypothesis (Carroll and Casagrande, 1958). However, Whorf assumed not only that language determined cognitive behavior, but also that it rendered the person incapable of making discriminations in the external world which were not relevant to its vocabulary or structure. He contended, in effect, that English-speaking people are incapable of discriminating the three kinds of snow separately designated by the Eskimo language. Brown and Lenneberg (IVA), however, are quick to point out that, despite the absence of equivalent terms in English, Whorf himself is apparently able to grasp the nature of the distinctions involved in the three varieties of snow. Otherwise how could he describe them with the longer-phrased names that he uses? A more parsimonious interpretation of the influence of language on cognition follows from their research: It is not that linguistic patterns actually modify or limit the cognitive capacities of the person, but rather that they direct these capacities toward certain aspects of the person's social environment and away from others.

Previously we took note of the fact that related languages differ to some degree in linguistic structure. One would expect, therefore, that the bilingual would encounter some interference in his use of the two languages. However, as Lambert, Havelka, and Crosby (IVA) point out, the extent of such interference will depend on the distinctiveness of the context in which the two languages were acquired. To say it another way, equivalent words of two languages, learned in the same or similar settings should evoke the same meaning for the bilingual; therefore, the use of one word should create interference by the other. On this basis these investigators predicted that bilinguals with distinctive or separated acquisition experiences would show comparatively greater differences in the meanings given to equivalent terms in the two languages. They studied bilingual students who spoke French and English and who could be distinguished in terms of three degrees of distinctiveness in the contexts in which these two languages were acquired. They found that those who had acquired the two languages in very different contexts showed the greatest variation in meaning attributed to equivalent words.

As Brown and Lenneberg point out, linguistic category systems applied to persons provide a basis for predicting how these individuals will behave. It is evident from the Katz and Braly (IVA) study that ethnic and racial membership is a significant category system in that respect. In selecting five traits they considered most characteristic of ten ethnic groups, college students showed agreements ranging from 50 to 84 percent. Given this degree of consistency in stereotyping racial and ethnic groups, it can only be concluded that these kinds of social categories are indeed important in how individuals on the American scene view each other. The psychological economy involved is evident. Wherever the racial or ethnic label fits, the person takes on the properties of the group and therefore his behavior can be "predicted." Linguistic categories are not mere abstractions but rather have concrete consequences for behavior that is of direct importance for social living.

The learning of a language is part of the *socialization* experiences of the child. Socialization is a pervasive and complex process by which approved modes of thought, affect, and behavior are inculcated in the child over time by the adult members of the society. The terms "child" and "adult" themselves reflect the organized character of the socialization practices of the society. In various contexts the role of the latter carries with it the right and responsibility of molding and modifying the conduct of the former. What does socialization mean from the child's point of view? It consists of his being immersed in a continuing sequence of social contexts—family, school, play group, and so on—in which he experiences people, objects, rewards, punishments, love, threats. As we indicated earlier, the child is not influenced by culture in the abstract, but rather by people in various culturally determined contexts who are the agents of culture. It is these social experiences which constitute the substantive basis of the socialization process.

The investigations reported here on the socialization of the child vary widely in the nature of the problems, settings, and individuals studied. By the same token, to an extent all of them reveal some of the basic characteristics of the socialization process that apply to any and all social settings. We have already indicated the significance of the special relationship between the child and adult in this process. It is also important to note that the child training practices of any society are always conditioned by the maturational development of the child. Although considerable variation is possible in the nature and timing of these practices from one cultural setting to the next, the physiological capacities of the child at various developmental levels set limits in all societies on when and how he will learn. For example, in the study by Whiting, Kluckhohn, and Anthony (IVB), severe initiation of the young male into the adult role was shown to be related to certain child training and sex-related practices of a society. It was assumed that these practices generate hostility toward the father and strong dependency on the mother, thereby making it necessary for the society to take means to reduce this potential threat to its existence. The investigators point out that "one function of the rites is to prevent open and violent revolt against parental authority at a time when physical maturity could make such revolt dangerous and socially disruptive." Even if we do not accept their explanation, the fact remains that the physical endurance tests undergone by the young male in these ceremonies—beatings, exposure to cold, thirst, and so on—occur at a time when he is capable of surviving these punishments, clearly a necessity if the society is to continue. If we turn to Piaget's conception of the moral development of the child (IVB), it is clearly evident that an increasing cognitive capacity is a necessary condition for the observed changes with age in the child's conception of the "rules of the game."

As we indicated above, socialization is a complex process that rests on the child's capacity to learn. It takes place by subtle and indirect means as well as by direct instruction given to the child in formal settings. What is not told to the child or what he is not permitted to observe is as important in his social development as what he experiences openly and directly. Although the family and school are social contexts in which formal learning occurs, informal influences pervade both settings that are no less significant in this development. The child's peers, siblings, family, neighbors, and relatives, as well as the mass media, are as much agents of his culture as are his parents, minister, and teacher.

The study by Horowitz (IIIA) reported in the previous section indicated that contact with the prevailing norm rather than direct experience with Negroes was primarily responsible for the white child's attitude toward the latter. Many other investigations have shown that this contact seldom involves direct instruction by the parent. However indirect these influences, parental and otherwise, the child not only learns the norm of his setting but learns it well. Furthermore, as the Clark and Clark (IVB) study vividly illustrates, the Negro child is no less subject to this influence than the white child. Not only is the Negro child aware of racial differences at an early age, but no differences are found in this respect between Negro children from Southern segregated schools and those from mixed Northern schools. Once again the prevalent attitude rather than direct experience with members of the other group seems to make the difference.

It can be argued, of course, that "racial differences" are taught to the Negro child by parents and other adults. Undoubtedly this is true. However, he also learns to accept the majority view that the white group is more desirable than his own. How else can we explain the fact that in general a majority of the Negro children in the investigation by the Clarks preferred a white doll and rejected a colored doll? It is not likely that he was taught directly that his own racial group was inferior to the white group.

When the norms, values, beliefs, and attitudes of a social system are internalized by the individual, then the efficacy of the socialization process is demonstrated. What was once external to the person is now internal, and it is in this sense that the person's concept of self reflects the general and specific nature of the social world in which he is reared. As we indicated in our discussion in Part II, the person himself becomes the focus of a cognitive structure that defines and evaluates who and what he is. The importance of the child's experience in his social setting in this respect is quite evident from the findings reported by the Clarks (IVB). If the young Negro child tends to prefer the white majority group to his own, then it follows that his self-evaluation must be something less than desirable. The fact that one third of the Negro children in the study chose a *white* doll when asked to identify themselves readily makes this clear.

It is important to stress that the growth of self in the life of the child is a continuing process that depends on the interaction between his cognitive capacities and his experiences in his social environment. For the child to internalize a rule or a social norm, he not only must be able to distinguish himself from others but also must be capable of taking the roles of these others. According to Piaget (IVB) moral development begins when rules are imposed on the child by grownups and older children (heteronomy) and ends when the child is guided by his own rules (autonomy). This final stage is only possible when the child's distinction between the self and the other is sufficiently clear for him to conceive of points of view other than his own. Important in this respect is the child's participation in games and other activities with age-mate groups on a cooperative basis. In time, egocentric relationships give way to reciprocal relationships, and through cooperative give-and-take the child comes to accept group norms as his own.

The effects of social class on the development of the child has been the subject of many investigations, to say the least. Typically, some measure of social class is used to distinguish groups of children, who are then compared in terms of their overt behavior, attitudes, self-conceptions, interests, motivations, or any other reasonable dependent variable. In the discussion of achievement motivation by Douvan (IIA) we noted differences in achievement motivation between middle- and lower-class high school students; and to this finding can be added differences in school performance, value orientations, ethnic attitudes, personality adjustment, attitudes toward parents, and others. What must be recognized, however, is that in order to understand how social class influences the behavior of the child it is necessary to identify the underlying social and psychological processes involved in these relationships. The task is one of identifying the intervening processes or events which can account for the observed variations in behavior as a consequence of class membership. The study by Winterbottom (IVB) and most of those cited by Bronfenbrenner (IVC) constitute attempts to achieve such understanding by examining the socialization practices of families at various levels in the social class hierarchy. Thus, the Winterbottom investigation (as well as others) provides evidence that middle-class mothers tend to emphasize mastery and independence training in the rearing of their sons to a greater extent than do lower-class mothers. This finding helps to explain the greater achievement motivation among middle-class boys than among lower-class ones.

On the other hand, Bronfenbrenner's thorough analysis of differences in child-rearing practices as a function of social class reveals considerable inconsistency in the findings of various investigations over two decades. A study by Davis and Havighurst (1948) first reported findings that middle-class parents tended to be stricter and to make greater demands in the rearing of their children than did lower-class parents. A later study by Maccoby and Gibbs (1954), on the other hand, found that the reverse was true—that, in general, middle-class parents were "more permissive" than those of the lower class. Studies undertaken before the Davis and Havighurst study tended to confirm their findings but those undertaken at a later period provide support for the findings reported by Maccoby and Gibbs. Aside from the usual methodological limitations involved in all these investigations, attempts to reconcile the two sets of findings must contend with differences in the time, place, and nature of the populations sampled, variations in the measures of social class, and differences in questions employed to determine the child-rearing practices of parents, as well as other factors. Yet, given these difficulties, Bronfenbrenner takes the position that these biases in sampling and method are not likely to operate in a consistent fashion over time or place. In effect, given any major trends in the comparison of the many studies involved, it might be possible to reconcile the two sets of findings. This, in fact, is what results from his analysis. In brief, both middle-class and lower-class parents have shifted in the pattern of their child-rearing practices, and these changes tend to reflect changes in the social order itself.

To the extent that two or more groups of individuals are hierarchically ordered on the basis of some set of socially valued criteria, a social class structure can be assumed to exist. Whatever the nature of the criteria employed, those groups higher in the hierarchy enjoy greater "rights and privileges" in terms of the reward structure of the social system than those groups lower down in it. The important controversial issue among stratification theorists concerns the kind of variables that should be emphasized in conceptualizing the class system. For some theorists the class structure is reflected in the *objective* properties by which individuals are ordered in various institutional structures of the society, for example, occupation, education, and the like. Standing in contrast are those theorists who maintain that the reality of social class structure is rooted in the cognitive orientations of the individual and therefore should be conceived of in *subjective* terms, that is, in how individuals conceive of or evaluate themselves in relation to others in the hierarchy. Finally, for still other theorists both objective and subjective variables are necessary for describing and explaining the existing class structure.

The social class analysis of "Old City" provided by Davis, Gardner, and Gardner (IVC) is based on a primarily subjective orientation to class developed by Warner (1941) and his associates. What is emphasized in this approach is the prestige of the person, which can be defined by the degree of deference and respect accorded to him by the other members of the community. The existence of a class system, in effect, is revealed in the mutually shared judgments by members of the community as to where individuals belong in the prestige structure. It is not only assumed that individuals rank themselves and others in this way, but that they tend to agree on the "styles" of living and thinking which characterize the members of the various class groups. A sample of community members in Old City were interviewed and observed in order to establish the class structure in these terms. On this basis the investigations revealed that there were three primary social classes in the community: "upper," "middle," and "lower," each of which could be further subdivided into "upper" and "lower" subgroups. Each of the six classes tended to share certain beliefs and overt behavior patterns, which were reflected in a unity of outlook and a sense of group solidarity. All of these social class groups recognized the existence of classes above or below them, or both; however, the greater the social distance between the person's class and the other classes the less precise were his perceptions of the differences between them. Furthermore, although classes immediately adjacent to the person's own class were viewed more clearly, he usually was not aware of the social distance actually maintained between his own class and those adjacent to it.

Although the Warner approach to social class is primarily subjective, it is important to note that it also relies on the objective characteristics of the individual as a means of establishing his class position. The respondent interviewed in Old City was placed in the class structure not only on the basis of how he and others viewed his class position, but also in terms of his observed behavior and mode of living. In a purely objective approach no consideration is given to how individuals conceive of themselves or others in the class structure. Of course, from a measurement point of view either approach is possible to the extent that objective class properties of individuals are closely correlated with their mutually shared judgments of themselves and others in the existing hierarchy. It is important to recognize at least one significant limitation in the Warner approach. In its focus on how individuals perceive themselves and others in the class structure, it is far more applicable to the smaller integrated community than to the very large urban metropolis such as New York. It assumes that class operates in personal-social contexts which allow individuals to view each other in these terms, and this is far more true of the former than of the latter.

Inherent in the class structure are sources of difficulty for individuals at all levels in the hierarchy, if for no other reason than that what is above one's own level is something to be achieved and what is below is to be avoided. It is reasonable to assume that how the person copes with these difficulties and others also will be class determined to some degree. The study by Hollingshead and Redlich (IVC) was predicated on this assumption. A number of hypotheses were tested concerning the relationship between the class structure and the development of mental illness in an urban community. It is interesting to note that class level in this instance was measured solely in terms of an objective index based on area of residence, occupation, and education. The findings revealed that the proportion of individuals under psychiatric care is significantly related to their social class status. Thus, although individuals in the lowest social class constituted some 18 percent of the population, approximately 37 percent of the individuals receiving psychiatric treatment were members of this class. It was also found that both type of psychiatric disorder and the kind of treatment received by the patient were significantly related to the person's social class position. Individuals at the lower class levels were more likely to present psychotic symptoms and receive organic treatment or no treatment at all, whereas neurotic manifestations and the use of psychotherapy were more characteristic of those at the upper end of the class structure.

The approach taken to social class by Centers (IVC) is clearly subjective in its orientation. Individuals are not only aware of their social class position but experience "class consciousness," that is, a sense of belonging and identification with other members of their class. Centers draws this conclusion from the fact that many individuals who see themselves as in the "middle class" tend to identify with the higher-status white-collar occupations; correspondingly, self-styled "working class" respondents are far more likely to identify themselves with skilled and unskilled manual workers. Also of significance is the fact that approximately half of all of Centers' respondents regarded another person's attitudes as the most important criterion in deciding whether or not he belonged to their class; 30 percent mentioned "education" and only 20 percent used "family" as the criterion.

According to this study, therefore, both what other people do in the occupational setting and what they think and believe serve as a basis for the class identifications of a majority of American white males. In this respect the most significant finding reported by Centers is the fact that where individuals in the *same* occupational groups vary in their class identifications, that is, "middle class" vs. "working class," their political and economic attitudes show corresponding differences. Those respondents, for example, in the business and professional group who consider themselves to be "working class" are more likely to express "radical" attitudes than those in the group who identify with the middle class, and are less likely than the latter to express "conservative" attitudes. These differences are only slightly less than what is found when high and low occupational groups are compared regardless of class identification. It would seem that class identification is no less important in determining these kinds of attitudes than the occupational status of the person.

However, the study by Converse (IVC) makes it abundantly clear that the relationship between social class status—whether in the sense of "class consciousness" or occupational level—and political attitudes is by no means an invariant one. The relatively strong relationships between these two variables found by Centers in

1945 showed a considerable weakening when they were measured again some ten years later by the Survey Research Center of the University of Michigan. The meaning of this finding should not be misconstrued. What the Converse study demonstrates is not that the significance of class as an influence on political attitudes and behavior was lessening, but rather that the degree of this influence is conditioned by the changing character of the social system in which the class structure is embedded. As a matter of fact, variations in the degree of this relationship, or what Converse calls "status polarization," are taken by him as a measure of relevant economic and political changes in the system.

Where status polarization is high, we should expect to find that groups at opposite ends of the class continuum have taken on strongly contrasting value positions in the politico-economic sphere. We should also expect to find increased class consciousness or identification among the members of each group. To account for the decrease in status polarization he found, Converse points to a number of factors. For example, his data suggest that domestic economic interests, as determinants of relevant political attitudes and behavior, may be dampened in individuals for whom the possibility of war or foreign policy issues are matters of focal concern. Similarly, such factors as a magnetic presidential candidate, and the extent to which the electorate can perceive differences in the economic programs of the two parties, may also reduce the role of economic or class interest factors in voting behavior.

References

CARROLL, J. B., and CASAGRANDE, J. B. The function of language classifications in behavior. In E. E. Maccoby, T. M. Newcomb, and E. L. Hartley (Eds.), *Readings in social psychology*, 3d Ed. New York: Holt, Rinehart and Winston, 1958.

DAVIS, A., and HAVIGHURST, R. J. Social class and color differences in child rearing. *Amer. sociol. Rev.*, 1948, *11*, 698-710.

KLUCKHOHN, C. Culture and behavior. In G. Lindzey (Ed.), *Handbook of social psychology*, Vol. 1. Reading, Mass.: Addison-Wesley, 1954.

MACCOBY, E. E., and GIBBS, P. K. Methods of child rearing in two social classes. In W. E. Martin and C. B. Standler (Eds.), *Readings in child development*. New York: Harcourt, Brace & World, 1954.

WARNER, W. L., and LUNT, P. S. *The social life of a modern community*. New Haven, Conn.: Yale Univer. Press, 1941.

WHORF, B. L. Science and linguistics. *Technology Rev.*, 1940, *44*, 229-231, 247, 248.

A. LANGUAGE AND MEANING

Studies in Linguistic Relativity ❧ Roger W. Brown

❧ Eric H. Lenneberg

Ethnocentrism is that state of mind in which the ways of one's own group seem natural and right for all human beings everywhere. Anthropologists are the natural antagonists of ethnocentrism. Their researches have long since taught us that the values of the American middle class are not dominant everywhere and that it is a kind of parochialism to suppose they ought to be. Nowadays everyone knows that life in Samoa is different from life in Boston, and at least as pleasant.

There is one kind of group practice, the use of a particular language, which we have always thought of as conventional rather than natural. On this matter we have seemed to need no instruction from anthropology. Who is not aware that there are many languages in the world and that one is no more natural to man than any other? However, the particular languages with which we are likely to have any close acquaintance all belong to the same historical family—the Indo-European. English, French, German, Italian, Spanish, Latin, Greek, and Sanskrit are all members of this family, which means

they are presumed to have a common linguistic ancestor. Because of their kinship these languages do not display the full range of variation to be found in human languages at large. To get some sense of that range we need to examine the anthropologists' descriptions of the languages of the Far East, of the American Indians, of the many peoples in the Pacific Ocean area. With this perspective Whorf (1956) finds the variations among the Indo-European languages to be so unimpressive that he lumps them together as "Standard Average European" and contrasts them as a group with various unrelated languages.

When unrelated languages are compared, cultural relativism takes on a new dimension. The differences between these languages suggest that people speaking different languages must experience the world in different ways.[1] It appears that "culture" includes, in addition to values and technology

[1] For early statements along this line see Boas (1911) and Sapir (1949). For more recent statements see Kluckhohn and Leighton (1946) and Whorf (1956).

This article was written by the authors especially for E. E. Maccoby, T. M. Newcomb, and E. L. Hartley (Eds.), *Readings in Social Psychology*, 3d Ed., New York: Holt, Rinehart and Winston, 1958, from previously published articles. Reprinted by permission of the authors, the publisher, the American Psychological Association, and John Wiley & Sons, Inc.

and religious practices, a particular cognitive structure. Children acquiring their first language learn more than a set of vocal skills; they take on the world view of their group. There are innumerable linguistic contrasts that suggest interesting cognitive differences. We offer here two examples, a difference of phonology or sound system and a difference of vocabulary. Through experiment and reasoning we have tried to find out what differences like these mean for social psychology.

A Difference of Phonology

The most obvious way in which one language differs from another is in the sequence of sounds used to convey any particular meaning. We say *city* where the Germans say *Stadt* and the French *ville*. Our first notion of comparative phonology may be that all languages make use of the same set of elementary sounds but make different selections and sequences for any particular meaning. This cannot be the whole story, however, since there are some sounds heard in French and German that never occur in English; e.g., the umlaut vowels and the uvular (*r*). Perhaps then we would do better to imagine a more inclusive repertoire of sounds, extending beyond English or any one language, to include all the sounds heard in all languages. The sounds of one particular language would be a selection from this source having more or less in common with the selection occurring in each other language.

A study of languages more remote than French or German shows that this conception of comparative phonology is inadequate. Not all differences of sound system involve the simple addition or subtraction of a few elementary sounds to an otherwise shared repertoire. There is a more interesting kind of difference in which two languages make use of the same sounds but put a different construction on them. In speaking English, for instance, we sometimes sound our vowels for a rather long time and sometimes we cut them short. Speakers of the Navaho language also produce both long and short vowels. However, this variation in speech does not have the same status in the two languages.

The linguistic scientist notices that the length of the vowel in English depends upon the consonant that follows it. The vowel of *bad* is like the vowel of *bat* except that it is longer; similarly with *mode, mote; fade, fate; halve, half,* etc. The rule is that the longer vowel is used before voiced consonants such as *d, v,* and *b* while the shorter form is heard before voiceless consonants like *t, f,* and *p*. No two words in English are differentiated by vowel length alone. The difference in vowel length is always accompanied by a difference of final consonant. For this reason the linguistic scientist describes the long and short vowels as two forms or varieties of the same basic sound (he would say two *allophones* of a single *phoneme*).

In Navaho the situation is different. The length of the vowel is not predictable from any other feature of the word in which it occurs. Many words of different meaning are exactly alike in form except that the vowel of one is short and the vowel of the other is long. A difference of duration of the vowel is used to signal a difference of meaning. In these circumstances the linguistic scientist classifies the long and short vowels as distinct phonemes. In so doing he says that this change in speech has the same status for the Navaho as a shift from *o* to *i* or from *i* to *a* has for the speaker of English.

All that we have said so far about long and short vowels belongs to descriptive linguistics. We should like to know something about the psychological implications of these phonological differences. Brown and Horowitz[2] have done a small experiment that clarifies the matter. They worked with a group of native speakers of Navaho and with a group of native speakers of English. The only special materials for the study

[2] This experiment was first reported in Brown (1956).

were eight precision-manufactured color chips. These eight colors were drawn from the Farnsworth-Munsell 100 Hue Test for Color Vision. The 100 Hue Test is made up of chips equally spaced around the hue dimension of the color circle. Saturation and brightness are constant throughout the series. The eight colors used by Brown and Horowitz were drawn from the reddish-violet region of the spectrum. There was the same very small perceptual gap between each adjacent pair of the eight.

Each subject was tested individually. He was first shown the whole series of chips in their proper order and told that the experimenter had a way of classifying the eight colors. It would be the subject's job to discover this classification. The experimenter then moved all the colors out of sight and, afterwards, exposed one at a time (in random order) naming each chip with a monosyllable that is not a color term in either English or Navaho. The subject simply watched this process until all eight had been named. He was then shown the full series once again and asked to group them as the experimenter had grouped them with his use of syllables.

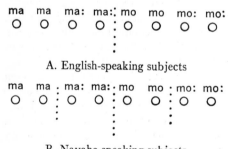

A. English-speaking subjects

B. Navaho-speaking subjects

Fig. 1. Categorizations of eight color chips by two groups of subjects.

As Figure 1 shows there were four groups of two chips each. The groups were respectively named *ma, ma:, mo,* and *mo:*. The syllables marked with a colon were pronounced with long vowels (as in *mode*) and the syllables without the color were pronounced with short vowels (as in *mote*). The change from *a* to *o* is a change from one vowel phoneme to another for both English and Navaho but the change of length is a change of vowel phoneme for Navaho only.

Fifteen Harvard students whose native language is English, after hearing each color named once, generally divided the colors into two groups of four chips each as in Figure 1. The line of division corresponds to the line of vowel phoneme change. They did not make a division where the vowels changed in length. Since the break into two groups does not correspond to any usual color grouping made in the vocabulary of English we may conclude that it was induced by the change in vowel phoneme.

Fifteen monolingual Navahos given exactly the same problem generally divided the colors into four classes of two colors each as marked by the division line in Figure 1. They made breaks at the points of change in vowel length and these are not points of division in the Navaho color vocabulary. As shown in Table 1 the English-

TABLE 1

THE NUMBER OF SUBJECTS IN EACH OF TWO GROUPS, BY TRIAL, WHO ARRANGED THE TEST COLORS INTO FOUR CATEGORIES

Group	Trial				
	1	*2*	*3*	*4*	*5 or More*
Navaho-speaking Subjects (N = 15)	11	1	—	2	1
English-speaking Subjects (N = 15)	—	1	—	—	14

speaking subjects generally persisted in their two-group classification, through four repetitions of the naming procedure, and the Navahos likewise held to their four-group classification.

Were the English-speaking subjects unable to hear the difference in vowel length, the difference to which the Navaho all responded? Brown and Horowitz tried rejecting the two-group classification as erroneous and found, when they did so, that the English-speaking subjects started to pay attention to the vowel change. Many of them then remarked that they had noticed the variations of length at the start but had assumed they were accidental. *We could have no better statement of the cognitive status of this speech variation for the speaker of English.* It is not purposeful and significant as is a change from *o* to *a*. It is not expected to signal a change of referent. The Navahos never thought of these variations as accidental. Both groups were perfectly able to hear the difference in question. Apparently, this test does not demonstrate a difference of auditory acuity in two societies but rather a difference in the range of potentially discriminable speech sounds customarily treated as equivalent.

When unrelated languages are compared this sort of phonological difference is ubiquitous. For instance, in English the consonant *p* is sometimes made with a resounding "pop" and is sometimes rather indolently produced. These variations do not change the phoneme; it remains a *p*. In Hopi and many other languages such a change in plosive force is a change of phoneme, like going from *p* to *b* for us. It is clear that different language communities sometimes put a different construction on the same range of experiences. Insofar as these experiences are only the sounds of speech no one but the student of perception or of language learning is likely to be greatly interested. But suppose the phenomena that can be variously construed go beyond speech to the referents named by speech, to the world of colors and textures, of persons and manners and places.

A Difference of Vocabulary

Foreign language textbooks commonly line up words in the new language directly opposite their English equivalents. This ar-

rangement strongly suggests that while English and the new language use different words, they name the same referents. Of course we know that one language sometimes has words that have no equivalents in the other language; e.g., classical Greek has no terms for nectarines and the movies as the speakers of that language had no referents for such terms. This kind of discrepancy in vocabulary should turn up whenever one community is acquainted with a kind of animal or flower or machine unknown to the other community. Insofar, however, as communities are exposed to the same world the familiar European languages suggest that this world imposes itself on the mind with a given structure that is the same for men everywhere.

When we look at more remote languages we find vocabulary differences that suggest another view. Lenneberg and Roberts (1956), for instance, compared the lexicon of color names possessed by native speakers of English with the lexicon of monolingual Zuñi Indians. Groups from the two language communities mapped out on elaborate color charts the semantic ranges of their color terms. A very striking discrepancy occurred in the region that English speakers divide into *yellow* and *orange;* the Zuñi made one category of this whole area and called it chupc?in:a. Whorf (1956) has pointed out that the Eskimo has words for three kinds of snow whereas all of these would be called *snow* in English [see Intro.]. There are four biologically distinct classes of kin called *aunt* in English: mother's sister, father's sister, mother's brother's wife, and father's brother's wife. Murdock (1949) in his study of kinship terminology in 250 societies found great variety in the manner of categorizing these kin, one lexicon having a distinct name for each, others grouping them together in various ways. These language differences are all the same type. A given region of experience familiar to both societies (colors, snows, kin, etc.) is differently categorized in the vocabularies of different languages.

We shall look closely now at one of these contrasts to determine its psychological significance. Where the Eskimo has words for three kinds of snow, we have just the single word *snow*. Apparently the Eskimo can and does name certain distinctions for which English seems to have no names. Yet Whorf, himself, does name these snows in English. He calls them "snow packed hard like ice," "falling snow," and "snow on the ground." The difference in the two languagss is not really one of a name and the lack of a name. It is rather a contrast between short single-word names and longer-phrase names. This is also true of all the other vocabulary contrasts of this kind. Murdock can name the four varieties of aunt, for instance, as *mother's sister, father's sister, mother's brother's wife,* and *father's brother's wife*. Other societies can use single words for one or another of these categories that we name with a phrase.

What psychological conclusions may we draw when a category is named with a short word in one society and with a long phrase in another society? We shall not want to say that the speaker of English is unable to distinguish the three varieties of snow named by the Eskimo. Whorf (a native speaker of English) appears to have grasped the nature of these distinctions and conveys them to us fairly well with simple line drawings. Is there then no difference in the psychological status of these three snows for the speakers of English and of Eskimo? We can make use, at this point, of a relationship discovered by the linguist George Zipf (1935). He has shown that there exists in many languages (all of those studied) a tendency for the length of a word to be negatively correlated with its frequency of occurrence. There are countless familiar examples of English words which have been abbreviated as they increased in frequency. The *automobile* has become the *car; television* is *TV; long-playing records* are *LP's*. In French the *cinématograph* became the *cinéma* and eventually the *ciné*. The failure of such phrases as *damp soft snow* or *father's brother's wife* to abbreviate to a word suggests that these phrases are not often used, these categories not often named in English. The language that has a word for a category, especially a short word, probably has now or has had in the past frequent occasion to make reference to that category. We will go further and propose that the frequency with which a category is named is an indication of the frequency with which the category is used in perception and thought.

Brown and Lenneberg[3] have expanded the simple difference between a long and a short name into the variable they call *codability*. They suspected that when a category has a single-word name, subjects from the same language community asked to name instances of the category ought to respond quickly, to be in close accord with one another on the name, and to agree with themselves from one occasion to another. Such a category could be said to be highly codable for the community in question. Where a category elicited a longer-phrase name, subjects asked to name instances of the category should respond more slowly, show some disagreement among themselves in their choice of a name, and some disagreement with themselves from one occasion to another. Such a category would have a low codability for the community in question. There should then be numerous indices of codability.

Brown and Lenneberg put this guesswork to test. Their subjects were 24 Harvard and Radcliffe students who spoke English as a native language and who were found to have normal color vision. Subjects were individually tested. They were shown controlled exposures of single Munsell colors (24 colors in all). They were asked to name each color as quickly as possible following its appearance. Five subjects were recalled after a month's time and put through the procedure a second time.

Four measures were drawn from the data: 1. the length of the naming response in syllables; 2. the average reaction time; 3. the

---

[3] This experiment was first reported in Brown and Lenneberg (1954).

degree of agreement among subjects on the naming responses; 4. the degree of agreement on two occasions for the same subjects. Table 2 presents the intercorrelations of

TABLE 2

INTERCORRELATIONS OF FOUR INDICES OF CODABILITY

Measure	1	2	3	4
1. No. of syllables				
2. Reaction time	.387			
3. Interpersonal agreement	−.630°	−.864°		
4. Intrapersonal agreement	−.355	−.649°	.773°	

° Significantly different from zero with $p < .05$.

these four measures. It can be seen that all are related to one another in the anticipated manner. Inconsistency within the group corresponds to inconsistency and hesitation in the individual. It is as though competing social tendencies are competing habits within the individual, a nice example of interiorized social norms. One measure, the amount of agreement between individuals, has higher correlations than does any of the others. It appears, therefore, to be the best single index of the factor all these measures have in common, the codability factor.

This expansion of the notion of codability into several measures suggests that its usefulness is not limited to cultural comparison. There seem to be three interesting cases to which it applies. There is, first of all, the cross-cultural case in which a particular category is more codable in one language than in another, e.g., *yellows* and *oranges* for English and *chupc?in:a* for Zuñi. In addition there are differences of codability within one language for different categories. Some collections of colors can be named in English with a single word, e.g., *red;* others require a phrase, e.g., *the blue-greens.* Finally, it should be possible to contrast groups and even individuals within one language community for their ability to encode the same category. What the meteorologist calls *cirrus clouds,* we may call *feathery, horsetail clouds;* what we call *schizoid traits,* the me-

teorologist may call *outlandish, antisocial tendencies.* For the first two cases where groups are being compared, the amount of agreement between individuals is probably the best index of codability. However, this index cannot be applied to the comparison of individuals. For this purpose we should want to use one of the other indices, probably reaction time (which) shows a very high correlation with the amount of agreement between individuals.

Having English codability scores for 24 colors (this is the second case to which codability applies, scores for different categories in one language) Brown and Lenneberg studied the association between these scores and the ability to recognize colors. From the Munsell collection 120 highly saturated colors were selected, including the 24 for which codability scores had been obtained, and the full set was mounted on a large white board. Subjects were used who had had no part in the earlier experiment, were native speakers of English, and had normal color vision. The basic procedure was to expose simultaneously four of the 24 colors for which codability was known and then ask the subject to point to the four colors he had just seen on the complete chart of 120.

In pretests subjects were asked how they managed to retain the four colors in memory after they had been removed from sight. Most subjects reported that they named the colors to themselves and "stored" the names. When a color elicits a considerable variety of names (low-codabililty score), the possibility of recovering the color from the name should not be very great. On the other hand colors that are almost always given the same name (high-codability score) ought to be recoverable from the name. This expectation was fulfilled by the experimental results; there was a rank-order correlation of .438 between codability and recognition scores.[4]

[4] The ability to recognize a color can also be affected by its inherent discriminability from the colors surrounding it on the large chart. For the correlations reported here discriminability was held constant through statistical control. A full discussion of this problem appears in the original article.

Since the reports of the pretest subjects indicated that colors were stored in linguistic code, it seemed plausible that the importance of codability scores would increase as the storage problem was maximized in the recognition situation. If, at one extreme, a single color were exposed, removed, and then identified with minimal delay, subjects might retain some direct trace of the color, conceivably as a mental image. Codability scores should, in these circumstances, have little relation to recognition scores. If, at the other extreme, the number of colors to be recognized were increased to four and a three-minute interval introduced between exposure and recognition during which the subject was occupied with some task, the importance of codability should be increased. Table 3 describes the experimental variations used. Groups A, B, C, D were believed to represent an order of increasingly difficult "storage" conditions. Group C is the major group for which results have already been described. The tasks which filled the interval for Group D were simple but absorbing, e.g., drawing a continuous line connecting in normal order a random array of numbers.

It can be seen in Table 3 that the correla-

is not large enough to be regarded as significantly different from zero.

In general, we propose that the more codable category is more frequently used in perception and thought than the less codable category. It is our notion that this principle will hold whether the codability comparison involves different languages, different speakers of one language, or different experiences for the same speakers. The various behavioral consequences of these differences in cognitive structure remain to be worked out, but it appears that performance on a recognition task is among them.

The Uses of the Named Category

We have come to similar conclusions concerning a kind of phonological difference and a kind of vocabulary difference. English speakers seem to have the same potentiality for distinguishing vowels by length as do persons born into the Navaho language community. The English speakers are easily able to make the distinction when there is some reason for them to do so. However, they are less prone to make this distinction than are native speakers of Navaho. Probably the two

TABLE 3

CORRELATIONS BETWEEN CODABILITY AND RECOGNITION SCORES FOR
FOUR RECOGNITION PROCEDURES

Group		No. of Colors Originally Exposed	Length of Interval	Content of Interval	Correlation
A	(N = 9)	1	7 seconds	—	.248
B	(N = 9)	4	7 seconds	—	.426°
C	(N = 16)	4	30 seconds	—	.438°
D	(N = 9)	4	3 minutes	tasks	.523°

° Significantly different from zero with $p < .05$.

tion between recognition and codability scores does increase as the importance of "storage" in the recognition task increases. The particular order obtained would occur by chance only once in 24 times. In the simplest recognition situation the correlation

groups do not differ in potential auditory acuity; they do differ in their habitual categorization of audible speech. Similarly, it seems probable that we are as capable as the Eskimo of discriminating varieties of snow but less prone than he to do so. In general it looks as if there is a potential for sensory discrimination characteristic of the whole human species. Language communities do not differ in this potential but rather in their manner of categorizing potentially discriminable experiences.

To treat potentially discriminable experiences as equivalent is to throw away information, and that may seem a surprising thing to do. Why should we call a number of different colors *red,* all sorts of different substances *snow,* all sorts of different people *Americans?* Why not keep track of all the attributes we can register? If we did so, we should experience very few recurrences in the world. What we think of as one person, for instance, proves on close examination to be continually changing—never precisely the same from one instant to another. A close examination of the sounds of speech shows that no two speakers of one language form their vowels and consonants in just the same way. What is more, no two pronunciations of the same speaker appear to be perfectly identical. If we noticed every detail our senses equip us to notice, life would be a stream of unique, never-recurring events.

We categorize because we want to know and need to know how to anticipate the future. It is a principal cognitive concern of every sort of higher animal to form expectancies and the terms of expectancies are categories. It is of no value to remember that on a particular day at a certain hour a change of hue in a light at a certain location was followed by a particular alteration in the pattern of traffic movement. This unique event will never come again. However, red lights (a category) regularly cause the facing traffic to halt (another category). It is of no use remembering that a particular person once said in a deep voice with his own peculiar inflection: "My name is Jed Prouty." That exact saying will never come again. Suppose we correctly categorize the name *Jed Prouty,* recognizing, for instance, that it does not matter how loudly the *p* is "popped" but it does make a difference if the voice is added to the initial consonant to

make *Brouty.* Categorized according to English phonology the name will recur and will stay with the man and can even be used as a surrogate for him. The phonology of a language describes the terms of significant recurrence in speech; the referents of a language are the terms of significant recurrence in the vast world outside speech.

A child spends years learning to make the correct matches between speech categories; learning to recognize dogs and call them *dog,* to recognize knives and call them *knife,* etc. This is an important part of culture transmission and it is prerequisite to a more important part. When one can identify the referents for words he can make use of the expectancies common in his culture. "Knives will cut," "sleeping dogs may bite if kicked," "if it rains before 7, it will be clear before 11," etc. These verbal formulations cannot be used for the guidance of action in the nonlinguistic world until the principal words can be "cashed" into referent categories. No one individual can, from his own experience, arrive at all the useful expectancies formulated by his culture. Furthermore, our language saves us a lot of disagreeable contact with bad-tempered dogs, poison ivy, and toadstools. In this sense, then, language is the repository of culture and the principal vehicle of culture transmission.

How does it happen that in their areas of common experience—vowels, snows, kin, colors, etc.—the languages of the world have not all hit upon the same categories? With the sounds of speech, variations in categorizing practice probably must be set down as accidental, but with referents this may not be so. Perhaps the case is analogous to differences of vocabulary and referent categories that exist within one community. Consider that important class of referents we call *persons.* A waitress may divide them into *cheapskates* and *good sports.* She is concerned with the prediction of tips and categorizes accordingly. Her categories are not relevant to the purposes of a physician (we trust). He is concerned with disease prognosis and treatment and categorizes patients into *diabetics* and *ulcer* cases and *hypochondriacs*. In our professional roles we focus on particular kinds of recurrences and categorize in the way that reveals these recurrences. Similarly, communities as a whole have their different purposes and, accordingly, their different vocabularies.

Even where purposes are the same, there is reason to expect some variation in categorizing practice. Everyone wants to predict what other people will do but we have no general consensus on the categories that are most useful for discovering general uniformities of behavior. Some people operate with ethnic categories; Negroes are expected to be superstitious and Turks to be cruel. Some people operate with physiognomic categories; nice faces go with nice behavior but look out for the evil eye. The behavioral sciences have not originated the interest in predicting human behavior; they have rather professionalized a prior general concern. The cognitive business of these sciences is essentially continuous with the business of the whole community; to find the categories in terms of which reliable important expectancies may be formed. The vocabularies of these sciences are a promise. If you will learn to categorize people as *marginal*, or as *socially mobile*, or as *compulsive*, you will find new and useful recurrences in the social world. Our predictions of behavior are not as good as we should like them to be and so we continue to recategorize and rename, looking for better expectancies.

The world around us is a human construction susceptible of more than one treatment. Various groups within our society—doctors, psychologists, bus drivers, skiers, philatelists—seize on different aspects of this common reality, aspects relevant to their peculiar purposes. Where our purposes are the same, we may still operate with a variety of categories because no really good set has been found. So long as we cannot predict all the things we should like to predict with the desired precision, the work of categorization is not finished. The languages of the world, like the professional vocabularies within one language, are so many different windows on reality. We should no more wish away the differences among languages than we should wish away the differences among ourselves.

References

BOAS, F. (Ed.). Introduction. *Handbook of American Indian Languages,* Part 1. Washington, D.C.: Government Printing Office, 1911.

BROWN, R. W. Language and categories. In J. S. Bruner, J. J. Goodnow, and G. A. Austin, *A study of thinking.* New York: Wiley, 1956.

BROWN, R. W., and LENNEBERG, E. H. A study in language and cognition. *J. abnorm. soc. Psychol.,* 1954, *49,* 454-462.

KLUCKHOHN, C., and LEIGHTON, D. *The Navaho.* Cambridge, Mass.: Harvard Univer. Press, 1946.

LENNEBERG, E. H., and ROBERTS, J. M. The language of experience. *Memoir of the intern. J. Amer. Linguistics,* 1956, *22,* No. 13.

MURDOCK, G. P. *Social structure.* New York: Macmillan, 1949.

SAPIR, E. *Selected writings of Edward Sapir.* D. G. Mandelbaum (Ed.). Berkeley, Calif.: Univer. of California Press, 1949.

WHORF, B. L. *Language, thought, and reality.* J. B. Carroll (Ed.). New York: Wiley, 1956.

WHORF, B. L. Science and linguistics, pp. 1-9 in E. E. Maccoby, T. M. Newcomb, and E. L. Hartley (Eds.), *Readings in social psychology,* 3d Ed. New York: Holt, Rinehart and Winston, 1958.

ZIPF, G. K. *The psycho-biology of language.* Boston: Houghton Mifflin, 1935.

Linguistic Determinism and

the Part of Speech ❧ Roger W. Brown

In recent years the anthropologists Whorf (1956), Lee (1938), and Hoijer (1954) have put forward the view that language is a determinant of perception and thought. The nature of the determining influence exerted by the vocabulary of a language is quite clear (Brown, 1956), but it is less easy to see how the grammatical features of a language can affect cognition. Yet it is just the grammatical differences between languages that are most striking and it is their determining force that the anthropologist has stressed. This paper undertakes to show how one kind of grammatical practice, the allocation of words to one or another part of speech, does affect cognition.

The words of a language can be collected into classes of formal equivalents which are called the parts of speech. Fries (1952) has shown that English nouns, for example, are words acceptable in sentence frames of the type "(The) ———— is (are) good." Native speakers of English will find it possible to insert "concert" or "cow" or "truth" in that frame but will find "very" or "of" grammatically impossible. Fries has used other sentence frames to separate out verbs, adjectives, and adverbs. In French, nouns can be further subdivided into formal gender classes. In Navaho there are more than 20 formal classes for words naming different kinds of objects. All of these word classes are defined by linguistic science in terms of the combinational possibilities of forms in a language without reference to the meanings of forms.

So long as these classes are defined in purely formal terms they do not suggest important cognitive differences. That suggestion comes in when we add the semantic correlates of the classes. The native speaker of English is likely to think of the parts of speech in semantic terms. Nouns name substances; verbs name processes; and adjectives name qualities. The genders of certain European languages are usually called masculine, feminine, and neuter, and these are semantic characterizations. The object classes of Navaho are usually described as words naming round objects, words naming long, thin objects, words naming granular substances, etc. The linguistic determinists in anthropology believe that the semantic character of the form classes fixes the fundamental conception of reality in a language community and that differences on this level correspond to different Weltanschauungen.

At the same time the science of descriptive linguistics refuses to define its word classes in semantic terms. Fries (1952) has shown that for the English parts of speech such definitions are always either unclear or overextended. We all know the English teacher's characterization of the noun as the name of a person, place, or thing. The terms "person" and "place" are reasonably clear, but do not apply to such nouns as "truth," "odor," and "thought." The meaning of "thing" is so unclear that we cannot tell whether or not odor and thought are things. No one has been able to provide clear semantic definitions that will serve to distinguish every English noun from every verb, adjective, and adverb. It is well known that

From the *Journal of Abnormal and Social Psychology*, 1957, 55, 1-5. Reprinted by permission of the author and the American Psychological Association. The gist of this paper was presented in a conference on "linguistic meaning" sponsored by the Social Science Research Council and held at Yale University, May 17-18, 1956. The Laboratory of Social Relations, Harvard University, financed the research.

the "masculine" and "feminine" genders in the European languages include names for objects having no sex. In Navaho, too, the object classes do not show perfect semantic consistency. In short, the semantic definitions of the form classes ignore many exceptions and are unsuitable for the purposes of linguistic science.

When the linguistic scientist sets up his descriptive categories he quite naturally looks for attributes of exceptionless validity, and there are not such semantic attributes for the English parts of speech. However, the layman may operate, in this area as in so many others, with conceptions that take account of probabilistic as well as certain associations. It may be that nouns *tend to have* a different semantic from verbs, and that the native speaker detects this tendency while he is in the process of learning the language. To answer these questions examination was made of the nouns and verbs of young children learning English to see whether there was a semantic distinction between the two parts of speech. The distinction proved to be much clearer than it is in the vocabulary of English-speaking adults. The second step was an experiment to find out whether the children were aware of the semantic distinction between nouns and verbs and whether they made any use of the distinction.

The Noun and Verb in Children's Speech

Harvard pre-school sessions were visited for about a month. There were eight children in each class; two of the classes were limited to children between four and five years while a third class accepted those between three and four. As an observer, the author sat on the side-lines and let the pre-school life swirl about him, recording verbatim all the conversation he could hear. From these records, he made vocabulary lists classified into the parts of speech. It was his impression, on examining this vocabulary, that the nouns and verbs of children were more nearly consistent with the classroom semantic definitions than are the nouns and verbs of adults. Nouns commonly heard were "truck," "blocks," and "teacher." There were no uses of "thought" or "virtue" or "attitude." These observations suggested that as the form classes grow larger they decline in semantic consistency. Perhaps children develop firm, and temporarily reliable, notions about the semantics of nouns and verbs. These notions may stay with them as adults even though they retain only a probabilistic truth.

To compare the character of adult and child vocabularies, the first thousand most frequent words from the Thorndike-Lorge (1944) list of adult usage were examined, and also the first thousand most frequent words from the Rinsland (1945) list of the vocabulary of children in the first grade. The Rinsland list is based on 4,630 pages of conversation, plus more than a thousand letters and stories. The Rinsland list is much the same as lists compiled independently by the Child Study Committee of the Kindergarten Union (1928) and by Horn (1925).

The first set of contrasts deals with two reduced lists; nouns found among the first thousand for adults but not for children, compared with nouns among the first thousand for children but not for adults. The set of nouns having clearest "thing" character would seem to be those that are called "concrete" and it is a commonplace to describe the language of children as more concrete than that of adults. One sense of the pair "concrete-abstract" is the same as "subordinate-superordinate." The more abstract term, the superordinate, includes in its denotation the denotation of the concrete or subordinate term, but extends beyond it. Superordinate-subordinate relations between the two lists were all in one direction. The adult list included "action," "article," "body," "experience," and at least seven others which were superordinate to many words on the children's list. There were no nouns on the children's list superordinate to those on the adult list.

The concrete noun with the smaller denotation is likely to be more picturable than its superordinate, and picturability is another common sense of "concrete." Of course the concrete noun, like the abstract, names a category rather than a particular instance. However, some categories have a more or less characteristic visual contour and size while others do not. Visual contour is a defining attribute for "table," but not for "thing" or "experience." Of the adult nouns 16% named categories having a characteristic visual contour, while 67% of the children's nouns were of this kind. Nouns like "apple," "barn," and "airplane" name categories for which size is a defining attribute, while nouns like "affair," "amount," and "action" do not. On the adult list, 39% of the nouns were of the former kind, while 83% of the children's nouns had size implications. It appears that children's nouns are more likely to name concrete things (in the sense of naming narrow categories with characteristic visual contour and size) than are the nouns of adults.

Two lists of verbs were compared: those among the first 1,000 for adults but not for children, and those among the first 1,000 for children but not for adults. The question here was the percentage of verbs naming animal (including human) movement. Of the adults' verbs, 33% were of this kind, while 67% of the children's verbs named actions. The common notion that verbs name actions seems to be truer for the vocabulary of children than for the vocabulary of adults.

These studies of word lists confirm the impression that the nouns and verbs used by children have more consistent semantic implications than those used by adults. It remains a question whether children are, in any sense, aware of these implications. There are many ways in which such awareness could be useful to one learning the language. Adults often try to convey the sense of a word by speaking it in the presence of the object or event named. All such single namings are ambiguous. The adult who says "water" while looking at a glass of water

may cause a child to attend to the glass itself as a container, to the glass as a transparent material, to the liquid character of its contents, to the height of the liquid, to the state of containment, and so on. Selection of the nonlinguistic attributes that govern proper denotative use of the word "water" cannot be guaranteed by a single naming. Repeated pointings can, of course, establish the invariant circumstances governing use of the word. If there were nothing to suggest to the child the probably relevant features of the nonlinguistic world, discovery of linguistic meanings would be a very laborious affair. However, a new word is ordinarily introduced in a way that makes its part-of-speech membership clear: "Look at the *dog*" or "See him *running*." If a part of speech has reliable semantic implications it could call attention to the kind of attribute likely to belong to the meaning of the word. A child who had absorbed the semantics of the noun and verb would know, the first time he heard the word "dog," that it was likely to refer to an object having characteristic size and shape, whereas "running" would be likely to name some animal motion. The part-of-speech membership of the new word could operate as a filter selecting for attention probably relevant features of the nonlinguistic world. It seemed that one could learn whether children experience any such filtering of attributes by introducing to them newly invented words assigned to one or another part of speech, and then inquiring about the meanings the words appeared to have.

In the children's speech that had been recorded, nouns and verbs were given proper grammatical treatment. In addition, the children made correct use of a subclass of nouns—the mass nouns. These are words like "dirt," "snow," "milk," and "rice" which are given different grammatical treatment from such particular nouns as "barn," "house," and "dog." For example, when "some" is used with "barn" the noun is in the plural—"some barns," whereas a mass noun would be in the singular—"some rice."

The semantic difference between these two classes of noun is suggested by the designations "mass" and "particular." Mass nouns usually name extended substances having no characteristic size or shape, while particular nouns name objects having size and shape. Many nouns can function in either a mass or particular way with attendant shifts in the speaker's view of the referent. "Some cake" is a chunk of a mass while "some cakes" are either cupcakes or layer cakes arranged in a row. Many words in the vocabulary of psychology have this double potentiality. Although the personologist deplores such usage, the layman speaks of someone having "a lot of personality" or "very little temperament." The professional insists that personality is not an undifferentiated substance of which one can have more or less. Personalities are like cupcakes—all of a size and one to a customer—with only their frostings to make them unique.

In the speech of the pre-school children "milk," and "orange juice," and "dirt" were the most common mass nouns. These were always given correct grammatical treatment. No one said "a milk" or "some dirts." It was decided to work with three functional classes: the particular noun, the mass noun, and the verb.

Method

The experiment involved three sets of four pictures each.[1] One of these sets will be described in detail. The first picture in the set shows a pair of hands performing a kneading sort of motion, with a mass of red confetti-like material which is piled into and overflowing a blue-and-white striped container that is round and low in shape. The important features of the picture are the kneading action, the red mass, and the blue-and-white round container. The motion would ordinarily be named with a verb (like

[1] The author is grateful to Dr. Susan Ervin for painting the pictures and for suggesting colors and forms that would please children.

"kneading") the mass with a mass noun (like "confetti"), and the container with a particular noun (like "container"). It was assumed that children would have no readily available names for any of these conceptions. Each of the remaining three pictures of this set exactly reproduced one of the three salient features of the first picture, either the motion, the mass, or the container. In order to represent the motion a second time it was necessary to show also a mass and a container. However, the mass was here painted yellow so as not to duplicate the original and the container was of a different size, shape, and color from the original. The other two sets of pictures involved different content, but always an action, a mass substance, and a particular object. In one case, the first picture showed hands cutting a mass of cloth with a strange tool. In the third set, hands were shown emptying an odd container of a slushy sort of material.

In overview, the following use was to be made of the three sets of pictures. Children were to be shown the first picture in conjunction with a new word identifiable either as a verb, a mass noun, or a particular noun. Then they would be shown the remaining three pictures of the set and asked to point out the one that pictured again what had been named in the first picture. It was anticipated that when the new word was a verb they would point to the picture of motion, when it was a particular noun they would point to the container, and when it was a mass noun they would point to the extended substance.

Three word stems were used: "niss," "sib," and "latt." If the stem was to function as a verb, X would begin by asking: "Do you know what it means to sib?" (Children do not always answer "no" as they ought.) "In this picture" (first picture of a set) "you can see sibbing. Now show me another picture of sibbing" (presenting the other three pictures of the set). If the stem was to function as a particular noun, X began: "Do you know what a sib is?" and proceeded in consistent fashion. If the word was to function as a mass noun, X began: "Have you ever seen any sib?" and went on accordingly.

Each child saw all three sets of pictures and heard each of the word stems; one of them as a particular noun, one as a mass noun, and one as a verb. The combinations of word stem, part-of-speech membership, picture set, and order of presentation were all randomly varied. There were 16 children in all, half of them between three and four years, and half between four and five. They were all acquainted with X by the time the experiment was performed. The procedure was very like the familiar business of looking at a picture book and naming the things seen and was accepted by the children as a kind of game. The game was always played with one child at a time.

Results and Discussion

When a new word was introduced as a verb, 10 of the 16 children picked out the picture of movement. When the word was a particular noun, 11 of 16 selected the picture of an object; and when the word was a mass noun, 12 of 16 selected the extended substance. Of the 15 responses that were not correct, four were simply failures to answer because of some distraction from the task. The results are summarized in Table 1.

TABLE 1

PICTURE SELECTIONS FOR WORDS
BELONGING TO VARIOUS PARTS OF SPEECH

Category Depicted	Verbs	Particular Nouns	Mass Nouns
Actions	10	1	0
Objects	4	11	3
Substances	1	2	12
No Response	1	2	1

A simple test was made to determine the significance of the differences in the pictures selected by children when the new word was a verb, when the word was a particular noun, and when it was a mass noun. For example, the selections made when the word was a verb were dichotomized into pictures of actions and all others. These frequencies for verbs were compared with like frequencies for the choices made when the words were either particular or mass nouns. In other words, the test was to determine whether action pictures were more likely to be selected as referents for new words introduced as verbs than for new words introduced as nouns. Comparable tests were made to see whether particular nouns were associated with pictures of objects and mass nouns with substances. All three of the resultant 2×2 tables yielded differences beyond the .005 level of significance when the Fisher-Yates test was applied.

It is well known that children will sometimes do what an adult wishes in a task of this kind though they do not understand the task as the adult does. Consequently, the qualitative results may be more persuasive than the quantitative. In the first trial with the first child, for instance, X showed the picture of cloth being cut by an odd tool and said that there was a "sib" in the picture. Then went on with: "Can you show me another sib?" and while X still fumbled with the other three pictures, his subject swung around and pointed to the steam valve on the end of the radiator saying, "There's a sib." The pictured tool looked very like the steam valve. In another case, X showed the picture of confetti-kneading and said, "There is some latt in this picture," whereupon his subject said: "The latt is spilling." And it was.

Recent experiments with phonetic symbolism (Brown, Black, and Horowitz, 1955) and metaphor (Brown, Leiter, and Hildum, 1957) indicate that semantic rules are not always arbitrary. A word can suggest its meaning because the sound is an echo of the sense or because the word had a prior meaning which is related to the new meaning. The present study suggests that most words have an additional kind of "appropriateness" stemming from their grammatical character. While the part-of-speech membership of a word does not give away the particular meaning, it does suggest the general type of that meaning, whether action, object, substance, or whatever. In learning a language, therefore, it must be useful to discover the semantic correlates of the various parts of speech; for this discovery enables the learner to use the part-of-speech membership of a new word as a first clue to its meaning. The present experiment with very young children who are learning English indicates that in this language, at least, the semantic implications of the verb, mass noun, and particular noun are discovered by native speakers. It now seems quite probable that speakers of other languages will also know about the semantics of their grammatical categories. Since these are strikingly different in unrelated languages, the speakers in question may have quite different cognitive categories. It remains to be determined how seriously and how generally thought is affected by these semantic distinctions.

Summary

Descriptive linguistics defines the parts of speech in strictly formal or syntactical terms. Nevertheless, the parts of speech usually have distinct semantic characteristics. These characteristics do not hold for all members of the various parts of speech, however, and so cannot serve to define the parts of speech for the purposes of linguistic science. Human beings are generally adept at picking up imperfect probabilistic implications, and so it may be the case that native speakers detect the semantic nature of the parts of speech of their language. It was shown that the nouns used by young English-speaking children were more reliably the names of things and their verbs more reliably the names of actions than is the case for the nouns and verbs used by English-speaking adults. It was shown experimentally that young English-speaking children take the part-of-speech membership of a new word as a clue to the meaning of the word. In this way, they make use of the semantic distinctiveness of the parts of speech. It seems likely that speakers of languages other than English will also have detected the semantic characters of their parts of speech. There is a sense, then, in which this grammatical feature of a language affects the cognition of those who speak the languages. Differences between languages in their parts of speech may be diagnostic of differences in the cognitive psychologies of those who use the languages.

References

BROWN, R. W. Language and categories. Appendix to J. S. Bruner, J. J. Goodnow, and G. A. Austin, A study of thinking. New York: Wiley, 1956.

BROWN, R. W., BLACK, A. H., and HOROWITZ, A. E. Phonetic symbolism in natural languages. J. abnorm. soc. Psychol., 1955, 50, 388-393.

BROWN, R. W., LEITER, R. A., and HILDUM, D. C. Metaphors from musical criticism. J. abnorm. soc. Psychol., 1957, 54, 347-352.

BUCKINGHAM, B. R., and DOLCH, E. W. A combined word list. Boston: Ginn, 1936.

FRIES, C. C. The structure of English. New York: Harcourt Brace & World, 1952.

HOIJER, H. (Ed.). Language in culture. Chicago: Univer. of Chicago Press, 1954.

HORN, E. The commonest words in the spoken vocabulary of children up to and including six years of age. In National Society for the Study of Education, Twenty-fourth yearbook. Bloomington, Ill.: Public School Publishing Company, 1925.

INTERNATIONAL KINDERGARTEN UNION, CHILD STUDY COMMITTEE. A study of the vocabulary of children before entering the first grade. Washington, D.C.: The Int. Kindergarten Union, 1928.

Lee, Dorothy D. Conceptual implications of an Indian language. *Phil. Sci.*, 1938, 5, 89-102.

Rinsland, H. D. *A basic vocabulary of elementary school children.* New York: Macmillan, 1945.

Thorndike, E. L., and Lorge, I. *The teacher's word book of 30,000 words.* New York: Bur. of Publ., Teachers College, Columbia Univer., 1944.

Whorf, B. L. *Language, thought, and reality: selected writings.* Cambridge, Mass.: Technology Press, 1956.

The Influence of Language-acquisition Contexts on Bilingualism

❊ W. E. Lambert

❊ J. Havelka

❊ C. Crosby

The bilingual person presumably must learn two different verbal responses for each referent, a requirement analogous to learning different responses to the same stimulus in experimental studies of negative transfer. It is of psychological interest, therefore, that bilinguals are so often able to communicate freely in either language without interference from the other. As yet, no adequate psychological theory has been offered to account for bilingualism. In his review of various limited explanations, Weinreich concludes that "a comprehensive psychological theory of bilingualism ought to account for both the effectively separated use of the two languages and for interference of the languages with one another" (Weinreich, 1953, p. 71). It is the purpose of the present investigation to contribute to such a theory by analyzing conditions that are presumed to affect both the "effectively separated use" of the bilingual's two languages and the "interference of the languages with one another."

As a first step, it may be profitable to apply certain principles derived from paired-associate learning and transfer phenomena to the case of learning two languages.[1] In the experimental study of retroactive inhibition, the learner must first link S_1 to R_1 and, in the later interpolated phase, S_1 to R_2. When alternative responses are associated with a common stimulus, interference between the two associations is the usual consequence. The bilingual is confronted with an analogous learning problem when, for example, the symbols "church" and "*église*" are both associated with the appropriate environmental event.

One general means of minimizing interference in learning situations is to increase the distinctiveness of the two tasks to be learned.[2] In studies of retroactive inhibition,

[1] In 1915, Epstein considered bilingualism in terms of such a psychological theory, but did not experimentally test its applicability.

[2] Essentially the same reasoning underlies the "direct method" of language teaching. The direct method theorists maintain that the acquired language should be learned directly from association with environmental events without the mediation of the native language. When learning French as a second language, one should never link "*pomme*" with "apple" but should link "*pomme*" directly with the perceived en-

From the *Journal of Abnormal and Social Psychology*, 1958, 56, 239-244. Reprinted by permission of the authors and the American Psychological Association. This research was supported in part by the Canadian Defence Research Board, Grant Number D77-94-01-10, and in part by N.R.C. Grant A.P. 17.

for example, interference is effectively minimized by increasing the degree of learning of original and interpolated tasks or by decreasing the associative similarity between the competing responses. Both these variations enhance the distinctiveness of the tasks. If distinctive secondary cues, such as differently colored backgrounds, are associated with the two tasks to be learned, the functional separation of the tasks should be increased.

Following the logic of interference theory, we can reason that response competition in bilingualism is functionally related to the distinctiveness of contexts in which the bilingual's two languages are acquired; the more "separated" the contexts of acquisition, the less the bilingual interference. Acquisition contexts are considered to be separated when the association between a symbol such as "church" and the appropriate environmental event has consistently taken place in a setting distinct from that in which the association between "*église*" and its corresponding environmental event occurs. On the other hand, in "fused" acquisition contexts, members of a linguistic community can and do use both symbols for any particular environmental event, thereby increasing the interchangeability of the symbols.

Recently, Ervin and Osgood (1954) attempted a theoretical interpretation of bilingualism that indicates the potential importance of language-acquisition contexts. They suggest that bilinguals could theoretically acquired "compound" or "coordinate" language systems. The compound system would be developed through experience in fused contexts, as with vocabulary training in school, or where the same family members use two languages interchangeably to refer to the same environmental events. The coordinate system would be developed

---

vironmental event. In contrast to the "indirect" method which utilizes translation as an aid in acquisition, the direct method is purported to develop "pure" bilingualism, the ability to move from one linguistic and semantic world of experience to another with comparatively little interference.

through experience in different linguistic communities where languages are rarely interchanged. They suggest that the alternative symbols in his two languages have a single meaning for the compound bilingual whereas the coordinate bilingual, presumably because of the distinctiveness of his language-acquisition contexts, develops separate meanings for each of his alternative symbols.

Accepting this theoretical position, we hypothesized that experience in "separated" language-acquisition contexts enhances the functional separation of the bilingual's two languages while experience in "fused" contexts reduces the functional separation of the two language systems. We predicted that bilinguals with experience in separated contexts would show comparatively greater semantic differences between symbols in one language and their translated equivalents in the other, more associative independence of translated equivalents in their two languages, and less facility of switching from one language to the other.

Method

CLASSIFICATION OF SUBJECTS

The Ss were college or university students with extensive experience in both English and French languages. Since all but four were either preparing for or actually in graduate schools, it can be assumed that the group was relatively homogeneous in intelligence. Each S was teted for extent of bilingualism (Lambert, 1955; Lambert, Havelka, and Gardner, 1959) and the 32 who met our criterion for bilingual "balance" will be discussed here. "Balance" implies a high level of second language competence, high enough, in fact, that no dominance of one language over the other is measurable with the technique employed.

Our primary task was to classify Ss according to their language-acquisition contexts and, to this end, detailed information was obtained from each S concerning how, when, and where his languages were acquired. Acquisition contexts were considered *separated* when one language was learned exclusively in the home and the other exclusively outside the home, when one parent consistently used one language and the other parent a different language, or when one language was acquired in a particular national or cultural setting distinct from that in which the second was acquired. Acquisition contexts were considered *fused* when both parents used the two languages indiscriminately, when both languages were used interchangeably inside and outside the home, or when an individual acquired his second language in a school system stressing vocabulary drill and translation and where the first or native language was used as the medium of instruction. This scheme of classification is derived from that used by Ervin and Osgood (1954) in their definitions of compound and coordinate systems. The actual classification of Ss as having separated or fused contexts for acquisition is essentially an arbitrary one in spite of the rather explicit criteria for placement. In five cases, for example, a problem arose in deciding whether to give credit for some experience with separated contexts when an S had early experience in a fused context, as when an English S acquired French in a school system but later used this language exclusively in France for some period of time. Our decision was to classify such an S as separated if he spent at least an entire year using the acquired language either exclusively or primarily. Using this scheme, 23 Ss were classified as "separated" and 9 as "fused." [3]

It was also possible to further subdivide the "separated" group according to the following line of reasoning. An S could be classified as "separated" if he had experience either in distinctive acquisition contexts within a particular national setting, as in Quebec, or in two geographically different cultures, as from living many years in France before coming to America. We predicted that separated contexts based on "bicultural" experiences, as in the latter example, would particularly enhance the distinctiveness of the two contexts. In this case, the environmental events themselves may often not be common for the two sets of symbols. For example, *"église"* could mean a gothic cathedral while "church" could mean a tall wooden building used on Sundays, and *"ami"* and "friend" could take on quite different meanings. A recent study by Ervin (1955) demonstrates how such environmental differences affect the perceptual and personality functionings of bilinguals. With these considerations in mind, the "separated" group was subdivided into 15 Ss with bicultural and 8 Ss with "unicultural" experiences.

BEHAVIORAL INDICES OF THE INFLUENCE OF ACQUISITION CONTEXTS

As a measure of the differences in meanings of concepts in the bilingual's two languages, we made use of Osgood's "semantic differential" (1952), a method of scaling stimulus-words on a standard set of meaning dimensions. For example, an S is presented with a stimulus-word, such as "house," and is asked to rate it along a seven-point dimension, such as "fast-slow" or "pleasant-unpleasant." In the present case, the stimulus-words were four common English concepts ("house," "drink," "poor," "me") and their French translations. They were presented in a fixed order so that any word was maximally separated from its translated pair. Ten standard dimensions (Osgood and Luria, 1954) were used and their order of presentation was continually changed to eliminate any patterning of ratings. The S might rate "house" at Position 3 on the "fast-slow" di-

[3] In view of our method of selecting Ss (Lambert, Havelka, and Gardner, 1959) where an attempt was made to draw equal numbers of both types, one may safely generalize that it is comparatively easier for bilinguals with separated acquisition contexts to attain bilingual balance.

mension, and later *"maison"* might be rated at Position 5 (more slow) on the same dimension, which had been translated into French. Since both stimulus-words and the anchors of each dimension were translated, we can only make statements about differences in meanings of both stimulus-words and dimensional attributes, or their interaction. The average degree of difference between the French and English semantic ratings for the four pairs of stimulus-words was determined for each S using Osgood's D score (1952); the larger the D score, the greater the semantic differences between translated equivalents in French and English. We predicted that Ss with experience in separated language-acquisition contexts would show comparatively greater semantic differences between translated equivalents in their two languages.

As a measure of the degree of associative independence of translated equivalents, we made use of the retroactive inhibition design. If an S learns list A, then list B, then relearns list A, one can determine the amount of associative interference imposed by the interpolated material. If the interpolation has no effect on the previously memorized material, then the two can be considered functionally independent. Interference and facilitation from the interpolated material may be thought of as indices of the functional dependence of the first-learned and interpolated tasks.

Each S learned a list of 20 commonly occurring English words by the anticipation method. A criterion of 8 correct responses out of 20 was chosen so as to permit improvement following the interpolated task. This was followed by three presentations of a list of 20 three-letter nonsense words. Then the English list was re-presented and the S's retention was measured. Finally, Ss were asked to relearn the nonsense list, but these data will not be discussed here. This preliminary test gives a measure of the associative interference or facilitation imposed by a meaningless task, one assumed to be semantically independent of the original

task. After a rest period, the same procedure was repeated, but this time a second, similar list of 20 English words, learned to the same criterion, was followed by a list of their exact translations in French, presented for three trials. A score was assigned to each S which indicated the degree of associative interference or facilitation imposed by the interpolated French material in relation to interpolated meaningless material. The following illustrative case indicates some facilitation from both interpolated tasks but more from the interpolated French. The number of correct responses for the criterion trials are placed in Column A, and the number of correct responses for retention trials are given in Column A′, for the English-Nonsense-English and the English-French-English series:

	A	I	A′	A — A′
Series I:	$E_1 = 10$	N (3 trials)	$E_1 = 11$	−1
Series II:	$E_2 = 10$	F (3 trials)	$E_2 = 15$	−5
		I − II = +4		

Positive scores indicate that the interpolated French translations facilitate retention of English words more than do interpolated nonsense words. Negative scores indicate that interpolated French translations interfere with the retention of English words. A zero score would indicate that the interpolated French translations offer no more facilitation than interpolated nonsense words. Following the reasoning outlined above, the closer the scores approach zero, the more associatively independent the translated equivalents. We predicted that Ss with experience in separated acquisition contexts would show more associative independence between translated equivalents in their two languages than those with experience in fused contexts.

Finally, we predicted that experience in fused as compared to separated contexts would express itself in a greater facility of switching from one language to the other.

As a measure of such facility, we made use of a speed of translation test described elsewhere (Lambert, Havelka, and Gardner, 1959). Each S, given 20 French and 20 English words to translate, was assigned a score for his average speed of translation from English to French and from French to English. Speed was measured by a voice key in circuit with a chronoscope.

Results and Discussion

As predicted, those bilinguals who acquired their languages in separated contexts showed a significantly greater difference in meanings of translated equivalents than did those who acquired their two languages in fused contexts (see Table 1). However, when a comparison was made between

function of experience in separated acquisition contexts. Experience in bicultural acquisition contexts, where there is a greater likelihood that the actual referents of translated symbols are different, does appear to affect the semantic aspects of the bilingual's two languages.

Bilinguals with experience in separated acquisition contexts also showed significantly more associative independence of translated equivalents in their two languages than did those with experience in fused contexts (see Table 2). An interpolated list of French translations had about the same influence for the separated group as an interpolated list of nonsense syllables; Ss in the fused group, on the other hand, clearly benefited from the interpolated French list.

These findings are consistent with those

TABLE 1

SEMANTIC DIFFERENTIAL COMPARISONS

Contexts	N	Mean English-French Profile Separations[a]	Variance	t Tests[b]		p Values
Fused (F)	9	3.19	0.38	F-S:	2.24	< .05
Separated (S)	23	3.93	1.23	F-B:	2.64	< .03
Bicultural (B)	15	4.22	1.47	F-U:	< 1	n.s.
Unicultural (U)	8	3.39	0.33	B-U:	2.13	< .06

[a] Entries are mean D scores (7). The larger the mean, the greater the semantic differences between languages.
[b] Where the variances were not homogeneous, p values were determined according to a formula suggested by Edwards (1954, p. 273 ff). All t tests in this and the following tables are 2-tailed tests of significance.

those who acquired their two languages in geographically distinct cultures (bicultural experience) and those who acquired both languages in separated contexts within one geographical region (unicultural experience), it became clear that bicultural experience accounted for the over-all difference between fused and separated groups. In fact, Ss with unicultural experience are not essentially different from either of the other two groups with respect to similarity of meanings of translated equivalents. It appears, therefore, that the difference in meanings of translated equivalents is not a simple

summarized above for semantic differences. Since translated equivalents were semantically more similar for the fused Ss, the interpolated translations in the learning problem were more like an extension of the original English list. It is logical therefore that these Ss were helped more by the interpolated French than were the separated Ss. Since translated equivalents have comparatively different meanings for the separated Ss, interpolated translations should have shown less associative facilitation and possibly more interference with the original English list, as was the case.

TABLE 2

ASSOCIATIVE-INDEPENDENCE COMPARISONS

Contexts	N	Mean Independence Indices[a]	Variance		t Tests	p Values
Fused (F)	9	+3.44	9.75	F-S:	2.65	< .02
Separated (S)	23	+0.13	11.23	F-B:	2.12	< .05
Bicultural (B)	15	+0.60	10.86	F-U:	2.55	< .02
Unicultural (U)	8	−0.75	12.28	B-U:	< 1	n.s.

[a] The closer the scores approach zero, the more between-language associative independence indicated. A constant of 8 was added to each score to eliminate negative values before variances were computed.

This interpretation has its limitations, however, since the data in Table 2 indicate that there is no difference in degree of associative independence between bilinguals with bicultural and those with unicultural experiences. In fact, both these subgroup means are significantly different from that of the fused group. This finding suggests that experience in separated contexts of either a bicultural or unicultural nature enhances the associative independence of translated equivalents in the bilingual's two languages, as compared to experience in fused acquisition contexts.

reliable, one may speculate that Ss in both groups have had equal experience in translating but possibly different types of experience. The fused Ss, by definition, have learned their two languages in contexts that encourage translation. On the other hand, a bilingual who has contacts with two separate linguistic communities may often be called on to recount his experiences with members of both communities. In a sense, he becomes the liaison between two linguistic communities and he may learn to use concepts which have meaningful equivalents for members of both communities.

TABLE 3

SWITCHING FACILITY COMPARISONS

Contexts	N	Mean Translation Speed[a]	Variance		t Test	p Values
Fused (F)[b]	7	125.08	112.43	F-S:	< 1	n.s.
Separated (S)	23	125.69	288.65	F-B:	< 1	n.s.
Bicultural (B)	15	124.59	303.42	F-U:	< 1	n.s.
Unicultural (U)	8	127.76	254.62	B-U:	< 1	n.s.

[a] Entries, in hundredths of a second, are group means. The larger the mean, the slower the group is in translating into French and into English.
[b] Two Ss were not available for this test.

Table 3 makes it clear that there were no differences between groups in facility of switching from one language to the other, a finding contrary to predictions. There is no immediately obvious interpretation for this lack of difference between groups, other than the possible lack of sensitivity of our measuring device. Accepting the finding as

When requested to translate, Ss in the two groups demonstrate similar facility to switch. In view of the other findings, however, the fused and separated Ss appear to make different use of the translation process. The fused Ss made use of the interpolated translations in the learning task and accordingly showed improvement in their retention scores. It is possible, although no attention was paid to this feature in the collection of data, that the separated Ss were less aware that actual translations were being interpolated than were the fused Ss. Stated differently, the fused Ss may have been more set to translate than were the separated Ss.

In conclusion, we have been able to demonstrate, within the limitations of the small sample of Ss studied, that language-acquisition context does influence the functional separation of the bilingual's two languages in certain respects. The theory of coordinate and compound language systems has been given empirical support and the defining characteristics of these systems have been extended. The coordinate bilinguals, in contrast to the compound bilinguals, in contrast to the compound bilinguals, appear to have more functionally independent language systems. If their coordinateness has been developed through experience in culturally distinctive contexts, they will have comparatively different meanings for concepts translated into their two languages. Coordinate and compound bilinguals, however, appear to have equal facility in switching from one language to the other.

Summary

Bilinguals were classified as having learned their two languages in either separated or fused contexts. It was hypothesized that experience in separated as compared with fused language-acquisition contexts comparatively enhances the effectively separated use of the bilingual's two languages.

It was found that experience in separated contexts comparatively increases the associative independence of translated equivalents in the bilingual's two languages. If the bilingual has learned his two languages in culturally distinctive contexts, the semantic differences between translated equivalents is comparatively increased. There was no difference found in facility to switch from one language to the other that can be attributed to contextual influences.

The findings were related to the theory of compound and coordinate bilingual language systems.

References

EDWARDS, A. L. *Statistical methods for the behavioral sciences.* New York: Holt, Rinehart and Winston, 1954.

EPSTEIN, I. *La pensée et la polyglossie.* Paris: Payot, approx. 1915.

ERVIN, S. M. The verbal behavior of bilinguals: the effect of the language of report upon the T.A.T. stories of adult French bilinguals. Unpublished dissertation, Univer. of Michigan, 1955.

ERVIN, S. M., and OSGOOD, C. E. Second language learning and bilingualism. In C. E. Osgood and T. A. Sebeok (Eds.), *Psycholinguistics. J. abnorm. soc. Psychol., Suppl.,* 1954, 139-146.

LAMBERT, W. E. Measurement of the linguistic dominance of bilinguals. *J. abnorm. soc. Psychol.,* 1955, *50,* 197-200.

LAMBERT, W. E., HAVELKA, J., and GARDNER, R. Linguistic manifestations of bilingualism. *Amer. J. Psychol.,* 1959, *72,* 77-82.

OSGOOD, C. E. The nature and measurement of meaning. *Psychol. Bull.,* 1952, *49,* 197-237.

OSGOOD, C. E., and LURIA, Z. A blind analysis of a case of multiple personality using the semantic differential. *J. abnorm. soc. Psychol.,* 1954, *49,* 579-591.

WEINREICH, U. *Languages in contact.* New York: Linguistic Circle of New York, 1953.

Verbal Stereotypes and ❧ Daniel Katz
Racial Prejudice ❧ Kenneth W. Braly

One outstanding result of investigations of racial prejudice is the uniformity in the patterns of discrimination against various races[1] shown by Americans throughout the United States. People in widely separated parts of the country show a high degree of agreement in their expressions of relative liking or disliking of different "foreign" groups.

In an early study Bogardus asked 110 businessmen and schoolteachers about the degrees of social intimacy to which they were willing to admit certain ethnic groups. The degrees of social distance employed were: to close kinship through marriage, to my club as personal chums, to my street as neighbors, to employment in my occupation, to citizenship in my country, to my country as visitors only, and exclusion from my country. By weighting these seven classifications Bogardus obtained the following preferential rating of 23 ethnic groups:

Canadians	22.51
English	22.35
Scotch	20.91
Irish	19.38
French	18.67
Swedes	16.20
Germans	14.95
Spanish	14.02
Italians	8.87
Indians	7.30
Poles	6.65

[1] The term *race* is here used in the popular, not the scientific, sense, and covers reference to racial, religious, and national groupings.

Russians	6.40
Armenians	6.16
German-Jews	5.45
Greeks	5.23
Russian-Jews	4.94
Mexicans	4.57
Chinese	4.12
Japanese	4.08
Negroes	3.84
Mulattoes	3.62
Hindus	3.08
Turks	2.91

The Bogardus study was carried out on the Pacific Coast but studies made in other parts of the United States indicate the same pattern of preferences for the various groups. In the Middle West, for example, Thurstone constructed a scale on the basis of the likes and dislikes of 239 students. The resulting rank order and scale values for 21 ethnic groups follow:

American	0.00
English	−1.34
Scotch	−2.09
Irish	−2.18
French	−2.46
German	−2.55
Swede	−2.90
South American	−3.64
Italian	−3.66
Spanish	−3.79
Jew	−3.92
Russian	−4.10
Pole	−4.41
Greek	−4.62

This article was written by the authors especially for T. M. Newcomb and E. L. Hartley (Eds.), *Readings in Social Psychology*, New York: Holt, Rinehart and Winston, 1947, from "Racial Stereotypes of 100 College Students," *Journal of Abnormal and Social Psychology*, 1933, 28, 280-290 and "Racial Prejudice and Racial Stereotypes," *ibid.*, 1935, 30, 175-193. Reprinted by permission of the authors, the publisher, and the American Psychological Association.

Armenian	−4.68
Japanese	−4.93
Mexican	−5.10
Chinese	−5.30
Hindu	−5.35
Turk	−5.82
Negro	−5.86

How is the agreement about "foreign" groups to be interpreted? The first possibility is that the foreign groups possess varying degrees of undesirable qualities upon which most Americans base their preferential ratings. But it is obvious that there are wide individual differences within any nationality group—that is, not all Englishmen are alike, nor are all Frenchmen, nor are all Russians. It is also obvious that few Americans have had much opportunity to know a large number of people from the many nationalities they dislike. It is also highly probable that if we were basing our judgments wholly upon what we know from actual contact with individual Spaniards, we would have differing impressions of what Spaniards are really like, because we would not all have met the same type of Spaniard. Hence a more valid interpretation of the agreement of Americans about foreign groups is that it represents the prejudgments or prejudices absorbed from the stereotypes of our culture.

Thus the preferential disliking reported by Bogardus and Thurstone may reflect attitudes toward race names and may not arise from animosity toward the specific qualities inherent in the real human beings bearing a given racial label. We have learned responses of varying degrees of aversion or acceptance to racial names and where these tags can be readily applied to individuals, as they can in the case of the Negro because of his skin color, we respond to him not as a human being but as a personification of the symbol we have learned to look down upon. Walter Lippmann has called this type of belief a stereotype—by which is meant a fixed impression which conforms very little to the facts it pretends to represent and results from our defining first and observing second.

The Present Study[2]

To explore the nature of racial and national stereotypes more fully, the following procedures were employed:

1. Twenty-five students were asked to list as many specific characteristics or traits as were thought typical of the following ten groups: Germans, Italians, Irish, English, Negroes, Jews, Americans, Chinese, Japanese, Turks. No traits were suggested to the students. This list was then supplemented by characteristics commonly reported in the literature. The result was a final check-list of 84 descriptive adjectives.
2. One hundred Princeton undergraduates were then asked to select the traits from this prepared list of 84 adjectives to characterize the ten racial and national groups. Specific directions used in the experiment follow in part:

   Read through the list of words on page one and select those which seem to you to be typical of the Germans. Write as many of these words in the following spaces as you think are necessary to characterize these people adequately. If you do not find proper words on page one for all the typical German characteristics, you may add those which you think necessary for an adequate description.

   This procedure was then repeated for other national and racial groups. When the student had finished this he was asked to go back over the ten lists of words which he had chosen and to mark the five words of each list which seemed most typical of the group in question.
3. Another group of students was asked to rate the list of adjectives on the basis of the desirability of these traits in friends and associates. The students making this judgment had no knowledge that the characteristics were supposed to describe racial groups. The traits or adjectives were rated from 1 to 10 on the basis of their desirability.

[2] This study was made in 1932.

TABLE 1

THE TWELVE TRAITS MOST FREQUENTLY ASSIGNED TO EACH OF VARIOUS RACIAL
AND NATIONAL GROUPS BY 100 PRINCETON STUDENTS

Traits Checked, Rank Order	No.	Percent	Traits Checked, Rank Order	No.	Percent
Germans			*Negroes*		
Scientifically-minded	78	78	Superstitious	84	84
Industrious	65	65	Lazy	75	75
Stolid	44	44	Happy-go-lucky	38	38
Intelligent	32	32	Ignorant	38	38
Methodical	31	31	Musical	26	26
Extremely nationalistic	24	24	Ostentatious	26	26
Progressive	16	16	Very religious	24	24
Efficient	16	16	Stupid	22	22
Jovial	15	15	Physically dirty	17	17
Musical	13	13	Naïve	14	14
Persistent	11	11	Slovenly	13	13
Practical	11	11	Unreliable	12	12
Italians			*Irish*		
Artistic	53	53	Pugnacious	45	45
Impulsive	44	44	Quick-tempered	39	39
Passionate	37	37	Witty	38	38
Quick-tempered	35	35	Honest	32	32
Musical	32	32	Very religious	29	29
Imaginative	30	30	Industrious	21	21
Very religious	21	21	Extremely nationalistic	21	21
Talkative	21	21	Superstitious	18	18
Revengeful	17	17	Quarrelsome	14	14
Physically dirty	13	13	Imaginative	13	13
Lazy	12	12	Aggressive	13	13
Unreliable	11	11	Stubborn	13	13
English			*Chinese*		
Sportsmanlike	53	53	Superstitious	34	35
Intelligent	46	46	Sly	29	30
Conventional	34	34	Conservative	29	30
Tradition-loving	31	31	Tradition-loving	26	27
Conservative	30	30	Loyal to family ties	22	23
Reserved	29	29	Industrious	18	19
Sophisticated	27	27	Meditative	18	19
Courteous	21	21	Reserved	17	17
Honest	20	20	Very religious	15	15
Industrious	18	18	Ignorant	15	15
Extremely nationalistic	18	18	Deceitful	14	14
Humorless	17	17	Quiet	13	13
Jews			*Japanese*		
Shrewd	79	79	Intelligent	45	48
Mercenary	49	49	Industrious	43	46
Industrious	48	48	Progressive	24	25
Grasping	34	34	Shrewd	22	23
Intelligent	29	29	Sly	20	21
Ambitious	21	21	Quiet	19	20
Sly	20	20	Imitative	17	18
Loyal to family ties	15	15	Alert	16	17
Persistent	13	13	Suave	16	17
Talkative	13	13	Neat	16	17
Aggressive	12	12	Treacherous	13	14
Very religious	12	12	Aggressive	13	14

Traits Checked, Rank Order	No.	Percent	Traits Checked, Rank Order	No.	Percent
Americans			*Turks*		
Industrious	48	48	Cruel	47	54
Intelligent	47	47	Very religious	26	30
Materialistic	33	33	Treacherous	21	24
Ambitious	33	33	Sensual	20	23
Progressive	27	27	Ignorant	15	17
Pleasure-loving	26	26	Physically dirty	15	17
Alert	23	23	Deceitful	13	15
Efficient	21	21	Sly	12	14
Aggressive	20	20	Quarrelsome	12	14
Straightforward	19	19	Revengeful	12	14
Practical	19	19	Conservative	12	14
Sportsmanlike	19	19	Superstitious	11	13

4. Still another group of students was asked to put in rank order the ten racial and national groups on the basis of preference for association with their members. The group which the subject most preferred to associate with was placed first and the group with which he preferred to associate least was placed tenth or last.

Results

STEREOTYPED CONCEPTIONS OF TEN ETHNIC GROUPS

Table 1 presents the twelve characteristics most frequently assigned to the ten races by the 100 students. This table summarizes the traits which students rechecked as the five most typical characteristics of each race.

The traits most frequently assigned to the Germans seem consistent with the popular stereotype to be found in newspapers and magazines. Their science, industry, ponderous and methodical manner, and intelligence were pointed out by over one fourth of the students. Scientifically-minded was the most frequently assigned characteristic, as many as 78 percent of the group ascribing this trait to the Germans.

Italians received the common characterization of the hot-blooded Latin peoples: artistic, impulsive, quick-tempered, passionate, musical, and imaginative. The greatest agreement was shown on the artistic qualities of the Italians with 53 percent of the students concurring in this belief.

The characteristics ascribed to the Negroes are somewhat similar to the picture of the Negro as furnished by the *Saturday Evening Post:* highly superstitious, lazy, happy-go-lucky, ignorant, musical, and ostentatious. The greatest degree of agreement for a single trait for any racial group was reached when 84 percent of the students voted the Negroes superstitious. Laziness was given as a typical characteristic by three fourths of the students, but the other traits mentioned above had much lower frequencies of endorsement. It may be noted in passing that for a Northern college, Princeton draws heavily upon the South for her enrollment so that this characterization of Negroes is not exclusively a Northern description.

In the case of the Irish no single trait of the 84 presented could be agreed upon as a typical Irish characteristic by half the students. Forty-five percent, however, thought pugnacity typical and 39 percent agreed upon quick-tempered. Witty, honest, very religious, industrious, and extremely nationalistic were the other adjectives selected by a fifth or more of the students.

The characterization of the English savors more of the English "gentleman" than of the general stereotype of John Bull. The leading characteristic is sportsmanship with an endorsement from 53 percent of the students. Forty-six percent of the students favored intelligence as typical of the English, 34 percent conventionality, 31 percent love of traditions, and 30 percent conservatism. Other adjectives were reserved, sophisticated, courteous, and honest.

The qualities of the competitive business world are used to describe the Jews. They are pictured as shrewd, mercenary, industrious, grasping, ambitious, and sly. Fifteen percent of the students did include Jewish loyalty to family ties. The greatest agreement (79 percent) was shown for shrewdness.

The traits ascribed to Americans show a certain objectivity on the part of the students in describing themselves, for the description given is not greatly at variance with the stereotype held by non-Americans. Americans are described as industrious, intelligent, materialistic, ambitious, progressive, and pleasure-loving. As in the case of the Irish the degree of agreement on these traits is relatively low. Almost one half did assign industry and intelligence to Americans, and a third gave materialistic and ambitious as the most descriptive adjectives.

Apparently the general stereotype for the Chinese among Eastern college students is fairly indefinite, for the agreement on typical Chinese characteristics is not great. Three of the 100 students could give no characteristics for the Chinese. Of the 97 who did respond 35 percent thought the Chinese superstitious, 30 percent thought them sly, 30 percent regarded them as conservative. The next most frequently ascribed traits were love of tradition, loyalty to family ties, industry, and meditation.

The picture of the Japanese seems more clear-cut with some recognition of the westernization of Japan. Emphasis was placed upon intelligence, industry, progressiveness, shrewdness, slyness, and quietness. The Japanese are the only group in which intelligence leads the list as the most frequently assigned characteristic. Forty-eight percent of the students filling in this part of the questionnaire gave intelligence as a typical Japanese trait.

Thirteen students could select no characteristics for the Turks. Fifty-four percent of those responding gave cruelty. Other traits selected described the Turks as very religious, treacherous, sensual, ignorant, physically dirty, deceitful, and sly.

PREFERENTIAL RANKING OF THE TEN GROUPS

The adjectives used to describe the ten groups are a rough index of the esteem in which they are held. More precise measures were furnished (1) by the direct ranking of the ten racial and national names in order of preference (Table 2), and (2) by the desirability of the typical traits attributed to the ten groups (Table 3).

TABLE 2

AVERAGE RANK ORDER OF TEN RACIAL GROUPS: PREFERENTIAL RANKING

Nationality	Average Rank Order
Americans	1.15
English	2.27
Germans	3.42
Irish	3.87
Italians	5.64
Japanese	5.78
Jews	7.10
Chinese	7.94
Turks	8.52
Negroes	9.35

TABLE 3

THE RANKING OF TEN RACES ON THE BASIS OF THE RATING OF THEIR ALLEGED TYPICAL TRAITS BY 65 STUDENTS

Nationality	Average Value of Assigned Traits
Americans	6.77
English	6.26
Germans	6.02
Japanese	5.89
Irish	5.42
Jews	4.96
Chinese	4.52
Italians	4.40
Negroes	3.55
Turks	3.05

The scores in Table 3 are the average total value of the traits assigned to the various races, computed as follows: For every race the average rating of a trait was multiplied by the number of times it was assigned to that race. The ratings of all the traits assigned to one race were added and divided by the total number of assignments of traits to that race. This division would have been unnecessary if all the 100 students in the original group assigning traits had assigned five traits to every race. In some cases, however, a student made less than five assignments.

When we compare the ranking of the ten groups on the basis of preference for association with their members with their standing based on the desirability of traits attributed to them, we find a few changes in relative placement. The Italians drop from fifth to eighth place; the Irish drop two places, while the Japanese move up two places; and the Jews, Chinese, and Negroes move up one place. In other words, the Italians are regarded more highly and the Japanese are held in lower esteem than the qualities imputed to them would justify.

It also is true that the ethnic groups are bunched much more closely together on the scores based on assigned traits than on the preference ranking. The preference ranking accorded to Americans is five times as desirable as that accorded to the Japanese, but the difference in rating Americans and Japanese on the basis of imputed characteristics is nowhere nearly as great. In part this is an artifact of our method, but in part it is due to the fact that prejudice exceeds the rationalization of undesirable racial characteristics. Nonetheless there is marked similarity between the relative ranking on the basis of preference for group names and the average scores representing an evaluation of typical traits.

Thus racial prejudice is part of a general set of stereotypes of a high degree of consistency and is more than a single specific reaction to a race name. The student is prejudiced against the label Negro because to him it means a superstitious, ignorant, shiftless person of low social status. The whole attitude is more than a simple conditioned response to the race name: it is a pattern of

rationalizations organized around the racial label.

This does not mean that the rationalized complex is justified by objective reality—that is, that Negroes really are the type of people described by the stereotype. In fact the clearness or vagueness of the stereotyped conception bear little relation to the degree of prejudice expressed against a group as determined by its preferential ranking.

RELATIVE CLEARNESS AND CONSISTENCY OF PATTERN OF STEREOTYPES

Table 4 shows the clearness of the stereotypes about the ten groups in terms of the degree of agreement in assigning typical characteristics to them.

TABLE 4

THE LEAST NUMBER OF TRAITS WHICH MUST BE TAKEN TO INCLUDE 50 PERCENT OF THE POSSIBLE ASSIGNMENTS FOR EACH RACE

Races, Rank Order	Number of Traits Required
Negroes	4.6
Germans	5.0
Jews	5.5
Italians	6.9
English	7.0
Irish	8.5
Americans	8.8
Japanese	10.9
Chinese	12.0
Turks	15.9

Table 4 lists the least number of traits which have to be included to find 50 percent of the 500 possible votes cast by the 100 students in the case of every racial and national group. It will be remembered that each student was allowed to select 5 of the 84 traits presented and that there were 100 students. If there were perfect agreement, 2.5 traits would have received 50 percent of the votes. Perfect disagreement or chance would mean that 42 traits would be necessary to give half of the votes. Table 4 shows that in the case of Negroes we can find 50 percent of the votes or selections of traits in 4.6 traits. The agreement here is very high and even in the case of the Turks where 15.9 traits must be included to give 50 percent of the possible 500 assignments or selections the voting is far from a chance selection.

Thus in Table 4 we have a comparison of the definiteness of the ten racial stereotypes. The most definite picture is that of the Negroes. The Germans and the Jews also give consistent patterns of response, while the Chinese, Japanese, and Turks furnish the least clear-cut stereotypes.

Though the belief in the undesirable qualities of a national group bolsters the prejudice against the group, it is not necessary to have a well worked out set of such rationalizations to obtain expressions of extreme prejudice. In fact Table 4 shows little relation between degree of disliking and the definiteness of the stereotyped picture. Negroes and Turks both are held in the lowest esteem, yet they represent opposite extremes in sharpness of stereotype. Students agreed among themselves most closely in characterizing Negroes and disagreed most in characterizing Turks. But they were in agreement in putting both groups at the bottom of the list as least desirable as companions or friends.

Summary

1. Ten ethnic groups were placed in rank order by Princeton students on the basis of preference for association with their members. The preferential ranking was similar in its main outline to the results reported by investigators in all parts of the United States. Minor exceptions occurred in the case of the Jews and Japanese, who were placed somewhat lower and higher, respectively, than in other studies.

2. Students not only agreed in their preferential ranking of ethnic groups, but they also agreed in the types of characteristics attributed to these groups. In fact the conception of "foreign" groups is so stereotyped that it cannot be based upon actual contact with or direct knowledge of the groups in question.

3. The clearness or definiteness of the stereotyped picture is not related to the degree of prejudice. The greatest prejudice is expressed against Negroes and Turks. The stereotyped picture of the Negro is very clear-cut while that of the Turk is the vaguest of any of the ten groups included in the study.

4. A list of 84 traits given as the typical characteristics of the ten nationalities by a group of students was rated by another group of students on the basis of their desirability in associates. From these ratings scores were assigned to the ten nationalities, the relative weight of which agreed closely with the preferential ranking. Racial prejudice is thus a generalized set of stereotypes of a high degree of consistency which includes emotional responses to race names, a belief in typical characteristics associated with race names, and an evaluation of such typical traits.

B. SOCIALIZATION OF THE

CHILD

Social Factors in Moral

Development ❧ Jean Piaget

Respect for the Group or Respect for Persons. Search for a Guiding Hypothesis

Before pursuing our analysis any further, it will be well to consider the results we have so far obtained in the light of the two principal hypotheses that have been brought forward concerning the psychological nature of respect and moral laws. If we refuse to accept Kant's view of respect as inexplicable from the point of view of experience,[1] only two solutions remain. Either respect is directed to the group and results from the pressure exercised by the group upon the individual or else it is directed to individuals and is the outcome of the relations of individuals amongst themselves. The first of these theses is upheld by Durkheim, the second by M. Bovet. The moment has not yet come for us to discuss these doctrines for their own sake, but at the same time we must, without anticipating our final critical

[1] I. Kant, *Metaphysics of Ethics*, pp. 9-10 and 104-113.

examination, develop a working hypothesis that will take account of all possible points of view. This is all the more indispensable since the discrepancy between results obtained by these authors is chiefly due, as will be shown later on, to differences of method. Now, a method is just what we are looking for at present in order to enable us to pass from the study of the rules of games to the analysis of moral realities imposed upon the child by the adult. It is only from the point of view of the right method to adopt that we shall here shortly touch upon the vexing question of the individual and society.

One way of attacking the problem is to analyze and explain the rules objectively, taking account of their connection with social groups defined by their morphology. This is the method which Durkheim used, and no one would think of denying his contribution to the subject of the evolution of moral realities. The mere fact of individuals living in groups is sufficient to give rise to new features of obligation and regularity in their lives. The pressure of the group upon the individual would thus explain the appearance of this *sui generis* feeling which we call respect and which is the source of all religion and morality. For the group could not impose itself upon the individual without surrounding itself with a halo of sanctity and without arousing in the individual the feeling of moral obligation. A rule is therefore nothing but the condition for the existence of a social group; and if to the individual conscience rules seem to be charged with obligation, this is because communal life alters the very structure of consciousness by inculcating into it the feeling of respect.

It is a striking fact, in this connection, that even such ephemeral groupings as those formed by children's societies or created primarily for the purpose of play have their rules and that these rules command the respect of individual minds. It is also curious to note how stable these rules remain in their main features and in their spirit throughout successive generations, and to what degree of elaboration and stylization they attain.

But, as we have shown above, rules, although their content continues to be the same, do not remain identical throughout the child's social development from the point of view of the kind of respect connected with them.

For very young children, a rule is a sacred reality because it is traditional; for the older ones it depends upon mutual agreement. Heteronomy and autonomy are the two poles of this evolution. Does Durkheim's method enable us to explain these facts?

No one has felt more deeply than Durkheim nor submitted to a more searching analysis the development and disappearance of obligatory conformity. In societies of a segmented type conformity is at its maximum: each social unit is a closed system, all the individuals are identical with each other except in the matter of age, and tradition leans with its full weight on the spirit of each. But as a society increases in size and density the barriers between its clans are broken down, local conformities are wiped out as a result of this fusion, and individuals can escape from their own people's supervision. And above all, the division of labor which comes as the necessary result of this increasing density differentiates the individuals from one another psychologically and gives rise to individualism and to the formation of personalities in the true sense. Individual heteronomy and autonomy would thus seem to be in direct correlation with the morphology and the functioning of the group as a whole.

Now, does this analysis apply to our children's societies? In many respects, undoubtedly, it does. There is certainly a resemblance between segmented or mechanical solidarity and the societies formed by children of 5 to 8. As in the organized clan so in these groups, temporarily formed and isolated in relation to each other, the individual does not count. Social life and individual life are one. Suggestion and imitation are all-powerful. All individuals are alike except for differences of prestige and age. The traditional rule is coercive and conformity is demanded of all.

As to the gradual disappearance of conformity as the child grows older, this too we could explain by some of the factors defined by Durkheim. To the increasing size and density of social groups and to the ensuing liberation of the individual we can compare the fact that our children, as they grow older, take part in an ever-increasing number of local traditions. The marble player of 10 or 12 will discover, for example, that there are other usages in existence besides those to which he is accustomed; he will make friends with children from other schools who will free him from his narrow conformity, and in this way a fusion will take place between clans which up till then had been more or less isolated. At the same time, the growing child detaches himself more and more from his family circle, and since at first he assimilates games to the duties laid down for him by adults, the more he escapes from family conformity, the greater change will his consciousness of rules undergo.

If, however, we are able to compare all these facts to the growth of societies in size and density, we can do so only from the point of view of the gradual diminution of the supervision exercised over individuals. In other words, the outstanding fact in the evolution of game rules is that the child is less and less dominated by the "older ones." There is little or no progressive division of labor among children; such differentiations as arise are psychological and not economic or political. If, therefore, children's societies do, in a sense, develop from the segmented to the more highly organized type, and if there is a correlative evolution from conformity to individualistic cooperation, or from heteronomy to autonomy, this process, though we may describe it in the objective terms of sociology, must be attributed first and foremost to the morphology and activity of the various age classes of the population.

In other words, the main factor in the obligatory conformity of very young children is nothing but respect for age—respect for older children, and, above all, respect for adults. And if, at a given moment, cooperation takes the place of constraint, or autonomy that of conformity, it is because the child, as he grows older, becomes progressively free from adult supervision. This came out very clearly in the game of marbles. Children of 11 to 13 have no others above them in this game, since it is one that is only played in the lower school. But apart from this, the boy begins at this age to feel himself more and more on the same level as adolescents and to free himself inwardly from adult constraint. As a result, his moral consciousness undergoes the alterations we have outlined above. There can be no doubt that this phenomenon is peculiar to our civilization and therefore falls under the Durkheimian scheme. In our societies the child of 13 escapes from the family circle and comes in contact with an ever-increasing number of social circles which widen his mental outlook. Whereas in so-called primitive communities, adolescence is the age of initiation, therefore of the strongest moral constraint, and the individual, as he grows older, becomes more and more dependent. But keeping in mind only our societies of children, we see that cooperation constitutes the most deep-lying social phenomenon, and that which has the surest psychological foundations. As soon as the individual escapes from the domination of age, he tends towards cooperation as the normal form of social equilibrium.

In short, if, putting other considerations aside for the moment, we seek only to find a working hypothesis, the methodological difficulty of Durkheimism seems to be the following with regard to the different kinds of respect. Durkheim argues as though differences from one age or from one generation to another were of no account. He assumes homogeneous individuals and tries to find out what repercussion different modes of grouping would have upon their minds. All that he gets at in this way is profoundly true, but it is incomplete. We have only to make the impossible supposition of a society where everyone would be of the same age, of a society formed by a single generation indefinitely prolonged, to realize the immense significance attaching to age relations and especially to the relations between adults and children. Would such a society ever have known anything of obligatory conformity? Would it be acquainted with religion or at any rate with the religions that taught transcendence? Would unilateral respect with all its repercussions upon the moral consciousness be observed in such a group as this? We only wish to ask these questions. Whichever way they are answered, there can be no doubt that cooperation and social constraint deserve to be far more sharply contrasted than they usually are, the latter being perhaps nothing more than the pressure of one generation upon the other, whereas the former constitutes the deepest and most important social relation that can go to the development of the norms of reason.

This influence exercised by age brings us to the second possible view of the psychology of rules, we mean that held by M. Bovet. Theoretically, and in his method, M. Bovet recognizes only individuals. Only, instead of becoming involved, as others have been in a barren discussion on the limits of what is social and what is individual, M. Bovet admits that respect, the feeling of obligation, and the making of rules presuppose the interaction of at least two individuals. On this point his method is parallel to Durkheim's and in no way opposed to it. For the real conflict lies between those who want to explain the moral consciousness by means of purely individual processes (habit, biological adaptation, etc.) and those who admit the necessity for an inter-individual factor. Once grant that two individuals at least must be taken into account if a moral reality is to develop, then it matters not whether you describe the facts objectively, as Durkheim did, or at least tried to do, or whether you describe them in terms of consciousness.[2] How, asks M. Bovet, does the sense of duty appear? Two conditions, he says, are necessary, and their conjunction sufficient. (1) The individual must receive a command from another individual; the obligatory rule is therefore psychologically different from the individual habit or from what we have called the motor rule. (2) The individual receiving the command must accept it, i.e., must respect the person from whom it came. M. Bovet differs on this point from Kant, since he regards respect as a feeling directed to persons and not to the rule as such. It is not the obligatory character of the rule laid down by an individual that makes us respect this individual, it is the respect we feel for the individual that makes us regard as obligatory the rule that he lays

[2] See R. Lacombe's conclusive remarks, *La Méthode sociologique de Durkheim.* Also, d'Essertier, *Psychologie et Sociologie*, Paris, Alcan, and many other contributions to the subject.

down. The appearance of the sense of duty in a child thus admits of the simplest explanation, namely that he receives commands from older children (in play) and from adults (in life), and that he respects older children and parents.

It will be seen that our results completely confirm this view of the matter. Before the intervention of adults or of older children there are in the child's conduct certain rules that we have called motor rules. But they are not imperative, they do not constitute duties but only spontaneous regularities of behavior. From the moment that the child has received from his parents a system of commands, however, rules and, in general, the world order itself seem to him to be morally necessary. In this way, as soon as the little child encounters the example of older children at marbles, he accepts these suggestions and regards the new rules discovered in this way as sacred and obligatory.

But the problem which faces us and which M. Bovet has himself clearly formulated and discussed is how this morality of duty will allow for the appearance of the morality of goodness.

The problem is two-fold. In the first place, the primitive consciousness of duty is essentially heteronomous, since duty is nothing more than the acceptance of commands received from without. How then, asks M. Bovet, will the child come to distinguish a "good" from a "bad" respect, and, after having accepted without distinction everything that was laid down for him by his environment, how will he learn to make his choice and to establish a hierarchy of values? In language which exactly recalls that in which Durkheim describes the effect of increasing social density on the minds of the individuals, M. Bovet points here to the effect of conflicting influences and even of contradictory commands: the child pulled in several directions at once is forced to appeal to his reason in order to bring unity into the moral material. Already we have autonomy, but since reason does not create new duties and can only choose from among the orders received, this autonomy is still only relative. In the second place, alongside of the sense of duty we must, according to M. Bovet, distinguish a sense of goodness, a consciousness of something attractive and not merely obligatory, a consciousness that is fully autonomous. In contrast to Durkheim who, while he fully recognized this dualism of duty and good nevertheless tried to trace them both to the same efficient cause, viz., pressure of the group, M. Bovet leaves the question open, and does so intentionally.

It is at this point, so it seems to us, that the part played by mutual respect comes in. Without going outside M. Bovet's fertile hypothesis, according to which all the moral sentiments are rooted in the respect felt by individuals for each other, we can, nevertheless, distinguish different types of respect. It seems to us an undeniable fact that in the course of the child's mental development, unilateral respect or the respect felt by the small for the great plays an essential part: it is what makes the child accept all the commands transmitted to him by his parents and is thus the great factor of continuity between different generations. But it seems to us no less undeniable, both in view of the results we have so far obtained and of the facts we shall examine in the rest of the book, that as the child grows in years the nature of his respect changes. In so far as individuals decide question on an equal footing—no matter whether subjectively or objectively—the pressure they exercise upon each other becomes collateral. And the interventions of reason, so rightly noted by M. Bovet, for the purpose of explaining the autonomy now acquired by morality, are precisely the outcome of this progressive co-operation. Our earlier studies led us to the conclusion that the norms of reason, and in particular the important norm of reciprocity, the source of the logic of relations, can only develop in and through cooperation. Whether cooperation is an effect or a cause of reason, or both, reason requires cooperation in so far as being rational consists in

"situating oneself" so as to submit the individual to the universal. Mutual respect therefore appears to us as the necessary condition of autonomy under its double aspect, intellectual and moral. From the intellectual point of view, it frees the child from the opinions that have been imposed upon him while it favors inner consistency and reciprocal control. From the moral point of view, it replaces the norms of authority by that norm immanent in action and in consciousness themselves, the norm of reciprocity in sympathy.

In short, whether one takes up the point of view of Durkheim or of M. Bovet, it is necessary, in order to grasp the situation, to take account of two groups of social and moral facts—constraint and unilateral respect on the one hand, cooperation and mutual respect on the other. Such is the guiding hypothesis which will serve us in the sequel and which will lead us in examining the moral judgments of children to dissociate from one another two systems of totally different origin. Whether we describe the facts in the terms of social morphology or from the point of view of consciousness (and the two languages are, we repeat, parallel and not contradictory) it is impossible to reduce the effects of cooperation to those of constraint and unilateral respect.

In conclusion, we find that the notions of justice and solidarity develop correlatively and as a function of the mental age of the child. In the course of this section, three sets of facts have appeared to us to be connected together. In the first place, reciprocity asserts itself with age. To hit back seems wrong to the little ones because it is forbidden by adult law, but it seems just to the older children, precisely because this mode of retributive justice functions independently of the adult and sets "punishment by reciprocity" above "expiatory punishment." In the second place, the desire for equality increases with age. Finally, certain features of solidarity, such as not cheating or not lying between children, develop concurrently with the above tendencies.

The Idea of Justice

To bring our enquiry to a close let us examine the answers given to a question which sums up all that we have been talking about. We asked the children, either at the end or at the beginning of our interrogatories, to give us themselves examples of what they regarded as unfair.[3]

The answers we obtained were of four kinds: (1) Behavior that goes against commands received from the adult—lying, stealing, breakages, etc.; in a word, everything that is forbidden. (2) Behavior that goes against the rules of a game. (3) Behavior that goes against equality (inequality in punishment as in treatment). (4) Acts of injustice connected with adult society (economic or political injustice). Now, statistically, the results show very clearly as functions of age.

Here are examples of the identification of what is unfair with what is forbidden.

AGE 6: "A little girl who has broken a plate," "to burst a balloon," "children who make a noise with their feet during prayers," "telling lies," "something not true," "it's not fair to steal," etc.

Category	Replies, Percent	
	6-8 Years	9-12 Years
Forbidden	64	7
Games	9	9
Inequality	27	73
Social injustice	—	11
Total	100	100

AGE 7: "Fighting," "disobeying," "fighting about nothing," "crying for nothing," "playing pranks," etc.
AGE 8: "Fighting each other," "telling lies," "stealing," etc.

Here are examples of inequalities:

AGE 6: "Giving a big cake to one and a little one to another." "One piece of chocolate to one and two to another."

[3] As a matter of fact this term is not understood by all, but it can always be replaced by "not fair" (Fr. *pas juste*).

AGE 7: "A mother who gives more to a little girl who isn't nice." "Beating a friend who has done nothing to you."
AGE 8: "Someone who gave two tubes [to two brothers] and one was bigger than the other" [taken from experience, this!]. "Two twin sisters who were not given the same number of cherries" [also experienced].
AGE 9: "The mother gives a [bigger] piece of bread to someone else." "The mother gives a lovely dog to one sister and not to the other." "A worse punishment for one than for the other."
AGE 10: "When you both do the same work and don't get the same reward." "Two children both do what they are told, and one gets more than the other." "To scold one child and not the other if they have both disobeyed."
AGE 11: "Two children who steal cherries: only one is punished because his teeth are black." "A strong man beating a weak one." "A master who likes one boy better than another, and gives him better marks."
AGE 12: "A referee who takes sides."

And some examples of social injustice:

AGE 12: "A mistress preferring a pupil because he is stronger, or cleverer, or better dressed." "Often people like to choose rich friends rather than poor friends who would be nicer." "A mother who won't allow her children to play with children who are less well dressed." "Children who leave a little girl out of their games, who is not so well dressed as they are."

The analysis of the child's moral judgments has led us perforce to the discussion of the great problem of the relations of social life to the rational consciousness. The conclusion we came to was that the morality prescribed for the individual by society is not homogeneous because society itself is not just one thing. Society is the sum of social relations, and among these relations we can distinguish two extreme types: relations of constraint, whose characteristic is to impose upon the individual from outside a system of rules with obligatory content, and relations of cooperation whose characteristic is to create within people's minds the consciousness of ideal norms at the back of all rules. Arising from the ties of authority and unilateral respect, the relations of constraint therefore characterize most of the features of society as it exists, and in particular the relations of the child to its adult surrounding. Defined by equality and mutual respect, the relations of cooperation, on the contrary, constitute an equilibrial limit rather than a static system. Constraint, the source of duty and heteronomy, cannot, therefore, be reduced to the good and to autonomous rationality, which are the fruits of reciprocity, although the actual evolution of the relations of constraint tends to bring these nearer to cooperation.

In the first place it should be noticed that the individual is not capable of achieving this conscious realization by himself, and consequently does not straight away succeed in establishing norms properly so called. It is in this sense that reason in its double aspect, both logical and moral, is a collective product. This does not mean that society has conjured up rationality out of the void, nor that there does not exist a spirit of humanity that is superior to society because dwelling both within the individual and the social group. It means that social life is necessary if the individual is to become conscious of the functioning of his own mind and thus to transform into norms properly so called the simple functional equilibria immanent to all mental and even all vital activity.

For the individual, left to himself, remains egocentric. By which we mean simply this—just as at first the mind, before it can dissociate what belongs to objective laws from what is bound up with the sum of subjective conditions, confuses itself with the universe, so does the individual begin by understanding and feeling everything through the medium of himself before distinguishing what belongs to things and other people from what is the result of his own particular intellectual and affective perspective. At this stage, therefore, the individual cannot be conscious of his own thought, since consciousness of self implies a perpetual comparison of the self with other people. Thus from the logical pont of view egocentrism would seem to involve a sort of alogicality, such that sometimes affectivity gains the ascendant over objectivity, and sometimes the relations arising from personal activity prove stronger than the relations that are independent of the self. And from the moral point of view, egocentrism involves a sort of anomy such that tenderness and disinterestedness can go hand in hand with a naïve selfishness, and yet child not feel spontaneously himself to be better in one case than the other. Just as the ideas which enter his mind appear from the first in the form of beliefs and not of hypotheses requiring verification, so do the feelings that arise in the child's consciousness appear to him from the first as having value and not as having to be submitted to some ulterior evaluation. It is only through contact with the judgments and evaluations of others that this intellectual and affective anomy will gradually yield to the pressure of collective logical and moral laws.

In the second place, the relations of constraint and unilateral respect which are spontaneously established between child and adult contribute to the formation of a first type of logical and moral control. But this control is insufficient of itself to eliminate childish egocentrism. From the intellectual point of view this respect of the child for the adult gives rise to an "annunciatory" conception of truth: the mind stops affirming what it likes to affirm and falls in with the opinion of those around it. This gives birth to a distinction which is equivalent to that of truth and falsehood: some affirmations are recognized as valid while others are not. But it goes without saying that although this distinction marks an important advance as compared to the anomy of egocentric thought, it is none the less irrational in principle. For if we are to speak of truth as rational, it is not sufficient that the contents of one's statements should conform with reality: reason must have taken active steps to obtain these contents and reason must be in a position to control the agreement or disagreement of these statements with reality. Now, in the case under discussion, reason is still very far removed from this autonomy: truth means whatever conforms with the spoken word of the adult. Whether the child has himself discovered the propositions which he asks the adult to sanction with his authority, or whether he merely repeats what the adult has said, in both cases there is intellectual constraint put upon an inferior by a superior, and therefore heteronomy. Thus, far from checking childish egocentrism at its source, such a submission tends on the contrary partly to consolidate the mental habits characteristic of egocentrism. Just as, if left to himself, the child believes every idea that enters his head instead of regarding it as a hypothesis to be verified, so the child who is submissive to the word of his parents believes without question everything he is told, instead of perceiving the element of uncertainty and search in adult thought. The self's good pleasure is simply replaced by the good pleasure of a supreme authority. There is progress here, no doubt, since such a transference accustoms the mind to look for a common truth, but this progress is big with danger if the supreme authority be not in its turn criticized in the name of reason. Now, criticism is born of discussion, and discussion is only possible among equals: cooperation alone will therefore accomplish what intellectual constraint failed to bring about. And indeed we constantly have occasion throughout our schools to notice the combined effects of this constraint and of intellectual egocentrism. What is "verbalism," for example, if not the joint result of oral authority and the syncretism peculiar to the egocentric language of the child? In short, in order really to socialize the child, cooperation is necessary, for it alone will succeed in delivering him from the mystical power of the word of the adult.

An exact counterpart of these findings about intellectual constraint is supplied by the observations on the effect of moral constraint contained in the present book. Just as the child believes in the adult's omniscience so also does he unquestioningly believe in the absolute value of the imperatives he receives. This result of unilateral respect is of great practical value, for it is in this way that there is formed an elementary sense of duty and the first normative control of which the child is capable. But it seemed to us clear that this acquisition was not sufficient to form true morality. For conduct to be characterized as moral there must be something more than an outward agreement between its content and that of the commonly accepted rules: it is also requisite that the mind should tend towards morality as to an autonomous good and should itself be capable of appreciating the value of the rules that are proposed to it. Now in the case under discussion, the good is simply what is in conformity with heteronomous commands. And as in the case of intellectual development, moral constraint has the effect of partly consolidating the habits characteristic of egocentrism. Even when the child's behavior is not just a calculated attempt to reconcile his individual interest with the letter of the law, one can observe (as we had occasion to do in the game of marbles) a curious mixture of respect for the law and of caprice in its application. The law is still external to the mind, which cannot therefore be transformed by it. Besides, since he regards the adult as the source of the law, the child is only raising up the will of the adult to the rank of the supreme good after having previously accorded this rank to the various dictates of his own desires. An advance, no doubt, but again an advance charged with doubtful consequences if cooperation does not come and establish norms sufficiently independent to subject even the respect due to the adult to this inner ideal. And indeed so long as unilateral respect is alone at work, we see a "moral realism" developing which is the equivalent of "verbal realism." Resting in part on the externality of rules, such a realism is also kept going by all the other forms of realism peculiar to the egocentric mentality of the child. Only cooperation will correct this attitude, thus showing that in the moral sphere, as in matters of intelligence, it plays a liberating and a constructive role.

Hence a third analogy between moral and intellectual evolution: cooperation alone leads to autonomy. With regard to logic, cooperation is at first a source of criticism; thanks to the mutual control which it introduces, it suppresses both the spontaneous conviction that characterizes egocentrism and the blind faith in adult authority. Thus, discussion gives rise to reflection and objective verification. But through this very fact cooperation becomes the source of constructive values. It leads to the recognition of the principles of formal logic in so far as these normative laws are necessary to common search for truth. It leads, above all, to a conscious realization of the logic of relations, since reciprocity on the intellectual plane necessarily involves the elaboration of those laws of perspective which we find in the operations distinctive of systems of relations.

In the same way, with regard to moral realities, cooperation is at first the source of criticism and individualism. For by comparing his own private motives with the rules adopted by each and sundry, the individual is led to judge objectively the acts and commands of other people, including adults. Whence the decline of unilateral respect and the primacy of personal judgment. But in consequence of this, cooperation suppresses both egocentrism and moral realism, and thus achieves an interiorization of rules. A new morality follows upon that of pure duty. Heteronomy steps aside to make way for a consciousness of good, of which the autonomy results from the acceptance of the norms of reciprocity. Obedience withdraws in favor of the idea of justice and of mutual service, now the source of all the obligations which till then had been imposed as incomprehensible commands. In a word, cooperation on the moral plane brings about transformations exactly parallel to those of which we have just been recalling the existence in the intellectual domain.

Is there any need, by way of conclusion, to point to the educational consequences of such observations? If education claims to be the direct application of what we know about Child Psychology, it would not be necessary. It is obvious that our results are as unfavorable to the method of authority as to purely individualistic methods. It is, as we said in connection with Durkheim, absurd and even immoral to wish to impose upon the child a fully worked-out system of discipline when the social life of children amongst themselves is sufficiently developed to give rise to a discipline infinitely nearer to that inner submission which is the mark of adult morality. It is idle, again, to try and transform the child's mind from outside, when his own taste for active research and his desire for cooperation suffice to ensure a normal intellectual development. The adult must therefore be a collaborator and not a master, from this double point of view, moral and rational. But conversely, it would be unwise to rely upon biological "nature" alone to ensure the dual progress of conscience and intelligence, when we realize to what extent all moral as all logical norms are the result of cooperation. Let us therefore try to create in the school a place where individual experimentation and reflection carried out in common come to each other's aid and balance one another.

If, then, we had to choose from among the totality of existing educational systems those which would best correspond with our psychological results, we would turn our methods in the direction of what has been called "Group Work" and "Self-government." [4] Advocated by Dewey, Sanderson, Cousinet, and by most of the promoters of the "Activity School," the method of work by groups consists in allowing the children to

[4] We refer the reader, on this point, to our "Rapport sur les procédés de l'Education morale," read at the Fifth International Congress on Moral Education in Paris, 1930.

follow their pursuits in common, either in organized "teams" or simply according to their spontaneous groupings. Traditional schools, whose ideal has gradually come to be the preparation of pupils for competitive examinations rather than for life, have found themselves obliged to shut the child up in work that is strictly individual: the class listens in common, but the pupils do their home work separately. This procedure, which helps more than all the family situations put together to reinforce the child's spontaneous egocentrism, seems to be contrary to the most obvious requirements of intellectual and moral development. This is the state of things which the method of work in groups is intended to correct. Cooperation is promoted to the rank of a factor essential to intellectual progress. It need hardly be said that this innovation assumes value only to the extent that the initiative is left to the children in the actual conduct of their work. Social life is here a complement of individual "activity" (in contrast to the passive repetition which characterizes the method of teaching by books), and it would have no meaning in the school except in relation to the renovation of the teaching itself.

As for self-government, the fine works of F. W. Foerster[5] and Ad. Ferrière[6] have rendered unnecessary the task of reminding our readers of its principles. M. Ferrière, in particular, has described with great care and with that proselytizing fervor which characterizes all his educational works the various modes of government of children by themselves. It is hard to read his book without

[5] F. W. Foerster, *L'École et le Caractère* (Saint-Blaise: Foyer Solid., 1910).
[6] Ad. Ferrière, *L'Autonomie des Écoliers* (Coll. des Actualités pédag. Delachaux et Niestlé).

being filled both with the hope of seeing the experiments he analyzes carried out more generally, and with the satisfaction at finding in the principles that characterize children's republics what we already know, thanks to the psycho-sociological study of the moral life.

As to F. W. Foerster, his moral pedagogy is still in our opinion too much tinged with the cult of authority or unilateral respect, and, above all, too much attached to the idea of expiatory punishment. But this makes the preoccupation with autonomy and self-government, which appears in the rest of his work, the more significant.

But pedagogy is very far from being a mere application of psychological knowledge. Apart from the question of the aims of education, it is obvious that even with regard to technical methods it is for experiment alone and not deduction to show us whether methods such as that of work in groups and of self-government are of any real value. For, after all, it is one thing to prove that cooperation in the play and spontaneous social life of children brings about certain moral effects, and another to establish the fact that this cooperation can be universally applied as a method of education. This last point is one which only experimental education can settle. Educational experiment, on condition that it be scientifically controlled, is certainly more instructive for psychology than any amount of laboratory experiments, and because of this experimental pedagogy might perhaps be incorporated into the body of the psycho-sociological disciplines. But the type of experiment which such research would require can only be conducted by teachers or by the combined efforts of practical workers and educational psychologists. And it is not in our power to deduce the results to which this would lead.

The Function of Male ❄ John W. M. Whiting
Initiation Ceremonies ❄ Richard Kluckhohn
at Puberty ❄ Albert Anthony

Our society gives little formal recognition of the physiological and social changes a boy undergoes at puberty. He may be teased a little when his voice changes or when he shaves for the first time. Changes in his social status from childhood to adulthood are marked by a number of minor events rather than by any single dramatic ceremonial observance. Graduation from grammar school and subsequently from high school are steps to adulthood, but neither can be considered as a *rite de passage*. Nor may the accomplishment of having obtained a driver's license, which for many boys is the most important indication of having grown up, be classed as one. Legally the twenty-first birthday is the time at which a boy becomes a man; but, except for a somewhat more elaborate birthday party this occasion is not ceremonially marked and, therefore, cannot be thought of as a *rite de passage*. Neither physiologically, socially, nor legally is there a clear demarcation between boyhood and manhood in our society.

Such a gradual transition from boyhood to manhood is by no means universal. Among the Thonga, a tribe in South Africa, every boy must go through a very elaborate ceremony in order to become a man.[1] When a boy is somewhere between ten and 16 years of age, he is sent by his parents to a "circumcision school" which is held every four or five years. Here in company with his age-mates he undergoes severe hazing by

[1] The following account is taken from Junod (1927, pp. 74-95).

the adult males of the society. The initiation begins when each boy runs the gauntlet between two rows of men who beat him with clubs. At the end of this experience he is stripped of his clothes and his hair is cut. He is next met by a man covered with lion manes and is seated upon a stone facing this "lion man." Someone then strikes him from behind and when he turns his head to see who has struck him, his foreskin is seized and in two movements cut off by the "lion man." Afterwards he is secluded for three months in the "yards of mysteries," where he can be seen only by the initiated. It is especially taboo for a woman to approach these boys during their seclusion, and if a woman should glance at the leaves with which the circumcised covers his wound and which form his only clothing, she must be killed.

During the course of his initiation, the boy undergoes six major trials: beatings, exposure to cold, thirst, eating of unsavory foods, punishment, and the threat of death. On the slightest pretext he may be severely beaten by one of the newly initiated men who is assigned to the task by the older men of the tribe. He sleeps without covering and suffers bitterly from the winter cold. He is forbidden to drink a drop of water during the whole three months. Meals are often made nauseating by the half-digested grass from the stomach of an antelope which is poured over his food. If he is caught breaking any important rule governing the ceremony, he is severely punished. For example, in one of these punishments, sticks are

This article was written especially for E. E. Maccoby, T. M. Newcomb, and E. L. Hartley (Eds.), *Readings in Social Psychology*, 3d Ed., New York: Holt, Rinehart and Winston, 1958. Reprinted by permission of the authors and publisher.

placed between the fingers of the offender, then a strong man closes his hand around that of the novice practically crushing his fingers. He is frightened into submission by being told that in former times boys who had tried to escape or who revealed the secrets to women or to the uninitiated were hanged and their bodies burnt to ashes.

Although the Thonga are extreme in the severity of this sort of initiation, many other societies have rites which have one or more of the main features of the Thonga ceremony. Of a sample of 55 societies[2] chosen for this study, 18 have one or more of the four salient features of the Thonga ceremony, e.g., painful hazing by adult males, genital operations, seclusion from women, and tests of endurance and manliness; the remaining 37 societies either have no ceremony at all or one which does not have any of the above features.[3]

Hypotheses

It is the purpose of this paper to develop a set of hypotheses concerning the function of male initiation rites which accounts for the presence of these rites in some societies and the absence of them in others. The theory that we have chosen to test has been suggested by previous explanations for the rites, particularly those of psychoanalytic

[2] The method of sample selection is discussed below.
[3] Seven of these societies have a minor ceremony which generally takes place during adolescence. In these societies the boy's change in status is announced by investing him with some symbol of manhood such as the donning of long pants which played such a role in our society in former years. Specifically these are tattooing— Maori and Ontong Javanese; tooth filling— Alorese, Balinese and Lakher; donning the "sacred thread"—Hindu (Khalapur Radjput). The Kwakiutl fall in a similar category. Their ceremony consists of a potlach given for the boy by his father. The ceremonies in these societies are so different in sociopsychological import from those to be described below that they will be classed hereafter with those societies which lack puberty ceremonies.

origin.[4] These explanations were modified to fit the problem of this research in two respects. First, certain of the concepts and hypotheses were restated or redefined so as to be coherent with the growing general behavioral theory of personality development,[5] and second, they were restated in such a way as to be amenable to cross-cultural test, i.e., cultural indices were specified for each variable.

We assume that boys tend to be initiated at puberty in those societies in which they are particularly hostile toward their fathers and dependent upon their mothers. The hazing of the candidates, as well as the genital operations, suggests that one function of the rites is to prevent open and violent revolt against parental authority at a time when physical maturity would make such revolt dangerous and socially disruptive. Isolation from women and tests of manliness suggest that another function of the rites is to break an excessively strong dependence upon the mother and to ensure identification with adult males and acceptance of the male role.

It is to be noted here that the educational and disciplinary functions of the initiation are not limited in time to the actual period of initiation. The boy knows all during childhood and latency about the initiation which he will face at puberty. While he is overtly not supposed to know any of the secrets of the rite, he actually knows almost everything that will happen to him. He is both afraid of what he knows will happen and also envious of the kudos and added status which his older friends have acquired through having successfully gone through this rite. Thus, through the boy's whole life the initiation ceremony serves as a conditioner of his behavior and his attitudes towards male authority, while at the same time emphasizing the advantages of becom-

[4] See, e.g., Freud (1939), Bettelheim (1954), and Mead (1949).
[5] See, e.g., Whiting and Child (1953), Sears, Maccoby, and Levin (1957), and Dollard and Miller (1950).

ing a member of the male group through initiation.

We assume that a long and exclusive relationship between mother and son provides the conditions which should lead to an exceptionally strong dependence upon the mother. Also, we assume that if the father terminates this relationship and replaces his son, there should be strong envy and hostility engendered in the boy which, although held in check during childhood, may dangerously manifest itself with the onset of puberty, unless measures are taken to prevent it.

As we indicated above, the hypothesis is derived from psychoanalytic theory. However, it should be noted that there are some modifications which may be important. First, no assumption is being made that the envy is exclusively sexual in character. We are making the more general assumption that if the mother for a prolonged period devotes herself to the satisfaction of all the child's needs—including hunger, warmth, safety, freedom from pain, as well as sex— he will become strongly dependent upon her. In accordance with this we believe rivalry may be based upon a competition for the fulfillment of any of these needs. Second, we do not propose, as most psychoanalysts do, that Oedipal rivalry is a universal, but rather we claim it is a variable which may be strong or weak depending upon specific relationships between father, mother, and son. Thus, we assume father-son rivalry may range from a value of zero to such high intensities that the whole society may be required to adjust to it.

An illustration of cultural conditions which should intensify the dependency of a boy on his mother and rivalry with his father is found in the following case.

KWOMA DEPENDENCY

The Kwoma,[6] a tribe living about 200 miles up the Sepik River in New Guinea,

[6] For a description of the Kwoma child-rearing reported here see Whiting (1941, pp. 24-64).

have initiation rites similar to those of the Thonga. Examination of the differences in the relationship of a mother to her infant during the first years of his life reveals some strong contrasts between the Kwoma and our own society. While in our society an infant sleeps in his own crib and the mother shares her bed with the father, the Kwoma infant sleeps cuddled in his mother's arms until he is old enough to be weaned, which is generally when he is two or three years old. The father, in the meantime, sleeps apart on his own bark slab bed. Furthermore during this period, the Kwoma mother abstains from sexual intercourse with her husband in order to avoid having to care for two dependent children at the same time. Since the Kwoma are polygynous and discreet extramarital philandering is permitted, this taboo is not too hard on the husband. In addition, it is possible that the mother obtains some substitute sexual gratification from nursing and caring for her infant.[7] If this be the case, it is not unlikely that she should show more warmth and affection toward her infant than if she were obtaining sexual gratification from her husband. Whether or not the custom can be attributed to this sex taboo, the Kwoma mother, while her cowife does the housework, not only sleeps with her infant all night but holds it in her lap all day without apparent frustration. Such a close relationship between a mother and child in our society would seem not only unbearably difficult to the mother, but also somewhat improper.

When the Kwoma child is weaned, a number of drastic things happen all at once. He is suddenly moved from his mother's bed to one of his own. His father resumes sexual

[7] This is, of course, difficult to determine and is a presumption based upon the following factors: (1) Kwoma informants reported that mothers had no desire for sexual intercourse as long as they were nursing the infant and (2) clinical evidence from women in our own society suggests that nursing is sexually gratifying to some women at least. See Benedek (1949), Deutsch (1944-1945), and Sears, Maccoby, and Levin (1957).

relations with his mother. Although the couple wait until their children are asleep, the intercourse takes place in the same room. Thus, the child may truly become aware of his replacement. He is now told that he can no longer have his mother's milk because some supernatural being needs it. This is vividly communicated to him by his mother when she puts a slug on her breasts and daubs the blood-colored sap of the breadfruit tree over her nipples. Finally he is no longer permitted to sit on his mother's lap. She resumes her work and goes to the garden to weed or to the swamp to gather sago flour leaving him behind for the first time in his life. That these events are traumatic to the child is not surprising. He varies between sadness and anger, weeping and violent temper tantrums.

It is our hypothesis that it is this series of events that makes it necessary, when the boy reaches adolescence, for the society to have an initiation rite of the type we have already described. It is necessary to put a final stop to (1) his wish to return to his mother's arms and lap, (2) to prevent an open revolt against his father who has displaced him from his mother's bed, and (3) to ensure identification with the adult males of the society. In other words, Kwoma infancy so magnifies the conditions which should produce Oedipus rivalry that the special cultural adjustment of ceremonial hazing, isolation from women, and symbolic castration, etc., must be made to resolve it.

If our analysis of the psychodynamics in Kwoma society is correct, societies with initiation rites should have similar child-rearing practices, whereas societies lacking the rite should also lack the exclusive mother-son sleeping arrangements and *post-partum* sexual taboo of the Kwoma.

Testing the Hypothesis

To test this hypothesis a sample of 56 societies was selected. First, the ethnographic

material on more than 150 societies was checked to determine whether or not there was an adequate description of our variables, e.g., sleeping arrangements, *post-partum* sex taboo, and initiation rites at puberty. Only half of the societies reviewed fulfilled these conditions. Although we had initially endeavored to select our cases so as to have maximum distribution throughout the world, we found that some areas were represented by several societies, while others were not represented by any. To correct for any bias that might result from this sample we made a further search of the ethnographic literature in order to fill in the gaps, and we thereby added several societies from areas previously not represented. Finally, to maximize diversity and to minimize duplication through selection of closely related societies, whenever there were two or more societies from any one culture area which had the same values on all our variables, we chose only one of them. Using these criteria, our final sample consisted of 56 societies representing 45 of the 60 culture areas designated by Murdock (1957).

The societies comprising our final sample range in size and type from small, simple, tribal groups to segments of large, complex civilizations such as the United States or Japan. In the latter case, our information has been drawn from ethnographic reports on a single delineated community.

When this sample had finally been chosen, the material relevant to our variables was first abstracted, and then judgments were made for each society as to the nature of the transition from boyhood to manhood, the sleeping arrangements, and the duration of the *post-partum* sex taboo To prevent contamination, the judgments on each variable were made at different times and the name of the society disguised by a code. All judgments were made by at least two persons and in every case where there was a disagreement (less than 15 percent of the cases for any given variable) the data were checked by one of the authors, whose judgment was accepted as final. Our findings with respect to initiation rites have been tabulated in Table 1 below.

We discovered that only five societies out of the total number had sleeping arrangements similar to our own, that is, where the father and mother share a bed and the baby sleeps alone. In only three societies did the mother, the father, and the baby each have his or her own bed. In the remaining 48, the baby slept with his mother until he was at least a year old and generally until he was weaned. In 24 of the latter, however, the father also shared the bed, the baby generally sleeping between the mother and father. The remaining 24 societies had sleeping arrangements like the Kwoma in which the mother and child sleep in one bed and the father in another. Often the father's bed was not even in the same house. He either slept in a men's club house or in the hut of one of his other wives leaving mother and infant not only alone in the same bed but alone in the sleeping room.

Similarly, the societies of our sample were split on the rules regulating the resumption of sexual intercourse following parturition. Twenty-nine, like our own, have a brief taboo of a few weeks to permit the mother to recover from her delivery. In the remaining 27, the mother did not resume sexual intercourse for at least nine months after the birth of her child, and in one instance, the Cheyenne, the ideal period adhered to was reported as ten years. The duration of the taboo generally corresponded to the nursing period and in many cases was reinforced by the belief that sexual intercourse curdles or sours the mother's milk, thus making it harmful for the infant. In other societies, like the Kwoma, the taboo is explicitly for the purpose of ensuring a desired interval between children where adequate means of contraception are lacking. In these societies the taboo is terminated when the infant reaches some maturational stage, e.g., "until the child can crawl," until the child can walk, or "until he can take care of himself."

For the 27 societies that have this taboo, more than a few weeks long, the average duration is slightly more than two years.

Results at the Cultural Level

Our hypothesis may now be restated in cultural terms as follows: *Societies which have sleeping arrangements in which the mother and baby share the same bed for at least a year to the exclusion of the father and societies which have a taboo restricting the mother's sexual behavior for at least a year after childbirth will be more likely to have a ceremony of transition from boyhood to manhood than those societies where these conditions do not occur (or occur for briefer periods).* For the purposes of this hypothesis, transition ceremonies include only those ceremonies characterized by at least one of the following events: painful hazing of the initiates, isolation from females, tests of manliness, and genital operations.

The test of this hypothesis is presented in Table 1. It will be observed from this table that of the 20 societies where both antecedent variables are present, 14 have initiation ceremonies and only six do not. Where both antecedent variables are absent only two of the 25 societies have the ceremonies. Thus, over 80 percent of the 45 pure cases correspond with the prediction.[8] Though our hypothesis was not designed for predicting the mixed cases, that is, where only one of the antecedent variables is present, it seems that they tended not to have the transition ceremonies.

Although the eight cases which are exceptional to our theory, the six in the upper

[8] Even though we made every effort to ensure at least a reasonable degree of independence for our cases, there are many instances of known historical connections among them. A statistical test of significance is therefore difficult to interpret. If the cases were independent, the probabilities are less than one in one thousand that this relationship could be obtained by chance ($x^2 < 18$).

TABLE 1

THE RELATIONSHIP BETWEEN EXCLUSIVE MOTHER-SON SLEEPING ARRANGEMENTS
AND A *Post-partum* SEX TABOO° AND THE OCCURRENCE
OF INITIATION CEREMONIES AT PUBERTY

| Customs in Infancy | | Customs at Adolescent Initiation Ceremonies | | |
Exclusive Mother-Son Sleeping Arrangements	*Post-partum Sex Taboo*	*Absent*	*Present*	
Long	Long		Azande	*hgs* †
			Camayura	*hs*
			Chagga	*hgs*
			Cheyenne	*ht*
			Chiricahua	*ht*
			Dahomeans	*hgs*
			Fijians	*gs*
			Jivaro	*ht*
		Ganda	Kwoma	*hgs*
		Khalapur (Rajput)	Lesu	*gs*
		Nyakyusa	Nuer	*hs*
		Tepoztlan	Samoans	*g*
		Trobrianders	Thonga	*hgs*
		Yapese	Tiv	*hgs*
	Short	Ashanti		
		Malaita	Cagaba	*ht*
		Siriono		
Short	Long	Araucanians	Kwakiutl	*s*
		Pilaga	Ojibwa	*t*
		Pondo	Ooldea	*hgs*
		Tallensi		
	Short	Alorese	Hopi	*hs*
		Balinese	Timbira	*hst*
		Druz		
		Egyptians (Silwa)		
		Eskimos (Copper)		
		French		
		Igorot (Bontoc)		
		Japanese (Suye Mura)		
		Koryak (Maritime)		
		Lakher		
		Lamba		
		Lapps		
		Lepcha		
		Maori		
		Mixtecans		
		Navaho		
		Ontong Javanese		
		Papago		
		Serbs		
		Tanala (Menabe)		
		Trukese		
		United States (Homestead)		
		Yagua		

° Both of a year or more duration.
† The letters following the tribal designations in the right-hand column indicate the nature of the ceremony—*h* = painful hazing, *g* = genital operations, *s* = seculsion from women, and *t* = tests of manliness.

left-hand column and the two in the lower right-hand column, may be simply misclass- ified through error of measurement, re- examination uncovers some other unantici- pated factor which may account for their placement.[9] This analysis turns out to be en- lightening.

Reviewing first the six cases in the upper left-hand column, that is, the societies which have both exclusive mother-son sleep- ing arrangements and a *post-partum* sex ta- boo but no initiation, we found that four of them (Khalapur, Trobrianders, Nyakusa, and Yapese) have an adjustment at adoles- cence which may serve as a psychological substitute for the initiation ceremony. The boys at this time leave the parental home and move to a men's house or a boys' village where they live until they are married. Mal- inowski (1927) observed this type of ad- justment amongst the Trobrianders. He wrote:

> But the most important change, and the one which interests us most is the partial break-up of the family at the time when the adolescent boys and girls cease to be permanent inmates of the parental home . . . a special institution . . . special houses inhabited by groups of adolescent boys and girls. A boy as he reaches puberty will join such a house. . . . Thus the parent home is drained completely of its adolescent males, though until the boy's marriage he will always come back for food, and will also con- tinue to work for his household to some extent. . . . [p. 67]
> At this stage, however, when the ado- lescent has to learn his duties, to be in- structed in traditions and to study his magic, his arts and crafts, his interest in his mother's brother, who is his teacher and tutor, is greatest and their relations are at their best. [p. 69]

This account suggests that this change of residence serves the same functions that we

have posited for initiation ceremonies, for example, by establishing male authority, breaking the bond with the mother, and en- suring acceptance of the male role. It is im- portant for our hypothesis, also, that there are only two other societies in our sample where such a change of residence occurs. One of these is the Malaita which has one but not both of our antecedent variables; the other is the Ashanti where the boy may move to the village of his mother's brother at or before puberty, but this is not mandatory and only half the boys do so. Thus, if we were to revise our hypothesis such that a change of residence was considered to be equivalent to initiation, the four societies mentioned should be moved over to the right-hand column and the exceptional cases would be reduced from eight to four.

Some comment should be made on the two remaining cases in the upper left-hand column. The Ganda are reported to have an interesting method of child rearing which may or may not be relevant to our theory. For the first three years of his life, a Ganda child sleeps exclusively with his mother and she is subject to a sexual taboo. At this point the boy is reported to be weaned and trans- ferred to the household of his father's brother by whom he is brought up from then on. It might be assumed that this event would obviate the need for later ceremonial initiation into manhood. Since several other societies that do have initiation also have a change of residence at weaning, however, this simple explanation cannot be accepted and the Ganda must remain an unexplained exception. Finally Lewis (1951) reports for the Tepoztlan that there was some disagree- ment among his informants as to the length of the taboo and exclusive sleeping arrange- ments. Since again there were other equally equivocal cases, we shall have to accept the verdict of our judges and let this case also remain an exception.

A reconsideration of the two exceptions in the lower right-hand column, the Hopi and the Timbira, which have the type of initia- tion into manhood required by our theory

[9] This procedure was suggested by Homans and Schneider (1955). It was used most effec- tively in their cross-cultural study of authority patterns and cross-cousin marriage.

but have neither exclusive sleeping arrangements nor a prolonged *post partum* sex taboo, also turns out to be fruitful. In neither of these societies does the father have authority over the children.[10] This is vested in the mother's brother who lives in another household.[11] That these societies should have an initiation rite, again, does not seem to contradict our general theory, even though it does contradict our specific hypothesis. From clinical studies in our own society it is clear that even with the lack of exclusive sleeping arrangements and a minimal *post partum* sex taboo, an appreciable degree of dependence upon the mother and rivalry with the father is generated. The cases here suggest that, although these motives are not strong enough to require ceremonial initiation into manhood if the father is present in the household and has authority over the child, this may be required if he lacks such authority.

But what of the cases which have but one of the antecedent variables? Taking into account the societies with exclusive sleeping arrangements but no *post-partum* sex taboo, our theory predicts that these conditions should produce dependency and rivalry. However, since the mother is receiving sexual satisfaction from her husband, she has less need to obtain substitute gratification from nurturing her infant, so that the dependency she produces in her child would be less intense and the need for initiation should be attenuated. Three of the four cases with exclusive sleeping arrangements but no taboo appear to fulfill these conditions. As we have reported above, the Ashanti and the Malaita practice a change of residence which, it could be argued, is somewhat less drastic than initiation. In any case this is permissive and not required for the Ashanti. When the Cagaba boy reaches

adolescence, he is given instruction in sexual intercourse by a priest and then sent to practise these instructions with a widow who lives with him temporarily in a specially built small hut. The boy is not allowed to leave this hut until he succeeds in having sexual intercourse with her. This trial is reported to be terrifying to the boy and it is often several days before he does succeed. This type of initiation, however, does not seem to compare with other societies which like the Thonga have a full-fledged ceremony. The Siriono, on the other hand, do not have any ceremonial recognition of the shift from boyhood to manhood and they must be regarded as an exception to our theory.

The final group of cases to consider are those that have a long *post-partum* sex taboo but not exclusive mother-son sleeping arrangements. For these, our theory would also predict an attenuated need for initiation ceremonies. Although the mothers of this group are presumed to gain substitute sexual gratification from being especially nurturant and loving toward their infants, they have less opportunity to do so than with those of societies where there are also exclusive sleeping arrangements.

As in the previous group of societies the ceremonies are, except for the Ooldea which will be discussed below, mild. The Kwakiutl have a ceremony which consists of a potlach given by the father for the son. There the boys undergo no hazing or genital operations but are secluded and expected to perform a dance. For the Ojibwa, the boy is expected to obtain a guardian spirit in a vision before he reaches maturity. Thus, generally when he is 11 or 12 years old, he goes alone into the forest where he stays often for several days without food, water, and generally without sleep until he either has a vision or returns home to recuperate before trying again. Again neither hazing or genital operations are involved.

The Ooldea, a tribe situated in southwestern Australia do, however, have a full-fledged initiation rite with hazing, isolation,

[10] A consideration of the influence of authority patterns was suggested by the work of Homans and Schneider (1955).
[11] This is also true of the Trobrianders discussed above, but of no other society in our sample about which we have information on authority patterns.

and a very painful genital operation. This apparently runs counter to our assumption that the rites should be mild if only one determinant is present.

Radcliffe-Brown, however, reports that in many Australian tribes

> the discipline of very young children is left to the mother and the other women of the horde. A father does not punish and may not even scold his infant children, but if they misbehave he will scold the mother and perhaps give her a blow with a stick. He regards the mother as responsible for misbehavior by very young children. When they are a little older, the father undertakes the education of the boys but leaves the education of the girls to the mother and the women of the horde. But the father behaves affectionately and is very little of a disciplinarian. Discipline for a boy begins when he approaches puberty and is exercised by the men of the horde. The big change comes with the initiation ceremonies when, in some tribes, the father, by a ceremonial (symbolic) action, hands over his son to the men who will carry out the initiation rites. During the initiation period of several years the boy is subjected to rigid and frequently painful discipline by men other than his father.[12]

If the Ooldea be one of those Austrialian tribes described above, they fall, along with the Trobrianders, Hopi, and Timbira, into the class of societies where the function of initiation is to make up for the lack of discipline exercised by a father over the boy during childhood.

A study of those societies without exclusive sleeping arrangements and with a long *post-partum* sex taboo which do not have the rites is interesting. In the first place both the Pondo and the Araucanians are reported to have had initiation ceremonies in the recent past, indicating that they are perhaps near the threshold of needing them. The Tallensi also are interesting. An observer

notes that the Tallensi should have invented the Oedipus-conflict theory since they are quite open and conscious of the strong rivalry and hostility between father and son, a conflict which remains strong and dangerous, guarded only by ritualized forms of etiquette, until the father dies and the son takes his place. Furthermore, family fissions are reported to occur frequently and the oldest son often leaves the family to establish a new lineage of his own.

Thus, the presence of a *post-partum* sex taboo alone seems to produce tension, which these societies commonly seek to resolve through initiation ceremonies. Societies in this group which do not have ceremonies either had them recently or show evidence of unresolved tension.

SUMMARY

The cross-cultural evidence indicates that:

1. A close relationship is established between mother and son during infancy as a consequence of either (a) their sleeping together for at least a year to the exclusion of the father, or (b) the mother being prohibited from sexual intercourse for at least a year after the birth of her child, or (c) both of these together having measurable consequences which are manifested in cultural adjustments at adolescence.

2. The cultural adjustments to the presence of the above factors are made when the boy approaches or reaches sexual maturity. These adjustments are either (a) a ceremony of initiation into manhood involving at least one and generally several of the following factors; painful *hazing* by the adult males of the society, tests of endurance and manliness, seclusion from women, and genital operations, or (b) a change of residence which involves separation of the boy from his mother and sisters and may also include some formal means for establishing male authority such as receiving instructions from and being required to be respectful to the mother's brother or the members of the men's house.

[12] Cited from a letter by A. R. Radcliffe-Brown to these authors in Homans and Schneider (1955, p. 41).

3. If both the factors specified in (1) are present, the consequences at adolescence tend to be more elaborate and severe than if only one is present.

4. The cultural adjustments specified in (2) also occur in societies where the father does not have the right to discipline his son, whether or not the conditions specified in (1) are present.

1. The more exclusive the relationship between a son and his mother during the first years of his life, the greater will be his emotional dependence upon her.

2. The more intensely a mother nurtures

TABLE 2

THE RELATIONSHIP OF INFANCY FACTORS TO CULTURAL ADJUSTMENTS AT ADOLESCENCE

Customs in Infancy and Childhood			Cultural Adjustment at Adolescence		
Authority of Father over Son	Exclusive Mother-Son Sleeping Arrangement	Post-partum Sex Taboo	None	Change of Residence	Initiation Ceremony
Present	Long	Long	2	3	14
		Short	1	2	1
	Short	Long	4	0	2
		Short	23	0	0
Absent			0	1	3

The evidence for these statements is summarized in Table 2.

The Sociopsychological Implications

So much for the manifest results at the cultural level. But what is the most reasonable sociopsychological interpretation of these relationships? What are the psychodynamics involved? We are not concerned with the bizarre rites of the Thonga or the peculiar life of a Kwoma infant, for their own sakes, but rather in discovering some general truths about human nature. We, therefore, wish to state what we believe to be the underlying processes that are involved. These are processes that we have not directly observed and which must be accepted or rejected on the grounds of their plausibility or, more important, on the basis of further research implied by our theory.

We believe that six sociopsychological assumptions are supported by our findings:

(loves) an infant during the early years of his life, the more emotionally dependent he will be upon her.

3. The greater the emotional dependence of a child upon a mother, the more hostile and envious he will be toward anyone whom he perceives as replacing him in her affection.[13]

4. If a child develops a strong emotional dependence upon his mother during infancy, and hostility toward and envy of his father in early childhood at the time of weaning and the onset of independence training, these feelings (although latent during childhood) will manifest themselves when he reaches physiological maturity in (a) open rivalry with his father and (b) incestuous approaches to his mother, unless measures are taken to prevent such manifestations.

5. Painful hazing, enforced isolation from women, trials of endurance or manliness, genital operations, and change of residence are effective means for preventing the dangerous manifestation of rivalry and incest.

[13] If, however, the mother herself is perceived by the child as the one responsible for terminating the early intense relationship, this should lead the boy to both envy her and identify with her. This should produce conflict with respect to his sex role identity, which initiation rites would serve to resolve.

6. Even a moderate or weak amount of emotional dependence upon the mother and rivalry with the father will be dangerous at adolescence if the father has no right to (or does not in fact) exercise authority over his son during childhood.

If these sociopsychological hypotheses are true, they have some interesting implications for individual differences in our own society.[14] It has long been known that there is an association between certain types of juvenile delinquency and broken homes.[15] We would predict that the probability of a boy becoming delinquent in such instances would be highest where the separation of the mother and father occurred during the early infancy of the boy and where she remarried when he was two or three years old. We would further predict that insofar as

[14] In a study of infant training William Sewell reports that "the children who slept with their mothers during infancy made significantly poorer showings on the self-adjustment, personal freedom, and family relations components of the California Test of Personality and suffered more sleep disturbances than did those who slept alone." W. H. Sewell, "Infant Training and the Personality of the Child," *Amer. J. Sociol.*, 1953, 58, 157.
[15] Cf., for example, Glueck and Glueck (1950) and Waltenberg and Balistrieri (1950).

there has been an increase in juvenile delinquency in our society, it probably has been accompanied by an increase in the exclusiveness of mother-child relationships and/or a decrease in the authority of the father. It is not unreasonable that industrialization and urbanization have done just this, but, of course, this matter should be investigated before such an interpretation is accepted.

Finally, if further research shows that juvenile delinquency in our society is in part a function of the early childhood factors that have been described in this paper, then it can be countered either by decreasing the exclusiveness of the early mother-child relationship, increasing the authority of the father during childhood, or instituting a formal means of coping wih adolescent boys functionally equivalent to those described in this paper. Change of residence would seem more compatible with the values of our society than an initiation ceremony. The Civilian Conservation Corps camps of the 1930's were an experiment which should provide useful data in this regard. The present institution of selective service would perhaps serve this purpose were the boys to be drafted at an earlier age and exposed to the authority of responsible adult males.

References

BENEDEK, T. Mother-child, the primary psychomatic unit. *Amer. J. Ortho-Psychiat.*, 1949, 19.

BETTELHEIM, B. *Symbolic wounds.* New York: The Free Press of Glencoe, 1954.

DEUTSCH, H. *The psychology of women.* Vols. I and II. New York: Grune & Stratton, 1944-1945.

DOLLARD, J., and MILLER, N. E. *Personality and psychotherapy.* New York: McGraw-Hill, 1950.

FREUD, S. *Moses and monotheism.* New York: Alfred A. Knopf, 1939.

GLUECK, E., and GLUECK, S. *Unravelling juvenile delinquency.* New York: Commonwealth Fund, 1950.

HOMANS, G. C., and SCHNEIDER, D. M. *Marriage, authority, and final causes: a study of unilateral cross-cousin marriage.* New York: The Free Press of Glencoe, 1955.

JUNOD, H. A. *The life of a South African tribe.* London: Macmillan & Co., 1927.

LEWIS, O. *Life in a Mexican village: Tepoztlan restudied.* Urbana, Ill.: Univer. of Illinois Press, 1951.

MALINOWSKI, B. *Sex and repression in savage society.* New York: Harcourt, Brace & World, 1927.

MEAD, M. *Male and female.* New York: William Morrow & Co., 1949.

MURDOCK, G. P. World ethnographic sample. *Amer. Anthropol.*, 1957, 59, 664-687.

SEARS, R. R., MACCOBY, ELEANOR E., and LEVIN, H. *Patterns of child rearing*. New York: Harper & Row, 1957.

WALTENBERG, W. W., and BALISTRIERI, J. J. Gang membership and juvenile misconduct. *Amer. Sociol. Rev.*, December 1950, 15, 744-752.

WHITING, J. W. M. *Becoming a Kwoma*. New Haven: Yale Univer. Press, 1941.

WHITING, J. W. M., and CHILD, I. L. *Child training and personality*. New Haven: Yale Univer. Press, 1953.

The Relation of Need
for Achievement
to Learning Experiences
in Independence and Mastery ❧ Marian R. Winterbottom

Research regarding the origins of the need for achievement has focused on the social conditions in which the growing person learns to be motivated for achievement. For example, McClelland and Friedman (1952) have found significant correlations between *n* Achievement scores obtained from the folk tales of eight American Indian tribes and the age and severity of independence training in those cultures. McClelland (1951a, 1951b) has derived from a theory of motivation a list of variables to be related to achievement motivation. His discussion directs attention to the number of experiences in independent mastery, the age at which the training is given, and the emotional accompaniments of the training as important conditions for the development of an achievement motive in the child.

In order to investigate further these hypotheses within an American community, the author studied a group of twenty-nine eight-year-old boys and their mothers, living in a small, middle-class, midwestern community in 1952. The group was relatively homogeneous economically and socially. The children all attended the same school and were in the same grade and same range of intelligence. The strength of *n* Achievement in the boys was related to dimensions of independence and mastery training as reported by their mothers in interviews conducted by the experimenter. Mothers were chosen as the initial group for study because of their close contact with children during the early formative years and because of the strong emotional ties of children to their mothers. Later in the paper we will discuss the importance of father and siblings in this learning, but the evidence presented will primarily be concerned with mothers and sons.

A somewhat abridged version of Chapter 33 from J. W. Atkinson, *Motives in Fantasy, Action, and Society*. Copyright © 1958, D. Van Nostrand Company, Inc., Princeton, N. J. Reprinted by permission of the author and publisher. The writer wishes to express her appreciation to Dr. J. W. Atkinson for his valuable guidance throughout the research.

The Hypotheses and Procedure

MOTHER'S STANDARDS OF TRAINING
IN INDEPENDENCE AND
MASTERY (DEMANDS)

The hypotheses relevant to this aspect of training state that mothers of boys who are high in n Achievement (a) will make a greater number of demands for independence and mastery, (b) that they will reward the child more frequently and more intensely, and (c) that they will give this training at an earlier age than mothers of boys who are low in n Achievement. These hypotheses are in accordance with McClelland's (1951a, 1951b) argument that as achievement cues are followed frequently by emotional changes, the cues take on the characteristic of arousing these emotional changes in an anticipatory way. McClelland has further specified that experiences early in life will be more decisive in this respect because there will be greater generalization of the learning and because emotional responses to parents are more intense at earlier ages.

Information regarding this aspect of training was obtained through interviews with each mother. The data presented comes from a questionnaire which each mother filled out and which included a list of twenty kinds of independence and mastery behaviors that she might consider as goals of her training. A mother was asked to put a check beside each item she considered to be a goal of her training and to indicate the age by which she expected her child to have learned the behavior. The demands were:

To stand up for his own rights with other children.
To know his way around his part of the city so that he can play where he wants without getting lost.
To go outside to play when he wants to be noisy or boisterous.
To be willing to try new things on his own without depending on his mother for help.

To be active and energetic in climbing, jumping, and sports.
To show pride in his own ability to do things well.
To take part in his parents' interests and conversations.
To try hard things for himself without asking for help.
To be able to eat alone without help in cutting and handling food.
To be able to lead other children and assert himself in children's groups.
To make his own friends among children his own age.
To hang up his own clothes and look after his own possessions.
To do well in school on his own.
To be able to undress and go to bed by himself.
To have interests and hobbies of his own. To be able to entertain himself.
To earn his own spending money.
To do some regular tasks around the house.
To be able to stay alone at home during the day.
To make decisions like choosing his clothes or deciding how to spend his money by himself.
To do well in competition with other children. To try hard to come out on top in games and sports.

The emotional consequences of the training were also assessed in the questionnaire. The hypotheses were that children who are more intensely and frequently rewarded for accomplishment are more highly motivated and that children who are more frequently and intensely punished for failure are more highly motivated. (There were some reservations about the latter part of this hypothesis, since it was expected that extreme punishment might lead ultimately to avoidance of thoughts and behavior related to achievement.)

Following the demands scale, there were two lists of alternative parental reactions to the child's behavior. One list is concerned with what the mother does when the child fulfills her expectations. The other list is concerned with what she does when he does not fulfill her demands. The list of alternative reactions to "good" performance in the child is made up of three rewarding reactions:

1. Kiss or hug him to show how pleased you are.
2. Tell him what a good boy he is. Praise him for being good.
3. Give him a special treat or privilege.

and three relatively neutral reactions:

4. Do nothing at all to make it seem special.
5. Show him you expected it of him.
6. Show him how he could have done better.

The list of alternative reactions to the "bad" performance in the child is made up of three punishment items:

1. Scold or spank him for not doing it.
2. Show him you are disappointed in him.
3. Deprive him of something he likes or expects, like a special treat or privilege.

and three relatively neutral items:

4. Don't show any feeling about it.
5. Point out how he should have behaved.
6. Just wait until he does what you want.

The items in each scale were randomized, and mothers were asked to make three choices among the six possibilities.

Two measures can be obtained from each scale. First, the number of rewards or punishments chosen from the six items. This measure can vary from zero to three. For example, a parent may make three choices all neutral, three choices all rewarding, or choices of one or two rewards. Second, the rewards and punishments are assumed to vary in intensity. It is assumed that direct physical rewards or punishments are affectively more intense than less personal reactions on the part of the mother. Verbal praise or punishment is assumed to be second in affective intensity; rewards or punishments which involve objects or privileges, least intense. The rewards and punishments

have been listed above in their assumed order of intensity.

The final part of the mothers' questionnaire listed the twenty independence or achievement activities again and asked the mothers to indicate the independence and success which their children had achieved relative to other children. Mothers were asked to rate their children as showing a particular behavior more, less, or to the same degree as other children the same age. This measure was included in order to obtain the mother's picture of the child's achievements. It was expected that the mothers of boys who are high in n Achievement would rate their sons higher than the mothers of boys who are low in n Achievement.

MOTHER'S RESTRICTIONS IN TRAINING FOR INDEPENDENCE AND MASTERY (RESTRICTIONS)

The discussion so far has been concerned with relating n Achievement to accomplishment in the positive sense, and except for the hypothesis that boys high in n Achievement will have experienced greater punishment for failure, the negative aspects of the training have not yet been considered.

In addition to failure to achieve mastery, there are certain aspects of independence and mastery that a mother may prohibit, and these prohibitions are likely to effect the achievement motivation of her child. To test the hypothesis that restrictions will have an effect opposite to that of demands, a list of twenty behaviors that a mother might want to discourage was added to the questionnaire. Each of these restrictions corresponded in content to one of the demand items. For example, the first demand on the above list, "standing up for his rights with other children," was converted to the restriction "not to fight with other children"; and the second, "knowing his way around his part of the city so that he can play where he wants without getting lost," to "not to play away from home without telling his parents where he is." As with demands, the mother was asked to check a restriction if she considered it a goal of her training and to indicate the age by which she expected it to be learned.

The restrictions were followed by a list of rewarding and punitive reactions identical to those following the demands. The specific hypotheses to be tested were that boys who are high in n Achievement experience fewer restrictions, later in training, and with less intense rewards and punishments.

The reader will note that for the two kinds of negative achievement-related experiences—failure to achieve in relation to parental demands and prohibitions on achievement behavior—we have offered different hypotheses. We predict the high n Achievement group will experience *more* intense punishment for failure to meet demands for achievement but *less* intense rewards and punishments for obeying restrictions. The reason for this difference in the hypotheses is evident if one considers the nature of the effect on the child of the two kinds of negative experience in training. Failure to meet a demand for independent accomplishment can be avoided in at least two ways: first, by not trying and leaving the situation physically or psychologically; second, by putting forth more effort and finally succeeding. We think a child is more likely to learn the former mode of resignation and giving up when failure is a terminal experience—that is, when success does not follow failure. If success often follows failure, then an experience of failure may itself contain cues which arouse anticipations of ultimate achievement. Failure is least likely to be a terminal experience when the mother has made demands which define positive achievement goals for the child. In this case the mother won't stop with failure but will insist that the child try until he succeeds. Extreme punishment for failure may lead to resignation, but moderate punishment probably serves as a goal to harder striving since the fear of failure and anticipation of pleasure in success are not channelled into the same mastery response. Achieving becomes the only sure way of avoiding failure.

On the other hand, if the child learns that a number of his attempts at independent mastery are wrong (i.e., punished) and there is no further definition of the correct response by the parent, he will be less likely to learn to want to achieve as a result of his failure experience. He will be more likely to fear attempting to achieve and will avoid thinking of it. Terminal failure experiences in the achievement training of the child are most likely to be introduced by a parent who phrases most of her goals in relation to independence training in terms of "don'ts," as wrong responses which she wants the child to inhibit. If she rewards the child for avoiding attempts at independence and mastery and if she punishes their occurrence, she is creating conditions which favor the development of a motive to avoid and inhibit achievement-directed thought and action. We expect this type of restrictive training to be reflected in a lower n Achievement score, since the score is primarily a function of the number of imaginative thoughts indicating continued striving towards achievement.

One consideration, however, must be taken into account. If a child has already learned the independent response (e.g., he can already dress or eat by himself), restrictions are less likely to lead to avoiding the situation completely since there will always be something he can do. It is important, then, to consider the sequence of demands and restrictions in studying the effects of restrictions on the strength of the motive to achieve. This is especially true when we consider the age at which restrictions are imposed. It is not age *per se* that is important, but what, if any, learning has preceded the imposition of restrictions. If no learning has preceded it, restrictive training will be more likely to contribute to a motive to avoid attempts at independence and mastery than if some mastery techniques have already been learned.

THE IMAGINATIVE MEASURE OF
n ACHIEVEMENT

Some young children showed that they often find it difficult to give imaginatively rich stories in four minutes (the standard time) when pictures are used to elicit thematic apperception. Lowell (McClelland, Atkinson, Clark, and Lowell, 1953) has used verbal cues with this age group with much more success and without the distracting description-provoking effects of pictures. Hence, two sets of verbal cues, similar but not identical to Lowell's, were used in this study. One set of four was given under what has been called Relaxed Orientation, where every effort is made to put the subject at ease and instructions are given to reduce as much as possible any "test atmosphere." The experimenter said: "What I have for you today is a sort of game. I'm interested in storytelling and I'd like you to tell some stories. It would be hard to make up stories about just anything, so I'm going to tell you what to make up a story about. I'll give you an idea, and you tell me a story about it. Make up a real story with a beginning and an end just like the ones you read. Tell me as much about your story as you can, and I'll write down what you say. Let's try one for practice. Tell me a story about a little boy who is in school."

During the practice story the experimenter asked leading questions similar to those usually printed on the story form when stories are written, i.e., What is happening in this story? What happened before? How did the story begin? What is the boy thinking about—how does he feel? What will happen—how will the story end?

At the end of the practice story, the experimenter said: "Now you have the idea. You can tell me the rest of your stories in the same way. I'll ask you what is happening, what happened before, how the people think and feel, and how the story ends. You can tell the story by answering my questions."

The verbal cues about which the child was to tell the story were: (1) A mother and her son. They look worried. (2) Two men standing by a machine. One is older. (3) A boy who has just left his house. (4) A young man sitting at a desk.

At the end of the "relaxed" stories, another condition was introduced: Achievement Orientation. The child was told that he would be given a puzzle test[1] which would tell how smart he was and on which he should try his best because he was to be compared to others in his class. After three minutes of work on the test and during a "rest period," a second set of stories was collected in response to the following verbal cues: (1) A father and son talking about something important. (2) Brothers and sisters playing. One is a little ahead. (3) A young man alone at night. (4) A young man with his head resting on his hands.

The stories were scored according to the criteria for achievement-related imagery developed by McClelland, Atkinson, Clark, and Lowell (1953). Scoring reliability was checked on twenty stories. These were scored by the experimenter and another person who had considerable experience with the scoring system. The product-moment correlation between the two scorings was .92. The over-all percentage agreement in scoring particular categories was 73 per cent.

The median *n* Achievement score of 5.0 for the 29 boys under Achievement Orientation was greater ($p < .06$ in the expected direction) than the median score of 3.8 under Relaxed Orientation. But since there is no evidence that the two forms of the measure were equivalent, little can be made of this difference except to note that it is in the expected direction.

TREATMENT OF THE DATA

For the analysis of results presented in this paper, the distributions of both Relaxed and Achievement-oriented *n* Achievement

[1] A form of the Carl Hollow Square test was used which was difficult enough so that no child completed it in three minutes.

scores are divided at the medians forming high and low n Achievement groups on each measure. Results are reported in terms of each of these measures and also in terms of another division of subjects into a group ($N = 10$) who were high (i.e., above the median scores) on both Relaxed and Achievement-oriented scores versus a group ($N = 10$) who were low (i.e., below the median scores) in both conditions. This particular breakdown isolates a group who, as Martire has argued elsewhere, show strong generalized motivation to achieve irrespective of the situation cues and a group who are relatively low in motivation to achieve irrespective of situation cues.

Results

n ACHIEVEMENT AND DEMANDS
FOR INDEPENDENCE AND MASTERY

The hypothesis that mothers of the high n Achievement group would report more demands was not confirmed. The median number of demands made by mothers of both high and low n Achievement groups was 19-20 in each of the comparisons, a result indicating that almost all of the mothers chose all of the items as goals of training by age ten.

However, the hypothesis that mothers of boys who are high in n Achievement would make these demands *earlier* is supported. By the age of eight, approximately half the de-

mands of the total group were made. If we consider the demands made before the age of eight as *early* demands, we can compare mothers of high and low n Achievement groups on the number of early demands they make. Table 1 shows the median number of early demands made by mothers of high and low n Achievement groups. It is clear in each of the three comparisons that the mothers of boys who had high n Achievement scores reported significantly more demands through the age of seven than the mothers of boys who were low in n Achievement.

Figure 1 shows the cumulative curves for demands over all ages by the mothers of the boys who were above and below the median n Achievement scores on both measures. This particular figure dramatizes an effect that is also apparent but slightly pronounced in cumulative curves drawn in terms of either Relaxed or Achievement-oriented n Achievement scores taken separately (Winterbottom, 1953).

When the number of demands made from age eight to ten are considered, the relationship is reversed. Mothers of boys who are high in n Achievement choose fewer items beyond the age of eight than mothers of boys who are low in n Achievement. This relationship is undoubtedly a function of the limited number of items to be chosen. The mothers of boys who are high in n Achievement have already used up significantly more of the items in the list by age eight

TABLE 1

MEDIAN NUMBER OF EARLY DEMANDS (THROUGH AGE SEVEN) REPORTED BY MOTHERS OF BOYS WHO WERE HIGH AND LOW IN n ACHIEVEMENT

n Achievement	Measure of n Achievement					
	Relaxed Orientation		Achievement Orientation		Both	
	N	MD.	N	MD.	N	MD.
High	15	10	14	11	10 (HH)	.002
Low	14	7	15	6	10 (LL)	15.5
p°		.01		.004		5.5

° Probability of the difference in predicted direction by Mann-Whitney U Test (Moses, 1952).

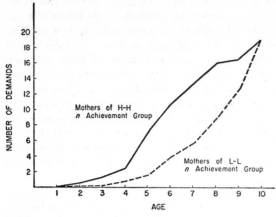

Fig. 1. Cumulative average number of demands for independence and mastery at each age (1-10 years) by mothers of boys who were high ($N = 10$) and low ($N = 10$) on both Relaxed and Achievement Orientation measures of n Achievement.

and hence there are fewer remaining to be chosen.

REWARDS FOR FULFILLED DEMANDS
AND n ACHIEVEMENT

The emotional consequences of demands training are summarized in Table 2. The hypotheses are that mothers of boys who are high in n Achievement will be more fre-

quently and intensely rewarding when demands for independence and mastery are fulfilled and will be more frequently and intensely punishing when these demands are not fulfilled.

More mothers of boys who are high in n Achievement report using all three types of rewards—verbal, object, and physical—than mothers of boys who are low in n Achievement ($p = .05-.10$). It is assumed

TABLE 2

Rewards and Punishments Administered in Connection with Demands for Independence as Reported by Mothers of Boys Who Are High and Low in n Achievement

	Measure of n Achievement					
	Relaxed Orientation		Achievement Orientation		Both	
n Achievement:	High	Low	High	Low	High-High	Low-Low
N	15	14	14	15	10	10
Reward						
Verbal	15	13	14	14	10	9
Object	11	8	8	11	6	7
Physical	11	5*	10	5*	9	3*
All Three Types	8	5	8	3*	6	1*
Punishment						
Verbal	15	12	13	14	7	10
Object	10	12	11	12	8	9
Physical	6	3	4	5	4	2
All Three Types	1	2	1	2	1	2

* $p < .05$ in predicted direction.
Note: Significance of differences tested by exact probabilities for 2 × 2 contingency tables.

that some form of physical affection like hugging or kissing is more intensely rewarding than either verbal praise or object rewards. There are no differences between mothers of high and low n Achievement boys in frequency of verbal or object rewards. However, mothers of high n Achievement boys report more physical affection as reward for fulfilled demands than mothers of low n Achievement boys ($p < .05$).

PUNISHMENTS FOR UNFULFILLED DEMANDS AND n ACHIEVEMENT

None of the comparisons between mothers of high and low n Achievement boys in use of punishment for unfilled demands reveals a significant difference. Apparently mothers of high and low n Achievement children are much the same in their reactions to the child's failure to fulfill demands, at least as we have measured these reactions.

Achievement will be more likely to rate their children as more skillful is confirmed. An index of the favorableness of each mother's judgments of her son was obtained by subtracting the number of times the son was rated worse than average from the number of times he was rated better than average on the list of twenty demands. A plus score indicates a predominance of positive judgments; a minus score indicates a preponderance of negative judgments. The median scores of mothers of high and low n Achievement boys are shown in Table 3. In each of the comparisons, the mothers of high n Achievement boys are more positive in their evaluations than mothers of low n Achievement boys ($p = .025$-$.05$).

It is difficult to say whether the difference in judgments corresponds to a real difference in achievement levels in the two groups, or whether the mother's own evaluation of her son's achievement has influenced the ratings. Several behavioral ratings made by the boys' teachers in another phase of

TABLE 3

JUDGMENTS OF MOTHERS CONCERNING THE SKILL OF THEIR SONS IN MASTERY AND INDEPENDENCE RELATIVE TO THE SKILL OF OTHER CHILDREN THE SAME AGE (NUMBER OF TIMES RATED MORE SKILLFUL THAN OTHERS MINUS NUMBER OF TIMES RATED LESS SKILLFUL THAN OTHERS)

	Measure of n Achievement					
	Relaxed Orientation		Achievement Orientation		Both	
n Achievement:	High	Low	High	Low	High-High	Low-Low
N	15	14	14	15	10	10
Md.	1.83	−1.00	2.87	−.50	2.50	−1.00
p*		.04		.005		.003

* Probability of difference between medians in the predicted direction obtained by the Mann-Whitney U Test (Moses, 1952).

MOTHER'S EVALUATION OF SON'S ACCOMPLISHMENTS

We may turn now to the mother's evaluation of her son's accomplishments in relation to those of other children. The hypothesis that mothers of boys who are high in n

this study provides some independent evidence of observable differences in the behavior of the two groups. According to the ratings of teachers, the boys who were high in n Achievement appeared significantly more motivated for success in school work, more independent, more successful in social groups (i.e., popular), and more pleased

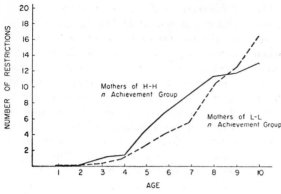

Fig. 2. Cumulative average number of restrictions upon independence and mastery at each age (1-10 years) by mothers of boys who were high ($N = 10$) and low ($N = 10$) on both Relaxed and Achievement Orientation measures of n Achievement.

when they did succeed than the boys who were low in n Achievement. But ratings of success in school work, sports and games, and in leadership did not discriminate significantly between the two motivation groups, although the trend always favored the high n Achievement group. However, there still may be some justification for considering the ratings of a mother as more indicative of her general evaluation of the child's performance. In this light, the data provide additional suggestive evidence that the mothers of boys who are high in n Achievement tend to be more rewarding, i.e., they take a more positive view of the child's behavior.

n ACHIEVEMENT AND RESTRICTIONS UPON INDEPENDENT ACTIVITY

The first hypothesis to be tested is that mothers of high n Achievement children are less restrictive than mothers of low n Achievement children. Table 4 shows that this hypothesis is confirmed. By the age of ten, mothers of the high n Achievement group have selected only 12 to 13 of the restrictions; mothers of the low n Achievement group have selected 16 to 17, significantly more in each of the three comparisons.

It was further hypothesized that the restrictions imposed by the mothers of the high n Achievement group would come later than the demands for independent accomplishment. A comparison between mothers of high and low n Achievement groups in making early restrictions, i.e., through the age of seven, shows that mothers of the high n Achievement boys actually impose more early restrictions than mothers of the low n Achievement group (Table 4 and Figure 2). But the questions is, Do the mothers of the high n Achievement group make more demands or restrictions at any early age?

TABLE 4

MEDIAN NUMBER OF TOTAL RESTRICTIONS (THROUGH AGE TEN) AND EARLY RESTRICTIONS (THROUGH AGE SEVEN) REPORTED BY MOTHERS OF BOYS WHO WERE HIGH AND LOW IN n ACHIEVEMENT

			Measure of n Achievement			
	Relaxed Orientation		Achievement Orientation		Both	
n Achievement:	High	Low	High	Low	High-High	Low-Low
N	15	14	14	15	10	10
Total restrictions	12.17	16.5°	13	16°	12.25	17.25°
Early restrictions	9.0	6.4	9.0	6.5°	10.25	6.25°

° p of difference $< .05$ in predicted direction by Mann-Whitney U Test (Moses, 1952).

TABLE 5

RELATIVE EMPHASIS UPON DEMANDS VERSUS RESTRICTIONS IN EARLY
TRAINING. NUMBER OF MOTHERS OF BOYS IN HIGH AND LOW n
ACHIEVEMENT GROUPS WHO MADE MORE DEMANDS FOR
INDEPENDENCE THAN RESTRICTIONS UPON INDEPENDENT
ACTIVITY BEFORE THE AGE OF EIGHT

	Measure of n Achievement					
	Relaxed Orientation		Achievement Orientation		Both	
n Achievement:	High	Low	High	Low	High-High	Low-Low
N	15	14	14	15	10	10
More Demands than Restrictions	10*	6	10*	5	8*	4

* $p < .05$ in the predicted direction.
Note: Tests for the high and low n Achievement groups were accomplished separately using the Wilcoxon Matched Pairs Signed Ranks test (Moses, 1952).

The number of demands and restrictions made by each mother through age seven was compared. Table 5 shows that mothers of boys who are high in n Achievement make more demands than restrictions during the early years ($p = .05$). But mothers of boys who are low in n Achievement do not. In other words, mothers of the high n Achievement boys report fewer restrictions through age ten but more early restrictions (through age seven) than mothers of boys who are low in n Achievement. However, the restriction training of the high n Achievement group does not precede their demand training; through age seven their training is characterized by a preponderance of positive demands.

REWARDS AND PUNISHMENTS
ADMINISTERED IN RESTRICTIVE
TRAINING

The emotional consequences of complying or failing to comply with restrictions are presented in Table 6. The pattern of rewards and punishments in connection with restrictions tends to be similar to the pattern for demands (Table 2) but is less consistent in the three comparisons. There is no evidence to support the hypothesis that the boys who are high in n Achievement experience less frequent and less intense reward and punishment in connection with restrictions. On the contrary, Table 6 shows that the mothers of boys who are high in n Achievement report administering all three types of rewards and using some form of physical affection to reward restrictive training more frequently than mothers of boys who are low in n Achievement. These differences are not significant, however, when the Achievement-Orientation score is the index of strength of n Achievement.

A NOTE ON THE RELATIONSHIP OF
n ACHIEVEMENT TO OVERT
BEHAVIOR IN THESE CHILDREN

This paper is primarily concerned with the relationship between n Achievement in children, as measured in thematic apperception, and childhood training as reported by their mothers. But a brief word is in order concerning some of the relationships discovered between n Achievement and overt behavior in these children. The question of whether or not the thematic apperceptive index of achievement motive has the same "meaning" for children as for the college-aged subjects of many other experiments is

TABLE 6

NUMBER OF MOTHERS OF BOYS HIGH AND LOW IN n ACHIEVEMENT
WHO REPORTED VARIOUS TYPES OF REWARDS AND PUNISHMENTS
IN CONNECTION WITH RESTRICTIONS PLACED UPON
INDEPENDENT ACTIVITY

	Relaxed Orientation		Measure of n Achievement Achievement Orientation		Both	
n Achievement:	High	Low	High	Low	High-High	Low-Low
N	15	14	14	15	10	10
Reward						
Verbal	15	12	13	14	10	9
Object	9	9	8	10	5	7
Physical	11	4°	9	6	8	3°
All Three Types	8	2†	6	4	5	1
Punishment						
Verbal	13	13	12	14	9	10
Object	12	12	10	14	8	10
Physical	6	4	5	5	4	2
All Three Types	1	2	1	2	1	2

° $p = .08$ (two-tail test).   † $p = .12$ (two-tail test).

best answered by a summary of the behavioral correlates of achievement motivation in these children. A description of the procedures and fuller discussion of these findings is presented elsewhere (Winterbottom, 1953).

Two kinds of behavior measures were obtained. The first consisted of ratings of the children by their teachers in school. The second consisted of observations made by the E during the child's performance under achievement orientation. The test situation had been especially contrived to enable the E to make observations of a number of achievement-related decisions and behaviors in the child.

The teachers used a five-point scale to rate children on the following questions. Each point on the scale was designated by an appropriate qualitative statement which represented a difference in degree from "most to least." The items were randomized in the list given teachers but are organized into several categories here.

Achievement Motivation

1. Generally, how much do you think he wants to do well?
2. How hard does he try to do well or win in sports or game (even though he may or may not win)?
3. How hard does he try to do well in schoolwork (even though he may or may not succeed)?

Objective Success

1. Generally, how successful is he?
2. How well does he do in schoolwork?
3. How popular a child is he with other children?
4. How well does he do in sports or games?
5. How much leadership does he show with other children?

Independence

1. Generally, how would you rate his overall independence?
2. How is he at entertaining himself or keeping himself occupied if necessary?

3. How well does he stand up for his rights with other children?
4. How is he about doing things in school on his own?
5. How well is he able to look after himself in eating, putting on his own clothes, coming and going from school, etc?

Two other questions asked about the degree of pleasure and pride the child took in success and the degree to which he persisted or gave up in the face of failure:

How does he react when he does well in something?
How does he react when he fails at something or has difficulty with a task?

The behaviors rated by the teachers were obviously selected on the theoretical presumption that they ought to be positively related to strength of *n* Achievement. In this respect it was found that from the teachers' point of view, the children who are high in *n* Achievement appear more independent in general ($p < .01$), as experiencing more pleasure and pride in success ($p < .01$), and, especially the group who were above the median score on both relaxed and achievement-oriented measures, more motivated for success, i.e. in general, in sports, and in school work ($p < .05$). The objective success of the two groups did not appear significantly different except in social relations where the high *n* Achievement group was demonstrably more popular ($p < .01$). More than a few of the remaining comparisons in independence were in the expected direction although not found to be statistically significant.

Now let us consider E's observations of children in the puzzle-solving situation. During the test period, each child was offered help and rest at intervals and could spontaneously ask for help if he wanted it. The results show that boys who are high in *n* Achievement on the stories told immediately after the puzzle-solution period (i.e., under achievement orientation) less frequently asked for help ($p < .05$) and more often refused an invitation to stop work and rest

($p < .05$) than boys who were low in *n* Achievement. And boys who were high in *n* Achievement on both relaxed and achievement-oriented measures more often refused help even when it was offered ($p < .05$).

Two different puzzles were used, one more difficult than the other. The high and low *n* Achievement groups did not differ in preference for easy versus more difficult task, as might have been expected. Nor did they differ in stated level of aspiration for the puzzle task. A statement of level of aspiration was obtained only once, and there is some doubt as to its value since the children were asked to estimate how long it would take them to do the puzzle. Time estimates may be particularly hard to make at this age.

A series of specific instructions were given at the beginning of the puzzle task with the intention of asking the child to recall them at the end. Some instructions were stated positively (as demands), others negatively (as restrictions) with a view to testing the hypothesis that the high *n* Achievement group would recall more positive and fewer negative instructions. There is no difference in recall of positive instructions, but the trend is as predicted for negative instructions ($p = .05$ on the relaxed index).

These results present some evidence that boys who are high in *n* Achievement appear more independent, more popular, and more motivated to succeed than boys who are low in *n* Achievement. The refusal of help and the offer to rest may be taken as indices of persistence at an achievement task. Assuming that scoring high on both relaxed and achievement-oriented measures of *n* Achievement indicates more generalized motivation to achieve, it makes sense that the teachers' ratings which must have been based on very general impressions should relate most clearly to the combined index of *n* Achievement. In general, these attempts to detect expressions of motivation to achieve in overt behavior show that we are measuring in fantasy an attribute of the child that is manifested both in specific tasks and in the kinds of general impressions which emerge from extensive observation of his behavior in a variety of settings.

Discussion

The data presented provide a basis for description of the differences in the learning experiences of boys who have relatively high or low n Achievement scores on the fantasy measure used. The high n Achievement group have earlier training in our list of independence and mastery behaviors. They have fewer experiences in being restricted in these areas, and though restriction training comes earlier for them, it has been preceded by a good deal of training in independence. Their mothers take a more positive view of their accomplishments and are more often and more affectively rewarding. There is no evidence that the high n Achievement group is more frequently punished. All of these conclusions are limited by the measures used. Interviews and questionnaires from mothers may not give an accurate representation of what actually went on during training. The sample of fantasy we used may often miss important kinds of fantasies which may relate to achievement behavior but which are not easily verbalized, or which are not elicited in this situation.

Though it is difficult to evaluate the meaning of our questionnaire data and how it relates to the actual behavior of the mother, there is some possibility of examining the stories of the two groups of children in order to understand the context of fantasy in which the achievement imagery occurs and what clues it may give to other determinants which we have not considered. In order to do this fairly systematically, though without any check on reliability, twenty-five stories that were scored for achievement imagery were selected from the lowest and highest scorers. These stories were analyzed for differences in the stories other than in achievement imagery itself.

Most of the stories were centered around

competitiveness. Both the high and low groups had nine stories each, involving competition with children though the resolutions of the stories were different. The high group resolved all the stories with someone winning. Four stories mentioned instances of aggression and cheating in the process of winning, though never leading to success. The low group had instances of resolution by the winner giving up the prize, or the loser refusing to play, or someone getting hurt or changing the theme of the story.

Competition between a young man and an older man occurred seven times in the stories of high n Achievers but not at all in the low group. The stories of the high group contained four references to aggression between the two, two references to someone being hurt, two references to helping each other, and no resolutions where the younger lost out. The low group, when they used the younger-older man theme, structured the stories twice as the older man helping the younger, once as the younger man admiring the older man's accomplishment, and three times as the young man being fired or worried about the possibility. There were no instances of aggression, bragging, or open competition.

These stories suggest that the context of the achievement imagery is limited more for the low group than the high group. Competitiveness is restricted to their own age group and does not get expressed with older men. Also cheating and aggression are not themes which accompany the achievement fantasy of the low group. It may be that the occurrence of such possibilities and subsequent avoidance of their expression may reduce the expressions of ambitions involving them. These stories lead one to believe that a son's relationship with his father may be as important an area to investigate as his relationship with his mother, especially in an attempt to understand the restriction of fantasies that may be present and unexpressed or avoided. The emotional meaning of achievement fantasies is not well understood and is likely far more complex than our data suggest. Investigation of the determinants of achievement motives that have their sources in the psychosexual nature of the child may be helpful.[2] The competitiveness with older men certainly suggests this as a direction for research. The age of independence and mastery training of the child would then be seen in relation to his developmental level. The results which indicate the importance of training before the age of eight do not justify the assertion that the earlier the training the more it contributes to the development of achievement motivation and fantasy. There may be particular age ranges during which an environment which encourages independence and achievement fits particularly well the needs of the growing child.

Another area for investigation is the parent's response to the child's fantasies, especially if the child expresses them in play or conversation. The parental response may be directly encouraging or inhibiting of certain types of fantasy. There is some suggestive evidence in a few cases that the n Achievement of parents (measured by using pictures) is related to the n Achievement of their children.[3] The available evidence, while not conclusive, reinforces the notion that certain kinds of fantasies are expressed in families and that these may vary and affect the child's expression of similar ideas.

The discussion of these other leads which require investigation indicates the author's belief that the determinants of n Achievement are undoubtedly very complex. Within the framework of all the possible determinants, this study has shown the importance of the nature of the child's experience in gaining independence and mastery as his learning is guided by his mother. The kinds of goals she chooses to train the child for, the age at which she wants them learned, and her general evaluation of her child's performance have been shown to be of some importance in contributing to the development of his motivation to achieve.

Summary and Conclusions

The results indicate that mothers of children with strong achievement motivation differ from mothers of children with weak achievement motivation in the following respects:

1. They make more demands before the age of eight.
2. They evaluate their children's accomplishments higher and are more rewarding.
3. The total number of restrictions made through age ten is less but the total number of restrictions made through age seven is greater.
4. Even though they make more restrictions through age seven the number of demands they make at this early age exceeds the number of restrictions.

No difference between the two groups was found in the total number of demands made, the number and intensity of punishments for demands and restrictions. It is concluded that early training in independence and mastery contributes to the development of strong achievement motivation.

[2] The lack of correspondence between the research on n Achievement in young men and women suggests this direction as well as an investigation of different methods of training.
[3] From the initial analysis of data collected by Miss Joanne Steger at Connecticut College, New London, Connecticut.

References

McClelland, D. C. *Personality*. New York: Wm. Sloane Associates, 1951a.

McClelland, D. C. Measuring motivation in phantasy: the achievement motive. In H. Guetzkow (Ed.), *Groups, leadership* and men. New York: Carnegie Press, 1951b, pp. 191-205.

McClelland, D. C., and Friedman, G. A. A cross-cultural study of motivation appearing in folk tales. In G. E. Swanson,

T. M. Newcomb, and E. L. Hartley (Eds.), *Readings in social psychology,* Rev. Ed. New York: Holt, Rinehart and Winston, 1952.

McCLELLAND, D. C., ATKINSON, J. W., CLARK, R. A., and LOWELL, E. L. *The achievement motive.* New York: Appleton-Century-Crofts, 1953.

MOSES, L. E. Non-parametric statistics for psychological research. *Psychol. Bull.,* 1952, *49,* 122-143.

WINTERBOTTOM, MARIAN R. The relation of childhood training in independence to achievement motivation. Unpublished doctoral dissertation, Univer. of Michigan, 1953.

Racial Identification and ❧ Kenneth B. Clark
Preference in Negro Children ❧ Mamie P. Clark

Problem

The specific problem of this study is an analysis of the genesis and development of racial identification as a function of ego development and self-awareness in Negro children.

Race awareness, in a primary sense, is defined as a consciousness of the self as belonging to a specific group which is differentiated from other observable groups by obvious physical characteristics which are generally accepted as being racial characteristics.

Because the problem of racial identification is so definitely related to the problem of the genesis of racial attitudes in children, it was thought practicable to attempt to determine the racial attitudes or preferences of these Negro children—and to define more precisely, as far as possible, the developmental pattern of this relationship.

Procedure

This paper presents results from only one of several techniques devised and used by the authors to investigate the development of racial identification and preferences in Negro children.[1] Results presented here are from the Dolls Test.

DOLLS TEST

The subjects were presented with four dolls, identical in every respect save skin color. Two of these dolls were brown with black hair and two were white with yellow hair. In the experimental situation these dolls were unclothed except for white diapers. The position of the head, hands, and legs on all the dolls was the same. For half of the subjects the dolls were presented in the order: white, colored, white, colored. For the other half the order of presentation was reversed. In the experimental situation the subjects were asked to respond to the following requests by choosing *one* of the dolls and giving it to the experimenter:

1. Give me the doll that you like to play with —(*a*) like best.
2. Give me the doll that is a nice doll.
3. Give me the doll that looks bad.

[1] Other techniques presented in the larger study include: (1) a coloring test; (2) a questionnaire and (3) a modification of the Horowitz line drawing technique. (Horowitz, 1939.)

This article was written by the authors especially for T. M. Newcomb and E. L. Hartley (Eds.), *Readings in Social Psychology,* New York: Holt, Rinehart and Winston, 1947. Reprinted by permission of the authors and publisher.

4. Give me the doll that is a nice color.
5. Give me the doll that looks like a white child.
6. Give me the doll that looks like a colored child.
7. Give me the doll that looks like a Negro child.
8. Give me the doll that looks like you.

Requests 1 through 4 were designed to reveal preferences; requests 5 through 7 to indicate a knowledge of "racial differences"; and request 8 to show self-identification.

It was found necessary to present the preference requests first in the experimental situation because in a preliminary investigation it was clear that the children who had already identified themselves with the colored doll had a marked tendency to indicate a preference for this doll and this was not necessarily a genuine expression of actual preference, but a reflection of ego involvement. This potential distortion of the data was controlled by merely asking the children to indicate their preferences first and then to make identifications with one of the dolls.

Subjects

Two hundred fifty-three Negro children formed the subjects of this experiment. One hundred thirty-four of these subjects (southern group) were tested in segregated nursery schools and public schools in Hot Springs, Pine Bluff, and Little Rock, Arkansas. These children had had no experience in racially mixed school situations. One hundred nineteen subjects (northern group) were tested in the racially mixed nursery and public schools of Springfield, Massachusetts.

AGE DISTRIBUTION OF SUBJECTS

Age, Years	North	South	Total
3	13	18	31
4	10	19	29
5	34	12	46
6	33	39	72
7	29	46	75
Total	119	134	253

SEX DISTRIBUTION OF SUBJECTS

Sex	North	South	Total
Male	53	63	116
Female	66	71	137

SKIN COLOR OF SUBJECTS

Skin Color	North	South	Total
Light[a]	33	13	46
Medium[b]	58	70	128
Dark[c]	28	51	79

[a] light (practically white).
[b] medium (light brown to dark brown).
[c] dark (dark brown to black).

All subjects were tested individually in a schoolroom or office especially provided for this purpose. Except for a few children who showed generalized negativism from the beginning of the experiment (results for these children are not included here), there was adequate rapport between the experimenter and all subjects tested. In general, the children showed high interest in and enthusiasm for the test materials and testing situation. The children, for the most part, considered the experiment somewhat of a game.

Results

RACIAL IDENTIFICATION

Although the questions on knowledge of "racial differences" and self-identification followed those designed to determine racial preference in the actual experimental situation, it appears more meaningful to discuss the results in the following order: knowledge of "racial differences," racial self-identification, and finally racial preferences.

The results of the responses to requests 5, 6, and 7, which were asked to determine the subjects' knowledge of racial differences, may be seen in Table 1. Ninety-four percent of these children chose the white doll when asked to give the experimenter the white doll; 93 percent of them chose the brown doll when asked to give the colored doll;

TABLE 1
CHOICES OF ALL SUBJECTS

Choice	Request 5 (for White)		Request 6 (for Colored)		Request 7 (for Negro)		Request 8 (for You)	
	No.	Percent	No.	Percent	No.	Percent	No.	Percent
Colored Doll	13	5	235	93	182	72	166	66
White Doll	237	94	15	6	50	20	85	33
Don't Know or No Response	3	1	3	1	21	8	2	1

and, 72 percent chose the brown doll when asked to give the Negro doll. These results indicate a clearly established knowledge of a "racial difference" in these subjects—and some awareness of the relation between the physical characteristic of skin color and the racial concepts of "white" and "colored." Knowledge of the concept of "Negro" is not so well developed as the more concrete verbal concepts of "white" and "colored" as applied to racial differences.

The question arises as to whether choice of the brown doll or of the white doll, particularly in response to questions 5 and 6, really reveals a knowledge of "racial differences" or simply indicates a learned perceptual reaction to the concepts of "colored" and "white." Our evidence that the responses of these children *do* indicate a knowledge of "racial difference" comes from several sources: the results from other techniques used (i.e., a coloring test and a questionnaire) and from the qualitative data obtained (children's spontaneous remarks) strongly support a knowledge of "racial differences." Moreover, the consistency of results for requests 5 through 8 also tends to support the fact that these children are actually making identifications in a "racial" sense.

The responses to request 8, designed to determine racial self-identification, follow the following pattern: 66 percent of the total group of children identified themselves with the colored doll, while 33 percent identified

themselves with the white doll. The critical ratio of this difference is 7.6.[2]

Comparing the results of request 8 (racial self-identification) with those of requests 5, 6, and 7 (knowledge of racial difference) it is seen that the awareness of racial differences does not necessarily determine a socially accurate racial self-identification—since approximately nine out of ten of these children are aware of racial differences as indicated by their correct choice of a "white" and "colored" doll on request, and only a little more than six out of ten make socially correct identifications with the colored doll.

AGE DIFFERENCES

Table 2 shows that when the responses to requests 5 and 6 are observed together, these subjects at each age level have a well-developed knowledge of the concept of racial difference between "white" and "colored" as this is indicated by the characteristic of skin color. These data definitely indicate that a basic knowledge of "racial differences" exists as a part of the pattern of ideas of Negro children from the age of three through seven years in the northern and southern communities tested in this study—and that this knowledge develops more definitely from year to year to the point of absolute stability at the age of seven.

[2] These results are supported by similar ones from the Horowitz line drawing technique.

TABLE 2

CHOICES OF SUBJECTS AT EACH AGE LEVEL*

Choice	3 Yr.		4 Yr.		5 Yr.		6 Yr.		7 Yr.	
	No.	Per-cent	No.	Per-cent	No.	Per-cent	No.	Per-cent	No.	Per-cent
Request 5 (for White)										
Colored Doll	4	13	4	14	3	7	2	3	0	
White Doll	24	77	25	86	43	94	70	97	75	100
Request 6 (for Colored)										
Colored Doll	24	77	24	83	43	94	69	96	75	100
White Doll	4	13	5	17	3	7	3	4	0	
Request 7 (for Negro)										
Colored Doll	17	55	17	59	28	61	56	78	64	85
White Doll	9	29	10	35	14	30	12	17	5	7
Request 8 (for You)										
Colored Doll	11	36	19	66	22	48	49	68	65	87
White Doll	19	61	9	31	24	52	23	32	10	13

*Individuals failing to make either choice not included, hence some percentages add to less than 100.

A comparison of the results of requests 5 and 6 with those of request 7, which required the child to indicate the doll which looks like a "Negro" child, shows that knowledge of a racial difference in terms of the word "Negro" does not exist with the same degree of definiteness as it does in terms of the more basic designations of "white" and "colored." It is significant, however, that knowledge of a difference in terms of the word "Negro" makes a sharp increase from the five- to the six-year level and a less accelerated one between the six- and seven-year levels. The fact that all of the six-year-olds used in this investigation were enrolled in the public schools seems to be related to this spurt. Since it seems clear that the term "Negro" is a more verbalized designation of "racial differences," it is reasonable to assume that attendance at public schools facilitates the development of this verbalization of the race concept held by these children.

In response to request 8 there is a general and marked increase in the percent of subjects who identify with the colored doll with an increase in age—with the exception of

the four- to five-year groups.[3] This deviation of the five-year-olds from the general trend is considered in detail in the larger, yet unpublished study.

IDENTIFICATION BY SKIN COLOR

Table 3 shows slight and statistically insignificant differences among the three skin-color groups in their responses which indicate a knowledge of the "racial difference" between the white and colored doll (requests 5 through 7).

It should be noted, however, that the dark group is consistently more accurate in its choice of the appropriate doll than either the light or the medium group on requests 5 through 7. This would seem to indicate that the dark group is slightly more definite in its knowledge of racial differences and that this definiteness extends even to the higher level of verbalization inherent in the use of the term "Negro" as racial designation. In this

[3] These results are supported by those from the use of the Horowitz line drawing technique.

TABLE 3

CHOICES OF SUBJECTS IN LIGHT, MEDIUM, AND DARK GROUPS°

Choice	Light		Medium		Dark	
	No.	Percent	No.	Percent	No.	Percent
Request 5 (for White)						
Colored Doll	2	5	8	6	3	4
White Doll	43	94	118	92	76	96
Request 6 (for Colored)						
Colored Doll	41	89	118	92	76	96
White Doll	4	9	8	6	3	4
Request 7 (for Negro)						
Colored Doll	32	70	91	71	59	75
White Doll	9	20	27	21	14	18
Request 8 (for You)						
Colored Doll	9	20	93	73	64	81
White Doll	37	80	33	26	15	19

° Individuals failing to make either choice not included, hence some percentages add to less than 100.

regard it is seen that 75 percent of the dark children chose the colored doll when asked for the doll which "looks like a Negro child" while only 70 percent of the light children and 71 percent of the medium children made this response. The trend of results for requests 5 and 6 remains substantially the same.

These results suggest further that correct racial identification of these Negro children at these ages is to a large extent determined by the concrete fact of their own skin color, and further that this racial identification is not necessarily dependent upon the expressed knowledge of a racial difference as indicated by the correct use of the words "white," "colored," or "Negro" when responding to white and colored dolls. This conclusion seems warranted in the light of the fact that those children who differed in skin color from light through medium to dark were practically similar in the pattern of their responses which indicated awareness of racial differences but differed markedly in their racial identification (responses to request 8 for the doll "that looks like you") only 20 percent of the light chil-

dren, while 73 percent of the medium children, and 81 percent of the dark children identified themselves with the colored doll.

It is seen that there is a consistent increase in choice of the colored doll from the light to the medium group; an increase from the medium group to the dark group; and, a striking increase in the choices of the colored doll by the dark group as compared to the light group.[4] All differences, except between the medium and dark groups, are statistically significant.

Again, as in previous work (Clark and Clark, 1939a, 1939b, 1940), it is shown that the percentage of the medium groups' identifications with the white or the colored representation resembles more that of the dark group and differs from the light group. Upon the basis of these results, therefore, one may assume that some of the factors and dynamics involved in racial identification are substantially the same for the dark and medium children, in contrast to dynamics for the light children.

[4] These results substantiate and clearly focus the trend observed through the use of the Horowitz line drawing technique.

NORTH-SOUTH DIFFERENCES

The results presented in Table 4 indicate that there are no significant quantitative

TABLE 4

CHOICES OF SUBJECTS IN NORTHERN (MIXED SCHOOLS) AND SOUTHERN (SEGREGATED SCHOOLS) GROUPS°

Choice	North, Percent	South, Percent
Request 5 (for White)		
Colored Doll	4	6
White Doll	94	93
Request 6 (for Colored)		
Colored Doll	92	94
White Doll	7	5
Request 7 (for Negro)		
Colored Doll	74	70
White Doll	20	19
Request 8 (for You)		
Colored Doll	61	69
White Doll	39	29

° Individuals failing to make either choice not included, hence some percentages add to less than 100.

differences between the northern and southern Negro children tested (children in mixed schools and children in segregated schools) in their knowledge of racial differences.

While none of these differences is statistically reliable, it is significant that northern children know as well as southern children which doll is supposed to represent a white child and which doll is supposed to represent a colored child. However, the northern children make fewer identifications with the colored doll and more identifications with the white doll than do the southern children. One factor accounting for this difference may be the fact that in this sample there are many more light colored children in the North (33) than there are in the South (13). Since this difference in self-identification is not statistically significant, it may be stated that the children in the northern mixed-school situation do not differ from children in the southern segregated schools in either their knowledge of racial differences or their racial identification. A more qualitative analysis will be presented elsewhere.

RACIAL PREFERENCES

It is clear from Table 5 that the majority of these Negro children prefer the *white* doll and reject the colored doll.

Approximately two thirds of the subjects indicated by their responses to requests 1 and 2 that they like the white doll "best," or that they would like to play with the white doll in preference to the colored doll, and that the white doll is a "nice doll."

Their responses to request 3 show that this preference for the white doll implies a concomitant negative attitude toward the brown doll. Fifty-nine percent of these children indicated that the colored doll "looks bad," while only 17 percent stated that the white doll "looks bad" (critical ratio 10.9).

TABLE 5

CHOICES OF ALL SUBJECTS

Choice	Request 1 (Play With)		Request 2 (Nice Doll)		Request 3 (Looks Bad)		Request 4 (Nice Color)	
	No.	Percent	No.	Percent	No.	Percent	No.	Percent
Colored Doll	83	32	97	38	149	59	96	38
White Doll	169	67	150	59	42	17	151	60
Don't Know or No Response	1	1	6	3	62	24	6	2

That this preference and negation in some way involve skin color is indicated by the results for request 4. Only 38 percent of the children thought that the brown doll was a "nice color," while 60 percent of them thought that the white doll was a "nice color" (critical ratio 5.0).

The importance of these results for an understanding of the origin and development of racial concepts and attitudes in Negro children cannot be minimized. Of equal significance are their implications, in the light of the results of racial identification already presented, for racial mental hygiene.

AGE DIFFERENCES

Table 6 shows that at each age from three through seven years the majority of these

established as a statistically significant fact (critical ratio 4.5).

Analyzing the results of requests 1 and 2 together, it is seen that there is a marked *increase* in preference for the white doll from the three- to the four-year level; a more gradual *decrease* in this preference from the four- to the five-year level; a further decrease from the five- to the six-year level; and a continued decrease from the six- to the seven-year level. These results suggest that although the majority of Negro children at each age prefer the white doll to the brown doll, this preference decreases gradually from four through seven years.

Skin color preferences of these children follow a somewhat different pattern of development. The results of request 4 show that while the majority of children at each

TABLE 6

CHOICES OF SUBJECTS AT EACH AGE LEVEL*

Choice	3 Yr.		4 Yr.		5 Yr.		6 Yr.		7 Yr.	
	No.	Per-cent	No.	Per-cent	No.	Per-cent	No.	Per-cent	No.	Per-cent
Request 1 (Play With)										
Colored Doll	13	42	7	24	12	26	21	29	30	40
White Doll	17	55	22	76	34	74	51	71	45	60
Request 2 (Nice Doll)										
Colored Doll	11	36	7	24	13	28	33	46	33	44
White Doll	18	58	22	76	33	72	38	53	39	52
Request 3 (Looks Bad)										
Colored Doll	21	68	15	52	36	78	45	63	32	43
White Doll	6	19	7	24	5	11	11	15	13	17
Request 4 (Nice Color)										
Colored Doll	12	39	8	28	9	20	31	43	36	48
White Doll	18	58	21	72	36	78	40	56	36	48

* Individuals failing to make either choice not included, hence some percentages add to less than 100.

children prefer the white doll and reject the brown doll. This tendency to prefer the white doll is not as stable (not statistically reliable) in the three-year-olds as it is in the four- and five-year-olds. On the other hand, however, the tendency of the three-year-olds to negate the brown doll ("looks bad") is

age below seven years prefer the skin color of the white doll, this preference increases from three through five years and decreases from five through seven years. It is of interest to point out that only at the seven-year level do the same number of children indicate a preference for the skin color of the colored doll as for that of the white doll.

The majority of these children at each age level indicate that the brown doll, rather than the white doll, "looks bad." This result shows positively the negation of the colored doll which was implicit in the expressed preference for the white doll discussed above.

The evaluative rejection of the brown doll is statistically significant, even at the three-year level, and is pronounced at the five-year level. The indicated preference for the white doll is statistically significant from the four-year level up to the seven-year level.

It seems justifiable to assume from these results that the crucial period in the formation and patterning of racial attitudes begins at around four and five years. At these ages these subjects appear to be reacting more uncritically in a definite structuring of attitudes which conforms with the accepted racial values and mores of the larger environment.

PREFERENCES AND SKIN COLOR

Results presented in Table 7 reveal that there is a tendency for the majority of these children, in spite of their own skin color, to prefer the white doll and to negate the brown doll. This tendency is most pronounced in the children of light skin color and least so in the dark children. A more intensive analysis of these results appears in a larger, yet unpublished study.

NORTH-SOUTH DIFFERENCES

From Table 8 it is clear that the southern children in segregated schools are less pronounced in their preference for the white doll, compared to the northern children's definite preference for this doll. Although still in a minority, a higher percentage of southern children, compared to northern, prefer to play with the colored doll or think that it is a "nice" doll. The critical ratio of this difference is not significant for request 1 but approaches significance for request 2 (2.75).

A significantly higher percentage (71) of the northern children compared to southern children (49) think that the brown doll looks bad (critical ratio 3.68). Also a slightly higher percent of the southern children think that the brown doll has a "nice

TABLE 7
Choices of Subjects in Light, Medium, and Dark Groups[*]

Choice	Light		Medium		Dark	
	No.	Percent	No.	Percent	No.	Percent
Request 1 (Play With)						
Colored Doll	11	24	41	32	31	39
White Doll	35	76	86	67	48	61
Request 2 (Nice Doll)						
Colored Doll	15	33	50	39	32	40
White Doll	31	67	72	56	47	60
Request 3 (Looks Bad)						
Colored Doll	31	67	73	57	45	57
White Doll	6	13	22	17	14	18
Request 4 (Nice Color)						
Colored Doll	13	28	56	44	27	34
White Doll	32	70	68	53	51	65

[*] Individuals failing to make either choice not included, hence some percentages add to less than 100.

color," while more northern children think that the white doll has a "nice color."

TABLE 8

CHOICES OF SUBJECTS IN NORTHERN (MIXED SCHOOLS) AND SOUTHERN (SEGREGATED SCHOOLS) GROUPS (REQUESTS 1 THROUGH 4)*

Choice	North, Percent	South, Percent
Request 1 (Play With)		
Colored Doll	28	37
White Doll	72	62
Request 2 (Nice Doll)		
Colored Doll	30	46
White Doll	68	52
Request 3 (Looks Bad)		
Colored Doll	71	49
White Doll	17	16
Request 4 (Nice Color)		
Colored Doll	37	40
White Doll	63	57

* Individuals failing to make either choice not included, hence some percentages add to less than 100.

In general, it may be stated that northern and southern children in these age groups tend to be similar in the degree of their preference for the white doll—with the northern children tending to be somewhat more favorable to the white doll than are the southern children. The southern children, however, in spite of their equal favorableness toward the white doll, are significantly less likely to reject the brown doll (evaluate it negatively), as compared to the strong tendency for the majority of the northern children to do so. That this difference is not primarily due to the larger number of light children found in the northern sample is indicated by more intensive analysis presented in the complete report.

SOME QUALITATIVE DATA

Many of the children entered into the experimental situation with a freedom similar to that of play. They tended to verbalize freely and much of this unsolicited verbalization was relevant to the basic problems of this study.

On the whole, the rejection of the brown doll and the preference for the white doll, when explained at all, were explained in rather simple, concrete terms: for white-doll preference—" 'cause he's pretty" or " 'cause he's white"; for rejection of the brown doll—" 'cause he's ugly" or " 'cause it don't look pretty" or " 'cause him black" or "got black on him."

On the other hand, some of the children who were free and relaxed in the beginning of the experiment broke down and cried or became somewhat negativistic during the latter part when they were required to make self-identifications. Indeed, two children ran out of the testing room, unconsolable, convulsed in tears. This type of behavior, although not so extreme, was more prevalent in the North than in the South. The southern children who were disturbed by this aspect of the experiment generally indicated their disturbance by smiling or matter of factly attempting to escape their dilemma either by attempted humor or rationalization.

Rationalization of the rejection of the brown doll was found among both northern and southern children, however. A northern medium six-year-old justified his rejection of the brown doll by stating that "he looks bad 'cause he hasn't got a eyelash." A seven-year-old medium northern child justified his choice of the white doll as the doll with a "nice color" because "his feet, hands, ears, elbows, knees, and hair are clean."

A northern five-year-old dark child felt compelled to explain his identification with the brown doll by making the following unsolicited statement: "I burned my face and made it spoil." A seven-year-old northern light child went to great pains to explain that he is actually white but: "I look brown because I got a suntan in the summer."

References

CLARK, K. B., and CLARK, MAMIE P. Segregation as a factor in the racial identification of Negro preschool children: a preliminary report. *J. exp. Educ.*, 1939a, *9*, 161-163.

CLARK, K. B., and CLARK, MAMIE P. The development of consciousness of self and the emergence of racial identification in Negro preschool children. *J. soc. Psychol.*, 1939b, *10*, 591-599.

CLARK, K. B., and CLARK, MAMIE P. Skin color as a factor in racial identification of Negro preschool children. *J. soc. Psychol.*, 1940, *11*, 159-169.

HOROWITZ, R. E. Racial aspects of self-identification in nursery school children. *J. Psychol.*, 1939, *7*, 91-99.

C. SOCIAL STRATIFICATION

The Class System ❉ Allison Davis
of the White Caste ❉ Burleigh B. Gardner
❉ Mary R. Gardner

The "caste line" defines a social gulf across which Negroes may not pass either through marriage or those other intimacies which Old City calls "social equality." A ritual reminder is omnipresent in all relationships that there are two separate castes—a superordinate white group and a subordinate Negro group. Within each of these separate social worlds there are other divisions: families, religious groups, associations, and a system of social classes.[1]

The most fundamental of these divisions within each caste is that of social class; and the researchers, both white and Negro, were initiated into the intricacies of class behavior at the same time that they were being taught how to act toward persons of the op-

posite caste. Whether it was a matter of accepting an invitation to a party, deciding to visit a family, or planning to attend a church, the participant-observers, who had been "adopted" by people of relatively high social status within their respective castes, were advised upon the important matter of "who" and "where." Certain people were to be approached, not as equals, but as subordinates. There were places where one "could not afford to be seen" having a "good time," or even worshipping, without loss of status unless it was for purposes of research.

There were many clues to assist in the "placing" of people within broad limits, some easily observable, such as peculiarities of speech, type of clothing worn, the manner of drinking and "carrying" liquor, or occupation. (Among Negroes there was the added factor of color evaluation.) Other criteria were far more subtle—genealogies and inner thoughts—which were ascertainable only after prolonged acquaintance with the society. "Stratifying" the inhabitants of Old City was, thus, one of the major research problems, that is, finding out the values

[1] As used here, a "social class" is to be thought of as the largest group of people whose members have intimate access to one another. A class is composed of families and social cliques. The interrelationships between these families and cliques, in such informal activities as visiting, dances, receptions, teas, and larger informal affairs, constitute the structure of a social class. A person is a member of that social class with which most of his participations, of this intimate kind, occur.

Reprinted from *Deep South: A Social Anthropological Study of Caste and Class* by A. Davis, B. B. Gardner, and M. R. Gardner by permission of The University of Chicago Press. Copyright © 1941 by The University of Chicago Press.

cherished by people of varying circumstances, checking their behavior against their beliefs about status, and finding a systematic way of describing the class structure of the society.

Social Stratification

As one becomes acquainted with the white people of Old City, he soon realizes that they are continually classifying themselves and others. There are "Negroes" and "whites"—the caste groups—a relatively simple dichotomy. There are also "leading families," "fine old families," "the four hundred," "the society crowd," "plain people," "nice, respectable people," "good people, but nobody," "po' whites," "red necks," etc. —all terms used to refer to different groups within the white caste. Not only do the whites frequently refer to these subdivisions within their own caste group, but they do so in such a manner as to indicate that they think in terms of a social hierarchy with some people at the "top," some at the "bottom"; with some people "equal" to themselves, and others "above" or "below" them. There are recurrent expressions such as: "He isn't our social equal," "She isn't our kind," "They are just nobody," "Those folk are the way-high-ups," "They're nothing but white trash!" "Oh, they're plain people like us." These expressions refer not only to individuals but also to groups, so that one may speak of superordinate and subordinate groups within the white society. And, most important of all, people tend to act in conformity with these conceptions of their "place" and the social position of others in the society.

When the individuals and groups so designated are studied, striking differences between them with regard to family relations, recreational behavior, standards of living, occupation and income, education, and other traits are immediately apparent. On the basis of these differences, it is possible to define the social classes within the white so-

ciety and to describe them in detail. It was soon evident that people at all levels were thinking in terms of, and often referring to, three broad social classes—"upper," "middle," and "lower"—although, when designating particular individuals, there were divergences of opinion as to their social position. There was some difference of opinion, too, as to the things that made one upper, middle, or lower; but an analysis of the relative social positions of the informants showed that these variations in conceptions of class status were, themselves, related to the social position of the informant. Thus, a "po' white," as defined by persons of the higher classes, conceived of the total structure in a somewhat different manner from an upper-class planter. In other words, the social perspective varied with the social position of the individual. People in the same social positions agreed, in the main, however, on the traits which characterized the classes, although the class traits did not apply to everyone within a class in absolute fashion. Thus, a member of a group defined by consensus as "superior" might have a few characteristics in common with a person of an "inferior" group; but when each group was considered as a whole, the differences were large and significant. Thus, "the society crowd," as a group, owns more property than the "po' whites," although some "society folks" own none at all; the "poor, but respectable" people, in the aggregate, are more church-minded than "trash," though some are not affiliated with churches.

The researchers were able to describe the structure of the society by interviewing a large number of informants drawn from various occupational, associational, and other status groups who "placed" individuals and stated their conceptions of class criteria. The observers were also alert to "off-the-record" remarks and to behavior in public places and in crisis situations, in order to ascertain the bearers of prestige, the wielders of power, and the persons who associated together on various occasions. The resulting picture of the society is that of a class system in operation, with a description of the way it appears to the people within it.

While generalized conceptions of the class structure were readily obtainable from interviewing, a detailed study of class characteristics depended upon a method of determining the social position of specific individuals. The first step was to establish a series of individuals distributed from the "top" of the society to the "bottom." This was done through interviewing, since almost any member of the society could point to some other individuals or groups whom he considered at the very top, at the very bottom, or "in between." Interviewing and observing the people who were thus placed resulted in the identification of a group of individuals who considered themselves either superordinate, subordinate, or equal in relationship to one another. Continuous interviewing of these informants made possible a detailed study of their ideology and behavior. Wide discrepancies in placement were studied as special cases, with the purpose of relating them to the system of relationships which was gradually emerging, and of accounting for the differing opinions of their social position. Thus, over a period of eighteen months, interviewing, coupled with observation of overt behavior, permitted the researchers to establish with certainty a sample of the personnel of the different social classes.

After identifying these individuals within the classes, it was possible to study their relationships and characteristics in detail and to correlate traits such as income, property, education, and church and associational memberships with social position and general behavior. An additional check was provided by interviewing for the "values" which people attributed to various types of behavior and class traits when they talked about them. It was thus possible to relate ideology to social class.

Because of the limitations of time, it was impossible to stratify every individual in the society by the interview-observation technique; but once the characteristics of the known individuals had been determined, criteria were available for placing any individual about whom some important facts were available.

Thus, when a person's participation could not be checked, if some pertinent facts about his job, his family, his education, and his children were known, one could state the participation potentialities which his social personality bore.

On the basis of the attitudes of many informants of various social positions, together with observations of many kinds of social behavior, the researchers concluded that the three main class divisions recognized by the society could be objectively described. Each of these was characterized by its particular behavior pattern and by a distinctive ideology. Closer study revealed the existence of subclasses within each of these three larger groups, and these are referred to in this study as the "upper-upper class," "lower-upper class," "upper-middle class," "lower-middle class," "upper-lower class," and the "lower-lower class." We shall examine, first, the conceptions of class which each of these groups holds, for the very way in which people conceive of the class divisions varies with their social position.

Class Perspective and the Class Structure

THE UPPER-UPPER CLASS

It was evident from the outset that certain persons were at the very top of the social hierarchy. They were accorded deference in nearly all types of relationships; people were anxious to associate with them; they belonged to the exclusive churches; their names were sought for patron's lists; they lived in imposing mansions inherited from Old City's "antebellum past" (or at least their parents did); and, on ritual occasions of high import, they dominated the scene and tended to organize community behavior. They were, without doubt, in almost everyone's eyes, members of the "upper-upper class." Neither whites nor Negroes questioned their position even when they resented it; and resentment, itself, tended to dissolve when they were functioning as symbols of the total community on such occasions as the annual Historical Week, when visitors from the entire nation came to Old City. It was this upper-upper class which made the finest distinctions when ranking or "stratifying" other people.

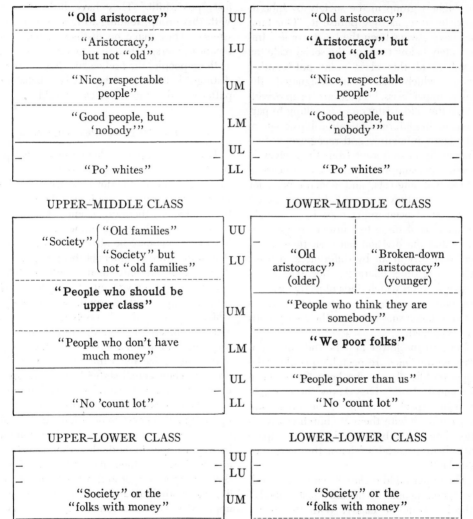

UPPER–UPPER CLASS

"Old aristocracy"	UU
"Aristocracy," but not "old"	LU
"Nice, respectable people"	UM
"Good people, but 'nobody'"	LM
	UL
"Po' whites"	LL

LOWER–UPPER CLASS

"Old aristocracy"	
"Aristocracy" but not "old"	
"Nice, respectable people"	
"Good people, but 'nobody'"	
"Po' whites"	

UPPER–MIDDLE CLASS

"Society"	"Old families"	UU
	"Society" but not "old families"	LU
"People who should be upper class"		UM
"People who don't have much money"		LM
		UL
"No 'count lot"		LL

LOWER–MIDDLE CLASS

"Old aristocracy" (older)	"Broken-down aristocracy" (younger)	
"People who think they are somebody"		UM
"We poor folks"		LM
"People poorer than us"		UL
"No 'count lot"		LL

UPPER–LOWER CLASS

	UU
	LU
"Society" or the "folks with money"	UM
"People who are up because they have a little money"	LM
"Poor but honest folk"	UL
"Shiftless people"	LL

LOWER–LOWER CLASS

"Society" or the "folks with money"	
"Way-high-ups," but not "Society"	
"Snobs trying to push up"	
"People just as good as anybody"	

Fig. 1. The social perspectives of the social classes.

Members of this highest status group rec-ognize five class divisions in the society (see Fig. 1). They visualize themselves at the top of the society, an *"old* aristocracy" whose superordination has its origin and stability in "time." They consider themselves the highest group in the society by inherit-ance, because, as they phrase it: "Our fam-ilies have always been the best people." Im-mediately below them on the social scale the members of this class point out another group, which has been designated the "lower-upper class." These are people with whom the "old aristocracy" is willing to par-ticipate in informal relationships, whom they know intimately and recognize as fun-damentally no different from themselves in income, consumption standards, education, intellectual interests, and general behavior pattern. But they are not *"old* aristocracy"; they haven't been upper class long enough. An analysis of these two upper groups indi-cates that the division between them is re-flected hardly at all by differences in overt behavior or other characteristics. It is a sub-jective division which finds objective expres-sion only in certain very intimate situations when antagonisms between the two groups are verbalized.

Beneath the lower uppers, the upper up-pers see the "nice, respectable people" (the upper-middle class) who have "never been prominent at all." They know these people by name, speak to them on the street, and may converse with them at church or associ-ational meetings; but they do not participate with them at social affairs of the more inti-mate kinds.

The upper-middle class is contrasted with the "good people" who are "just nobody" (the lower-middle class). With the lower-middle class, the upper uppers have only formal and definitely limited relations, usu-ally economic in nature, such as those of employer-to-employee or merchant-to-customer. The type of behavior in such rela-tionships is explicitly delimited; and, in gen-eral, upper-upper individuals resent the social mobility of lower-middle-class per-sons, probably because such a movement involves a change in these relatively imper-sonal economic relationships and the corre-sponding traditional behavior pattern.

Finally, at the very bottom of the society are the people whom the upper uppers call the "working class," "the poorer class," or just "po' white." They have little contact with this group, tending to ignore their ex-istence. They make no distinction between tenant-farmers, fishermen, factory workers, as these people, themselves, do. Nor do they distinguish between other variant behavior patterns within this lower-class world.

THE LOWER-UPPER CLASS

The lower uppers, whom the upper up-pers call "aristocracy, but not *old*," make the same general distinctions between social groups. They do not emphasize the distinc-tion between themselves and the upper uppers so much as the upper uppers do, however. This may be attributed to the fact that most of the members of this group have, during their lifetime, been socially mobile, and they have moved into the upper class from the upper-middle group. Consequently, while they recognize themselves as a group apart from, and below, the upper uppers, they tend to ally themselves with this group and to minimize the value of family back-ground. Their actual status is evident, how-ever, in their individual relations and in their verbally expressed antagonisms toward the upper uppers on certain occasions. In several cases, lower uppers resisted subordination by upper-upper individuals through face-to-face criticisms of their ancestry; Thus, Mrs. Bowley, upper upper and proud of her fam-ily, was both hurt and indignant at lower-upper Mrs. Duncan's remarks about her an-cestry:

I said something to Mrs. Duncan about being related to the Montgomerys. She said; "Well, that is nothing to be proud of. I wouldn't brag about it!" I said I didn't see why not; my father had always taught me to be proud of the Montgomery blood in my veins. Then she said that the first Montgomery was nothing but a gambler, and that that was nothing to be proud of. Well, that isn't true! He wasn't *really* a gambler. . . .

Similarly, the lower uppers' definition of the upper-middle class, as a group, is both vague and reluctant. Directly questioned, they frequently deny that persons stratified as upper middle are really below them on the social scale, or they will attempt an evasion. (Their overt behavior, however, belies their words.) They will say, for instance: "I don't mean that Mrs. Atkins and people like that aren't nice and all that. She is. She is very nice, and well-thought-of here. We just don't happen to know her very well, and *she doesn't enjoy the same things we do.*" This hesitancy about actually identifying persons as upper-middle class is probably related to the fact that they, themselves, have rather recently moved out of the upper-middle stratum, and many of them still have kinsmen in this social position. (Equally logical, perhaps, are attempts by some persons to overestimate the social distance between themselves and the class from which they came.)

The lower-middle class, on the other hand, is clearly defined by these ascending uppers. In general, they have the same limited contact with the lower-middle class as the upper uppers have; but they seem less inclined to resent the rise of lower middles into the upper-middle class, or their economic improvement. This is, perhaps, due to the fact that specific limited relations with these persons, and a corresponding behavior pattern, are less well established and less fixed by tradition than in the case of upper-upper relations with the lower middles.

Toward the lower class, as a whole, lower uppers present the same indifference and lack of precise definition that their upper-upper associates display.

THE UPPER-MIDDLE CLASS

Stratification of the society by persons immediately below the upper class (here designated the "upper-middle class") is fre-

quently associated with an expression of moral attitudes and with definite conceptions of the positive value and important role of wealth. These persons are often unable to reconcile the existing social hierarchy with a hierarchy that "should be." In their thinking, their own class group "should be" the highest group in the society, since it is the wealthiest group and the one whose behavior reflects most precisely the traditional teachings of the Protestant church. In spite of this condemnatory attitude, however, they conceive of the upper class as a group separate from themselves. Its superordination in the existing scheme of things is generally acknowledged, albeit somewhat reluctantly. Occasionally, certain persons whom upper uppers place as lower uppers are not included in this group by the upper-middle class. But the "*old* aristocracy" is quite definitely assigned its place at the top; its ascendancy is resented; and the group is condemned for its "immoral behavior."

Upper-middle class individuals who are attempting to rise in the social scale point out beneath them the "lower middles" as a separate class group and almost invariably attempt to exaggerate their social distance from it. Behavior and attitudes of these mobile middle-class individuals toward the subordinate lower middles are similar to those of the upper class, and their relationships with this group tend to be formal and economic. Stable upper middles, however, know many lower middles and sometimes participate with them informally, especially in the younger age ranges. In general, they attribute this differentiation more to the lower economic position of these people than to other traits. They do not try to maintain great social distance between lower middles and themselves.

Like members of the upper-class groups, upper middles make no distinctions within the lower-class group, although they seem somewhat more aware of the presence of this group at the bottom of the white society. While they do have somewhat more frequent contact with them than uppers, especially in employer-employee relationships, all of the lower class is thought of as "just the working class," the "poorer class."

THE LOWER-MIDDLE CLASS

"We poor folks and the other poor people like us" make up the lower-middle class. But, "it shouldn't be that way," they think. "The people who are up are there mainly because they have money," they insist. Persons in this group have rather strong class feelings. Above them they see the upper middles, people like themselves, but with more money. Above the upper middles, they recognize an "aristocracy." Within this "aristocracy" (upper upper and lower upper together) they distinguish between the older persons who have established their superiority through the possession of great wealth in the past and younger individuals, on the other hand, who are not now wealthy or who never have been. These latter have no claim to the position of "upper class," they say; yet they are there. They are just a "broken-down aristocracy." Lower middles think in terms of "younger" and "older" aristocrats, rather than in terms of an upper-upper and lower-upper class, with all age ranges within each group.

Toward the upper middles they level a frequent taunt, "They think they *are* somebody"; and, as a group, lower middles prefer not to recognize the social distance between themselves and such people. They resent all attempts by this class to express any social distance. In general, too, they seem to resent mobility from the upper-middle class into the upper class more than they do mobility from their own ranks into the upper-middle class.

Here, for the first time, a group subdivides the lower class. There is one group, immediately below them, for whom the lower middles have pity but whom they do not condemn or scorn. These are people "even poorer than us," the upper lowers, who are definitely distinguished from the "po' whites," the "no-count," and the "worthless"—the lower lowers.

THE UPPER-LOWER CLASS

Members of the upper-lower class have a sense of solidarity and speak often of "people like us" as distinct both from the lower-middle class above them and the lower lowers below them. Like the middle classes, they think of social stratification in Old City as an absolute hierarchy of wealth. (They are less accurately informed of the actual economic status of individuals above them, however, than one would infer from their conversation.) Their interpretation of class differences is less often tinged with moral concepts than in the case of the middle class.

At the top of the social world, as they see it, is "Society," composed of nearly all those persons who are upper upper, lower upper, and upper middle. All these people are said to be "wealthy." Their high social position is thus recognized and accepted as a fact. Beneath "Society," the upper-lower class recognizes the members of the lower-middle class, whose assumption of social superiority they resent. They are sure that these people occupy a superordinate position simply because they have more wealth.

Between themselves and the lower-lower class, upper lowers make a very careful distinction in their verbalizations, although in actual overt behavior little social distance is maintained. They visit and borrow, exchange domestic services, and converse on the street and in the stores, although such relations are not so frequent as with members of their own group. Thus, while they participate as equals with lower lowers in many one-to-one, face-to-face relations, they do not, as a group, wish to be identified with those whom they consider inferior, unkempt, and improvident.

THE LOWER-LOWER CLASS

The lower lowers, like the upper lowers, also see "Society" at the top, a vague category for persons above the lower-middle position. Lower-lower-class women occasionally refer to the "very wealthy ladies" in this group. Sometimes, even a few lower-middle-class individuals are included in "Society"; more often, however, lower-middle-class individuals are recognized as a separate group with "some money, but not Society." The small shopkeepers with whom they trade, some policemen, artisans with whom they have some contact, and other members of the lower-middle class are spoken of as "way high up" but distinct from "Society." Lower lowers resent the position of the upper-lower class, the members of which are thought to be socially ambitious and snobbish. Their attempts at refinement are generally ridiculed. The upper lowers' claim to a higher social position is thought to be unjustified and to be based entirely on their economic superiority, their better jobs, and more adequate housing.

SUMMARY

Members of any one class thus think of themselves as a group and have a certain unity of outlook. This is indicated by their frequent reference to "people like us" and to persons "not our kind." Expressions of this group solidarity are particularly prevalent when individuals are discussing groups immediately above and below them. When expressing resentment at exclusion from the class above and antagonism toward mobility from the class below, social classes betray unconsciously their sense of solidarity and "we-ness." It will be seen subsequently, too, that members of these classes and subclasses have a further unity through a common set of beliefs, a common pattern of overt behavior, and other traits which function as symbols of status.

While members of all class groups recognize classes above and below them, or both, the greater the social distance from the other classes the less clearly are fine distinctions made. Although an individual recognizes most clearly the existence of groups immediately above and below his own, he is usually not aware of the social distance ac-

tually maintained between his own and these adjacent groups. Thus, in all cases except that of members of the upper-lower class the individual sees only a minimum of social distance between his class and the adjacent classes. This is illustrated by the dotted lines in Figure 1. Almost all other class divisions, however, are visualized as definite lines of cleavage in the society with a large amount of social distance between them.

In general, too, individuals visualize class groups above them less clearly than those below them; they tend to minimize the social differentiations between themselves and those above. This difference in perspective is partly explained by the fact that class lines in the society are not permanent and rigid and that upward mobility is fairly frequent. It is, further, due to the natural tendency in such a status system to identify with "superiors." In view of this situation it is not surprising that individuals in the two upper strata make the finest gradations in the stratification of the whole society and that class distinctions are made with decreasing precision as social position becomes lower.

Not only does the perspective on social stratification vary for different class levels, but the very bases of class distinction in the society are variously interpreted by the different groups. People tend to agree as to where people are but not upon why they are there. Upper-class individuals, especially upper uppers, think of class divisions largely in terms of time—one has a particular social position because his family has "always had" that position. Members of the middle class interpret their position in terms of wealth and time and tend to make moral evaluations of what "should be." Both middle-class groups accept the time element as an important factor in the superordinate position of the "old aristocracy," but for the rest of the society they consider only individual wealth and moral behavior as differentiating factors. Lower-class people, on the other hand, view the whole stratification of the society as a hierarchy of wealth. The lower lowers think that all those above them on the social scale are progressively wealthy and that their own subordination is dependent upon this economic factor alone. While upper lowers have a similar idea of those above them, they frequently add a moral note in explaining the subordinate position of lower lowers.

The identity of a social class does not depend on uniformity in any one or two, or a dozen, specific kinds of behavior but on a complex pattern or network of interrelated characteristics and attitudes. Among the members of any one class, there is no strict uniformity in any specific type of behavior but rather a range and a "modal average." One finds a range in income, occupation, educational level, and types of social participation. The "ideal type" may be defined, however, for any given class—the class configuration—from which any given individual may vary in one or more particulars. Also, two individuals may belong to the same association, fall in the same occupational category, belong to the same church, or have the same ideas about local politics; but identity in any one or two such particulars does not necessarily indicate that both individuals belong to the same social class. Class position is determined rather by the configuration of traits which an individual possesses.

An important aspect of this configuration is "ideology"—the set of concepts and the complex of attitudes toward individuals and institutions which individuals exhibit. The members of any one class or subclass share the same general attitudes and beliefs—that is, the same ideology. The conceptions of class which have been described in this section represent one aspect of the class ideologies.

The American Class Structure:
A Psychological Analysis ❉ Richard Centers

In the summer of 1945, a public attitude survey was conducted which attempted to combine the approaches of Kornhauser (1939) and Cantril (1943) by studying both attitudes with respect to various major economic and social issues and to class identification. Interviewers questioned a representative cross section of the adult white male population (1,100 persons), with respect to their subjective class identification, their opinions on major social, economic, and political issues, their adherence to certain traditional attitudes and beliefs typically regarded as parts of the American ideology, and various background factors such as occupation, religious affiliation, national-ity, etc.[1] A battery of six questions designed to test conservative-radical orientations was included in the interview. These were as follows (numbers refer to the position of the items in the interview schedule):

1. Do you agree or disagree that America is truly a land of opportunity and that people get pretty much what's coming to them in this country?
4. Would you agree that everybody

[1] A survey was carried out through the facilities of the Office of Public Opinion Research of the Department of Psychology at Princeton University.

This article was written especially for T. M. Newcomb and E. L. Hartley (Eds.), *Readings in Social Psychology*, New York: Holt, Rinehart and Winston, 1947. It appeared in a larger study, *The Psychology of Social Classes* by Richard Centers, copyright © 1949 by Princeton University Press. Reprinted by permission of the author and Princeton University Press.

would be happier, more secure, and more prosperous if the working people were given more power and influence in government, or would you say we would all be better off if the working people had no more power than they have now?

5. As you know, during this war, many private businesses and industries have been taken over by the government. Do you think wages and salaries would be fairer, jobs more steady, and that we would have fewer people out of work if the government took over and ran our mines, factories, and industries in the future, or do you think things would be better under private ownership?

6. Which one of these statements do you most agree with?
   (1) The most important job for the government is to make it certain that there are good opportunities for each person to get ahead on his own.
   (2) The most important job for the government is to guarantee every person a decent and steady job and standard of living.

7. In strikes and disputes between working people and employers do you usually side with the workers or with the employers?

14a. Do you think working people are usually fairly and squarely treated by their employers, or that employers sometimes take advantage of them?

These questions had all been pretested for comprehensibility by the writer. Their validity and the internal consistency of the battery have been discussed fully elsewhere.[2]

In describing the results of this test, individuals are assigned to one or another of five different categories, viz.: Ultraconservative, Conservative, Indeterminate, Radical, and Ultraradical, in accordance with the consistency with which their answers to the six questions adhered to either extreme of conservatism-radicalism.

In such terms our results show a fairly even division of the male population of America in attitude. Fifty percent are either conservative or ultraconservative. The other 50 percent are nonconservative (i.e., indeterminate, radical, or ultraradical). The differences in attitude of several occupational strata, however, are our main interest here. These are shown in Figure 1.[3] An ex-

[2] See Centers (1949).
[3] Those interested in the exact figures and the statistical significance of differences should refer to the original source, Centers (1949).

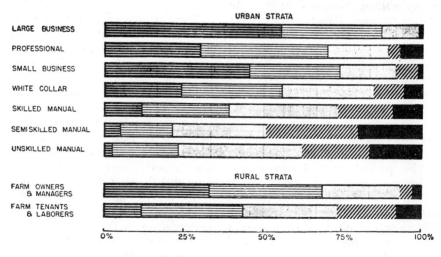

Fig. 1. Attitude differences of occupational strata, conservatism-radicalism.

amination of these differences can leave little doubt that peoples' politico-economic orientations are closely associated with their statuses and roles in the economic order. Persons who stand at the top and dominate that order are clearly its stanchest defenders. *Less than 2 percent of large business owners and managers are either radical or ultraradical.* Adherence to the status quo decreases in frequency consistently as one examines lower and lower status levels of the occupational· hierarchy. *The laboring groups are conspicuously nonconservative, and they are the most radical of all the groups in the whole array.*

Conservatism is not entirely absent among them, to be sure, but the contrasts between these groups and the business-owning and managing and professional strata are striking. More of the laboring strata than others, again, show such marked inconsistency of allegiance or opposition to the existing order that they can only be classified as "indeterminates," in terms of our scale. It is impossible to describe them as clearly radical, yet impossible to categorize them as conservative either. It is much as if they wavered, torn between conflicting desires, unable to reach a decision. (In times of political or economic conflict the persuasion of these "marginal" cases might well decide the issue. Twenty-seven percent of the total cross section are of this character.)

Striking contrasts between occupational strata not only exist with respect to the conservatism-radicalism scale as a whole, but also for individual items of the battery. Some of these are illustrated in Figure 2. The differences between the top and bottom occupational strata scarcely require comment. The opposed points of view are nowhere better exemplified than with respect to question 6, which required the respondent to choose between two opposed philosophies of government—an individualistic one and a collectivistic one. *This is the central issue of all today's politico-economic strife.* It is in terms of it that the largest contrasts in attitudes of occupational strata are found.

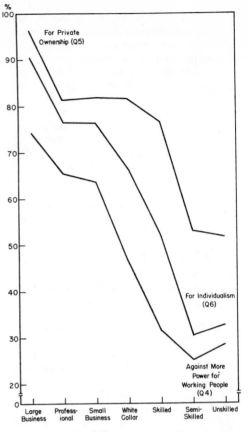

Fig. 2. Attitude differences of urban occupational strata.

There is little need to dwell upon these findings. They are clear and unambiguous evidence that persons occupying different positions with respect to the economy of production and exchange tend to have the differing orientations presumed by an interest-group theory of class.

But are people of these strata that differ so much also class conscious and in a way that conforms with their politico-economic orientations? This is one of the crucial questions that the class theorist must answer.

The previous attempts to assess the status of class consciousness have been uniformly unsatisfactory, in the sense that they tended to find no differences in class identification that agreed with the sort of differences described above. The most obvious defect has been that those studying identification seem to have assumed that class-conscious persons of the manual labor strata *should* differentiate themselves from the business and professional groups by use of the term *lower class* to describe their group. Lower class, however, is not a flattering term. The writer has rarely heard anyone use it to designate his class. He has, however, often heard the term *working class* used.

The people we interviewed were asked: "If you were asked to use one of these four names for your social class, which would you say you belonged in: the middle class, lower class, working class, or upper class?" The results for the national cross section are shown in Table 1.

TABLE 1

PERCENTAGES OF THE POPULATION AFFILIATING WITH EACH SOCIAL CLASS

Upper Class	3
Middle Class	43
Working Class	51
Lower Class	1
Don't Know	1
Don't Believe in Classes	1

These figures make it obvious that Americans in heavy majority do not belong to one big middle class as formerly believed. *A majority are now found to affiliate themselves with the working class.* This is not at all surprising, since the majority of our male breadwinners *are* workingmen. Such a class term more or less accurately characterizes their social role. We have more than such easy generalizations as this to testify to the social meaning of classes, however. We asked our respondents to define them. If they are more than just names they should demarcate definite sectors or groups of the population in terms of some objective criterion such as occupation, standard of living, function or role in the economic order, education or the like. It is in terms of such criteria that the meaning of classes to the population may be learned.

In order to discover the social definitions of the several classes, the members of each

class were asked which of the several occupational groups listed below belonged to their classes.

Big business owners and executives
Small business owners and operators
Factory workers
Office workers
Doctors and lawyers
Servants
Farmers
Laborers, such as miners, truck drivers and shopworkers
Store and factory managers
Waiters and bartenders
Salesmen

Individuals, of course, each named several occupational groups they conceived to belong to their classes, and their individual definitions of membership vary somewhat. By pooling the individual definitions of persons in a given class, however, we obtain a composite definition that tells us *who belongs to that class,* and hence, *what sort of people an individual is identifying himself with,* when he identifies himself with a given class. The definitions of the two major social classes are given in Figures 3 and 4.[4] These indicate the distinctive patterns of occupational membership characteristic of each group. Despite a considerable confusion and blurring of class lines, the patterns of membership are unmistakably different. It is clear that the middle class is a business, professional, and white-collar group, equally clear that the working class is a manual one. The blurring merely suggests that though occupation serves well as a criterion of class distinction, it may not be the only one in actual use.

It was suspected that several other criteria might be important, and to gain some knowledge of their relative significance we asked each person: "In deciding whether a

[4] Because such small numbers of the 1,100 people we interviewed identified themselves with the upper and lower classes, the numbers defining these classes are very small for each of them, and lacking statistical adequacy, these definitions are omitted here. Interested readers are advised to see the larger report, Centers (1949).

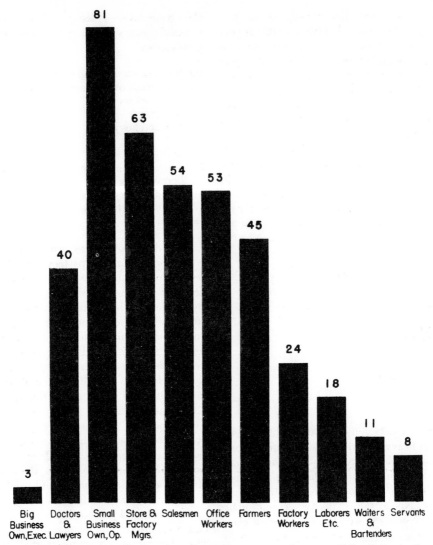

Fig. 3. Occupational composition of the middle class according to middle-class specifications of the occupational membership. Numbers at the top of each bar represent the percent of people in the middle class who include the given occupational group in the middle class.

person belongs to your class or not, which of these other things do you think is most important to know: Who his family is; how much money he has; what sort of education he has; or how he believes and feels about certain things?"

The results are summarized in Table 2. *Nearly half the people of our cross section*

said, "how he believes and feels about certain things." The implications of this for an interest-group theory are so plain as to make much additional comment superfluous. Common attitudes and beliefs are distinctive characteristics of social classes.

Let us turn now to another important question. How do people of different occu-

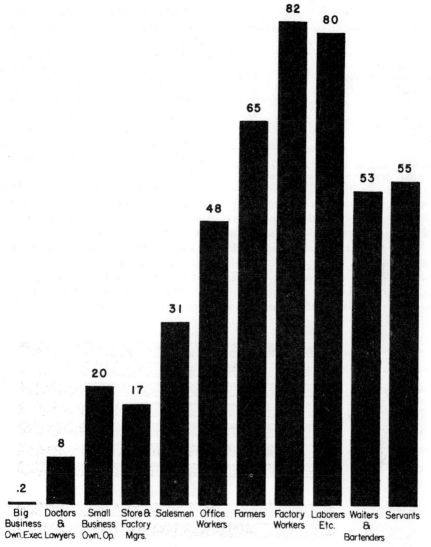

Fig. 4. Occupational composition of the working class according to working-class specifications of the occupational membership. Numbers at the top of each bar represent the percent of people in the working class who include the given occupational group in the working class.

pational strata differ in their class affiliations, and are such differences of affiliation in a direction to be expected on the basis of the interest-group concept? The answers to such questions can be gained from an examination of Figure 5. *The differences are in the expected direction.* Just as occupational groups were found to differ before in conservatism-radicalism, so now they differ with respect to class allegiances also. The business-owning and managing groups and professional and white-collar people are all predominantly middle class. Considered all together about three quarters of them say they belong to this group. The manual-labor strata are, in contrast, predominantly work-

TABLE 2

CRITERIA FOR OWN CLASS MEMBERSHIP
OTHER THAN OCCUPATION

Percent Saying:[a]	
Beliefs and Attitudes	47.4
Education	29.4
Family	20.1
Money	17.1
Other Answers	5.6
Don't Know	9.1

[a] Percentages add to more than 100 percent. People often gave more than one answer.

ing class in subjective class membership. Seventy-nine percent of all such persons profess such an identification. The differences for the two rural strata are less striking (as were also their attitude differences), but they too display a cleavage of loyalties in the direction to be expected from their differing socio-economic statuses and roles.

pected to minimize consciousness of differences in class, as well as might the fact that much less differentiation of wealth and power exists among them. However this may be, it is significant to note that *their conceptions of the classes with which they identify themselves are strikingly like the conceptions that urban people have of these classes*. In Figure 6, persons of the middle class whose residences (and occupations) differ are seen to define the middle class in quite similar ways except for the frequency of inclusion of farmers in that class. Figure 7 shows the two definitions of the urban and rural sections of the working class. Again the similarities are evident.

Thus far the data cited certainly support an interest-group concept of class structure, but the comparisons have been primarily of an indirect sort. Occupational strata have been seen to manifest the same trends of be-

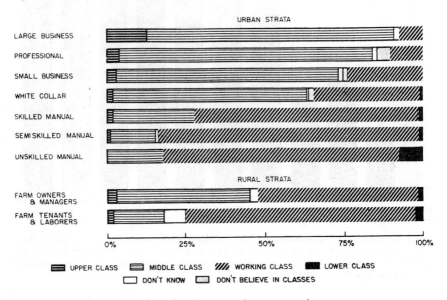

Fig. 5. Class identifications of occupational strata.

The differences between upper- and lower-farm strata are less sharp, probably because of several related factors. Space limitations forbid detailed discussion here, but such circumstancs as their both being tool users and productive workers might be ex-

havior with respect to both politico-economic orientation and class identification, but we need a more direct comparison of these dual aspects of class feeling. Let us contrast the politico-economic orientations of our two major social classes themselves.

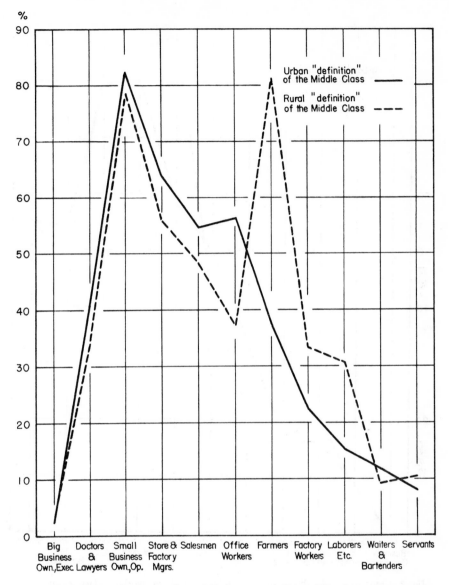

Fig. 6. Comparison of urban and rural definitions of the middle class. Points on the lines above each occupational category indicate the percentage of persons who say members of that occupational category are members of the middle class.

Figure 8 affords this contrast. The attitudes certainly differ in a substantial way. *The middle class is by far the more conservative group, while the working class is beyond question the more radical.* This is true not only for the classes as wholes, but also true for the urban and rural portions of the two classes considered separately.

Numerous other comparisons can be made which show the consistency with which class identification and conservatism-radicalism vary together. But only one more,

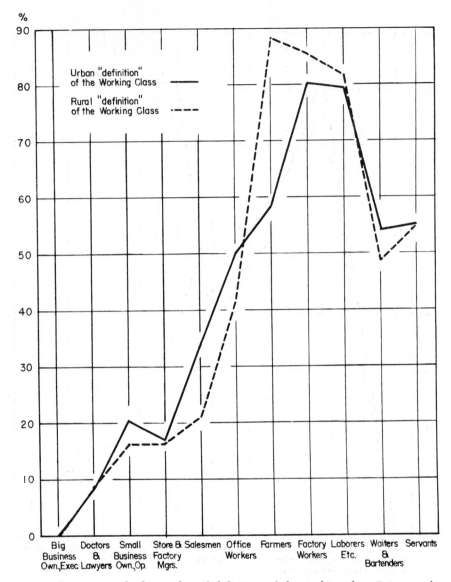

Fig. 7. Comparison of urban and rural definitions of the working class. Points on the lines above each occupational category indicate the percentage of persons who say members of that occupational category are members of the working class.

which will serve to bring out several important points, will be given here. In Figure 9 the attitudes of persons of similar occupational strata, but of different class affiliation, are shown contrasted. It can be seen at once that if people of a given occupational stratum differ in a class membership they tend to differ also in attitude. Those identifying with the middle class are more often conservative than those who identify themselves with the working class. The latter tend to be more often radical. *If people's class identifications are the same, their attitudes tend to be similar even though their*

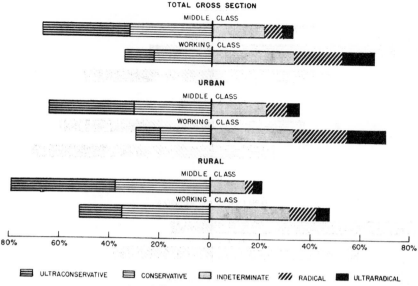

Fig. 8. Class differences in conservatism-radicalism.

objective occupational positions are differ-ent.

It is obvious also that the person's occupational stratum is an even better index to his attitude than is subjective class affiliation. Further, where objective position and subjective identification "coincide"—as we might express it where manual workers are identified with the working class and where business, professional, and white-collar workers are identified with the middle class —the attitude differences are greater than ever, greater, that is, than they would be if either class identification or occupational stratum were considered alone. *Both objective and subjective factors work in the same direction; two indices to conservatism-radicalism are better than one.* If we know a person's occupation we can predict something about his attitude from that knowledge alone, and if we know only his class identification we can also predict something about attitude; but if both occupation and class identification are known, our prediction of his attitude can be even more definite.

It should not, of course, be assumed that

class identification is, by such a comparison, implied to be a cause of attitude differences over and above *all* socio-economic factors. It may well be, but further data (which cannot be included here) indicate that other socio-economic factors such as standard of living and dominance-subordination in productive and exchange activities "summate" or combine with occupational position to determine, in the main, both class identification and conservatism-radicalism. For example, the middle-class affiliates in Figure 9 who are found in the manual stratum may be somewhat better off than most manual workers as far as income or authority over others is concerned. Such factors are known to be associated with identification with a "higher" class. Also, those (in Fig. 9) of the business, professional, and white-collar stratum who are found identified with the working class may be so identified for a variety of reasons, two of which are known to be comparative poverty and subordinate, i.e., employee, status.

The contrasting of separate portions of classes, as in Figure 9, can also serve to answer still another very important question.

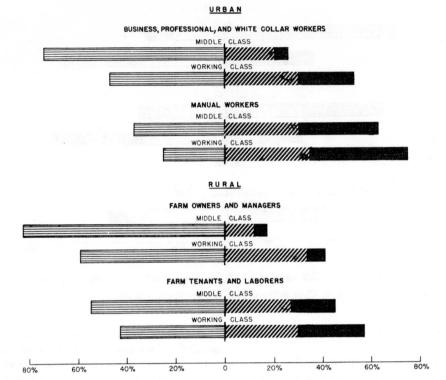

Fig. 9. Stratum and class differences in conservatism-radicalism.

How can we know that people of the business, professional, and white-collar stratum who say they are members of the working class are really identifying themselves with a predominantly manual group? *If they are doing this, then they should define the working class in essentially the same way as it is defined by the manual workers of that class.* As can be seen in Figure 10, this is approximately what they do. Their definition is biased in the direction of including members of their own strata in the working class more frequently than manual workers do, but they are, nevertheless, *despite their own higher status,* identifying themselves with a preponderantly manual group. A similar comparison can be made for different sectors of the middle class. In Figure 11 it is to be seen that persons of different occupational strata but of like class affiliation tend to define their class in essentially similar occupational terms. Manual workers who affiliate with the middle class are identifying themselves with primarily nonmanual occupational strata.

Social classes differ with respect to many other psychological characteristics in addition to those mentioned above. Some outstanding differences are those that relate to such matters as satisfaction and discontent with the various circumstances of life and work. Others concern their desires and motives. Extended consideration of these cannot, however, be encompassed here.

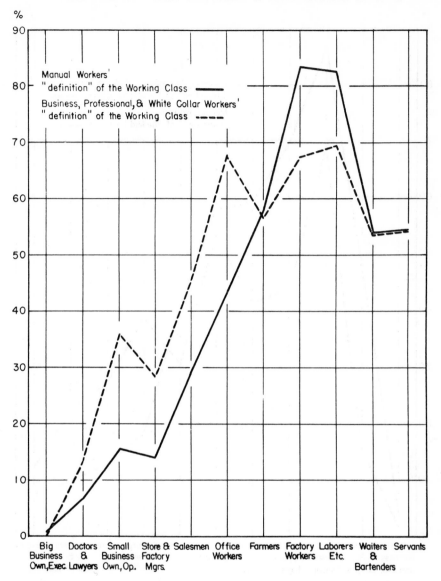

Fig. 10. Comparison of two definitions of the working class. Points on the lines above each occupational category indicate the percentage of persons who say members of that occupational category are members of the working class.

Summary

Several findings of a recent study concerned with the nature of social classes have been reviewed in the foregoing discussion, with particular emphasis being placed upon the significance of these in relation to an economic interest group theory of class structure. The politico-economic orientations of occupational strata as well as the class identifications of these strata were described. The American class structure as

Fig. 11. Comparison of two definitions of the middle class. Points on the lines above each occupational category indicate the percentage of persons who say members of that occupational category are members of the middle class.

people in America themselves define it was discussed, and the definitions of the two major social classes of the system were depicted. A series of tests of the interest group concept of social classes was briefly reviewed. In each case clear and substantial support for the theory was found.

On the basis of the evidence reported, social classes may be tentatively described as psycho-social groupings of the population of persons whose socio-economic positions are objectively similar, in the main, and whose politico-economic interests tend to coincide. Similarities of socio-economic position of only one kind, namely occupation, were described above because of limitations of space. Other factors, such as standard of living and dominance-subordination in the productive and exchange relations, are also known to be important determinants of class

consciousness. Coincidences of interests also are not confined to those of a political and economic sort alone, but these are so striking as to permit us to describe them as major characteristics of social classes.

References

CANTRIL, H. Identification with social and economic class. *J. abnorm. soc. Psychol.*, 1943, 38, 74-80.

CENTERS, R. C. *The psychology of social classes.* Princeton, N.J.: Princeton Univer. Press, 1949.

KORNHAUSER, A. W. Analysis of "class" structure in contemporary American society. In G. W. Hartmann and T. Newcomb (Eds.), *Industrial conflict: a psychological interpretation.* New York: Holt, Rinehart and Winston, 1939.

The Shifting Role of Class in
Political Attitudes and Behavior ❦ Philip E. Converse

The first studies of social class to use the new techniques of large-scale sampling documented a number of relationships between status and politico-economic attitudes. Such empirical demonstration was a valuable, if not always surprising, contribution. We learned, for example, that people lodged in different strata of the social system have tended to hold somewhat different attitudes regarding the benevolence of the existing social order, much as interest-group theory and classical views on stratification had postulated. We became familiar, furthermore, with the finding that different status groups may implement these beliefs in differential voting behavior. Thus, over the last 25 years, high-status persons in the United States have favored the Republican party while the less fortunately placed have subscribed instead to the Democratic party.

Although some particulars of these findings have been subject to controversy, their broad outlines have been so completely absorbed into the basic lore of attitude research as to become commonplace. We have come to consider them, implicitly at least, as relationships of roughly constant magnitude and, hence, diminishing fascination. However, the passage of time now permits us to evaluate the extent to which changes can occur in the role played by social class in political opinions and behavior.

It is only such observation of stability and change over a lengthening period of our national history that can provide an empirical test for some of the more important hypotheses as to the significance of social class in a modern society. The first round of survey studies in this area served for the most part to document only a static description of class differences. There was found to be indeed a visible divergence of opinion on mat-

This article was written especially for E. E. Maccoby, T. M. Newcomb, and E. L. Hartley (Eds.), *Readings in Social Psychology*, 3d Ed., New York: Holt, Rinehart and Winston, 1958. Reprinted by permission of the author and publisher.

ters of economic interest between members of different class levels. But the grand dynamic models of the classic-stratification theories received little empirical support or challenge in these materials. Marx, for example, had taken the existence of social strata with divergent interests as a postulate, self-evident beyond need for proof, and proceeded to spin a theory concerning the social and economic conditions under which class consciousness might be expected to vary as modern industrial society developed. However obsolete his speculations may appear today, it can be fairly said that we have yet to exploit modern research vehicles toward a more adequate understanding of the dynamic role which status plays in the political life of a modern state as it passes through depression, war, and prosperity.

It is our theses that in the United States the strength of relationships between status and political variables is subject to more short-term variation than is generally recognized. Yet we hold that this instability need not be a source of dismay to the student of social class; if we accept the strength of these relationships as a critical variable in its own right and seek its determinants in the major events which impinge upon the social system, we shall have taken a first step toward putting a dynamic view of social class and its political consequences on an empirical footing.

Such analysis requires comparative measurement over time. A national sample survey conducted by the Survey Research Center (SRC) of the University of Michigan during October and November of 1956 permits a detailed comparison of class attitudes in 1956 with those encountered by Richard Centers in his 1945 study.[1] A cross-sect'onal sample of 1,772 respondents, chosen by strict probability methods from all adult cit-

izens living in private households in the United States, was interviewed just prior to the 1956 presidential election and again just subsequent to it. Since the 1945 survey involved a sample of 1,097 adult white males, the following comparison is based upon the 728 white male respondents interviewed in the 1956 study.[2]

Centers' detailed description of the assignment of respondents to an occupational status in his pioneering study allowed us to make a matching array within our sample. The second measure of status, the repondent's self-assignment to a social class, was obtained in 1956 through an elaboration of the original question devised for this purpose by Centers.[3] Each person interviewed was asked: "There's quite a bit of talk these days about different social classes. Most people say they belong either to the middle class or to the working class. Do you ever think of yourself as being in one of these classes?" If the response was affirmative, the respondent was simply asked "Which one?" If the response was negative, the ensuing question was "Well, if you had to make a choice, would you call yourself middle class or working class?" In both cases, the respondent was then asked, "Would you say you are about an average (class selected) person or that you are in the upper part of the (class selected)?"

The results of the class identification

---

[1] The 1956 study was carried out at the Survey Research Center under the direction of Angus Campbell and Warren E. Miller. It was supported by a grant from the Rockefeller Foundation. A more detailed report of the study is available in Campbell, Converse, Miller, and Stokes (1960). The 1945 study is fully reported in Centers (1949).

[2] It might be noted, however, that the findings to be presented here hold generally for the total cross-sectional sample. While certain factors such as the relative indeterminacy of the occupation status of many women act to reduce slightly the clarity of some of the relationships reported, our data for females look substantially like those for males. On the other hand, inclusion of nonwhite respondents would, if anything, serve to sharpen relationships, as such racial groups fall at an extreme of the status continuum and manifest opinions and political behavior appropriate to this extreme. Nevertheless, our interest in the specific magnitude of relationships over time legislated against treatment here of any elements of the sample not directly comparable with the 1945 data.

[3] This question was phrased: "If you were asked to use one of these four names for your social class, which would you say you belonged in: the middle class, lower class, working class, or upper class?"

TABLE 1

Subjective Class Identification of White Males

	SRC 1956 Aware of Social Class	SRC 1956 Unaware of Social Class	Total	SRC 1952	SRC 1952 Total	Centers 1945 Total
Average Working Class	50%	42%	47%	(Lower class)	2%	1%
Upper Working Class	11	+10	11	(Working class)	59	51
Working-class Total	61	52	58		61	52
Average Middle Class	33	34	33	(Middle class)	35	43
Upper Middle Class	6	5	5	(Upper class)	1	3
Middle-class Total	39	39	38		36	46
Reject Idea of Class		5	2		1	1
Don't Know, Not Ascertained	❃	4	2		2	1
	(N = 456)	(N = 272)	(N = 728)		(N = 666)	(N = 1097)

❃ Less than one half of one percent.

question are shown in Table 1. Although three rebellious spirits—all women—assigned themselves to the "upper class" despite the wording of the question, it will be noted that we have sacrificed the differentiation of the handful of people who chose "upper" or "lower" class in the 1945 study to subdivide each major class into an "average" or "upper" segment more susceptible to detailed analysis. If, however, we restrict our attention to gross comparisons between frequencies in the two major classes, we find a sizeable shift from choice of middle class to choice of working class, by comparison with the 1945 distribution.

It is impossible to judge whether these differences are a result of a shift in underlying parameters in the interim, or whether more mechanical discrepancies are involved. The quota sample design used in the Princeton study may have been vulnerable to a systematic upward shift in economic status of respondents chosen. It seems fairly safe to say, however, that the differences in distribution of class identification are not a result of the change in question wording, since we see that the Centers question repeated verbatim from a 1952 SRC study produced a distribution which coincides almost exactly

with that found by the SRC using the revised wording in 1956 (Table 1).

As a final point of comparison, we find that the subjective choice of class affiliation as obtained with the 1956 question related to status as objectively determined by occupation in much the same fashion as it did within the 1945 data. Among the nonfarm portion of the sample, we find some tendency for higher-status respondents in 1956 to place themselves more frequently in the working class. Nonetheless, the correlation between the two modes of status measurement in 1956 ($\tau_\beta = .46$) is very close to that represented in the earlier study ($\tau_\beta = .49$).[4]

[4] The tau-beta statistic due to Kendall will be used throughout this analysis to fulfill the need for a measure of degree of association between variables. Such coefficients have been computed from the bivariate distributions published by Centers as well as for our own data. This statistic is derived from a rank-order correlation technique which handles any number of ranked categories or ties. The tau-beta tends to produce coefficients which are lower in magnitude than corresponding Pearson-product-moment coefficients computed from the same data. Therefore, the absolute magnitude of the coefficients may appear somewhat conservative to the reader accustomed to the Pearson r, and considerably more conservative than the tetrachoric r originally used by Centers.

In sum, then, there seems to be little question about the comparability of measurement between the two studies with regard to the primary independent variables. Therefore, it seems reasonable to assume that any notable differences which we may find in relationships between these status measures and political variables after the lapse of a decade are due to actual changes in the American scene.

Social Class and Political Attitudes in 1956

Politico-economic attitudes constituted a major type of dependent variable for the 1945 study. From a large battery of questions concerning governmental policy asked in the 1956 SRC study we have chosen three which appear most closely related in content to the items employed by Centers in forming his scale of "conservatism-radicalism." These agree-disagree items are as follows:

(b) "The government in Washington ought to see to it that everyone who wants to work can find a job;"
(d) "The government ought to help people get doctors and hospital care at low cost;"
(k) "The government should leave things like electric power and housing for private businessmen to handle."

These questions have as a common core the distinction between what Centers referred to in 1949 as "two opposed philosophies of government—an individualistic one and a collectivistic one." Centers considers this "the central issue of all today's politico-economic strife" and the locus of the largest differences in class attitude.[5]

It would be dangerous to make comparisons of absolute response distributions for questions similar in spirit though not in letter. However, if the empirical situation is like

[5] See Swanson, Newcomb, and Hartley (1952, p. 301).

that which Centers encountered, we would have a right to expect these basic politico-economic orientations to relate clearly to status variables much as they did in 1945. Instead, we find a general decline in the strength of these relationships (see Figure 1).

Each of our three questions shows a lower order of relationship with both subjective class and occupational status than Centers' data show for 1945. If we draw a trend line between the questions from the two studies which are most closely matched in content the contrasts are striking.[6] Assuming an equivalence between the questions, we find the employment-guarantee issue more highly related to both subjective and objective status than the free-enterprise issue in 1956, exactly as it was in 1945. But by 1956 both relationships have receded and the respective slopes of their decline are very close to parallel.

We cannot conclude that politico-economic attitudes are no longer significantly associated with statuses and self-perceptions in the economic order. Indeed, when we introduce more refined measurement, such as the distinction between the "average" and "upper part" of the two major subjective classes, we find that we can restore at least a part of the old strength of relationship which Centers treats. But if we can assume that the two gross classes and the politico-economic attitudes as measured

[6] This matching equates our question (b) with Centers' question (6): "Which one of these statements do you most agree with? (1) The most important job for the government is to make it certain that there are good opportunities for each person to get ahead on his own. (2) The most important job for the government is to guarantee every person a decent and steady job and standard of living." The 1956 item (k) is likewise paired with question (5) in the Princeton study: "As you know, during this war, many private businesses and industries have been taken over by the government. Do you think wages and salaries would be fairer, jobs more steady, and that we would have fewer people out of work if the government took over and ran our mines, factories, and industries in the future, or do you think things would be better under private ownership?"

in 1956 may be legitimately compared with those of Centers in 1945, it is beyond dispute that a sizable decline in the association between them has occurred in the interim.

Social Class and Political Behavior in 1956

A prime behavioral outlet for class consciousness is the act of voting. Centers acknowledges the relevance of the vote by employing it as a validity criterion for his scale of conservatism-radicalism and by describing its familiar relationships to various definitions of status.[7] The relationship between status and vote allows a more extensive test of the assertion that status differentials fluctuate considerably in their degree of impact on mass political behavior. The series of presidential election studies at the Survey Research Center provides material for status-trend lines similar to those we have used for attitudes, yet with more frequent data.[8] By prefixing computations from Centers' tables on status and the vote, we can thus observe a span of four presidential elections.

Figure 2 reveals a striking range of variation in the strength of the status-vote relationship since the last Roosevelt election in 1944. The degree to which people of self-designated middle- or working-class status have given their votes to the presidential candidates of the Republican and Democratic parties respectively has fluctuated widely over little more than a decade.

In the face of this variation, two regularities which emerge from the data become most noteworthy. The first is the degree of coincidence between the objective and subjective variants of the status-vote relationship over time. As we have seen, class identification, while strongly related to occupation status, still enjoys considerable variation

[7] See Centers (1949, pp. 45-47, 115).
[8] Moreover, while the comparability of attitudinal items used in the two studies is not perfect, the act of voting provides nearly identical behaviors for comparison.

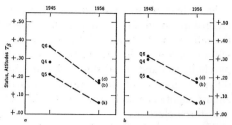

Fig. 1. Status and attitudes,* 1945 and 1956, showing (a) the relationships between attitudes and occupation status, and (b) the relationships between attitudes and subjective class. (Letters and numbers in parentheses refer to attitude items on the 1945 and 1956 questionnaires.†

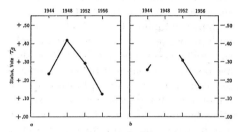

Fig. 2. Status and presidential vote,* 1944 through 1956, showing (a) the relationships between vote and occupational status, and (b) the relationships between vote and subjective class.

* We have followed the usage of the 1945 study in removing farm occupations from the basic occupation–status array. For purposes of comparability, therefore, all coefficients in Figures 1 and 2 are based on a subsample of white males reporting nonfarm occupations. The 1945 coefficients in Figure 1 represent an N ranging from 758 to 835, while the N for the 1956 coefficient varies between 525 and 574. In Figure 2, elimination of nonvoters reduces the N in 1945 to about 700, to 141 in 1948, 455 in 1952, and 480 in 1956. In all cases, the addition of white females to the Survey Research Center data would more than double the number of cases without any substantial effect on the coefficients involved.

† Question 4 in the 1945 study was "Would you agree that everybody would be happier, more secure, and more prosperous if the working people were given more power and influence in government, or would you say we would all be better off if the working people had no more power than they have now?" For questions 5 and 6, see footnote [6].

independent of it.[9] One form of the relationship could, for example, lag behind the other in its temporal cycles, or vary within narrower limits. Instead, we find psychological and social status, despite their differing division of the sample, producing almost identical relationships with the vote over three elections.

The second regularity is apparent if we compare Figures 1 and 2. The decline in the status-attitude relationships between 1945 and 1956 matches the two terminal points of the status-vote trend in provocative fashion. Unfortunately, we lack comparable attitudinal material for the intervening period with which to fill out Figure 1. We have, of course, no guarantee that status-vote relationships need follow the fluctuation of relationships between status and certain relevant politico-economic attitudes. We shall have occasion to comment below on some of the factors which may disrupt direct translation of crystallized economic interest into voting behavior. Nevertheless, the congruence between the status-vote and status-attitude trends lends strong support to the conclusion that we are dealing with variation in an important property of a social system.

We suggest, therefore, that the *strength of relationship* between status and relevant politico-economic variables may be taken as a fairly reliable measure of such a system property at a point in time. For easy reference, we shall label this relational concept *status polarization.*[10]

By definition, status polarization is a group-level concept. It should indicate the degree to which groups at opposing ends of the status continuum have taken up mutually antagonistic value positions in the politico-economic sphere. We may imagine that as polarization increases it is likely to become manifest in values less immediately bound up with economic self-interest and public policy, so that a more salient and generalized antagonism exists between class groups. Its limiting case is class war.

The counterpart of status polarization at the individual level would be, therefore, the familiar concept of class consciousness. The fit is not perfect. We can imagine a mild divergence of beliefs between various class subcultures without any of the visible loyalty to a class group or hostility toward another class which we associate with full-fledged class consciousness. But in a rough way, the polarization of a social system is taken to reflect the extent and intensity of class consciousness measured over a representative portion of its members.

Richard Centers was concerned with the measurement of class consciousness and his demonstration of the psychological reality of class is a move in this direction. However, his implication that "self-affiliation" alone is sufficient to distinguish the "internally cohesive . . . social groupings" which we tend to associate with class consciousness is not entirely convincing.[11] The claim is compounded by the use of the label "class identification" for the self-affiliation procedure. We can take "identification" to refer to a sense of belongingness with a group, a usage which accords fairly well with the concept of class consciousness. Or—and this is closer to the Centers procedure—we can take it to refer merely to the nominal assignment of an object to a category.

The interview question with which we

---

[9] For example, if we were to make the arbitrary assumption that people of nonmanual occupation were a "true" middle class, with the manual occupations constituting the working class, we would find roughly equivalent portions of the sample, amounting to more than a quarter of the total, indulging in "misclassification" upward or downward. Given such slippage between the two definitions of status, we might expect more differential variation between each of them and the vote.

[10] It should be emphasized that it is difficult to attach any unequivocal meaning at this point to the *absolute magnitude* of coefficients of the relationship between status and attitudes or the vote. Given its operational definition, status

polarization can show a hypothetical variation between .00 and 1.00. However, it is clear that the absolute magnitude of any coefficient is a function of the dependent variables employed.

[11] See Centers (1949, p. 28. See also pp. 74-76).

prefaced our requests for self-assignment to a class was less an attempt to sort out respondents who were class-conscious in the old militant sense than to improve upon the Centers technique by distinguishing a group for whom the notion of class was most salient and self-allocation most nearly habitual. With this limited objective in mind, we shall speak of "class awareness" rather than "class consciousness." However, it seems reasonable to suppose that we have to some degree "tightened the ring" on a small group of people who may be sufficiently class-conscious to merit the term: we would expect the two thirds of our sample who admitted class awareness to contain most of them. Therefore, we may take our measure of awareness as a serviceable individual measure relating to status polarization.

We lack the data from earlier samples requisite to test the hypothesis that fluctuation in our measure of status polarization would be directly reflected in variation in class awareness over a period of time. But with minimal inference we may substitute a cross-sectional test for a longitudinal one. If our measure of awareness is reliable and our concept of status polarization meaningful, we should expect higher status-attitude and status-vote relationships within the group of people who are aware of class than within the group who are unaware.

Table 2 provides some support for this proposition. While the low general level of relationships between status and our dependent variables coupled with the large proportion of the sample who reported being "aware" imposes a ceiling on variation, there is indication that lack of awareness of class reduces the likelihood that the respondent will hold beliefs and will vote along lines most "appropriate" for his subjective class group. A more differential measure of awareness might show bigger differences in relationships between these groups. However, it seems reasonable to suppose that status polarization in a society will reflect, over time, the varying extent and intensity of awareness of social class among its members.

Some Determinants of Status Polarization

We turn now to the consideration of some of the factors that may account for variations in status polarization. Without a more adequate accumulation of data, we cannot pursue the argument closely at an empirical level. However, initial and cursory speculation will serve to mark out directions for investigation.

We assume that status polarization in a society reflects concern about the allocation of rewards and deprivations across the sta-

TABLE 2

STATUS-VOTE AND STATUS-ATTITUDE RELATIONSHIPS FOR WHITE MALES
ACCORDING TO AWARENESS OF SOCIAL CLASS*

		Attitudes, 1956		
		Item (b)		
	1956	Government	Item (d)	Item (k)
	Presidential Vote	Guarantee of Employment	Government Medical Aid	Government vs. Private Industry
Aware of Social Class	.20	.17	.22	.08
	(N = 358)	(N = 430)	(N = 416)	(N = 388)
Unaware of Social Class	.07	.09	.12	−.01
	(N = 207)	(N = 228)	(N = 227)	(N = 203)

* The cell entry indicates the τ_β for the relationship between subjective status and vote or attitudes: the number of cases is included for each coefficient.

tus continuum. In modern western democracies this concern has been primarily economic, directed at the distribution of wealth. Under prevailing expectations the inequity represented by a bimodal distribution of wealth would undoubtedly be accompanied by status polarization as well. Conversely, in the United States the expansion of a middle class engaged in service occupations which fail to fit the old ownership-proletariat cleavage may currently be functioning to set upper limits on the polarization potential of the society.

In the shorter term, given a fairly constant pattern of wealth distribution, we would predict that polarization would increase in time of depression and decrease in periods of prosperity. The net decline of status polarization which we have seen in relevant attitudes between 1945 and 1956 lends credence to such a proposition, if we consider the general increase in prosperity which has characterized the period since the depression of the 1930's.

However, the sharp crest attained by status-vote relationships in 1948 suggests that this decline in attitude polarization may not have been monotonic during the intervening period. On the other hand, the mild levelling of the economy in the reconversion period between the end of the war boom and the recession of 1949 would hardly seem sufficient, in itself, to generate the rapid increase in polarization suggested by our data. We conclude that a single-factor theory is oversimplified and that we must cope with a more complex explanatory burden.

Consideration of the effects which war may have on status polarization is an obvious first step toward explanation of our data and consequent modification of our theory. Even an overseas war, it must be conceded, has a major impact on any population involved; yet this impact, in contrast to that of a depression, is less clearly distributed along status lines. Pressing questions of foreign policy eclipse those concerns of domestic economics which lead so directly to cleavage among status-interest groups. There-

fore, we would propose that war and the preeminence of foreign policy considerations may act to reduce status polarization temporarily. For the case in point we would suggest that polarization tendencies carrying over from the depression were dampened by the national crisis imposed by World War II but rebounded toward their prewar level after that conflict was concluded.

The temporary evaporation of the most burdensome foreign problems, along with the sudden unleashing of pent-up class-relevant actions, particularly the great postwar strikes in major industries, the struggle in Congress to place legislative controls on the activities of labor unions, and the development of first anxieties concerning an "inevitable" postwar depression, all must have contributed to a rise in the relative salience of domestic economic issues which had remained dormant during the war. After the 1948 peak of status polarization, we may speculate that the renewal of the threat of global war along with the outbreak of hostilities in Korea ought to have acted, in concert with increasing prosperity, to depress the level of status polarization once again.

If war and the consequent prominence of foreign-policy concerns do in fact work toward a reduction of polarization, we should be able to find traces of this effect in our 1956 sample, who were interviewed at a time when many voters were still apprehensive about war. It would follow from our argument that respondents showing marked concern over foreign policy could not be expected to vote in accordance with their subjective class position, whether or not they were aware of that position. On the other hand, respondents who were aware of their self-assigned status and for whom domestic policy controversies were more salient than foreign affairs and the possibility of war should show a higher status-vote relationship than that found in the total sample.

In the 1956 interview a series of open-ended questions which enabled the respondent to volunteer comments on aspects of the current political scene which were important for him permitted us to test th's proposition. Table 3 bears out our specula-

TABLE 3

Status-vote Relationships for White Males According to Relative Concern over Domestic or Foreign Issues[°]

	Higher Domestic Issue Concern	Equiva- lent Concern	Higher Foreign Issue Concern
Aware of Social Class	.25 (N=191)	.20 (N=105)	.00 (N=62)
Unaware of Social Class	.04 (N=99)	.14 (N=74)	−.02 (N=34)

[°] The cell entry indicates the τ_β for the relationship between subjective status and vote or attitudes; the number of cases is included for each coefficient.

tions rather well. While it represents once again a cross-sectional rather than a longitudinal test, we can infer that, other things equal, status polarization will vary inversely with the salience of war over a period of time.

Other political factors in addition to the intrusion of foreign policy may affect the level of polarization or act to disturb the correspondence between attitudinal polari-

zation and the status-vote relationship. For example, rapid changes in degree of attitudinal polarization may be reflected only imperfectly in voting behavior due to loyalties which have grown up between the voter and a particular political party. Thus, theories of voting behavior which imply, by suggesting that status can affect the vote only as an expression of economic self-interest, that the level of attitudinal polarization is an upper limit for a status-vote relationship, are not entirely adequate; we can imagine conditions under which party identifications born in time of polarization could conserve a status-vote relationship after relevant status attitudes had faded.

Other prominent elements in the election situation may tend to mitigate the simple expression of economic interest. A magnetic presidential candidate can have a broad public appeal which defies status lines. It is at least suggestive that three of the four elections recorded in Figure 2 were dominated by such personalities, while it is the remaining election in 1948 which produced the high-water point of the status-vote trend line. Once again we may turn to our 1956 data for evidence concerning the degree to which the personal characteristics of the candidates may draw the attention of the voters away from domestic economic concerns and thereby weaken status voting. Table 4, constructed on the basis of volun-

TABLE 4[°]

Status-vote Relationships for White Males According to Relative Concern over Domestic Issues as Opposed to Interest in the Candidates

	High Domestic Issue Concern	Balanced Candidate Interest and Domestic Issue Concern	High Candidate Interest
Aware of Social Class	.30 (N = 87)	.21 (N = 103)	.17 (N = 159)
Unaware of Social Class	.06 (N = 47)	.10 (N = 76)	.04 (N = 81)

[°] The cell entry indicates the τ_β for the relationship between subjective status and vote or attitudes; the number of cases is included for each coefficient.

teered comments similar to those in Table 3, offers some support for this proposition, although the differences generated are less sharp than in the case where the intruding factor is concern over foreign affairs.[12]

Another type of political factor which must serve to set varying limits on the status-vote relationship over time is the convergence and divergence of the domestic-policy positions of the two major parties. However high the level of attitudinal polarization in the society, the impact of status on vote decision is dependent on the degree to which the political parties proffer clear and equally polarized policy alternatives. Where party differences with regard to economic philosophy are not perceived by the electorate, political translations from attitude to vote will lose any discernible status significance.

It is likely that differences between the parties on status-relevant economic issues had by 1956 reached a decade's low. However, since, our respondents were asked for each of our three questions on economic policy whether or not they saw differences in the way in which the two parties would handle the problem, we can inquire whether the status-vote relationship is not highest among people in the sample who still perceive these differences between the parties.

If we include the variable of class awareness as a precondition for meaningful status voting, we find the coefficients in Table 5 which clearly support the general argu-

ment.[13] Of course, discrimination between the two parties with regard to domestic policy may accompany high salience of domestic isues, both at the objective policy level and in the reflection of these differences in perceptions of an interested segment of the electorate. Therefore, Table 5 is, in conjunction with Tables 3 and 4, part of a larger whole. If the salience of domestic issues rests at a constant level over a period of time, any tendency for the two parties to climb on the same domestic-policy bandwagon in appealing for public support must act as a force reducing status polarization of the vote.

By reflecting on some of the factors which must influence status polarization, we have

TABLE 5*

STATUS-VOTE RELATIONSHIPS FOR WHITE MALES ACCORDING TO PERCEPTION OF DIFFERENCES BETWEEN THE PARTIES ON THREE DOMESTIC ISSUES

	Perceived No Differences	Perceived Differences on One or More Issues
Aware of Social Class	.04 (N = 94)	.26 (N = 263)
Unaware of Social Class	.08 (N = 75)	.03 (N = 131)

* The cell entry indicates the τ_β for the relationship between subjective status and vote or attitudes; the number of cases is included for each coefficient.

been able to sort out of our 1956 sample a group for whom status remains a significant determinant of vote, despite the general decline of predictive efficacy of status over the

[12] It is interesting to note that further combination of political orientations of this sort can produce a "purified" group for whom the status-vote relationship is extremely high. Another category of volunteered response not subsumed under the domestic-issue comments treated above covers those cases in which a party or a candidate is seen to support or discriminate against—in economic terms—some group in the society such as the "working man," the "aged," etc. If we isolate an extreme group of 60 "aware" voters who gave the most frequent group references and domestic-issue comments, while giving a minimum of responses concerning foreign issues or the candidates, we find a τ_β of .49 between subjective status and vote, in contrast with the coefficient of .16 for white male voters over the total sample in 1956.

[13] Similar differences are evident in data from the Survey Research Center study of the 1952 election, although we lack in this case the variable of class awareness with which to sharpen the findings. Among people who saw differences between the two parties on general policy with regard to the degree of government welfare activity, the status-vote relationship was .41 (τ_β as opposed to .19 among those who failed to discriminate between the parties at this point.

total sample. Some of these factors, such as the intrusion of war, are likely to reduce the general level of polarization in the society as a whole. Others which we have discussed may intervene to disturb the direct translation of economic attitudes into political action. Both types of factors must be examined in detail if we are to piece together an understanding of the varying role of status differences in public life over time.

Summary

By replicating, after the lapse of a decade, the Richard Centers study of relationships between objective and psychological status on the one hand and certain attitudes and the vote on the other, we have demonstrated considerable variability in the strength of these relationships. We have proposed that such variability be exploited as a tool by investigators who wish to bring some empirical "reality testing" to dynamic theories of class and status. Toward this end, we have tried to show the clear relationships between this "status polarization" as a property of a social system and the concept of individual class consciousness prominent in such dynamic theory.

Finally, we have taken recent variation in status polarization as the basis for a preliminary discussion of some of the factors which seem to determine its level, as measured by either status-attitudes or status-vote relationships at any point in time. We assume that investigation proceeding along such lines may increase our general understanding of the long-term effect of status position on political attitudes and behavior.

References

CAMPBELL, A., CONVERSE, P. E., MILLER, W. E., and STOKES, D. E. *The American voter.* New York: Wiley, 1960.

CENTERS, R. *The psychology of social classes.* Princeton, N.J.: Princeton Univer. Press, 1949.

SWANSON, G. E., NEWCOMB, T. M., and HARTLEY, E. L. (Eds.). *Readings in social psychology,* Rev. Ed. New York: Holt, Rinehart and Winston, 1952.

Socialization and Social Class through Time and Space ❧ Urie Bronfenbrenner

I. Background and Resources

During the past two decades, a class struggle has been taking place in American social psychology—a struggle, fortunately, not *between* but *about* social classes. In the best social revolutionary tradition the issue was joined with a manifesto challenging the assumed superiority of the upper and middle classes and extolling the neglected virtues of the working class. There followed a successful revolution with an overthrow of the

This article has been adapted by the author especially for this book from E. E. Maccoby, T. M. Newcomb, and E. L. Hartley (Eds.), *Readings in Social Psychology,* 3d Ed., New York: Holt, Rinehart and Winston, 1958. Reprinted by permission of the author and publisher.

established order in favor of the victorious proletariat, which then reigned supreme—at least for a time. These dramatic changes had, as always, their prophets and precursors, but they reached a climax in 1948 with the publication of Davis and Havighurst's influential paper on "Social Class and Color Differences in Child Rearing"(1948). The paper cited impressive statistical evidence in support of the thesis that middle-class parents "place their children under a stricter regimen, with more frustration of their impulses than do lower-class parents." For the next eight years, the Davis-Havighurst conclusion was taken as the definitive statement of class differences in socialization. Then, in 1954, came the counterrevolution; Maccoby and Gibbs published the first report (1954) of a study of child-rearing practices in the Boston area which, by and large, contradicted the Chicago findings: in general, middle-class parents were found to be "more permissive" than those in the lower class.

In response, one year later, Havighurst and Davis (1955) presented a reanalysis of their data for a subsample more comparable in age to the subjects of the Boston study. On the basis of a careful comparison of the two sets of results, they concluded that "the disagreements between the findings of the two studies are substantial and large" and speculated that these differences might be attributable either to genuine changes in child-rearing practices over time or to technical difficulties of sampling and item equivalence.

A somewhat different view, however, was taken by Sears, Maccoby, and Levin (1957) in their final report of the Boston study. They argued that Davis and Havighurst's interpretation of the Chicago data as reflecting greater permissiveness for the working-class parent was unwarranted on two counts. First, they cited the somewhat contrasting results of still another research— that of Klatskin (1952) in support of the view that class differences in feeding, weaning, scheduling, and toilet training "are not very stable or customary." Second, they contended that the Chicago findings of greater freedom of movement for the lower-class child were more properly interpreted not as "permissiveness" but as "a reflection of rejection, a pushing of the child out of the way." Such considerations led the Boston investigators to conclude (Sears, Maccoby, and Levin, 1957, 446-447):

This re-examination of the Chicago findings suggests quite clearly the same conclusion that must be reached from Klatskin's study and from our own: the middle-class mothers were generally more permissive and less punitive toward their young children than were working-class mothers. Unfortunately, the opposite interpretation, as presented by Davis and Havighurst, has been widely accepted in education circles during the past decade. This notion of working-class permissiveness has been attractive for various reasons. It has provided an easy explanation of why working-class children have lower academic achievement motivation than do middle-class children —their mothers place less restrictive pressure on them. It has also provided a kind of compensatory comfort for those educators who have been working hard toward the goal of improving educational experiences for the noncollege-oriented part of the school population. In effect, one could say, lower-class children may lack the so highly desirable academic motivation, but the lack stems from a "good" reason—the children were permissively reared.

It would appear that there are a number of unresolved issues between the protagonists of the principal points of view—issues both as to the facts and their interpretation. At such times it is not unusual for some third party to attempt a reappraisal of events in a broader historical perspective with the aid of documents and information previously not available. It is this which the present writer hopes to do. He is fortunate in having at his disposal materials not only from the past and present, but also seven manuscripts unpublished at the time of this writing, which report class differences in child-rearing practices at four different places and five points in time. To begin with, Bayley and Schaefer (1957) have re-analyzed data from the Berkeley Growth Study to provide information on class differences in maternal-behavior ratings made from 1928 to 1932, when the children in the study were under three years old, and again from 1939 to 1942, when most of them were about ten years old. Information on maternal behavior in this same locale as of 1953 comes from a recent report by Martha Sturm White (1957) of class differences in child-rearing practices for a sample of preschoolers in Palo Alto and environs. Miller and Swanson have made available relevant data from their two comprehensive studies of families in Detroit, one based on a stratified sample of families with children up to 19 years of age (1958), the other a specially selected sample of boys, ages 12 to 14 years (1960). Limited information on another sample of adolescent boys comes from Strodtbeck's investigation of "Family Interaction, Values, and Achievement" (1958). Also, Littman, Moore, and Pierce-Jones (1957) have recently completed a survey of child-rearing practices in Eugene, Oregon, for a random sample of parents with children from two weeks to 14 years of age. Finally, Kohn (1957) reports a comparison of child-training values among working and middle-class mothers in Washington, D.C.

In addition to these unpublished sources, the writer has made use of nine published researches.[1] In some instances—notably for the monumental and regrettably neglected Anderson report (1936)—data were reanalyzed and significance tests computed in order to permit closer comparison with the results of other investigations. A list of all the studies utilized in the present review appears in Table 1. Starred items designate the researches which, because they contain reasonably comparable data, are used as the principal bases for analysis.

[1] Anderson (1936), Baldwin, Kalhorn, and Breese (1945), Boek, Lawson, Yankhauser, and

II. Establishing Comparable Social-class Groupings

Although in most of the studies under consideration the investigators have based their classification of socioeconomic status (SES) explicitly or implicitly on the criteria proposed by Warner (1949), there was considerable variation in the number of social-class categories employed. The majority, however, following the precedent of Havighurst and Davis, differentiated two levels only—middle vs. lower or working class. As a result, both necessity and wisdom call for dropping to the lowest common denominator and reanalyzing the results of the remaining researches in terms of a two-level classification of socioeconomic status.

In most instances, the delicate question of where to establish the cutting point was readily resolved. The crux of the distinction between middle and working class in all four of the studies employing this dichotomous break lies in the separation between white- and blue-collar workers. Fortunately, this same differentiation was made at some point along the scale in each of the other researches included in the basic analysis.

In some instances it was, of course, necessary to compute anew percentages and average scores for the two class levels and to calculate tests of significance. All other figures and significance tests cited are taken from the original reports.

The effort to make the division between middle and working class at similar points for the basic samples, however successful it may have been, does not eliminate many other important sources of difference among the several researchers.

Many factors, some known and many more unknown, may operate to produce differences in results from one sample to the

Sussman (1957), Davis and Havighurst (1948), Duvall (1946-1947), Klatskin (1952), Maccoby and Gibbs (1954), McClelland, Rindlisbacher, and DeCharms (1955), Sears, Maccoby, and Levin (1957).

TABLE 1
DESCRIPTION OF SAMPLES

Sample	Principal Investigator Source	Date of Field Work	Age	No. of Cases Total	Middle Class	Working Class	Description of Sample
National Cross Section,° I	Anderson	1932	0-1	494	217	277	National sample of white families "having child between 1 and 5 years of age" and "representing each major geographic area, each size of community and socioeconomic class in the United States." About equal number of males and females. SES (seven classes) based on Minnesota Scale for Occupational Classification.
II			1-5	2420	1131	1289	
III			6-12	865	391	474	
IV			1-12	3285	1522	1763	
Berkeley, Cal., I-II	Bayley and Schaefer	1928-32 / 1939-42	1-3 / 9-11	31 / 31	Information Not Available		Subjects of both sexes from Berkeley Growth Study, "primarily middle class but range from unskilled laborer, relief, and three-years education to professional, $10,000 income and doctoral degrees." SES measures include education, occupation (Taussig Scale), income, home and neighborhood rating, and composite scale.
Yellow Springs, Ohio	Baldwin	1940	3-12	124	Information Not Available		Families enrolled in Fels Research Institute Home Visiting Program. "Above average" in socioeconomic status but include "a number of uneducated parents and from the lower economic levels." No SES index computed but graphs show relationships by education and income.
Chicago, Ill., I°	Davis and Havighurst	1943	5 (approx.)	100	48	52	Middle-class sample "mainly" from mothers of nursery-school children; lower class from "areas of poor housing." All mothers native born. Two-level classification SES following Warner based on occupation, education, residential area, type of home, etc.
Chicago, Ill., II	Duvall	1943-44	5 (approx.)	433	230	203	Negro and white (Jewish and non-Jewish) mothers. Data collected at "regular meetings of mothers' groups." SES classification (four levels) following Warner.
New Haven, Conn., I°	Klatskin	1949-50	1 (approx.)	222	114	108	Mothers in Yale Rooming-in Project returning for evaluation of baby at one year of age. SES classification (three levels) by Hollingshead, following Warner.
Boston, Mass.°	Sears, et al.	1951-52	4-6	372	198	174	Kindergarten children in two suburbs. Parents American born, living together. Twins, adoptions, handicapped children, and other special cases eliminated. Two-level SES classification follows Warner.

Location	Author(s)	Years	Age	N			Description
New Haven, Conn., II	Strodtbeck	1951-53	14-17	48	24	24	Third-generation Jewish and Italian boys representing extremes of under- and over-achievement in school. Classified into three SES levels on basis of occupation.
Detroit, Mich., I*	Miller and Swanson	1953	12-14	112	59	53	Boys in grades 7-8 above borderline intelligence within one year of age for grade, all at least third-generation Americans, Christian, from unbroken, nonmobile families of Northwest European stock. SES (four levels) assigned on basis of education and occupation.
Detroit, Mich., II*	Miller and Swanson	1953	0-18	479	Information Not Available		Random sample of white mothers with child under 19 and living with husband. Step-children and adoptions eliminated. SES (four levels) based primarily on U.S. census occupation categories.
Palo Alto, Cal.,*	White	1953	2½-5½	74	36	38	Native-born mothers of only one child, the majority expecting another. Unbroken homes in suburban area SES (two levels) rated on Warner scale.
Urban, Connecticut	McClelland, et al.	1953-54	6-18	152	Information Not Available		Parents between 30-60 having at least one child between six and eighteen and representing four religious groups, "Rough check on class status" obtained from educational level achieved by parent.
Upstate New York	Boek, et al.	1955-56	3-7 months	1432	595	837	Representative sample of N.Y. State mothers of newborn children, exclusive of unmarried mothers. SES classification (five levels) as given on Warner scale.
Eugene, Oregon*	Littman, et al.	1955-56	0-14	206	86	120	Random sample of children from preschool classes and school rolls. Two SES levels assigned on same basis as in Boston study.
Washington, D.C.	Kohn and Clausen	1956-57	10-11	339	174	165	Representative samples of working- and middle-class mothers classified by Hollingshead's index of social position.

* Denotes studies used as principal basis for the analysis.

next. It is hardly likely, however, that these manifold influences will operate in a consistent direction over time or space. The possibility of obtaining interpretable findings, therefore, rests on the long chance that major trends, if they exist, will be sufficiently marked to override the effects of bias arising from variations in sampling and method. This is a rash and optimistic hope, but— somewhat to our own surprise—it seems to have been realized, at least in part, in the analyses that follow. . . .

IV. Social-class Differences in Infant Care, 1930–1955

In interpreting reports of child-rearing practices it is essential to distinguish between the date at which the information was obtained and the actual period to which the information refers. This caution is particularly relevant in dealing with descriptions of infant care for children who (as in the Eugene or Detroit studies) may be as old as 12, 14, or 18 at the time of the interview. In such instances it is possible only to guess at the probable time at which the practice occurred by making due allowances for the age of the child. The problem is further complicated by the fact that none of the studies reports SES differences by age. The best one can do, therefore, is to estimate the median age of the group and from this approximate the period at which the practice may have taken place. For example, the second Detroit sample, which ranged in age from birth to 18 years, would have a median age of about nine. Since the field work was done in 1953, we estimate the date of feeding and weaning practices as about 1944. It should be recognized, however, that the practices reported range over a considerable period extending from as far back as 1935 to the time of the interview in 1953. Any marked variation in child-rearing practices over this period could produce an average figure which would in point of fact be atypical for the middle year 1944.

We shall have occasion to point to the possible operation of this effect in some of the data to follow.

If dates of practices are estimated by the method outlined above, we find that the available data describe social-class differences in feeding, weaning, and toilet training for a period from about 1930 to 1955. The relevant information appears in Tables 2 and 3.

GENERAL TRENDS

We may begin by looking at general trends over time irrespective of social-class level. These appear in column 6 of Tables 2 and 3. The data for breast feeding are highly irregular, but there is some suggestion of decrease in this practice over the years.[2] In contrast, self-demand feeding is becoming more common. In both instances the trend is more marked (column 8) in the middle class; in other words, it is they especially who are doing the changing. This fact is reflected even more sharply in column 9 which highlights a noteworthy shift. Here we see that in the earlier period—roughly before the end of World War II—both breast feeding and demand feeding were less common among the middle class than among the working class. In the later period, however, the direction is reversed; it is now the middle-class mother who more often gives her child the breast and feeds him on demand.

Data[3] on duration of breast feeding and on the timing of weaning and bowel training simply confirm, somewhat less reliably, the above general trends. All the figures on timing point to the same generalization. In the earlier period, middle-class mothers were

[2] As indicated below, we believe that these irregularities are largely attributable to the highly selective character of a number of the samples (notably, New Haven I and Palo Alto) and that the downward trend in frequency of breast feeding is probably more reliable than is reflected in the data of Table 2.

[3] These data are cited in the original publication (Bronfenbrenner, 1958).

TABLE 2

FREQUENCY OF BREAST FEEDING

1. Sample	2. Approx. Date of Practice	No. of Cases Reporting			Percentage Breast Fed			9.
		3. Total Sample	4. Middle Class	5. Working Class	6. Total Sample	7. Middle Class	8. Work- ing Class	Difference*
National I	1930	1856	842	1014	80	78	82	—4†
National II	1932	445	201	244	40	29	49	—20†
Chicago I	1939	100	48	52	83	83	83	0
Detroit I	1941	112	59	53	62	54	70	—16
Detroit II	1944	200	70	130	Percentages Not Given			+
Eugene	1946-47	206	84	122	46	40	50	—10
Boston	1947-48	372	198	174	40	43	37	+6
New Haven I	1949-50	222	114	108	80	85	74	+11†
Palo Alto	1950	74	36	38	66	70	63	+7
Upstate New York	1955	1432	594	838	24	27	21	+6†

* Minus sign denotes lower incidence for middle class than for working class.
† Denotes difference significant at 5-percent level of confidence or better.

TABLE 3

SCHEDULED VERSUS SELF-DEMAND FEEDING

1. Sample	2. Approx. Date of Practice	No. of Cases Reporting			Percentage Fed on Demand			9.
		3. Total Sample	4. Middle Class	5. Working Class	6. Total Sample	7. Middle Class	8. Work- ing Class	Difference*
National I	1932	470	208	262	16	7	23	—16†
Chicago I	1939	100	48	52	25	4	44	—40†
Detroit I	1941	297	52	45	21	12	53	—41†
Detroit II	1944	205	73	132	55	51	58	—7
Boston	1947-48	372	198	174	Percentages Not Given			—
New Haven I	1949-50	191	117	74	65	71	54	+17
Palo Alto	1950	74	36	38	59	64	55	+9

* Minus sign denotes lower incidence of self-demand feeding in middle class.
† Denotes difference significant at 5-percent level of confidence or better.

exerting more pressure; they weaned their children from the breast and bottle and carried out bowel and bladder training before their working-class counterparts. But in the last ten years the trend has been reversed— it is now the middle-class mother who trains later.

These consistent trends take on richer significance in the light of Wolfenstein's impressive analysis (1953) of the content of successive editions of the United States Children's Bureau bulletin on *Infant Care*.[4] She describes the period 1929-38 (which corresponds to the earlier time span covered by our data) as characterized by:

> . . . a pervasive emphasis on regularity, doing everything by the clock. Weaning and introduction of solid foods are to be

[4] Similar conclusions were drawn in an earlier report by Stendler surveying 60 years of child-training practices as advocated in three popular women's magazines. (Stendler, 1950.)

accomplished with great firmness, never yielding for a moment to the baby's resistance. . . . bowel training . . . must be carried out with great determination as early as possible . . . The main danger which the baby presented at this time was that of dominating the parents. Successful child training meant winning out against the child in the struggle for domination.

In the succeeding period, however,

. . . all this was changed. The child became remarkably harmless . . . His main active aim was to explore his world . . . When not engaged in exploratory undertakings, the baby needs care and attention; and giving these when he demands them, far from making him a tyrant, will make him less demanding later on. At this time mildness is advocated in all areas: thumbsucking and masturbation are not to be interfered with; weaning and toilet training are to be accomplished later and more gently. (Wolfenstein, 1953, p. 121)

The parallelism between preachment and practice is apparent also in the use of breast feeding. Up until 1945, "breast feeding was emphatically recommended," with "warnings against early weaning." By 1951, "the long-term intransigence about breast feeding is relaxed." States the bulletin edition of that year: "Mothers who find bottle feeding easier should feel comfortable about doing it that way."

One more link in the chain of information completes the story. There is ample evidence that, both in the early and the later period, middle-class mothers were much more likely than working-class mothers to be exposed to current information on child care. Thus Anderson cites table after table showing that parents from higher SES levels read more books, pamphlets, and magazines, and listen to more radio talks on child care and related subjects. This in 1932. Similarly, in the last five years, White, in California, and Boek, in New York, report that middle-class mothers are much more likely

than those in the working class to read Spock's best-seller, *Baby and Child Care* (1957) and similar publications.

Our analyses suggest that the mothers not only read the books but take them seriously, and that their treatment of the child is affected accordingly. Moreover, middle-class mothers not only read more but are also more responsive; they alter their behavior earlier and faster than their working-class counterparts.

In view of the remarkably close parallelism in changes over time revealed by Wolfenstein's analysis and our own, we should perhaps not overlook a more recent trend clearly indicated in Wolfenstein's report and vaguely discernible as well in the data we have assembled. Wolfenstein asserts that, since 1950, a conservative note has crept into the child-training literature; "there is an attempt to continue . . . mildness, but not without some conflicts and misgivings . . . May not continued gratification lead to addiction and increasingly intensified demands?" (Wolfenstein, 1953, p. 121). In this connection it is perhaps no mere coincidence that the difference in the last column of Table 2 shows a slight drop after about 1950); the middle class is still more "relaxed" than the working class, but the differences are not so large as earlier. Once again, practice may be following preachment—now in the direction of introducing more limits and demands—still within a permissive framework. We shall return to a consideration of this possibility in our discussion of class differences in the training of children beyond two years of age.

Taken as a whole, the correspondence between Wolfenstein's data and our own suggests a general hypothesis extending beyond the confines of social class as such: *child-rearing practices are likely to change most quickly in those segments of society which have closest access and are most receptive to the agencies or agents of change (e.g., public media, clinics, physicians, and counselors)*. From this point of view, one additional trend suggested by the available data is

TABLE 4

Permissiveness toward Impulse Expression

Sample	Approx. Date of Practice	No. of Cases Reported	Direction of Trend for Middle Class			
			Oral Behavior	Toilet Accidents	Sex	Aggression
National I	1932	470			More infants allowed to play on bed unclothed.*	
Chicago	1943	100		Treated by ignoring,* reasoning or talking, rather than slapping,* scolding, or showing disgust.*		More children allowed to "fight so long as they don't hurt each other badly." *
Detroit II	1946	70-88	Less often disciplined for thumb sucking.		Less often discipline. for touching sex organs.	
New Haven	1949-50	216	Less often disapproved for thumb sucking, eating habits, mannerisms, etc.*			
Eugene	1950	206		Less often treated by spanking or scolding	More permissive toward child's sexual behavior.*	Fewer children allowed "to fight so long as they don't hurt each other badly." More permissiveness toward general aggression.
Boston	1951-52	372	Less restriction on use of fingers for eating.*	Less severe toilet training.*	Higher sex permissiveness (general index).*	More permissive of aggression toward parents,* children† and siblings. Less punishment of aggression toward parents.*
Palo Alto	1953	73		Less severe toilet training.*		More permissive of aggression toward parents.* Less severe punishment of aggression toward parents.

* Indicates difference between classes significant at the 5-percent level or better.
† The difference between percentages is not significant but the difference between ratings is significant at the 5-percent level or better.

worthy of note: rural families appear to "lag behind the times" somewhat in their practices of infant care. For example, in Anderson's beautifully detailed report, there is evidence that in 1932 farm families (Class IV in his sample) were still breast feeding their children more frequently but being less flexible in scheduling and toilet training than nonfarm families of roughly comparable socioeconomic status. Similarly, there are indications from Miller and Swanson's second Detroit study that, with SES held constant, mothers with parents of rural background adhere to more rigid techniques of socialization than their urban counterparts. Finally, the two samples in our data

most likely to contain a relatively high proportion of rural families—Eugene, Oregon, and Upstate New York—are also the ones which are slightly out of line in showing smaller differences in favor of middle-class permissiveness.

In general, our findings point to the conclusion that American mothers—especially in the middle class—are becoming increasingly permissive in their feeding and toilet-training practices during the first two years of the child's life. The question remains whether this tendency is equally apparent in the training of the child as he becomes older. We turn next to a consideration of this issue.

TABLE 5
Restriction on Freedom of Movement

Sample	Approx. Date of Practice	No. of Cases Reported	Age	Item	Direction of Relationship*
National II	1932	2289	1-5	Play restricted to home yard	—
				Play restricted to block	+
				Play restricted to neighborhood	+†
				No restriction on place of play	+†
National III	1932	669	6-12	Child goes to movie with parents	+
				Child goes to movie with other children	+
National IV	1932	2414	1-12	Child goes to bed earlier	+
Chicago	1943	100	5	Age at which child is allowed to go to movie alone or with other children	+†
				Age at which child is allowed to go downtown	—†
				Time at which children are expected in at night	+†
New Haven I	1949-50	211	1	Definite bed time	—†
Boston	1951-52	372	5	Restriction on how far child may go from home	—
				Frequency of checking on child's whereabouts	—**
				Strictness about bed time	—†
				Amount of care taken by persons other than parents	—†
Detroit II	1953	136	0-18	Child supervised closely after 12 years of age	—†
Palo Alto	1953	74	2½-5½	Extent of keeping track of child	0

* Plus sign denotes greater restriction for middle class.
† Denotes difference significant at 5-percent level or better.
** The difference between percentages is not significant but the difference between mean ratings is significant at the 5-percent level or better.

V. Class Differences in the Training of Children beyond the Age of Two

Once we leave the stage of infancy, data from different studies of child training become even more difficult to compare. There are still greater variations in the questions asked from one research to the next, and results are reported in different types of units.

Such considerations combine to restrict severely our ability to identify changes in practices over time. Accordingly, the absence of evidence for such changes in some of the data is perhaps more properly attributed to the limitations of our measures than to the actual course of events.

PERMISSIVENESS AND RESTRICTION OF FREEDOM OF MOVEMENT

The areas of impulse expression documented in Table 4 reflect a continuity in treatment from babyhood into early childhood. With only one minor, statistically insignificant exception, the results depict the middle-class parent as more permissive in all four spheres of activity: oral behavior, toilet accidents, sex, and aggression. There is no suggestion of a shift over the somewhat truncated time span. The now-familiar trend reappears, however, in the data on restriction of freedom of movement shown in Table 5.

In Table 5 we see a gradual shift over time with the middle class being more restrictive in the 1930's and early 1940's but becoming more permissive during the last decade.

TRAINING FOR INDEPENDENCE AND ACHIEVEMENT

Thus far, the trends that have appeared point predominantly in one direction—

increasing leniency on the part of middle-class parents. At the same time, careful consideration of the nature of these data reveals that they are, in a sense, one-sided: they have been concerned almost entirely with the parents' response to the expressed needs and wishes of the child. What about the child's response to the needs and wishes of the parent, and the nature of these parental demands? The results[5] are of especial interest since they shed light on all three aspects of the problem. What is more, they signal a dramatic departure from the hitherto unchallenged trend toward permissiveness.

It is important to distinguish between two types of questions that have been asked with respect to independence training. The first is of the kind we have been dealing with thus far; for example, the Boston investigators inquired about the mother's reaction to the child's expression of dependence (hanging on to the mother's skirt, demanding attention, etc.). The results for this sort of query are consistent with previous findings for the postwar period; middle-class mothers are more tolerant of the child's expressed needs than are working-class mothers. The second type of question deals with the mother's expectations for the child.

Here the previously consistent trend reverses itself. By and large, the middle-class mother expects more of her child than her working-class counterpart. This tendency is especially pronounced in the area of parental aspirations for the child's academic progress. In ten out of eleven studies, middle-class mothers exacted significantly higher expectations than lower-class mothers. The only exception to the highly reliable trend is in itself noteworthy. In the Boston study, more middle-class mothers expected their children to go to college, but they were less likely to say that it was important for their child to do well in school. Are these mothers merely giving what they consider to be the socially acceptable response, or do they really, as Sears and his colleagues sug-

[5] Presented in full in the original publication (Bronfenbrenner, 1958).

gest, have less cause for concern because their children are living up to expectations?

The preceding question raises an even broader and more significant issue. Our data indicate that middle-class parents are becoming increasingly permissive in response to the child's expressed needs and desires. Yet, these same parents have not relaxed their high levels of expectations for ultimate performance. Do we have here a typical instance of Benedict's "discontinuity in cultural conditioning" (Benedict, 1938), with the child first being encouraged in one pattern of response and then expected to perform in a very different fashion? If so, there are days of disappointment ahead for middle-class fathers and mothers. Or, are there other elements in the parent-child relationship of the middle-class family which impel the child to effort despite, or, perhaps, even *because of,* his early experiences of relatively uninhibited gratification? The data on class differences in techniques of discipline shed some light on this question.

TECHNIQUES OF DISCIPLINE

The most consistent finding documented in Table 6 is the more frequent use of physical punishment by working-class parents. The middle class, in contrast, resort to reasoning, isolation, and what Sears and his colleagues have referred to as "love-oriented" discipline techniques. These are methods which rely for their effect on the child's fear of loss of love. Miller and Swanson referred to substantially the same class of phenomena by the term "psychological discipline," which for them covers such parental behaviors as appeals to guilt, expressions of disappointment, and the use of symbolic rather than direct rewards and punishments. Table 6 shows all available data on class differences in the use of corporal punishment, reasoning, isolation, and "love-oriented" techniques. Also, in order to minimize the risks involved in wearing theoretical blinders, we have listed in the last column of the table all other significant class differences in techniques of discipline reported in the studies we have examined.

From one point of view, these results highlight once again the more lenient policies and practices of middle-class families. Such parents are, in the first place, more likely to overlook offenses, and when they do punish, they are less likely to ridicule or inflict physical pain. Instead, they reason with the youngster, isolate him, appeal to guilt, show disappointment,—in short, convey in a variety of ways, on the one hand, the kind of behavior that is expected of the child; on the other, the realization that transgression means the interruption of a mutually valued relationship.

These consistent class differences take on added significance in the light of the finding, arrived at independently both by the Boston and Detroit investigators, that "love-oriented" or "psychological" techniques are more effective than other methods for bringing about desired behavior. Indeed, both groups of researchers concluded on the basis of their data that physical punishment for aggression tends to increase rather than decrease aggressive behavior. From the point of view of our interest, these findings mean that middle-class parents, though in one sense more lenient in their discipline techniques, are using methods that are actually more compelling. Moreover, the compelling power of these practices, rather than being reduced, is probably enhanced by the more permissive treatment accorded to middle-class children in the early years of life. The successful use of withdrawal of love as a discipline technique implies the prior existence of a gratifying relationship: the more love present in the first instance, the greater the threat implied in its withdrawal.

In sum, to return to the issue posed in the preceding section, our analysis suggests that middle-class parents are in fact using techniques of discipline which are likely to be effective in evoking the behavior desired in the child. Whether the high levels of expectation held by such parents are actually

TABLE 6

TECHNIQUES OF DISCIPLINE

| Sample | Approx. Date of Practice | No. of Cases Reporting | Age | Direction of Relationship* | | | | Nature of Love-Oriented Technique | Other Significant Trends for Middle Class |
				Physical Punishment	Reasoning	Isolation	Love-Oriented Technique		
National II	1932	1947	1-5	−†					Infractions more often ignored.† More children deprived of pleasure as punishment.
National III	1932	839	6-12			+†			
National IV	1932	3130	1-12		+†				
Chicago I	1943	100	5	+		−	+†	Praise for good behavior.	Soiling child more often ignored,† rather than spanked † or shown disgust.
Detroit I	1950	115	12-14	−†			+†	Mother expresses disappointment or appeals to guilt.	
Detroit II	1950	222	0-19	−			+	Mother uses symbolic rather than direct rewards and punishments.	
Eugene	1950	206	0-18	−	0	+†			
Boston	1951-52	372	5	−†	+	+	0	No difference in over-all use of praise or withdrawal of love.	Less use of ridicule,† deprivation of privileges** or praise for no trouble at the table.†

* Plus sign indicates practice was more common in middle class than in working class.
† Denotes difference between classes significant at 5-percent level or better.
** The difference between percentages is not significant but the difference between mean ratings is significant at the 5-percent level or better.

achieved is another matter. At least, there would seem to be some measure of functional continuity in the way in which middle-class parents currently treat their children from infancy through childhood.

Before we leave consideration of the data of Table 6, one additional feature of the results deserves comment. In the most recent study reported, the Boston research, there were three departures from the earlier general trend. First, no class difference was found in the over-all use of praise. Second, working-class parents actually exceeded those of the middle class in praising good behavior at the table. Third, in contrast to earlier findings, the working-class mother more frequently punished by withdrawing privileges. Although Sears *et al.* did not classify "withdrawal of privileges" as a love-oriented technique, the shift does represent a change in the direction of what was previously a method characteristic of the middle-class parent. Finally, there is no clear trend in the differential use of love-oriented techniques by the two social classes. If we view the Boston study as reflecting the most recent trends in methods of discipline, then either middle-class mothers are beginning to make less use of techniques they previously relied upon, or the working class is starting to adopt them. We are inclined toward the latter hypothesis in the belief that the working class, as a function of increasing income and education, is gradually reducing its "cultural lag." Evidence from subsequent studies, of course, would be necessary to confirm this speculative interpretation, since the results cited may merely be a function of features peculiar to the Boston study and not typical of the general trend.

OVER-ALL CHARACTER OF THE PARENT-CHILD RELATIONSHIP

The material considered so far has focused on specific practices employed by the parent. A number of researches document class differences as well in variables of a more molar sort—for example, the emotional quality of the parent-child relationship as a whole.

The results of these studies[6] are noteworthy in a number of respects. First, we have clear confirmation that, over the entire 25-year period, middle-class parents have had a more acceptant, equalitarian relationship with their children. In many ways, the contrast is epitomized in Duvall's distinction between the "developmental" and "traditional" conceptions of mother and child. Duvall (1946-1947) asked the mother in her sample to list the "five things that a good mother does" and the "five things that a good child does." Middle-class mothers tended to emphasize such themes as "guiding and understanding," "relating herself lovingly to the child," and making sure that he "is happy and contented," "shares and cooperates with others," and "is eager to learn." In contrast, working-class mothers stressed the importance of keeping house and child "neat and clean," "training the child to regularity," and getting the child "to obey and respect adults."

What is more, this polarity in the value orientation of the two social classes appears to have endured. In data secured, Kohn (1957) reports that working-class mothers differ from those of the middle class in their choice of characteristics most desired in a child; the former emphasize "neatness, cleanliness, and obedience," while the latter stress "happiness, considerateness, and self-control."

Yet, once again, it would be a mistake to conclude that the middle-class parent is exerting less pressure on his children. Thus, the data show that a higher percentage of middle-class children are punished in some manner, and there is more "necessary" discipline to prevent injury or danger. In addition, though the middle-class father typically has a warmer relationship with the child, he is also likely to have more authority and status in family affairs.

Although shifts over time are difficult to

[6] Presented in detail in the original publication (Bronfenbrenner, 1958).

appraise when the data are so variable in specific content, one trend is sufficiently salient to deserve comment. In the early Berkeley data the working-class parent is more expressive of affection than his middle-class counterpart. But in the follow-up study of the same children eight years later the trend is reversed. Perhaps the same mothers behave differently toward younger and older children. Still, the item "Baby picked up when cries" yields a significant difference in favor of the working-class mother in 1932 and a reliable shift in the opposite direction in 1953. *Sic transit gloria Watsoniensis!*

Especially in studies of this kind, one must be concerned with the possibility that the data document primarily not actual behavior but the middle-class mother's superior knowledge of the socially acceptable response. Undoubtedly, this factor operates to inflate the reported relationships. But there are several reassuring considerations. First, although the items investigated vary widely in the intensity of their value connotations, all show substantially the same trends. Second, four of the studies reported are based not on the mother's responses to an interview but on observation of actual interaction among family members. It seems highly unlikely, therefore, that the conclusions we have reached apply only to professed opinions and not to real behavior as well.

VI. Retrospect and Prospect

It is interesting to compare the results of our analysis with the traditional view of the differences between the middle- and lower-class' styles of life, as documented in the classic descriptions of Warner (1942; 1949), Davis (1941), Dollard (1937), and the more recent accounts of Spinley (1953), Clausen (1957), and Miller and Swanson (1958). In all these sources the working class is typically characterized as impulsive and uninhibited, the middle class as more rational, controlled, and guided by a broader perspective in time. Thus Clausen writes:

The lower class pattern of life . . . puts a high premium on physical gratification, on free expression of aggression, on spending and sharing. Cleanliness, respect for property, sexual control, educational achievement—all are highly valued by middle class Americans—are of less importance to the lower class family or are phrased differently. (1957, p. 42)

To the extent that our data even approach this picture, it is for the period before World War II rather than for the present day. The modern middle class has, if anything, extended its time perspective so that the tasks of child training are now accomplished on a more leisurely schedule. As for the lower class the fit is far better for the actual behavior of parents rather than for the values they seek to instill in their children. As reflected in the data of Table 6, the lower-class parent—though he demands compliance and control in his child—is himself more aggressive, expressive, and impulsive than his middle-class counterpart. Even so, the picture is a far cry from the traditional image of the casual and carefree lower class. Perhaps the classic portrait is yet to be seen along the skid rows and Tobacco Roads of the nation, but these do not lie among the well-trodden paths of the survey researcher. He is busy ringing doorbells, no less, in the main section of the lower-class district, where most of the husbands have steady jobs and, what is more important, the wife is willing to answer the door and the interviewer's questions. In this modern working-class world there may be greater freedom of emotional expression, but there is no laxity or vagueness with respect to goals of child training. Consistently over the past 25 years, the parent in this group has emphasized what are usually regarded as the traditional middle-class virtues of cleanliness, conformity, and control, and although his methods are not so effective as those of his middle-class neighbors, they are perhaps more desperate.

Perhaps this very desperation, enhanced by early exposure to impulse and aggression, leads working-class parents to pursue new goals with old techniques of discipline. While accepting middle-class levels of aspiration he has not yet internalized sufficiently the modes of response which make these standards readily achievable for himself or his children. He has still to learn to wait, to explain, and to give and withhold his affection as the reward and price of performance.

As of 1957, there are suggestions that the cultural gap may be narrowing. Spock has joined the Bible on the working-class shelf. If we wish to see the shape of the future, we can perhaps do no better than to look at the pages of the newly revised edition of this ubiquitous guidebook. Here is a typical example of the new look—a passage not found in the earlier version:

> If the parent can determine in which respects she may be too permissive and can firm up her discipline, she may, if she is on the right track, be delighted to find that her child becomes not only better behaved but much happier. Then she can really love him better, and he in turn responds to this. (1957, p. 326)

Apparently "love" and "limits" are both watchwords for the coming generation of parents. As Mrs. Johnson, down in the flats, puts away the hairbrush and decides to have a talk with her unruly youngster "like the book says," Mrs. Thomas, on the hill, is dutifully striving to overcome her guilt at the thought of giving John the punishment she now admits he deserves. If both ladies are successful, the social scientist may eventually have to look elsewhere in his search for everlarger F's and t's.

Such speculations carry us beyond the territory yet surveyed by the social scientist. Perhaps the most important implication for the future from our present analysis lies in the sphere of method rather than substance. Our attempt to compare the work of a score of investigators over a score of years will have been worth the labor if it but convinces future researchers of the wastefulness of such uncoordinated efforts. Our best hope for an understanding of the differences in child rearing in various segments of our society and the effects of these differences on personality formation lies in the development of a systematic long-range plan for gathering comparable data at regular intervals on large samples of families at different positions in the social structure. We now have survey organizations with the scientific competence and adequate technical facilities to perform the task. With such hopes in mind, the author looks ahead to the day when the present analysis becomes obsolete, in method as well as substance.

References

ANDERSON, H. E. (Chairman). *The young child in the home.* Report of the Committee on the Infant and Preschool Child, White House Conference on Child Health and Protection. New York: Appleton-Century-Crofts, 1936.

BALDWIN, A. L., KALHORN, J., and BREESE, F. H. Patterns of parent behavior. *Psychol. Monogr.*, 1945, 57, No. 3 (Whole No. 268).

BAYLEY, N., and SCHAEFER, E. S. Relationships between socioeconomic variables and the behavior of mothers toward young children. Unpublished manuscript, 1957.

BENEDICT, R. Continuities and discontinuities in cultural conditioning. *Psychiat.*, 1938, *1*, 161-167.

BOEK, W. E., LAWSON, E. D., YANKHAUSER, A., and SUSSMAN, M. B. *Social class, maternal health, and child care.* Albany: New York State Department of Health, 1957.

BRONFENBRENNER, U. *Socialization and social class through time and space.* In E. E. Maccoby, T. M. Newcomb, and E. L. Hartley (Eds.), *Readings in social psychology*, 3d Ed. New York: Holt, Rinehart and Winston, 1958.

CLAUSEN, J. A. Social and psychological

factors in narcotics addiction. *Law and Contemporary Problems*, 1957, *22*, 34-51.

DAVIS, A., GARDNER, B. B., and GARDNER, M. R. *Deep south*. Chicago: University of Chicago Press, 1941.

DAVIS, A., and HAVIGHURST, R. J. Social class and color differences in child rearing. *Amer. Sociol. Rev.*, 1948, *11*, 698-710.

DOLLARD, J. *Caste and class in a southern town*. New Haven: Yale University Press, 1937.

DUVALL, E. M. Conceptions of parenthood. *Amer. J. Sociol.*, 1946-1947, *52*, 190-192.

HAVIGHURST, R. J., and DAVIS, A. A comparison of the Chicago and Harvard studies of social class differences in child rearing. *Amer. Sociol. Rev.*, 1955, *20*, 438-442.

KLATSKIN, E. H. Shifts in child care practices in three social classes under an infant care program of flexible methodology. *Amer. J. Orthopsychiat.*, 1952, *22*, 52-61.

KOHN, M. L. Social class and parental values. Paper read at the annual meeting of the American Sociological Society, Washington, D.C., Aug. 27-29, 1957.

LITTMAN, R. A., MOORE, R. A., and PIERCE-JONES, J. Social class differences in child rearing: a third community for comparison with Chicago and Newton, Massachusetts. *Amer. Sociol. Rev.*, 1957, *22*, 694-704.

McCLELLAND, D. C., RINDLISBACHER, A., and DeCHARMS, R. Religious and other sources of parental attitudes toward independence training. In D. C. McClelland (Ed.), *Studies in motivation*. New York: Appleton-Century-Crofts, 1955.

MACCOBY, E. E., GIBBS, P. K., and the staff of the Laboratory of Human Development at Harvard University. Methods of child rearing in two social classes. In W. E. Martin and C. B. Standler (Eds.), *Readings in child development*. New York: Harcourt, Brace & World, 1954.

MILLER, D. R., and SWANSON, G. E. *Inner conflict and defense*. New York: Holt, Rinehart and Winston, 1960.

MILLER, D. R., and SWANSON, G. E. *The changing American parent*. New York: Wiley, 1958.

SEARS, R. R., MACCOBY, E. E., and LEVIN, H. *Patterns of child rearing*. New York: Harper & Row, 1957.

SPINLEY, B. M. *The deprived and the privileged: personality development in English society*. London: Routledge & Kegan Paul, 1953.

SPOCK, B. *Baby and child care*. New York: Pocket Books, 1957.

STENDLER, C. B. Sixty years of child training practices. *J. Pediatrics*, 1950, *36*, 122-134.

STRODTBECK, F. L. Family interaction, values, and achievement. In A. L. Baldwin, U. Bronfenbrenner, D. C. McClelland, and F. L. Strodtbeck, *Talent and society*. Princeton, N.J.: D. Van Nostrand Co., 1958.

WARNER, W. L., and LUNT, P. S. *The social life of a modern community*. New Haven: Yale University Press, 1942.

WARNER, W. L., MEEKER, M., and others. *Social class in America*. Chicago: Science Research Associates, 1949.

WHITE, M. S. Social class, child rearing practices, and child behavior. *Amer. Sociol. Rev.*, 1957, *22*, 704-712.

WOLFENSTEIN, M. Trends in infant care. *Amer. J. Orthopsychiat.*, 1953, *23*, 120-130.

Social Stratification and ❄ August B. Hollingshead
Psychiatric Disorders ❄ Frederick C. Redlich

The research reported here grew out of the work of a number of men, who, during the last half century, have demonstrated that the social environment in which individuals live is connected in some way, as yet not fully explained, to the development of mental illness (Rosanoff, 1916; Stern, 1913; Sutherland, 1901; etc.). Medical men have approached this problem largely from the viewpoint of epidemiology (Braatoy, 1937; Gerard and Siegel, 1950; Hyde and Kingsley, 1944; etc.). Sociologists, on the other hand, have analyzed the question in terms of ecology (Faris and Dunham, 1939; Dunham, 1947; Felix and Bowers, 1948; etc.) and of social disorganization (Faris, 1934; 1944). Neither psychiatrists nor sociologists have carried on extensive research into the specific question we are concerned with, namely, interrelations between the class structure and the development of mental illness. However, a few sociologists and psychiatrists have written speculative and research papers in this area.[1]

The present research, therefore, was designed to discover whether a relationship does or does not exist between the class system of our society and mental illnesses. Five general hypotheses were formulated in our research plan to test some dimension of an assumed relationship between the two. These hypotheses were stated positively; they could just as easily have been expressed either negatively or conditionally. They were phrased as follows:

I. The *expectancy* of a psychiatric disorder is related significantly to an individual's position in the class structure of his society.

II. The *types* of psychiatric disorders are connected significantly to the class structure.

III. The type of *psychiatric treatment* administered is associated with patient's positions in the class structure.

IV. The *psycho-dynamics* of psychiatric disorders are correlative to an individual's position in the class structure.

V. *Mobility* in the class structure is neurotogenic.

Each hypothesis is linked to the others, and all are subsumed under the theoretical assumption of a functional relationship between stratification in society and the prevalence of particular types of mental disorders among given social classes or strata in a specified population. Although our research was planned around these hypotheses, we have been forced by the nature of the problem of mental illness to study *diagnosed* prevalence of psychiatric disorders, rather than *true* or *total* prevalence.

Methodological Procedure

The research is being done by a team of four psychiatrists,[2] two sociologists,[3] and a

---

[1] Extensive bibliographical sources are provided by the authors for the various approaches noted above. The reader is referred to the original publication.

[2] F. C. Redlich, B. H. Roberts, L. Z. Freedman, and Leslie Schaffer.

[3] August B. Hollingshead and J. K. Myers.

From *American Sociological Review*, 1953, 18, 163-167. Reprinted by permission of the authors and the American Sociological Association. The research reported here is supported by a grant from the National Institute of Mental Health of the United States Public Health Service to Yale University under the direction of Dr. F. C. Redlich, Chairman, Deparment of Psychiatry, and Professor August B. Hollingshead, Department of Sociology. Reprinted by permission of the authors and publisher.

clinical psychologist.[4] The data are being assembled in the New Haven urban community, which consists of the city of New Haven and surrounding towns of East Haven, North Haven, West Haven, and Hamden. This community had a population of some 250,000 persons in 1950.[5] The New Haven community was selected because the community's structure has been studied intensively by sociologists over a long period. In addition, it is served by a private psychiatric hospital, three psychiatric clinics, and 27 practicing psychiatrists, as well as the state and Veterans Administration facilities.

Four basic technical operations had to be completed before the hypotheses could be tested. These were: the delineation of the class structure of the community, selection of a cross-sectional control of the community's population, the determination of who was receiving psychiatric care, and the stratification of both the control sample and the psychiatric patients.

August B. Hollingshead and Jerome K. Myers took over the task of delineating the class system. Fortunately, Maurice R. Davie and his students had studied the social structure of the New Haven community in great detail over a long time span (Davie, 1937; Kennedy, 1944; McConnell, 1937; etc.) Thus, we had a large body of data we could draw upon to aid us in blocking out the community's social structure.

The community's social structure is differentiated *vertically* along racial, ethnic, and religious lines; each of these vertical cleavages, in turn, is differentiated *horizontally* by a series of strata or classes. Around the socio-biological axis of race two social worlds have evolved: A Negro world and a white world. The white world is divided by ethnic origin and religion into Catholic, Protestant, and Jewish contingents. Within these divisions there are numerous ethnic

groups. The Irish hold aloof from the Italians, and the Italians move in different circles from the Poles. The Jews maintain a religious and social life separate from the gentiles. The *horizontal* strata that transect each of these vertical divisions are based upon the social values that are attached to occupation, education, place of residence in the community, and associations.

The vertically differentiating factors of race, religion and ethnic origin, when combined with the horizontally differentiating ones of occupation, education, place of residence and so on, produce a social structure that is highly compartmentalized. The integrating factors in this complex are twofold. First, each stratum of each vertical division is similar in its cultural characteristics to the corresponding stratum in the other divisions. Second, the cultural pattern for each stratum or class was set by the "Old Yankee" core group. This core group provided the master cultural mold that has shaped the status system of each sub-group in the community. In short, the social structure of the New Haven community is a parallel class structure within the limits of race, ethnic origin, and religion.

This fact enabled us to stratify the community, for our purposes, with an *Index of Social Position*.[6] This *Index* utilizes three scaled factors to determine an individual's class position within the community's stratificational system: ecological area of residence, occupation, and education. Ecological area of residence is measured by a six point scale; occupation and education are each measured by a seven point scale. To obtain a social class score on an individual we must therefore know his address, his occupation, and the number of years of school he has completed. Each of these factors is given a scale score, and the scale score is multiplied by a factor weight determined by a standard regression equation. The factor weights are as follows: Ecological area of

---

[4] Harvey A. Robinson.
[5] The population of each component was as follows: New Haven, 164,443; East Haven, 12,-212; North Haven, 9,444; West Haven, 32,010; Hamden, 29,715; and Woodbridge, 2,822.

[6] A detailed statement of the procedures used to develop and validate this Index is described in Hollingshead and Redlich (1958).

residence, 5; occupation, 8; and education, 6. The three factor scores are summed, and the resultant score is taken as an index of this individual's position in the community's social class system.

This *Index* enabled us to delineate five main social class strata within the horizontal dimension of the social structure. These principal strata or classes may be characterized as follows:

Class I. This stratum is composed of wealthy families whose wealth is often inherited and whose heads are leaders in the community's business and professional pursuits. Its members live in those areas of the community generally regarded as "the best"; the adults are college graduates, usually from famous private institutions, and almost all gentile families are listed in the New Haven *Social Directory*, but few Jewish families are listed. In brief, these people occupy positions of high social prestige.

Class II. Adults in this stratum are almost all college graduates; the males occupy high managerial positions, many are engaged in the lesser ranking professions. These families are well-to-do, but there is no substantial inherited or acquired wealth. Its members live in the "better" residential areas; about one-half of these families belong to lesser ranking private clubs, but only 5 per cent of Class II families are listed in the New Haven *Social Directory*.

Class III. This stratum includes the vast majority of small proprietors, white-collar office and sales workers, and a considerable number of skilled manual workers. Adults are predominately high school graduates, but a considerable percentage have attended business schools and small colleges for a year or two. They live in "good" residential areas; less than 5 per cent belong to private clubs, but they are not included in the *Social Directory*. Their social life tends to be concentrated in the family, the church, and the lodge.

Class IV. This stratum consists predominately of semi-skilled factory workers. Its adult members have finished the elementary grades, but the older people have not completed high school. However, adults under thirty-five have generally graduated from high school. Its members comprise almost one-half of the community; and their residences are scattered over wide areas. Social life is centered in the family, the neighborhood, the labor union, and public places.

Class V. Occupationally, Class V adults are overwhelmingly semi-skilled factory hands and unskilled laborers. Educationally most adults have not completed the elementary grades. The families are concentrated in the "tenement" and "cold-water flat" areas of New Haven. Only a small minority belong to organized community institutions. Their social life takes place in the family flat, on the street, or in neighborhood social agencies.

The second major technical operation in this research was the enumeration of psychiatric patients. A Psychiatric Census was taken to discover the number and kinds of psychiatric patients in the community. Enumeration was limited to residents of the community who were patients of a psychiatrist or a psychiatric clinic, or were in a psychiatric instituton on December 1, 1950. To make reasonably certain that all patients were included in the enumeration, the research team gathered data from all public and private psychiatric institutions and clinics in Connecticut and nearby states, and all private practitioners in Connecticut and the metropolitan New York area. It received the cooperation of all clinics and institutions, and of all practitioners except a small number in New York City. It can be reasonably assumed that we have data comprising at least 98 per cent of all individuals who were receiving psychiatric care on December 1, 1950.

Forty-four pertinent items of information were gathered on each patient and placed on a schedule. The psychiatrists gathered material regarding symptomatology and diagnosis, onset of illness and duration, referral to the practitioner and the institution, and the nature and intensity of treatment. The sociologists obtained information on age, sex, occupation, education, religion, race and ethnicity, family history, marital experiences, and so on.

The third technical research operation was the selection of a control sample from the normal population of the community. The sociologists drew a 5 per cent random sample of households in the community from the 1951 New Haven *City Directory*. This directory covers the entire communal area. The names and addresses in it were compiled in October and November, 1950— a period very close to the date of the Psychiatric Census. Therefore there was comparability of residence and date of registry between the two population groups. Each household drawn in the sample was interviewed, and data on the age, sex, occupation, education, religion, and income of family members, as well as other items necessary for our purposes were placed on a schedule. This sample is our Control Population.

Our fourth basic operation was the stratification of the psychiatrc patients and of the control population with the *Index of Social Position*. As soon as these tasks were completed, the schedules from the Psychiatric Census and the 5 per cent Control Sample were edited and coded, and their data were placed on Hollerith cards. The analysis of these data is in process.

Selected Findings

Before we discuss our findings relative to Hypothesis I, we want to reemphasize that our study is concerned with *diagnosed* or *treated* prevalence rather than *true* or *total* prevalence. Our Psychiatric Census included only psychiatric cases under treatment, diagnostic study, or care. It did not include individuals with psychiatric disorders who were not being treated on December 1, 1950, by a psychiatrist. There are undoubtedly many individuals in the community with psychiatric problems who escaped our net. If we had *true* prevalence figures, many findings from our present study would

be more meaningful, perhaps some of our interpretations would be changed, but at present we must limit ourselves to the data we have.

Hypothesis I, as revised by the nature of the problem, stated: *The diagnosed prevalence of psychiatric disorders is related significantly to an individual's position* in the class structure. A test of this hypothesis involves a comparison of the normal population with the psychiatric population. If no significant difference between the distribution of the normal population and the psychiatric patient population by social class is found, Hypothesis I may be abandoned as unproved. However, if a significant difference is found between the two populations by class, Hypothesis I should be entertained until more conclusive data are assembled. Pertinent data for a limited test of Hypothesis I are presented in Table 1. The data included show the number of individuals in the normal population and the psychiatric population, by class level. What we are concerned with in this test is how these two populations are distributed by class.

TABLE 1

DISTRIBUTION OF NORMAL AND PSYCHIATRIC POPULATION BY SOCIAL CLASS

Social Class	Normal Population*		Psychiatric Population	
	Number	Per Cent	Number	Per Cent
I	358	3.1	19	1.0
II	926	8.1	131	6.7
III	2500	22.0	260	13.2
IV	5256	46.0	758	38.6
V	2037	17.8	723	36.8
Unknown†	345	3.0	72	3.7
Total	11,422	100.0	1,963	100.0

Chi square = 408.16, P less than .001.
* These figures are preliminary. They do not include Yale students, transients, institutionalized persons, and refusals.
† The unknown cases were not used in the calculation of chi square. They are individuals drawn in the sample, and psychiatric cases whose class level could not be determined because of paucity of data.

When we tested the reliability of these population distributions by the use of the chi square method, we found a *very significant* relation between social class and treated prevalence of psychiatric disorders and in the New Haven community. A comparison of the percentage distribution of each population by class readily indicates the direction of the class concentration of psychiatric cases. For example, Class I contains 3.1 per cent of the community's population but only 1.0 per cent of the psychiatric cases. Class V, on the other hand, includes 17.8 per cent of the community's population, but contributed 36.8 per cent of the psychiatric patients. On the basis of our data Hypothesis I clearly should be accepted as tenable.

Hypothesis II postulated a significant connection between the *type* of psychiatric disorder and social class. This hypothesis involves a test of the idea that there may be a functional relationship between an individual's position in the class system and the type of psychiatric disorder that he may present. This hypothesis depends, in part, on the question of diagnosis. Our psychiatrists based their diagnoses on the classificatory system developed by the Veterans Administration (1947). For the purposes of this paper, all cases are grouped into two categories: the neuroses and the psychoses. The results of this grouping by social class are given in Table 2.

TABLE 2

DISTRIBUTION OF NEUROSES AND PSYCHOSES
BY SOCIAL CLASS

Social Class	Neuroses		Psychoses	
	Number	Per Cent	Number	Per Cent
I	10	52.6	9	47.4
II	88	67.2	43	32.8
III	115	44.2	145	55.8
IV	175	23.1	583	76.9
V	61	8.4	662	91.6
Total	449		1,442	

Chi square = 296.45, P less than .001.

A study of Table 2 will show that the neuroses are concentrated at the higher levels and the psychoses at the lower end of the class structure. Our team advanced a number of theories to explain the sharp differences between the neuroses and psychoses by social class. One suggestion was that the low percentage of neurotics in the lower classes was a direct reaction to the cost of psychiatric treatment. But as we accumulated a series of case studies, for tests of Hypotheses IV and V, we became skeptical of this simple interpretation. Our detailed case records indicate that the social distance between psychiatrist and patient may be more potent than economic considerations in determining the character of psychiatric intervention. This question therefore requires further research.

The high concentration of psychotics in the lower strata is probably the product of a very unequal distribution of psychotics in the total population. To test this idea, Hollingshead selected schizophrenics for special study. Because of the severity of this disease it is probable that very few schizophrenics fail to receive some kind of psychiatric care. This diagnostic group comprises 44.2 per cent of all patients, and 58.7 per cent of the psychotics, in our study. Ninety-seven and six-tenths per cent of these schizophrenic patients had been hospitalized at one time or another, and 94 per cent were hospitalized at the time of our census. When we classify these patients by social class we find that there is a very significant inverse relationship between social class and schizophrenia.

Hollingshead decided to determine, on the basis of these data, what the probability of the prevalence of schizophrenia by social class might be in the general population. To do this he used a proportional index to learn whether or not there were differentials in the distribution of the general population, as represented in our control sample, and the distribution of schizophrenics by social class. If a social class exhibits the same proportion of schizophrenia as it comprises of the general population, the index for that class is 100. If schizophrenia is disproportionately prevalent in a social class the index is above 100; if schizophrenia is disproportionately low in a social class the index is below 100. The index for each social class appears in the last column of Table 3.

in the lower classes. The same finding applies to organic treatment. Psychotherapy, on the other hand, was concentrated in the higher classes. Within the psychotherapy category there were sharp differences between the types of psychotherapy adminis-

TABLE 3

COMPARISON OF THE DISTRIBUTION OF THE NORMAL POPULATION WITH SCHIZOPHRENICS
BY CLASS, WITH INDEX OF PROBABLE PREVALENCE

| Social Class | Normal Population | | Schizophrenics | | Index of Prevalence |
	No.	Per Cent	No.	Per Cent	
I	358	3.2	6	.7	22
II	926	8.4	23	2.7	33
III	2,500	22.6	83	9.8	43
IV	5,256	47.4	352	41.6	88
V	2,037	18.4	383	45.2	246
Total	11,077	100.0	847	100.0	

The fact that the Index of Prevalence in class I is only one-fifth as great as it would be if schizophrenia were proportionately distributed in this class, and that it is two and one-half times as high in class V as we might expect on the basis of proportional distribution, gives further support to Hypothesis II. The fact that the Index of Prevalence is 11.2 times as great in class V as in class I is particularly impressive.

Hypothesis III stipulated that the type of psychiatric treatment a patient receives is associated with his position in the class structure. A test of this hypothesis involves a comparison of the different types of therapy being used by psychiatrists on patients in the different social classes. We encountered many forms of therapy but they may be grouped under three main types; psychotherapy, organic therapy, and custodial care. The patient population, from the viewpoint of the principal type of therapy received, was divided roughly into three categories: 32.0 per cent received some type of psychotherapy; 31.7 per cent received organic treatments of one kind or another; and 36.3 per cent received custodial care without treatment. The percentage of persons who received no treatment care was greatest

tered to the several classes. For example, psychoanalysis was limited to classes I and II. Patients in class V who received any psychotherapy were treated by group methods in the state hospitals. The number and percentage of patients who received each type of therapy is given in Table 4. The data clearly support Hypothesis III.

At the moment we do not have data available for a test of Hypotheses IV and V. These will be put to a test as soon as we complete work on a series of cases now under close study. Preliminary materials give us the impression that they too will be confirmed.

Conclusions and Interpretations

This study was designed to throw new light upon the question of how mental illness is related to social environment. It approached this prolem from the perspective of social class to determine if an individual's position in the social system was associated significantly with the development of psychiatric disorders. It proceeded on the theoretical assumption that if mental illnesses were distributed randomly in the popula-

TABLE 4

DISTRIBUTION OF THE PRINCIPAL TYPES OF THERAPY BY SOCIAL CLASS

Social Class	Psychotherapy		Organic Therapy		No Treatment	
	Number	Per Cent	Number	Per Cent	Number	Per Cent
I	14	73.7	2	10.5	3	15.8
II	107	81.7	15	11.4	9	6.9
III	136	52.7	74	28.7	48	18.6
IV	237	31.1	288	37.1	242	31.8
V	115	16.1	234	32.7	367	51.2

Chi square = 336.58, P less than .001.

tion, the hypotheses designed to test the idea that psychiatric disorders are connected in some functional way to the class system would not be found to be statistically significant.

The data we have assembled demonstrate conclusively that mental illness, as measured by diagnosed prevalence, is not distributed randomly in the population of the New Haven community. On the contrary, psychiatric difficulties of so serious a nature that they reach the attention of a psychiatrist are unequally distributed among the five social classes. In addition, types of psychiatric disorders, and the ways patients are treated, are strongly associated with social class position.

The statistical tests of our hypotheses indicate that there are definite connections between particular types of social environments in which people live, as measured by the social class concept, and the emergence of particular kinds of psychiatric disorders, as measured by psychiatric diagnosis. They do not tell us what these connections are, nor how they are functionally related to a particular type of mental illness in a given individual. The next step, we believe, is to turn from the strictly statistical approach to an intensive study of the social environments associated with particular social classes, on the one hand, and of individuals in these environments who do or do not develop mental illnesses on the other hand. Currently the research team is engaged in this next step but is not yet ready to make a formal report of its findings.

References

BRAATOY, T. Is it probable that the sociological situation is a factor in schizophrenia? *Psychiatrica et Neurologica,* 1937, *12,* 109-138.

DAVIE, M. R. The pattern of urban growth. Murdock, G. P. (Ed.) in *Studies in the science of society.* New Haven: 1937, 133-162.

DUNHAM, H. W. Current status of ecological research in mental disorder. *Soc. Forces,* 1947, *25,* 321-326.

FARIS, R. E. L. Cultural isolation and the schizophrenic personality. *Amer. J. Sociol.,* 1934, *39,* 155-169.

FARIS, R. E. L. Reflections of social disorganization in the behavior of a schizophrenic patient. *Amer. J. Sociol.,* 1944, *50,* 131-141.

FARIS, R. E. L., and DUNHAM, H. W. *Mental disorders in urban areas.* Chicago: University of Chicago Press, 1939.

FELIX, R. H., and BOWERS, R. V. Mental hygiene and socio-environmental factors. *The Milbank Memorial Fund Quarterly,* 1948, *26,* 125-147.

GERARD, D. L., and SIEGEL, J. The family background of schizophrenia. *Psychiatric Quart.,* 1950, *24,* 47-73.

HOLLINGSHEAD, A. B., and REDLICH, F. C. *Social class and mental illness: a community study.* New York: John Wiley & Sons, 1958.

HYDE, R. W., and KINGSLEY, L. V. Studies in medical sociology, I: The relation of mental disorders to the community socioeconomic level. *The New England J. Medicine*, 1944, *231*, 543-548, No. 16.

KENNEDY, J. R. Single or triple melting-pot: intermarriage trends in New Haven, 1870-1940. *Amer. J. Sociol.*, 1944, 39, 331-339.

McCONNELL, J. W. The influence of occupation upon social stratification. Unpublished Ph.D. thesis, Sterling Memorial Library, Yale University, 1937.

ROSANOFF, A. J. *Report of a survey of mental disorders in Nassau County, New York*. New York: National Committee for Mental Hygiene, 1916.

STERN, L. *Kulturkreis und Form der Geistigen Erkrankung*. Sammlung Zwanglosen Abhandlungen aus dem Gebiete der Nerven-und-Geiteskrankheiten, 10, No. 2. Halle a. S:C. Marhold, 1913, 1-62.

SUTHERLAND, J. F. Geographical distribution of lunacy in Scotland. *Brit. Assoc. for Advancement of Science*. Glasgow, 1901.

VETERANS ADMINISTRATION. *Psychiatric disorders and reactions*. Washington, D.C.: Technical Bulletin 10A-78, October, 1947.

Patterning

of Social

Interaction

PART V

in Groups

and

Organizations

INTRODUCTION

Man's capacity to interact in a meaningful way with other men lies at the foundation of every human society. The primary ingredient of the individual's social environment is the existence of other individuals who act toward him and toward whom he, in turn, reacts. The present discussion is focused primarily on the structure of these interactions or, more concretely, on the human *relationships* which both determine and are determined by the interaction process. It should be evident that these relationships express the group character of much of the person's existence. As we shall see, the individual's group memberships have important consequences for his behavior. Yet, it should be stressed that both the formation and maintenance of all social groups are rooted in the social interactions between individuals.

In our earlier discussion of the role of groups in attitude formation and change, we used the concept "group" in a special sense. It is now important to make this meaning explicit. Most social psychologists use the term to refer to two or more individuals who can be collectively characterized as follows: they share a common set of norms, beliefs, and values and they exist in implicitly or explicitly defined relationships to one another such that the behavior of each has consequences for the others. These properties in turn emerge from and have consequences for the interaction of individuals who are similarly motivated with respect to some specific objective or goal. It should be evident that a family, a gang, a congressional committee, and a local political club are examples of groups meeting these criteria. On the other hand, individuals riding the same bus or people waiting in line to buy a theater ticket do not constitute a group in this sense. In the discussion that follows we shall simply use the term "group" to refer to groups with these properties. However, wherever necessary we shall take note of those studies of groups where the normative and structural aspects of the groups are minimal.

Some groups are functionally related to each other in the pursuit of some super-ordinate objective, and thereby also share to some extent a common ideology. The term "social organization" is used to designate these larger systems of social inter-action, for example, an industrial corporation. Within any social organization we can expect to find both formal and informal groups. Formal groups are usually established by a social organization for specific purposes and with specified structural characteristics, for example, the various committees of the United States Senate. It is also true, however, that within a social organization individuals may spontaneously form stable informal groups to satisfy some common needs, say, for friendship, anxiety reduction, and the like; and quite often these groups may be organized along lines that cut across the formal organizational structure. Informal groups of this kind are no less demanding on the individual despite the fact that their purposes, norms, and structures are very often implicit rather than explicit. Furthermore, within the organizational setting the individual may be subjected by the formal organization to pressures to behave that run counter to what is expected of him by the members of his informal group.

In the introduction to Part III we noted that the norms of a group are the standards against which the behavior and thought of each member can be evaluated as appropriate or inappropriate. Some of these norms specify the behavior expected from all the group members, whereas others apply only to individuals in specific group roles, for example, leader. In either case the norms of any group can be expected to vary in importance. Those that are less relevant to the purposes and values of the group usually allow for a greater range of behavior, and bring less intense pressures for individuals to conform, than do those standards which are highly relevant to the functioning of the group.

How can we account for the emergence of group norms? Festinger (1950) has proposed a number of factors. First, in order for a group to maintain its identity there must be some uniformity in the attitudes and behavior of the members. He also suggests that the achievement of a group's objectives may often depend on the extent to which the activities of its members are coordinated. Norms that determine who does what, and when and how, are important for group achievement. Finally, the norms of a group may provide a basis for "social reality" for its members. Some of the beliefs of a person cannot be validated by objective means or by logical criteria. The truth of these beliefs is established by consensual agreement; the fact that others hold similar beliefs attests to their validity. Norms, then, may often serve as the "facts" that sustain the values and objectives of the group. That norms may evolve in just this sense seems indicated by the now classic study reported by Sherif (VB). Individuals made judgments in a setting where they were unable to determine whether their answers were right or wrong. When the subjects first made their judgments in isolation from each other there was a wide range of individual differences. However, when they later made their judgments in the presence of one another, there was a convergence toward a "group norm." No less significant was the fact that when they again judged in isolation, their final judgments reflected the "norm" established in the previous group situation.

Up to this point we have been talking about group norms as a source of pressures toward uniformity. The members of a group exert direct influence on each other to think and behave in appropriate ways. Yet both the Sherif (VB) and the Asch (VA) investigations suggest that similarities in the responses of individuals may not always be a function of the operation of group norms. The subjects in both studies simply made their judgments in the presence of other subjects (or experimental confederates) without any direct interaction taking place. Relatively speaking, there were no explicitly defined relationships among the subjects nor were they pursuing a common objective. The fact remains, however, that uniformity of response did occur despite the relative lack of these group properties.

The theoretical orientations of Asch (1952) and Festinger (1954) led each of them to suggest that uniformity of response may occur because of one's need for an accurate picture of his external world. Where discrepencies exist between what the individual perceives or thinks and what others perceive or think, then, as Asch puts it, "the 'pull' toward the group becomes understandable" (p. 484). Under these circumstances it is not any direct influence brought to bear by the group members that create the "pull," but rather the conflicts experienced by the person because of these observed discrepancies. It is on this basis that Deutsch and Gerard (VA) distinguish between *normative social influence* and *informational social influence*.

In the Asch (VA) study each subject was required to match the length of a given line with one of three unequal lines in the presence of seven other "subjects." All eight individuals involved were college students except that seven of them were experimental confederates who had been instructed to make the same wrong response at various times in a series of judgments. Thus, the actual subject was presented with a clear conflict between the evidence of his own senses and the responses of a group of his peers. Some three quarters of all the subjects tested (50) showed some errors in their judgments in the direction of the distorted estimates of the majority. However, of the total number of judgments made by all subjects, 68 percent were correct. Finally, a wide range of individual differences was found. One quarter of the subjects showed no distortion at all, but another one third made errors in the direction of the majority in at least half of their trials.

As we noted earlier, the subjects in the Asch experiment were not group members in any obvious way. However, the shifts toward the majority that occurred can probably be attributed both to informational social influences and to normative pressures. Other findings reported by Asch shed light on the factors or conditions that determine the extent to which the individual will conform to others when he experiences cognitive conflict. He will conform more if he is confronted with a unanimity of belief that dissents from his own. He will be less influenced, however, if at least one other person agrees with him and hence he is not alone in his dissent. It was also found that conformity increased with a decrease in the clarity of the stimulus situation to be judged. Finally, the wide range of individual differences found by Asch points to the importance of personality factors.

The study by Deutsch and Gerard (VA) compared the relative effects of normative and informational social influence. With certain modifications and variations these investigators duplicated the Asch situation: each subject made his judgments in a face-to-face situation in the manner of Asch's subjects; other subjects made their judgments without being seen by each other; and, finally, still other subjects also made their judgments privately but as members of a group pursuing a group goal. In general, the results confirm and add to those reported by Asch. They not only demonstrated the tendency to conform when the subject experienced cognitive conflict but also showed that such conformity was greater when the subject made his judgments publicly rather than privately. Furthermore, and perhaps of greater importance, Deutsch and Gerard found greater conformity when the individual was a member of a group than when he was not normatively involved with others.

What determines the extent to which the members of a group can influence each other? We can expect the intensity and effectiveness of normative influences to vary with a host of factors ranging from the unique personality characteristics of the individual to specific properties of the group itself. Cartwright and Zander (1960) single out a number of factors for which there is some degree of empirical support. Important in this respect is the *cohesiveness* of a group, which is generally defined as the degree to which the members are attracted to the group. The more cohesive the group the greater its control over the behavior of its members. Individuals are attracted to a group if it serves (or can serve) as a source of satisfaction for their needs. Although the needs involved may vary from one group member to the next, as long as the group has value for the person in this respect it can exert influence over this thought and action.

Back (VA) varied the strength and nature of group cohesiveness in two-person groups in the laboratory setting. The experimental task required that the two subjects first interpret a set of three pictures independently, then they had to discuss them as a group in order to improve their interpretations, and subsequently, each had to make a final independent interpretation. The nature and extent of cohesiveness were varied by means of appropriate experimental instructions in which the attributes of the group partner, the character of the task, or the prestige of the group was presented so as to create either high or low attractiveness for the group. Back's findings clearly demonstrate greater pressures toward uniformity in the high-cohesive groups. Members of these groups made more effort to reach agreement or to influence each other, and these influence attempts were more effective than those made in the low-cohesive groups. As one might expect, the nature of the interactions between the members of the group varied as a function of the kind of attraction it held for them. For example, where cohesiveness was based on group prestige, the patterns of communication and interaction involved efficient task performance rather than sociable interaction—the latter occurred more in high-cohesive groups where members were attracted to each other.

The study by Festinger, Schachter, and Back (VB), in contrast to the Back investigation, dealt with the relationship between the strength of group norms and the degree of cohesiveness in a field setting involving two housing projects. By means of repeated interviewing the investigators were able to determine the attitudes of the residents toward a tenant organization and the extent of cohesiveness in various courts and buildings in the projects. They found that the residents in the more cohesive courts were more uniform in their attitudes toward the tenant organization and in the extent to which they participated in the organization. If the strength of norms is greater in more cohesive groups one would expect that those who deviate from these norms would experience greater rejection by other group members. Thus it was found that deviants in the high-cohesive courts were less likely to be accepted as friends by others living there than deviants in the low-cohesive courts. A laboratory study by Schachter (1951) also demonstrated stronger rejection of deviants in groups with high cohesiveness.

In addition to the level of cohesiveness of the group, Cartwright and Zander (1960) cite a number of other determinants of the strength and effectiveness of group influences on its members. Thus the salience or importance of the group for the individual will determine how much influence it will have over him. It is also evident that pressures toward uniformity will be stronger if the group members perceive that similar behaviors are required for the group to achieve its goals. Another factor concerns the extent to which members believe that deviation will bring punishment from the group. Greater certainty in this respect will mean a great likelihood of conformity by the group member—at least in his overt responses. By the same token, group members who believe that conformity will result in rewards are more likely to be less resistant to group pressures. Finally, Cartwright and Zander indicate the importance of the self-confidence of the person in determining the extent to which he will be influenced by group pressures. The study by Deutsch and Gerard (VA) revealed that the certainty the person had in the correctness of his judgment determined his susceptibility to both normative and informational influences.

Psychotherapists are the first to admit that changing the basic dispositions of the individual is by no means a simple task. History tells us that the task is no less difficult when it comes to changing the established practices of a group or a community. Of course, group norms do change but not simply or easily. A number of investigations have attempted to determine the conditions under which such changes will occur.

During World War II, Lewin (VA) and his associates attempted to induce housewives to increase their consumption of meats that were in general not preferred, for example, kidneys, sweetbreads, and beef hearts. Two methods for inducing change were employed. Some groups attended lectures on the attractiveness, taste, and preparation of these foods, but in other groups these same topics were discussed by the housewives with the aid of a nutrition expert. At the end of the discussion period, the housewives were asked to indicate by a show of hands whether they intended to serve these meats. In a follow-up of these women, it was found that 32 percent of those in the discussion groups, as compared with 3 percent in the lecture groups, had served one of the three meats. A second investigation comparing the two methods for inducing change confirmed the superiority of the group discussion method.

Although the evidence is clear concerning the efficacy of the group decision method in changing established behavior, the specific factors underlying its superiority are not revealed in the studies by Lewin and his associates. The purpose of the Pelz (VA) investigation was to determine the significance of the following factors, which were systematically varied: group discussion vs. lecture, decision vs. no decision, the degree of public commitment to adopt the recommended behavior, and the degree of actual or perceived consensus to act on the recommendation. Pelz found that the group discussion and public commitments elements involved in making a group decision were not important in determining subsequent behavior. On the other hand, the act of making a decision and the degree of perceived consensus were sufficient to account for the changes brought about by group decision reported by Lewin and his associates.

Innovations in the industrial setting designed to improve worker production may often have just the opposite effect. Anxiety and uncertainty over the new requirements, as well as group pressures to maintain certain standards, lead to considerable resistance to management-initiated changes. On the basis of a preliminary theory, Coch and French (VA) tested certain group methods of reducing the resistance to such change. In general, groups of workers who participated in making decisions about how the changes were to be carried out were compared with other groups who were simply notified that such changes would occur. Those workers participating in the discussions of the changes not only showed a rapid rate of recovery in their production levels immediately following the change, but in many instances increased their production over what it had been before the change. The uninvolved groups showed a sharp decline in their production rate after the change and within the period they were studied never returned to their original level of output.

In certain respects the findings of Coch and French (VA) parallel those of the Western Electric researches reported by Homans (VD). Groups of girls in a wire assembly shop expressed their grievances against management by establishing a standard output rate which was below the expected rate of management. Strong pressures were brought to bear on any girl who exceeded the rate. On the other hand, much higher production rates were found among small groups of girls who were set apart from their co-workers in order to participate in a number of experiments. A steady and continuing increase in output occurred over a whole year which could not be attributed solely to the changes in work procedures. In fact, near the end of the study, for a twelve-week period, the girls were subjected to the original work procedures; yet output rose to a higher point than ever before. As Homans suggests, the involvement of the girls in an experiment which brought them special attention from management, a sense of participation, and a new common purpose undoubtedly contributed to this change. This is not unlike what the workers in the Coch and French study must have experienced in their group discussions of how management's changes could best be carried out.

We pointed out earlier that some norms of the group do not apply to all its members. Individuals often occupy different *positions* in a group (for example, group leader and group member) or in an institutional structure (for example, factory owners and factory workers) so that different sets of standards may apply to each. The expectations shared by the members of a group regarding the pattern of behavior and thought required of a person in a given position constitute the *role* of that position. Failure of the person to meet these expectations brings pressures from the other members for him to conform. It should be stressed that a role always prescribes a person's behavior in relation to other individuals whose own roles prescribe just how they should behave toward him. The several roles of a group are interdependent—each one is defined in terms of its relationship to other roles. The role of teacher, for example, requires that the child be instructed in given ways; the pupil role, in turn, requires that the child listen to and be guided by what the teacher says.

Roles (and role systems) vary in the specificity of their definitions. In a formalized work setting the roles associated with various positions usually involve highly specialized functions that are spelled out in detail. Informal groups are more likely to be characterized by roles that are more general in their definition and that are implicitly rather than explicitly recognized. It is true, however, that regardless of the degree of specificity of a role, its interpretation and therefore the actual *role behavior* exhibited will vary to some degree with the individual occupying its associated position. Role behavior is always determined by personality and situational factors as well as by the specifications of the role. We would expect, however, greater variation in the role behavior of individuals in the same informal role— because it tends to be defined more generally—than in the role behavior of persons in the same formal role.

Individuals occupy positions in the major institutional structures that organize a society—age-sex, family-kinship, occupation, and so on. For each of these positions there is an appropriate role, so that the person has not one but a number of roles that determine his behavior in relation to different individuals in different situations. Some of the roles are determined by who and what he is at birth—sex and social class position are examples—whereas others are achieved by his own efforts, say his occupational status. In any single day an adult male may act in the roles of employee, father, club member, husband, union member, as well as others.

In the introduction to Part III we noted the consequences of social class for the development of the individual with respect to his attitudes, values, interests, self-esteem, and other personality attributes. Obviously the sex role of the person as well as those roles that come later in his life—his occupation is one—are also important determinants of his behavior. Indeed, studies of sex and occupational groups have revealed significant effects resulting from the variations in these roles (Friedman and Havighurst, 1954; Komarovsky, 1946). The relationship between role and personality, however, is clearly a reciprocal one. Role behavior has consequences for personality development, but it is also evident that personality factors will influence in varying degrees many of the person's role behaviors.

It is generally recognized that many of the different roles of the person make inconsistent or contradictory demands on him. The role of adolescent son is in many ways incompatible with the role of adolescent clique member. The aggressive and shrewd practices demanded of the businessman stand in sharp contrast to the role demands made on him as father and churchgoer. Although many other examples could be given, the fact remains that individuals do manage to function skillfully and efficiently in handling what would otherwise seem to be mutually exclusive patterns of thought and action. This is possible for at least two reasons.

First, in many instances individuals are unaware or are only vaguely aware of the contradictions in their behaviors and beliefs. And, second, seldom is the individual directly confronted with these inconsistencies. Each role becomes salient for the person in its relevant group setting, and these settings vary in time and space as well as in the individuals who are involved.

Of course, individuals do experience role conflict. In some instances the individual's position in a social organization involves him in overlapping group memberships. If the role expectations for these groups are in conflict with each other he is confronted with a serious dilemma: meeting the role demands of one may mean that sanctions are invoked against him by the others. The familiar example is the foreman in the industrial setting who at the same time is a representative of management and a member of a work crew.

How are such conflicts resolved? Gross, McEachern, and Mason (VB) tested a theory of role conflict resolution on a random sample of school superintendents in Massachusetts in 1952-1953. Role conflict is inevitable in this position: the superintendent is not only a member of the school board but a member of the faculty. As the study demonstrates, he perceives many other groups and individuals making conflicting demands on him—the union, the chamber of commerce, his friends, the PTA, his wife, to name some. With respect to salary increases, for example, a large majority of the respondents (88 percent) perceived that they were exposed to conflicting demands from these individuals and groups. In support of the theory it was found that such conflicts were resolved by the school superintendents in one of three ways: some, who were "Moralists," primarily evaluated the legitimacy or illegitimacy of the various expectations; others, the "Expedients," gave far greater emphasis to the possible sanctions to be expected if the demands of certain groups were not met; and finally, the "Moral-Expedients" balanced both factors and attempted compromise solutions.

Ordinarily, the multigroup memberships of the individual do not create problems of role conflict for him. In most instances he remains unaware of the "cross-pressures" involved in his various roles since they do not overlap. Under catastrophic conditions, however, the individual may find himself in the unenviable position of having to make a choice among his many group loyalties. As the investigation by Killian (VB) vividly demonstrates, latent role conflicts are suddenly transformed into conscious dilemmas for the person. He must choose, for example, between giving help and comfort to his family and lending assistance to his fellow workers. Killian found that each person attempted to aid the group that was most attractive to him, which was usually either his family or, to a lesser extent, his friendship groups. It would seem that loyalty to primary groups, as one might expect, had the highest priority, but there were exceptions which seemed to be a function of the previous training of the individual and particular situational factors.

A change in the individual's position in a given social setting—and therefore, in his required role—should result in corresponding changes in his attitudes and behavior. A natural field experiment was undertaken by Lieberman (VB) in a factory setting in which some workers were made foremen and others became union stewards. Earlier, all the workers had filled out questionnaires dealing with management and the union. After fifteen months they were readministered to the men who had changed positions and to a matched control group of workers whose positions in the factory had not changed. A comparison of the "before and after" attitudes of these two groups revealed systematic attitude changes in the former but little or no changes in the attitudes of those workers whose status had remained the same. Workers who were promoted to foremen tended to become more favorable to management, whereas those who were made stewards tended to become more favorable to the union; the changes among the foremen, however, were greater than those found among the stewards. Furthermore, when some of these men reverted to their original status as workers, their attitudes tended to change once again in the direction of what they had been originally.

Whenever and wherever groups emerge, the problem of leadership emerges with it. Few problems have commanded as much attention from behavioral scientists, social planners, and responsible officials alike. Their great and continuing concern is understandable. Although other factors in group life must be considered, who leads and how has important consequences for the functioning of a group and, therefore, for the behavior and experience of its members. If various group contexts define and circumscribe the life of the individual, then it follows that in no small measure his social fate lies in the hands of those who exert influence as leaders.

The research literature on leadership reveals two quite different orientations to this problem. By far the older of the two approaches conceives of leadership as a property of the person. For those confronted with the task of selecting leaders the essential problem is one of identifying the characteristics of leaders which distinguished them from nonleaders. A major review by Bird (1940) of the relevant investigations indicates that any number of studies have been undertaken to measure in a variety of situations the physical, social, intellectual, and tempermental traits of those who lead and those who follow. One implication of this approach, of course, is that certain traits or constellation of traits characterizes all leaders. Bird's review makes it quite clear that there is little agreement in this respect in the findings of these studies, and, furthermore, that in many instances the results are contradictory—some leaders are aggressive and other leaders are mild. A later review of research by Stodgill (1950) still reports contradictory findings, although there is fairly good agreement that leaders are superior to nonleaders in socioeconomic status, intelligence, scholarship, dependability and responsibility, and activity and social participation. It is patent, however, that although these minimal attributes may be required of all leaders, they are undoubtedly shared widely by nonleaders as well.

Because of the apparent futility of identifying the universal characteristics of leaders, a new approach has evolved in recent years. Leadership is not a property of persons but rather of groups. Although there are differences in theoretical orientation, the general conception is the same: leadership is conceived of as a set of goal achievement and group maintenance functions that are determined by the internal and external properties of the group. A number of implications follow from this general approach. First, and perhaps most important, it indicates that the traits of a leader necessary for the effective functioning of a group will vary with these properties. Different groups or the same group under two different sets of conditions may require different kinds of leaders and leadership activity. Second, to the extent that any person in the group contributes to achieving the group's goals or its maintenance, he will be involved to that degree in a leadership role. Finally, it also follows from this approach that formal leadership is to be distinguished from functional leadership. Not all officially appointed leaders are necessarily involved in the leadership functions of a group. It is what a person does in a group and not who he is that determines whether he is a leader.

Although the functional approach to leadership characterizes the thinking of many theorists, they clearly differ from each other in what is emphasized as uniquely leadership functions. Cattell (1951) takes a broad approach: any member behavior that moves a group closer to its goals is a leadership function. All members are leaders to a greater or lesser extent. Krech, Crutchfield, and Ballachey (1962), on the other hand, employ the concept of leadership in a more restrictive sense and point to a set of fourteen functions that, depending on the group and its circumstances, may characterize the role of a leader: "Executive," "Planner," "Father Figure," "Policy Maker," "Scapegoat," and so on. Which functions will be emphasized or even appear, as well as the ways in which they will be performed, depends on the internal and external properties of the group. Redl (1942), taking a psychoanalytic point of view, introduces the concept of "central" person and distinguishes ten different kinds of emotional relationships (leadership function) between the central person and other group members. Still other conceptions are evident in the relevant literature.

Actually, many of these conceptions as well as the findings of empirical investigations point to the importance of two basic types of leadership function: *goal achievement* and *group maintenance*. Some activities of the leader or leaders are focused on accomplishing the group's tasks or achieving its objectives—"makes information available," "plans the work," and so on, whereas others are directly concerned with the stability and harmony of the group itself—"reduces member conflict," "gives encouragement," and so on. It should be clear that any number of different behaviors can serve each of these primary functions; in fact, any single behavior can serve both of them. Furthermore, any member of the group can behave in ways that will help the group achieve its goals and/or maintain itself. It should be noted, however, that leadership functions tend to be concentrated in the hands of a few individuals, especially in groups that have been in existence for some time. In his study of small informal discussion groups Bales (1953) found that over time the members elevate to positions of leadership a "task specialist" and a "socio-emotional" specialist. The former moves the group toward the solution of its problem in an aggressive fashion and is usually disliked; the latter resolves group tensions and conflicts within the group and is usually liked a great deal.

Studies of formal groups have also revealed goal achievement and group maintenance functions in the behavior of leaders. Halpin and Winer (1957) studied the leader behavior of air-crew commanders and report that "consideration" (group maintenance) and "initiating and directing" (goal achievement) taken together accounted for 83 percent of the variation in leader behavior. "Consideration" involved leader behavior which indicated respect, mutual trust, and friendship; the "initiating and directing" orientation was associated with leader behavior which defined the members' roles, established organizational patterns, and concentrated on getting the job done. It is important to keep in mind, however, that which of these two basic functions will be emphasized, how they will be expressed, and who will be responsible for them will depend on what the group is, on the point it has reached in its existence, and on the nature of its immediate situation. For example, where conflicts within a group reach a level that threatens its existence, we can expect group maintenance functions to dominate the behavior of its leaders as well as its members. In fact, it is quite likely that under these circumstances new leaders will emerge.

The excerpt reported here from Whyte's (VC) study of street-corner gangs clearly indicates that both group maintenance and goal achievement functions characterized the role of the gang leader. He initiated and directed the group's activities, provided needed material resources, served as the expert, arbitrated the conflicts in the group, and represented the interests of the group to other groups in the community. It is also evident that the particular leadership behaviors and qualities necessary to carry out these functions were determined by the goals of the gang and the setting in which it moved. Not unlike other studies of leadership, we learn from Whyte's study that leadership is not a "one-way street." Group leaders influence the behavior of the members, but at every turn the leader is expected to "measure up" by fulfilling the demands of the leadership role as perceived by the members.

The emergence of leadership in informal groups was also studied by Jennings (VC) by means of Moreno's (1934) sociometric technique. Underprivileged girls at a state training school were asked to choose from among the other girls those they would prefer to be associated with in various activities—in work, in recreation, and so on. The girls in each cottage were classified in terms of their choice scores, and it was found that the "overchosen" girls actually held formal leadership positions in the community. Jennings also gathered personality data on the overchosen girls and interviewed the other girls regarding their reasons for choosing them. Two important findings emerge. First, the girls who were overchosen varied in their "styles" of leadership, thereby suggesting that the different leaders appealed to different patterns of needs and interests in the girls who chose them. Second, evident in the personality descriptions of the leaders and the reasons given by others for choosing them are behaviors or abilities that are important for goal achievement and group maintenance leadership functions.

Both the Whyte and the Jennings studies suggest that who becomes a leader depends on the characteristics of the individual in relation to the needs of the members and the objectives of the group. Here we should take note of the fact that in informal groups there are many other factors that determine whether a person will or will not engage in leadership behavior or become a leader. For example, even if the person has the "right" characteristics for the group, he may be unwilling to lead because he is low in confidence, achievement motivation, or motivation for power (Veroff, 1957). Nor should we overlook the fact that a person is more likely to assume a leadership function when existing leaders, formal or informal, prove to be inadequate (Kahn and Katz, 1960). Still another factor concerns the existing position or role of the person in the group. Those high in the hierarchy or those who feel that what they are already doing in the group is important are usually more willing to engage in leadership activity than those who are of low status or who feel "left out."

There has been considerable discussion over whether leadership responsibility should be in the hands of a few or many group members. Some have argued that concentrated leadership is necessary in order to maximize efficiency and prevent chaos. Others have taken the opposing view and point out that such leadership lowers morale and creates leader-follower conflict. The study by Leavitt (VD) and others by Bavelas (1960) suggest that the concentration of leadership results in both efficient group performance and lower morale. However, Cartwright and Zander (1960) suggest that if these groups had lasted for a longer period of time lower morale might have resulted in reduced efficiency. The original question has also been stated in terms of whether leadership should be democratic or authoritarian. In the case of the authoritarian leader all significant group functions are in his hands and only he in fact wields power in the group. The democratic leader also has power but he exercises it differently. He seeks to spread responsibility or leadership functions to others.

The now famous study by Lippitt and White (VC) investigated the effects of democratic, authoritarian, and laissez-faire leadership on the behavior of young children. Actual task groups were set up that were led by adults who were trained to play each of these leadership roles. The children were engaged in various activities, for example, mask making, and they met regularly over a period of weeks. Differences in the behavior of the children under the various leadership conditions were striking. In comparison with authoritarian leadership, under a "democratic regime" the children were less aggressive, more interested, friendlier toward the leader, more unified as a group, less domineering toward each other, and more constructive. It is important, however, to view these findings in their proper perspective. For example, not all the children in the Lippitt and White investigation reacted unfavorably to authoritarian leadership. Some children came from homes which were autocratic in structure and apparently functioned more effectively in the task groups when taking orders from others. Furthermore, it is essential to stress the fact that the superiority of the democratic leadership has been demonstrated on individuals who have been reared in a democratic culture. Similar studies in other cultures may well produce very different findings.

We must also take note of the fact that some studies have shown that some individuals—students, for example—may oppose democratic leadership (Bailey, 1953). There is also some evidence that under conditions of threat or severe anxiety persons may be more attracted to authoritarian leadership (Lanzetta, 1955; Peak, 1945). What appears to emerge is the basic assumption of the functional approach to leadership: that the relative effectiveness of authoritarian and democratic leadership practices will depend on the internal and external properties of the group. The investigation by Fiedler (VC) provides considerable support for this assumption.

By the use of appropriate measures Fiedler was able to distinguish leaders on a continuum extending from high person-orientation (permissive, accepting, democratic) to high task-orientation (directive, controlling, autocratic). It is evident that the distinction between the two leadership approaches is similar to the "consideration" and "initiating and directing" categories reported by Halpin and Winer (1957). In correlating scores on this dimension with group effectiveness in many different groups, Fiedler found no consistency in the obtained relationships. In other words, for some group situations, the person-oriented leader was effective, and in others a task-oriented leadership made for more effective group performance. To reconcile these findings Fiedler provides a theoretical analysis of the various group situations in terms of their "task-structure," "leader-member relations," and "position power" properties. Thus, some group situations involve a structured task, favorable leader-member relations, and a leadership position with power. Others are very low in all these respects, and still others fall in between the two extremes. By re-examining his earlier findings and by means of new research, Fiedler is able to show that groups that are either very high or very low in all three of these attributes perform more effectively with a directive, task-oriented leader than with a permissive, person-oriented one. The latter, in turn, is more effective with groups which have these properties only to a moderate degree.

Earlier in the discussion we noted that individuals in groups occupy different positions, which determine how they will behave toward each other. Each position "locates" the individual who occupies it with respect to other individuals in other positions. The differentiated system of positions that characterizes a group constitutes the *structure* of the group. In most instances persons form groups because their common objective cannot be achieved by any one of them alone. To ensure greater efficiency and therefore to maximize the possibility of goal attainment, each individual takes or is given responsibility for some part of the task. Involved in the emergence of the group structure, however, are not only the demands of a complex task which require a division of responsibility, but also the fact that individuals desire to and are able to do some things and not others. Differences in motivations and skills of the group members also contribute to the development of a differentiated system of positions. Finally, society also makes distinctions among individuals—sex, age, race, social class are examples of these—so that when individuals meet as a group for the first time, a minimum basis for the emergence of a group structure has already been established.

Throughout the present discussion we have employed the term "position" to characterize the individual's place in the structure of a group. It is apparent from our discussion of leadership, however, that the various positions of a group also have "connections" with each other. In effect, to talk about a supervisor, his foreman, and the foreman's workers, means that these connections are being described in terms of the authority relations among these individuals. Both the positions and the relations among them make up the structure of a group. However, we see from the investigation by Leavitt (VD) that it is also possible to characterize the "connections" or relations among positions in terms of the lines of communication which exist among them. Cartwright and Zander (1960) indicate that in addition to the authority and communication relations among positions, relations involving the "flow of work" and "the mobility of people" have also been used for describing the structure of a group. Of course, in any group these four types of relations among the members may involve very similar structures, but this need not be the case.

The study by Leavitt (VD) varied the communication structures in five-person problem-solving groups. The subjects in a group were separated from each other by partitions and could communicate with one another only by means of written messages. By controlling who could send messages to whom, Leavitt was able to establish various communication networks. In the "chain," for example, the only communication links permitted are A-B, B-C, C-D, and D-E, which means that C occupies the most central position and A and E the most peripheral ones. In the "circle," on the other hand, each person can communicate with each individual adjacent to him, which means that no one person is central or peripheral. Clearly opposite to the circle groups are "wheel" groups, in which A, B, D, and E can communicate with each other only through C. Here centrality reaches a maximum level.

In general, Leavitt's findings show that networks with more central positions— in other words, wheel groups—lead to more efficient group performances and a greater recognition of specific persons as leaders than those with less central positions. The circle groups, in effect, exhibited the poorest performances and the least recognition of a particular person as a leader. When the morale of the individuals in the various types of networks was considered, the findings were just the reverse. Groups with the fewest central positions showed higher member satisfaction than did those with more central positions. Furthermore, within networks in which positions varied in their degree of centrality, individuals in the least central positions were far less satisfied with their jobs and the tasks accomplished than those in the most central positions. Other studies have confirmed these findings, and various hypotheses have been proposed to explain them.

We have already noted that a group's leadership and structure (as well as other factors) have important consequences for a member's satisfactions in the group. It stands to reason that where member satisfaction is low, the group members will be less willing to work for the specified goals of the group. A study by Fouriezos, Hutt, and Guetzkow (1950), for example, showed that the extent of self-oriented-need behavior (motives leading to behavior not directed toward the goals of the group) correlated negatively with the degree of member satisfaction. In addition, measures of productivity in the groups were inversely related to the amount of self-oriented-need behavior exhibited by the members. Obviously, where members become increasingly preoccupied with their own concerns rather than with those of the group, we would also expect the amount of cooperative interaction among them to decline. Indeed, they should actually compete with each other if—as is very likely the case—their self-oriented needs are similar, for example, the need for recognition, for power, and the like.

The study by Deutsch (VD) investigated the effects of cooperative and competitive situations on group structure and process. In the cooperative situation the subjects were told that their performance in the tasks would be evaluated on a group basis in comparison with the performance of other groups. The competitively organized subjects also worked together on a common task, but they were informed that each of them would be evaluated on the basis of his individual contribution to the solutions obtained for the various tasks given to the group. Five pairs of matched groups of subjects were set up, each group meeting for a three-hour period every week for six weeks. It was found that the cooperative groups, in comparison with the competitive ones, exhibited a higher quantity and quality of task solutions, a greater division of labor and integration of individual efforts, less difficulty in member communication, greater friendliness among the members, and greater satisfaction with the group and its performance.

References

Asch, S. E. *Social psychology.* Englewood Cliffs, N.J.: Prentice-Hall, 1952.

Bailey, J. C. A classroom evaluation of the case method. In K. R. Andrews (Ed.), *Case method of teaching human relations and administration.* Cambridge, Mass.: Harvard Univer. Press, 1953.

Bales, R. F. The equilibrium problem in small groups. In T. Parsons, R. F. Bales, and E. A. Shils, *Working papers in the theory of action.* New York: The Free Press of Glencoe, 1953.

Bavelas, A. Communication patterns in task-oriented groups. In D. Cartwright and A. Zander (Eds.), *Group dynamics,* 2d Ed. New York: Harper & Row, 1960.

Bird, C. *Social psychology.* New York: Appleton-Century-Crofts, 1940.

Cartwright, D., and Zander, A. *Group dynamics,* 2d Ed. New York: Harper & Row, 1960.

Cattell, R. B. New concepts for measuring leadership in terms of group syntality. *Hum. Relat.,* 1951, 4, 161-184.

Festinger, L. Informal social communication. *Psychol. Rev.,* 1950, 57, 271-282.

Festinger, L. A theory of social comparison processes. *Hum. Relat.,* 1954, 7, 117-140.

Fouriezos, N. T., Hutt, M. L., and

Guetzkow, H. Measurement of self-oriented needs in discussion groups. *J. abnorm. soc. Psychol.,* 1950, 45, 682-690.

Friedman, E., and Havighurst, R. J. *The meaning of work and refinement.* Chicago: Univer. of Chicago Press, 1954.

Halpin, A. W., and Winer, B. J. A factorial study of the leader behavior descriptions. In R. M. Stodgill and A. E. Coons (Eds.), *Leader behavior: its description and measurement.* Bur. Bus. Res. Monogr. 88. Columbus: Ohio State Univer., 1957.

Kahn, R. L., and Katz, D. Leadership practices in relation to productivity and morale. In D. Cartwright and A. Zander (Eds.), *Group dynamics,* 2d Ed. New York: Harper & Row, 1960.

Komarovsky, M. Cultural contradictions and sex roles. *Amer. J. Sociol.,* 1946, 52, 184-189.

Krech, D., Crutchfield, R. S., and Ballachey, E. L. *Individual in society.* New York: McGraw-Hill, 1962.

Lanzetta, J. T. Group behavior under stress. *Hum. Relat.,* 1955, 8, 29-52.

Linton, R. *The study of man.* New York: Appleton-Century-Crofts, 1936.

Moreno, J. L. *Who shall survive?* Washington, D.C.: Nervous and Mental Disease Publ. Co., 1934.

PEAK, H. Observation on the characteristics and distribution of German Nazis. *Psychol. Monogr.*, 1945, *59*, No. 276.

REDL, F. Group emotion and leadership. *Psychiat.*, 1942, *5*, 573-596.

SCHACHTER, S. Deviation, rejection, and communication. *J. abnorm. soc. Psychol.*, 1951, *46*, 190-207.

STODGILL, R. Leadership, membership and organization. *Psychol. Bull.*, 1950, *47*, 1-14.

VEROFF, J. Development and validation of a projective measure of power motivation. *J. abnorm. soc. Psychol.*, 1957, *54*, 1-8.

A. INTERPERSONAL INFLUENCE

Effects of Group Pressure
upon the Modification
and Distortion of Judgments ✶ S. E. Asch

We shall here describe in summary form the conception and first findings of a program of investigation into the conditions of independence and submission to group pressure.[1]

Our immediate object was to study the social and personal conditions that induce individuals to resist or to yield to group pressures when the latter are perceived to be *contrary to fact*. The issues which this problem raises are of obvious consequence for society; it can be of decisive importance whether or not a group will, under certain conditions, submit to existing pressures. Equally direct are the consequences for individuals and our understanding of them, since it is a decisive fact about a person whether he possesses the freedom to act independently, or whether he characteristically submits to group pressures.

The problem under investigation requires the direct observation of certain basic processes in the interaction between individuals, and between individuals and groups. To clarify these seems necessary if we are to make fundamental advances in the understanding of the formation and reorganization of attitudes, of the functioning of public opinion, and of the operation of propaganda. Today we do not possess an adequate theory of these central psycho-social processes. Empirical investigation has been predominantly controlled by general propositions concerning group influence which have as a rule been assumed but not tested. With few exceptions investigation has relied upon descriptive formulations concerning the operation of suggestion and prestige, the inadequacy of which is becoming increasingly obvious, and upon schematic applications of stimulus-response theory.

[1] The earlier experiments out of which the present work developed and the theoretical issues which prompted it are discussed in S. E. Asch, *Social Psychology* (Englewood Cliffs, N.J.: Prentice-Hall, Inc., 1952), Ch. 16. A full account of the procedures and data on which the present report is based can be found in S. E. Asch, "Studies of independence and submission to group pressure: I. A minority of one against a unanimous majority." *Psychol. Monogr.*, 1956, 70.

This article was adapted by the author especially for G. E. Swanson, T. M. Newcomb, and E. L. Hartley (Eds.), *Readings in Social Psychology*, Rev. Ed., New York: Holt, Rinehart and Winston, 1952, from H. Guetzkow (Ed.), *Groups, Leadership and Men* (Pittsburgh: Carnegie Press, 1951). Reprinted by permission of the author and publishers.

Basic to the current approach has been the axiom that group pressures characteristically induce psychological changes *arbitrarily*, in far-reaching disregard of the material properties of the given conditions. This mode of thinking has almost exclusively stressed the slavish submission of individuals to group forces, has neglected to inquire into their possibilities for independence and for productive relations with the human environment, and has virtually denied the capacity of men under certain conditions to rise above group passion and prejudice. It was our aim to contribute to a clarification of these questions, important both for theory and for their human implications, by means of direct observation of the effects of groups upon the decisions and evaluations of individuals.

The Experiment and First Results

To this end we developed an experimental technique which has served as the basis for the present series of studies. We employed the procedure of placing an individual in a relation of radical conflict with all the other members of a group, of measuring its effect upon him in quantitative terms, and of describing its psychological consequences. A group of eight individuals was instructed to judge a series of simple, clearly structured perceptual relations—to match the length of a given line with one of three unequal lines. Each member of the group announced his judgments publicly. In the midst of this monotonous "test" one individual found himself suddenly contradicted by the entire group, and this contradiction was repeated again and again in the course of the experiment. The group in question had, with the exception of one member, previously met with the experimenter and received instructions to respond at certain points with wrong—and unanimous—judgments. The errors of the majority were large (ranging between ½" and 1¾") and of an order not encountered under control conditions. The outstanding person—the critical subject—whom we had placed in the position of a *minority of one* in the midst of a *unanimous majority*—was the object of investigation. He faced, possibly for the first time in his life, a situation in which a group unanimously contradicted the evidence of his senses.

This procedure was the starting point of the investigation and the point of departure for the study of further problems. Its main features were the following: (1) The critical subject was submitted to two contradictory and irreconcilable forces—the evidence of his own experience of a clearly perceived relation, and the unanimous evidence of a group of equals. (2) Both forces were part of the immediate situation; the majority was concretely present, surrounding the subject physically. (3) The critical subject, who was requested together with all others to state his judgments publicly, was obliged to declare himself and to take a definite stand *vis-à-vis* the group. (4) The situation possessed a self-contained character. The critical subject could not avoid or evade the dilemma by reference to conditions external to the experimental situation. (It may be mentioned at this point that the forces generated by the given conditions acted so quickly upon the critical subjects that instances of suspicion were infrequent.)

The technique employed permitted a simple quantitative measure of the "majority effect" in terms of the frequency of errors in the direction of the distorted estimates of the majority. At the same time we were concerned to obtain evidence of the ways in which the subjects perceived the group, to establish whether they became doubtful, whether they were tempted to join the majority. Most important, it was our object to establish the grounds of the subject's independence or yielding—whether, for example, the yielding subject was aware of the effect of the majority upon him, whether he abandoned his judgment deliberately or compulsively. To this end we constructed a comprehensive set of questions which served as the basis of an individual interview immediately following the experimental period. Toward the conclusion of the interview each subject was informed fully of the purpose of the experiment, of his role and of that of the majority. The reactions to the disclosure of the purpose of the experiment became in fact an integral part of the procedure. The information derived from the interview became an indispensable source of evidence and insight into the psychological structure of the experimental situation, and in particular, of the nature of the individual differences. It should be added that it is not justified or advisable to allow the subject to leave without giving him a full explanation of the experimental conditions. The experimenter has a responsibility to the subject to clarify his doubts and to state the reasons for placing him in the experimental situation. When this is done most subjects react with interest, and some express gratification at having lived through a striking situation which has some

bearing on them personally and on wider human issues.

Both the members of the majority and the critical subjects were male college students. We shall report the results for a total of fifty critical subjects in this experiment. In Table 1 we summarize the successive comparison trials and the majority estimates. The reader will note that on certain trials the majority responded correctly; these were the "neutral" trials. There were twelve critical trials on which the responses of the majority responded incorrectly.

The quantitative results are clear and unambiguous.

1. There was a marked movement toward the majority. One third of all the estimates in the critical group were errors identical with or in the direction of the distorted estimates of the majority. The significance of this finding becomes clear in the light of the virtual absence of errors in the control group, the members of which recorded their estimates in writing.

TABLE 1

LENGTHS OF STANDARD AND COMPARISON LINES

Trial	Length of Standard Line (in Inches)	Comparison Lines (in Inches)			Correct Response	Group Response	Majority Error (in Inches)
		1	2	3			
1	10	8¾	10	8	2	2	—
2	2	2	1	1½	1	1	—
3	3	3¾	4¼	3	3	1°	+¾
4	5	5	4	6½	1	2°	−1.0
5	4	3	5	4	3	3	—
6	3	3¾	4¼	3	3	2°	+1¼
7	8	6¼	8	6¾	2	3°	−1¼
8	5	5	4	6½	1	3°	+1½
9	8	6¼	8	6¾	2	1°	−1¾
10	10	8¾	10	8	2	2	—
11	2	2	1	1½	1	1	—
12	3	3¾	4¼	3	3	1°	+¾
13	5	5	4	6½	1	2°	−1.0
14	4	3	5	4	3	3	—
15	3	3¾	4¼	3	3	2°	+1¼
16	8	6¼	8	6¾	2	3°	−1¼
17	5	5	4	6½	1	3°	+1½
18	8	6¼	8	6¾	2	1°	−1¾

° Starred figures designate the erroneous estimates by the majority.

The relevant data of the critical and control groups are summarized in Table 2.

TABLE 2

DISTRIBUTION OF ERRORS IN EXPERIMENTAL
AND CONTROL GROUPS

Number of Critical Errors	Critical Group* (N = 50) F	Control Group (N = 37) F
0	13	35
1	4	1
2	5	1
3	6	
4	3	
5	4	
6	1	
7	2	
8	5	
9	3	
10	3	
11	1	
12	0	
Total	50	37
Mean	3.84	0.08

* All errors in the critical group were in the direction of the majority estimates.

2. At the same time the effect of the majority was far from complete. The preponderance of estimates in the critical group (68 percent) was correct despite the pressure of the majority.
3. We found evidence of extreme individual differences. There were in the critical group subjects who remained independent without exception, and there were those who went nearly all the time with the majority. (The maximum possible number of errors was 12, while the actual range of errors was 0-11.) One fourth of the critical subjects was completely independent; at the other extreme, one third of the group displaced the estimates toward the majority in one half or more of the trials.

The differences between the critical subjects in their reactions to the given conditions were equally striking. There were subjects who remained completely confident throughout. At the other extreme were those who became disoriented, doubt-ridden, and experienced a powerful impulse not to appear different from the majority.

For purposes of illustration we include a brief description of one independent and one yielding subject.

INDEPENDENT

After a few trials he appeared puzzled, hesitant. He announced all disagreeing answers in the form of "Three, sir; two, sir"; not so with the unanimous answers on the neutral trials. At Trial 4 he answered immediately after the first member of the group, shook his head, blinked, and whispered to his neighbor: "Can't help it, that's one." His later answers came in a whispered voice, accompanied by a deprecating smile. At one point he grinned embarrassedly, and whispered explosively to his neighbor: "I always disagree—darn it!" During the questioning, this subject's constant refrain was: "I called them as I saw them, sir." He insisted that his estimates were right without, however, committing himself as to whether the others were wrong, remarking that "that's the way I see them and that's the way they see them." If he had to make a practical decision under similar circumstances, he declared, "I would follow my own view, though part of my reason would tell me that I might be wrong." Immediately following the experiment the majority engaged this subject in a brief discussion. When they pressed him to say whether the entire group was wrong and he alone right, he turned upon them defiantly, exclaiming: "You're *probably* right, but you *may* be wrong!" To the disclosure of the experiment this subject reacted with the statement that he felt "exultant and relieved," adding, "I do not deny that at times I had the feeling: 'to heck with it, I'll go along with the rest.'"

YIELDING

This subject went with the majority in 11 out of 12 trials. He appeared nervous and somewhat confused, but he did not attempt to evade discussion; on the contrary, he was helpful and tried to answer to the best of his ability. He opened the discussion with the statement: "If I'd been first I probably would have responded differently"; this was his way of stating that he had adopted the majority estimates. The primary factor in his case was loss of confidence. He perceived the majority as a decided group, acting without hesitation: "If they had been doubtful I probably would have changed, but they answered with such confidence." Certain of his errors, he explained, were due to the doubtful nature of the comparisons; in such instances he went with the majority. When the object of the experiment was explained, the subject volunteered: "I suspected about the middle—but tried to push it out of my mind." It is of interest that his suspicion did not restore his confidence or diminish the power of the majority. Equally striking is his report that he assumed the experiment to involve an "illusion" to which the others, but not he, were subject. This assumption too did not help to free him; on the contrary, he acted as if his divergence from the majority was a sign of defect. The principal impression this subject produced was of one so caught up by immediate difficulties that he lost clear reasons for his actions, and could make no reasonable decisions.

A First Analysis of Individual Differences

On the basis of the interview data described earlier, we undertook to differentiate and describe the major forms of reaction to the experimental situation, which we shall now briefly summarize.

Among the *independent* subjects we distinguished the following main categories:

1. Independence based on *confidence* in one's perception and experience. The most striking characteristic of these subjects is the vigor with which they withstand the group opposition. Though they are sensitive to the group, and experience the conflict, they show a resilience in coping with it, which is expressed in their continuing reliance on their perception and the effectiveness with which they shake off the oppressive group opposition.

2. Quite different are those subjects who are independent and *withdrawn*. These do not react in a spontaneously emotional way, but rather on the basis of explicit principles concerning the necessity of being an individual.

3. A third group of independent subjects manifests considerable tension and doubt, but adhere to their judgment on the basis of a felt necessity to deal adequately with the task.

The following were the main categories of reaction among the *yielding* subjects, or those who went with the majority during one half or more of the trials.

1. *Distortion of perception* under the stress of group pressure. In this category belong a very few subjects who yield completely, but are not aware that their estimates have been displaced or distorted by the majority. These subjects report that they came to perceive the majority estimates as correct.

2. *Distortion of judgment.* Most submitting subjects belong to this category. The factor of greatest importance in this group is a decision the subjects reach that their perceptions are inaccurate, and that those of the majority are correct. These subjects suffer from primary doubt and lack of confidence; on this basis they feel a strong tendency to join the majority.

3. *Distortion of action.* The subjects in this group do not suffer a modification of perception nor do they conclude that they are wrong. They yield because of an overmastering need not to appear different from or inferior to others, because of an inability to tolerate the appearance of defectiveness in the eyes of the group. These subjects suppress their observations and voice the majority position with awareness of what they are doing.

The results are sufficient to establish that independence and yielding are not psychologically homogeneous, that submission to group pressure and freedom from pressure can be the result of different psychological conditions. It should also be noted that the categories described above, being based exclusively on the subjects' reactions to the experimental conditions, are descriptive, not presuming to explain why a given individual responded in one way rather than another. The further exploration of the basis for the individual differences is a separate task.

Experimental Variations

The results described are clearly a joint function of two broadly different sets of conditions. They are determined first by the specific external conditions, by the particular character of the relation between social evidence and one's own experience. Second, the presence of pronounced individual differences points to the important role of personal factors, or factors connected with the individual's character structure. We reasoned that there are group conditions which would produce independence in all subjects, and that there probably are group conditions which would induce intensified yielding in many, though not in all. Secondly, we deemed it reasonable to assume that behavior under the experimental social pressure is significantly related to certain characteristics of the individual. The present account will be limited to the effect of the surrounding conditions upon independence and submission. To this end we followed the procedure of experimental variation, systematically altering the quality of social evidence by means of systematic variation of the group conditions and of the task.

THE EFFECT OF NONUNANIMOUS MAJORITIES

Evidence obtained from the basic experiment suggested that the condition of being exposed *alone* to the opposition of a "compact majority" may have played a decisive

role in determining the course and strength of the effects observed. Accordingly we undertook to investigate in a series of successive variations the effects of *nonunanimous* majorities. The technical problem of altering the uniformity of a majority is, in terms of our procedure, relatively simple. In most instances we merely directed one or more members of the instructed group to deviate from the majority in prescribed ways. It is obvious that we cannot hope to compare the performance of the same individual in two situations on the assumption that they remain independent of one another; at best we can investigate the effect of an earlier upon a later experimental condition. The comparison of different experimental situations therefore requires the use of different but comparable groups of critical subjects. This is the procedure we have followed. In the variations to be described we have maintained the conditions of the basic experiment (e.g., the sex of the subjects, the size of the majority, the content of the task, and so on) save for the specific factor that was varied. The following were some of the variations studied:

1. *The presence of a "true partner."* (*a*) In the midst of the majority were *two* naïve, critical subjects. The subjects were separated spatially, being seated in the fourth and eighth positions, respectively. Each therefore heard his judgments confirmed by one other person (provided the other person remained independent), one prior to, the other after announcing his own judgment. In addition, each experienced a break in the unanimity of the majority. There were six pairs of critical subjects. (*b*) In a further variation the "partner" to the critical subject was a member of the group who had been instructed to respond correctly throughout. This procedure permits the exact control of the partner's responses. The partner was always seated in the fourth position; he therefore announced his estimates in each case before the critical subject.

The results clearly demonstrate that a disturbance of the unanimity of the majority markedly increased the independence of the critical subjects. The frequency of promajority errors dropped to 10.4 percent of the total number of estimates in variation (a), and to 5.5 percent in variation (b). These results are to be compared with the frequency of yielding to the unanimous majorities in the basic experiment, which was 32 percent of the total number of estimates. It is clear that the presence in the field of *one other* individual who responded correctly was sufficient to deplete the power of the majority, and in some cases to destroy it. This finding is all the more striking in the light of other variations which demonstrate the effect of even small minorities provided they are unanimous. Indeed, we have been able to show that a unanimous majority of 3 is, under the given conditions, far more effective than a majority of 8 containing 1 dissenter. That critical subjects will under these conditions free themselves of a majority of 7 and join forces with one other person in the minority is, we believe, a result significant for theory. It points to a fundamental psychological difference between the condition of being alone and having a minimum of human support. It further demonstrates that the effects obtained are not the result of a summation of influences proceeding from each member of the group; it is necessary to conceive the results as being relationally determined.

2. *Withdrawal of a "true partner."* What will be the effect of providing the critical subject with a partner who responds correctly and then withdrawing him? The critical subject started with a partner who responded correctly. The partner was a member of the majority who had been instructed to respond correctly and to "desert" to the majority in the middle of the experiment. This procedure permits the observation of the same subject in the course of the transition from one condition to another. The withdrawal of the partner produced a powerful and unexpected result. We had assumed that the critical subject, having gone through the experience of opposing the majority with a minimum of support, would maintain his independence when alone. Contrary to this expectation, we found that the experience of having had and then lost a partner restored the majority effect to its full force, the proportion of errors rising to 28.5 percent of all judgments, in contrast to the preceding level of 5.5 percent. Further experimentation is needed to establish whether the critical subjects were responding to the sheer fact of being alone, or to the fact that the partner abandoned them.

3. *Late arrival of a "true partner."* The critical subject started as a minority of 1 in the midst of a unanimous majority. Toward the conclusion of the experiment one member of the majority "broke" away and began announcing correct estimates. This procedure, which reverses the order of conditions of the preceding experiment, permits the observation of the transition from being alone to being a member of a pair against a majority. It is obvious that those critical subjects who were independent when alone would continue to be so when joined by a partner. The variation is therefore of significance primarily for those subjects who yielded during the first phase of the experiment. The appearance of the late partner exerts a freeing effect, reducing the level of yielding to 8.7 percent. Those who had previously yielded also became markedly more independent, but not completely so, continuing to yield more than previously independent subjects. The reports of the subjects do not cast much light on the factors responsible for the result. It is our impression that some subjects, having once committed themselves to yielding, find it difficult to change their direction completely. To do so is tantamount to a public admission that they had not acted rightly. They therefore follow to an extent the precarious course they had chosen in order to maintain an outward semblance of consistency and conviction.

4. *The presence of a "compromise partner."* The majority was consistently extremist, always matching the standard with the most unequal line. One instructed subject (who, as in the other variations, preceded the critical subject) also responded incorrectly, but his estimates were always intermediate between the truth and the

majority position. The critical subject therefore faced an extremist majority whose unanimity was broken by one more moderately erring person. Under these conditions the frequency of errors was reduced but not significantly. However, the lack of unanimity determined in a strikingly consistent way the *direction* of the errors. The preponderance of the errors, 75.7 percent of the total, was moderate, whereas in a parallel experiment in which the majority was unanimously extremist (i.e., with the "compromise" partner excluded), the incidence of moderate errors was 42 percent of the total. As might be expected, in a unanimously moderate majority, the errors of the critical subjects were without exception moderate.

THE ROLE OF MAJORITY SIZE

To gain further understanding of the majority effect, we varied the size of the majority in several different variations. The majorities, which were in each case unanimous, consisted of 2, 3, 4, 8, and 10-15 persons, respectively. In addition, we studied the

and often hiding it from the experimenter. To examine the range of effects it is capable of inducing, decisive variations of conditions are necessary. An indication of one effect is furnished by the following variation in which the conditions of the basic experiment were simply reversed. Here the majority, consisting of a group of 16, was naïve; in the midst of it we placed a single individual who responded wrongly according to instructions. Under these conditions the members of the naïve majority reacted to the lone dissenter with amusement. Contagious laughter spread through the group at the droll minority of 1. Of significance is the fact that the members lacked awareness that they drew their strength from the majority, and that their reactions would change radically if they faced the dissenter individually. These observations demonstrate the role of social support as a source of power and stability, in contrast to the preceding investigations which stressed the effects of social opposition. Both aspects must be explicitly considered in a unified formulation of the

TABLE 3
ERRORS OF CRITICAL SUBJECTS WITH UNANIMOUS MAJORITIES OF DIFFERENT SIZE

Size of Majority	Control	1	2	3	4	8	10-15
N	37	10	15	10	10	50	12
Mean Number of Errors	0.08	0.33	1.53	4.0	4.20	3.84	3.75
Range of Errors	0-2	0-1	0-5	1-12	0-11	0-11	0-10

limiting case in which the critical subject was opposed by one instructed subject. Table 3 contains the mean and the range of errors under each condition.

With the opposition reduced to 1, the majority effect all but disappeared. When the opposition proceeded from a group of 2, it produced a measurable though small distortion, the errors being 12.8 percent of the total number of estimates. The effect appeared in full force with a majority of 3. Larger majorities did not produce effects greater than a majority of 3.

The effect of a majority is often silent, revealing little of its operation to the subject,

effects of group conditions on the formation and change of judgments.

THE ROLE OF THE STIMULUS-
SITUATION

It is obviously not possible to divorce the quality and course of the group forces which act upon the individual from the specific stimulus-conditions. Of necessity the structure of the situation molds the group forces and determines their direction as well as their strength. Indeed, this was the reason that we took pains in the investigations described above to center the issue between the individual and the group around an elementary matter of fact. And there can be no doubt that the resulting reactions were directly a function of the contradiction between the observed relations and the majority position. These general considerations are sufficient to establish the need to vary the stimulus-conditions and to observe their effect on the resulting group forces.

Accordingly we have studied the effect of increasing and decreasing the discrepancy between the correct relation and the position of the majority, going beyond the basic experiment which contained discrepancies of a relatively moderate order. Our technique permits the easy variation of this factor, since we can vary at will the deviation of the majority from the correct relation. At this point we can only summarize the trend of the results which is entirely clear. The degree of independence increases with the distance of the majority from correctness. However, even glaring discrepancies (of the order of 3-6") did not produce independence in all. While independence increases with the magnitude of contradiction, a certain proportion of individuals continues to yield under extreme conditions.

We have also varied systematically the structural clarity of the task, employing judgments based on mental standards. In agreement with other investigators, we find that the majority effect grows stronger as the situation diminishes in clarity. Concurrently, however, the disturbance of the subjects and the conflict-quality of the situation decrease markedly. We consider it of significance that the majority achieves its most pronounced effect when it acts most painlessly.

Summary

We have investigated the effects upon individuals of majority opinions when the latter were seen to be in a direction contrary to fact. By means of a simple technique we produced a radical divergence between a majority and a minority, and observed the ways in which individuals coped with the resulting difficulty. Despite the stress of the given conditions, a substantial proportion of individuals retained their independence throughout. At the same time a substantial minority yielded, modifying their judgments in accordance with the majority. Independence and yielding are a joint function of the following major factors: (1) The character of the stimulus situation. Variations in structural clarity have a decisive effect: with diminishing clarity of the stimulus-conditions the majority effect increases. (2) The character of the group forces. Individuals are highly sensitive to the structural qualities of group opposition. In particular, we demonstrated the great importance of the factor of unanimity. Also, the majority effect is a function of the size of group opposition. (3) The character of the individual. There were wide and, indeed, striking differences among individuals within the same experimental situation.

A Study of Normative

and Informational Social Influences ❧ Morton Deutsch

upon Individual Judgment ❧ Harold B. Gerard

By now, many experimental studies (Asch, 1951; Bovard, 1951; Sherif, 1935) have demonstrated that individual psychological processes are subject to social influences. Most investigators, however, have not distinguished among different kinds of social influences; rather, they have carelessly used the term "group" influence to characterize the impact of many different kinds of social factors. In fact, a review of the major experiments in this area—e.g., those by Sherif (1935), Asch (1951), Bovard (1951)—would indicate that the subjects (Ss) in these experiments as they made their judgments were *not* functioning as *members* of a group in any simple or obvious manner. The S, in the usual experiment in this area, made perceptual judgments in the physical presence of others after hearing their judgments. Typically, the S was *not* given experimental instructions which made him feel that he was a member of a group faced with a common task requiring cooperative effort for its most effective solution. If "group" influences were at work in the foregoing experiments, they were subtly and indirectly created rather than purposefully created by the experimenter.

Hypotheses

The purpose of this paper is to consider two types of social influence, "normative" and "informational," which we believe were operative in the experiments mentioned

above, and to report the results of an experiment bearing upon hypotheses that are particularly relevant to the former influence. We shall define a *normative social influence* as an influence to conform with the positive expectations[1] of another.[2] An *informational social influence* may be defined as an influence to accept information obtained from another as *evidence* about reality. Commonly these two types of influence are found together. However, it is possible to conform behaviorally with the expectations of others and say things which one disbelieves but which agree with the beliefs of others. Also, it is possible that one will accept an opponent's beliefs as evidence about reality even though one has no motivation to agree with him, per se.

Our hypotheses are particularly relevant to normative social influence upon individual judgment. We shall not elaborate the theoretical rationales for the hypotheses, since they are for the most part obvious and they follow from other theoretical writings (Deutsch, 1949; Festinger, 1950).

[1] By positive expectations we mean to refer to those expectations whose fulfillment by another leads to or reinforces positive rather than negative feelings, and whose nonfulfillment leads to the opposite, to alienation rather than solidarity; conformity to negative expectations, on the other hand, leads to or reinforces negative rather than positive feelings.

[2] The term *another* is being used inclusively to refer to "another person," to a "group," or to one's "self." Thus, a normative social influence can result from the expectations of oneself, or of a group, or of another person.

From the *Journal of Abnormal and Social Psychology*, 1955, *51*, 629-636. Reprinted by permission of the authors and the American Psychological Association. This research was conducted under a grant from the Office of Naval Research.

HYPOTHESIS I

Normative social influence upon individual judgments will be greater among individuals forming a group than among an aggregation of individuals who do not conpose a group.[3]

That is, even when susceptibility to informational social influence is equated, we would predict that the greater susceptibility to normative social influence among group members would be reflected in the greater group influence upon individual judgment. This is not to say that individuals, even when they are not group members, may not have some motivation to conform to the expectations of others—e.g., so as to ingratiate themselves or so as to avoid ridicule.

HYPOTHESIS II

Normative social influence upon individual judgment will be reduced when the individual perceives that his judgment cannot be identified or, more generally, when the individual perceives no pressure to conform directed at him from others.

HYPOTHESIS III

Normative social influence to conform to one's own judgment will reduce the impact

[3] Generally one would also expect that group members would be more likely to take the judgments of other group members as trustworthy evidence for forming judgments about reality and, hence, they would be more susceptible to informational social influence than would nongroup members. The greater trustworthiness usually reflects more experience of the reliability of the judgments of other members and more confidence in the benevolence of their motivations. However, when group members have had no prior experience together and when it is apparent in both the group and nongroup situations that the others are motivated and in a position to report correct judgments, there is no reason to expect differential susceptibility to informational social influence among group and nongroup members.

of the normative social influence to conform to the judgment of others.

HYPOTHESIS IV

Normative social influence to conform to one's own judgment from another as well as from oneself will be stronger than normative social influence from oneself.

Normative social influence from oneself to conform to one's own judgment may be thought of as an internalized social process in which the individual holds expectations with regard to his own behavior; conforming to positive self-expectations leads to feelings of self-esteem or self-approval while nonconformity leads to feelings of anxiety or guilt. In general, one would expect that the strength of these internalized self-expectations would reflect the individual's prior experiences with them as sources of need satisfaction—e.g., by conforming to his own judgments or by self-reliance he has won approval from such significant others as his parents. As Hypothesis IV indicates, we believe that contemporaneous social pressure to conform to one's own judgment may supplement, and perhaps be even stronger than, the individual's internalized pressure to conform to his own judgment.

Two additional hypotheses, dealing with the effect of difficulty of judgment, are relevant to one of the experimental variations. They follow:

HYPOTHESIS V

The more uncertain the individual is about the correctness of his judgment, the more likely he is to be susceptible to both normative and informational social influences in making his judgment.

HYPOTHESIS VI

The more uncertain the individual is about the correctness of the judgment of others, the less likely he is to be susceptible to informational social influence in making his judgment.[4]

Method

SUBJECTS

One hundred and one college students from psychology courses at New York University were employed as Ss. The study was defined for the Ss as an experimental study of perception.

PROCEDURE

We employed the experimental situation developed by Asch (1951) with certain modifications and variations which are specified below. For detailed description of the procedures utilized by Asch and replicated in this experiment, Asch's publication should be consulted. The basic features of the Asch situation are: (a) the Ss are instructed that they are participating in a perceptual experiment, wherein they have to

[4] Although we have no data relevant to this hypothesis, we present it to qualify Hypothesis V and to counteract an assumption in some of the current social psychological literature. Thus, Festinger (1950) has written that where no physical reality basis exists for the establishment of the validity of one's belief, one is dependent upon social reality (i.e., upon the beliefs of others). Similarly, Asch (1952) has indicated that group influence grows stronger as the judgmental situation diminishes in clarity. The implication of Hypothesis VI is that if an individual perceives that a situation is objectively difficult to judge—that others as well as he experience the situation in the same way (i.e., as being difficult and as having uncertainty about their judgments)—he will not trust their judgments any more than he trusts his own. It is only as his confidence in their judgments increases (e.g., because he deems that agreement among three uncertain judges provides more reliable evidence than one uncertain judge) that the judgments of others will have informational social influence. However (at any particular level of confidence in the judgment of others), one can predict that as his confidence in his own judgment decreases he will be more susceptible to normative social influence. With decreasing self-confidence there is likely to be less of a commitment to one's own judgment and, hence, less influence not to conform to the judgments of others.

match accurately the length of a given line with one of three lines; (b) correct judgments are easy to make; (c) in each experimental session there is only one *naive S*, the other participants, while ostensibly Ss, are in fact "stooges" who carry out the experimenter's instructions; (d) each participant (i.e., the naive S and the stooges) has to indicate his judgments publicly; (e) on 12 of the 18 perceptual judgments the stooges announce wrong and unanimous judgments, the errors of the stooges are large and clearly in error; (f) the naive S and the stooges are in a face-to-face relationship and have been previously acquainted with one another.[5]

[5] Inspection of the Asch situation would suggest that informational social influence would be strongly operative. As Asch has put it (1952, p. 461):

The subject knows (a) that the issue is one of fact; (b) that a correct result is possible; (c) that only one result is correct; (d) that the others and he are oriented to and reporting about the same objectively given relations; (e) that the group is in unanimous opposition at certain points with him.

He further perceives that the others are motivated to report a correct judgment. In such a situation, the subject's accumulated past experience would lead him to expect that he could reply on the judgments of others, especially if they all agreed. That is, even if his eyes were closed he might feel that he could safely risk his life on the assumption that the unanimous judgments of the others were correct. This is a strong informational social influence and one would expect it to be overriding except for the fact that the subject has his eyes open and receives information from a source which he also feels to be completely trustworthy—i.e., from his own perceptual apparatus. The subject is placed in strong conflict because the evidences from two sources of trustworthy information are in opposition.

In the Asch situation, it is apparent that, in addition to informational social influence, normative social influence is likely to be operating. The naive S is in a face-to-face situation with acquaintances and he may be motivated to conform to their judgments in order to avoid being ridiculed, or being negatively evaluated, or even possibly out of a sense of obligation. While it may be impossible to remove completely the impact of normative social influence upon any socialized being, it is evident that the Asch situation allows much opportunity for this type of influence to operate.

To test the hypotheses set forth in the foregoing section, the following experimental variations upon Asch's situation were employed:

1. *The Face-to-face Situation.* This was an exact replication of Asch's situation except for the following minor modifications: (a) Only three stooges, rather than eight, were employed[6]; (b) the S and the stooges were unacquainted prior to the experiment; and (c) two series of 18 judgments were employed. In one series (the visual series), the lines were physically present when the S and the stooges announced their judgments; in the other series (the memory series), the lines were removed before anyone announced his judgment. In the memory series, approximately three seconds after the lines were removed the first stooge was asked to announce his judgment. The sequences of visual and memory series were alternated so that approximately half the Ss had the memory series first and half had the visual series first.

2. *The Anonymous Situation.* This situation was identical with the face-to-face situation except for the following differences: (a) Instead of sitting in the visual presence of each other, the Ss were separated by partitions which prevented them from talking to each other or seeing one another. (b) Instead of announcing their judgments by voice, the Ss indicated their judgments by pressing a button. (c) No stooges were employed. Each S was led to believe he was Subject No. 3, and the others were No. 1, No. 2, and No. 4. He was told that when the experimenter called out "Subject No. 3" he was to indicate his judgment by pressing one of three buttons (A, B, or C) which corresponded to what he thought the correct line was. When an S pressed a given button, a corresponding bulb lit on his own panel and on a hidden master panel. Presumably the appropriate bulb also lit on the panels of each of the other Ss, but, in fact, the bulbs

on any S's panel were not connected to the buttons of the other Ss. When the experimenter called for the judgments of Subject No. 1, of Subject No. 2, and of Subject No. 4, a concealed accomplice manipulated master switches which lit bulbs on each of the S's panels that corresponded to judgments presumably being made by these respective Ss. Subjects No. 1, No. 2, and No. 4 were, in effect, "electrical stooges" whose judgments were indicated on the panels of the four naive Ss (all of whom were Subject No. 3) by an accomplice of the experimenter who manipulated master switches controlling the lights on the panels of the naive Ss. The pattern of judgments followed by the "electrical stooges" was the same as that followed by the "live stooges" in the face-to-face situation. (d) In providing a rationale for being labeled Subject No. 3 for each of the naive Ss, we explained that due to the complicated wiring setup, the S's number had no relation to his seating position. Implicitly, we assumed that each S would realize that it would be impossible for the others to identify that a judgment was being made by him rather than by any of two others. However, it is apparent from postexperiment questionnaires that many of the Ss did not realize this. It seems likely that if we had made the anonymous character of the judgments clear and explicit to the Ss, the effects of this experimental variation would have been even more marked.

3. *The Group Situation.* This situation was identical to the anonymous situation except that the subjects were instructed as follows:

This group is one of twenty similar groups who are participating in this experiment. We want to see how accurately you can make judgments. We are going to give a reward to the five best groups—the five groups that make the fewest errors on the series of judgments that you are given. The reward will be a pair of tickets to a Broadway play of your own choosing for each member of the winning group. An error will be

---

[6] Asch found that three stooges were about as effective in influencing the Ss as eight.

counted any time one of you makes an incorrect judgment. That is, on any given card the group can make as many as four errors if you each judge incorrectly or you can make no errors if you each judge correctly. The five groups that make the best scores will be rewarded.

4. *The Self-commitment Variation.* This variation was employed in both the face-to-face and anonymous situations. In it, each S was given a sheet of paper on which to write down his judgment before he was exposed to the judgments of the others. He was told not to sign the sheet of paper and that it would not be collected at the end of the experiment. After the first series of 18 judgments, the Ss threw away their sheets. The Ss did not erase their recorded judgments after each trial as they did in the Magic Pad self-commitment variation.

4A. *The Magic Pad Self-commitment Variation.* This variation was employed in the anonymous situation. In it, each S was given a Magic Writing Pad on which to write down his judgment before he was exposed to the judgments of the others. After each S had been exposed to the judgment of the others and had indicated his own judgment, he erased his judgment on the Magic Writing Pad by lifting up the plastic covering. It was made convincingly clear to the S that only he would ever know what he had written down on the pad.

5. *The Public Commitment Variation.* This variation was employed in both the face-to-face situation and in the anonymous situation. In it, the Ss followed the same procedure as in the self-commitment variation except that they wrote down their initial judgments on sheets of paper which they signed and which they knew were to be handed to the experimenter after each series of 18 judgments.

Results

The primary data used in the analysis of the results are the errors made by the Ss which were in the direction of the errors made by the stooges. We shall present first the data which are relevant to our hypotheses; later we shall present other information.

HYPOTHESIS I

The data relevant to the first hypothesis are presented in Table 1. The table presents

TABLE 1

Mean Number of Socially Influenced Errors in Individual Judgment Among Group Members and Among Nonmembers

Experimental Treatment	N	Memory Series	Visual Series	Total
Group, Anonymous, No Commitment	15	6.87	5.60	12.47
Nongroup, Anonymous, No Commitment	13	3.15	2.77	5.92

	p Values*	
.01	.05	.001

* Based on a *t* test, using one tail of the distribution.

a comparison of the anonymous situation in which the individuals were motivated to act as a group with the anonymous situation in which there was no direct attempt to induce membership motivation; in both situations, no self or public commitment was made. The data provide strong support for the prediction that the normative social influence upon individual judgments will be greater among individuals forming a group than among individuals who do not compose a group. The average member of the group made more than twice as many errors as the comparable individual who did not participate in the task as a member of a group.

Qualitative data from a postexperimental questionnaire, in which we asked the S to describe any feelings he had about himself or about the others during the experiment, also support Hypothesis I. Seven out of the fifteen Ss in the "group" condition spontaneously mentioned a felt obligation to the other group members; none of the individuals in the nongroup condition mentioned any feeling of obligation to go along with the others.

HYPOTHESIS II

To test the second hypothesis, it is necessary to compare the data from the face-to-face and anonymous situations among the individuals who were otherwise exposed to similar experimental treatments. Tables 2 and 3 present the relevant data. It is apparent that there was less social influence upon individual judgment in the anonymous as compared with the face-to-face situation. This lessening of social influence is at the .001 level of statistical confidence even when the comparisons include the "commitment variations" as well as both the visual and the memory series of judgments. The interaction between the commitment variations and the anonymous, face-to-face variations, which is statistically significant, is

such as to reduce the over-all differences between the anonymous and face-to-face situation; the differences between the face-to-face and the anonymous situations are most strongly brought out when there is no commitment. Similarly, if we compare the anonymous and face-to-face situations, employing the memory rather than the visual series, the effect of the normative influence upon judgments in the face-to-face situation is increased somewhat, but not significantly. That is, as we eliminate counter-normative influences (i.e., the "commitment") and as we weaken reality restraints (i.e., employ the "memory" rather than "visual" series), the normative influences in the face-to-face situation operate more freely.

The support for Hypothesis II is particularly striking in light of the fact that, due to faulty experimental procedure, the "anonymous" character of the anonymous situation was not sufficiently impressed on some of the Ss. For these Ss, the anonymous situation merely protected them from the immediate, visually accessible pressure to conform arising from the lifted eyebrows and expressions of amazement by the stooges in the face-to-face situation. Complete feeling of anonymity would probably have strengthened the results.

HYPOTHESES III AND IV

Tables 4, 5, and 6 present results showing the influence of the different commitment variations. The public and the self-commitment variations markedly reduce the socially influenced errors in both the face-to-face

TABLE 2

MEAN NUMBER OF SOCIALLY INFLUENCED ERRORS IN INDIVIDUAL JUDGMENT IN THE ANONYMOUS AND IN THE FACE-TO-FACE SITUATIONS

| Situation | No Commitment | | | | Self-commitment | | | | Public Commitment | | | |
	Visual	Mem-ory	Total	N	Visual	Mem-ory	Total	N	Visual	Mem-ory	Total	N
Face-to-face	3.00	4.08	7.08	13	.92	.75	1.67	12	1.13	1.39	2.52	13
Anonymous	2.77	3.15	5.92	13	.64	.73	1.37	11	.92	.46	1.38	13

TABLE 3

p VALUES° FOR VARIOUS COMPARISONS OF SOCIALLY INFLUENCED ERRORS IN THE ANONYMOUS AND FACE-TO-FACE SITUATIONS

Comparison	Total Errors
A vs. F	.001
A vs. F, No Commitment	.001
A vs. F, Self-commitment	.10
A vs. F, Public Commitment	.001
Interaction of Commitment with A-F	.01

° p values are based on t tests, using one tail of distribution, derived from analyses of variance.

TABLE 4

p Values* for Various Comparisons of Socially Influenced
Errors in the Different Commitment Treatments

Comparison	Total Errors	Errors on Visual Series	Errors on Memory Series
No Commitment vs. Public Commitment, F	.001	.01	.001
No Commitment vs. Self-commitment, F	.001	.01	.001
Self-commitment vs. Public Commitment, F	.01	NS	NS
No Commitment vs. Self-commitment, A	.001	.01	.01
No Commitment vs. Public Commitment, A	.001	.01	.002
Self-commitment vs. Public Commitment, A	NS	NS	NS

* p values are based on t tests, using one tail of the distribution, and derived from the analyses of variation.

and anonymous situations. In other words, the data provide strong support for Hypothesis III which asserts that normative social influence to conform to one's own judgment will reduce the impact of the normative influence to conform to the judgment of others.

The data with regard to the influence of self-commitment are ambiguous in implication since the results of the two self-commitment variations—i.e., the "Magic Pad self-commitment" and the "self-commitment"—are not the same. The first self-commitment variation produced results which are essentially the same as the public commitment variation, markedly reducing socially influenced errors. The Magic Pad self-commitment variation produced results which were different from the no commitment variation, reducing the errors to an

TABLE 5

Mean Number of Socially Influenced Errors in Judgments in the
Anonymous Situation as Affected by the Commitment Variations

No Commitment				Magic Pad Self-commitment				Self-commitment				Public Commitment			
Visual	Memory	Tot.	N	Visual	Memory	Tot.	N	Visual	Memory	Tot.	N	Visual	Memory	Tot.	N
2.77	3.15	5.92	13	1.63	2.27	3.90	11	.64	.73	1.37	11	.92	.46	1.38	13

TABLE 6

p Values* for Various Comparisons of Socially Influenced
Errors in the Different Commitment Variations

Comparison	Total Errors	Errors on Visual Series	Errors on Memory Series
No Commitment vs. Magic Pad Self-commitment	.05	NS	NS
Magic Pad Self-commitment vs. Self-commitment	.005	NS	.05
Magic Pad Self-commitment vs. Public Commitment	.001	NS	.01

* p values are based on t tests using one tail of the distribution.

extent which is statistically significant; however, unlike the first self-commitment variation, the Magic Pad self-commitment was significantly less effective than the public commitment in reducing socially influenced errors.

Our hunch is that the Ss in the first self-commitment variation perceived the commitment situation as though it were a public commitment and that this is the explanation of the lack of differences between these two variations. That is, writing their judgments indelibly supported the belief that "others can see what I have written." The Ss in the Magic Pad self-commitment variation, on the other hand, were literally wiping their initial judgments away in such a manner that they would be inaccessible to anyone. Hence, in the Magic Pad variation, the normative influences to conform to one's own judgment had to be sustained by the S himself. Normative influences from the S's self (to be, in a sense, true to himself) were undoubtedly also operating in the noncommitment variation. What the Magic Pad did was to prevent the S from distorting his recollection of his independent judgment after being exposed to the judgments of the others. Further, there is a theoretical basis for assuming that the commitment to a judgment or decision is increased following the occurrence of behavior based upon it. Hence, the behavior of writing one's judgment down on the Magic Pad makes the original decision less tentative and less subject to change. However, it is apparent that this internally sustained influence to conform with one's own judgment was not as strong as the combination of external and self-motivated influences. These results support our fourth hypothesis.

HYPOTHESIS V

Table 7 presents a comparison of the errors made on the visual and on the memory series of judgments. It is apparent that the Ss were less influenced by the judgments of others when the judgments were made on a visual rather than on a memory basis. It is

TABLE 7

SOCIALLY INFLUENCED ERRORS IN INDIVIDUAL JUDGMENTS AS AFFECTED BY THE STIMULUS TO BE JUDGED (VISUAL OR MEMORY)

	N	Mean Number of Errors	"p" Value
Errors on Visual Series	99	2.20 ⎫	
Errors on Memory Series	99	2.60 ⎭	.005*
Total Errors When Visual Series Was First	51	4.12 ⎫	
Total Errors When Memory Series Was First	48	5.71 ⎭	.005

* Based on a *t* test of differences between visual and memory series for each subject.

also evident from the data of Table 2 that the differences between the visual and memory series were reduced or disappeared when the Ss wrote down their initial, independent judgments. These results support our fifth hypothesis which asserts that the more uncertain the individual is about the correctness of his judgment, the more likely he is to be susceptible to social influences in making his judgment. Further support comes from the questionnaire data. Out of the 90 Ss who filled out questionnaires, 51 indicated that they were more certain of their judgment when the lines were visually present, 2 were more certain when they were absent, and 39 were equally certain in both instances.

Being exposed first to the memory series rather than the visual series had the effect of making the Ss more susceptible to social influence upon their judgments throughout both series of judgments. In other words, an S was more likely to make socially influenced errors on the memory series and, having allowed himself to be influenced by the others on this first series of judgments, he was more likely to be influenced on the visual series than if he had not previously participated in the memory series. It is as though once having given in to the social influence (and it is easier to give in when one is less certain about one's judgment), the S is more susceptible to further social influences.

Discussion

A central thesis of this experiment has been that prior experiments which have been concerned with "group" influence upon individual judgment have, in fact, only incidentally been concerned with the type of social influence most specifically associated with groups, namely "normative social influence." Our results indicate that, even when normative social influence in the direction of an incorrect judgment is largely removed (as in the anonymous situation), more errors are made by our Ss than by a control group of Ss making their judgments when alone.[7] It seems reasonable to conclude that the S, even if not nomatively influenced, may be influenced by the others in the sense that the judgments of others are taken to be a more or less trustworthy source of information about the objective reality with which he and the others are confronted.

It is not surprising that the judgments of others (particularly when they are perceived to be motivated and competent to judge accurately) should be taken as evidence to be weighed in coming to one's own judgment. From birth on, we learn that the perceptions and judgments of others are frequently reliable sources of evidence about reality. Hence, it is to be expected that if the perceptions by two or more people of the same objective situation are discrepant, each will tend to re-examine his own view and that of the others to see if they can be reconciled. This process of mutual influence does not necessarily indicate the operation of normative social influence as distinct from informational social influence. Essentially the same process (except that the influence is likely to be unilateral) can go on in interaction with a measuring or computing machine. For example, suppose one were to judge which of two lines is longer (as in the Müller-Lyer illusion) and then were given

information that a measuring instrument (which past experience had let one to believe was infallible) came up with a different answer; certainly one might be influenced by this information. This influence could hardly be called a normative influence except in the most indirect sense.

While the results of prior experiments of "group" influence upon perception can be largely explained in terms of non-normative social influence, there is little doubt that normative influences were incidentally operative. However, these were the casual normative influences which can not be completely eliminated from any human situation, rather than normative influences deriving from specific group membership. Our experimental results indicate that when a group situation is created, even when the group situation is as trivial and artificial as it was in our groups, the normative social influences are grossly increased, producing considerably more errors in individual judgment.

The implications of the foregoing result are not particularly optimistic for those who place a high value on the ability of an individual to resist group pressures which run counter to his individual judgment. In the experimental situation we employed, the S, by allowing himself to be influenced by the others, in effect acquiesced in the distortion of his judgment and denied the authenticity of his own immediate experience. The strength of the normative social influences that were generated in the course of our experiment was small; had it been stronger, one would have expected even more distortion and submission.

Our findings, with regard to the commitment variations, do, however, suggest that normative social influences can be utilized to buttress as well as to undermine individual integrity. In other words, normative social influence can be exerted to help make an individual be an individual and not merely a mirror or puppet of the group. Groups can demand of their members that they have self-respect, that they value their own experience, that they be capable of act-

---

[7] Asch (1952) reports that his control group of Ss made an average of considerably less than one error per S.

ing without slavish regard for popularity. Unless groups encourage their members to express their own, independent judgments, group consensus is likely to be an empty achievement. Group process which rests on the distortion of individual experience undermines its own potential for creativity and productiveness.

Summary and Conclusions

Employing modifications of the Asch situation, an experiment was carried out to test hypotheses concerning the effects of normative and informational social influences upon individual judgment. The hypotheses received strong support from the experimental data.

In discussion of our results, the thesis was advanced that prior studies of "group" influence upon individual judgment were only incidentally studies of the type of social influence most specifically associated with groups—i.e., of normative social influence. The role of normative social influence in buttressing as well as undermining individual experience was considered.

References

Asch, S. E. Effects of group pressure upon the modification and distortion of judgments. In H. Guetzkow (Ed.), *Groups, leadership and men.* Pittsburgh: Carnegie Press, 1951, 177-190.

Asch, S. E. *Social psychology.* Englewood Cliffs, N.J.: Prentice-Hall, 1952.

Bovard, E. W. Group structure and perception. *J. abnorm. soc. Psychol.*, 1951, 46, 398-405.

Deutsch, M. A theory of cooperation and competition. *Hum. Relat.*, 1949, 2, 129-152.

Festinger, L. Informal social communication. *Psychol. Rev.*, 1950, 57, 271-282.

Sherif, M. A study of some social factors in perception. *Arch. Psychol.*, 1935, 27, No. 187.

Influence through
Social Communication ❊ Kurt W. Back

Introduction

The experiment described in this paper investigates a property of groups which has been given various names but will be called here "cohesiveness," following the use in a study by Festinger, Schachter, and Back (1950). Cohesiveness was defined by them as the resultant forces which are acting on the members to stay in a group; in other words, cohesiveness is the attraction of membership in a group for its members. In the study cited, it was found that under certain conditions there will be increased pressure toward uniformity within a group with increase in cohesiveness. In the present ex-

From the *Journal of Abnormal and Social Psychology,* 1951, 46, 9-23. Reprinted by permission of the author and the American Psychological Association. For brevity, several of the more detailed technical passages have been omitted. The reader is referred to the original article for this material.

periment, a laboratory situation was created in which the consequences of this relationship could be studied in detail.

From the relationship between the forces to remain in the group and pressure to agree on important topics, some other relationships can be deduced.

1. The increase in pressure toward uniformity should show itself in a discussion between members. Either members will attempt to influence each other more in highly cohesive groups, or they will be more receptive to influence.
2. The basis for participation in a discussion of group members lies partly in individual motives, which may vary among individuals, and pressure arising from the group, which affects all members. Since the factor which is common to all members is larger in highly cohesive groups than in less cohesive groups, we would expect less individual differences in participation in these groups.
3. As the pressure toward uniformity in highly cohesive groups is stronger, the activities of the groups—discussion, for example—should have a greater effect on the members than activities of less cohesive groups.
4. Weak pressures toward uniformity in less cohesive groups can therefore lead only to little changes in individual members. Hence, the preferred outcome should be a compromise solution where all members change their positions slightly and equally. In highly cohesive groups, individual members may change considerably. Agreement can be established at any point with little consideration given the degree to which some individuals may have to change.

Individuals may want to belong to a group because they like the other members, because being a member of a group may be attractive in itself (for example, it may be an honor to belong to it), or because the group may mediate goals which are important for the members. All these are bases for attractiveness of a group. In the experiment, groups were established on all three bases.

The strength of cohesiveness for each basis was varied.

The main purpose of the experiment was to measure the effect of strength of cohesiveness on the pressure toward uniformity within groups and the consequences of this effect. At the same time the effect of different bases of cohesiveness could be studied.

The Method of the Experiment

INTRODUCTION

The experiment included the following features:

1. The topic of discussion was the interpretation of a set of pictures. This was an unusual task on which hardly any group standards could have been established outside the experimental situation.
2. The pictures depicted a simple situation which could be discussed in a few minutes. They were so unclear that a change in interpretation was easily possible.
3. Each subject received a set of three pictures, believing that all sets were identical. Actually, there were slight differences among the sets which led to different interpretations. The differences were too slight to be detected in a discussion without seeing the photographs again. This device was successful, and subjects never realized that there were differences (see Figure 1 for the two sets).
4. The experiment was introduced as a cooperative working situation; the eventual outcome, however, consisted of the independent products of each subject. The discussion was introduced as an opportunity to improve their own stories. Necessity for influence was specifically denied, and both length and manner of the discussion were left to the subjects.
5. In order to trace influence to one person only, the experimental groups consisted of pairs.
6. Although most of the subjects attended the same class (of about 250 students), each member of a pair attended a different discussion section of this class. After the session, each subject was asked whether he had known his partner pre-

viously, and if he had, the results of this group were discarded. As the subjects were recruited for a single session of one experiment, they did not expect any prolonged existence of the group.

GENERAL PROCEDURE

After the subjects were introduced to each other, each of them was taken to a different room and given the following instructions:

> Your task is to write a story from a set of three photographs which depict quite a commonplace incident. This gives you an opportunity to give play to your imagination, although the story should be plausible and supported by features of the pictures. The pictures, being taken from a film strip, form a sequence which you will have to reconstruct. Then you will write a story connecting the pictures. Right now you will write a preliminary story. Then you will talk over your ideas with your partner, and afterward you will write a final story. Remember, you should write a good story, but it is important to make it plausible by the use of the available clues.

In addition, they were given the special instructions appropriate to their experimental conditions, which will be explained later. Then they received the pictures and wrote the preliminary story. There was no time limit.

When they were finished they came together to discuss their stories. At the start of the discussion, the subjects were reminded that its object was to help them to improve their own stories. They were cautioned that it was not necessary to conclude with a common story and that they could stop the discussion at any time that they saw its usefulness at an end. The amount and manner of communication was therefore left to the subjects.

After the discussion, the subjects returned to their separate rooms to write their final stories. They were instructed: "Write what you now think to be the best story." They

could not see the pictures again; therefore, they could not check information which they had received from their partners.

After the completion of the experiment, the subjects were told the significant features of the set-up, and all their questions were answered truthfully. In conclusion, they were asked not to discuss the experiment and were thanked for their cooperation.

INTRODUCTION OF THE
EXPERIMENTAL VARIABLES

The experiment was designed to differentiate the pairs by the attractiveness of the group and on the basis of this attractiveness. Three sources of attractiveness were introduced: (1) attraction to the partner, (2) mediation of other goals (task direction), and (3) prestige of the group itself. Each of these variables was introduced in two different strengths. The combination of strength and type gave six different experimental treatments. A seventh treatment was introduced in which any force toward the group was kept at a minimum. The execution of this design required a technique which started at the time the subjects were recruited.

When the subjects signed up in their classes, they were told only that they were going to participate in a group experiment. The sign-up blank included a few questions which were ostensibly going to help in making up the groups. Some questions asked for self-description and self-ratings. The concluding questions read: "You will be paired with another student of your own sex. As we want people together who are congenial, can you describe the type of person you want to work with?" and "What would be the most objectionable traits in a person you would work with?"

Personal Attraction. The questionnaire aided in controlling the personal attraction the subjects had for each other when they entered the discussion. In the treatments where attraction was to be the basis of cohesiveness, the experimenter referred to the questionnaire after giving the instructions and reported on the effectiveness of the matching.

To create weak cohesiveness, he said, "You remember the questions you answered when you signed up in class? We tried to find a partner with whom you could work best. Of course, we couldn't find anybody who would fit the description exactly, but we found a fellow who corresponded to the main points, and you probably will like him. You should get along all right."

To create strong cohesiveness, he said, 'You remember the questions you answered in class about the people you would like to work with? Of course, we usually cannot match people the way they want, but for you we have found almost exactly the person you described. As a matter of fact, the matching was as close as we had expected to happen once or twice in the study, if at all. You'll like him a lot. What's even more, he described a person very much like you. It's quite a lucky coincidence to find two people who are so congenial, and you should get along extremely well."

Task Direction. In the treatments where the group was to mediate goals, the *outcome of the task was stressed.* The experiment was introduced as a test; the importance of its result for the subject was varied to create different degrees of cohesiveness. The questionnaire was mentioned in passing as an unsuccessful attempt to match partners.

For low cohesiveness: "This is a part of a study of the way people use their imaginations. We developed a somewhat special procedure to test this ability." After the instructions for the task were given, the experimenter continued, "In this way, you will have the best chance to show your ability and get a high score in the test—you know, we had some idea of putting people together who were congenial. But that didn't work because of schedule difficulties; so all we could do was to take into account the objections you stated."

For high cohesiveness, the same introduction to the task was given. After the instruc-

tions, the experimenter continued, "Remember, the whole test shows how well you can use your imagination: your product will be judged in comparison with that of other people. We intend, for instance, to compare students from this and other universities, and men and women. The group you are in is a special prize group. There are ten such groups, and the two members who produce the best story get $5 each. You know, we had some idea of putting people together who were congenial, but that didn't work out because of schedule difficulties. All we could do was to take into account the objections you stated."

Group Prestige. Another way in which cohesiveness was produced was by *stressing the value of belonging to the group.* This was done by making selection for this particular group an important achievement. The rarity of this achievement was varied to create different strengths of cohesiveness. Here, too, the idea of being matched by personality was played down.

For low cohesiveness, the experiment was introduced: "This is part of a study in the use of imagination. We are trying to compare good groups and bad groups in this type of work, and your lab section instructor told us you would be particularly good material for a good group. You know, we had some idea of putting people together who were congenial, but that didn't work out because of schedule difficulties. All we could do was to take into account the objections you stated." Then the instructions were given.

For high cohesiveness, the experimenter stated: "This is part of a study in the use of imagination. We select at first the pairs of people to work together by means of the questionnaire you filled out in class (although the part about putting congenial people together didn't work out because of schedule difficulties; all we could do was to take into account the objections you stated). We try to put people together who should be especially good at this kind of task. We checked on assignments with your lab instructor. From all we could learn, you have all the qualifications which have been set up to be good in this task: you two should be about the best group we have had. So we want to use you as a model group after which we can train other people to be more productive in this task." Then the instructions were given.

Negative Treatment. To minimize all forces to belong to the group, the attraction to the partner, the outcome of task, and the pleasure of the discussion itself were put in a dim light.

> After the instructions were given, the experimenter said, "I am sorry, but the idea of putting people together who are congenial didn't work. Especially in your case we had some trouble because of scheduling. So the fellow you are going to work with may irritate you a little, but I hope it will work out all right. The trouble is that the whole thing is quite frustrating and the conversation somewhat strained, so we would have preferred to have you with a person you liked. But anyway, do the best you can."

In addition to the talk by the experimenter, some treatments were stressed by the headings of the paper on which the subjects wrote their stories—for instance, "prize group" for task-directed and "model group" for prestige high-cohesive groups.

Ten groups were used in each treatment. Both members of each pair were of the same sex. In each treatment, seven pairs were male and three female. Assignment of a pair to a treatment was a matter of chance, independent of the answers to the questionnaire. One exception in discarding the questionnaire results had to be made: subjects were assigned to a condition where personal attraction was important, only if they had made a reasonable amount of specification about their partners.

MEASUREMENT

The Measurement of Influence. Influence could be measured by the change from the preliminary story to the final story. In order to arrive at a numerical measure of the change, the stories were broken down into small units, and the amount of change could be measured by the change of these elements.

The changes were determined only by comparison of the codes without going back to the original stories. Any difference in the coded stories, omissions or additions, were considered changes. These could then be separated into those toward the partner's position and independent changes.

Changes toward the partner were considered those which tended toward the position the partner had shown in either his first or final story. All changes which did not meet these criteria were considered to be independent changes.

The Recording of the Communication. The communication process itself was recorded by two observers, who afterward rated the total discussion.

One observer noted all the communication. His observation blank contained 20 categories, which fell into three groups:

One group contained all the methods which could be used to influence the partner.

The second group contained the reactions to attempted influence. There were five such categories, arranged along an acceptance-rejection dimension. They were given arbitrary weights from 1 to 5; from them a mean level of reaction could be computed.

The categories which were not concerned with influence attempts made up the last group.

The second observer noted only the attempts to influence. From his observations the strength of attempted influence could be measured. He classified the attempts used into 17 categories, such as assertion, hypothetical example, rhetorical question, and exhortation. One sentence was scored as a unit.

Weighting factors were assigned to the different categories by having each observer (five observers alternated in this task) rate the influence attempts which he noted on a four-point scale of intensity. The amount of influence attempted by one person during a period of time was computed as the number of units scored weighted by the factors of the categories in which they occurred.

Reliability of this measure was checked in three different groups by having two observers rate the same meeting and then comparing the values they obtained for "number of observations" and "strength of attempted influence" for each partner, minute by minute. For the number of observations the correlations are $+.91$, $+.78$, and $+.64$, and for strength of attempted influence, $+.87$, $+.68$, and $+.61$.

After the meeting both observers attempted to characterize the whole discussion by a pattern of discussion. Although they were permitted to distinguish five patterns for purposes of analysis, these were reduced to two main types, active patterns and withdrawing patterns:

Active patterns implied acceptance of the discussion situation where the main emphasis of the discussion was on discovering the important facts in the pictures, on reaching an agreement, or on arguing for argument's sake.
Withdrawing patterns implied little involvement in the situation. They included discussion which consisted mainly of telling the stories without additional comments or of agreeing that the problem was too indefinite.

A specific type of pattern was assigned to a group when both observers checked the same one. Agreement was reached in sixty-three of the seventy groups.

Inasmuch as the observers administered the instructions, they always knew which type of group they were observing. They were, however, mainly unaware of the nature of the hypotheses under investigation. Therefore, it is unlikely that they would have biased the results. The principal measure derived from the observation—strength of attempted influence—was derived so indirectly from the actual observations that any bias is excluded for the measure. The categories could only be weighted after all experimental sessions had been concluded.

Other Measures. Additional ratings and questions used will be discussed in the next section.

A sociometric scale was designed to measure the effects of the experimental situation on interpersonal relationships. The scale consisted of seven questions which were known to correspond to different strengths of attraction. The questions were scaled by an abbreviated Thurstone technique (Thurstone and Chave, 1929). The questions used were selected from a set of forty original questions by a group of judges which consisted of seventeen students in social psychology. Each judge divided the statements into seven groups according to the desire for intimacy expressed. The questions which showed the smallest dispersion, and for which medians corresponded to the seven integers, were used in the scale (scale value in parentheses), as follows:

I would like to see him around campus sometime (1)
I would want to have him in the same lab section (2)
I would enjoy talking to him (3)
I would enjoy an animated discussion with him (4)
I would like to discuss serious general problems with him (5)
I would want him to come to me with his problems (6)
I would discuss important personal problems with him (7)

In the course of the experiment it was found that 71 percent of the 140 subjects gave a perfect scale pattern (that is, a "yes" answer to any question implied a "yes" to any question with a lower scale value). An additional 16 percent gave scale patterns which were only one point off. It seemed justified to take the total number of "yes" answers as the score assigned by the scale.

Results

STRENGTH OF COHESIVENESS

Effects on Communication. In a high cohesive group, it is our hypothesis that the members will try to come to an agreement on differences in point of view. Discussion on relevant topics, then, should be sought, and its importance should be accepted.

The patterns of discussion provide a first test of this hypothesis. In the low cohesive groups, the withdrawing patterns predominate. Of twenty-six of these groups, nineteen were rated as having withdrawing patterns. In twenty-seven high cohesive groups only eleven showed withdrawing patterns, while sixteen showed active patterns. (In four low cohesive and three high cohesive groups, no agreement between the observers could be reached.) This difference is significant at the 2-percent level (chi-square test). The dominant behavior in the active class— arguing, seeking agreement, and seeking facts—implies a considerable attempt to influence the partner. This over-all measure indicates that low cohesive groups react to realization of difference by withdrawing from the situation, while high cohesive groups tend to eliminate the difference.

On the more molecular level, the importance of the discussion for the partners is indicated by the reaction to the partners' attempts at influence. An average reaction level could be computed for the five categories in which the observation of reaction was recorded, as the mean of all the values of these observations.

Table 1 shows that the level of reaction was higher in the more cohesive groups.

TABLE 1

LEVEL OF REACTION

Group	Personal Attraction	Task Direction	Group Prestige	Negative
Low Cohesive	2.10	2.22	2.38	2.25
High Cohesive	2.49	2.85	2.50	

$$F = \frac{V \text{ strength}}{V \text{ within groups}} = 3.91; \ df = 1 \text{ and } 54;$$

$$p < .06$$

These groups tend more toward argument and serious consideration of the partner's position than the less cohesive groups. It

may seem surprising that the more cohesive groups show more outward signs of resistance, like objecting to the partner's story. From our interpretation of the reaction level, however, it may be suggested that argument against the partner is not a real indicator of resistance; rejecting the group as a reference group would imply polite agreement as a means of avoiding entering the discussion at all. Giving expression to disagreement suggests a more important role for the discussion and offers opportunities for later agreement.

This interpretation derives some support if we consider the extremes of reactions with different strengths of cohesiveness. Taking the mean of the most "accepting" reactions occurring in each group, we find no difference between high and low cohesive groups. The mean value of these "minimum" reactions is 1.47 for low cohesive and 1.43 for high cohesive groups. The difference is pronounced, however, if the mean of the most "objecting" reactions in each group is used. This is 3.83 for high and 3.10 for low cohesive groups. There is just as much agreement in both types of groups, but in the high cohesive groups it is accompanied by serious argument, while in the low cohesive groups, it seems to mean mere politeness.

Self-ratings on resistance confirm the interpretation that the more argumentative level in the high cohesive groups does not mean greater resistance to the partner's arguments. These ratings show a slight decrease in resistance, not statistically significant, with all three bases of cohesiveness.

Observation has shown that more influence is being exerted in the more cohesive groups. Conversely, the participants feel that more pressure has been exerted on them. In postsession interviews the subjects were asked, "Did you think that your partner tried to influence you?" Less than half (21 of 45) of the members of the low cohesive groups reported that they felt some pressure, while more than two thirds (36 of 51) of the members of the high cohesive groups did so. The remainder did not answer adequately for coding. This difference is significant at the 2-percent level (chi-square test).

Acceptance of the discussion group as a meaningful reference point means more, however, than a stronger effort to come to an agreement with the partner. It should be manifested also by a great acceptance of the partner as a participant in the discussion. In general, we can assume that, because of individual differences, one person will be more interested than another in convincing his partner of the superiority of his story. But if pressures from the group are great, they will affect both members strongly, and the ultimate effect of individual differences will be less pronounced. Further, the partners should try to adjust to each other, and give each other a greater opportunity to press their points. The total effect would be that influence attempts are more evenly distributed in high cohesive than in low cohesive groups.

TABLE 2

PERCENTAGE OF ATTEMPTED INFLUENCE
IN HIGHER INDUCER

Group	Personal Attraction	Task Direction	Group Prestige	Negative
Low Cohesive	62.4	64.6	60.2	
				60.0
High Cohesive	58.9	54.9	56.7	

$$F = \frac{V \text{ strength}}{V \text{ within cells}} = 6.98; \, df = 1 \text{ and } 54;$$

$$p < .02$$

Table 2 confirms this hypothesis: the mean percentage of attempted influence for the higher "inducer" is above 60 percent in all low cohesive conditions, while it falls to 54-59 percent in the high cohesive groups. In only nine of the thirty high cohesive groups does one partner account for more than 60 percent of attempted influence, while this occurred in more than half of the low cohesive groups.

In line with the hypothesis that attempted influence is a question of personal preference in low cohesive groups while it is made necessary by the pressures toward uniformity in high cohesive groups, we can expect members of high cohesive groups to accept their partner's greater share of influence attempts. We can test this by comparing the scores on the sociometric scale given to high and low inducers in the different treatments. In Table 3, we see that the lower inducers like their partners less than do the higher inducers in the low cohesive groups, while no such differences are shown in the high cohesive groups.

Until now, we have limited the discussion to the six treatments in which some degree of cohesiveness was created. In the negative condition, on the other hand, the forces toward the group were kept at a minimum. Without any forces of this kind, there was no pressure toward uniformity within the group. But acceptance of the experimental situation, interest in the problem itself, and a desire to help the experimenter combined to make the subjects try to make something of the discussion.

The reaction level of the negative groups is 2.25, which is close to the average reaction level (2.33) of the low cohesive groups (Table 1). The high inducers in these groups account for 60 percent of the total attempted influence, just as the percentages in the low cohesive groups were 60 percent or more (Table 2). They agree, too, with the low cohesive groups in that the high inducers were more attracted to partners than were the low inducers (Table 3).

The members of negative groups, however, attempted more influence than those of the low cohesive groups. Six of the 10 discussions in these groups were rated as having "active" patterns. In the same way, nine of 15 subjects in this treatment reported that the partner tried to influence them. This, too, is a similar proportion to that of the high cohesive groups.

The foregoing can be interpreted as indicating that in the negative groups there was little acceptance of the other member of the pair as a partner in the discussion; the sub-

TABLE 3

EXTENT TO WHICH HIGH AND LOW INDUCERS LIKE THEIR PARTNERS

Group	Personal Attraction		Task Direction		Group Prestige		Negative	
	High Inducer	Low Inducer	High Inducer	Low Inducer	High Inducer	Low Inducer	High Inducer	Low Inducer
Low Cohesive	4.7	3.8	4.60	3.20	4.55	3.90	4.55	3.90
High Cohesive	4.25	4.35	3.90	4.15	4.50	4.40		

Low cohesive groups: $F = \dfrac{V \text{ strength of inducers}}{V \text{ within cells}} = 6.097$; $df = 1$ and 54; $p < .03$

High cohesive groups: F not significant

jects do not seem to consider the discussion as a serious step in establishing an idea about the stories. But, on the other hand, they are much freer in expressing their opinions and pushing their own ideas.

Effects on Influence. Table 4 shows the amount of influence which was shown by both partners. There is a definite increase in change toward features of the partners' stories when cohesiveness increases. That this represents influence and not increased motivation, and hence a greater willingness to change and improve the story, can be seen from a comparison with changes which were not in the partner's direction. These

TABLE 4

CHANGES INFLUENCED BY THE PARTNER

Group	Personal Attraction	Task Direction	Group Prestige	Negative
Low Cohesive	7.9	8.9	6.7	8.5
High Cohesive	10.5	11.0	8.3	

$$F = \frac{V \text{ strength}}{V \text{ within cells}} = 3.13; \; df = 1 \text{ and } 54;$$

$$p < .11$$

changes (which cannot be ascribed to the influence of the partner) increase slightly only in two of three conditions. The mean of the low cohesive groups is 5.3, of the high cohesive groups 5.7; this difference is statistically not significant. It would seem, there-

fore, that the change in Table 4 does represent influence and not a greater desire to improve the story.

The increase in total change within the group does not give an adequate picture of the manner in which influence changes with an increase in cohesiveness. We have shown before how uneven distribution of change within the group can be taken as a sign of strong pressures toward uniformity. In line

TABLE 5

CHANGE TOWARD THE PARTNER: HIGHER CHANGERS AND LOWER CHANGERS

(a) *Higher Changers*

Group	Personal Attraction	Task Direction	Group Prestige	Negative
Low Cohesive	5.0	5.6	4.8	7.0
High Cohesive	7.3	7.3	6.1	

(b) *Lower Changers*

Group	Personal Attraction	Task Direction	Group Prestige	Negative
Low Cohesive	2.9	3.3	1.9	1.5
High Cohesive	3.2	3.7	2.2	

High changers: $F = \dfrac{V \text{ strength}}{V \text{ within cells}} = 4.78$;

$df = 1$ and 54; $p < .05$

Low changers: F not significant

with this, Table 5 shows how much the partner who changed more and the partner who changed less were influenced in each treatment. We can see that almost the total increase in influence is the function of one member of the pair. As we expected, the greater pressure toward uniformity in the high cohesive groups results in the possibility that some members can be influenced quite strongly; as long as the agreement is reached at some point, perhaps close to the original position of one of the partners, it does not matter whether some members will show much change and some only a little. In low cohesive groups, however, both partners can merely show small and approximately equal changes.

The negative groups show an average amount of change which is mainly borne by one member of the group. This result seems surprising, as it would make the negative groups very similar to the high cohesive groups. But we shall see later that the meaning of change is different in these groups and that different members of the group are primarily affected.

The data presented in this section show that cohesiveness can indeed be considered as a unitary concept, although the increase in cohesiveness corresponded to very different operations in the various treatments. We could predict the same effect in each case by deriving the consequences of increasing the attraction of the group.

THE BASIS OF COHESIVENESS

We shall attempt now to explore further the meaning of the different conditions of attractiveness.

If an individual is attracted to a group because he wants to be with some of the members, he will consider the group activity mainly a means of meeting them. We should expect therefore that he will try to be pleasant and active with less regard to the performance of the group activity as such.

If an individual enters the group to achieve ulterior goals, we can expect him to try to perform the required task as efficiently and as fast as possible. There should be less effort to establish a relationship with the other group members except insofar as it is necessary to perform the work successfully.

If an individual enters a group because membership as such is attractive, we can expect that he will be concerned about his behavior in order to stay in the favored position. His behavior toward the other group members will be determined by his perception of them as parts of the environment in which he has to succeed. He should adjust quickly to their attitude toward him; we should expect, therefore, rapid development of complementary personal roles and a conscious effort to show good behavior.

The Effects of Personal Attraction. Several signs in the observations of the personal-attractiveness treatment suggest that the discussion gave more attention to influences as such and was more related to interpersonal relationship than in the other conditions.

From the observations of the discussion we find some evidence of the increased attention to the process of influence. One measurement of this tendency is the number of groups in which the category "asks to be influenced" was coded by the observer who recorded all communications. Statements of this kind occurred quite rarely. But they were noted in ten of the twenty groups in the personal attraction treatment and in only five of the other fifty groups.

The types of attempted influence, which the same observer recorded, give evidence in the same direction. The personal attraction groups favor the more direct approach while the most distant method—"stating one's own position"—is less represented than in the other conditions.

A further suggestion on how personal the influence process becomes in this treatment is shown in the analysis of the sociometric scores. With high personal attraction, the high changer likes his partner less than his partner likes him. This difference amounts to two steps on the sociometric scale. This difference is significant at the 1-percent level.

The Effects of Task Direction. The relationship created by setting up a goal which can be reached by the group activity tends to have somewhat opposite effects from those of the personal attraction relationship. Group activity is seen as a necessity which is to be completed as quickly and as efficiently as possible.

The intent toward accomplishment is shown in the average decrease of 95 seconds in the time taken for the discussion when cohesiveness increases (Table 6). This shortening of interaction does not mean any withdrawal from the situation; however, the discussion becomes more intense. This is indicated by the strength of attempted influence per minute. It increases correspondingly to the decrease in time between the low and high conditions. This increase is almost statistically significant (11-percent level). There is no comparable increase in the other conditions. There, attempted influence increases with cohesiveness because the time of discussion increases, while in the task-direction condition, the intensity increases.

TABLE 6
TIME OF DISCUSSION (SECONDS)

Group	Personal Attraction	Task Direction	Group Prestige	Negative
Low Cohesive	412.5	415.5	307	
				330
High Cohesive	449	321.5	362.5	

t not significant	t = 2.91	t = 3.65
	p < .01	p < .01

The Effects of Group Prestige. We have suggested before that cohesiveness based on group prestige will have the following implications: Members will be careful of their own behavior, guiding their actions by some general notions of how they are supposed to act. As they focus their attention on their own proper behavior, the partner becomes the background in this situation, though a very important one. They will therefore adjust quickly to their partners' behavior, and

a mutual adjustment of personal roles will result.

We should expect that the feeling of being "on the spot" would result in wariness during the experimental situation. We saw that in these conditions the discussion tended to be short—an average of 335 seconds (Table 6). Further, relatively little change occurred. Table 7 shows the combined changes, both toward the partner and

TABLE 7
CHANGES OF ALL KINDS

Group	Personal Attraction	Task Direction	Group Prestige	Negative
Low Cohesive	13.2	14.5	11.6	
				13.4
High Cohesive	16.5	17.7	12.7	

$$F = \frac{V \text{ types}}{V \text{ within cells}} = 2.33; \, df = 2 \text{ and } 54;$$

$$p < .08$$

independently, and we see that the prestige groups clung most to the original story. This may be interpreted as an avoidance of the discussion situation.

If the complementary relationship between the partners is established here, it should result in an unequal distribution of influence. We have seen that there is a general tendency in this direction in the high cohesive groups. Evidence is given in Table 8 that, in the prestige groups, this differentiation is a function of the amount of attempted influence by the group members. We see that in groups of this kind, especially with high cohesiveness, the low inducer changes more than the higher inducer. This would suggest that, in this treatment, making the larger change corresponds to a submissive role.

It would be reasonable to suppose that under the stress of the group-prestige situation, a conscious effort was made to let the partner have his say, particularly by the member who felt in control of the situation. If we assume that this effort will be made

TABLE 8

Changes of High and Low Inducers

Group	Personal Attraction		Task Direction		Group Prestige		Negative	
	High Inducer	Low Inducer	High Inducer	Low Inducer	High Inducer	Low Inducer	High Inducer	Low Inducer
Low Cohesive	4.0	3.9	4.0	4.9	2.4°	4.3°		
							6.6‡	1.9‡
High Cohesive	5.3	5.2	5.9	5.2	2.7†	5.6†		

° $t = 1.36, p < .20$ † $t = 2.42, p < .05$ ‡ $t = 3.38, p < .02$
Remaining differences not significant. Note: Two groups with tied scores of attempted influence excluded.

after the relationship is established, we could expect that the difference in attempted influence in the first part of the discussion would be quite large but would vanish during the later part. Analysis of the difference in attempted influence in the first and second half of the discussions bears out this hypothesis. Of all conditions, only the high prestige group showed an appreciable difference between the first and second half of the discussion. The difference between the partners dropped from 8.3 "attempt units" to virtual equality between the partners (0.9 units). This is the closest the two partners came to equality in any of the treatments. The difference between the two parts of the discussion in these groups is significant at the 5-percent level.

Table 8 shows the negative condition in striking contrast to the high prestige condition. Here the higher inducer changes most. No genuine interaction seems to be involved but, rather, two people acting independently and convincing only themselves that they should change.

Conclusions

Within this setting the results show that an increase in cohesiveness, independent of its nature, will produce the following consequences:

1. In the high cohesive groups the members made more effort to reach an agreement. Both the ratings of the total discussion and direct observation showed more serious effort to enter the discussion in highly cohesive groups. The subjects' own statements also confirmed the high pressures in these groups.

2. Behavior in the highly cohesive groups was more affected by the situation than in the low cohesive groups. The amount of attempted influences measured in highly cohesive groups showed less individual differences, and those differences which did exist were not considered on a personal level.

3. In the highly cohesive groups the discussion was more effective in that it produced influence—that is, group members changed more toward the partners' positions than they did in the less cohesive groups.

4. In the highly cohesive groups the change was quite unevenly distributed between the members, while in the less cohesive groups the changes were more evenly distributed. On the average, one member of the highly cohesive groups changed more than either member of the less cohesive groups; and the other member of the highly cohesive group was nearly the same as one member of the less cohesive groups.

The four points summarize the effects of the forces to belong to the group, of cohesiveness considered as a unitary concept. The differences among the ways in which cohesiveness was produced led to the following interpretations about patterns of communication and influence:

1. If cohesiveness was based on personal attraction, group members wanted to transform the discussion into a longish, pleas-

ant conversation. The discussion was taken as a personal effort, and rejection of persuasion tended to be resented.

2. If cohesiveness was based on the performance of a task, group members wanted to complete the activity quickly and efficiently; they spent just the time necessary for performance of the task, and they tried to use this time for the performance of the task only. They tended to participate in the discussion only as much as they thought it valuable to achieve their purposes.

3. If cohesiveness was based on group prestige, group members tried to risk as little as possible to endanger their status: they acted cautiously, concentrated on their own actions, and adjusted to their part-

ners as the social environment. One partner would easily assume a dominant role, and the submissive member was influenced more, without their actually trying to establish this relationship.

Finally, with cohesiveness at a minimum, the members of the pair acted independently and with little consideration for each other. As the subjects did not try to adjust to the other member of the pair, each member was concerned only with his own discussion. Influence, accordingly, did not depend on the action of the partner but on the interest of the member himself in entering the group activity.

References

FESTINGER, L., SCHACHTER, S., and BACK, K. *Social pressure in informal groups.* New York: Harper & Row, 1950.

THURSTONE, L. L., and CHAVE, E. J. *The measurement of attitudes.* Chicago: University of Chicago Press, 1929.

Group Decision and Social Change ❈ Kurt Lewin

The following experiments on group decision have been conduced during the last four years. They are not in a state that permits definite conclusions. But they show the nature of the problems and the main factors concerned. They also indicate the type of concepts to which the attempt to integrate cultural anthropology, psychology, and sociology into one social science may lead.

Social Channels and Social Perception

The meaning and the over-all effect of a group decision depends upon the nature of

the process itself, and upon the position of the group, within the total social field. In regard to these broader questions we will consider two aspects of social steering, namely, steering through gatekeepers and the function which reality perception should have.

CHANNELS, GATES, AND GATEKEEPERS

Food Habits and Food Channels. The first experiment on group decision was part of a larger study on food habits. Its main objective was a comparison of different ethnic and economic groups in a midwestern town. The favorite family food was studied,

This article is slightly abridged from the original, which was written especially for T. M. Newcomb and E. L. Hartley (Eds.), *Readings in Social Psychology*, New York: Holt, Rinehart and Winston, 1947. Reprinted by permission of Mrs. Gertrud Lewin and the publisher.

what food was considered essential, what main frame of reference and values guided the thinking of these groups about foods, and what authorities were seen as standing behind these standards and values. Children at different ages were included to indicate the process of acculturation of the individual in regard to food. Since this study was part of a larger problem of changing food habits in line with war needs, we were in-. terested in including an attempt to bring about some of the desired changes at least on a small scale.

The data acquired give considerable insight into the existing attitudes and practices of the various groups. However, in this, as in many other cases, such data about a present state of affairs do not permit many conclusions in regard to how to proceed best to bring about a change. Should one use radio, posters, lectures, or what other means and methods for changing efficiently group ideology and group action? Should one approach the total population of men, women, and children who are to change their food habits, or would it suffice and perhaps be more effective to concentrate on a strategic part of the population? Obviously the housewife plays some particular role in food habits. What are the underlying assumptions?

Food which comes to the family table is likely to be eaten by someone in the family since little is thrown away. If this is correct, to consider methods of changing family food habits we have first to ask: how does food come to the table?

Food comes to the table through different channels, such as the Buying Channel or the Gardening Channel.[1] After the food has been bought, it might be placed in the icebox or put in the pantry to be either cooked later or prepared directly for the table (Fig. 1). Similarly, the food moves through the garden channel in a step-by-step fashion.

[1] For quantitative data, see Lewin (1943).

To understand what comes on the table we have to know the forces which determine what food enters a channel. Whether food enters the channel to the family table or not is determined in the buying situation. The buying situation can be characterized as a conflict situation. Food 1 (Fig. 1) might be attractive, that is, the force ($f_{P,EF}$) toward eating is large but at the same time the food might be very expensive and therefore the opposing force ($f_{P,Sp.M}$) against spending money is large too. Food 2 might be unattractive but cheap. In this case the conflict would be small. The force toward buying might be composed of a number of components, such as the buyer's liking for the food, his knowledge of his family likes and dislikes, or his ideas about what food is "essential."

The opposing forces might be due to the lack of readiness to spend a certain amount of money, a dislike of lengthy or disagreeable form of preparation, unattractive taste, lack of fitness for the occasion, etc. Food is bought if the total force toward buying becomes greater than the opposing forces (Food 3) until the food basket is filled. Food of type 1 can be called conflict food.

It is culturally significant that the average conflict rating is considerably higher in the middle group (7.44) than in the high (4.35) or the low economic group (5.62). This conflict is probably the result of the greater discrepancy between the standards this group would like to keep up and their ability to do so in a situation of rising prices.

In comparing the conflict rating of different foods for the same group, one finds that meat stands highest for the low group, whereas it is second for the middle and third for the high economic group. That probably means that the conflict between "like" and "expense" in the low group is most outspoken for meat. The high conflict rating of vegetables for the high and middle economic group is probably an expression of the fact that vegetables are desirable as

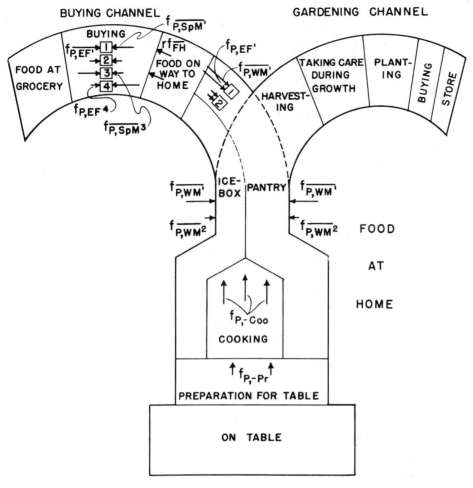

Fig. 1. Channels through which food reaches the family table.

health food but not well liked and not easily prepared. The rates are:

Food	High Group	Middle Group	Low Group
Vegetables	.89	1.44	.57
Milk	.70	.89	.33
Meat	.65	1.28	.95
Butter	.30	.94	.67
Fruits	.43	.94	.62
Potatoes	. . .	.33	.76

The Gate. It is important to know that once food is bought some forces change its direction. Let us assume the housewife has finally decided to buy the high conflict Food 1. The force against spending money, instead of keeping the food out of the channel, will then make the housewife doubly eager not to waste it. In other words, the force $(f_{P,WM})$ against wasting money will have the same direction as the force toward eating this food or will have the character of a force against leaving the channel.

This example indicates that a certain area within a channel might function as a "gate": The constellation of the forces before and after the gate region are decisively different in such a way that the passing or not passing of a unit through the whole channel depends to a high degree upon what happens in the gate region. This holds not only for food channels but also for the traveling of a news item through certain communication channels in a group, for movements of goods, and the social locomotion of individuals in many organizations. A university, for instance, might be quite strict in its admission policy and might set up strong forces against the passing of weak candidates. Once a student is admitted, however, the university frequently tries to do everything in its power to help everyone along. Many business organizations follow a similar policy. Organizations which discriminate against members of a minority group frequently use the argument that they are not ready to accept individuals whom they would be unable to promote sufficiently.

The Gatekeeper. In case a channel has a gate, the dominant question regarding the movements of materials or persons through the channel is: who is the gatekeeper and what is his psychology?

The study of the high, middle, and low groups, as well as of a group of Czechs and of Negroes in a midwestern town, revealed that all channels except gardening were definitely controlled by the housewife.

We can conclude from this that changes of food habits in the family finally depend on changes of the psychology of the housewife in the buying situation. Changes of the attitudes and desires of children and husbands will affect actual food habits only to the degree they affect the housewife.

Similar considerations hold for any social constellation which has the character of a channel, a gate, and gatekeepers. Discrimination against minorities will not be changed as long as the forces are not changed which determine the decisions of the gatekeeper. Their decision depends partly on their ideology, that is, the system of values and beliefs which determines what they consider to be "good" or "bad," partly on the way they perceive the particular sit- uation. This latter point will be considered more closely by discussing problems of planning.

PLANNING, FACT-FINDING, AND EXECUTION

Planning usually starts with something like a general idea. For one reason or another it seems desirable to reach a certain objective. Exactly how to circumscribe this objective and how to reach it is frequently not too clear. The first step, then, is to examine the idea carefully in the light of the means available. Frequently more fact-finding about the situation is required. If this first period of planning is successful, two items emerge: an "over-all plan" of how to reach the objective and a decision in regard to the first step of action. Usually this planning has also somewhat modified the original idea.

The next period is devoted to executing the first step of the over-all plan. In highly developed fields of social management, such as modern factory management or the execution of a war, this second step is followed by certain fact-findings. For example, in the bombing of Germany a certain factory may have been chosen as the first target after careful consideration of various priorities and of the best means and ways of dealing with this target. The attack is pressed home and immediately a reconnaissance plane follows with the one objective of determining as accurately and objectively as possible the new situation.

This reconnaissance or fact-finding has four functions: It should evaluate the action by showing whether what has been achieved is above or below expectation. It should serve as a basis for correctly planning the next step. It should serve as a basis for modifying the "over-all plan." Finally, it gives the planners a chance to learn, that is, to gather new general insight, for instance, regarding the strength and weakness of certain weapons or techniques of action.

The next step again is composed of a

circle of planning, executing, and reconnaissance or fact-finding for the purpose of evaluating the results of the second step, for preparing the rational basis for planning the third step, and for perhaps modifying again the over-all plan.

Rational social management, therefore, proceeds in a spiral of steps each of which is composed of a circle of planning, action, and fact-finding about the result of the action.

In most social areas of management and self-management of groups, such as conducting a conference and committee meeting, family life, or the improvement of intergroup relations within and between nations, we are still lacking objective standards of achievement. This has two severe effects: (1) People responsible for social management are frequently deprived of their legitimate desire for reconnaissance on a realistic basis. Under these circumstances, satisfaction or dissatisfaction with achievement becomes mainly a question of temperament. (2) In a field that lacks objective standards of achievement, no learning can take place. If we cannot judge whether an action has led forward or backward, if we have no criteria for evaluating the relation between effort and achievement, there is nothing to prevent us from coming to the wrong conclusions and encouraging the wrong work habits. Realistic fact-finding and evaluation is a prerequisite for any learning.

Group Decision

LECTURE COMPARED WITH GROUP DECISION (RED CROSS GROUPS)

A preliminary experiment in changing food habits[2] was conducted with six Red Cross groups of volunteers organized for

[2] The studies on nutrition discussed in this article were conducted at the Child Welfare Research Station of the State University of Iowa for the Food Habits Committee of the National Research Council (Executive Secretary, Margaret Mead).

home nursing. Groups ranged in size from 13 to 17 members. The objective was to increase the use of beef hearts, sweetbreads, and kidneys. If one considers the psychological forces which kept housewives from using these intestinals, one is tempted to think of rather deep-seated aversions requiring something like psychoanalytical treatment. Doubtless a change in this respect is a much more difficult task than, for instance, the introduction of a new vegetable such as escarole. There were, however, only 45 minutes available.

In three of the groups attractive lectures were given which linked the problem of nutrition with the war effort, emphasized the vitamin and mineral value of the three meats, giving detailed explanations with the aid of charts. Both the health and economic aspects were stressed. The preparation of these meats was discussed in detail as well as techniques for avoiding those characteristics to which aversions were oriented (odor, texture, appearance, etc.). Mimeographed recipes were distributed. The lecturer was able to arouse the interest of the groups by giving hints of her own methods for preparing these "delicious dishes," and her success with her own family.

For the other three groups Mr. Alex Bavelas developed the following procedure of group decision. Again the problem of nutrition was linked with that of the war effort and general health. After a few minutes, a discussion was started to see whether housewives could be induced to participate in a program of change without attempting any high-pressure salesmanship. The group discussion about "housewives like themselves" led to an elaboration of the obstacles which a change in general and particularly change toward sweetbreads, beef hearts, and kidneys would encounter, such as the dislike of the husband, the smell during cooking, etc. The nutrition expert offered the same remedies and recipes for preparation which were presented in the lectures to the other groups. But in these groups preparation techniques were offered after the groups had become sufficiently involved to be interested in knowing whether certain obstacles could be removed.

In the earlier part of the meeting a census was taken on how many women had served any of these foods in the past. At the end of the meeting, the women were asked by a showing of hands who was willing to try one of these meats within the next week.

A follow-up showed that *only 3 percent* of the women who heard the lectures served one of the meats never served before, whereas after group decision *32 percent* served one of them.

If one is to understand the basis of this striking difference, several factors may have to be considered.

1. Degree of Involvement. Lecturing is a procedure in which the audience is chiefly passive. The discussion, if conducted correctly, is likely to lead to a much higher degree of involvement. The procedure of group decision in this experiment follows a step-by-step method designed (*a*) to secure high involvement and (*b*) not to impede freedom of decision. The problem of food changes was discussed in regard to "housewives like yourselves" rather than in regard to themselves. This minimized resistance to considering the problems and possibilities in an objective, unprejudiced manner, in much the same way as such resistance has been minimized in interviews which use projective techniques, or in a socio-drama which uses an assumed situation of role playing rather than a real situation.

2. Motivation and Decision. The prevalent theory in psychology assumes action to be the direct result of motivation. I am inclined to think that we will have to modify this theory. We will have to study the particular conditions under which a motivating constellation leads or does not lead to a decision or to an equivalent process through which a state of "considerations" (indecisiveness) is changed into a state where the individual has "made up his mind" and is ready for action, although he may not act at that moment.

The act of decision is one of those transitions. A change from a situation of undecided conflict to decision does not mean merely that the forces toward one alternative become stronger than those toward the other alternative. If this were the case, the resultant force should frequently be extremely small. A decision rather means that the potency of one alternative has become zero or is so decidedly diminished that the other alternative and the corresponding forces dominate the situation. This alternative itself might be a compromise. After the decision people may feel sorry and change their decision. We cannot speak of a real decision, however, before one alternative has become dominant so far as action is concerned. If the opposing forces in a conflict merely change so that the forces in one direction become slightly greater than in the other direction, a state of blockage or extremely inhibited action results rather than that clear one-sided action which follows a real decision.

Lecturing may lead to a high degree of interest. It may affect the motivation of the listener. But it seldom brings about a definite decision on the part of the listener to take a certain action at a specific time. A lecture is not often conducive to decision.

Evidence from everyday experience and from some preliminary experiments by Bavelas in a factory indicate that even group discussions, although usually leading to a higher degree of involvement, as a rule do not lead to a decision. It is very important to emphasize this point. Although group discussion is in many respects different from lectures, it shows no fundamental difference on this point.

Of course, there is a great difference in asking for a decision after a lecture or after a discussion. Since discusson involves active participation of the audience and a chance to express motivations corresponding to different alternatives, the audience might be more ready "to make up its mind," that is, to make a decision after a group discussion than after a lecture. A group discussion gives the leader a better indication of where the audience stands and what particular obstacles have to be overcome.

In the experiment on hand, we are dealing with a group decision after discussion. The decision, itself, takes but a minute or two. (It was done through raising of hands as an answer to the question: Who would like to serve kidney, sweetbreads, beef hearts next week?) The act of decision, however, should be viewed as a very important process of giving dominance to one of the alternatives, serving or not serving. It has an effect of freezing this motivational constellation for action. We will return to this point later.

3. *Individual versus Group.* The experiment does not try to bring about a change of food habits by an approach to the individual, as such. Nor does it use the "mass approach" characteristic of radio and newspaper propaganda. Closer scrutiny shows that both the mass approach and the individual approach place the individual in a quasi-private, psychologically isolated situation with himself and his own ideas. Although he may, physically, be part of a group listening to a lecture, for example, he finds himself, psychologically speaking, in an "individual situation."

The present experiment approaches the individual as a member of a face-to-face group. We know, for instance, from experiments in level of aspiration (Lewin, 1946) that goal setting is strongly dependent on group standards. Experience in leadership training and in many areas of re-education, such as re-education regarding alcoholism or delinquency (Lewin and Grabbe, 1945), indicates that it is easier to change the ideology and social practice of a small group handled together than of single individuals. One of the reasons why "group carried changes" are more readily brought about seems to be the unwillingness of the individual to depart too far from group standards; he is likely to change only if the group changes. We will return to this problem.

One may try to link the greater effectiveness of group decision procedures to the fact that the lecture reaches the individual in a more individualistic fashion than group discussion. If a change of sentiment of the group becomes apparent during the discussion, the individual will be more ready to come along.

It should be stressed that in our case the decision which follows the group discussion does not have the character of a decision in regard to a group goal; it is rather a decision about individual goals in a group setting.

4. *Expectation.* The difference between the results of the lectures and the group decision may be due to the fact that only after group decision did the discussion leader mention that an inquiry would be made later as to whether a new food was introduced into the family diet.

5. *Leader Personality.* The difference in effectiveness may be due to differences in leader personality. The nutritionist and the housewife who did the lecturing were persons of recognized ability, experience, and success. Still, Mr. Bavelas, who led the discussion and subsequent decision, is an experienced group worker and doubtless of unusual ability in this field.

To determine which of these or other factors are important, a number of systematic variations have to be carried out. To determine, for instance, the role of the decision as such, one can compare the effect of group discussion with and without decision. To study the role of group involvement and the possibility of sensing the changing group sentiment, one could introduce decisions after both, lecture and discussion, and compare their effects.

The following experiments represent partly analytical variations, partly repetitions with somewhat different material.

LECTURE VERSUS GROUP DECISION
(NEIGHBORHOOD GROUPS)

Dana Klisurich, under the direction of Marian Radke, conducted experiments with 6 groups of housewives composed of 6-9 members per group. She compared the effect of a lecture with that of group decision. The topic for these groups was increasing home consumption of milk, in the form of fresh or evaporated milk or both (Radke and Klisurich).

The procedure followed closely that described above. Again there was no attempt at high-pressure salesmanship. The group discussion proceeded in a step-by-step way, starting again with "what housewives in general might do" and only then leading to the individuals present. The lecture was kept as interesting as possible. The knowledge transmitted was the same for lecture and group decision.

A check-up was made after two weeks and after four weeks. As in the previous experiments, group decision showed considerably greater effectiveness, both after two weeks and after four weeks and for both fresh and evaporated milk (Figs. 2 and 3).

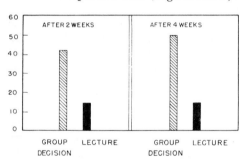

Fig. 2. Percentage of mothers reporting an increase in the consumption of fresh milk.

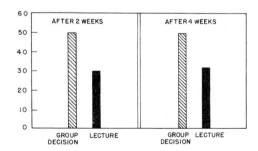

Fig. 3. Percentage of mothers reporting an increase in the consumption of evaporated milk.

This experiment permits the following conclusions:

1. It shows that the greater effectiveness of the group decision in the first experiment is not merely the result of the personality or training of the leader. The leader was a lively person, interested in people, but she did not have particular training in group work. She had been carefully advised and had had a try-out in the group decision procedure. As mentioned above, the leader in lecture and group decision was the same person.

2. The experiment shows that the different effectiveness of the two procedures is not limited to the foods considered in the first experiment.

3. It is interesting that the greater effectiveness of group decision was observable not only after one week but after two and four weeks. Consumption after group decision kept constant during that period. After the lecture it showed an insignificant increase from the second to the fourth week. The degree of permanency is obviously a very important aspect of any changes in group life. We will come back to this point.

4. As in the first experiment, the subjects were informed about a future check-up after group decision but not after the lecture. After the second week, however, both groups knew that a check-up had been made and neither of them was informed that a second check-up would follow.

5. It is important to know whether group decision is effective only with tightly knit groups. It should be noticed that in the second experiment the groups were composed of housewives who either lived in the same neighborhood or visited the nutrition information service of the community center. They were not members of a club meeting regularly as were the Red Cross groups in the first experiment. On the other hand, a good proportion of these housewives knew each other. This indicates that decision in a group setting seems to be effective even if the group is not a permanent organization.

INDIVIDUAL INSTRUCTION VERSUS
GROUP DECISION

For a number of years, the state hospital in Iowa City has given advice to mothers on feeding their babies. Under this program, farm mothers who have their first child at the hospital meet with a nutritionist for from 20-25 minutes before discharge from the hospital to discuss feeding. The mother receives printed advice on the composition of the formula and is instructed in the importance of orange juice and cod liver oil.

There had been indication that the effect of this nutrition program was not very satisfactory. An experiment was carried out by Dana Klisurich under the direction of Marian Radke to compare the effectiveness of this procedure with that of group decision (Radke and Klisurich).

With some mothers individual instruction was used as before. Others were divided into groups of six for instruction on and discussion of baby feeding. The manner of reaching a decision at the end of this group meeting was similar to that used in the previous experiments. The time for the six mothers together was the same as for one individual, about 25 minutes.

After two weeks and after four weeks, a check was made on the degree to which each mother followed the advice on cod liver oil and orange juice. Figures 4 and 5 show the percentage of individuals who completely followed the advice. The group decision method proved far superior to the individual instruction. After four weeks every mother who participated in group decision followed exactly the prescribed diet in regard to orange juice.

The following specific results might be mentioned:

1. The greater effect of group decision in this experiment is particularly interesting. Individual instruction is a setting in which the individual gets more attention from the instructor. Therefore, one might expect the individual to become more

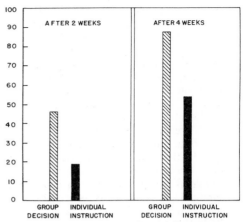

Fig. 4. Percentage of mothers following completely group decision or individual instruction in giving cod liver oil.

deeply involved and the instruction to be fitted more adequately to the need and sentiment of each individual. After all, the instructor devotes the same amount of time to one individual as he does to six in group decision. The result can be interpreted to mean either that the amount of individual involvement is greater in group decision or that the decision in the group setting is itself the decisive factor.

2. Most of the mothers were not acquainted with each other. They returned to farms

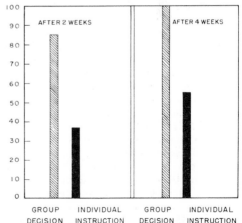

Fig. 5. Percentage of mothers following completely group decision or individual instruction in giving orange juice.

which were widely separated. Most of them had no contact with each other during the following four weeks. The previous experiment had already indicated that the effectiveness of group decision did not seem to be limited to well-established groups. In this experiment the absence of social relations among the mothers before and after the group meeting is even more clearcut.

3. The data thus far do not permit reliable quantitative, over-all comparisons. However, they point to certain interesting problems and possibilities. In comparing the various experiments concerning the data two weeks after group decision, one finds that the percentage of housewives who served kidneys, beef hearts or sweetbreads is relatively similar to the percentage of housewives who increased the consumption of fresh milk or evaporated milk or of mothers who followed completely the diet of cod liver oil with their babies. The percentages lie between 32 and 50. The percentage in regard to orange juice for the baby is clearly higher, namely, 85 percent. These results are surprising in several respects. Mothers are usually eager to do all they can for their babies. This may explain why a group decision in regard to orange juice had such a strong effect. Why, however, was this effect not equally strong on cod liver oil? Perhaps, giving the baby cod liver oil is hampered by the mothers' own dislike of this food. Kidneys, beef hearts, and sweetbreads are foods for which the dislike seems to be particularly deep-seated. If the amount of dislike is the main resistance to change, one would expect probably a greater difference between these foods and, for instance, a change in regard to fresh milk. Of course, these meats are particularly cheap and the group decision leader was particularly qualified.

4. The change after lectures is in all cases smaller than after group decision. However, the rank order of the percentage of change after lectures follows the rank order after group decision, namely (from low to high), glandular meat, fresh milk, cod liver oil for the baby, evaporated milk for the family, orange juice for the baby.

The constancy of this rank order may be interpreted to mean that one can ascribe to each of these foods—under the given circumstances and for these particular populations—a specific degree of "resistance to change." The "force toward change" resulting from group decision is greater than the force resulting from lecture. This leads to a difference in the amount (or frequency) of change for the same food without changing the rank order of the various foods. The rank order is determined by the relative strength of their resistance to change.

5. Comparing the second and the fourth week, we notice that the level of consumption remains the same or increases insignificantly after group decision and lecture regarding evaporated or fresh milk. A pronounced increase occurs after group decision and after individual instruction on cod liver oil and orange juice, that is, in all cases regarding infant feeding. This seems to be a perplexing phenomenon if one considers that no additional instruction or group decision was introduced. On the whole, one may be inclined to expect weakening effect of group decision with time and therefore a decrease rather than an increase of the curve. To understand the problems involved, it is essential to formulate the question of condition of social change on a more theoretical level.

QUASI-STATIONARY SOCIAL EQUILIBRIA AND THE PROBLEM OF PERMANENT CHANGE

1. The Objective of Change. The objective of social change might concern the nutritional standard of consumption, the economic standard of living, the type of group relation, the output of a factory, the productivity of an educational team. It is important that a social standard to be changed does not have the nature of a "thing" but of a "process." A certain standard of consumption, for instance, means that a certain action—such as making certain decisions, buying, preparing, and canning certain food in a family—occurs with a certain frequency within a given period. Similarly, a certain type of group relations means that within a given period certain friendly and hostile actions and reactions of a certain degree of severity occur between the members of two groups. Changing group relations or changing consumption means changing the level at which these multitude of events proceed. In other words, the "level" of consumption, of friendliness, or of productivity is to be characterized as the aspect of an ongoing social process.

Any planned social change will have to consider a multitude of factors characteristic for the particular case. The change may require a more or less unique combination of educational and organizational measures; it may depend upon quite different treatments or ideology, expectation and organization. Still, certain general formal principles always have to be considered.

2. *The Conditions of a Stable Quasistationary Equilibrium.* The study of the conditions for change begins appropriately with an analysis of the conditions for "no change," that is, for the state of equilibrium.

From what has been just discussed, it is clear that by a state of "no social change" we do not refer to a stationary but to a quasistationary equilibrium; that is, to a state comparable to that of a river which flows with a given velocity in a given direction during a certain time interval. A social change is comparable to a change in the velocity or direction of that river.

A number of statements can be made in regard to the conditions of quasi-stationary equilibrium. (These conditions are treated more elaborately elsewhere (Lewin, 1947).)

(A) The strength of forces which tend to lower that standard of social life should be equal and opposite to the strength of forces which tend to raise its level. The resultant of forces on the line of equilibrium should therefore be zero.

(B) Since we have to assume that the strength of social forces always shows variations, a quasi-stationary equilibrium presupposes that the forces against raising the standard increase with the amount of raising and that the forces against lowering increase (or remain constant) with the amount of lowering. This type of gradient which is

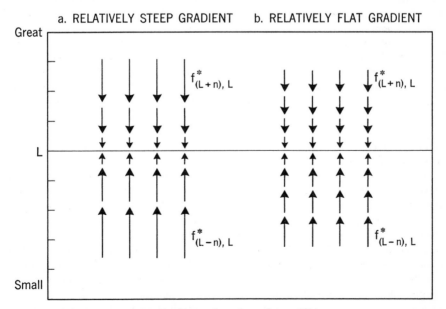

a. RELATIVELY STEEP GRADIENT   b. RELATIVELY FLAT GRADIENT

Great

$f^*_{(L+n), L}$

L

$f^*_{(L-n), L}$

Small

Fig. 6. Gradients of resultant forces (f°).

characteristic for a "positive central force field" (Lewin, 1947) has to hold at least in the neighborhood of the present level (Fig. 6).

(C) It is possible to change the strength of the opposing forces without changing the level of social conduct. In this case the tension (degree of conflict) increases.

3. *Two Basic Methods of Changing Levels of Conduct.* For any type of social management, it is of great practical importance that levels of quasi-stationary equilibria can be changed in either of two ways: by adding forces in the desired direction, or by diminishing opposing forces. If a change from the level L_1 to L_2 is brought about by increasing the forces toward L_2 the secondary effects should be different from the case where the same change of level is brought about by diminishing the opposing forces.

In both cases the equilibrium might change to the same new level. The secondary effect should, however, be quite different. In the first case, the process on the new level would be accompanied by a state of relatively high tension; in the second case, by a state of relatively low tension. Since increase of tension above a certain degree is likely to be paralleled by higher aggressiveness, higher emotionality, and lower constructiveness, it is clear that as a rule the second method will be preferable to the high pressure method.

The group decision procedure which is used here attempts to avoid high pressure methods and is sensitive to resistance to change. In the experiment by Bavelas on changing production in factory work (as noted below), for instance, no attempt was made to set the new production goal by majority vote because a majority vote forces some group members to produce more than they consider appropriate. These individuals are likely to have some inner resistance. Instead a procedure was followed by which a goal was chosen on which everyone could agree fully.

It is possible that the success of group decision and particularly the permanency of the effects is, in part, due to the attempt to bring about a favorable decision by removing counterforces within the individuals rather than by applying outside pressure.

The surprising increase from the second to the fourth week in the number of mothers giving cod liver oil and orange juice to the baby can probably be explained by such a decrease of counterforces. Mothers are likely to handle their first baby during the first weeks of life somewhat cautiously and become more ready for action as the child grows stronger.

4. *Social Habits and Group Standards.* Viewing a social stationary process as the result of a quasi-stationary equilibrium, one may expect that any added force will change the level of the process. The idea of "social habit" seems to imply that, in spite of the application of a force, the level of the social process will not change because of some type of "inner resistance" to change. To overcome this inner resistance, an additional force seems to be required, a force sufficient to "break the habit," to "unfreeze" the custom.

Many social habits are anchored in the relation between the individuals and certain group standards. An individual P may differ in his personal level of conduct (L_P) from the level which represents group standards (L_{Gr}) by a certain amount. If the individual should try to diverge "too much" from group standards, he would find himself in increasing difficulties. He would be ridiculed, treated severely and finally ousted from the group. Most individuals, therefore, stay pretty close to the standard of the groups they belong to or wish to belong to. In other words, the group level itself acquires value. It becomes a positive valence corresponding to a central force field with the force $f_{P,L}$ keeping the individual in line with the standards of the group.

5. *Individual Procedures and Group Procedures of Changing Social Conduct.* If the resistance to change depends partly on the value which the group standard has for the individual, the resistance to change should diminish if one diminishes the strength of the value of the group standard or changes

the level perceived by the individual as having social value.

This second point is one of the reasons for the effectiveness of "group carried" changes (Maier, 1946) resulting from procedures which approach the individuals as part of face-to-face groups. Perhaps one might expect single individuals to be more pliable than groups of like-minded individuals. However, experience in leadership training, in changing of food habits, work production, criminality, alcoholism, prejudices, all indicate that it is usually easier to change individuals formed into a group than to change any one of them separately (Lewin and Grabbe, 1945). As long as group standards are unchanged, the individual will resist

changes more strongly the farther he is to depart from group standards. If the group standard itself is changed, the resistance which is due to the relation between individual and group standard is eliminated.

6. *Changing as a Three-step Procedure: Unfreezing, Moving, and Freezing of a Level.* A change toward a higher level of group performance is frequently short lived: after a "shot in the arm," group life soon returns to the previous level. This indicates that it does not suffice to define the objective of a planned change in group performance as the reaching of a different level. Permanency of the new level, or permanency for a desired period, should be included in the objective. A successful change

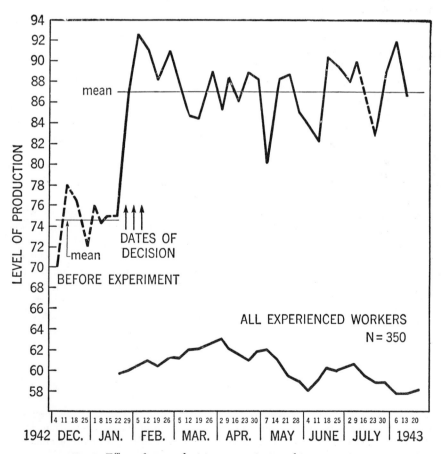

Fig. 7. Effect of group decision on sewing-machine operators.

includes therefore three aspects: unfreezing (if necessary) the present level L_1, moving to the new level L_2, and freezing group life on the new level. Since any level is determined by a force field, permanency implies that the new force field is made relatively secure against change.

The "unfreezing" of the present level may involve quite different problems in different cases. Allport (1945) has described the "catharsis" which seems to be necessary before prejudices can be removed. To break open the shell of complacency and self-righteousness, it is sometimes necessary to bring about deliberately an emotional stir-up.

Figure 7 presents an example of the effect of three group decisions of a team in a factory reported by Bavelas (Maier, 1946) which illustrates an unusually good case of permanency of change measured over nine months.

The experiments on group decision reported here cover but a few of the necessary variations. Although in some cases the procedure is relatively easily executed, in others it requires skill and presupposes certain general conditions. Managers rushing into a factory to raise production by group decisions are likely to encounter failure. In social management as in medicine there are no patent medicines and each case demands careful diagnosis.

One reason why group decision facilitates change is illustrated by Willerman.[3] Figure 8 shows the degree of eagerness to have the members of a students' eating cooperative change from the consumption of white bread to whole wheat. When the change was simply requested the degree of eagerness varied greatly with the degree of personal preference for whole wheat. In case of

[3] See Lewin (1943).

group decision the eagerness seems to be relatively independent of personal preference; the individual seems to act mainly as a "group member."

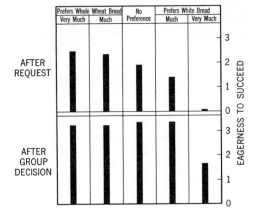

Fig. 8. Relation between own food preferences and eagerness to succeed.

Summary

Group decision is a process of social management or self-management of groups. It is related to social channels, gates and gate-keepers; to the problem of social perception and planning; and to the relation between motivation and action, and between the individual and the group.

Experiments are reported in which certain methods of group decision prove to be superior to lecturing and individual treatment as means of changing social conduct.

The effect of group decision can probably be best understood by relating it to a theory of quasi-stationary social equilibria, to social habits and resistance to change, and to the various problems of unfreezing, changing and freezing social levels.

References

ALLPORT, G. W. Catharsis and the reduction of prejudice. In K. Lewin and P. Grabbe (Eds.), Problems of re-education. *J. soc. Issues,* 1945, *1*, 3-10.

LEWIN, K. Behavior and development as a function of the total situation. In L. Carmichael (Ed.), *Manual of child psychology.* New York: Wiley, 1946, 791-844.

SOME FACTORS IN "GROUP DECISION" ❧ 437

LEWIN, K. Forces behind food habits and methods of change. *Bull. Nat. Res. Coun.*, 1943, *108*, 35-65.

LEWIN, K. Frontiers in group dynamics: concept, method, and reality in social science; social equilibria and social change. *Hum. Relat.*, 1947, *1*, 5-42.

LEWIN, K., and GRABBE, P. (Eds.). Prob-

lems of re-education. *J. soc. Issues*, 1945, *1*, 3-10.

MAIER, N. R. F. *Psychology in industry*. Boston: Houghton Mifflin Co., 1946.

RADKE, M., and KLISURICH, D. Experiments in changing food habits. Unpublished Manuscript.

Some Factors in "Group Decision" ❧ Edith Bennett Pelz

The major historical antecedents of this experiment were three studies reported by Kurt Lewin[1] and performed under his direction in the 1940's, comparing the effectiveness of a procedure Lewin named "group decision" with that of another method used to induce a change in food habits.

By "group decision" Lewin meant a group discussion about the desirability of a particular action to be taken by members of the group *as individuals*. The discussion always ended with the leader's request for individual decisions regarding intended action. This experiment also focused upon individuals under inducement to reach a personal decision in a group setting. This use of the term should be clearly differentiated from one involving collective solutions of group problems in which action decisions have implications for the discussion participants as group members rather than as individuals.

The first of the Lewinian studies, performed by Bavelas, Festinger, Woodward, and Zander, found that a method of group decision was vastly superior to the lecture method in persuading housewives to serve

intestinal meats. The second experiment, by Radke and Klisurich (1947), again compared group decision to lecture, improving on the previous design by holding the factor of leader personality constant over both methods. Group decision again was shown superior to lecture in increasing housewives' use of fresh and evaporated milk. The third study cited by Lewin—Radke and Klisurich (1947)—compared the effectiveness of group decision and individual instruction in persuading mothers to supplement infant diets with orange juice and cod-liver oil. Again results were favorable to the group decision method, though differences this time were not as striking as in the previous studies. Neal Miller succinctly summarized both the significance and the limitations of the Lewinian researches (1951, p. 468):

The investigators found that a group of housewives who participated in a discussion, made a public decision by raising their hands, and were told that there would be a follow-up study to check on what they did were much more likely to serve the nonpreferred meat than another group who listened to a lecture without making a public decision and

[1] See K. Lewin, preceding article.

This article was adapted by the author especially for E. E. Maccoby, T. M. Newcomb, and E. L. Hartley (Eds.), *Readings in Social Psychology*, 3d Ed., New York: Holt, Rinehart and Winston, 1958, from E. B. Bennett, "Discussion, Decision, Commitment and Consensus in 'Group Decision,'" *Human Relations*, 1955, 8, 251-274. Reprinted by permission of the author and publisher.

without being told to expect a follow-up study. In this pioneer stage these investigators have tended to lump together a number of factors such as hearing the views of other group members, having a chance to express one's objections, being required to make some immediate public or private decision, etc.

The present experiment was designed to analyze further the operation of group decision as used by Lewin and his coworkers by breaking it down into several separate factors which could be individually assessed.

Group decision, in the Lewinian experiments, consisted of group discussions concluding with a request for decision. These discussions yielded 100-percent positive decisions which were made publicly. In addition, they always included a specifically stated time period within which the requisite action was to be taken (and after which experimental effects were measured), as well as the information that a follow-up would be made. The contrasted approaches, lecture and individual instruction, were similar *only* in so far as the same information was conveyed. On every other variable they differed.

A specific time limit and knowledge of follow-up were entirely eliminated from the present experiment. Four factors were thus isolated for study in the research reported here:

1. *Group discussion* as a means of conveying information;
2. *Decision* to perform a specific action;
3. *Commitment*—the degree to which the decision is indicated publicly;
4. *Degree of consensus* by the group in reaching the requested decision.

In addition to the separation of these four factors, an important improvement over previous designs was the provision of an *objective action criterion*.

Hypotheses

For each of the four major variables a hypothesis, testable without reference to the

effectiveness of the remaining factors, was formulated.

Hypothesis I: Group discussion, as an influence technique, is a more effective inducement to action than is the lecture method or no persuasion attempt at all.

Hypothesis II: The process of coming to a decision regarding future action raises the probability of the execution of the action.

Hypothesis III: Where a decision is made, a more public commitment or indication of the decision is more effective in assuring the execution of such action than is a less public one.

Hypothesis IV: A high degree of group consensus on intention to act raises the probability that individual members of the group will execute the action above the probability of action by members of groups in which there was a low degree of consensus.

Experimental Procedures

The experimental manipulations attempted to raise the willingness of University of Michigan students in a beginning psychology course to volunteer as subjects in behavioral-science experiments.

Three types of "influence-attempt" and four "decision and commitment" variations were combined to create twelve experimental treatments [as shown in Table 1].

The four variations along the vertical axis represent two of the experimental variables relevant to the testing of two of the hypotheses: (1) The "no-decision" variation is differentiated from all of the other three with reference to the factor of reaching a decision; (2) decision levels II, III, and IV differ with reference to the degree of anonymity with which decisions were indicated.

Thirty-six groups of eight to 16 students were assembled and three groups were assigned to each of the 12 experimental variations. Three male graduate students with teaching experience were trained in practice discussions with subjects comparable to the experimental population. On the basis of the

TABLE 1

TWELVE EXPERIMENTAL VARIATIONS
(with total number of Ss participating in each)

| Commitment Level | Influence Attempt | | | Total |
	Discussion	Lecture	Control	
I. No Decision	39	44	52	135
II. Anonymous Decision	40	35	37	112
III. Partially Anonymous Decision	46	32	35	113
IV. Public Commitment	40	33	40	113
Total	165	144	164	473

practice discussion, they prepared common lecture outlines and discussion objectives. Leader personality was held constant by assigning each man to lead one of the three groups in each of the experimental variations.

In the discussion groups all possible expectations about participating in experiments were elicited and discussed—fears and distrust as well as individual and social gains. Lectures covered the same topics. The control groups heard no arguments pro or con.

Decision-level I groups were dismissed after influence attempts. Control groups at decision-level I were not contacted at this stage of the experiment. In Type II groups students wrote anonymous statements about their willingness to volunteer if asked. In Type III groups those who thought they would volunteer in the future raised their hands. The most public commitment, Type IV, involved raising hands and publicly giving names to the leader, who openly recorded them.

Several days after the completion of experimental sessions, a letter was sent to all subjects announcing the establishment of a "central file" of prospective volunteers by the "Committee for Recruiting Experimental Subjects." They were invited to appear at a specified place during a limited-time period, to make their names, telephone numbers, etc. available to experimenters. Subjects who came to sign up fulfilled the criterion of having "taken action." A week after the volunteering period a questionnaire was administered during class session, yielding further

information on the reported commitments (Did you decide to volunteer?), perceived consensus (How many from your group would you estimate signed up?), and reported action (Did you actually go to sign up?) [2]

Results

I. GROUP DISCUSSION AS A FACTOR

Hypothesis I stated that group discussion, as an influence technique, would have a significantly greater effect upon action than would the lecture method or no influence attempt at all. This prediction was not satisfied by results on the objective-action criterion. Table 2 shows no difference between the influence variations in the proportion of subjects who signed up with the "central file."

One of the postexperimental questionnaire measures, however, does show a striking difference in the influence-attempt groups: In all treatments fewer subjects reported having made a positive decision than had actually done so during the experimental sessions. But, while there had been no differences in the proportion of positive decisions (experimental commitment) in the discussion, lecture and control groups, the reported commitment data show the greatest divergence between the two figures for

[2] The interested reader is referred to E. B. Bennett, op. cit., and Bennett (1952). These sources give fuller descriptions of procedures in equating groups, training leaders, and experimental manipulations.

TABLE 2

NUMBER AND PROPORTION OF SUBJECTS
EXPOSED TO EACH OF THE INFLUENCE
ATTEMPTS WHO FULFILLED THE
ACTION CRITERION

	Total No.	No. Acting	Percentage Acting
Discussion	165	34	21
Lecture	144	31	22
Control	164	31	19

$$\chi^2 = .374 \quad p = .84^*$$

* Probabilities reported throughout this paper are two-tailed chance probabilities. However, where a hypothesis correctly predicts the *direction* of deviation from expected frequencies, the probability of chance occurrence of results is smaller than that read from the table of chi square; e.g., one half as great for a two-by-two analysis (see A. M. Mood and W. J. Dixon, "A Method for Obtaining and Analyzing Sensitivity Data," *J. Amer. Stat. Assn.*, 1948, 43, 109-126). Such cases arise later in this paper.

discussion subjects, the smallest for control subjects. A distortion phenomenon which is especially strong among participants in a group discussion has clearly emerged here.

The Lewinian experiments demonstrated the greater likelihood of action on the part of subjects who had been asked to reach a decision than on the part of those who had not been exposed to a decision request. This approach to the hypothesis is taken in Table

TABLE 4

NUMBER AND PROPORTION OF "ACTORS"
AMONG SUBJECTS WHO WERE AND
WERE NOT ASKED TO REACH A
DECISION

	Total No.	No. Acting	Percentage Acting
No Decision	135	20	15
Decision	338	76	22

$$\chi^2 = 3.509 \quad p = .07$$

4 in which subjects who were not asked to come to a decision (decision-level I) are compared with those from all other decision variations. The results are in the predicted direction and of respectable magnitude (cf. footnote to Table 2).

TABLE 3

NUMBER AND PROPORTION OF SUBJECTS EXPOSED TO EACH
OF THE INFLUENCE ATTEMPTS WHO . . .

	When asked to reach a decision made a positive one			Responded *yes* to later question, *Did you decide to volunteer?*			Percentage Difference
	Total	N	Percent	Total	N	Percent	
Discussion	126	95	75	104	45	44	31
Lecture	92*	70	76	83	46	55	21
Control	112	80	71	90	54	60	11
	$\chi^2 = .604; \quad p = .73$			$\chi^2 = 5.853; \quad p = .06$			

* This datum was lost for eight subjects in the lecture-III variation. The reduced totals for questionnaire data were caused by normal absenteeism in beginning psychology courses.

II. DECISION AS A FACTOR

Hypothesis II stated that the process of coming to a decision on future action would raise the probability that such a decision would be executed. This hypothesis was tested in two ways.

The second interpretation of the decision hypothesis was not testable in the pioneer "group-decision" experiments, in which 100 percent positive decisions were always the goal and the outcome. In the present experiment some subjects who were asked to make a decision did *not* decide to volunteer as research subjects. This fact makes possible a comparison of action by positive and negative deciders (regardless of experimental variation). Here, not a single subject who had responded negatively to a request for decision took the action step.

If failure to indicate a positive decision can be interpreted as a decision *not* to act, Table 5 reveals that such negative decisions

TABLE 5
FREQUENCY OF POSITIVE AND NEGATIVE DECISIONS AMONG THOSE WHO DID AND DID NOT FULFILL THE ACTION CRITERION

	Positive Decision	Negative Decision	Total
Actors	76	0	76
Nonactors	169	85	254
Total	245	85	330

$$\chi^2 = 34.322 \quad p < .001$$

were consistently executed. The hypothesis identifying decision as an effective factor in "group decision" has been substantially confirmed, with reference to both positive and negative deciders.

III. PUBLIC COMMITMENT AS A FACTOR

Hypothesis III stated that a more public commitment to an action decision would be more effective in assuring the execution of the action than a less public one. This hypothesis was tested by comparing results with the three different manners of indicating decisions.

It had been predicted that the number who actually carried out their decision at each commitment level would be in the order: level IV greater than III greater than II, on the basis of the proposition that giving one's name to the leader is a more public commitment than raising one's hand. Nevertheless, results showing either of the "decision-plus" variations to be more effective

than "pure decision" could be accepted as evidence tending to confirm the commitment hypothesis.

The obtained results, however, directly

TABLE 6
NUMBER AND PROPORTION OF SUBJECTS IN EACH COMMITMENT VARIATION WHO FULFILLED THE ACTION CRITERION

	Total No.	No. Acting	Percentage Acting
II. Anonymous Decision	112	32	29
III. Partially Anonymous Decision	113	22	19
IV. Public Commitment	113	22	19

$$\chi^2 = 3.542 \quad p = .18$$

contradict even the less stringent interpretation of Hypothesis III.

The commitment hypothesis, thus, was not supported by the data.

IV. GROUP CONSENSUS AS A FACTOR

Hypothesis IV stated that a high degree of consensus in a group regarding intention to act would raise the probability of action by individual group members.

A. Objective Consensus. Analyses reported here consider the action data in terms of individual group sessions (three in each experimental cell) rather than in terms of experimental variations. A new classification, "high" and "low" positive decision, is introduced here.

For this analysis, the nine groups (level I) who were not asked to make a decision are omitted. In the other 27 groups, subjects were asked to make a decision, and groups varied considerably in the proportion of members who made a positive decision. The group proportions ranged from 100 percent to 41 percent with a mean of 72.5 percent.

Groups with above- and below-average proportions of positive decisions were separated; 13 "high" and 14 "low" groups were thus identified.[3] "High" as well as "low" categories represented subjects exposed to all three sets of treatments on the influence attempt and commitment axes. In this analysis, experimental treatment—the manner in which given levels of consensus were stimulated—may be considered to have been held constant.

In view of the finding (Table 5) that negative deciders did not act and the fact that by definition·there are more committed subjects in the "high" than in the "low" groups, Hypothesis IV had to be tested by a comparison of action and nonaction among committed subjects only (that is, among those who decided to act). Differences in Table 7 lie in the predicted direction but do

TABLE 7

NUMBER AND PROPORTION OF SUBJECTS IN "HIGH" AND "LOW" CONSENSUS GROUPS WHO SUBSEQUENTLY ACTED[*]

	No. Committed	No. Acting	Percentage Acting
High	131	45	34
Low	112	31	28
	$\chi^2 = 1.233$	$p = .27$	

[*] This table includes only those who made a positive decision.

not support the hypothesis with a very high degree of confidence.

B. Perception of Consensus. The dichotomy employed above was based on the objectively measured reactions of subjects to the decision request. Another approach to the hypothesis involves considering group members' perception of these reactions and their belief that action would follow the commitments.

The postexperimental questionnaire item, "How many from your group would you estimate signed up with the central file?" was

[3] These were rechecked for their pre-experimental comparability with each other and the nine "no-decision" groups. No original differences were found. See E. B. Bennett, *op. cit.*

used to check the assumption that seeing others make a commitment is equivalent to believing that they will act. A comparison between objective consensus and answers to this question corroborated this assumption with a relationship significant at the .01 level of confidence.

Perceived consensus could then be tested for its effect on a group member's tendency to act. A separate comparison was made of actors' and nonactors' estimates of the action of others in the "high" consensus, "low" consensus and "no-decision" groups. The 13 individual group sessions within the "high" classification (in each of which consensus was, of course, objectively identical for all participants) were then inspected for actors' and nonactors' estimates of the action of others. In ten of these 13 sessions, people who actually did go to sign up with the central file assumed that more of their fellow group members had also done so than was the case for the nonactors.

C. Consensus and Reported Action. At this point it was interesting to look at reports of action (postexperimental questionnaire item: "Did you go to sign up?"). There were only ten subjects who had not actually met the action criterion but reported having done so.

A disproportionate number of those came from the groups in which there was high consensus ($p = .14$, and cf. footnote to Table 2).

Hypothesis IV, then, received a measure of support. Where a decision request yielded a high proportion of positive decisions and where members of the group perceived this high degree of consensus, the data showed some probability that members would (a) carry out the action themselves, or (b) report having done so, more often than members of groups with smaller proportions of positive decisions.

V. A REDEFINITION OF "GROUP DECISION"

The preceding sections have reported results that rejected Hypotheses I and III and gave support to II and IV. That is, group discussion *per se* was not found to be a variable heightening the probability of action nor was public commitment found to be an effective variable.

The factor of decision, on the other hand, was found to account for significant differences in action. A high degree of actual and perceived consensus regarding intention to carry out an action also showed some relation to action and reported action.

In the Lewinian experiments, it will be remembered, "group decisions" were invariably obtained with 100 percent unanimity. Action (or reported action) from such groups was, in all cases, compared with that of subjects who had been exposed to no request for decision. Populations from our study might now be selected in such a manner as most closely to approximate the populations in the three Lewinian experiments with respect to only those variables that were, here, demonstrated to have an effect on action.

Subjects most like Lewin's "group-decision" participants were those who had been asked to make a decision and themselves decided to volunteer in the setting of groups in which a high proportion of positive decisions had been indicated. There are 131 cases fitting these criteria (cf. Table 7).

Subjects most like Lewin's contrasted groups, in terms of the two effective variables, were, of course, the 135 students who had been exposed to no decision request at all (cf. Table 4).

A comparison of the number who fulfilled the action criterion finds 34 percent in the former group and only 15 percent in the latter, a difference at the significance level $p = < .001$.

Of course, this highly significant result represents a combination of two effects previously established and not an independent confirmation of a virgin hypothesis. Nevertheless, the impressive differences obtained between two experimental conditions in the Lewinian experiments could be said, in this manner, to have been reproduced. This reproduction permits a much clearer identification of the variables to which their large differences can be attributed.

The line of argument followed here indicates that results that have been associated with "group decision" do not need the group-discussion technique. The factors of decision and objective or perceived group consensus alone have been shown to be as effective in increasing the probability of action as "group decision" in the Lewinian experiments.

Conclusions

The purpose of this experiment was the assessment of the contribution of four variables to previously demonstrated effects of a set of experimental conditions termed "group decision." Two of the factors—group discussion as an influence technique and public commitment—were found not to be essential to the reproduction of previously obtained results.

It was further shown that the combination of the two other variables—the process of making a decision and the degree to which group consensus is obtained and perceived—was alone capable of generating differences as large as those reported in the classic experiments of Lewin's co-workers.

The reports of both the Lewinian studies and the present one have referred to "group discussion" and "lecture" as simple, self-evident operations. Yet, there undoubtedly exist tremendous qualitative variations in both. Variables such as leadership technique, salience of subject matter, group cohesiveness, etc., would certainly be expected to affect the influence of the manipulations on subsequent action by participants.

The results of this experiment, then, need not imply a blanket rejection of the usefulness of group discussion and public commitment. The experiment was designed, rather, to test the overgeneralizations that have, at times, been drawn from the dramatic results of the Lewinian studies.

The label "group decision" is, actually, still consistent with the procedures here demonstrated to be effective in influencing behavior of group members. The use of the term, however, is now likely to create more confusion than it has in the past. The same term is widely used in the field of human relations to refer to a genuine group solution of problems involving commonly perceived obstacles to group goals. Since the publication of the results of the Lewinian experiments in the immediate area of decision about individual goals in a group setting, the term "group decision" has also become associated with a procedural requirement of conducting a group discussion before the introduction of a stimulus for decision.

In the light of the findings here reported, therefore, "group decision" might profitably be redefined as "decision about individual goals in a setting of shared norms regarding such goals."

References

BAVELAS, A., FESTINGER, L., WOODWARD, P., and ZANDER, A. The relative effectiveness of a lecture method and a method of group decision for changing food habits. *Bulletin of the committee on food habits*. National Research Council.

BENNETT, EDITH B. *The relationship of group discussion, decision, commitment and consensus to individual action*. Ann Arbor, Mich.: Univer. of Michigan Press, 1952.

MILLER, N. E. Learnable drives and rewards. In S. S. Stevens (Ed.), *Handbook of experimental psychology*. New York: Wiley, 1951.

RADKE M., and KLISURICH, D. Experiments in changing food habits. *J. Amer. Dietetic Assn.*, 1947, 24, 403-409.

Overcoming Resistance ❅ Lester Coch
to Change ❅ John R. P. French, Jr.

Introduction

It has always been characteristic of American industry to change products and methods of doing jobs as often as competitive conditions or engineering progress dictates. One of the most serious production problems faced at the Harwood Manufacturing Corporation has been the resistance of production workers to the necessary changes in methods and jobs. This resistance expressed itself in several ways, such as grievances about the piece rates that went with the new methods, high turnover, very low efficiency, restriction of output, and marked aggression against management.

Efforts were made to solve this serious problem by the use of a special monetary allowance for transfers, by trying to enlist the cooperation and aid of the union, by making necessary layoffs on the basis of efficiency, etc. In all cases, these actions did little or nothing to overcome the resistance to change. On the basis of these data, it was felt that the pressing problem of resistance to change demanded further research for its

This article was adapted by the authors especially for G. E. Swanson, T. M. Newcomb, and E. L. Hartley (Eds.), *Readings in Social Psychology*, Rev. Ed., New York: Holt, Rinehart and Winston, 1952, from *Human Relations*, 1948, *1*, 512-532. Reprinted by permission of the authors and Tavistock Publications, Ltd.

solution. From the point of view of factory management, there were two purposes to the research: (1) Why do people resist change so strongly? and (2) What can be done to overcome this resistance?

Starting with a series of observations about the behavior of changed groups, the first step in the over-all program was to devise a preliminary theory to account for the resistance to change. Then on the basis of the theory, a field experiment was devised and conducted within the context of the factory situation. Finally, the results of the experiment were interpreted in the light of the preliminary theory and the new data.

Background

The main plant of the Harwood Manufacturing Corporation, where the present research was done, is located in the small town of Marion, Virginia. The plant produces pajamas and, like most sewing plants, employs mostly women. The plant's population is about 500 women and 100 men. The workers are recruited from the rural, mountainous areas surrounding the town, and are usually employed without previous industrial experience. The average age of the workers is 23; the average education is eight years of grammar school.

The policies of the company in regard to labor relations are liberal and progressive. A high value has been placed on fair and open dealing with the employees, and they are encouraged to take up any problems or grievances with the management at any time. Every effort is made to help foremen find effective solutions to their problems in human relations, using conferences and role-playing methods. Carefully planned orientation, designed to help overcome the discouragement and frustrations attending entrance upon the new and unfamiliar situation, is used. Plant-wide votes are conducted where possible to resolve problems affecting the whole working population. The company has invested both time and money in employee services, such as industrial music, health services, lunchroom, and recreation programs. As a result of these policies, the company has enjoyed good labor relations since the day it commenced operations.

Harwood employees work on an individual incentive system. Piece rates are set by time study and are expressed in terms of units. One unit is equal to 1 minute of standard work: 60 units per hour equal the standard efficiency rating. Thus, if on a particular operation the piece rate for one dozen is 10 units, the operator would have to produce 6 dozen per hour to achieve the standard efficiency rating of 60 units per hour. The skill required to reach 60 units per hour is great. On some jobs, an average trainee may take thirty-four weeks to reach the skill level necessary to perform at 60 units per hour. Her first few weeks of work may be on an efficiency level of 5 to 20 units per hour.

The amount of pay received is directly proportional to the weekly average efficiency rating achieved. Thus, an operator with an average efficiency rating of 75 units per hour (25 percent more than standard) would receive 25 percent more than base pay. However, there are two minimum wages below which no operator may fall. The first is the plant-wide minimum, the hiring-in wage; the second is a minimum wage based on six months' employment and is 22 percent higher than the plant-wide minimum wage. Both minima are smaller than the base pay for 60 units per hour efficiency rating.

The rating of every piece worker is computed every day, and the results are published in a daily record of production which is shown to every operator. This daily record of production for each production line carries the names of all the operators on that line arranged in rank order of efficiency rating, with the highest rating girl at the top of the list. The supervisors speak to each operator each day about her unit ratings.

When it is necessary to change an operator from one type of work to another, a transfer bonus is given. This bonus is so designed that the changed operator who relearns at an average rate will suffer no loss in earnings after change. Despite this allowance, the general attitudes toward job changes in the factory are markedly negative. Such expressions as, "When you make your units (standard production), they change your job," are all too frequent. Many operators refuse to change, preferring to quit.

The Transfer Learning Curve

An analysis of the after-change relearning curves of several hundred experienced operators rating standard or better prior to change showed that 38 percent of the changed operators recovered to the standard efficiency rating of 60 units per hour. The other 62 percent either became chronically substandard operators or quit during the relearning period.

The average relearning curve for those who recover to standard production on the simplest type job in the plant reaches 60 units per hour after eight weeks and, when smoothed, provides the basis for the transfer bonus. The bonus is the percent difference between this expected efficiency rating and the standard of 60 units per hour. It is interesting to note that this relearning period of an experienced operator is longer than the learning period for a new operator. This is true despite the fact that the majority of transfers—the failures who never recover to standard—are omitted from the curve. However, changed operators rarely complain of "wanting to do it the old way," etc., after the first week or two; and time and motion studies show few false moves after the first week of change. From this evidence it is deduced that proactive inhibition or the interference of previous habits in learning the new skill is either nonexistent or very slight after the first two weeks of change.

An analysis of the relearning curves for forty-one experienced operators who were changed to very difficult jobs, compared the recovery rates for operators making standard or better prior to change with those below standard prior to change. Both classes of operators dropped to a little below 30 units per hour and recovered at a very slow but similar rate. These curves show a general (though by no means universal) phenomenon: that the efficiency rating prior to change does not indicate a faster or slower recovery rate after change.

A Preliminary Theory of Resistance to Change

The fact that relearning after transfer to a new job is so often slower than initial learning on first entering the factory would indicate, on the face of it, that the resistance to change and the slow relearning is primarily a motivational problem. The similar recovery rates of the skilled and unskilled operators tend to confirm the hypothesis that skill is a minor factor and motivation is the major determinant of the rate of recovery. Earlier experiments at Harwood by Alex Bavelas demonstrated this point conclusively. He found that the use of group-decision techniques on operators who had just been transferred resulted in very marked increases in the rate of relearning, even though no skill training was given and there were no other changes in working conditions (Lewin, 1947).

Interviews with operators who have been transferred to a new job reveal a common pattern of feelings and attitudes which are distinctly different from those of successful nontransfers. In addition to resentment against the management for transferring them, the employees typically show feelings of frustration, loss of hope of ever regaining their former level of production and status in the factory, feelings of failure, and a very low level of aspiration. In this respect these transferred operators are similar to the chronically slow workers studied previously.

Earlier unpublished research at Harwood

has shown that the nontransferred employees generally have an explicit goal of reaching and maintaining an efficiency rating of 60 units per hour. A questionnaire administered to several groups of operators indicated that a large majority of them accept as their goal the management's quota of 60 units per hour. This standard of production is the level of aspiration according to which the operators measure their own success or failure; and those who fall below standard lose status in the eyes of their fellow employees. Relatively few operators set a goal appreciably above 60 units per hour.

The actual production records confirm the effectiveness of this goal of standard production. The distribution of the total population of operators in accordance with their production levels is by no means a normal curve. Instead there is a very large number of operators who rate 60 to 63 units per hour and relatively few operators who rate just above or just below this range. Thus we may conclude that:

1. There is a force acting on the operator in the direction of achieving a production level of 60 units per hour or more. It is assumed that the strength of this driving force (acting on an operator below standard) increases as she gets nearer the goal —a typical goal gradient.

On the other hand restraining forces operate to hinder or prevent her from reaching this goal. These restraining forces consist among other things of the difficulty of the job in relation to the operator's level of skill. Other things being equal, the faster an operator is sewing the more difficult it is to increase her speed by a given amount. Thus we may conclude that:

2. The strength of the restraining force hindering higher production increases with increasing level of production.

In line with previous studies, it is assumed that the conflict of these two opposing forces—the driving force corresponding to the goal of reaching 60 and the restraining force of the difficulty of the job— produces frustration. In such a conflict situation, the strength of frustration will depend on the strength of these forces. If the restraining force against increasing production is weak, then the frustration will be weak. But if the driving force toward higher production (i.e., the motivation) is weak, then the frustration will also be weak. Probably both of the conflicting forces must be above a certain minimum strength before any frustration is produced; for all goal-directed activity involves some degree of conflict of this type, yet a person is not usually frustrated so long as he is making satisfactory progress toward his goal. Consequently we assume that:

3. The strength of frustration is a function of the weaker of these two opposing forces, provided that the weaker force is stronger than a certain minimum necessary to produce frustration (French, 1944).

From propositions 1, 2, and 3 we may derive that the strength of frustration: (a) should be greater for operators who are below standard in production than for operators who have already achieved the goal of standard production; (b) should be greater for operators on difficult jobs than for operators on easy jobs; (c) should increase with increasing efficiency rating below standard production. Previous research would suggest the hypothesis that:

4. One consequent of frustration is escape from the field (French, 1944).

An analysis of the effects of such frustration in the factory showed that it resulted, among other things, in such forms of escape from the field as high turnover and absenteeism. The rate of turnover for successful operators with efficiency ratings above standard was much lower than for unsuccessful operators. Likewise, operators on the more difficult jobs quit more frequently than those on the easier jobs. Presumably the effect of being transferred is a severe frustration which should result in similar attempts to escape from the field.

In line with this theory of frustration, and the finding that job turnover is one resultant of frustration, an analysis was made of the turnover rate of transferred operators as compared with the rate among operators who had not been transferred recently. For the year September 1946 to September 1947 there were 198 operators who had not been transferred recently—that is, within the thirty-four-week period allowed for relearning after transfer. There was a second group of 85 operators who had been transferred recently—that is, within the time allowed for relearning the new job. Each of these two groups was divided into seven classifications according to their unit rating at the time of quitting. For each classification the percent turnover per month, based on the total number of employees in that classification, was computed.

The results are given in Figure 1. Both the levels of turnover and the form of the curves are strikingly different for the two groups. Among operators who have not been transferred recently the average turnover per month is about 4½ percent; among recent transfers the monthly turnover is nearly 12 percent. Consistent with the previous

studies, both groups show the predicted very marked drop in the turnover curve after an operator becomes a success by reaching 60 units per hour or standard production. However, the form of the curves at lower unit ratings is markedly different for the two groups. As predicted the nontransferred operators show a gradually increasing rate of turnover up to a rating of 55 to 59 units per hour. The transferred operators, on the other hand, show a high peak at the lowest unit rating of 30 to 34 units per hour, decreasing sharply to a low point at 45 to 49 units per hour. Since most changed operators drop to a unit rating of around 30 units per hour when changed and then drop no further, it is obvious that the rate of turnover was highest for these operators just after they were changed and again much later just before they reached standard. Why?

It is assumed that the strength of frustration for an operator who has *not* been transferred gradually increases because both the driving force toward the goal of reaching 60 and the restraining force of the difficulty of the job increase with increasing unit rating. This is in line with hypotheses 1, 2, and 3 above. For the transferred operator, on the other hand, the frustration is greatest

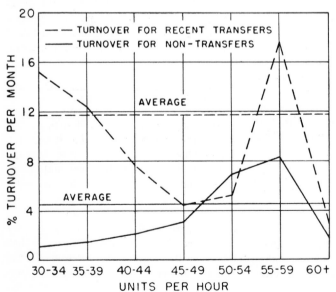

Fig. 1. The rate of turnover at various levels of production for transfers as compared with nontransfers.

immediately after transfer when the contrast of her present status with her former status is most evident. At this point the strength of the restraining forces is at a maximum because the difficulty is unusually great due to proactive inhibition. Then as she overcomes the interference effects between the two jobs and learns the new job, the difficulty and the frustration gradually decrease and the rate of turnover declines until the operator reaches 45-49 units per hour. Then at higher levels of production the difficulty starts to increase again, and the transferred operator shows the same peak in frustration and turnover at 55-59 units per hour.

Though our theory of frustration explains the forms of the two turnover curves in Figure 1, it hardly seems adequate to account for the markedly higher level of turnover for transfers as compared to nontransfers. On the basis of the difficulty of the job, it is especially difficult to explain the higher rate of turnover at 55-59 units per hour for transfers. Evidently additional forces are operating.

Another factor which seems to affect recovery rates of changed operators is the cohesiveness of the work group. Observations seem to indicate that a strong psychological subgroup with negative attitudes toward management will display the strongest resistance to change. On the other hand, changed groups with high cohesiveness and positive cooperative attitudes are the best relearners. Collections of individuals with little or no cohesiveness display some resistance to change but not so much as the groups with high cohesiveness and negative attitudes toward management.

An analysis of turnover records for changed operators with high cohesiveness showed a 4-percent turnover rate per month at 30 to 34 units per hour, not significantly higher than in unchanged operators but significantly lower than in changed operators with little or no cohesiveness. However, the acts of aggression are far more numerous among operators with high than among operators with low cohesiveness. Since both types of operators experience the same frustration as individuals but react to it so differently, it is assumed that the effect of the in-group feeling is to set up a restraining force against leaving the group and driving forces toward staying in the group. In these circumstances, one would expect some alternative reaction to frustration rather than escape from the field. This alternative is aggression. Strong cohesiveness provides strength so that members dare to express aggression which would otherwise be suppressed.

One common result in a cohesive subgroup is the setting of a group standard concerning production. Where the attitudes toward management are antagonistic, this group standard may take the form of a definite restriction of production to a given level. This phenomenon of restriction is particularly likely to happen in a group that has been transferred to a job where a new piece rate has been set; for they have some hope that if production never approaches the standard, the management may change the piece rate in their favor.

A group standard can exert extremely strong forces on an individual member of a small subgroup. That these forces can have a powerful effect on production is indicated in the production record of one presser during a period of forty days.

In the Group	
Days	Efficiency Rating
1-3	46
4-6	52
7-9	53
10-12	56
Scapegoating Begins	
13-16	55
17-20	48
Becomes a Single Worker	
21-24	83
25-28	92
29-32	92
33-36	91
37-40	92

For the first twenty days she was working in a group of other pressers who were producing at the rate of about 50 units per hour.

Starting on the thirteenth day, when she reached standard production and exceeded the production of the other members, she became a scapegoat of the group. During this time her production decreased toward the level of the remaining members of the group. After twenty days the group had to be broken up, and all the other members were transferred to other jobs leaving only the scapegoat operator. With the removal of the group, the group standard was no longer operative; and the production of the one remaining operator shot up from the level of about 45 to 96 units per hour in a period of four days. Her production stabilized at a level of about 92 and stayed there for the remainder of the twenty days. Thus it is clear that the motivational forces induced in the individual by a strong subgroup may be more powerful than those induced by management.

The Experiment

On the basis of the preliminary theory that resistance to change is a combination of an individual reaction to frustration with strong group-induced forces, it seemed that the most appropriate methods for overcoming the resistance to change would be group methods. Consequently an experiment was designed employing three degrees of participation in handling groups to be transferred. The first variation involved *no participation* by employees in planning the changes, though an explanation was given to them. The second variation involved *participation through representation* of the workers in designing the changes to be made in the jobs. The third variation consisted of *total participation* by all members of the group in designing the changes. Two experimental groups received the total participation treatment. The four experimental groups were roughly matched with respect to: (1) the efficiency ratings of the groups before transfer; (2) the degree of change involved in the transfer; (3) the amount of cohesiveness observed in the groups.

In no case was more than a minor change in the work routines and time allowances made. The no-participation group, the eighteen hand pressers, had formerly stacked their work in one-half-dozen lots on a flat piece of cardboard the size of the finished product. The new job called for stacking their work in one-half-dozen lots in a box the size of the finished product. The box was located in the same place the cardboard had been. An additional two minutes per dozen was allowed (by the time study) for this new part of the job. This represented a total job change of 8.8 percent.

The group treated with participation through representation, the thirteen pajama folders, had formerly folded coats with prefolded pants. The new job called for the folding of coats with unfolded pants. An additional 1.8 minutes per dozen was allowed (by time study) for this new part of the job. This represented a total job change of 9.4 percent.

The two total participation groups, consisting of eight and seven pajama examiners respectively, had formerly clipped threads from the entire garment and examined every seam. The new job called for pulling only certain threads off and examining every seam. An average of 1.2 minutes per dozen was subtracted (by time study) from the total time on these two jobs. This represented a total job change of 8 percent.

The no-participation group of hand pressers went through the usual factory routine when they were changed. The production department modified the job, and a new piece rate was set. A group meeting was then held in which the control group was told that the change was necessary because of competitive conditions, and that a new piece rate had been set. The new piece rate was thoroughly explained by the time-study man, questions were answered, and the meeting dismissed.

The group which participated through representatives was changed in a different manner. Before any changes took place, a group meeting was held with all the operators to be changed. The need for the change was presented as dramatically as possible, showing two identical garments produced in the factory; one was produced in 1946 and had sold for 100 percent more than its fellow in 1947. The group was asked to identify the cheaper one and could not do it. This demonstration effectively shared with the group the entire problem of the necessity of cost reduction. A general agreement was reached that a savings could be effected by removing the "frills" and "fancy" work from the garment without affecting the folders' opportunity to achieve a high efficiency rating. Management then presented a plan to set the new job and piece rate:

1. Make a check study of the job as it was being done.
2. Eliminate all unnecessary work.
3. Train several representative operators in the correct methods.
4. Set the piece rate by time studies on these specially trained operators.
5. Explain the new job and rate to all the operators.
6. Train all operators in the new method so they can reach a high rate of production within a short time.

The group approved this plan (though no formal group decision was reached), and chose the operators to be specially trained. A submeeting with the "special" operators was held immediately following the meeting with the entire group. They displayed a co-operative and interested attitude and immediately presented many good suggestions. This attitude carried over into the working out of the details of the new job; and when the new job and piece rates were set, the "special" operators referred to the resultants as "our job," "our rate," etc. The new job and piece rates were presented at a second group meeting to all the operators involved. The "special" operators served to train the other operators on the new job.

The total participation groups went through much the same kind of meetings. The groups were smaller, and a more intimate atmosphere was established. The need for a change was once again made dramatically clear; the same general plan was presented by management. However, since the groups were small, all operators were chosen as "special" operators—that is, all operators were to participate directly in the designing of the new jobs, and all operators would be studied by the time-study man. It is interesting to note that in the meetings with these two groups, suggestions were immediately made in such quantity that the stenographer had great difficulty in recording them. The group approved of the plans, but again no formal group decision was reached.

RESULTS

The results of the experiment are summarized in graphic form in Figure 2. The

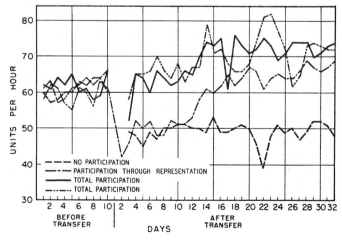

Fig. 2. The effects of participation through representation (Group I) and of total participation (Groups II and III) on recovery after an easy transfer.

gaps in the production curves occur because these groups were paid on a time-work basis for a day or two. The no-participation group improved little beyond their early efficiency ratings. Resistance developed almost immediately after the change occurred. Marked expressions of aggression against management occurred, such as conflict with the methods engineer, expression of hostility against the supervisor, deliberate restriction of production, and lack of cooperation with the supervisor. There were 17 percent quits in the first forty days. Grievances were filed about the piece rate, but when the rate was checked, it was found to be a little "loose."

The group treated with participation through representation showed an unusually good relearning curve. At the end of fourteen days, the group averaged 61 units per hour. During the fourteen days, the attitude was cooperative and permissive. They worked well with the methods engineer, the training staff, and the supervisor. (The supervisor was the same person in the cases of the first two groups.) There were no quits in this group in the first forty days. This group might have presented a better learning record if materials had not been scarce during the first seven days. There was one act of aggression against the supervisor recorded in the first forty days. It is interesting to note that the three special representative operators recovered at about the same rate as the rest of their group.

OVERCOMING RESISTANCE TO CHANGE

The total participation groups recovered faster than the other experimental groups. After a slight drop on the first day of change, the efficiency ratings returned to a prechange level and showed sustained progress thereafter to a level about 14 percent higher than the prechange level. No additional training was provided them after the second day. They worked well with their supervisors, and no indications of aggression

were observed from these groups. There were no quits in either of these groups in the first forty days.

A fifth experimental group, composed of only two sewing operators, was transferred by the total-participation technique. Their new job was one of the most difficult jobs in the factory, in contrast to the easy jobs for the four other experimental groups. As expected, the total participation technique again resulted in an unusually fast recovery rate and a final level of production well above the level before transfer.

In the first experiment, the no-participation group made no progress after transfer for a period of thirty-two days. At the end of this period the group was broken up, and the individuals were reassigned to new jobs scattered throughout the factory. Two and a half months after their dispersal, the thirteen remaining members of the original group, having regained standard production, were again brought together as a group for a second experiment.

This second experiment consisted of transferring the group to a new job, using the total participation technique. The new job was a pressing job of comparable difficulty to the new job in the first experiment. On the average it involved about the same degree of change. In the meetings no reference was made to the previous behavior of the group on being transferred.

The results of the second experiment were in sharp contrast to the first (see Figure 3). With the total-participation technique, the same group now recovered rapidly to their previous efficiency rating, and, like the other groups under this treatment, continued on beyond it to a new high level of production. There was no aggression or turnover in the group for nineteen days after change, a marked modification of their previous behavior after transfer. Some anxiety concerning their seniority status was expressed, but this was resolved in a meeting of their elected delegate, the union business agent, and a management representative.

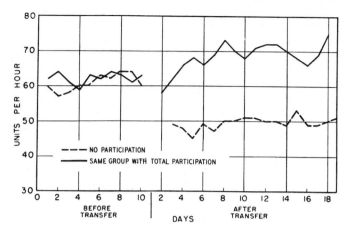

Fig. 3. A comparison of the effect of no participation with the different participation procedures on the same group.

Interpretation

The purpose of this section is to explain the drop in production resulting from transfer, the differential recovery rates of the three experimental treatments, the increases beyond their former levels of production by the participating groups, and the differential rates of turnover and aggression.

The first experiment showed that the rate of recovery is directly proportional to the amount of participation, and that the rates of turnover and aggression are inversely proportional to the amount of participation. The second experiment demonstrated more conclusively that the results obtained depended on the experimental treatment rather than on personality factors like skill or aggressiveness, for identical individuals yielded markedly different results in the no-participation treatment as contrasted with the total-participation treatment.

Apparently total participation has the same type of effect as participation through representation, but the former has a stronger influence. In regard to recovery rates, this difference is not unequivocal because the experiment was unfortunately confounded. Right after transfer, the latter group had insufficient material to work on for a period of seven days. Hence their slower recovery during this period is at least in part due to insufficient work. In succeeding days, however, there was an adequate supply of work,

and the differential recovery rate still persisted. Therefore, we are inclined to believe that participation through representation results in slower recovery than does total participation.

Before discussing the details of why participation produces high morale, we will consider the nature of production levels. In examining the production records of hundreds of individuals and groups in this factory, one is struck by the constancy of the level of production. Though differences among individuals in efficiency rating are very large, nearly every experienced operator maintains a fairly steady level of production, given constant physical conditions. Frequently the given level will be maintained despite rather large changes in technical working conditions.

As Lewin has pointed out, this type of production can be viewed as a quasi-stationary process—in the ongoing work the operator is forever sewing new garments, yet the level of the process remains relatively stationary (1947). Thus there are constant characteristics of the production process permitting the establishment of general laws.

In studying production as a quasi-stationary equilibrium, we are concerned with two types of forces: (1) forces on production in a downward direction, (2) forces on production in an upward direction. In this situation we are dealing with a variety of both upward forces tending to increase the level of production and downward forces tending to decrease the level of production. However, in the present experiment we have no method of measuring independently all of the component forces either downward or upward. These various component forces upward are combined into one resultant force upward. Likewise the several downward component forces combine into one resultant force downward. We can infer a good deal about the relative strengths of these resultant forces.

Where we are dealing with a quasi-stationary equilibrium, the resultant forces upward and the forces downward are opposite in direction and equal in strength at the equilibrium level. Of course, either resultant forces may fluctuate over a short period of time, so that the forces may not be equally balanced at a given moment. However, over a longer period of time and on the average the forces balance out. Fluctuations from the average occur, but there is a tendency to return to the average level.

Just before being transferred, all the groups in both experiments had reached a stable equilibrium level at just above the standard production of 60 units per hour. This level was equal to the average efficiency rating for the entire factory during the period of the experiments. Since this production level remained constant, neither increasing nor decreasing, we may be sure

that the strength of the resultant force upward was equal to the strength of the resultant force downward. This equilibrium of forces was maintained over the period of time when production was stationary at this level.[1] But the forces changed markedly after transfer, and these new constellations of forces were distinctly different for the various experimental groups.

For the no-participation group the period after transfer is a quasi-stationary equilibrium at a lower level, and the forces do not change during the period of thirty days. The resultant force upward remains equal to the resultant force downward and the level of production remains constant. The force field for this group is represented schematically in Figure 4. Only the resultant forces are shown. The length of the vector represents the strength of the force; and the point of the arrow represents the point of application of the force—that is, the production level and the time at which the force applies. Thus the forces are equal and opposite only at the level of 50 units per hour. At higher levels of production the forces downward are greater than the forces upward; and at lower levels of production the forces upward are stronger than the forces downward. Thus there is a tendency for the equilibrium to be maintained at an efficiency rating of 50.

[1] See Lewin (1947, p. 29).

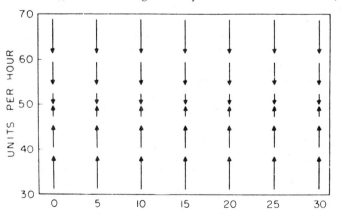

Fig. 4. A schematic diagram of the quasi-stationary equilibrium for the control group after transfer.

The situation for the other experimental groups after transfer can be viewed as a quasi-stationary equilibrium of a different type. Figure 5 gives a schematic diagram of the resultant forces for all the participation groups. At any given level of production, such as 50 units per hour or 60 units per hour, both the resultant forces upward and the resultant forces downward change over the period of thirty days. During this time the point of equilibrium, which starts at 50 units per hour, gradually rises until it reaches a level of over 70 units per hour after thirty days. Yet here again the equilibrium level has the character of a "central force field" where at any point in the total field the resultant of the upward and the downward forces is in the direction of the equilibrium level.

influencing production in a downward direction: (1) the difficulty of the job; (2) a force corresponding to avoidance of strain; (3) a force corresponding to a group standard to restrict production to a given level. The resultant force upward in the direction of greater production is composed of three additional component forces: (1) the force corresponding to the goal of standard production; (2) a force corresponding to pressures induced by the management through supervision; (3) a force corresponding to a group standard of competition. Let us examine each of these six component forces.

1. JOB DIFFICULTY

For all operators the difficulty of the job is one of the forces downward on production.

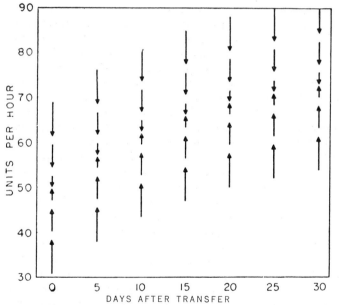

Fig. 5. A schematic diagram of the quasi-stationary equilibrium for the experimental groups after transfer.

To understand how the differences among the experimental treatments produced the differences in force fields represented in Figures 4 and 5, it is not sufficient to consider only the resultant forces. We must also look at the component forces for each resultant force.

There are three main component forces

The difficulty of the job, of course, is relative to the skill of the operator. The given job may be very difficult for an unskilled operator but relatively easy for a highly skilled one. In the case of a transfer a new element of difficulty enters. For some time the new job is much more difficult, for the operator is unskilled at that particular job. In addition to the difficulty experienced by any learner, the transfer often encounters the added difficulty of proactive inhibition. Where the new job is similar to the old job there will be a period of interference between the two similar but different skills required. For this reason a very efficient operator whose skills have become almost unconscious may suffer just as great a drop as a much less efficient operator. Except for Group V, the difficulty of these easy jobs does not explain the differential recovery rates because both the initial difficulty and the amount of change were equated for these groups. The two operators in Group V probably dropped further and recovered more slowly than any of the other three groups under total participation because of the greater difficulty of the job.

2. STRAIN AVOIDANCE

The force toward lower production corresponding to the difficulty of the job (or the lack of skill of the person) has the character of a restraining force—that is, it acts to prevent locomotion rather than as a driving force causing locomotion. However, in all production there is a closely related driving force toward lower production, namely "strain avoidance." We assume that working too hard and working too fast is an unpleasant strain; and corresponding to this negative valence there is a driving force in the opposite direction, namely towards taking it easy or working slower. The higher the level of production the greater will be the strain and, other things being equal, the stronger will be the downward force of strain avoidance. Likewise, the greater the difficulty of the job the stronger will be the force corresponding to strain avoidance. But the greater the operator's skill the smaller will be the strain and the strength of the force of strain avoidance. Therefore:

5. The strength of the force of strain avoidance =

$$\frac{\text{job difficulty} \times \text{production level}}{\text{skill of operator}}$$

The differential recovery rates of the three experimental groups in Experiment I cannot be explained by strain avoidance because job difficulty, production level, and operator skill were matched at the time immediately following transfer. Later, however, when the participation treatments had produced a much higher level of production, these groups were subjected to an increased downward force of strain avoidance which was stronger than in the no-participation group in Experiment I. Evidently other forces were strong enough to overcome this force of strain avoidance.

3. THE GOAL OF STANDARD PRODUCTION

In considering the negative attitudes toward transfer and the resistance to being transferred, there are several important aspects of the complex goal of reaching and maintaining a level of 60 units per hour. For an operator producing below standard, this goal is attractive because it means success, high status in the eyes of her fellow employees, better pay, and job security. On the other hand, there is a strong force against remaining below standard because this lower level means failure, low status, low pay, and the danger of being fired. Thus it is clear that the upward force corresponding to the goal of standard production will indeed be strong for the transfer who has dropped below standard.

It is equally clear why any operator shows such strong resistence to being changed. She sees herself as becoming a failure and losing status, pay, and perhaps the job itself. The result is a lowered level of aspiration and a weakened force toward the goal of standard production.

Just such a weakening of the force toward 60 units per hour seems to have occurred in the no-participation group in Experiment I. The participation treatments, on the other hand, seem to have involved the operators in designing the new job and setting the new piece rates in such a way that they did not lose hope of regaining the goal of standard production. Thus the participation resulted in a stronger force toward higher production. However, this force alone can hardly account for the large differences in recovery rate between the no-participation group and the other experimental groups; certainly it does not explain why the latter increased to a level so high above standard.

4. MANAGEMENT PRESSURE

On all operators below standard the management exerts a pressure for higher production. This pressure is no harsh and autocratic treatment involving threats. Rather it takes the form of persuasion and encouragement by the supervisors. They attempt to induce the low-rating operator to improve her performance and to attain standard production.

Such an attempt to induce a psychological force on another person may have several results. In the first place the person may ignore the attempt of the inducing agent, in which case there is no induced force acting on the person. On the other hand, the attempt may succeed so that an induced force on the person exists. Other things being equal, whenever there is an induced force acting on a person, the person will locomote in the direction of the force. An induced force, which depends on the power field of an inducing agent—some other individual or group—will cease to exist when the inducing power field is withdrawn. In this respect it is different from an "own" force which stems from a person's own needs and goals.

The reaction of a person to an effective induced force will vary depending, among other things, on the person's relation to the inducing agent. A force induced by a friend may be accepted in such a way that it acts more like an "own" force. An effective force induced by an enemy may be resisted and rejected so that the person complies unwillingly and shows signs of conflict and tension. Thus in addition to what might be called a "neutral" induced force, we also distinguish an *accepted* induced force and a

rejected induced force. Naturally the acceptance and the rejection of an induced force can vary in degree from zero (i.e., a neutral induced force) to very strong acceptance or rejection. To account for the difference in character between the acceptance and rejection of an induced force, we make the following assumptions:

6. The acceptance of an induced force sets up additional "own" forces in the same direction.
7. The rejection of an induced force sets up additional "own" forces in the opposite direction.

The grievances, aggression, and tension in the no-participation group in Experiment I indicate that they rejected the force toward higher production induced by the management. The group accepted the stereotype that transfer is a calamity, but the no-participation procedure did not convince them that the change was necessary, and they viewed the new job and the new piece rates set by management as arbitrary and unreasonable. The other experimental groups, on the contrary, participated in designing the changes and setting the piece rates so that they spoke of the new job as "our job" and the new piece rates as "our rates." Thus they accepted the new situation and accepted the management-induced force toward higher production.

From the acceptance by the participation groups and the rejection by the no-participation group of the management-induced forces, we may derive [by (6) and (7) above] that the former had additional "own" forces toward higher production whereas the latter had additional "own" forces toward lower production. This difference helps to explain the better recovery rate of the participation groups and the fact that they exceeded their original level of production.

5. GROUP STANDARDS

Probably the most important force affecting the recovery under the no-participation procedure was a group standard, set by the group, restricting the level of production to 50 units per hour. Evidently this explicit agreement to restrict production is related to the group's rejection of the change and of the new job as arbitrary and unreasonable. Perhaps they had faint hopes of demonstrating that standard production could not be attained and thereby obtain a more favorable piece rate. In any case there was a definite group phenomenon which affected all the members of the group.

We have already noted the striking example of the presser whose production was restricted in the group situation to about half the level she attained as an individual. In the no-participation group, too, we would expect the group to induce strong forces on the members. The more a member deviates above the standard, the stronger would be the group-induced force to conform to the standard, for such deviations both negate any possibility of management's increasing the piece rate and at the same time expose the other members to increased pressure from management. Thus individual differences in levels of production should be sharply curtailed in this group after transfer.

An analysis was made for all groups of the individual differences within the group in levels of production. In Experiment I the forty days before change were compared with the thirty days after change; in Experiment II the ten days before change were compared to the seventeen days after change. As a measure of variability, the standard deviation was calculated each day for each group. The average daily standard deviations *before* and *after* change were as follows:

Group	Variability	
	Before Change	*After Change*
Experiment I		
No Participation	9.8	1.9
Participation through Representation	9.7	3.8
Total Participation	10.3	2.7
Total Participation	9.9	2.4
Experiment II		
Total Participation	12.7	2.9

There is indeed a marked decrease in individual differences within the no-participation group after their first transfer. In fact the restriction of production resulted in a lower variability than in any other group. Thus we may conclude that the group standard at 50 units per hour set up strong group-induced forces which were important components in the central-force field shown in Figure 4. It is now evident that for this group the quasi-stationary equilibrium after transfer has a steep gradient around the equilibrium level of 50 units per hour—the strength of the forces increases rapidly above and below this level. It is also clear that the group standard to restrict production is a major reason for the lack of recovery in the no-participation group.

The table of variability also shows that the experimental treatments markedly reduced variability in the other four groups after transfer. In participation by representation this smallest reduction of variability was produced by a group standard of individual competition for improvement in efficiency rating. Competition among members of the group was reported by the supervisor soon after transfer. This competition was a force toward higher production which resulted in good recovery to standard and continued progress beyond standard.

The total participation groups showed a greater reduction in variability following transfer. These two groups in Experiment I under total participation were transferred on the same day. Each group tried to set a better record for improvement than the other group. This group competition, which evidently resulted in stronger forces on the members than did the individual competition, was an effective group standard. The standard gradually moved to higher and higher levels of production with the result that the groups not only reached but far exceeded their previous levels of production.

Probably a major determinant of the strength of these group standards is the cohesiveness of the group (Festinger, Back, Schachter, Kelley, and Thibaut, 1950). Whether this power of the group over the members was used to increase or to decrease productivity seemed to depend on the use of participation (Schachter, Ellertson, Mc-Bride, and Gregory, 1951).

TURNOVER AND AGGRESSION

Returning now to our preliminary theory of frustration, we can see several revisions. The difficulty of the job and its relation to skill and strain avoidance has been clarified in proposition (5). It is now clear that the driving force toward 60 is a complex affair; it is partly a negative driving force corresponding to the negative valence of low pay, low status, failure, and job insecurity. Turnover results not only from the frustration produced by the conflict of these two forces but also as a direct attempt to escape from the region of these negative valences. For the members of the no-participation group, the group standard to restrict production prevented escape by increasing production, so that quitting their jobs was the only remaining escape. In the participation groups, on the contrary, both the group standards and the additional "own" forces resulting from the acceptance of management-induced forces combined to make increasing production the distinguished path of escape from this region of negative valence.

In considering turnover as a form of escape from the field, it is not enough to look only at the psychological present; one must also consider the psychological future. The employee's decision to quit the job is rarely made exclusively on the basis of a momentary frustration or an undesirable present situation; she usually quits when she also sees the future as equally hopeless. The operator transferred by the usual factory procedure (including the no-participation group) has in fact a realistic view of the probability of continued failure because, as we have already noted, 62 percent of transfers do in fact fail to recover to standard production. Thus the higher rate of quitting for transfers as compared to nontransfers results from a more pessimistic view of the future.

The no-participation procedure had the effect for the members of setting up management as a hostile power field. They rejected the forces induced by this hostile power field, and group standards to restrict production developed within the group in opposition to management. In this conflict between the power field of management and the power field of the group, the group attempted to reduce the strength of the hostile power field relative to the strength of their own power field. This change was accomplished in three ways: (1) the group increased its own power by developing a more cohesive and well-disciplined group, (2) they secured "allies" by getting the backing of the union in filing a formal grievance about the new piece rate, (3) they attacked the hostile power field directly in the form of aggression against the supervisor, the time-study engineer, and the higher management. Thus the aggression was derived not only from individual frustration but also from the conflict between two groups. Furthermore, this situation of group conflict both helped to define management as the frustrating agent and gave the members strength to express any aggressive impulses produced by frustration.

Conclusions

It is possible for management to modify greatly or to remove completely group resistance to changes in methods of work and the ensuing piece rates. This change can be accomplished by the use of group meetings in which management effectively communicates the need for change and stimulates group participation in planning the changes.

Such participation results in higher production, higher morale, and better labor-management relations.

Harwood's management has long felt that such field experiments are the key to better labor-management relations. It is only by discovering the basic principles and applying them to the true causes of conflict that an intelligent, effective effort can be made to correct the undesirable effects of the conflict. In addition to these practical values, therefore, this experiment also contributes to our theories of group productivity, group processes, and intergroup relations.

A Cross-cultural Replication

This experiment was replicated in a similar Norwegian factory in 1956, although necessarily using somewhat different operational definitions (French, Israel, and As, 1958). Nine 4-man groups were changed to producing new products with a new piece rate. The four control groups had low participation in planning the changes, but the five experimental groups were given more participation through a series of meetings which were similar to the "total participation" procedures in the previous experiment. However, this treatment probably produced somewhat weaker psychological participation (defined as the amount of influence which the person perceives that he exerts on a jointly made decision which affects all participants).

The effects of participation on several dimensions of labor-management relations and on job satisfaction were measured by a questionnaire. It was predicted that these effects would increase with increasing legitimacy of participation and with decreasing resistance to the methods of introducing the change.

Compared to the control groups, the experimental groups showed trends in the direction of greater job satisfaction and more favorable attitudes toward management. As predicted these effects became significant when we controlled for the legitimacy of participation and for the amount of resistance to change as measured by the questionnaire. Thus participation produces improved morale only to the extent that it is legitimate (i.e., the workers feel they have as much influence as they should have). Likewise participation produces improved morale only to the extent that there is no strong resistance to the methods of introducing change.

There was no difference between the experimental and the control groups in the level of production, probably because the participation was less relevant and because there were stronger group standards restricting production.

The revised theory, specifying the conditioning variables, accounts for the results of both experiments and also for individual differences in reactions to participation.

References

FESTINGER, L., BACK, K., SCHACHTER, S., KELLEY, H., and THIBAUT, J. *Theory and experiment in social communication.* Ann Arbor, Mich.: Edwards Bros., 1950.

FRENCH, J. R. P., JR. The behavior of organized and unorganized groups under conditions of frustration and fear, studies in topological and vector psychology, III. *University of Iowa Studies in Child Welfare,* 1944, 20, 229-308.

FRENCH, J. R. P., JR., ISRAEL, J., and AS, D. An experiment on participation in a Norwegian factory: interpersonal dimensions of decision-making. *Hum. Relat.,* 1960, 13, 3-19.

LEWIN, K. Frontiers in group dynamics. *Hum. Relat.,* 1947, 1, 5-41.

SCHACHTER, S., ELLERTSON, N., McBRIDE, D., and GREGORY, D. An experimental study of cohesiveness and productivity. *Hum. Relat.,* 1951, 4, 229-238.

B. NORMS, ROLES,

AND ROLE CONFLICT

Formation of Social Norms:

The Experimental Paradigm ⁊ Muzafer Sherif

Problem of Norm Formation

Now, coming to concrete life situations, we find norms wherever we find an organized society, primitive or complicated. . . . We shall consider customs, traditions, standards, rules, values, fashions, and all other criteria of conduct which are standardized as a consequence of the interaction of individuals, as specific cases of "social norms." . . . These norms serve as focal points in the experience of the individual, and subsequently as guides for his actions. This need not always be a conscious function; many times it is effective without our awareness of it. We see the evidence of its effectiveness by its results, that is, in the behavior of the individual. The daily routine of everyday life is regulated to a large extent by the social norms in each society. As long as life with its many aspects is well settled and runs more or less smoothly from day to day, very few doubt the validity of the existing norms; very few challenge their authority. And the few who challenge them are considered to be doubting Thomases, eccentrics, trouble makers, or lunatics, and are reacted against with varying degrees of scorn or violence.

But when social life becomes difficult and there are stresses and tensions in the lives of many people in the community, the equilibrium of life ceases to be stable, and the air is pregnant with possibilities. . . . Under these delicate conditions the strength of the norms incorporated in the individual becomes uncertain and liable to break down. Such a delicate, unstable situation is the fertile soil for the rise of doubts concerning the existing norms, and a challenge to their authority. The doubt and the challenge which no one would listen to before, now become effective. These are times of transition from one state to another, from one norm or set of norms to another. The transition is not simply from the orderliness of one set of norms to chaos, but from one set of norms to a new set of norms, perhaps through a stage of uncertainty, confusion, and at times even violence. . . .

As a result of the strain and stress, of the confusion and uncertainty and feeling of insecurity, there may be action and reaction,

This article has been adapted by the author especially for this book from *The Psychology of Social Norms*, New York: Harper & Row, Publishers, Inc., 1936. Reprinted by permission of the author and publisher.

apparent stability followed by fresh instability. The outcome is the final emergence or establishment of a stable set of norms having the status of standards. . . .

The study of the process of emergence or standardization of norms in actual life situations is an extremely complicated task. There are so many variables involved that cannot be directly observed. It may, therefore, pay us in the long run to start first with the study of the psychology of norm formation in a general way in a well-controlled laboratory situation. Yet what we shall undertake is really the study of the general psychological process involved in the formation of any norm, and not simply the explanation of the psychology of one particular norm. The test for such an approach lies in the applicability of the principle reached to the description and explanation of norms found in actual social life. Whether or not this is just one more psychological abstraction or laboratory artifact, which does not have anything to do with the true psychology of the formation of norms that are effective in everyday life, can be decided after it has met facts in the fresh and wholesome air of actualities. . . .

Hypothesis to Be Tested

We have seen that if a reference point is lacking in the external field of stimulation, it is established internally as the temporal sequence of presentation of stimuli goes on. Accordingly we raise the problem: What will an individual do when he is placed in an objectively unstable situation in which all basis of comparison, as far as the external field of stimulation is concerned, is absent? In other words, what will he do when the external frame of reference is eliminated, insofar as the aspect in which we are interested is concerned? Will he give a hodgepodge of erratic judgments? Or will he establish a point of reference of his own? *Consistent* results in this situation may be taken as the index of a subjectively evolved frame of reference.

We must first study the tendency of the individual. We must begin with the individual in order to do away with the dualism between "individual psychology" and "social psychology." In this way we can find the differences between individual responses in the individual situation and in the group situation.

Coming to the social level we can push our problem further. What will a group of people do in the same unstable situation? Will the different individuals in the group give a hodgepodge of judgments? Or will they establish a collective frame of reference? If so, of what sort? If every person establishes a norm, will it be his own norm and different from the norms of others in the group? Or will there be established a common norm peculiar to the particular group situation and depending upon the presence of these individuals together and their influence upon one another? If they in time come to perceive the uncertain and unstable situation which they face in common in such a way as to give it some sort of order, perceiving it as ordered by a frame of reference developed among them in the course of the experiment, and if this frame of reference is peculiar to the group, then we may say that we have at least the prototype of the psychological process involved in the formation of a norm in a group.

The Autokinetic Effect: Its Possibilities for Our Problem

With these considerations clearly in mind, our first task has been to find objectively unstable situations that would permit themselves to be structured in several ways, depending on the character of the subjectively established reference points. From among other possible experimental situations that could be used to test our hypothesis, we chose to use the situation that is suitable to produce autokinetic effects, as meeting the requirements demanded by our hypothesis.

The conditions that produce the autokinetic effect afford an excellent experimental situation to test our hypothesis. We can easily get the autokinetic effect. In complete darkness, such as is found in a closed room that is not illuminated, or on a cloudy night in the open when there are no other lights visible, a single small light seems to move, and it may appear to move erratically in all directions. If you present the point of light repeatedly to a person, he may see the light appearing at different places in the room each time, especially if he does not know the distance between himself and the light. The experimental production of the autokinetic effect is very easy and works without any exception, provided, of course, that the person does not use special devices to destroy the effect. For in a completely dark room a single point of light *cannot* be localized definitely, because there is nothing in reference to which you can locate it. The effect takes place even when the person looking at the light knows perfectly well that the light is not moving. These are facts which are not subject to controversy; any one can easily test them for himself. In this situation not only does the stimulating light appear erratic and irregular to the subject, but at times the person himself feels insecure about his spatial bearing. This comes out in an especially striking way if he is seated in a chair without a back and is unfamiliar with the position of the experimental room in the building. Under these conditions some subjects report that they are not only confused about the location of the light; they are even confused about the stability of their own position.

The autokinetic effect is not a new artificial phenomenon invented by the psychologists. It is older than experimental psychology. Since it sometimes appears in the observation of the heavenly bodies, the astronomers[1] had already noticed it and offered theories to explain it.

We have studied the influence of such social factors as *suggestion* and the *group situation* on the extent and direction of the experimental movement. The study of the extent of the experienced movement permits a quantitative study for the approach to the formation of norms. We shall therefore report on the extent of movement.

Procedure

We have studied the extent of the movement experienced in two situations: (1) when alone, except for the experimenter (in order to get the reaction of the individual unaffected by other experimentally introduced social factors, and thus to gain a basic notion about the perceptual process under the circumstances); and (2) when the individual is in a group situation (in order to discover modifications brought about by membership in the group).

The subject was introduced into the group situation in two ways: (1) He was brought into a group situation after being experimented upon when alone. This was done to find out the influence of the group situation after he had an opportunity to react to the situation first in accordance with his own tendencies and had ordered it subjectively in his own way. (2) He was first introduced to the situation in the group, having no previous familiarity with the situation at all, and afterwards experimented upon individually. This was done to find out whether the perceptual order or norm that might be established in the group situation would continue to determine his reaction to the same situation when he faced it alone. This last point is crucial for our problem. The others lead up to it and clarify its implications.

The subjects, apparatus, and procedures used will be only briefly outlined here. They are reported in full elsewhere (Sherif, 1935). The experiments were carried on in

[1] For a concise history of the autokinetic effect as a scientific problem, see Adams (1912). Several theories have also been advanced by psychologists to explain the nature of the autokinetic effect. These are immaterial for our present problem. The important fact for us to remember is that the autokinetic effect is produced whenever a visual stimulus object lacks a spatial frame of reference.

dark rooms in the Columbia University psychological laboratory. The subjects were graduate and undergraduate male students at Columbia University and New York University. They were not majoring in psychology. They did not know anything about the physical stimulus setup, or the purpose of the experiment. There were 19 subjects in the individual experiments; 40 subjects took part in the group experiments.

Individual Experiments

The stimulus light was a tiny point of light seen through a small hole in a metal box. The light was exposed to the subject by the opening of a small shutter controlled by the experimenter. The distance between the subject and the light was five meters. The observer was seated at a table on which was a telegraph key. The following instructions were given in written form: "When the room is completely dark, I shall give you the signal *Ready*, and then show you a point of light. After a short time the light will start to move. As soon as you see it move, press the key. A few seconds later the light will disappear. Then tell me the distance it moved. Try to make your estimates as accurate as possible."

These instructions summarize the general procedure of the experiment. A short time after the light was exposed following the *Ready* signal, the subject pressed the key; this produced a faint but audible ticking in the timing apparatus indicating that the subject had perceived the (autokinetic) movement. The exposure time, after the subject pressed the key to indicate that he had begun to experience the movement, was two seconds in all cases. The light was physically stationary during the entire time and was not moved at all during any of the experiments.

After the light had disappeared, the subject reported orally the distance through which it had moved as he experienced it. The experimenter recorded each judgment

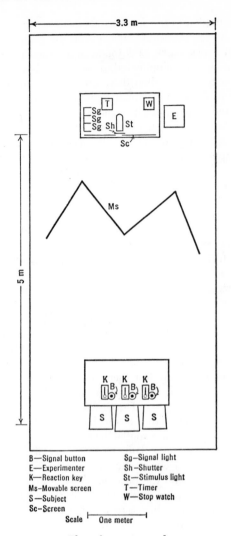

B—Signal button   Sg—Signal light
E—Experimenter   Sh—Shutter
K—Reaction key   St—Stimulus light
Ms—Movable screen   T—Timer
S—Subject   W—Stop watch
Sc—Screen

Scale   One meter

Fig. 1. Plan of experimental room.

as soon as it was spoken by the subject, writing each one on a separate sheet of a small paper pad. One hundred judgments were obtained from each subject. The subjects reported their estimates in inches (or fractions of inches).

The quantitative results are reported elsewhere. Here we shall present only the conclusions reached on the basis of these quantitative results, and give some important introspections that clarify these conclusions further.

The results unequivocally indicate that when individuals perceive movements which lack any other standard of comparison, *they subjectively establish a range of extent and a point (a standard or norm) within that range which is peculiar to the individual,* that may differ from the range and point (standard or norm) established by other individuals. In other words, when individuals repeatedly perceive movement which offers no objective basis for gauging the extent of movement, there develops within them, in the course of a succession of presentations, a standard (norm or reference point). This subjectively established standard or norm serves as a reference point with which each successive experienced movement is compared and judged to be short, long, or medium—within the range peculiar to the subject.

To express the point more generally, we conclude that in the absence of an objective range or scale of stimuli and an externally given reference point or standard, each individual builds up a range of his own and an internal (subjective) reference point within that range, and each successive judgment is given within that range and in relation to that reference point. The range and reference point established by each individual are peculiar to himself when he is experimented upon alone.

In the second series of the individual experiments, it was found that once a *range*, and a point of reference within that range, is established by an individual, there is a tendency to preserve these in the experiments on subsequent days. A second and third series of 100 judgments each show a median score for a given subject which is very similar to that found in the first series, but with a reduced variability.

The written introspective reports obtained from every observer at the end of the experiment further corroborate these conclusions based upon the quantitative results. Introspections of the following sort, which are typical, show that the subjects first found it hard to estimate distance because

of the lack of externally given reference points or standards:

"Darkness left no guide for distance."

"It was difficult to estimate the distance the light moved, because of the lack of visible neighboring objects."

There was no fixed point from which to judge distance."

Introspections of the following sort indicate that the subjects developed standards of their own in the absence of objective ones:

"Compared with previous distance."

"Used first estimate as standard."

This reveals once more the general psychological tendency to experience things in relation to some frame of reference. What we did in the group experiments was to carry this finding of experimental psychology into social psychology and note how it operates when the individual is in a group situation.

Group Experiments

On the basis of the results given, the problem which we must study in the group situation becomes self-evident. The individual experiences the external field of stimulation in relation to a frame of reference. When a frame of reference is given in the objective situation, this will usually determine in an important way the structural relationships of the experience; in such cases all other parts will be organized as determined or modified by it. But at times such an objective frame of reference is lacking— the field of stimulation is unstable, vague, and not well structured. In this case the individual perceives the situation as shaped by his own internally evolved frame of reference. The questions that arise for the experiment in the group situation, then, are the following:

How will an individual who is found in the group situation perceive the stimulus field? Will there evolve in him again a range and a standard (norm) within that range that will be peculiar to him, as was the case when individuals were experimented on alone? Or will group influences prevent him from establishing any well-defined range and reference point within that range, and thus spoil his capacity to perceive the uncertain situation in any sort of order? Or will the individuals in the group act together to establish a range, and a reference point within that range, which are peculiar to the group? If such a range and reference point are established, what will be the influence of such a group product on the individual member when he subsequently faces the same stimulus situation alone?

The questions outlined above represent more or less pure cases. There are, of course, other possibilities that lie between these pure cases.

With these questions, we face directly the psychological basis of social norms. We must admit that we have reduced the process to a very simple form. But the first fundamental psychological problem is the way an individual perceives a stimulus situation. The behavior follows upon this perception rather than upon the bald physical presence of the stimulus. There is no simple and direct correlation between the stimulus and the subsequent behavior, especially on the level of behavior with which we are dealing. A simple perceptual situation is the first requirement for experimental analysis of the problem.

We purposely chose a stimulus situation in which the external factors are unstable enough, within limits, to allow the internal factors to furnish the dominating role in establishing the main characteristics of organization. This enables us to say that any consistent product in the experience of the individual members of the group, differing from their experience as isolated individuals, is a function of their interaction in the group.

We do not face stimulus situations involving other people, or even the world of nature around us, in an indifferent way; we are charged with certain modes of readiness, certain established norms, which enter to modify our reactions. This important consideration shaped the planning of the group experiments. We studied the differences between the reactions (a) when the individuals first faced our stimulus situation in the group, and (b) when they faced the group situation after first establishing their individual ranges and norms in the individual situation. Accordingly, twenty of the subjects began with the individual situation and were then put into groups in subsequent experimental sessions; the other twenty started with group sessions and ended with individual sessions.

This rotation technique enabled us to draw conclusions regarding the following important questions: How much does the individual carry over from his individually established way of reacting to a later situation when facing the same stimulus in the group? How much will he be influenced by his membership in the group after once his range and norm have been established individually when alone? How will he experience the situation when alone, after a common range and norm have been established peculiar to the group of which he is a member? In short, will the common product developed in the group serve as a determining factor when he subsequently faces the same situation *alone?*

The experimental setting was in general the same as in previous experiments. Of course, additional techniques were necessary to handle two or more members of a group at the same time. One major addition was the use of signal lights. As the subjects were new to the experimenter, he could not tell from the voice alone who was giving a judgment. So as each subject gave his judgment aloud, he pressed a push button connected with a dim signal light of a particular color by which the experimenter might know who the speaker was.

There were eight groups of two subjects each and eight groups of three subjects each. Four groups in each of the two categories started with the individual situation (one whole session for each individual), and then functioned as groups. Four groups in each category started in group situations for the first three sessions on three different days (all subjects of each group being present), and were then broken up and studied in the individual situation.

In order to make the relation of individual members to one another as natural as possible, within the limits of the experimental setting, the subjects were left free as to the order in which they would give their judgments. In fact, they were told at the start to give their judgments in random order as they pleased. Whether the judgments of the person who utters his first have more influence than the others becomes a study in leadership, which is a further interesting problem. Perhaps such studies will give us an insight into the effect of polarization on the production of norms in a group situation. But from the examination of our results, we can say that the reporting of the judgments has a gradual cumulative effect; aside from whatever influence the first judgment may have on the second or third at a given moment, the judgments of the third individual at a given presentation are not without effect on the subsequent judgments of the first subject in the round of presentations following. Thus the production of an established group influence is largely a temporal affair and not the outcome of this or that single presentation. We shall refer to this point again later.

Besides the quantitative judgments obtained during the experiments, the subjects were asked at the end of each experimental session to write down their introspections. Questions were asked which aimed at finding whether they became conscious of the range and norm they were establishing subjectively. These questions were: "Between what maximum and minimum did the distances vary?" "What was the most frequent distance that the light moved?"

Certain facts stand out clearly from our results. We may summarize these facts in a few paragraphs.

When an individual faces this stimulus situation, which is unstable and not structured in itself, he establishes a range and norm (a reference point) within that range. The range and norm that are developed in each individual are peculiar to that individual. They may vary from the ranges and norms developed in other individuals in different degrees, revealing consistent and stable individual differences. The causes of these individual differences are difficult problems in themselves, the understanding of which may prove to be basic to a satisfactory understanding of our problem. But for the time being it may be worth while to work on our main theme.

When the individual, in whom a range and a norm within that range are first developed in the individual situation, is put into a group situation, together wth other individuals who also come into the situation with their own ranges and norms established in their own individual sessions, the ranges and norms tend to converge. But the convergence is not so close as when they first work in the group situation, having less opportunity to set up stable individual norms. (See left-hand graphs, Figures 2 and 3.)

When individuals face the same unstable, unstructured situation as members of a group for the first time, a range and a norm (standard) within that range are established which are peculiar to the group. If, for the group, there is a rise or fall in the norms established in successive sessions, it is a group effect; the norms of the individual members rise and fall toward a common norm in each session. To this the objection may be raised that one subject may lead, and be uninfluenced by other members of the group; the group norm is simply the leader's norm. To this only possible empirical reply is that in our experiments the leaders were constantly observed to be influenced by their followers—if not at the moment, then later in the series and in subsequent series. Even if the objection has occasional force, the statement regarding group norms is in general true. Even if the group norm gravitates toward a dominating per-

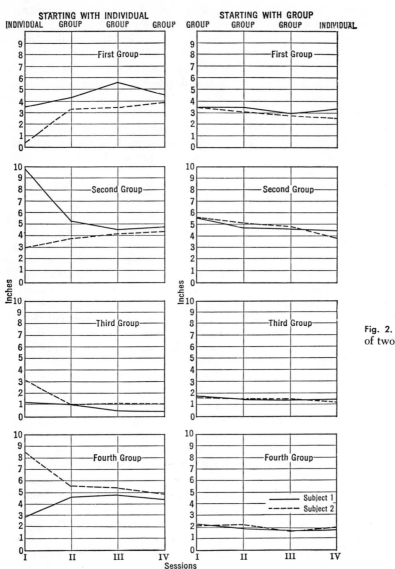

Fig. 2. Medians in groups of two subjects.

son, the leader represents a polarization in the situation, having a definite relationship toward others which he cannot change at will. If the leader changes his norm after the group norm is *settled* he may *cease thereupon to be followed,* as occurred several times strikingly in our experiments. In general, such cases of complete polarization are, however, exceptional. (See right-hand graphs, Figures 2 and 3.)

The fact that the norm thus established is peculiar to the group suggests that there is a factual psychological basis in the contentions of social psychologists and sociologists who maintain that new and supra-individual qualities arise in the group situations. This

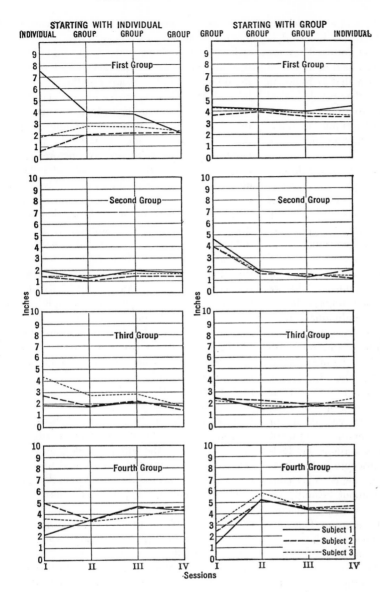

Fig. 3. Medians in groups of three subjects.

is in harmony with the facts developed elsewhere in the psychology of perception.

When a member of a group faces the same situation subsequently *alone*, after once the range and norm of his group have been established, he perceives the situation in terms of the range and norm that he brings from the group situation. This psychological fact is important in that it gives a psychological approach to the understanding of the "social products" that weigh so heavily in the problem of the stimulus situation.

Discussion of Results

The experiments, then, constitute a study of the formation of a norm in a simple laboratory situation. They show in a simple way the basic psychological process involved in the establishment of social norms. They are an extension into the social field of a general psychological phenomenon that is found in perception and in many other psychological fields, namely, that our experience is organized around or modified by frames of reference participating as factors in any given stimulus situation.

In our experimental situation, within certain limits, there is no "right" or "wrong" judgment. One subject demonstrated this spontaneously during the experiment, in spite of the fact that he was not supposed to talk: "If you tell me once how much I am mistaken, all my judgments will be better." Not being sure about the correctness of his judgments, the subject feels uneasy. This we know from the introspective reports. In the individual situation, the individual structures the unstructured situation by furnishing his own peculiar range and reference point. In the group situation the members of the group tend to structure the situation by converging toward a common norm in their judgments. If in the beginning of the experimental situation they start with divergent judgments, in the course of the experiment they come together, the divergent one feeling uncertain and even insecure in the deviating position of his judgments. This convergence is not brought about instantly by the direct influence of one or two judgments of the other members of the group. It exhibits a temporal pattern. The following introspection of a member of one of the groups, written in answer to the question, "Were you influenced by the judgments of the other persons during the experiments?" illustrates our point clearly. This subject wrote, "Yes, but not on the same observation. My judgment in each case was already made, and I did not change to whatever the other person said. But on subsequent observations my judgments were adjusted to their judgments. After a number of observations, the previous agreement or lack of it influenced me in adjusting my own perspective."

Despite the above case, every individual need not be aware of the fact that he is being influenced in the group situation, or that he and the other members are converging toward a common norm. In fact, the majority of the subjects reported not only that their minds were made up as to the judgment they were going to give before the others spoke, but that they were not influenced by the others in the group. This fact is in harmony with many observations in the psychology of perception; we know that the general setting in which a stimulus is found influences its properties, and that unless we take a critical and analytic attitude toward the situation we need not be aware that its properties are largely determined by its surroundings. This is the general principle underlying the psychology of "illusions."

It must be said that in our experimental setting the subjects are not moved by a common interest or drive such as is found in a group that faces a common danger, such as starvation or the cruel authority of a tyrant. In these vital situations there is a certain gap that has to be filled. Until this gap is properly filled, the instability of the situation continues. If the norms and slogans that arise under the stress of a tense and uncertain situation that requires a solution do not meet the situation adequately, the instability is not removed, and new norms and new slogans are likely to arise until the tension is removed. For example, in a hungry mass of people searching for food, a leader or a small party may standardize certain norms or slogans as guides to an outlook upon the situation and as guides to action. If these norms do not lead to the satisfaction of hunger, other leaders or interested parties may spring up and standardize other norms or slogans. This (dialectic) dynamic process moves on and on until the appropriate norms or slogans are reached that meet the situation best.

References

ADAMS, H. F. Autokinetic sensations. *Psychol. Monogr.*, 1912, No. 59, 32-44.

SHERIF, M. A study of some social factors in perception. *Arch. Psychol.*, 1935, No. 187.

The Operation ❦ Leon Festinger
of Group Standards ❦ Stanley Schachter

❦ Kurt Back

The term *group standard*, or *group norm*, has been used freely either to describe or to explain the rather well substantiated finding that members of the same face-to-face group exhibit relative uniformity with respect to specified opinions and modes of behavior. The use of the term, whether in a descriptive or an explanatory manner, has generally carried with it the meaning that this observed uniformity derives in some manner from influences which the group is able to exert over its members. The fact that members of some social set all have relatively similar tastes in, for example, selecting recreational activities, has generally been explained on the basis of interindividual or group influences rather than on the basis of similar circumstances producing similar but independent reactions in a number of people.

There is no question any longer that individuals and groups do exert influences on others which can and do result in uniform opinions and behavior patterns. There have been many studies which have demonstrated the existence and importance of this phenomenon. The classic experiment by Sherif (1936) clearly demonstrated that, at least in a situation which was almost com-

pletely unstructured, the individual was virtually entirely dependent upon the group for forming a stable mode of response. The strength of the group influence was plainly sufficient to override most individual factors.

It has also been shown, by a series of independent studies (Lewin et al., 1944), that people's aspirations and goal-setting behavior are strongly influenced by information they possess about how others behave and their relationship to these others. All of these influences produce changes in the individual's behavior which result in his being more similar to other members of the group to which he feels he belongs.

Once we depart from the well-controlled laboratory situation it is no longer easy to claim unequivocally that observed uniformity is due to group influence. Newcomb (1943), for example, in his study of a college community which had a reputation for being liberal found that students consistently became more liberal with increasing length of attendance at the college. It is possible plausibly to maintain that these changing attitudes resulted from group pressures and influences once the student became a member of the community. It would also, however, be possible to main-

This article has been adapted by the authors especially for this book from Chapters 5 and 6 of *Social Pressures in Informal Groups*, New York: Harper & Row, Publishers, Inc., 1950. Reprinted by permission of the authors.

tain that these changes occurred in different people independently as a result of the similar experiences, curricular and otherwise, to which they were all subjected in the rather unique college. The demonstration that a group standard existed would indeed be difficult. Such demonstration would have to rest upon a series of empirical facts concerning the means by which the group enforces the standard, the relation between the pattern of conformity and the group structure, and the relationship to the group of members who deviate from the standard.

The study to be reported here undertook to investigate the nature and operation of group standards in two housing projects. These two projects, Westgate and Westgate West, were occupied by families of students of the Massachusetts Institute of Technology. The homes in Westgate were houses arranged in U-shaped courts. Those in Westgate West were apartments in rows of two-story barracklike structures. The same tenants' organization served both projects. The court in Westgate, and the building in Westgate West, had become the unit of social life in these projects by the time of the study. Friendship groups formed mainly within the court and within the building. The backgrounds and interests of the residents were relatively homogeneous throughout both projects and the assignment of houses or apartments to particular people had not been made on any kind of selective basis. It was also clear that there had been no differential treatment of courts or of buildings. The study of group standards might consequently be pursued fruitfully by carefully examining the reasons for differences in behavior among these social units where such differences emerged.

It was found that differences between courts did exist to a rather marked extent on matters concerning the Westgate tenants' organization. This organization was, at least potentially, of equal relevance and importance to all residents of Westgate and of Westgate West, and all residents were urged to support it. Representation in the Westgate Council was on the basis of courts

and buildings, and consequently called for action from each court and each building. Yet, in spite of this equality of relevance, some courts and buildings supported the organization, others were overtly hostile, while still others were indifferent. We shall proceed to examine the determinants of these differences among courts and among buildings to see whether group standards were or were not operating and, if they were, how they made themselves effective.

Attitudes toward the Westgate Council

By May of 1947, when interview data concerning the attitudes of residents toward the Westgate organization were collected, the Council had almost completed the first semester of active existence. Since the turnover in residents occurred mainly at the break between semesters, practically all residents who were living there at the time of the interview had been living in the project when the Council started its active program.

All of the 100 Westgate families and 166 of the 170 Westgate West families were asked, as part of a larger interview, "We understand there is a tenants' organization here. What do you think of it? Are you active in it?" The interviewers were instructed to follow these questions with nondirective probes until they were satisfied that they had obtained an adequate picture of the attitude toward the organization and the degree and kind of participation in its activities. These data were then categorized in the following way:

Attitudes toward the Organization
FAVORABLE

People who considered the organization primarily a good thing. Usually they endorsed both the idea of organization as such and some aims of the Council. Statements ranged from warm approval, "I am definitely in favor of it. It's a worth-while project. It's functioning well," to a vaguely approving, "It's all right."

NEUTRAL

People who mentioned specific good and bad points about the organization so that no definitely favorable or unfavorable attitude could be assigned. In effect, this category included border-line people who had some basic attitude, but saw many points contrary to it. Examples are: "I guess it's all right if they accomplish something—I don't think they have as yet." "It's a good idea, but there are not too many problems for the community to deal with."

APATHETIC

People who said they had not been interested enough to find out anything about the organization. In a sense this is a mildly unfavorable attitude—the organization did not concern them. On the other hand, they did not express any directly unfavorable opinion: "Don't know anything about it. Haven't been to any of the meetings or anything. Not knowing, I wouldn't want to say anything."

UNFAVORABLE

People who expressed a definitely unfavorable opinion about the organization, saying that it was a waste of time, that the people in it were objectionable, that they never would achieve anything. "A large majority of the members are reactionary. They give no attention to wider aspects." "It's unnecessary and highschoolish."

Activities in the Organization

ACTIVE LEADER

People who took a definite part in the activities of the Council as a whole, as representatives, committee members, or doing volunteer work. "We've been to meetings as delegates two or three times. I volunteered

as bartender for the block party." "I am one of the court representatives. I'm a member of the welcoming committee greeting new residents."

ACTIVE FOLLOWER

People who, though not active in the sense of the previous category, had attended more than one court meeting. They cooperated with the Council as it was set up on the court level. They went to the meetings in which the representatives were elected. They listened to the representatives' reports of the Council's actions and gave their suggestions and complaints to be taken up in the next meeting. They were, therefore, a necessary working part of the organization, although they took no part in the workings of the Council as such. "We have been to the building meetings; that's as far as it goes." "We go to the meetings. Everybody goes to them."

INACTIVE

People who did not make any effort to keep in contact with the organization. This included both the people who belonged (that is, they considered themselves represented by the Council) and those who did not feel even a formal connection with the Council. From the point of view of actual behavior, these two groups are indistinguishable. "To be truthful, I'm not active. Splendid idea, but I'm too busy." The principal answer from this group was a curt "No." These people did not even attend court meetings.

The questions about attitudes and activity measure two different aspects of a person's relation to the organization. His attitude may stem from a variety of interests and beliefs. He may view the Council as a way of having certain needs satisfied, as a way to meet his fellow tenants, as unrelated to his needs, or as a childish pastime. It is clear that some of these ways of looking at the Council will lead more readily to activity than others. But a resident's actual activity will also depend on other factors— whether he has time, whether a neighbor draws him into some work, whether he sees something that he personally can do. It is therefore possible that attitude and activity may occur together in all combinations, although some are more likely than others. They are distinct, though correlated, variables.

Patterns of Attitude and Activity

There were differences from one court to another in attitude toward and activity in the tenants' organization. This implies that within any one court there was relative homogeneity with respect to both of these factors. In the extreme case, where all members of a court coincided exactly on both of these dimensions, the demonstration of homogeneity would be a simple matter. This extreme case does not occur, of course, and some method must be devised for describing the pattern within any court both with respect to the content of the pattern and the degree of homogeneity. That is, is it a favorable and active court or is it an unfavorable and inactive court? Do 80% of the court members show this behavior and attitude combination, or do only 60% of the court members show it?

It seemed feasible, from the nature of the data, to distinguish four possible types of court patterns: namely, favorable-active, favorable-inactive, unfavorable-active, and unfavorable-inactive. Once it was determined in which of these categories a court was located, the number of people in the court who conformed to or deviated from the court pattern could then be easily computed. When this was done it would be possible to proceed to a careful examination of whether or not the observed degree of homogeneity within courts was worthy of note, and whether or not it could be attributed to the existence of group standards.

If only these four types of patterns are to be distinguished we must, for this purpose,

do some additional combining of the original categories into which the data were classified. This presents no problem for the activity dimension. Clearly the active leader and active follower categories should both be called active; but the combination of the attitude categories presents somewhat more of a problem. The extreme categories, favorable and unfavorable, clearly fall into their proper place. The categories of apathetic and neutral are not quite so clear. It was reasoned that the apathetic people were at least mildly unfavorable to the organization, since they either did not care to know about it or else had simply remained sufficiently out of things not to have heard about what was going on. On the basis of this reasoning, the apathetic people were classed as unfavorable.

The few residents who were classified as neutral were really borderline cases. To some extent they were favorable and to some extent unfavorable. Whatever the court pattern happens to be, in this sense they both conform to and deviate from it on the attitude dimension. In accordance with this view, the neutral people were not considered in determining the court pattern. In any event there were too few people thus categorized to have affected this determination much. Once the court pattern was determined, these neutrals were regarded as conformers if they fell into the proper activity category and were, of course, considered deviates if they did not.

We shall describe the method used for determining the court pattern by using Tolman Court as an example. Looking first at the activity dimension, we found that 12 residents were active and only one was not. On the attitude dimension, nine residents were favorable and two were unfavorable. The classification of this court, then, is "favorable-active." In this case, following our procedure for neutrals, we shall consider anybody who was neutral and active as conforming to the group standard. Of the two neutrals in the court, one followed the group standard and the other did not. The conformers include everybody who was favorable or neutral and active. There were 10 conformers and three deviates from the pattern.

A different type of pattern is shown in Main Court. Here six of the seven residents were inactive, while five were either apathetic or unfavorable. The pattern is therefore "unfavorable-inactive." As the only neutral resident was active, he cannot be considered as conforming to the pattern; he and the favorable inactive resident were deviates. The five inactive residents, who were either apathetic or unfavorable, conformed to the pattern.

This procedure was carried out for each of the nine Westgate courts and for each of the 17 Westgate West buildings. In Westgate, five of the courts showed a favorable-active pattern, one court showed a favorable-inactive pattern, and three courts showed an unfavorable-inactive pattern. Wide differences did exist among the courts. Also, within each court there was relative homogeneity. Five of the nine courts had a small proportion of deviates. In all but one of the courts the majority conformed to the court pattern.

In Westgate West the degree of homogeneity within the building was perhaps even more striking. Only four of the 17 buildings had as many as 40% deviates from the building pattern, and nine of the buildings had only one or two such deviates. In contrast to Westgate, however, there were no marked differences among the patterns in different buildings. Thirteen of the buildings had favorable-active patterns and four of them had favorable-inactive patterns. There were no buildings with an unfavorable pattern. While in Westgate there was evidence for homogeneity within the court and heterogeneity among the courts, in Westgate West there seems to have been the same amount of homogeneity among buildings as was found within the building.

If we combine all courts into an over-all Westgate pattern, and all buildings into an over-all Westgate West pattern, this difference between the projects emerges even more clearly. These over-all patterns for the two projects are shown in Table 1. In Westgate, no homogeneous over-all pattern exists. Favorable attitudes were displayed by 54% of the residents, unfavorable or apa-

TABLE 1

ATTITUDE-ACTIVITY DISTRIBUTIONS (PERCENTAGE)

	Active Leaders	Active Followers	Inactive	Unclassified	Total
		a. Westgate ($N = 100$)			
Favorable	22	14	18		54
Neutral	2	6	4		12
Apathetic		1	15		16
Unfavorable	2	2	13		17
Unclassified			1		1
Total	26	23	51		100
		b. Westgate West ($N = 166$)			
Favorable	16	38	24	1	79
Neutral		2	1		3
Apathetic	1	2	8		11
Unfavorable	1		3		4
Unclassified		2	1		3
Total	18	44	37	1	100

NOTE: Significance of difference between Westgate and Westgate West: Attitude $\chi^2 = 37.86$; $p = .01$. Activity $\chi^2 = 12.42$; $p = .01$.

thetic attitudes by 33%, while 49% were active and 51% inactive. If we use the same criteria for determining the over-all pattern here as was used for the individual courts, we would conclude that Westgate had a favorable-inactive pattern from which 78% of the residents deviated. Clearly, the greatest concentrations were in the favorable-active and the unfavorable-inactive quadrants. Even if we depart from our rigorous method of determining patterns and regard the pattern in Westgate as favorable-active, we still find that a majority (56%) of the residents were deviates.

The situation in Westgate West is clearly different. Here 79% of the residents were favorable and only 15% were unfavorable or apathetic, while 62% of the residents were active and 37% were inactive. The over-all pattern is favorable-active. Most of the deviation that did occur from this pattern was on the activity dimension, with little deviation on the attitude dimension.

What may we conclude from this analysis of the patterns within Westgate and within Westgate West? Do we as yet have any evidence for asserting the existence or nonexistence of group standards? With regard to Westgate we can clearly say that there was no group standard for the project as a whole. There were obviously opposing subgroups within Westgate with regard to both attitude and activity. Can one, however, maintain that there were group standards within each court? At this point this conclusion would seem plausible, although it is by no means unequivocally demonstrated. We must, however, find some explanation why different courts, each composed of the same kinds of people in similar circumstances, reacted so differently from each other toward the organization and why, in spite of different reactions from different courts, there was relatively homogeneous behavior within each court. We at least are led to suspect that group standards or group norms were operating.

In Westgate West, however, we cannot come to the same conclusions. Here it is possible that a group standard existed for the project as a whole; it is possible that group standards existed within each building; and it is possible that no group standards or norms existed at all, but the obtained high degree of uniformity was due to similar independent reactions of the residents to the same state of affairs. As we have pointed out before, the hypothesis that the uniformity in Westgate West resulted from similar independent reactions of the residents seems probable on the basis of several considerations: Unlike the residents of Westgate, who had been living there up to 15 months and had had four months' actual experience with the organization, the residents of Westgate West were all relative newcomers. The oldest residents of Westgate West had only been living there about five months, and their contact with the Westgate organization had been limited. It was only about one month prior to the collection of these data that Westgate West actually joined the organization. We might expect, then, that in Westgate West, where the social groupings had not had time to form into cohesive units, and where the contact with the tenants' organization was only recent, group norms would not have developed to any considerable degree. The tenants, however, all in the same situation and pretty much the same kinds of people, tended individually to react favorably to the organization.

The Evidence for Group Standards

On the basis of an examination of the actual distribution of conformity to and deviation from patterns of majority behavior, we have arrived at hypotheses concerning the reasons behind the observed degree of uniformity. It has seemed reasonable to suppose that group standards existed in the Westgate courts but that none existed in Westgate West. If this is true, there should be other differences between these two projects which would support these hypotheses. One derivation may immediately be made. If the behavior in Westgate was determined largely by group influences while the behavior in Westgate West was determined largely by individual reactions, then individual differences on relevant factors should show more relationship to attitude and activity in Westgate West than in Westgate.

The personal reasons which residents of the two projects gave for their attitudes, and for whether or not they participated in the activities of the organization, were numerous and varied. Some people had special interests which were aided by the organization; some did not believe in organized activities in general; some said they had no time; some felt that their efforts would be fruitless for the short time that remained for them to stay in the project. All these factors, and others of the same kind, were influences acting on the individual, independently of the group to which he belonged. It would have been desirable, but almost impossible, to obtain reliable indications as to whether or not each of these factors was operating on a particular individual.

Reliable data are at hand, however, concerning the length of time they expected to remain in the project. This, of course, coincided with the length of time they expected to remain in school and was fairly frequently mentioned as a reason for not participating in the activities of the tenants' organization. These data reveal that there was hardly any difference in attitude between long-term and short-term residents in either Westgate or Westgate West.

The breakdown by activity tells a different story. In Westgate, again, little difference was found. The shortest time group—those moving out in June—could not be affected by any medium of long-range program of the Council. In spite of this, 9 out of 16 cooperated with the Council. The group expecting the longest residence—those who intended to stay at least for a year and were frequently indefinite about how much longer—cooperated even a little less with the Council; only 14 out of 29 fell into these categories. The differences are not statistically significant.

In the activity ratings of the Westgate West residents, however, we find that length of expected residence made a difference. Among the short-term residents, 50% were actively cooperating with the Council, while 72% of the long-term residents were. The median expected residence for the active leaders was 17 months; for the inactive residents 12 months. These differences are significant at the 5% level.

We thus find our derivation borne out. The data support our hypotheses concerning the difference between Westgate and Westgate West. In Westgate West, where individuals were reacting more or less independently in terms of their own needs and preferences, we find a significant and appreciable degree of relationship between how much longer they expected to stay in the project and whether or not they became active in the affairs of the tenants' organization. In Westgate, group influences were important. A major determinant of an individual's activity was whether or not others in his group were active. There was, consequently, no relationship at all between how long one expected to stay there, or how much benefit one would derive from the organizational activities, and whether or not one became active. We may reaffirm our hypotheses with somewhat more confidence now and look for the next testable derivation which we can make.

To be able to create and maintain group standards, a group must have power over its members. This power, the ability to induce forces on its members, has been called cohesiveness. If the group uses this power to make the members think and act in the same way, that is, if there are group standards, the homogeneity of the attitude and activity patterns should be related to the cohesiveness of the group. Correspondingly, if no relation exists between cohesiveness and homogeneity of the pattern, the group does not use its power to induce the members to conform, and we may take it as indicative of the absence of group standards.

The power of a group may be measured

by the attractiveness of the group for the members. If a person wants to stay in a group, he will be susceptible to influences coming from the group, and he will be willing to conform to the rules which the group sets up.

The courts and buildings in Westgate and Westgate West were mainly social groups. The attractiveness of the group may, therefore, be measured by the friendships formed within the group. If residents had most of their friends within the court, the group was more attractive to them than if they had few friends within the court. The former situation will imply a more cohesive court, which should be able to induce stronger forces on its members. This should result in greater homogeneity within the more cohesive court than within the less cohesive one.

The necessary measures for determining the relationship between the cohesiveness of the court and the effectiveness of the group standard are easily obtained. Sociometric data from a question regarding who the residents saw most of socially may be used here. Thus, if the members of one court give a total of 30 choices, 18 of which are given to others in their own court, the percentage of "in-court" choices is 60. This court is then

considered more cohesive than some other court which gives a total of 32 choices, only 16 of which are to others in the same court. The homogeneity of the court, or how effective the group standard is, may be measured simply by the percentage of members of the court who deviate from the court pattern. The more effective the group standard and the more homogeneous the court, the lower will be the percentage of members who deviate. The second and third columns of Tables 2 and 3 show the percentage of deviates and the proportion of "in-court" choices for each court in Westgate and for each building in Westgate West.

From our hypotheses concerning the existence of group standards in the Westgate courts and the absence of group standards in the Westgate West buildings, we would expect to find an appreciable negative correlation in Westgate and no correlation in Westgate West between the percentage of deviates and the proportion of "in-court" choices. In Table 2 it may be seen that the correlation is −.53 in Westgate. Here, the more cohesive the court (that is, the greater the proportion of "in-court" choices) the smaller the proportion of people who deviated from the court standard. As we ex-

TABLE 2

COHESIVENESS OF COURT AND STRENGTH OF GROUP STANDARD (WESTGATE)

Court and N of Residents		% Deviates	Choices in Court Total Choice	Choices in Court —½ Pairs Total Choice
Tolman	13	23	.62	.529
Howe	13	23	.63	.500
Rotch	8	25	.55	.523
Richards	7	29	.47	.433
Main	7	29	.67	.527
Freeman	13	38	.48	.419
Williams	13	46	.53	.447
Miller	13	46	.56	.485
Carson	13	54	.48	.403
R.O. Correlation with % Deviates			−.53	−.74
t^*			1.65	2.92
p			.15	.02

* Testing significance of file and rank order correlation as suggested by Kendall, M. G., *The Advanced Theory of Statistics*. London: Charles Griffin and Co., Limited, Vol. I, 1943, p. 401.

TABLE 3

COHESIVENESS OF BUILDING AND STRENGTH OF GROUP STANDARD
(WESTGATE WEST)

Building	% Deviates	Choices in Building *Total Choices*	Choices in Building—½ Pairs *Total Choices*
211-20	10	.58	.50
221-30	10	.66	.59
201-10	11	.60	.54
231-40	20	.80	.64
241-50	20	.70	.61
251-60	20	.74	.63
281-90	20	.80	.68
311-20	20	.66	.53
261-70	25	.57	.46
271-80	30	.47	.38
341-50	30	.62	.50
351-60	30	.85	.76
321-30	33	.62	.52
361-70	40	.67	.56
291-300	50	.59	.50
301-10	50	.72	.64
331-40	70	.42	.35
R.O. Correlation with % Deviates		—.20	—.27
t		.79	1.09
p		Not Significant	

pected, this correlation is virtually zero in Westgate West (Table 3). Here the proportion of people who deviated from the building pattern had little or nothing to do with the cohesiveness of the building group.

The measure of cohesiveness which we have used may, however, be considerably improved. The major uncertainty in the measure, as it stands, lies in our inability to distinguish between the cohesiveness of the whole group and the cohesiveness of subgroups. For example, a group of eight people all making choices within the group might or might not have high cohesiveness as a total group. As an extreme illustration, there conceivably might be two subgroups of four people each, every member within each subgroup choosing every other member, but without any choices at all between the subgroups. In this case each of the subgroups may have great cohesiveness, but the cohesiveness of the group as a whole would

be low. Similarly, if in a group of eight or ten people there is a subgroup of three, the total group would be less cohesive than if no subgroup existed. It appears that if a strongly knit subgroup includes a large majority of the group, the cohesiveness of the whole group may still be high.

This effect of tendencies toward subgroup formation may be taken into account in our measure by correcting for the number of mutual choices which occurred. If there were no tendencies at all toward subgroup formation within a group, then the number of mutual choices which we would expect to occur would be quite low. In a group of ten people with each person giving, say, two choices within the group, we would only expect to obtain two mutual choices in the complete absence of tendencies toward subgroup or pair formation. As the tendencies toward subgroup formation increase, we shall expect to find more and more mutual choices. Thus, the existence of mutual choices to some extent decreases the cohesiveness of the group as a whole.

We may check further on whether or not this relationship was a property of the group as a whole. A corrected measure of cohesiveness, obtained by subtracting half of the number of mutual pairs of choices, is certainly meaningful only as a measure of the group as a whole. The fact that mutual choices occurred ,certainly does not detract from the personal attractiveness of the individuals involved in these mutual choices. We should then expect the correlation with the measure of prestige of the subgroup to increase when the corrected measure of cohesiveness is used. This correlation in Westgate is .75, representing an appreciable increase in relationship. In Westgate West, where the buildings did not constitute really functional social units, the correlation remains unchanged—still very close to zero.

The Social Status of the Deviate

What are the conditions which produce deviates? When pressures and influences are being exerted on people to adopt a certain way of thinking or a certain pattern of behavior, some people conform quite readily while others are able entirely to resist these influences. The mere knowledge that these "individual differences" exist does not explain the reasons for them or the factors which are responsible for producing deviates. To learn this, we must examine the means by which group influences may be resisted.

The pressure which a group exerts on its members may be overt and sometimes even formalized. Laws, rules, mores, etiquette, and so on exemplify some of these overt pressures. The pressures which induce men to open doors for women, to dress in certain special ways on certain special occasions, or to enter their fathers' businesses are all overt and recognized. It is likely, of course, that before a group norm or standard can become thus openly formalized it must be in

existence for a long time, or else must be of such a nature that deviation from the standard is harmful to the group. Such open pressures are generally also accompanied by open punishment for deviation in the form of censure, overt disapproval, or even rejection from the group.

On the other hand, the pressures which a group exerts on its members may be subtle and difficult to locate. The weight of others' opinions, the gradual change in one's ideas of what is the "normal" thing to do simply because everyone else does it, the mutual influences of people who share their ideas and their attitudes, also serve effectively as pressures toward conformity with the behavior pattern of the group. Under these circumstances the consequences of nonconformity are also more subtle. These consequences may merely be a tendency to prefer those people who are not "difficult."

There is no indication that in Westgate there was any overt or formalized pressure on court members to conform to the court standard. Many of the residents realized that the people in their court were different from the people in some other court, but the influences which created and maintained these differences among courts were indirect and nonovert. Members of the courts were being influenced in their opinions and behavior merely by virtue of their association with others in their courts, without any formalized "group intent" to influence.

The strength of the influence which the group can exert in this manner depends partly upon the attractiveness of the group for the member and partly on the degree to which the member is in communication with others in the group. No matter how attractive the group is to a particular person, it will be impossible for the group to exert any influence on him if he is never in communication with the group. We may now examine some of the conditions under which individuals will be able to resist these influences.

1. The group may not be sufficiently attractive to the member. Under these circum-

stances, the relatively weak influence which the group exerts cannot overcome personal considerations which may happen to be contrary to the group standard. An example will illustrate this phenomenon:

(*Mr. and Mrs. C, in Williams Court.*) We don't have any opinion at all about the organization. We're bad ones for you to interview. We have no need for an organization because we're pretty happy at home. We're socially self-sufficient. Others in the court feel it is wonderful and we discovered many that felt that way. We have friends in this and other courts but our main interests are in the home.

2. There may not be sufficient communication between the member and others in the group. Under these conditions the pressures from the group are simply not brought to bear on the member although, if they had been exerted, they might have been very effective. In such instances the deviate may not even be aware of the fact that he is different from most of the others in his group. An example of this type of deviate follows:

(*Mr. and Mrs. S, in Freeman Court.*) The organization is a good idea, but the trouble with people like us is that we don't have time. That's why we haven't had anything to do with it. I think it's the consensus of opinion that people here don't have the time. [Actually the majority of the people in the court were active.] There are wonderful people living here, but it seems peculiar to Westgate that people are hard to get to know. A lot of people come here expecting to make friends without any trouble, and then finds it isn't so easy. It would be a good thing if the organization helped people to get acquainted.

3. The influence of some other group to which the people belong may be stronger than the influence which the court group is able to exert on them. Under these conditions the person who appears as a deviate is a deviate only because we have chosen, somewhat arbitrarily, to call him a member of the court group. He does

deviate from his own court, but he conforms to some other group to which he actually feels he belongs. Such a group may, of course, be outside of Westgate altogether. There are instances, however, of people belonging to groups other than their own court, but still within the limits of Westgate:

(*Mr. and Mrs. M, in Carson Court.*) We think the organization is fine and Mrs. M is the chairman of the social committee which is holding its first big event tomorrow night. I don't see much of the others in this court. My real friends are in the next court over there, in Tolman Court. There are only two people living in this court that do anything for the organization, myself and one other person. It's generally understood that the others have different interests. The people in Tolman Court are more active. Carson Court people aren't as sociable as people in Tolman Court.

The Deviate in Westgate

These three types of conditions do, then, appear to produce deviates; at least we were able to locate deviates who seemed to exhibit such patterns of relationship between themselves and the group. If these are the major factors which make for nonconformity, we should also be able to demonstrate their relevance for all of the deviates rather than for a few selected examples. The two variables, attractiveness of the group for the member and amount of communication between the member and the group, should be reflected in the sociometric choices which people gave and received. We should expect that deviates would give fewer choices to others in their court and would receive fewer choices from them. Whether ths happened because they were not in full communication with the group or because the group was not attractive to them, the result in the sociometric choices should be essentially the same—the deviates should be sociometric isolates in their court.

Table 4 shows the average number of "in-court" choices given and received by the 36 deviates and the 64 conformers in Westgate. It is readily apparent that the deviates were more isolated sociometrically than were the conformers. They both gave and received fewer choices than did the conformers.[1] Moreover, the conformers tended to receive more choices than they gave, while the deviates tended to receive fewer choices than they gave. Deviates tended to choose conformers more than conformers chose deviates. This might be called relative rejection by the conformers.

TABLE 4
AVERAGE NUMBER OF "IN-COURT" CHOICES OF DEVIATES AND CONFORMERS IN WESTGATE

	N	Choices Given	Choices Received
Deviates	36	1.25	1.11
Conformers	64	1.53	1.61

Deviate status, then, was accompanied by a smaller degree of association with others in the court. It is still possible, however, that these deviates were not true isolates, but merely members of groups other than the court group. In our case studies we saw two examples of this sort. An examination of all sociometric choices exchanged with people outside the court, however, reveals that this was not true of the deviates as a whole. Table 5 shows the average number of "out-court" choices given and received by the deviates and conformers. It is clear that the deviates, in the main, were not members of groups other than those of their own court. They gave only as many choices to people outside their own court as did the conformers, but received considerably fewer choices

---

[1] The significance of the differences in this and the following tables was computed by taking the means for each court and comparing the distributions of these means. This was done because the effects of group standards made the group, not the individual, the unit of sampling. This difference is significant at the 7% level of confidence for choices given. Significance is at the 17% level of confidence for choices received.

from outside than the conformers.[2] We must conclude that these deviates, who had fewer associations within their own court, also had fewer associations with others in Westgate —at least, insofar as this is reflected by the number of choices they received.

TABLE 5
AVERAGE NUMBER OF "OUT-COURT" CHOICES OF DEVIATES AND CONFORMERS IN WESTGATE

	N	Choices Given	Choices Received
Deviates	36	1.14	.89
Conformers	64	1.16	1.55

Choices given by deviates to people outside their own court tended to be given to the conformers in other courts. These conformers tended not to reciprocate the choices. The deviate, who was perceived as being different from the others in his court, was not as often chosen by outsiders. This is consistent with our knowledge that the court is perceived as the basis for social grouping in Westgate. People who were on the fringes of their own group were also on the fringe of social life between courts. While conformers in Westgate received an average of 3.16 choices from others, the deviates received an average of only 2.00 such choices. The deviates were relative isolates. It is clear that this isolation was not wholly voluntary on the part of the deviates, since they gave only slightly fewer choices than the conformers.

It is possible to examine the situation of the deviate more closely if we restrict ourselves to the six full-size courts in Westgate. Ten of the houses in these six courts faced onto the street rather than into the court-yard area, so that the people living in these houses had fewer contacts with others in the court. Of the other 68 people living in these courts only 34% were deviates, while 7 of the 10 corner-house residents were deviates. It appears that the isolated geographical po-

---

[2] Significant at the 2% level of confidence.

sition in which these 10 found themselves, and the resultant lack of contact between them and the rest of the court, made it difficult for the court to exert influence on them. The lack of contact suggests that mainly chance factors would determine whether they would show the pattern of attitude and behavior that had become the standard in the court.

Table 6 shows the "in-court" choices for these six full-size courts with the corner-

TABLE 6

AVERAGE NUMBER OF "IN-COURT" CHOICES OF DEVIATES AND CONFORMERS FOR THE SIX LARGE COURTS IN WESTGATE

	N	Choices Given	Choices Received
Deviates in Corner Houses	7	.57	.43
Deviates in Inner Houses	23	1.52	1.39
Conformers	48	1.52	1.60

house deviates separated from the others. The lack of contact between the court and the deviates in these corner houses is readily apparent. They both gave and received only about one-third as many choices as did the others in the court.[3] It is not surprising that they had remained uninfluenced by the group standard in their particular court.

The other deviates in the court did not suffer from such lack of contact. They gave as many choices to the others in the court as did the conformers. As was true for all the deviates in Westgate, however, they tended to receive fewer than they gave, while the conformers tended to receive more choices than they gave.[4]

Table 7, again, shows that these inner-house deviates were not members of groups other than the court group. They gave only as many choices to people outside their own

[3] For all comparisons this is significant, at least at the 3% level of confidence.
[4] Not statistically significant.

TABLE 7

AVERAGE NUMBER OF "OUT-COURT" CHOICES OF DEVIATES AND CONFORMERS FOR THE SIX LARGE WESTGATE COURTS

	N	Choices Given	Choices Received
Deviates in Corner Houses	7	1.29	1.14
Deviates in Inner Houses	23	1.13	.87
Conformers	48	1.17	1.58

court as did the conformers and, again, received many fewer.

The deviates stood out as relative isolates, not only within their own court, but in Westgate as a whole. The corner-house deviates received, from all sources, an average of only 1.57 choices, the other deviates received an average of 2.26 choices, while the conformers received an average of 3.18 choices. The conformers were more closely involved with the social life in Westgate than were the deviates. Whether relative isolation brings about deviate status (as seems to be the case for those living in corner houses), or whether deviate status tends to bring about isolation through "rejection by others" (as might be the case with the deviates living in inner houses), the two things seem to go hand in hand.

The Deviate in Westgate West

We concluded above that there was no relation in Westgate West between the uniformity of behavior within a building and the cohesiveness of the building, and that group standards were not operating in Westgate West. The opinions of the people about the tenants' organization and their degree of activity in it would, consequently, not be determined by pressures or influences from the group. The behavior of the individual would be more a matter of individual reaction and influence from other individuals than of group pressures.

We may well examine the sociometric status of those people who were different from the majority in their building, although we should not expect the isolation which we found among the deviates in Westgate. These people were deviates only in the sense that they reacted differently from most of the residents, and not in the sense of having successfully resisted group pressures to conform.

Few people in Westgate West expressed unfavorable attitudes toward the organization. Consequently, few people differed from the pattern of their building on the attitude dimension. The great majority of the deviates differed only on the activity dimension from the others in their building. Thirteen of the seventeen buildings had "favorable-active" patterns, and most of the deviates were people who felt favorably inclined, but had merely not attended the meetings of their building. It is plausible to expect, then, that we would find these deviates not to be isolates in the community despite their absence from building meetings. The data corroborate these expectations. Altogether, deviates and conformers both gave an average of about two and one-half choices, and both received an average of about two and one-half choices. We may thus conclude that in the absence of strong group formation, and in the absence of group standards, being different from the people in the group did not result in isolation.

Summary

In order to conclude that observed uniformity in behavior of a number of individuals is the result of the operation of group standards or the existence of "social norms," we must be able to show the existence of psychological groups which are enforcing such standards. A collection of individuals with a relatively high number of sociometric linkages among them may constitute such a psychological group, or may merely constitute a series of friendship relationships with no real unification of the group as a whole. It is highly likely, of course, that such a series of friendship relationships among a number of people will in time make for the development of a cohesive group. In Westgate West, where there had not been time for this process really to develop, evidence indicating the absence of group standards was found.

When a cohesive group does exist, and when its realm of concern extends over the area of behavior in which we have discovered uniformity among the members of the group, then the degree of uniformity must be related to the degree of cohesiveness of the group, if a group standard is operative. The more cohesive the group, the more effectively it can influence its members. Thus we have found that in the more cohesive groups in Westgate there were fewer deviates from the group pattern of behavior. The cohesiveness of the court group as a whole was the important determinant of the number of deviates. Subgroup formation within the larger group, no matter how cohesive these subgroups may have been, tended to disrupt the cohesiveness of the larger unit.

Although, on the basis of the data available to us, we have not been able to separate clearly the different means by which people can resist group influences and thus become deviates, there is abundant evidence that the attractiveness of the group and the amount of communication between the member and the group are major determinants. It also would seem likely that these two factors would generally not occur separately, but would operate together in most situations. The sociometric status of the deviate is clearly different from that of the conformer—isolation seems to be both a cause and an effect of being a deviate.

References

LEWIN, K. et al. Level of aspiration. In J. McV. Hunt (Ed.), *Personality and the behavior disorders.* Vol. I. New York: Ronald, 1944.

NEWCOMB, T. M. *Personality and social*

change. New York: Holt, Rinehart and Winston, 1943.

SHERIF, M. *The psychology of social norms.* New York: Harper & Row, 1936.

The Effects of Changes in Roles
on the Attitudes of
Role Occupants ❊ Seymour Lieberman

Problem

One of the fundamental postulates of role theory, as expounded by Newcomb (1950), Parsons (1951), and other role theorists, is that a person's attitudes will be influenced by the role that he occupies in a social system. Although this proposition appears to be a plausible one, surprisingly little evidence is available that bears directly on it. One source of evidence is found in common folklore. "Johnny is a changed boy since he was made a monitor in school." "She is a different woman since she got married." "You would never recognize him since he became foreman." As much as these expressions smack of the truth, they offer little in the way of systematic or scientific support for the proposition that a person's attitudes are influenced by his role.

Somewhat more scientific, but still not definitive, is the common finding, in many social-psychological studies, that relationships exist between attitudes and roles. In

other words, different attitudes are held by people who occupy different roles. For example, Stouffer *et al.* (1949) found that commissioned officers are more favorable toward the Army than are enlisted men. The problem here is that the mere existence of a relationship between attitudes and roles does not reveal the cause and effect nature of the relationship found. One interpretation of Stouffer's finding might be that being made a commissioned officer tends to result in a person's becoming pro-Army—i.e., the role a person occupies influences his attitudes. But an equally plausible interpretation might be that being pro-Army tends to result in a person's being made a commissioned officer—i.e., a person's attitudes influence the likelihood of his being selected for a given role. In the absence of longitudinal data, the relationship offers no clear evidence that roles were the "cause" and attitudes the "effect."

The present study was designed to examine the effects of roles on attitudes in a par-

This article has been adapted by the author especially for this book from *Human Relations,* 1956, 9, 385-402. Reprinted by permission of the author and publisher. This study was one of a series conducted by the Human Relations Program of the Survey Research Center, Institute for Social Research, at the University of Michigan. The author wishes to express a special debt of gratitude to Dr. Gerald M. Mahoney and Mr. Gerald Gurin, his associates on the larger study of which the present one was a part, and to Dr. Daniel Katz, Dr. Theodore M. Newcomb, and Dr. Eugene Jacobson for their many useful suggestions and contributions.

ticular field situation. The study is based on longitudinal data obtained in a role-differentiated, hierarchical organization. By taking advantage of natural role changes among personnel in the organization, it was possible to examine people's attitudes both before and after they underwent changes in roles. Therefore, the extent to which changes in roles were followed by changes in attitudes could be determined, and the cause and effect nature of any relationships found would be clear.

Method: Phase 1

The study was part of a larger project carried out in a medium-sized Midwestern company engaged in the production of home appliance equipment. Let us call the company the Rockwell Corporation. At the time that the study was done, Rockwell employed about 2,500 factory workers and about 150 first-level foremen. The company was unionized and most of the factory workers belonged to the union local, which was an affiliate of the U.A.W., C.I.O. About 150 factory workers served as stewards in the union, or roughly one steward for every foreman.

The study consisted of a "natural field experiment." In September and October 1951, attitude questionnaires were filled out by virtually all factory personnel at Rockwell—2,354 workers, 145 stewards, and 151 foremen. The questions dealt for the most part with employees' attitudes and perceptions about the company, the union, and various aspects of the job situation. The respondents were told that the questionnaire was part of an overall survey to determine how employees felt about working conditions at Rockwell.

Between October 1951 and July 1952, twenty-three workers were made foremen and thirty-five workers became stewards. Most of the workers who became stewards during that period were elected during the annual steward elections held in May 1952,

replacing stewards who did not choose to run again or who were not re-elected by their constituents. The workers who became foremen were promoted at various points in time as openings arose in supervisory positions.

In December 1952, the same forms that had been filled out by the rank-and-file workers in 1951 were readministered to the two groups of workers who had changed roles and to two matched control groups of workers who had not changed roles. Each control group was matched with its parallel experimental group on a number of demographic, attitudinal, and motivational variables. Therefore, any changes in attitudes that occurred in the experimental groups but did not occur in the control groups could not be attributed to initial differences between them.

The employees in these groups were told that the purpose of the follow-up questionnaire was to get up-to-date measures of their attitudes in 1952 and to compare how employees felt that year with the way that they felt the previous year. The groups were told that, instead of studying the entire universe of employees as was the case in 1951, only a sample was being studied this time. They were informed that the sample was chosen in such a way as to represent all kinds of employees at Rockwell—men and women, young and old, etc. The groups gave no indication that they understood the real bases on which they were chosen for the "after" measurement or that the effect of changes in roles were the critical factors being examined.[1]

Results: Phase 1

The major hypothesis tested in this study was that people who are placed in a role

[1] Some of the top officials of management and all of the top officers of the union at Rockwell knew about the nature of the follow-up study and the bases on which the experimental and control groups were selected.

TABLE 1

QUESTIONS USED TO MEASURE ATTITUDES TOWARD MANAGEMENT AND THE UNION

Management

Question 1.	How is Rockwell as a place to work?
Question 2.	How does Rockwell compare with other companies?
Question 3.	If things went bad for Rockwell, should the workers try to help out?
Question 4.	How much do management officers care about the workers at Rockwell?

Union

Question 5.	How do you feel about labor unions in general?
Question 6.	How much say should the union have in setting standards?
Question 7.	How would things be if there were no union at Rockwell?
Question 8.	How much do union officers care about the workers at Rockwell?

Management-Sponsored Incentive System

Question 9.	How do you feel about the principle of an incentive system?
Question 10.	How do you feel the incentive system works out at Rockwell?
Question 11.	Should the incentive system be changed?
Question 12.	Is a labor standard ever changed just because a worker is a high producer?

Union-Sponsored Seniority System

Question 13.	How do you feel about the way the seniority system works out here?
Question 14.	How much should seniority count during lay-offs?
Question 15.	How much should seniority count in moving to better jobs?
Question 16.	How much should seniority count in promotion to foreman?

will tend to take on or develop attitudes that are congruent with the expectations associated with that role. Four attitudinal areas were examined: (1) attitudes toward management and officials of management; (2) attitudes toward the union and officials of the union; (3) attitudes toward the management-sponsored incentive system (whereby workers are paid according to the number of pieces they turn out); and (4) attitudes toward the union-sponsored seniority system (whereby workers are promoted according to the seniority principle). The questions used to tap these four attitudinal areas are listed in Table 1.

The data support the hypothesis that being placed in the foreman and steward roles will have an impact on the attitudes of the role occupants. As shown in Tables 2 and 3, both experimental groups—those who became foremen and those who became stewards—underwent systematic changes in atti-

tudes, in the predicted directions, from the "before" situation to the "after" situation. In the control groups, either no attitude changes occurred, or less marked changes occurred, from the "before" situation to the "after" situation.

Although a number of the differences are not statistically significant, almost all which are significant are in the expected directions and most of the non-significant differences are also in the expected directions. New foremen, among other things, came to see Rockwell as a better place to work, developed more positive perceptions of top management officers, and became more favorably disposed toward the principle and operation of the incentive system. New stewards came to look upon labor unions in general in a more favorable light, developed more positive perceptions of the top union officers at Rockwell, and came to prefer seniority over ability as a criterion of what

TABLE 2

EFFECT OF FOREMAN ROLE ON ATTITUDES TOWARD MANAGEMENT AND THE UNION

	New Foremen (23)	Control Group° (46)	p
% Becoming More Favorable toward Management			
Question 1 †	70%	47%	< .10
Question 2	52	24	< .05
Question 3	17	17	N.S.
Question 4	48	15	< .05
% Becoming More Critical of the Union			
Question 5	22	15	N.S.
Question 6	74	24	< .01
Question 7	52	22	< .05
Question 8	9	7	N.S.
% Becoming More Favorable toward Management-Sponsored Incentive System			
Question 9	57	15	< .01
Question 10	65	37	< .05
Question 11	39	11	< .05
Question 12	48	11	< .01
% Becoming More Critical of Union-Sponsored Seniority System			
Question 13	35	17	< .15
Question 14	39	17	< .10
Question 15	39	26	N.S.
Question 16	13	33	< .10

° Workers who did not change roles, matched with future foremen on demographic and attitudinal variables in the "before" situation.
† Question numbers refer to the question numbers of the attitudinal items in Table 1.

should count in moving workers to better jobs. In general, the attitudes of workers who became foremen gravitated in a pro-management direction and the attitudes of workers who became stewards shifted in a pro-union direction.

A second kind of finding has to do with the relative *amount* of attitude change that took place among new foremen in contrast to the amount that took place among new stewards. On the whole, more pronounced and more widespread attitude changes occurred among those who were made foremen than among those who were made stewards. This can probably be accounted for in large measure by the fact that the change from worker to foreman represented a more fundamental change in roles than the change from worker to steward. For one

thing, the foreman role was a relatively permanent position, while many stewards took the steward role as a "one-shot" job and even if they wanted to run again their constituents might not re-elect them. Secondly, the foreman role was a full-time job, while stewards spent only a few hours a week in the performance of their steward functions and spent the rest of the time carrying out their regular rank-and-file jobs. Thirdly, workers who were made foremen had to give up their membership in the union and become surrogates of management, while workers who were made stewards retained the union as a reference group and simply took on new functions and responsibilities as representatives of it.

A third finding has to do with the *kinds* of attitude changes which occurred among

TABLE 3

EFFECT OF STEWARD ROLE ON ATTITUDES TOWARD MANAGEMENT AND THE UNION

	New Stewards (35)	Control Group° (35)	p
	% Becoming More Critical of Management		
Question 1 †	23%	11%	N.S.
Question 2	11	11	N.S.
Question 3	0	17	< .05
Question 4	9	0	N.S.
	% Becoming More Favorable toward the Union		
Question 5	54	29	< .05
Question 6	31	20	N.S.
Question 7	14	11	N.S.
Question 8	57	26	< .01
	% Becoming More Critical of Management-Sponsored Incentive System		
Question 9	29	29	N.S.
Question 10	23	26	N.S.
Question 11	23	20	N.S.
Question 12	14	9	N.S.
	% Becoming More Favorable toward Union-Sponsored Seniority System		
Question 13	23	9	< .15
Question 14	29	29	N.S.
Question 15	34	17	< .15
Question 16	31	17	N.S.

° Workers who did not change roles, matched with future stewards on demographic and attitudinal variables in the "before" situation.
† Question numbers refer to the question numbers of the attitudinal items in Table 1.

workers who changed roles. As expected, new foremen became more pro-management and new stewards became more pro-union. Somewhat less expected was the finding that new foremen became more anti-union but new stewards did not become more anti-management. New foremen showed statistically significant shifts in an anti-union direction on a number of items dealing with the union and the union-sponsored seniority system, while new stewards did not show any statistically significant shifts on any of the items dealing with management and the management-sponsored incentive system. This may be related to the fact that workers who became foremen had to relinquish their membership in the union, while workers who became stewards retained their status as employees of management. New foremen, subject to one main set of loyalties and called on to carry out a markedly new set of functions, tended to develop negative attitudes toward the union as well as positive attitudes toward management. New stewards, subject to over-lapping group membership and still dependent on management for their livelihoods, tended to become more favorable toward the union but did not turn against management, at least not within the relatively limited time period covered by the present research project.

Method: Phase 2

One of the questions that may be raised about the results that have been presented up to this point concerns the extent to which the changed attitudes displayed by new foremen and new stewards were internalized by the role occupants. Were the changed attitudes expressed by new foremen and new stewards relatively stable, or were they ephemeral phenomena to be held only as long as they occupied the foreman and steward roles? An unusual set of circumstances at Rockwell enabled the researchers to glean some data on this question.

A short time after the 1952 re-survey, the nation suffered an economic recession. In order to meet the lessening demand for its products, Rockwell, like many other firms, had to cut its work force. This resulted in many rank-and-file workers being laid off and a number of the foremen being returned to non-supervisory jobs. By June 1954, eight of the twenty-three workers who had been promoted to foremen had returned to the worker role and only twelve were still foremen. (The remaining three respondents had voluntarily left Rockwell by this time.)

Over the same period, a number of role changes had also been experienced by the thirty-five workers who had become stewards. Fourteen had returned to the worker role, either because they had not sought re-election by their work groups or because they had failed to win re-election, and only six were still stewards. (The other fifteen respondents, who composed almost half of this group, had either voluntarily left Rockwell or had been laid off as part of the general reduction in force.)

Once again, in June 1954, the researchers returned to Rockwell to readminister the questionnaires that the workers had filled out in 1951 and 1952. The instructions to the respondents were substantially the same as those given in 1952—i.e., a sample of employees had been chosen to get up-to-date measures of employees' attitudes toward working conditions at Rockwell and the same groups were selected this time as had been selected last time in order to lend greater stability to the results.

TABLE 4

EFFECTS OF ENTERING AND LEAVING THE FOREMAN ROLE ON
ATTITUDES TOWARD MANAGEMENT AND THE UNION

	Workers Who Became Foremen and Stayed Foremen (N = 12)			Workers Who Became Foremen and Were Later Demoted (N = 8)		
	(W) 1951	(F) 1952	(F) 1954	(W) 1951	(F) 1952	(W) 1954
% Who Feel Rockwell Is a Good Place to Work	33	92	100	25	75	50
% Who Feel Management Officers Really Care about the Workers at Rockwell	8	33	67	0	25	0
% Who Feel the Union Should Not Have More Say in Setting Labor Standards	33	100	100	13	63	13
% Who Are Satisfied with the Way the Incentive System Works Out at Rockwell	17	75	75	25	50	13
% Who Believe a Worker's Standard Will Not Be Changed Just Because He Is a High Producer	42	83	100	25	63	75
% Who Feel Ability Should Count More than Seniority in Promotions	33	58	75	25	50	38

TABLE 5

EFFECTS OF ENTERING AND LEAVING THE STEWARD ROLE ON
ATTITUDES TOWARD MANAGEMENT AND THE UNION

	Workers Who Were Elected Stewards and Were Later Re-elected ($N=6$)			Workers Who Were Elected Stewards But Were Not Later Re-elected ($N=14$)		
	(W) 1951	(S) 1952	(S) 1954	(W) 1951	(S) 1952	(W) 1954
% Who Feel Rockwell Is a Good Place to Work	50	0	0	29	79	36
% Who Feel Management Officers Really Care about the Workers at Rockwell	0	0	0	14	14	0
% Who Feel the Union Should Not Have More Say in Setting Labor Standards	0	17	0	14	14	14
% Who Are Satisfied with the Way the Incentive System Works Out at Rockwell	17	17	0	43	43	21
% Who Believe a Worker's Standard Will Not Be Changed Just Because He Is a High Producer	50	50	17	21	43	36
% Who Feel Ability Should Count More than Seniority in Promotions	67	17	17	36	36	21

In this phase of the study, the numbers of cases with which we were dealing in the various groups were so small that the data could only be viewed as suggestive, and systematic statistical analysis of the data did not seem to be too meaningful. However, the unusual opportunity to throw some light on an important question suggests that a reporting of these results may be worthwhile.

Results: Phase 2

The principal question examined here was: on those items where a change in roles resulted in a change in attitudes between 1951 and 1952, how were these attitudes influenced by a reverse change in roles between 1952 and 1954?

The most consistent and widespread attitude changes noted between 1951 and 1952 were those that resulted when workers moved into the foreman role. What were the effects of moving out of the foreman role be-

tween 1952 and 1954? The data indicate that, in general, most of the "gains" that were observed when workers became foremen were "lost" when they became workers again. The results on six of the items, showing the proportions who took pro-management positions at various points in time, are presented in Table 4. On almost all of the items, the foremen who remained foremen either retained their favorable attitudes toward management or became even more favorable toward management between 1952 and 1954, while the demoted foremen showed fairly consistent drops in the direction of re-adopting the attitudes they held when they had been in the worker role. On the whole, the attitudes held by demoted foremen in 1954, after they had left the foreman role, fell roughly to the same levels as they had been in 1951, before they had ever moved into the foreman role.

The results on the effects of moving out of the steward role are less clear-cut. As shown in Table 5, there was no marked tendency for ex-stewards to revert to earlier-held attitudes when they returned from the steward role to the worker role. At the same time, it should be recalled that there had not been particularly marked changes in their attitudes when they initially moved from the worker role to the steward role. These findings, then, are consistent with the interpretation offered earlier that the change in roles between worker and steward was less significant than the change in roles between worker and foreman.

One final table is of interest here. Table 6 compares the attitudes of two groups of respondents: (1) the twelve employees who were rank-and-file workers in 1951, had been selected as foremen by 1952, and were still foremen in 1954; and (2) the six employees who were rank-and-file workers in 1951, had been elected as stewards by 1952, and were still stewards in 1954. At each time period, for each of the sixteen questions cited in Table 1, the table shows (1) the proportion of foremen or future foremen who took a pro-management position on these questions; (2) the proportion

TABLE 6

EFFECTS OF FOREMAN AND STEWARD ROLES OVER A THREE-YEAR PERIOD: BEFORE CHANGE IN ROLES, AFTER ONE YEAR IN NEW ROLES AND AFTER TWO–THREE YEARS IN NEW ROLES

% Who Take a Pro-management Position on the Following Questions:	Before Change in Roles (1951)			After 1 Year in New Roles (1952)			After 2-3 Years in New Roles (1954)		
	Workers Who Became Foremen	Workers Who Became Stewards	D%°	Workers Who Became Foremen	Workers Who Became Stewards	D%°	Workers Who Became Foremen	Workers Who Became Stewards	D%°
Question 1†	33	50	−17	92	0	+92	100	0	+100
Question 2	33	33	0	75	33	+42	67	17	+50
Question 3	92	83	+9	100	100	0	100	50	+50
Question 4	8	0	+8	33	0	+33	67	0	+67
Question 5	67	100	−33	67	17	+50	33	17	+16
Question 6	33	0	+33	100	17	+83	100	0	+100
Question 7	8	0	+8	50	0	+50	58	0	+58
Question 8	75	67	+8	75	50	+25	58	17	+41
Question 9	33	83	−50	83	17	+66	83	0	+83
Question 10	17	17	0	75	17	+58	75	0	+75
Question 11	17	17	0	25	0	+25	67	0	+67
Question 12	42	50	−8	83	50	+33	100	17	+83
Question 13	58	50	+8	100	17	+83	100	17	+83
Question 14	33	67	−34	50	17	+33	75	17	+58
Question 15	33	0	+33	58	0	+58	67	0	+67
Question 16	67	33	+34	67	33	+34	67	67	0
No. of Cases	12	6		12	6		12	6	
Mean D%			−0.1			+47.8			+62.4

° Percentage of workers who became foremen who take a pro-management position minus percentage of workers who became stewards who take a pro-management position.
† Question numbers refer to the question numbers of the attitudinal items in Table 1.

of stewards or future stewards who took a pro-management position on these questions; and (3) the difference between these proportions. The following are the mean differences in proportions for the three time periods:

1. In 1951, while both future foremen and future stewards still occupied the rank-and-file worker role, the mean difference was only −0.1 per cent, which means that practically no difference in attitudes existed between these two groups at that time. (The minus sign means that a slightly, but far from significantly, larger proportion of future stewards than future foremen expressed a pro-management position on these items.)
2. In 1952, after the groups had been in the foremen and steward roles for about one year, the mean difference had jumped to +47.8 per cent, which means that a sharp wedge had been driven between them. Both groups had tended to become polarized in opposite directions, as foremen took on attitudes consistent with being a representative of management and stewards took on attitudes appropriate for a representative of the union.
3. In 1954, after the groups had been in the foreman and steward roles for two to three years, the mean difference was +62.4 per cent, which means that a still larger gap had opened up between them. Although the gap had widened, it is interesting to note that the changes that occurred during this later and longer 1952 to 1954 period are not as sharp or as dramatic as the changes that occurred during the initial and shorter 1951 to 1952 period.

The data indicate that changes in attitudes occurred soon after changes in roles took place. And inside a period of three years those who had remained in their new roles had developed almost diametrically opposed sets of attitudinal positions.

Summary

This study was designed to test the proposition that a person's attitudes will be influenced by the role he occupies in a social system. This is a commonly accepted postulate in role theory but there appears to be little in the way of definitive empirical evidence to support it. Earlier studies have generally made inferences about the effects of roles on attitudes on the basis of correlational data gathered at a single point in time. The present study attempted to measure the effects of roles on attitudes through data gathered at three different points in time.

The first phase of the study centered around two groups of rank-and-file workers who underwent role changes in a factory situation: one group of workers who were promoted to foremen and a second group of workers who were elected as union stewards. Both groups manifested systematic changes in attitudes after they moved into their new roles. The workers who were made foremen tended to become more favorable toward management, and the workers who were made stewards tended to become more favorable toward the union. The changes were more marked among new foremen than among new stewards, which can be probably accounted for by the fact that the change from worker to foreman was a more significant and more meaningful change in roles than the change from worker to steward.

The second phase of the study explored what happened at a later point in time when several foremen and stewards reverted to the rank-and-file worker role. Some of the foremen were cut back to non-supervisory positions during a period of economic recession, and some of the stewards either did not run again or failed to be re-elected during the annual steward elections. The findings indicated that foremen who were demoted tended to revert to the attitudes they had previously held while they were in the worker role, while foremen who remained in the foreman role either maintained the attitudes they had developed when they first became foremen or moved even further in that direction. The results among stewards who left the steward role were less consistent and less clear-cut, which parallels the smaller and less clear-cut attitude changes that took place when they first became stewards.

The study results support the proposition that a person's role will have an impact on attitudes relevant to the carrying out of that role. In both phases of the study reported here—when rank-and-file workers moved into the foreman and steward roles and again when some of them moved back into their former roles—the respondents' attitudes were sharply molded by the roles which they occupied at a given point in time.

References

NEWCOMB, T. M. *Social psychology.* New York: Holt, Rinehart and Winston, 1950.

PARSONS, T. *The social system.* New York: The Free Press of Glencoe, 1951.

STOUFFER, S. A., SUCHMAN, E. A., DeVIN-NEY, L. C., STAR, S. A., and WILLIAMS, R. M., JR. *The American soldier: adjustment during Army life* (Vol. 1). Princeton, N.J.: Princeton University Press, 1949.

Role Conflict ❧ Neal Gross

and Its Resolution ❧ Alexander W. McEachern

❧ Ward S. Mason

In certain situations an individual may find himself exposed to conflicting expectations: some people expect him to behave in one way, others in another, and these expectations are incompatible. How will individuals behave when faced with such conflicts? This is the problem with which our paper is concerned. Later we shall offer a theory of role-conflict resolution and present a test of its usefulness. Before doing this it is necessary to try, first, to clarify the meaning of role conflict and introduce definitions of the concepts we shall employ; second, to present the methods we used in a study of role conflicts of school superintendents; and third, to describe their behavior when they perceived their exposure to conflicting expectations.

Concepts

An examination of the literature concerned with "role conflict" reveals that this term has been given different meanings by different social scientists. Some have used it to denote incompatible expectation situations to which an actor is exposed, whether he is aware of the conflict or not. Other social scientists use "role conflict" to mean situations in which the actor *perceives* incompatible expectations. A foreman's subordinates and his boss may hold quite opposite expectations for his behavior but he may or may not be aware of this discrepancy.

Some formulations of role conflict specify

This article was adapted by the authors especially for E. E. Maccoby, T. M. Newcomb, and E. L. Hartley (Eds.), *Readings in Social Psychology*, 3d Ed., New York: Holt, Rinehart and Winston, 1958, from N. Gross, W. S. Mason, and A. McEachern, *Explorations in Role Analysis: Studies of the School Superintendency Role*, New York: John Wiley & Sons, Inc., 1957. Reprinted by permission of the authors and publishers.

that the actor must be exposed to conflicting expectations that derive from the fact that he occupies two or more positions simultaneously. For example, a young man may occupy simultaneously the positions of a son and a member of a fraternity, and his father and his fraternity brothers may hold contradictory expectations for his "drinking behavior." Other formulations include in role conflict those contradictory expectations that derive from an actor's occupancy of a single position. A professor may be expected to behave in one way by his students, in another way by his dean.

Some writers limit role conflict to situations in which an actor is exposed to conflicting *legitimate* expectations or "obligations" whereas others do not make this restriction.

In view of these differences it is necessary to specify the way we defined and limited our problem. First, our interest was in role conflicts which were *perceived* by the individuals subject to them. Second, we were concerned with incompatible expectations resulting from an actor's occupancy of single as well as of multiple positions; *intra-role* as well as *inter-role* conflicts were within the focus of inquiry. Third, the analysis was not restricted to incompatible expectations which were perceived as legitimate. Attention was directed to situations involving both legitimate and illegitimate incompatible expectations.

Limiting the problem in this way the following definitions of basic concepts were used. A *role congruency* is a situation in which an actor as the incumbent of one or more positions perceives that the same or highly similar expectations are held for him. A school superintendent who perceived that his teachers, principals, students, and school board all expected him to handle a discipline problem in the same way would be confronted with a role congruency.

There are situations, however, in which an actor perceives that he is exposed to expectations which are incompatible. A school superintendent may think teachers and parents hold conflicting expectations for his behavior in dealing with a truant child. Any situation in which the incumbent of a position perceives that he is confronted with incompatible expectations will be called a *role conflict.*

The person for whom an expectation is held may consider it to be *legitimate* or *illegitimate*. A legitimate expectation is one which the incumbent of a position feels others have a right to hold. An illegitimate expectation is one which he does not feel others have a right to hold. An expectation which is felt to be legitimate will be called a *perceived obligation*. One which is felt to be illegitimate will be called a *perceived pressure.*

A *sanction* is either a reward or a punishment, conditional on how an individual behaves. For our analysis we will not be concerned with negative sanctions, nor will we be concerned with *actual* sanctions, but rather with an individual's *perceptions* of the sanctions others may apply to him. Whether or not the perceived and actual sanctions are the same in any given situation is an empirical problem which will not be relevant to these analyses.

Methodology

One hundred and five school superintendents were included in the study. They represented a 48 percent stratified random sample of all school superintendents in Massachusetts in 1952-53. The data to be reported were obtained from each of these superintendents in the course of an eight-hour interview conducted in the staff research offices.

After considerable experimentation with various methods of isolating the role conflicts to which superintendents were exposed, the following procedure was developed. Four situations were presented to the superintendent, each involving problems with which all superintendents must deal and which, on the basis of the pretests, were judged likely to arouse incompatible expectations. They concerned (1) the hiring and promotion of teachers, (2) the superintendent's allocation of his after-office hours, (3) salary increases for teachers, and (4) the priority the superintendent gives financial or educational needs in drawing up the school budget. For each situation we offered three alternative expectations that incumbents of relevant counterpositions might hold. For example, in the situation which is concerned with teachers' salaries these three expectations were described:

A. Expect me to recommend the highest possible salary increases for teachers so that their incomes are commensurate with their professional responsibilities.
B. Expect me to recommend the lowest possible salary increases for teachers.
C. Have no expectations one way or another.

Eighteen potentially relevant groups or individuals were then listed, and each of the superintendents was asked to indicate which of the three statements most nearly represented what each of the groups or individuals expected the superintendent to do in the situation. If he said that one or more individuals held expectation A and one or more held expectation B, then he was reporting incompatible expectations from incumbents of positions counter to his own.

In addition, the superintendents were asked whether or not they felt that the expectations they said others held were "legitimate." Furthermore, if incompatible expectations were perceived by the superintendent, the interviewer probed with open-end questions to discover how much anxiety was thus created, how the conflict was resolved, and what sanctions the superintendent thought would result from selecting one or the other of the incompatible alternatives.

An example of a city superintendent's re-

TABLE 1

A SAMPLE QUESTIONNAIRE—THREE ATTITUDES OF VARIOUS GROUPS AND INDIVIDUALS WHICH ONE SUPERINTENDENT PERCEIVED IN HIS COMMUNITY

	A	B	C			A	B	C
1. Politicians		×		12. Fraternal Organizations				×
2. Church or Religious Groups		×		13. Veterans' Organizations				×
3. Farm Organizations			×	14. Individual School-Committee Members	×	×	
4. Business or Commercial Organizations			×	15. Town Finance Committee		×	
5. Labor Unions	×			16. My Wife, Family	×		
6. Parents (PTA)	×	×		17. Chamber of Commerce			×
7. Teachers	×			18. The Press		×	
8. Personal Friends	×	×		19. Other			
9. Taxpayers' Association		×					
10. Individuals Influential for Economic Reasons		×					
11. Service Clubs	×	×					

DIRECTIONS: For each group or individual listed above please check the box which most nearly represents what they think you should do about this:
A. Expect me to recommend the *highest* salary increases possible for teachers so that their incomes are commensurate with their professional responsibilities.
B. Expect me to recommend the *lowest* possible salary increases for teachers.
C. Have no expectations one way or another.

sponses to the role conflict instrument illustrates the exact method of securing the data for this analysis. Table 1 summarizes the responses of this superintendent to the question of which groups or individuals held which expectations for him with respect to salary increases for teachers.

It is clear that he perceived incompatible expectations. He perceived that labor unions, the Parent-Teacher Association (PTA) and parent groups, some teachers, some of his personal friends, some service clubs, some of the school-board members, and his family expect him to recommend the highest possible salary increases. A number of other groups and individuals hold the contrary expectation; these are politicians, religious groups, some parents, some personal friends, taxpayers' association, economic influentials, service clubs, some school-board members, the town finance committee and the press.

In four cases some members of a given category held one expectation, according to the superintendent, while others in the same category held the contrary expectation. School-board members, parents, personal friends, and service clubs were all described by the superintendent in this way.

The Incidence and Resolution of Role Conflict

In view of space limitations it is necessary to limit consideration of the incidence and resoluton of role conflict to only one of the four situations studied. The teacher-salary issue will be used. An examination of this potential area of role conflict will serve as a background to the theory of role-conflict resolution and yield part of the data with which one test of it can be made.

TABLE 2

PERCENTAGE OF SUPERINTENDENTS WHO PERCEIVED PARTICULAR EXPECTATIONS FROM SPECIFIED GROUPS AND INDIVIDUALS WITH RESPECT TO THEIR SALARY RECOMMENDATIONS

Group or Individual	A. High Salary Expectation (Percent)	B. Low Salary Expectation (Percent)	C. Mixed Expectation (Percent)	D. No Expectation (Percent)	N °
1. Politicians	14	51	6	29	105
2. Church or Religious Groups	34	6	3	57	104
3. Farm Organizations	12	17	2	69	62
4. Business or Commercial Organizations	15	34	4	47	105
5. Labor Unions	63	2	2	33	53
6. Parents (PTA)	78	1	9	12	105
7. Teachers	99	0	1	0	105
8. Personal Friends	57	1	5	37	105
9. Taxpayers' Association	9	77	4	11	61
10. Individuals Influential for Economic Reasons	11	45	7	37	105
11. Service Clubs	35	7	7	50	87
12. Fraternal Organizations	19	3	3	74	93
13. ·Veterans' Organizations	27	5	4	64	104
14. Individual School-Committee Members	70	14	14	2	105
15. Town Finance Committee or City Council	18	60	11	10	103
16. My Wife, Family	71	0	0	29	103
17. Chamber of Commerce	20	27	7	47	65
18. The Press	28	25	2	45	88

° When N is less than 105 it is usually because the group or individual did not exist in a number of communities; the "no answers" when the group or individual did exist are also excluded.

That the teacher-salary issue is a fertile source of role conflict is clear from the fact that 88 percent of the superintendents perceived that they were exposed to conflicting expectations in this area. Table 2 reports the proportions of superintendents who perceived that incumbents of each of the listed counterpositions held: (1) the expectation that he recommend the highest salary increases possible; (2) the expectation that he recommend the lowest salary increases possible; (3) mixed expectations (that is, some held the A and others the B expectation); (4) no expectations regarding this issue.

Whereas 99 percent of the superintendents perceived that their teachers expected them to recommend the highest salary increases possible, 75 percent of those with taxpayers' associations in their communities reported that these associations held the opposite expectation (column 2). Similarly a majority of the superintendents said that their town finance committee or city council and local politicians expected them to minimize salary increases for teachers. In addition to reporting that their teachers expected them to recommend the highest possible salary increases, a majority of the superintendents reported that labor organizations, parents and the PTA, personal friends, individual school-board members, and their wives held the same expectation. Relatively few superintendents, however, are confronted with the "mixed" expectation from members of the same group or category, school-board members obtaining the highest percentage (14 percent in column 3) and town finance-committee members the next highest (12 percent in column 3).

From these data it is possible to conclude not only that superintendents are frequently confronted with role conflicts with respect to their teacher salary recommendations, but also that these conflicts may stem from different groups and individuals or from groups and individuals of the same kind. For the 88 percent of the superintendents who perceived that they were exposed to incompatible expectations, there is clearly a problem which must be resolved. How do

superintendents act when they perceive that some groups or individuals expect them to behave in a contradictory manner?

When a superintendent had indicated that he was exposed to incompatible expectations, he was asked how he resolved the dilemma implied by this condition. Of the 92 superintendents (88 percent) who were exposed to role conflict in this situation (13 were not), seven gave insufficient information to permit coding their behavior, 54 conformed to the expectation of recommending the highest possible salary increases (64 percent of the 85 who told us what they did), eight recommended the lowest possible increases (9 percent of 85), and 23 (27 percent of 85) adopted some kind of strategy which did not require them to make an unequivocal choice between the two incompatible alternatives. Before we turn to an effort to predict which people will resolve the conflict in which way, let us examine briefly the different resolution techniques of those 23 superintendents who did not make a definite choice but developed a procedure whereby they could to some degree satisfy (18 or 21 percent) or ignore (5 or 6 percent) both demands.

One of the five superintendents who ignored both demands was not yet on tenure and perceived that his school board members, the town finance committee, the taxpayers' association, and individuals who were economically influential all expected him to recommend the lowest possible salary increases, whereas his teachers held the contrary expectation. He described his situation in this way:

> I put it all in the hands of the school committee. It's a hot potato so I let the school committee handle it. The teachers feel I should represent them; the school committee feels I should represent them: I'd hang myself by getting involved. But I go along with the school committee recommendation one hundred percent, whatever they decide.

Four of the 18 superintendents who compromised assumed the position of negotiator when confronted with this dilemma. They apparently worked on the assumption that, although the expectations they face conflict, it is their duty to negotiate "a settlement" that will be most satisfactory to everyone. One superintendent perceived that his teachers, the school board, and the PTA expected him to recommend high salary increases to hold and attract competent personnel, while the town finance committee and taxpayers' association expected him to recommend the lowest increases, because they felt that the town was approaching a financial crisis. This superintendent says: "I use the salesman's technique. I tell the town, 'You don't want cheap teachers if you want a good school system.' I tell the teachers they have to be reasonable, that there has to be a compromise . . . if I completely agreed with the teachers, I'd be out of a job."

Three of the superintendents who compromise rejected both sets of expectations and substituted a new criterion in making their recommendations. They took the position that since they could not fully conform to both sets of expectations they try to develop a defensible rationale for their recommendations which is independent of the incompatible expectations of others. One of the superintendents recommended that the salary increases be contingent on a cost of living index. The others recommended an increase that would keep their school system in a competitive position with those of comparable size and wealth. One superintendent said he tried ". . . to do what's fair in light of what other communities are doing. I don't want my teachers to be at a disadvantage, but neither do I want our system to be a leader in the salaries we pay."

Ten of the 18 superintendents who compromised resolved the salary dilemma by trying to modify the conflicting expectations of one group so that they more nearly approximated the expectations of other groups. This technique differs from that of the superintendents who tried to adopt the position of negotiator, in that no attempt was made by these ten to modify both sets of expectations, and additionally, once one

group's expectation had been modified, the superintendents gave their clear support to it. One superintendent told his teachers that if they gave him ". . . a reasonable request, I'll fight for it. If it's unreasonable, I won't. Then I tell them what I think is reasonable according to the town's ability to pay. . . . It's the realistic way to support the profession."

The remaining superintendent who compromised combined several of the previously described strategies. His primary objective was to obtain the maximum salary increases possible. According to his assessment, however, the way to do this was a little at a time. This superintendent said that he worked on this principle: "He who fights and runs away, lives to fight another day." He went on to say that ". . . it's a give and take matter. If your goal isn't damned you haven't lost. I have friends operating for better salaries for teachers who are on the town finance committee. This is the effective way to get results over time, if done consistently. You have to make compromises, and get part of what you want one year and part the next. You can't move too fast. The idea is to make steady progress."

The above excerpts from interviews have illustrated strategies of compromise or avoidance. We saw earlier that while some superintendents compromised, others made a clear choice between the two kinds of behavior expected of them. What determines the choice an individual will make in resolving role conflict?

The Theory

The starting point for this theory of role-conflict resolution is the actor's definition of the situation. We assume that actors will have perceptions of whether or not the expectations to which they are exposed are legitimate. Furthermore, we assume that they will have perceptions of the sanctions to which they would be exposed if they did not conform to each of the expectations. In addition, we assume that individuals may be differentiated into three types according to whether they are primarily oriented toward legitimacy or sanctions in making decisions.

The first type characterizes the person who, when faced with a role conflict, gives most weight to the legitimacy of expectations. His definition of the situations places stress on *the right* of others to hold their expectations and de-emphasizes the sanctions he thinks will be applied to him for nonconformity to them. We shall say such a person has a *moral* orientation to expectations. He will be predisposed to behave in a role-conflict situation in such a way that he can fulfill legitimate expectations and reject illegitimate ones. If one of the incompatible expectations is viewed as legitimate and the other is not, he will be predisposed to conform to the legitimate expectation, regardless of what sanctions are involved. If both

are legitimate he will adopt a compromise behavior in order to conform, at least in part, to both of them. If both are perceived as illegitimate, he will be predisposed to conform to neither of them and will adopt in consequence some type of avoidance behavior. In short, for an individual with a moral orientation to expectations we will ignore his perceptions of the probable sanctions in making predictions about his behavior. From his definition of the legitimacy of the expectations we can make predictions about his behavior, and in Table 3 these predictions are specified.

The second type of orientation to expectations may be called *expedient*. An individual who has this orientaton is one who gives priority to the sanctions others will bring to bear if he does not conform to their expectations. Such a person, we will assume, will

TABLE 3

PREDICTED AND ACTUAL BEHAVIORS OF MORALISTS IN 16 TYPES OF ROLE CONFLICT

Types of Role Conflict				Predicted Behavior°	Number of Moral Superintendents Exposed to Each Type of Conflict	Frequency of Actual Behavior	Proportion of Correct Predictions
Superintendent's Perception of:							
Expectation A		*Expectation B*					
IS IT LEGITIMATE?	SANCTIONS FOR NONCONFORMITY?	IS IT LEGITIMATE?	SANCTIONS FOR NONCONFORMITY?				
1. Yes	Yes	Yes	Yes	*c*	2	*c* = 2	2/2
2. Yes	No	Yes	Yes	*c*	1	*c* = 1	1/1
3. Yes	Yes	Yes	No	*c*	0	—	—
4. Yes	No	Yes	No	*c*	0	—	—
5. Yes	Yes	No	Yes	*a*	4	*a* = 3; *c* = 1	3/4
6. Yes	No	No	Yes	*a*	4	*a* = 4	4/4
7. Yes	Yes	No	No	*a*	7	*a* = 7	7/7
8. Yes	No	No	No	*a*	1	*a* = 1	1/1
9. No	Yes	Yes	Yes	*b*	0	—	—
10. No	No	Yes	Yes	*b*	0	—	—
11. No	Yes	Yes	No	*b*	0	—	—
12. No	No	Yes	No	*b*	0	—	—
13. No	Yes	No	Yes	*d*	0	—	—
14. No	No	No	Yes	*d*	0	—	—
15. No	Yes	No	No	*d*	0	—	—
16. No	No	No	No	*d*	0	—	—
			Total:		19		18/19 (.95)

° The abbreviations used in this column are as follows: *a* = conformity to expectation *A*, *b* = conformity to expectation *B*, *c* = compromise, and *d* = avoidance.

act so as to minimize the negative sanctions involved in the role-conflict situation. He will try to provide the best defense for himself in view of the relative severity of the sanctions he feels others will apply to him for noncomformity to their expectations. Whether others have a right to hold certain expectations is irrelevant or of secondary importance to him. When he perceives strong sanctions for nonconformity to one expectation and weaker sanctions for nonconformity to the other, he will conform to the expectation which would result in the stronger sanctions for nonconformity. If he perceives that equally strong sanctions result from both, he will compromise in order to minimize sanctions. If he perceives no sanctions for nonconformity to either of the expectations, then the sanctions dimension will be of no value as a predictor of his behavior. Under this condition the other factor

in the model, the legitimacy dimension, would be the only basis for predicting his behavior. In Table 4 the predictions for expedients are specified.

A third type of orientation to expectations will be called *moral-expedient*. A person who has this orientation does not give primacy to either the legitimacy or sanctions dimensions but takes both relatively equally into account and behaves in accordance with the perceived "net balance." For some role-conflict situations the decisions of an individual with a moral-expedient orientation are relatively simple since both the legitimacy and sanctions elements lead him to the same behavior. If, for example, expectation A is perceived as legitimate and expectation B illegitimate and if he perceives greater sanctions for nonconformity to expectation A than for nonconformity to B, he will conform to expectation A. In general, if

TABLE 4

PREDICTED AND ACTUAL BEHAVIORS OF EXPEDIENTS IN 16 TYPES OF ROLE CONFLICT

Types of Role Conflict				Predicted Behavior°	Number of Expedient Superintendents Exposed to Each Type of Conflict	Frequency of Actual Behavior	Proportion of Correct Predictions
Superintendent's Perception of:							
Expectation A		Expectation B					
IS IT LEGITIMATE?	SANCTIONS FOR NONCONFORMITY?	IS IT LEGITIMATE?	SANCTIONS FOR NONCONFORMITY?				
1. Yes	Yes	Yes	Yes	c	3	c = 1; d = 2	1/3
2. Yes	No	Yes	Yes	b	2	b = 2	2/2
3. Yes	Yes	Yes	No	a	2	a = 2	2/2
4. Yes	No	Yes	No	c	0	—	—
5. Yes	Yes	No	Yes	c	3	c = 3	3/3
6. Yes	No	No	Yes	b	4	b = 4	4/4
7. Yes	Yes	No	No	a	7	a = 7	7/7
8. Yes	No	No	No	a	0	—	—
9. No	Yes	Yes	Yes	c	0	—	—
10. No	No	Yes	Yes	b	0	—	—
11. No	Yes	Yes	No	a	0	—	—
12. No	No	Yes	No	b	0	—	—
13. No	Yes	No	Yes	c	1	c = 1	1/1
14. No	No	No	Yes	b	0	—	—
15. No	Yes	No	No	a	1	a = 1	1/1
16. No	No	No	No	d	0	—	—
			Total:		23		21/23 (.91)

° The abbreviations used in this column are as follows: a = conformity to expectation A, b = conformity to expectation B, c = compromise, and d = avoidance.

the legitimacy dimension leads him to the same behavior indicated by the sanctions dimension, no problem exists for him. Either criterion leads him to the same behavior.

By comparing Tables 3 and 4 and observing which types of role conflict lead moralists and expedients to the same behavior we can easily isolate all the nonproblematic situations for the moral-expedients.

What is required as a basis for predicting his behavior in the remaining types of role conflict? A person with a moral-expedient orientation is one who takes both the legitimacy and sanctions dimensions into account and is predisposed to adopt a behavior that emerges from a balancing of these two dimensions. Thus, if expectations A and B are both viewed as legitimate but he perceives greater negative sanctions for noncomformity to A than to B, he will conform to expectation A. Weighing the two dimensions would result in clear-cut resolutions of the role conflict in types 2, 3, 5, 9, 14, and 15 of Table 5. In each of these instances on the basis of the sanctions and legitimacy dimensions there are two predispositions to one of the behaviors and only one to the other.

How would a moral-expedient behave when the sanctions and legitimacy dimensions lead him to conform to opposite expectations, as in types 6 and 11? In type 6, the legitimacy dimension would require conformity to expectation A, but the sanctions dimension would lead to conformity to expectation B. Since the actor is a moral-expedient he will try to do both or compromise because this seems to be the best balancing of the two dimensions when they lead to opposite behaviors; he is predisposed to do A on the basis of legitimacy and B on

TABLE 5

PREDICTED AND ACTUAL BEHAVIORS OF MORAL-EXPEDIENTS IN 16 TYPES
OF ROLE CONFLICT

Types of Role Conflict				Pre-dicted Behav-ior°	Number of Moral-Expedient Super-intendents Exposed to Each Type of Conflict	Frequency of Actual Behavior	Proportion of Correct Predictions
Superintendent's Perception of:							
Expectation A		*Expectation B*					
IS IT LEGITI-MATE?	SANCTIONS FOR NON-CON-FORMITY?	IS IT LEGITI-MATE?	SANCTIONS FOR NON-CON-FORMITY?				
1. Yes	Yes	Yes	Yes	c	6	c = 5; d = 1	5/6
2. Yes	No	Yes	Yes	b	2	b = 2	2/2
3. Yes	Yes	Yes	No	a	6	a = 6	6/6
4. Yes	No	Yes	No	c	1	c = 0; d = 1	0/1
5. Yes	Yes	No	Yes	a	4	a = 3; c = 1	3/4
6. Yes	No	No	Yes	c	3	c = 2; d = 1	2/3
7. Yes	Yes	No	No	a	20	a = 19; c = 1	19/20
8. Yes	No	No	No	a	1	a = 1	1/1
9. No	Yes	Yes	Yes	b	0	—	—
10. No	No	Yes	Yes	b	0	—	—
11. No	Yes	Yes	No	c	0	—	—
12. No	No	Yes	No	b	0	—	—
13. No	Yes	No	Yes	c	0	—	—
14. No	No	No	Yes	b	0	—	—
15. No	Yes	No	No	a	0	—	—
16. No	No	No	No	d	0	—	—
			Total:		43		38/43 (.88)

° The abbreviations used in this column are as follows: a = conformity to expectation A, b = conformity to expectation B, c = compromise, and d = avoidance.

the basis of sanctions, and is, therefore, predisposed to both *A* and *B*, or to a compromise of the two.

We are left with one additional type in Table 5, type 13. In this case neither of the expectations is viewed as legitimate but nonconformity to both is perceived as leading to strong negative sanctions. The legitimacy dimension leads him to an avoidance behavior and the sanctions dimension suggests a compromise. It seems clear that he will not conform to expectation *A* or to *B*. To minimize sanctions he would compromise or try to conform to both *A* and *B*, and to emphasize legitimacy he would avoid or fail to conform to both *A* and *B*. It is clear that an avoidance reaction does not conform at all to either *A* or *B*; but it seems equally clear that a compromise fails to conform in part to both *A* and *B* and, therefore, is partially an avoidance. Consequently, the most probable resolution of situations of this kind by moral-expedients would be a compromise, which in part avoids and in part conforms to both expectations.

In Table 5 the predictions made on the basis of legitimacy and sanctions for "moral-expedients" are specified. Tables 3, 4, and 5 together describe all of the predictions made on the basis of the theory.

THE DATA FOR A TEST OF
THE THEORY

If the superintendent's responses to the salary instrument revealed that contradictory expectations were held for his behavior, we designated the situation as a role conflict. On the basis of his answers to the interview questions, each of the superintendents was then coded on (1) his perception of the legitimacy or illegitimacy of the expectations, (2) the perceived sanctions for noncompliance with each expectation, and (3) how he resolved the role conflict.

The remaining element of the theory that requires consideration is the superintendent's orientation to expectations, that is, whether he was a moralist, expedient or moral-expedient. The superintendent's responses to another and completely independent instrument provided the data used for this catagorization. Each item in this instrument refers to expectations that could be applied to a superintendent. For the 37 items in this instrument, he was asked: "As a school superintendent, what obligation do you feel that you have to do or not to do the following things?" The response categories were: absolutely must; preferably should; may or may not; preferably should not; absolutely must not.

We reasoned that a person who would typically react to expectations in terms of "it depends" is one who possesses an *expedient* orientation to expectations. In operational terms he would respond to the expectation items with the "preferably should," "preferably should not," or "may or may not" response categories.

On the other hand, a person whose typical response is not a contingent one but is in terms of "absolutely must" or "absolutely must not" carry out expectations is one who is primarily oriented toward their rectitude. He does not think in terms of factors in the situation that would lessen his obligations. Such a person would be predisposed "to honor" legitimate expectations regardless of the sanctions involved in the situations. Such a person would be a moralist.

One who shows no "typical" response to expectations but vacillates between the conditional and mandatory categories in his reactions to expectations would possess the characteristic required for the moral-expedient orientation. This lack of consistency in orientation to expectations suggests that he is the type of person who would tend to take *both* the sanctions and legitimacy dimensions into account in reacting to perceived expectations.

This line of reasoning led to the following procedure. Each superintendent was given a score of 1 for each item in this instrument for which he gave a mandatory response (absolutely must, or absolutely must not). This provided a range of scores from 1 through 30 for the 37 items in the instrument. The estimated reliability of these scores is .884. These scores were then split into the following three categories: 1-9, 10-18, and 19-30. On the reasoning outlined above those superintendents who fell into the low mandatoriness group (1-9) were defined as expedients, those who fell into the high mandatoriness group (19-30) were considered moralists, and those who fell in the middle category (10-18) were categorized as moral-expedients.

A Test of the Theory

If we accept each of these operational indexes as adequately representing the variables and conditions described by the theory of role-conflict resolution, we can use our data to perform an exploratory test of the theory. We have 48 possible "types" of situations. That is, the moralists, expedients, and moral-expedients can each be subdivided into four groups according to their judgments about the legitimacy of the expectations directed toward them (i.e., both expectations legitimate; both illegitimate; A legitimate and B illegitimate, and A illegitimate and B legitimate). Each of the resulting 12 groups can be further subdivided into four categories according to whether the subject believed sanctions would be forthcoming for nonconformity to A, B, both, or neither.

By comparing the behavior predicted on the basis of the theory for each of these 48 types with the actual behavior of the superintendents who fell within these categories, we may say whether or not the theory has led in each case to the correct prediction.

As can be seen in Tables 3, 4, and 5 for 77 (91 percent) of the 85 role-conflict cases the theory led to the correct prediction. In order to test the theory it is necessary to ask whether the proportion of correct predictions obtained could have occurred by chance. To answer this question, the numbers of correct and of incorrect predictions

were compared with the numbers expected on the basis of chance. Statistical details are presented elsewhere.[1] The theory led to significantly more correct predictions than would be expected by chance (at the .01 level). We are consequently led to the conclusion that the findings provide significant support for the theory in the teacher-salary role-conflict situation.

A review of the predictions made for moralists, moral-expedients, and expedients will reveal that for many of the types of role conflict the theory leads to exactly the same prediction no matter what the orientation of the individual involved. It is particularly interesting, therefore, to ask how well the theory does in the "difficult" cases. How well will the theory do in predicting the behavior in only those cases of role conflict where it makes a difference (according to the theory) what the orientation of the individual is? It would be inappropriate to apply a significance test to only those cases, but it is nevertheless revealing of the power of the theory to consider them separately.

Let us consider those cases for moralists and those for expedients in which the theory makes a prediction which differs from the one made in the case of the moral-expedient orientation. In types 2, 6, 11, 13, 14, and 15 of the moralist orientation and types 5, 6, 9, and 11 of the expedient orientation the theory leads to a prediction which differs from the one to which it leads for the moral-expedients. There were 12 school superintendents with either a moralist or expedient orientation who experienced role conflicts of these types. For how many of these did the theory lead to the correct prediction? For how many would the correct prediction have been made by assuming that their resolution of role conflict would be the same as that of moral-expedients? The answer is that in all 12 cases (as may be verified by reviewing the appropriate types of conflict in

[1] See Neal Gross, Ward S. Mason, and Alexander McEachern, *Explorations in Role Analysis: Studies of the School Superintendency Role* (New York: Wiley, 1957).

Tables 3 and 4) the theory led to the correct prediction, and in none of these cases would the correct prediction have been made on the basis of the assumption that these moral or expedient individuals resolved their conflicts in the same way as do moral-expedients.

In this paper we have not been able to consider a number of questions that the crit-ical reader would ask about the theory. How does this theory differ from others? What accounts for the errors in the predictions? Have we ignored certain variables which affect the resolution of certain types of role-conflict situations? We have tried to consider these problems elsewhere.[2]

[2] *Ibid.*

The Significance of Multiple-group
Membership in Disaster ✴ Lewis M. Killian

Although the importance of multiple-group membership as one of the salient features of modern social life is widely recognized by sociologists and psychologists, the task of exploring its many implications has only just been begun. Cooley, a pioneer in the study of the importance of group membership for the individual, recognized the existence of multiple-group memberships, describing the individual in modern society as a point through which numerous arcs, representing different group memberships, pass.[1] Before him, William James declared that a man has "as many social selves . . . as there are distinct groups of persons about whose opinions he cares."[2]

In recent years other students have begun a more systematic exploration of the implications of identification with several different groups for the individual and for the society of which he is a part. The creation of psychological problems for the individual and the development of new strata in the social structure as the result of some types of multiple-group membership are discussed in the work of Robert E. Park (1928), Everett Stonequist (1937), and E. C. Hughes (1945). Hughes has demonstrated that possession of contradictory roles in different groups may create "dilemmas and contradictions of status" for the individual.

Muzafer Sherif, in his elaboration of the concepts of "membership group" and "reference group," has furnished valuable conceptual tools for the analysis of multiple-group identifications and conflicting group loyalties.[3] He suggests, furthermore, that identification with numerous different reference groups and the lack of a unitary ego are the keys to the understanding of inconsistencies in certain types of behavior, such as inter-group relations.[4]

In a study of the reactions of people in four Southwestern communities to physical disasters—explosions and tornadoes—made by the University of Oklahoma Research Institute, it was found that conflicting group loyalties and contradictory roles resulting

[1] See Cooley (1900, p. 114).
[2] See James (1890, p. 294).

[3] See Sherif (1948, pp. 122-125).
[4] See Sherif (1949).

Reprinted from the *American Journal of Sociology*, 1952, 57, 309-314, by permission of The University of Chicago Press. Copyright © by The University of Chicago Press.

from multiple-group membership were significant factors affecting individual behavior in critical situations. The dilemmas created by the disasters also brought to light latent contradictions in roles not ordinarily regarded as conflicting.

In spite of the fact that multiple-group memberships do create dilemmas and inconsistencies, the majority of people in modern urban society manage to function efficiently as members of many groups, often being only vaguely aware of contradictions in their various roles. Sherif points out that the individual is often not aware of the derivation of the "cross-pressures" which cause inconsistent behavior.[5] Newcomb declares that many role prescriptions are "relatively nonconflicting" and says:

> Most of us, most of the time, manage to take quite different roles, as prescribed by the same or by different groups, without undue conflict. . . . Indeed, it is rather remarkable how many different roles most of us manage to take with a minimum of conflict.[6]

He points out that many roles are "nonoverlapping." A man may play the role of a businessman, acting in terms of the work situation, during most of the day. For a few hours in the evening he may play the role of "the family man," leaving his work at the office. In a small community he may, on certain occasions, act as a functionary of the town government, as a volunteer fireman or as a town councilman. Simultaneously, he has other group memberships which call for certain behavior—in a social-class group, in a racial group, in the community of which he is a citizen, and in "society-at-large."[7]

When catastrophe strikes a community many individuals find that the latent conflict between ordinarily nonconflicting group loyalties suddenly becomes apparent and that they are faced with the dilemma of making an immediate choice between various roles. In his classic study of the Halifax disaster, S. H. Prince noted this conflict when he wrote:

> But the earliest leadership that could be called social, arising from the public itself, was that on the part of those who had no family ties, much of the earliest work being done by visitors in the city. The others as a rule ran first to their homes to discover if their own families were in danger.[8]

People who had been present in the explosion port of Texas City and in three Oklahoma tornado towns during disasters were asked, among other questions, "What was the first thing you thought of after the disaster struck?" and "What was the first thing you did?" Their answers revealed not only the conflict between loyalties to the family and to the community, described by Prince, but also dilemmas arising from conflicting roles derived from membership in other groups. The individuals concerned were not always conscious of the dilemmas or of the existence of "cross-pressures," but even in such cases the choice of roles which the person made was significant in affecting the total pattern of group reaction to the disaster. In some cases subjects indicated that they recognized *after* the emergency that their reaction had been of critical social importance. On the basis of the experiences of people involved in these four community disasters it is possible to suggest the types of groups between which dilemmas of loyalty may arise in modern communities. Tentative generalization as to how these dilemmas will be resolved and as to their significance for *group* reactions to disaster may also be formulated.

The choice required of the greatest number of individuals was the one between the family and other groups, principally the employment group or the community. Especially in Texas City, many men were at work away from their families when disaster

---

[5] See Sherif (1949, p. 37).
[6] In Newcomb (1950, p. 449).
[7] See Newcomb (1950, p. 544).

[8] In Prince (1921, p. 61).

struck and presented a threat to both "the plant" and "the home." In all the communities there were individuals, such as policemen, firemen, and public utilities workers, whose loved ones were threatened by the same disaster that demanded their services as "trouble-shooters." Even persons who had no such definite roles to play in time of catastrophe were confronted with the alternatives of seeing after only their own primary groups or of assisting in the rescue and relief of any of the large number of injured persons, regardless of identity. Indeed, only the unattached person in the community was likely to be free of such a conflict.

How these conflicts between loyalty to the family group and loyalty to other membership groups, including the community and "society-at-large," were resolved was of great significance for the reorganization of communities for rescue, relief, and prevention of further disaster. In Texas City, at the time of the first ship explosion, many men were working in oil refineries, where failure to remain on the job until units were shut down could result in additional fires and explosions. In all the communities studied, failure of community functionaries, such as firemen and policemen, to perform the duties appropriate to their positions could result in the absence of expected and badly needed leadership in a disorganized group. This, in turn, could cause costly delay in the reorganization of the community for emergency rescue, traffic control, and fire-fighting activity. Preoccupation of large numbers of able survivors with their own small primary groups could result in the atomization of the community into small, unco-ordinated groups, again delaying reorganization into a relatively well-integrated, unified, large group. As Prince indicated in his statement, quoted above, this would increase the dependence of the community on outside sources of leadership.

The great majority of persons interviewed who were involved in such dilemmas resolved them in favor of loyalty to the family or, in some cases, to friendship groups.

Much of the initial confusion, disorder, and seemingly complete disorganization reported in the disaster communities was the result of the rush of individuals to find and rejoin their families. Yet in none of the four communities studied did the disastrous consequences contemplated above seem to have materialized. In the first place, there were important exceptions to the tendency to react first in terms of the family. Most of the refinery workers in Texas City did stay on the job until their units were safely shut down, as they had been trained to do. The significance of conflicting group loyalties in a disaster situation is underlined, however, by the importance of the actions taken by a few exceptional individuals in each town who were not confronted with such conflicts. In Texas City the chief of police remained at his post from the moment of the first explosion until seventy-two hours later, never returning to his home during the entire period and playing a vital part in the reorganization of the community. He ascribed his ability to give undivided attention to his official duties to the fact that he knew that his family was safely out of town, visiting relatives, at the time of the explosion. One member of the volunteer fire department of a tornado town told of the thin margin by which his community escaped a disastrous fire following the "twister":

I was at my home, right on the edge of where the storm passed, when it hit. Neither me nor my wife was hurt. The first thing I thought of was fires. I knew there'd be some, so I went to the fire station right away. On the way I could see that there was a fire right in the middle of the wreckage—a butane tank had caught fire. I got out of the truck, drove over there, and fought the fire by myself until the army got there to help me.

All the rest of the firemen had relatives that were hurt, and they stayed with them. Naturally they looked after them. If it hadn't been that my wife was all right, this town probably would have burned up. It's hard to say, but I kind of believe I would have been looking after my family, too.

Devotion to the family as the primary object of loyalty did not always redound to the detriment of aid to other groups, however. Many people who served as rescue workers, assisting injured people whom they did not even know, were drawn to the areas of heavy casualties because of concern for members of their own families whom they believed to be there. Apparently they found their identification with society-at-large and the emphasis of American culture upon the importance of human life too great to permit them to pass an injured stranger without assisting him. Hence, many stayed to assist in the common community task of rescuing the injured in both Texas City and in the tornado towns. In one of the latter a man sensed the approach of the tornado only minutes before it struck. In spite of great personal danger he rushed through the storm to a theater where his children were attending a movie. There he prevented the frightened audience from pouring forth into the storm by holding the doors closed. Later he was acclaimed as a hero whose quick action had saved the lives of many of his fellow citizens. He himself denied that he had any thought of taking the great risk that he took for the sake of the anonymous audience itself; he was thinking only of his own children.

A second, but less common, type of conflict was found in the case of people who were confronted with the alternatives of playing the "heroic" role of rescue worker and of carrying out what were essentially "occupational roles." In terms of group loyalty, they were impelled, on the one hand, to act as sympathetic, loyal members of society-at-large and to give personal aid to injured human beings. On the other hand, they were called to do their duty as it was indicated by their membership in certain occupational groups.

One such person was a minister in Texas City who, upon hearing the explosion, started for the docks with the intention of helping in the rescue work. On the way he became conscious of the choice of roles which confronted him. He said:

After I heard the first explosion my first impulse was to go down to the docks and try to help there. But on the way down I saw two or three folks I knew who had husbands down there. I saw then that my job was with the families—not doing rescue work. I had a job that I was peculiarly suited for, prepared for, and I felt that I should do that.

More important for the reorganization of a tornado-stricken town was the choice made by a state patrolman between his role as a police officer and his role as friend and neighbor to the people of the community in which he was stationed. His story was:

As I drove around town after the tornado had passed I realized that the best thing I could do was to try to make contact with the outside and get help from there. I started out to drive to the next town and try to call from there. As I drove out of town people I knew well would call me by name and ask me to help them find their relatives. Driving by and not stopping to help those people who were looking to me as a friend was one of the hardest things I ever had to do.

As a result of this difficult decision this man became the key figure in the development of organized rescue work, after he recruited and organized a large force of rescue workers in a nearby community.

A similar dilemma faced many public utilities workers who were forced to disregard the plight of the injured if they were to perform their task of restoring normal community services. Unlike the minister and the patrolman, these workers reported no awareness of a conflict of roles, regarding it as a matter of course that they concentrated on their often quite dangerous jobs. Some indicated that preoccupation with the job was so intense that they were scarcely aware of what went on around them. Yet the instances of devotion to prosaic duty cited above were exceptional. Many policemen, firemen, and other functionaries acted heroically but quite outside the framework and discipline of their organizations.

For people whose usual occupational roles bore little or no relationship to the needs created by a disaster, identification with the community as a whole and disregard of their occupational roles came still more easily. Many merchants and clerks rushed from their stores to aid in rescue work, leaving both goods and cash on the counters. The postmaster in one tornado town left the post office completely unguarded, even though the windows were shattered and mail was strewn about the floor. This was, it is true, an extreme case of abandonment of the occupational role.

A third type of conflict of loyalties was that between the loyalty of employees to "the company" as an organization and to fellow employees as friends and human beings. It might seem that the choice, essentially one between life and property, should have been an easy one; but the fact that different choices were made by men with different degrees of identification with other workers reveals that a basic conflict was present. In Texas City many plant officials were also residents of the community and friends of the workers. After the explosions, in which several top executives were killed, some men found themselves suddenly "promoted" to the position of being in charge of their company's damaged property. At the same time men with whom they had worked daily for several years were injured or missing. The most common, almost universal, reaction was to think of the men first and of the plant later. One plant official, active in rescue work in spite of a broken arm and numerous lacerations, described his reaction to the sudden, dramatic conflict between loyalty to the company and loyalty to the workers as follows:

Property! Nobody gave a damn for property! All that was important was life.

I've often wondered just how it would be to walk off and let a plant burn up. That was the way it was. We didn't even consider fighting the fire.

In sharp contrast to this reaction, however, was that of a man in charge of a neighboring plant. While he was in Texas City at the time of the first blast, he had never lived in the community and scarcely knew his workers. He described his first reaction in the following words:

I got in my car and drove over to another refinery to find out what had happened. The assistant superintendent told me that their top men had been killed and asked me what I thought he should do. I told him, "You should take charge of the company's property. That's what the president of your company would tell you if he were here. You look after the property. I'm going over to Galveston to call our president, and I'll call yours at the same time."

While this reaction was exceptional, it is significant as suggesting an alternate way of resolving the conflict between loyalty to "the company" and "the men."

Finally, some individuals suddenly discovered, in the face of disaster, that there was a conflict between loyalty to the community and loyalty to certain extra-community groups. At the time of two of the disasters telephone workers in the Southwest were on strike. In both communities the striking workers were allowed to return to duty by union leaders but were ordered to walk out again a few days later. In both cases the union officials considered the emergency to be over sooner than did the townspeople of the stricken communities. In one town the workers obeyed the union's orders only to find themselves subjected to harsh criticism by their fellow townsmen. In the other community the workers resigned from the union rather than forsake their loyalty to their other membership group. It was almost a year before union officials were able to reorganize the local in this town, and some workers never rejoined.

As was pointed out earlier, the individual may, under normal circumstances, carry out roles appropriate to membership in several groups without having to make a choice between basically conflicting group loyalties. He may even do so without seriously impairing his performance of any of his roles. The worker may wish that he could spend more time at home with his family but resigns himself to the fact that he cannot if he is to keep the job he wants. On his way to work he may pass the scene of a fire and be vaguely conscious that, as a citizen, he is indirectly responsible for the protection of life and property; but he assumes that the limit of his direct responsibility for action extends only to notifying the fire department, if it is not already there. The employer may, within certain limits, think of the workers as persons and friends and still not be disloyal to the company's interests. In the crisis induced by disaster, however, these individuals may find that it is impossible to serve two masters, to act in two roles. An immediate choice is demanded, but it may be difficult because the demands of the competing groups may appear equally urgent. The nature of the choice made by the individual, particularly if one of his roles is associated with a key position in the community, may have important consequences for the reorganization of the community. Large-scale reorganization, coordination, and direction of efforts are necessary to speedy rescue work and the restoration of normalcy. Activities carried on in terms of the demands of many diverse, competing groups act as an impediment to this reorganization.

Further research is needed to make possible the prediction of the choices that will be made by individuals in these conflicts. The frequency with which individuals thought and acted first in terms of family and close friends suggests that loyalty to primary groups stands first in the hierarchy of group loyalties, as might be expected. On the other hand, important exceptions in which persons played relatively impersonal roles as leaders or working with matériel, rather than people, indicate that some factors, such as training or feelings of responsibility, may predispose the individual to adhere to secondary-group demands even in a disaster. Knowledge of what these factors are and how they may be induced would contribute to greater understanding of group reactions to disorganization and of methods of facilitating group reorganization.

References

COOLEY, C. H. *Human nature and the social order.* New York: Charles Scribner's Sons, 1900.

HUGHES, E. C. Dilemmas and the contradictions of status. *Amer. J. Sociol.,* 1945, *50,* 353-359.

JAMES, W. *Principles of psychology.* Vol. I. New York: Holt, Rinehart and Winston, 1890.

NEWCOMB, T. M. *Social psychology.* New York: Holt, Rinehart and Winston, 1950.

PARK, R. E. Human migration and the marginal man. *Amer. J. Sociol.,* 1928, *33,* 881-893.

PRINCE, S. H. *Catastrophe and social change.* Columbia University Studies in History, Economics, and Public Law, *94.* New York: Columbia Univer. Press, 1921.

SHERIF, M. *An outline of social psychology.* New York: Harper & Row, 1948.

SHERIF, M. The problems of inconsistency in intergroup relations. *J. soc. Issues,* 1949, *5,* 32-37.

STONEQUIST, E. *The marginal man.* New York: Charles Scribner's Sons, 1937.

C. LEADERSHIP

Leadership and Sociometric

Choice ❊ Helen Hall Jennings

Leadership phenomena "happen" in a human setting where people get into interaction on the basis of feeling, or *tele*. As Moreno demonstrates, the tele process of attraction and repulsion must be considered dependent upon *both* individuals in a relationship (even though the flow of feeling on the part of one individual toward another may be unknown by the second), since its direction is not random but depends upon the second person. The tele is not, therefore, viewed merely as the subjective, independent product of a single person (Moreno, 1934; Moreno and Jennings, 1938).

The existence of tele relationships may be observed in terms of the expressions of choices on the part of individuals for each other. The choice process in a community occurs in a particularized fashion, along the lines of association for work or for living which are important to its population. These may be called *sociogroups*, since association is founded on a collective criterion. In *psychegroups*, on the other hand, association, though equally real and important, is strictly a private matter; choices for mem-

bers of such groups have a private, personalized basis. (I, as Mary Jones, feel toward you, as Sally Smith, thus and so. . . .) Choices within the sociogroup have a collective, impersonal basis freer of the uniqueness of private personality aspects of response. (I, an unemployed woman holding membership in this union, feel toward you, as an employed woman also holding membership in this union, thus and so. . . .) The membership of a given psychegroup may also overlap and be a part of a sociogroup, but while functioning as sociogroup members, the individuals apparently expect to relinquish roles appropriate in psychegroup membership.

By psychegroup is not meant, in sociological terms, the same thing as a face-to-face group or a primary group. There are such groups which never become either totally or in part what is here meant by the term psychegroup. The psychegroup is an interpersonal structure where the uniqueness of the individual as a personality is appreciated and allowed for, with varying degrees of spontaneous indulgence and affection. It is

Prepared by the author from data more fully reported in *Leadership and Isolation*, 2d Ed., New York: David McKay Company, 1950. Reprinted by permission.

where one counts "altogether" as a person, not merely as an individual or as a member of a sociogroup. In industry it springs up in the informal grouping that comes to exist as men work side by side. But in such psychegroup formations, as these develop inside sociogroups, the individual must consider his participation separately from his participation as a sociogroup member. In a particular sociogroup, only certain aspects of personality are appreciated by other members, as only certain aspects are appropriate to the tasks important in the specific sociogroup life. Within the sociogroup, there may be many members chosen by others as sociogroup members who at the same time are rejected or unchosen by these same individuals in the latters' several psychegroups.

It is the confusion between a sociogroup and a psychegroup, or the lack of a clear-cut delineation between them, that has complicated the study of leadership phenomena. It is necessary to ask: Leadership in what respect? For whom? In what sort of group? What kind of psychological position in respect to the given population did the individual showing leadership have at the time he displayed it?

The Nature of the Investigation

The laboratory of the research was the New York State Training School for Girls, a closed community comprising over 400 girls committed by the Children's Courts of the state. The population represents a cross section of the socially and economically underprivileged in the state. To be admitted, the girl must be over 12 and under 16 years of age, and of normal intelligence.

The sociometric test, devised by Moreno (1934), discloses the feelings which individuals have toward each other in respect to membership in the groups in which they are at a given moment (ideally, all groups in which they are or could be). It is an *action* test. The criterion for choice must have explicit meaning for the subject, and offer him

the specific opportunity to give information for reconstruction or retention of the situations which he is in. The results are put into operation to the optimal satisfaction of *all* subjects (Moreno, 1934; Moreno and Jennings, 1947). Thus, in respect to the criterion of the group's formation, the psychological position of every member in the composition of the group structure is brought to light. By periodic testing, changes in this structure can be traced, followed, and evaluated.

The following excerpt from the test instructions[1] illustrates the simplicity and directness of the approach used:

> You will notice that your paper is divided into eight squares or boxes. In the first Yes box, marked "Live with," write the names of whatever girls there are anywhere on the campus or in your own house whom you would prefer to live with. In the No box marked "Live with," write the names of whatever girls there are anywhere on the campus or in your own house whom you would prefer not to live with. Do the same for the "Work with" boxes. Then, those you would prefer not to work with, place in the No box for work. Next, do your "Recreation or Leisure," and then your "Study or School" boxes, having in mind the same instructions. . . . The No boxes should contain only the names of those, *if any,* whom you definitely *don't* want in your group for the particular function or functions which it happens to be. The Yes boxes should contain only the names of those, *if any,* whom you definitely *do* want in your group for the particular function or functions which it happens to be. . . . Do the boxes in any other order than that suggested, if you prefer.

As previously employed, the sociometric test has been found to have an average reliability of .95, based on tests given on four successive weeks with five choices allowed on the criterion of tentmates in a summer camp (Newstetter, Feldstein, and New-

[1] The complete protocol appears in Jennings (1943).

comb, 1938). At the college level, using also five choices and one criterion (membership in a discussion group), reliability coefficients ranging from .93 to .95 are reported from tests given on successive days (Zeleny, 1938). These coefficients are based on the extent to which the subject is chosen by others on two or more occasions; they relate to the choices individuals *receive from others*. The more stringent comparison of the present study, by use of unlimited choices and a much longer retest interval, also reveals that even under these conditions there is a fairly high correlation. A comparison of the individual's self-consistency on separate occasions (his extent of expenditure of choices), with unlimited choices allowed, reveals that the individual shows a *characteristic repertoire* in choice expression for others. At the same time, a comparison of choice expression towards the individual on separate occasions with unlimited choices allowed reveals that the individual shows a characteristic *stimulus-value* for others.

Thus, it is found that as the individual invests his affection in others, the extent and quality of these investments appear by early adulthood to be stabilized into what can be called his *emotional repertoire*. The repertoire represents his characteristic range for reacting by choice and rejection to others. Similarly, by early adulthood, he is shown to be characterized by consistency in his *stimulus-value* for arousing choice and rejection from others. These findings do not mean that the individual's interpersonal situation in respect to choice and rejection becomes so definite as to be unchangeable by adulthood; they indicate rather that the individual's intrapsychic organization is not subject to random variation to changes in interpersonal setting, nor, in turn, is the individual randomly reacted to. These findings mean also that an individual's future is being created as he moves through his past and, in a quite specific sense, even *what pattern* will differentiate his interpersonal reflection is being created.

The first thing to be noted about this pattern is that the individual's consistency in use of the choice process involves both his use of choice *and* rejection as expressions of *one* process, and similarly as the focus of one process directed upon him. It is notable also that the individual who is relatively more or relatively less expansive towards others will react to them independently of the length of time he is in association with them.

The individual's extent of emotional expansiveness towards others is seen to be his *individual* characteristic which finds consistent expression without relation to the environmental factors which may exert pressure for or against its fulfillment.[2] These findings are confirmed in research on other populations, disclosing that, while they hold for a stable community, the individual tends to retrench from maintaining his full repertoire and to "drop" others who are unlike him in religion and race when the community in which he is living undergoes rapid population change (Deutschberger, 1946). Thus, in a very broad sense, the nature of the social setting of the individual *does* affect his expansiveness—perhaps, in the instance cited, the individual reacting as in shock, fear, or grief, by temporarily emotionally holding back.

The average repertoire of positive expansiveness, as measured by the number of other individuals the individual includes in his life situation by positive choice for associating with them, is found to be about eight, when common situations are explored (working, etc.), and this number is increased to about four more when the setting of leisure time is explored; but as about one-third of the latter overlaps with the former, the average size of positive repertoire is somewhat less in number than twelve other

[2] It may be postulated that the concept of need comes nearer to describing emotional expansiveness than does the concept of trait, as the individual is actually expressing how many persons he feels *the need for* in his life situation and is neither consciously displaying consistency nor necessarily aware of it.

individuals. Upon retest eight months later, no significant differences are found.

It becomes apparent not only that choice is not distributed by chance but upon analysis it is found that the whole constellation of relationships centered in and emanating from a given individual shows characteristic patterns (Moreno and Jennings, 1938). Moreover the incidence of patterns at one time and a later time in the same community appears as a relatively constant factor in the structure of attractions and rejections which characterize it, and reflects the fact that the choice process operates in particular ways.

The first tests were given during the last week of December 1937. The test population included all individuals (443) comprising the school population as of that date. Retests were given during the first week of September 1938, to all individuals (457) comprising the population at that time.

The method of analysis is a comparison of the number of *different* individuals reacted to positively (chosen) or negatively (rejected) by the subjects, with the number of different individuals reacting positively or negatively to the subjects. The data used in the analysis include all choices and rejections, either on the criterion of living or on the criterion of working, given to or received by 133 subjects present for both tests and occupying the same housing units on both occasions.

The problem of this report is to note the relation between behavior shown in interaction with others and the sociometric choice status of the individual. In order to examine behavior at different levels of choice status, "under-chosen" is defined as placing one standard deviation or more below the mean of the 133 subjects, "over-chosen" as placing one standard deviation or more above the mean, and "average-chosen" as placing approximately at the mean, in number of individuals choosing the subject. The number of under-chosen positions is 41 (19 on Test I and 22 on Test II); the number of over-

chosen positions is 43 (22 on Test I and 21 on Test II). For purposes of comparison, 41 other positions placing nearest the mean on either test were selected.

Among other evidence which might be cited, the following is offered to show that high choice status is closely related to leadership in this community. Elections to a House Council were held in the fall of 1937. The individual receiving the highest number of votes automatically became a member of the Community Council. The election was held under the supervision of the Club Director, and the ballots were closed. Four members were elected to the Council from each house. For the purpose of comparing membership in the Councils with rank in positive sociometric choices received from others, only data for the two members in each living unit receiving the highest and second highest number of votes were used. This comparison reveals that of the 20 such Council members (two from each of the ten housing units of this study), 18 or 90 percent place among the over-chosen, as here defined. The two Council members who do not so rank place just below this point. When allowance is made for the difference between being chosen from a community-wide base and being elected from the limited house population, it is evident that there is practically a one-to-one relationship between being elected to represent the house body in matters concerning the group and being chosen by community members on the sociometric criteria of living and/or working with them.

Observation of the personalities of the over-chosen subjects and study of the motivations given for choice provide the following clues to their choice status. Each over-chosen subject, to a greater or less extent:

enlarges her social space, for interchange of ideas and activities;
secures more and more responsibilities to be held by members in her work groups, her housing unit, and in the community as a whole;

takes definite stands on what she considers right, and will "fight for it";

aids the average-chosen individuals to broaden their conceptions of their potential capacities; shows faith in their abilities by taking it for granted that they can and want to contribute to their own development and to the life of the community;

shows ability to establish rapport quickly and effectively with a wide range of other personalities and to win their confidence in varying circumstances;

insists on an impersonal fairness, and succeeds in gaining respect for this level of interaction between members;

raises the level of conduct of average members by demanding considerate behavior towards the less able (in the sense of less contributing) members;

calls to account individuals who attempt to exclude participation by the relatively noncontributing or destructively contributing members; shows towards them protective behavior;

exhibits anger and censuring almost exclusively towards only those members whom they consider "should know better," rather than towards all alike; controls the destiny of nonadjusting members (i.e., nonadjusting to the kind of regime instituted by such behaviors as listed above) by influencing other members to aid them, by blocking their possible satisfactions in nonadjusting behaviors, and by obliging other members to show respect for them in the community as a whole (e.g., not to carry unfavorable reports about them into the "networks" by telling out-group members of occurrences which would prejudice their standing in the community);

causes others to feel that she aids them to meet their problems.

These behavior tendencies are confirmed and further expanded when housemother reports commending or complaining of the individual's behavior are examined in relation to the individual's choice-status. To the over-chosen, as compared with the average-chosen, are attributed three times as many incidences of initiatory behavior in making innovations without permission, twice as many incidences showing planning and organization, four times as many occasions showing initiative in starting new projects, over four times as frequent behavior exhibiting ingenuity in changing conduct of "problem" members or fostering understanding between new members and others, and about twice as many rebellious behaviors. In these reports, the incidences for the under-chosen range from none to half as many as for the average-chosen.

To the under-chosen are attributed twelve times as many incidences of actively or passively interfering with the group's activities, as to the over-chosen, while such incidences are practically missing for the average-chosen. For the over-chosen are reported *almost three times* as great an incidence of retaliatory behavior (among other over-chosen) as for average-chosen, and this behavior is rare for under-chosen. (Could this reflect less earnest competition to give occasion for such behavior among the latter members?)

On the other hand, the most often spontaneously given "praise" of the housemother by the over-chosen is for her listening to and considering the members' opinions in planning; such comment is made only a third as often by the average-chosen and not at all by the under-chosen.

Thus, it appears that the under-chosen show in common many varieties of behaviors the effect of which may tend to separate and draw individuals apart rather than to bring them together. The average-chosen show somewhat less than half as great an incidence of such behaviors, and about twice as great an incidence of behaviors the effect of which may tend to bring individuals into constructive relationship with one another. Further, in the very behaviors in which the average-chosen outrank the under-chosen, the over-chosen in turn are found to exceed the average citizen by approximately twice as great an incidence. And in those behaviors which "make new events happen" or "enlarge the kind and extent of activity" the over-chosen surpass the average citizen by over four times as great an incidence.

Just as isolated-from-choice positions and over-chosen positions are but two ends of one continuum, so behaviors when analyzed in relation to such choice-status of the individual (at the time he has the particular choice-status) appear as forming extremes on another continuum—at one end showing expressions disruptive (or "clogging") to the life of the group, and at the other, expressions conducive to an expanding life for the group. Sociometric choice for the individual thus appears to depend directly upon the nature of the group *in which he is to be functioned with.*

For the citizen who would earn choice, it appears as much a matter of what behaviors she rarely exhibits as of those she frequently shows which will determine what choice status she will hold in a sociogroup for working or living. The average citizens of this study are not in any sense average in all constructive behaviors; the incidence of behaviors having a negative import for interpersonal exchange (in common work and living) appears to offset those having a positive import sufficiently, in the case of such individuals, to hold them down to an average-status.

Leadership and isolation appear, from this study, as phenomena which arise out of individual differences in interpersonal capacity for sociogroup participation and as phenomena which are *indigenous to the specific milieu of the sociogroup* or sociogroups *in which they are produced.*

Individuals who emerge as leaders in one sociogroup may or may not emerge in a similar role in another community, or even in another sociogroup in the same community. Likewise, individuals who classify as isolates in terms of choice from their associates in one sociogroup in a given community may or may not change in choice-status in another sociogroup in the same or another community.

Nevertheless, it is a reasonable hypothesis that when certain qualities have become pronounced and integrated in the personality expression of the individual (such a quality as relatively great freedom from self-concern, sufficient to enable him to be concerned with matters affecting many others than himself), these are likely to persist, for they reflect a high level of emotional growth and maturity, and thus may be expected to act favorably upon his future relationships with persons in other sociogroups.

It would also appear, similarly, that certain qualities (such a quality as relative inability to observe and orient one's actions to the elements of a situation and the persons comprising it) may, unless outgrown, continue to act unfavorably upon the individual's future relationships.

The "why" of leadership appears, however, not explainable by any personality quality or constellation of traits. Some individuals are found who are as emotionally mature and as resourceful in ideas as the leader-individuals of this study, yet they were not allowed a role of leadership, nor chosen more than the average citizen in the community. The why of leadership appears to reside in the interpersonal contribution of which the individual becomes capable in a specific setting eliciting such contribution from him. Similarly, isolation appears as but the opposite extreme on this continuum of interpersonal sensitivity between the membership and the individual in the sociogroup.

The over-chosen personalities showing certain behaviors in common differ markedly from one another in the "style" of these behaviors and the "style" they show *in contact with* specific other individuals. As persons, they are very unlike. (Similarly, isolates and near-isolates differ greatly from each other.) An analysis of their ways of behaving shows the leadership they exert to be definable as *a manner of interacting with others*—a manner which moves others in directions apparently desired by the latter, even though they may be doing little themselves towards attaining such directions. It is as if these individuals recognize and think more of the needs of others than others think of their own needs. The leader-individuals often take actions in behalf of others whom they do not choose and who do not know of the effort made for them. For example, three times as frequently the over-chosen individual, as compared with the average-chosen subject, made "unasked-for-suggestions to the psychologist for the welfare of others." Further, "visits to the psychology office in behalf of another individual (instead of self)" were made approximately seven times as often by the over-chosen individuals as by the average-chosen, and not at all by the under-chosen. Such actions by the average individuals almost invariably involve others whom they choose and thus may be inferred to be of more personalized interest to them.

While the varieties of styles of leadership (and of isolation) are many, nevertheless, a number of characteristics of leader-individuals stand out as common attributes. The social milieu is "improved" from the point of view of the membership through the efforts of each leader. Each widens the area of social participation for others (and indirectly his own social space) by his unique contribution to this milieu. Each leader seems to sense spontaneously when to censure and when to praise, apparently is intellectually and emotionally uncomfortable when others are "left out," and acts to foster tolerance on the part of one member towards another. At the same time they may give little quarter to other leaders. (By contrast, the isolates and near-isolates appear relatively "self-bound," behaving in ways which tend to show little capacity to identify with others or to bridge the gap between their own personalities and others as members of the sociogroup.)

The leadership thus exhibited in the community by various members appears, in each instance, to reflect a "style" of leadership—a particularized way of behaving, derived from the personality attributes of the individual in an over-chosen position. Actually, however, the success of several "types" of personality in achieving leadership status through their ways of behaving while a member of the population appears to depend, in turn, upon the fact that the population itself is comprised of so great a variety of personalities that no one personality has a constellation of attributes necessary to win an exclusive position in esteem and influence necessary to a role of exclusive leadership. Each leader makes a contribution *to some parts* of the membership which all members do not equally want or need. There may be very little overlap between the individuals who support one leader and those who support another.

Leadership appears as a process in which no one individual has a major role but in which relatively many share. The superior capacity which one individual may have to recognize and respond to the needs of others does not show itself as a generalized capacity which may relate him to all other individuals. It appears in the special sensitivity between the individual and *specific* other persons, resulting in interaction between them.

The choice-status of the individual appears directly attributable to the capacities he shows *in interaction* with colleagues to lessen or augment the satisfactions of the common group life. In this sense, choice is found to be evoked towards him or withheld from him, more or less in proportion to *how he carries* his role *in relation* to other members' roles, or, to state it more precisely, in proportion to how others perceive him to interact with them for the benefit of their common-group regime.

In contrast, no such function and no such "judgment" can be discerned in respect to the sheer quantity of choice "earned" by the individual on the sociometric criterion of leisure-time association. In the latter, not only is sheer quantity of choice received by the individual *not* an index to his role *in the informal milieu* in which he is a member, but the role which *any* individual appears to play within it has very much in common with the roles which other individuals play within it.

No one individual aids many others in the leisure-time milieu, so far as evidenced in this study, in the ways characteristic of the living-working groups. Likewise, no one individual wins from a great number of other individuals in the population their choice for him as a leisure-time associate.

Likewise, in contrast to the exceptionally great "group service" which is implied in the behaviors of those found to be most chosen in the living-working structure of the community, the interaction of even these same individuals in the informal leisure-choice structure may be said to be a highly *mutual* interindividual expression, emotionally supportive to the individuals *as persons* rather than as group members and at the same time *remarkably reciprocal* in its function— rather than reflecting extreme exertion on the part of some members as is found in the official groupings. It may be premised that insofar as "service" enters, it appears to be a service which renders each individual about equally indebted to the other and not many indebted to the few who show extraordinary effort in their behalf.

In the first study, under military auspices, to analyze choice data for psychegroup and sociogroup components, Maucorps (1949) finds a "general factor" which appears to operate throughout the choice expression but least in the data resulting from a psychegroup criterion; he calls this general factor "efficiency" in collective work situations and notes that "this distinction between subjective attraction and objective efficiency"

is, of course, not absolute and "must not be drawn too far." [3]

The psychological structure resulting from choice behavior on the part of the members of the test-community, this research finds, may be most accurately envisioned as *an equilibrium in flux*. The movements which take place continually within it are compensatory movements which do not disturb the total structure viewed as a totality. The total structure tends to retain its characteristics from one time to another *even though the respective positions of its carriers* (the members of the population) alter from time to time. The shifts "upward" and "downward" that are shown in the choice-status of the individuals in the population are, so to speak, bound to occur since interaction cannot be static. The reasons for this stability and this slowness of flux within the structure appear in the behaviors distinguishing choice-status. A social process of interaction *by and towards* the individuals respectively isolated or lifted to leadership is found to form the very basis of the isolation and of the leadership. Personality *per se,* insofar as it is reflected in social structure, is the capacity for interplay with other personalities, for responding to and being responded to, in a reciprocal situation, in which the individual is in common with other individuals.

---

[3] It is of interest that the sociometric data of the United States Office of Strategic Services resulted from applying both bases of criteria and hence could be given a similar analysis; also that, similarly, as in the present study, individual differences in expansiveness on different criteria could be compared as no limit was placed on the number of choices permitted; see Office of Strategic Services Assessment Staff (1948, p. 184).

References

DEUTSCHBERGER, P. Interaction patterns in changing neighborhoods. *Sociometry,* 1946, 9, 303-315.

JENNINGS, H. H. A sociometric study of emotional and social expansiveness. In R. G. Barker, J. S. Kounin, and H. F. Wright

(Eds.), *Child behavior and development.* New York: McGraw-Hill, 1943.

MAUCORPS, P. H. A sociometric inquiry in the French Army. *Sociometry,* 1949, *12,* 46-80.

MORENO, J. L. *Who shall survive? A new approach to the problem of human inter-relations.* Washington, D.C.: Nervous and Mental Disease Monograph Series, 1934, No. 58.

MORENO, J. L., and JENNINGS, H. H. Statistics of social configurations. *Sociometry,* 1938, *1,* 342-374.

MORENO, J. L., and JENNINGS, H. H. Sociometric control studies of grouping and re-grouping. *Sociometry Monogr.,* 1947, No. 7.

NEWSTETTER, W. I., FELDSTEIN, M., and NEWCOMB, T. M. *Group adjustment.* Cleveland: Western Reserve University, 1938.

Office of Strategic Services Assessment Staff. *Assessment of men.* New York: Holt, Rinehart and Winston, 1948.

ZELENY, L. D. Sociometry of morale. *Amer. Sociol. Rev.,* 1938, *4,* 799-808.

Leader-Follower Relations
in Street-corner Society ❧ William Foote Whyte

The stable composition of the group and the lack of social assurance on the part of its members contribute toward producing a very high rate of social interaction within the group. The group structure is a product of these interactions.

Out of such interaction there arises a system of mutual obligations which is fundamental to group cohesion. If the men are to carry on their activities as a unit, there are many occasions when they must do favors for one another. The code of the corner boy requires him to help his friends when he can and to refrain from doing anything to harm them. When life in the group runs smoothly, the obligations binding members to one another are not explicitly recognized. Once Doc asked me to do something for him, and I said that he had done so much for me that I welcomed the chance to reciprocate. He objected: "I don't want it that way. I want you to do this for me because you're my friend. That's all."

It is only when the relationship breaks down that the underlying obligations are brought to light. While Alec and Frank were friends, I never heard either one of them discuss the services he was performing for the other, but when they had a falling-out over the group activities with the Aphrodite Club, each man complained to Doc that the other was not acting as he should in view of the services that had been done him. In other words, actions which were performed explicitly for the sake of friendship were revealed as being part of a system of mutual obligations.

Not all the corner boys live up to their obligations equally well, and this factor partly accounts for the differentiation in status among them. The man with a low status may violate his obligations without much change in his position. His fellows know that he has failed to discharge certain obligations in the past, and his position reflects his past performances. On the other hand, the leader is depended upon by all the members to meet his personal obligations. He cannot fail to do so without causing confusion and endangering his position.

The relationship of status to the system of mutual obligations is most clearly revealed when one observes the use of money. During the time that I knew a corner gang called the Millers, Sam Franco, the leader, was out of work except for an occasional odd job; yet, whenever he had a little money, he spent it on Joe and Chichi, his closest friends, who were next to him in the structure of the group. When Joe or Chichi had money, which was less frequent, they reciprocated. Sam frequently paid for two members who stood close to the bottom of his group and occasionally for others. The two men who held positions immediately below Joe and Chichi were considered very well off according to Cornerville standards. Sam said that he occasionally borrowed money from them, but never more than fifty cents at a time. Such loans he repaid at the earliest possible moment. There were four other members with lower positions in the group, who nearly always had more money than Sam. He did not recall ever having borrowed from them. He said that the only time he had obtained a substantial sum from anyone around his corner was when he borrowed eleven dollars from a friend who was the *leader* of another corner gang.

The situation was the same among the Nortons. Doc did not hesitate to accept money from Danny, but he avoided taking any from the followers.

The leader spends more money on his followers than they on him. The farther down in the structure one looks, the fewer are the financial relations which tend to obligate the leader to a follower. This does not mean that the leader has more money than others or even that he necessarily spends more—though he must always be a free spender. It means that the financial relations must be explained in social terms. Unconsciously, and in some cases consciously, the leader refrains from putting himself under obligations to those with low status in the group.

The leader is the focal point for the organization of his group. In his absence, the members of the gang are divided into a number of small groups. There is no common activity or general conversation. When the leader appears, the situation changes strikingly. The small units form into one large group. The conversation becomes general, and unified action frequently follows. The leader becomes the central point in the discussion. A follower starts to say something, pauses when he notices that the leader is not listening, and begins again when he has the leader's attention. When the leader leaves the group, unity gives way to the divisions that existed before his appearance.

The members do not feel that the gang is really gathered until the leader appears. They recognize an obligation to wait for him before beginning any group activity, and when he is present they expect him to make their decisions. One night when the Nortons had a bowling match, Long John had no money to put up as his side bet, and he agreed that Chick Morelli should bowl in his place. After the match Danny said to Doc, "You should never have put Chick in there."

Doc replied with some annoyance, "Listen, Danny, you yourself suggested that Chick should bowl instead of Long John."

Danny said, "I know, but you shouldn't have let it go."

The leader is the man who acts when the situation requires action. He is more resourceful than his followers. Past events have shown that his ideas were right. In this sense "right" simply means satisfactory to the members. He is the most independent in judgment. While his followers are undecided as to a course of action or upon the character of a newcomer, the leader makes up his mind.

When he gives his word to one of his boys, he keeps it. The followers look to him for advice and encouragement, and he receives more of their confidences than any other man. Consequently, he knows more about what is going on in the group than anyone else. Whenever there is a quarrel among the boys, he hears of it almost as soon as it happens. Each party to the quarrel may appeal to him to work out a solution; and, even when the men do not want to compose their differences, each one takes his side of the story to the leader at the first opportunity. A man's standing depends partly upon the leader's belief that he has been conducting himself properly.

The leader is respected for his fair-mindedness. Whereas there may be hard feelings among some of the followers, the leader cannot bear a grudge against any man in the group. He has close friends (men who stand next to him in position), and he is indifferent to some of the members; but, if he is to retain his reputation for impartiality, he cannot allow personal animus to override his judgment.

The leader need not be the best baseball player, bowler, or fighter, but he must have some skill in whatever pursuits are of particular interest to the group. It is natural for him to promote activities in which he excels and to discourage those in which he is not skillful; and, insofar as he is thus able to influence the group, his competent performance is a natural consequence of his position. At the same time his performance supports his position.

The leader is better known and more respected outside his group than are any of his followers. His capacity for social movement is greater. One of the most important functions he performs is that of relating his group to other groups in the district. Whether the relationship is one of conflict, competition, or cooperation, he is expected to represent the interests of his fellows. The politician and the racketeer must deal with the leader in order to win the support of his followers. The leader's reputation outside the group tends to support his standing within the group, and his position in the group supports his reputation among outsiders.

The leader does not deal with his followers as an undifferentiated group. Doc explained:

> On any corner you would find not only a leader but probably a couple of lieutenants. They could be leaders themselves, but they let the man lead them. You would say, "They let him lead because they like the way he does things." Sure, but he leans upon them for his authority. Many times you find fellows on a corner that stay in the background until some situation comes up, and then they will take over and call the shots. Things like that can change fast sometimes.

The leader mobilizes the group by dealing first with his lieutenants. It was customary for the Millers to go bowling every Saturday night. One Saturday Sam had no money, so he set out to persuade the boys to do something else. Later he explained to me how he had been able to change the established social routine of the group. He said:

> I had to show the boys that it would be in their own interests to come with me—that each one of them would benefit. But I knew I only had to convince two of the fellows. If they start to do something, the other boys will say to themselves, "If Joe does it—or if Chichi does it—it must be a good thing for us too." I told Joe and Chichi what the idea was, and I got them to come with me. I didn't pay no attention to the others. When Joe and Chichi came, all the other boys came along too.

Another example from the Millers indicates what happens when the leader and his lieutenant disagree upon group policy. This is Sam talking again:

> One time we had a raffle to raise money to build a camp on Lake Blank [on property lent them by a local businessman]. We had collected $54, and Joe and I were holding the money. That week I knew Joe was playing pool, and he lost three or four dollars gambling. When Saturday came, I says to the boys, "Come on, we go out to Lake Blank. We're gonna build that camp on the hill."
>
> Right away, Joe said, "If yuz are gonna build the camp on the hill, I don't come. I want it on the other side."

All the time I knew he had lost the money, and he was only making up excuses so he wouldn't have to let anybody know. Now the hill was really the place to build that camp. On the other side, the ground was swampy. That would have been a stupid place. But I knew that if I tried to make them go through with it now, the group would split up into two cliques. Some would come with me, and some would go with Joe. So I let the whole thing drop for a while. After, I got Joe alone, and I says to him, "Joe, I know you lost some of that money, but that's all right. You can pay up when you have it and nobody will say nothin'. But, Joe, you know we shouldn't have the camp on the other side of the hill because the land is not good there. We should build it on the hill."

So he said, "All right," and we got all the boys together, and we went out to build the camp.

Disagreements are not always worked out so amicably. I once asked Doc and Sam to tell me who was the leader of a corner gang that was familiar to both of them. Sam commented:

Doc picked out Carmen. He picked out the wrong man. I told him why he was wrong—that Dominic was the leader. But that very same night, there was almost a fight between the two of them, Dominic and Carmen. And now the group is split up into two gangs.

Doc said:

Sometimes you can't pick out one leader. The leadership may be in doubt. Maybe there are a couple of boys vying for the honors. But you can find that out.

The leadership is changed not through an uprising of the bottom men but by a shift in the relations between men at the top of the structure. When a gang breaks into two parts, the explanation is to be found in a conflict between the leader and one of his former lieutenants.

This discussion should not give the impression that the leader is the only man who proposes a course of action. Other men frequently have ideas, but their suggestions must go through the proper channels if they are to go into effect.

In one meeting of the Cornerville S. and A., Dodo, who held a bottom ranking, proposed that he be allowed to handle the sale of beer in the clubrooms in return for 75 percent of the profits. Tony spoke in favor of Dodo's suggestion but proposed giving him a somewhat smaller percentage. Dodo agreed. Then Carlo proposed to have Dodo handle the beer in quite a different way, and Tony agreed. Tony made the motion, and it was carried unanimously. In this case Dodo's proposal was carried through, after substantial modifications, upon the actions of Tony and Carlo.

In another meeting Dodo said that he had two motions to make: that the club's funds be deposited in a bank and that no officer be allowed to serve two consecutive terms. Tony was not present at this time. Dom, the president, said that only one motion should be made at a time and that, furthermore, Dodo should not make any motions until there had been opportunity for discussion. Dodo agreed. Dom then commented that it would be foolish to deposit the funds when the club had so little to deposit. Carlo expressed his agreement. The meeting passed on to other things without action upon the first motion and without even a word of discussion on the second one. In the same meeting, Chris, who held a middle position, moved that a member must be in the club for a year before being allowed to hold office. Carlo said that it was a good idea, he seconded the motion, and it carried unanimously.

The actions of the leader can be characterized in terms of the origination of action in pair and set events. A pair event is one which takes place between two people. A set event is one in which one man originates action for two or more others. The leader frequently originates action for the group without waiting for the suggestions of his followers. A follower may originate action for the leader in a pair event, but he does not originate action for the leader and other followers at the same time—that is, he does not originate action in a set event which includes the leader. Of course, when the leader is not present, parts of the group are mobilized when men lower in the structure originate action in set events. It is through observation of such set events when the top men are not present that it is possible to determine the relative positions of the men who are neither leaders nor lieutenants.

Each member of the corner gang has his own position in the gang structure. Although the positions may remain unchanged over long periods of time, they should not be conceived in static terms. To have a position means that the individual has a customary way of interacting with other members of the group. When the pattern of interactions changes, the positions change. The positions of the members are interdependent, and one position cannot change without causing some adjustments in the other positions. Since the group is organized around the men with the top positions, some of the men with low standing may change positions or drop out without upsetting the balance of the group. For example, when Lou Danaro and Fred Mackey stopped participating in the activities of the Nortons, those activities continued to be organized in much the same manner as before, but when Doc and Danny dropped out, the Nortons disintegrated, and the patterns of interaction had to be reorganized along different lines.

An Experimental Study of ❀ Ronald Lippitt
Leadership and Group Life ❀ Ralph K. White

The study here reported, conducted in 1939 and 1940, attempted in an exploratory way to discover the extent to which various aspects of leadership behavior and of total group life could be fruitfully studied by experimental procedures of controlled matching and planned variation in conditions. The study had as its objectives:

1. To study the effects on group and individual behavior of three experimental variations in adult leadership in four clubs of eleven-year-old children. These three styles may be roughly labeled as "democratic," "authoritarian" and "laissez-faire."
2. To study the group and individual reactions to shifts from one type of leadership to another within the same group.
3. To seek relationships between the nature

and content of other group memberships, particularly the classroom and family, and the reactions to the experimental social climates.
4. To explore the methodological problems of setting up comparative "group test situations," to develop adequate techniques of group process recording, and to discover the degree to which experimental conditions could be controlled and manipulated within the range of acceptance by the group members.

The major experimental controls may be described briefly as follows:

1. Personal characteristics of group members. Because a large group of volunteers were available from which to select each of the small clubs, it was possible to ar-

This article was written especially for T. M. Newcomb and E. L. Hartley, *Readings in Social Psychology,* New York: Holt, Rinehart and Winston, 1947. Reprinted by permission of the authors and publisher.

range for comparability of group members on such characteristics as intelligence, and on such social behaviors (measured by teachers' ratings) as obedience, amount of social participation, leadership, frequency of quarreling, amount of physical energy, etc.

2. The interrelationship pattern of each club. In each group, by the use of a sociometric questionnaire in each classroom, it was possible to select groups which were very closely matched in terms of patterns of rejection, friendship, mutuality of relationship, and leadership position.

3. Physical setting and equipment. All clubs met in the same clubroom setting, two at a time in adjacent meeting spaces, with a common equipment box.

4. Activity interests. It was important to know the extent to which initial interest in the planned activities might be responsible for differences in degree of involvement in activity during the experiment. Therefore it was ascertained in the beginning that all groups of boys were comparably interested in the range of craft and recreational activities in which they would later be engaged.

5. Activity content. It is clear that the structure and content of an activity often exerts a powerful influence on the patterns of interdependence, cooperation, competition, etc. in group life. Therefore, it was important that activity content should be equated in these three types of leadership situations. In order to insure this, the clubs under democratic leadership met first in time during the week, and the activities which were selected by those clubs were automatically assigned to the parallel clubs under authoritarian leadership. In the laissez-faire situation, there were a number of potential activities of the same type as that selected by the "democratic clubs."

6. The same group under different leadership. The experimental design also made it possible to have a perfect matching of club personnel on the same analysis by comparing the same club with itself under three different leaders.

Experimental Variations

In the beginning the experimenters had planned for only two major variations in adult leader behavior: an authoritarian pattern and a democratic pattern. Later it was decided that it would be more fruitful to add a third variation of "laissez-faire" adult behavior, although with the four available clubs it would make the experimental design less rigorous. The method of systematic rotation can be noted in the accompanying chart, which refers to the earlier experiment (the same method was followed in the later experiment).

The three types of planned variation were as follows:

	Period I (7 Weeks)	Period 2 (7 Weeks)	Period 3 (7 Weeks)
Treatment Club Leader	Autocracy Sherlock Holmes I	Autocracy Sherlock Holmes IV	Democracy Sherlock Holmes II
Treatment Club Leader	Autocracy Dick Tracy II	Democracy Dick Tracy III	Autocracy Dick Tracy I
Treatment Club Leader	Democracy Secret Agents III	Autocracy Secret Agents II	Democracy Secret Agents IV
Treatment Club Leader	Democracy Charlie Chan IV	Democracy Charlie Chan I	Autocracy Charlie Chan III

1. The sequence of social climates. A number of the hypotheses focused upon the effect of a particular type of group history in determining the reactions of a group to a present pattern of leadership. The chart indicates the variety of group history sequences which were selected for exploratory study.
2. "Leader role" and "leader personality." There was a question as to the extent to which certain basic personality characteristics of the adult leaders would be important determinants in the individual and group behavior patterns which resulted. To study this variable, four adults with very different personality patterns were selected as leaders and all of them after proper indoctrination took two or three different leadership roles with different groups during the course of the experiment as indicated on the chart. This made it possible to discover whether certain of the leaders induced common reaction patterns which could be traced to their "personality" as contrasted to their "leadership role."
3. The three planned leadership roles. The three variations in leader role which were worked through in careful detail by the four club leaders may be summarized as follows:

Plan for authoritarian leadership role. Practically all policies as regards club activities and procedures should be determined by the leader. The techniques and activity steps should be communicated by the authority, one unit at a time, so that future steps are in the dark to a large degree. The adult should take considerable responsibility for assigning the activity tasks and companions of each group member. The dominator should keep his standards of praise and criticism to himself in evaluating individual and group activities. He should also remain fairly aloof from active group participation except in demonstrating.

Plan for the democratic leadership role. Wherever possible, policies should be a matter of group decision and discussion with active encouragement and assistance by the adult leader. The leader should attempt to see that activity perspective emerges during the discussion period with the general steps to the group goal becoming clarified. Wherever technical advice is needed, the leader should try to suggest two or more alternative procedures from which choice can be made by the group members. Everyone should be free to work with whomever he chooses, and the divisions of responsibility should be left up to the group. The leader should attempt to communicate in an objective, fact-minded way the bases for his praise and criticism of individual and group activities. He should try to be a regular group member in spirit but not do much of the work (so that comparisons of group productivity can be made between the groups).

Plan for laissez-faire leadership role. In this situation, the adult should play a rather passive role in social participation and leave complete freedom for group or individual decisions in relation to activity and group procedure. The leader should make clear the various materials which are available and be sure it is understood that he will supply information and help when asked. He should do a minimum of taking the initiative in making suggestions. He should make no attempt to evaluate negatively or positively the behavior or productions of the individuals or the group as a group, although he should be friendly rather than "stand-offish" at all times.

The data below will indicate the extent to which these planned variations were carried out and the pattern of social stimulation which was represented by the leader behavior in each of the clubs.

The Three Patterns of Leader Behavior

From the great variety of observations recorded on the behavior of each leader it was possible to compute quantitative profiles of leader performance which could be compared to see the extent to which the three different types of leadership role were different and the degree to which the adults carrying out the same role were comparable in their behavior patterns. Figure 1 illustrates some of the major differences in the

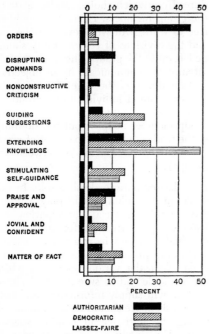

Fig. 1. Comparison of behavior of average authoritarian, democratic, and laissez-faire leader.

patterns of behavior of the three leadership roles. Most of the comparisons on the graph meet the test of statistical significance. The "average leader" comparisons are based on four democratic, four authoritarian, and two laissez-faire leader roles. The first three classifications of behavior, "leader orders," "disrupting commands" and "nonconstructive criticism," may be thought of as representing adult behavior which has a limiting effect upon the scope and spontaneity of child activity. About 60 percent of all of the behavior of the average authoritarian leader was of these types as compared to 5 percent for the democratic and laissez-faire leaders. The data show that the authoritarian leader usually initiated individual or group activity with an order, often disrupted on-going activity by an order which started things off in

the new direction not spontaneously chosen, and fairly frequently criticized work in a manner which carried the meaning, "It is a bad job because I say it is a bad job" rather than, "It is a poor job because those nails are bent over instead of driven in."

The next three behavior classifications, "guiding suggestions," "extending knowledge," "stimulating self-guidance," may be thought of as extending individual and group freedom and abilities. We note here some of the major differences between the democratic and the laissez-faire leadership role. Whereas the democratic leader took the initiative (where he felt it was needed in making guiding suggestions) much more frequently than the laissez-faire leader, a major proportion of the latter leadership role was giving out information when it was asked for. It is clear, however, that the democratic leader did not take initiative for action away from the group as indicated by the fact that the average democratic leader showed a greater proportion of "stimulating self-guidance" than even the laissez-faire leader. The category of "stimulating self-guidance" was made up of three main items: "leader's requests for child's opinions on individual and group plans," "use of child judgment as criterion," and "taking consensus of opinion." The data indicate that the democratic leaders stimulated child independence eight times as often as the authoritarian leader and about twice as often as the laissez-faire leader, although the latter two types of adults showed about the same proportion of this behavior in their total pattern of activity.

The classification on the graph entitled "praise and approval" is made up of such behavior items as "praising," "giving credit," "giving O.K.'s," etc. It indicates largely the functioning of the adult as a dispenser of social recognition. The authoritarian adult was significantly more active in this regard than either of the other two types of leaders.

The extent to which the adult discussed personal matters unrelated to the club situation (home, school, etc.), and also joked on a friendly basis with the club members, is indicated by the "jovial and confident" classification. The democratic leader had social interactions of this type with the group members about eight times as often as either the authoritarian or laissez-faire leaders. This is perhaps one of the best indices of the extent to which the democratic leaders were "on the same level" as the club members.

The last classification on Figure 1, "matter of fact," indicates one measurement of the extent to which the various social atmospheres were "fact-minded" as compared to "personal-minded" as far as the behavior of the adults was concerned.

The degree to which all the adult leaders, delegated to assume a given leadership role, behaved in a comparable fashion on these major aspects of leadership role is indicated by the fact that, on all comparisons differentiating major characteristics of the three roles, there is no overlapping of the behavior of any representative of one role with any representative of a different role. Thus it is possible to conclude that three clearly different leadership patterns were created with a much smaller range of individual differences in leader behavior within each pattern than between the patterns.

LEADERSHIP ROLE AND PERSONALITY
STYLE

An examination of the behavior patterns of the different leadership roles by the same individuals (see chart on page 526) reveals that on the items of leader behavior there is no greater similarity between the different performance patterns of the same individual than between those of different individuals. If we turn to the data of the three interviews with each club member in which at each transition stage in their club life they compared their leaders and talked very fully about them, we find again that there is no evidence of any adult personalities being rated favorably or unfavorably independently of their particular leadership role (i.e., authoritarian, democratic, laissez-faire). All

leaders stood high as well as low for one group or another and all the comments about their "personalities" were concerned with attributes of their leadership roles which had been measured.

The following excerpts from interviews of club members who had just completed six months of club life which included an authoritarian, a laissez-faire, and a democratic leader (in that sequence) indicate rather clearly the aspects of "leadership personality" which were perceived as important.

"RW (democratic) was the best leader and DA (laissez-faire) was the poorest. RW has good ideas and goes right to the point of everything . . . and always asked us what to do next time the club met, which was very nice. . . . DA gave us no suggestions like RW did, and didn't help us out at all, though he was very nice to us . . . but let us figure things out too much. I liked RL (authoritarian) pretty well for that kind of work."

"RL (authoritarian) was best, and then RW (democratic) and DA (laissez-faire). RL was the strictest and I like that a lot. DA and RW let us go ahead and fight, and that isn't good, though RW didn't do it as much as DA did. DA just didn't give us much to do. RW was OK, but he didn't have so many ideas as RL did. RW wanted to do what we did; RL didn't want to go with us lots of times, and he decided what we were to do."

"I liked RW (democratic) best, then DA (laissez-faire) and then RL (authoritarian). RW was a good sport, works along with us and helps us a lot; he thinks of things just like we do and was just one of us—he never did try to be the boss, and wasn't strict at all, but we always had plenty to do (the golden mean). DA didn't do much, just sat and watched; there wasn't much I didn't like about him, but he didn't help us much . . . not like with RW when we had regular meetings and that was very good. RL was all right mostly; he was sort of dictator like, and we had to do what he said pretty nearly; he helped us work but he was sort of bossy."

"I liked RW (democratic) the best and RL

(authoritarian) the least. RW was in between DA and RL, I like everything about him. I once said I didn't want to change from DA but I'm glad we changed. We could do what we pleased with DA but he was too easy going, not hard enough nearly, but he's a real nice person. With RL we always had something to do, and we did get a lot of things done, but I didn't like anything about him; he was much too strict. He was not cross, but very direct."

"I'd take RW (democratic) for a club leader, and DA (laissez-faire) was the worst. RW is just the right sort of combination; RL (authoritarian) was just about as good as RW, but he was kind of cross once in a while. RW had interesting things to do, he was just about right in everything. DA was too easy; he didn't know anything about the club—didn't know about its ways. He didn't understand us boys at all. . . . I didn't like him as well as RL because he had too few things for us to do." [1]

Another indirect indication that individual personality characteristics were not of any great significance in influencing group life in this study might be inferred from the finding that the total patterns of group reactions of different clubs to the same atmosphere tend to be remarkably homogeneous in spite of differences in adult leadership.

Data Collection and Analysis

Before continuing to summarize the individual and group behaviors which resulted from these three variations in leadership role, we will indicate briefly the types of data collection and analysis in the total study.

Eight types of club records were kept on each group, of which the four most impor-

[1] Besides indicating the leadership characteristics perceived as important by the boys, the reader will note that one boy in this club (an army officer's son) preferred his authoritarian leader and that the other four split in that two preferred their authoritarian leader second best and two liked their laissez-faire leader second best.

tant were kept by four different observers as follows.

1. A quantitative running account of the social interactions of the five children and the leader, in terms of symbols for directive, compliant, and objective (fact-minded) approaches and responses, including a category of purposeful refusal to respond to a social approach.
2. A minute-by-minute group structure analysis giving a record of activity subgroupings, the activity goal of each subgroup, whether the goal was initiated by the leader or spontaneously formed by the children, and rating on degree of unity of each subgrouping.
3. An interpretive running account of strikingly significant member actions and changes in the atmosphere of the group as a whole.
4. Continuous stenographic records of all conversation.

These data were synchronized at minute intervals so that placed side by side they furnished quite a complete and integrated picture of the on-going life of the group.

Five other types of data covering the lives of the club members were collected, the three most important being:

1. Interviews with each child by a friendly "non-club" person during each transition period from one kind of group atmosphere and leader to another. These interviews elicited comparisons of the various club leaders with one another, with the teacher and with parents as well as other data about how the club could be run better, who were the best and poorest types of club members, what an ideal club leader would be like, etc.
2. Interviews with the parents, concentrating on kinds of discipline used in the home, status of the child in the family group, personality ratings on the same scales used by the teachers, discussion of the child's attitude toward the club, school and other group activities.
3. Talks with the teachers concerning the transfer to the schoolroom of behavior patterns acquired in the club and vice versa.

The reliability of the eleven trained observers ranged from .78 to .95 with an average reliability of .84. Another reliability computation on the coding of three thousand units of conversation into twenty-three categories of behavior showed a percent agreement of 86. The analyses of what constituted a "group life unit" showed reliabilities ranging from .90 to .98. A number of methodological researches carried on since the date of this study seem to suggest that it is possible to get much more meaningful and reliable observation data than has been generally believed if much more time and effort are spent on a careful "calibration" of psychologically well-trained observers.

COMPARATIVE GROUP TEST

SITUATIONS

The experimenters also postulated that a fruitful way to discover some of the major differences between the three types of group atmosphere would be to arrange comparable "test episodes" in each club. So at regular intervals the following situations occurred:

1. Leader arrives late.
2. Leader called away for indeterminate time.
3. Stranger ("janitor" or "electrician") arrives while leader out and carries on critical attack of work of individual group member, then of group as a whole.

The Four Resultant Styles of Group Life

Some of the major findings, summarized from stenographic records and other case material which are elsewhere reproduced, are as follows: Two distinct types of reaction were shown to the same pattern of authoritarian leadership. All of the data, including the documentary films, indicate that three of the clubs responded with a dependent leaning on the adult leader, relatively low levels of frustration tension, and practically no capacity for initiating group action,

while the fourth club demonstrated considerable frustration and some degree of channelized aggression toward the authoritarian leader. (This latter pattern is much more comparable to the behavior of the club under authoritarian leadership in a previous experimental study of two clubs.[2])

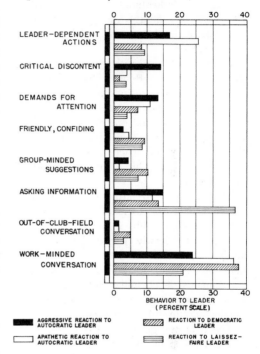

Fig. 2. Four patterns of group reaction to the three different types of leadership.

Figure 2 indicates the major differences in the relations which developed between the group members and the adult leaders in the four resultant social atmospheres. In both types of authoritarian atmosphere the members were markedly more dependent upon the leader than in either the democratic or laissez-faire situations, dependence being somewhat greater in the more passive clubs. All other clubs showed a somewhat greater feeling of discontent in their rela-

[2] See Ronald Lippitt, "An Experimental Study of Authoritarian and Democratic Group Atmospheres" in *Studies in Topological and Vector Psychology, I, University of Iowa Studies in Child Welfare*, 1940, No. 16.

tions with the adult leader than did the members of the democratic clubs, members of the "aggressive autocracy" being outstanding in their expression of rebellious feelings. There is evidence from other sources that the actual "felt discontent" in the "apathetic autocracies" was somewhat higher than indicated by the conversation which was considerably more restricted than was that of the democratic and laissez-faire club members.

In both types of authoritarian situations the demands for attention from the adult were greater than in the other atmospheres. It seemed clear that getting the attention of the adult represented one of the few paths to more satisfactory social status in the authoritarian situation where all of the "central functions" of group life were in the hands of the dominator.

The category "friendly, confiding" indicates that the members of the democratic and laissez-faire clubs initiated more "personal" and friendly approaches to their adult leaders, and the data on "out-of-club-field conversation" further indicate the more spontaneous exchanging of confidences about other parts of one's life experience in the democratic club atmosphere.

The data on "group-minded suggestions" to the leader show that the members in the democratic atmosphere felt much freer and more inclined to make suggestions on matters of group policy than in the other three group atmospheres. It is clear from other data that the lower level of suggestions in the laissez-faire situation is not because of any feeling of restricted freedom but because of a lack of a cooperative working relationship between the adult and the other group members.

The much greater responsibility of the members of the laissez-faire clubs to get their own information is shown by the fact that about 37 percent of their behavior toward their leader consisted of asking for information, as compared to about 15 percent in the other three club situations.

The final category in Figure 2, "work-minded conversation," indicates that a con-siderably larger proportion of the initiated approaches of the club members to their leaders were related to on-going club activity in the democratic and in the apathetic authoritarian situations than in the other two types of social climate.

RESULTANT RELATIONSHIPS OF CLUB MEMBERS

The relationships between the club members also developed along quite different lines in the four social climates. Expressions of irritability and aggressiveness toward fellow members occurred more frequently in both the authoritarian atmospheres and the laissez-faire situation than in the democratic social climates. Unlike the relationships of high interpersonal tension and scapegoating which developed in the previous aggressive autocracy[3] the club in this experiment seemed to focus its aggression sufficiently in other channels (toward the leader and toward the out-group) so that in-group tension did not rise to a dangerously high point.

There were more requests for attention and approval from fellow club members to each other in the democratic and laissez-faire situations than in the two authoritarian climates. It seems clear that the child members depended upon each other to a great extent for social recognition and were more ready to give recognition to each other in the democratic and laissez-faire situations.

It is interesting to find nearly as high a level of interpersonal friendliness in the authoritarian situations as in the democratic and laissez-faire atmospheres. The underlying spirit of rebellion toward the leader and cooperation in out-group aggression seem to be the "cohesive forces" in aggressive autocracy, while in apathetic autocracy with its much lower level of felt frustration, the shared submissiveness seemed to do away with all incentive to competition for social status.

Intermember suggestions for group action and group policy were significantly lower in

3 *Ibid.*

both types of autocracy than in the laissez-faire and democratic atmospheres. The dissatisfactions arising from any lack of feeling of real progress in the laissez-faire situation led to a high frequency of expression of ideas about "something we might do." Contrary to the democratic situation, these suggestions seldom became reality because of the lack of the social techniques necessary for group decision and cooperative planning. The group achievement level, as contrasted to the "wish level," was far lower in laissez-faire than in any of the other three atmospheres.

OTHER DIFFERENCES

By having the leaders arrive a few minutes late at regular intervals in each club life, it was possible to discover that in the five authoritarian situations no group initiative to start new work or to continue with work already under way developed, as contrasted with the democratic situations where leaders who arrived late found their groups already active in a productive fashion. The groups under the laissez-faire leaders were active but not productive. Figure 3 shows the percentage of total club time in each of

the four social atmospheres which was spent in giving major attention to some planned club project. For each atmosphere there is a comparison between the time when the leader was in the room, the time when the leader had been called out for planned experimental periods, and the unit of time just after the leader returned. The data here give striking evidence of the extent to which work motivation was leader-induced in the two types of authoritarian situation. "Working time" dropped to a minimum with the leader out, and most of what was done was in the minutes just after the leader had left the room. We see that in the democratic atmosphere the absence or presence of the leader had practically no effect. The apparent increase in group productive time with the laissez-faire leader out of the room may or may not be a meaningful result. Two or three times it was noted that when the adult left, one of the boys exerted a more powerful leadership and achieved a more coordinated group activity than when the relatively passive adult was present.

The behavior of the groups under authoritarian domination after their transition to a freer social atmosphere provided a very interesting index of unexpressed group tension. In Figure 4 it can be noted that both of

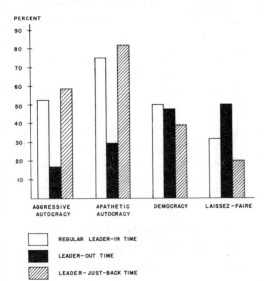

Fig. 3. Percent of time spent in high activity involvement.

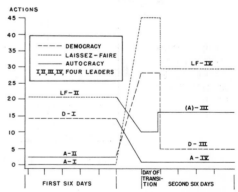

Fig. 4. Horseplay.

these apathetic authoritarian clubs showed great outbursts of horseplay between the members on the first day of their transitions to a laissez-faire and a democratic group situation. This need to "blow off steam" disappeared with more meetings in the freer atmosphere.

It will be recalled that in certain situations all groups were subject to the same frustration of hostile criticism by a strange adult (e.g., "janitor") while the adult leader was gone. Under the different types of leaders, •the groups handled these frustrations differently. Members of the apathetic au-

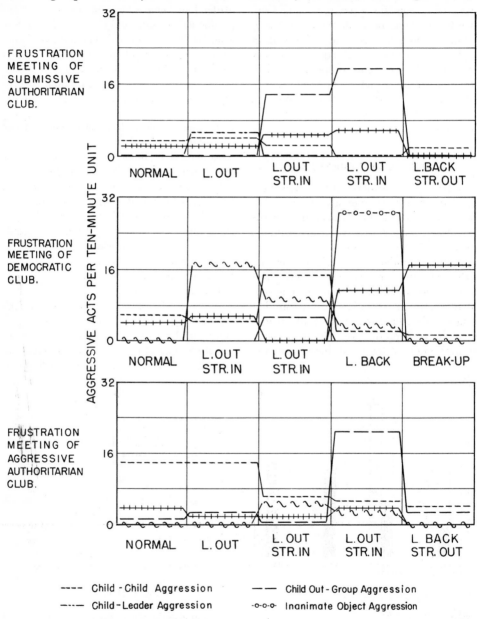

Fig. 5. Channels of group tension release in clubs of eleven-year-old boys under different types of leadership.

thoritarian clubs tended to accept individually and to internalize the unjust criticism or, in one or two cases, they "blew off steam" in aggressive advances toward an out-group (the other club meeting in the adjacent clubroom; see Figure 5). In the aggressive authoritarian situation, the frustration was typically channeled in aggression toward the out-group, although in several cases there was some direct reaction to the source of frustration, the hostile stranger (see Figure 5). In the democratic atmospheres there was evidence of a greater readiness to unite in rejection of the real source of frustration, the stranger, and to resist out-group aggression. Figure 5 shows an interesting case of a democratic club which first expressed its aggression directly against the stranger, then showed a slight rise in intermember tension, followed by an aggressive outburst against a sheet of three-ply wood with hammer and chisels accompanied by a striking rise in ingroup friendliness and a quick return to cooperative harmony. It was particularly interesting to discover that the clubs under democratic leaders resisted scapegoating as a channel of aggressive release.

The data indicate that the democratic type of adult role resulted in the greatest expression of individual differences, and that some type of uniformity-producing forces brought about a slightly lessened individual variability in the laissez-faire situation, and a much reduced range of individuality in the authoritarian clubs. Figure 6 gives an example of this analysis for the same group of individuals under three different leaders.

Individual Differences and the Group Atmospheres

We now come to the question of to what extent it is correct to report the data as though all individuals and all groups under the same type of adult leadership role reacted with a high degree of uniformity to the induced social climate. Before turning to the final section of interpretation of individual differences in reaction to the same social

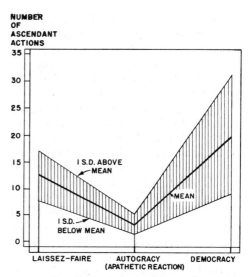

Fig. 6. The effect of changed atmosphere upon the range of individual differences within the same group.

climate, it will be interesting to look at the various club lives and see the extent to which the personalities making up each club or the different social atmospheres in which they lived seemed to be the most determining influence in the resulting behavior patterns. Two of the clubs had all three types of leadership. For these two groups it was possible by the techniques of analysis of variance to compare the effects of differences in child personnel and differences in all three experimental treatments. All four clubs were compared in the same way on various items of behavior for the two treatments of autocracy and democracy. It can be reported that in nearly all cases differences in club behavior could be attributed to differences in the induced social climate rather than to constant characteristics of the club personnel. One club showed a consistent variation from the rest through all atmospheres in level of friendliness between members, and one group showed a consistently lower level of social interaction which was not related wholly to their particular club environment.

We have already indicated [somewhat earlier] that boys in the same club indicated quite different social perceptions of the behavior of the same leader and also made differing comparative judgments about their preferred leaders after having had two or three. Although all but one boy preferred the democratic leader to the other two types, there was quite a split in the population as to whether they preferred as a second choice the laissez-faire or authoritarian type of adult. To get some clues as to the basis for these differences the experimenters made an attempt to study the personality structure of each individual boy as it showed itself in his reactions to the other boys, to his adult leaders, and to his school and home environments. The records taken during the experiments constituted a type of data which is infrequently found in other approaches to personality study. The most commonly used techniques for studying an individual include interviews, questionnaires, Rorschachs, thematic apperception tests, psychoanalytic free association, and the social case history, consisting of interviews with parents and relatives, but not direct observations of social behavior.

It is not felt, of course, that such records are more useful than interviews, social case histories, or other customary techniques, but only that *when combined* with other techniques they are a valuable part of the total picture and are an extremely useful addition to the toolchest of the clinical psychologist, the educator, the vocational counselor, and others who want to understand and to help a particular individual.

To show this concretely, one condensed case study is summarized below. Like our other case studies, it is based primarily upon club behavior data with much less interview material and home study data than would be found in a first class clinical analysis, but with enough of these data to suggest how the club behavior data can be combined with other sorts in the building up of an integrated personality structure.

The case chosen is one of two extremes, not in a single trait only, but in the large structure of intercorrelated traits, which has been found to be more important than any other trait cluster in our data. This cluster includes such variables as not being aggressive, not demanding attention, high work-mindedness, contentment in the strict but orderly atmosphere of autocracy, discontent in the free but disorderly atmosphere of laissez-faire, consistency of discipline in the home, and warmth of emotional relationship to parents. [4] These variables are statistically correlated to a marked degree; that is, the boys who show one of them usually show most of the others also. The reader can form his own judgment as to an approximate name for the cluster. The boys who stand low in the cluster as a whole would often be called "bad" by the exasperated adults who have to deal with them, while those who stand high in it would be called "good." Goodness, then, or conscientiousness, might be as good a name as any. It should be noticed, though, that the cluster includes some things, such as liking autocracy better than laissez-faire, which are not included in the ordinary connotations of the word "conscientious." It should be noticed too that the boys who stand low in the cluster—boys like Reilly[5] who is described here—are not necessarily "bad" or antagonistic to adult values and requirements; they may be only heedless and relatively indifferent to those values. In groups such as ours, which contain only healthy "normal" children, with no actual delinquents, it would do violence to common usage to call any of the boys "bad." [6]

For these and other reasons the rather cumbersome term "adult-value-centeredness" seems more accurate than "conscientiousness" as a name for the cluster.

[4] A factor-analysis of the data will be published elsewhere; its technical character makes it unsuitable for this brief report.

[5] Names and other identifying data have been changed here.

[6] The Freudian concept of the "super-ego" is relevant here; a "weak super-ego" does not necessarily mean active "badness" or antisocial tendencies. It may be noticed also that the cluster found in our data is similar to one which seems to have been discovered independently by a number of other investigators. It closely resembles Webb's "w" factor, which Thurstone renamed "conscientiousness."

Reilly

CLUB PERSONALITY

Reilly was the most talkative, the most conspicuous, and the most popular member of the Charlie Chan club. He was also one of the most irritating to those of his adult leaders who found themselves unable to cope with him. It was Reilly, for instance, who gleefully shouted, "Let's make war!" at the beginning of the first big water battle with the Secret Agents; it was Reilly whose vociferousness, as much as Fred's and Leonard's more aggressive horseplay, led to the complete disintegration of the group under laissez-faire leadership; and it was Reilly who led the "sitdown strike" against the autocratic leader, which was the one instance in any of the clubs of more or less organized rebellion against authority.

While he was so heedless of adult values and adult wishes, he was at the same time very popular with the other boys. He was the best-liked boy in his schoolroom, as determined by a sociometric questionnaire, and he had been elected president of his class. Yet he asserted his personality as vigorously in competition with other boys as in competition with adults. His personality contrasts sharply with that of Eddie, who was the best-liked boy in the other schoolroom from which our club members were selected. Where Eddie was conscientious, quiet, unassuming, and genuinely friendly with everyone, Reilly was exuberant, self-advertising, constantly bombarding the eyes and ears of others with his demands for attention, and, as the statistics showed, relatively low in both friendly and group-minded conversation. He was not actually a leader in the sense that he showed any planning or organizing ability; he was too impatient and too lacking in time-perspective for that. He was a leader only in the sense that he was liked, and also, perhaps, in the sense that his headlong, self-centered activity was imitated by others in the group.

It is interesting to find that, unlike the other two boys who stood with him at the bottom of the total group in the trait-cluster of "conscientiousness," he was never sullen, hostile, or maliciously mischievous. His scores in aggression were only about average, and his aggression (i.e., criticisms of other boys and playful collective aggression) was never really hostile in character. Even toward adults he was competitive rather than hostile. He ranked highest among the seventeen boys[7] in the proportion of his adult-contacts which had an attention-demanding character. Characteristically, he would loudly interrupt when the adult was talking to some other club member, and vociferously demand that the adult pay attention to him rather than to the other boy. The absolute frequency of this behavior was also very high, as evidenced by the fact that he also ranked highest, out of 17, in the absolute volume of his verbal contacts with the adult leader, in both autocracy and democracy. (The motivation behind these contacts, to be sure, was probably rather different in the two atmospheres. In autocracy it seems to have been almost entirely an expression of competition for power—perhaps in order to win boy-admiration—while in democracy it was also an expression of genuine man-to-man friendliness.) It would seem, then, that his somewhat paradoxical popularity was not due to the kind of warm liking which drew other boys to the quiet and unassuming Eddie. Rather, it seems to have been due to the fact that he was so successful in getting a rather gullible public to accept him at his own valuation, while at the same time the absence of malice in his self-assertion kept it from arousing hostility in others. In spite of his competitiveness and essential self-centeredness, the group accorded him a sort of hero worship, perhaps largely because each of them would have liked to be the sort of vital and self-confident person—completely uncowed by adults—which he unquestionably was.

[7] All statistics are based on a population of 17 rather than 20, since there were three boys about whom there was not an adequate amount of home background information.

The statistical club-behavior data and interview data support this impressionistic picture. In additon to the quantitative data already mentioned, we find that he had unusually high scores in volume of conversation (with boys as well as with the adult leader) and in percent of "out-of-field" conversation, which in his case represented such things as bragging about his father's hardware store, his own chemistry set at home, etc. In the interviews he expressed a preference for his laissez-faire leader as compared with his autocratic leader, indicating, probably, that his need for orderliness was less than his need for free self-assertion. He also showed unusual frankness in his avowed preference for the boy-valued activity of "fighting," as compared with the adult-valued activity of working. In describing his autocratic leader he said, "We didn't have any fun then—we didn't have any fights."

Summarizing his club personality, we can say first that he was not noticeably motivated by any of the adult-sponsored values which were conspicuous in the conscientious boys—obedience, respectfulness, nonaggression, order, self-control, hard work; second, that his primary goal in the club situation was apparently competition, or *superiority* in the eyes of the other boys; and third, that he tended to perceive adults, not as objects of obedience, respect, or hostility, but as equals, with whom he could compete (or be friendly, as he was with his democratic leader) on very much the same basis as with any of the other boys. These more basic characteristics of his present personality-structure, and not the peripheral behavior-traits of talkativeness, attention-demanding, etc., are what must be especially taken into account, whether our interest is the practical interest of the adult group-leader who has to cope with him, or the scientific interest of the clinical investigator who wants to race the origins of his present personality-structure in his home background and the behavior of his parents.

HOME BACKGROUND

His indifference to adult-sponsored values becomes intelligible when we discover that neither of his parents seems to have given him any incentive—neither fear of punishment nor hope of loving approval—to develop these values. His indulgent father apparently enjoyed his company (in a man-to-man relationship which offers a clue to his warm reaction to his democratic club leader), but his father was extremely busy and apparently accepted little or no responsibility for his training. His mother apparently disliked him, but felt helpless in relation to him; in the constant feud between them, there was neither the warmth which might have made him want to win her love by being "good," nor the firmness which might have made him fear her restrictions when he was "bad." These two attitudes, rejection and a feeling of helplessness, repeatedly came out in the interview with his mother. According to her, he is impudent, he is irresponsible, he is lazy, he is impatient and unable to stay long at one thing, he continually quarrels with his older brother and teases his younger brother. She blurted out these criticisms in a weary but almost defiant way. According to her, "punishment doesn't do him any good. I used to lose my temper and whip him; I was pretty mean, I guess," but he would be just as bad or worse afterward, so that now she doesn't ever punish him. "He sasses me back, and I can't stand a sassy child." Sometimes he argues for hours at a time; "maybe it's because I've given in to him several times," and he knows it's a good way to get things. For a while he had an allowance, but "he'd borrow on the next week's allowance and then expected to get it just the same," so the plan was discontinued. He now gets money for movies at least twice a week; if she tells him he can't go, he often goes to his father and gets the money from him.

Not only his indifference to adult values,

but also his desire for superiority and his tendency to perceive adults as equals now seem more intelligible. Since his father does not try to exert much authority, and his mother lets the authority situation become a feud in which he often gets the upper hand, he naturally tends to look upon adults as equals. Since his father's affection is always present and his mother's never is, his life is not geared to the winning of affection; the goal of superiority, first of all in relation to his mother and his brothers, has tended to take its place. And, finally, his exuberant vitality and absence of hostility, which were noted as major reasons for his popularity, now make sense in the light of the fact that his home life contains no major frustrations, and no repressed hostilities. Though his personality-structure may bring him trouble later in life, his existence at the moment is full of affection from his father, triumph over his mother, and exciting, successful competition with other boys.

Interpretive Summary

The foregoing condensed and highly selective research report has attempted to show some of the interdependencies of leadership role, group composition, group history, and membership personality structure in this study of four experimental clubs of preadolescent boys.

The leader-induced social atmosphere of the group, together with the group history (the preceding club atmospheres), established a hierarchy of channels of expression of response to frustration. Whereas the "aggressive autocracy" club was more ready to express its frustrations in interclub wars, the "apathetic autocracies" were more prone to internalize the aggression, and the "democratic" and "laissez-faire" groups to react against the source of frustration.

Passive acceptance by the group of the socially induced frustrations of authoritarian leadership was found in some cases to mean a nonfrustrated acceptance of a dependent relationship, and in other cases to mean a frustrated hopelessness in the face of overwhelming power. When a transition to a freer atmosphere occurred these latter cases gave evidence by their "blow-off" behavior of their previous frustrations.

The adult restrictiveness of the benevolent authoritarian role and the environmental unstructuredness of the laissez-faire situation were both found to inhibit greatly genuine "psychological freedom" as contrasted to "objective freedom."

The adult-leader role was found to be a very strong determiner of the pattern of social interaction and emotional development of the group. Four clear-cut types of social atmosphere emerged, in spite of great member differences in social expectation and reaction tendency due to previous adult-leader (parent, teacher) relationships.

It was clear that previous group history (i.e., preceding social climates) had an important effect in determining the social perception of leader behavior and reaction to it by club members. A club which had passively accepted an authoritarian leader in the beginning of its club history, for example, was much more frustrated and resistive to a second authoritarian leader after it had experienced a democratic leader than a club without such a history. There seem to be some suggestive implications here for educational practice.

It was found in this exploratory study that the process of small-group life could be experimentally manipulated in a satisfactory way for scientific study and could be recorded adequately for meaningful quantitative analysis. There emerged a variety of meaningful clusters of correlations between member case history, member social perception of the group situation, member and group behavior, and leader behavior.

The Contingency Model: A Theory
of Leadership Effectiveness ❊ Fred E. Fiedler

Leadership, as a problem in social psychology, has dealt primarily with two questions, namely, how one becomes a leader, and how one can become a *good* leader, that is, how one develops effective group performance. Since a number of excellent reviews (e.g., Stogdill, 1948; Gibb, 1954; Mann, 1959; Bass, 1960) have already dealt with the first question we shall not be concerned with it in the present paper.

The second question, whether a given leader will be more or less effective than others in similar situations, has been a more difficult problem of research and has received correspondingly less attention in the psychological literature. The theoretical status of the problem is well reflected by Browne and Cohn's (1958) statement that "leadership literature is a mass of content without coagulating substances to bring it together or to produce coordination. . . ." McGrath (1962), in making a similar point, ascribed this situation to the tendency of investigators to select different variables and to work with idiosyncratic measures and definitions of leadership. He also pointed out, however, that most researchers in this area have gravitated toward two presumably crucial clusters of leadership attitudes and behaviors. These are the critical, directive, autocratic, task-oriented versus the democratic, permissive, considerate, person-oriented type of leadership. While this categorization is admittedly oversimplified, the major controversy in this area has

been between the more orthodox viewpoint —reflected in traditional supervisory training and military doctrine that the leader should be decisive and forceful, that he should do the planning and thinking for the group, and that he should coordinate, direct, and evaluate his men's actions—and the other viewpoint—reflected in the newer human-relations-oriented training and in the philosophy behind nondirective and brain-storming techniques—which stresses the need for democratic, permissive, group-oriented leadership techniques. Both schools of thought have strong adherents and there is evidence supporting both points of view (Gibb, 1954; Hare, 1962).

While one can always rationalize that contradictory findings by other investigators are due to poor research design, or different tests and criteria, such problems present difficulties if they appear in one's own research. We have, during the past thirteen years, conducted a large number of studies on leadership and group performance, using the same operational definitions and essentially similar leader attitude measures. The inconsistencies which we obtained in our own research program demanded an integrative theoretical formulation which would adequately account for the seemingly confusing results.

The studies which we conducted used as the major predictor of group performance an interpersonal perception or attitude score which is derived from the leader's descrip-

This article was written especially for this book while the author was a Ford Faculty Research Fellow at the University of Louvain, Belgium (1963-1964). The present paper is based mainly on research conducted under the Office of Naval Research Contracts 170-106, N6-ori-07135 (Fred E. Fiedler, Principal Investigator) and RN177-472, Nonr 1834 (36) (Fred E. Fiedler, C. E. Osgood, L. M. Stolurow, and H. C. Triandis, Principal Investigators). The writer is especially indebted to his colleagues, A. R. Bass, L. J. Cronbach, M. Fishbein, J. E. McGrath, W. A. T. Meuwese, C. E. Osgood, H. C. Triandis, and L. R. Tucker, who offered invaluable suggestions and criticisms at various stages of the work.

tion of his most and of his least preferred co-workers. He is asked to think of all others with whom he has ever worked, and then to describe first the person with whom he worked best (his most preferred co-worker) and then the person with whom he could work least well (his least preferred co-worker, or LPC). These descriptions are obtained, wherever possible, before the leader is assigned to his team. However, even where we deal with already existing groups, these descriptions tend to be of individuals whom the subject has known in the past rather than of persons with whom he works at the time of testing.

The descriptions are typically made on 20 eight-point bipolar adjective scales, similar to Osgood's Semantic Differential (Osgood, et al., 1957), e.g.,

| Pleasant | 8 | : | 7 | : | 6 | : | 5 | : | 4 | : | 3 | : | 2 | : | 1 | Unpleasant |
| Friendly | 8 | : | 7 | : | 6 | : | 5 | : | 4 | : | 3 | : | 2 | : | 1 | Unfriendly |

These items are scaled on an evaluative dimension, giving a score of 8 to the most favorable pole (i.e., Friendly, Pleasant) and a score of 1 to the least favorable pole. Two main scores have been derived from these descriptions. The first one, which was used in our earlier studies, is based on the profile similarity measure D (Cronbach and Gleser, 1953) between the descriptions of the most and of the least preferred co-worker. This score, called the Assumed Similarity between Opposites, or ASo, indicates the degree to which the individual perceives the two opposites on his co-worker continuum as similar or different. The second score is simply based on the individual's description of his least preferred co-worker, LPC, and indicates the degree to which the subject evaluates his LPC in a relatively favorable or unfavorable manner. The two measures are highly correlated (.80 to .95) and will here be treated as interchangeable.

We have had considerable difficulty in interpreting these scores since they appear to be uncorrelated with the usual personality

and attitude measures. They are, however, related to the Ohio State University studies' "Initiation of structure" and "Consideration" dimensions (Stogdill and Coons, 1957). Extensive content analyses (Julian and McGrath, 1963; Morris, 1964) and a series of studies by Hawkins (1962) as well as still unpublished research by Bass, Fiedler and Krueger have given consistent results. These indicate that the person with high LPC or ASo, who perceives his least preferred co-worker in a relatively favorable, accepting manner, tends to be more accepting, permissive, considerate, and person-oriented in his relations with group members. The person who perceives his most and least preferred co-workers as quite different, and who sees his least preferred co-worker in a very unfavorable, rejecting manner tends to be directive, controlling, task-oriented, and managing in his interactions.

ASo and LPC scores correlated highly with group performance in a wide variety of studies, although, as mentioned above, not consistently in the same direction. For example, the sociometrically chosen leader's ASo score correlated $-.69$ and $-.58$ with the percentage of games won by high school basketball teams and $-.51$ with the accuracy of surveying of civil engineer teams (Fiedler, 1954), and the melter foreman's ASo score correlated $-.52$ with tonnage output of open-hearth shops (Cleven and Fiedler, 1956). These negative correlations indicate that *low* ASo or LPC scores were associated with good group performance, i.e., that these groups performed better under managing, directive leaders than under more permissive, accepting leaders. However, while the ASo score of the sociometrically accepted company managers also correlated negatively $(-.70)$ with the net income of consumer cooperatives, the board chairman's ASo score under the same circumstances correlated

+.62 (Godfrey, Fiedler, and Hall, 1959). Thus, groups with different tasks seemed to require different leader attitudes. In a more recent study of group creativity in Holland, the leader's LPC score correlated with performance +.75 in religiously homogeneous groups with formally appointed leaders, but −.72 in religiously heterogeneous groups; and while the correlation was +.75 in homogeneous groups with appointed leaders it was −.64 in homogeneous groups having emergent (sociometrically nominated) leaders (Fiedler, Meuwese, and Oonk, 1961).

The results of these investigations clearly showed that the direction and magnitude of the correlations were contingent upon the nature of the group-task situation which confronted the leader. The problem resolved itself then into (a) developing a meaningful system for categorizing group-task situations; (b) inducing the underlying theoretical model which would integrate the seemingly inconsistent results obtained in our studies; and (c) testing the validity of the model by adequate research.

Development of the Model

KEY DEFINITIONS

We shall here be concerned with "interacting" rather than "co-acting" task groups. By an interacting task group we mean a face-to-face team situation (such as a basketball team) in which the members work *interdependently* on a common goal. In groups of this type, the individual's contributions cannot readily be separated from total group performance. In a co-acting group, however, such as a bowling or a rifle team, the group performance is generally determined by summing the members' individual performance scores.

We shall define the leader as the group member who is officially appointed or elected to direct and coordinate group action. In groups in which no one has been so designated, we have identified the informal leader by means of sociometric preference questions

such as asking group members to name the person who was most influential in the group, or whom they would most prefer to have as a leader in a similar task.

The leader's effectiveness is here defined in terms of the group's performance on the assigned primary task. Thus, although a company manager may have, as one of his tasks, the job of maintaining good relations with his customers, his main job, and the one on which he is in the final analysis evaluated, consists of the long-range profitability of the company. Good relations with customers, or high morale and low labor turnover may well contribute to success, but they would not be the basic criteria by this definition.

THE CATEGORIZATION OF
GROUP-TASK SITUATIONS

Leadership is essentially a problem of wielding influence and power. When we say that different types of groups require different types of leadership we imply that they require a different relationship by which the leader wields power and influence. Since it is easier to wield power in some groups than in others, an attempt to categorize groups might well begin by asking what conditions in the group-task situation will facilitate or inhibit the leader's exercise of power. On the basis of our previous work we postulated three important aspects in the total situation which influence the leader's role.

1. Leader-Member Relations. The leader who is personally attractive to his group members, and who is respected by his group, enjoys considerable power (French, 1956). In fact, if he has the confidence and loyalty of his men he has less need of official rank. This dimension can generally be measured by means of sociometric indices or by group atmosphere scales (Fiedler, 1962) which indicate the degree to which the leader experiences the group as pleasant and well disposed toward him.

2. Task Structure. The task generally implies an order "from above" which incorporates the authority of the superior organization. The group member who refuses to comply must be prepared to face disciplinary action by the higher authority. For example, a squad member who fails to perform a lawful command of his sergeant may have to answer to his regimental commander. However, compliance with a task order can be enforced only if the task is relatively well structured, i.e., if it is capable of being programmed. One cannot effectively force a group to perform well on an unstructured task such as developing a new product or writing a good play.

Thus, the leader who has a structured task can depend on the backing of his superior organization, but if he has an unstructured task the leader must rely on his own resources to inspire and motivate his men. The unstructured task thus provides the leader with much less effective power than does the highly structured task.

We operationalized this dimension by utilizing four of the aspects which Shaw (1962) recently proposed for the classification of group tasks. These are (a) decision *verifiability,* the degree to which the correctness of the solution can be demonstrated objectively; (b) *goal clarity,* the degree to which the task requirements are clearly stated or known to the group; (c) *goal path multiplicity,* the degree to which there are many or few procedures available for performing the task (reverse scoring); and (d) *solution specificity,* the degree to which there is one rather than an infinite number of correct solutions (e.g., solving an equation vs. writing a story). Ratings based on these four dimensions have yielded interrater reliabilities of .80 to .90.

3. *Position Power.* The third dimension is defined by the power inherent in the position of leadership irrespective of the occupant's personal relations with his members. This includes the rewards and punishments which are officially or traditionally at the leader's disposal, his authority as defined by the group's rules and bylaws, and the organizational support given to him in dealing with his men. This dimension can be opera-

tionally defined by means of a check list (Fiedler, 1964) containing items such as "Leader can effect promotion or demotion," "Leader enjoys special rank and status in real life which sets him apart from, and above, his group members." The median interrater agreement of four independent judges rating 35 group situations was .95.

A THREE-DIMENSIONAL GROUP CLASSIFICATION

Group-task situations can now be rated on the basis of the three dimensions of leader-member relations, task structure, and position power. This locates each group in a three-dimensional space. A rough categorization can be accomplished by halving each of the dimensions so that we obtain an eight-celled cube (Fig. 1). We can now determine whether the correlations between leader attitudes and group performance within each of these eight cells, or octants, are relatively similar in magnitude and direction. If they are, we can infer that the group classification has been successfully accomplished since it shows that groups falling within the same octant require similar leader attitudes.

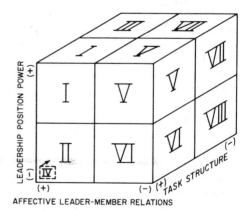

Fig. 1. A model for the classification of group-task situations.

A previous paper has summarized 53 group-task situations which are based on our previous studies (Fiedler, 1964). These 53 group-task situations have been ordered into the eight octants. As can be seen from Table 1, groups falling within the same octant show correlations between the leader's ASo or LPC score and the group performance criterion which are relatively similiar in magnitude and direction. We can thus infer that the group classification has been accomplished with at least reasonable success.

tions. In the present instance we have postulated that the most important dimension in the system is the leader-member relationship since the highly liked and respected leader is less in need of position power or the power of the higher authority incorporated in the task structure. The second most important dimension is the task structure, since a leader with a highly structured task does not re-

TABLE 1

MEDIAN CORRELATION BETWEEN LEADER LPC AND GROUP PERFORMANCE
IN VARIOUS OCTANTS

	Leader-Member Relations	Task Structure	Position Power	Median Correlation	Number of Relations Included in Median
Octant I	Good	Structured	Strong	−.52	8
Octant II	Good	Structured	Weak	−.58	3
Octant III	Good	Unstructured	Strong	−.41	4
Octant IV	Good	Unstructured	Weak	.47	10
Octant V	Mod. Poor	Structured	Strong	.42	6
Octant VI	Mod. Poor	Structured	Weak		0
Octant VII	Mod. Poor	Unstructured	Strong	.05	10
Octant VIII	Mod. Poor	Unstructured	Weak	−.43	12

Consideration of Figure 1 suggests a further classification of the cells in terms of the effective power which the group-task situation places at the leader's disposal, or more precisely, the favorableness of the situation for the leader's exercise of his power and influence.

Such an ordering can be accomplished without difficulty at the extreme poles of the continuum. A liked and trusted leader with high rank and a structured task is in a more favorable position than is a disliked and powerless leader with an ambiguous task. The intermediate steps pose certain theoretical and methodological problems. To collapse a three-dimensional system into an undimensional one implies in Coombs' terms a partial order or a lexicographic system for which there is no unique solution. Such an ordering must, therefore, be done either intuitively or in accordance with some reasonable assump-

quire a powerful leader position. (For example, privates or noncommissioned officers in the army are at times called upon to lead or instruct officers in certain highly structured tasks—such as demonstrating a new weapon or teaching medical officers close order drill—though not in unstructured tasks—such as planning new policies on strategy.) This leads us to order the group-task situations first on leader-member relations, then on task structure, and finally on position power. While admittedly not a unique solution, the resulting ordering constitutes a reasonable continuum which indicates the degree of the leader's effective power in the group.[1]

[1] Another cell should be added which contains real-life groups which reject their leader. Exercise of power would be very difficult in this situation and such a cell should be placed at the extreme negative end of the continuum. Such cases are treated in the section on validation.

A Contingency Model for Predicting Leadership Performance

As was already apparent from Table 1, the relationship between leader attitudes and group performance is contingent upon the accurate classification of the group-task situation. A more meaningful model of this contingency relationship emerges when we now plot the correlation between LPC or ASo and group performance on the one hand, against the octants ordered on the effective power or favorableness-for-the-leader dimension on the other. This is shown in Figure 2. Note that each point in the plot is a *correlation* predicting leadership performance or group effectiveness. The plot therefore represents 53 *sets of groups* totaling over 800 separate groups.

As Figure 2 shows, managing, controlling, directive (low LPC) leaders perform most

effectively either under very favorable or under very unfavorable situations. Hence we obtain negative correlations between LPC and group performance scores. Considerate, permissive, accepting leaders obtain optimal group performance under situations intermediate in favorableness. These are situations in which (a) the task is structured, but the leader is disliked and must, therefore, be diplomatic; (b) the liked leader has an ambiguous, unstructured task and must, therefore, draw upon the creativity and cooperation of his members. Here we obtain positive correlations between LPC and group performance scores. Where the task is highly structured and the leader is well liked, nondirective behavior or permissive attitudes (such as asking how the group ought to proceed with a missile count-down) is neither appropriate nor beneficial. Where the situation is quite unfavorable, e.g., where the dis-

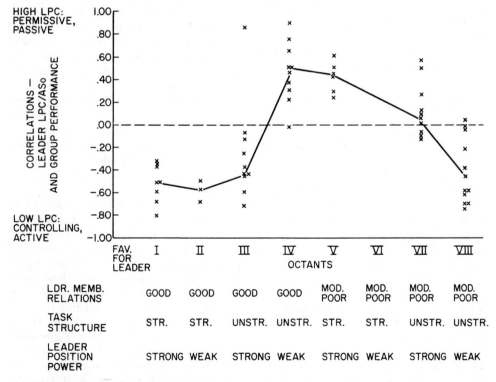

Fig. 2. Correlations of leader LPC and group performance plotted against octants, that is, favorableness of group-task situation for leader.

liked chairman of a volunteer group faces an ambiguous task, the leader might as well be autocratic and directive since a positive, non-directive attitude under these conditions might result in complete inactivity on the part of the group. This model, thus, tends to shed some light on the apparent inconsistencies in our own data as well as in data obtained by other investigators.

Empirical Tests: Extension of the Model

The basic hypothesis of the model suggests that the directive, controlling, task-oriented (low LPC) leader will be most successful in group-task situations which are either very favorable or else very unfavorable for the leader. The permissive, considerate, human-relations-oriented (high LPC) leader will perform best under conditions which are intermediate in favorableness. This hypothesis was tested by reanalyzing data from previous studies as well as by a major experiment specifically designed to test the model. Both are briefly described below.

REANALYSES OF PREVIOUS STUDIES

As we indicated before, there is reason to believe that the relationship between the leader and his members is the most important of the three dimensions for classifying group-task situations. The problem of exercising leadership will be a relatively easy one in group-task situations in which the leader is not only liked by his crew and gets along well with his group, but in which the task is structured and the leader has a relatively powerful position. The situation will be somewhat more difficult if the leader under the latter circumstances has an only moderately good relationship with his group members, and it will be quite difficult if the leader-member relations are very poor, i.e., if the group members reject or actively dislike the leader. Ordinarily this does not occur in

laboratory studies. It does happen, however, that real-life groups strongly reject leaders —sometimes to the point of sabotaging the task. Since such a situation would present a very difficult problem in leadership, we would expect better performance from the task-oriented, controlling leader, and hence a negative correlation between the leader's ASo of LPC score and his group's performance. This result appeared in one study of bomber crews for which we already had the appropriate data, and it was tested by new analyses in two other studies.

Bomber Crew Study. A study of B-29 bomber crews was conducted (Fiedler, 1955) in which the criterion of performance consisted of radar bomb scores. This is the average circular error or accuracy of hitting the target by means of radar procedures. The crews were classified on the basis of the relationship between the aircraft commander and his crew members. The crews were ordered on whether or not (a) the aircraft commander was the most chosen member of the crew, and (b) the aircraft commander sociometrically endorsed his key men on his radar bombing team (the radar observer and navigator).

The results of this analysis are presented in Table 2. It can be seen that the correlations between ASo and crew performance are highly negative in crews having very good and very poor leader-group relations, but they tend to be positive in the intermediate range.

Antiaircraft Artillery Crews. A second set of data came from a study of antiaircraft artillery crews (Hutchins and Fiedler, 1960). The criterion of crew performance consisted of scores indicating the "location and acquisition" of unidentified aircraft. These crews were subdivided on the basis of leader-crew relations by separately correlating the leader's LPC score with group performance (a) for the ten crews which most highly chose their crew commander, (b) the ten which were in the intermediate range, and (c) the ten crews which gave the least favorable sociometric choices to their leader. Correla-

TABLE 2

CORRELATIONS BETWEEN AIRCRAFT COMMANDER'S (AC's) ASo SCORE AND RADAR
BOMB SCORES UNDER DIFFERENT PATTERNS OF SOCIOMETRIC CHOICES
IN B-29 BOMBER CREWS

	Rho	N
AC is most preferred crew member and chooses keymen (K)	−.81	10
AC is most preferred crew member and is neutral to K	−.14	6
AC is most preferred crew member and does not choose K	.43	6
AC is not most preferred crew member but chooses K	−.03	18
AC is not most preferred crew member and is neutral to K	−.80	5
AC is not most preferred crew member and does not choose K	−.67	7

tion coefficients (Rho) of −.34, +.49, and −.42 were obtained respectively for the three sets of artillery crews. Here again there is a clear indication that controlling and directive leaders perform most effectively under very favorable or unfavorable leader-group relations (negative correlations between LPC and group performance), whereas more permissive and accepting leaders obtain optimal group performance when leader-group relations are intermediate in favorableness (positive correlations between LPC and group performance).

Consumer Cooperative Companies. Finally we reanalyzed data from a study of 31 consumer cooperatives (Godfrey, Fiedler, and Hall, 1959) in which the criterion of performance consisted of the percentage of company net income over a three-year period. The companies were subdivided into those in which the general manager was sociometrically chosen (a) by his board of directors as well as by his staff of assistant managers, (b) by his board but not his staff, or (c) by his staff but not his board, and (d) the companies in which the general manager was rejected, or not chosen, by both board of directors and staff. The findings shown in

Table 3 are clearly consistent with those reported above for the two studies of military personnel.

The results of these three investigations are summarized in Figure 3. It can be seen that

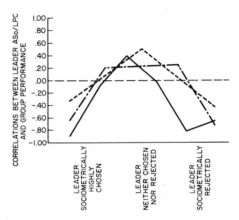

Fig. 3. Correlations between leader LPC or ASo scores and group performance under three conditions of leader acceptance by the group in studies of bomber crews, antiaircraft artillery crews, and consumer cooperatives.

the task-oriented, managing, low LPC leaders performed best under very favorable and

TABLE 3

CORRELATIONS BETWEEN GENERAL MANAGER'S ASo SCORE
AND COMPANY NET INCOME

	Rho	N
Gen. Mgr. is chosen by board and staff (ASo Perf.)	−.67	10
Gen. Mgr. is chosen by board, but rejected by staff	.20	6
Gen. Mgr. is rejected by board, but chosen by staff	.26	6
Gen. Mgr. is rejected by board and staff	−.75	7

under very unfavorable situations, while the permissive, considerate leaders performed best under conditions intermediate in favorableness. These data, therefore, clearly support the hypothesis derived from the model.

Experimental Test of the Contingency Model

In cooperation with the Belgian naval forces we recently conducted a major study which served in part as a specific test of the model. Only aspects immediately relevant to the test are here described. The investigation was conducted in Belgium where the French- and Dutch-speaking (or Flemish) sectors of the country have been involved in a long-standing and frequently acrimonious dispute. This conflict centers about the use of language, but it also involves a host of other cultural factors which differentiate the 60 percent Flemish- and 40 percent French-speaking population groups in Wallonie and Brussels. This "linguistic problem," which is rooted in the beginning of Belgium's natural history, has in recent years been the cause of continuous public controversy, frequent protest meetings, and occasional riots.

The linguistic problem is of particular interest here since a group consisting of members whose mother tongue, culture, and attitudes differ will clearly present a more difficult problem in leadership than a group whose members share the same language and culture. We were thus able to test the major hypothesis of the model as well as to extend the research by investigating the type of leadership which linguistically and culturally heterogeneous groups require.

Design. The experiment was conducted at the naval training center at Ste. Croix-Bruges.[2] It utilized 48 career petty officers

and 240 recruits who had been selected from a pool of 546 men on the basis of a pretest in which we obtained LPC, intelligence, attitude, and language comprehension scores.

The experiment was specifically designed to incorporate the three major group classification dimensions shown in Figure 1, namely, leader-member relations, position power, and task structure. It also added the additional dimension of group homogeneity vs. heterogeneity. Specifically, 48 groups had leaders with high position power (petty officers) while 48 had leaders with low position power (recruits); 48 groups began with the unstructured task, while the other 48 groups began with the two structured tasks; 48 groups were homogeneous, consisting of three French- or three Dutch-speaking men, while the other 48 groups were heterogeneous, consisting of a French-speaking leader and two Flemish members, or a Dutch-speaking, Flemish leader and two French-speaking members. The quality of the leader-member relations was measured as in our previous studies by means of a group atmosphere scale which the leader completed after each task session.

Group Performance Criteria. Two essentially identical structured tasks were administered. Each lasted 25 minutes and required the groups to find the shortest route for a ship which, given certain fuel capacity and required ports of call, had to make a round trip calling at respectively ten or twelve ports. The tasks were objectively scored on the basis of sea miles required for the trip. Appropriate corrections and penalties were assigned for errors.

[2] This investigation was conducted in collaboration with Dr. J. M. Nuttin (Jr.) and his students while the author was a Ford Faculty Research Fellow at the University of Louvain, 1963-1964. The experiment, undertaken with permission of Commodore L. Petitjean, then Chief of Staff of the Belgian naval forces, was carried out at the Centre de Formation Navale,

Ste. Croix-Bruges. The writer wishes to express his special gratitude and appreciation to the commandant of the center, Captain V. Van Laethem, who not only made the personnel and the facilities of the center available to us, but whose active participation in the planning and the execution of the project made this study possible. We are also most grateful to Dr. U. Bouvier, Director of the Center for Social Studies, Ministry of Defense, and to Capt. W. Cafferata, USN, of the U.S. Military Assistance and Advisory Group, and to Cmdr. J. Robison, U.S. Naval Attaché in Brussels, who provided liaison and guidance.

The unstructured task required the groups to compose a letter to young men of 16 and 17 years, urging them to choose the Belgian navy as a career. The letter was to be approximately 200 words in length and had to be completed in 35 minutes. Each of the letters, depending upon the language in which it was written, was then rated by Dutch- or by French-speaking judges on style, the use of language, as well as interest value, originality, and persuasiveness. Estimated reliability was .92 and .86 for Dutch- and French-speaking judges, respectively.

It should be noted in this connection that the task of writing a letter is not as unstructured as might have been desirable for this experiment. The form of any letter of this type is fairly standardized, and its content was, of course, suggested by the instructions. The navy officers with whom we consulted throughout the study considered it unwise, however, to give a highly unstructured task, such as writing a fable or proposing a new policy, since tasks of this nature were likely to threaten the men and to cause resentment and poor cooperation. High and low task structure is, therefore, less well differentiated in this study than it has been in previous investigations.

Results. The contingency model specifies that the controlling, managing, low LPC leaders will be most effective either in very favorable or else in relatively unfavorable group-task situations, while the permissive, considerate, high LPC leaders will be more effective in situations intermediate in difficulty.

The basic test of the hypothesis requires, therefore, that we order the group-task situations represented in this experiment in terms of the difficulty which they are likely to present for the leader. Since there are 16 cells in the design, the size of the sample within each cell (namely, 6 groups) is, of course, extremely small. However, where the conditions are reasonably replicated by other cells, the relationship can be estimated from the median rank-order correlations.

The hypothesis can be tested more readily with correlations of leader LPC and group

performance in homogeneous groups on the more reliably scorable second structured task. These conditions approximate most closely those represented in Figure 3, on bomber and antiaircraft crews and consumer cooperatives. We have here made the fairly obvious assumption that the powerful leader or the leader who feels liked and accepted faces an easier group-task situation than low-ranking leaders and those who see the groups as unpleasant and tense. Each situation is represented by two cells of six groups each. Arranging the group-task situations in order of favorableness for the leader then gives us the following results:

High group atmosphere and high position power . . . $-.77$, $-.77$

High group atmosphere and low position power . . . $+.60$, $+.50$

Low group atmosphere and high position power . . . $+.16$, $+.01$

Low group atmosphere and low position power . . . $-.16$, $-.43$

These are, of course, the trends in size and magnitude of correlations which the model predicts. Low LPC leaders are again most effective in favorable and unfavorable group-task situations; the more permissive, considerate, high LPC leaders were more effective in the intermediate situations.

Extending the model to include heterogeneous groups requires that we make a number of additional assumptions for weighting each of the group-task dimensions so that all 48 cells (i.e., 16 cells × 3 tasks) can be reasonably ordered on the same scale. We have here assigned equal weights of 3 to the favorable poles of the major dimension, i.e., to homogeneity, high group atmosphere, and high position power. A weight of 1 was assigned to the first structured task, and a weight of 2 to the second structured task on the assumption that the structured task makes the group-task situation somewhat more favorable than the unstructured task, and that the practice and learning effect inherent in performing a second, practically identical, task will make the group-task situation still more favorable for the leader. Finally, a weight of 1 was given to the "second presentation," that is, the group task which occurred toward the end of the session, on the assumption that the leader by that time had gotten to know his group members and had learned to work with them more effectively, thus again increasing the favorableness of his group-task situation to a certain extent.

The resulting weighting system leads to a scale from 12 to 0 points, with 12 as the most favorable pole. If we now plot the median correlation coefficients of the 48

group-task situations against the scale indicating the favorableness of the situation for the leader, we obtain the curve presented in Figure 4.

As can be seen, we again obtain a curvilinear relationship which resembles the one shown in Figure 2. Heterogeneous groups with low position power and/or poor leader-member relations fall below point .00 on the scale, and thus tend to perform better with controlling, directive, low LPC leaders. Only under otherwise very favorable conditions do heterogeneous groups perform better

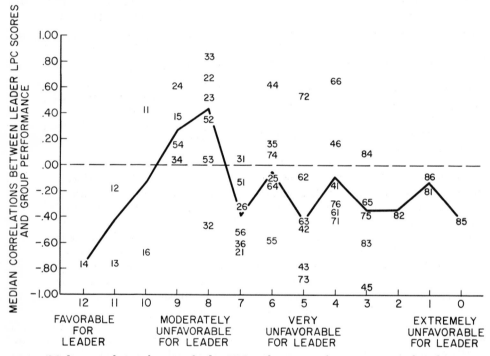

Fig. 4. Median correlations between leader LPC and group performance scores plotted against favorableness-for-leader scale in the Belgian Navy study. The code is explained in the table.

CODE IN FIG. 4

Compo-sition	Pos. Pow.	High Group Atmos.	Low Group Atmos.	Task	1st Pres.	2d Pres.
		1st Digit			2d Digit	
Homo.	High	1	5	Str. I	1	2
Homo.	Low	2	6	Str. II	3	4
Het.	High	3	7	Unstr.	5	6
Het.	Low	4	8			

with permissive, considerate, high LPC leaders, that is, in group-task situations characterized by high group atmosphere as well as high position power, four of the six correlations (66%) are positive, while only five of eighteen (28%) are positive in the less favorable group-task situations.

It is interesting to note that the curve is rather flat and characterized by relatively low negative correlations as we go toward the very unfavorable end of the scale. This result supports Meuwese's (1964) recent study which showed that correlations between leader LPC as well as between leader intelligence and group performance tend to become attenuated under conditions of relative stress. These findings suggest that the leader's ability to influence and control the group decreases beyond a certain point of stress and difficulty in the group-task situation.

Discussion

The contingency model seeks to reconcile results which up to now had to be considered inconsistent and difficult to understand. We have here attempted to develop a theoretical framework which can provide guidance for further research. While the model will undoubtedly undergo modifications and elaboration as new data become available, it provides an additional step toward a better understanding of leadership processes required in different situations. We have here tried to specify exactly the type of leadership which different group-task situations require.

The model has a number of important implications for selection and training as well as for the placement of leaders and organizational strategy. Our research suggests, first of all, that we can utilize a very broad spectrum of individuals for positions of leadership. The problem becomes one of placement and training rather than of selection since both the permissive, democratic, human-relations-oriented and the managing, autocratic, task-oriented leader can be effectively utilized. Leaders can be trained to recognize their own style of leadership as well as the conditions which are most compatible with their style.

The model also points to a variety of administrative and supervisory strategies which the organization can adopt to fit the group-task situation to the needs of the leader. Tasks can, after all, be structured to a greater or lesser extent by giving very specific and detailed, or vague and general, instructions; the position power of the group leader can be increased or decreased and even the congeniality of a group and its acceptance of the leader can be affected by appropriate administrative action, e.g., increasing or decreasing the group's homogeneity.

The model also throws new light on phenomena which were rather difficult to fit into our usual ideas about measurement in social psychology. Why, for example, should groups differ so markedly in their performance on nearly parallel tasks? The model—and our data—show that the situation becomes easier for the leader as the group moves from the novel to the already known group-task situations. The leaders who excel under relatively novel and therefore more difficult conditions are not necessarily those who excel under those which are more routine, or better known, and therefore more favorable. Likewise, we find that different types of task structure require different types of leader behavior. Thus, in a research project's early phases the project director tends to be democratic and permissive: everyone is urged to contribute to the plan and to criticize all aspects of the design. This situation changes radically in the more structured phase when the research design is frozen and the experiment is underway. Here the research director tends to become managing, controlling, and highly autocratic and woe betide the assistant who attempts to be creative in giving instructions to subjects, or in his timing of tests. A similar situation is often found in business organization where the routine operation tends to be well structured and calls for a managing, directive leadership. The situation becomes suddenly unstructured when a crisis occurs. Under these conditions the number of discussions, meetings, and conferences increases sharply so as to give everyone an opportunity to express his views.

At best, this model is of course only a partial theory of leadership. The leader's intellectual and task-relevant abilities, and the members' skills and motivation, all play a role in affecting the group's performance. It is to be hoped that these other important aspects of group interaction can be incorporated into the model in the not too distant future.

References

BASS, B. M. *Leadership, psychology and organizational behavior.* New York: Harper & Row, 1960.

BROWNE, C. G., and COHN, T. S. (Eds.). *The study of leadership.* Danville, Ill.: Interstate Printers and Publishers, 1958.

CLEVEN, W. A., and FIEDLER, F. E. Interpersonal perceptions of open hearth foremen and steel production. *J. appl. Psychol.,* 1956, 40, 312-314.

CRONBACH, L. J., and GLESER, GOLDENE, C. Assessing similarity between profiles. *Psychol. Bull.,* 1953, 50, 456-473.

FIEDLER, F. E. Assumed similarity measures as predictors of team effectiveness. *J. abnorm. soc. Psychol.,* 1954, 49, 381-388.

FIEDLER, F. E. The influence of leader-keymen relations on combat crew effectiveness. *J. abnorm. soc. Psychol.,* 1955, 51, 227-235.

FIEDLER, F. E. Leader attitudes, group climate, and group creativity. *J. abnorm. soc. Psychol.,* 1962, 65, 308-318.

FIEDLER, F. E. A contingency model of leadership effectiveness. In L. Berkowitz (Ed.), *Advances in experimental social psychology,* New York: Academic Press, 1964.

FIEDLER, F. E., and MEUWESE, W. A. T. The leader's contribution to performance in cohesive and uncohesive groups. *J. abnorm. soc. Psychol.,* 1963, 67, 83-87.

FIEDLER, F. E., MEUWESE, W. A. T., and OONK, SOPHIE. Performance of laboratory tasks requiring group creativity. *Acta Psychologica,* 1961, 18, 100-119.

FRENCH, J. R. P., JR. A formal theory of social power. *Psychol. Rev.,* 1956, 63, 181-194.

GIBB, C. A. Leadership. In G. Lindzey (Ed.), *Handbook of social psychology,* Vol. 2. Reading, Mass.: Addison-Wesley, 1954.

GODFREY, ELEANOR P., FIEDLER, F. E., and HALL, D. M. *Boards, management, and company success.* Danville, Ill.: Interstate Printers and Publishers, 1959.

HARE, A. P. *Handbook of small group research.* New York: The Free Press of Glencoe, 1962.

HAWKINS, C. A study of factors mediating a relationship between leader rating behavior and group productivity. Unpublished Ph.D. dissertation, Univer. of Minnesota, 1962.

HUTCHINS, E. B., and FIEDLER, F. E. Task-oriented and quasi-therapeutic role functions of the leader in small military groups. *Sociometry,* 1960, 23, 293-406.

JULIAN, J. W., and MCGRATH, J. E. *The influence of leader and member behavior on the adjustment and task effectiveness of negotiation groups.* Urbana, Ill.: Group Effectiveness Research Laboratory, Univer. of Illinois, 1963.

MCGRATH, J. E. *A summary of small group research studies.* Arlington, Va.: Human Sciences Research Inc., 1962 (Litho.).

MANN, R. D. A review of the relationship between personality and performance in small groups. *Psychol. Bull.,* 1959, 56, 241-270.

MEUWESE, W. A. T. The effect of the leader's ability and interpersonal attitudes on group creativity under varying conditions of stress. Unpublished doctoral dissertation, Univer. of Amsterdam, 1964.

MORRIS, C. G., II. The effects of leader attitudes on the behavior of problem solving groups and their leaders. Unpublished MA thesis, Univer. of Illinois, 1964.

Osgood, C. E., Suci, G. A., and Tannenbaum, P. H. *The measurement of meaning.* Urbana, Ill.: Univer. of Illinois Press, 1957.

Shaw, M. E. Annual Technical Report, 1962. Gainesville, Fla.: Univer. of Florida, 1962 (Mimeo.).

Stogdill, R. M. Personal factors associated with leadership: a survey of the literature. *J. Psychol.*, 1948, 25, 35-71.

Stogdill, R. M., and Coons, A. E. Leader behavior: its description and measurement. Columbus, Ohio: Ohio State University, *Res. Monogr. No. 88*, 1957.

D. GROUP STRUCTURE

AND PROCESS

The Effects of Cooperation and
Competition upon Group Process ❧ Morton Deutsch

The concept of *cooperation* and the interrelated concept of *competition* are rarely missing in discussions of interpersonal and intergroup relations. Implicitly, they play a key role in the writings of many social theorists. Yet, despite the obvious significance of these concepts for the understanding and control of social process, there has been little in the way of explicit theorizing and virtually no experimental work with respect to the effects of cooperation and competition upon social process. The work in this area has largely been concerned with the effects of the individual's motivation to achieve under the two different conditions. None of the experimental studies has investigated the interactions between individuals, the group process that emerges as a consequence of the cooperative or competitive social situation.

The purpose of this article is to sketch out a theory of the effects of cooperation and competition upon small (face-to-face) group functioning and to present the results of an experimental study of such effects.

Part I—A Conceptualization of the Cooperative and Competitive Situations with a Development of Some of Its Logical and Psychological Implications

In a *cooperative social situation* the goals for the individuals or subunits in the situation under consideration have the following characteristics: the goal regions for each of the individuals or subunits in the situation are defined so that a goal region can be entered (to some degree) by any given individual or subunit only if all the individuals or subunits under consideration can also enter their respective goal regions (to some degree). For convenience's sake, the phrase *promotively interdependent goals* will be used to identify any situation in which the individuals or subunits composing it have their goals interrelated by the characteristic defined above.

In a *competitive social situation* the goals for the individuals or subunits in the situation under consideration have the following characteristic: the goal regions for each of the individuals or subunits in the situation are defined so that, if a goal region is entered by any individual or subunit (or by any given portion of the individuals or subunits under consideration), the other individuals or subunits will, to some degree, be unable to reach their respective goals in the social situation under consideration. For convenience's sake, the phrase *contriently interdependent goals* will be used to identify any situation in which the individuals or subunits composing it have their goals interrelated by the characteristic defined immediately above.

It should, perhaps, be noted that there are probably very few, if any, real-life situations which, according to the definitions offered above, are "purely" cooperative or competitive. Most situations of everyday life involve a complex set of goals and subgoals. Consequently, it is possible for individuals to be promotively interdependent with respect to one goal and contriently interdependent with respect to another goal. Thus, for example, the members of a basketball team may be cooperatively interrelated with respect to winning the game, but competitively interrelated with respect to being the "star" of the team.

It is also rather common for people to be promotively interdependent with respect to subgoals and contriently interdependent with respect to goals, or vice versa. For instance, advertising concerns respresenting different cigarette companies may be cooperatively interrelated with respect to the subgoal of increasing the general consumption of cigarettes but competitively interrelated with respect to the goal of increasing both the relative and absolute sales of a specific brand of cigarette.

No attempt will be made here to describe and analyze further the wide variety of "impure" cooperative and competitive situations which are found in everyday life. The theoretical development to be presented will be primarily concerned with "pure" cooperative and competitive situations. However, it is believed that in many circumstances not much theoretical extrapolation is necessary to handle the more complex situations.

From the definitions of promotively and contriently interdependent goals, it appears to follow that (*a*) any person, X, who has promotively interdependent goals with persons A, B, C, etc., will come to have promotively interdependent locomotions in the direction of his goal with persons A, B, C, etc.; (*b*) any person, Y, who has contriently interdependent goals with persons A, B, C, etc., will come to have contriently interdependent locomotions in the direction of his goal with persons A, B, C, etc.

The above statements are based on the following considerations. Locomotion in the direction of the goal, from any point not in the goal region, may be thought of as a condition for entry into the goal region. Entry into the goal region may be thought of as a part of locomotion in the direction of the goal, entry being the final step in locomotion. It follows that a locomotion by X or Y in the direction of his goal can be considered to be promotively or contriently interdependent with the locomotions of A, B, C, etc., in the direction of their goals, the nature of the interdependence with respect to locomotions depending upon the nature of the interdependence with respect to goal regions.

Several major differences reveal themselves as inherent in the distinctions between the cooperative and competitive social situations. The analysis of the cooperative situation reveals that all the individuals in such a setting occupy the same relative positions with respect to their goals. If any one individual locomotes, the others must also locomote in the same direction. In the competitive situations, the various individuals may occupy the same or different positions with respect to their goals. Locomotion by any individual has no necessary effect on the locomotions of others, though it may affect the relative positions of the various individuals.

Up to this point we have stated some of the consequences logically inherent in the conceptualizations of simple cooperative and competitive situations. No statements have been made which have a direct psychological reference, i.e., a reference in terms of individual life spaces. The statements have had reference only to an objectively defined social space.

The next step called for is to derive psychological implications from these statements by introducing additional psychological assumptions which will somehow relate these statements about events in objective social space to events in individual life spaces. It should be apparent that very complex assumptions are required to make any rigorously derived predictions about behavior from an analysis of the characteristics of an objective social situation. However, as this problem relates to the specific conditions of the experiment to be reported here, we shall make the relatively simple assumption that the perceptions and expectations of an individual are likely to be veridical to his environment if he has had enough experience with the situation, if he has intelligence, and if the situation is simple enough.

We may now proceed to state certain specific hypotheses.

Basic Hypotheses

Hypothesis 1. Individuals who are exposed to the cooperative social situation (*Indiv coop*) will perceive themselves to be more promotively interdependent (in relation to the other individuals composing their group) with respect to goal, locomotions, facilitations, and similar matters, than will individuals who are exposed to the competitive social situation (*Indiv comp*).

Hypothesis 1a. *Indiv comp* will perceive themselves to be more contriently interdependent (in relation to the other individuals composing their group) with respect to such matters as goal, locomotions, and facilitations than will *Indiv coop*.

For convenience's sake, let us direct our attention to the psychological implications of locomotion in the cooperative and the competitive situations. Let us analyze a hypothetical instance with respect to locomotion in the direction of the goal, in which A locomotes in the direction of his goal and the other individuals in the social situation perceive that A is locomoting.

1. THE COOPERATIVE SITUATION

Under these conditions X would be likely to perceive that he has locomoted toward his goal as a consequence of A's actions. Several implications seem directly to follow, if we accept certain additional psychological assumptions:

Substitutability. Since X has locomoted toward his goal as a consequence of A's actions, there is no longer any necessity for X to perform any action which is similar to A's.

Positive Cathexis. If we make a rather widely accepted assumption that an entity will acquire positive valence or cathexis if that entity is seen to be promotively related to need satisfaction, it is possible to derive that A's action (which results in locomotion in the direction of the goal) will be positively cathected by X. That is, X is likely to accept, like, or reward A's action.

Positive Inducibility. Let us assume that inducibility derives from the fact that the inducible person perceives the inducing entity to be such that it can cause the intensification, continued persistence, or lowering of need tension within himself. Positive inducibility[1] occurs when the inducing entity is seen to be promotive rather than contrient with respect to tension reduction (or when the inducing entity is seen as capable of producing even more tension than before).

Making the above assumption, one can

---

[1] Positive inducibility is meant to include two related phenomena, (*a*) the production of additional *own* forces in the direction induced, and (*b*) the channeling of existing *own* forces in the direction induced.

derive that X will stand in the relationship of positive inducibility to A insofar as A's action contributes towards X's locomotion in the direction of his goal.

Facilitations and Hinderings. If X facilitates the locomotion of A in the direction of his goal, he also facilitates his own locomotion. Thus, X's facilitations of others are likely to result in his own locomotion and therefore are also likely to result in tension reduction with respect to that locomotion. His own actions of facilitation (helpfulness) will become positively cathected and will be likely to be manifested in appropriate situations. By similar reasoning, we conclude that acts hindering locomotion in the direction of the goal (obstructiveness) will be negatively cathected and will be avoided.

2. THE COMPETITIVE SITUATION

Under conditions of competition essentially opposite conclusions to those above are to be drawn:

Substitutability. It is evident that there will be no substitutability.

Negative Cathexis. The assumption here is parallel to that made in deriving positive cathexis. An entity will acquire negative cathexis if that entity is seen to be contriently related to need satisfaction (and therefore is seen to decrease the probability of need satisfaction). A's locomotions in the direction of his goal will, therefore, be negatively cathected by Y.

Negative Inducibility. Assuming that negative inducibility[2] occurs when the inducing entity is seen as contrient with respect to tension reduction, one can derive that Y will stand in the relationship of negative inducibility to A insofar as A's actions lead to locomotions by A which decrease Y's probability of reaching his goal. However,

[2] Negative inducibility is meant to include two related phenomena, (*a*) the production of additional *own* forces, and (*b*) channeling existing *own* forces in the direction opposite to that desired by the inducer.

another factor, cognitive in nature, may come into play making Y's relation to B one of ambivalence or noninducibility—the cognition that going in a direction opposite to or away from A's would be going in a direction opposite to or away from his own goal.

Facilitations and Hinderings. When others locomote in the direction of the goal, helpfulness will become negatively cathected, obstructiveness positively cathected. The converse should be true for locomotion in a direction opposite to that of the goal.

We can, with the same kinds of assumptions, analyze a hypothetical instance in which B locomotes in a direction away from his goal. Without detailing the analysis, it is evident that in the cooperative situation, substitutability is not expected, but one would expect negative cathexis and negative inducibility. The competitive situation is not so unequivocal. Here one would expect positive cathexis and ambivalent inducibility or noninducibility.

Our statements about substitutability, cathexis, inducibility, and helpfulness are somewhat different in the two social situations, depending upon whether locomotions are made in the direction of the goal or away from it. To test the theory experimentally, it is necessary, therefore, to make some assumption about the incidence of these two directions of locomotion. We assume that, under the experimental conditions set up to test the theory, in both social situations there will be more locomotions in the direction of the goal than in a direction away from the goal. From this assumption and the foregoing analysis it is possible to assert the following hypotheses:

Hypothesis 2. There will be greater substitutability for similarly intended actions among *Indiv coop* as contrasted with *Indiv comp*.

Hypothesis 3. There will be a larger percentage of actions by fellow members positively cathected by *Indiv coop* than by *Indiv comp*.

Hypothesis 3a. There will be a larger percentage of actions by fellow members negatively cathected by *Indiv comp* than by *Indiv coop.*

Hypothesis 4. There will be greater positive inducibility with respect to fellow members among *Indiv coop* than among *Indiv comp.*

Hypothesis 4a. There will be greater internal (self) conflict among *Indiv comp* than among *Indiv coop.*

Hypothesis 5. There will be more helpfulness towards one another among *Indiv coop* than among *Indiv comp.*

Hypothesis 5a. There will be more obstructiveness towards one another among *Indiv comp* than among *Indiv coop.*

Implications for Group Functioning

Let us turn now to the next step, that of applying some of the psychological implications of the hypotheses derived in the preceding section to the functioning of small face-to-face groups.

ORGANIZATION

From Hypothesis 4 (positive inducibility), it seems evident that one would expect greater coordination of effort, as well as more frequent interrelationship of activity, among *Indiv coop* than among *Indiv comp.*

Hypothesis 6. At any given time there will be more coordination of efforts (working together, interrelation of activities) among *Indiv coop* than among *Indiv comp.*

Hypothesis 6a. Over a period of time, there will be more frequent coordination of efforts among *Indiv coop* than among *Indiv comp.*

If we assume that the individuals composing the various groups in both the cooperative and competitive situations differ from one another with respect to ability or personal inclinations to contribute, it is possible from the substitutability hypothesis (Hyp. 2) to derive:

Hypothesis 7. There will be more homogeneity with respect to amount of contributions or participations among *Indiv comp* than among *Indiv coop.*

The above hypothesis follows from the consideration that the contribution of an *Indiv coop* can substitute for similarly intended contributions by another *Indiv coop.* This does not hold for *Indiv comp.* In the cooperative situation, if any individual has ability and contributes, there is less need for another individual to contribute, producing greater heterogeneity in amount of contributions.

Making the same kinds of assumptions as above, plus the additional ones that the individuals comprising the various groups differ in respect to either ability, interest, or both, in performing the various functions necessary for successful task completion, it is possible from the substitutability hypothesis to derive:

Hypothesis 8. There will be greater specialization of function (i.e., different individuals fulfilling different functions) among *Indiv coop* than among *Indiv comp.*

If we assume some time or achievement pressure, from the substitutability hypothesis it is also possible to derive:

Hypothesis 9. There will be greater specialization with respect to content or activity (i.e., different individuals takng different aspects of the task and working on them simultaneously) among *Indiv coop* than among *Indiv comp.*

The structure of certain kinds of tasks makes it extremely difficult for this type of specialization to take place. Thus, one would expect fewer differences between *Indiv coop* and *Indiv comp* on some tasks than on others.

If specialization of function occurs, and we assume that expectations are established as a result of this specialization and that these expectations act as a determinant of behavior, we would expect:

Hypothesis 10. There will be greater structural stability (from like situation to like situation) with respect to functions assumed among *Indiv coop* than among *Indiv comp*. This difference will increase with time.

From the lack of substitutability among *Indiv comp* one can derive a rigidity, each individual always trying to fulfill all the functions. Stability of structure among *Indiv coop* may result in some perseverance but there does not seem to be any reason to equate rigidity and stability.

Hypothesis 11. In the face of changing circumstances, more organizational flexibility (change of roles to adapt to circumstances) will be manifested among *Indiv coop* than among *Indiv comp*.

MOTIVATION

From the hypothesis about positive inducibility one can expect:

Hypothesis 12. The direction of the forces operating on *Indiv coop* will be more similar than the direction of the forces operating on *Indiv comp*.

From this hypothesis one would expect more rapid locomotions, i.e., more rapid decisions and reaching of agreements by cooperative groups. Another point to be considered here is that of the frame of reference with respect to locomotion in the cooperative and competitive situations. In the latter situation, the individual is oriented to locomotions relative to those of other individuals with whom he is competing; in the cooperative situation, meaningful locomotion units are defined in relation to task completion. One can therefore expect:

Hypothesis 13. The directions of the forces on *Indiv coop* will be more toward task closure than will the forces on *Indiv comp*, i.e., there is more achievement pressure on *Indiv coop*.

From the hypothesis of positive inducibility we can assert that a force on any *Indiv coop* is likely to be paralleled by a force on other *Indiv coop*. Thus, if we define *group motivation* as some complex function of the strength of forces that operate simultaneously on all individuals in the group, there follows:

Hypothesis 14. The group force in the direction of the goal in a cooperative group will be stronger than such a group force in a competitive group.

From positive inducibility we would expect more additional own forces to be induced on *Indiv coop* once he is exposed to induction by other members. In the competitive situation, due to combined negative and positive induction, one would also expect the production of additional own forces. If to the concept of the sum of the strength of forces operating on an individual we coordinate interest, or involvement, there does not seem to be any clear-cut rationale for predicting differences between the situations.

Hypothesis 15. There will not be a significant difference in the total strength of the forces (interest, involvement) operating on *Indiv coop* and *Indiv comp*.

COMMUNICATION

From the substitutability hypothesis and the additional assumptions that (a) it is perceived that locomotion takes place either through the utterance of many good ideas, i.e., the production of many signs that will be evaluated highly, or through the frequent persuasion or informing of others via communication; (b) quantitative efforts do not seriously interfere with quality or that, if they do, quantity is seen to be as important as or more important than quality; and (c) the time available allows for more production of signs than are necessary for optimal solution of any problem, it is possible to derive:

Hypothesis 16. When the task structure is such that production in quantity of observable signs is perceived to be a means for locomotion, there will be a greater total of signs produced per unit of time by *Indiv comp* than by *Indiv coop*.

From the hypothesis about the coordination of effort in tasks (Hyps. 6 and 6a), one would expect:

Hypothesis 17. When the task structure is such that locomotion is possible without the production of observable signs, there will be a greater total production of such signs per unit time by *Indiv coop* than by *Indiv comp*.

If from the communicator's point of view communication can be considered a locomotion or a means of locomotion, the state of receptivity, i.e., the readiness to be aroused, in the communicatee can potentially facilitate or hinder the locomotions of the communicator. From the hypotheses concerning helpfulness and obstructiveness (Hyps. 5 and 5a) one can derive:

Hypothesis 18. There will be less attentiveness to one another's productions of signs among *Indiv comp* than among *Indiv coop*.

If attentiveness is a condition for the arousing of common significata, there follows:

Hypothesis 19. The production of signs will less frequently result in common significata among *Indiv comp* than among *Indiv coop*.

Even when attentiveness is present, there probably will be a greater likelihood of distortion by communicatees in the competitive situation, since in this situation locomotion is likely to be perceived in terms of its effect on relative position, while in the cooperative situation the locomotion of any individual is likely to be perceived as resulting in the locomotion of the others. The consequence of this difference is that the expressive characteristics of the production of signs are likely to be more significant to *Indiv comp*. A sign is expressive if the fact of its production is itself a sign to its interpreter of something about the producer of the sign.

Hypothesis 20. Common signification, even when attentiveness is optimal, will be less prevalent among *Indiv comp* than *Indiv coop*.

From the hypothesis of positive inducibility, there follows directly:

Hypothesis 21. There will be more common appraisals (mutual agreements and acceptances) of communications by communicators and communicatees among *Indiv coop* than among *Indiv comp*.

ORIENTATION

From the hypothesis about communication, one can assert:

Hypothesis 22. *Indiv coop* will have more knowledge about other active members than will *Indiv comp*.

Group orientation, as we define it, exists to the extent that there is commonality of perception among the members. It can be assessed in relation to goals, position at a given time, direction to the goal, or steps in the path to the goal. From the hypotheses concerning communication and positive inducibility, one can derive:

Hypothesis 23. There will be more group orientation among *Indiv coop* than among *Indiv comp*.

GROUP PRODUCTIVITY

From the hypothesis with respect to strength of group motivation (Hyp. 14), assuming that locomotion will proceed more rapidly the stronger the motivation, one can derive:

Hypothesis 24. *Indiv coop* as a group will produce more per unit of time than will *Indiv comp* as a group.
Hypothesis 24a. It will take less time for *Indiv coop* as a group to produce what *Indiv comp* as a group produce.

Let us assume that any or all of the following are negatively related to group productivity in respect to quality of product: lack of coordination, communication difficulties, persisting internal conflict, and lack of group orientation. We can then derive:

Hypothesis 25. The qualitative productivity of *Indiv coop* as a group will be higher than that of *Indiv comp* as a group.

From the hypotheses about communication and about positive inducibility, with the additional assumption that the individuals in the various groups have information and experience that can benefit the others, it is possible to derive:

Hypothesis 26. *Indiv coop* will learn more from one another than will *Indiv comp*. (The more knowledgeable and experienced of *Indiv coop* will, of course, learn less than the not so well-informed *Indiv coop*.)

INTERPERSONAL RELATIONS

From the hypotheses about cathexis (Hyps. 3 and 3a), we expect the actions of fellow members to be more positively cathected among *Indiv coop* than among *Indiv comp*. We also expect the perceived source of these actions to acquire, to some extent, a cathexis similar to that held with respect to the actions. Thus, there follows:

Hypothesis 27. There will be more friendliness among *Indiv coop* than among *Indiv comp*.

By similar reasoning, it follows that the cathexis will be generalized to the products of the joint actions of fellow members and oneself, i.e., the group products. Thus, we propose:

Hypothesis 28. The group products will be evaluated more highly by *Indiv coop* than by *Indiv comp*.

If we define *group functions* as any actions which are intended to increase the solidarity of the group, or to maintain and regulate the group so that it functions smoothly, and assert that group functions are seen to be helpful, from the hypothesis about helpfulness (Hyp. 5a) there follows:

Hypothesis 29. There will be a greater per-

centage of group functions among *Indiv coop* than among *Indiv comp*.

If we define *individual functions* as any actions of the individual which are not immediately directed toward task solution and which are not group functions (actions which are obstructive, blocking, aggressive, or self-defensive are individual functions), from the hypothesis about obstructiveness (Hyp. 5a) there follows:

Hypothesis 30. There will be a greater percentage of individual functions among *Indiv comp* than among *Indiv coop*.

From the hypothesis concerning communication, it was developed (Hyp. 22) that over a period of time *Indiv coop* should know more than *Indiv comp* about the attitudes of (active) fellow members. Using the same reasoning, and making the assumption that the communication difficulty with respect to this content is also greater for *Indiv comp*, there follows:

Hypothesis 31. The perception of the attitudes of the others towards aspects of one's own functioning in the group by *Indiv coop* should be more realistic than such perceptions by *Indiv comp*.

From the hypothesis about inducibility, there also follows:

Hypothesis 32. The attitudes of any individual with respect to his own functioning should be more similar to the attitudes of the others with respect to his functioning among *Indiv coop* than among *Indiv comp*.

From Hypothesis 31 and the hypothesis about cathexis, we can derive with respect to *Indiv coop* that he has a favorable effect on the others in the group. If we make the assumption of *autistic hostility*, that is, that hostile impulses under conditions of reduced communication tend to create the expectation of counter-hostility, we can demonstrate:

Hypothesis 33. *Indiv coop* will perceive himself as having more favorable effects on fellow members than will *Indiv comp*.

The term *attitude of the generalized other* refers to an internalized structure which is developed as a result of introjecting the mutually interacting attitudes of those with whom one is commonly engaged in a social process. From our preceding discussion, it is clear that the development of the attitude of the generalized other requires communication and positive inducibility. There follows, then:

Hypothesis 34. Incorporation of the attitude of the generalized other will occur to a greater extent in *Indiv coop* than in *Indiv comp*.

For present purposes, the *feeling of obligation* to other members will be taken as an operational definition of the degree of internalized attitude of the generalized other.

Part II—An Experimental Study of the Effects of Cooperation and Competition upon Group Process

The Experimental Design

In setting up the experiment to test the hypotheses it was necessary to have the following: (*a*) intelligent and reasonably well-adjusted subjects who would regularly attend experimental sessions over a period of time; (*b*) some degree of control over the goals the subjects strove for (to be able, through manipulations of these goals, to place the subjects in cooperative or competitive situations); and (*c*) a readily observable situation.

The somewhat unorthodox Introductory Psychology course offered by the Industrial Relations Section at the Massachusetts Institute of Technology appeared to provide the needed conditions. Through the excellent cooperation of the Industrial Relations Section, it became possible to make the experimental sessions an integral part of the course. Regular attendance was thus assured. The experimenter-instructor's control over grades and assignments also provided the needed degree of control over the goals of the subjects.

At the first meeting of the various sections, it was announced that the department was interested in doing research on the course and wanted to form some small sections to be composed of five students and one instructor. These sections would meet once weekly as a substitute for the regularly scheduled three one-hour meetings. Nothing was stated about the research except that it had the purpose of improving the course. Volunteers were requested and over 50 were obtained, which was more than enough. The volunteers were then formed into 10 tentative groups on the basis of their available meeting times. Though this very much limited the possibility of matching personalities as well as groups, some flexibility still remained because of the large overlappings of time schedules.

All the volunteers were administered the following tests: The A-S Reaction Study, Wide Range Vocabulary Test, and the University of California ideology questionnaires. On the basis of these tests and other face-sheet data about the individuals, the most deviant students were eliminated as subjects. The time schedules of the remaining subjects did not allow for further shifting of subjects from group to group.

The next step was to match pairs of groups. Each group, at its first meeting together, was told, "You are to be constituted as a board of human relations experts. As experts, each week you will be presented a human relations problem. Your job is to analyze and discuss the problem and to formulate, in letter form, some written recommendations." They were then given a human relations problem having to do with a question of discipline in a children's camp. A total of 50 minutes for the discussion and writing of recommendations was allowed. Each of the groups was rated by the experimenter on a nine-point scale in terms of the productivity of their discussion of the problem. Groups were then paired off in terms of these ratings, and by a random procedure one of each pair was assigned to the cooperative treatment and the other to the competitive treatment.

Experimental Procedures

Instructions designed to produce the cooperative or the competitive situation were given at the beginning of the second meeting to the appropriate groups. The two sets of instructions are presented below.[3]

INSTRUCTIONS TO
COOPERATIVE GROUPS

Puzzle Problems. Every week you will be given a puzzle to solve as a group. These puzzles are, in effect, tests of your ability to do clear, logical thinking as a group. Your effectiveness in handling the problem will be evaluated by ranking you as a group in comparison with four other groups who will also tackle the same problems. Each of the five groups will be ranked. The group that works together most effectively will receive a rank of 1, the next most effective group will receive a rank of 2, the least effective group will receive a rank of 5. The ranks that each group receives on the weekly problems will be averaged. At the end of it all, we should be able to have a pretty good picture of each group's ability to do clear, logical thinking.

To motivate you to contribute your best efforts, we will have a reward. The group that comes out with the best average will be excused from one term paper and will receive an automatic *H* for that paper. That is, if your group receives the highest rank, all of you will receive an automatic *H*.[4]

You are to come out with one solution as a group. When you have decided as a group that you have reached a solution,

let me know by handing me your answer written on this answer sheet.

Human Relations Problems. There are two principal factors determining your grade for this course: (*a*) the discussions in class of the human relations problems, and (*b*) the papers you hand in periodically.

Your grade for the discussions in class will be determined in the following manner:

Each week the plans or recommendations that the group comes out with as a result of discussion will be judged and evaluated by ranking them in comparison with the efforts of four other similar groups. The group whose discussions and recommendations are judged to be best (in terms of both quality and quantity of ideas) will receive a rank of 1, the next best group a rank of 2, and so on; the worst group will receive a rank of 5.

Every member of the group will be given the rank that his group receives. That is, all members of a group will receive the same rank, the rank being determined by how good their group discussions and recommendations are.

The ranks that are received weekly will be averaged and used in making up that part of the grade which is based on class discussion.

Thus, in effect, you are to consider the discussions of these human relations problems presented to you weekly as a test in which your group rank or grade is determined by your ability to effectively apply insight to these problems. Remember, the group whose discussions and recommendations are best in quality and quantity will get the highest grade; the group whose discussions and recommendations are worst will get the lowest grade.

In this meeting, as in all the other meetings, you will consider yourself to be a board of human relations experts. As such, you have been presented with the following problem which I will read to you. You may glance at your copies of the problem as I read, if you wish to do so. (*The problem was then read by the experimenter.*)

You will be allowed a total of 50 minutes for both the discussion and the writing of recommendations. You are to write

[3] "Pure" cooperative and competitive situations were not created by the instructions. Other goals, related to such needs as recognition and affiliation, made it possible for these instructions to produce only relative differences of cooperation and competition.

[4] An *H* at M.I.T. is the highest grade obtainable.

your recommendations in letter style, on this form which I have provided.

You will be notified when you have only 20 minutes, 10 minutes, and 5 minutes left.

INSTRUCTIONS TO COMPETITIVE GROUPS

Puzzle Problems. Every week you will be given a puzzle to solve as a group. These puzzles are, in effect, tests of your individual abilities to do clear, logical thinking. The contributions that each of you make to solving the weekly puzzle will be ranked, so that the person who contributes most to the solution will receive a rank of 1, the one who contributes next most will receive a rank of 2, etc. The one who contributes least will receive a rank of 5. The ranks that each of you receive on the weekly problems will be averaged. At the end of it all, we should have a pretty good picture of each individual's ability to do clear, logical thinking.

To motivate you to contribute your best individual efforts, we will have a reward for the individual who comes out with the best average. He will be excused from one term paper and will receive an automatic *H* for that paper.

You are to come out with one solution as a group. When you have decided as a group that you have reached a solution, let me know by handing me your answer written on this answer sheet.

Human Relations Problem. There are two principal factors determining your grade for this course: (*a*) the discussions in class of the human relations problems, and (*b*) the papers you hand in periodically.

Your grades for the discussion in class will be determined in the following manner:

Each week the contributions that each of you makes to the plan of recommendations that the group comes out with as a result of discussion will be ranked so that the individual contributing the most (in terms of both quality and quantity of ideas) to the group plan will receive a rank of 1, the individual contributing next most will get a 2, and so on; the individual who contributes least will get a 5.

The ranks that each individual receives from week to week will be averaged and will be used in making up that part of his grade which is based on class discussion.

Thus, in effect, you are to consider the discussions of these human relations problems presented to you weekly as a test, in which each of you is being ranked and graded on your individual ability to effectively apply insight to these problems. Remember, the individual who contributes most in quality and quantity to the discussions and recommendations will get the highest grades; the individual who contributes least will get the lowest grades.

In this meeting, as in all the other meetings, you will consider yourself to be a board of human relations experts. As such, you have been presented with the following problem which I will read to you. You may glance at your copies of the problem as I read, if you wish to do so. (*The problem was then read by the experimenter.*)

You will be allowed a total of 50 minutes for both the discussion and the writing of recommendations. You are to write your recommendations in letter style, on this form which I have provided.

You will be notified when you have only 20 minutes, 10 minutes, and 5 minutes left.

The cooperation of the subjects in not discussing problems and procedures outside of the group meetings was solicited. The same instructions were repeated at each group meeting. Subjects in both the cooperative and competitive groups were not informed about their weekly grades until the end of the experiment.

During the five weeks of experimentation, each of the groups met once weekly for a period of approximately three hours. The schedule of a meeting was as follows: (*a*) The experimenter read the appropriate instructions for the puzzles. (*b*) The group undertook the solution of the puzzle. (c) The students filled out a brief questionnaire while the observers made various ratings. (d) The experimenter read the appropriate instructions for the human relations problem. (e) The group was allowed a total of 50 minutes for the discussion and writing of recommendations. (f) The students then filled out a lengthy questionnaire. (g) There was a 10-15 minute break. (h) The rest of the three hours the experimenter lectured, encouraging active discussion, on psychological principles such as are involved in "need theory," "level of aspiration," and "conflict." Each of the 10 groups received the same informal lectures in any given week.

It should be clear that the discussion and solution of both the puzzles and the human relations problems were undertaken by the various groups without the participation of the experimenter-instructor. During these discussions he sat at a table with the other observers and functioned as an observer.

It should be emphasized that the only differences introduced into the three-hour meetings by the experimenter-instructor were the differences in instructions read to the cooperative and competitive groups. The experimenter-instructor tried to create a friendly, informal, but impersonal relationship with all groups.

THE PROBLEMS

The background considerations previously outlined dictated that human relations problems be used as group tasks. In addition, for comparative purposes, it was thought that it would be interesting to have the groups confronted with problems of a rather different type. The human relations problems are tasks in which there are no clearly discernible objective criteria of locomotion; they are tasks in which the group itself, through consensus, provides the criteria for judging locomotion. In addition, the content of these problems is likely to evoke strongly held personal value systems. The puzzle problems were, for convenience, chosen for contrast. Due to their objective (i.e., logically demonstrable) solutions, locomotion could take place without group consensus. This, of course, provided the possibility for relatively more individual work in the puzzles than in the human relations problems. The relative lack of ideological relevance of the content of the puzzle problems also made conflict more likely in the human relations problems.

It is possible that the sequence in which the problems were presented might influence the results obtained. Care was taken, therefore, to control this influence. With the limited number of subjects and groups available it was decided that a latin-square design would be most appropriate. This design makes it possible to vary systematically from group to group the sequence in which the different problems were presented. It permits the effective elimination and estimation (by statistical methods) of the effect of differences among groups, due to the effect of sequence in which the problems are presented, and the effect of different kinds of problems.

Measuring Instruments
INSTRUMENTS USED BY THE OBSERVERS

For most of the experiment there were four observers. Two major tasks, among others, were assigned to the different observers.

1. The Functions Observations Sheet.
The job of the observer was to categorize each participation of the members in terms of the following: (a) who spoke (or gestured), (b) to whom the remark was addressed, (c) the intent of the participant, and (d) the length of the participation. Arbitrarily it was decided to use the *utterance* to define a unit of participation, with the exception that if more than one function distinctly occurred in any utterance two or more categorizations would be made. To provide the possibility of cross-analysis with

other instruments, a new *functions sheet* was used for each 5-minute period. To facilitate tabulation no attempt was made to retain sequence of utterances or the linkage "who-to-whom."

The categories used in the Functions Observation Sheet were divided into three broad groupings:[5]

Task functions include participations which are directed toward the task with which the group is confronted. These functions have as their immediate purpose the facilitation of problem solution. Included in this grouping are such functions as "initiator-contributor," "information-giver," "position-stater," "elaborator," "co-ordinator," "orientor," "evaluator-critic," "energizer," and "information-seeker."

Group functions include participations which are directed toward the functioning of the group. They have for their immediate purpose the maintenance, strengthening, regulation, or perpetuation of the group. Included here are such functions as "en-courager-rewarder," "harmonizer-mediator," "good group member," "gate-keeper," "standard-setter," "follower," and "group observer."

Individual functions include participations which are directed toward the satisfaction of the participant's individual needs. They have for their immediate purpose the reaching of an individual goal which is neither task nor group relevant. The goal is individual in the sense that the satisfaction aimed at by the participant cannot be participated in by the others, either at all or in the same way. Such functions are grouped here as "play-boy," "sympathy-seeker," "aggressor," "domi-nator," "blocker," "recognition-seeker," "self-defender," and "self-observer."

The observer, using this instrument, was trained for approximately 30 hours before

observing the experimental group meetings.

2. *The Over-all Rating Scales.* These are a series of nine-point rating scales which were rated by each observer at the end of each problem. They covered such things as group-discussion productivity, group orientation, self-centeredness, involvement, communication difficulties, attentiveness, and acceptance-rejection. All the rating scales apply to the entire discussion of any given problem.

In considering the various ratings, we should keep in mind that it was impossible to maintain any absolute standards. The ratings more or less presumed a standard of judgment based on experience with groups of introductory psychology students. Thus, the emphasis throughout will be primarily on the direction of the obtained differences rather than on size of differences between the two types of groups.

The results themselves give prima-facie evidence that the observing instruments have sufficient reliability for many of the present purposes. The validity of the observations and ratings, however, cannot be directly determined from the results. One of the primary questions that may arise with respect to the validity of the observations may be concerned with a possible bias among the observers. Thus, if the observers were disposed to see the cooperative groups as being better than the competitive groups, any significant results might be a reflection of this predisposition rather than of real differences.

There is no simple way to insure that the observers had no such predispositions. However, two kinds of evidence support the belief that the observers did not bias their observations in terms of any preconceptions about cooperation and competition:[6] (*a*) The observers made impromptu statements to the effect that, if they were allowed to keep the instructions in mind, they would

---

[5] This classification was developed by the present author in conjunction with this research project. It was also used by the National Training Laboratory in Group Development and was the basis for an article appearing under the authorship of Benne and Sheats. For fuller description of this system of classification, see the article by Benne and Sheats, 1948.

[6] The observers were never informed by the experimenter of the hypotheses being investigated.

have a better interpretive frame of reference for their observations. (b) The second kind of evidence is indirect but, nevertheless, quite convincing. Data collected from the subjects strongly agree with the results from data collected by observers. Since there is no reason to suspect the subjects of bias (they did not know what the experiment was about), this is good indication of lack of bias in the observers.

INSTRUMENTS USED BY THE SUBJECTS

1. *The Weekly Questionnaire.* At each meeting after the discussion of the human relations problems, the subjects filled out a questionnaire. The items on the questionnaire consisted for the most part of rating scales which roughly paralleled those in the observers' Over-all Rating Scales. In addition to such scales as attentiveness, communication difficulties, and acceptance-rejection, the subjects rated interest, group-feeling, amount of group cooperation, group productivity, individual productivity, and anticipated reactions of the others to their own contributions.

2. *The Postexperimental Questionnaire.*[7] One week after the last experimental group meeting, the subjects filled out a lengthy questionnaire covering a range of topics. The questionnaire attempted to get at such things as (a) when first and last names were learned; (b) amount and kinds of social activities mutually engaged in by group members outside of class hours; (c) reactions to the small group meetings, the instructor, and the course; (d) the importance of different factors in motivating the subjects to achieve during the solution of the problems; (e) reaction to the grading system; and (f) reaction to being observed.

Experimental Results

EFFECTIVENESS OF INSTRUCTIONS

It is perhaps important to start out by inquiring about the reactions of the subjects to the two different sets of instructions. Clearly, if the instructions never "got over," one could reasonably question their efficacy in producing differences.

All subjects, when requested (D)[8] to "describe the method by which you were being graded on the human relations problems," responded with an appropriate description. That is, each subject understood and could recall the essentials of the instructions.

In answer to the question (D), "If you had had completely free choice as to the method of grading discussion in class, which would you have preferred?" the following results were obtained:

Grading Method Preferred	Co-operative	Com-petitive	No Preference
By *Indiv coop*	11	6	2
By *Indiv comp*	6	11	3

Assuming these differences did not exist at the beginning of the experiment, one can conclude that roughly the same percentage of individuals were satisfied with the method of grading to which they were exposed.

Clearly, then, the instructions "got over" to the subjects in both kinds of groups and in such a way as to seem satisfactory to approximately the same percentage in both groups.

PERCEIVED INTERDEPENDENCE

Hypothesis 1 asserts that *Indiv coop* will perceive themselves to be more promotively

---

[7] Due to unavoidable circumstances, this questionnaire was given to only four cooperative groups, totaling 19 subjects, and four competitive groups, totaling 20 subjects.

[8] From this point on, (A) will refer to the *Over-all Rating Scales,* (B) to the *Functions Observations Sheet,* (C) to the *Weekly Questionnaire* filled out by subjects, and (D) to the *Postexperimental Questionnaire.*

interdependent than will *Indiv comp*. Table 1 presents some relevant data.

Group-centeredness (we-feeling) was rated by the observers to be considerably higher in the cooperative groups for both the puzzles and the human relations problems. The ratings of the subjects, in the questionnaire pertaining to the human relations problems, give the same results. *Indiv coop* give themselves credit for more "group feeling" than do *Indiv comp*. These differences with respect to group-centeredness and group-feeling are significant at the 1% level for both the puzzles and human relations problems. Thus, the evidence gives

contriently interdependent than will *Indiv coop*) is partly supported by the same evidence. Thus, the competitive group members were rated to be more self-centered by the observers. Likewise, *Indiv comp* rated themselves as being more self-oriented than did *Indiv coop*. "Perceived contrient interdependence," however, seems to include, in addition to "self-centeredness," the notion of "I" versus "the others." To measure this component, the subjects were asked (C), in reference to the human relations problem, "How competitive with the other members in your group did you feel you were, during the discussion?"

TABLE 1

Differences between Cooperative and Competitive Groups on Data
Relevant to Hypotheses of Perceived Promotive and
Contrient Interdependence[9]

Variable	Problem Type	Total	
		M diff	p
Group-centeredness (A)	H. R.	+2.98	.001
Group-centeredness (A)	P	+2.54	.001
Group-feeling (C)	H. R.	+1.20	.01
Competitiveness (C)	H. R.	−.37	*
Desire to Excel Others (D)	H. R.	−2.30	.03
Desire to Excel Others (D)	P	−2.20	.01

* The differences for three of the pairs are in the same direction as the total mean difference; these differences have p values of .01, .01, and .13 respectively. The differences for the other two pairs are in an opposite direction; these differences have p values of .14 and .23.

support to the first part of the hypothesis (perceived promotive interdependence).

The second part of the hypothesis (*Indiv comp* will perceive themselves to be more

[9] The following symbols are being used in the various tables: P = Puzzles; H. R. = Human Relations problems; (A), (B), (C), or (D) = the measuring instrument (see footnote 8); Total M diff = average of the differences (cooperative minus competitive) between each of the five paired groups for each of the five experimental weeks. A plus sign indicates that the cooperative groups had more of the variable than did the competitive groups. Total p = the p value obtained by combining the p values for each of the five pairs. A combined value is given only when the direction of the differences for all five pairs is the same as that of the total mean difference.

The results obtained here are not so conclusive, though they tend to support the hypothesis (see Table 1, competitiveness). It seems probable that the lack of clean-cut results is a reflection of the differing interpretations placed on the word *competitiveness* by *Indiv coop*. This interpretation is supported by the fact that when the question was phrased, "How much did you desire to excel others?" on the Postexperimental Questionnaire, significant differences were obtained in the predicted direction.

To sum up, the data support the predictions that perceived promotive interdependence would be greater among *Indiv coop*

TABLE 2

DIFFERENCES BETWEEN COOPERATIVE AND COMPETITIVE GROUPS ON DATA
RELEVANT TO THE HYPOTHESIS CONCERNING COORDINATION OF EFFORT

Variable	Problem Type	Total	
		M diff	p
Working-together (A)	H. R.	+2.42	.001
Working-together (A)	P	+2.68	.001
Degree of Coordination (A)	H. R.	+2.62	.001
Degree of Coordination (A)	P	+2.57	.001
Group Cooperation (C)	H. R.	+1.18	.001

and that perceived contrient interdependence would be greater among *Indiv comp*.[10]

ORGANIZATION

Coordination of Efforts. Hypothesis 6 asserted that there would be greater degree of coordination of efforts and that coordination would occur more frequently among *Indiv coop* than among *Indiv comp*. Table 2 presents the relevant evidence.

The observers rated that the cooperative groups worked together more frequently (A) and were more highly coordinated (A)

[10] We proposed in our theoretical discussion that *Indiv coop* has greater unity as a *sociological group* than does *Indiv comp*. Also, *psychological unity as a group, cohesiveness of a group,* and *strength of membership motives* were defined to be direct functions of the degree of perceived promotive interdependence. Thus, it is possible to state the results here more generally. The data support the hypothesis that a sociological group with greater unity will possess more psychological unity than a sociological group with lesser unity. In further comparisons of *Indiv coop* and *Indiv comp*, one should keep in mind the possibility of making similar more general statements.

than were the competitive groups. In answer to the question (C), "How cooperatively did the group work together on this problem?" the ratings of *Indiv coop* indicated more working together than did the ratings of *Indiv comp*.

Thus the data give rather definite support to the coordination hypothesis.

Homogeneity of Participation. Hypothesis 7 states that there will be less homogeneity with respect to amount of contribution among *Indiv coop* than among *Indiv comp*. The data presented in Table 3 provide the evidence relevant to this hypothesis. The variance in amount of contributions among members has been used as the measure of homogeneity. The differences between variances of paired groups were then entered as scores in the latin square and the customary statistical treatment was made.

The data give support for the hypothesis, although the results are not conclusive. In both the puzzles and human relations problems, there is greater homogeneity of participation within competitive groups. Four out of the five pairs in the human relations prob-

TABLE 3

DIFFERENCES IN HOMOGENEITY OF AMOUNT OF PARTICIPATION BETWEEN
COOPERATIVE AND COMPETITIVE GROUPS

Variable	Problem Type	Total	
		M diff	p
Homogeneity of Participation (B)	H. R.	−2593	°
Homogeneity of Participation (B)	P	−518	.16

° The differences for four of the pairs are in the same direction as the total mean difference; these differences have p values of .005, .07, .13, and .67 respectively. The pair going in the opposite direction has a p value of .16.

lem and all of the five pairs in the puzzles go in the direction predicted by the hypothesis.

Further support is given the hypothesis by some additional data which are directly relevant to the basic substitutability hypothesis. On the Weekly Questionnaire the subjects were asked to indicate the reasons they had for not offering suggestions or thoughts to the group discussion. Of the reasons checked by *Indiv coop*, 47% were in the category "Somebody else said pretty much the same thing," compared to 33% for *Indiv comp*.

Thus, though the results are not conclusive, support is given to the hypothesis that there will be more homogeneity in amount of participation among *Indiv comp* than among *Indiv coop*.

Specialization. A cursory inspection of the data collected on the Functions Observations Sheets revealed a low reliability of the data needed to test Hypothesis 8 (specialization with respect to function). In the statistical tests that were made the data revealed no clear-cut significance (though with respect to all functions there is, on the average, greater specialization of functioning within cooperative groups than within competitive groups).

The evidence relevant to specialization with respect to content or activity (Hyp. 9) is much more clear-cut. Table 4 presents the data. The results definitely indicate that

with respect to the job of writing the letter of recommendations, asked for in the human relations problems, there were significantly more instances of division of labor in the cooperative groups. Faced with the problem of achievement in a limited amount of time, cooperative members were able to organize themselves so as not to duplicate one another's efforts. Substitutability of one for the other permitted the members to divide up the job into its different aspects and allowed the various members to work on these components simultaneously. In the competitive situation, writing procedure generally followed either of two extremes: (*a*) One man was assigned the job, usually on the basis of a rotation scheme, and the other members took an active part in supervising the writing. The getting of ideas into written form was seen as a path, thus everyone was actively concerned with what was being written. Since the number of pages, always less than five, prevented the possibility of any compromise—"we each do one"—it was necessary for all to focus on the same activity. As a consequence, it was rare that two members were writing simultaneously. When two or more recorders are shown in the competitive groups, their time of writing did not overlap much. (*b*) A conscientious member took the form and wrote up recommendations while the others discussed. The discussants showed no interest in the write-up, never examining it, their whole attention

TABLE 4

AVERAGE NUMBER OF PERSONS SIMULTANEOUSLY ENGAGED IN WRITING RECOMMENDATIONS FOR THE DIFFERENT HUMAN RELATIONS PROBLEMS IN COOPERATIVE AND COMPETITIVE GROUPS

	Barber Shop	Cheating	WW II Vet	Negro Workers	Supervisors †
Coop*	1.8	2.4	2.0	2.8	2.8
Comp	1.2	1.0	1.2	1.8	1.2

* In none of the 25 paired experimental sessions were there more members simultaneously engaged in writing in a competitive group than in its paired cooperative group. In sixteen of the sessions there were more members in cooperative groups engaged in simultaneous writing; in the remaining nine sessions there were no differences between the paired groups.
† For all problems but the Supervisors, only three persons could write simultaneously; it was possible for four persons to write simultaneously on this one.

being directed to the discussion. The written product was, more or less, considered to be an irrelevant side issue for some conscientious soul to handle. It was not seen as a necessary path, thus it was perfectly permissible for anyone who wished to do so to take over the function of writing.

MOTIVATION

Hypothesis 12 asserts that the directions of the forces operating on *Indiv coop* should be more similar than the directions of the forces on *Indiv comp*. If this hypothesis is correct, one should expect greater speed in group locomotion for the cooperative groups. The data with respect to locomotion are presented under the heading of *Productivity* below. The data give strong support to the hypothesis.

The validity of the hypothesis presupposes the validity of the basic hypothesis with respect to positive inducibility. The following questions (C), "How did you react to the ideas or suggestions of others?" and "How frequently was your own thinking or reaction affected by what the others were saying?" are relevant. Table 5 indicates that *Indiv coop* were affected by the ideas of others significantly more often than were *Indiv comp*. Table 7 indicates, further, that *Indiv coop* were markedly more agreeable and acceptant towards the ideas initiated by

others. These two sets of facts provide direct support for the basic hypothesis with respect to positive inducibility and indirect evidence for Hypothesis 12.

From Hypothesis 13 one would predict that there would be more pressure for achievement in the cooperative groups than in the competitive ones. The ratings of the observers and of the subjects both produce significant differences in the predicted direction for the human relations problem. The direction of the differences obtained for the puzzles is in line with the hypothesis, but the size of the differences is not significant.

Hypothesis 15 states that there is nothing inherent in the cooperative or competitive situations which should produce differences in the strength of force operating on individuals in the two situations. *Interest* or *involvement* is considered to be an operational measure of total situationally relevant forces. The data of Table 5 clearly provide no basis for rejecting the hypothesis. The differences between cooperative and competitive groups with respect to involvement or interest in the problems at hand were negligible.

COMMUNICATION

Hypotheses 16 and 17 assert that the volume of participation of the cooperative as contrasted with the competitive groups will

TABLE 5

DIFFERENCES BETWEEN COOPERATIVE AND COMPETITIVE GROUPS ON DATA
RELEVANT TO THE MOTIVATION HYPOTHESES

Variable	Problem Type	Total	
		M diff	p
Effect of Other's Ideas (C)	H. R.	+.78	.001
Achievement Pressure (A)	H. R.	+1.00	.01
Achievement Pressure (A)	P	+.49	*
Strength of Motivation to Achieve (D)	H. R.	+.83	.01
Strength of Motivation to Achieve (D)	P	+.20	Not Sig.
Involvement (A)	H. R.	+.15	Not Sig.
Involvement (A)	P	+.23	Not Sig.
Interest (C)	H. R.	−.10	Not Sig.

* The differences for four of the five pairs are in the same direction as the mean differences; these differences have p values of .04, .13, .24, and .68. The p value for the pair going in the opposite direction is .66.

TABLE 6

DIFFERENCES IN PARTICIPATION VOLUME, ATTENTIVENESS, AND COMMUNICATION DIFFICULTIES BETWEEN COOPERATIVE AND COMPETITIVE GROUPS

Variable	Problem Type	Total	
		M diff	p
Participation Volume* (B)	H. R.	−22.8	†
Participation Volume (B)	P	+118	.001
Attentiveness (A)	H. R.	+1.04	.01
Attentiveness (A)	P	+1.50	.001
Attentiveness (C)	H. R.	+.42	‡
Communication Difficulties (A)	H. R.	−1.94	.001
Communication Difficulties (A)	P	−1.39	.01
Difficulty in Communicating to Others (C)	H. R.	−.81	.001
Difficulty in Understanding Others (C)	H. R.	−.67	.001

* *Participation Volume* has the meaning of total number of participations per 45 minutes. Thus, all participation volumes are equaled in terms of a constant time unit.
† The differences for three pairs are in the same direction as the total mean difference; these differences have *p* values of .007, .06, and .20. The other two pairs go in the opposite direction; these differences have *p* values of .12 and .73.
‡ The differences for three pairs are in the same direction as the total mean difference; these differences have *p* values of .03, .04, and .72. The other two pairs, in the opposite direction, both have *p* values of .83.

be (Hyp. 16) smaller for the human relations problems, and (Hyp. 17) greater for the puzzles. The relevant data are presented in Table 6.

The observers rated that there were significantly fewer communication difficulties among *Indiv coop* than among *Indiv comp* for both the human relations problems and puzzles. Further support for Hypothesis 19 is obtained from the subjects. In answer to the question (C), "Did you find that you had difficulty in getting your ideas across to others?" the ratings of *Indiv coop* expressed significantly less difficulty than did the ratings of *Indiv comp*. The same results were obtained in answers to the following question (C), "Did you find that you had difficulty in trying to follow or get the point of what the others were saying?" Thus, the competitive subjects experienced more difficulty with respect to the spread of common signification, both in the roles of communicators and communicatees.

Hypothesis 21 asserts that there will be more common appraisals of communications in the cooperative groups than in the competitive groups. Table 7 presents the evidence for the hypothesis.

The observers rate greater acceptance of one another's ideas in the cooperative groups than in the competitive groups in both kinds of tasks. The subjects' ratings also strongly support the hypothesis. In answer to the questions (C), "How did you react to the suggestions of others?" and "How did the others tend to react to your ideas or suggestions?" the ratings made by *Indiv coop*, as contrasted with those of *Indiv comp*, indicate both significantly more agreement with the ideas and suggestions of others and perception of more agreement from other group members.

Two categories on the Functions Observation Sheets, "evaluator-critic" and "follower," also provide some relevant data, although it should be kept in mind that both categories may contain a few items which are not specifically related to the notion of *common appraisal*. Thus, "evaluator-critic" probably contains some items which are positive evaluations and "follower" includes some items which connote understanding

TABLE 7

DIFFERENCES BETWEEN COOPERATIVE AND COMPETITIVE GROUPS ON DATA
RELEVANT TO THE HYPOTHESIS ABOUT COMMON APPRAISALS
OF COMMUNICATIONS

Variable	Problem Type	Total	
		M diff	p
Acceptance of Each Other's Ideas (A)	H. R.	+1.80	.001
Acceptance of Each Other's Ideas (A)	P	+.95	.01
Agreement with Others (C)	H. R.	+.81	.001
Agreement by Others (C)	H. R.	+.61	❀
Follower (B)	H. R.	+4.34	.01
Follower (B)	P	+2.05	.25
Evaluator-critic (B)	H. R.	−3.36	.04
Evaluator-critic (B)	P	−.95	Not Sig.

❀ The differences for four of the five pairs are in the same direction as the total
mean difference; these differences have p values of .01, .02, .04, and .38. The
other pair, in the opposite direction, has a p value of .92.

but not necessarily agreement. Nevertheless, for both categories there are significant differences between the cooperative and competitive groups on the human relations problems in the direction of the hypothesis. The differences with respect to the puzzles are in the predicted direction but are not significant.

ORIENTATION

Hypothesis 23 asserts that there will be more commonality of perception with respect to position and direction to the goal among *Indiv coop* than among *Indiv comp*. The relevant data are presented in Table 8.

According to the observers' ratings the cooperative groups were significantly more oriented ("aware of where they are and where they are going") than the competitive groups for both kinds of tasks. The hypothe-

sis is also given indirect support by the observers' ratings which indicate that the cooperative groups were also significantly more orderly and systematic in their approach to the various problems.

PRODUCTIVITY

Hypothesis 24 asserts that, since speed of locomotion will be greater in cooperative groups, quantitative productivity per unit of time will be less in the competitive groups. The evidence in Table 9 provides striking support. Cooperative groups solve the puzzle problems more rapidly than do the competitive groups and they also produce more on the human relations problems (number of words written in the recommendations are taken as a crude measure of quantity of productivity).

Hypothesis 25 states that qualitative pro-

TABLE 8

DIFFERENCES IN DEGREE OF ORIENTATION AND ORDERLINESS BETWEEEN
COOPERATIVE AND COMPETITIVE GROUPS

Variable	Problem Type	Total	
		M diff	p
Orientation (A)	H. R.	+1.70	.001
Orientation (A)	P	+1.92	.01
Orderliness (A)	H. R.	+1.99	.001
Orderliness (A)	P	+1.96	.001

TABLE 9

DIFFERENCES BETWEEN COOPERATIVE AND COMPETITIVE GROUPS ON
VARIOUS MEASURES OF PRODUCTIVITY

Variable	Problem Type	Total	
		M diff	p
Discussion Productivity (A)	H. R.	+1.86	.001
Discussion Productivity (A)	P	+1.90	.01
Discussion Insight (A)	H. R.	+1.25	.001
Discussion Insight (A)	P	+1.72	.02
Time per Solution	P	−7.35	.01
		Minutes	
Number of Words in Written Product	H. R.	+2.99	.001
		Words	
Average Individual Productivity (A)	H. R.	+.15	Not Sig.
Average Individual Productivity (A)	P	+.58	.07
Learning from Discussion (C)	H. R.	+.25	°
Grades on Term Paper		+2.85	.18

° Differences for three pairs are in the same direction as the total mean difference; these differences have p values of .07, .07, and .39. The two pairs, in the opposite direction, have p values of .30 and .45.

ductivity will be higher for the cooperative groups. Clear support is given to this hypothesis by the observers' ratings of discussion productivity (Table 9) and by the judges' ratings of written recommendations for the human relations problems (Table 10). According to observer ratings, the discussions of the cooperative groups not only came out with more fruitful ideas for handling the problem presented to them, but also their group discussions showed more insight and understanding of the nature of the problem being posed to them. These differences with respect to group productivity and group insight are significant for both kinds of tasks.

Average individual productivity must not be confused with group productivity. Group productivity ratings referred to the ideas that were agreed upon and accepted as a basis for action by the group. The ratings of average individual productivity show no significant difference for the cooperative and competitive groups on the human relations problems. For the puzzles, there is a difference approaching significance favoring *Indiv coop*. The latter result is probably explained by the fact that the greater communication within cooperative groups meant that in-

dividuals were less likely to stay in blind alleys for long periods of time.

Table 10 presents the ratings of each group for each of the five different problems, as made by three different judges. Although it is evident that there is a considerable unreliability in the ratings, it is also clear that despite this there are significant differences between the paired cooperative and competitive groups.

Hypothesis 26 states that *Indiv coop* will learn more from one another than will *Indiv comp*. Table 9 indicates that the cooperative group members in three of the five pairs rated themselves as learning more from the discussion of the human relations problem than did the competitive members rate themselves.

The same kind of results are obtained when one examines the grades obtained by the individuals exposed to each of the experimental conditions. The grades being considered were those obtained on the first term paper handed in by all the subjects. The paper was due on the final week of the experiment. Statistical analysis reveals that the differences are in the predicted direction but not statistically significant.

Thus, the hypotheses predicting greater

TABLE 10

DATA RELEVANT TO HYPOTHESIS THAT QUALITATIVE PRODUCTIVITY WILL BE HIGHER
IN COOPERATIVE GROUPS

Correlations among Ratings of Group Products by Three Judges			
Judges 1 & 2	*Judges 1 & 3*	*Judges 2 & 3*	*Average of Correlations*
.42	.46	.61	.50

Differences between Cooperative and Competitive Groups on Mean of Judges' Ratings						
	Total	*Pair 1*	*Pair 2*	*Pair 3*	*Pair 4*	*Pair 5*
Mean difference	+2.04					
p	.001	.02	.001	.54	.01	.05

group productivity for the cooperative groups have received strong support from the data, but the evidence with respect to the hypothesis predicting greater learning for *Indiv coop* is far from conclusive. It should be noted that the discussions took place at the very beginning of an introductory psychology course. Perhaps at such an early stage the subjects were not particularly ready to have cognitive changes induced by fellow members under either of the two conditions.

INTERPERSONAL RELATIONS

From the basic hypothesis with respect to cathexis, it was derived that *Indiv coop* would be more friendly towards one another in the group meetings than would *Indiv comp* (Hyp. 27). Table 11 presents the relevant data.

Observers' ratings reveal that *Indiv coop* were significantly more friendly than *Indiv comp* during discussions of both types of problems. The hypothesis receives additional

TABLE 11

DIFFERENCES BETWEEN COOPERATIVE AND COMPETITIVE GROUPS IN
FRIENDLINESS AND OTHER RELATED DATA

Variable	Problem Type	Total	
		M diff	p
Friendliness (A)	H. R.	+1.26	.001
Friendliness (A)	P	+.89	.01
How Good Were Contributions of Others (C)	H. R.	+.70	*
Encourager (B)	H. R.	+.96	†
Encourager (B)	P	+.20	Not Sig.
Aggressor (B)	H. R.	−1.16	.01
Aggressor (B)	P	−.64	Not Sig.
Time Taken to Learn Last Names (D)		−.20	.06
Correctness of Spelling of Last Names (D)		+5.3	.11

* Differences for four pairs are in the same direction as the total mean difference; these differences have p values of .005, .01, .01, and .07. The other pair, in the opposite direction, has a p value of .87.
† Differences for four pairs are in the same direction as the total mean difference; these differences have p values of .001, .18, .57, and .62. The other pair has a p value of .57.

support from the observation of functions during discussion of the human relations problems. A greater percentage of encouraging or rewarding remarks was made in cooperative groups, and a significantly larger proportion of aggressive remarks was made in the competitive groups. The puzzle problems yielded such a low frequency of all emotionally laden functions that no significant differences could be established between groups.

The cooperative subjects in answer to the question (C), "How good were the contributions of others?" rated one another's contributions to be better than did the competitive subjects. This result can also be taken to indicate greater positive cathection among *Indiv coop*.

The next question of interest has to do with the extent of the generalization of the friendliness shown during the experimental meetings. The question (D), "How much did the weekly small group meetings stand out for you in contrast with the other classes you attend during the week?" is the only relevant measure. The average responses for the cooperative and the competitive groups were not significantly different. On the average, the subjects rated the weekly meetings as, "Thought about some—more prominent in my thinking than some of my other courses, but not more prominent than most of my other courses." Since the experimental sessions were not especially prominent in the lives of the subjects, there is little reason to expect much generalization of cathexis to other areas.

Various measures were taken to test the extent of generalization: ratings of fellow members with respect to desirability as a friend, rating of amount of friendly feeling toward others, time taken to learn first and last names, correctness of spelling of last names, amount of time spent together in outside activities and kinds of activities jointly engaged in outside of class. Table 11 presents most of the evidence.

Indiv coop learned one another's last names sooner than did *Indiv comp* (as re-

ported on the final questionnaire). They also spelled one another's names more nearly correctly, but the size of this difference is significant at only the 11% level of confidence. No differences were obtained with regard to learning first names nor in the frequency or kinds of outside activities undertaken together. At the end of the experiment, *Indiv coop* rated themselves as being more friendly towards one another than did *Indiv comp*. These differences, however, are clearly not statistically significant. The data thus indicate that little generalization of cathexis occurred. The relative lack of generalization was probably due to (a) the relative lack of importance of the goals involved in the experiment and (b) strong restraining forces against any inclinations toward increased sociability which might have resulted from the experimental situation.

Hypothesis 28 states that the group and its products will be evaluated more highly by *Indiv coop* than by *Indiv comp*. Table 12 presents the relevant data. In answer to the question (C), "Did the group help your thinking?" the ratings revealed significantly more help among the cooperative than among the competitive members. Similar results were obtained from the question (C), "How good do you think the group's product was?"

According to Hypotheses 29 and 30 there should be a greater precentage of group functions among *Indiv coop* and a greater percentage of individual functions among *Indiv comp*. The data in Table 12 support these hypotheses with respect to the human relations problems but not the puzzles. The lack of difference for the puzzles suggests that (a) the objectively demonstrable solution of the puzzles makes it more difficult for individuals to produce the rationalizations necessary for "civilized" blocking or aggressive behavior, and (b) a demonstrable solution compels a certain degree of agreement and acceptance, making group functions more likely. Thus, the competitive groups have a significantly greater percentage of

TABLE 12

DIFFERENCES BETWEEN COOPERATIVE AND COMPETITIVE GROUPS ON KINDS
OF FUNCTIONS PERFORMED AND EVALUATIONS OF THE GROUP

Variable	Problem Type	Total	
		M diff	p
Group Help to Thinking (C)	H. R.	+1.03	.001
How Good Was Group Product (C)	H. R.	+1.22	.01
Total Group Functions (B)	H. R.	+4.64	*
Total Group Functions (B)	P	+.08	Not Sig.
Total Individual Functions (B)	H. R.	−3.87	.05
Total Individual Functions (B)	P	−2.10	Not Sig.
Blocker (B)	H. R.	−1.40	.01
Blocker (B)	P	−.25	Not Sig.
Self-defender (B)	H. R.	−1.03	.05
Self-defender (B)	P	−.10	Not Sig.

* Differences for four pairs are in the same direction as the total mean difference;
these differences have p values of .001, .001, .01, and .01. The other pair, in the
opposite direction, has a p value of .05.

group functions in the puzzles than in the human relations problems and a slightly smaller percentage of individual functions in the puzzles. Similar, but less marked, differences are found for the cooperative groups on the two kinds of problems.

Hypothesis 33 states that *Indiv coop* will perceive themselves as having more favorable effects on fellow members than will *Indiv comp*. Table 13 indicates that the cooperative subjects saw their fellow members as reacting more positively to their ideas,

the competitive members perceived that their ideas were being ignored more frequently, and the cooperative members felt that their contributions would be evaluated more highly.

Hypothesis 34 asserts that there will be greater internalization of the attitude of the generalized other by *Indiv coop* than by *Indiv comp*. Most of the experimental data already discussed are relevant to this hypothesis, but, in the more restricted sense of identification with the attitudes of others,

TABLE 13

DIFFERENCES BETWEEN COOPERATIVE AND COMPETITIVE GROUPS IN
PERCEPTION OF EFFECTS ON OTHERS AND IN FEELING OF
OBLIGATION TO OTHER MEMBERS

Variable	Problem Type	Total	
		M diff	p
How Did Others React to Your Ideas? (C)	H. R.	+.61	.01
How Frequently Did Others React? (C)	H. R.	+.49	.10
How Will Others Rate Your Contributions? (C)	H. R.	+.49	.09
Strength of Feeling of Obligation to Others (D)	H. R.	+2.80	.001
Strength of Feeling of Obligation to Others (D)	P	+1.55	*
Strength of Desire to Win Respect of Others (D)	H. R.	+1.53	†
Strength of Desire to Win Respect of Others (D)	P	+2.38	‡

* Four pairs are in the same direction as the total mean difference; the differences for these pairs have p values of .01, .04, .12, and .38. The other pair has a p value of .92.
† Four pairs are in the same direction as the total mean difference, with p values of .01, .03, .04, and .18. The other pair has a p value of .02.
‡ Four pairs are in the same direction as the total difference, with p values of .01, .02, .06, and .28. The other pair has a p value of .33.

two complementary measures, the feeling of obligation to others and the desire to win the respect of others, are especially pertinent. Table 13 presents data which indicate that *Indiv coop* felt more obligated as members of a group to participate in joint effort than did *Indiv comp*. The desire to win the respect of the other members also played more of a role in the motivation of *Indiv coop* than *indiv comp*.

Summary and Conclusions

BASIC HYPOTHESES

The evidence for the basic hypotheses is, for the most part, indirect. Data collected to test the more specific hypotheses about group functioning also, in effect, test the basic hypotheses.

The experimental findings give support to the following hypotheses:

1. *Indiv coop* will perceive themselves to be more promotively interdependent and *Indiv comp* will perceive themselves to be more contriently interdependent (Hyp. 1).
2. There will be greater substitutability for similarly intended actions among *Indiv coop* than *Indiv comp*. This hypothesis is supported by data obtained in connection with Hypotheses 7 and 9, but the data are ambiguous with respect to Hypotheses 8 and 16.
3. A larger percentage of actions of others will be positively cathected among *Indiv coop;* a larger percentage of actions of others will be negatively cathected among *Indiv comp* (Hyp. 3).
4. There will be a greater positive inducibility among *Indiv coop* than among *Indiv comp* (Hyp. 4).

5. *Indiv coop* will exhibit more helpfulness and *Indiv comp* will exhibit more obstructiveness (Hyp. 5).

Thus, all in all, the theory of cooperation and competition has been given considerable backing by the present experimental investigation.

GROUP FUNCTIONING

The results, with respect to aspects of group functioning, indicate that *Indiv coop* showed more of the following characteristics than did *Indiv comp*: (*a*) coordination of efforts; (*b*) diversity in amount of contributions per member; (*c*) subdivision of activity; (*d*) achievement pressure; (*e*) production of signs in the puzzle problem; (*f*) attentiveness to fellow members; (*g*) mutual comprehension of communication; (*h*) common appraisals of communication; (*i*) orientation and orderliness; (*j*) productivity per unit time; (*k*) quality of product and discussions; (*l*) friendliness during discussions; (*m*) favorable evaluation of the group and its products; (*n*) group functions; (*o*) perception of favorable effects upon fellow members; and (*p*) incorporation of the attitude of the generalized other.

Indiv comp showed more (*a*) production of signs in the human relations problem, and (*b*) individual functions.

No significant differences were found in the (*a*) amount of interest or involvement, (*b*) amount of specialization of function, and (*c*) amount of learning (though the trend is in favor of *Indiv coop*). Nor did the data reveal any striking development differences with time.

References

BARNARD, C. I. *The functions of the executive.* Cambridge, Mass.: Harvard Univer. Press, 1938.

BENNE, K. D., and SHEATS, P. Functional roles and group members. *J. soc. Issues,* 1948, *4,* 41-49.

KOFFKA, K. *Principles of gestalt psychology.* New York: Harcourt, Brace & World, 1935.

NEWCOMB, T. M. Autistic hostility and social reality. *Hum. Relat.,* 1947, *1,* 69-86.

Some Effects of Certain
Communication Patterns
on Group Performance ❧ Harold J. Leavitt

It was the purpose of this investigation to explore experimentally the relationship between the behavior of small groups and the patterns of communication in which the groups operate. It was our further purpose to consider the psychological conditions that are imposed on group members by various communication patterns, and the effects of these conditions on the organization and the behavior of its members. We tried to do this for small groups of a constant size, using two-way written communication and a task that required the simple collection of information.

SOME CHARACTERISTICS
OF COMMUNICATION STRUCTURES

The stimulus for this research lies primarily in the work of Bavelas,[1] who considered the problem of defining some of the dimensions of group structures. In his study, the structures analyzed consist of cells connected to one another. If we make persons analogous to "cells" and communications channels analogous to "connections," we find that some of the dimensions that Bavelas defines are directly applicable to the description of communication patterns. Thus, one way in which communication patterns vary can be described by the sum of the neighbors that each individual member has, neighbors being defined as individuals

[1] See A. Bavelas, "A mathematical model for group structures," *Appl. Anthropol.*, 1948, 7, 16-30.

to whom a member has communicative access. So, too, the concept of *centrality*, as defined by Bavelas, is of value in describing differences within and between structures. The most central position in a pattern is the position closest to all other positions. Distance is measured by number of communicative links which must be utilized to get, by the shortest route, from one position to another. The use of these particular four channels yields pattern C (Fig. 1). The original seven-link pattern (A) can be used as a four-link pattern in various ways. For instance, each of the four Ss diagrammatically labeled c, b, a, and e might send his item of information to d who would organize the items, arrive at the answer, and send it back to each respectively. Use of these particular four channels would yield the pattern B in Figure 1. The problem could also be solved by the Ss using five, six, or all of the seven potential channels.

Operational Flexibility. Secondly, with the specification that a given number of links be used, any pattern can be operated in a variety of ways. Thus the pattern D (Fig. 1), which has no pattern flexibility, can be used as shown in D-1, with information funneled into C and the answer sent out from C. It is also possible to use it, as in D-2, with E as the key position; or as in D-3. These are operational differences that can be characterized in terms of the roles taken by the various positions. Thus in D-1, C is the decision-making position. In D-2, it is E or A. Some patterns can be operated with two or three decision-makers.

From the *Journal of Abnormal and Social Psychology*, 1951, 46, 38-50, with slight abridgment. Reprinted by permission of the author and the American Psychological Association.

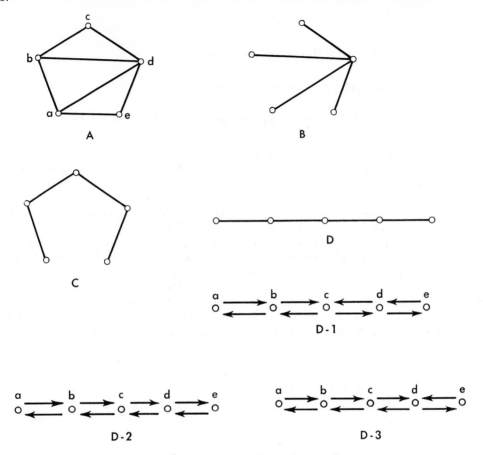

Fig. 1. Communication patterns (see text).

THE DEFINITION OF MAXIMUM THEORETICAL EFFICIENCY

Before going further it may be helpful to state the task used in this research. To each S, labeled by color, was given a card on which there appeared a set of five (out of six possible) symbols. Each S's card was different from all the others in that the symbol lacking, the sixth one, was a different symbol in each case.

Thus, in any set of five cards there was only one symbol in common. The problem was for every member to find the common symbol. To accomplish this each member was allowed to communicate, by means of written messages, with those other members of the group to whom he had an open channel (a link in our diagrams). Every separate

written communication from one S (A) to another (B) was considered one message. An S who had discovered the answer was allowed to pass the answer along.

Minimum Number of Communications For any pattern of n Ss, the minimum number of communications, C, is given by $C = 2(n-1)$.

Theoretically, then, with *number of messages as the sole criterion*, any pattern of n Ss is as efficient as any other n-sized pattern.

The Minimum Time Required for Solution. If we assume "standard" Ss, all of whom work, think, and write at the same speed, it is possible to calculate the limit set by the communication pattern on the speed with which the problem can be solved. Toward this end, we can arbitrarily define a *time unit* as the time required to complete any message, from its inception by any S to its reception by any other.

For any n not a power of 2 and *with unrestricted linkage*, when $2^x < n < 2^{x+1}$ and x is a power of 2, $x + 1$ equals the minimum possible time units for solution of the problem. Thus, for a five-man group we have $2^x < 5 < 2^{x+1}$ becoming $2^2 < 5 < 2^3$, and $x + 1 = 3$ time units. *No* five-man pattern can be done in less than three time units, although several require more than three time units. When n is an even power of 2, the formula $2^x = n$ holds, and $x =$ minimum time.[2]

It will be noted that, although some patterns require fewer time units than others, they may also require more message (m) units. This phenomenon, effectively the generalization that it requires increased messages to save time units, holds for all the patterns we have examined. It is, however, true that certain patterns requiring different times can be solved in the same number of message units.

Bavelas also introduced a *sum of neighbors* measure—sum of neighbors being a summation, for the entire pattern, of the number of positions one link away from each position. Similarly, *sum of distances* is the summation, for all positions, of the shortest distances (in links) from every position to every other one.

Unfortunately, these dimensions we have mentioned do not in themselves uniquely define a pattern of communication. What defines a pattern is the *way* the cells are connected, regardless of how they are represented on paper. In essence, our criterion is

[2] This is an empirical generalization derived chiefly from an analysis of a four-man square pattern. In such a pattern, A and B, and C and D may swap information in one time unit. Then A and C, and B and D may swap in two time units to yield a complete solution. For an eight-man ladder pattern the same simultaneous swapping process yields a minimum time. For the intervening n's at least "part" of a time unit is required, in addition to the minimum time for the four-man pattern. A detailed account of this analysis may be found in a paper, as yet unpublished, by J. P. Macy, Jr.

this: if two patterns cannot be "bent" into the same shape without breaking a link, they are different patterns. A more precise definition of unique patterns would require the use of complex topological concepts.

SOME OPERATIONAL CHARACTERISTICS OF COMMUNICATION PATTERNS

Consider the pattern depicted as A in Figure 1. If at each dot or cell (lettered a, b, etc.) we place a person; if each link (line between dots) represents a two-way channel for written communications; and if we assign to the five participants a task requiring that *every* member get an answer to a problem which can be solved only by pooling segments of information originally held separately by each member, then it is possible a priori to consider the ways in which the problem can be solved.

Pattern Flexibility. First we note that the subjects (Ss) need not always use all the channels potentially available to them in order to reach an adequate solution of the problem. Although pattern A (Fig. 1) contains potentially seven links or channels of communication, it can be solved as follows with three of the seven channels ignored:

Step 1: a and e each send their separate items of information to b and d respectively.

Step 2: b and d each send their separate items of information, along with those from a and b respectively, to c.

Step 3: c organizes all the items of information, arrives at an answer, and sends the answer to b and then to d.

Step 4: b and d then send the answer to a and e respectively.

SOME POSSIBLE EFFECTS OF VARIOUS PATTERNS ON THE PERFORMANCE OF INDIVIDUALS

There are two general kinds of reasons which dictate against our theoretically perfect performance from real people. The first of these is the obvious one that people are not standardized. There are also the forces set up by the patterns themselves to be considered. The problem becomes one of analyzing the forces operating on an individual in any particular position in a communication pattern and then predicting how the effects of these forces will be translated into behavior.

It is our belief that the primary source of differential forces will be *centrality*. Centrality will be the chief (though perhaps not the sole) determinant of behavioral differences because centrality reflects the extent to which one position is strategically located relative to other positions in the pattern.

Our selection of centrality derives from the belief that availability of information necessary for the solution of the problem will be of prime importance in affecting one's behavior. Centrality is a measure of one's closeness to all other group members and, hence, is a measure of the availability of the information necessary for solving the problem.

Availability of information should affect behavior, in turn, by determining one's role in the group. An individual who can rapidly collect information should see himself and be seen by others in a different way from an individual to whom vital information is not accessible. Such roles should be different in the extent to which they permit independence of action, in the responsibility they entail, and in the monotony they impose. Finally, differences in independence, in responsibility, and in monotony should affect the speed, the accuracy, the aggressiveness, and the flexibility of behavior.

Method

THE PROBLEM TO BE SOLVED

We have already described the task to be given our Ss—a task of discovering the single common symbol from among several symbols. When *all five* men indicated that they knew the common symbol, a trial was ended.

Another set of cards, with another common symbol, was then given to the Ss, and another trial was begun. Each group of Ss was given fifteen consecutive trials.

THE APPARATUS

The Ss were seated around a circular table so that each was separated from the next by a vertical partition from the center to six inches beyond the table's edge. The partitions had slots permitting subjects to push written message cards to the men on either side of them.

To allow for communication to the other men in the group, a five-layered pentagonal box was built and placed at the center of the table. The box was placed so that the partitions just touched each of the five points of the pentagon. Each of the five resulting wedge-shaped work spaces was then painted a different color. The Ss were supplied with blank message cards whose colors matched that of their work spaces. Any message sent from a booth had to be on a card of the booth's color. On the left wall of each partition, 16 large symbol cards, representing 16 trials, were hung in loose-leaf fashion. The cards were placed in order with numbered backs to S. At the starting signal, S could pull down the first card and go to work.

In addition, each work space was provided with a board in which were mounted six switches. Above each switch appeared one of the six symbols. When S got an answer to the problem, he was to throw the proper switch, which would turn on an appropriate light on a master board of 30 lights in the observer's room. When five lights (whether or not they were under the correct symbol), representing five different Ss, were lit, the observer called a halt to the trial. The observer could tell by a glance at the light panel whether (*a*) five different Ss had thrown their switches, (*b*) whether all five had decided on the same answer, and (*c*) whether the answer decided on was right or wrong. The same detailed instructions were given to all Ss.

A preliminary series of four problems, in which each S was given all the information required for solution, was used. This was done to note the extent of differences among Ss in the time required to solve such problems.

THE PROCEDURE

One hundred male undergraduates of M.I.T.,[3] drawn from various classes at the Institute, served as Ss for these experiments. These 100 were split up into 20 groups of five men each. These 20 groups were then further subdivided so that five groups could be tested on each of four experimental patterns.

Each group was given 15 consecutive trials on *one* pattern, a process which required one session of about fifty minutes. These Ss were *not used again*. The order in which we used our patterns was also randomized. Just in case the color or geographical position of one's work space might affect one's behavior we shifted positions for each new group. After a group had completed its 15 trials, and before members were permitted to talk with one another, each member was asked to fill out a questionnaire.

THE PATTERNS SELECTED

The four five-man patterns selected for this research are shown in Figure 2.

These four patterns represented extremes

[3] Data on female graduate students are being gathered at M.I.T. by Smith and Bavelas, and the indications are that their behavior differs in some ways from the behavior of our male Ss.

in centrality (as in the circle vs. the wheel), as well as considerable differences in other characteristics (Table 1).

Results

The data which have been accumulated are broken down in the pages that follow into (a) a comparison of total patterns and (b) a comparison of positions within patterns.

A. DIFFERENCES AMONG PATTERNS

It was possible to reconstruct a picture of the operational methods actually used by means of: (a) direct observation, (b) post-experimental analysis of messages, and (c) postexperimental talks with Ss.

The *wheel* operated in the same way in all five cases. The peripheral men funneled information to the center where an answer decision was made and the answer sent out. This organization had usually evolved by the fourth or fifth trial and remained in use throughout.

The Y operated so as to give the most central position, C (see Fig. 2 and Table 1), complete decision-making authority. The next-most-central position, D (see Fig. 2), served only as a transmitter of information and of answers. In at least one case, C transmitted answers first to A and B and only then to D. Organization for the Y evolved a little more slowly than for the wheel, but, once achieved, it was just as stable.

In the *chain* information was usually funneled in from both ends to C, whence the an-

TABLE 1

CHARACTERISTICS OF THE EXPERIMENTAL PATTERNS

Pattern	No. of Links	Most Central Position	Sum of Neighbors	Sum of Distances	Min. Time Units	Min. Messages
Chain	4	C (6.7)	8	40	5 (8m)	8 (5t)
Y	4	C (7.2)	8	36	4 (8m)	8 (4t)
Wheel	4	C (8.0)	8	32	5 (8m)	8 (5t)
Circle	5	All (5.0)	10	30	3 (14m)	8 (5t)

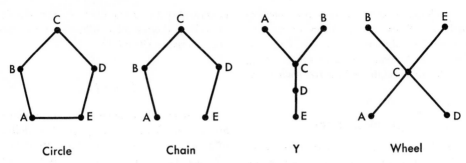

Fig. 2. The experimental patterns.

swer was sent out in both directions. There were several cases, however, in which B or D reached an answer decision and passed it to C. The organization was slower in emerging than the Y's or the wheel's, but consistent, once reached.

The *circle* showed no consistent operational organization. Most commonly messages were just sent in both directions until any S received an answer or worked one out. In every case, all available links were used at some time during the course of each trial.

DIRECT MEASURES OF DIFFERENCES AMONG PATTERNS

Time. The curves in Figure 3 are for *correct* trials only—that is, for trials in which all five switches represented the correct common symbols. In most cases, the

medians shown are for distributions of five groups, but in no case do they represent less than three groups.

The variability of the distributions represented by these medians is considerable. In the fifteenth trial, the distribution for the circle has a range of 50-96 seconds; for the chain, 28-220 seconds; for the Y, 24-52 seconds; and for the wheel, 21-46 seconds. Moreover, much of the time that went to make up each trial was a constant consisting of writing and passing time. Any differences attributable to pattern would be a small fraction of this large constant and would be easily obscured by accidents of misplacing or dropping of messages.

Despite all these factors, one measure of speed did give statistically significant differences. A measure of the *fastest single trial* of each group indicates that the wheel was con-

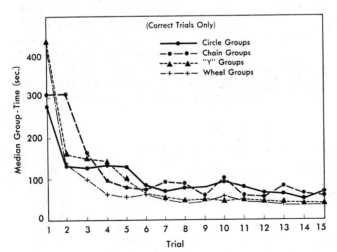

Fig. 3. Median group times per trial.

TABLE 2
FASTEST SINGLE CORRECT TRIAL

	Circle	Chain	Y	Wheel	Diff.	$p°$
Mean	50.4	53.2	35.4	32.0	Ci-W	< .01
Median	55.0	57.0	32.0	36.0	Ch-W	< .10
Range	44-59	19-87	22-53	20-41	Ci-Y	< .05
					Ch-Y	< .20

° Significance of differences between means were measured throughout by t-tests. The p-values are based on distributions of t which include both tails of the distribution (see Freeman, H., *Industrial statistics*. New York: Wiley, 1942). Where differences are between proportions, p is derived from the usual measure of significance of differences between proportions. Ci-W means the circle-wheel difference, and so on.

siderably faster (at its fastest) than the circle (Table 2).

Messages. The medians in Figure 4 represent a count of the number of messages sent by each group during a given (correct) trial. It seems clear that the circle pattern used more messages to solve the problem than the others.

Errors. An error was defined as the throwing of any incorrect switch by an S during a trial. Errors that were *not* corrected before the end of a trial are labeled "final errors"; the others are referred to as "corrected errors."

It should be pointed out that the error figures for the *wheel* in Table 3 are distorted by the peculiar behavior of one of the five wheel groups. The center man in this group took the messages which he received to be *answers* rather than simple information, and, in addition to throwing his own switch, passed the information on *as an answer*. This difficulty was cleared up after a few trials, and the figures for the last 8 trials are probably more representative than the figures for the full 15 trials.

In addition to the differences in errors, there are differences in the proportion of total errors that were corrected. Although more errors were made in the circle pattern than in any other, a greater proportion of them (61 percent) were corrected than in any other pattern. Too, the frequency of unanimous five-man final errors is lower, both absolutely and percentage-wise, for the circle than for the chain.

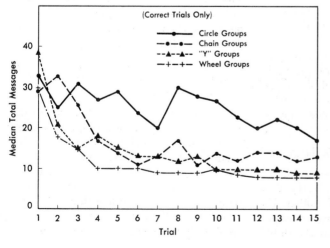

Fig. 4. Median messages per trial.

TABLE 3

ERRORS

Pattern	Total Errors (15 Trials)		Total Errors (Last 8 Trials)		Final Errors		Mean No. of Trials with At Least
	Mean	Range	Mean	Range	Mean	Range	One Final Error
Circle	16.6	9-33	7.6	1-18	6.4	2-14	3.4
Chain	9.8	3-19	2.8	0-11	6.2	1-19	1.8
Y	2.6	1-8	0	0	1.6	0-5	.8
Wheel	9.8	0-34	0.6	0-2	2.2	0-7	1.2

p Values Ci-Y $< .02$

QUESTIONNAIRE

RESULTS

1. *Did your group have a leader? If so, who?"*

Only 13 of 25 people who worked in the circle named a leader, and those named were scattered among all the positions in the circle. For all patterns, the total frequency of people named increased in the order *circle, chain, Y, wheel.* Similarly, the unanimity of opinion increased in the same order so that, for the wheel pattern, all 23 members who recognized any leader agreed that position C was that leader.

2. *"Describe briefly the organization of your group."*

The word "organization" in this question was ambiguous. Some of the *Ss* understood the word to mean pattern of communication, while others equated it with their own duties or with status difference.

These differences in interpretation were not random, however. Sixteen people in the wheel groups fully reproduced the wheel structure in answer to this question, while only one circle member reproduced the circle pattern.

3. *"How did you like your job in the group?"*

In this question *Ss* were asked to place a check on a rating scale marked "disliked it" at one end and "liked it" at the other. For purposes of analysis, the scale was translated into numerical scores from 0 at the dislike end to 100. Each rating was estimated only to the closest decile.

Again, we find the order *circle, chain, Y, wheel,* with circle members enjoying their jobs significantly more than the wheel members.

4. *"See if you can recall how you felt about the job as you went along. Draw the curve below."*

The *Ss* were asked to sketch a curve into a space provided for it. We measured the height of these curves on a 6-point scale at trials 1, 5, 10, and 15. These heights were averaged for each group, and the averages of the group averages were plotted.

Although the differences between groups are not statistically significant, trends of increasing satisfaction in the circle and decreasing satisfaction in the wheel seem to corroborate the findings in the question on satisfaction with one's job. Except for a modest Y-chain reversal, the order is, as usual, from circle to wheel.

5. *"Was there anything, at any time, that kept your group from performing at its best? If so, what?"*

The answers to this question were categorized as far as possible into several classes.

None of the circle members feels that "nothing" was wrong with his group; a fact that is suggestive of an attitude different from that held by members of the other patterns. So, too, is the finding that insufficient knowledge of the pattern does not appear as an obstacle to the circle member but is mentioned at least five times in each of the other patterns.

6. *"Do you think your group could improve its efficiency? If so, how?"*

Circle members place great emphasis on *organizing* their groups, on working out a "system" (mentioned 17 times). Members of the other patterns, if they felt that any improvement at all was possible, emphasized a great variety of possibilities.

7. *"Rate your group on the scale below."*

For purposes of analysis, these ratings (along a straight line) were transposed into numbers from 0, for "poor," to 100.

The same progression of differences that we have already encountered, the progression *circle, chain, Y, wheel,* holds for this question. Once again the circle group thinks less well of itself (Mean = 56) than do the other patterns ($M_{ch} = 60$; $M_y = 70$; $M_w = 71$).

MESSAGE ANALYSIS

The messages sent by all Ss were collected at the end of each experimental run and their contents coded and categorized. Some of these categories overlapped with others, and hence some messages were counted in more than one category.

The now familiar progression, *circle, chain, Y, wheel,* continues into this area. Circle members send many more informational messages than do members of the other patterns ($M_{ci} = 283$; $M_w = 101$). Circle members also send more answers ($M_{ci} = 91$; $M_w = 65$).

The same tendency remains in proportion to total errors as well as absolutely. The circle has a mean of 4.8 recognition-of-error messages for a mean of 16.6 errors; the chain has a mean of 1 recognition-of-error messages for a mean of 9.8 errors.

We were concerned, before beginning these experiments, lest Ss find short cuts for solving the problem, thus making certain comparisons among patterns difficult. One

such short cut we have called "elimination." Instead of taking time to write their five symbols, many Ss, after discovering that only six symbols existed in all, wrote just the missing symbol, thus saving considerable time. This method was used by at least one member in two of the circle groups, in all the chain groups, in three of the Y groups, and in four of the wheel groups. In *both* the circle cases, the method was used by *all five members* during final trials. In the chain, though present in every group, elimination was used only once by all five members, twice by three members, and twice by just one member. In the Y, the method was adopted once by four members (the fifth man was *not* the center) and twice by two members. There was at least one case (in the wheel) in which a member who suggested the use of elimination was ordered by another member not to use it.

The questions raised here are two. Is the idea of elimination more likely to occur in some patterns than in others? Is an innovation like elimination likely to be more readily accepted in some patterns than in others? To neither of these questions do we have an adequate answer.

B. A POSITIONAL ANALYSIS OF THE DATA

Observation of the experimental patterns indicates that every position in the circle is indistinguishable from every other one. No one has more neighbors, is more central, or is closer to anyone than anyone else. In the wheel, the four peripheral positions are alike, and so on. Despite our inability to differentiate these positions from one another, we have set up the data in the following sections as if all positions in each pattern were actually different from one another.

DIRECT OBSERVATIONS

Messages. The most central positions, it will be seen from Table 4, send the greatest

TABLE 4

NUMBER OF MESSAGES SENT BY EACH POSITION

Group		A	B	C	D	E	Diff.	p
Circle	Mean	78.4	90.0	83.6	86.2	81.0	A-B	< .30
	Range	64-101	63-102	60-98	60-122	72-90		
Chain	Mean	24.8	70.8	82.4	71.8	27.6	C-E	< .01
	Range	20-34	43-112	45-113	42-101	22-43		
Y	Mean	28.0	23.8	79.8	63.8	25.6	A-C	< .01
	Range	20-44	21-28	65-104	43-78	21-37	D-C	< .20
							D-E	< .01
Wheel	Mean	29.4	26.2	102.8	26.6	30.2	C-E	< .01
	Range	19-48	17-40	78-138	17-39	22-43		

number of messages; the least central ones send the fewest.

Errors. The analysis of total errors made in each position showed nothing of significance.

QUESTIONNAIRE RESULTS BY POSITION

1. *"How much did you enjoy your job?"*

The most central positions in other patterns enjoy their jobs more than any circle position. Peripheral positions, on the other hand, enjoy the job less than any circle position (Table 5).

2. *"See if you can recall how you felt about the job as you went along. Draw the curve below."*

The data for this question are gathered after all most-peripheral and all most-central positions are combined. Peripheral positions were: positions A and E, in the chain; position E in the Y; and positions A, B, D, and E in the wheel. Central positions were all C positions with the exception of C in the circle. The data thus combined highlight the trend toward higher satisfaction with increasing centrality. The central positions progress from a mean of 2.1 at trial 1 to a mean of 3.9 at trial 15. Peripheral positions decline from 3.9 to 2.3.

TABLE 5

ENJOYMENT OF THE JOB

Group		A	B	C	D	E	Diff.	p
Circle	Mean	58.0	64.0	70.0	65.0	71.0	A-E	< .70
	Range	0-100	0-100	20-100	40-100	25-100		
Chain	Mean	45.0	82.5	78.0	70.0	24.0	C-E	< .02
	Range	25-55	50-100	50-100	40-100	0-70	C-AE	< .01
Y	Mean	46.0	49.0	95.0	71.0	31.0	C-A	< .02
	Range	0-100	25-100	75-100	30-100	0-75	C-AB	< .01
							D-E	< .10
							B-C	< .01
Wheel	Mean	37.5	20.0	97.0	25.0	42.5	C-E	< .02
	Range	0-50	0-40	85-100	0-75	0-100	ABED-C	< .01

MESSAGE ANALYSIS BY POSITION

One of the things that immediately stand out from an examination of the messages is an apparent peculiarity in the *informational message* category. Although the most central man in the chain sends more informational messages (52) than the other positions in that pattern, the same is not true of the most central men in the Y and the wheel. In the Y, it is position *D*, the next-most-central position, that sends most; while in the wheel all positions are about equal. This peculiarity becomes quite understandable if we take into account (*a*) the kind of organization used in each pattern and (*b*) the fact that these figures represent the entire 15 trials, some of which occurred before the group got itself stably organized. In the wheel, the Y, and the chain, the center man really needed to send *no* informational messages, only answers; but in the *early* trials, before his role was clarified, he apparently sent enough to bring his total up to or higher than the level of the rest.

It can also be noted that the number of *organizational messages* (messages which seek to establish some plan of action for future trials) is negatively correlated with positional centrality. The most peripheral men send the greatest numbers of organizational messages, the most central men least.

Discussion

Patternwise, the picture formed by the results is of differences almost always in the order *circle, chain, Y, wheel*.

We may grossly characterize the kinds of differences that occur in this way: the circle, one extreme, is active, leaderless, unorganized, erratic, and yet is enjoyed by its members. The wheel, at the other extreme, is less active, has a distinct leader, is well and stably organized, is less erratic, and yet is unsatisfying to most of its members.

There are two questions raised by these behavioral differences. First, what was wrong with our a priori time-unit analysis?

The results measured in clock time do not at all match the time-unit figures. And second, to what extent are behavioral differences matched by centrality differences?

THE TIME UNIT

It was hypothesized earlier that the time taken to solve a problem should be limited at the lower end by the structure of the pattern of communication. If pattern does set such a limitation on speed, the limitation is not in the direction we would have predicted. Our analysis (Table 1), based on a theoretical time unit, led us falsely to expect greatest speed from the circle pattern.

There are three outstanding reasons for the failure of the time-unit analysis to predict clock time. First, the time unit, itself, was too gross a measure. We defined the time unit as the time required for the transmission of one message from its inception to its reception. In actuality, different kinds of messages required very different clock times for transmission. Ss could send two messages simultaneously. They could also lay out and write several messages before sending any.

A second reason for the failure of the time-unit analysis was the assumption that Ss would gravitate to the theoretically "best" operating organization. Only the wheel groups used the theoretically "best" method (the minimum time method) consistently.

Finally, it should be pointed out that differences in speed among patterns were subject to major fluctuations for reasons of differences in writing speed, dexterity in passing messages, and other extraneous factors.

THE RELATION OF THE CENTRALITY MEASURE TO BEHAVIOR

Our second and more important question is: Are the behavioral differences among patterns and among positions related consistently to the centrality index? An examination of Table 1 indicates that the centrality index shows the same progression, *circle, chain, Y, wheel,* as do most of the behavioral differences. On a positional basis, centrality also differentiates members of a pattern in the same order that their behavior does.

Because such a relationshp does exist between behavior and centrality, a more detailed consideration of the centrality concept is in order.

The central region of a structure is defined by Bavelas as "the class of all cells with the smallest p to be found in the structure." The quantity, p, in turn, is defined as the largest distance between one cell and any other cell in the structure. Distance is measured in link units. Thus the distance from A to B in the chain is one link; from A to C the distance is two links. The most central position in a pattern is the position that

is closest to all other positions. Quantitatively, an index of the centrality of position A in any pattern can be found by (a) summing the shortest distances from *each* position to every other one and (b) dividing this summation by the total of the shortest distances from position A to every other position.

Centrality, then, is a function of the size of a pattern as well as of its structure. Thus in a five-man circle, the centrality of each man is 5.0. In a six-man circle, the centrality of each man jumps to 6.0. The two most peripheral men in a five-man chain each have a centrality of 4.0. But in a seven-man chain, the two most peripheral men have centralities of 5.3.

In Figure 5 are given the centralities of each position in each of our four test patterns. The sum of centralities is also given.

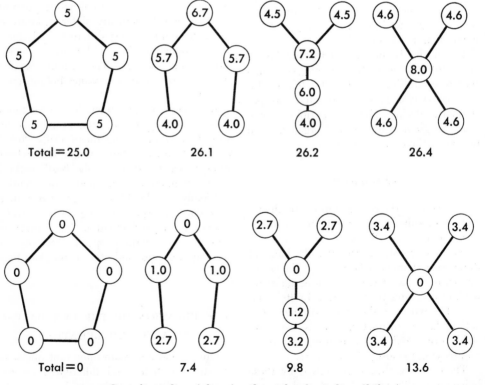

Fig. 5. Centrality indices (above) and peripherality indices (below).

Both total centrality and distribution of centralities fall in the order *circle, chain, Y, wheel*.

These centrality figures correlate with the behavior we have observed. But it seems unreasonable to assume that the correlation would hold for larger *n*'s. Certainly we would not expect *more* message activity or *more* satisfaction from peripheral positions in a chain of a larger *n* than from a five-man chain.

To obviate this difficulty, a measure we have called "relative peripherality" may be established. The relative peripherality of any position in a pattern is the difference between the centrality of that position and the centrality of the most central position in that pattern. Thus, for the two end men in a five-man chain, the peripherality index is 2.7 (the difference between their centralities of 4.0 and the centrality of the most central position, 6.7). For a total pattern, the peripherality index may be taken by summating all the peripherality indices in the pattern (Fig. 5).

Examination of the data will show that observed differences in behavior correlate positively with these peripherality measures. *By total pattern*, messages, satisfaction, and errors (except for the wheel) vary consistently with total peripherality index. Similarly, by position, messages and satisfaction vary with peripherality. Errors, however, show no clear relationship with peripherality of position, a finding which is discussed in detail later in this section.

Recognition of a leader also seems to be a function of peripherality, but in a somewhat different way. A review of our leadership findings will show that leadership becomes more clear-cut as the differences in peripherality *within a pattern become greater*. Recognition of a leader seems to be determined by the extent of the difference in centrality between the most central and next-most-central man.

There arises next the question: What is the mechanism by which the peripherality of a pattern or a position affects the behavior of persons occupying that pattern or position?

A reconstruction of the experimental situation leads us to this analysis of the peripherality-behavior relationship:

First, let us assume standard S*s*, motivated to try to solve our experimental problem as quickly as possible. Let them be "intelligent" S*s* who do not send the same information more than once to any neighbor. Let them also be S*s* who, given several neighbors, will send, with equal probability, their first message to any one of those neighbors.

Given such standard S*s*, certain specific positions will probably get an answer to the problem before other positions. In the chain, position *C* will be most likely to get the answer first, but, in the circle, all positions have an equal opportunity.

To illustrate, consider the chain pattern (see Fig. 2): During time unit 1, *A* may send only to *B*. *B* may send either to *C* or to *A*. *C* may send either to *B* or to *D*. *D* may send either to *C* or to *E*. *E* may send only to *D*. No matter where *B*, *C*, and *D* send their messages, *B* and *D* will have, at the end of one time unit, *A*'s and *E*'s information. During the second time unit, if *B* and/or *D* have sent to *C* the first time, they will now send to *A* and *E*. If they sent to *A* and *E* the first time, they will send to *C*, and *C* will have the answer. Even if *B* and *D* do not send to *C* until the third time unit, *C* will get the answer either before or simultaneously with *B* and *D*. In *no* case can any position beat *C* to the answer. In the wheel, *C* cannot even be tied in getting an answer. He will *always* get it first.

Our second concern is with S*s*' perceptions of these answer-getting potentials. We suggest that these random differences in answer-getting potentials rapidly structure members' perceptions of their own roles in the group. These differences affect one's independence from, or dependence on, the other members of the group. In the wheel, for example, a peripheral S perceives, at first, only that he gets the answer and information from C and can send only to C. C perceives that he gets information from everyone and must send the answer to everyone. The recognition of roles is easy. The peripheral men are dependent on C. C is autonomous and controls the organization.

In the circle, an S's perception must be very different. He gets information from both sides; sometimes he gets the answer, sometimes he sends it. He has two channels of communication. He is exclusively dependent on no one. His role is not clearly different from anyone else's.

Thirdly, having closed the gap between structural pattern and Ss' perceptions of their roles in the group, the problem reduces to one purely psychological. The question becomes: How do differences in one's perception of one's own dependence or independence bring about specific behavior differences of the sort we have observed?

Differences in satisfaction level are relatively easy to relate to independence. In our culture, in which needs for autonomy, recognition, and achievement are strong, it is to be expected that positions which limit independence of action (peripheral positions) would be unsatisfying.

A fairly direct relationship between centrality (and, hence, independence) and the speed with which a group gets organized is also perceptible. In the wheel, unless Ss act "unintelligently," an organization, with C as center, is forced on the wheel groups by the structural pattern. In the circle, no such differences in role and, hence, in organization are forced on the group.

Message-activity can also be related to centrality by means of the independence-of-action concept. A peripheral person in any pattern can send messages to only one other position. Only one informational message is called for. Extra messages would be repetitious. Central positions, however, are free to send more than one nonrepetitious informational message until an organization evolves.

Once the most central man perceives that he is most central, he need send no informational messages. But so long as the most central man does not perceive his own position, it is intelligent to send informational messages to whomever he feels may require some information. It is in keeping with this analysis that the circle should yield maximum messages and the wheel minimum messages.

If the behavior of one of the wheel groups can be discounted, then an explanation, in terms of peripherality, is also possible for both differences in tendencies to correct errors and total error differences.

If peripherality determines one's independence of action, it seems very likely that positions most limited in independence should begin to perceive themselves as subordinates whose sole function is to send information and await an answer. That they should then uncritically accept whatever answer they receive is perfectly in keeping with their subordinate, relatively unresponsible positions—hence, very little correction of errors in the patterns in which there are great differences in peripherality.

Total errors, it will be recalled, were correlated with total peripherality indices but showed no clear relationship with the relative peripherality of particular positions. A consideration of our definition of error may shed some light on this apparent anomaly.

The "errors" that we recorded were signals from the S that indicated a wrong answer. But these wrong answers derived from a variety of sources. First, Ss might wrongly interpret the correct information they received. They might also make errors in throwing switches; and they might also correctly interpret wrong information. In all three cases, "errors" were recorded.

We submit that this broad definition of error should yield a total pattern relationship with peripherality, but no positional relationship. Our reasoning can be illustrated by an example. Suppose that the central man in the wheel wrongly interprets information sent to him, and, hence, throws an incorrect switch. This is a "real" error. He then funnels out the wrong answer to the other members. At least three of these intelligently conclude that the answer sent them is correct and also throw the wrong switches. We then have three "false" errors consequent to our single "real" one. When several independent answer decisions are made (as in the circle), we should expect several real errors, multiplication of these by a factor of about 3, and a larger total of errors. This process should lead to a correlation between total pattern behavior and peripherality but not to a correlation between positional behavior and peripherality. The process simply multiplies real errors more or less constantly for a whole pattern but obscures positional differences because the "real" and the "false" errors are indistinguishable in our data.

We submit, further, that pattern differences in real errors, if such there be, may be attributable to "overinformation"; too much information to too many members which, under pressure, leads to errors. Central positions or positions which are no less central than others in the pattern should be the ones to yield the greatest number of real errors, while peripheral positions, which require no such rapid collation of information, should be the false error sources. Such a hypothesis would be in keeping with our total pattern findings and might also clarify our positional findings. Only an experiment designed to differentiate real from false errors can answer this question.

It is in keeping with this peripherality-independence analysis, also, that we should find the recognition of a single leader occurring most frequently in the wheel and Y groups. It is also to be expected that we should find circle members emphasizing need for organization and planning and seldom giving a complete picture of their pattern. Perhaps, too, it is reasonable to expect that the whole group should be considered good in the highly organized wheel (and

not so good in the unorganized circle) even though one's own job is considered poor.

In summary, then, it is our feeling that centrality determines behavior by limiting independence of action, thus producing differences in activity, accuracy, satisfaction, leadership, recognition of pattern, and other behavioral characteristics.

Summary and Conclusion

Within the limits set by the experimental conditions—group size, type of problem, source of Ss—these conclusions seem warranted:

1. The communication patterns within which our groups worked affected their behavior. The major behavioral differences attributable to communication patterns were differences in accuracy, total activity, satisfaction of group members, emergence of a leader, and organization of the group. There may also be differences among patterns in speed of problem-solving, self-correcting tendencies, and durability of the group as a group.

2. The positions which individuals occupied in a communication pattern affected their behavior while occupying those positions. One's position in the group affected the chances of becoming a leader of the group, one's satisfaction with one's job and with the group, the quantity of one's activity, and the extent to which one contributed to the group's functional organization.

3. The characteristic of communication patterns that was most clearly correlated with behavioral differences was *centrality*. Total pattern differences in behavior seemed to be correlated with a measure of centrality we have labeled the *peripherality index*. Positional differences in behavior seemed to be correlated with the positional peripherality indices of the various positions within patterns.

4. It is tentatively suggested that centrality affects behavior via the limits that centrality imposes upon independent action. Independence of action, relative to other members of the group, is, in turn, held to

be the primary determinant of the definition of who shall take the leadership role, total activity, satisfaction with one's lot, and other specific behaviors.

More precisely, it is felt that where centrality and, hence, independence are evenly distributed, there will be no leader, many errors, high activity, slow organization, and high satisfaction. Whatever frustration occurs will occur as a result of the inadequacy of the group, not the inadequacy of the environment.

Where one position is low in centrality relative to other members of the group, that position will be a follower position, dependent on the leader, accepting his dictates, falling into a role that allows little opportunity for prestige, activity, or self-expression.

Group Factors

in Worker Productivity ❊ George Caspar Homans

In April, 1927, six girls were selected from a large shop department of the Hawthorne works. They were chosen as average workers, neither inexperienced nor expert, and their work consisted of the assembling of telephone relays. A coil, armature, contact springs, and insulators were put together on a fixture and secured in position by means of four machine screws. The operation at that time was being completed at the rate of about five relays in six minutes. This particular operation was chosen for the experiment because the relays were being assembled often enough so that even slight changes in output rate would show themselves at once on the output record. Five of the girls were to do the actual assembly work; the duty of the sixth was to keep the others supplied with parts.

The test room itself was an area divided from the main department by a wooden partition eight feet high. The girls sat in a row on one side of a long workbench. The bench and assembly equipment were identical with those used in the regular department, except in one respect. At the right of each girl's place was a hole in the bench, and into this hole she dropped completed relays. It was the entrance to a chute, in which there was a flapper gate opened by the relay in its passage downward. The opening of the gate closed an electrical circuit which controlled a perforating device, and this in turn recorded the completion of the relay by punching a hole in a tape. The tape moved at the rate of one-quarter of an inch a minute and had space for a separate row of holes for each operator. When punched, it thus constituted a complete output record for each girl for each instant of the day. Such records were kept for five years.

In this experiment, then, as in the earlier illumination experiments, great emphasis was laid on the rate of output. A word of caution is needed here. The Western Electric Company was not immediately interested in increasing output. The experiments were not designed for that purpose. On the other hand, output is easily measured, i.e., it yields precise quantitative data, and experience suggested that it was sensitive to at least some of the conditions under which the employees worked. Output was treated as an index. In short, the nature of the experi-

From Chapter 4 of *Fatigue of Workers: Its Relation to Industrial Production* by the Committee on Work in Industry of the National Research Council, New York: Reinhold Publishing Corporation, 1941. Reprinted by permission of the author and publisher.

mental conditions made the emphasis on output inevitable.

From their experience in the illumination experiments, the investigators were well aware that factors other than those experimentally varied might affect the output rate. Therefore arrangements were made that a number of other records should be kept. Unsuitable parts supplied by the firm were noted down, as were assemblies rejected for any reason upon inspection. In this way the type of defect could be known and related to the time of day at which it occurred. Records were kept of weather conditions in general and of temperature and humidity in the test room. Every six weeks each operator was given a medical examination by the company doctor. Every day she was asked to tell how many hours she had spent in bed the night before and, during a part of the experiment, what food she had eaten. Besides all these records, which concerned the physical condition of the operators, a log was kept in which were recorded the principal events in the test room hour by hour, including among the entries snatches of conversation between the workers. At first these entries related largely to the physical condition of the operators: how they felt as they worked. Later the ground they covered somewhat widened, and the log ultimately became one of the most important of the test room records. Finally, when the so-called Interviewing Program was instituted at Hawthorne, each of the operators was interviewed several times by an experienced interviewer.

The girls had no supervisor in the ordinary sense, such as they would have had in a regular shop department, but a "test room observer" was placed in the room, whose duty it was to maintain the records, arrange the work, and secure a cooperative spirit on the part of the girls. Later, when the complexity of his work increased, several assistants were assigned to help him.

When the arrangements had been made for the test room, the operators who had been chosen to take part were called in for an interview in the office of the superintendent of the Inspection Branch, who was in general charge of the experiment and of the researches which grew out of it. The superintendent described this interview as follows: "The nature of the test was carefully explained to these girls and they readily consented to take part in it, although they were very shy at the first conference. An invitation to six shop girls to come up to a superintendent's office was naturally rather startling. They were assured that the object of the test was to determine the effect of certain changes in working conditions, such as rest periods, midmorning lunches, and shorter working hours. They were expressly cautioned to work at a comfortable pace, and under no circumstances to try and make a race out of the test." This conference was only the first of many. Whenever any experimental change was planned, the girls were called in, the purpose of the change was explained to them, and their comments were requested. Certain suggested changes which did not meet with their approval were abandoned. They were repeatedly asked, as they were asked in the first interview, not to strain but to work "as they felt."

The experiment was now ready to begin. Put in its simplest terms, the idea of those directing the experiment was that if an output curve was studied for a long enough time under various changes in working conditions, it would be possible to determine which conditions were the most satisfactory. Accordingly, a number of so-called "experimental periods" were arranged. For two weeks before the operators were placed in the test room, a record was kept of the production of each one without her knowledge. In this way the investigators secured a measure of her productive ability while working in the regular department under the usual conditions. This constituted the first experimental period. And for five weeks after the girls entered the test room no change was made in working conditions. Hours remained what they had been before. The investigators felt that this period would be long enough to reveal any changes in output incidental merely to the transfer. This constituted the second experimental period.

The third period involved a change in the method of payment. In the regular department, the girls had been paid according to a scheme of group piecework, the group consisting of a hundred or more employees. Under these circumstances, variations in an individual's total output would not be immediately reflected in her pay, since such variations tended to cancel one another in such a large group. In the test room, the six operators were made a group by themselves. In this way each girl received an amount more nearly in proportion to her individual effort, and her interests became more closely centered on the experiment. Eight weeks later, the directly experimental changes began. An outline will reveal their general character: Period IV: two rest pauses, each five minutes in length, were established, one occurring in midmorning and the other in the early afternoon. Period V: these rest pauses were lengthened to ten minutes each. Period VI: six five-minute rests were established. Period VII: the company provided each member of the group with a light lunch in the midmorning and another in the midafternoon, accompanied by rest pauses. This arrangement became standard for subsequent Periods VIII through XI. Period VIII: work stopped a half-hour earlier every day —at 4:30 P.M. Period IX: work stopped at 4 P.M. Period X: conditions returned to what they were in Period VII. Perod XI: a five-day work week was established. Each of these experimental periods lasted several weeks.

Period XI ran through the summer of 1928, a year after the beginning of the experiment. Already the results were not what had been expected. The output curve, which had risen on the whole slowly and steadily throughout the year, was obviously reflecting something other than the responses of the group to the imposed experimental conditions. Even when the total weekly output had fallen off, as it could

hardly fail to do in such a period as Period XI, when the group was working only five days a week, daily output continued to rise. Therefore, in accordance with a sound experimental procedure, as a control on what had been done, it was agreed with the consent of the operators that in experimental Period XII a return should be made to the original conditions of work, with no rest pauses, no special lunches, and a full-length working week. This period lasted for twelve weeks. Both daily and weekly output rose to a higher point than ever before: the working day and the working week were both longer. The hourly output rate declined somewhat but it did not approach the level of Period III, when similar conditions were in effect.

The conclusons reached after Period XII may be expressed in terms of another observation. Identical conditions of work were repeated in three different experimental periods: Periods VII, X, and XIII. If the assumptions on which the study was based had been correct, that is to say, if the output rate were directly related to the physical conditions of work, the expectation would be that in these three experimental periods there would be some similarity in output. Such was not the case. The only apparent uniformity was that in each experimental period output was higher than in the preceding one. In the Relay Assembly Test Room, as in the previous illumination experiments, something was happening which could not be explained by the experimentally controlled conditions of work.

The question remains:

With what facts, if any, can the changes in the output rate of the operators in the test room be correlated? Here the statements of the girls themselves are of the first importance. Each girl knew that she was producing more in the test room than she ever had in the regular department, and each said that the increase had come about without any conscious effort on her part. It seemed easier to produce at the faster rate in the test room than at the slower rate in the regular department. When questioned further each girl stated her reasons in slightly different words, but there was uniformity in the answers in two respects. First, the girls liked to work in the test room; "it was fun." Secondly, the new supervisory relation or, as they put it, the absence of the old supervisory control, made it possible for them to work freely without anxiety.

For instance, there was the matter of conversation. In the regular department, conversation was in principle not allowed. In practice it was tolerated if it was carried on in a low tone and did not interfere with work. In the test room an effort was made in the beginning to discourage conversation, though it was soon abandoned. The observer in charge of the experiment was afraid of losing the cooperation of the girls if he insisted too strongly on this point. Talk became common and was often loud and general. Indeed, the conversation of the operators came to occupy an important place in the log. T. N. Whitehead has pointed out that the girls in the test room were far more thoroughly supervised than they ever had been in the regular department. They were watched by an observer of their own, an interested management, and outside experts. The point is that the character and purpose of the supervision were different and were felt to be so.

The operators knew that they were taking part in what was considered an important and interesting experiment. They knew that their work was expected to produce results —they were not sure what results—which would lead to the improvement of the working conditions of their fellow employees. They knew that the eyes of the company were upon them. Whitehead has further pointed out that although the experimental changes might turn out to have no physical significance, their social significance was always favorable. They showed that the management of the company was still interested, that the girls were still part of a valuable piece of research. In the regular department, the girls, like the other employees, were in the position of responding to changes the

source and purpose of which were beyond their knowledge. In the test room, they had frequent interviews with the superintendent, a high officer of the company. The reasons for the contemplated experimental changes were explained to them. Their views were consulted and in some instances they were allowed to veto what had been proposed. Professor Mayo has argued that it is idle to speak of an experimental period like Period XII as being in any sense what it purported to be—a return to the original conditions of work. In the meantime, the entire industrial situation of the girls had been reconstructed.

Another factor in what occurred can only be spoken of as the social development of the group itself. When the girls went for the first time to be given a physical examination by the company doctor, someone suggested as a joke that ice cream and cake ought to be served. The company provided them at the next examination, and the custom was kept up for the duration of the experiment. When one of the girls had a birthday, each of the others would bring her a present, and she would respond by offering the group a box of chocolates. Often one of the girls would have some good reason for feeling tired. Then the others would "carry" her. That is, they would agree to work especially fast to make up for the low output expected from her. It is doubtful whether this "carrying" did have any effect, but the important point is the existence of the practice, not its effectiveness. The girls made friends in the test room and went together socially after hours. One of the interesting facts which has appeared from Whitehead's analysis of the output records is that there were times when variations in the output rates of two friends were correlated to a high degree. Their rates varied simultaneously and in the same direction—something, of course, which the girls were not aware of and could not have planned. Also, these correlations were destroyed by such apparently trivial events as a change in the order in which the girls sat at the workbench.

Finally, the group developed leadership

and a common purpose. The leader, self-appointed, was an ambitious young Italian girl who entered the test room as a replacement after two of the original members had left. She saw in the experiment a chance for personal distinction and advancement. The common purpose was an increase in the output rate. The girls had been told in the beginning and repeatedly thereafter that they were to work without straining, without trying to make a race of the test, and all the evidence shows that they kept this rule. In fact, they felt that they were working under less pressure than in the regular department. Nevertheless, they knew that the output record was considered the most important of the records of the experiment and was always closely scrutinized. Before long they had committed themselves to a continuous increase in production. In the long run, of course, this ideal was an impossible one, and when the girls found out that it was, the realization was an important element of the change of tone which was noticeable in the second half of the experiment. But for a time they felt that they could achieve the impossible. In brief, the increase in the output rate of the girls in the Relay Assembly Test Room could not be related to any changes in their physical conditions of work, whether experimentally induced or not. It could, however, be related to what can only be spoken of as the development of an organized social group in a peculiar and effective relation with its supervisors.

Many of these conclusions were not worked out in detail until long after the investigators at Hawthorne had lost interest in the Relay Assembly Test Room, but the general meaning of the experiment was clear at least as early as Period XII. A continuous increase in productivity had taken place irrespective of changing physical conditions of work. In the words of a company report made in January 1931 on all the research which had been done up to that date: "Upon analysis, only one thing seemed to show a continuous relationship with this improved output. This was the mental attitude of the operators. From their conversations with each other and their comments to the test observers, it was not only clear that their attitudes were improving but it was evident that this area of employee reactions and feelings was a fruitful field for industrial research."

At this point the attention of the investigators turned sharply from the test room to the regular shop department from which the girls had come. Why was the mental attitude of the girls different in the test room from what it had been in the department? In their conversations with one another and in their comments to the observers, the girls were full of comparisons between the test room and the department, very much to the disadvantage of the latter. They felt relief from some form of constraint, particularly the constraint of supervision. They were exceedingly disparaging about the supervisors in the department, although management felt that the department had particularly good supervisory personnel. These facts suggested that the management of the company really knew very little about the attitudes which employees took toward conditions in the plant and very little also about what constituted good supervisory methods. Such was the atmosphere in which the so-called Interviewing Program, the third phase of the work at Hawthorne, was planned. So far the interests of the investigators had been centered on the question of what were good physical conditions of work. Now they shifted definitely in the direction of a study of human relations.

Finally, the investigators discovered, in the course of the regular interviews, evidence here and there in the plant of a type of behavior which strongly suggested that the workers were banding together informally in order to protect themselves against practices which they interpreted as a menace to their welfare. This type of behavior manifested itself in (a) "straight-line" output, that is, the operators had adopted a standard of what they felt to be a proper day's work and none of them exceeded it by very much; (b) a resentment of the wage incentive system under which they worked —in most cases, some form of group piecework; (c) expressions which implied that group piecework as a wage incentive plan was not working satisfactorily; (d) informal practices by which persons who exceeded the accepted standard, that is, "rate killers," could be punished and "brought into line"; (e) informal leadership on the part of individuals who undertook to keep the working group together and enforce its rules; (f) feelings of futility with regard to promotions; and (g) extreme likes and dislikes toward immediate superiors, according to their attitude toward the behavior of the operators. The investigators felt that this complex of behavior deserved further study.

In view of these considerations, the decision was taken in May, 1931, to assign selected interviewers to particular groups of employees and allow them to interview the employees as often as they felt was necessary. The story of one of these groups is characteristic of the findings reached by this new form of interviewing. The work of the employees was the adjustment of small parts which went into the construction of telephone equipment. The management thought that the adjustment was a complicated piece of work. The interviewer found that it was really quite simple. He felt that anyone could learn it, but that the operators had conspired to put a fence around the job. They took pride in telling how apparatus which no one could make work properly was sent in from the field for adjustment. Then telephone engineers would come in to find out from the operators how the repairs were made. The latter would fool around, doing all sorts of wrong things and taking about two hours to adjust the apparatus, and in this way prevented people on the outside from finding out what they really did. They delighted in telling the interviewer how they were pulling the wool over everybody's eyes. It followed that they were keeping the management in ignorance as to the amount of work they could do. The output of the group,

when plotted, was practically a straight line.

Obviously this result could not have been gained without some informal organization, and such organization in fact there was. The group had developed leadership. Whenever an outsider—engineer, inspector, or supervisor—came into the room, one man always dealt with him. Whenever any technical question was raised about the work, this employee answered it. For other purposes, the group had developed a second leader. Whenever a new man came into the group, or a member of the group boosted output beyond what was considered the proper level, this second leader took charge of the situation. The group had, so to speak, one leader for dealing with foreign and one for dealing with domestic affairs. The different supervisors were largely aware of the situation which had developed, but they did not try to do anything about it because in fact they were powerless. Whenever necessary, they themselves dealt with the recognized leaders of the group.

Finally, the investigator found that the group was by no means happy about what it was doing. Its members felt a vague dissatisfaction or unrest, which showed itself in a demand for advancements and transfers or in complaints about their hard luck in being kept on the job. This experience of personal futility could be explained as the result of divided loyalties—divided between the group and the company.

In order to study this kind of problem further, to make a more detailed investigation of social relations in a working group, and to supplement interview material with direct observation of the behavior of employees, the Division of Industrial Research decided to set up a new test room. But the investigators remembered what happened in the former test room and tried to devise an experiment which would not be radically altered by the process of experimentation itself. They chose a group of men—nine wiremen, three soldermen, and two inspectors— engaged in the assembly of terminal banks for use in telephone exchanges, took them out of their regular department, and placed them in a special room. Otherwise no change was made in their conditions of work, except that an investigator was installed in the room, whose duty was simply to observe the behavior of the men. In the Relay Assembly Test Room a log had been kept of the principal events of the test. At the beginning it consisted largely of comments made by the workers in answer to questions about their physical condition. Later it came to include a much wider range of entries, which were found to be extremely useful in interpreting the changes in the output rate of the different workers. The work of the observer in the new test room was in effect an expansion of the work of keeping the log in the old one. Finally, an interviewer was assigned to the test room; he was not, however, one of the population of the room but remained outside and interviewed the employees from time to time in the usual manner. No effort was made to get output records other than the ones ordinarily kept in the department from which the group came, since the investigators felt that such a procedure would introduce too large a change from a regular shop situation. In this way the experiment was set up which is referred to as the Bank Wiring Observation Room. It was in existence seven months, from November 1931 to May 1932.

The method of payment is the first aspect of this group which must be described. It was a complicated form of group piecework. The department of which the workers in the observation room were a part was credited with a fixed sum for every unit of equipment it assembled. The amount thus earned on paper by the department every week made up the sum out of which the wages of all the men in the department were paid. Each individual was then assigned an hourly rate of pay, and he was guaranteed this amount in case he did not make at least as much on a piecework basis. The rate was based on a number of factors, including the nature of the job a worker was doing, his efficiency, and his length of service with the company.

Records of the output of every worker were kept, and every six months there was a rate revision, the purpose of which was to make the hourly rates of the different workers correspond to their relative efficiency.

The hourly rate of a given employee, multiplied by the number of hours worked by him during the week, was spoken of as the daywork value of the work done by the employee. The daywork values of the work by all the employees in the department were then added together, and the total thus obtained was subtracted from the total earnings credited to the department for the number of units of equipment assembled. The surplus, divided by the total daywork value, was expressed as a percentage. Each individual's hourly rate was then increased by this percentage, and the resulting hourly earnings figure, multiplied by the number of hours worked, constituted that person's weekly earnings.

Another feature of the system should be mentioned here. Sometimes a stoppage which was beyond the control of the workers took place in the work. For such stoppages the workers were entitled to claim time out, being paid at their regular hourly rates for this time. This was called the "daywork allowance claim." The reason why the employees were paid their hourly rate for such time and not their average hourly wages was a simple one. The system was supposed to prevent stalling. The employees could earn more by working than they could by taking time out. As a matter of fact, there was no good definition of what constituted a stoppage which was beyond the control of the workers. All stoppages were more or less within their control. But this circumstance was supposed to make no difference in the working of the system, since the assumption was that in any case the workers, pursuing their economic interests, would be anxious to keep stoppages at a minimum.

This system of payment was a complicated one, but it is obvious that there was a good logical reason for every one of its features. An individual's earnings would be affected by changes in his rate or in his output and by changes in the output of the group as a whole. The only way in which the group as a whole could increase its earnings was by increasing its total output. It is obvious also that the experts who designed the system made certain implicit assumptions about the behavior of human beings, or at least the behavior of workers in a large American factor. They assumed that every employee would pursue his economic interest by trying to increase not only his own output but the output of every other person in the group. The group as a whole would act to prevent slacking by any of its members. One possibility, for instance, was that by a few weeks' hard work an employee could establish a high rate for himself. Then he could slack up and be paid out of all proportion with the amount he actually contributed to the wages of the group. Under these circumstances, the other employees were expected to bring pressure to bear to make him work harder.

Such was the way in which the wage incentive scheme ought to have worked. The next question is how it actually did work. At first the workers were naturally suspicious of the observer, but when they got used to him and found that nothing out of the ordinary happened as a result of his presence in the room, they came to take him for granted. The best evidence that the employees were not distrustful of the observer is that they were willing to talk freely to him about what they were doing, even when what they were doing was not strictly in accord with what the company expected. Conversation would die down when the group chief entered the room, and when the foreman or the assistant foreman entered everyone became serious. But no embarrassment was felt at the presence of the observer. To avoid misunderstanding it is important to point out that the observer was in no sense a spy. The employees were deliberately and obviously separated from their regular department. The observer did not, and could not, pass himself off as one of them. And if only from the fact that a special interviewer was assigned to them, the members of the group knew they were under investigation.

The findings reached by the observer were more detailed but in general character the same as those which had emerged from the early interviews of other groups. Among the employees in the observation room there was a notion of a proper day's work. They felt that if they had wired two equipments a day they had done about the right amount. Most of the work was done in the morning. As soon as the employees felt sure of being able to finish what they considered enough for the day, they slacked off. This slacking off was naturally more marked among the faster than among the slower workmen.

As a result, the output graph from week to week tended to be a straight line. The employees resorted to two further practices in order to make sure that it should remain so. They reported more or less output than they performed and they claimed more daywork allowances than they were entitled to. At the end of the day, the observer would make an actual count of the number of connections wired—something which was not done by the supervisors—and he found that the men would report to the group chief sometimes more and sometimes less work than they actually had accomplished. At the end of the period of observation, two men had completed more than they ever had reported, but on the whole the error was in the opposite direction. The theory of the employees was that excess work produced on one day should be saved and applied to a deficiency on another day. The other way of keeping the output steady was to claim excessive daywork allowance. The employees saw that the more daywork they were allowed, the less output they would have to maintain in order to keep the average hourly output rate steady. The claims for daywork allowance were reported by the men to their group chief, and he, as will be seen, was in no position to make any check. These practices had two results. In the first place, the departmental efficiency records did not represent true efficiency, and therefore decisions as to grading were subject to errors of considerable importance. In the second place, the group chief was placed in a distinctly awkward position.

The findings of the observer were confirmed by tests which were made as a part of the investigation. Tests of intelligence, finger dexterity, and other skills were given to the workers in the room, and the results of the tests were studied in order to discover whether there was any correlation between output on the one hand and earnings, intelligence, or finger dexterity on the other. The studies showed that there was not. The output was apparently not reflecting the native intelligence or dexterity of the members of the group.

Obviously the wage incentive scheme was not working in the way it was expected to work. The next question is why it was not working. In this connection, the observer reported that the group had developed an informal social organization, such as had been revealed by earlier investigations. The foreman who selected the employees taking part in the Bank Wiring Observation Room was cooperative and had worked with the investigators before. They asked him to produce a normal group. The men he chose all came out of the same regular shop department, but they had not been closely associated in their work there. Nevertheless, as soon as they were thrown together in the observation room, friendships sprang up and soon two well-defined cliques were formed. The division into cliques showed itself in a number of ways: in mutual exclusiveness, in differences in the games played during off-hours, and so forth.

What is important here is not what divided the men in the observation room but what they had in common. They shared a common body of sentiments. A person should not turn out too much work. If he did, he was a "rate-buster." The theory was that if an excessive amount of work was turned out, the management would lower the piecework rate so that the employees

would be in the position of doing more work for approximately the same pay. On the other hand, a person should not turn out too little work. If he did, he was a "chiseler"; that is, he was getting paid for work he did not do. A person should say nothing which would injure a fellow member of the group. If he did, he was a "squealer." Finally, no member of the group should act officiously.

The working group had also developed methods of enforcing respect for its attitudes. The experts who devised the wage incentive scheme assumed that the group would bring pressure to bear upon the slower workers to make them work faster and so increase the earnings of the group. In point of fact, something like the opposite occurred. The employees brought pressure to bear not upon the slower workers but upon the faster ones, the very ones who contributed most to the earnings of the group. The pressure was brought to bear in various ways. One of them was "binging." If one of the employees did something which was not considered quite proper, one of his fellow workers had the right to "bing" him. Binging consisted of hitting him a stiff blow on the upper arm. The person who was struck usually took the blow without protest and did not strike back. Obviously the virtue of binging as punishment did not lie in the physical hurt given to the worker but in the mental hurt that came from knowing that the group disapproved of what he had done. Other practices which naturally served the same end were sarcasm and the use of invectives. If a person turned out too much work, he was called names, such as "Speed King" or "The Slave."

It is worth while pointing out that the output of the group was not considered low. If it had been, some action might have been taken, but in point of fact it was perfectly satisfactory to the management. It was simply not so high as it would have been if fatigue and skill had been the only limiting factors.

In the matter of wage incentives, the actual situation was quite different from the assumptions made by the experts. Other activities were out of line in the same way. The wiremen and the soldermen did not stick to their jobs; they frequently traded them. This was forbidden, on the theory that each employee ought to do his own work because he was more skilled in that work. There was also much informal helping of one man by others. In fact, the observation of this practice was one means of determining the cliques into which the group was divided. A great many things, in short, were going on in the observation room which ought not to have been going on. For this reason it was important that no one should "squeal" on the men.

A group chief was in immediate charge of the employees. He had to see that they were supplied with parts and that they conformed to the rules and standards of the work. He could reprimand them for misbehavior or poor performance. He transmitted orders to the men and brought their requests before the proper authorities. He was also responsible for reporting to the foreman all facts which ought to come to his attention. The behavior of the employees put him in an awkward position. He was perfectly well aware of the devices by which they maintained their production at a constant level. But he was able to do very little to bring about a change. For instance, there was the matter of claims for daywork allowance. Such claims were supposed to be based on stoppages beyond the control of the workers, but there was no good definition of what constituted such stoppages. The men had a number of possible excuses for claiming daywork allowance: defective materials, poor and slow work on the part of other employees, and so forth. If the group chief checked upon one type of claim, the workers could shift to another. In order to decide whether or not a particular claim was justified, he would have to stand over the group all day with a stop watch. He did not have time to do that, and in any case refusal to honor the employees' claims would imply doubt of their integrity and would arouse

their hostility. The group chief was a representative of management and was supposed to look after its interests. He ought to have put a stop to these practices and reported them to the foreman. But if he did so, he would, to use the words of a short account of the observation room by Roethlisberger and Dickson, "lose sympathetic control of his men, and his duties as supervisor would become much more difficult." [1] He had to associate with the employees from day to day and from hour to hour. His task would become impossible if he had to fight a running fight with them. Placed in this situation, he chose to side with the men and report unchanged their claims for daywork. In fact there was very little else he could do, even if he wished. Moreover he was in a position to protect himself in case of trouble. The employees always had to give him a reason for any daywork claims they might make, and he entered the claims in a private record book. If anyone ever asked why so much daywork was being claimed, he could throw the blame wherever he wished. He could assert that materials had been defective or he could blame the inspectors, who were members of an outside organization. In still another respect, then, the Bank Wiring Observation Room group was not behaving as the logic of management assumed that it would behave.

Restriction of output is a common phenomenon of industrial plants. It is usually explained as a highly logical reaction of the workers. They have increased their output, whereupon their wage rates for piecework have been reduced. They are doing more work for the same pay. They restrict their output in order to avoid a repetition of this experience. Perhaps this explanation holds good in some cases, but the findings of the Bank Wiring Observation Room suggest

[1] F. J. Roethlisberger and W. J. Dickson, "Management and the worker," *Bus. Res. Stud.*, No. 9 (Cambridge, Mass.: Harvard Business School, Division of Research, 1939). (All quotations relating to the Western Electric researches are from this study as well as from the book of the same title by the same authors.)

that it is too simple. The workers in the room were obsessed with the idea that they ought to hold their production level "even" from week to week, but they were vague as to what would happen if they did not. They said that "someone" would "get them." If they turned out an unusually high output one week, that record would be taken thereafter as an example of what they could do if they tried, and they would be "bawled out" if they did not keep up to it. As a matter of fact, none of the men in the room had ever experienced a reduction of wage rates. What is more, as Roethlisberger and Dickson point out, "changes in piece rates occur most frequently where there is a change in manufacturing process, and changes in manufacturing process are made by engineers whose chief function is to reduce unit cost wherever the saving will justify the change. In some instances, changes occur irrespective of direct labor cost. Moreover, where labor is a substantial element, reduction of output tends to increase unit costs and instead of warding off a change in the piece rate may actually induce one."

What happened in the observation room could not be described as a logical reaction of the employees to the experience of rate reduction. They had in fact had no such experience. On the other hand, the investigators found that it could be described as a conflict between the technical organization of the plant and its social organization. By technical organization the investigators meant the plan, written or unwritten, according to which the Hawthorne plant was supposed to operate, and the agencies which gave effect to that plan. The plan included explicit rules as to how the men were to be paid, how they were to do their work, what their relations with their supervisors ought to be. It included also implicit assumptions on which the rules were based, one of the assumptions being that men working in the plant would on the whole act so as to further their economic interests. It is worth while pointing out that the assumption was in fact implicit, that the experts

who devised the technical organization acted upon the assumption without ever stating it in so many words.

There existed also an actual social situation within the plant: groups of men, who were associated with one another, held common sentiments and had certain relations with other groups and other men. To some extent this social organization was identical with the technical plan and to some extent it was not. For instance, the employees were paid according to group payment plans, but the groups concerned did not behave as the planners expected them to behave.

The investigators considered the relations between the technical organization and the social. A certain type of behavior is expected of the higher levels of management. Their success is dependent on their being able to devise and institute rapid changes. Roethlisberger and Dickson describe what happens in the following terms: "Management is constantly making mechanical improvements and instituting changes designed to reduce costs or improve the quality of the product. It is constantly seeking new ways and new combinations for increasing efficiency, whether in designing a new machine, instituting a new method of control, or logically organizing itself in a new way." The assumption has often been made that these changes are designed to force the employee to do more work for less money. As a matter of fact, many of them have just the opposite purpose: to improve the conditions of work and enable the employee to earn higher wages. The important point here, however, is not the purpose of the changes but the way in which they are carried out and accepted.

Once the responsible officer has decided that a certain change ought to be made, he gives an order, and this order is transmitted "down the line," appropriate action being taken at every level. The question in which the investigators were interested was this: What happens when the order reaches the men who are actually doing the manual work? Roethlisberger and Dickson made the following observations: "The worker occupies a unique position in the social organization. He is at the bottom of a highly stratified organization. He is always in the position of having to accommodate himself to changes which he does not originate. Although he participates least in the technical organization, he bears the brunt of most of its activities." It is he, more than anyone, who is affected by the decisions of management, yet in the nature of things he is unable to share management's preoccupations, and management does little to convince him that what he considers important is being treated as important at the top—a fact which is not surprising since there is no adequate way of transmitting to management an understanding of the considerations which seem important at the work level. There is something like a failure of communication in both directions—upward and downward.

The worker is not only "asked to accommodate himself to changes which he does not initiate, but also many of the changes deprive him of those very things which give meaning and significance to his work." The modern industrial worker is not the handicraftsman of the medieval guild. Nevertheless, the two have much in common. The industrial worker develops his own ways of doing his job, his own traditions of skill, his own satisfactions in living up to his standards. The spirit in which he adopts his own innovations is quite different from that in which he adopts those of management. Furthermore, he does not do his work as an isolated human being, but always as a member of a group, united either through actual cooperation on the job or through association in friendship. One of the most important general findings of the Western Electric researches is the fact that such groups are continually being formed among industrial workers, and that the groups develop codes and loyalties which govern the relations of the members to one another. Though these codes can be quickly destroyed, they are not formed in a moment. They are the product

of continued, routine interaction between men. "Constant interference with such codes is bound to lead to feelings of frustration, to an irrational exasperation with technical change in any form, and ultimately to the formation of a type of employee organization such as we have described—a system of practices and beliefs in opposition to the technical organization."

The Bank Wiring Observation Room seemed to show that action taken in accordance with the technical organization tended to break up, through continual change, the routines and human associations which gave work its value. The behavior of the employees could be described as an effort to protect themselves against such changes, to give management the least possible opportunity of interfering with them. When they said that if they increased their output, "something" was likely to happen, a process of this sort was going on in their minds. But the process was not a conscious one. It is important to point out that the protective function of informal organization was not a product of deliberate planning. It was more in the nature of an automatic response. The curious thing is that, as Professor Mayo pointed out to the Committee, these informal organizations much resembled formally organized labor unions, although the employees would not have recognized the fact.

Roethlisberger and Dickson summarize as follows the results of the intensive study of small groups of employees: "According to our analysis the uniformity of behavior manifested by these groups was the outcome of a disparity in the rates of change possible in the technical organization, on the one hand, and in the social organization, on the other. The social sentiments and customs of work of the employees were unable to accommodate themselves to the rapid technical innovations introduced. The result was to incite a blind resistance to all innovations and to provoke the formation of a social organization at a lower level in opposition to the technical organization."

It is curious how, at all points, the Relay

Assembly Test Room and the Bank Wiring Observation Room form a contrast. In the former, the girls said that they felt free from the pressure of supervision, although as a matter of fact they were far more thoroughly supervised than they ever had been in their regular department. In the latter, the men were afraid of supervision and acted so as to nullify it. The Bank Wiremen were in the position of having to respond to technical changes which they did not originate. The Relay Assemblers had periodic conferences with the superintendent. They were told what experimental changes were contemplated; their views were canvassed, and in some instances they were allowed to veto what had been proposed. They were part of an experiment which they felt was interesting and important. Both groups developed an informal social organization, but while the Bank Wiremen were organized in opposition to management, the Relay Assemblers were organized in cooperation with management in the pursuit of a common purpose. Finally, the responses of the two groups to their industrial situation were, on the one hand, restriction of output and, on the other, steady and welcome increase of output. These contrasts carry their own lesson.

PART VI

Stress and Conflict in Group Life

INTRODUCTION

Tightly woven into the cultural and organizational fabric of a complex society are many fundamental social problems. We have already alluded to ethnic prejudice, mental illness, and labor-management strife in the previous discussions, and to this list can be added international conflict, political extremism, economic poverty, drug addiction, as well as many others. In this section we shall consider a number of investigations directly relevant to some of these problems. In each case the investigator has attempted to cast some light on the social-psychological factors underlying the emergence of a particular social problem. Before turning to these studies, it is important to clarify a number of issues regarding research endeavors directed at the social ills of a society.

In no sense should it be assumed that the social problems of a society are atypical phenomena which can be divorced or isolated from the more acceptable social realities of its existence. Human behavior expresses itself in a variety of ways, and whether it is condemned or condoned by the members of the society in no way alters its status as a significant phenomenon to be explained by the social psychologist and other behavioral scientists. As a number of theorists have noted, most social problems, even the worst of them, are functionally related to the acceptable values and institutions of a society. Given the emphasis on status and achievement in American society—and these are clearly acceptable values—it is little wonder that the norms of particular groups of individuals involve prejudicial attitudes and discriminatory behavior with respect to one or more minority groups.

The fact that a particular social problem is inherent in the structure of a social system in no way reduces its significance as a potential threat to the existence of that system. It is for this reason, among others, that increasing demands have been made on the social psychologist to direct his research efforts at these problems in order to help solve them. During the last two decades the number of such investigations has multiplied manyfold, and in the process, significant advances in theory and method in social psychology have taken place. It is important, however, not to exaggerate the role of the social psychologist in his effort to solve these problems. His function is clearly a limited one in at least two respects. First, any one of these problems is rooted in a host of other factors beside those that are psychological in nature, and in this respect the contributions of other behavioral scientists are needed to understand it fully. Furthermore, even if we had such understanding at the present time, the ultimate solution of the problem lies in the hands of many other individuals in the society: legislators, social planners, government officials, and, indeed, the members of the society itself. Knowing the factors that underlie a given social problem and the changes needed to eliminate it is one thing; bringing about such changes is still another. As we have already observed, it is by no means a simple matter to effect changes in the established norms, values, and behaviors of a group. The fact that the recommended changes have a firm empirical basis— as in the case of recommended health practices—in no way guarantees that the task of bringing about change will be any easier.

It was not uncommon at one time to describe investigations of social problems as "applied" research in contrast to so-called pure research. An important implication of the distinction was that applied research was directed at solving specific practical problems determined by others, and, therefore, in contrast to pure research, had much less to offer by way of establishing a body of general concepts and principles for explaining man's social behavior. In recent years the validity of this implication has been seriously questioned by many social psychologists. Science does not exist in a social vacuum. The pure scientist no less than his applied colleague conducts his research in a given society and, therefore, is no less influenced in the problems he selects for study by the values and pressures of that society. Research, whether pure or applied, costs money, and those who are ready to offer it for this purpose exert considerable influence on what problems are to be selected for study. The forces that shaped developments in research on atomic energy were as much social as they were scientific—a fact only recently grasped by many physical scientists.

What should be stressed is that pure and applied research in social psychology are interdependent scientific endeavors. Each has a contribution to make to the other and each is a necessary ingredient for the development of a science. Without general concepts and principles, the analysis of a particular social problem in a given situation falls back on traditional, common-sense ways of viewing it. On the other hand, the validity of any abstract theoretical system rests on its ability to explain social events in concrete situations. Investigations of a social problem in a given setting can be both theoretically meaningful and socially useful. Such investigations, under appropriate circumstances, can serve as a source of new facts and hypotheses and can provide the opportunity for testing existing theoretical conceptions.

Although it is simple enough to describe the contributions that can be made by applied research to the development of a body of principles in social psychology, it should not be assumed that such a description is the usual consequence of an applied investigation. The fact that demands are made on the services of the social psychologist to "solve" an immediate social problem is no guarantee that he will be able to formulate his research in terms of existing concepts and principles. In fact, both the urgency of the problem and the tendency of the social practitioner to conceive of it in familiar and practical terms very often preclude this possibility. What are often desired are ready-made schemes for changing attitudes, increasing morale, or reducing supervisor-worker conflict. From the practitioner's point of view, the pressing need is to get immediate and practical answers, not to establish the conceptual properties of the specific problem that will relate it to other quite different problems. Of course, this is not always the case and, where it is not, research, as we noted above, may be both theoretically meaningful and socially useful.

To what extent can we expect changes in the attitudes and behavior of individuals under conditions of severe restraint directed at producing such changes? Two of the papers in the present section provide some tentative answers to this question. The study by Schein (VIA) focuses on the "brainwashing" techniques employed by the Chinese Communists during the Korean conflict in their attempt to convert UN prisoners of war to the Communist ideology. The analysis by Bettelheim (VIA) deals with the experiences of political prisoners in Nazi concentration camps where the primary purpose was to "break the prisoners as individuals." Broadly conceived, the approaches taken in the two prison settings to produce changes in behavior and attitudes were similar. Prisoners were exposed to intense physical and psychological stress in an environment that was completely controlled in almost every detail by their captors. The same underlying assumption was involved: in order to produce effective and enduring changes in thought and action it was necessary to demolish the self-identity of the individual. By subjecting him to continual stress, his ability to resist such changes would be considerably weakened. And by undermining his social relationships and his group memberships—both of which provide the necessary consensual validation for his standards, attitudes, and values—established ways of thinking and acting would soon be discarded.

As we indicated above, however, the essential objectives of the Chinese Communists and the Nazis were not the same. The ultimate goal of the latter was to change the individual from an active antagonist to a completely docile slave laborer. The adult was to become the child once again, standing in awe of the omnipotent parent whose every wish had to be obeyed. The Chinese Communists, on the other hand, aimed at replacing one adult self-identity with another, with substituting the ideology of the Western democracies with the values and belief systems of the Communist viewpoint. The objective was true conversion and not subjugation. Given this essential difference in purpose, we find corresponding differences in the methods used in the two settings. In the concentration camp not only was the use of physical and psychological torture carried to its extreme, but punitive treatment was the primary if not the only method employed to change the individual. The only reward was the eventual reduction of these punishments over time if the prisoner survived and in fact gave indications of his complete docility and subjugation.

The Red Chinese, in their concern with ideological conversion, made a greater use of psychological pressures than of physical ones. Their approach was systematic and thorough in that almost every known device for changing attitudes and behavior was employed: lectures, group discussions, interrogations, self-criticism, confessions, mass media, and others. What should be emphasized is that rewards as well as punishments were employed to control the behavior of the men. In fact, the approach leaned heavily toward a policy of "leniency" in which the prisoners were treated as individuals in need of "education." Only the prisoners who showed themselves to be "reactionary" were treated punitively.

The essence of the method involved, on the one hand, eliminating group ties and social interactions that sustained the old attitudes, beliefs, and values, and, on the other, creating new interactions and emotional ties that would increase the probability of the internalization of the new ideology. Each prisoner was permitted to have contacts only with others whose views were entirely different from his own, and on this basis there was a strong possibility that a growing attraction to some of them would lead to his identifying with them and subsequently adopting their views. One is immediately reminded of the Asch (VA) investigation in which the greatest conformity occurred when the critical subject found the evidence of his senses unanimously contradicted by a group of his peers.

From his interviews with some prisoners and from other sources of information, Schein concludes that the Chinese had little success in actually changing beliefs and attitudes. Conversion to Communism was the exception rather than the rule. With respect to collaboration, however, the Chinese clearly had far more success. Some 10 to 15 percent of the men were chronic collaborators in that they gave lectures, wrote and broadcast propaganda, signed petitions, informed on fellow prisoners, and so on. A larger proportion of prisoners engaged in some collaborative activities at one time or another. Individuals collaborated for one of a number of reasons. Some cooperated because of the material benefits or rewards which resulted; others because they could not withstand the physical and psychological rigors. Kelman's concept of changes in behavior or attitudes based on compliance seems relevant to these two groups of collaborators (IIIA). There is public conformity because rewards are to be gained and punishments avoided. Other prisoners were tricked into collaboration and then rationalized their continued involvement with the Chinese with the belief that they could help the UN forces in this way. Finally, men of low status in this society as well as various malcontents and minority group members were actually attracted to the ideological appeal of Communism.

There were, however, other men who continually resisted and obstructed the Chinese attempts at indoctrination. And among these individuals there were also differences in the factors underlying their resistance. Finally, the largest proportion of prisoners, Schein points out, were those who established a compromise between their own beliefs and values and the demands of their captors. It is clearly evident that how individuals behave under conditions of severe stress is as much a function of their personality dispositions and past history as it is of the nature of the stress-producing situation itself.

On the basis of Bettelheim's analysis of the concentration camp situation it seems evident that greater success was achieved by the Nazis. In the light of their simpler objective—to reduce the individual to an "infantile" state by brutal treatment—this is to be expected. Undoubtedly, the alternative to complete subjugation was death. Most revealing was the fact that in time the prisoners tended to identify with the punitive authority figures of the camp and to internalize many of the values they held. They imitated their style of dress and speech, curried their favor, and attempted to coerce other prisoners to follow the camp rules strictly.

In our previous discussions we focused almost exclusively on the behavior of individuals as members of face-to-face groups that were normative in character. The fundamental significance of these group memberships in an understanding of the social existence of the individual has already been indicated. Social scientists, however (as well as laymen) have also been very much interested in more transient interaction situations involving larger numbers of individuals, or what is generally referred to as "mass phenomena" (Brown, 1954). The nexus of this interest has been less on the usual or commonplace mass-behavior situation, for example, a group of persons passively watching a fire or a typical theater audience, and more on the unusual or extreme interaction situation exemplified by a mob bent on destruction, a riot at a sports event, or a widespread panic during a crisis. In general, attempts have been made to distinguish audiences, crowds, and mobs. Audiences are considered more passive groups usually involved in ritualized responses to some focal event, whereas crowds are regarded as more spontaneous and emotional groups. When crowds move into action, they take on the properties of mobs.

According to Brown (1954) mobs may be distinguished in terms of their predominant behavior tendency. "Aggressive" mobs are bent on the destruction of individuals or property—lynchings, riots, and so on. When faced with extreme danger, groups of individuals may panic and thereby take on the character of an "escape" mob. Mobs may also be "acquisitive" in their orientation as exemplified by the "bank run," or the rush of housewives to secure foods believed to be in low supply. Finally, groups of individuals primarily involved in emotional release are characterized as "expressive" mobs; an example is the religious revival.

Attempts to explain mob action have usually involved two rather distinct issues. The first concerns the conditions or factors which lead to this kind of mass response. In most instances, a specific precipitating incident can be identified, but as Lee and Humphrey (1943) point out in their analysis of the Detroit race riots in 1943, the occurrence of these riots cannot be explained solely by the event that set them off. The event itself derived its potency from a set of conflict-producing conditions involving Negroes and whites that were in operation long before the riots occurred. In their analysis the investigators point to such factors as the influx of Southern Negroes and whites in the previous years, congested housing and recreational facilities, resentment by the Negroes because of continued segregation while many of their race were fighting in the war, and others. The importance of examining the properties of the larger social context as a basis for understanding mob action cannot be stressed too strongly.

A second issue concerns the general properties of a mob once it has been set into action. Mobs have urgent and focused objectives that are pursued by their members in an atmosphere of intense emotionality. Furthermore, the members of a mob show considerable homogeneity in their thought and action, and in many instances these responses are marked by an irrational quality. Any number of theorists have attempted to explain these properties of the mob (Brown, 1954). Le Bon, for example, invoked the concepts of "contagion" and "suggestion" to explain the uniformity of behavior in a mob; McDougall, on the other hand, spoke of "primitive sympathy," while for Park the critical term was "rapport." Still other concepts can be cited. Unfortunately, when these concepts are laid bare, they all turn out to be more elaborate descriptions of the tendency of individuals in a crowd to behave like one another.

In recent years investigators have paid considerable attention to the behavior of individuals in disaster situations—fires, tornados, and so on. A number of studies illuminate the conditions that provoke a panic reaction ("escape" mob), in contrast to those that lead to coordinated efforts to combat the danger. In his analysis of reactions to disasters in a number of communities in the Southwest, Killian (1954) found that panic was likely to occur when there was ambiguity concerning the possibility of escape. Regarding the now-famous "Invasion from Mars" broadcast, Cantril (1952) reports that panic occurred among those listeners who, once having accepted the broadcast as factual, then perceived that any delay in the attempt to escape would mean certain destruction. Fritz and Marks (1954) studied an actual disaster and found that the more warning time given so as to allow for preparation, the less likelihood there would be of a panic response. If the warning was too brief to allow for such preparation, then the individual would be no better off than if he received no warning at all. Panic is also less likely to occur in a crisis situation if effective communication exists among the individuals involved.

The study by Mintz (VIA) points to still another important condition responsible for panic behavior: the breakdown in cooperative behavior. He argues that panic is likely to occur during disaster when individuals perceive that their own safety is no longer contingent on the safety of others. Once cooperative or coordinated behavior breaks down, individuals compete with each other to survive and hence panic results. The selfish needs of the individual take precedence over the needs of the group. Mintz tested his formulation in a laboratory study in which each of a number of individuals had to remove an aluminum cone from a large bottle. Each cone had a string attached to it and only one cone could be drawn out of the bottle at a time; hence without cooperation, jamming would occur at the neck of the bottle. When subjects were told that they would receive rewards or punishments for their performance, jamming occurred quite often, and this was true even when the subjects were allowed to make a preliminary plan as a group. Under nonincentive conditions the task was simply described as a study of cooperative activity and subjects were allowed to draw up a plan of action. No serious jamming took place under these conditions.

Ethnic prejudice exists when the members of one ethnic group hold negative or unfavorable attitudes toward the members of another ethnic group. The term "ethnic group" is used in the general sense of any collection of people who are identified by themselves and others in terms of their racial origin, religion, national origin, or language and cultural traditions. It should be apparent that all individuals in the United States are members of more than one ethnic group.

Ethnic prejudice continues to be a critical social problem on the American scene. Few other social problems have been subjected to as much theoretical analysis and systematic investigation by social psychologists and sociologists. This is as it should be. Ethnic prejudice is a complex social phenomenon that cannot be explained in terms of some simple cause and effect relationship. In the introduction to Part III we emphasized the fact that attitudes toward the same object vary in terms of their structural properties and the kinds of needs they may satisfy in the individual. On this basis alone it is evident that prejudice undoubtedly takes many forms rather than a single form; hence not one but several methods will be required to change these attitudes.

A review of the literature on ethnic prejudice reveals that many theoretical conceptions have been applied to the problem. Considering that prejudice, like any other social problem, has many causal factors, we would expect different theorists to stress the importance of different determinants or classes of determinants. Indeed, this is the case, which means that in general these theories are not mutually exclusive interpretations, but rather are interlocking or complementary conceptions, all of which are necessary for an understanding of the problem. The need for an eclectic approach is stressed by Allport (1954): "By far the best view to take toward this multiplicity of approaches is to admit them all. Each has something to teach us" (p. 218).

In general, the many theories of prejudice reflect two broad fundamental orientations. The first focuses on factors that are external to the individual: cultural and group norms, conflict and competition between groups, intergroup contacts, status mobility, parental influences, and others. The significance of some of these factors in the development of attitudes generally has been stressed a number of times in the previous discussions. It will be recalled, for example, that Horowitz (IIIA) found that the attitudes of white children toward Negroes was a function of contact with the prevalent attitude rather than of experiences with members of this minority group. The second orientation to be found in theories of prejudice stresses determinants within the individual: frustration and displaced hostility, projection, cognitive function, personality structure, and others. External influences are by no means denied, but greater concern is given to the psychological consequences of these influences in terms of the nature of prejudicial attitudes and their functional significance for the person. In the remaining discussion we will have occasion to consider some of the viewpoints representing the two major orientations.

By means of intensive interviews Bettelheim and Janowitz (VIB) studied the ethnic attitudes of a group of war veterans. The importance of a person's economic and social status as a determinant of these attitudes has long been emphasized. Yet the data of these investigators show that it is not the present status of the person which regulates prejudice but rather the changes in his status, that is, his upward or downward social mobility. They found both anti-Semitism and anti-Negro attitudes most frequent among those veterans whose economic status had declined from its prewar position. Those who had shown economic improvement were more friendly toward both groups than those whose status had remained the same.

Displaced aggression as a factor in ethnic prejudice has long been stressed by psychoanalytically oriented theorists. This approach, which is one version of the "scapegoat" theory of prejudice, assumes the following: first, that frustration arouses aggression; second, that because direct expression of the aggression has been blocked, it is displaced to existing minority group targets; and, finally, that the displaced aggression is rationalized by stereotyping, blaming, and so on. Thus, the greater prejudice found by Bettelheim and Janowitz (VIB) among the veterans who had shown downward social mobility could be interpreted in this fashion. However, they actually provide a more direct test of the relationship between experienced frustration and minority group prejudice. They found that, among veterans who experienced frustration in the army, almost five times as many were intolerant as tolerant; whereas for those veterans exposed to more or less the same objective conditions without experiencing frustration, the majority were tolerant. Further support for the displacement of aggression hypothesis is provided by Campbell (1947), Gough (1951), and Morse (1947). Campbell found, for example, that anti-Semitism is high when job satisfaction is low.

Other findings of the Bettelheim and Janowitz study suggest that ethnic prejudice may also be related to the individual's ability to control his aggressive tendencies. The latter, in turn, would be reflected in the extent to which the person accepts the values of his society. Where these values or the authority figures who symbolize them were openly rejected, it was assumed that control over aggressive tendencies was low. It was found that where such rejection occurred, ethnic intolerance was high. Taken together the findings of this study point to the importance of personality factors as well as sociocultural factors in the development of ethnic prejudice.

The study by Frenkel-Brunswik, Levinson, and Sanford (VIB) deals directly with fundamental personality dispositions or character structure as a basis for hostility toward members of minority groups. The assumption is made, as we noted in the introduction to Part III, that social attitudes may operate as "symptoms" of deeper underlying personality conflicts. Unacceptable, and therefore unconscious, hostile and sexual impulses are projected onto socially acceptable targets, thereby providing some satisfaction for these impulses without the individual's experiencing the pain of recognizing them as his own.

Studying large numbers of non-Jewish, white, native-born, middle-class Americans, Frenkel-Brunswik, Levinson, and Sanford were able to demonstrate high positive correlations among attitude scores involving a number of ethnic groups.

On this basis they intensively studied and compared a group of women who were extremely high on ethnocentrism with another group who were extremely low in this respect. The subjects in the two groups were clinically interviewed, and administered the Rorschach and the Thematic Apperception Tests. The highly ethnocentric women, in contrast to those low in ethnocentrism, were found to idealize their parents as authority figures, to be conventionally moralistic toward others, to be materialistic and exploitative toward the opposite sex, to think in dichotomous terms, to be impersonal and punitive in their aggression, and to be concerned with status and power relationships. These characteristics in turn are explained in terms of a childhood in which rigid discipline, conditional love, and clearly defined roles of dominance and submission were primary features. The unconscious conflict involving fear of and dependency on the parents, on the one hand, and strong feelings of hatred and suspicion of them, on the other, is contained by an authoritarian personality structure that finds an outlet for these hostile feelings in negative attitudes toward minority groups.

The study by Christiansen (VIC) sheds further light on the influence of personality factors on ethnic attitudes; in particular, on attitudes toward national groups. The investigation was undertaken in Norway with applicants to and students of two military academies. By employing appropriate instruments, the investigator measured the following: the degree to which the subjects expressed aggressive reactions in everyday conflict situations and in international conflict situations; the amount of conflict involved in the handling of psychosexual impulses, which was employed as a measure of latent aggression; and, finally, the extent of their knowledge of the international situation and their nationalistic feelings. It was found that the degree of underlying conflict or latent aggression was positively associated with aggressive solutions to international conflict situations ($r = .33$). Of greater significance is the fact that it was also evident that the tendency to displace aggression in this way depended on the degree to which the individual was nationalistic. Christiansen concludes that nationalism may be a mediating factor "for the degree to which latent personality factors are likely to colour a person's international attitudes." Another significant finding was that individuals expressing aggression in everyday conflict situations tended to generalize this aggression to international conflict situations ($r = .42$). However, this was most likely to occur in individuals who were relatively free of latent aggression and who were highly nationalistic. One other more tentative finding is worth noting: There is some indication that when latent aggression is pronounced, the person is less likely to express it in the international sphere if he "drains" it off in everyday conflict situations.

In contrast to the emphasis given to personality factors in ethnic prejudice, other theorists stress the group membership of the individual in relation to conflict and competition between his group and others. The analysis of the Detroit race riots by Lee and Humphrey (1943) we cited earlier is a case in point. Different ethnic groups may become economic competitors through geographical migration as well as through upward social mobility. The paper by Sherif (VIC), although not directly concerned with ethnic attitudes, illustrates the importance of rivalry and conflict between groups as a basis for the formation of negative feelings, beliefs, and action tendencies in the members of one group toward the members of the other. The two groups in question were artificially formed at a boys' camp, but each group developed strong in-group solidarity and became very important for its members through a succession of group activities. After the groups were well established a program of intergroup competition was initiated, with the result that the members of each group developed hostile feelings and unfavorable stereotypes toward the other group and its members. Each group avoided the other and open conflict in the form of raids, name-calling, and the like was evident.

It was at this stage in each of his investigations that Sherif attempted to reduce intergroup conflict by means of a number of methods including friendly social contacts between the rival groups and the use of superordinate goals which required cooperative interaction between them. The former was found to be ineffective, whereas the latter proved to be successful in reducing intergroup conflict. The superordinate goal condition presented both groups with a common and compelling problem which could be solved only by cooperative action on the part of members of both groups. Data collected before and after the successive use of problems of this kind, which in each case led to cooperative action between the two groups, revealed a decrease in name-calling, more favorable feelings toward and less stereotyping of out-group members, less glorification of one's own group, and an increase in sociometric preferences for out-group members.

In considering other methods of reducing intergroup conflict, Sherif points out that the use of group leaders meeting alone to negotiate the problem is not an effective technique. Each leader is still dependent on the prevailing attitudes and orientations of his membership; if he deviates too far from their expectations in arriving at a settlement he is likely to lose his role as leader. Blake and Mouton (VIC) tested the hypothesis that where group representatives meet under conditions where compromise is not possible, that is, where one must win and the other lose, then the meetings are more likely to end in deadlock than in capitulation based on a logical evaluation of which of the two positions is better. Not unlike Sherif's line of reasoning, it was assumed that under these circumstances representatives are not free to engage in a logical analysis of the problem or to engage in compromise since group members would interpret such a solution as a defeat. Some 520 persons, including supervisory and executive personnel as well as college students, were set up in 62 groups that engaged in the same sequence of in-group and intergroup activities. Groups were then set in competition with each other, with the outcome of the win-lose competition depending on the negotiations of the representatives from each of these groups. The results indicated that only 2 of the 62 representatives gave in to the opposition, thereby suggesting that in-group loyalty worked against a logical analysis of the problem.

The "well-earned reputation" theory of prejudice holds that ethnic prejudice evolves out of differences in the objective characteristics of the members of different groups which are observed in the course of interactions between them. We have already noted that prejudice develops in the absence of contact between members of different groups (Horowitz, IIIA); still another argument against this view is the fact that common stereotypes of various ethnic groups seldom correspond to the actual characteristics of their members. Furthermore, in many instances simultaneously held stereotypes about a particular group are often incompatible; and it has been shown that stereotypes change over time without changes in the actual attributes of the group to which they refer. Of course, this does not mean that personal contact does not play a role in the formation of ethnic attitudes. Not only does such contact increase the salience of the individual's attitude toward another group; repeated observations of the group may contribute to the development of particular stereotypes about them. The Sherif (VIC) study suggests that under conditions of intergroup contact, it is not the objective characteristics of the members that are of primary importance, but rather the nature of the relationships between the two groups, that is, competitive vs. cooperative (Harding, Kutner, Proshansky, and Chein, 1954).

We would expect, therefore, that, under appropriate conditions of intergroup contact, negative ethnic attitudes would become more positive. The remaining three investigations in Part VI provide considerable support for this assumption. In the study by Star, Williams, and Stouffer (VIB) a majority of the white officers (93 percent) and the enlisted men (60 percent) who were in companies which included Negro platoons, indicated that white and Negro soldiers got along "very well" together; the remainder stated that they got along "fairly well." This occurred despite the fact that two thirds of each group, according to their own retrospective report, began the experience with relatively unfavorable attitudes toward serving in a mixed company. More revealing is the fact that the closer soldiers came to a mixed-company organization the less opposition they showed to it. Thus, infantrymen in a company that had a Negro platoon approved of it most; men in larger units in which there were no mixed companies were least favorable toward it; while men in all-white companies within a regiment or division containing mixed companies held intermediate opinions. It should be noted that the white officers and enlisted men in mixed companies overwhelmingly endorsed the performance of Negro soldiers in combat. Intergroup contact between majority and minority group members is likely to result in a reduction of prejudice if the two groups are in a cooperative, equal-status situation in which the behavior of the latter does not conform to the stereotypes held by the dominant group.

The findings reported by Deutsch and Collins (VIB) on the effects of residential contact on interracial attitudes provide considerable support for this conclusion. They compared the attitudes and behavior of housewives living in segregated housing projects with those of housewives living in integrated projects. It was found that living in an integrated project resulted in more frequent and more intimate interpersonal experiences involving Negroes and whites than living in a segregated one. Over 95 percent of the women in two integrated projects reported that a person living in the project would get to know some Negroes living there; on the other hand, the majority of the housewives living in the two segregated projects were convinced that this was not likely to occur. Only a very small percentage of the respondents in the segregated projects indicated they knew any Negro people well enough to call them by their first names, whereas this degree of intimacy was true of approximately half the women in one integrated project, and over three quarters in the other.

Using a variety of measures, Deutsch and Collins also found that housewives in the integrated projects were less prejudiced against Negroes than were those in the segregated ones. This was true of measures of attitudes toward Negroes in general, as well as of those that focused on Negroes in the projects. There were probably some differences in initial attitude toward Negroes among housewives in the two types of project, but the investigators were able to show that these differences could not have accounted for more than a small part of the difference in attitude found after several years of living in the projects. In their conclusions they point to the specific conditions that are required in intergroup contacts if they are to foster a reduction in prejudice, some of which we have already noted.

Yarrow, Campbell, and Yarrow (VIB) studied the behavior and attitudes of white and Negro children living in racially integrated camps for two-week periods. Comparable information was obtained from racially segregated camps to provide a baseline for evaluating the effects of the interracial contacts. Boys and girls between the ages of eight and thirteen from low-income families were studied in the two settings by means of interviews, detailed behavior observations, counselor ratings, and other techniques. It was found that although radical shifts in longstanding interracial orientations did not occur, both Negro and white children in the integrated setting showed an immediate adaptation to the demands of the situation. In effect, the social distance between the two groups was reduced, and race as a criterion of friendship exerted less influence at the end of the two-week period. A major factor which determined the new standards of conduct and feeling was the consistent expectation of equality that characterized the behavior of the counselors toward the children and that was reflected in the integrated culture of Negro and white counselors. Here again intergroup contact between racial groups was effective in changing attitudes and behavior in an equal-status setting in which cooperative relationships between the members of the two groups were emphasized.

References

ALLPORT, G. W. *The nature of prejudice.* Reading, Mass.: Addison-Wesley, 1954.

BROWN, R. W. Mass phenomena. In G. Lindzey (Ed.), *Handbook of social psychology*, Vol. 2. Reading, Mass.: Addison-Wesley, 1954.

CAMPBELL, A. A. Factors associated with attitudes toward Jews. In T. M. Newcomb and E. L. Hartley (Eds.), *Readings in social psychology.* New York: Holt, Rinehart and Winston, 1947.

CANTRIL, H. The invasion from Mars. In G. E. Swanson, T. M. Newcomb, and E. L. Hartley (Eds.), *Readings in social psychology*, Rev. Ed. New York: Holt, Rinehart and Winston, 1952.

FRITZ, C. E., and MARKS, E. S. The NORC studies of human behavior in disaster. *J. soc. Issues*, 1954, 10, 26-41.

GOUGH, H. G. Studies of social intolerance: I. Some psychological and sociological correlates of anti-Semitism. *J. soc. Psychol.*, 1951, 33, 237-246.

HARDING, J., KUTNER, B., PROSHANSKY, H., and CHEIN, I. Ethnic prejudice. In G. Lindzey (Ed.), *Handbook of social psychology*, Vol. 2. Reading, Mass.: Addison-Wesley, 1954.

KILLIAN, L. M. Some accomplishments and some needs in disaster study. *J. soc. Issues*, 1954, *10*, 66-72.

LEE, A. M., and HUMPHREY, N. D. *Race riot*. New York: Holt, Rinehart and Winston, 1943.

MORSE, N. C. Anti-Semitism: a study of its causal variables and other associated variables. Unpublished doctoral dissertation, Syracuse Univer., 1947.

A. THE INDIVIDUAL

UNDER STRESS

Nonadaptive Group Behavior ❧ Alexander Mintz

Theoretical Considerations

It is common knowledge that groups of people frequently behave in a way which leads to disastrous consequences not desired or anticipated by the members of the group. At theater fires, people often block the exits by pushing, so that individuals are burned or trampled. Since it normally takes only a few minutes for a theater to be emptied, the strikingly nonadaptive character of this behavior is obvious.

In the explanations for the occurrence of such behavior offered by social psychologists, intense emotional excitement resulting from mutual facilitation (or "contagion" or "suggestion") and leading to interference with thinking, adaptive behavior, and the operation of moral codes, has tended to be viewed as the decisive factor. Ultimately they stem from the theories of the nature of crowd behavior of Le Bon (1916), who has been an extremely influential figure in the thinking on social issues of the past fifty years.

Material will be presented in this paper suggesting that violent emotional excitement is not the decisive factor[1] in the nonadaptive behavior of people in panics and related situations. Instead, it appears to be possible to explain the nonadaptive character of such behavior in terms of [people's] perception of the situation and their expectation of what is likely to happen.

What are the reasonable expectations of people at a theater fire or in similar circumstances in which a panic is apt to develop? Situations of this type tend to have a characteristically unstable reward structure, which has been generally overlooked by social scientists as a factor in panics. Cooperative behavior is required for the common good but has very different consequences for the individual depending on the behavior of others. Thus at a theater fire, if everyone leaves in an orderly manner, everybody is safe, and an individual waiting for his turn is not sacrificing his interests. But, if the cooperative pattern of behavior is disturbed, the usual advice, "Keep your head, don't

[1] Its existence is not denied.

From the *Journal of Abnormal and Social Psychology*, 1951, *46*, 150-159. Reprinted by permission of the author and the American Psychological Association.

push, wait for your turn, and you will be safe," ceases to be valid. If the exits are blocked, the person following this advice is likely to be burned to death. In other words, if everybody cooperates, there is no conflict between the needs of the individual and those of the group. However, the situation changes completely as soon as a minority of people cease to cooperate. A conflict between the needs of the group and the selfish needs of the individual then arises. An individual who recognizes this state of things and who wants to benefit the group must sacrifice his own selfish needs.

It is suggested here that it is chiefly the reward structure of the situations which is responsible for nonadaptive behavior of groups at theater fires and similar situations. People are likely to recognize the threats to themselves, as they appear, and behave accordingly. These situations may be compared to states of unstable equilibrium in mechanics; a cone balanced on its tip is not likely to remain in this position a long time because a slight initial displacement of its center of gravity allows the force of gravity to make it fall all the way. Similarly, cooperative behavior at a theater fire is likely to deteriorate progressively as soon as an initial disturbance occurs. If a few individuals begin to push, the others are apt to recognize that their interests are threatened; they can expect to win through to their individual rewards only by pressing their personal advantages at the group's expense. Many of them react accordingly, a vicious circle is set up, and the disturbance spreads. Competitive behavior (pushing and fighting) may result as, e.g., at theater fires, or the group may disperse as in military panics. There is another factor which makes for further disintegration. As the behavior of the group becomes increasingly disorderly, the amount of noise is apt to increase, and communication may then become so difficult that no plan for restoring order can emerge.

This interpretation is almost the reverse of the conventional ones which ascribe nonadaptive group behavior to emotional facilitation and to the supposed alterations of personality in group situations.

The existence of mutual emotional facilitation is not denied; its operation can be readily observed, e.g., in college students during final examinations, in audiences at sports events, etc. However, it is not believed that emotional excitement as such is responsible for nonadaptive group behavior. There are many situations in which intense emotional excitement is the rule, and yet no nonadaptive group behavior appears. Thus it has been reported that intense fear is practically universally present in soldiers about to go into battle, and yet no panic need develop. Similarly, participants in an athletic contest are apt to be so emotionally excited that vomiting is common; no markedly nonadaptive group behavior appears to develop as a result of this kind of intense excitement.

The assumption of personality alterations of people due to crowd membership appears to be entirely unsubstantiated in the case of panics. On the contrary, the competitive behavior or dispersal occurring in panics suggests that group cohesion disappears and that people begin to behave purely as individuals in accordance with their selfish needs.[2] Rather similarly Freud has explained certain types of panics in terms of the disappearance of the libidinal ties between individuals (1910).

As a first step toward the verification of the proposed theory, a set of laboratory experiments was devised. It was thought that if the theory were correct, it should be possible to illustrate its functioning in the laboratory. If not substantiated by laboratory findings, the theory would have to be discarded.

Experimental Design

The experiments were conducted with groups of people, 15 to 21 subjects in each

[2] I am indebted to Dr. M. Scheerer for pointing out this inference from the suggested theory.

group. The subjects had the task of pulling cones out of a glass bottle; each subject was given a piece of string to which a cone was attached. Cooperation on the part of the subjects was required if the cones were to come out; the physical setup made it easy for "traffic jams" of cones to appear at the bottle neck. Only one cone could come out at a time; even a near tie between two cones at the bottle neck prevented both from coming out because the narrow apex of the second cone, wedged into the bottle neck, blocked the path for the wide base of the cone ahead of it. The cones had to arrive at the bottle neck in order, one at a time.

EXPERIMENTAL SITUATIONS

1. One of the experimental setups was designed to show that it was possible to produce disorganized, uncooperative, nonadaporative group behavior resulting in "traffic jams" by duplicating the essential features of panic-producing situations, as explained in the theoretical section of this paper. The experimental situation was represented to the subjects as a game in which each participant could win or lose money. A subject could win or lose depending on how successful he was in pulling out his cone. Success was defined in terms of arbitrary time limits in some experiments. In other experiments water was made to flow into the bottle through a spout near the bottom, and the subject was successful if his cone came out of the bottle untouched by the water. Inasmuch as the rewards and fines were offered to individuals, depending on what would happen to their particular cones, it was thought that the cooperative pattern of behavior, required for group success, would be easily disrupted; a momentary "traffic jam" at the bottle neck would be perceived by some of the subjects as threatening them with loss in the game as a result of the anticipated failure of cooperative behavior. These subjects would be tempted to save themselves from the loss by pulling out of turn. Some of them would probably do so, and thus the situation could be expected

rapidly to deteriorate after an initial disturbance occurred.

In order that subjects who recognized that full success was out of their reach should not stop trying, intermediate steps between full success and full failure were announced. The details and the amounts of rewards and fines are summarized in the table of results in the original source. The monetary rewards and fines were very small, the rewards for full success ranging from 10 to 25 cents, the fines for full failure from 1 to 10 cents. The very small fines were decided upon because it was intended to show that the characteristically inefficient, nonadaptive features of group behavior such as occurs in panics can be reproduced in a situation in which there was no opportunity for fear. It was not thought that the small rewards and fines were likely to constitute real financial incentives for college students. They were introduced to emphasize the nature of the experimental situation as a game in which individuals could win or lose.

2. In the contrasting experimental setups there were no individual rewards or fines, and there was no flow of water except for a few control experiments. The experiments were described as attempts to measure the ability of groups of people to behave cooperatively. Good performances of other groups were quoted. It was expected that under these conditions no "traffic jams" would develop. Subjects had no motivation to disregard any plan that might be devised by the group; the only incentive offered was membership in a group of people who were going to show their ability to cooperate effectively with each other.[3] Thus the reward structure was the principal experimental variable studied in these two experimental situations.

3. Another variable investigated was the excitement built up by mutual facilitation.

[3] The need to belong has been particularly emphasized as an important motive, among others, by Fromm (1941) and Sherif (1948). The important role which group membership plays in industry has been investigated particularly in the Hawthorne studies; see, for example, Whitehead (1938).

In a number of "no-reward" experiments several subjects were asked to act as accomplices. They were secretly instructed, before the experiment began, to scream, behave excitedly, swear, and make as much noise as possible. To limit their influence to emotional facilitation they were asked not to give specific bad advice nor to disturb the workings of any plan the group might decide upon. It was expected that the added emotional excitement, which is the major factor in Le Bon's and similar theories of panics, would not have much effect on results.

4. In certain of the reward-and-fine experiments an attempt was made to minimize the opportunities for mutual emotional facilitation by largely preventing the subjects from seeing each other. This was accomplished by a circular screen with holes for eyes and arms and with vertical partitions on the outside, placed around the glass bottle. Each subject stood in an individual "stall" hiding him from his neighbors; he saw the bottle standing on the floor through the eye hole; only his arm and eyes could be seen by the other subjects, and the eyes were not likely to be seen because the subjects were mainly looking at the bottle tied to the floor. In order to prevent excited screams, the subjects were asked to remain silent after the experiment began, which request was largely complied with. It was expected that the results would be essentially the same as those in the other reward-and-fine experiments.

5. A third variable which was introduced in a few of the experiments was interference with the opportunity to arrive at a plan of action. In most of the experiments the subjects were not prevented from conducting preliminary discussions; in almost all instances either they started such a discussion immediately or asked for permission to do so, which was given. Only twice did a group fail to discuss and agree upon a plan when discussion was not explicitly forbidden. On the other hand, in two of the reward-and-fine experiments conducted early in the study the subjects were forbidden to talk to

each other both before and during the experiment; in one reward-and-fine experiment conducted immediately after three no-reward experiments with the same group, the subjects were prevented from having a preliminary discussion so that no plan could be agreed upon beforehand, but were allowed to talk during the experiment.

APPARATUS AND PROCEDURE

Figure 1 gives the shapes and dimensions of the cones and of the bottle and shows

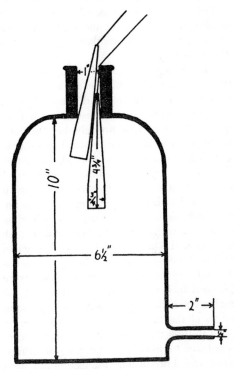

Fig. 1. Cross section of the glass bottle with two cones shown blocking the bottle neck. Main dimensions of the equipment are given.

where the pieces of string were attached. The cones were made of wood in the early experiments. Later, aluminum cones were substituted[4] because the wooden one tended to become tightly forced into the bottle neck

[4] Postwar shortages prevented the use of smooth plastic material, as had been intended.

and had to be loosened by hand (which was done promptly by the experimenter). In the experiments with the aluminum cones the glass bottle had too large an opening, which was remedied by the insertion of a cylinder with a 1-inch hole bored through it. This cylinder, made of aluminum, had rubber tape wound on the outside. It was forced tightly into the bottle neck and was tied down with wire. In addition to cutting down the opening of the bottle to the desired diameter, it also protected the glass from the impact of the aluminum cones. A sponge rubber pad was cemented to the bottom of the glass bottle. A rubber tube could be attached to the spout and lead either to a water faucet or to another similar bottle placed high up.

The screen was made of corrugated cardboard. Two strips 23.5 feet in length were cut off a 3-foot-wide roll and glued together, so that a strip 6 feet wide resulted. The ends of the strip could be brought together and the strip could be made to stand on edge in .he shape of a cylinder around the bottle. Pieces of corrugated cardboard, 3 feet by 1 foot, were attached to the screen at intervals of 1 foot 3 inches, subdividing the space immediately around the screen into individual stalls. The rectangular eye holes cut in each stall were 1.5 inches high, 5 inches wide; their bottoms were 4 feet 8 inches above the ground; the roughly circular arm holes were about 5 inches in diameter and 3 feet 1.5 inches from the ground, near the right-hand edges of the stalls. There were 18 stalls.

In putting the cones into the bottle, care was taken to prevent the tangling of strings; as an added precaution, the fishing line used as string was waxed in later experiments. In the early experiments the bottle was tied to the legs of a table on which it was placed. In the later experiments it was placed on the floor and tied to nails driven into the floor like tent stakes.

The instructions were not rigidly standardized. The rewards were always larger than the fines, ranging from 10 to 25 cents in different experiments. The fines ranged from 1 to 5 cents. Examples of the two main types of instructions and other details of the experiment follow:

1. *A reward-and-fine experiment.* "I need volunteers for an experiment which is set up as a game in which you can win up to a quarter or lose up to 2 cents [or 5 or 10 cents as the case may have been]." Then, after the volunteers (sometimes after some urging) assembled: "As I said, this is going to be like a game. Each of you will receive a cone with an attached piece of string. All cones will be placed into the bottle. The object of the game is to get your cone out before it gets wet. You may start pulling when I give the signal, 'ready-go!' but only one cone can come out at a time. If two get into the bottle neck, neither comes out (demonstration). Simultaneously, I shall start water flowing into the bottle. If your cone comes out dry you get a quarter. If less than a third of it is wet, you get nothing; if more than a third but less than two thirds of it gets wet, you pay a penny fine. If the cone is more than two-thirds wet, you pay a two-cent fine. The fines will be contributed to the Student Council." Then the students were asked to put their cones in the bottle. While they were doing it, a discussion of a plan of action generally started and was not interfered with by the experimenter.

The signal to begin was given after an agreement was reached by the subjects. When in doubt, the experimenter asked the group whether they were ready.

2. *A no-reward experiment.* "This is going to be an experiment in which your ability to cooperate with each other will be measured. I need volunteers." Then, after the subjects assembled around the bottle, the procedure continued exactly as in the reward-and-fine experiments except that no rewards were offered, the rubber tube was not attached, and no reference to water was made. Instead, after the possibility of "traffic jams" was demonstrated, the experimenter said: "In spite of the smallness of the opening, a group of students from the University of Nevada succeeded in cooper-

ating with each other so well that they got all their cones out in 10.5 seconds. See if you can do as well as the Westerners!"

Results

Forty-two experiments with 26 groups of subjects were performed altogether, including some preliminary and control experiments conducted to investigate potential sources of error. One experiment (R_1) was conducted before the procedure was fully developed; there were no fines and only one reward level was announced. No "traffic jam" resulted.

There were 16 experiments with rewards and fines. In three of them (RF_1 to RF_3) discussion was interfered with before the experiment, so that the subjects had no opportunity to devise a plan of action. In all three experiments "traffic jams" developed. In only one of them did the subjects succeed in pulling *any* cones out of the bottle—two cones out of 19 in 40 seconds; these same subjects had successfully pulled out *all* cones in 18.6 seconds and 23 seconds in two immediately preceding trials in which they had had the opportunity to agree upon a plan of action.

In the other 13 reward-and-fine experiments (RF_4 to RF_{16}) discussion was not interfered with. In eight of these experiments (RF_4 to RF_6, RF_9, RF_{10}, RF_{12}, RF_{13}, and RF_{16}) there were serious "traffic jams," the large majority of the cones failing to be pulled out of the bottle within times ranging from 1 to approximately 2 minutes. In another experiment almost half of the cones were in the bottle after 1 minute (RF_{15}). In two of these experiments (RF_{15} and RF_{16}) the factor of mutual emotional facilitation was minimized by the use of the screen. The results were much the same as in most of the other reward-and-fine experiments, suggesting that this factor was not primarily responsible for the results.

In four of the reward-and-fine experiments (RF_7, RF_8, RF_{11}, RF_{14}) there were no serious "traffic jams"; all or almost all of the cones came out of the bottle in less than a minute. In three of these experiments the experimenter was unable to persuade the winners to take the rewards; apparently the subjects had failed to accept the situation as a game with winners and losers. In one of these experiments there was an additional factor which probably interfered with "traffic jams"; immediately before this experiment (RF_{14}) these subjects had participated in another (NR_5) in which no rewards had been offered and in which the fastest time of any group was achieved (10 seconds). The subjects knew the time of this trial; the time allowance for winning exceeded it by 5 seconds, so that the chances of losing must have been recognized as slight by the subjects.

In the remaining 25 experiments there were no rewards or fines. Twenty of these experiments were described to the subjects as measures of cooperation. These experiments fell into three groups. Experiments NR_1 to NR_5 were conducted with groups of subjects who had not been previously exposed to similar experiments, and under "natural" conditions, i.e., without the experimenter entering into a conspiracy with accomplices. Experiments NR_6 to NR_{12} were similar but were conducted immediately after experiments with accomplices. Experiments ANR_1 to ANR_8 were the experiments with accomplices who had been instructed to make noise and to stir up excitement in the group.

No serious "traffic jam" developed in any of these experiments, not in those with new subjects, nor in those with accomplices, nor in those preceded by experiments with accomplices. The times for taking *all* cones out of the bottle ranged in these three groups of experiments from 10 to 22 seconds, from 10.5 to 30 seconds, and from 13.4 to 59 seconds.

The experimenter's accomplices were generally able to stir up excitement, but this excitement failed to disrupt the cooperative behavior of the group to an extent comparable to that of the effect of the individual rewards and fines. In most of the reward-and-fine experiments the majority of the cones were still in the bottle after a minute or longer had elapsed.

Did the accomplices have any effect? The mean times of the two groups of the no-reward, no-accomplice experiments were 16.8 seconds (NR_1 to NR_5) and 19.6 seconds (NR_6 to NR_{12}); the mean time of the accomplice experiments was 34.4 seconds. The difference between the times of the two groups of experiments without accomplices is very small and not statistically significant. In the accomplice experiments the mean time was longer, significantly so at the .01 level of confidence, suggesting that the accomplices did have some disrupting effect. However, a closer examination of the data shows that the two longest times in the accomplice experiments were obtained when some of the accomplices had misunderstood the instructions and gave bad advice to the group. If the results of these two experiments (ANR_1 and ANR_8) are eliminated, the mean time drops to 26.4 seconds, and the critical ratio (Fisher's t for small, uncorrelated samples) indicates that the difference between this time and that of the no-accomplice experiments is too small to reach the conventional standards of statistical significance ($t = 1.82$, $d.f. = 16$, $P > .05$). Thus it was not established with certainty that the accomplices who made noise and stirred up excitement without giving bad advice had a disrupting effect on group cooperation. They may have had; the evidence was inconclusive. More experiments would have been needed to establish this point. The experiments with accomplices were designed merely to discover whether an additional opportunity for mutual emotional facilitation would seriously disrupt group cooperation. They served their purpose in showing that it did not.

There were several additional no-reward experiments (PC_1 to PC_5). One of these was described to the subjects as a preliminary trial conducted in order to determine the proper conditions for the next experiment in which rewards were to be offered. This was the only no-reward experiment in which a serious "traffic jam" developed; there was no organized plan for action in this group, probably because the subjects were not sufficiently motivated to devise one before the experiment began. The remaining four experiments were described to the subjects, who had previously participated in reward-and-fine experiments as control experiments conducted in order to demonstrate to the group what were the effects of the rewards. In view of the common claim of the subjects that the flow of water was primarily responsible for the "traffic jams," water was made to flow in three of them. No serious "traffic jam" developed in any of the control experiments. On the other hand, three out of the four times were distinctly slow ones as compared to those in the other no-reward experiments. It is not clear whether this finding was due to fluctuations of random sampling ("chance"), whether the subjects were inadequately motivated in these "control" experiments, or whether the earlier reward-and-fine experiments had continued bad effects on the cooperative behavior of the subjects. The matter was not investigated at this time.

After each experiment or group of experiments the subjects were told by the experimenter about the true nature of the experiment and about the results obtained so far. The explanations were followed by discussions. In the groups which had failed to pull out the cones from the bottle, marked tendencies toward rationalization appeared during these discussions. Subjects tended to explain the bad results of their group in terms of supposedly tangled strings, effects of the water, or insufficient time for the formulation of a plan, disregarding the fact that these failed to produce "traffic jams" in no-reward experiments.

Discussion

The experiments provide laboratory demonstrations for our hypothesis and partially verify the hypothesis. The behavior of the subjects did not tend toward inefficiency unless the reward structure of the situation provided them with incentives to behave uncooperatively after the cooperative pattern of group behavior was disturbed. There were no "traffic jams" in the no-reward experiments. Emotional excitement produced by the experimenter's accomplices interfered with the efficiency of group behavior only to a minor extent, if at all, compared to the effects of individual rewards and fines. On the other hand, there were inefficient behavior and "traffic jams" in more than half the reward-and-fine experiments, in which the subjects were confronted with the probability of individual failure as soon as the bottle neck was temporarily blocked. This result was obtained without any more serious threat to the individuals than the loss of 10 cents at most and probably a mild feeling of failure in a game. Thus intense fear was not found to be an essential condition of chaotic, nonadaptive group behavior analogous to that occurring in panics.

"Traffic jams" did not occur in all the reward-and-fine experiments and were not expected to. In an experiment with 15 to 20 subjects one cannot be certain that one or a few subjects will create a disturbance within the short time available. With larger groups the percentage of "traffic jams" should be larger; the more people there are, the more likely it becomes that one uncooperative individual will create the initial disturbance which leads to deterioration of the situation.

The theory presented here, if correct, appears to apply to many situations and to contribute to the understanding of a number of social and economic phenomena. Situations with reward structures resembling those of panics and the reward-and-fine ex-

periments reported here seem to be numerous. Tendencies toward nonadaptive group behavior are clearly present in many such situations, regardless of the presence or absence of face-to-face contacts between people and opportunities for mutual emotional facilitation. There are situations in which the appearance of danger does not provide incentives for antisocial behavior, and no chaotic nonadaptive behavior of groups seems to occur in spite of the catastrophic nature of the danger and ample opportunity for face-to-face contacts. There seem to be no panics when people are so trapped that there can be no struggle for an exit, e.g., submarine and mine disasters.[5]

The experiments reported here belong also in a second theoretical context. In these experiments a system of individual rewards resulted in strikingly inefficient behavior, while the goal of demonstrating the ability of the group to cooperate produced much more orderly action. These findings may be compared with those of the type reported by Maller (1929) and Sims (1928), who found that individual competition led to greater efficiency than group competition. It should be noted that the structure of the tasks in these earlier experiments and those reported here differed. In the former the subjects worked separately and could not interfere with each other as readily as in our experiments. Thus the experiments provide an additional illustration for the caution that any generalization pertaining to the effect of competition on behavior is limited not only by the prevalent social norms and personality characteristics but also by the nature of the task.

[5] Dying miners wrote notes to their families as deadly gas crept in on them in an Illinois pit. *New York Times,* March 31, 1947, p. 8.

References

FREUD, S. *Group psychology and analysis of the ego.* London: Hogarth Press, 1910, 45-48.

FROMM, E. *Escape from freedom.* New York: Holt, Rinehart and Winston, 1941.

LE BON, G. *The crowd.* London: Unwin, 1916.

MALLER, J. B. Cooperation and competition. New York: Columbia Univer. Press. *Teach. Coll. Contr. Educ.,* 1929, No. 384.

SHERIF, M. *An outline of social psychology.* New York: Harper & Row, 1948.

SIMS, V. M. The relative influence of two types of motivation on improvement. *J.* *educ. Psychol.*, 1928, *19*, 480-484.

WHITEHEAD, T. N. *The industrial worker,* Vol. I. Cambridge, Mass.: Harvard Univer. Press, 1938.

Individual and Mass Behavior

in Extreme Situations ✳ Bruno Bettelheim

The author spent the year 1938-39 in the two German concentration camps at Dachau and at Buchenwald. In these camps the prisoners were deliberately tortured; they suffered from extreme malnutrition but had to perform hard labor. Every single moment of their lives was strictly regulated and supervised. The prisoners did not know why they were imprisoned nor for how long. This may explain why the prisoners were persons finding themselves in an "extreme" situation.

The acts of terror committed in these camps aroused in the minds of civilized persons justified emotions which led them to overlook that terror was used by the Gestapo only as a means for attaining certain ends. The results which the Gestapo tried to obtain by means of the camps were varied. Among them were: *to break the prisoners as individuals* and to change them into docile masses from which no individual or group act of resistance could arise; *to spread terror among the rest of the population* by using the prisoners as hostages and by demonstrating what happens to those who oppose the Nazi rulers; *to provide the Gestapo members with a training ground* in which they were educated to lose all human emotions; *to provide the Gestapo with an experimental laboratory* in which to study the effective means for breaking civilian resistance, the minimum food requirements needed to keep prisoners able to perform hard labor when the threat of punishment takes the place of other incentives, and the influence on performance if the prisoners are separated from their families.

In this short paper, an effort is made to deal with *the concentration camp as a means of producing changes in the prisoners which will make them more useful subjects of the Nazi state.*

These changes were produced by exposing the prisoners to extreme situations which forced them to adapt themselves entirely and with the greatest speed. This adaptation produced interesting types of private, individual, and mass behavior. "Private" behavior originates in a subject's particular background and personality, rather than in the experiences to which the Gestapo exposed him, although they were instrumental in bringing it about. "Individual" behavior is developed by individuals independently of one another, although it is the result of experiences common to all prisoners. "Mass" behavior were those phenomena which could be observed *only* in a group of prisoners when functioning as a mass. Although these three types of behavior were over-

This article was adapted by the author especially for G. E. Swanson, T. M. Newcomb, and E. L. Hartley (Eds.), *Readings in Social Psychology,* Rev. Ed., New York: Holt, Rinehart and Winston, 1952, from the *Journal of Abnormal and Social Psychology*, 1943, *38,* 417-452. Reprinted by permission of the author and the American Psychological Association.

lapping, the subdivision seems advisable. The discussion is restricted mainly to individual and mass behavior. One example of private behavior is discussed below.

The purpose of changing the prisoners into useful subjects of the Nazi state was attained by exposing them to extreme situations. During this process different stages could be recognized. The first of them centered around *the initial shock of finding oneself unlawfully imprisoned.* The main event of the second stage was *the transportation into the camp and the first experiences in it.* Next was a slow process of change in the prisoner's life and personality: *the adaptation to the camp situation.* The final stage was reached when *the prisoner had adapted himself to the camp;* it was characterized by a definitely changed attitude to, and evaluation of, the Gestapo.

Why the Material Was Collected

Before discussing these stages of a prisoner's development a few remarks on *why the material was collected* seems advisable. This study was a mechanism developed by the author *ad hoc* in order to retain some intellectual interests and thus be better equipped to endure life in the camp. His observing and collecting of data was a particular type of defense, individually developed, not enforced by the Gestapo, and based on his training and interests. It was developed to protect him against a disintegration of his personality. It is an example of private behavior. Private behaviors follow characteristically the individual's former life interests.

Since it is the only example of a *private behavior* presented in the paper, how it developed deserves mention. During the first days in the camp, the writer realized that he behaved differently from the way he used to. He observed, for instance, the split in his person into one who observes and one to whom things happen, a typical psychopathological phenomenon. He also observed that his fellow prisoners, who had been normal persons, now behaved like pathological liars, were unable to restrain themselves and to make objective evaluations. Thus the question arose, "How can I protect myself against disintegration?" The answer was: to find out what changes occurred in the prisoners and why they took place. By occupying myself with interviewing prisoners, by pondering my findings while forced to perform exhausting labor, I succeeded in killing the time in a way which seemed constructive. As time went on, the enhancement of my self-respect due to my ability to continue to do meaningful work despite the contrary efforts of the Gestapo became even more important than the pastime.

The Initial Shock

The initial psychological shock of being unlawfully locked into a prison may be separated from the shock originating in the torture to which the prisoners were exposed. The prisoners' reactions on being brought into prison can best be analyzed on the basis of two categories: their socio-economic class and their political education. These categories can be separated only for the purposes of presentation.

The *politically educated prisoners* sought support for their self-esteem in the fact that the Gestapo had singled them out as important enough to take revenge on. In their imprisonment they saw a demonstration of how dangerous for Nazis their former activities had been.

The *nonpolitical middle-class prisoners* were a small minority among the prisoners. They were least able to withstand the initial shock. They found themselves utterly unable to comprehend what happened to them. In their behavior became apparent the dilemma of the politically uneducated German middle classes when confronted with the phenomenon of National Socialism. They had no consistent philosophy which would protect their integrity as human beings. They had obeyed the law handed down by the ruling classes without questioning its wisdom. And now the law-enforcing agencies turned against them, who always had been their stanchest supporters. They could not question the wisdom of law and police. Therefore what was wrong was that *they* were made objects of a persecution which in itself *must* be right, since it was carried out by the authorities. Thus they were convinced that it must be a "mistake."

These prisoners resented most to be treated "like ordinary criminals." After some time they could not help realizing their actual situation. Then they disintegrated. Suicides were practically confined to this group. Later on, they were the ones who behaved in an antisocial way; they cheated their fellow prisoners; a few turned spies. They lost their middle-class sense of propriety and their self-respect; they became shiftless and disintegrated as autonomous persons.

Members of *the upper classes* segregated themselves as much as possible. They seemed unable to accept what was happening to them. They expressed their conviction that they would be released within the shortest time because of their importance. This conviction was absent among the middle-class prisoners. Upper-class prisoners remained aloof even from the upper classes. They looked down on all other prisoners nearly as much as they despised the Gestapo. In order to endure life in the camp they developed such a feeling of superiority that nothing could touch them.

The *political prisoners* used another psychological mechanism at a later time, which might already have played some part in the initial development. It seems that many political leaders had some guilt-feeling that they had fallen down on the job of preventing the rise of Nazi power. This guilt-feeling was relieved to a considerable degree by the fact that the Nazis found them important enough to bother with. It might be that prisoners managed to endure living in the camp because their punishment freed them from their guilt-feeling. Indications

are found in remarks with which prisoners responded when reprimanded for undesirable behavior. They asserted that one cannot behave normally when living under such circumstances and that after liberation they would again act in civilized ways.

Thus it seems that most prisoners tried to protect themselves against the initial shock by mustering forces helpful in supporting their badly shaken self-esteem. Those groups which found in their past life some basis for the erection of such a buttress to their endangered egos seemed to succeed.

The Transportation into the Camp and the First Experiences in It

During the transportation into the camp, the prisoners were exposed to constant tortures. Corporal punishment intermingled with shooting and wounding with the bayonet alternated with tortures the goal of which was extreme exhaustion. For instance, the prisoners were forced to stare into glaring lights or to kneel for hours. Several were killed; the injured were not permitted to take care of their wounds. The guards also forced the prisoners to hit one another, and to defile their most cherished values. They were forced to curse their God, to accuse themselves of vile actions and their wives of prostitution. This continued for many hours. The purpose of the tortures was to break the resistance of the prisoners, and to assure the guards that they were superior.

It is difficult to ascertain what happened in the minds of the prisoners while they were exposed to this treatment. Most of them became so exhausted that they were only partly conscious of what happened. In general, prisoners did not like to talk about what they had felt and thought during the time of torture. The few who volunteered information made vague statements which sounded like devious rationalizations, invented for justifying that they had endured treatment injurious to their self-respect without trying to fight back. The few who had tried to fight back could not be interviewed; they were dead.

The writer recalls his extreme weariness, resulting from a bayonet wound and a heavy blow on the head. He recalls, nevertheless, his thoughts and emotions. He wondered that man can endure so much without committing suicide or going insane; that the guards tortured prisoners in the way it had been described in books on the concentration camps; that the Gestapo was so simpleminded as to enjoy forcing prisoners to defile themselves. It seems that he gained emotional strength from the following facts: that things happened according to expectation; that, therefore, his future in the camp was at least partly predictable from what he already was experiencing and from what he had read; and that the Gestapo was more stupid than he had expected. He felt pleased that the tortures did not change his ability to think or his general point of view. In retrospect these considerations seem futile, but they ought to be mentioned because, if asked to sum up what was his main problem during the time he spent in the camp, he would say: *to safeguard his ego in such a way that, if he should regain liberty, he would be approximately the same person he was when deprived of liberty.*

The writer feels that he was able to endure the transportation and what followed, because he convinced himself that these horrible and degrading experiences somehow did not happen to "him" as a subject, but only to "him" as an object. The importance of this attitude was corroborated by statements of other prisoners. They couched their feelings usually in such terms as, "The main problem is to remain alive and unchanged." What should remain unchanged was individually different and roughly covered the person's general attitudes and values.

The author's thoughts and emotions during the transportation were extremely detached. It was as if he watched things happening in which he only vaguely partici-

pated. Later he learned that many prisoners developed this same feeling of detachment, as if what happened really did not matter to oneself. It was strangely mixed with a conviction that "this cannot be true, such things do not happen." Not only during the transportation but all through the time spent in camp, the prisoners had to convince themselves that this was real and not just a nightmare. They were never wholly successful. The feeling of detachment which rejected the reality of the situation might be considered a mechanism safeguarding the integrity of the prisoners' personalities. They behaved in the camp as if their life there could have no connection with their "real" life. Their evaluation of their own and other persons' behavior differed from what it would have been outside of camp. The separation of behavior patterns and schemes of values inside and outside of camp was so strong that it could hardly be touched in conversation; it was one of the many "taboos" not to be discussed. The prisoners felt that what they were doing at camp and what happened to them there did not count; everything was permissible as long as it contributed to helping them to survive.

During the transportation no prisoner fainted. To faint meant to get killed. In this particular situation fainting was not protective against intolerable pain; it endangered a prisoner's existence because anyone unable to follow orders was killed.

The Adaptation to the Camp Situation

DIFFERENCES IN THE RESPONSE TO EXTREME AND TO SUFFERING EXPERIENCES

It seems that camp experiences which remained within the normal frame of reference of a prisoner's life experience were mastered by normal psychological mechanisms. For mastering experience which transcended this frame of reference, new psychological mechanisms were needed. The transportation was only one of the experiences transcending the normal frame of reference and the reaction to it may be described as "unforgettable, but unreal."

Attitudes similar to those developed toward the transportation could be observed in other extreme situations. On a terribly cold winter night, all prisoners were forced to stand at attention without overcoats for hours. They were threatened with having to stand all through the night. After about 20 prisoners had died from exposure the threats of the guards became ineffective. To be exposed to the weather was a terrible torture; to see one's friends die without being able to help, and to stand a good chance of dying, created a situation similar to the transportation. Open resistance was impossible. A feeling of utter indifference swept the prisoners. They did not care whether the guards shot them; they were indifferent to acts of torture committed by the guards. It was as if what happened did not "really" happen to oneself. There was again the split between the "me" to whom it happened, and the "me" who really did not care and was a detached observer.

After more than 80 prisoners had died, and several hundred had their extremities so badly frozen that they had later to be amputated, the prisoners were permitted to return to the barracks. They were completely exhausted, but did not experience the feeling of happiness which some had expected. They felt relieved that the torture was over, but felt at the same time that they no longer were free from fear.

The psychological reactions to events which were within the sphere of the normally comprehensible were different from those to extreme events. Prisoners dealt with less extreme events in the same way as if they had happened outside of the camp. A slap in one's face was embarrassing, and not to be discussed. One hated the individual guards who kicked, slapped, or abused much more than the guard who wounded one seriously. In the latter case one hated

the Gestapo as such, but not the individual inflicting the punishment. This differentiation was unreasonable, but inescapable. One felt deeper and more violent aggressions against particular Gestapo members who had committed minor vile acts than one felt against those who had acted in a more terrible fashion. Thus it seems that experiences which might have happened during the prisoner's "normal" life history provoked a "normal" reaction. Prisoners seemed particularly sensitive to punishments similar to those which a parent might inflict on his child. To punish a child was within their "normal" frame of reference, but that they should be the object of punishment destroyed their adult frame of reference. So they reacted to it not in an adult, but in a childish way—with shame and violent, impotent, unmanageable emotions directed, not against the system, but against the person inflicting the punishment. It seems that if a prisoner was cursed, slapped, pushed around "like a child" and if he was, like a child, unable to defend himself, this revived in him behavior patterns and psychological mechanisms which he had developed in childhood. He was unable to see his treatment in its general context. He swore that he was going "to get even," well knowing that this was impossible. He could not develop an objective evaluation which would have led him to consider his suffering as minor when compared with other experiences. The prisoners as a group developed the same attitude to minor sufferings; they did not offer help and blamed the prisoner for not having made the right reply, for letting himself get caught, in short, accused him of behaving like a child. So the degradation of the prisoner took place not only in his mind, but also in the minds of his fellow prisoners. This attitude extended to details. A prisoner did not resent being cursed by the guards during an extreme experience, but was ashamed of it when it occurred during some minor mistreatment. As time went on the difference in the reaction to minor and major sufferings slowly disappeared. This change in reaction was only one of many differences between old and new prisoners.

DIFFERENCES IN THE PSYCHOLOGICAL ATTITUDES OF OLD AND NEW PRISONERS

In the following discussion the term "new prisoners" designates those who had not spent more than one year in the camp; "old" prisoners are those who have spent at least three years in the camp.

All the emotional efforts of the new prisoners seemed to be directed toward returning to the outer world as the same persons who had left it. Old prisoners seemed mainly concerned with the problem of how to live well within the camp. Once they had reached this attitude, everything that happened to them, even the worst atrocity, was "real" to them. No longer was there a split between one to whom things happened and the one who observed them. When they reached this stage the prisoners were afraid of returning to the outer world. Moreover, they then hardly believed they would ever return to it. They seemed aware that they had adapted themselves to the life in the camp and that this process was coexistent with ·a basic change in their personality. There was considerable variation among individuals in the time it took them to make their peace with the idea of having to spend the rest of their lives in the camp. How long it took a prisoner to cease to consider life outside the camp as real depended to a great extent on the strength of his emotional ties to his family and friends. Some of the indications for the changed attitude were: scheming to find a better place in the camp rather than trying to contact the outer world, avoiding speculation about one's family or world affairs, concentrating all interest on events taking place inside of the camp. Some of the old prisoners admitted that they no longer could visualize themselves living outside the camp, making free decisions, taking care of themselves and their families.

Other differences between old and new prisoners could be recognized in their hopes for their future lives, in the degree to which they regressed to infantile behavior, and in many other ways.

CHANGES IN ATTITUDES TOWARD ONE'S FAMILY AND FRIENDS

The new prisoners received most signs of attention. Their families were trying everything to free them. Nevertheless, they accused them of not doing enough, of betraying them. They would weep over a letter telling of the efforts to liberate them, but curse in the next moment when learning that some of their property had been sold without their permission. Even the smallest change in their former private world attained tremendous importance. This ambivalence seemed due to their desire to return exactly the person who had left. Therefore they feared any change, however trifling, in their former situation. Their worldly possessions should be secure and untouched, although they were of no use to them at this moment.

It is difficult to say whether the desire that everything remain unchanged was due to their realization of how difficult it might be to adjust to an entirely changed home situation or to some sort of magical thinking running along the following lines: If nothing changes in the world in which I used to live, then I shall not change, either. In this way they might have tried to counteract their feeling that they were changing. The violent reaction against changes in their families was then the counterpart of the realization that they were changing. What enraged them was probably not only the fact of the change, but also the change in their status within the family which it implied. Their families had been dependent on them for decisions; now they were dependent. The only chance they saw for becoming again the head of the family was that the family structure remain untouched despite their absence. The question arises as to how they could blame their families for changes which occurred in them, and whose cause they were. It might be that the prisoners took so much punishment that they could not accept any blame. They felt that they had atoned for any past shortcomings in their relations to their families and friends, and for any changes which might occur in them. Thus they felt free to hate other people, even their own families, for their defects.

The feeling of having atoned for all guilt had some real foundation. When the concentration camps were established the Nazis detained in them their more prominent foes. Soon there were no more prominent enemies left. Still, an institution was needed to threaten the opponents of the system. Many Germans were dissatisfied with the system. To imprison all of them would have interrupted the functioning of the industrial production. Therefore, if a group of the population got fed up with the Nazi regime, a selected few members of the group were brought into the concentration camp. If lawyers, for instance, became restless, a few hundred lawyers were sent to the camp. The Gestapo called such group punishments "actions." During the first of them only the leaders of the opposing group were punished. That led to the feeling that to belong to a rebellious group as a member only was not dangerous. Soon the Gestapo revised its system and punished a cross section of the different strata of the group. This procedure had not only the advantage of spreading terror among all members of the group, but made it possible to destroy the group without necessarily touching the leader if that was for some reason inopportune. Though prisoners were never told why they were imprisoned, those imprisoned as representatives of a group came to know it. Prisoners were interviewed by the Gestapo to gain information about their friends. During these interviews prisoners were told that if their fate did not teach the group to behave better they would get a chance to meet them in

the camp. So the prisoners rightly felt that they were atoning for the rest of the group.

Old prisoners did not like to be reminded of their families and former friends. When they spoke about them, it was in a very detached way. A contributing factor was the prisoners' hatred of all those living outside of the camp, who "enjoyed life as if we were not rotting away." The outside world which continued to live as if nothing had happened was in the minds of the prisoners represented by those whom they used to know, namely, by their relatives and friends. But even this hatred was subdued in the old prisoners. It seemed that, as much as they had forgotten to love their kin, they had lost the ability to hate them. *They had learned to direct a great amount of aggression against themselves so as not to get into too many conflicts with the Gestapo, while the new prisoners still directed their aggressions against the outer world, and—when not supervised—against the Gestapo.* Since the old prisoners did not show much emotion either way, they were unable to feel strongly about anybody.

Old prisoners did not like to mention their former social status; new prisoners were rather boastful about it. New prisoners seemed to back their self-esteem by letting others know how important they had been. Old prisoners seemed to have accepted their state of dejection, and to compare it with their former splendor was probably too depressing.

HOPES ABOUT LIFE AFTER LIBERATION

Closely connected with the prisoners' attitudes toward their families were their hopes concerning their life after release from camp. Here they embarked a great deal on individual and group daydreams. To indulge in them was one of the favorite pastimes if the general emotional climate in the camp was not too depressed. There was a marked difference between the daydreams of the new and the old prisoners. *The longer the time a prisoner had spent in camp, the less true to reality were his daydreams;* so much so that the hopes and expectations of the old prisoners often took the form of eschatological or messianic hopes. They were convinced that out of the coming world war and world revolution they would emerge as the future leaders of Germany at least, if not of the world. This was the least to which their sufferings entitled them. These grandiose expectations were coexistent with great vagueness as to their future private lives. In their daydreams they were certain to emerge as the future secretaries of state, but they were less certain whether they would continue to live with their wives and children. Part of these daydreams may be explained by the fact that they seemed to feel that only a high public position could help them to regain their standing within their families.

The hopes and expectations of the new prisoners were truer to reality. Despite their open ambivalence about their families, they never doubted that they were going to continue to live with them. They hoped to continue their public and professional lives in the same way as they used to.

REGRESSION INTO INFANTILE BEHAVIOR

Most of the adaptations to the camp situation mentioned so far were more or less individual behaviors. The regression to infantile behavior was a mass phenomenon. It would not have taken place if it had not happened in all prisoners. The prisoners did not interfere with another's daydreams or his attitudes to his family, but they asserted their power as a group over those who objected to deviations from normal adult behavior. Those who did not develop a childlike dependency on the guards were accused of threatening the security of the group, an accusation which was not without foundation, since the Gestapo punished the group for the misbehavior of the individual. The regression into childlike behavior was more inescapable than other types of behavior imposed on the individual by the impact of the conditions in the camp.

The prisoners developed types of behavior characteristic of infancy or early youth. Some of them have been discussed, such as ambivalence to one's family, despondency, finding satisfaction in daydreaming rather than in action. During the transportation the prisoners were tortured in a way in which a cruel and domineering father might torture a helpless child; at the camp they were also debased by techniques which went much further into childhood situations. They were forced to soil themselves. Their defecation was strictly regulated. Prisoners who needed to eliminate had to obtain the permission of the guard. It seemed as if the education to cleanliness would be once more repeated. It gave pleasure to the guards to hold the power of granting or withholding the permission to visit the latrines. This pleasure found its counterpart in the pleasure the prisoners derived from visiting them, because there they could rest for a moment, secure from the whips of the overseers.

The prisoners were forced to say "thou" to one another, which in Germany is indiscriminately used only among small children. They were not permitted to address one another with the many titles to which middle- and upper-class Germans are accustomed. On the other hand, they had to address the guards in the most deferential manner, giving them all their titles.

The prisoners lived, like children, only in the immediate present; they lost the feeling for the sequence of time; they became unable to plan for the future or to give up immediate pleasure satisfactions to gain greater ones in the near future. They were unable to establish durable object-relations. Friendships developed as quickly as they broke up. Prisoners would, like adolescents, fight one another tooth and nail, only to become close friends within a few minutes. They were boastful, telling tales about what they had accomplished in their former lives, or how they succeeded in cheating guards. Like children they felt not at all set back or ashamed when it became known that they had lied about their prowess.

Another factor contributing to the regression into childhood behavior was the work the prisoners were forced to perform. Prisoners were forced to perform nonsensical tasks, such as carrying heavy rocks from one place to another, and back to the place where they had picked them up. They were forced to dig holes in the ground with their bare hands, although tools were available. They felt debased when forced to perform "childish" and stupid labor, and preferred even harder work when it produced something that might be considered useful. There seems to be no doubt that the tasks they performed, as well as the mistreatment by the Gestapo which they had to endure, contributed to their disintegration as adult persons.

The Final Adjustment to the Life in the Camp

A prisoner had reached the final stage of adjustment to the camp situation when he changed his personality so as to accept as his own the values of the Gestapo. A few examples may illustrate this.

The prisoners suffered from the steady interference with their privacy on the part of the guards and other prisoners. So a great amount of aggression accumulated. In new prisoners it vented itself in the way it might have done in the world outside the camp. But slowly prisoners accepted, as expression of their verbal aggressions, terms which definitely were taken over from the vocabulary of the Gestapo. From copying the verbal aggressions of the Gestapo to copying their form of bodily aggressions was one more step, but it took several years to make it. Old prisoners, when in charge of others, often behaved worse than the Gestapo be-

cause they considered this the best way to behave toward prisoners in the camp.

Most old prisoners took over the Gestapo's attitude toward the so-called unfit prisoners. Newcomers presented difficult problems. Their complaints about life in camp added new strain to the life in the barracks; so did their inability to adjust to it. Bad behavior in the labor gang endangered the whole group. Thus newcomers who did not stand up well under the strain tended to become a liability for the other prisoners. Moreover, weaklings were those most apt eventually to turn traitors. Therefore old prisoners were sometimes instrumental in getting rid of the unfit, thus shaping their own behavior in the image of Gestapo ideology. This was only one of the many situations in which old prisoners molded their way of treating other prisoners according to the example set by the Gestapo. Another was the treatment of traitors. Self-protection asked for their destruction, but the way in which they were tortured for days and slowly killed was copied from the Gestapo.

Old prisoners tended to identify with the Gestapo not only in respect to aggressive behavior. They tried to arrogate to themselves old pieces of Gestapo uniforms. If that was not possible, they tried to sew and mend their uniforms so that they would resemble those of the guards. When asked why they did it they admitted that they loved to look like one of the guards.

The satisfaction with which old prisoners boasted that, during the twice daily counting of the prisoners, they had stood well at attention can be explained only by their having accepted as their own the values of the Gestapo. Prisoners prided themselves on being as tough as the Gestapo members. This identification with their torturers went so far as copying their leisure-time activities. One of the games played by the guards was to find out who could stand to be hit longest without uttering a complaint. This game was copied by old prisoners.

Often the Gestapo would enforce nonsensical rules, originating in the whims of one of the guards. They were usually forgotten as soon as formulated, but there were always some old prisoners who would continue to follow these rules and try to enforce them on others long after the Gestapo had forgotten about them. These prisoners firmly believed that the rules set down by the Gestapo were desirable standards of human behavior, at least in the camp situation. Other areas in which prisoners made their peace with the values of the Gestapo included the race problem, although race discrimination had been alien to their previous scheme of values.

Among the old prisoners one could observe other developments which indicated their desire to accept the Gestapo along lines which definitely could not originate in propaganda. It seems that, since they returned to a childlike attitude toward the Gestapo, they had a desire that at least some of those whom they accepted as all-powerful father-images should be just and kind. They divided their positive and negative feelings—strange as it may be, they had positive feelings—toward the Gestapo in such a way that all positive emotions were concentrated on a few officers who were high up in the hierarchy of camp administrators, but hardly ever on the governor of the camp. They insisted that these officers hid behind their rough surfaces a feeling of justice and propriety; they were supposed to be genuinely interested in the prisoners and even trying, in a small way, to help them. Since these supposed feelings never became apparent, it was explained that they hid them effectively because otherwise they would not be able to help the prisoners. For in-

stance, a whole legend was woven around the fact that of two officers inspecting a barrack one had cleaned his shoes before entering. He probably did it automatically, but it was interpreted as a rebuff to the other officer and a clear demonstration of how he felt about the concentration camp.

After so much has been said about the old prisoners' tendency to identify with the Gestapo, it ought to be stressed that this was only part of the picture. Old prisoners who identified with the Gestapo at other moments also defied it, demonstrating extraordinary courage in doing so.

Summary

The concentration camp had an importance reaching far beyond its being a place where the Gestapo took revenge on its enemies. It was the training ground for young Gestapo soldiers who were planning to rule Germany and all conquered nations; it was the Gestapo's laboratory for developing methods for changing free citizens into serfs who in many respects accept their masters' values while they still thought that they were following their own life goals and values. The system was too strong for an individual to break its hold over his emotional life, particularly if he found himself within a group which had more or less accepted the Nazi system. It seemed easier to resist the pressure of the Gestapo if one functioned as an individual; the Gestapo knew it and therefore insisted on forcing all individuals into groups which they supervised. The Gestapo's main goal was to produce in the subjects childlike attitudes and childlike dependency on the will of the leaders.

Reaction Patterns to Severe,
Chronic Stress
in American Army Prisoners of War
of the Chinese ❊ Edgar H. Schein

In this paper I will outline some of the constellations of stress which prisoners of war faced during the Korean conflict, and describe some of the reaction patterns to these stresses. Rather than presenting a complete catalogue of their experiences (Schein, 1956), I have selected those aspects which seem to me to throw some light on the problem of collaboration with the enemy. I will give particular emphasis to the *social* psychological factors, because the Chinese approach to treatment of prisoners seemed to emphasize control over groups, rather than individuals.

My material is based on a variety of sources. I was in Korea during the repatriation, and had the opportunity to interview extensively 20 unselected repatriates. This basic material was supplemented by the information gathered by three psychiatrists, Drs. Harvey Strassman, Patrick Israel, and Clinton Tempereau, who together had seen some 300 men. On board ship returning to the United States, I also had the opportunity to sit in on bull sessions among repatriates in which many of the prison experiences were discussed. Additional details were obtained from the Army dossiers on the men.

The typical experience of the prisoner of war must be divided into two broad phases. The first phase lasted anywhere from one to six months beginning with capture, followed by exhausting marches to the north of Korea and severe privation in inadequately equipped temporary camps, terminating in assignment to a permanent prisoner of war camp.

The second phase, lasting two or more years, was marked by chronic pressures to collaborate and to give up existing group loyalties in favor of new ones. Thus, while physical stresses had been outstanding in the first six months, psychological stresses were outstanding in this second period.

The reactions of the men toward capture were influenced by their overall attitude toward the Korean situation. Many of them felt inadequately prepared, both physically and psychologically. The physical training, equipment, and rotation system all came in for retrospective criticism, though this response might have been merely a rationalization for being captured. When the Chinese entered the war they penetrated into rear areas, where they captured many men who were taken completely by surprise. The men felt that when positions were overrun, their leadership was often less than adequate. Thus, many men were disposed to blame the UN command for the unfortunate event of being captured.

On the psychological side, the men were not clearly aware of what they were fighting for or what kind of enemy they were oppos-

From the *Journal of Social Issues*, 1957, *13*, 21-30. Reprinted by permission of author and publisher. This work was completed while the author was a captain, U.S. Army Medical Service Corps, assigned to the Walter Reed Institute of Research. The author would like to acknowledge the invaluable help and guidance of Dr. David McK. Rioch and Capt. Harold Williams as well as the staff of the Neuropsychiatric Division of the Walter Reed Army Institute of Research.

ing. In addition, the reports of the atrocities committed by the North Koreans led most men to expect death, torture, or non-repatriation if captured.

It was in such a context that the soldier found his Chinese captor extending his hand in a friendly gesture and saying "Welcome" or "Congratulations, you've been *liberated.*" This Chinese tactic was part of their "lenient policy" which was explained to groups of prisoners shortly after capture in these terms: because the UN had entered the war illegally and was an aggressor, all UN military personnel were in fact war criminals, and *could* be shot summarily. But the average soldier was, after all, only carrying out orders for his leaders who were the real criminals. Therefore, the Chinese soldier would consider the POW a "student," and would teach him the "truth" about the war. Anyone who did not cooperate by going to school and by learning voluntarily could be reverted to his "war criminal" status and shot, particularly if a confession of "criminal" deeds could be obtained from him.

In the weeks following capture, the men were collected in large groups and marched north. From a physical point of view, the stresses during these marches were very severe: there was no medicine for the wounded, the food was unpalatable and insufficient, especially by our standards, clothing was scarce in the face of severe winter weather, and shelter was inadequate and overcrowded. The Chinese set a severe pace and showed little consideration for weariness that was the product of wounds, diarrhea, and frostbite. Men who were not able to keep up were abandoned unless they were helped by their fellows. The men marched only at night, and were kept under cover during the day, ostensibly as protection against strafing by our own planes.

From a psychological point of view this situation is best described as a recurring cycle of fear, relief, and new fear. The men were afraid that they might die, that they might never be repatriated, that they might never again have a chance to communicate with the outside, and that no one even knew they were alive. The Chinese, on the other hand, were reassuring and promised that the men would be repatriated soon, that conditions would improve, and that they would soon be permitted to communicate with the outside.

One of the chief problems for the men was the disorganization within the group itself. It was difficult to maintain close group ties if one was competing with others for the essentials of life, and if one spent one's resting time in overcrowded huts among others who had severe diarrhea and were occasionally incontinent. Lines of authority often broke down, and with this, group cohesion and morale suffered. A few men attempted to escape, but they were usually recaptured in a short time and returned to the group. The Chinese also fostered low morale and the feeling of being abandoned by systematically reporting false news about United Nations defeats and losses.

In this situation goals became increasingly short-run. As long as the men were marching, they had something to do and could look forward to relief from the harsh conditions of the march. However, arrival at a temporary camp was usually a severe disappointment. Not only were physical conditions as bad as ever, but the sedentary life in overcrowded quarters produced more disease and still lower morale.

What happened to the men under these conditions? During the one- to two-week marches they became increasingly apathetic.[1] They developed a slow, plodding gait, called by one man a "prisoners' shuffle." Uppermost in their minds were fantasies of food: men remembered all the good meals they had ever had, or planned detailed menus for years into the future. To a lesser extent they thought of loved ones at home, and about cars which seemed to them to symbolize freedom and the return home.

[1] A more detailed discussion of the apathy reaction may be found in Strassman, Thaler, and Schein (1956).

In the temporary camps disease and exposure took a heavy toll in lives. But it was the feeling of many men, including some of the doctors who survived the experience, that some of these deaths were not warranted by a man's physical condition. Instead, what appeared to happen was that some men became so apathetic that they ceased to care about their bodily needs. They retreated further into themselves, refused to eat even what little food was available, refused to get any exercise, and eventually lay down as if waiting to die. The reports were emphatic concerning the lucidity and sanity of these men. They seemed willing to accept the prospect of death rather than to continue fighting a severely frustrating and depriving environment.

Two things seemed to save a man who was close to such "apathy" death: getting him on his feet and doing something, no matter how trivial, or getting him angry or concerned about some present or future problem. Usually it was the effort of a friend who maternally and insistently motivated the individual toward realistic goals which snapped him out of such a state of resignation. In one case such "therapy" consisted of kicking the man until he was mad enough to get up and fight.

Throughout this time, the Chinese played the role of the benevolent but handicapped captor. Prisoners were always reminded that it was their *own* Air Force bombing which was responsible for the inadequate supplies. Furthermore, they were reminded that they were getting treatment which was just as good as that which the average Chinese was getting. One important effect of this was that a man could never give *full* vent to his hostility toward the Chinese, even in fantasy. In their *manner* and *words* they were usually solicitous and sympathetic. The Chinese also implied that conditions could be better for a prisoner if he would take a more "cooperative" attitude, if he would support their propaganda for peace. Thus a man was made to feel that he was himself responsible for his traumatic circumstances.

Arrival at a permanent camp usually brought relief from many of these physical hardships. Food, shelter, and medicine, while not plentiful, appeared to be sufficient for the maintenance of life and some degree of health. However, the Chinese now increased sharply their efforts to involve prisoners in their own propaganda program, and to undermine loyalties to their country. This marks the beginning of the second phase of the imprisonment experience.

The Chinese program of subversion and indoctrination was thoroughly integrated into the entire camp routine and involved the manipulation of the entire social milieu of the prison camp. Its aims appeared to be to manage a large group of prisoners with a minimum staff of guards, to indoctrinate them with the Communist political ideology, to interrogate them to obtain intelligence information and confessions for propaganda purposes, and to develop a corps of collaborators within the prisoner group. What success the Chinese had stemmed from their *total* control of the environment, not from the application of any one technique.

The most significant feature of Chinese prisoner camp control was the systematic destruction of the prisoners' formal and informal group structure. Soon after arrival at a camp, the men were segregated by race, nationality, and rank. The Chinese put their own men in charge of the platoons and companies, and made arbitrary selections of POW squad leaders to remind the prisoners that their old rank system no longer had any validity. In addition, the Chinese attempted to undermine *informal* group structure by prohibiting any kind of group meeting, and by systematically fomenting mutual distrust by playing men off against one another. The most effective device to this end was the practice of obtaining from informers or Chinese spies detailed information about someone's activities, no matter how trivial, then calling him in to interrogate him about it. Such detailed surveillance of the men's activities made them feel that their own ranks were so infiltrated by spies and informers that it was not safe to trust anyone.

A similar device was used to obtain information during interrogation. After a man had resisted giving information for hours or days, he would be shown a signed statement by one of his fellow prisoners giving that same information. Still another device was to make prisoners who had not collaborated look like collaborators, by bestowing special favors upon them.

A particularly successful Chinese technique was their use of testimonials from other prisoners, such as the false germ-warfare confessions, and appeals based on familiar contexts, such as peace appeals. Confessions by prisoners or propaganda lectures given by collaborators had a particularly demoralizing effect, because only if resistance had been *unanimous* could a man solidly believe that his values were correct, even if he could not defend them logically.

If the men, in spite of their state of social disorganization, did manage to organize any kind of group activity, the Chinese would quickly break up the group by removing its leaders or key members and assigning them to another camp.

Loyalties to home and country were undermined by the systematic manipulation of mail. Usually only mail which carried bad news was delivered. If a man received no mail at all, the Chinese suggested that his loved ones had abandoned him.

Feelings of social isolation were increased by the complete information control maintained in the camps. Only the Communist press, radio, magazines, and movies were allowed.

The weakening of the prisoner group's social structure is particularly significant because we depend to such an extent on consensual validation in judging ourselves and others. The prisoners lost their most important sources of information and support concerning standards of behavior and beliefs. Often men who attempted to resist the Chinese by means other than *outright* obstruction or aggression failed to obtain the active support of others, often earning their suspicion instead.

At the same time, the Chinese did create a situation in which meaningful social relationships could be had through common political activity, such as the "peace" committees which served as propaganda organs. The Chinese interrogators or instructors sometimes lived with prisoners for long periods of time in order to establish close personal relationships with them.

The Communist doctrines were presented through compulsory lectures followed by compulsory group discussions, for the purpose of justifying the conclusions given at the end of the lectures. On the whole, this phase of indoctrination was ineffective because of the crudeness of the propaganda material used in the lectures. However, its constant repetition seemed eventually to influence those men who did not have well-formed political opinions to start with, particularly because no counter-arguments could be heard. The group discussions were effective only if their monitor was someone who could keep control over the group and keep it on the topic of discussion. Attempts by the Chinese to use "progressive" POWs in the role of monitors were seldom successful because they aroused too much hostility in the men.

The Chinese also attempted to get prisoners to use mutual criticism and self-criticism in the fashion in which it is used within China.[2] Whenever a POW was caught breaking one of the innumerable camp rules, he was required to give an elaborate confession and self-criticism, no matter how trivial the offense. In general, the POWs were able to use this opportunity to ridicule the Chinese by taking advantage of their lack of understanding of slang and American idiom. They would emphasize the wrong parts of sentences or insert words and phrases which

[2] See the paper by Robert J. Lifton (1957).

made it apparent to other prisoners that the joke was on the Chinese. Often men were required to make these confessions in front of large groups of other prisoners. If the man could successfully communicate by a linguistic device his lack of sincerity, this ritual could backfire on the Chinese by giving the men an opportunity to express their solidarity (by sharing a communication which could not be understood by the Chinese). However, in other instances, prisoners who viewed such public confessions felt contempt for the confessor and felt their own group was being undermined still further by such public humiliation.

Various tales of how prisoners resisted the pressures put on them have been widely circulated in the press. For example, a number of prisoners ridiculed the Chinese by playing baseball with a basketball, yet telling the Chinese this was the correct way to play the game. Such stories suggest that morale and group solidarity was actually quite high in the camps. Our interviews with the men suggest that morale climbed sharply during the last *six* to *nine months* of imprisonment when the armistice talks were underway, when the compulsory indoctrination program had been put on a voluntary basis, and when the Chinese were improving camp conditions in anticipation of the repatriation. However, we heard practically no stories of successful group resistance or high morale from the first year or so in the camps when the indoctrination program was seriously pursued by the Chinese. (At that time the men had neither the time nor the opportunity to play any kind of games, because all their time was spent on indoctrination activities or exhausting labor).

Throughout, the Chinese created an environment in which rewards such as extra food, medicine, special privileges, and status were given for cooperation and collaboration, while threats of death, non-repatriation, reprisal against family, torture, decreases in food and medicine, and imprisonment served to keep men from offering much resistance. Only imprisonment was consistently used as an actual punishment. *Chronic* resistance was usually handled by transferring the prisoner to a so-called "reactionary" camp.

Whatever behavior the Chinese attempted to elicit, they always *paced* their demands very carefully, they always required some level of *participation* from the prisoner, no matter how trivial, and they *repeated* endlessly.

To what extent did these pressures produce either changes in beliefs and attitudes, or collaboration? Close observation of the repatriates and the reports of the men themselves suggest that the Chinese did not have much success in changing beliefs and attitudes. Doubt and confusion were created in many prisoners as a result of having to examine so closely their own way of thinking, but very few changes, if any, occurred that resembled actual *conversion* to Communism. The type of prisoner who was most likely to become *sympathetic* toward Communism was the one who had chronically occupied a low status position in this society, and for whom the democratic principles were not very salient or meaningful.

In producing collaboration, however, the Chinese were far more effective. By collaboration I mean such activities as giving lectures for the Communists, writing and broadcasting propaganda, giving false confessions, writing and signing petitions, informing on fellow POWs, and so on; none of these activities required a personal change of belief. Some 10 to 15 per cent of the men chronically collaborated, but the dynamics of this response are very complex. By far the greatest determinant was the amount of pressure the Chinese put on a particular prisoner. Beyond this, the reports of the men permit one to isolate several sets of motives that operated, though it is impossible to tell how many cases of each type there may have been.

1. Some men collaborated for outright opportunistic reasons; these men lacked any kind of stable group identification, and exploited the situation for its material

benefits without any regard for the consequences to themselves, their fellow prisoners, or their country.

2. Some men collaborated because their egos were too weak to withstand the physical and psychological rigors; these men were primarily motivated by fear, though they often rationalizd their behavior; they were unable to resist any kind of authority figure, and could be blackmailed by the Chinese once they had begun to collaborate.

3. Some men collaborated with the firm conviction that they were infiltrating the Chinese ranks and obtaining intelligence information which would be useful to the UN forces. This was a convenient rationalization for anyone who could not withstand the pressures. Many of these men were initially tricked into collaboration or were motivated by a desire to communicate with the outside world. None of these men became ideologically confused; what Communist beliefs they might have professed were for the benefit of the Chinese only.

4. The prisoner who was vulnerable to the ideological appeal because of his low status in this society often collaborated with the conviction that he was doing the right thing in supporting the Communist peace movement. This group included the younger and less intelligent men from backward or rural areas, the malcontents, and members of various minority groups. These men often viewed themselves as failures in our society, and felt that society had never given them a chance. They were positively attracted by the immediate status and privileges which went with being a "progressive," and by the promise of important roles which they could presumably play in the peace movement of the future.

Perhaps the most important thing to note about collaboration is the manner in which the social disorganization contributed to it. A man might make a slanted radio broadcast in order to communicate with the outside, he might start reading Communist literature out of sheer boredom, he might give information which he knew the Chinese already had, and so on. Once this happened, however, the Chinese rewarded him, increased pressure on him to collaborate, and blackmailed him by threatening exposure. At the same time, in most cases, his fellow prisoners forced him into further collaboration by mistrusting him and ostracizing him. Thus a man had to stand entirely on his own judgment and strength, and both of these often failed. One of the most common failures was a man's lack of awareness concerning the effects of his own actions on the other prisoners, and the value of these actions for the Chinese propaganda effort. The man who confessed to germ warfare, thinking he could repudiate such a confession later, did not realize its immediate propaganda value to the Communists.

A certain percentage of men, though the exact number is difficult to estimate, exhibited chronic resistance and obstructionism toward Chinese indoctrination efforts. Many of these men were well integrated with secure, stable group identifications who could withstand the social isolation and still exercise good judgment. Others were chronic obstructionists whose histories showed recurring resistance to any form of authority. Still others were idealists or martyrs to religious and ethical principles, and still others were anxious, guilt-ridden individuals who could only cope with their own strong impulses to collaborate by denying them and over-reacting in the other direction.

By far the largest group of prisoners, however, established a complex compromise between the demands of the Chinese and their own value system. This adjustment, called by the men "playing it cool," consisted primarily of a physical and emotional withdrawal from the whole environment. These men learned to suspend their feelings and to adopt an attitude of watching and waiting, rather than hoping and planning. This reaction, though passive, was not as severe as the apathy described earlier. It was a difficult adjustment to maintain because some concessions had to be made to the Chinese in the form of trivial or well-timed collaborative acts, and in the form of a feigned interest in the indoctrination program. At the same time, each man had to be prepared to deal with the hostility of his buddies if he made an error in judgment.

Discussion

This paper has placed particular emphasis on the social psychological factors involved in "brainwashing" because it is my opinion that the process is primarily concerned with social forces, not with the strengths and weaknesses of individual minds. It has often been asserted that drugs, hypnotic techniques, refined "mental tortures" and, more recently, implanted electrodes can make the task of the "brainwasher" much easier by rendering the human mind submissive with a minimum of effort.[3] There is little question that such techniques can be used to elicit confessions or signatures on documents prepared by the captor; but so can withdrawal of food, water, or air produce the same results. The point is that the Chinese Communists do not appear to be interested in obtaining merely a confession or *transient* submission. Instead, they appear to be interested in producing changes in men which will be lasting and self-sustaining. A germ-warfare confession alone was not enough—the POW had to "testify" before an international commission explaining in detail how the bombs had been dropped, and had to tell his story in other prison camps to his fellow POWs.

There is little evidence that drugs, posthypnotic suggestion, or implanted electrodes can now or ever will be able to produce the kind of behavior exhibited by many prisoners who collaborated and made false confessions. On the other hand, there is increasing evidence (Hinkle and Wolff,

[3] For example, see the paper by Miller (1957).

1956; Lifton, 1956) that Russian and Chinese interrogation and indoctrination techniques involve the destruction of the person's social ties and identifications, and the partial destruction of his ego. If this is successfully accomplished, the person is offered a new identity for himself and given the opportunity to identify with new groups. What physical torture and deprivation are involved in this process may be either a calculated attempt to degrade and humiliate a man to destroy his image of himself as a dignified human being, or the product of fortuitous circumstances, i.e., failure of supply lines to the prison, loss of temper on the part of the interrogator, an attempt to inspire fear in other prisoners by torturing one of them, and so on. We do not have sufficient evidence to determine which of these alternatives represents Communist intentions; possibly all of them are involved in the actual prison situation.

Ultimately that which sustains humans is their personality integration born out of secure and stable group identifications. One may be able to produce temporary submission by direct intervention in cortical processes, but only by destroying a man's self-image and his group supports can one produce any lasting changes in his beliefs and attitudes. By concerning ourselves with the problem of artificially creating submission in man, we run the real risk of overlooking the fact that we are in a genuine struggle of ideas with other portions of the world and that man often submits himself directly to ideas and principles.

To understand and combat "brainwashing" we must look at those social conditions which make people ready to accept new ideas from anyone who states them clearly and forcefully, and those social conditions which give people the sense of integrity which will sustain them when their immediate social and emotional supports are stripped away.

References

HINKLE, L. E., and WOLFF, H. C. Communist interrogation and indoctrination of "enemies of the state." *Arch. Neurol. Psychiat.*, 1956, *76*, 115-174.

LIFTON, R. J. "Thought reform" of Western civilians in Chinese communist prisons. *Psychiat.*, 1956, *19*, 173-198.

LIFTON, R. J. Thought reform of Chinese intellectuals: a psychiatric evaluation. *J. soc. Issues*, 1957, *13*, 5-20.

MILLER, J. G. Brainwashing: present and future. *J. soc. Issues*, 1957, *13*, 48-55.

SCHEIN, E. H. The Chinese indoctrination program for prisoners of war. *Psychiat.*, 1956, *19*, 149-172.

STRASSMAN, H. D., THALER, MARGARET, and SCHEIN, E. H. A prisoner of war syndrome: apathy as a reaction to severe stress. *Amer. Psychiat.*, 1956, *112*, 998-1003.

B. PREJUDICE AND INTERGROUP TENSION

The Effect of Public
Policy in Housing Projects upon ❊ Morton Deutsch
Interracial Attitudes ❊ Mary Evans Collins

There have been very few studies which have centered about changing prejudices.[1] Not only have there been few such studies, but most of them have been limited to the investigation of influences (such as a college course, a motion picture, a visit to a Negro hospital) "which were probably relatively minor in relation to other influences in the subject's social milieu" (Williams, 1947). The often discouraging and inconclusive results of such investigations may well reflect the comparatively superficial nature of the influences being studied. The strength of the social and psychological barriers to democratic race relations as well as the pervasiveness of discrimination and prejudice suggests that a reduction in prejudices will require strong influences.

The social scientist is rarely in the position where he, himself, has the opportunity to create these influences. He has neither the political power nor the financial resources to produce of his own accord a major social experiment. Nevertheless, social

[1] For a good summary of such studies, see Rose (1947).

"experiments" are going on all the time; or, perhaps more accurately, major attempts at producing social and psychological changes of one sort or another are a commonplace.

With the aid of scientific controls, the social scientist may occasionally be able to convert an attempt at social change into a social experiment. This is the purpose of our study. *We wish to investigate the effects upon prejudice of what is perhaps one of the most important "social experiments" in the area of race relations—the establishment of publicly supported non-segregated interracial housing projects.* Unfortunately, as in most "social experiments," social scientists did not participate in the design of the "experiment." The problem we face, then, is to convert, *ex post facto*, a "social change" into a scientific "social experiment."

THE SIGNIFICANCE OF INTERRACIAL HOUSING

There are many reasons why residential segregation can be considered to be of central importance to intergroup relations in

This article was adapted by the author especially for G. E. Swanson, T. M. Newcomb, and E. L. Hartley (Eds.), *Readings in Social Psychology*, Rev. Ed., New York: Holt, Rinehart and Winston, 1952, from *Interracial Housing: A Psychological Evaluation of a Social Experiment* by Morton Deutsch and Mary E. Collins, the University of Minnesota Press, Minneapolis. Copyright © 1951 by the University of Minnesota.

general. First of all, residential segregation brings with it, as a natural consequence, segregation in many other areas of living. If Negro and white people do not live near each other, ". . . they cannot—even if they otherwise would—associate with each other in the many activities founded on common neighborhood" (Myrdal, 1944). Segregated racial neighborhoods tend to bring with them segregation in schools, recreational centers, shopping districts, playgrounds, theaters, hospitals, leisure-time facilities, etc. Thus, one result of residential segregation is that prejudiced whites have little opportunity to see Negroes in social contexts which bring out the fundamental *condition humaine* of Negroes and whites. They do not see the Negroes, for example, as school children disliking homework, as expectant mothers in their first pregnancy, as tenants complaining about their landlords, or as breadwinners facing a contracting labor market.

Residential segregation, in yet another way, is of central importance. Next to employment discrimination, segregation is probably the most significant way by which Negroes, as a group, are disadvantaged. Residential segregation for Negroes in the North has always resulted in increased competition for a limited number of dwelling units, with the consequence that Negroes have invariably paid higher rentals for poorer accommodations. With limited incomes, high rentals have resulted in severe overcrowding and rapid physical deterioration. The economic and psychological burdens resulting from these housing conditions have contributed notably to a high incidence of delinquency, broken homes, emotional instability, and the general brutalization of life. These characteristics of Negro ghettos also tend to support the rationales for prejudice, helping to perpetuate the vicious circle which Myrdal and others have fully documented.

With a few exceptions and apart from run-down neighborhoods or areas in a process of racial transition, the only major instances of a break with the traditional practices of resi-dential segregation in the United States have occurred in public housing. However, even in public housing the common pattern is complete segregation; Negroes and whites live in separate housing projects. But there are important exceptions. These exceptions and the variations among them, in effect, provide a natural social experiment which permits those engaged in carefully controlled social research to gather valuable information about the conditions which affect interracial attitudes.

The Research Problem

To orient ourselves to the various factors which might influence race relations in public housing projects and to determine the social urgencies and vital issues, we interviewed officials with experience in interracial housing throughout the country. From our survey of expert opinion and from other social-science knowledge, it was apparent that one of the most crucial influences affecting race relations in housing communities is the *occupancy pattern*. To determine the impact of different occupancy patterns, we decided to do a comparative study of race relations in two types of housing projects: the *integrated interracial* project (families are assigned to apartments without consideration of race) and the *segregated bi-racial* project (Negro and white families live in the same project but are assigned to different buildings or to different parts of the project).

We obtained the cooperation of two large housing authorities[2] in neighboring cities, Newark and New York, which differ in policy with respect to the type of occupancy pattern in interracial public housing projects. In Newark, the projects, which house both Negro and white families, have a segregated occupancy pattern; in New York

[2] We wish to express gratitude to both the Newark and New York Housing Authorities for their constructive cooperation throughout the study. Without their objectivity and their concern with the broadening of knowledge this study would not have been possible.

the pattern is integrated. In each city two projects were selected for study. Realizing that the ratio of Negro to white families might be an important influence on race relations, we selected projects in the two cities that had approximately the same ratios. In one project in each of the two cities, there are about 70 Negro families to 30 white families; in the other project in Newark the ratio is 50-50, while the second project in New York has 60 white to every 40 Negro families.

Of course, other factors in addition to the ratio of Negro to white families may influence race relations. Fortunately the projects we were comparing are similar in many relevant respects: they all are low-income projects containing families who had to meet similar eligibility requirements in order to move in; they were all built at about the same time, just before World War II, the neighborhoods surrounding the various projects are much alike—all of them are predominantly Negro neighborhoods, and one of the projects in each city is located in a neighborhood that is considerably deteriorated and characterized by much delinquency; the staffs in each of the four projects include both Negro and white personnel; the project managers have all had considerable experience in interracial public housing projects; etc. The projects differ somewhat, as one would expect, e.g., one New York project is larger and the other smaller than the corresponding projects with similar racial ratios in Newark. Also, it should be indicated that population differences exist that act to enhance some of the results reported below. However, statistical analysis reveals that these population differences are by no means sufficient to "explain away" the differences we attribute to the effects of occupancy pattern.

The data for this study were collected primarily through systematic interviewing of white housewives. The home is, after all, largely the domain of the woman. She spends more time in it than anyone else; she is, by and large, the initiator of activities and contacts that develop directly out of the home. Whether or not she "wears the pants in the family," she is the key person in activities centered about the place of residence.

The funds at our disposal made it unfeasible to interview both Negro and white housewives in equal proportion. We decided to interview more white housewives as a result of our conviction that prejudiced interracial attitudes are more socially crucial among whites than among Negroes, since the practices of segregation and discrimination are enforced by the white and not by the Negro segment of the population.

We interviewed approximately 100 white and 25 Negro housewives in each of the four projects. In addition, a total of 24 Negro and white adolescent boys and girls were interviewed in one project in each of the two cities. The interviewees were selected by a random procedure.

The Interview

The interview was long and intensive; on the average, it lasted about one and a quarter hours. Some interviews ran over two hours. In the course of the interview, data were obtained about five major areas:

1. *The attitudes of the housewife toward living in the project:* What she liked most and least about the project; her feelings about public housing, the neighborhood, the apartment, etc.; the anticipations she had before moving into the project; her future plans; and her feeling toward people in the project.
2. *Attitudes toward Negroes:*[3] A series of questions attempted to uncover the attitudes of the housewife toward Negroes, her feelings about them, her "knowledge" and beliefs about them, and her feelings about living in an interracial project.
3. *The amount and intimacy of contact with other women in the project:* Questions were asked about neighborly contacts (such as visiting, shopping together, minding children, going to movies to-

[3] Essentially the same questions were asked of the Negro housewives but, of course, we asked them about white people.

gether), friendships, how one gets to know people, etc. Information was obtained about the types of contacts with Negro women.

4. *The social supports for attitudes:* The housewife was asked, for example, to tell how her relatives, friends, people in the project, management staff, etc., would react to her being friendly with Negro people.

5. *The characteristics of the housewife:* A miscellaneous assortment of questions was asked about the housewife: her age, number of children, her activities, her education, her religion, her interests, etc., to obtain information about the comparability of the populations in the projects we were studying.

The interview, for the most part, encouraged the respondent to answer freely in her own words rather than restricting her to "yes" or "no" answers. Interviewing was done in the respondent's home.

Research Results

In an *ex post facto* experiment such as we are here reporting, there is always need to be cautious in making causal inferences. One must inevitably face the critical question, "Which came first?" That is, did the attitudinal differences between the housewives in the integrated interracial and the segregated bi-racial projects exist prior to their residence in public housing and perhaps *cause* them to move into the one or the other type project? Or did the differences in attitudes *result* from their living in the different types of projects? In the book from which this article is adapted and condensed considerable indirect evidence is brought to bear upon these questions. This evidence, for which we do not have space here, leads us to believe that the differences primarily reflect the effects of the different occupancy patterns. The evidence is of several sorts: (1) an examination of the socio-psychological situation of prospective tenants; (2) an examination of refusal rates and voluntary move-outs; (3) an examination of the housewives' prior interracial experiences;

(4) the reports of the housewives about their prior attitudes; (5) comparison of housewives who did or did not know about the nature of the occupancy pattern before they made their applications; (6) a comparison of housewives in the different projects who were equated for education, religion, and political beliefs. All these types of evidence give credence to the interpretation that the occupancy pattern had causal efficacy.

GETTING TO KNOW EACH OTHER

As our knowledge about the development of prejudice has increased, it has become more and more evident that prejudice rarely originates in personal experiences with the members of a minority group. We know that many people who are extremely prejudiced against Negroes or Jews have never known a Negro or a Jew.

Further, we know that the nature of prejudice is such that it results in a reduction of intimate, equal-status contacts with the objects of prejudice. Prejudices combine with social custom to prevent the bigot from having the types of experiences, with Negro people, for example, which would destroy his prejudices. Hence, the main source of information about Negroes comes to be the "experiences," beliefs, and feelings of other prejudiced members of his own group. As a consequence, members of the prejudiced group, through contact with each other, tend mutually to confirm and support one another's prejudices. A vicious circle or a "socially shared autism" [4] is established whereby, without personal experience with members of a minority group, contact with the prevailing attitude toward them provides the "experience" to support a prejudice.

---

[4] Gardner Murphy has originated the term "socially shared autism" to refer to phenomena such as these in which members of a social group develop considerable confidence in their belief about something with which they no longer have contact, as a consequence of their mutual reinforcement of each other's beliefs. See Murphy (1947).

Perhaps the first problem that faces the person who wishes to change the attitudes of a prejudiced individual is that of breaking through this vicious circle so as to bring to bear upon the bigoted the experiences necessary to a change in attitudes. Something must be done to "prevent" the prejudiced person from selectively avoiding the experiences which might disrupt his prejudices. One method of accomplishing this objective would be to "compel" him to get to know Negro people in equal-status contacts of a sufficiently intimate and extended nature to resist perceptual or memorial distortion. This latter qualification must be inserted because we know that attitudes tend to select and distort experiences so as to maintain themselves. However, persistent, intense experiences that are. repeated are likely to survive attitudinal distortion, if only because of the individual's need to accept the reality of his own senses and experiences.[5]

One of the basic hypotheses of the study

[5] It is important to emphasize the strength of the motivation to accept as real one's perception and experiences. If they were not customarily accepted, the individual would be in a continuous state of insecurity and indecision.

is that *the greater physical and functional proximity of Negro and white families in the integrated interracial projects will result in more frequent and more intimate contacts between Negroes and whites in these projects as contrasted with the segregated bi-racial projects.* Let us consult the data.

In the interview, we asked the housewife to indicate whether she thought that a person who moved into the project would "be likely to get to know any colored people in the project." The differences in responses of the housewives in the two types of projects are striking. More than 95 percent of the women in each of the two integrated projects assert that a person will get to know some Negro people in the project; the few dissenters voice the opinion that "it depends upon you." In contrast, only a minority (30 percent in one and 21 percent in the other) of the housewives in the segregated bi-racial projects feel that there is any chance of getting to know Negro people; the majority are quite convinced that no such likelihood exists.

Clearly, then, the opportunity to get to know Negro people is considerably greater in the integrated than in the segregated project. Table 1 helps to explain why there

TABLE 1

PERCENTAGES OF HOUSEWIVES INDICATING THEIR MOST LIKELY CONTACTS
WITH NEGRO PEOPLE

Meeting Place	Integrated Interracial Projects		Segregated Bi-racial Projects	
	Koaltown°	Sacktown°	Bakerville°	Frankville°
As Neighbors in the Building	60	53	0	0
Through Laundry Facilities Located in or near Building	13	17	0	0
Outside on Benches	46	64	7	21
In Office, etc.	2	1	7	17
At Tenant Meetings	2	17	28	28
Shopping in Stores, in the Streets around Project	12	13	81	60
Through the Children's Schools	1	3	14	0
Total Cases †	102	86	43	42

° The project names are pseudonyms.
† Only the people who responded "yes" or "uncertain" to the question of getting to know Negro people are included. The percentage figures add up to more than 100 because many people named more than one place.

is such a striking difference in this respect between the two types of projects. The most frequently mentioned places of contact with Negro people for white residents in the integrated projects are the buildings in which they live, laundry facilities located in or near their buildings, or outside on benches. (People in the projects, for the most part, during the warm season customarily sit on benches located near their buildings.) It seems evident that the major source of Negro-white contact—contacts that arise from living in the same building—is not available to residents of a segregated bi-racial project.

Several of our questions in the interview of the housewives had the purpose of finding how intimate the contacts were with Negro women in the two types of projects. Only 3 percent of the housewives in each of the two segregated projects report "knowing any Negro people in the project pretty well —well enough to call them by their first names"; in contrast 77 percent of the housewives in one and 49 percent in the other integrated project report having at least this degree of intimacy. The tenants were also asked to tell us the five people in the project they know best. Table 2 indicates the percentage of persons "known best" who are Negro. None of the women in the segregated projects include Negro people among those they know best in the project. In contrast, 27 percent of the women in Koaltown and 62 percent in Sacktown indicate that at least one of the women they knew best is Negro.

Similar differences obtain in "neighborly"

activities, such as *visiting back and forth; helping one another out,* for example, with shopping or taking care of the children or when somebody is sick; *informal club activities,* such as "card" clubs, sewing or ironing clubs, and going out together, such as going to the movies, shopping together, or going "downtown" together. Only a very small percentage (1 percent and 4 percent) of white housewives in the segregated projects engage in any such activities with Negro women; in the integrated projects many of the white women (39 percent and 72 percent in the two projects, respectively) engage in such activities with their Negro neighbors.

To sum up, the data we have presented so far have demonstrated that the likelihood of white tenants getting to know Negro people and of having intimate social relationships with them is considerably less in the segregated than in the integrated projects. Our interviews with Negro housewives and with children of both races give the same results. Further, when we compare people in the two types of projects of the same religion or of similar educational backgrounds, or with similar political attitudes (or people who are similar in all three respects—religion, education, and political attitudes) it is still strikingly clear that the occupancy pattern markedly affects interracial contact. . . . The integrated project is, thus, considerably more successful in stimulating unprejudiced behavior toward Negroes among the white people in the project. Many more white people in the integrated

TABLE 2

PERCENTAGE OF PERSONS KNOWN BEST WHO ARE NEGRO

Percentage of Negroes among People "Known Best"	Integrated Interracial Projects		Segregated Bi-racial Projects	
	Koaltown	Sacktown	Bakerville	Frankville
0	73	38	100	100
20-39	19	18	0	0
40-59	6	23	0	0
60 or Over	2	21	0	0
Total Cases	96	84	99	98

than in the segregated projects violate, in actual behavior, the social prejudices and social customs which have the consequence of preventing intimate, equal-status contacts between Negroes and whites. In effect, living in the integrated projects produces a *behavioral* change with respect to race relations for many of the white people.

SOCIAL STANDARDS FOR BEHAVIOR WITH PEOPLE OF THE OTHER RACE

A housing project may be seen as composed of many informal groups organized around various types of goals. These groups are intricately connected through the overlapping memberships of individuals within each group. Within this complex network it is likely that group standards or social norms will develop with regard to issues which are collectively important to the interconnected groups. In a society where prejudice is commonplace and where interracial association is a possibility, race relations will be such an issue. It is our hypothesis that *the social norms in the intergrated projects will be more favorable to friendly interracial relations than will the corresponding social norms in the segregated projects.*

There are several reasons for advancing the foregoing hypothesis. First of all, it has long been recognized that people tend to behave as they are expected to behave. The expectations of others in a social situation, particularly if these others are important to the individual, help to define what is the appropriate behavior. There is little doubt that a public housing authority looms importantly in the life of residents in public housing projects, since it controls their only means of obtaining decent housing at a low rental. Thus, to the people who live in the projects, the action of a housing authority in establishing a policy of integration or of segregation is not likely to be without significance. Further, the policy of integration or segregation is an "official" decision implicitly carrying public sanction, and as such it

may set up standards for what one "should" or "should not" do. The policy of segregation may be seen as implying the notion that Negroes and whites should be kept apart; the policy of integration, that race should *not* be a criterion for distinguishing among tenants.

In addition to the direct psychological impact of official policy decision in shaping social norms, the policy decision has indirect effects upon social norms through the physical environment that it creates for race relations. In the previous section, we have seen how interracial contact is promoted or hindered by the physical nature of the occupancy pattern. The differences in interracial behavior resulting from the different occupancy patterns are likely to have consequences for the social norms which emerge in the projects. Thus, a housewife in the integrated projects is more likely to have friendly relations with Negroes, as well as to see other housewives as having similar relations. These differences combined with the inclination to moralize one's own behavior (to rationalize the status quo) and with the tendency to conform to and to accept as "right" the behavior of one's peers would work in the direction of producing more favorable social norms in the integrated projects. Another factor working in the same direction would be the comparatively greater number of cooperative relationships between Negroes and whites in the integrated projects.

Several questions were designed to determine whether and to what extent the decision with respect to occupancy pattern by a public authority and the fact of occupancy pattern do establish a standard for interracial conduct. Such a standard, we felt, would be reflected in the housewife's description of how "the other people in the project would react if she were friendly with Negro people" and in her answer to questions about whether it would influence her reputation in the project if she had much to do with the colored people.

The evidence strongly indicates that the housewife in the integrated project expects more approval than disapproval from others in the project if she is friendly with the Negro people. She thinks it is better rather than not better for her "to have much to do with the colored people." In contrast, the housewife in the segregated project expects to be socially ostracized by the other white women if she is friendly with the Negro people, and asserts that it is better not to have much to do with them. Thus, one woman in a segregated project said: "They'd think you're crazy if you had a colored woman visit you in your home. They'd stare at you and there'd be a lot of talk." Another said, "I used to be good friends with a colored woman who worked with me at the factory before I moved here. She lives in the other side of the project but I never have her over to my side of the project—it just isn't done. Occasionally, I go over and visit her."

Perhaps the most striking evidence as to the effects of occupancy pattern in creating guides for behavior comes from interviews with the children. The children in Bakerville (a segregated project) go to unsegregated elementary schools, where Negro and white children mix freely. As a consequence of meeting in the schools, they all have at least speaking acquaintances with members of the other race. Many of them play games together and belong to the same clubs. Yet in no single instance among the children interviewed in Bakerville do they engage in such activities with children of the other race in the project. The children in Bakerville implicitly understand that different standards with respect to interracial association exist in the school and in the housing project. In contrast, the children in Sacktown (an integrated project) play together at the project as well as in the school, visiting in each other's homes freely.

Some examples will illustrate the effects of social norms on children in Bakerville (a segregated bi-racial project):

One twelve-year-old white girl stated that she had made friends with a Negro girl at camp and she thought the girl was very nice. The girl lived in the project, but they never saw each other.

A Negro girl who feels that she is friendly with a number of white children stated, "I play with them at school and go to the movies with them. In the project, I have nothing to do with them."

Thus, it is clear that the occupancy pattern brings along with it a frame of reference which helps to establish expectations and values with respect to race relations within the project. Since this frame of reference is *shared* by other housewives with whom one is interacting, it can be said that a consequence of moving into one or another project is that the housewife becomes exposed to one rather than another social norm with respect to being friendly with the Negro people in the project. It is apparent that the social norm that one is exposed to as a result of moving into an integrated project is more likely to favor friendly interracial association than the norm of the segregated project; the latter is more likely to favor avoidance (with the more or less inevitable connotation in American society that interracial association brings trouble or that it is socially degrading).

The fact that the tenants in the various projects are exposed to "shared frames of reference," as Newcomb (1950) calls them, rather than merely their isolated individual experiences, is a matter of some significance. Lewin and Grabbe have pointed out that "only by anchoring his own conduct in something as large, substantial, and super-individual as the culture of the group can the individual stabilize his new beliefs sufficiently to keep them immune from day-by-day fluctuations of moods and influences to which he, as an individual, is subject" (1945). This is why attempts to change significant social attitudes must be directed not only at the individual but also at the social institutions and social norms which determine the individual's values and which help to induce the goals for which he strives.

THE EFFECTS UPON INTERRACIAL ATTITUDES

So far, the results have indicated that the integrated occupancy pattern creates more opportunities for close contact with members from the other race, an atmosphere more favorable to friendly interracial associations, and friendlier interracial relations.

Let us now make the assumption that the tenants who moved into the two types of projects had, like most people of similar education and circumstance, rather prejudiced attitudes toward Negroes. If this were the case, one would expect many of the tenants in the integrated projects, through their experiences and relationships with Negro neighbors, to shift their attitudes in a more favorable direction; few of the tenants in the segregated projects could be expected to change. That is to say, we hypothesize that *the differences between the two types of projects with respect to interracial contacts and social norms which have already been indicated would result in attitudinal differences between the residents in the two types of projects.* These attitudinal differences would be most directly reflected in attitudes toward the Negro people in the project; they might be generalized somewhat to include Negro people in general, and perhaps might even extend to other minority groups.

In our data we have many different indicators of attitudes toward the Negro people in the project; some of the measures of interracial association and interracial contact may be so considered. All give the same results: the attitudes of the housewives in the integrated projects are considerably less prejudiced than those of the women in the segregated bi-racial projects. Almost three times as many women in the segregated projects (36 percent and 31 percent as compared with 13 percent and 10 percent) in describing the Negro people spontaneously use words like "aggressive," "dangerous,"

"trouble-makers." There are approximately *two* housewives who want to be friendly *to every one* who wishes to avoid contact with Negroes in the integrated projects; in the segregated developments there is approximately only *one* who wishes to be friendly to *every ten* who wish to avoid relationships.

We also obtained many different indicators about attitudes toward *Negro people in general:* reactions to social-distance questions, acceptance of stereotypes about Negroes, interviewer ratings, reports of the housewives about their own attitudinal change, etc. Again, all provide the same result. The attitudes of the housewives in the integrated projects are considerably more favorable than those of the women in the segregated developments. We can infer that the *changes* in attitudes toward Negroes in general among the women in the integrated projects have been considerable. In other words, many of the women in this type of development have not only come to respect and like the Negro people with whom they have associated, but they have also changed their notions about Negroes in general. Their experiences in the project with Negro people have become partially *generalized,* so that they now have more favorable attitudes toward Negroes as a group.

Perhaps the most striking data come from the reports of the housewives themselves about their own attitude changes toward Negroes in general.[6] We asked the housewives a series of questions which included: "Can you remember what you thought colored people were like before you moved into the project?" "How much have your ideas about colored people changed since you have lived in the project?" (If some change occurred) "In what ways have they changed?" And, "What do you think made you change your ideas?"

Results which cannot be presented in full

[6] To be sure, such reports must always be evaluated with caution because of distorting effects in recall. We have examined the data to see if differential distortion between the two types of project has occurred and could find no such indications.

here indicate that the *net gain* (percent of housewives reporting favorable changes minus percent reporting unfavorable changes) for the two integrated projects among housewives who indicated that they were initially highly prejudiced is 71 percent and 78 percent; for the housewives reporting moderate prejudice initially, it is 46 percent and 61 percent; for housewives reporting favorable initial attitudes it is 13 percent and 28 percent. In the two segregated projects, the corresponding net gains are much smaller: for those reporting much initial prejudice it is 26 percent and 19 percent; for those indicating moderate initial prejudice, it is 18 percent and 2 percent; for those reporting that they were originally unprejudiced, there is a net gain of 15 percent in one and *a net loss* of 18 percent in the other segregated project.

The interview material provides dramatic illustration of the nature of the attitudinal changes that occurred among many of the housewives in the integrated projects. Thus one woman, when asked to tell how she felt about living in the project, said: "I started to cry when my husband told me we were coming to live here. I cried for three weeks. . . . I didn't want to come and live here where there are so many colored people. I didn't want to bring my children up with colored children, but we had to come; there was no place else to go. . . . Well, all that's changed. I've really come to like it. I see they're just as human as we are. They have nice apartments; they keep their children clean, and they're very friendly. I've come to like them a great deal. I'm no longer scared of them. . . . I'd just as soon live near a colored person as a white; it makes no difference to me."

Another woman put it quaintly: "I thought I was moving into the heart of Africa. . . . I had always heard things about how they were . . . they were dirty, drink a lot . . . were like savages. Living with them my ideas have changed altogether. They're just people . . . they're not any different."

Another one said: "I was prejudiced when I moved in here but not any more. . . . I find there is no such thing as 'my kind.' . . . I was under the impression that every colored man that looked at you wanted to rape you or was going to pull out a razor. . . . I don't feel that way any more. . . . I know the people. I have been in their homes . . . been to church with them. . . . I know they're not dirty. My doctor is colored . . . my dentist is colored. He's a surgeon and he's wonderful."

In contrast with the above, the following remarks express typical findings in the segregated projects: "I don't have anything to do with the colored people . . . they don't bother me . . . I don't mingle with them. I guess I don't like them because they're colored . . . the Bible says 'God created them equal' so I guess they're equal, but I don't like them. I don't like living so close to them. I think they ought to be in separate projects. Let them live their lives and let us live ours. . . . My ideas haven't changed any since I've lived here. . . . They're colored and I'm white. They don't like us and we don't like them."

Conclusions

Our results provide considerable evidence to discredit a notion that has characterized much of social-science thinking in the field of race relations: the notion originating with William S. Sumner that "stateways cannot change folkways." The implication of our study is that official policy, executed without equivocation, can result in large changes in behavior and attitudes despite initial resistance to that policy. Thus it is clear from our data that although most of the white housewives in the integrated projects we studied did not, upon moving into the projects, like the idea of living in the same buildings with Negro families (and certainly the community as a whole did not favor it), a considerable change has taken place in their beliefs and feelings as well as in their behavior. *It is evident that from the point of view of reducing prejudice and of creating harmonious democratic intergroup relations, the net gain resulting from the integrated projects is considerable; from the same point of view, the gain created by the segregated bi-racial projects is slight.*

Further, our results are consistent with the growing body of evidence about the effects of equal-status contacts, under certain conditions, upon prejudiced attitudes. Studies by Allport and Kramer (1946), by Brophy (1946), by the Information and Education Division of the U.S. War Department (1952), by Mackenzie (1948), among others, all support the notion that prejudices are likely to be diminished when prejudiced persons are brought into situations which compel contacts between them and the objects of prejudice, provided:

(a) that the behavior of the objects of prejudice is such as not to conform with the beliefs of the prejudiced. That is, the Negroes with whom the prejudiced person has contact are not "lazy," "ignorant," "delinquent," etc.

(b) that the intimacy and amount of contact with objects of prejudice not conforming to the stereotypes of the prejudiced are such as to result in experiences which are sufficiently compelling to resist marked perceptual and memorial distortion.

(c) that the contact takes place under conditions which make the nonconforming behavior seem relevant to the basis on which the objects of prejudice are grouped together. Thus, if a Negro attendant is seen to be clean and honest, there may be little effect on stereotypes if the perception of cleanliness and honesty is connected primarily with the requirements of the situation, with the classification of the individual as an attendant rather than as a Negro or Negro attendant." [7]

(d) that the prejudiced person has values or is exposed to social influences (e.g., democratic values or the social influences emanating from a policy of an official, public body) which would strongly conflict with the unabashed retention of unrationalized prejudices.

In addition, if the contact situation is such that it encourages the development of new sentiments to replace prejudiced sentiments either as a result of the experience of cooperative activity with the objects of prejudice or as a result of the internalization of the social norms of an unprejudiced group, the reduction of prejudiced sentiments will be much facilitated.

[7] Just as there is likely to be little effect upon prejudiced beliefs if "good" behavior on the part of the objects of prejudice is seen to result from the requirements of the situation rather than from the person or from the person's membership in a minority group, so too, one can expect a reduction in prejudice if "bad" behavior upon their part comes to be seen as emanating from their circumstances rather than from their personality or minority-group membership. This is why changes in theories of behavior (from a genetic to an environmental emphasis) may have a subtle influence even upon prejudice.

References

ALLPORT, G. W., and KRAMER, B. M. Some roots of prejudice. *J. Psychol.*, 1946, 22, 9-39.

BROPHY, I. N. The luxury of anti-Negro prejudice. *Publ. Opin. Quart.*, 1946, 9, 456-466.

Information and Education Division, U.S. War Department. Opinions about Negro infantry platoons in white companies of seven divisions. In G. E. Swanson, T. M. Newcomb, and E. L. Hartley (Eds.), *Readings in social psychology*, Rev. Ed. New York: Holt, Rinehart and Winston, 1952.

LEWIN, K., and GRABBE, P. Conduct, knowledge, and the acceptance of new values. *J. soc. Issues*, 1945, 1, 53-64.

MACKENZIE, B. K. The importance of contact in determining attitudes toward Negroes. *J. abnorm. soc. Psychol.*, 1948, 43, 417-441.

MURPHY, G. *Personality: a biosocial approach*

to origin and structure. New York: Harper & Row, 1947.

MYRDAL, G. The American dilemma. New York: Harper & Row, 1944.

NEWCOMB, T. M. Social psychology. New York: Holt, Rinehart and Winston, 1950.

ROSE, A. Studies in the reduction of prejudice. Chicago: American Council on Race Relations, 1947.

SWANSON, G. E., NEWCOMB, T. M., and HARTLEY, E. L. Readings in social psychology, Rev. Ed. New York: Holt, Rinehart and Winston, 1952.

WILLIAMS, R. M., JR. The reduction of intergroup tensions. Soc. Sci. Res. Coun. Bull. No. 57. New York: Social Science Research Council, 1947.

Interpersonal Dynamics ✲ Marian Radke Yarrow

in Racial Integration ✲ John D. Campbell

✲ Leon J. Yarrow

This is a study of social change, a study of racial integration at a time when this issue is of great importance in the American culture. When integration occurs, what are the experiences of the individual Negro and white children involved? What happens when attitudes built up over a lifetime dictate one course of action, while the new situation requires different behavior? This is a basic social psychological question posed by integration.

It was with this question in mind that we undertook to study the children in a racially integrated summer camp. We attempted to examine the *process* of integration by studying the actions, feelings, and perceptions of the campers from their first day in the integrated camp to the time of their departure. To provide a base line for evaluating the effects of interracial contact we also obtained comparable information from racially segregated camps. We assumed at the outset that two kinds of factors would be important in understanding how the children reacted to integration: the customs and attitudes in the homes and communities from which these children came, and the demands of the immediate situation in which they found themselves.

It is more than likely that, in their home environment, most children in the study had learned certain racial stereotypes and certain customary modes of interacting with members of the other race which were based on a policy of segregation. There were many indications of this learning in unsolicited comments. When such a background is brought into an integrated camp situation, it appears inevitable that integration initially will certainly present confusion, if not conflict, to the child. New face-to-face contacts will confront him with many uncertainties regarding his behavior and his expectations of others' behavior toward him. Not all children will have the same degree and kind of conflict, however. Quite possibly, there will be differences in the socialization pressures impinging on Negro and white children or on boys as compared with girls. Since we assume that early socialization experiences

This article was written especially for E. E. Maccoby, T. M. Newcomb, and E. L. Hartley, (Eds.), Readings in Social Psychology, 3d Ed., New York: Holt, Rinehart and Winston, 1958. Reprinted by permission of the authors and publisher.

(particularly those related to the expression of aggression, nurturance, and dominance) influence how a child thinks and feels about, as well as behaves toward, others, it is possible that one race or one sex might be especially facilitated, or especially handicapped, in functioning in a racially mixed group.

The kind of situation in which racial contacts occur is known to be significant. To a marked degree the camp situation was well defined in advance. Integration was a *fait accompli*. The children were matter-of-factly assigned to racially mixed cabins; all activities were mixed; the authority of the counselors stood behind the "rules of the game," rules prescribing equal-status participation for white and Negro children.

Research Design: Setting and Sample

Only minor adjustments to the requirements of research were necessary to create a uniquely controlled situation out of a natural setting. Children from low-income families with Southern and border-state backgrounds were studied in two summer camps. Both camps were under the direction of the same agency and had essentially similar facilities and leadership. Children came to the camp for two-week sessions. For the first three sessions of the summer, the camps were racially segregated; the children in one camp were Negro, in the other, white. The last two sessions were racially integrated. The same Negro and white adult leaders served as counselors in both the segregated and the integrated sessions.

Thirty-two cabin groups and their adult counselors were studied. Children, aged eight to 13, who had had no prior acquaintance with one another were assigned to a cabin. Approximately eight were in each cabin. The groups were homogeneous in age and sex: 131 boys and girls in 16 segregated cabins and 136 in 16 racially integrated cabins. White and Negro children were in equal numbers in the integrated cabins.

We obtained information about each child from the following sources: (1) detailed behavior observations, (2) individual interviews with children, (3) interviews with counselors, (4) ratings of the children by their counselors, and (5) journal records by participant observers—members of the research staff living in the cabins.[1]

Children were interviewed in the first days of camp. Questions focused on the child's impressions and feelings about his cabin mates and his counselor. (Photographs of each child and the counselor permitted ready identification and helped to hold the respondent's interest.) Early in the interview each child was asked to choose one of his new acquaintances about whom he felt he knew the most. He was encouraged to tell all that he knew about him (as if he were telling a friend back home) and to tell how he learned what he had described. Since the aim was to capture the child's impressions in terms of the attributes that were salient to *him*, predetermined questions were not imposed at this point.

Excerpts from the impressions of 11-year-old Rosemary show the nature of replies:

> Betty is little. Children always blame her. When we clean, kids make her sweep the floor. She plays with me when I have no one to play with. She's scared of everyone in the cabin. . . . They pick on her. She was sitting at the supper table and kicked Rosy by mistake. Rosy said she's going to get her and Betty started crying. Doris told Betty, "You better not let people pick on you, or you will all your life. Fight back." . . . I'm scared too [like Betty, but] I know I can fight back."

Free descriptions were followed by "guess-who" questions, which asked the child to pick a cabin mate who best fitted a given

[1] The writers wish to acknowledge their indebtedness to the following persons who assisted in the various phases of data gathering: Florence Christopher, Ruth Greene, Erwin Linn, John Lucas, Gladys Morris, Frances Polen, and Olive W. Quinn.

description of behavior. Characteristics such as aggressiveness, submissiveness, leadership, and anxiety were tapped. To assess spontaneous racial stereotyping, the research worker clearly must not ask his questions in such a way as to impose, or imply, a stereotype. In our research, the child was never required to respond to abstract racial classifications. In his own description of another, the child was completely free to evaluate and appraise in the terms he found most relevant. On the "guess-who" questions, he could freely choose any one of his cabin mates (or himself) as best fitting behavior categories. Other questions in the interview explored friendship choices within the cabin, the child's views of his counselor, and his expectations about camp. At the end of the two-week session essentially the same interview was repeated.

Counselors were interviewed at the beginning and end of each session. Interviews dealt with (1) the counselor's appraisal of individual children and relationships in the cabin, (2) his assessments of his own relationship to the group, and (3) his expectations and attitudes about serving as leader in a racially integrated group. Further, at the beginning and end of each session the counselor rated his children on aspects of behavior that paralleled the "guess-who" items in the children's interview.

Systematic observations of behavior were made in 20 cabins. Beginning on the first day, series of five-minute samples were taken at specified times during the two-week session. Observations were recorded in the form of detailed running accounts. In addition to these scheduled observations, the research member living in the cabin served as a participant observer, keeping a journal record of the counselor's functioning and characteristics of group interaction.[2]

2 Personality factors are recognized as significant but are not included in this analysis. Similarly, specific racial attitudes held by the child or his parents are important. But for reasons which are apparent, the research did not specifically ask the children their attitudes toward Negroes and whites. Children in segregated and

Interpersonal Relations in Segregation

The first problem with which we are concerned is whether there are characteristic differences between Negro and white children in patterns of interaction with their peers in *segregated* situations. Do the children differ in ways that would lead one to anticipate that their standards of behavior would be incompatible when they are brought together and required to interact? To answer this question, observed behavior and children's descriptions of their cabin mates in segregated camps were analyzed in terms of categories such as nurturance, dominance, dependence, aggression, etc.

During the first days at camp, as the children became acquainted and established themselves among their peers, similarities in the behavior of Negro and white children in segregated groups were more striking than differences. However, in culturally significant areas relating to control and expression of aggression and dominance-deference patterns, small but consistent subgroup differences appeared. As can be seen in Table 1, aggressive-dominant behavior occurred with highest frequency among the Negro boys (25 percent of their total behavior was coded in these categories); this occurred least frequently among white girls (15 percent and 10 percent at beginning and end of camp respectively), while white boys and Negro girls were in intermediate positions. Consistent with their high proportion of aggression, Negro boys showed the lowest proportion (11 percent) of nurturant and affiliative behavior toward their peers while Negro girls showed the highest proportion of such acts (24 percent).

These subgroup differences also appeared

integrated groups were drawn from the same population and, it is assumed, held similar attitudes. Parents opposing integration, with the choice of an integrated camp or no camp for their child, more often chose the former, sometimes admonishing the child, as he departed for camp, not to play with children of the other race.

TABLE 1
CHILDREN'S BEHAVIOR IN SEGREGATED CABINS°

| Behavior Category | Initial Phases (Percent of Behavior Units) | | | | Later Phases (Percent of Behavior Units) | | | |
| | Negro | | White | | Negro | | White | |
	GIRLS	BOYS	GIRLS	BOYS	GIRLS	BOYS	GIRLS	BOYS
Dominance, Aggression, Nonconformity	18	25	15	19	22	25	10	22
Fearful Submission	5	2	3	0	3	1	3	2
Mild Dependence	6	6	12	9	5	9	11	7
Conformity	2	3	5	3	5	2	3	5
Sociability	34	39	27	36	29	27	34	27
Affiliation and Nurturance	24	11	21	21	16	15	19	16
Assertive Leading	11	14	17	12	20	23	20	21

° This table summarizes peer-directed behavior. It excludes children's solitary actions and their behavior directed toward adults. The latter types constitute 41 percent of the 2,909 behavior units recorded in initial observations of children in segregated cabins and 35 percent of the 3,753 units in observations made during later phases of segregated camping.

in the descriptions children gave of the cabin mate they felt they knew best. Negro boys, in addition to behaving more aggressively, were more alerted to dominance, aggression, and nonconformity. That is, they, more often than the other children, described their cabin mates in these terms. (Initially, Negro boys referred to aggression in 50 percent of the cases; the other subgroups, in approximately 12 percent.) Girls of both races, more than boys, appraised other children in terms of their nurturant qualities (girls, 44 percent; boys, 32 percent).

Although race and sex groups did not differ profoundly from one another in either their behavior or their perceptual sensitivities in segregated settings, the areas in which differences did occur have psychological significance for integration. The expression of aggression, nurturance, dominance, and deference are critical areas in Negro-white relationships. Will these small differences make a difference in racially mixed groups? Possibly because they are "sensitive" areas in intergroup relations, they are likely to take on added meaning in a mixed setting by being interpreted "racially." If slightly more overt acting out of aggression occurs in Negro boys, will it be seized upon by white children as aggression along racial

lines or as evidence supporting a stereotype they may hold of Negroes? Will slightly more overt nurturing behavior (such as expression of affection) in Negro girls be given a racial interpretation in interaction by the white girls? Will both white and Negro children behave in an integrated situation as they did when segregated?

Interpersonal Relations in Integration

It would be difficult to grow up in our culture unaware of racial stereotyping and tensions. Such awareness is a part of the social learning brought by the children to interracial groups. A question of interest for our research is, then, to see to what extent stereotyping and tensions emerge in the Negro and white children's perceptions of one another in this face-to-face experience, and in their interactions with one another.

To answer this question we have compared segregated and integrated groups in the ways in which they develop a mode of living together, and the ways in which individuals judge one another and establish their own positions in the groups. Secondly, we have examined in integration the relationships among children of like race and of unlike race, and the self-analyses of children of each racial group.

BEHAVIOR IN SEGREGATED AND INTEGRATED GROUPS

The behavior of children in segregated and integrated groups was markedly similar within the first days of the groups' development and over the two-week period studied. A high rate of interaction was generally maintained or developed in integration, both within and across racial lines. Affiliative, submissive, fearful, and aggressive interactions occurred with similar frequencies in both settings. In segregation, 18 percent of the units of recorded interactions fell into categories of negative, nonconforming behavior; 55 percent in categories of friendly,

supportive, social interactions. The comparable percentages in integration were 16 percent and 52 percent.

Within these similarities were also differences. Boys, particularly Negro boys, began integration with a somewhat lower amount of interaction with other boys than they showed in segregation. Among the Negro boys, the proportion of solitary activity and passive observations was 14 percent greater in integration than in segregation. Over time, however, the amount of interaction in the boys' groups increased and did not differ from that observed under segregation.

The Negro boys, who displayed slightly higher proportions of aggressive and disruptive behavior in segregation than did white boys, continued to do so when integrated (see Table 2). They directed these actions

TABLE 2

CHILDREN'S BEHAVIOR IN INTEGRATED CABINS

A. Initial Phases of Camp (Percent of Behavior Units)

Behavior Category	Actions by Negro Girls Directed toward		Actions by White Girls Directed toward		Actions by Negro Boys Directed toward		Actions by White Boys Directed toward	
	Negro	White	Negro	White	Negro	White	Negro	White
Dominance, Aggression, Nonconformity	15	13	19	12	27	25	20	21
Fearful Submission	2	0	1	0	0	1	0	0
Mild Dependence	11	8	13	7	12	14	7	13
Conformity	3	4	2	4	0	5	6	9
Sociability	32	34	29	36	28	17	22	18
Affiliation and Nurturance	24	29	21	25	12	23	26	14
Assertive Leading	13	12	15	16	21	15	19	25

B. Later Phases of Camp (Percent of Behavior Units)

Behavior Category	Actions by Negro Girls Directed toward		Actions by White Girls Directed toward		Actions by Negro Boys Directed toward		Actions by White Boys Directed toward	
	Negro	White	Negro	White	Negro	White	Negro	White
Dominance, Aggression, Nonconformity	29	19	24	13	25	23	21	24
Fearful Submission	1	1	1	1	1	1	0	2
Mild Dependence	9	9	6	8	5	8	7	10
Conformity	5	3	3	5	8	6	7	6
Sociability	19	26	26	30	26	28	26	22
Affiliation and Nurturance	20	22	19	25	9	15	17	14
Assertive Leading	17	20	21	18	26	19	22	22

to white and Negro boys alike. The white boys' aggressive and nonconforming acts did not increase in frequency in integration nor was either race the preferred target. Friendly and supportive actions were as frequent in integration and segregation. They were initially directed across racial lines more often than toward members of a child's own race.

Girls' groups showed no differences between segregation and integration in amount of interaction with others and no gross alterations in frequencies of negative and positive forms of behavior. But, in integration, actions directed within and across racial lines differed.

In the boys' behavior, there appeared to be emerging a pattern of cautious but equal-status "give-and-take." The behavior of the girls suggested a status differential. White girls directed more of their aggressive and less of their friendly actions toward Negro than toward white girls. Negro girls followed the white pattern; that is, they directed more aggressive behavior toward girls of their own race and more friendly sociability toward white girls. In each instance the differences were small.

These assessments of the children's behavior were based on the samples of interaction recorded systematically on each cabin group at specified times. Other less quantifiable behavioral evidence of the children's adjustments to integration was provided by the journal records of the participant observers. For example, just how did the social groupings look in the camp at large—in the dining hall, at the council ring, on the playground? What behavioral evidences of anxiety appeared?

Throughout camp, the children of the two races intermingled in all activities. The amount of this intermingling varied, however. The factors of former acquaintance and kinship make it difficult to evaluate precisely the meaning of spontaneous mixing and separation. In activities for which the entire camp rather than the cabin group was the unit, some children quickly sought out precamp acquaintances, who were most often of the same race. Some instances of segregated grouping occurred at the camp fires, ball games, etc. However, this spontaneous segregation never included all the children, nor were camp issues clearly defined along racial lines.

Whether it be segregated or integrated, camp away from home is likely to bring out anxious behavior in children. The usual variety of overt signs was observed in both camp settings—attempts to "leave the field" physically or symbolically, fearful or withdrawn behavior, minor accidents and physical complaints, bed-wetting, and disruptive, overt acting-out behavior. Children whom observers noted as particularly anxious indulged in substitute behavior. For example, one boy tended to withdraw from the group and kept with him a small toad that he petted, cuddled, and talked to. It is difficult to determine the extent to which such anxious behavior is intensified in integration. There is evidence suggesting, however, that such anxiety indicators appear more frequently in integration. For example, one such symptom, "leaving the field," is most literally represented by those children who, for one reason or another, left camp prior to the scheduled ending of the session. Of the 267 children studied, only ten fell in this category and seven of these ten were children from integrated groups. The existence of such anxieties and the anticipation of underlying tensions also modify the way the adult leaders function in the integrated groups. (The leader's role is discussed later.)

Although the psychological environment was most certainly altered by integration for children without prior experience in racially mixed association, their overt behavior in camp continued to present a picture of overwhelming conformity to the requirements of the situation. The effectiveness of the setting in evoking conforming and compatible behavior in segregated and integrated groups alike would appear to stem from the newness of the situation (new peers and adults with whom to become acquainted, new living routines to learn) and from the explicit and implicit demands for equalitarian behavior. To throw further light on the psychological environment of the children, we turn to their perceptions of interpersonal relationships and associates in camp.

PERCEPTION IN SEGREGATED AND INTEGRATED GROUPS

The descriptive details that the child selects to relate about his peers almost always concern social relationships and behavior. These he gives as predictions or expectations, as much as observations of past performance. When he says that Jack is always causing trouble, he has the future as much in mind as the past. Seldom does he report characteristics such as appearance, skills, home background, and the like.

Rarely did the total descriptions of other children in integration sound like racial stereotypes (with a few children excepted). To this extent, the expression of the familiar racial stereotypes in face-to-face appraisals was rare. However, the indirect effects of these stereotypes were apparent in a perceptual sensitivity to those behaviors which cluster around domination and aggression. These effects were reflected both in the findings for segregation and integration and in differences in Negro and white children's perceptions of one another in integration.

A comparison of cabin-mate descriptions in segregated and integrated groups shows that both Negro and white children came to the integrated situation with a heightened concern about aggressive, disruptive behavior of their peers, but that the object of their concern differed. In white children, this increased sensitivity was seen chiefly in their assessments of Negro children. With the Negro children, concern was directed toward their own race. Aggression was important in the white children's descriptions of their peers in 12 percent of the cases in segregation and in 19 percent in integration, but in their evaluations of Negro children the frequency rose to 39 percent. Thirty-one percent of the segregated Negro children mentioned aggressiveness in their cabin-mate descriptions; in integration, 43 percent did so with regard to Negroes, 27 percent with regard to white peers. This suggests that Negro children were more anxious about control of aggression in their own group than about aggression from the white children.

An interesting comparison is provided by the children's answers to the "guess-who" questions. When asked to choose which child best fitted the description of a child who "gets mad easily," 25 percent of the segregated Negro girls and 16 percent of the segregated Negro boys chose themselves. In integration, none of the Negro girls and only 8 percent of the Negro boys viewed themselves in this light. Furthermore, in integration, 25 percent of the Negro children named themselves as the child who "helps others out," while in segregation only 7 percent did so. Thus we see that as Negro children seem more concerned about aggression in *other* Negro children in the integrated situation, they are less likely to see this trait in themselves—a reaction which would be consistent with the interpretation that their anxiety over aggression from Negroes to whites has led to a denial of their own aggressive impulses.

In integration, power relationships are important for both the white and Negro children. Roughly half the white children interpreted peer behavior in terms of accomplished or attempted leadership or domination. These interpretations were introduced less frequently (30 percent) by the Negro children. On the other hand, Negro children (particularly the girls) were more concerned about the behavior in themselves that was complementary to leadership and dominance, namely, fearfulness and submission.

On "guess-who" questions, race-linked roles stressed similar components of behavior (see Table 3). Negro girls were seen by white and Negro cabin mates as fearful and anxious, as lacking leadership skills and social sensitivity. White girls were cast in a

TABLE 3

PERCENT OF CHILDREN IN INTEGRATED CABINS SELECTING A NEGRO CHILD IN "GUESS-WHO" RESPONSES

"Guess-who" Items	Initial Interview				Final Interview			
	Girls		Boys		Girls		Boys	
	NEGRO	WHITE	NEGRO	WHITE	NEGRO	WHITE	NEGRO	WHITE
"Does what he is told"	28	53	49	58	57	46	64	32
"Helps, is kind"	34	43	62	61	47	50	72	44
"Good leader"	28	40	54	47	40	39	69	47
"Good at 'sizing up' others"	17	23	57	25	37	28	55	44
"Gets mad easily"	45	33	54	58	40	32	58	65
"Bosses others"	45	47	43	55	40	36	53	65
"Afraid, shy"	58	67	43	33	74	68	36	50
	(N = 29)	(N = 30)	(N = 37)	(N = 36)	(N = 30)	(N = 28)	(N = 36)	(N = 34)

mold characterized by social competence and ascendance, again by both Negroes and whites. Negro boys were selected for descriptions emphasizing assertive and helpful behavior. The white boys were not clearly typed. (Statistical tests confirm the general patterns described.) The influence of sex in determining racial role typing is crucial. When sex groups were combined, the systematic picture of racial role assignments was obscured.

Since precamp background and the immediate camping situation were not congruent with respect to race relations, integration presented to both Negro and white children a situation in which there was greater ambiguity and greater conflict, initially, than in segregation. Evidences of this changed psychological environment were found in increased anxiety manifestations (discussed earlier) and also in an increased tendency for children to seek out cues to lessen ambiguity. Intensified cue-seeking, we suggest, should result in perceptions of other children which are more complex in integration than in segregation and which search out explanations and draw inferences about what is observed in the "other."

The less complex descriptions, those consisting of unrelated bits of behavior or global descriptions, were rated at the lower end of a seven-point scale. For example, a low rating was given the following: "She sleeps next to me. I know her name. She has kind of brown complexion. She's nice." Where there was a more thorough assessment of peer relationships and various aspects of behavior were interrelated and motivational inferences were made, as in the excerpt from Rosemary's interview (p. 658), a high rating was given. The ratings of children's impressions of their peers were higher in integration than in segregation. The median rating of initial descriptions in the segregated groups was 3.96, in the integrated, 4.58. One would expect that chance differences between the two groups of this magnitude would occur less than ten percent of the time.

Differences in complexity of interpersonal perceptions appeared in cross-race and in-race descriptions. White children made more searching appraisals of Negro than of white cabin mates. The other race, presenting the greater ambiguity in face-to-face interactions, called out the greater alertness to cues. Negro children, on the other hand, made fuller descriptions of members of their *own* race in the beginning of the camp session. That is in line with the findings presented earlier, which we have interpreted as pointing to the Negro children's initial hyperconcern regarding their own behavior in a racially mixed setting. However, at the end of camp, they, too, were attending more closely to the characteristics of children of the other race.

INTERRACIAL FRIENDSHIP

So far we have discussed how campers actually behaved toward one another in the segregated and integrated settings and how they perceived each other's characteristics. Equally important is the question of affective relationships—how feelings of liking and disliking find expression in friendship groupings. Sociometric research and social distance questionnaires have repeatedly documented racial cleavage in children's groups. Our study provided a picture of the kinds of interpersonal attraction that develop when background factors such as neighborhood and family ties do not guide friendship pairing.

Each child was asked, after one day in camp, to rank his cabin mates on friendship potential, beginning with his choice of best friend and continuing in order of his preference. In addition, he was asked to choose the children whom he would like to have with him if he could set up a new cabin. When each child's average friendship ranking of white children was compared with his

average ranking of his Negro peers, the evidence is abundantly clear that significantly higher friendship rankings were given to white than to Negro children (see Table 4). The underchoosing of Negro children was somewhat more pronounced among the Negro children themselves. Negro girls stood as a group apart, markedly underchoosing members of their own race.

A similar pattern of racial preference appeared in the selection of children for hypothetical cabins. However, this opportunity to compose a new group seldom resulted in hypothetical segregated cabins. None of the Negro and only eight percent of the white campers set up such cabins. Quite the reverse composition, in which the chooser makes himself the only member of his race, occurred among 13 percent of the Negro and 14 percent of the white campers.

The underlying motivations for patterns of friendship and cabin-mate choice were doubtless varied. Clearly some of these children were consciously choosing on racial lines; thus, their selection of desired cabin mates may have represented an attempt at direct control of potential power relationships and subgrouping possibilities. This conscious choice was sometimes expressed: "There would be five whites in one room and five colored in the other. They could talk their way, and we could talk ours." For

TABLE 4

FRIENDSHIP PREFERENCES IN INTEGRATED CABINS

| Average Friendship Appraisal | Initial Interview (Percent) | | | | Final Interview (Percent) | | | |
| | Negro | | White | | Negro | | White | |
	GIRLS	BOYS	GIRLS	BOYS	GIRLS	BOYS	GIRLS	BOYS
Higher Average Ranking to Negro Cabin Mates	14	32	37	34	24	31	48	39
Same Average Ranking to Negro and White	10	18	7	6	21	11	7	12
Highe Average Ranking to White Cabin Mates	76	50	56	60	55	58	45	49
	(N = 29)	(N = 38)	(N = 30)	(N = 35)	(N = 29)	(N = 36)	(N = 28)	(N = 33)

many others, race as a criterion for choice may have intruded more indirectly and unconsciously. In other instances, however, children showed an awareness of race, yet consciously rejected it as an adequate basis for selecting friends. Thus one girl, in naming her best friend, stressed interests shared in common, "even though we are different colors and everything."

RACE- AND SEX-LINKED PATTERNS
IN INTEGRATION

The interactive effects of race and sex have appeared in each set of data examined thus far. The meaning of being white or Negro and the impact of integration are not the same for boys as they are for girls, nor are the relationships among behavior, attitudes, and perceptions identical for each race and sex group. As we have noted, status relationships and the expression and control of aggression are significant areas in Negro-white relations, and in these areas sex differences enter quite crucially. Social norms and socialization practices grant boys more freedom for expression of aggression than is the case for girls. The relevance of this difference became apparent in the adaptation of white and Negro boys to integration. They tested each other aggressively but without clearly patterning this behavior along racial lines. Their behavior suggested that they were able to act out interracial hostilities and apprehensions which they may have felt within the limits tolerated in the boys' culture of their particular social class.

The Negro boys were required to come to terms with two conflicting codes regarding aggression. As *boys*, aggression within limits is permitted, but, as *Negro boys*, they must learn control of hostility toward whites. Their initial concern about hostile acts was not only high, but it was especially focused on such behavior in their own race. At the end of two weeks, the Negro boys showed a decrease in awareness of aggression in their own race, with a corresponding increase in sensitivity to it in white children. This may

have reflected a shift from a pervasive anxiety about control of their own aggressive impulses to a greater sensitivity to the behavior of others toward them.

White boys, we have noted, were more concerned about aggression in their Negro peers than in their own group. We have noted, too, some basis for their concern in the actual higher frequency of aggressive actions by Negro boys. In giving more prominence to aggression in their perceptions of Negro boys, the white boys, therefore, may have been perceiving "accurately" as well as out of stereotyped expectations regarding Negroes.

In each of the indices we have used, race has been different and probably more important in the thought-patterns and behavior of the girls than of the boys. Girls' groups, while generally conforming to the equality requirements of the situation, showed more frequent deviation in their behavior in temporary and partial cleavages. Further, concepts of the self and others and the meaning of the total situation were quite different for the girls of the two races.

Segregated white girls displayed least overt aggression toward their peers, which we have interpreted as being in line with cultural prescriptions of greater conformity for girls. When integrated, however, their aggressive actions toward Negro girls were much less inhibited. Their more hostile behavior was also echoed in their expressed negative feelings and opinions about the Negro girls and was further underscored by their preferential regard for other white girls.

What was the reality basis in the immediate situation for their reaction? What were the underlying dynamics? Negro girls did not counter aggression with aggression; in fact, they directed less aggression toward their white cabin mates than toward other Negro girls. They did not counter the white girls' expression of rejection. In other words, their reactions were not adequate to evoke the negative responses of their white peers. To the extent that behavior and feelings of the white girls were out of line with the approved model for girls and were in accord neither with the prescriptions of equality in the immediate situation nor with the general behavior of members of the other group, one would suppose that white girls had feelings of conflict and guilt.

The Negro girls came to integration with elements of self-rejection, with awareness of the favored position of the white girls, and with tightened control over their own behavior. In the integrated camp, they experienced at first hand equalitarian living with white children, which in a large measure was successful. But they experienced, too, the undercurrent of the white girls' resistance. What did these diverse aspects of the experience add up to for the Negro girls? The picture was not simple, but it pointed to evidence of change. By the end of camp there was lessened self-rejection among the Negro girls. Yet they did not, at the same time, harbor clearly developed negative stereotypes concerning white girls. The camp situation had provided sufficient supports to permit Negro girls to feel somewhat freer to express aggression at the end of the camp session, although such hostile acts were less characteristic of their relations with white girls than with Negro girls. The barrier of race remained, inhibiting and channeling patterns of action.

It might be noted that the nature of the sex differences in this study is in line with expectations regarding adult role relationships. Negro and white males from the lower socioeconomic status levels may find themselves side by side, engaged in the same type of work; the culturally imposed status differential does not preclude this relationship. For Negro women, the extent to which such nearly equal-status contact with white women is possible has been considerably more limited, at least in the past. To a noticeable degree contact between white and Negro women in occupational spheres would typically involve marked status differences, with the Negro a servant and the white woman her employer.

CHANGES IN INTERGROUP RELATIONS

Under conditions of intensive, equal-status contacts in an atmosphere supporting favorable interracial relations, it is relevant to ask whether changes occurred over the two-week period. The question ordinarily asked in "change experiments" is simply whether there has been a shift from unfavorable to favorable attitudes. Seldom is it known, when such a measured change is reported, whether or how the total constellation of the individual's beliefs and motivations and behavior is similarly altered. Yet only by knowing this are predictions regarding stability of change and consequences of change possible. Our study, of course, does not provide all the information that would be needed to approach this ideal; however, we can examine changes occurring in behavior and perception as well as in attitudes toward the opposite race.

In the two weeks of living in the integrated setting, radical shifts in long-standing interracial orientations did not occur. However, there was a rapid initial behavioral adjustment to the situation, a quick establishment of a behavioral equilibrium, which was overwhelming conformity to what was expected in the immediate situation but which also incorporated within the conformity varying degrees and manifestations of tension and resistance.

Small changes occurred over time with a slight drop in over-all social and friendly interactions and a slight rise in disruptive interactions. These shifts, however, are not greatly unlike time changes in segregated groups and cannot be assumed to have special significance in integration.

Concurrent with the behavioral adaptation that takes place in integrated groups, are there changes in friendship choices and perceptions? If the experience of integration is successful in reducing social distance between racial groups, one would expect that race as a criterion (conscious or unconscious) for assessing friendship should exert less influence at the end of the two weeks.

The findings support this. Although the children still tended to prefer their white cabin mates as friends at the close of camp, there was a statistically significant drop in the extent to which they were the favored group.

The white children's shifts over time were primarily in friendship choices. The roles the white girls attributed to girls of both races remained relatively unchanged. The white boys, neither at the beginning nor at the end of the two weeks, made stereotyped role assignments.

The Negro children showed greater change effects than the white children on each of the levels of response. Initially, as we have seen, they tightened the reins of control over their behavior. With the passage of time they permitted themselves greater freedom of action. More often at the end of camp than initially they assigned socially valued roles to cabin mates of their own race. This suggests an altered evaluation of their own group. One should not lose sight of the fact, however, that the changes for the Negro girls did not result in a conflict-free situation. Although their self-regard by some indicators had improved, they nevertheless held the white girls as their models of persons they want to be like. The Negro girls' constellation of responses pointed to this subgroup as the one facing the greatest difficulties in resolving self-other attitudes in the integrated setting.

The specific measures of interracial behavior, perception, and attitudes that have been discussed in this paper cannot, by themselves, fully show the total impact on the individual participant of the two-week experience of around-the-clock integration. It would be important to know how this experience effects the acceptance of the *idea* of integration and the individual's anxious anticipations regarding intergroup relationships. Children coming to an interracial setting for the first time bring with them, as we have indicated, certain anxieties about coping with the new situation. If these anxieties are not supported by the actualities of sub-

sequent experience, the participants may more fully accept the total situation. This increased acceptance may be necessary, in itself, to provide a climate in which attitude change can take place. In general, the experience of integrated camping was viewed favorably by the children. A significantly greater proportion of children in integrated than in segregated sessions indicated at the end that they would have liked to extend the camping period. Under integration, 76 percent wanted to "stretch it out"; 64 percent of those under segregation so signified. Thus, the two-week experience of integration should probably be viewed not as completing the process of change in intergroup relations but as providing the necessary first steps in a long-term process of reorganizing beliefs and feelings.

INFLUENCE AGENTS IN INTEGRATION

Although many of the standards of home and school were carried over into the new camp setting, it is likely that, initially, patterns of approved and expected interracial behavior were not fully clear to the camper. In an ego-relevant ambiguous situation such as this, the participants seek clarification of appropriate behavior. The ambiguities lend themselves to structuring by any influence agent. Our study points to the crucial role of the adult leader in this respect, both as a formal, institutionally accepted leader and as an individual participant whose motives, attitudes, and feelings have a subtle impact on the total atmosphere. While the present report is not intended as an analysis of the leader role, a number of leader influences may be mentioned.

The leaders directly influenced the children's responses to the experience of integration by: (1) defining equalitarian behavior, both explicitly and by example, as the behavior that is expected; (2) manipulating the situation to enforce equal status; and (3) directly controlling the degree of freedom of action permitted in the interracial situation. Leaders reflected increased anxiety and strong motivation for the success of integration by exhibiting tighter control over their groups than had been the case in segregation. Tighter control was evident by their more explicit definition of acceptable and unacceptable behavior and by their quick reactions to the slightest indication of interracial tension. (For example, in integration, 62 percent of the counselor interactions with the children were of a directive nature as compared to 46 percent in the segregated situation.)

We found a strong tendency for the counselors to deny the existence of any interracial tensions among the children and, in fact, to be unaware of obvious tension signs. This probably stemmed partly from their desire for integration to succeed and partly from their anxiety. Preceding desegregation the counselors were freer to admit and express their uncertainties and anxieties than they were when they became involved in the new situation. For the leader who consciously wants to participate in a racially integrated setting, it is clear that his is a dual role; he is an influence agent with respect to the children and he is himself influenced by the situation.

Conclusions

Our study consistently points to the importance of the immediate situation in channeling behavior. We might hypothesize that new standards of behavior, such as those so quickly established in the camp, are more readily inculcated in a situation where new elements predominate over the familiar. The consistent expectation of equality, as conveyed by a racially integrated adult culture (counselors), enforced by the leader in his control techniques, and expressed in his behavior toward the children, were of overwhelming importance in setting the tone of the situation.

A short period of equalitarian contact is not sufficient to bring about marked and enduring alterations of attitudes or perceptions towards others and oneself. Yet, within a limited time span and with favorable situational supports, the beginnings of such changes have been noted. Should such a group experience be continued over a longer period of time, more pronounced and lasting changes might be anticipated. That these might prove to be limited solely to the situation experienced is possible. Yet the broad range of contact experienced in the supervised group living suggests the likelihood that more basic and enduring changes resulted than would be the case in more situation-specific experiences.

Adjustment of the individual child to membership in an integrated group and the nature of group functioning are conditioned by the social sex roles of the children of the minority and majority groups. Influences of significance in this respect probably stem from child-rearing differences for boys and girls in the expression and control of impulses and from the special racial roles of each subgroup (including not only their racial roles as children but also their anticipated adult roles). These sex-linked aspects of integration warrant more systematic study.

The effects of change in intergroup relations are most often conceived of in terms of changed responses toward the out-group. It was the minority child's changed self-evaluation which even the short period of integration appeared to influence most. Change in the evaluation of one's own membership group is an integral aspect of the integration process.

The Authoritarian Personality ❊ Else Frenkel-Brunswik

❊ Daniel J. Levinson

❊ R. Nevitt Sanford

Introduction

The present research was guided by the conception of an individual whose thoughts about man and society form a pattern which is properly described as antidemocratic and which springs from his deepest emotional tendencies. Can it be shown that such a person really exists? If so, what precisely is he like? What goes to make up antidemocratic thought? What are the organizing forces within the person? If such a person exists, how commonly does he exist in our society? And what have been the determinants and what the cause of his development?

Although the antidemocratic individual may be thought of as a totality, it is nevertheless possible to distinguish and to study separately (*a*) his ideology and (*b*) his underlying personality needs. Ideology refers to an organization of opinions, attitudes, and values. One may speak of an individual's total ideology or of his ideology with respect to different areas of social life: politics, economics, religion, minority groups, and so forth. Ideologies have an existence independent of any single individual, those existing at a particular time being results both of historical processes and of contemporary social events. These ideologies, or the more particular ideas within them, have for different individuals different degrees of appeal, a matter that depends upon the individual's needs and the degree to which these needs are being satisfied or frustrated.

The pattern of ideas that the individual takes over and makes his own will in each case be found to have a function within his over-all adjustment.

Although ideological trends are usually expressed more or less openly in words, it is important to note that, in the case of such affect-laden questions as those concerning minority groups, the degree of openness with which a person speaks will depend upon his situation. At the present time, when antidemocratic sentiments are officially frowned upon in this country, one should expect an individual to express them openly only in a guarded way or to a limited extent. This most superficial level of expression would afford a poor basis for estimating the potential for fascism in America. We should know, in addition, what the individual will say when he feels safe from criticism, what he thinks but will not say at all, what he thinks but will not admit to himself, and what he will be disposed to think when this or that appeal is made to him. In short, it is necessary to know the individual's *readiness* for antidemocratic thought and action, what it is that he will express when conditions change in such a way as to remove his inhibitions. Antidemocratic propaganda, though it makes some appeal to people's real interests, addresses itself in the main to emotional needs and irrational impulses, and its effectiveness will depend upon the susceptibility existing in the great mass of people.

This article was written especially for T. M. Newcomb and E. L. Hartley (Eds.), *Readings in Social Psychology*, New York: Holt, Rinehart and Winston, 1947. It appeared as "The Antidemocratic Personality." The research was subsequently reported in T. W. Adorno, E. Frenkel-Brunswik, et al., *The Authoritarian Personality*, New York: Harper & Row, 1950. Reprinted by permission of the authors and publishers.

THE AUTHORITARIAN PERSONALITY

To know that antidemocratic trends reside in the personality structure is to raise the further question of how this structure develops. According to the present theory, the major influences upon personality development arise in the course of child training as carried forward in a setting of family life. The determinants of personality, in other words, are mainly social; such factors as the economic situation of the parents, their social, ethnic, and religious group memberships, and the prevailing ideology concerning child training might be factors of crucial significance. This means that broad changes in social conditions and institutions will have a direct bearing upon the kinds of personalities that develop within a society. It does not mean, however, that such social changes would appreciably alter the personality structures that already exist.

It was necessary to devise techniques for surveying surface expression, for revealing ideological trends that were more or less inhibited, and for bringing to light unconscious personality forces (Frenkel-Brunswik and Sanford, 1945; Levinson and Sanford, 1944). Since the major concern was with *patterns* of dynamically related factors, it seemed that the proper approach was through intensive individual studies. In order to gauge the significance and practical importance of such studies, however, it was necessary to study groups as well as individuals and to find ways and means for integrating the two approaches.

Individuals were studied by means of (*a*) intensive clinical interviews and (*b*) a modified Thematic Apperception Test; groups were studied by means of questionnaires. It was not hoped that the clinical studies would be as complete or profound as some which have already been performed, primarily by psychoanalysts, nor that the questionnaires would be more accurate than any now employed by social psychologists. It was hoped, however—indeed it was necessary to our purpose—that the clinical material could be conceptualized in such a way as to permit its being quantified and carried over into group studies, and that the questionnaires could be brought to bear upon areas of response ordinarily left to clinical study. The attempt was made, in other words, to bring methods of traditional social psychology into the service of theories and concepts from the newer dynamic theory of personality, and in so doing to make "depth psychological" phenomena more amenable to mass-statistical treatment, and to make quantitative surveys of attitudes and opinions more meaningful psychologically.

In order to study antidemocratic individuals, it was necessary first to identify them. Hence a start was made by constructing a questionnaire and having it filled out anonymously by a large group of people. This questionnaire contained, in addition to numerous questions of fact about the subject's past and present life, and a number of open-answer ("projective") questions, several opinion-attitude scales containing a variety of antidemocratic (anti-Semitic, ethnocentric, reactionary, profascist) statements with which the subjects were invited to agree or disagree. A number of individuals (identified by indirect means) who showed the greatest amount of agreement with these statements were then studied by means of clinical tehniques, and contrasted with a number of individuals showing strong disagreement. On the basis of these individual studies, the questionnaire was revised, and the whole procedure repeated. The study began with college students as subjects, and then was expanded to include a variety of groups from the community at large. The findings are considered to hold fairly well for non-Jewish, white, native-born, middle-class Americans.

The Study of Ideology

Anti-Semitism was the first ideological area studied. Anti-Semitic ideology is regarded as a broad system of ideas including: *negative opinions* regarding Jews (e.g., that they are unscrupulous, dirty, clannish, power-seeking); *hostile attitudes* toward them (e.g., that they should be excluded, restricted, suppressed); and *moral values* which permeate the opinions and justify the attitudes.

In what senses, if any, can anti-Semitic ideology be considered irrational? What are the main attitudes in anti-Semitism—segregation, suppression, exclusion—for the solution of "the Jewish problem"? Do people with negative opinions generally have hostile attitudes as well? Do individuals have a general readiness to accept or oppose a broad pattern of anti-Semitic opinions and attitudes?

These questions led to and guided the construction of an opinion-attitude scale for the measurement of anti-Semitic ideology. This scale provided a basis for the selection of criterion groups of extreme high and low scorers, who could then be subjected to intensive clinical study. The source material for the scale included: the writings of virulent anti-Semites; technical, literary, and reportorial writings on anti-Semitism and fascism; and, most important, everyday American anti-Semitism as revealed in parlor discussion, in the discriminatory practices of many businesses and institutions, and in the literature of various Jewish "defense" groups trying vainly to counter numerous anti-Semitic accusations by means of rational argument. In an attempt to include as much as possible of this type of content in the scale, certain rules were followed in its construction.

Each item should be maximally rich in ideas, with a minimum of duplication in wording or essential content. In order to reflect the forms of anti-Semitism prevalent in America today, the statements should not be violently and openly anti-democratic; rather, they should be pseudodemocratic, in the sense that active hostility toward a group is somewhat tempered and disguised by means of a compromise with democratic ideals. Each statement should have a familiar ring, should sound as it had been heard many times in everyday discussions and intensive interviews.

The 52-item scale contained five subscales—not statistically pure dimensions but convenient and meaningful groupings of items—the correlations among which should provide partial answers to some of the questions raised above. (*a*) Subscale "Offensive" (12 items) deals with imagery (opinions) of Jews as personally unpleasant and disturbing. Stereotypy is most explicit in the item: "There may be a few exceptions, but in general Jews are pretty much alike." To agree with this statement is to have an image of "the Jew" as a stereotyped model of the entire group. (*b*) Subscale "Threatening" (10 items) describes the Jews as a dangerous, dominating group. In various items the Jews are regarded as rich and powerful, poor and dirty, unscrupulous, revolutionary, and so on. (*c*) Subscale "Attitudes" (16 items) refers to programs of action. The specific hostile attitudes vary in degree from simple avoidance to suppression and attack, with intermediate actions of exclusion, segregation, and suppression. The social areas of discrimination covered include employment, residence, professions, marriage, and so on. (*d*) and (*e*) Subscales "Seclusive" and "Intrusive" deal with opposing stands on the issue of assimilation. The "Seclusive" subscale accuses the Jews of being too foreign and clannish; it implies that Jews can themselves eliminate anti-Semitism (a problem of their own making, so to speak) by greater assimilation and conformity to American ways. The "Intrusive" subscale, on the other hand, accuses the Jews of overassimilation, hiding of Jewishness, prying, seeking power and prestige. These items imply that Jews ought to keep more to themselves and to develop a culture, preferably even a nation of their own.

The total scale is intended to measure the individual's readiness to support or oppose anti-Semitic ideology as a whole. This ideology is conceived as involving stereotyped negative opinions describing Jews as threatening, immoral, and categorically different from non-Jews, and of hostile attitudes urging various forms of restriction. Anti-Semitism is conceived, then, not as a specific attitude (jealousy, blind hate, religious disapproval, or whatever) but rather as a general way of thinking and feeling about Jews and Jewish-Gentile relations.

For two groups, the reliabilities were at least .92 for the total A-S scale, and between .84 and .94 for all subscales ("Intrusive," second group only), except for "Seclusive," for which .71 was obtained (second group only). The correlations among the subscales "Offensive," "Threatening," and "Attitudes" are .83 to .85, while each of these correlates .92 to .94 with the total scale.

These correlations seem to reveal that each person has a rather general tendency to accept or reject anti-Semitic ideology as a whole. The correlations of subscale "Seclusive" with "Intrusive" (.74) and with "Attitudes" (also .74) reveal basic contradictions in anti-Semitic ideology. (All the raw coefficients, if corrected for attenutation, would be over .90.) Most anti-Semites are, apparently, willing to criticize both Jewish assimilation and Jewish seclusion. This is further testimony to the irrationality of anti-Semitism. Also irrational is the stereotyped image of "the Jew" (the item about Jews being all alike was very discriminating), an image which is intrinsically self-contradictory, since one person cannot be simultaneously rich and poor, dirty and luxurious, capitalistic and radical.

The question then presents itself: Are the trends found in anti-Semitic ideology—its generality, stereotyped imagery, destructive irrationality, sense of threat, concern with power and immorality, and so on—also expressed in the individual's social thinking about group relations generally? Can it be that what was found in anti-Semitism is not specific to prejudice against Jews but rather is present in prejudice against all groups?

Considerations such as these led to the study of ethnocentrism, that is, ideology regarding in-groups (with which the individual identifies himself), out-groups (which are "different" and somehow antithetical to the in-group), and their interaction. A 34-item Ethnocentrism scale was constructed along lines similar to those employed for the A-S scale. There were three subscales: (a) A 12-item subscale deals with Negroes and Negro-white relations. The items refer to Negroes as lazy, good-natured, and ignorant; also aggressive, primitive, and rebellious, and so on. (b) Minorities. These 12 items deal with various groups (other than Jews and Negroes), including minority political parties and religious sects, foreigners, Oklahomans (in California), zoot-suiters, criminals, and so on. (c) "Patriotism." These 10 items deal with America as an in-group in relation to other nations as out-groups. The items express the attitude that foreign, "inferior" nations should be subordinate; they include a value for obedience and a punitive attitude toward value-violators, and, finally, they express regarding permanent peace a cynicism which is rationalized by moralistic, hereditarian theories of aggressive, threatening out-group nations.

The reliabilities for the subscales ranged from .80 to .91; and for the total E scale .91. These figures, considered together with the correlations of .74 to .83 among the subscales, and the subscale-total E scale correlations of .90 to .92, indicate a generality in ethnocentric ideology that is almost as great as and even more remarkable than that found in A-S.

The correlations of A-S with E complete the picture. The A-S scale correlates .80 with the E scale, and from .69 to .76 with the subscales. Through successive revisions there finally emerged a single E scale of 10 items (including 4 A-S items) which had reliabilities of .7 to .9 in different groups of subjects. It is clear that an attempt to understand prejudice psychologically must start with the total pattern of ethnocentric thinking, including both general outgroup rejection and in-group submission-idealization.

Space does not permit a detailed discussion of the study of politics and religion. Ethnocentrism is related, though not very closely, to political conservatism ($r = .5$) and to support of the more conservative political groupings. In the responses of individuals scoring high on the conservatism scale, two patterns could be distinguished: a traditional *laissez-faire* conservatism as opposed to "pseudoconservatism" in which a profession of belief in the tenets of traditional conservatism is combined with a readiness for violent change of a kind which would abolish the very institutions with which the individual appears to identify himself. The latter appeared to contribute more to the correlation between E and conservatism than did the former. The nonreligious are less ethnocentric on the average than the religious, although such sects as the Quakers and Unitarians made low E scale means (nonethnocentric).

The Study of Personality

The main variables underlying the various ideological areas above represent personality trends expressed in ideological form. A primary hypothesis in this research is that an individual is most receptive to those ideologies which afford the fullest expression to his over-all personality structure. Thus, a person clinically described as strongly authoritarian, projective, and destructive is likely to be receptive to an antidemocratic ideology such as ethnocentrism —ultimately fascism as the total social objectification of these trends—because it expresses his needs so well.

The attempt at a quantitative investigation of personality variables underlying ethnocentric ideology led to the construction of a personality scale. It was called, for convenience, the F scale because it was intended to measure some of the personality trends which seemed to express a predisposition or deep-lying receptivity to fascism.

The items are statements of opinion and attitude in nonideological areas (not dealing with formal groups or social institutions) such as self, family, people in general, sex, personal values, and so on; they are not tied by official statement or surface meaning to items in the other scales. Any consistency in response to the F and E scales, as indicated by the correlation between them, must be due primarily to the fact that both scales express the same underlying trends, since their surface content is quite different. The main difference between the scales is that the F items are less openly ideological.

Ten main variables guided scale construction, each variable being represented by a cluster of several items. The clusters were partially overlapping, since several items were intended to express more than a single variable. In three successive forms the scale contained 38, 34, than 30 items, but the 10 main variables were always represented.

The cluster variables were as follows: conventional values, authoritarian submission, authoritarian aggression, anti-intraception, superstition-stereotypy, pseudotoughness, power, cynicism, projectivity, and sex.

Three of these clusters may be discussed to illustrate the general approach. "Authoritarian submission" refers to an inability seriously to criticize, reject, or actively rebel against one's main in-group (particularly the family) figures and values. There is a highly moralized and idealized conception of authority-representatives and a submissive relation to them. Examples: "No sane, normal, decent person could ever think of hurting a close friend or relative"; "Every person should have complete faith in some supernatural power whose decisions he obeys without question."

"Anti-intraception" involves opposition to a psychological, insightful view of people and oneself. This includes a rejection of emotion and of attempts to look into one's deeper motives and conflicts. Personal inquiries tend to be regarded as prying, and there is often an exaggerated idea of how much prying is going on. Work and keeping

busy are emphasized as ways of "not thinking about yourself." Examples: "When a
person has a problem or worry, it is best for
him not to think about it but to keep busy
with more cheerful things"; "Nowadays
more and more people are prying into matters that should remain personal and private."

"Projectivity" refers to the disposition to
imagine strange, evil, dangerous, destructive
forces at work in the outer world; these im-
aginings have only the smallest basis in reality but can be understood as projections of
the individual's deep-lying sexual and aggressive strivings. Examples: "Wars and social troubles may someday be ended by an
earthquake or flood that will destroy the
whole world"; "Nowadays when so many
different kinds of people move around and
mix together so much, a person has to protect himself especially carefully against
catching an infection or disease from them";
"The wild sex life of the old Greeks and Ro-
mans was tame compared to some of the
goings-on in this country, even in places
where people might least expect it."

The successive forms of the F scale involved elimination, modification, and addition of items, based on both statistical considerations and on theoretical requirements
of richness of ideas and over-all inclusive-
ness. The reliability of the scale increased
from an average of .74 for the first form to
.85 on the last. Each high quartile scorer is
high on most items and clusters; on each
item and cluster the difference between
high scorers (total scale) and low scorers is
statistically significant.

Correlations of F with A-S and E increased from an average of about .6 to about
.75 in later forms, that is, higher than the
correlation of .50 with the conservatism
scale. This correlation, in conjunction with
the clinical findings reported below, gives
evidence of the functional role of personality
trends in organizing and giving meaning to
surface attitudes, values, and opinions.

Does ethnocentrism help the individual
avoid conscious ambivalence toward his

family by displacing the hostility onto out-
groups (the morally "alien") and thus leave
in consciousness exaggerated professions of
love toward family and authority? Do high
scorers on the F scale (who are usually also
ethnocentric) have an underlying anticon-
ventionalism, in-group- and family-directed
hostility, a tendency to do the very things
they rigidly and punitively oppose in others?
What impels an individual to feel, for example, that aggression against his family is
unthinkable and yet to agree that "homosex-
uals should be severely punished" and (during the war) that the "Germans and Japs
should be wiped out"? Such contradictions
suggest that the deeper personality trends of
high scorers are antithetical to their conscious values, opinions, and attitudes. The
clinical studies reported below investigate
further these and other questions.

The so-called "projective questions" are
intermediate between the scales and the intensive clinical techniques. As part of the
questionnaire they are used in group studies
in order to determine how common in larger
populations were the relationships discovered in clinical studies. They are open questions to be answered in a few words or lines;
each question deals with events or experiences which are likely to have emotional
significance for the individual. The original
set of about 30 questions was gradually reduced to 8, which were both statistically
differentiating and theoretically inclusive.
These deal with "what moods are unpleasant," "what desires are hard to control,"
"what great people are admired," "what
would drive a person nuts," "what are the
worst crimes," "what moments are embarrassing," "how to spend your last six
months," "what is most awe-inspiring."

The responses of the entire high and low
quartiles on the A-S (later the total E) scale
were contrasted. For each question "high"
and "low" scoring categories were made; a
"high" category expresses a personality
trend which seems most characteristic of
ethnocentrists and which can be expected
significantly to differentiate the two groups.

A scoring manual, giving the specific categories (usually two to six) for each item, was the basis on which two independent raters scored each response (not knowing the actual A-S or E score of the subjects). Each response was scored "high," "low," or "neutral"—the neutral category being used when the response was omitted, ambiguous, or when it contained "high" and "low" trends equally. Less than 10 percent of the responses received neutral scores.

The scoring agreement for the battery of items averaged 80 to 90 percent on a variety of groups (total, 200 to 300). The high quartiles received an average of 75-90 percent "high" scores, as compared with 20-40 percent "high" scores for the low quartiles. Almost never was an individual ethnocentrist given more than 50 percent low scores, and conversely for the anti-ethnocentrists. For each item the difference between the two groups was always significant at better than the 1 percent level.

The differences between the ethnocentric and anti-ethnocentric groups may be illustrated by the scoring of the item "What experiences would be most awe-inspiring for you?" The "low" categories are: (a) Values which refer to personal achievement (intellectual, esthetic, scientific), contribution to mankind, the realization of democratic goals by self and society, and so on. (b) "Power," as exemplified in man's material-technological achievements and in nature. (c) Intense nature experiences in which there are clear signs of esthetic, sensual-emotional involvement.

The "high" categories for this item, in contrast, are: (a) "Power" in the form of deference and submission toward powerful people; emphasis on a generally authoritarian and ritualized atmosphere (military, superficial religious, patriotic, etc.). (b) Personal power in self, with others playing a deferent role. (c) Destruction-harm of people (e.g., "death of a close relative"; no open hostility). (d) Values which refer to conventionalized sex, material security, ownership, vague sense of virtue, and so on.

(e) Dilute nature experiences which differ from those of the low-scorers in that they are matter-of-fact, unspecific, surface descriptions with no indication of sensual-emotional involvement.

Some other general differences between these two groups were found. Deeplying trends such as hostility, dependency, sexuality, curiosity, and the like exist in both groups, but in the unprejudiced group they are more ego-integrated, in the sense of being more focal, more tied to other trends, more complex affectively, and with fewer defenses. This group is also more aware of inner conflicts, ambivalence, and tendencies to violate basic values. Their inner life is richer if more troubled; they tend to accuse themselves of faults, while the prejudiced group externalizes and engages more in idealization of self and family.

Clinical Analysis of Interview Material

As mentioned above, those scoring extremely high or extremely low on the overt ethnocentrism scale of the questionnaire were further subjected to clinical interviews and to projective tests.

The interviews covered the following major fields: vocation, income, religion, politics, minority groups, and clinical data. The directives given to the interviewer listed in each field both the kinds of things it was hoped to obtain from the subject and suggestions as to how these things might indirectly be ascertained by questioning. The former were the "underlying questions"; they had reference to the variables by means of which the subject was eventually to be characterized. The "manifest questions," those actually put to the subject, were framed in such a way as to conceal as much as possible the real purpose of the interview and yet elicit answers that were significant in terms of over-all hypotheses. The manifest questions used to obtain material bearing on a given underlying question were allowed to vary greatly from subject to subject, depending in each case on the subject's ideology, surface attitudes, and defenses. Nevertheless a number of manifest questions, based on general theory and experience, were formulated for each underlying question. Not all of them were asked each subject.

Examples of manifest questions, taken from the area of Income are: "What would you do with (expected or desired) income?" and "What would it mean to you?" The corresponding underlying issues are the subject's aspirations and phantasies as to social status, as to power as a means to manipulate others, as to (realistic or neurotic) striving for security, as to lavish and exciting living, the readiness really to take chances, and so forth.

It was the task of the interviewer subtly to direct the course of the interview in such a way that as much as possible would be learned about these underlying attitudes without giving away to the subject the real foci of the inquiry.

In attempting to achieve a crude quantification of the interview material, so that group trends might be ascertained, there was developed an extensive set of scoring categories, comprising approximately a hundred headings. An attempt was made to encompass as much as possible of the richness and intricacy of the material. The complexity of the categories introduced inferential and subjective elements, but, as it turned out, this did not prevent adequate interrater reliability and validity. The categories were arrived at on the basis of a preliminary study of the complete interviews and of all the other available material pertaining to the same subjects. These categories represent, in fact, the hypotheses as to which clinical characteristics go with presence or absence of prejudice.

In order to test all the categories, passages of the interview protocols referring directly to political or social issues and all other data that might indicate the subject's identity or ideological position were care-

fully removed before two clinically trained scorers undertook the evaluation of the protocols.

Interviews of 40 women were thus evaluated. (A later report will present results from a group of men.) Three kinds of judgments were used for each category: (1) whether the interview revealed attitudes tentatively classified as "high" or as "low"; (2) whether no decision could be reached; or, more often, (3) whether no material was available on the issue in question. A number of categories proved nondiscriminating either because "high" and "low" statements appeared with equal frequency in the interviews of those found "high" and of those found "low" on the questionnaire, or because of a large proportion of "neutral" responses.

Some of the most discriminating categories included the following. Of the 15 interviewed women who were extremely low on ethnocentrism, 0 (none) displayed a conventional "idealization" of the parents, the variable previously assumed to be characteristic of ethnocentrism, whereas 12 showed an attitude of objective appraisal of the parents.[1] On the other hand, of the 25 women interviewees extremely high on ethnocentrism, 11 clearly displayed the "high" and only 6 the "low" variant (the remaining 8 being "neutral"). This distribution of attitudes toward parents is in line with the general glorification of and submission to ingroup authority, on the surface at least, by the high scorers on ethnocentrism. In fact,

---

[1] In view of the small number of cases (40) and the frequency of the neutral categories (about 30 percent), these differences between the high and low scorers must be regarded as tentative. However, there is additional evidence that these differences would be found in a large sample. (1) Even with this small number of cases the differences are very striking. (2) The data on men appear to reveal similar differences. This not only provides an independent confirmation, but it will provide a sample twice as large as the present one. (3) The variables considered here are similar to those found to be differentiating in the ideological material, the Thematic Apperception Test, and the projective questions.

the corresponding figures on the category "submission to parental authority and values (respect based on fear)" vs. "principled independence" are 1 to 7 for the "low" subjects as against 9 to 0 for the "high" subjects.

The "high" women emphasize sex as a means for achieving status; they describe their conquests and—as they do in other fields as well—rationalize rather than admit failures and shortcomings, whereas the "lows" do not shrink from open admission of inadequacies in this respect (8 to 3 for "highs"; 1 to 8 for "lows"). In the same vein we find in "highs" underlying disrespect and resentment toward the opposite sex, typically combined with externalized, excessive, and counteractive "pseudoadmiration," vs. "genuine respect and fondness for opposite sex" in the "lows" (11 to 4 for "highs"; 2 to 7 for "lows"). Similarly, the attitude toward the opposite sex in the "high" women is power-oriented, exploitative, manipulative, with an eye on concrete benefits hiding behind superficial submission as contrasted with a warm, affectionate, and love-seeking attitude on the part of the "lows." Thus, the traits desired in men by "high" women are: hard-working, energetic, go-getting, moral, clean-cut, deferent, "thoughtful" toward the woman; the desiderata mentioned by the "low" women, on the other hand, are: companionship, common interests, warmth, sociability, sexual love, understanding, and liberal values. (For the entire pattern just described the figures are 14 to 4 for the "highs" and 2 to 10 for the "lows.")

As to attitudes toward people in general, the "highs" tend to assume an attitude of "moralistic condemnation" vs. the "permissiveness" shown toward individuals by the lows (14 to 3 for the "highs," 2 to 10 for the "lows"). Of special importance for the problem discussed here is the "hierarchical conception of human relations" in the "highs" as compared with an "equalitarianism and mutuality" in the "lows" (13 to 2 in the "highs" and 1 to 10 in the "lows").

All through the material it was frequently observed that the difference between the high and low subjects does not lie so much in the presence or absence of a basic tendency but rather in the way of dealing with such tendencies. As an illustration from the field of interpersonal relationships, we may refer to the category of Dependence. Whereas the dependence of the high subjects tends to be diffuse, ego-alien, and linked to an infantile desire to be taken care of, the dependence of the lows is focal and love-seeking as can be expected in cases where a real object relationship has been established (11 to 1 in the highs; 1 to 7 in the lows). The traits desired in friends are in many ways similar to those desired in the opposite sex (see above); we find emphasis on status, good manners, and so forth in the highs as compared with intrinsic values in the lows (9 to 2 for highs, 0 to 10 for lows.)

In the high scorer's attitude toward the Self, we find self-glorification mixed with feelings of inferiority which are not faced as such, conventional moralism, the belief in a close correspondence between what one is and what one wishes to be, and the "denial of genuine causality" (e.g., an explanation of one's traits or symptoms in terms of hereditary or accidental factors), as contrasted to opposite attitudes in the lows, with figures generally as discriminatory or better than those mentioned above for the other fields.

In the case of more general categories pertaining to personality dynamics an unusually large proportion were found to be discriminating. This might be due to the fact that the scoring of these categories was based on the over-all impression of the subject rather than on a specific piece of information. High-scoring women tend to give particular evidence of "rigid-moralistic anal reaction-formations" as ends in themselves, e.g., totalitarian-moralistic conceptualization of two kinds of people—"clean and dirty"—and overemphasis on propriety and kindliness, often with underlying aggression. The women with low scores show more evidence of "oral character structure"; and when such values as cleanliness and kindliness are present they are of a more functional nature.

As far as aggression is concerned, the high-scoring women tend toward a diffuse, depersonalized, moralistic, and punitive type of aggression, whereas the aggression of the low-scoring women is more focal and personalized, and more often it seems to be elicited by violation of principles or as a response to rejection by a loved object.

Ambivalence, e.g., toward the parents, is not admitted into consciousness by the "high" subjects but is rather solved by thinking in terms of dichotomies and by displacement onto out-groups. The ambivalence of the "lows" is more often expressed against the original objects (e.g., parents) or representatives, in reality, of the original objects, e.g., real authority.

There is a strong tendency in the high-scoring women to display "femininity" exclusively, whereas the low-scoring women are more ready to accept and to sublimate their masculine traits.

Some of the categories scored under the tentative assumption of their relevance to prejudice did not prove discriminating. Among these are various "childhood events," e.g., death or divorce of parents, number of siblings, and order of birth. The conception of one's own childhood, e.g., image of father and mother, proved only slightly discriminating, mostly because of the great number of neutral scores due often to lack of information in these categories. The fact that some of the categories were not discriminating may be taken as evidence that the raters were at least partially successful in their attempt to eliminate halo effect.

As was mentioned above, the over-all contrast between the highly prejudiced and the tolerant women hinges less than originally expected on the existence or absence of "depth" factors such as latent homosexuality, but rather, as seen here again, on the way they are dealt with in the personality: by acceptance and sublimation in our tolerant extremes, by repression and defense measures in our prejudiced extremes.

It is because of their repressions, it may be supposed, that the high scorers are found to be outstanding on such formal characteristics as rigidity, anti-intraception, pseudo-scientific thinking, and so forth.

The differences between high and low scorers revealed by the several independent techniques of the study reported here are consistent one with another and suggest a pattern which, embracing as it does both personality and ideology, may be termed the "antidemocratic personality."

References

FRENKEL-BRUNSWIK, ELSE, and SANFORD, R. N. Some personality correlates of anti-Semitism. *J. Psychol.*, 1945, 20, 271-291.

LEVINSON, D. J., and SANFORD, R. N. A scale for the measurement of anti-Semitism. *J. Psychol.*, 1944, 17, 339-370.

Negro Infantry Platoons ❧ Shirley A. Star

in White Companies ❧ Robin M. Williams, Jr.

❧ Samuel A. Stouffer

During World War II, a number of all-Negro platoons were introduced into white infantry companies with white officers and white noncommissioned officers. Since many activities in the Army—mess, recreation, housing, for example—were on a company basis, this arrangement meant a limited amount of integration.

Shortly after VE Day, a survey was undertaken by the Research Branch (Information and Education Division, War Department) in Europe to evaluate this program. Seven of the 11 divisions containing Negro platoons were visited, and interviews were conducted with officers and enlisted men. The sample included three highly experienced divisions and four with less combat experience. Two of the divisions were predominantly Southern in background. The range of experience sampled was thought to be representative of what would have been found if all 11 divisions had been investigated.

At the outset, one must keep in mind the fact that the Negro platoons were *volunteers* for combat, and to say this is to imply a difference from the rank and file of Negroes in orientation and motivation, even though they came from the same service branches and the same sorts of relatively unskilled jobs as those who did not volunteer. No data on the attitudes of these Negro volunteers exist, but it is safe to assume that they were motivated by convictions about the war, and by desires to prove the ability of their race and to make this "experiment in race relations succeed," as well as by the many individual motives which led men to choose combat. The Negro infantry volunteers were, like other volunteers, younger on the average than white infantrymen. More important, probably, for their subsequent relationships with white infantrymen, the Negro volunteers were somewhat better educated than Negro troops generally and had somewhat better Army General Classification Test (AGCT) scores. These differences, however, can easily be exaggerated; compared with the greater differences between white infantrymen and the Negro volunteers, they represent only minor fluctuations:

	Percentage Who Were High School Graduates	Percentage with AGCT Scores of I, II, or III
White Riflemen in ETO °	41	71
Negro Riflemen in White Companies	22	29
All Negroes in ETO	18	17

° ETO refers to European Theater of Operations.

In the companies in which Negro platoons served, the overwhelming majority of white officers and men gave approval to their performance in combat. This is shown in Table 1. As some of the respondents indicated in their comments, the Negro troops were fighting for a relatively short time dur-

TABLE 1

EVALUATION OF NEGRO INFANTRYMEN BY WHITE OFFICERS AND ENLISTED MEN
SERVING IN SAME COMPANIES WITH THEM (EUROPE, JUNE 1945)

	White Company Officers (Percent)	White Platoon Sergeants and Other Enlisted Men (Percent)
Question: *How well did the colored soldiers in this company perform in combat?*		
Very Well	84	81
Fairly Well	16	17
Not So Well	—	1
Not Well At All	—	—
Undecided	—	1
Question: *With the same Army training and experience, how do you think colored troops compare with white troops as infantry soldiers?*		
Better than White Troops	17	9
Just the Same as White Troops	69	83
Not as Good as White Troops	5	4
No Answer	9	4
	(N = 60)	(N = 195)

ing the closing, victorious stages of the war and did not have to meet the test of long, continued stalemate fighting with heavy casualties, but the same was true of some of the white troops with whom they fought and were compared. There was some indication in the data that the performance of Negro troops was rated highest by the officers and men in the companies in which the colored platoons had had the most severe fighting. The comments of their leaders indicated again and again, however, that in bestowing this praise, they were strongly aware that these men, as volunteers, were special cases. For example, as a company commander from Pennsylvania said: "Would do equally well with the best of the whites. Our men are good because they are volunteers, but an average of Negroes would probably do as well as the average of white soldiers." And a platoon sergeant from North Carolina commented: "I don't think you can say that about all of them. These are volunteers, and most colored men wouldn't be as willing to fight. These here are just the same as we are in combat."

As might be expected from these results,

almost all the officers and enlisted men endorsed the idea of having Negroes used as infantry, sometimes with qualifications like "if they are volunteers" or "only while we're in combat, but not in garrison," a point which will be discussed more fully later. These men favored the organization they then had of separate Negro platoons within the same company as the best arrangement for the utilization of Negro infantrymen. These facts are shown in Table 2. It should be remembered, however, that not all the white support of using Negroes as infantrymen necessarily reflected "democratic" or "pro-Negro" attitudes. It could be simply a reflection of the desire of combat men to have their own burden lightened by letting others do part of the fighting; it might even conceal the most extreme attitudes of racial superiority leading to the reasoning that inferior Negro lives should be sacrificed before white lives. Moreover, the Negroes were still in separate platoons, which, to some Southern respondents, preserved at least the principle of segregation.

In fact, the reasons advanced for favoring the "separate-platoon, same-company" pat-

TABLE 2

ATTITUDES OF WHITE OFFICERS AND ENLISTED MEN SERVING IN SAME COMPANIES
WITH NEGRO PLATOONS TOWARD THE UTILIZATION OF NEGRO INFANTRYMEN
(EUROPE, JUNE 1945)

	Officers (Percent)	Enlisted Men (Percent)
Question: *On the whole, do you think it is a good idea or a poor idea to have colored soldiers used as infantry troops?*		
Good Idea		
Unqualified statement	55	72
Qualified statement*		
"In combat, yes; but not in garrison"	25	26
"If volunteers," "If like the ones we have now"	15	—
Undecided	5	—
Poor Idea	—	2
Question: *If colored soldiers are used as infantry, do you think they should be set up by platoons as they are here or would some other way be better?*		
In Same Platoon with White Soldiers	7	1
In a Platoon within the Company	64	85
In Separate Companies	19	12
In Separate Battalions or Larger Organizations	10	2
	(N = 60)	(N = 195)

* These percentages represent the number of men who *volunteered* comments. If direct questions had been asked on these two qualifications, the percentages endorsing them might well have been considerably higher.

tern of organization clearly show that there were at least two points of view involved. The five leading reasons, in order of their frequency, were:

1. *Competition-emulation* ("encourages friendly competition, each tries to make a good showing"; "gives them something to come up to").
2. *Avoidance of friction* ("saves any chance of trouble to have them in their own platoon," "because of the old feeling of boys from the South").
3. *Better discipline and control among the Negro soldiers* ("whites have a steadying influence on them"; "colored boys feel more secure in combat this way").
4. *Feeling of participation or nondiscrimination on part of the Negro soldiers* ("gives them the feeling of being with the white boys"; "avoids that feeling of being set apart and discriminated against").
5. *Improved interracial understanding* ("work close enough together so they can

get to know the other better and see what they can do").

It may be seen here that some men accepted the platoon idea and assimilated it to usual white views by regarding it as a form of separation, as compared with mixing within the platoon, and justifying the interracial contacts it did bring in terms of the inferiority of the Negro and his need for white supervision. Other men, however, were in favor of it for opposite reasons: because it seemed to them to do away with enforced separation and encourage understanding.

But, though motives might vary, the white and Negro infantrymen did get along together amicably. Both white officers and fellow enlisted men reported that the white and Negro soldiers got along well together (93 percent of the officers and 60 percent of the enlisted men said "very well"; everyone else said "fairly well"), in spite of the fact that two thirds of each group had begun, according to their own retrospective reports, with relatively unfavorable attitudes toward serving in a mixed company. In a similar fashion, the bulk of both groups (77 percent) reported that their feeling had become more favorable since serving in the same unit with Negro soldiers. As a platoon sergeant from South Carolina said,

> When I heard about it, I said I'd be damned if I'd wear the same shoulder patch they did. After that first day when we saw how they fought, I changed my mind. They're just like any of the other boys to us.

However, many took occasion to note that relationships were better in combat than they were in the garrison situation. Not that there was serious overt friction between Negro and white soldiers. Such instances were, as far as is known, confined to isolated cases and involved white soldiers from other units who did not know the combat record of the Negro men. There were, however, some tensions in companies stationed where friendly contact with liberated populations was possible, and there was some expression of preference for separation in garrison. Some typical comments were:

> *Company commander from Nevada:* Relations are very good. They have their pictures taken together, go to church services, movies, play ball together. For a time there in combat our platoons got so small that we had to put a white squad in the colored platoon. You might think that wouldn't work well, but it did. The white squad didn't want to leave the platoon. I've never seen anything like it.

> *Company commander from Tennessee:* Good cooperation in combat. They were treated as soldier to soldier. Now they play ball, joke, and box together. The colored go to company dances—we've had no trouble, but some of the white boys resent it. In garrison the strain on both parties is too great.

> *First sergeant from Georgia:* Got along fine in combat. But we don't like to mix too much now and I think they should be pulled out if we're going to stay in garrison.

> *Platoon sergeant from Indiana:* They fought and I think more of them for it, but I still don't want to soldier with them in garrison.

As some of these comments imply, relationships in combat could be regarded as working relationships rather than social relationships. More precisely, they could be confined more narrowly to a functionally specific basis than could the contacts involved in community living. In particular, the combat situation was exclusively masculine, and issues of social relationships between men and women did not appear as they did in garrison. Far from being a "test case" in ordinary Negro-white relations, the combat setting may be regarded as a special case making for good relationships, for the sense of common danger and common obligation was high, the need for unity was at a maximum, and there was great consciousness of shared experience of an intensely emotional kind. In many respects the experience of fighting together is analogous to the kind of informal working together that results from any community crisis or disaster: fighting a forest fire or fighting a flood.

Relationships between white and Negro infantrymen turned out to be far better than their officers had expected: 96 percent of the officers questioned on this point reported themselves agreeably surprised. However, the comments made by the officers indicate that in some instances special precautions were taken. For example, one regimental commander said:

> I'm from the South—most of us here are —and I was pretty dubious as to how it would work out. But I'll have to admit we haven't had a bit of trouble. I selected the best company commander I had to put over them.

And a platoon commander from Texas said:

> We all expected trouble. Haven't had any. One reason may be that we briefed the white boys in advance—told them these men were volunteers coming up here to fight, and that we wouldn't stand for any foolishness.

In other words, in at least some of these cases there was careful selection of officers and orientation of the white troops. In some instances, the white officers or noncoms who were later to lead the colored platoons went back to the replacement depots and trained the men for combat, thus getting to know and work with their men before they were thrust into combat.

In spite of the qualifications introduced— the volunteer character of the Negro platoons, the fact that the war was in its final successful stages, the peculiar nature of the combat situation, the special reasons for and the precautions taken to insure smooth functioning—there can be little question that these Negro troops performed well by the criteria applied to white troops. Nor can there be any doubt that, *under the conditions specified*, Negro-white relations were harmonious. Of more interest than this historical conclusion, however, is the question of how far, in the face of these limitations, one can generalize from these data.

From this point of view, perhaps the most illuminating piece of data coming out of the study was the finding, shown in Figure 1, that the closer men approached to the mixed company organization, the less opposition there was to it. That is, men actually in a company containing a Negro platoon were most favorable toward it, men in larger units in which there were no mixed companies were least favorable, while men in all-white companies within a regiment or division containing mixed companies held intermediate opinions. When we note that the proportion of men having no experience with mixed companies who say "they would dislike the arrangement very much" is almost exactly the same (62 percent) as the two-thirds proportion of white enlisted men in mixed companies who were previously noted as reporting retroactively that they were initially opposed to the idea, we can get some conception of the revolution in at-

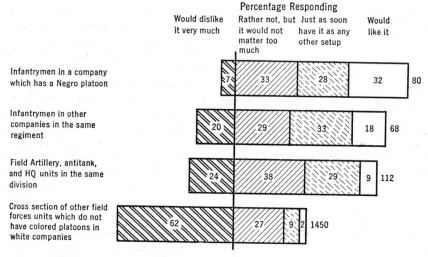

Fig. 1. Question: *Some Army divisions have companies which include Negro platoons and white platoons. How would you feel about it if your outfit was set up like that?* Attitudes toward serving in a company containing Negro and white platoons among men who have done so and men who have not (Europe, June, 1945). The numbers following the bars are the number of cases on which percentages are based.

titudes that took place among these men as a result of enforced contacts.

Though this still leaves unanswered the question of whether whites would ultimately adjust to and come to accept enforced inter-racial contacts under other circumstances, it does show that integration between Negro volunteers and whites could be achieved under the stress of combat. Extensions of

[1] Another experiment in the integration of Negroes and whites into the same units is sympathetically reported in John Beecher's *All brave sailors: the story of the S.S. Booker T. Washington* (New York: L. B. Fischer Corp., 1945), about a merchant marine ship with a Negro captain and racially mixed crew. Here the whites as well as the Negroes would appear to have volunteered specifically to demonstrate the feasibility of such interracial cooperation.

this sort of experimentation[1] could show how successfully Negro troops in general could be integrated in white units in combat and how far such integration could be extended into noncombat situations.[2] The results of this experiment suggest that efforts at integration of white and colored troops into the same units may well be more successful when attention is focused on concrete tasks or goals requiring common effort than when it is focused on more abstract considerations of justice or of desirable policy which emphasize the "race issue" and arouse traditional prejudices.

[2] At the time of this writing, racial integration in the United States armed forces had not yet been accomplished. (Ed.)

Ethnic Tolerance: A Function of ❊ Bruno Bettelheim
Social and Personal Control ❊ Morris Janowitz

In this study of ethnic intolerance we attempt to throw light on the principles of group hostility in general and on ethnic hostility as a special subtype.

The four main hypotheses that the research sought to test were based on sociological theory and dynamic psychology. They were: (1) hostility toward outgroups is a function of the hostile individual's feeling that he has suffered deprivations in the past; (2) such hostility toward out-groups is a function of the hostile individual's anxiety in anticipation of future tasks; (3) the individual blames out-groups for his failure at mastery and projects undesirable characteristics denied in himself upon members of the out-group because of inadequate personal and social controls which favor irrational discharge and evasion rather than rational action; (4) ethnic intolerance can be viewed in terms of the individual's position within

the social structure either statically or dynamically. It was assumed that ethnic intolerance was related more to the individual's dynamic movement within the structure of society than to his position at a particular moment. No claim is made that these hypotheses are universally applicable, but they seemed useful in understanding hostility in modern industrialized communities.

A major premise of the study was that persons who believe they have undergone deprivations are disposed to ethnic intolerance. It seemed plausible to study ex-soldiers, since they had suffered deprivations in varying degrees and might be especially responsive to the appeal of intolerance. A random sample of 150 male war veterans, all residents of Chicago, was studied. Former officers were eliminated from the study, since their experiences were at variance with those of enlisted men and since most of them came

Reprinted from the *American Journal of Sociology*, 1949, 55, 137-145, by permission of The University of Chicago Press. Copyright © by The University of Chicago Press. The study was later published as *The Dynamics of Prejudice*, New York: Harper & Row, 1950.

from social and economic backgrounds which differed from those of enlisted men. Hence the sample tended more adequately to represent the economic lower and lower-middle classes. Members of those major ethnic groups toward which hostility is projected were not included—that is, Negroes, Jews, Chinese, Japanese, and Mexicans.

The data were obtained through intensive interviews in which free associations were always encouraged. The interviewers were psychiatrically trained social workers, experienced in public-opinion surveying. The wide range of personal data sought and the special problems of building rapport before gathering data on ethnic attitudes required long interviews which took from four to seven hours and in several cases were carried on in two sessions. The veterans were offered ample opportunity to express personal views on many issues and to recount their wartime experiences before ethnic minorities were mentioned.

On the basis of an exploratory study we found it necessary to distinguish four types of veterans with respect to their ethnic attitudes. For the sake of brevity, only the four types of anti-Semite are mentioned, but a parallel classification as regards anti-Negro attitudes was also developed. These four types of anti-Semite were designated as *intensely anti-Semitic, outspoken anti-Semitic, stereotyped anti-Semitic,* and *tolerant* toward Jews and were characterized as follows: (1) The *intensely anti-Semitic* veteran was spontaneously outspoken in expressing a preference for restrictive action against the Jews even before the subject was raised. (2) The *outspoken anti-Semitic* man revealed no spontaneous preference for restrictive action against the Jews. Instead, outspoken hostility toward the Jews emerged only toward the end of the interview when he was directly questioned. As in the case of the intensely anti-Semitic veteran, his thinking contained a wide range of unfavorable stereotypes. (3) The *stereotyped anti-Semitic* man expressed no preference for hostile or restrictive action against the Jews even when questioned directly. In-

stead, he merely expressed a variety of stereotyped notions about the Jews, including some which were not necessarily unfavorable from his point of view. (4) The *tolerant* veteran revealed no elaborately stereotyped beliefs about the Jews (among the statements of even the most tolerant veterans isolated stereotypes might from time to time be found). Moreover, not even when questioned directly did he advocate restrictive action against the Jews.

TABLE 1
DISTRIBUTION OF INTOLERANCE

	Anti-Semitic		Anti-Negro	
	No.	Percent	No.	Percent
Tolerant	61	41	12	8
Stereotyped	42	28	40	27
Outspoken	41	27	74	49
Intense	6	4	24	16
Total	150	100	150	100

The interview situation was so constructed that the responses to questions would permit a clear discrimination between these four types of ethnic intolerance. The first portion of the interview was designed to offer the men an opportunity for spontaneous expression of hostility against minorities without bringing this subject to their attention. In a second portion, especially in connection with Army experiences, ample opportunity was offered to display sterotyped thinking by asking, for example, who the "gold-brickers" or troublemakers had been. Only the last portion contained direct questions on ethnic minorities. There the stimuli "Negro" and "Jew" were introduced to determine which men were consistently tolerant. First it was asked what kinds of soldiers they made, next what the subject thought of social and economic association with them, and then what his views were on possible changes in the current patterns of interethnic relations[1] Table 1 shows the distribution of degrees of intolerance.

[1] The full methodological and statistical details of the procedure will be found in the 1950 publication.

TABLE 2
CORRELATES OF ANTI-SEMITISM IN PERCENT

Total Cases	Tolerant (61)	Stereotyped (42)	Outspoken and Intense (47)	Total (150)	No.
Age:					
Under 28	44	27	29	100	94
29-36	34	30	36	100	56
Education:					
Did not complete high school	35	31	34	100	65
Completed high school	39	28	33	100	46
Some college or more	51	23	26	100	39
Religion:°					
Catholic	40	28	32	100	103
Protestant	48	25	27	100	33
No present religious denomination	33⅓	33⅓	33⅓	100	12
Current Salary:					
Up to $2500	39	33	28	100	59
$2500 to $3000	39	24	37	100	43
$3000 and over	43	18	39	100	28
Not applicable	45	35	20	100	20
Socio-economic Status:					
Top four groups	42	24	34	100	70
Semiskilled and unskilled	38	33	29	100	80

° Two cases of Greek Orthodox not included.

We tried to determine whether the men's social and economic history could account for their ethnic intolerance. Among the characteristics studied were age, education, religion, political affiliation, income, and social status. But the data indicate that—subject to certain limitations—these factors of themselves do not seem to account for differences in the degree or nature of intolerance.

Table 2, for example, shows that no statistically significant relation exists between income and socio-economic status, on the one hand, and intensity of anti-Semitism, on the other.[2] The same was true for such other categories as education, age, and religious affiliation. Which newspaper, magazine, or radio program the men favored was also unrelated to the intensity of ethnic hostility. The pattern of anti-Negro distribution was similar.

[2] Where a significant difference is reported, it is at least at the 0.01 confidence limit.

SOCIAL MOBILITY

The picture changes, however, if a static concept of social status is replaced by the dynamic concept of social mobility. It was possible to gather precise data on the social mobility of 130 veterans. They were rated as having experienced downward mobility or upward mobility if they had moved at least one grade up or down on the Alba Edward's socio-economic scale when compared with their previous civilian employment.

Table 3 shows that ethnic hostility was most highly concentrated in the downwardly mobile group, while the pattern was *significantly* reversed for those who had risen in their social position. Those who had experienced no change presented a picture somewhat in the middle; the relationship between ethnic intolerance and social mobility (as defined in this study) was also present when educational level was held constant.

The group which was static showed the

TABLE 3

INTOLERANCE AND MOBILITY

	Downward Mobility		No Mobility		Upward Mobility		Total	
	No.	Percent	No.	Percent	No.	Percent	No.	Percent
Anti-Semitic:								
Tolerant	2	11	25	37	22	50	49	38
Stereotyped	3	17	26	38	8	18	37	28
Outspoken and intense	13	72	17	25	14	32	44	34
Anti-Negro:								
Tolerant and stereotyped	5	28	18	26	22	50	45	34
Outspoken	5	28	40	59	17	39	62	48
Intense	8	44	10	15	5	11	23	18
Total	18	100	68	100	44	100	130	100

highest concentration of sterotyped opinions —that is, they were "middle-of-the-roaders" with regard to anti-Semitism. Over 70 percent of the sterotyped anti-Semites were found in this middle category. This illuminates the relation between mobility and intolerance. On the other hand, the no-mobility group was most generally in the outspokenly anti-Negro category. This supplies another crude index of the limits of intolerance toward minority groups in a northern urban industrial community. In the case of the Jew the social norms were most likely to produce merely stereotyped thinking, while it was correspondingly "normal" to be outspoken in one's hostility toward the Negro.

In view of the association between upward social moblity and tolerance, the few cases (14) who displayed both upward mobility and were outspokenly anti-Semitic warrant special attention. The actual income gains associated with upward mobility reveal that the men who were both outspokenly anti-Semitic and upwardly mobile tended to be considerably more mobile than the others. This may be tentatively explained by the fact that sharp upward mobility is likely to be associated with marked aggressiveness in general. The data, particularly on those in the group downwardly mobile, suggest that to understand intolerance it is less important to concentrate on the social and economic background of the individual than to investigate the character of his social mobility.

FEELING OF DEPRIVATION

Whatever their social and economic life-histories had been, all the men interviewed had one common experience—the Army. Reactions to comparable wartime deprivations thus afforded a unique opportunity to examine the hypothesis that the individual who suffers deprivation tries to restore his integration and self-control by the expression of hostility, one form of which may be ethnic hostility. But here a sharp distinction must be introduced between *actual* deprivations experienced and his *feelings* of deprivation. Whether the men reacted favorably to Army life primarily because they experienced relief from the insecurities of civilian life was also pertinent.

Army experiences which involved *objective* deprivations were found not related to differential degrees of ethnic intolerance (combat versus noncombat service, wounds, length of service, etc.). On the other hand, a clear association emerged between the display of *feelings* of deprivation and outspoken or intense anti-Semitic and anti-Negro attitudes.

On the basis of a content analysis it was found that it was possible to make reliable decisions as to whether the veterans (1) accepted it in a matter-of-fact way, (2) were

TABLE 4

ACCEPTANCE OF ARMY

	Tolerant		Stereotyped		Outspoken and Intense		Total	
	No.	Percent	No.	Percent	No.	Percent	No.	Percent
Accepted Army Life	44	81	21	64	6	17	71	50
Embittered toward Army Life	6	11	7	21	20	56	33	35
Attached to or Gratified by Army Life	4	8	5	15	10	27	19	15
Total	54	100	33	100	36	100	123	100

embittered about Army life, or (3) were attached to it or gratified by it. The overwhelming majority of those who were tolerant, regardless of the specific content of their wartime experience, had an attitude of acceptance toward Army life, while the intolerant veteran presented a completely reversed picture (see Table 4). The latter were overwhelmingly embittered by Army life. In addition, those who declared themselves particularly attached to Army life displayed a high concentration of intolerance.

The judging of one's war experiences as depriving or not is a function of the individual's total personality and of the adequacy of his adjustive mechanisms. The interview records of those who seemed gratified by Army life revealed that they were also the men who described themselves as economically and socially deprived before induction; they seem to have been poorly adjusted to civilian society and to have found gratification and release in the particular adventure and comradeship of Army life.

CONTROLS FOR TOLERANCE

There seems little doubt that frustrating social experiences and the inability to integrate them account to a large degree for those aggressions which are vented in ethnic hostility. While our investigation could not ascertain which particular experiences accounted for the men's frustration, it permitted us to ascertain their readiness to submit in general to the existing controls by society. If, by and large, they accepted social institutions, it seems reasonable to assume that such acceptance implied a willingness to control their own aggressive tendencies for the sake of society. Or, oversimplifying complex emotional tendencies, one might say that those men who felt that society fulfilled its task in protecting them against unavoidable frustrations were also those who, in return, were willing to come to terms with society by controlling their aggressive tendencies as society demands. Hence, the hypothesis correlating the men's acceptance or rejection of society with their ethnic attitudes had to be tested. The Army is only one of many social institutions. The postulated association between intolerance and the rejection of social controls, which was central in terms of this study, had to be investigated for a number of other institutions as well.

Control, technically speaking, is the ability to store tension internally or to discharge it in socially constructive action rather than in unwarranted hostile action. The predominant mechanisms of control which a person uses for dealing with inner tensions are among the most important elements characterizing his personality. Each of these mechanisms of control is more or less adequate for containing a particular type of aggression generated in the individual by anxiety. These controls or restraints remain adequate only if the level of tension does not become overpowering, thereby creating unmasterable anxiety. It will not suffice to investigate the association between control and tolerance in general; it is necessary to discriminate between tolerance as it relates to three types of control over hostile tendencies: (1) external or social control, (2) superego or conscience control, and (3) rational self-control or ego control.

Religion may serve as the prototype of an institution, the acceptance of, or submission to, which was found to be related to tolerance. Unquestioning acceptance of religious values indicates that the individual tends to rely on a type of control in which he is guided by traditional and nonrational external social forces. In contrast, control is exercised not by the minister or the priest but originates within the person, although such inner control may have come initially from their teachings. If the moral teachings of the church are accepted by the individual not through fear of damnation or of societal disapproval but because he considers them absolute standards of behavior independent of external threats of approval, then we say that the individual has "internalized" these moral precepts. They have become an internal control, but a control which is still only partially conscious and only partly rational. Such control is exercised over the individual by his "conscience," or, technically speaking, by his superego.

Markedly different from *external* control through outside institutions and from *superego* control, which also depends for its effectiveness on props in the external world (such as parental images or institutionalized religion), is the rational control of irrational tendencies which forces them into consciousness and then deals with them along purely rational lines. The latter may be termed "ego control." In actuality, the three types of control are nearly always coexistent, and in each individual case control will depend in varying degrees on all three—external, superego, and ego control. In the men studied, wherever control was present it was overwhelmingly the result of a combination of external and superego control, with the first being dominant. Only a few men were also motivated by ego control, and in even fewer was ego control dominant over

superego or external control. Hence a study of external, i.e., societal, control was the only one which promised to permit insight into the correlation between acceptance of, or submission to, social control and ethnic intolerance for this particular group.

The analysis of religious attitudes indicated that veterans who had stable religious convictions tended to be the more tolerant. When the political party system was viewed as another norm-setting institution, a similar relationship of at least partial acceptance or consensus with this basic institution was found to be associated with tolerance. Whether the veteran was Democratic or Republican was in no way indicative of his attitude toward minorities. But the veteran who rejected or condemned both parties ("they are both crooks") tended to be the most hostile toward minorities.

Thus not only greater stability in societal status but the very existence of stable religious and political affiliations as well proved to be correlated with tolerance. These phenomena are indicative of the tolerant individual's relatively greater control over his instinctual tendencies, controls which are strong enough to prevent immediate discharge of tension in asocial action. Such delay in the discharge of tension permits its canalization into socially more acceptable outlets.

To explore more fully this relationship between tolerance and control, the responses to other symbols of societal authority which signify *external* control of the individual were also investigated. Two groups of institutions were analyzed separately. The first group, that of Army control through discipline and officers' authority, is discussed below. The second group was composed of significant representatives of civilian authority to which the men were relatively subject at the time of the interview.

Four institutions were singled out as being most relevant. They were: (1) the administration of veterans' affairs; (2) the political party system; (3) the federal government; and (4) the economic system, as defined by the subjects themselves.

TABLE 5
ATTITUDES TOWARD THE JEW AND TOWARD CONTROLLING INSTITUTIONS

Attitude	Tolerant		Stereotyped		Outspoken and Intense		Total	
	No.	Percent	No.	Percent	No.	Percent	No.	Percent
Accept	41	67	20	48	11	23	72	48
Intermediate	15	25	17	40	13	28	45	30
Reject	5	8	5	12	23	49	33	22
Total	61	100	42	100	47	100	150	100

The veterans' views of each of these institutions were quite complex and in some respects ambivalent. Nevertheless, it was possible to analyze attitudes toward them on a continuum of acceptance, rejection, or intermediate.

When acceptance or rejection of the four representative institutions was compared with the degree of anti-Semitism (Table 5), it appeared that only an insignificant percentage of the tolerant men rejected them, while nearly half the outspoken and intense anti-Semites did so. This is in marked contrast, for example, to studies of certain types of college students, in whom radical rejection of authority is combined with liberalism toward minority groups.

Controls, it may be said, are not internalized by merely accepting society. On the contrary, general attitudes of accepting existing society and its institutions are the result of previous internalization of societal values as personally transmitted by parents, teachers, and peers. Hence the acceptance of individuals who are representatives of societal values should have been more closely related to internal control than the acceptance of discipline in general, which is more characteristic of external control. Attitudes

toward officers seemed suitable gauges for the individual's attitudes toward control. Incidentally, most of the men evaluated their officers on the basis of personal quality, their moral authority, and not on the basis of their punitive power.

The tolerant veteran appeared able to maintain better relations with his officers; he was more willing to accept the authority and discipline of the Army as represented by them. In general, his attitude was reasonable. When queried as to how the fellows in their outfits got along with the officers, tolerant veterans were significantly more prone to claim they got along well than were the intolerant men.

In the case of the Negro (Table 6), societal controls exercise a restraining influence only on what would be classified as violent, as "intense," intolerance. Violence is generally disapproved of by the controlling institutions, while they approve, if not enforce, stereotyped and outspoken attitudes. The men who were strongly influenced by external controls were, in the majority, stereotyped and outspoken but not intense in their intolerance toward Negroes, as the present data show.

The division between those who rejected

TABLE 6
ATTITUDES TOWARD THE NEGRO AND TOWARD CONTROLLING INSTITUTIONS

Attitude	Tolerant		Stereotyped		Outspoken		Intense		Total	
	No.	Percent	No.	Percent	No.	Percent	No.	Percent	No.	Percent
Acceptance	9	75	19	48	38	51	6	25	72	48
Intermediate	2	17	16	40	23	31	4	17	45	30
Rejection	1	8	5	12	13	18	14	58	33	22
Total	12	100	40	100	74	100	24	100	150	100

and those who accepted external control came between outspoken and intense attitudes toward Negroes. To score "high" on the index of rejection for the four controlling institutions meant that an individual was likely to fall in the intensely anti-Negro category. Thus acceptance of external controls not only was inadequate in conditioning men to be tolerant of the Negroes but was not even enough to prevent them from holding outspoken views in that regard. It served only to restrain demands for violence.

STEREOTYPED THINKING

Precisely because most of the men in the sample based their restraint of aggressive tendencies on societal controls rather than on inner integration, some aggression remained uncontrolled. This the men needed to explain to themselves—and to others. For an explanation they fell back again on what society, or rather their associates, provided in the way of a justification for minority aggression. It has already been mentioned that most of the men voiced their ethnic attitudes in terms of sterotypes. The use of these sterotypes reveals a further influence —if not control—by society on ethnic attitudes and should therefore at least be mentioned.

One of the hypotheses of this study is that intolerance is a function of anxiety, frustration, and deprivation, while the intolerant person's accusations are ways to justify his aggression. While the rationalizations for this intolerance must permit a minimum of reality testing, they will also condition the ways in which hostile feelings are discharged.

All intolerant veterans avoided reality testing to some degree, and each of them made statements about minorities which showed that he neglected the individual's uniquely personal characteristics—in short, he used stereotypes. As was to be expected, those who were only moderately biased retained more ability to test reality. They were more able to evaluate correctly the in-

dividuals whom they met, but they clung to stereotyped thinking about the rest of the discriminated group. In this way it remained possible to retain the stereotyped attitudes which permitted discharge of hostility despite actual experiences to the contrary. Such a limited amount of reality testing did not seem to be available to strongly biased individuals.

Because the intolerant person's rationalizations are closely, although not obviously, connected with his reasons for intolerance, he must take care to protect them. On the other hand, they also reveal the nature of the anxieties which underlie them.

An examination of the five most frequent Negro and five most frequent Jewish stereotypes reveals strikingly different results, each set of which presents a more or less integrated pattern (see Tables 7 and 8).

TABLE 7

STEREOTYPES CHARACTERIZING JEWS

Stereotype	No. of Veterans Mentioning Stereotypes
They Are Clannish; They Help One Another	37
They Have the Money	26
They Control Everything (or Have an Urge to Control Everything); They Are Running the Country	24
They Use Underhanded or Sharp Business Methods	24
They Do Not Work; They Do Not Do Manual Labor	19

The composite pattern of sterotypes about Jews does not stress personally "obnoxious" characteristics. In the main, they are represented in terms of a powerful, well-organized group which, by inference, threatens the subject.

On the other hand, the stereotypes about the Negro stress the individual, personally "offensive" characteristics of the Negro. As the stereotypes of the group characteristics of Jews implied a threat to the values and well-being of the intolerant white, so, too, those about the Negro were used to describe a conception of the Negro as a threat, particularly because the Negro was "forcing out the whites."

TABLE 8

STEREOTYPES CHARACTERIZING NEGROES

Stereotype	No. of Veterans Mentioning Stereotypes
They Are Sloppy, Dirty, Filthy	53
They Depreciate Property	33
They Are Taking Over; They Are Forcing Out the Whites	25
They Are Lazy; They Are Slackers in Work	22
They Are Ignorant; Have Low Intelligence	18
They Have Low Character; They Are Immoral and Dishonest	18

A comparison of the distribution of stereotypes applied to Jews and Negroes, as indicated by this enumeration, with those used by the National Socialists in Germany permits certain observations. In Germany the whole of the stereotypes, which in the United States were divided between Jews and Negroes, were applied to the Jews. Thus in the United States, where two or more ethnic minorities are available, a tendency emerges to separate the stereotypes into two sets and to assign each of them to one minority group. One of these two sets indicates feelings of being anxious because of one minority's (the Jews') assumed power of overwhelming control. The other set of stereotypes shows feelings of anxiety because of the second minority's (the Negroes') assumed ability to permit itself the enjoyment of primitive, socially unacceptable forms of gratification. Thus, of two minority groups which differ in physical characteristics, such as skin color, the minority showing greater physical difference is used for projecting anxieties associated with dirtiness and sex desires. Conversely, the minority whose physical characteristics are more similar to those of the majority become a symbol for anxieties concerning overpowering control. If we apply the frame of reference of dynamic psychology to these observations, then these stereotypes permit further emphasis on the relation between tolerance and control. The individual who has achieved an integration or an inner balance between superego demands and instinctual, asocial strivings does not need to externalize either of them in a vain effort to establish a control that he does not possess. The intolerant man who cannot control his superego demands or instinctual drives projects them upon ethnic minorities as if, by fighting them in this way or by at least discharging excessive tension, he seeks to regain control over unconscious tendencies.

Actual experiences later in life, once the personality has been formed, seem relatively incapable of breaking down this delusional mechanism. Questioning revealed, for example, that, although Army experience threw the men into new and varied contacts with Jews and frequently with Negroes, the stereotypes applied to the service of Jews and Negroes in the Army proved largely an extension of the conceptions of civilian life into Army experiences.

It seems reasonable to assume that, as long as anxiety and insecurity persist as a root of intolerance, the effort to dispel stereotypes by rational propaganda is at best a half measure. On an individual level only greater personal integration combined with social and economic security seems to offer hope for better interethnic relations. Moreover, those who accept social controls are the more tolerant men, while they are also, relatively speaking, less tolerant of the Negro because Negro discrimination is more obviously condoned, both publicly and privately. This should lead, among other things, to additional efforts to change social practice in ways that will tangibly demonstrate that ethnic discrimination is contrary to the mores of society, a conviction which was very weak even among the more tolerant men.

C. GROUP CONFLICT
AND INTERNATIONAL TENSION

Superordinate Goals in the Reduction

of Intergroup Conflicts ⁕ Muzafer Sherif

In the past, measures to combat the problems of intergroup conflicts, proposed by social scientists as well as by such people as administrators, policy-makers, municipal officials, and educators, have included the following: introduction of legal sanctions; creation of opportunities for social and other contacts among members of conflicting groups; dissemination of correct information to break down false prejudices and unfavorable stereotypes; appeals to the moral ideals of fair play and brotherhood; and even the introduction of rigorous physical activity to produce catharsis by releasing pent-up frustrations and aggressive complexes in the unconscious. Other measures proposed include the encouragement of co-operative habits in one's own community, and bringing together in the cozy atmosphere of a meeting room the leaders of antagonistic groups.

Many of these measures may have some value in the reduction of intergroup conflicts, but, to date, very few generalizations have been established concerning the circumstances and kinds of intergroup conflict in which these measures are effective. Today measures are applied in a somewhat

trial-and-error fashion. Finding measures that have wide validity in practice can come only through clarification of the nature of intergroup conflict and analysis of the factors conducive to harmony and conflict between groups under given conditions.

The task of defining and analyzing the nature of the problem was undertaken in a previous publication (Sherif and Sherif, 1953). One of our major statements was the effectiveness of superordinate goals for the reduction of intergroup conflict. "Superordinate goals" we defined as goals which are compelling and highly appealing to members of two or more groups in conflict but which cannot be attained by the resources and energies of the groups separately. In effect, they are goals attained only when groups pull together.

Intergroup Relations and the Behavior of Group Members

Not every friendly or unfriendly act toward another person is related to the group membership of the individuals involved. Ac-

Reprinted from the *American Journal of Sociology*, 1958, *63*, 349-356, by permission of The University of Chicago Press. Copyright © by The University of Chicago Press.

cordingly, we must select those actions relevant to relations between groups.

Let us start by defining the main concepts involved. Obviously, we must begin with an adequate conception of the key term—"group." A group is a social unit (1) which consists of a number of individuals who, at a given time, stand in more or less definite interdependent status and role relationships with one another and (2) which explicitly or implicitly possesses a set of values or norms regulating the behavior of individual members, at least in matters of consequence to the group. Thus, shared attitudes, sentiments, aspirations, and goals are related to and implicit in the common values or norms of the group.

The term "intergroup relations" refers to the relations between two or more groups and their respective members. In the present context we are interested in the acts that occur when individuals belonging to one group interact, collectively or individually, with members of another in terms of their group identification. The appropriate frame of reference for studying such behavior includes the functional relations between the groups. Intergroup situations are not voids. Though not independent of relationships within the groups in question, *the characteristics of relations between groups cannot be deduced or extrapolated from the properties of in-group relations.*

Prevalent modes of behavior within a group, in the way of co-operativeness and solidarity or competitiveness and rivalry among members, need not be typical of actions involving members of an out-group. At times, hostility toward out-groups may be proportional to the degree of solidarity within the group. In this connection, results presented by the British statistician L. F. Richardson are instructive. His analysis of the number of wars conducted by the major nations of the world from 1850 to 1941 reveals that Great Britain heads the list with twenty wars—more than the Japanese (nine wars), the Germans (eight wars), or the United States (seven wars). We think that this significantly larger number of wars engaged in by a leading European democracy has more to do with the intergroup relations involved in perpetuating a far-flung empire than with dominant practices at home or with personal frustrations of individual Britishers who participated in these wars (Pear, 1950, p. 126).

In recent years relationships between groups have sometimes been explained through analysis of individuals who have endured unusual degrees of frustration or extensive authoritarian treatment in their life-histories. There is good reason to believe that some people growing up in unfortunate life-circumstances may become more intense in their prejudices and hostilities. But at best these cases explain the intensity of behavior in a given dimension (Hood and Sherif, 1955). In a conflict between two groups—a strike or a war—opinion within the groups is crystallized, slogans are formulated, and effective measures are organized by members recognized as the most responsible in their respective groups. The prejudice scale and the slogans are not usually imposed on the others by the deviate or neurotic members. Such individuals ordinarily exhibit their intense reactions within the reference scales of prejudice, hostility, or sacrifice established in their respective settings.

The behavior by members of any group toward another group is not primarily a problem of deviate behavior. If it were, intergroup behavior would not be the issue of vital consequence that it is today. The crux of the problem is the participation by group members in established practices and social-distance norms of their group and their response to new trends developing in relationships between their own group and other groups.

On the basis of his UNESCO studies in India, Gardner Murphy concludes that to be a good Hindu or a good Moslem implies belief in all the nasty qualities and practices attributed by one's own group—Hindu or Moslem—to the other. Good members remain deaf and dumb to favorable information concerning the adversary. Social contacts and avenues of communication serve, on the whole, as vehicles for further conflicts not merely for neurotic individuals but for the bulk of the membership (Murphy, 1953).

In the process of interaction among members, an in-group is endowed with positive qualities which tend to be praiseworthy, self-justifying, and even self-glorifying. Individual members tend to develop these qualities through internalizing group norms and through example by high-status members, verbal dicta, and a set of correctives standardized to deal with cases of deviation. Hence, possession of these qualities, which reflect their particular brand of ethnocentrism, is not essentially a problem of deviation or personal frustration. It is a question of participation in in-group values and trends by good members, who constitute the majority of membership as long as group solidarity and morale are maintained.

To out-groups and their respective members are attributed positive or negative qualities, depending on the nature of functional relations between the groups in question. The character of functional relations between groups may result from actual harmony and interdependence or from actual incompatibility between the aspirations and directions of the groups. A number of field studies and experiments indicate that, if the functional relations between groups are positive, favorable attitudes are formed toward the out-group. If the functional relations between groups are negative, they give rise to hostile attitudes and unfavorable stereotypes in relation to the out-group. Of course, in large group units the picture of the out-group and relations with it depend very heavily on communication, particularly from the mass media.

Examples of these processes are recurrent in studies of small groups. For example, when a gang "appropriates" certain blocks in a city, it is considered "indecent" and a violation of its "rights" for another group to carry on its feats in that area. Intrusion by another group is conducive to conflict, at

times with grim consequences, as Thrasher showed over three decades ago (1927).

When a workers' group declares a strike, existing group lines are drawn more sharply. Those who are not actually for the strike are regarded as against it. There is no creature more lowly than the man who works while the strike is on (Hiller, 1928). The same type of behavior is found in management groups under similar circumstances.

In time, the adjectives attributed to out-groups take their places in the repertory of group norms. The lasting, derogatory stereotypes attributed to groups low on the social-distance scale are particular cases of group norms pertaining to out-groups.

As studies by Bogardus show, the social-distance scale of a group, once established, continues over generations, despite changes of constituent individuals, who can hardly be said to have prejudices because of the same severe personal frustrations or authoritarian treatment (1947).

Literature on the formation of prejudice by growing children shows that it is not even necessary for the individual to have actual unfavorable experiences with out-groups to form attitudes of prejudice toward them. In the very process of becoming an in-group member, the intergroup delineations and corresponding norms prevailing in the group are internalized by the individual (Horowitz, 1944).

A Research Program

A program of research has been under way since 1948 to test experimentally some hypotheses derived from the literature of intergroup relations. The first large-scale intergroup experiment was carried out in 1949, the second in 1953, and the third in 1954.[1] The conclusions reported here briefly

[1] The experimental work in 1949 was jointly supported by the Yale Attitude Change Project and the American Jewish Committee. It is summarized in Sherif and Sherif (1953, chaps. IX and X). Both the writing of that book and the experiments in 1953-54 were made possible by

are based on the 1949 and 1954 experiments and on a series of laboratory studies carried out as co-ordinate parts of the program.[2]

The methodology, techniques, and criteria for subject selection in the experiments must be summarized here very briefly. The experiments were carried out in successive stages: (1) groups were formed experimentally; (2) tension and conflict were produced between these groups by introducing conditions conducive to competitive and reciprocally frustrating relations between them; and (3) the attempt was made toward reduction of the intergroup conflict. This stage of reducing tension through introduction of superordinate goals was attempted in the 1954 study on the basis of lessons learned in the two previous studies.

At every stage the subjects interacted in activities which appeared natural to them at a specially arranged camp site completely under our experimental control. They were not aware of the fact that their behavior was under observation. No observation or recording was made in the subjects' presence in a way likely to arouse the suspicion that they were being observed. There is empirical and experimental evidence contrary to the contention that individuals cease to be mindful when they know they are being observed and that their words are being recorded.[3]

In order to insure validity of conclusions, results obtained through observational methods were cross-checked with results obtained through sociometric technique, stereotype ratings of in-groups and out-groups, and through data obtained by techniques adapted from the laboratory. Unfortunately, these procedures cannot be elaborated here.

a grant from the Rockefeller Foundation. The 1953 research is summarized in Sherif, White, and Harvey (1955). The 1954 experiment was summarized in Sherif, Harvey, White, Hood, and Sherif (1954). For a summary of the three experiments see chaps. VI and IX in Sherif and Sherif (1956).

[2] For an overview of this program see Sherif (1954).

[3] E.g., see Miller (1954) and Wapner and Alper (1952).

The conclusions summarized briefly are based on results cross-checked by two or more techniques.

The production of groups, the production of conflict between them, and the reduction of conflict in successive stages were brought about through the introduction of problem situations that were real and could not be ignored by individuals in the situation. Special "lecture methods" or "discussion methods" were not used. For example, the problem of getting a meal through their own initiative and planning was introduced when participating individuals were hungry.

Facing a problem situation which is immediate and compelling and which embodies a goal that cannot be ignored, group members *do* initiate discussion and *do* plan and carry through these plans until the objective is achieved. In this process the discussion becomes *their* discussion, the plan *their* plan, the action *their* action. In this process discussion, planning, and action have their place, and, when occasion arises, lecture or information has its place, too. The sequence of these related activities need not be the same in all cases.

The subjects were selected by rigorous criteria. They were healthy, normal boys around the age of eleven and twelve, socially well adjusted in school and neighborhood, and academically successful. They came from a homogeneous sociocultural background and from settled, well-adjusted families of middle or lower-middle class and Protestant affiliations. No subject came from a broken home. The mean I.Q. was above average. The subjects were not personally acquainted with one another prior to the experiment. Thus, explanation of results on the basis of background differences, social maladjustment, undue childhood frustrations, or previous interpersonal relations was ruled out at the beginning by the criteria for selecting subjects.

The first stage of the experiments was designed to produce groups with distinct structure (organization) and a set of norms which could be confronted with intergroup problems. The method for producing groups from unacquainted individuals with similar background was to introduce problem situations in which the attainment of the goal depended on the co-ordinated activity of all individuals. After a series of such activities, definite group structures or organizations developed.

The results warrant the following conclusions for the stage of group formation: When individuals interact in a series of situations toward goals which appeal to all and which require that they co-ordinate their activities, group structures arise having hierarchical status arrangements and a set of norms regulating behavior in matters of consequence to the activities of the group.

Once we had groups that satisfied our definition of "group," relations between groups could be studied. Specified conditions conducive to friction or conflict between groups were introduced. This negative aspect was deliberately undertaken because the major problem in intergroup relations today is the reduction of existing intergroup frictions. (Increasingly, friendly relations between groups is not nearly so great an issue.) The factors conducive to intergroup conflict give us realistic leads for reducing conflict.

A series of situations was introduced in which one group could achieve its goal only at the expense of the other group—through a tournament of competitive events with desirable prizes for the winning group. The results of the stage of intergroup conflict supported our main hypotheses. During interaction between groups in experimentally introduced activities which were competitive and mutually frustrating, members of each group developed hostile attitudes and highly unfavorable stereotypes toward the other group and its members. In fact, attitudes of social distance between the groups became so definite that they wanted to have nothing further to do with each other. This we take as a case of experimentally produced "social distance" in miniature. Conflict was manifested in derogatory name-calling and invectives, flare-ups of physical conflict, and raids on each other's cabins and territory. Over a period of time, negative stereotypes and unfavorable attitudes developed.

At the same time there was an increase in in-group solidarity and co-operativeness. This finding indicates that co-operation and democracy within groups do not necessarily lead to democracy and co-operation with out-groups, if the directions and interests of the groups are conflicting.

Increased solidarity forged in hostile encounters, in rallies from defeat, and in victories over the out-group is one instance of a more general finding: Intergroup relations, both conflicting and harmonious, *affected the nature of relations within the groups involved.* Altered relations between groups produced significant changes in the status arrangements *within* groups, in some instances resulting in shifts at the upper status levels or even a change in leadership. Always, consequential intergroup relations were reflected in new group values or norms which signified changes in practice, word, and deed within the group. Counterparts of this finding are not difficult to see in actual and consequential human relations. Probably many of our major preoccupations, anxieties, and activities in the past decade are incomprehensible without reference to the problems created by the prevailing "cold war" on an international scale.

Reduction of Intergroup Friction

A number of the measures proposed today for reducing intergroup friction could have been tried in this third stage. A few will be mentioned here, with a brief explanation of why they were discarded or were included in our experimental design.

1. Disseminating favorable information in regard to the out-group was not included. Information that is not related to the goals currently in focus in the activities of groups is relatively ineffective, as many

studies on attitude change have shown (Williams, 1947).

2. In small groups it is possible to devise sufficiently attractive rewards to make individual achievement supreme. This may reduce tension between groups by splitting the membership on an "every-man-for-himself" basis. However, this measure has little relevance for actual intergroup tensions, which are in terms of group membership and group alignments.

3. The resolution of conflict through leaders alone was not utilized. Even when group leaders meet apart from their groups around a conference table, they cannot be considered independent of the dominant trends and prevailing attitudes of their membership. If a leader is too much out of step in his negotiations and agreements with out-groups, he will cease to be followed. It seemed more realistic, therefore, to study the influence of leadership within the framework of prevailing trends in the groups involved. Such results will give us leads concerning the conditions under which leadership can be effective in reducing intergroup tensions.

4. The "common-enemy" approach is effective in pulling two or more groups together against another group. This approach was utilized in the 1949 experiment as an expedient measure and yielded effective results. But bringing some groups together against others means larger and more devastating conflicts in the long run. For this reason, the measure was not used in the 1954 experiment.

5. Another measure, advanced both in theoretical and in practical work, centers around social contacts among members of antagonistic groups in activities which are pleasant in themselves. This measure was tried out in 1954 in the first phase of the integration stage.

6. As the second phase of the integration stage, we introduced a series of superordinate goals which necessitated co-operative interaction between groups.

The social contact situations consisted of activities which were satisfying in themselves—eating together in the same dining room, watching a movie in the same hall, or engaging in an entertainment in close physical proximity. These activities, which were satisfying to each group, but which did not involve a state of interdependence and co-operation for the attainment of goals, were not effective in reducing intergroup tension. On the contrary, such occasions of contact were utilized as opportunities to engage in name-calling and in abuse of each other to the point of physical manifestations of hostility.

The ineffective, even deleterious, results of intergroup contact without superordinate goals have implications for certain contemporary learning theories and for practice in intergroup relations. Contiguity in pleasant activities with members of an out-group does not necessarily lead to a pleasurable image of the out-group if relations between the groups are unfriendly. Intergroup contact without superordinate goals is not likely to produce lasting reduction of intergroup hostility. John Gunther, for instance, in his survey of contemporary Africa, concluded that, when the intergroup relationship is exploitation of one group by a "superior" group, intergroup contact inevitably breeds hostility and conflict (Gunther, 1955).

Introduction of Superordinate Goals

After establishing the ineffectiveness, even the harm, in intergroup contacts which did not involve superordinate goals, we introduced a series of superordinate goals. Since the characteristics of the problem situations used as superordinate goals are implicit in the two main hypotheses for this stage, we shall present these hypotheses:

1. When groups in a state of conflict are brought into contact under conditions embodying superordinate goals, which are compelling but cannot be achieved by the efforts of one group alone, they will tend to co-operate toward the common goals.

2. Co-operation between groups, necessi-

tated by a series of situations embodying superordinate goals, will have a cumulative effect in the direction of reducing existing conflict between groups.

The problem situations were varied in nature, but all had an essential feature in common—they involved goals that could not be attained by the efforts and energies of one group alone and thus created a state of interdependence between groups: combating a water shortage that affected all and could not help being "compelling"; securing a much-desired film, which could not be obtained by either group alone but required putting their resources together; putting into working shape, when everyone was hungry and the food was some distance away, the only means of transportation available to carry food.

The introduction of a series of such superordinate goals was indeed effective in reducing intergroup conflict: (1) when the groups in a state of friction interacted in conditions involving superordinate goals, they did co-operate in activities leading toward the common goal and (2) a series of joint activities leading toward superordinate goals had the cumulative effect of reducing the prevailing friction between groups and unfavorable stereotypes toward the out-group.

These major conclusions were reached on the basis of observational data and were confirmed by sociometric choices and stereotype ratings administered first during intergroup conflict and again after the introduction of a series of superordinate goals. Comparison of the sociometric choices during intergroup conflict and following the series of superordinate goals shows clearly the changed attitudes toward members of the out-group. Friendship preferences shifted from almost exclusive preference for ingroup members toward increased inclusion of members from the "antagonists." Since the groups were still intact following co-operative efforts to gain superordinate goals, friends were found largely within one's group. However, choices of out-group members grew, in one group, from practically none during intergroup conflict to 23 per cent. Using chi square, this difference is significant ($P < .05$). In the other group, choices of the out-group increased to 36 per cent, and the difference is significant ($P < .001$). The findings confirm observations that the series of superordinate goals produced increasingly friendly associations and attitudes pertaining to out-group members.

Observations made after several superordinate goals were introduced showed a sharp decrease in the name-calling and derogation of the out-group common during intergroup friction and in the contact situations without superordinate goals. At the same time the blatant glorification and bragging about the in-group, observed during the period of conflict, diminished. These observations were confirmed by comparison of ratings of stereotypes (adjectives) the subjects had actually used in referring to their own group and the out-group during conflict with ratings made after the series of superordinate goals. Ratings of the out-group changed significantly from largely unfavorable ratings to largely favorable ratings. The proportions of the most unfavorable ratings found appropriate for the out-group—that is, the categorical verdicts that "all of them are stinkers" or ". . . smart alecks" or ". . . sneaky"—fell, in one group, from 21 per cent at the end of the friction stage to 1.5 per cent after interaction oriented toward superordinate goals. The corresponding reduction in these highly unfavorable verdicts by the other group was from 36.5 to 6 per cent. The over-all differences between the frequencies of stereotype ratings made in relation to the out-group during intergroup conflict and following the series of superordinate goals are significant for both groups at the .001 level (using chi-square test).

Ratings of the in-group were not so exclusively favorable, in line with observed decreases in self-glorification. But the differences in ratings of the in-group were not statistically significant, as were the differences in ratings of the out-group.

Our findings demonstrate the effectiveness of a series of superordinate goals in the reduction of intergroup conflict, hostility, and their by-products. They also have implications for other measures proposed for reducing intergroup tensions.

It is true that lines of communication between groups must be opened before prevailing hostility can be reduced. But, if contact between hostile groups takes place without superordinate goals, the communication channels serve as media for further accusations and recriminations. When contact situations involve superordinate goals, communication is utilized in the direction of reducing conflict in order to attain the common goals.

Favorable information about a disliked out-group tends to be ignored, rejected, or reinterpreted to fit prevailing stereotypes. But, when groups are pulling together toward superordinate goals, true and even favorable information about the out-group is seen in a new light. The probability of information being effective in eliminating unfavorable stereotypes is enormously enhanced.

When groups co-operate in the attainment of superordinate goals, leaders are in a position to take bolder steps toward bringing about understanding and harmonious relations. When groups are directed toward incompatible goals, genuine moves by a leader to reduce intergroup tension may be seen by the membership as out of step and ill advised. The leader may be subjected to severe criticism and even loss of faith and status in his own group. When compelling superordinate goals are introduced, the leader can make moves to further co-operative efforts, and his decisions receive support from other group members.

In short, various measures suggested for the reduction of intergroup conflict—disseminating information, increasing social contact, conferences of leaders—acquire new significance and effectiveness when they become part and parcel of interaction processes between groups oriented toward superordinate goals which have real and compelling value for all groups concerned.

References

Bogardus, E. S. Changes in racial distances. *Int. J. opin. att. Res.,* 1947, *1,* 55-62.

Gunther, J. *Inside Africa.* New York: Harper & Row, 1955.

Hiller, E. T. *The strike.* Chicago: Univer. of Chicago Press, 1928.

Hood, W. R., and Sherif, M. Personality oriented approaches to prejudice. *Sociol. soc. Res.,* 1955, *40,* 79-85.

Horowitz, E. L. Race attitudes. In Otto Klineberg (Ed.), *Characteristics of the American Negro,* part 4. New York: Harper & Row, 1944.

Miller, F. B. "Resistentialism" in applied social research. *Hum. Org.,* 1954, *12,* 5-8.

Murphy, G. *In the minds of men.* New York: Basic Books, 1953.

Pear, T. H. *Psychological factors of peace and war.* New York: Philosophical Library, 1950.

Sherif, M. Integrating field work and laboratory in small group research. *Amer. sociol. Rev.,* 1954, *19,* 759-771.

Sherif, M., Harvey, O. J., White, B. J., Hood, W. R., and Sherif, Carolyn W. *Experimental study of positive and negative intergroup attitudes between experimentally produced groups: robbers cave study.* Norman, Okla.: Univer. of Oklahoma, 1954 (Multilithed).

Sherif, M., and Sherif, Carolyn W. *Groups in harmony and tension.* New York: Harper & Row, 1953.

Sherif, M., and Sherif, Carolyn W. *An outline of social psychology,* Rev. Ed. New York: Harper & Row, 1956.

Sherif, M., White, B. J., and Harvey, O. J. Status in experimentally produced groups. *Amer. J. Sociol.,* 1955, *60,* 370-379.

Thrasher, F. M. *The gang.* Chicago: Univer. of Chicago Press, 1927.

WAPNER, S., and ALPER, T. G. The effect of an audience on behavior in a choice situation. *J. abnorm. soc. Psychol.*, 1952, 47, 222-229.

WILLIAMS, R. M. *The reduction of intergroup tensions.* Soc. Sci. Res. Coun. Bull. 57. New York, 1947.

Loyalty of Representatives
to Ingroup Positions during ❧ Robert R. Blake
Intergroup Competition ❧ Jane S. Mouton

A representative of a group may meet a representative of an opposing group to decide an issue under conditions which give victory to one of the sides and defeat to the other. International negotiation frequently takes this form, as do typical negotiations between labor and management in our own economic system. Military situations often arise in which the same pattern is present. Opposing groups seek a resolution of differences through interactions between representatives *within* the managerial branches of industrial, political and governmental units as well.

Resolution of intergroup conflict is sought most commonly through negotiations carried on by representatives. The rationale is that a spokesman is a *member* of the group he represents and, therefore, he knows the problem from an ingroup point of view (Blake, 1959).

Yet, a critical limitation is placed on a representative when intergroup relations are on a competitive basis or when they take a win-lose turn. From the standpoint of his own group membership, he is not entirely "free" to act in accord with fact or even to engage in compromise, for to do so would be interpreted by group members as bringing

them "defeat." A previous study (Blake and Mouton, 1961) has shown that the representative who exerts influence on the opposing representative, and in doing so obtains acceptance of his group's position, is accorded a "hero" reaction, and thereafter he enjoys increased status within his group. The representative who capitulates and thereby brings defeat to his group is treated as disloyal or traitorous by its members.

Examined from another point of view, in the negotiation situation, logical considerations may require that a representative renounce his group's prior position in order to gain a valid resolution of the intergroup problem. But acting against the exercise of a logical and factually analytical attitude are group ties that require him to gain victory and, at whatever cost, to defend a point of view which protects his membership position.

The present study is designed to investigate the loyalty v. logic issue. The hypothesis is that, under conditions of win-lose competition, if the resolution of differences through representatives must result in acceptance of one position as "better" and another as "poorer" (no compromise possible), then it will more frequently end in deadlock

From *Sociometry*, 1961, 24, 177-184. Reprinted by permission of the authors and the American Sociological Association. Studies reported concerned with intergroup behavior were partially supported by Grant M-2447 c1, Behavior of Group Representatives under Pressure, National Institutes of Health, and by a grant from Esso Division, Humble Oil and Refining Company.

(i.e., loyalty to a party line) than in capitulation (i.e., the application of logic in evaluating which position is better).

Procedure

SETTING AND SUBJECTS

All studies were undertaken in connection with human relations training programs (The Human Relations Training Laboratory, 1960), with laboratory populations ranging between 18 and 36 people each. A total of 520 participants served as members of 62 groups which engaged in a parallel sequence of activities centering on intergroup competition. The competition took place between pairs, trios and quartets of groups which ranged each in size from seven to twelve members.

Forty-six groups were composed of adults aged from 25 to 55, who were engaged in executive or supervisory positions. All were attending two-week human relations laboratory programs in which the experiment to be described was inserted to help participants gain insight regarding group action and the dynamics of intergroup relations under competitive conditions.

The remaining 16 groups were composed of junior and senior college students, both male and female, enrolled in social psychology. The sequence of activities paralleled those for the adult groups. All groups were matched in educational and occupational level for adult groups, and in class level and sex for college groups.

SEQUENCE OF INTERACTIONS

The arrangements for creating intergroup competition were:

Development of Autonomous Groups. Ten to twelve hours, divided into five or six two-hour sessions occurring over a three-day period, were devoted to autonomous ingroup activity. The purpose of having individuals meet together was to study decision making in groups through developing and

then evaluating their own ingroup structures. The kind of group action involved in human relations training programs is described more fully elsewhere (Blake and Mouton, 1960)

This basis of group organization was suitable for investigating intergroup conflict. First the grouping was intrinsically meaningful, since participants were engaged in studying internal group processes under their own responsibility and initiative. Cohesion generated quickly. Pride in membership was evidenced in quantitative measures of solidarity, which showed an increasing trend over the entire series of meetings. In addition, members sensed that their ability to perform as a group and their status as an effective unit were challenged when they were confronted with competition which would lead to victory or defeat. The result was a strong motive to win, shown by the fact that, when asked to indicate prospects of victory on a nine-point scale, all groups uniformly reported that they considered their own chance of victory better than the groups against whom they were pitted.

Creating Intergroup Competition. After completion of the first phase, each group had three hours to develop its own approach to the solution of an assigned problem. The problem, to be solved in the form of a two-page, double-spaced, typewritten memorandum, always concerned some basic issue with which members of the contending groups were equally familiar.

In the adult groups the problem used varied from occasion to occasion, but it always was related to an organizational situation, and typically it involved developing a statement of ways to improve the operation of the organization with respect to some specific issue, such as labor-management negotiations, relations between technical and practical personnel, the improvement of communications through levels within the organization hierarchy, and so on. For college groups the problem involved topics such as how to handle a deviant in a group, ways to deal with the integration issue, or developing a set of recommendations for the resolution of intergroup conflict.

Group members uniformly accepted the proposition that their performance provided an indication of their effectiveness as a problem-solving unit. The possibility of resolving differences between solutions by compromise or through an emergent product approach was unavailable. Group members were committed to the superiority of their own products, as shown by significant differences between ratings of the quality of their own solution and ratings of the quality of their solution by the opposing groups.

Clarification of Group Positions. On completion of the assigned task, the solutions were reproduced and exchanged for purposes of comparison. One to two hours were spent in ingroup discussion and evaluation of the merits of each solution. During this phase members were urged to increase their understanding of the position of the other group by noting similarities and differences between it and their own, and points needing clarification or elaboration.

At the beginning of this phase, representatives were elected by each group through a rank-ordering procedure. After the ingroup discussion, each representative explained and clarified his own group's solution in response to questions raised by the representative of the other group. The explanation and clarification phase lasted an additional two to four hours, depending on circumstances. This phase led to intensification of competition and to further elevation of estimates of the quality of one's own group's solution and devaluation of the solution of the competing group.

Winner and Loser Determined. Finally, through public interactions, the representatives attempted to reach a decision as to which solution was more adequate, and, therefore, the winner. Discussion between representatives continued until a decision was reached. If their efforts resulted in *deadlock*, impartial judges, either two or three in number, who had not participated in the earlier phases of competition and who

did not know which groups produced which solutions, rendered the verdict. Before doing so, the judges had had a full opportunity to study the two solutions and then to gain any needed clarification from the representatives; these conferred in private and then answered queries in a "mechanical" order, so as to conceal the "ownership" of the solutions. The formal competition phase was completed after the verdict was announced.

Results

The data summarized in Figure 1 show that it is extremely rare under the conditions described for a representative to capitulate.

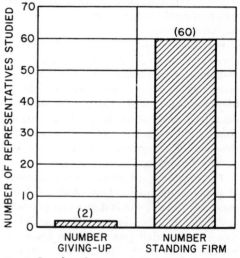

Fig. 1. Loyalty of representatives to their groups during intergroup competition.

Only two out of 62 representatives voted against their group's position. The other 60 remained steadfastly loyal to their own group's point of view and deadlocked. In each case, impartial judges were able to decide upon a clear-cut winner. The repetitiveness of the phenomenon across competitions—on a probability basis, attributable to chance in only 1 in 10,000 times—demonstrates the strength of the motivation to win experienced by the person into whose hands is placed his group's fate. These results confirm that loyalty to an ingroup position replaces the exercise of logic when two group positions are evaluated under win-lose conditions.

The findings reported are generalizable to situations integrated around a win-lose outcome. Comparable results have also been obtained when representatives interacted in secrecy rather than under conditions where their behavior could be observed, and when representatives had no realistic basis for anticipating that the outcome of their interactions would be known to the group from which they came. In other words, confidence can be placed in these data as typifying a basic situation under which members from two autonomous groups confront one another when a win-lose outcome is to be expected from their interactions.

Discussion

If relations between groups are on a win-lose basis, as happens when preferred positions have been publicly announced in advance, then the quest for a resolution by representatives is replete with obstacles.

The core of the difficulty seems to be in the fact that representatives are "committed" people. From the standpoint of their own group membership they do not appear to be free to apply a logical analysis, to weigh facts and balance relative units in developing a win-lose judgment. Rather, representatives act on loyalty and are motivated to win, or at least to avoid defeat, even though a judgment which would resolve an intergroup problem is sacrificed in the process. Where there is conflict of interest between groups, the situation is such that ingroup loyalty overwhelms logic. If a representative cannot win, then, through deadlocking, traitorous action can be avoided, and group defeat forestalled. In all but two of the competitive situations studied here, deadlock occurred. Judges had to be used to break the impasse.

Situations of competition in which mutu-

ally exclusive positions are taken are exceedingly common. The inability of representatives of groups to adjudicate differences in points of view has resulted in a number of "neutral" groups whose function is to give an impartial judgment. The use of a judge to render a verdict is one example. Within industry, stalemates between representatives of management and the union lead to the use of arbitration and mediation as a basis for resolving differences. When interaction, discussion, and problem solving between representatives of governments fail, alternatives to violence include Cold War and recourse to the United Nations.

In view of the results presented here, one question that might be posed is: What conditions are more conducive to representative interaction which will result in decisions rather than deadlock? Several suggestions can be made. The examples given above, as well as the experimental conditions, constitute situations where public positions are taken by *groups* in advance of negotiation, which is a routine procedure. Taking a position lays the groundwork for competition to enter, even when the groups would be expected to interact in a collaborative manner. For a representative to deviate from a fixed position means he is going against his group. If negotiations between representatives were to occur before a fixed position was taken, the possibility of reaching an acceptable solution might be increased (Rusk, 1955). Another method of obtaining a resolution of differences in positions is through the use of superordinate goals (Sherif and Sherif, 1953). The superordinate goal approach aims at changing a win-lose situation into one where all parties stand to gain through the actions of each. Both of these procedures provide possible alternative approaches to resolving the sharply drawn conflict of interests representatives face when they are called upon to negotiate differences between groups within a logical frame of reference while at the same time remaining loyal to their own group's point of view.

Summary

Five hundred and twenty persons, participating as members of 62 groups in human-relations training programs, engaged in a parallel sequence of ingroup and intergroup activities. Groups were placed in competition in pairs, trios and quartets, with the outcome of the win-lose competition resting on the negotiations of representatives from each of the groups. Results demonstrate that ingroup loyalty prevented the application of "objective" logic and only two of the 62 representatives capitulated to the opposition.

We interpret these data as supporting the proposition that negotiations by representatives can be an ineffectual basis for resolving a win-lose situation between contending groups.

References

BLAKE, R. R. Psychology and the crisis of statesmanship. *Amer. Psychologist,* 1959, *14,* 87-94.

BLAKE, R. R., and MOUTON, JANE S. Heroes and traitors: two patterns of representing groups in a competitive situation. *Int. J. Sociometry,* 1961.

BLAKE, R. R., and MOUTON, JANE S. *Training for decision-making in groups.* New York: Putnam, 1960.

The Human Relations Training Laboratory. *Proceedings.* Austin, Tex.: The Univer. of Texas, 1960.

RUSK, D. Parliamentary diplomacy—debate versus negotiation. *World Affairs Interpreter,* 1955, *26,* 121-138.

SHERIF, M., and SHERIF, CAROLYN W. *Groups in harmony and tension.* New York: Harper & Row, 1953.

Attitudes towards Foreign Affairs

as a Function of Personality ❈ Bjorn Christiansen

The Channelization Hypothesis: A Preliminary Analysis

The Channelization Hypothesis contends that various psychological conditions are of decisive importance for the degree to which deeper personality layers will influence a person's attitudes towards foreign affairs. We have previously discussed three such conditions: nationalism, international knowledge, and manifest reaction tendencies in everyday situations.

In what follows we shall take as our point of departure our previous demonstration of a positive correlation between psychodynamic conflicts and aggressive attitudes towards foreign affairs. We shall consider this correlation as supporting the fact that latent, character-conditioned aggression has a tendency to become displaced on to the sphere

This article has been adapted by the editors for this book primarily from Chapters 5 and 12 of *Attitudes towards Foreign Affairs as a Function of Personality, Universitetsforlaget,* Oslo, Norway: 1959. Reprinted by permission of the author and publisher. It should be noted that the descriptions given in the present selection under "Variables And Measuring Instruments" were adapted from a number of other chapters in the volume, and represent highly condensed versions of otherwise detailed accounts of the nature, development, and properties of the measuring instruments employed in the research.

of foreign affairs, and investigate the degrees to which such displacement is related to nationalism (patriotism), international knowledge, and aggressive everyday ways of reacting.

Next we shall start out with our earlier demonstration of a positive correlation between aggressive everyday and international reaction patterns, and investigate the degree to which this correlation is related to psychodynamic conflicts (latent aggression), nationalism (patriotism), and international knowledge respectively.

The latter proposition perhaps falls outside what should strictly be described as the Channelization Hypothesis. However, it can at any rate be said to complement it, since it often seems to be assumed that a lack of displacement of aggression implies an independent and rational stand in foreign affairs. In our opinion a lack of displacement will provide a basis for increased generalization of aggression unless tendencies in this direction are counterbalanced by other psychological conditions.

A. *Procedure*

SUBJECTS

Applicants to and students of the Military Academy and the Naval Academy in Oslo were used as subjects. The empirical data were collected in two stages: in August and the beginning of September 1952, and at the end of January 1954. In the first session which lasted approximately three hours for each subject, various attitude-scales and questionnaires as well as projective methods were administered. In the second session, which lasted approximately one hour for each subject, two projective techniques and a sociometric scale were given.

In the first stage a total of 103 applicants to the Military Academy and 64 students at the Naval Academy were used. The subjects were divided into groups, with 15-20 persons in each group. The students of the Naval Academy worked under completely anonymous conditions. The applicants to the Military Academy were given repeated assurances that all answers would be strictly confidential, that no names would be mentioned, and that their responses would have no bearing on their admission to the Academy—which they had the opportunity to verify through their own representatives.

The samples of Military Academy applicants had an average age of 23 years. The majority, 84 or 82%, were between 21 and 24 years of age, and the total ranged from 20 to 30 years. We have no complete specification of the age-distribution for the students of the Naval Academy. However there are many indications that there is no great difference between them and the Military Academy applicants.

The second stage of our data collection occurred exactly a year and a half after the first. This time we used 70 students of the Military Academy in Oslo as subjects. The sample represented a part of our original sample of subjects, specifically, those of the previous applicants who had been accepted by the Academy. The sample included practically all of the students in the second year of training, and the investigation was again based on groups. We worked with three groups in all—three classes—consisting of 21, 24, and 25 students respectively. These three classes were studied successively, and we have every reason to assume that none of the subjects had any prior knowledge of the tests and instruments applied.

In other words, our sample of subjects consists exclusively of men in their twenties. They come from all over the country. They have a similar educational background, all having completed gymnasium.[1] Unquestionably the most striking characteristic is the subjects' specific occupational position.

The fact that they all wanted military training and had roughly the same previous educational background undoubtedly limits considerably the possible variation in group

[1] Secondary school to university entrance standard.

membership. Our subjects represent a very homogeneous sample in many ways; but at the same time—psychologically speaking—a less homogeneous sample than one might be inclined to assume. In informal interviews with some of the subjects, for example, it was clearly evident that their occupational motivations were highly varied. In certain cases distinct signs of "authoritarian" traits could be discerned, the wish to defend King and Fatherland, conventionalism, authoritarian submission and identification with strong leaders. In other cases these motives did not seem to occur at all. The desire for a relatively well-paid and diversified occupation, one offering unique opportunities for exercise and outdoor living, was usually in evidence.

We will not deny the fact that a certain homogeneity exists. Our sample of respondents is by no means representative of the Norwegian population, nor of Norwegian men, nor of Norwegian men of the same age-group and the same general educational background.

VARIABLES AND MEASURING INSTRUMENTS

1. *Aggressive Reactions in Foreign Affairs* (*E Score of the IR Scale*). Types of reactions to international incidents which threaten Norwegian interests were measured by the forty-item IR scale. Each item described a conflict for Norway created by either the United States or the Soviet Union or nations oriented to either side of the East-West controversy, or nations or events which were neutral to this controversy. Choosing from among six alternatives, the subject indicated his strongest preference and his next strongest preference in the action he would prefer Norway to take in the conflict. Each alternative could be classified in terms of the direction of the reaction (inward, outward, or passive) and its form (threat-oriented or problem-oriented), thereby providing six types of possible reaction patterns to international conflict. Scores

were obtained for each of these patterns based on an appropriate weighting of the subject's first and second choices from the six alternatives for each of the forty items. Of concern in the present study is the E score which measures the degree to which the subject's reactions to international conflict are threat-oriented in an outward direction, that is, they indicate aggressive reactions toward other nations. A reliability coefficient of .86 was obtained for this measure.

2. *Aggressive Reactions in Everyday Situations* (*E Score of the ER Scale*). Measures of reaction patterns to conflict situations in everyday life were obtained by means of the ER scale, which, except for its item content, was identical in design and approach to the IR scale. The everyday situations involved incidents which could happen to anyone in an ordinary day's activity, e.g., splattered by dirty water by a passing car, etc. The items covered relationships between the subject and the conflict-producing object which were either impersonal, intimate, formal, or involved the subject in conflict with a child. Here again the subject made two choices from the six alternatives provided for each item, indicating what he would be most likely to do and next most likely to do in the situation. His choices reflected particular directions and forms of response as noted above for the IR scale. The E score of the ER scale therefore provided a measure of aggressive reaction tendencies in everyday situations which corresponded to the measure of aggression in international situations, i.e., the E score of the IR scale. A reliability measure of .86 was obtained for the E score of the ER scale.

3. *Latent Aggression as a Function of Psychodynamic Conflicts* (*Blacky Test*). The extent of conflict in connection with psychosexual impulses was measured by means of a modified form of the Blacky Test (Blum, 1949; 1950), a projective technique in which a family of dogs consisting of a puppy *Blacky*, Blacky's parents, and a sibling

is depicted cartoon style in a variety of situations. The eleven pictures (slides) in the test were designed to detect conflict with respect to various psychosexual dimensions, e.g., oral eroticism, sibling jealousy, etc., based on the spontaneous stories told by the subject about each picture as well as his responses to a series of questions (the inquiry) presented immediately following his story about the picture. In order to adapt the test to both the Norwegian setting and the requirements of the immediate research problem, appropriate translations from English to Norwegian were made, only the four pictures focused on early psychosexual development were used, the test was group administered rather than given on an individual basis, as well as other minor changes in the details of administering the test being made. The scoring of the test was also modified with greatest emphasis placed on the spontaneous stories which were scored for the extent to which they reflected conflict-free or conflict-charged manifestations in the handling of basic psychosexual impulses. Scoring reliabilities in assessing the presence or absence of such conflict in the stories told for each of the four pictures were in the order of 86 to 99 per cent rater agreement involving two reliability studies.

4. *National Patriotism (NP Scale).* National patriotism is defined as a general tendency to see one's own nation as superior to the rest of mankind. A prominent trait would be a superordinate loyalty to one's own nation in relation to other reference and membership groups. Loyalty to one's own nation will take priority over loyalty to (a) national sub-groups, (b) supra-national organizations, (c) national outgroups, and (d) humanity as a whole. To measure patriotism of this kind a nine-item scale was constructed reflecting the "loyalty dimensions" listed above. The subjects were asked to give their opinions about each of the statements by indicating the extent to which they agreed or disagreed with it on a five-point evaluation scale extending from "strong agreement" to "strong disagree-

ment" Each statement was numerically scored for the degree of patriotism indicated by the subject's extent of agreement or disagreement with it, and on this basis a total patriotism score for the nine-item scale was obtained.

5. *International Knowledge (IK Scale).* International knowledge refers to the degree of accuracy in the subject's perceptions of how Norway compares with "most other nations" with respect to a series of twenty national attributes, e.g., "General Education," "Artistic Standards," "Educational Facilities," etc. The subject judged each attribute on a five-point scale extending from the view that Norway had this trait to a considerably greater degree than other nations, to the view that it had this trait to a considerably lesser degree than these other nations. These judgements were then compared with the average corresponding judgements made by a panel of three experts. In establishing the judgements of the latter as criteria for accuracy, it was found that the judgements of the experts never involved more than one expert disagreeing with the others concerning a trait, and except for one case the deviation was never more than one scale interval in the five-point scale. The sum of the differences in intervals between the subject's judgements and the average judgements of the panel for the twenty national traits provided a total deviation score. The lower the score the less the deviation from the accuracy criteria and therefore the greater the international knowledge.

METHOD OF ANALYSIS

To obtain a survey of the effect of various factors on tendencies towards generalization and displacement of aggression, we proceeded in the following manner: first we examined the score distribution on the factor whose effect we wished to study, and isolated the approximately highest, middle, and lowest third of the distribution. On the basis of this delimitation we undertook a division of the subjects into three sub-samples and calculated the trend towards generalization (or displacement) in each of the sub-samples. Finally we compared the sub-samples and examined the differences among them.

B. Results

There follows a statistical analysis of the connection of various factors with tendencies towards displacement of aggression, after which we shall present a parallel analysis of the connection of various factors with tendencies towards generalization of aggression. In both cases the analyses will be based on a comparison of fairly small groups since our total sample included a comparatively small number of subjects. On the whole the results will serve rather as a basis for elaborating hypotheses than providing material for final conclusions.

DISPLACEMENT OF AGGRESSION IN RELATION TO NATIONALISM

For our total sample we found a significant positive correlation between "number of conflict scores" on the Blacky test and the E category of the IR scale ($r = .33$). We have interpreted this as indicating that there is a connection between latent aggression and aggressive international reaction patterns.

To investigate the degree to which nationalism (patriotism) influences the connection between these two factors, we isolated the subjects who had answered both the IR scale and the Blacky Pictures, and

divided the sample approximately into three groups according to the individual scores on the NP scale. We delimited three sub-samples: those who had achieved a score in the highest, middle, and west third of the score distribution on the NP scale. We then calculated for each sub-sample the correlation between "number of conflict scores" on the Blacky test and the E category of the IR scale.

Table 1 presents the correlation coefficients in these three cases, showing that there are respectively highest and lowest correlations in the sub-sample with the highest and lowest scores on the NP scale. A comparison between the samples with the highest and lowest scores shows a difference between correlations of .38. Because of the small samples, however, the difference does does not achieve statistical significance ($p = .18$).[2] In spite of this fact our data suggest that displacement tendencies might be associated with the degree of nationalism in the sense of patriotism. The correlation only achieves a satisfactory statistical significance in the sub-sample with the highest scores on the NP scale ($p = .007$).[3] In other words a certain degree of nationalism seems to be a prerequisite for the displacement of aggression on to the international sphere. Our data thus tend to support Durbin and Bowlby's view of nationalism as a channelizing factor (1939).

[2] If a one-tail criterion is applied, the difference obtains an approximate statistical significance ($p < .10$).
[3] In testing the significance of an obtained correlation in sub-samples where N is less than 30, the r to z transformation has consistently been used.

TABLE 1

CORRELATION (r) BETWEEN THE E CATEGORY OF THE IR SCALE AND CONFLICT SCORES ON THE BLACKY TEST IN SAMPLES WITH DIFFERENT SCORES ON THE NP SCALE

Score Intervals on NP Scale	N	r	p
19-26 (Least Nationalistic)	20	.18	.45
27-29 (Moderately Nationalistic)	21	.26	.26
30-38 (Most Nationalistic)	21	.56	.01

DISPLACEMENT OF AGGRESSION IN RELATION TO EVERYDAY AGGRESSION

To investigate the degree to which manifest aggressive reaction tendencies in everyday situations influence the connection between latent aggression and aggressive international reaction patterns, we proceeded in the same way as above and undertook a triple division of the total sample according to the scores of the individual subjects on the E category of the ER scale.

Table 2 surveys the correlation coefficients in these three instances.

The table shows highest correlation in the sub-sample with medium scores on the ER scale, and lowest correlation in the sub-sample with the highest scores. Only in the sub-sample with medium scores does the correlation achieve statistical significance ($p < .05$).

In spite of the fact that the difference between correlations in the sub-samples does not achieve statistical significance it is interesting to note that high scores on the ER scale's E category are associated with a comparatively smaller displacement tendency than low and medium scores. This is exactly what we might expect from the point of view of the "drainage theory": that aggressive tendencies in everyday situations function as a draining of latent aggression, so that less remains for international situations. An argument against such a view is the higher correlation in the sub-sample with medium scores than in the sub-sample with the lowest scores on the ER scale's E category. This does not necessarily mean that the "drainage theory" is untenable, but

that it must be complemented by other considerations. A view which is opposite in the present connection is that inhibitions of everyday aggression—if sufficiently strong —may be transferred or generalized to affect aggressive international tendencies. If this were the case we should in fact expect greatest displacement to occur when more moderate inhibition of aggression is present. In those cases where we are dealing with a generalized inhibition of aggression we should further expect, from a depth psychological point of view, a comparatively greater tendency towards hypochondria and somatization. No examination was undertaken on this point. Some support for such a view is found in the fact that the frequency of certain heart and circulatory diseases (and also of certain mental diseases) was considerably reduced in Norway during the occupation period from 1940-45, compared with pre- and post-war periods.[4] An intense positive sanctioning and encouragement of aggressive social attitudes may possibly under certain circumstances be positively stimulating and "health bringing" for strongly affect-inhibited persons. Here we are faced with an extremely interesting hypothesis which invites further exploration.[5]

[4] A personal communication from H. J. Ustvedt.

[5] An observation relevant in the present context is that aggressive persons by and large seem to be in a much better state of physical health that people of similar age taken from the general population. E.g., in an American investigation of paranoid patients, nearly all diagnosed as dementia praecox, paranoid type, it was found that the manifestation of arteriosclerosis, including cerebral arteriosclerosis, was less frequent than in the general population. (See H. S. Alpert, et

TABLE 2

CORRELATION (r) BETWEEN THE E CATEGORY OF THE IR SCALE AND CONFLICT SCORES ON THE BLACKY TEST IN SAMPLES WITH DIFFERENT SCORES ON THE E CATEGORY OF THE ER SCALE

Score Intervals on the ER Scale	N	r	p
0-10 (Least Aggressive)	23	.32	.14
12-22 (Moderately Aggressive)	23	.43	.04
24-45 (Most Aggressive)	20	.22	.36

DISPLACEMENT OF AGGRESSION IN RELATION TO INTERNATIONAL KNOWLEDGE

In investigating the effect of international knowledge on the connection between latent aggression and international attitudes we proceeded in the same way as above, dividing the total sample into three sub-samples according to the individual subjects' scores on the IK scale.

Table 3 surveys the correlation coefficients in this case. The table shows that there is comparatively little difference between the sub-samples. The highest correlation turns out to be in the sub-sample with medium scores on the IK scale, the lowest correlation in the sub-sample with the highest scores. The fact that we find the least displacement of aggression to occur in the sub-sample characterized by least international knowledge is in accordance with a point of view previously referred to, that the influence of latent personality layers presupposes an orientation towards international relations. The very slight trend which exists in the direction of a lower displacement tendency in the case of most as compared to moderate knowledge, or the mere fact that here we do not find a corresponding higher displacement tendency in the case of most knowledge, fits in with the viewpoint that

---

al., "Central arteriosclerosis in the paranoid state," *Psychiat. Quart.,* 1947, *21,* 305-313.) Since the paranoid is a personality type who continually acts out his hostilities, the data indirectly support the hypothesis that repressed hostility often is a causal factor of hypertension and somatization.

international knowledge may contribute in keeping character-conditioned aggression under control.

The differences found between the three sub-samples are much too small to verify these hypotheses. The differences achieve no statistical significance and the reason for the above comments is therefore mainly to indicate some lines for future research on more heterogeneous samples of subjects.

GENERALIZATION OF AGGRESSION IN RELATION TO LATENT AGGRESSION

As we have previously stated we found a significant positive correlation ($r = .42$) between the E categories of the ER and IR scales. We interpreted this as indicating that a generalization of aggressive reaction tendencies takes place from everyday to international situations.

In order to investigate the degree to which latent aggression (psychodynamic conflicts) affects tendencies towards the generalization of aggression, we delineated the subjects who had given complete responses on both the ER and IR scales, and divided the sample into approximately three groups according to the individuals' "number of conflict scores" on the Blacky test.

Table 4 surveys the correlation between the E categories in the sub-samples with 2 or less, 3, and 4 conflict scores on the Blacky test. The table shows that the highest and lowest correlations occur in the sub-sample having the lowest and highest "number of conflict scores" respectively on the Blacky test.

TABLE 3

CORRELATION (r) BETWEEN THE E CATEGORY OF THE IR SCALE AND CONFLICT SCORES ON THE BLACKY TEST IN SAMPLES WITH DIFFERENT SCORES ON THE IK SCALE

Score Intervals on IK Scale	N	r	p
14-21 (Least Knowledge)	24	.26	.22
11-13 (Moderate Knowledge)	15	.39	.15
4-10 (Most Knowledge)	26	.37	.06

TABLE 4

CORRELATION (r) BETWEEN THE E CATEGORIES OF THE IR AND ER
SCALES IN SAMPLES WITH DIFFERENT SCORES ON THE BLACKY TEST

Score Intervals on the Blacky Test	N	r	p
0-2 (Least Conflict Charged)	23	.69	.001
3 (Moderately Conflict Charged)	14	.56	.04
4 (Most Conflict Charged)	29	.29	.13

While the correlation in the sub-sample with most conflict scores achieves a very limited statistical significance ($p = .13$), the correlation in the sub-sample with least conflict scores shows a significance well below the 1% level ($p \approx .001$). The difference between correlations in these two samples is .40 and statistically significant at the 6% level.[6] The frequency of conflicts in connection with basic impulse patterns thus seems to be approximately significantly associated with a lack of generalization of aggression. The less the amount of latent aggression the greater the generalization tendency which seems to be present.[7]

Our empirical material thus supports the view we previously put forward, that lack of repression of aggression does not necessarily lead to attitudes towards foreign affairs independent of personality factors, but to an increased generalization, unless tendencies in this direction are counteracted by other factors.

GENERALIZATION OF AGGRESSION
IN RELATION TO NATIONALISM

We proceeded in the same fashion as above in investigating the degree to which nationalism (patriotism) affects the correlation between aggressive everyday and international reaction patterns, by making a triple division of the total sample according to the individual scores on the NP scale.

Table 5 shows the correlation between the E categories in the three sub-samples.

The table shows that the highest and lowest correlations occur in the sub-sample with the highest and lowest scores respectively on the NP scale. The difference between correlations in these two sub-samples is .39 and statistically significant below the 5% level ($p = .02$). We may therefore conclude that the score values on the NP scale are significantly associated with a tendency towards generalization of aggression. The more the patriotism present, the greater appears to be the tendency towards generalization.

[6] If a one-tail criterion is used the difference reaches a statistical significance at the 3% level.

[7] In concluding our empirical investigation of the Generalization Hypothesis it was pointed out that the hypothesis cannot explain why aggressive reactions do not show highest generalization despite the fact that this reaction type seems to be more consistent than others both in everyday and international situations. It is not inconceivable that this discrepancy might be abolished were we to concentrate on subjects who were unburdened by latent aggression.

TABLE 5

CORRELATION (r) BETWEEN THE E CATEGORIES OF THE IR AND ER
SCALES IN SAMPLES WITH DIFFERENT SCORES ON THE NP SCALE

Score Intervals on NP Scale	N	r	p
16-25 (Least Nationalistic)	50	.23	.11
26-29 (Moderately Nationalistic)	56	.55	.001
30-40 (Most Nationalistic)	47	.62	.001

Our data indicate on the whole that nationalism (patriotism) co-varies with tendencies towards displacement as well as towards generalization; in other words, it probably facilitates the influence of various personality factors on international attitudes.

GENERALIZATION OF AGGRESSION IN RELATION TO INTERNATIONAL KNOWLEDGE

In examining the degree to which international knowledge affects the connection between aggressive everyday and international reaction patterns we proceeded in the same manner as above, dividing the total sample according to the individuals' scores on the IK scale.

Table 6 surveys the correlation between the E categories of the ER and IR scales in the three sub-samples. The table shows highest correlation in the sub-sample with the highest scores on the IK scale, and least correlation in the sub-sample with medium scores. The difference between correlations in these two samples is .16, but it achieves no statistical significance ($p = .36$).

Our data give no basis for any definite conclusion, but there is a certain tendency for the greatest generalization to occur in the case of most and least international knowledge. In the two latter sub-samples only we find correlation coefficients obtaining a statistical significance below the 1% level. However, the difference between correlations in these two samples and the sample with moderate scores on the IK scale does not achieve statistical significance ($p = .33$).

In spite of the obvious shortcomings of the IK scale it nevertheless may be worth while to venture some speculations concerning our results: the relatively higher correlation coefficient in the sub-sample with the lowest scores on the IK scale (those with most knowledge), than in the sub-sample with medium scores, is in accordance with the aforementioned hypothesis: that the effect of personal values (*in casu* such values as are reflected in everyday reaction patterns) on a person's attitudes towards foreign affairs will be the greater, the greater the international knowledge present. The same hypothesis is, however, weakened by our findings of a relatively higher correlation coefficient in the sub-sample with the highest scores on the IK scale, than in the sub-sample with the medium scores. The latter relationship supports the hypothesis that little international knowledge implies small ability to differentiate between everyday and international situations, and that tendencies towards generalization are greater the less a person differentiates between different situations.

On the whole our data do not weaken the hypothesis that a curvilinear correlation exists between international knowledge and tendencies towards generalization. Furthermore, a comparison between Tables 3 and 6 suggests an inverse relationship between the influence of international knowledge on tendencies towards generalization and displacement respectively. Among the subjects characterized by least knowledge, the correlation between the R scales ("generalization") is somewhat higher than the correlation between the Blacky test and the IR scale ("displacement"), while the opposite is true in the rest of the sample. Here again

TABLE 6

CORRELATION (r) BETWEEN THE E CATEGORIES OF THE IR AND ER
SCALES IN SAMPLES WITH DIFFERENT SCORES ON THE IK SCALE

Score Intervals on the IK Scale	N	r	p
15-23 (Least Knowledge)	56	.46	.001
11-14 (Moderate Knowledge)	45	.30	.05
2-10 (Most Knowledge)	59	.43	.001

interesting prospects open up for later empirical research on more heterogeneous samples of subjects based upon a more adequate method for registering international knowledge.

C. Summary and Conclusion

The intention of our investigation was the clarification of the influence of various psychological factors on tendencies towards generalization and displacement of aggression. We have previously shown that both these psychological mechanisms seem to have a certain validity as regards the explanation of aggressive reaction patterns towards foreign affairs.

By *generalization* we refer to the fact that a person reacts similarly to everyday and international situations, in other words, that a person's preference with regard to his nation's ways of reacting in international conflict situations are connected with his own reaction patterns in everyday conflict situations. The greater the correlation present in this area, the greater the generalization.

For the registration of ways of reacting to everyday and international situations we made use of two parallel attitude scales, the ER and IR scales. In the present investigation we concentrated entirely on the generalization of aggressive ways of reacting, that is, on the E categories of these two scales.

By *displacement* we refer to the fact that reaction tendencies which are repressed in relation to certain objects or situations find an outlet towards other objects or in other situations. In the present thesis we have concentrated exclusively on displacement of latent reaction tendencies on to international matters. We have said that greater displacement occurs the higher the correlation between a person's way of reacting to international conflict situations and his latent tendencies. In this chapter we have dealt with displacement of aggression only. To register the latter factor we made use of a shortened version of Blum's Blacky Pictures, and presumed that the frequency of

conflicts in connection with basic psychosexual impulse patterns gives an approximate measure of the degree of latent aggression present.

As well as investigating how far latent aggression (or psychodynamic conflicts) influence tendencies towards generalization of aggression, and how far aggressive ways of reacting in everyday situations influence tendencies towards displacement of aggression, we concentrated on the influence of nationalism in the sense of patriotism and international knowledge respectively. For registering these last two factors we made use of two scales called the NP and IK scales.

The results of our investigation give support to the following statements:

A certain degree of nationalism (patriotism) is generally a necessary precondition for the displacement of aggression towards foreign affairs. In spite of the fact that our data do not give any conclusive evidence, on the whole there seems to be a closer connection between latent aggression and aggressive attitudes towards foreign affairs the more a person identifies himself with his own nation. Nationalism therefore seems to represent a mediating factor of importance for the degree to which latent personality layers are likely to colour a person's international attitudes.

There is no direct (linear) connection between aggressive ways of reacting in everyday situations and tendencies towards the displacements of aggression. Our data give no basis for concluding that tendencies towards aggressive ways of reacting to everyday situations represent a mediating factor of importance for the degree to which latent personality layers are likely to colour a person's attitudes towards foreign affairs; they nevertheless indicate hypothetically that extremely strong as well as extremely weak tendencies towards everyday aggression are associated with less pronounced displacement than moderate everyday aggression.

There is no direct (linear) connection between international knowledge and tendencies towards the displacement of latent aggression. Due to the inadequacy of our research instrument this statement must be considered with great cautiousness. As a hypothesis for later studies we may propose that displacement of aggression increases with increased knowledge up to a certain point, after which it decreases or remains approximately constant.

There exists an inverse connection between latent aggression (psychodynamic conflicts) and generalization of everyday aggressive reaction patterns. Our data indicate that there is a closer connection between aggressive ways of reacting to everyday and international conflict situations the more basic psychosexual impulse patterns are conflict-free and assimilated. Latent aggression seems to represent a mediating factor of importance for the degree to which everyday reaction patterns are likely to colour a person's attitudes towards foreign affairs.

A direct connection exists between nationalism (patriotism) and generalization of everyday aggressive reaction patterns. Our data indicate that there is a closer connection between aggressive reaction patterns towards everyday and international conflict situations the more a person is characterized by patriotic attitudes.

Nationalism in the sense of patriotism therefore seems to represent a mediating factor of importance for the degree to which everyday aggression is likely to colour a person's attitudes towards foreign affairs.

No direct (linear) connection exists between international knowledge and generalization of everyday aggressive reaction patterns. Here too we wish to stress the shortcomings of our measurement of international knowledge. As a hypothesis for further investigations we wish to point to the possibility that extremely great as well as extremely little international knowledge may be associated with greater generalization than moderate international knowledge.

We can summarize the above conclusions by stressing that the following three factors at least should be considered in attempting a psychological explanation of aggressive reaction patterns towards foreign affairs: 1) tendencies towards everyday aggressive ways of reacting, 2) scope of latent aggression or degree of psychodynamic conflicts; and 3) degree of nationalism or patriotism.

References

BLUM, G. S. A study of the psychoanalytic theory of psycho-sexual development. *Genet. Psychol. Monogr.*, 1949, 3, 3-99.

BLUM, G. S. *The Blacky Pictures: a technique for the exploration of personality dynamics.* New York: Psychological Corp., 1950.

DURBIN, E. F. M., and BOWLBY, J. *Personal aggressiveness and war.* New York: Columbia Univer. Press, 1939.

INDEX

A

Abstract conceptions, 11
Abstract variables, 14
Acceptance, social, desire for, 101-104,
    121, 123-125, 138-139, 212-213
Acceptance-rejection, of induced forces,
    82, 457, 458
  of stands, 186-196
Achievement motivation, development
    of, 294-308
  social status and, 28-30, 58-64, 239-240,
    359-360
Acquisitive mobs, 611
Action beliefs, 98, 99
Adams, H. F., 471
Adaptive acculturation, socialization
    and, 62
Adorno, T. W., 83, 94, 123, 128, 226, 230
Advice-givers, 199, 200
Adviser-advisee dyad, 200-202
Affective associations, 100
Affective elements of attitudes, 23, 98-
    100, 130, 132, 133, 139, 149-156
Affiliation, need for, 29, 30, 124, 214

Aggression, 157, 158, 170, 171
  authoritarian, 674
  cohesiveness, effect of on, 449
  in conflict situations, everyday, 615,
    708, 711
    intergroup, control of, 689
    international, 615, 706-716
  displacement of, 614, 706-707, 709-712,
    715
    in relation to everyday aggression,
    711
    in relation to international knowl-
    edge, 712
    in relation to nationalism, 710
  generalization of, 707, 709-710, 715
    in relation to international knowl-
    edge, 714-715
    in relation to latent aggression, 712-
    713
    in relation to nationalism, 713-714
  latent, 615, 706-709, 712-713
  in resistance to change, 449, 452, 453,
    457, 459
Aggressive mobs, 611
Alexander, F., 158, 174

Allport, G. W., 4, 5, 9-10, 23-24, 57, 97,
109, 206, 208, 436, 613, 618, 656
Alper, T. G., 39, 47, 702
Ambiguity, rumor spreading and, 48
American Soldier, The, 211, 212
Americans, stereotyped conceptions of,
269-272
Anchor effect, 187
Anderson, H. E., 351, 356, 358, 364
Aneshansel, J., 11, 24, 39
Anthony, A., 238, 283
Anthropology, 4, 5, 9, 28, 233-234, 244,
253, 423
Antidemocratic trends, 670-671, 674, 679
Anti-intraception, 674-675
Anti-Semitism, 614, 671-673, 686-687
See also Jews
Anti-Semitism scale, 41
Anxiety, 29, 30
arousal of, 157-174
As, D., 460
Applied research, 608-609
Approval, social, desire for, 101-104, 121,
123-125, 138-139, 212-213
in stimulus persons, evaluation of, 71-
84
Arapesh, 234
Argumentation, 106-107, 125, 167-170,
172-174, 183
Army, Negroes in, attitudes toward, 680-
685
Asch, S. E., 3, 7, 17, 26, 31, 65-67, 70, 122-
123, 128, 175, 185, 379, 391, 393,
402, 404-405, 411, 610
Ashanti, male initiation ceremonies of,
289, 290
Aspirations, 471, 695
Assimilation, 24, 54-56
Assimilation-contrast effects, 186-195
Assumptions, 11, 15
Atkinson, J. W., 29, 31, 59-60, 64, 71, 81,
298, 308
Attitude change, 8, 14, 97, 100, 104-109

Bennington College study on, 100, 103,
215-225
cognitive structure and, 123, 149-156
compliance process in, 26, 81-83, 88-93,
109, 141-148, 610
identification process in, 109, 142-148
influences on, communication (*see*
Communication)
fear, 98, 108, 157-174
membership groups, 102-104, 210,
225-230, 377
needs, 83, 102, 104, 107, 121-123,
125, 379, 380, 613
See also Needs
norms (*see* Group norms)
reference groups (*see* Reference
groups)
reward and punishment, 101, 104-
109, 121-125, 141, 212-213, 609-
610
role occupancy, 485-494
social status, 26, 614
value systems, 100, 105, 108, 109,
124, 125, 142
values, 100-102, 104, 105, 108, 135-
137, 142
See also Values
internalization process in, 109, 142-
148, 231, 239, 575, 611, 690
levels of, 141
motivating patterns in, 104-105, 108-
109, 121-129
adaption of procedures to, 124-129
direct interpretation, 126
permissive catharsis, 108, 125-126
rational approach in, 124, 125
rational persuasion, 108-109, 124-
128
ego defense, 104-105, 108-109, 122-
123
reward and punishment, 121-125
search for meaning, 121-123
nature of, 140-141

Attitude change (*continued*)
 opposite-direction, 105, 106, 186-187, 192-195
 predictions of, 123-125, 140-142, 145-146, 335
 resistance to, 123, 125, 158, 170, 172, 174
 theoretical analysis of, 141-143
Attitudes, 97-109
 adaptive significance of, 97
 affective elements of, 23, 98-100, 130, 132, 133, 139, 149-156
 aggressive (*see* Aggression)
 and behavior, relationship between, 100, 101, 125-126, 141-143
  See also Behavior
 behavioral components of, 23, 98, 99
 and beliefs, structural relationship between, 99, 149, 155
  See also Beliefs
 clustering of, 100-101
 cognitive components of, 23, 98, 99, 130, 132, 133, 139
 toward Communism, 104, 133, 138, 150-156
 consistency and differentiation in, balance between, 138
 differences in, determination of, 28
 ego-defensive, 104-105, 108-109, 122-123
 ego-involved, 107, 186-196
 evaluative character of, 98
 functional bases of, 104, 105, 135
 hierarchical organization of, 131, 136
 induced, 141-148
 influence of, on behavior (*see* Behavior)
  on beliefs (*see* Beliefs)
  on learning, 24, 39-47
  on motivation (*see* Motivation)
  on recall, 44
 informational context of, 132-133, 136-137
 intellectualized, 100

international, 99, 129-141, 615, 706-716
interrelatedness of, 100-101, 105, 210
toward Jews (*see* Jews)
negative, 99, 100, 105, 108, 186, 613, 615, 617
toward Negroes (*see* Negro children; Negroes)
objects of, response to, 23, 98-100, 130, 132, 133, 139, 149-156
and opinions, structural relationship between, 98-99
 See also Opinions
political (*see* Political attitudes)
positive, 99, 100, 105, 108
toward prohibition, 107, 186-196
referents of, distortion of, 123
religious, 97, 98, 100, 690
toward Russia, 99, 129-139
toward sex, 97, 674, 678
socio-economic, 332, 335, 338-340, 351, 385
value-expressive, 104, 108
 See also Attitude change
Attitudinal learning, 149, 155-156
Attitudinal polarization, 347-348
Attributes, social, 25, 26
Australian tribes, child-rearing practices among, 290-291
Authoritarian aggression, 674
Authoritarian character structure, F scale of, 126, 127
Authoritarian leadership, 388-389, 523-537
Authoritarian personality, 24, 105, 670-679
Authoritarian submission, 674, 708
Authoritarian suggestion, rational persuasion and, 126-127
Authoritarianism, 24, 226-229
 measurement of, 83, 92, 126-127
Autistic hostility, 559
Autism, 39-40, 45, 57
 socially shared, 649

Autokinetic effect, 462-470
Autonomy, 239, 274, 280-282, 590

B

Baby and Child Care, 356
Back, K., 380-381, 411, 423, 458, 460, 471
Bailey, J. C., 388, 391
Balance theories, 30-31
Baldwin, A. L., 364
Bales, R. F., 10, 17, 386, 391
Ballachey, E. L., 3, 6, 7, 17, 386, 391
Barlow, M. F., 128
Barnard, C. I., 576
Bartlett, F. C., 22, 32, 43, 57, 58
Bass, B. M., 538, 539, 550
Bavelas, A., 338, 391, 427-429, 434, 436,
        444, 446, 557, 579
Bayley, N., 351, 364
Behavior, 4-17
    aggressive (*see* Aggression)
    and attitudes, relationship between,
        100, 101, 125-126, 141-143
        See also Attitude change; Attitudes
    cognitive, language as determinant of,
        236-237, 244-265
    communication patterns, effects of on,
        390, 577-592
    competitive, 621
    contradictions in, self-awareness of,
        383-384
    cooperative, breakdown in, 612-613,
        620-628
    culture as determinant of, 234
    established, change of, group decision
        method in, 381-382, 423-444, 446
        resistance to, 382, 602-604
            overcoming of, 444-460
    mob (*see* Mobs)
    motivational (*see* Motivation)
    nonadaptive, 612-613, 620-628
    perception, effect of on, 71

See also Perception
    predictions of, 29, 42-46, 100, 101, 237,
        252
    in role conflict, 501-505
    role, 382
    self-oriented need, 390-391
    study of, empirical method in (*see*
        Research)
    voting (*see* Political attitudes)
Behavioral components, of attitudes, 23,
        98, 99
    of perception, 21-27
Belgium, experimental test of contin-
        gency model in, 546-549
Beliefs, 23, 98-101, 105
    acquisition of, influences on, 124
    action, 98, 99
    and attitudes, structural relationship
        between, 99, 149, 155
        See also Attitude change; Attitudes
    change of, 140
    contradictions in, self-awareness of,
        383-384
    internalization of, 239
    negative, 99, 615-616
    about objects, 149, 155
    policy orientation and, 132-134, 138
    religious, 98, 100, 133
    validity of, establishment of, 378
Bender Gestalt test, 127
Benedek, T., 293
Benedict, R., 360, 364
Benne, K. D., 576
Bennett, E. B., 444
Bennington College study on attitude
        change, 100, 103, 215-225
Bentham, Jeremy, 4, 234
Berelson, B., 102, 110, 197-199, 201, 203,
        204, 207-209
Berkeley Growth Study, 351, 362
Bettelheim, B., 99, 109, 293, 609, 611, 614,
        628, 685
Bicultural experiences, 261, 263, 264
Bilingualism, 237, 259-265

Biological drives, 28, 235, 285
Bird, C., 385, 391
Birney, R. C., 16, 17
Black, A. H., 257, 258
Black, K., 208-209
Blacky test, 708-709
Blake, R. R., 616, 702, 703, 706
Blau, P. M., 208
Blum, G. S., 708, 716
Boas, F., 32, 39, 252
Boek, W. E., 356, 364
Bogardus, E. S., 266, 267, 696, 701
Bogardus social distance scale, 127, 266, 696
Bogey rumors, 48, 49
    See also Rumors
"Boomerang effect," 186, 187
Bovard, E. W., 402, 411
Bovet, M., 273, 276, 277
Bowers, R. V., 366, 372
Bowlby, J., 710, 716
Braatoy, T., 366, 372
Brainwashing techniques, 108, 609-611, 638-645
Braly, K. W., 65, 70, 99, 237, 266
Breese, F. H., 364
Bronfenbrenner, U., 240, 349, 364
Brophy, I. N., 656
Brown, R. W., 63, 64, 236, 237, 244-249, 253, 257, 258, 611, 612, 618
Browne, C. G., 538, 550
Bruner, J. S., 71, 81
Buckingham, B. R., 258

C

Cagaba, male initiation ceremonies of, 290
California ethnocentric scale, 41
California F-scale, 83, 85, 92, 128
Campbell, A., 106, 109, 349, 614, 618
Cantril, H., 326, 339, 612, 618

"Captive" audience, 170, 184
Carlson, E. R., 108, 109, 125, 128, 153, 156
Carroll, J. B., 236, 243
Cartwright, D., 9, 17, 149, 156, 380, 381, 390, 391 .
Casagrande, J. B., 236, 243
Caste line, 318
Categorizing, 237, 250-252, 254, 255
Catharsis, permissive, 108, 125-126, 436
Cathexis, negative, 555-556
    positive, 554-556, 559
Cattell, R. B., 10, 17, 386, 391
Causality, direction of, interpretation of, difficulties in, 14-15
    locus of, 88-90
    multi-, 5
    perception of, determinants and consequences of, 26, 81-94
Cause and effect relationships, perception of, 25
Centers, R., 12, 59, 63, 64, 242-243, 339, 345, 349
Centrality, 577, 580, 587-592
Change, attitude (see Attitude change)
    of established practices, group decision method in, 381-382, 423-444, 446
    resistance to, 382, 602-604
        overcoming of, 444-460
    in roles, effects of on attitudes of role occupants, 485-494
Channelization hypothesis, 706-707
Chave, E. J., 416, 423
Chein, I., 109, 617
Cheyenne, sexual taboos among, 287
Child development, maturational, 238
    moral, 239
        social factors in, 273-282
Child-rearing practices, 237-240
    achievement motivation, development of, 294-308
    discipline, techniques of, 360-362, 615
    feeding, 350, 354-356, 358
        breast, 354-356, 358

Child-rearing practices (*continued*)
  freedom of movement, permissiveness in, 350, 356-360, 364
  independence-mastery training, 28, 240, 294-308, 359-360
  physical punishment, application of, 360
  among primitive tribes, 283-293
  social status and, 28-30, 58-64, 239-240, 349-365
  toilet training, 350, 354-356, 358
  weaning, 350, 354-356
Children's camps, integration in, 618, 657-669
Chinese Communists, brainwashing techniques employed by, 108, 609-611, 638-645
Chinese people, accommodation of, questionnaire on, 101
  stereotyped conceptions of, 268, 270-272
Christiansen, B., 615, 706
Circumcision school, primitive, 283-284
Civil Conservation Corps, 293
Clark, K. B., 39, 47, 238-239, 308, 312, 317
Clark, M. P., 238-239, 308, 312, 317
Clark, R. A., 29, 31, 59-60, 64, 298, 308
Class affiliation, 331-332, 335, 341, 344
Class awareness, 345, 348
Class consciousness, 242, 328-329, 333, 339, 340, 344-345
Class identification, 242, 326, 328-335, 340-341, 343-344
Class structure, 240-243, 318-339
  interest-group theory of, 328, 331-332, 337-339
  politico-economic orientations in, 326-328, 331-335, 337, 339, 342-344
  psychological analysis of, 326-339
  socio-economic factors in, 332, 335, 338-340, 351
  See also Social status
Clausen, J. A., 363-365

Cleven, W. A., 539, 550
Coch, L., 12, 382, 444
Codability of colors, 236, 248-250
Cognition, 21-23
  See also Perception
Cognitive behavior, language as determinant of, 236-237, 244-265
Cognitive components of attitudes, 23, 98, 99, 130, 132, 133, 139
Cognitive conflict, 379, 380
Cognitive consistency, need for, 30
Cognitive distortions, 23-24
Cognitive object, 123, 124
Cognitive structure, 22-23, 25, 30, 124, 239, 244-245, 250
  and attitudinal affect, 149-156
Cognitive styles, 24
Cohesiveness (*see* Group cohesiveness)
Cohn, T. S., 538, 550
Coleman, A. L., 209
Coleman, J. S., 209
Collins, M. E., 12, 617-618, 646
Colors, codability of, 236, 248-250
Columbia University, 197, 463-464
"Common-enemy" approach, 699
Communication, decision-making influences from, 102, 196-209
  effectiveness of, source credibility as factor in, 8, 106, 175-185
  emotional interference in, 157-158, 170-172
  fear-arousing, effects of, 108, 157-174
  group, competition and cooperation, effects of on, 557-559, 569-571
  instrumental, 81-82
  mass media, 8, 102, 104, 106, 206-207, 238
  one-sided, 106
  and opinion change, time interval between, 14, 175, 181-185
  patterns in, effects of on group behavior, 390, 577-592
  perception of, differences in, 178-180
  persuasive, 106, 107, 157-174, 186

Communication (*continued*)
reactions to, assimilation and contrast effects in, 186-195
"sleeper effect" in, 175, 181-185
two-sided, 106-107, 125, 167-170, 172-174, 183
two-step flow hypothesis of, 102, 196-209
Communicator power, 142-148
Communism, attitudes toward, 104, 133, 138, 150-156
Communists, Chinese, brainwashing techniques employed by, 108, 609-611, 638-645
Community, social structure of, 367
Competition, economic, 615-616
effects of on group process, 552-576
intergroup, 615-617, 695, 697
loyalty of representatives during, 702-706
and resistance to change, 458
Competitive behavior, 621
Compliance, 26, 81-83, 109, 141-148, 610
causal locus for, 88-93
Concentrated leadership, 388
Concentration camps, Chinese Communist, 108, 609-611, 638-645
Nazi, 609-611, 628-637
Conceptions, 11, 26
self, 30, 239
stereotyped, of ethnic groups, 55, 122, 237, 252, 266-272, 616-617, 663, 671-673, 692-693, 696
Condemnation, moralistic, 678
Conflict(s), aggression in (*see* Aggression)
cognitive, 379, 380
intergroup, 5-6, 8, 98, 125, 614-617
aggression in, control of, 689
reduction of, superordinate goals in, 615-616, 694-701
See also Racial prejudice
psychodynamic, 706-709, 712-713, 715
role, 8, 9, 384

in disaster situations, 384, 505-510
latent, 384, 506
resolution of, 384, 494-505
Conflicting expectations, 495, 498, 499
Conservative-radical orientations, 326-328, 331-335, 342, 343
Conservatism, political, 674
Contingency model, 538-551
Contradictory expectations, 495, 497, 503
Contrast and assimilation effects, 186-195
Contravaluant material, learning and utilization of, 24, 39-47
Control population, 12, 369
Controls, tolerance, 689-692
Conventional values, 674
Converse, P. E., 242-243, 339, 349
Cook, S. W., 5, 17
Cooley, C. H., 505, 510
Coons, A. E., 539, 551
Cooperation, effects of on group process, 572-576
intergroup, 615, 616, 618, 694-701
and resistance to change, 449, 452
Cooperative behavior, breakdown in, 612-613, 620-628
See also Mobs
Counterarguments, 41-45
Counterpropaganda, 106-107, 167-170, 172-174
Crises, mob reactions in, 611-613, 620-623, 627
role conflict in, 384, 505-510
Cronbach, L. J., 539, 550
Crosby, C., 237, 259
Cross-pressures, 384, 506
Crutchfield, R. S., 3, 5-7, 17, 70, 386, 391
Cultural causation, 124
Cultural comparison, 249
Cultural relativism, 124, 235, 244-245
Culture, 22
as behavior determinant, 234
implicit, 234
influence of, 233-235

Culture (*continued*)
  inner, 233-234
Culture transmission, 251

D

Darwinian theory, 28
Data collection, 12-16
  See also Research
Davie, M. R., 367, 372
Davis, A., 12, 58, 62-64, 240, 241, 243, 318, 350, 351, 363, 365
Decatur study on decision-making influences, 197, 200-203, 205-207
DeCharms, R., 365
Decision, group, social change and, 381-382, 423-444, 446
Decision-making, influences on, 102, 196-209
Defensive-avoidance hypothesis, 171-173
Democratic leadership, 388-389, 523-538
Dental hygiene, communication on, fear appeal in, 158-174
Depressions, status polarization and, 346
Desires (*see* Needs)
Determinants, interaction of, 5
Detroit, race riots in, 611-612, 615
Deutsch, H., 293
Deutsch, M., 5, 12, 17, 379-381, 391, 402 411, 552, 617-618, 646
Deutschberger, P., 513, 518
DeVinney, L. C., 494
Dewey, John, 281
Dickson, W. J., 601-603
Direct interpretation, 126
Disaster situations, mob reactions in, 611-613, 620-623, 627
  role conflict in, 384, 505-510
Discipline, child, 360-362, 615
Dislikes (*see* Prejudice)
Displaced hostility, 126, 613
Displacement of aggression, 614, 706-707, 709-712, 715

in relation to everyday aggression, 711
in relation to international knowledge, 712
in relation to nationalism, 710
Distances, sum of, 579
Distortion, of attitude referent, 123
  cognitive, 23-24
  facilitative, 71, 79-80
  fear, influence of on, 23, 24
  of judgments, group influence and, 378-380, 393-401
  needs, influence of on, 23, 24
  of perception, 23-24, 397
    determinants of, 71-81
  in rumors (*see* Rumors)
DiVesta, F. J., 156
Doctors, influences among, 197, 202-208
Dolch, E. W., 258
Dollard, J., 158, 171-172, 174, 293, 363, 365
Domestic-policy positions, status polarization and, 348
Doob, L. W., 44, 47
Douvan, E., 28, 29, 58, 64, 239
Draft-evasion charges against Jews, 48, 49, 52
Drug addiction, 607
Drug diffusion, influences on, 197, 202-208
Drug research, placebo, use of in, 15
Duke University, 40
Dunham, H. W., 366, 372
Durbin, E. F. M., 710, 716
Durkheim, E., 273-277, 281
Duvall, E. M., 58, 64, 362, 365

E

Ebbinghaus curve, 52
Ecology, 366
Economic competition, 615-616
Economic poverty, 607
Edwards, A. L., 39, 47, 265

Ego control, 690
Egocentrism, 239, 279-282
Ego-defensive attitudes, 104-105, 108-109, 122-123
Ego-enhancement, motives of, 45
Ego-involving issues, attitudes toward, 107, 186-196
Eisenstadt, S. N., 208
Ellertson, N., 459-460
Elmira study on voting-decision influences, 197-199, 201, 203, 204, 206
Embedding process, 56-58
Emotional expansiveness, 513
Emotional facilitation, 621, 623, 627
Emotional interference in communication, 157-158, 170-172
Emotional repertoire, 513
English people, stereotyped conceptions of, 269-272
Environment, geographical, language acquisition and, 261, 263, 264
social (*see* Social environment)
Epidemiology, 366
Epstein, I., 265
Ericson, M. C., 58, 64
Ervin, S. M., 260, 261, 265
Escape mobs, 611, 612
Eskimo language, 236, 247, 248, 250
Established behavior, change of, group-decision method in, 381-382, 423-444, 446
resistance to, 382, 602-604
overcoming of, 444-460
Ethical hedonism, 234
Ethnic groups, stereotyped conceptions of, 55, 122, 237, 252, 266-272, 616-617, 663, 671-673, 692-693, 696
Ethnic intolerance, 614, 685-693
Ethnic labels, 65, 237
Ethnic origin, differentiating factors of, 367
Ethnic prejudice (*see* Racial prejudice)

Ethnocentrism, 244, 615, 673-679, 696
Everyday conflict situations, aggression in, 615, 708, 711
Expansiveness, positive, 513-514
Expectations, conflicting, 495, 498, 499
contradictory, 495, 497, 503
illegitimate, 495
incompatible, 494-498
legitimate, 495, 496
orientation to, expedient, 500-501, 503-504
moral, 500, 503-504
moral-expedient, 501-504
perceived, 494-499
about war, 132, 133
Experimental learning theory, 27, 30-31
Expressive mobs, 611
Extrapunitive reaction, 137
Extremism, political, 607

F

Facilitation, emotional, 621, 623, 627
Facilitative distortion, 71, 79-80
Factual information, source credibility and, 8, 106, 175-185
Family-directed hostility, 675
Faris, R. E. L., 366, 372
Farnsworth-Munsell 100 hue test, 246, 248-249
Fashion decisions, influences on, 197, 201-202, 205, 207
Fear, appeal to, 108, 157-174
influence of, on attitudes, 98, 108, 157-174
on distortion, 23, 24
on motivation, 27
Fear rumors, 48
See also Rumors
Feldstein, M. J., 66, 71, 512-513, 519
Felix, R. H., 366, 372
Fenichel, O., 158, 174

Ferrière, Ad., 282
Feshbach, S., 108, 157
Festinger, L., 30, 31, 81, 94, 140, 148, 208-209, 378-381, 391, 402, 411, 423, 437, 444, 460, 471
Fiedler, F. E., 389, 538-541, 544, 545, 550
Field investigations, 10-16
    See also Research
Fine, B. J., 190, 196
First impressions, warm-cold variables in, 26-27, 65-70
Fisher, S., 187, 196
Fisher-Yates test, 257
Foerster, F. W., 282
Food habits, efforts to change, 381, 423-438
Force, induced, acceptance-rejection of, 82, 457, 458
Foreign affairs, attitudes toward, 99, 129-141, 615, 706-716
Foreign policy, status polarization and, 346-348
Fouriezos, N. T., 390, 391
French, J. R. P., Jr., 12, 148, 187, 195, 382, 444, 447, 460, 540, 550
French, T. M., 158, 174
French language, 245, 248
    bilingualism and, 259-265
Frenkel-Brunswik, E., 71, 81, 83, 94, 123, 126, 128, 226, 230, 614-615, 670, 671, 679
Freud, S., 293, 621, 627
Friedman, E., 383, 391
Friedman, G. A., 294, 307-308
Friedson, E., 209
Friendly-authority situation, 73-74
Friendly-hostile situation, 13, 73
Friendly-neutral situation, 73
Fries, C. C., 253, 258
Fritz, C. E., 612, 618
Fromm, E., 627
Frustration, 5-6, 108, 137, 445, 447-450, 459, 613, 614, 689, 695, 696
Functional leadership, 386, 388-389

G

Ganda, child-rearing practices of, 289
Gangs, street-corner, 377, 696
    leadership in, 387, 519-523
Gardner, B. B., 12, 241, 318, 365
Gardner, M. R., 12, 241, 318, 365
Gardner, R., 260, 263, 265
Gaudet, H., 102, 110, 197-199, 204, 209
General psychology, 6-9, 16, 29
Generalization of aggression, 707, 709-710, 715
    in relation to international knowledge, 714-715
    in relation to latent aggression, 712-713
    in relation to nationalism, 713-714
Geographical environment, language acquisition and, 261, 263, 264
Gerard, D. L., 366, 372
Gerard, H. B., 379-381, 402
German language, 245
Germans, hostility toward, 49
    stereotyped conceptions of, 268-272
Gestalt, 54, 55
Gestalt school, perceptual model of, 121
Gestapo, 628-637
Ghettos, Negro, 647
Gibb, C. A., 538, 550
Gibbs, P. K., 240, 243, 350, 365
Gilbert, E., 101, 110
Gilchrist, J. C., 81, 94
Gleser, G., 539, 550
Glock, C. Y., 209
Glueck, E., 293
Glueck, S., 293
Godfrey, E. P., 539-540, 545, 550
Goldberg, S. C., 187, 195
Goodman, C. C., 71, 81
Gough, H. G., 226, 230, 614, 618
Grabbe, P., 429, 435-437, 653
Gregory, D., 458-460
Grievances, worker, 444, 445, 452, 457
Gross, N., 206, 209, 384, 494

Group cohesiveness, 8, 81, 344, 380-381, 411-423
  disappearance of, panics as result of, 621
  and group norms, relationship between, 478-480, 484
  resistance to change and, 449, 458-459
  in street-corner gangs, 519
Group contexts, 30, 385
Group-decision method in social change, 381-382, 423-444, 446
Group goals, 8
  achievement of, 104, 378, 380, 385-387, 389, 390
  contriently interdependent, 553
  promotively interdependent, 552-553
  reference groups and, 213
  superordinate, 615-616, 694-701, 705, 709
Group identification, 102-106, 695
Group influence, 101-106
  cohesiveness and, 411-423
  comparison, 103, 104
  on distortion of judgments, effects of, 378-380, 393-401
  leadership (*see* Leadership)
  normative and informational, 103-104, 379-381
    on individual judgment, 402-411
Group norms, 9, 101, 377, 378
  attitude change and, 101-104, 121, 124-125, 138-139, 212-214, 225-230, 378-381
  and cohesiveness, relationship between, 478-480, 484
  emergence of, reasons for, 378, 461-470
  in housing projects, operation and nature of, 472-485
  importance of, variations in, 378, 380-381
  internalization of, 239, 696
  for production, 449-450, 456-458
  social habits and, 434-435

Group prestige, 380, 413-415, 421-422
Group process, effects of cooperation and competition on, 552-576
  communication, 557-559, 569-571
  interpersonal relations, 559-560, 573-576
  motivation, 557, 569
  organization, 556-557, 567-568
  orientation, 558, 571
  productivity, 558-559, 571-573
Group representatives, loyalty of during intergroup competition, 702-706
Group standards (*see* Group norms)
Group-task situations, 389, 538-550
Groups, characteristics of, 377
  formal, 378, 386-387
  formation of, 377, 389, 698
  informal, 378, 383, 387-388
  maintenance of, 377, 385-389
    See also Leadership
  membership, 102-104, 210, 225-230, 377
  positions in, 382-384, 389-390
  reference (*see* Reference groups)
  structural aspects of, 377, 389-390
Guetzkow, H., 390, 391
Guilt feelings, 125, 157
Gunther, J., 699, 701
Gurin, G., 106, 109

H

Hall, D. M., 539-540, 545, 550
Halo effect, 67
Halpin, A. W., 386-387, 389, 391
Handel, L. A., 209
Hanfmann, E., 158, 174
Harding, J., 109, 617, 618
Hare, A. P., 538, 550
Hartley, E. L., 349, 657
Hartmann, G. W., 39, 47
Harvard University, 85-93, 246, 248, 254
Harvey, O. J., 107, 186, 701

Harwood Manufacturing Company, 444-460
Havelka, J., 237, 259, 260, 263, 265
Havighurst, R. J., 240, 243, 350, 351, 365, 383, 391
Hawkins, C. A., 539, 550
Hedonism, ethical, 234
Heider, F., 25, 30, 31, 82, 94
Heintz, R., 187, 195
Heteronomy, 239, 274, 280, 281
Hildum, D. C., 257, 258
Hiller, E. T., 696, 701
Hilliard, A. E., 149, 156
Hinkle, L. E., 644, 645
Hobbs, Thomas, 4, 234
Hoijer, H., 253, 258
Hollingshead, A. B., 12, 63, 64, 242, 366, 367, 370, 372
Homans, G. C., 13, 81, 94, 293, 382, 592
Homosexuality, 675
  latent, 679
Hood, W. R., 695, 701
Hopi, child-rearing practices of, 289-291
Hopi language, 235-236, 247
Horn, E., 254, 258
Horowitz, A. E., 245-247, 257, 258
Horowitz, E. L., 99, 102, 111, 155, 156, 238, 613, 616, 696, 701
Hostile impulses, projection of, 105, 123, 614, 675
Hostility, autistic, 559
  displaced, 126, 613
  family-directed, 675
  intergroup, 5-6, 8, 98, 125, 614, 616, 695, 698-700
    See also Intergroup conflicts
  reactive, 171
  replaced, 126
  toward therapist, 158
Hostility rumors, 48-49, 55, 56
  See also Rumors
Housing projects, group norms in, operation and nature of, 472-485
  interracial, 617-618, 646-657

Hovland, C. I., 11, 14, 17, 98, 106, 107, 109, 174, 175, 181-187, 190-194, 196
Hughes, E. C., 505, 510
Human Relations Training Laboratory, The, 703, 706
Humphrey, N. D., 611, 615, 619
Hunger, 28, 235, 285
Hutchins, E. B., 544, 550
Hutt, M. L., 390, 391
Hyde, R. W., 366, 373
Hyman, H. H., 210-214
Hypotheses, concepts, use of in, 11
  empirical tests of, 3-4, 11-13
  revision of, 10

I

Identification process in attitude change, 109, 142-148
Ideological conversion, efforts toward, in Nazi concentration camps, 609-611, 628-637
  in Red Chinese prison camps, 108, 609-611, 638-645
Ideological trends, 670-671
Illegitimate expectations, 495
Impulses, hostile, projection of, 105, 123, 614, 675
  psychosexual, handling of, conflict in, 615, 708-709
  sexual, projection of, 105, 614, 675
  unconscious, expression of, 122
Impunitive reaction, 137
Incentive wage systems, 445-446, 487, 594, 597-602
Incest, 292
Incompatible expectations, 494-498
Independence-mastery training, 28, 240, 294-308, 359-360
Index of Social Position, 367-369
Induced attitudes, 141-148
Induced conceptions, 11

Induced force, 82, 457, 458
Inducibility, negative, 555-556
  positive, 554-558
Influence(s), acceptance of, 141-148
  from communication (*see* Communi-
      cation)
  on decision-making, 102, 196-209
  determinants of, 142
  group (*see* Group influence)
  personal, impact of, 197-199, 203-204
  social, 103-104, 379-381
    on individual judgment, 402-411
Influential-influencee dyads, 208
Information, factual, source credibility
      and, 8, 106, 175-185
Inhibition, proactive, 449, 456
  retroactive, 259-260, 262
Initiation ceremonies, male, among prim-
      itive tribes, 283-293
Instinct theory, 28, 235
Instrumentality, perceived, 150-156
Integration, in armed forces, 680-685
  in children's camps, 618, 657-669
  friendship preferences and, 665-666
  influence agents in, 668-669
  interpersonal perceptions in, 663-665
  interpersonal relations in, 660-661
  power relationships in, 663
  race- and sex-linked patterns in, 666-
      667
  residential, 617-618, 646-657
  school, 12, 40-47, 107, 143-148
Intellectualized attitudes, 100
Interest-group theory of class structure,
      328, 331-332, 337-339
Interests, 23
  influence of on rumors, 24
Intergroup competition, 615-617, 695, 697
  loyalty of representatives during, 702-
      706
Intergroup conflicts, 5-6, 8, 98, 125, 614-
      617
  aggression in, control of, 689
    See also Aggression

reduction of, superordinate goals in,
      615-616, 694-701
  See also Racial prejudice
Intergroup cooperation, 615, 616, 618,
      694-701
Intergroup hostility, 5-6, 8, 98, 125, 614,
      616, 695, 698-700
  See also Intergroup conflicts
Internalization process in attitude
      change, 109, 142-148, 231, 239,
      575, 611, 690
International attitudes, 99, 129-141, 615,
      706-716
International Kindergarten Union, 254,
      258
International knowledge, 707, 709
  displacement of aggression in relation
      to, 712
  generalization of aggression in relation
      to, 714-715
Interracial housing projects, 617-618,
      646-657
Intolerance, ethnic, 614, 685-693
Intrapunitive reaction, 137
"Invasion from Mars" broadcast, 612
Irish people, stereotyped conceptions of,
      268-272
Israel, J., 460
Israel, Patrick, 638
Italians, stereotyped conceptions of,
      268-272

J

Jahoda, M., 5, 17, 148
James, William, 505, 510
Janis, I. L., 98, 106-110, 157, 169-170,
      174, 190, 196
Janowitz, M., 99, 109, 209, 614, 685
Japanese, hostility toward, 49
  stereotyped conceptions of, 55, 268,
      270, 271

Jennings, H. H., 387, 511, 512, 514, 518, 519

Jews, attitudes toward, 41, 614, 649, 671-673, 686-687

   intolerance studies on, 614, 685-693

   draft-evasion charges against, 48, 49, 52

   stereotyped conceptions of, 268, 270-272, 671-673, 692-693

Jonckheere, A. R., 228-230

Jones, E. E., 11, 24, 39, 94

Judgment(s), distortion of, effects of group influence on, 378-380, 393-401

   of lifted weights, 187

   normative and informational social influences on, 402-411

Julian, J. W., 539, 550

Junod, H. A., 36, 39, 293

Justice, children's ideas of, 278-282

Juvenile delinquency, 293

Kluckhohn, C., 233, 243, 252

Kluckhohn, R., 238, 283

Knapp, R. H., 48, 58

Knower, F. H., 186, 196

Knowledge, international, 707, 709

   displacement of aggression in relation to, 712

   generalization of aggression in relation to, 714-715

Koffka, K., 576

Kohn, M. L., 351, 362, 365

Komarovsky, M., 383, 391

Korchin, S. J., 39, 47

Kornhauser, A. W., 326, 339

Kramer, B. M., 656

Krech, D., 3, 5-7, 17, 70, 386, 391

Kutner, B., 101, 109, 110, 617, 618

Kwakiutl, 234

   male initiation ceremony of, 290

Kwoma, child-rearing practices of, 285-287, 292

K

Kahn, R. L., 388, 391

Kalhorn, J., 364

Kant, Immanuel, 273, 276

Katz, D., 65, 70, 99-109, 121, 237, 266, 388, 391

Katz, E., 196, 197, 201-203, 206, 207, 209

Kelley, H. H., 26-27, 65, 70, 81, 94, 98, 103, 106, 107, 109, 190, 196, 210, 458, 460

Kelman, H. C., 109, 140, 148, 610

Kennedy, J. R., 367, 372

Khalapur, male initiation ceremonies of, 289

Killian, L. M., 384, 505, 612, 619

Kingsley, L. V., 366, 373

Kitt, A. S., 210, 211, 214

Klatskin, E. H., 350, 365

Klisurich, D., 429-431, 437, 444

L

Labels, ethnic, 65, 237

   rumor, 53

   stimulus-person, 65, 69

Laboratory investigations, 6, 11-16

   natural experiment, 12-13

   See also Research

Laird, D. A., 39, 47

Laissez-faire conservatism, 674

Laissez-faire leadership, 388, 523-537

Lambert, W. E., 237, 259, 260, 263, 265

Language, cognitive behavior and, 236-237, 244-265

Language-acquisition contexts, bilingualism and, 237, 259-265

Language differences (*see* Linguistic differences)

Lanzetta, J. T., 388, 391

LaPiere, R. T., 101, 110, 117, 121

Latent aggression, 615, 706-709, 712-713
Latent homosexuality, 679
Latent role conflict, 384, 506
Lawson, E. D., 364
Lazarsfeld, P. F., 102, 110, 197-199, 201, 203, 204, 206-209
Leadership, 8, 378, 382, 385-391, 511-551
  authoritarian, 388-389, 523-537
  centrality and, 589, 591-592
  concentrated, 388
  democratic, 388-389, 523-538
  effective, theory of, 385-388
    contingency model, 538-551
  in formal groups, 386-387
  functional, 386, 388-389
  in informal groups, 387-388
  laissez-faire, 388, 523-537
  opinion, 102, 196-201, 205-207, 210
  person-oriented, 389, 538
  and sociometric choice, 511-519, 524, 539-540
  in street-corner gangs, 387, 519-523
  task-oriented, 389, 538-550
Learning, attitudinal, 149, 155-156
  bilingual, language-acquisition contexts and, 237, 259-265
  of contravaluant material, 24, 39-47
  influences on, attitudes, 24, 39-47
    values, 24
  interference theory in, 259-260
  meaningful, autistic nature of, 39-40, 45
  paired-associate, 259-260
  See also Recall
Learning theory, experimental, 27, 30-31
Leavitt, H. J., 388, 390, 577
Le Bon, E., 612, 620, 623, 627
Lee, A. M., 611, 615, 619
Lee, D. D., 253, 259
Legitimate expectations, 495, 496
Leighton, D., 252
Leiter, R. A., 257, 258
Lenneberg, E. H., 236, 237, 244, 247-249, 252

Leveling process, 24, 51-52
Levin, H., 350, 365
Levine, J. M., 24, 31, 39, 47
Levinson, D. J., 83, 94, 123, 128, 226, 230, 614-615, 670, 671, 679
Lewin, K., 28, 31, 71, 81, 381, 382, 423, 429, 433-440, 443, 446, 453, 460, 471, 485, 653
Lewis, H. B., 175, 185
Lewis, O., 289, 293
Lieberman, S., 12, 384-385, 485
Lifton, R. J., 644, 645
Likert-type scale, 40, 216
Lindquist, E. F., 42, 47
Linguistic categories, 237, 250-252, 254, 255
Linguistic determinism, 253-259
Linguistic differences, 235-237, 244-252
  color codability and, 236, 248-250
  phonological, 236, 245-247
  semantic, 253-258, 260, 262, 263, 265
  vocabulary, 236, 247-250
Linguistic habits, assimilation to, 55
Linton, R., 391
Lippitt, R., 11, 388, 523
Lippman, Walter, 267
Lipset, S. M., 209
Littman, R. A., 351, 365
Lorge, I., 254, 259
Love-oriented discipline, 360-362
Lowell, E. L., 29, 31, 59-60, 64, 298, 308
Loyalty, national (see Nationalism)
  of representatives during intergroup competition, 702-706
Lubin, A., 187, 196
Luchins, A. S., 66, 70
Lumsdaine, A. A., 106-107, 109, 110, 174, 175, 181-185
Lund, F. H., 107, 110
Lunt, P. S., 241, 243, 365
Luria, Z., 261, 265
Lynd, H. M., 63, 64
Lynd, R. S., 63, 64

M

McBride, D., 458-460

McClelland, D. C., 29, 31, 59-60, 64, 71, 81, 294, 295, 298, 307-308, 365

McClintock, C., 104-106, 108, 121

Maccoby, E. E., 240, 243, 350, 365

McConnell, J. W., 367, 373

McEachern, A. W., 384, 394

McGrath, J. E., 538, 539, 550

McGuire, W. J., 107, 110

MacKenzie, B. K., 99, 110, 656

MacLeod, R. B., 22, 31

McPhee, W. N., 197, 201, 203, 204, 207, 208

Magic-pad self commitment, 406, 408-409

Maier, N. R. F., 435-437

Majority opinion, shift to, 379, 394-401

Malaita, male initiation ceremonies of, 289, 290

Male initiation ceremonies among primitive tribes, 283-293

Malinowski, B., 289, 293

Maller, J. B., 627

Management-initiated changes, resistance to, 382, 602-604
  overcoming of, 444-460

Mann, R. D., 538, 550

Mann-Whitney test, 220

Manske, A. J., 186, 196

Marketing decisions, influences on, 102, 197, 205

Marks, E. S., 612, 618

Marsh, C. P., 209

Marx, Karl, 340

Mason, W. S., 384, 394

Mass media, 8, 102, 106, 238
  opinion leaders and, 102, 206-207

Mass phenomena, 611
  See also Mobs

Massachusetts Institute of Technology, 66, 472, 560, 581

Maucorps, P. H., 518, 519

Maximum theoretical efficiency, 578-579

Mayo, E., 595

Mead, M., 293

Meeker, M., 365

Membership groups, 102-104, 210, 225-230, 377

Memory (see Recall)

Mensh, I. N., 66, 70-71

Mental illness, social status and, 242, 366-373

Menzel, H., 197, 202, 209

Merton, R. K., 200, 205, 209-212, 214

Meuwese, W. A. T., 540, 549, 550

Michigan, University of, 126, 150, 243, 340, 438

Michigan completion test, 126-128

Michigan State Teachers College, 127, 150

Michotte, A., 82, 94

Miller, D. R., 351, 358, 360, 363, 365

Miller, F. B., 701

Miller, J. G., 645

Miller, N. E., 158, 171-172, 174, 293, 437, 444

Miller, W. E., 106, 109, 349

Minard, R. D., 101, 110, 117, 121

Mintz, A., 612-613, 620

Mobility, social, intolerance and, 687-688

Mobs, 611-612
  acquisitive, 611
  aggressive, 611
  escape, 611, 612
  expressive, 611
  panic reactions in, 611-613, 620-623, 627
  thought and action of, homogeneity in, 612
  "contagion" concept in, 612, 620
  "suggestion" concept in, 612, 620

Mood, A. E., 156

Moore, R. A., 351, 365

Moral development of child, 239
  social factors in, 273-282

Moralistic condemnation, 678

Moreno, J. L., 209, 387, 391, 511, 512, 514, 519
Morris, C. G., 539, 550
Morse, N. C., 614, 619
Moses, L. E., 308
Motivating patterns in attitude change, 104-105, 108-109, 121-129
Motivation, 7, 13, 21, 23, 126
 achievement, development of, 294-308
  social status and, 28-30, 58-64, 239-240, 359-360
 content of, 29-30
 effects of on estimation of power and approval, 71-81
 group, cooperation and competition, effects of on, 557, 569
 influences on, 27-30
  See also Attitude change; Attitudes
 in learning of contravaluant material, 39-47
 problem of, focal nature of, 27
  fundamental aspect of, 27-28
 reference groups and, 213-214
 self-, 213
 thinking on, influences on, 30-31
 understanding of, approaches in, 27-31
  genetic, 28-29
  situational, 29
Mouton, J. S., 616, 702, 703, 706
Movie-going decisions, influences on, 197, 205
Mowrer, O. H., 171-172, 174
Müller-Lyer illusion, 410
Multicausality, 5
Multiple-group membership, disaster and, 384, 505-510
Munsell colors, 246, 248-249
Murdock, G. P., 247, 248, 252, 286, 293
Murphy, G., 24, 31, 39, 47, 186, 196, 656-657, 695-696, 701
Murphy, L. B., 186, 196
Murray, H. A., 71, 81, 150, 156
Mutual emotional facilitation, 621, 623, 627

Myers, J. K., 367
Myrdal, G., 647, 657

N

Name-calling, 616, 700
Nationalism, 615, 706-707
 displacement of aggression in relation to, 710
 generalization of aggression in relation to, 713-714
 measurement of, 709
Natural laboratory experiment, 12-13
 See also Research
Navaho language, 245-247, 250
Nazi concentration camps, 609-611, 628-637
Nazis, attitudes toward, 49
Needs, affiliation, 29, 30, 124, 214
 arousal of, 30
 differences in, determination of, 28
 influence of, on attitudes, 83, 102, 104, 107, 121-123, 125, 379, 380, 613
 on distortion, 23, 24
 on motivation, 28-30
 situational analysis of, 29
Negative attitudes, 99, 100, 105, 108, 186, 613, 615, 617
 See also Attitude change; Attitudes
Negative cathexis, 555-556
Negative inducibility, 555-556
Negro children, attitudes of white children toward, 99, 102, 111-121, 613, 618
 integration and (see Integration; Segregation)
 racial identification in, 239, 308-317
Negroes, attitudes toward, 28, 124-128, 155, 238-239, 613-614, 618
 in Army, 680-685
 in housing projects, 617-618, 646-657
 intolerance studies on, 614, 685-693
 hostility rumors about, 48, 49, 55, 56

Negroes (*continued*)
   stereotyped conceptions of, 55, 122,
       252, 268-272, 663, 673, 692-693
Neighbors, sum of, 577, 579
New York State Training School for
       Girls, 512
New York University, 404, 464
Newcomb, T. M., 3, 12, 16, 17, 30, 31, 66,
       70, 71, 100, 103, 186, 196, 210,
       211, 214, 215, 349, 471, 485, 494,
       506, 510, 512-513, 519, 576, 653,
       657
Newstetter, W. I., 66, 71, 512-513, 519
Nonadaptive group behavior, 612-613,
       620-628
   See also Mobs
Nonsense words, 236, 262, 263
Norms (*see* Group norms)
North Carolina, University of, 84-93
Norway, studies in, on international at-
       titudes, 615, 706-716
   on resistance to change, 460
Nyakusa, male initiation ceremonies of,
       289

O

Object(s), of attitudes, response to, 23,
       98-100, 130, 132, 133, 139, 149-
       156
   beliefs about, 149, 155
   cognitive, 123, 124
   social, perception of, 25
   See also Perception
Obligation, perceived, 495
Obligatory conformity, 273-277
Observable events, 11
Occupational strata, politico-economic
       orientations of, 326-328, 331-
       335, 337, 339, 342-344
Oedipus rivalry in primitive tribes, 285,
       286, 290-292
Ohio State University, 539

Oklahoma, University of, 505
Old City, social class analysis of, 241,
       318-326
Ooldea, male initiation ceremonies of,
       290-291
Oonk, S., 540, 550
Opinion change (*see* Attitude change)
Opinion leadership, 102, 196-201, 205-
       207, 210
Opinions, and attitudes, structural re-
       lationship between, 98-99
   direction of, beliefs and, 132-134, 138
   majority, shift to, 379, 394-401
   in primary groups, homogeneity in, 204
   public, personal setting of, 129-139
     policy orientation of, 99, 130-134,
       138, 139
   See also Attitudes
Organizations, social, 378
Ort, R. S., 59, 64
Osgood, C. E., 260-262, 265, 539, 551

P

Paired-associate learning, 259-260
Panics, 611-613, 620-623, 627
Park, R. E., 505, 510
Parsons, T., 485, 494
Parts of speech, 253-258
Past experience, influence of on percep-
       tion, 22-23
Patriotism, 615, 706-707
   displacement of aggression in relation
       to, 710
   generalization of aggression in relation
       to, 713-714
   measurement of, 709
Peak, H., 126, 388, 392
Pear, T. H., 695, 701
Pearl Harbor rumors, 47-49
   See also Rumors
Pelz, E. B., 381-382, 437
People's Choice, The, 196-201, 203, 206

Pepitone, A., 13, 23, 26, 71
Perceived expectations, 494-499
Perceived instrumentality, 150-156
Perceived obligation, 495
Perceived sanctions, 495, 499-503
Perceptions, 7, 21, 27, 65-94
  behavioral components of, 21-27
  of causality, determinants and conse-
     quences of, 26, 81-94
  of cause and effect relationships, 25
  of communication, differences in, 178-
     180
  distortion of, 23-24, 397
    determinants of, 71-81
  interpersonal, in integrated and segre-
     gated groups, 663-665
  past experience, influence of on, 22-23
  of social objects, 25
  stimulus factors in, 21-27
  warm-cold variables in, 26-27, 65-70
Perceptual defense, 40
Perceptual selectivity, 45
Perceptual vigilance, 40
Peripherality, 581, 586-591
Permissive catharsis, 108, 125-126, 436
Permissiveness, in child-rearing practices,
    350, 356-360, 364
  resistance to change and, 452
Person-oriented leadership, 389, 538
Personal influence, impact of, 197-199,
    203-204
Persuasion, in communication, 106, 107,
    157-174, 186
  See also Communication
  rational, 108-109, 124-128
Phenomena, 3
  empirical and conceptual relationships
    among, 9, 10
  study of, selection for, 11
Phonological differences, 236, 245-247
Physical punishment, application of in
    child-rearing practices, 360
Physicians, influences among, 197, 202-
    208

Physiognomic categories, 252
Piaget, J., 239, 273
Piece-rate wage plans, 445-446, 487, 594,
    597-602
Pierce-Jones, J., 351, 365
Pipe-dream rumors, 48
  See also Rumors
Placebo, use of, 15
Policy orientation, 99, 130-134, 138, 139
Political attitudes, 14-15, 97, 100, 139
  influences on, 102, 197-199, 201, 203,
    204, 206
    social status, 242-243, 339-349
    politico-economic, 326-328, 331-335,
     337, 339, 342-344
Political conservatism, 674
Political and economic progressivism
    scale (PEP), 216-217
Political extremism, 607
Politico-economic attitudes, 326-328,
    331-335, 337, 339, 342-344
Polygamy, 285
Positive attitudes, 99, 100, 105, 108
  See also Attitude change; Attitudes
Positive cathexis, 554-556, 559
Positive expansiveness, 513-514
Positive inducibility, 554-558
Postman, L. F., 23-24, 46, 47, 206, 208
Post-partum sexual taboos, 286-291
Poverty, economic, 607
Power, communicator, 142-148
  need for, 30
  in stimulus persons, evaluation of, 71-
    94
Practices, established, change of, group
    decision method in, 381-382,
    423-444, 446
  resistance to, 382, 602-604
  overcoming of, 444-460
Predictions, attitude change, 123-125,
    140-142, 145-146, 335
  behavior, 29, 42-46, 100, 101, 237, 252
  in role conflict, 501-505
  compliance, 82-83

Predictions (*continued*)
  empirical tests of, 3-4
  language acquisition, 260-265
  leadership effectiveness, 543-544
Prejudice, 5-6, 9, 13
  assimilation to, 56
  influence of, on attitudes (*see* Attitude
      change; Attitudes)
    on motivation, 27
  racial (*see* Racial prejudice)
Prestige studies, 175, 184, 216-217, 393
  group, 380, 413-415, 421-422
Primitive tribes, child-rearing practices
      among, 283-293
Prince, S. H., 506, 507, 510
Princeton University, 267-269
Prison camps, Nazi, 609-611, 628-637
  Red Chinese, 108, 609-611, 638-645
Pritzker, H. A., 107, 109, 187, 194, 196
Proactive inhibition, 449, 456
Production methods, change of, resist-
      ance to, 382, 602-604
  overcoming of, 444-460
Productivity, cooperation and competi-
      tion, effects of on, 558-559, 571-
      573
  group factors in, 382, 592-604
Prohibition, attitudes toward, 107, 186-
      196
Projection of impulses, 105, 123, 614, 675
Projectivity, 674, 675
Propaganda, 123, 155, 156, 175, 393
  in Communist Chinese prison camps,
      610, 640-644
  counteracting, 106-107, 167-170, 172-
      174
Proshansky, H. M., 71, 81, 109, 617, 618
Pseudoconservatism, 674
Pseudotoughness, 674
Psychegroups, 511-512, 518
Psychiatric disorders, social status and,
      242, 366-373
Psychoanalytic theory, 27, 28, 30-31, 158,
      283, 284

Psychodynamic conflicts, 706-709, 712-
      713, 715
Psychosexual impulses, handling of, con-
      flict in, 615, 708-709
Psychotherapy, 125-126, 158, 170
Puberty, male, primitive initiation cere-
      monies at, 283-293
Public opinion, personal setting of, 129-
      139
  policy orientation of, 99, 130-134, 138,
      139
Public policy, interracial housing and,
      617-618, 646-657
Pure research, 608

Q

Quasi-stationary social equilibria, 432-
      436, 453-455

R

Race riots, 611-612, 615
Racial identification in Negro children,
      239, 308-317
Racial prejudice, 613-618
  eclectic approach in, 613
  intolerance studies on, 614, 685-693
  stereotypes and, 55, 122, 237, 252, 266-
      272, 616-617, 663, 671-673, 692-
      693, 696
  theories of, orientations in, 613
  "well-earned-reputation" theory of, 616
  See also Intergroup conflicts; Jews;
      Negro children; Negroes
Radcliffe-Brown, A. R., 291
Radical-conservative orientations, 326-
      328, 331-335, 342, 343
Radke, M., 429-431, 437, 444
Rational persuasion, 108-109, 124-128
Reactive hostility, 171

Recall, 21
  accuracy of, attitude as factor in, 44
  of contravaluant material, 24, 39-47
  cultural and past experiences, influence
      of on, 22-23
  delayed, 39
  of factual information, source credi-
      bility and, 181-185
  immediate, 39
  by males and females, studies on, 39
  repeated reproduction method in, 32-
      34
  serial reproduction method in, 34-35
  social factors in, 32-39
  See also Learning
Redl, F., 386, 392
Redlich, F. C., 12, 242, 372
Reference groups, 102-104, 210-230
  comparison function of, 103, 104, 213-
      214
  current usages of term, 211-212
  first use of term, 210
  and motivation, 213-214
  negative, 103, 211
  normative, 103, 104, 212-214, 611
  positive, 103, 211
  theory of, 210-214
Relative peripherality, 589
Religious attitudes, 97, 98, 100, 690
Religious beliefs, 98, 100, 133
Religious values, 100, 690
Remembering (*see* Recall)
Remmers, H. H., 186, 196
Repeated reproduction, method of, 32-34
Replaced hostility, 126
Representatives, group, loyalty of during
      intergroup competition, 702-
      706
Research, 9-17
  applied, 608-609
  artificiality of, defense of, 14
  data collection for, 12-16
  drug, placebo, use of in, 15
  field investigations, 10-16

  generalizations in, 13-14
  laboratory, 6, 11-16
    natural experiment, 12-13
  problems in, 14-16
  pure, 608
  unintended influences in, 15-16
  variables in, control of, 12-15
Residential segregation, 617-618, 646-657
Resistance to change, of attitudes, 123,
      125, 158, 170, 172, 174
  of established practices, 382, 602-604
  overcoming of, 444-460
Retroactive inhibition, 259-260, 262
Reward and punishment, attitude change
      and, 101, 104-109, 121-125, 141,
      212-213, 609-610
  in independence-mastery training, 295-
      297, 300-304, 306
  self-delivery of, 213
Richardson, L. F., 695
Riecken, H. W., 15, 17, 26, 81, 83, 94
Riesman, D., 209
Riley, J. A., 209
Riley, M., 209
Rindlisbacher, A., 365
Rinsland, H. D., 254, 259
Riots, race, 611-612, 615
Rivalry, Oedipus, in primitive tribes, 285,
      286, 290-292
  See also Competition
Roberts, J. M., 247, 252
Robertson, I. V., 186, 196
Roethlisberger, F. J., 601-603
Rogers, S., 187, 196
Role behavior, 382
Role conflict, 8, 9, 384
  in disaster situations, 384, 505-510
  latent, 384, 506
  resolution of, 384, 494-505
Role congruency, 495
Role occupancy, 382-385
  attitude change and, 485-494
Roosevelt, F. D., 47-48, 216, 343
Rorschach test, 534, 615

Rosanoff, A. J., 366, 372
Rose, A., 657
Rosenberg, M. J., 104, 125, 128-129, 149, 156
Rosenzweig, S., 137, 139
Rovere study on decision-making influences, 197, 199-200, 205, 207
Rumors, 47-58
  bogey, 48, 49
  fear, 48
  hostility, 48-49, 55, 56
  Pearl Harbor, 47-49
  pipe-dream, 48
  spreading of, experiment on, 49-50
    interests as factor in, 24
    mechanisms in, 51-58
      assimilation, 24, 54-56
      embedding, 56-58
      leveling, 24, 51-52
      sharpening, 24, 42-54
    reasons for, 49
  wartime, 47-49, 53
  wish, 48
Rusk, D., 705, 706
Russell, D. H., 186, 196
Russia, attitudes toward, 99, 129-139
  rumors about, 48, 52
Ryan, B., 206, 209

S

Saenger, G., 101, 110
Sanctions, perceived, 495, 499-503
Sanford, R. N., 71, 81, 83, 94, 123, 128, 226, 230, 614-615, 670, 671, 679
Sapir, E., 252
Sarnoff, I., 104-106, 108, 121
Saturday Evening Post, 269
Scapegoating, 48, 49, 126, 386, 450, 614
Schachter, S., 29-31, 208-209, 380-381, 392, 411, 423, 458-460, 471
Schaefer, E. S., 351, 364
Schein, E. H., 108, 609-611, 638, 645

Schizophrenia, social status and, 370-372
Schneider, D. M., 293
School segregation, 40-47, 107, 143-148
Sears, R. R., 350, 359-360, 362, 365
Seeleman, V., 71, 81
Segregation, in children's camps, 618, 657-669
  interpersonal perceptions in, 663-665
  interpersonal relations in, 659-660
  residential, 617-618, 646-657
  school, 40-47, 107, 143-148
Self-concept, 30, 239
Self-evaluation, 30, 211-214, 239-241
Self-insight, rational persuasion and, 108-109, 127-128
Self-motivation, 213
Self-oriented-need behavior, 390-391
Selltiz, C., 5, 17
Semantic differences, 253-258, 260, 262, 263, 265
Semantic differential, 261-263, 539
Senders, V. L., 46, 47
Serial reproduction, method of, 34-35
Sex, 28, 235, 285
  attitudes toward, 97, 674, 678
Sex-linked patterns in integration, 666-667
Sexual impulses, projection of, 105, 614, 675
Sexual taboos among primitive tribes, 283-291
Sexuality, 676
Sharpening process, 24, 52-54
Shaw, M. E., 541, 551
Sheats, P., 576
Sheffield, F. D., 106, 109, 175, 181-185
Sherif, C. W., 3, 5, 17, 225, 230, 694, 701, 705, 706
Sherif, M., 3, 5, 11, 17, 107, 175, 185-187, 191, 193, 196, 210, 211, 214, 225, 230, 378, 379, 402, 411, 461, 463, 471, 485, 505, 510, 615-617, 628, 694, 695, 701, 705, 706
Siegel, A. E., 103
Siegel, J., 366, 372

Siegel, S., 103, 225, 226, 228, 230
Sims, V. M., 627, 628
"Sleeper effect," 175, 181-185
Smith, Adam, 234
Smith, M. B., 99, 100, 129, 149, 156
"Snowball" interviews, 201, 208
Social acceptance, desire for, 101-104,
     121, 123-125, 138-139, 212-213
Social attributes, 25, 26
Social causality (see Causality)
Social class structure (see Class struc-
     ture)
Social environment, control of, 83
  perception of, effects of on behavior, 71
  substantive elements of, 233
  See also Class structure; Social status
Social influences, normative and informa-
     tional, 103-104, 379-381
  on individual judgment, 402-411
  See also Group influence
Social mobility, intolerance and, 687-688
Social objects, perception of, 25
  See also Perception
Social organizations, 378
Social psychology, 3-17
  and anthropology, 4, 5, 9, 28
  approaches in, cognitive, 9, 10
    empirical, 3-4, 9-11
    factor analytic, 10
    reinforcement, 9
    scientific, 10, 16
    sociological, 16-17
    theoretical, 10-11
  birth of, 4
  definitions of, 3-4
  and general psychology, 6-9, 16
  research methods in (see Research)
  as scientific discipline, 3, 4
  and sociology, 4-6, 9, 16, 28
  theoretical developments in, 3-4, 8-11
  advances in, 607, 608
Social status, influence of, areas of,
     achievement motivation, 28-30,
     58-64, 239-240, 359-360
    attitude change, 26, 614

child-rearing practices, 28-30, 58-
    64, 239-240, 349-365
    Communistic appeal, 610
    mental illness, 242, 366-373
    political attitudes, 242-243, 339-349
Social stratification (see Class structure;
    Social status)
Socialization, 22, 237-240, 273-317, 349-
    365
  and adaptive acculturation, distinction
    between, 62
  See also Child-rearing practices
Socially shared autism, 649
Socio-economic attitudes, 332, 335, 338-
    340, 351, 385
Sociogroups, 511-512, 516, 518
Sociology, 4-6, 9, 16, 28
Sociometric choice, 481-484, 616, 697, 700
  leadership and, 511-519, 524, 539-540
Source credibility, 8, 106, 175-185
Speech categories, 251
Spinley, B. M., 363, 365
Spock, B., 356, 364, 365
Standards, group (see Group norms)
Stands, 133
  acceptance-rejection of, 186-196
Star, S. A., 494, 617, 680
Statements, counterarguments used as,
    41-45
Status polarization, 243, 344-349
Steiner, I., 62, 64
Stendler, C. B., 365
Stereotypes, racial prejudice and, 55,
    122, 237, 252, 266-272, 616-617,
    663, 671-673, 692-693, 696
Stern, L., 366, 373
Stimulus factors in perception, 21-27
Stimulus persons, approval in, evaluation
    of, 71-84
  interaction with, first impressions in,
    27, 65-70
  labels attached to, 65, 69
  power in, evalution of, 71-94
Stimulus-response theory, 393
Stimulus-words, 261-262

Stodgill, R. M., 385, 392, 538, 539, 551
Stoker, D. E., 349
Stonequist, E., 505, 510
Stotland, E., 100, 101, 109
Stouffer, S. A., 211, 214, 485, 495, 617, 680
Strain avoidance, 456, 459
Strassman, H. D., 638, 645
Street-corner gangs, 377, 696
    leadership in, 387, 519-523
Strodtbeck, F. L., 351, 365
Stycos, J. M., 209
Submission, authoritarian, 674, 708
Suchman, E. A., 494
Suci, G. A., 551
Suggestion, authoritarian, rational persuasion and, 126-127
Sum of distances, 579
Sum of neighbors, 577, 579
Sumner, W. S., 655
Super-ego control, 690
Superordinate goals, 615-616, 694-701, 705, 709
Superstition-stereotypy, 674
Sussman, M. B., 364
Sutherland, J. F., 366, 373
Swanson, G. E., 349, 351, 358, 360, 363, 365, 657

T

Taboos, sexual, among primitive tribes, 283-291
Tallensi, child-rearing practices of, 291
Tannenbaum, P. H., 551
Task direction, cohesiveness and, 380, 413, 414, 420-421
Task-oriented leadership, 389, 538-550
Taub, D., 187, 196
Tele relationships, 511
Tempereau, Clinton, 638
Tension, 108, 125, 158-159, 170, 171, 173, 457, 461
    controlling mechanisms for, 689-690
    international, 706-716

reduction of, superordinate goals in, 697, 699, 701
    See also Intergroup conflicts
Tepoztlan, child-rearing practices of, 289
Thaler, M., 645
Thematic apperception test, 534, 615
Theoretical efficiency, maximum, 578-579
Thibaut, J. W., 26, 81, 83, 94, 458, 460
Thonga, child-rearing practices of, 283-285, 290, 292
Thorndike, E. L., 254, 259
Thrasher, F. M., 696, 701
Thurstone, L. L., 266, 267, 416, 423
Tolerance, ethnic, 614, 685-693
Tolman, E. C., 149, 156
"Traffic jams," 622, 625-627
Threats (see Reward and punishment)
Timbira, child-rearing practices of, 289-291
Trobrianders, male initiation ceremonies of, 289, 291
Trow, M. A., 209
Turks, stereotyped conceptions of, 252, 269-272
Turnover and aggression, differential rates of, 459

U

Unicultural experiences, 261, 263, 264

V

Value-expressive attitudes, 104, 108
Value-importance measure, 150-156
Value systems, 100, 105, 108, 109, 142
    restructuring of, 124, 125
Values, 23
    blocking of, 149, 152, 155
    conventional, 674
    influence of, on attitudes, 100-102, 104, 105, 108, 142
        toward Russia, 135-137

Values (*continued*)
  on learning, 24
  on motivation, 28
 intensity of, 149
 internalization of, 239, 611, 690
 religious, 100, 690
Variables, control of, 12-15
Veroff, J., 388, 392
Veterans Administration, 367, 370, 373
Vocabulary differences, 236, 247-250
Voting behavior (*see* Political attitudes)

W

Wage incentive plans, 445-446, 487, 594,
    597-602
Wagman, M., 126, 129
Walsh, W. B., 133, 139
Wapner, S., 702
War, effects of on status polarization, 346,
    349
 expectations about, 132, 133
Warm-cold variables, 26-27, 65-70
Warner, W. L., 241, 243, 351, 363, 365
Wartime rumors, 47-49, 53
 See also Rumors
Watson, W. S., 39, 47
Wealth distribution, 346
Weinrich, U., 259, 265
Weiss, W., 11, 14, 106, 175, 190, 196
"Well-earned-reputation" theory of preju-
    dice, 616
Western Electric Company, 382, 592-604
Westgate and Westgate West, housing
    projects in, 472-484
White, B. J., 701
White, M. S., 128, 129, 356, 365
White, R. K., 11, 150, 156, 388, 523
White caste, class system of, 318-326
White children, attitudes of toward
    Negro children, 99, 102, 111-
    121, 613, 618
 integration and (*see* Integration;
    Segregation)

Whitehead, T. N., 595, 628
Whiting, J. W. M., 238, 283
Whorf, B. L., 236-237, 243, 244, 247, 248,
    252, 253, 259
Whyte, W. F., 12, 63, 64, 387, 519
Wilke, W. H., 186, 196
Wilkins, C., 101, 110
Williams, A. C., 186, 196
Williams, R. M., Jr., 186, 196, 494, 617,
    646, 657, 680, 698-699, 702
Winer, B. J., 386-387, 389, 391
Winterbottom, M. R., 28, 240, 294, 299,
    304
Wishner, J., 66, 70-71
Wolfenstein, M., 355, 356, 365
Wolff, H. C., 644, 645
Woodruff, A. D., 149, 156
Woodward, P., 437, 444
Worker production methods, change of,
    resistance to, 382, 602-604
 overcoming of, 444-460
Worker productivity, cooperation and
    competition, effects of on, 558-
    559, 571-573
 group factors in, 382, 592-604

Y

Yale University, 177
Yankhauser, A., 364
Yapese, male initiation ceremonies of,
    289
Yarrow, L. J., 618, 657
Yarrow, M. R., 618, 657
Yarrow, P. R., 101, 110

Z

Zander, A., 9, 17, 380, 381, 390, 391, 437,
    444
Zeleny, L. D., 513, 519
Zipf, G., 248, 252
Zuñi, 247, 249